Modern Photoshop Color Workflow

The Quartertone Quandary, the PPW, and Other Ideas for Speedy Image Enhancement

DAN MARGULIS

MCW PUBLISHING
www.moderncolorworkflow.com

MCW Publishing
http://www.moderncolorworkflow.com

ISBN: 978-0-9882808-0-9
10 9 8 7 6 5 4 3 2 1

Manufactured in the United States of America.

Table of Contents

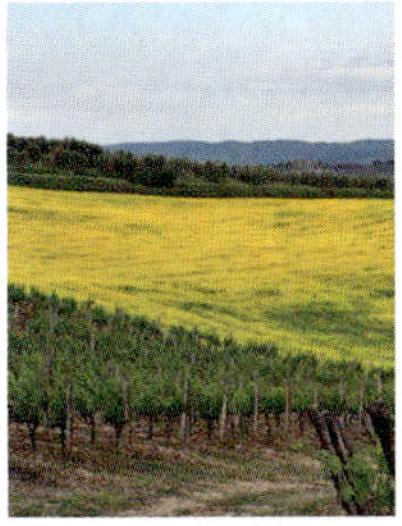
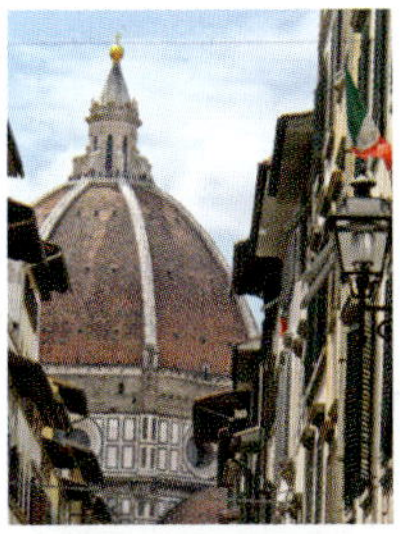
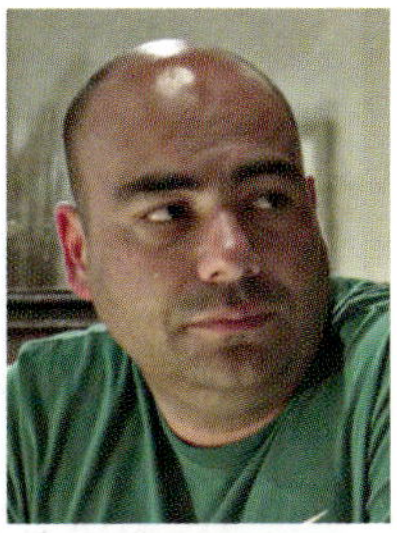
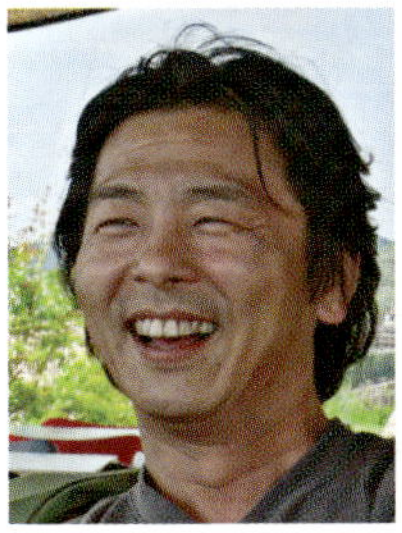
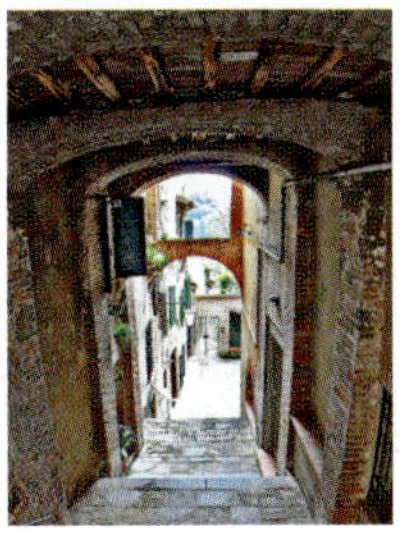
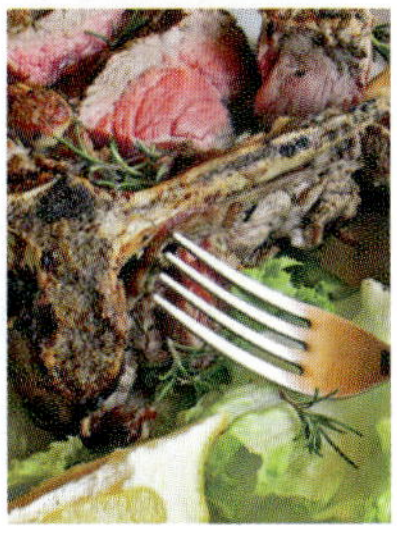

Introduction

A modern color workflow isn't easy to summarize briefly. According to this book's beta readers, six pictures are worth six thousand words. Come join their spirited discussion, and welcome to the adventure.

1

A Philosophy and a Preview

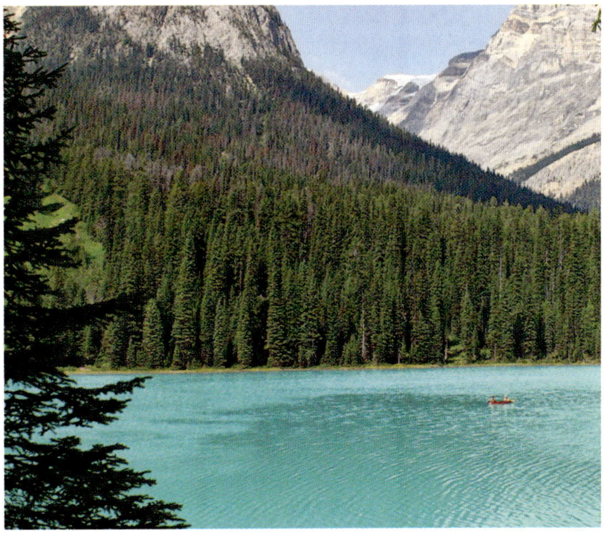

One image is taken from start to finish—with three different assumptions on how much time is available.

2 Five Lessons About Human Perception

This chapter studies two pictures in depth to show how the workflow can be used—or abused.

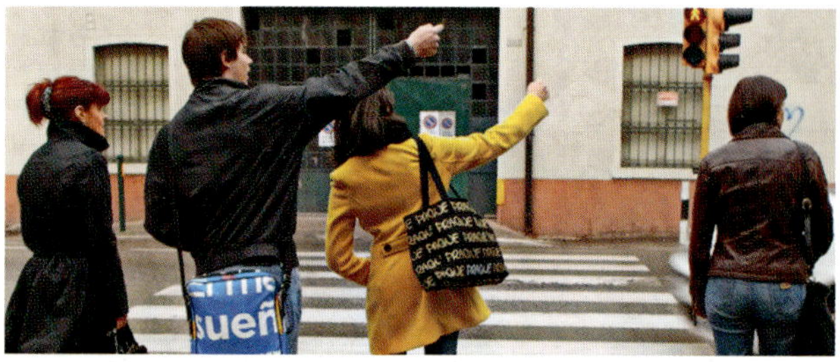

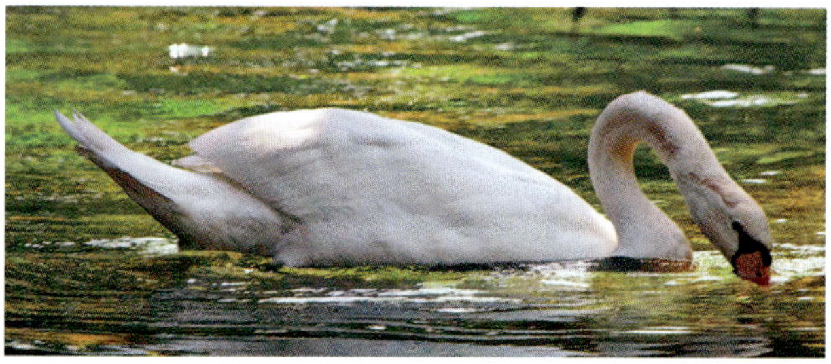

3 Once for Color: Early Detective Work

The first step is the toughest: don't try to achieve the right colors, just make sure that they aren't wrong.

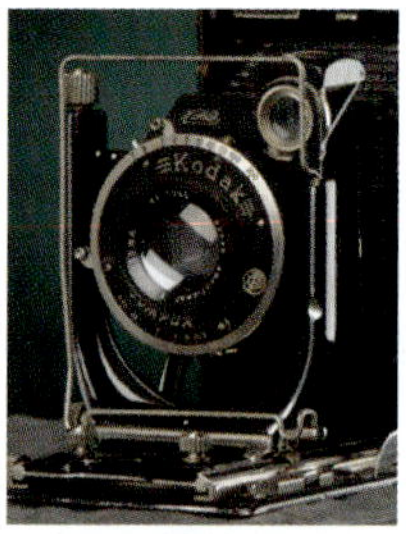

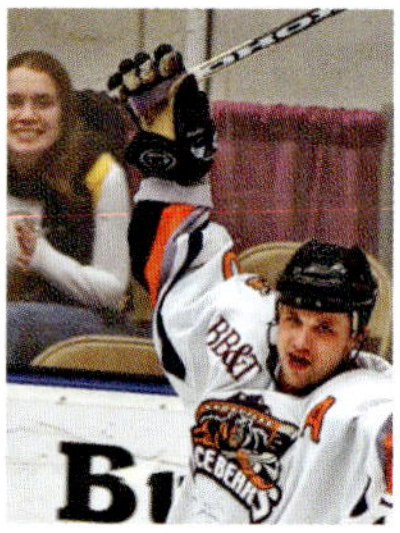

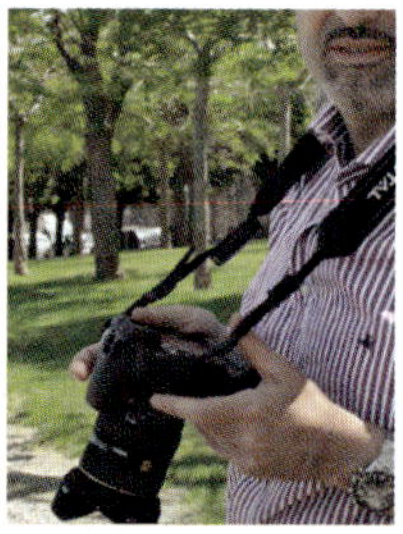

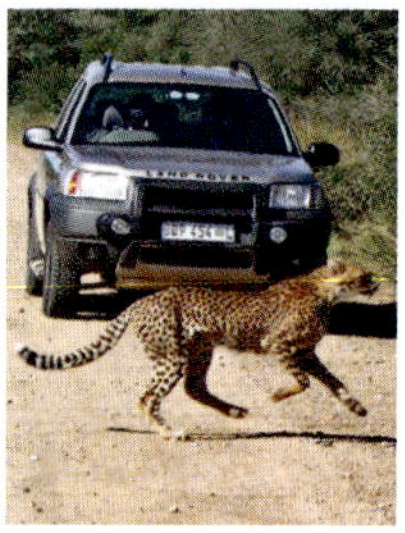

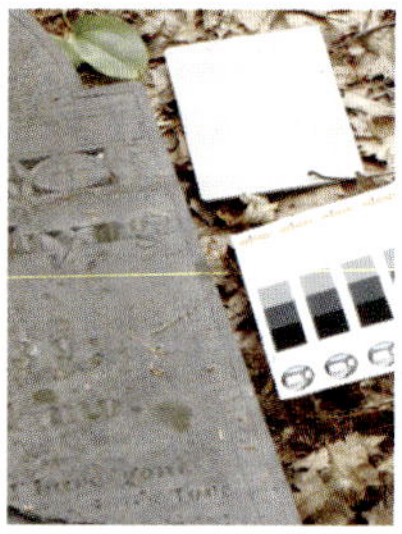

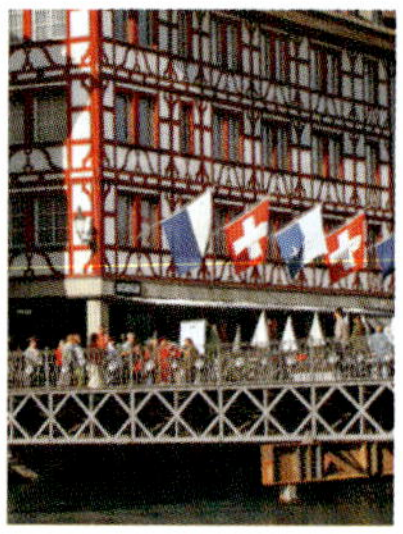

4 Once for Contrast

Working with channel blending and curves, without the need to worry about color issues, can make a whole that is more than the sum of its parts.

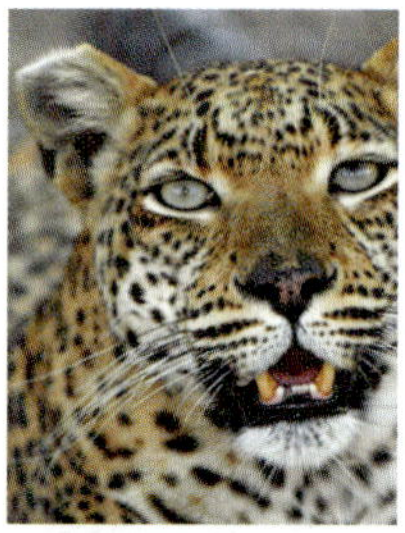

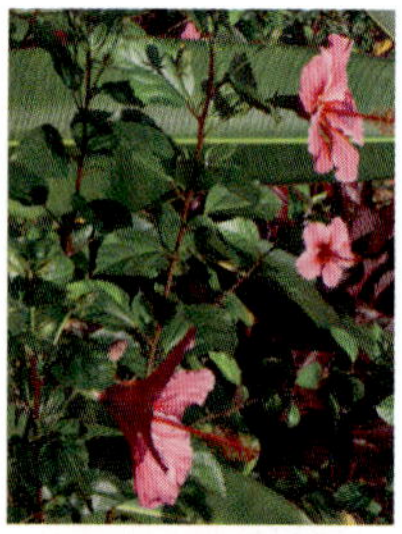

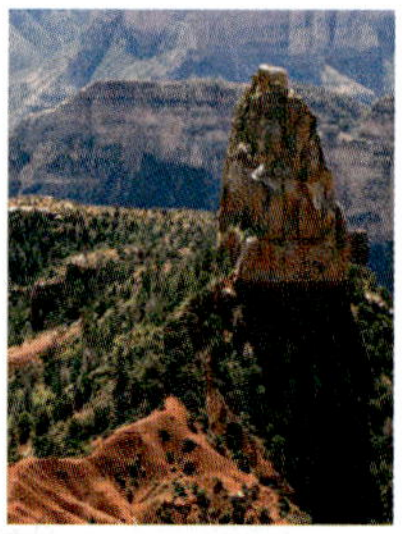

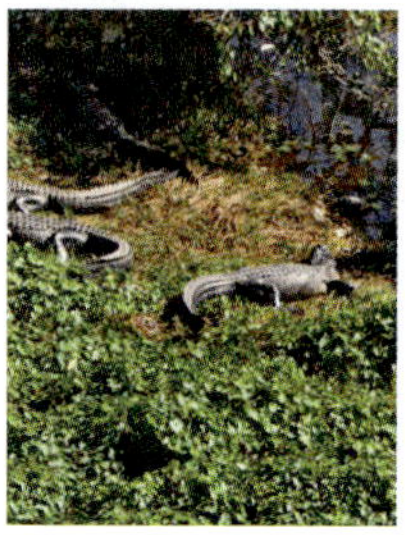

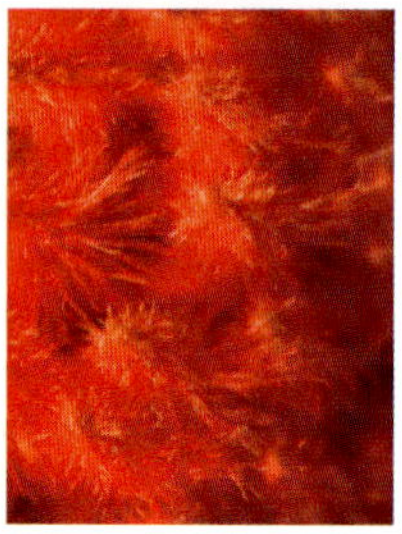

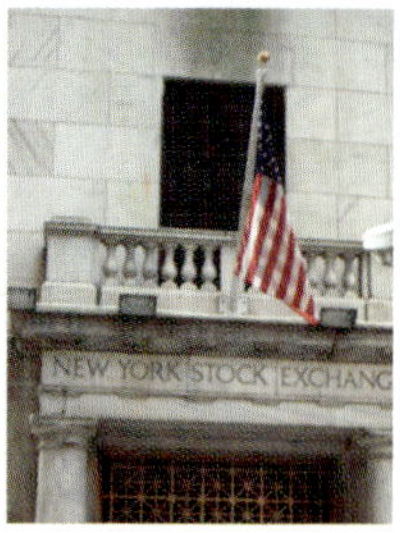

5 Once More for Color

The concept is counterintuitive, the results spectacular. Incorporate far too much color, then decide on the most graceful way to back off.

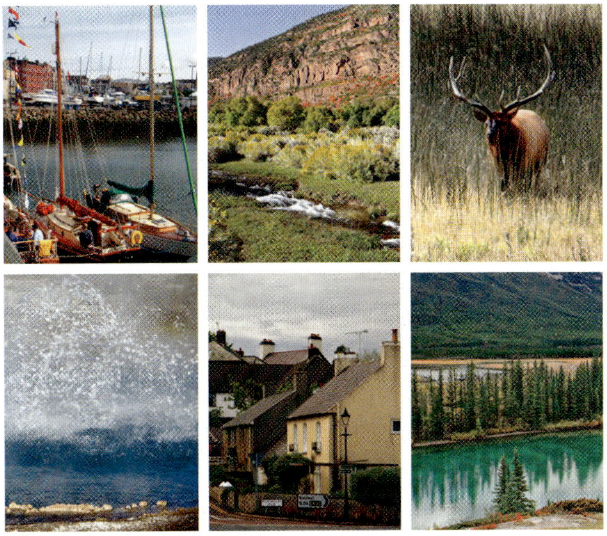

6 The Modern Man From Mars

A bogus selection, an ancient command, and a 60-step action make for compelling variation.

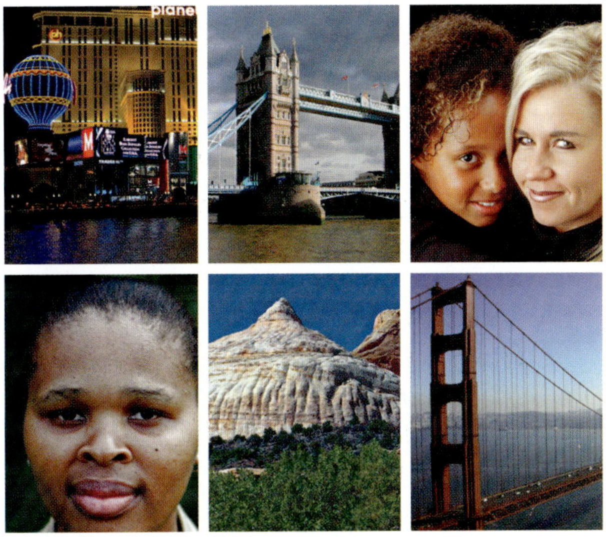

7 Shadows/Highlights

The terminology is confusing, but the concept is easy: do you think that the lightest and or darkest areas of the picture could use more detail?

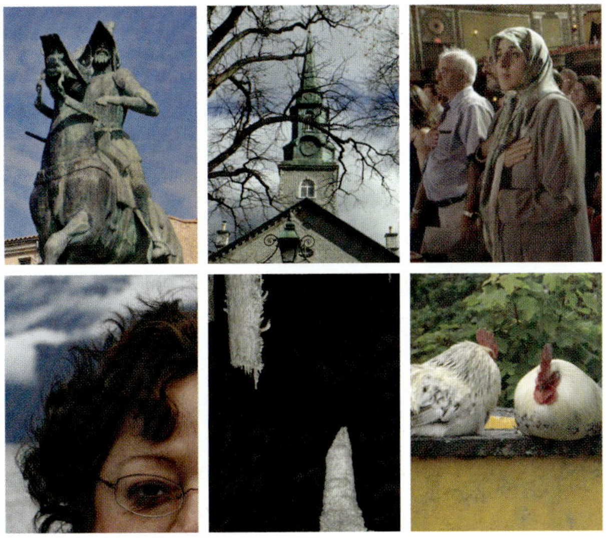

8

The Sky's No Limit

Skies don't behave like other objects. We often want them darker, but would object to adding detail or bright color. The solution: automate.

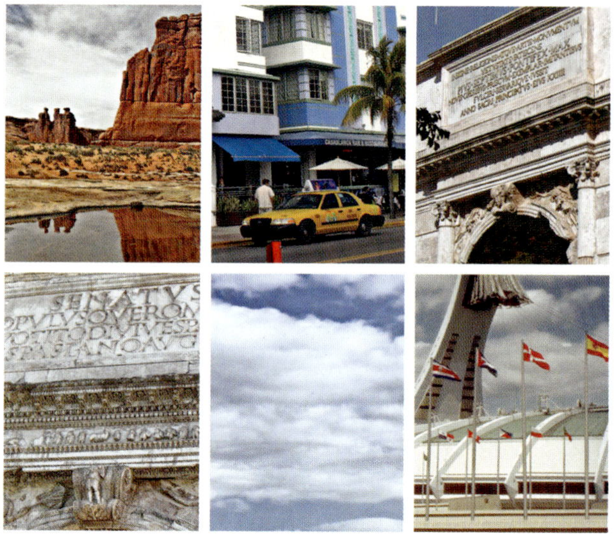

9

A Face Is Like a Sky

Extra detail makes a person look older, and extra redness is ugly. The solution: an action that pre-empts future color issues.

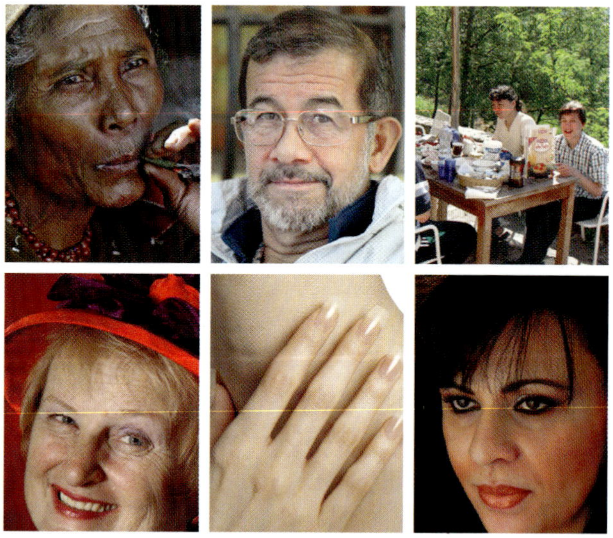

10

The Bigger Hammer

Exceptional images demand exceptional technique. When highlight detail is critical, we need something that packs a punch.

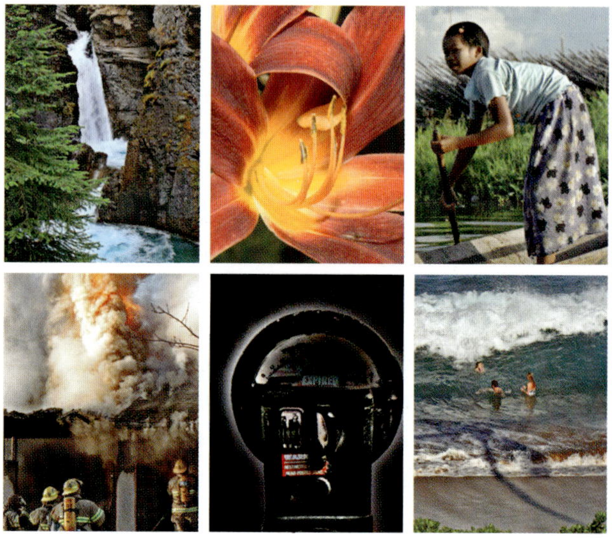

11

Of Bridges and Blurs

Introducing a theoretical, although not very practical, solution to the issue of sun vs. shade: multiplication through a blurred layer mask.

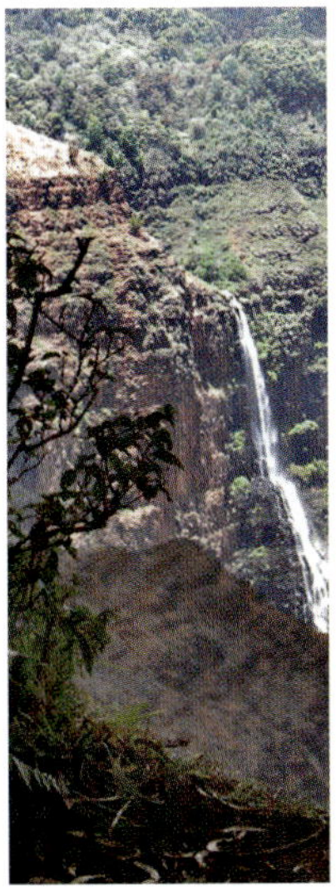
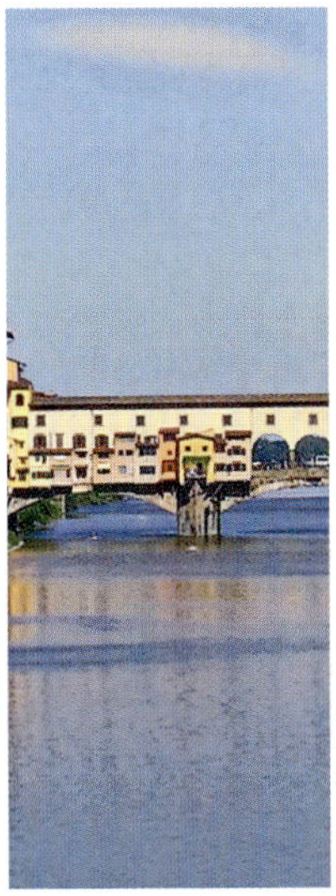
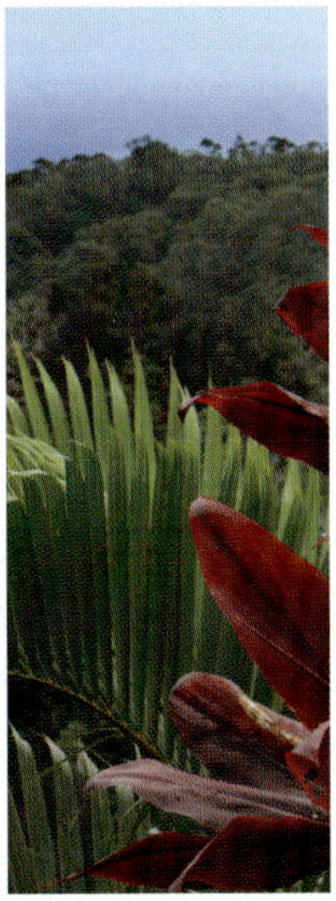

12

When the Story Has Two Sides

The technique of Chapter 11 explodes into relevance when a missing piece is added.

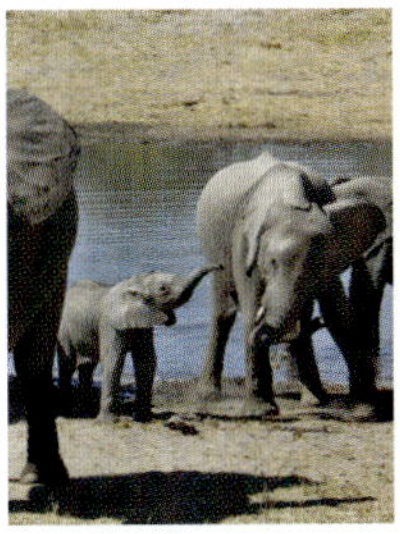
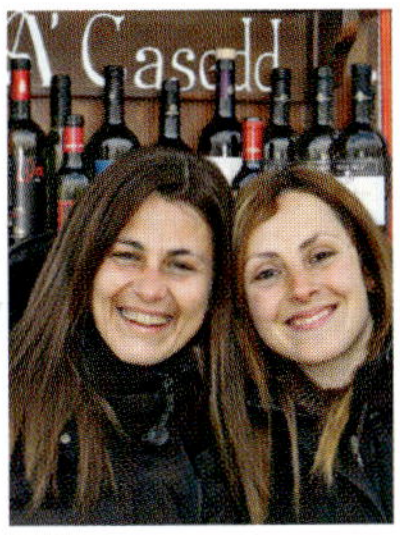
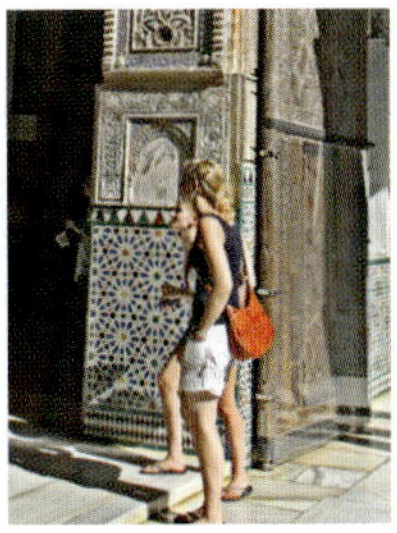
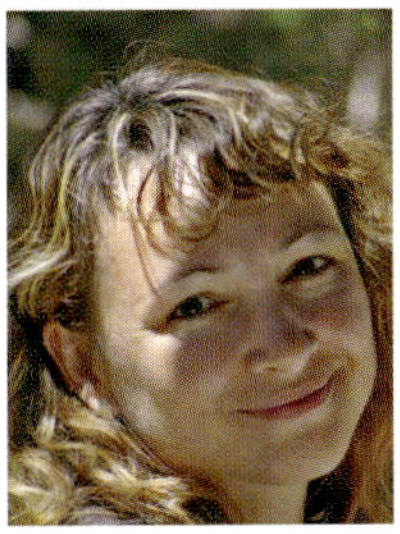
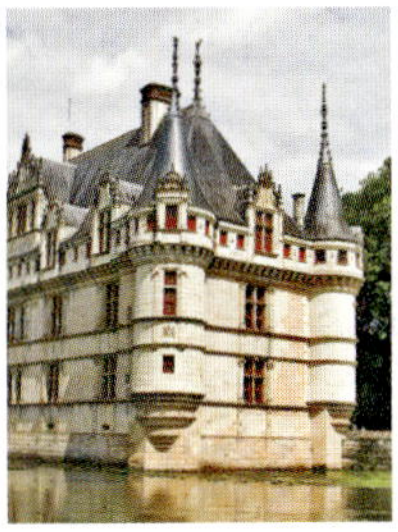
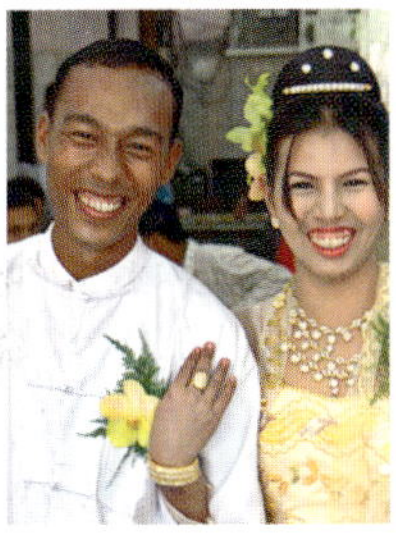

13

The Black Art of Color Enhancement

Darkening and/or desaturating near-neutrals can add depth and emphasize more brilliant colors.

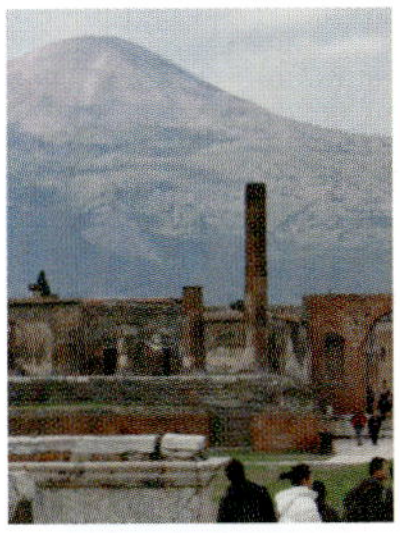
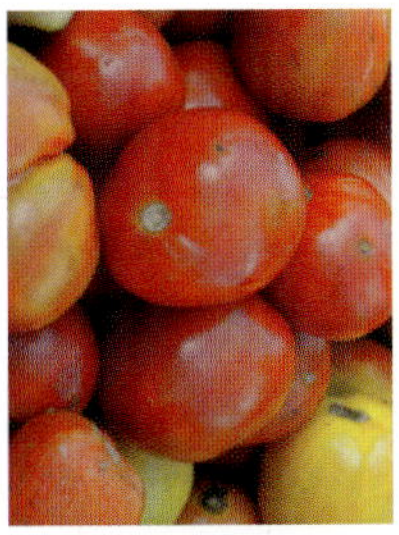
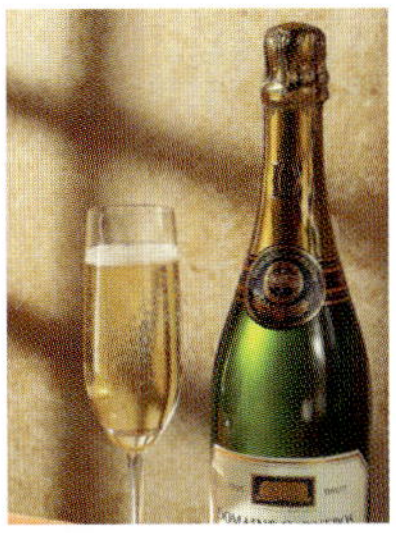
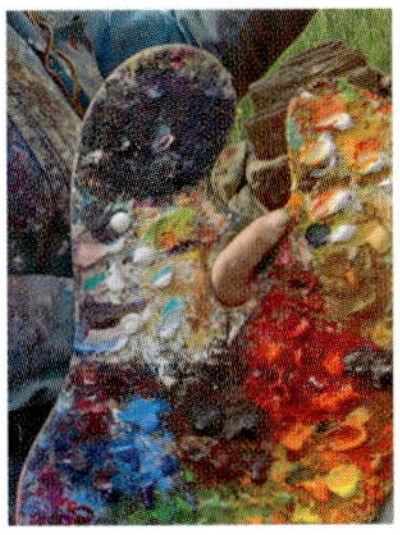
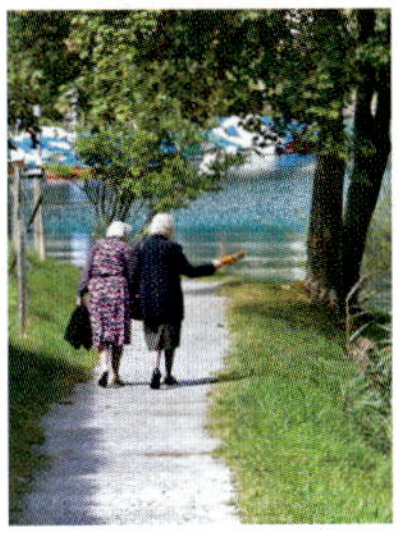
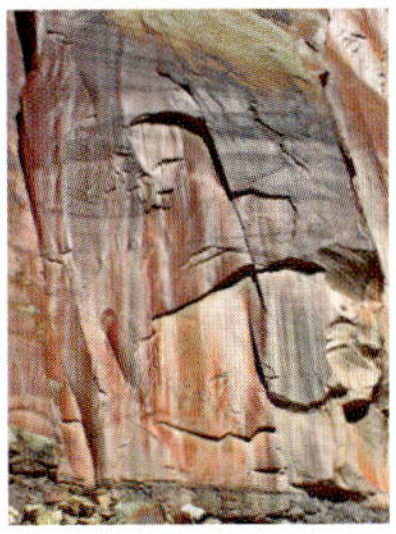

14 etaoin shrdlu and Its Progeny

Raw modules have advantages, but often impose a modern interface on dated methods. Here's how to cope.

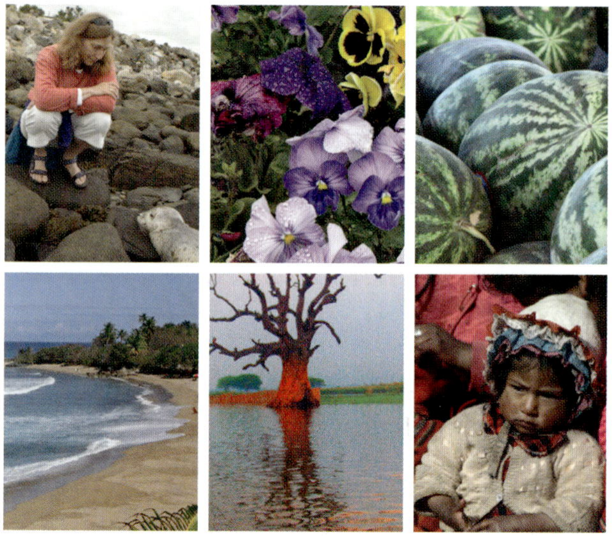

15 110 Steps to A Sharper Image

PPW doesn't require a particular sharpening method, but here's a powerful and configurable one.

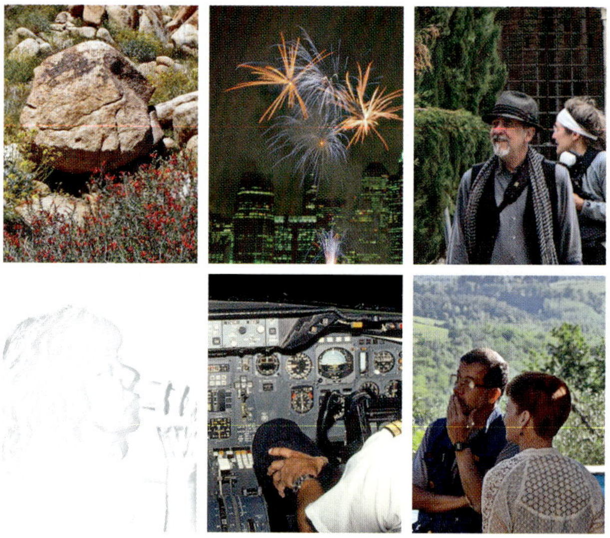

Introduction

Traditional color workflows became traditional because they were effective. If they are to be discarded it should not be because they are old, but because we have something that can do better in less time. This book proposes such an alternative—a modern one, because it would not have been technically possible until recently. It's the workflow I now recommend to just about anyone interested in image quality.

It may seem counterintuitive to suggest that someone processing a slew of photos from an iPhone should use the same procedure that a professional retoucher working on a full-page magazine advertisement would. To see why the concept holds requires understanding some history.

Speed and Quality

In the early days of digital color, computers were so slow and so expensive that the whole process was reserved for commercial advertising and other situations justifying a high price for color correction.

Today this is no longer true. People routinely correct pictures, often lots of them, that nobody would have bothered with in the past. Time becomes a major limitation.

I've taught and written about color correction for nearly twenty years. The techniques I've advocated have changed greatly, but until recently the basic approach has been based on yesterday's realities, dating from an era when the user's own time was unimportant in the context of the overall job.

I am not much of a photographer, and this is not a book about photography. I do understand that things have changed somewhat since the turn of the century, that cost of film is no longer a consideration, that cameras of superlative quality are available at low prices and poorer ones are included free in cell phones, that the cost of file storage is now infinitesimal, that the result can be sent around the world with a single click.

All these factors suggest that a radically different workflow is now in order. And as nearly as I can tell, that is indeed what has happened in the photographic industry—but not in the discipline described in this book.

Professionals who process digital images have not had to absorb anything as revolutionary as the development of digital cameras has been for photographers, but in other respects the pace of change has been faster. Increased computing speeds and cheaper memory, for example, benefit retouchers even more than they do photographers.

At the turn of the century, photographers had a good understanding of how to take a picture. Retouchers, on the other hand, were still groping for the best techniques. Meanwhile, the market for purchasing processing services has changed more drastically than that for buying photography.

Yet in color correction, the workflow has not changed very much. It needs rethinking, and for the last decade or so I've been doing a lot of it. What is the best way to get good quality if you are limited to spending an average of five minutes per image? What if the average must be one minute?

In asking these questions I made some wrong assumptions. I took for granted that a five-minute time limit implied a quality hit. As it turned out, I was mistaken: the workflow described in this book usually gives better results than older, slower ones.

And I assumed that the likely images for the new workflow would be travel shots, pictures of property for sale, personal stuff for posting on the web, and so on. Such pictures invite bright, happy colors. Absolute fidelity to the original scene is not usually important; a positive feeling is. This, also, turned out to be an incorrect assumption: the workflow is generally applicable to any type of image.

On its introduction in 2007, I called it Picture Postcard Workflow (PPW henceforth) because it often produced the type of deep, rich, pleasant feeling associated with such postcards. The name turned out to be a poor choice for cultural reasons: Americans put a positive spin on the words *picture postcard,* but several countries feel differently: the term is understood to suggest cheap-looking imagery. Too late to change now, though.

What Is the Workflow?

PPW, then, is the name, for better or worse. It departs from past practice in that color and contrast are always handled separately.

The approach is disciplined. After two introductory chapters, each step is laid out in the order in which it would be applied, including a statement of how difficult each is and how often it is used.

The workflow can be heavily automated, and a lot of that automation is yours for the downloading, at least as of this writing, including 14 actions. Some are so complex that they *have* to be in action form, as doing things manually would take much too long.

A free PPW panel installs these actions with one click, offers many variations on them and includes a mountain of documentation. I wrote the actions, but the sophisticated scripting of this panel is beyond my capabilities. Instead, it was developed and encouraged by some of my Italian friends.

My books historically have a long life—say four or five versions of Photoshop. Actions have a long life, too. As far as I know, the actions that our panel loads work in any version of Photoshop released in the last decade.

So far, however, panels for one version of Photoshop don't work in any other. Our installer detects whether you have Photoshop CS5 or CS6; it is incompatible with anything earlier. We intend to continue development for future Photoshop releases, but can offer no guarantees and no technical support.

Therefore, the panel's importance is downplayed in the text. Instead, we've prepared several videos that show how its options work and should convince you of how much speed the panel adds. We even have one video where the development team talks about how the panel came about.

Originally this workflow took about five minutes an image on average. That's now down to three, thanks largely to the panel's efficiency. But what if you don't have three minutes? And what if it's an important image and you're willing to spend more time?

The three basic workflow steps are color-contrast-color. First we eliminate color that is clearly incorrect, next we adjust contrast, and finally in the fun part, we establish pleasing, exciting color. The steps are separated because the first two are more effective in RGB while the third works better in LAB.

If you must get the time down to one minute, then eliminate those first two steps. The final LAB action can serve as a semi-complete workflow, with better results than any equally quick alternate method.

The above is a cost/benefit analysis. The one-minute result would likely be better, often much better, if the omitted steps were restored, but we have decided that the gain isn't worth the extra two minutes.

The same considerations apply to the basic three-minute PPW. Certain steps, certain adjustments are omitted, even if they could improve the image slightly. The PPW philosophy is that they don't do enough to warrant the additional time to execute them.

You would think that for images worthy of more than three minutes, we should just restore these omitted embellishments, to get the improvements that are admittedly possible. At one time, I thought so too. It seems only logical. But it's wrong. It is dead wrong, absolutely, positively wrong.

If you have more time, pretend you don't. Go through the three-minute workflow just as if other options didn't exist. Then, when you finish, do the work again from scratch. And, if time permits, a third version after that.

Even if your only choice were to accept one version or the other as is—and there are many other options—your odds of making a big improvement this way are much greater than if you fritter the time away by making small improvements in certain settings.

The PPW is volatile. It leaves a lot of room for user judgment. Do the work a second time and the results will be quite different. This is particularly true if you are satisfied with your first try and are willing to experiment the next time by altering certain steps.

I do not like fast food, but I like fast color correction. Alternate versions can be blended in ways that emphasize the best points of each. The improvement can be huge. That multiple quick versions are superior to a single careful one is the most important thing I've learned about image processing in the last several years.

Who Should Read This Book?

Parts of the PPW, particularly the final establishment of color, are beginner-friendly. But this is no collection of recipes. If you have read my previous books, you know the drill. If not, be aware that your way of thinking will be challenged. Google discussions about those books, and you will find one person after another advising that they must be read more than once.

Saying that about a book does it great honor. I am not aware of any other book written in the last hundred years, regardless of discipline, with such near-unanimity about the need to re-read.

In principle, the inexperienced should look elsewhere for their reading pleasure, because this book is tough. In practice, history shows that the ambitious ones won't. To these brave souls I offer two concessions, one old, one new.

First, the chapter structure is as in my earlier *Photoshop LAB Color:* first half accessible to everyone, second half geekier. Note, though, that *accessible* means only that among the many things that might derail you, lack of knowledge of Photoshop will not be one. The first halves assume that you know how to make adjustment layers and change their opacity and not much more.

Complex color concepts, however, don't require Photoshop expertise. They require a brain and a willingness to use it. I have no hesitation in including this difficult material in the first halves of chapters. It is one thing to know where you want to go with an image, and another how to get there. Many amateurs can manage the first but not the second; many experts are the other way around.

Consequently there is a case to be made that the most important part of the book has little to do with technique, and the more prepublication comments I get the more I see the point. For example, later in this Introduction, as I try to explain one of my own mistakes in execution, I go off into a riff on how such errors occur. It provoked two comments that this one page justifies the price of the book, because the readers had not considered my point previously and now agree with it. Near the end of this Introduction you'll get a recommendation from another reader as to how you should approach the book. The recommendation surprised me as I assume it will you, but it has to do very much with the idea that technique is not the most important thing being discussed.

The second concession is video support. My previous books have all contained CDs, for which there is no longer a need. Today's high bandwidth and essentially free online storage has allowed us to post however much we want.

Given a choice between print and video, I prefer the former, because it allows more depth. But why choose one, when we can have both? Video has advantages. Readers have complained that sometimes they draw a blank on certain simple explanations. If they could only see somebody demonstrating what I was talking about!

This time, therefore, some friends and I have recorded videos, to clarify points chapter by chapter. Sometimes this consists of redoing a certain image, sometimes exploring different directions. Many videos demonstrate the use of the PPW panel and its options. We plan to add updates when appropriate. Topics that were recorded by press time are listed in the Notes & Credits section, which begins on Page 431.

In short, this book is designed to be quite a bullet train. If you decide to hop on board, heed the warnings—but enjoy the ride.

Who Is the Nominal Author?

As pointed out earlier, I have written about this subject for a long time. Knowledge has advanced so rapidly throughout that period that whatever reputation I have for things I said in 1995 or 2005 is of little value today.

Even so, I have unique qualifications.

Some evaluation of image quality is subjective. Some is not. Most people have great difficulty understanding which is which. Getting it right is critical, at least if you're an author, teacher, or supervisor of others who do this type of work. If close to 100 percent of viewers dislike a certain effect, it is fair to describe it as an error. If, on the other hand, a certain percentage of people like it although you or I do not, then it's just personal preference. We cannot impose our taste on other people—the problem is to know when we are inadvertently doing so. All of us have blind spots where we cannot imagine that somebody else may see merit in a certain version, whereupon we condemn it for being "wrong" when in fact it is a matter of opinion.

I make this mistake occasionally, but not as often as other people. I have taught hundreds of three-day, small-group classes. Every student works on the same image and then the results are compared and discussed. I have participated in about 10,000 such group discussions—every class features more than 20 of them. When I state my own position, I now have an excellent, if still imperfect, idea of when a group is going to agree with it unanimously, and when there will be dissent. If I tell you that a certain result is a mistake that would be overwhelmingly rejected by impartial observers, you should give that statement a bit more than normal credence.

The same applies to claims that a certain image correction is a good one. This is a tough thing to know for sure when the only thing you have to compare it to is the original or another version that you have made yourself. It is easy to assume that something that looks great next to the original is in fact great—until you see someone else's file that is obviously much better.

This problem afflicts me, too; you'll see proof of it at various times. But if I have any doubt, I can assign an image as a classroom exercise and get scores if not hundreds of competing versions from people who are serious about color. Not every image in this book has been so tested by fire, but many have. As to those, if I say that the version being shown is a good one, it doesn't mean that it is perfect or that you couldn't do better yourself. It means that a whole lot of qualified people have tried the same image and the result being shown is competitive with the best of theirs.

Finally, I have a resource that no one else can match: the ability to assemble a group of competent people to represent your interests while this book was being written.

Who Was Behind the Scenes?

The entire book was carefully vetted by a group of beta readers. As with my previous titles, they were chosen from more than 50 volunteers from my appliedcolortheory group, after filling out a questionnaire designed to produce diversity. An enormous amount of work was required of them. It is an amazing honor that so many people volunteered for this difficult duty.

The twelve people I chose said the following about themselves:

- Two are currently professional photographers, two were professional photographers once upon a time, five described themselves as *serious* amateur photographers, and three people said none of the above.
- Eight people described themselves as Photoshop experts.
- Six claimed professional educational experience, Photoshop or otherwise.
- Four said they had professional writing experience.
- Seven said they typically spend half or more of their working time in Photoshop.
- Six said they retouch professionally.
- All twelve had experimented with the PPW panel.
- Eight people claimed a background in the hard sciences.
- Six claimed a background in fine art.
- Seven knew me personally, five did not.
- Seven said that their work normally commences with a file in a raw format.
- Six said that their final file is almost always RGB; three that it is almost always CMYK; three that it might be either.
- Ten completed the full program and have had input on every single page. Four of these hail from the United States, two from Italy, and one each from Australia, Canada, Portugal, and the United Kingdom.

This is the third book I've written with the aid of such beta readers. A Facebook group made this readership step more effective this time around. Chapter drafts went to the group over a period of three months, deadlines were announced, and each member sent me an annotated PDF reaction. In-group discussion of any chapter was prohibited until everyone had submitted these private comments. The readers had access to all original files and sometimes produced their own alternate corrections.

Their feedback defined this book. Every chapter had significant changes and four, plus this Introduction, were so heavily overhauled that the group had to read and comment on a complete second draft.

Naturally, the readers liked certain chapters more than others. In fact, the book almost died in its infancy when there was an icy reaction to Chapter 1 and parts of Chapter 2. Fortunately it was a while before the next unpopular chapter turned up.

You will be hearing from many of these readers by name later in this Introduction and throughout the book.

The Images in This Introduction

The beta readers found fault with Chapter 1 for a number of reasons that have been duly addressed. However, they also pointed out a difficulty with the overall concept. I wanted to show a start-to-finish correction as a preview of the workflow. Good idea, but what to choose for the example?

I thought it should be an amateur photo of reasonable quality, of an outdoor scene, where nobody would be likely to complain if the colors came out a bit more intense than they are in nature. Hence, the scene of Emerald Lake that still is the focus of the chapter.

Some readers argued that the original should have been shot by a professional, because this is a book aimed at professionals even if most potential buyers aren't. Others advised choosing a worse original so that the corrected version would seem more impressive. Several, understanding how fast the

Terms and Acronyms

Here is a list of some of the acronyms and specialized nomenclature that appear frequently in this book.

Bigger Hammer: A technique for drastically enhancing highlight and/or shadow contrast. We have it as an action. It is described in Chapter 10.

Channel blending: merging parts of channels to create better contrast, discussed in Chapter 4.

Color Boost: an action that is one of the principal PPW color enhancements. Discussed in Chapter 5.

Color mode preserves detail on layers below it.

CR-CS5 and CR-CS6 are used to differentiate the improved Camera Raw structure introduced in Photoshop CS6 from that of previous versions.

Darken and Darker Color modes prohibit lightening but otherwise behave like Normal mode. Darken works channel by channel, Darker Color overall.

False profile: a way of tricking Photoshop into seeing a lighter image. Uses are shown in Chapter 12.

H-K: An action described in Chapter 13. It downplays dull colors to prevent competition with brighter ones.

H/S: The Hue/Saturation command.

HDR: High Dynamic Range, an amorphous term now used to describe extreme color and contrast effects.

Lighten and Lighter Color modes prevent darkening but otherwise behave like Normal mode. Lighten works channel by channel, Lighter Color overall.

Luminosity mode preserves color on layers below it.

MMM: The Modern Man from Mars action, described in Chapter 6, creates color and contrast variation.

Multiply mode darkens everything except where one of the sources is pure white or pure black.

Overlay mode lightens the target where the overlay is light, and darkens it where the overlay is dark. The power behind the Bigger Hammer.

PPW: The Picture Postcard Workflow.

S/H: The Shadows/Highlights command.

SWAG: A Scientific Wild Ass Guess.

Soft Light mode is a relative of Overlay, used in the Bigger Hammer when shadows are the main target.

USM: Unsharp mask, discussed in Chapter 15.

workflow is, said that explaining each step so thoroughly made it seem as though each correction would take an hour. Still others found fault with the subject of the picture, that there should be people in it, and on and on.

In reply, I noted that so many photographers have kindly handed over their work with permission to use it for educational purposes that I now have about a terabyte's worth of professional shots, and that I doubted that among them could be found a single one that would satisfy this beta group's criteria.

A consensus developed. The group wanted, and got, a Workflow Summary at the end of the book, starting on Page 439. Meanwhile, Chapter 1's format requires close examination of one, and only one, file. Yet one picture cannot summarize the workflow. To compensate, I should, the group opined, add half a dozen "somewhat typical" PPW results here in the Introduction, commenting only about aesthetics and not matters of technique.

Fortunately, I had a good source of somewhat typical originals. In May 2012 I threw a month-long party to celebrate retirement, old age and several other excuses. My wife and I rented a large villa in Tuscany, and invited my best friends from all over the world to come for a week apiece. At the end of the month I had gained ten pounds and ten thousand photos, because all guests let me copy their cards before checking out.

I cut the ten thousand down to about six hundred, which I corrected and distributed. Already you should be able to see the connection. This is the type of work for which the PPW was designed. Quality is important, because the recipients of these files know who processed them and have, harrumph, certain expectations. On the other hand, I'm not getting paid. Yes, I would like to do a good job, but I'll be dipped if I'm going to take more than two days doing it. That implies three minutes an image, on average, and zero local retouching, global changes only.

These pictures featured every type of subject. They were shot by people from twelve different countries. Lighting conditions were anywhere from optimal to abysmal. Skill level ranged from some of the best photographers in the world, to retouchers who are great at processing photos but poor at exposing them, to personal friends who wouldn't know an SLR from an SUV because they have no connection to the graphic arts.

Accordingly, I drafted this Introduction with the six pairs of images you're about to see. As usual, it went out for group comment, and as usual, certain infelicities of style, substance, and organization were found and zapped. Then the fun began.

The annotated files that came back generally dealt with text matters. Some readers, however, also commented about the images. It wasn't a big enough sampling to prove much, but it was clear that the group agreed on certain things and not on others. A light bulb went off in my head.

I noted earlier that specialized experience lets me predict response to a given version rather more accurately than the average bear. Being able to gauge how people will judge our work is critical to our success. If a person disagrees with us we need to know whether it is simply because tastes differ or because we have made some kind of mistake.

So, I said to myself, here is a rare opportunity. The group is chosen because it cares deeply about image quality, but also for its diversity. Members are technically qualified to comment; as a group they are more representative than would be, say, any organization of professional photographers or of retouchers.

The readers were enthusiastic about the idea of sharing their views on the images with you. I therefore asked each of them to prepare a memo about every one of these six corrections, trying to talk about overall impression, specifics of what made the execution good or bad, and what it said for or against the workflow. I also asked them to predict whether the rest of the group would agree with them. Several people went further and made their own versions of the images, as I had given them access to the originals.

I incorporated their views into an expanded second draft, which the group reviewed again. I am sorry to add so many pages to an Introduction, but I think their comments make fascinating and instructive reading and hope you feel the same way.

The Past, the Present and the Future

At the turn of the millennium, I wrote a long magazine column about graphic arts history. I said that the twentieth century was an excellent one for the advancement of imaging knowledge but that it had to take second place to the fabulous fifteenth, when Leonardo, Botticelli, and similar luminaries were showing the rest of the world how it was done, all without the benefit of Photoshop.

I'd now say that progress in the last quarter-century beats anything at any time in the past. Knowledge has exploded and the number of people who possess it has increased astronomically. In my classes, images that were too difficult even for experts five years ago are now cannon fodder for intermediate users—you'll see some proof of that statement later in the book.

Evolution is natural for the PPW and any other novel workflow. About three years ago, I recorded three PPW videos for my friends at Kelby Training. They're still available and still popular. There was no PPW panel back then and I wasn't using actions, but the content regarding initial color correction in the first installment would be almost unchanged today. The second video, contrast enhancement, is still basically correct but I have since added several refinements. The third, on finalizing color, was effective enough in its day but the techniques shown in Chapters 5 and 6 of this book make most of it obsolete.

Three of the six corrections shown in this Introduction would not have been possible with the PPW of three years ago. One wasn't even possible before writing this book; I know, because I was dissatisfied with my results on a certain category of images, decided that a new technique was in order, and found one with experimentation.

When files for the following examples arrived in a raw format, what is shown as the original was acquired using the defaults of the version of Camera Raw introduced with Photoshop CS6, except for one case in which highlights were enhanced. Otherwise the original came as a JPEG. The show is about to start. I suggest that you grab a piece of paper, go through the six before reading about them, write down your thoughts, then compare them to the group reaction.

I–1 Yellow Flowers in Tuscan Field

From the First Draft of This Introduction: The PPW specializes in this type of image. The yellow flowers should be brilliant. The technical problem is that the greenery has a big yellow component, too. Brightening the flowers may make it hard to avoid overwhelming the viewer with vivacity. The enhancement techniques shown in Chapter 5 and 6 handle this gracefully. Meanwhile, there is realistic detail throughout, and an action shown in Chapter 8 has deepened the sky.

- *The Beta Readers* thought on the whole that this was the most successful correction of the six, and correctly anticipated that there would be broad agreement.

John Jacobs: "This has the 'wow' factor that is so indicative of the PPW. The sky, distant hills, and yellow field are beautifully rendered. The vineyards are aggressive in the separation of detail and if it was not being used as a postcard, could be easily brought back a bit by use of a slider."

Alessandro Bernardi: "Detail is everywhere and looks natural without any excess of local contrast. Also what I like very much is the way you have differentiated the yellow flowers from the greenery, but above all the way you have kept all the subtle colors in the sky while retaining the shape. If I have to find a defect probably I would like to see the ground just a little bit warmer with slightly more yellow."

Marco Olivotto: "I know from experience that this kind of photograph can be a serious problem: introducing variation and shape in the yellow area is very difficult with traditional methods, and sometimes hopeless unless one is very good at dealing with local contrast, or willing to try out exotic blends. This is, to me, the perfect example of what PPW can do."

- *The Aftermath.* No photo is ever considered perfect by every viewer. Some would have liked this picture a bit less colorful. Others wanted even more, looking for the effect now often described as HDR.

These are valid desires but not valid criticisms of the method. The PPW has a step that deliberately introduces excessive color. At one point, all six example images were much more colorful than shown on these pages. The user (that's me) had to make a judgment as to how far to back off this wild color, and whether to do so uniformly or in a way that emphasized certain things.

Taking color out is contrary to traditional practice, which is to force extra color in until satisfied. The PPW method is more manageable, when you think about it. More importantly, if you believe that any of these pictures are too colorful, or not colorful enough, all it means is that you would have made a different decision than I did when the time came to back off. No extra step would have been required. You would have had the result you like in the same amount of time.

I'm giving you the technique to get where you want to go, not trying to force my own personal views of how much of it to use down your throat.

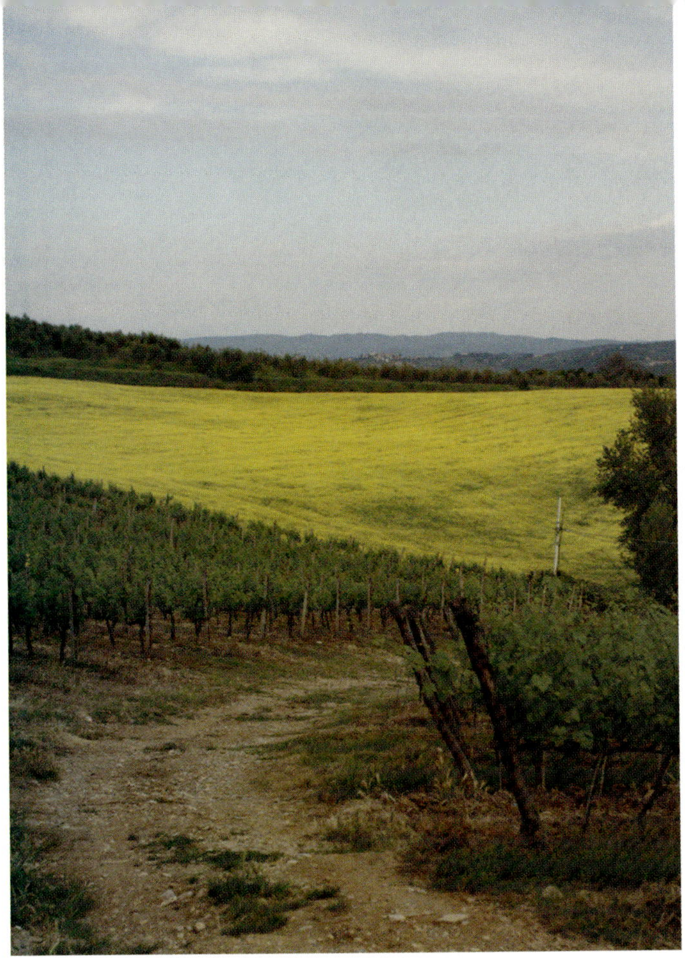

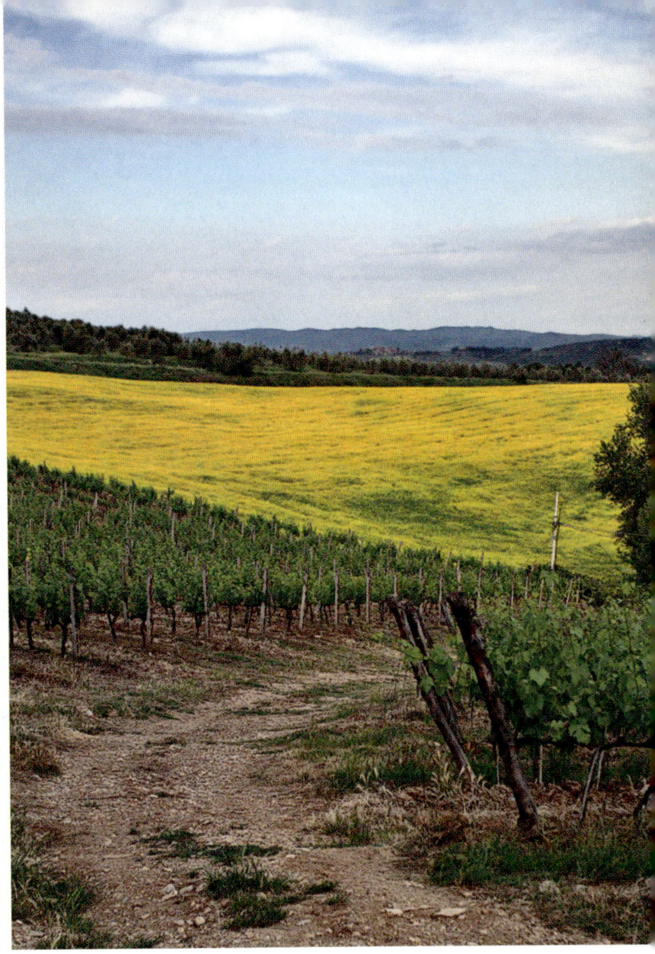

***Postcard I–1** The Picture Postcard Workflow in action. All six photos shown in this Introduction were produced quickly, with no selections or hand retouching. The originals (or reasonable acquisitions from a raw module) come from people of widely varying skill levels; all were taken in Tuscany in May 2012. Here, the problem is how to suggest the brilliance of the yellow flowers without making the entire image too colorful. This sort of thing is covered in Chapters 5 and 6. Also, the sky was enhanced using methods discussed in Chapter 8.*

I–2 Florence Street Scene, With Duomo

From the First Draft: Here the key interest area dates from that fabulous fifteenth century. Unlike the yellow flowers that were the most important part of Postcard I–1, Brunelleschi's dome can only absorb so much color. On the other hand, unless small objects such as the street signs, clothing, and flags are colorful, the photo may resemble a black and white. The key step in arranging this was an action described in Chapter 13, aimed at suppressing duller color.

• *The Readers* thought this one was as successful technically as the first, but the opinion was hidden by a barrage of commentary about what we ought to try to achieve and indeed whether this photo should even have been shot. Or whether all of it should print.

James Gray: "An absolutely amazing improvement in a mediocre image. It reminds me of the problem with many of my travel images. I do like the sky in the original better than in the post processed image. I think that the color in the sky and building is a skosh too green. I think that all will agree that the postcard is a vast improvement over the original. I would have liked to see more contrast in the dome. I would have cropped most of the people out of the bottom."

The flowery field was a scene that must be taken in its entirety. This one is not; it has one object that is far more important than the rest of the picture. The same is true in many product shots. Postcard I–6, which showcases a beefsteak, is another example.

When confronted with a picture falling

into this category, skilled people are reluctant to add too much color or other activity elsewhere, fearing that they may distract from the object the viewer should be focusing on. Unsurprisingly, some readers complained that I had made the street too busy—too much contrast, too much color.

These complaints state a good general rule. According to me, however, that general rule needs an exception here. The huge cathedral so dominates the photo that *nothing* can distract from it. Putting the activity in the foreground just makes the scene more real.

- *The Aftermath.* As indicated at the outset, this book assumes that each photo has already been taken and that we have been asked to work on it. If the photo is technically sound and artistically meritorious, so much the better. Neither factor, however, has an impact on what we have to do. So I could just dismiss as irrelevant the comments on whether this photo is worth working on. I will cast a vote nevertheless.

Brunelleschi's dome is one of the most photographed objects in the world. Pictures of it in isolation are a dime a dozen. Showing its great beauty is not a problem. Its architectural merit is plain to those who understand such things. But the dome is also known for its enormity. That such a monster could be built more than half a millennium ago is hard to believe. Most photographs can't capture its scale. Distant shots can do it, but tend to make the rest of the area look like a kind of Disneyland. This photo puts the size in the context of a major city.

I therefore disagree with many group members about the merits of the original. I share the views of Frederick Yocum: "The flatness of the original has disappeared. The stronger colors separate the foreground from the bulky muted presence of the Duomo and turn what could have been a snapshot into a statement about the omnipresence of the church in the landscape of Florence."

I–3 In a Darkened Restaurant

From the First Draft: Now comes a series of three with lighting problems. Postcard I–3, shot in a dark restaurant, starts with an awful cast and no detail in the faces. The PPW has little difficulty with the excessive darkness, but the cast reduction is nasty in any workflow. After seeing a lot of these sorts of images from this trip, I came up with a new method, discussed in Chapter 9. And speaking of new techniques, it is fitting to have a picture of beta reader Adriano Esteves, shown here with his wife Catarina Morgado. Adriano developed an important modification of the MMM action shown in Chapter 6. His contribution is now an option within the PPW panel.

- *The Readers' View* was summarized by James Gray: "I think that if I were Adriano or Catarina I would not like the image even after it is processed. I do not yet grasp the advanced techniques that I assume you used. The postcard is a big improvement over the original and does create a distinct separation of the people from the background. However, I do not like the color variation in Catarina's face. The redness in her cheeks and nose is too much. It seems that most of the improvement in the image is in the background and not in the faces. I think there is too much variation in the color of Adriano's face as well. His chin and neck seem to have a green cast while his right ear looks too red."

Everyone agreed. The redness was described by one reader as "not flattering" to Catarina and by two less diplomatic ones as making her look drunk.

Marco Olivotto brought up another point: "The woman's skin seems too pink, which suggests a cold environment; but the man's T-shirt says it can't be cold, so I'd err a bit on the warmer side. The walls are portrayed as very neutral, and I wouldn't be 100% sure about this—what can be seen of the mirror and shelf suggests not a very modern place, so a hint of yellow may be appropriate."

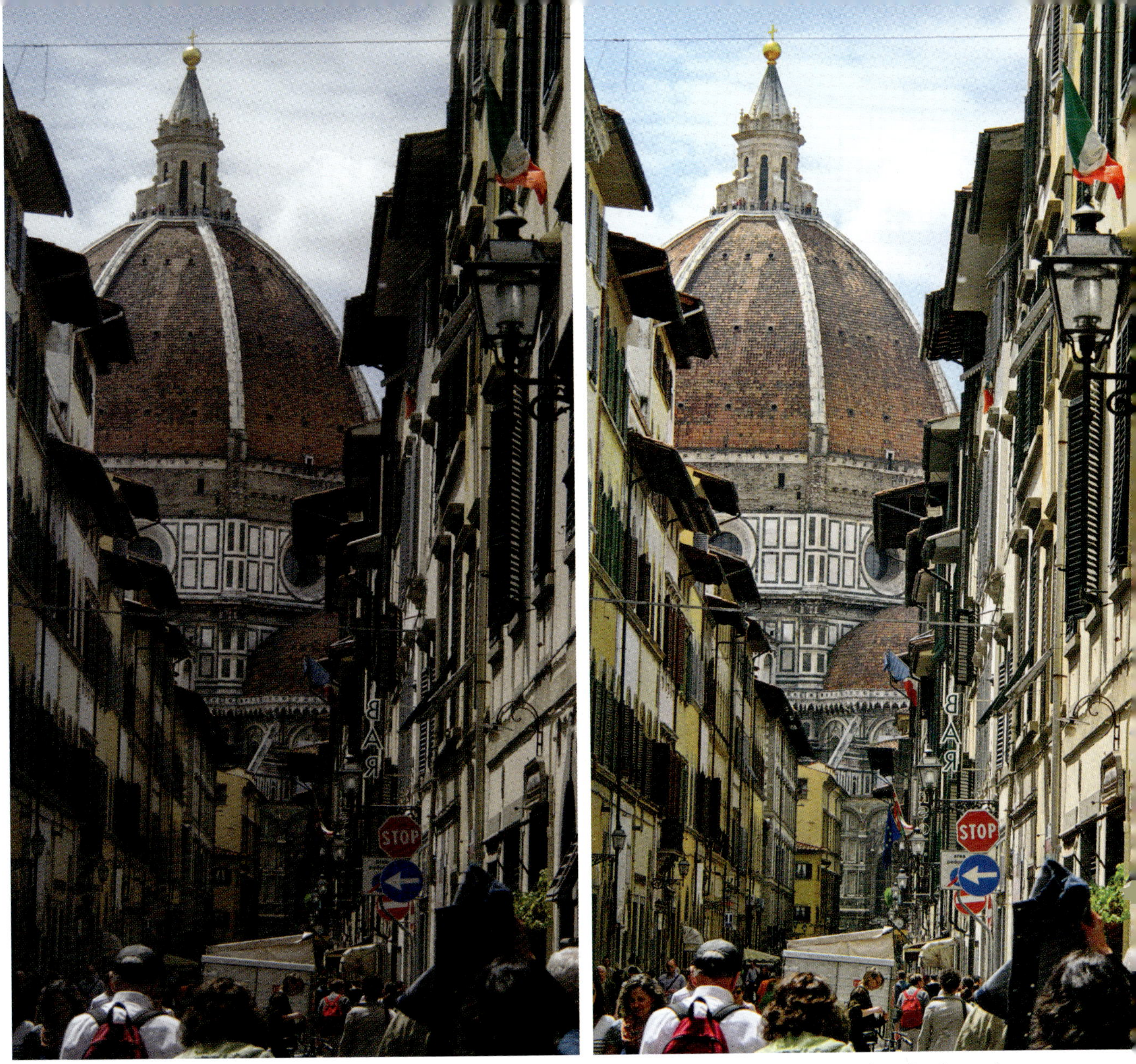

***Postcard I–2** The foreground needs to be lightened here, using techniques shown in Chapter 12. Also, the dome dates from the fifteenth century, so there is a limit to how much color it can take. But without the brightly colored objects in the street the picture looks dead. Chapter 13 describes a method that discriminates against duller colors, keeping them subdued so as to emphasize purer ones.*

Others criticized leaving the reflection on Adriano's head, but this is not fair because local retouching was prohibited by the rules of engagement.

Those predicting the outcome correctly foresaw that this would be the least popular of the six. That may not be fair either. Two people reported trying this image out for themselves, without success with the lighting issue. Adriano himself said, "This photo is one of the difficult category where the original is very weak but we must do the best we can with it because for some reason it's important. And I fail miserably, so this is a good exercise to include in the book—it represents reality in that we all handle photos like it."

In other words, these readers trashed my effort even though I did better with this picture than they could. Life is full of injustices—and lessons.

- *The Aftermath.* Recall how some thought that the flowery scene of Postcard I–1 was too colorful, but others did not, and still others thought it was not colorful enough. These differing opinions justify use of the phrase *a matter of taste.*

In this picture, however, nobody likes the redness in Adriano's ear or Catarina's cheeks. I don't like it either, now that attention has been called to it. That means it cannot be described as a matter of taste. The appropriate term is *an error.* How it came about has ramifications that go well beyond imaging.

Errors are inevitable during every phase of graphic arts work. Hopefully they get caught and corrected before the client or whoever the final judge is sees them. Therefore, in every area of our discipline there is some form of inspection. Sometimes that inspector is us, as when we check a final image to make sure that highlight and shadow are correct. There can also be a person whose main job is catching errors: a proofreader, a plate inspector, or the like.

Supervising this inspection process in large companies was an important part of my prepress work for many years. I was successful in reducing the error rate, but never to zero. When the company did release work containing an error, I would investigate why it happened. Often I felt that it was not so much the inspector's fault as that of people earlier in the process who failed to take actions that would have made a subsequent error almost impossible.

When the error *was* totally the fault of the inspector, though, I detected a disturbing pattern that I should have remembered when working on this picture, and that you should take to heart.

In a surprisingly high number of cases where the inspectors let an error through, they had already detected a major snafu.

You have to be sympathetic. I certainly was. Here were these people who had just saved themselves and the company a peck of trouble by finding and fixing a terrible error. Is it any wonder that they felt good enough about it to cause their attention to lag?

I have repeated over and over, to employee after employee, and now to you, that when you have found and fixed one big problem, pay extra attention, because you are more likely than ever to overlook another—such as obviously excessive fleshtone variation.

In this particular image the elimination of the cast and introduction of shape in the faces justified my feeling pleased—but not turning off normal evaluation processes. *If this had been an easier original, no way would I have missed the problem in the faces.*

On a happier note, I can report that Catarina was *not* drinking on this occasion, for the best of reasons. A few months later, she and Adriano celebrated the birth of their first child, Matilde, to whom we all wish a long life of many highlights and few shadows.

I–4 Dining al Fresco

From the First Draft: On to a different restaurant, with faces deeply in shadow. Previous iterations of the PPW could handle this situation fairly well, but a new feature of the panel made for a dramatic improvement. Chapter 10 has an action called the Bigger Hammer, used for pictures in desperate need of highlight and/or shadow detail. Postcard I–4 seems a questionable candidate, and in fact the action's defaults do poorly with it. Investigating alternative ways to use the action used to take too much time. Now, however, the panel allows quick previews of different Bigger Hammer settings, and I found one that I thought worked well.

• *The Readers' Response:* "This will be the most controversial of the six," predicted Adriano. "Some will love it, some hate it." He incidentally, identified himself as one of those who loved it, citing its "alien HDR look", which I am not certain is a compliment.

His prediction did not come true. There were no extreme views. The main area of

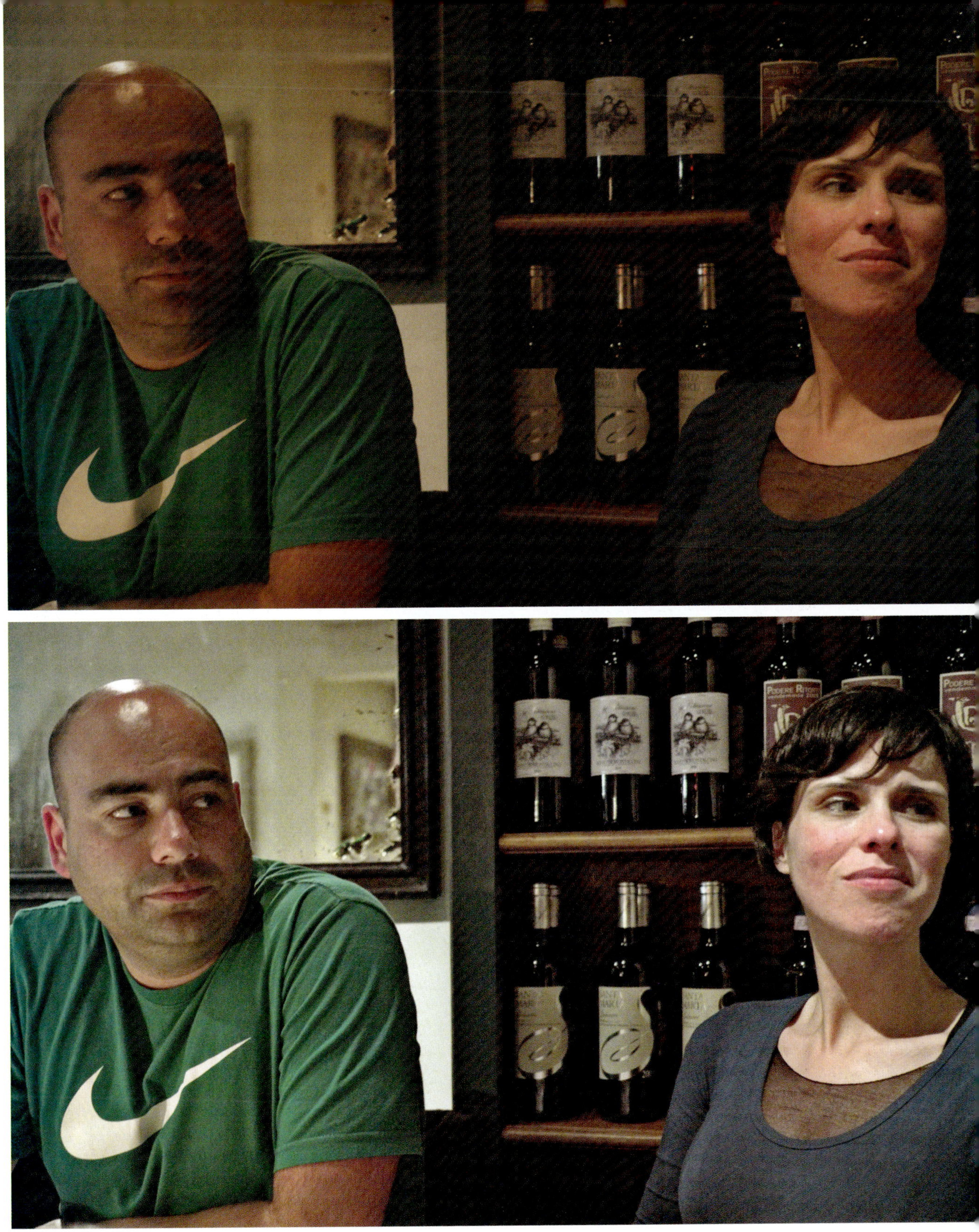

Postcard I–3 *An evening in a Florence restaurant with dim lighting. The resulting orange cast is difficult to manage with traditional methods. A technique shown in Chapter 9 uses the complementary color to minimize the cast and create more distinct separation of the people from the background.*

agreement was that this sort of picture happens more often than many think and so having an example of it is useful. Mike Demyan: "Typical snapshot taken from 'inside to outside'. The camera exposes for the 'outside' and underexposes the 'inside' people. Good exercise for fixing this type of shot."

Some liked my neutral-to-pink skintones; others wanted them yellower. The most common comment, as always, dealt with how far to take the PPW effect.

John Jacobs: "This is the most severe change from the original of any of the six. Standing alone, it would be a good holiday shot, capturing the mood and moment. Overall, it is too bright and I believe the average viewer would be fine with the whole image darker. This would help make sense of the roof over the subjects and give more of an impression of inside-outside."

Frederick Yocum: "Often when photographing people, we don't get to pick the best moment. This leaves us with only bad choices. Lose the background or leave the foreground murky? The final photograph has an embarrassment of riches when it comes to detail. It feels a little overprocessed with no place for the eye to rest, but there is a lot of animation in the subject and it all seems to work together."

And now a couple of comments that bear on the workflow itself.

Russ Brown: "I have to admit to still not being a big fan of the workflow for people pictures, however Postcards I–3 and I–4 do demonstrate that a big improvement as well as an acceptable result is obtainable easily by using the workflow. A similar and perhaps better result would be achieveable in other ways but would probably take much more time, effort and skill."

John Pavel: "Fine as snapshot for personal use. Processed version a definite improvement. Faces are very slightly on the sculpted side of realistic."

The "sculpted" look that John describes is a common result of this workflow and can be avoided if need be. For example, if this had been a picture of two women rather than two men I would likely not have used this effect, preferring smoother faces.

• *The Aftermath.* I don't agree with Russ that traditional techniques would get something equivalent here, with or without additional time. I think they'd be more likely to be competitive on the next image, Postcard I–5. Other than that, nothing about these comments surprised me. Mike submitted an alternate version that I liked better than mine. The basic difference was that he had the faces slightly darker than I did. The neutrality of my faces suggests the shadow from whence they came. If I left them so light I should have added a more golden fleshtone. Or I could have taken Mike's approach and kept my own color without lightening so much.

I–5 Sunlight and Shadow in Siena

From the First Draft: Taken with a fisheye in the streets of Siena, this one is an even more extreme sun-and-shade exercise. Chapter 12 shows how to handle this kind of image.

• *The Readers* liked it almost as well as the flowery fields of Postcard I–1. Russ Brown: "This alleyway is, I think, the best of the six. This really shows how a picture which might otherwise be discarded as unfixable can be turned into a dramatic and interesting shot."

Agreeing, Adriano Esteves: "My favorite before/after of the entire Introduction. Detail, color, highlight recovery, good photo. Who the hell turned on the lights?"

James Gray adds, "This is an awesome improvement. It is really a great demonstration of what can be done using the techniques of Chapter 12. The effect is almost magical. How can anyone not love it? A skosh more color might have been even better. I assume everyone will agree about this one."

Those finding fault generally said I had

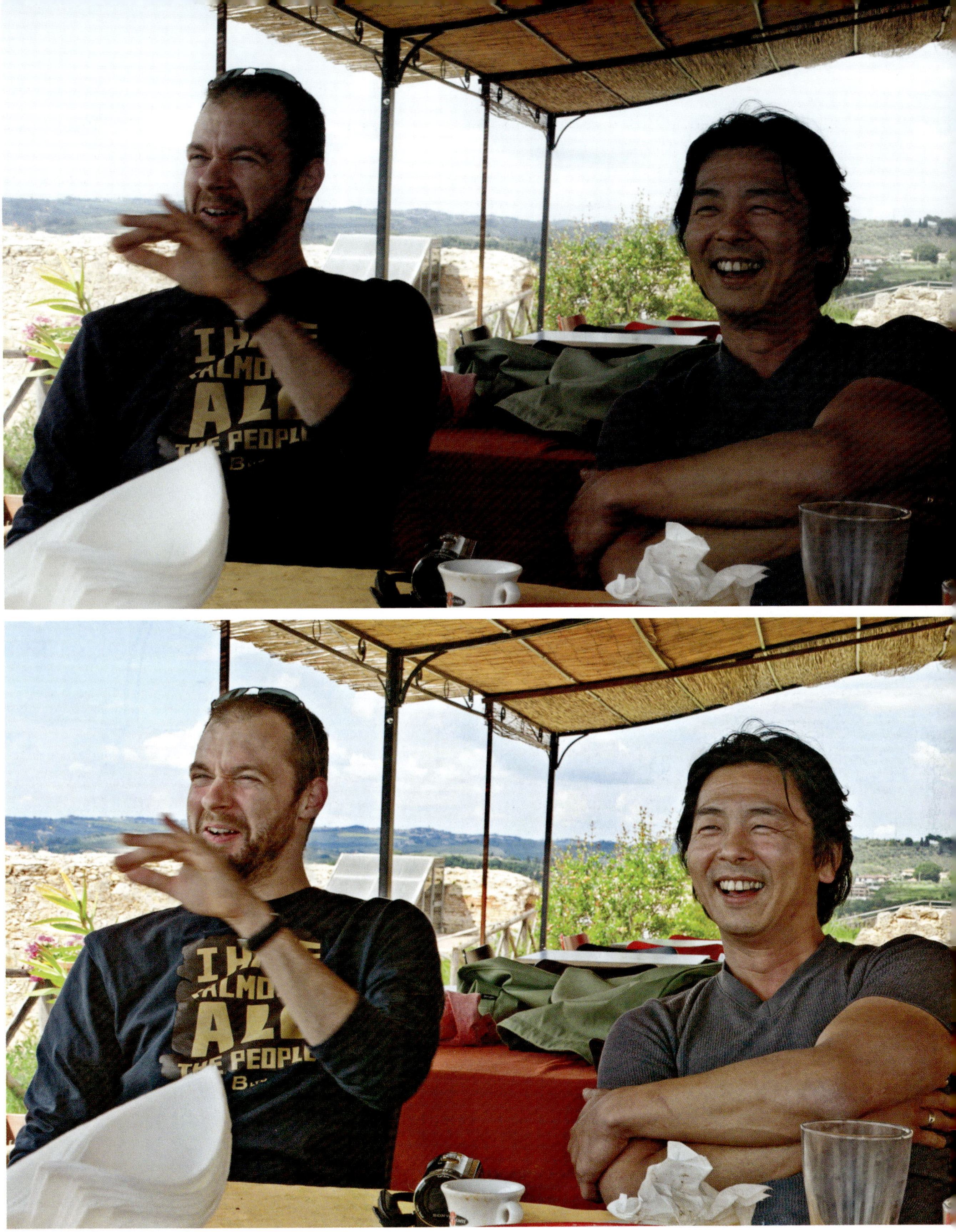

Postcard I–4 *The al fresco meal is an Italian custom. The subjects are squinting in the sunlight, but the canopy has put the faces in shadow. The Bigger Hammer action introduced in Chapter 10 corrects the lighting.*

gone too far. Taking the opposite view, Alessandro Bernardi joined James in saying it should be *more* colorful. He also suggested moving the whole picture toward yellow.

Representing the hard-bitten prepress specialist, Clarence Maslowski rained on the parade. As might be expected, he assigned more of the blame to the photographer than to me, saying, "This image comes up a little short. It is my considered opinion that any photographer should expose for the highlights and let me worry about the shadow end of things. I can fix 'em. This image could have been infinitely superior if there were better detail in the sunlit area at the base of the stairs. This image does show the power of the PPW technique. And we can see the interior of the alleyway. I do think you went just a little too far in lightening the darker tones. You quoted Ansel Adams in Chapter 15: *I believe there is nothing more disturbing than a sharp image of a fuzzy concept.* Is this validation? I would think that the professionals on our team would agree with me."

- *The Aftermath.* This is actually the easiest of the six exercises, which is why some of the opinions weren't as enthusiastic as they were about the more difficult Postcard I–1.

Many PPW techniques are more effective when the photo isn't as gray and monotonous as this one. Two readers, understanding this, prepared versions in Camera Raw and Lightroom, respectively. 2012 additions to these modules make it possible to get similar contrast effects to what's shown in this particular image, although previous releases could not. The remaining PPW advantage on this picture is color variation.

I–6 The Controversy: Where's the Beef?

From the First Draft: Finally, back to normal lighting for one of the great meals of the world, bistecca fiorentina. This thick cut is always served rare. Ask for it cooked medium and the chef is likely to refuse and say something in Italian that you are better off not understanding. Menus often have a snooty line stating that they will not prepare the meat any other way and if you don't like it, order something else. This note is in English, of course, no need to inform the Italians. Anyway, the added depth and color variation underscores the PPW's suitability for food shots.

- *The Readers* went ballistic. You may wish to duck before reading their exchanges, as the crossfire is rather intense.

John Jacobs: "Great! Love it! Especially the life that comes from the improved color and texture. The best correction of the six."

Marco Olivotto: "On a scale of one to five, this is a one. If you point a gun at the head of an Italian and tell him to choose one of these two, I could foresee 95% of the votes going to the original. The final version is amazing, but it would look inedible to many people."

Shall we try another pair? Mike Demyan: "Good food photo example. Your correction shows how to bring out the 'taste' of the entree. Makes my mouth water—mmmm!"

Alessandro Bernardi: "I don't think that anyone would like to eat something like this. If you show your version to the chef, I suspect he will try to kill you. It's clear that the steak has a cold cast that must be corrected, but in the final version the color of the cooked part of the meat is too grayish, while the bloody areas are too magenta, purple, compared to the cooked ones."

The rest of the group divided evenly between those enthusiastic about the correction and those finding it slightly too colorful—though not the wrong color. Those predicting group response said they expected a near unanimous favorable rating. I'd have predicted that myself.

- *The Aftermath.* What you just read is why I asked every group member to comment on each image. When I sent out the request, I tried to avoid biasing anyone. All I said was that the comments so far indicated that the

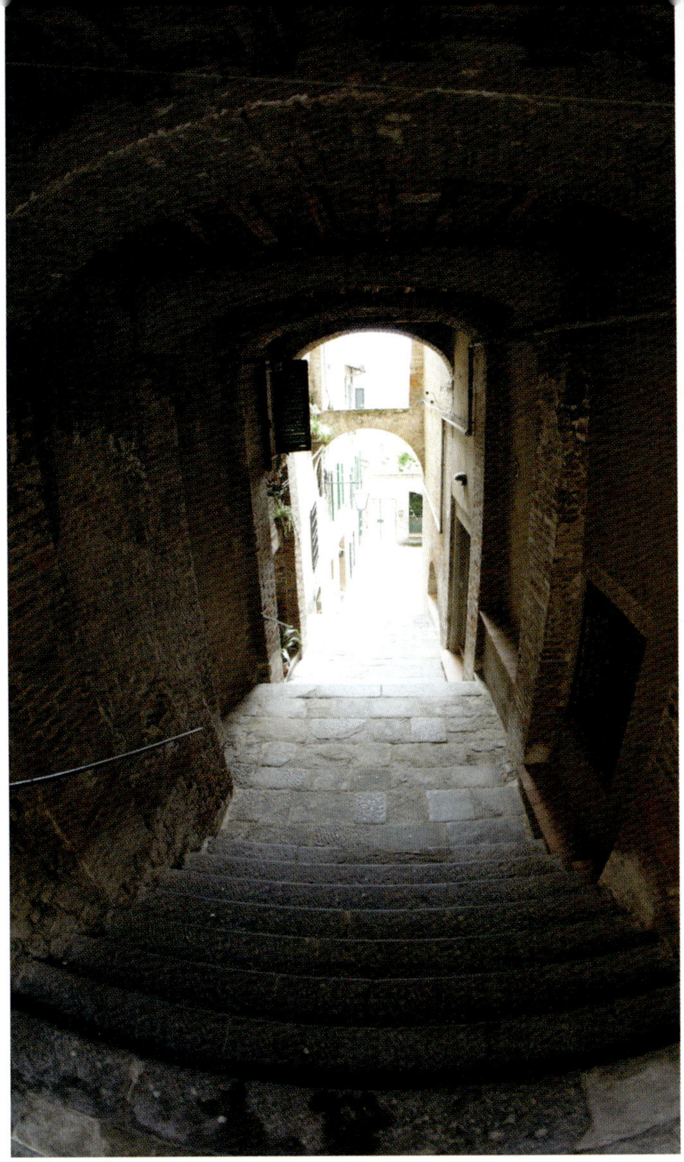

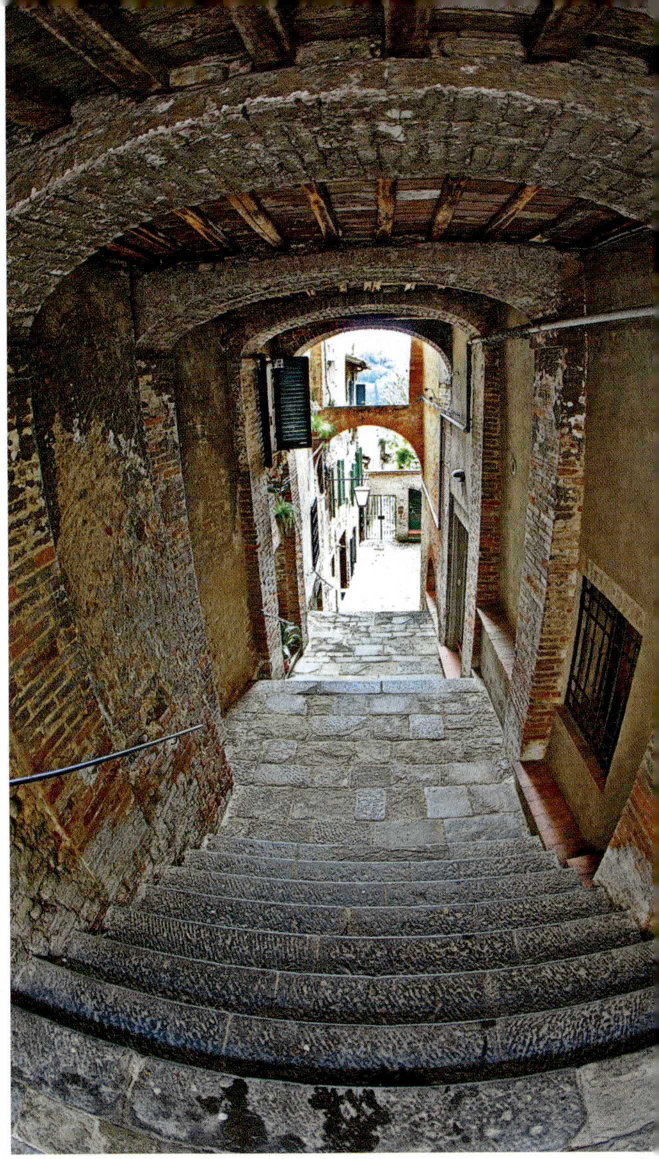

***Postcard I–5** An alleyway in Siena shows a common photographic hazard in regions with strong sunlight: the dark parts are plugged, the light ones almost blown out. Techniques shown in Chapter 12 bring the two halves closer together.*

group saw eye to eye in some cases and not in others, and that a certain result was considered the best of the six by some and the worst by others. But I did not reveal which it was.

My coyness did not fool Marco. Not only did he realize what image I was likely referring to, he made an astounding, but correct prediction: he said that Italians would hate the picture and everyone else would like it. Here's part of his reasoning:

"To me, this is a cultural problem...we have some very colorful mosaics in Italy, some dating back more than a thousand years, but the most vivid of them are tame with respect to what you may find, say, in India. Same goes for food: my feeling is that there is a more aggressive idea of what the food should look like in America than in the Mediterranean area. Your version is not objectionable on the technical side, but my feeling is that it would fall flat, aesthetically, in my country. If McDonald's decided to include florentine steaks in their menu, so be it—but this is not how a luxury recipe book in Italy would wish to depict the steak."

There is likely some truth in the explanation, but a general Italian preference for subdued color is belied by previous comments. Marco and Alessandro themselves strongly endorsed the very colorful flowers of Postcard

I–1. And in the Siena scene of Postcard I–5, Alessandro was one of only two readers to say that my version was not colorful enough.

Food, however, appears to be different. My view is that Italians are more fanatical about their food than just about anybody—as witness the irate refusal to cook meat to any other than the Correct degree of doneness.

The violent negative reaction shows how quickly our work can backfire if we provide unacceptable color. Note this does not mean *too much* color—that can always be adjusted. Marco and Alessandro may believe that there is too much color here but they also say it is the *wrong* color. Alessandro explains:

"In food work it's commonly accepted that a warm cast makes everything more inviting, especially if we talk about meat. Google "bistecca fiorentina" and you'll get a lot of images. The best ones will be more or less always the same: reddish in the bloody areas, not purple, while featuring a yellow or warm cast in the meat. So I'd suggest to add some warmth to the image, otherwise it looks unreal or unattractive."

Memory plays a critical role, and memories are sometimes biased. I have eaten a lot of bistecca fiorentina in my time. Postcard I–6 represents my memory of what it looks like, since I had not imported a steak and a Tuscan chef and kitchen to look at while I worked. Then again, as Alessandro never tires of reminding me, I am not Italian. My memory of the color is influenced by American preconceptions of what rare beef looks like. Is he right that in reality it's more red, or even orange? Possibly so, but that's not how I recall it.

Also, you shouldn't take Marco's rhetoric too literally. Nobody is holding a gun to anybody's head. We don't have to choose one or another. Creating something that strikes people as being over-the-top is an occupational hazard of the PPW. The solution is to have a conservative version available. The original image qualifies. It's not exciting, but it's reasonable. It can be blended with my version in many different ways, and the degree of blending is up to the individual. I believe Marco when he says that some people might prefer the original to the corrected version, but I would not believe anyone who said that they would prefer the original to a new version that had a third of mine averaged in.

Frederick Yocum gets the last word. "This exercise is not about rescue. If you saw the original you would be satisfied. It is in focus, well lit and adequately records a beautiful plate of food. The corrected version does not sacrifice any part of the original, just gives us more. Is it too much? It depends on how hungry you are."

* * *

I hope the extended discussion of these six images has been enlightening about what makes people like pictures, and especially how to distinguish matters of taste from outright errors. And even though little technique or procedure was discussed, I hope you get the idea of what the PPW does—that it offers a very quick way to produce striking imagery, with the flexibility to decide how colorful an image you want.

I trust, also, that you grasp why this book is different from others on similar topics. For one thing, it's wide-ranging. In principle it's about a specific workflow but you may find that the most valuable sections have nothing to do with it and are concepts only.

Moreover, a committed group of highly qualified beta readers changes everything. This extended Introduction would never have happened without their discussions. They had a clear feeling that something like this was necessary. Was this the best way to

***Postcard I–6** (opposite) One of the world's great dishes, the Florentine beefsteak, is always served rare. The redness is therefore correct, at least in the opinion of some. Methods of enhancing contrast in the meat and the darker bone are discussed in Chapters 4 and 7.*

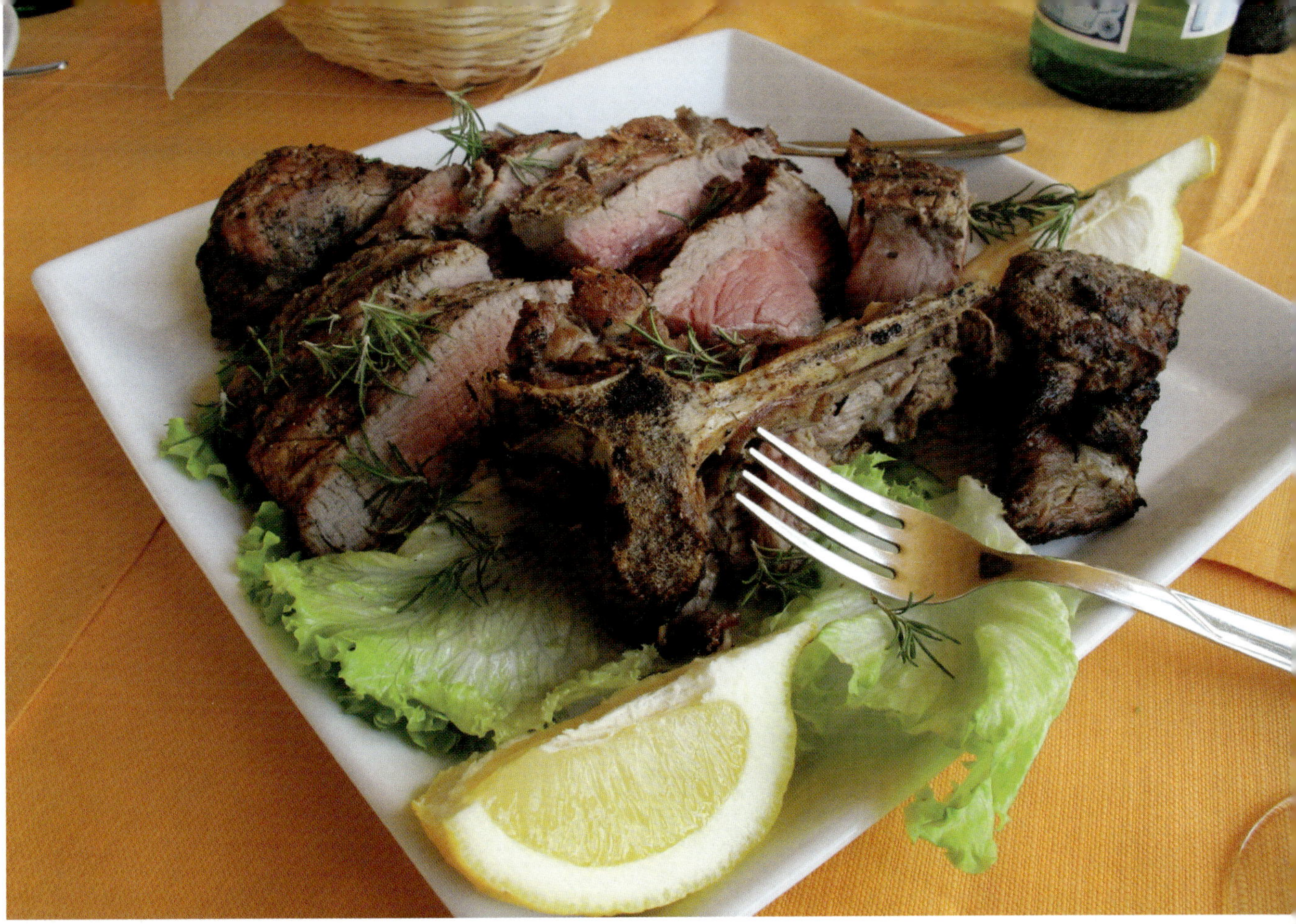

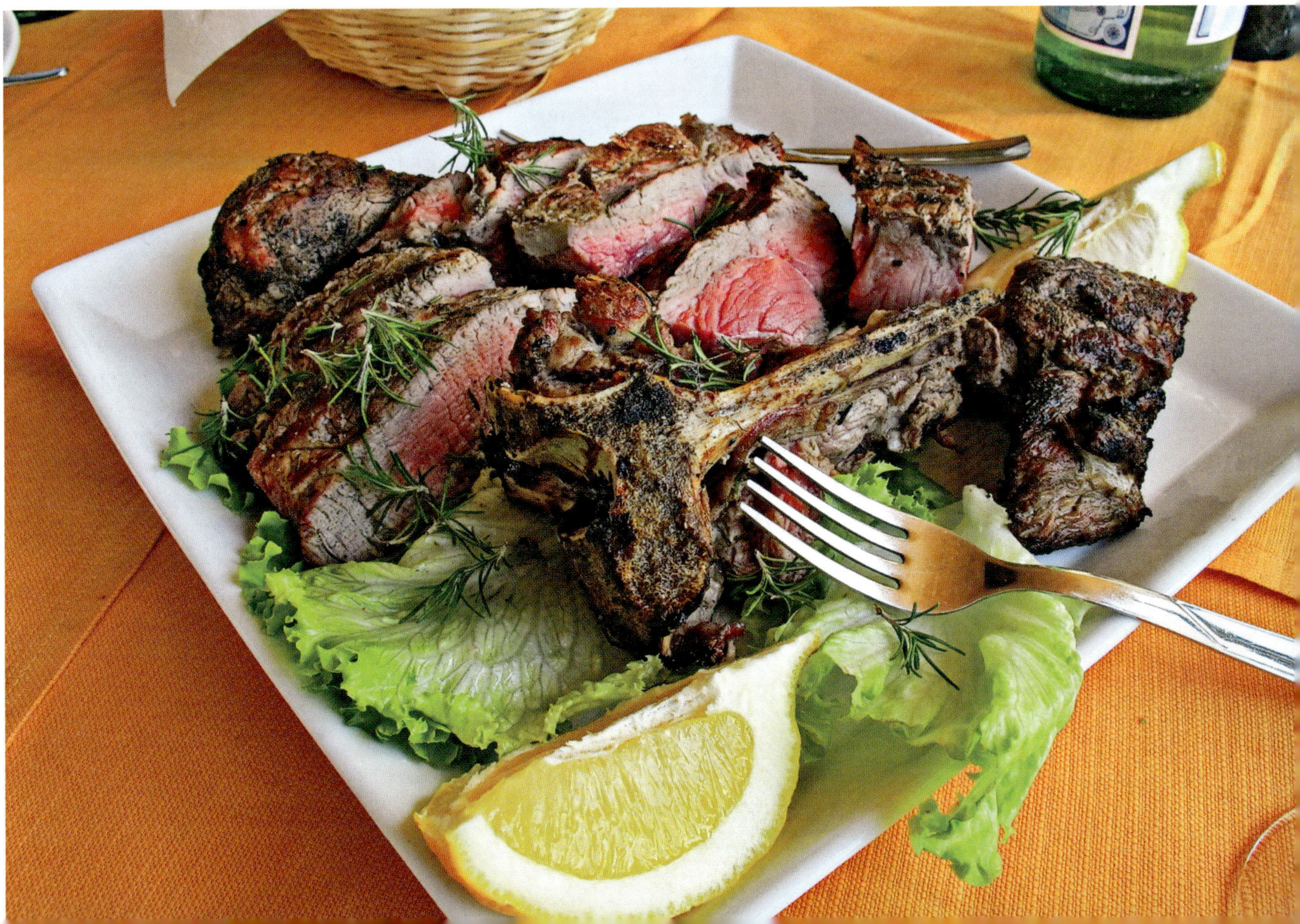

implement it? I don't know, but I know that without these readers, there would be nothing of the kind here.

Finally, I hope you can now visualize both the frustrations and the accessibility of this book. Parts are highly technical, difficult even for expert retouchers. On the other hand, certain extended discussions are quite challenging but don't require any particular background. In reviewing this Introduction I can't find any reason why a reader would even need to know how to launch Photoshop to understand what's being said—yet some of these concepts would baffle color experts.

Adriano is one of those experts. After completing his read of the entire book, he asked to offer you some extraordinary advice. I'm not sure I agree, but here it is:

"I would add that everyone's first reading of the book should be without Photoshop and computer. I've done this with all Dan's previous books and this one is no exception.

"Every book from Dan has so many layers of information that if you follow in Photoshop you will lose the plot and start concentrating on the process. I've seen several designers in my company starting the books and never finishing because of this.

"So, read it like you don't own Photoshop."

* * *

This, then, is the current state of the Picture Postcard Workflow, including some changes during the course of writing this book. Unless you think that we already know all there is worth knowing, that change will continue.

I bought my first Macintosh 25 years ago. Half a decade later, I was correcting images professionally in Photoshop.

The big advances since then have been related to hardware, not software. We were ignorant back then because there wasn't anyone to teach us. Experimentation was difficult to impossible. To store all the images I worked on to prepare for this book would have required an investment of a quarter of a million dollars or more in hard drives alone. To get all these images into digital form would have required huge expenditures for scanning the film (you remember film, don't you?) Even assuming that I had the money and the inclination, I could only have tested a small fraction because each experiment would have taken fifty times as long.

Hardware has thus driven the accelerating vehicle of knowledge, which in turn has changed our taste. Now that the capability exists to create photos with wildly unrealistic brilliance, many people have decided that they like that look, leaving me somewhat of a centrist. The surrealistic look is known today as HDR; a few years ago the same acronym was used to describe results similar to those shown in this book.

With all this change, one thing has remained the same. We do things the best way we know how given the tools we have to work with. It is entirely appropriate that the most significant tool introduced here, the one that can't be duplicated at all with other methods, depends not on some recently revised raw module, but on a command so ancient that I and every other expert wrote it off as useless in the early 1990s, and which hasn't been heard of since. Read about it in the second half of Chapter 6 if you don't believe me.

Is the idea of separating color and contrast completely, with the improvements we expect to continue, the workflow of the future? I don't know, but would assert that in the year 2013, it is the most reliable and the quickest way to assure top image quality. Time will tell whether I was right.

Modern Photoshop Color Workflow

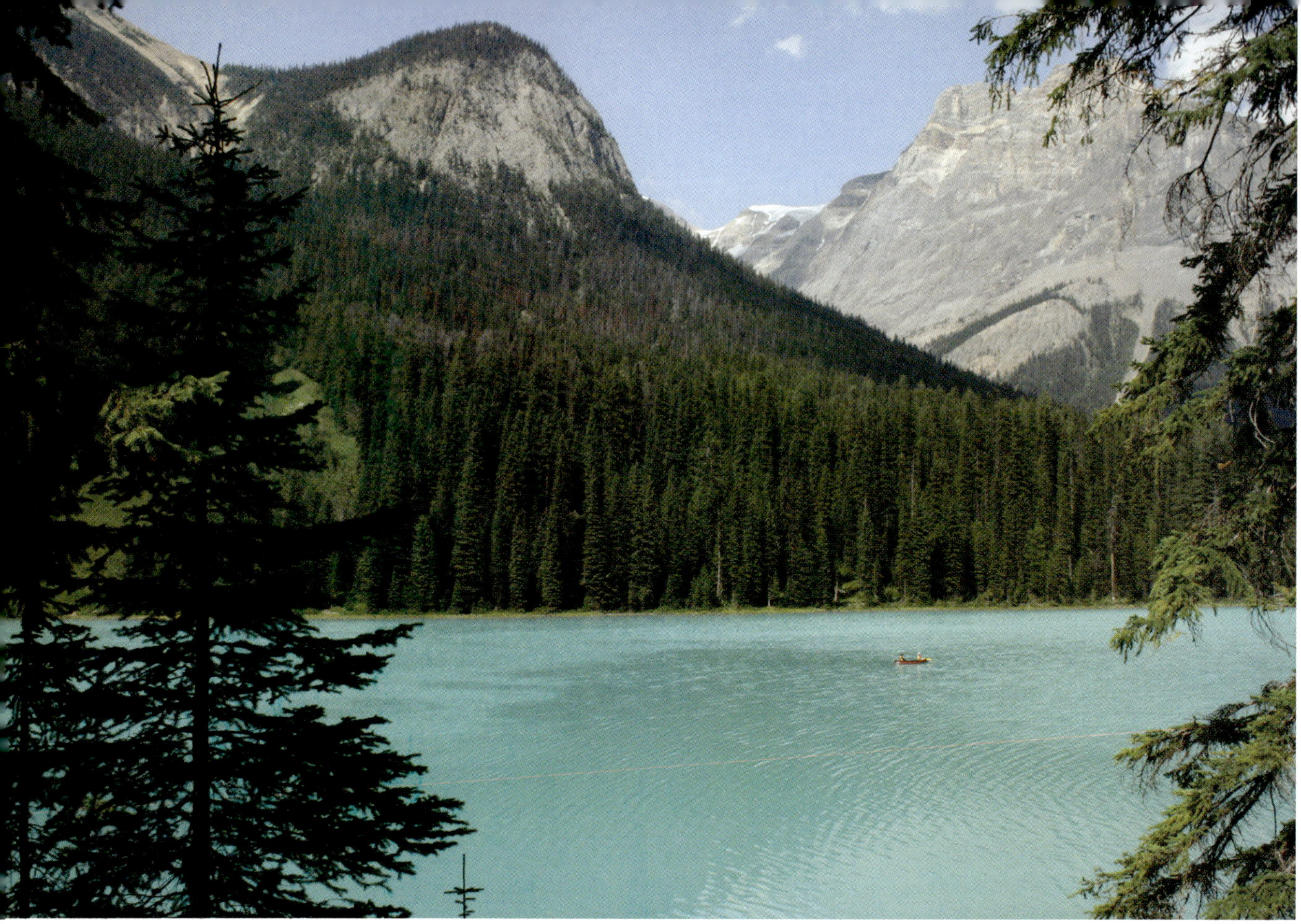

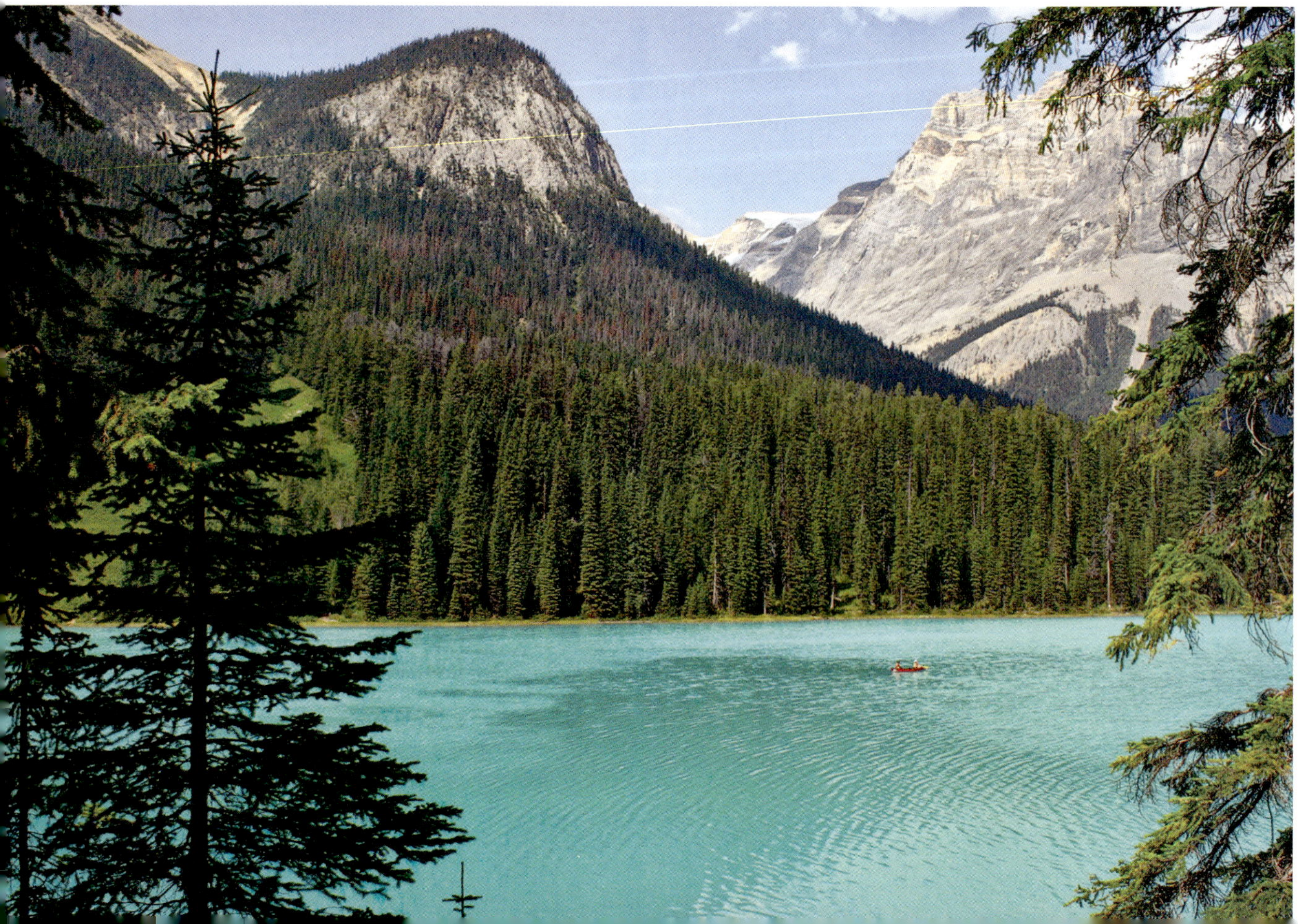

1

A Philosophy and a Preview

The Picture Postcard Workflow consists of several interlocking steps. Three are fundamental, the remainder optional. The journey starts with an overview, discussing what the workflow tries to achieve and why. We follow a single correction from start to finish, under three different assumptions as to how much time is permitted.

The saying is as old as the color industry itself: Price. Speed. Quality. Choose any two.

This book's objective is to disprove the saying, by offering a new and faster color correction workflow that happens to increase quality as well.

Now, down to business. Do you prefer the bottom version of the photograph on the facing page?

If you represent a tourism board, or any other group interested in promoting this region of British Columbia, yes. If you've just been there on vacation and want a little keepsake, yes. If you'd like to send a copy of the picture to your friends to make them envious, yes. Postcard 1.1 showcases depth, definition, and richness—and not necessarily a whole lot of fidelity to what many would call the *real* colors.

But what does *real* mean? Take a copy of this book to Emerald Lake, and you'll find that the original, not the bottom version, is closer to the true color. The glacial sediment found in this water has given it a surrealistic cyan-green hue rarely seen elsewhere. The original portrays water of an unusual color, just as the lake's name suggests.

But is the original what we recall? In real life the lake is the most brilliant object in its immediate vicinity. It's an unexpected color, it seems greener because of the dullness of the background trees, and there are other stimuli, such as the clean pine scent of the forest, and a gaggle of photographers snapping away, awed by the beauty. On the printed page, or on the web, all this context is missing. The lake's color gets compared

***Postcard 1.1** Emerald Lake, British Columbia, Canada, before and after application of the Picture Postcard Workflow.*

not to duller things but to brighter ones. The trees we recall as romantically green are now gray. We find them boring—and unrealistic.

Some History, and an Invitation

I developed the Picture Postcard Workflow, hereinafter PPW, in 2006 for this type of image. There was a clear need for something faster than traditional professional methods, such as the ones I've been writing about for nearly twenty years. The hope was that a disciplined, compressed approach would not lose too much quality as a price for its speed.

Unexpectedly, the quality turned out to be *better.* I keep archives of corrections done by both me and my students, so a comparison of how the new way stacks up to that of past years is possible. The results are convincing: a clear superiority in about a third of images.

Also, I get feedback from those who have adopted this workflow. We know now that it isn't just for postcards. We know that it's easier to learn than traditional methods and easier to operate once mastered. I have never heard of anyone going back to the old way after becoming comfortable with this one.

Think of it from the perspective of the expensive hotel on the lake's shore. For advertising purposes, management would naturally prefer the more intense look of the bottom version.

If the hotel were located on top of a garbage dump instead of in one of the most romantic spots in the world, the objectives would be the same. Greater depth and more vivid colors are appropriate not just for travel pictures but for almost everything we process. The only question is one of degree. Viewers have more tolerance for wild color when the photo is of a landscape than when the subject is a person, or food. If the general look of the corrected Emerald Lake photo can somehow be retained without producing beet-red fleshtones or radioactive vegetables, everybody will be happy.

The rest of the chapter is devoted to correcting this one image. It is meant as an overview of the workflow. In the Introduction to this book I presented six before-and-after images, without explaining anything about the process. This chapter should give an idea about how it was done—it mentions, briefly, all the steps and some of their variants. Of course, it doesn't qualify you to go out and start applying this workflow. If it could do that, there would be no need for the 14 chapters that follow.

If you don't think you need this kind of overview before plunging ahead, you'll get no argument from me. This is the first of many times in this book that I'll point out that a

Support Materials

Resources for this book are available at http://www.moderncolorworkflow.com and at http://www.ledet.com/margulis/ppw.

What will be there in future years is unknown, but a treasure chest is there now. It includes the PPW panel, which installs its own documentation and actions. At present the panel only works in Photoshop CS5 and CS6; if you work with earlier versions you can download the actions and documentation separately.

A series of videos explore various topics or review procedures. They are organized by chapter. Similarly, most of the original images for this book are available (private use only, please) if you wish to try your hand at correcting them yourself.

The site also contains miscellaneous items such as links to my other writings or PDFs of other support materials. For example, early drafts of this book had a couple of lengthy technical sections that the beta readers and I decided were too intense for general consumption, yet of interest to a few, so we've posted those sections.

Everything mentioned above is free. A summary of the things that were planned for posting at press time is at the end of each chapter's summary in the Notes & Credits section, commencing on page 431.

certain part can be skipped. It's a long book, and not exactly bedtime reading. I'll try to help you get through it in the most efficient way for you—which may not be the most efficient way for the next person. I wouldn't skip Chapter 2, which discusses our goals, but you've heard what we're about to do in this one, and if it doesn't sound good to you, move on. Besides, there's a full summary of the workflow in the back of the book, starting on Page 439.

In the Introduction, you met a group of beta readers who pored over drafts of this book. Here is their first of many major contributions. En masse, they pointed out that spending more than a dozen pages explaining how to correct this Emerald Lake image was not likely to persuade anybody that this is a three-minute process. In response, I've tried to talk more about speed in this chapter, to the point that the beta readers now complain that I'm emphasizing it too much.

It is true that it's easier to do this overview in a classroom or video than it is in a book. I've therefore recorded a video in which I do this correction from scratch. I did not review the chapter before beginning, so that I would not remember how I had done it previously and was therefore certain to proceed in a slightly different way. It's good fun. As with all of our videos, it's available in the sites indicated in the box on Page 4.

What's the Hardest Part?

Here are some points to bear in mind as our adventure begins.

- It's faster to do it than to read about it. The description in the rest of the chapter sounds like a lot of steps. But because the approach is disciplined and easily automated, the time from start to finish can be reduced to three to five minutes per image on average.
- Everybody accepts that the final result is what counts, not some intermediate version. Never before, however, have we either sabotaged image appearance temporarily or refused to accept changes that would clearly make the picture look better. The PPW commonly does both.

"I would say this is the most difficult concept to assimilate," says beta reader Adriano Esteves, "especially to understand how an image that is thoroughly messed up colorwise can serve as a luminosity layer."
- Most important of all, in my view: the first step is the most difficult. It is also the one with the least obvious benefit. Trying to learn that first step can be discouraging and may lead to an alarming dropout rate.

"Absolutely agreed!" says Marco Olivotto, who, like me, teaches small-group, multi-day color correction classes. "This has been my pièce de résistance since I started talking about the PPW, and it is the most difficult thing to drill into the students' heads. I guess it's because they equate RGB with easy, which is not true. I suggest you drop the words *in my view*. It is the most important of all, period."

Adriano and Marco were commenting on the first draft of this chapter. There was a second. When he saw the two comments above, James Gray added one of his own: "I find some of this confusing. Adriano says the second step is the most difficult for him. Yet you and Marco are talking about the first step being the most difficult. Maybe you're just trying to illustrate how the PPW is difficult to wrap your brain around as a whole. I happen to agree with Marco and not Adriano on this. In fact I almost dropped out of using the PPW before I got the panel because of that first color adjustment step. Personally I find the idea of the second step, working on contrast at the expense of color, fits into my scientific mind—as in manipulating one variable at a time and holding others constant."

* * *

The dropout rate that Marco, James, and I refer to is why we don't begin with a chapter about that frustrating first workflow step.

Is that first step really the hardest? Possibly, but in reading between the lines of what the beta readers had to say, I'm no longer so sure. The hardest part, in my opinion, is grasping the overall logic of doing things this way. The readers feel that if you can get through Chapter 4 then all the rest is downhill and the merits will be obvious. The question is how to get you there. This is why the readers insisted on the extensive Introduction, on two major rewrites of this chapter, and an overhaul of the next one as well.

Color, Contrast, Color Again

All correction methods strive for better detail and more pleasing color. Traditional workflows try to achieve both simultaneously. Until the mid-1990s, even if somebody had wanted to do things a different way, it wouldn't have been possible because computers were too slow. So, whether using a drum scanner, a dedicated retouching system such as those manufactured by Scitex, or an early version of Photoshop, the idea was to analyze the original and apply a single set of curves that would resolve all color issues while adding snap.

The method worked most of the time, but sometimes color problems could not be addressed without hurting contrast, and vice versa. Some professionals began to treat color and contrast as separate entities in certain cases.

Still, the basic curves approach remained. An original is called *flat* when it lacks contrast. Usually, the cause is that the lightest point isn't light enough, or the darkest not dark enough, or both. A snootier way of saying this is that the picture lacks *tonal range.*

A definition is in order, as we will speak of *range* frequently. The term can apply to the image as a whole, or to specific objects in it. It refers to the difference, or you might say the space, or the interval, between the lightest and darkest points.

That definition can therefore be ambiguous, and so can five words that often accompany it. *Highlight, Quartertone, Midtone, Three-Quartertone,* and *Shadow* divide the image into lightest-to-darkest zones. There is no precision in these terms. Nobody knows the difference between a dark midtone and a light three-quartertone. Worse, we sometimes use *the highlight* and *the shadow* to describe specific points. Plus, there is always the potential for confusion because many pictures contain objects known in English as *shadows,* which may or may not be the literally darkest areas of the picture.

Greater tonal range equates to more detail. Skilled people don't permit flat images; they force in a light and a dark point, thus improving contrast. Coincidentally, doing so also makes for more pleasing color.

Killing two birds with one stone sounds attractive, until we ask ourselves whether we really like the idea of having pleasing color appear by accident rather than design.

* * *

The Picture Postcard Workflow almost never mixes color and contrast. We set light and dark points in more or less the traditional way. When we do so in RGB, we still get more pleasing color, but we treat that improvement as we would an offer for a new credit card, or an e-mail advising that we have just won a sweepstakes. We decline with thanks—but we accept the increased contrast.

Turning down that apparent gain leaves us with a dishwater-dull file halfway through the process. But it will be our secret—nobody else will ever see that version. Accepting randomly better color now is likely to preempt the intelligent introduction of color later.

The seemingly perverse refusal to accept something obviously better is one reason that nobody thought of a strictly segregated workflow. A second is that it isn't clear whether the color or contrast step should come first.

A third reason: if we commit to treating

color separately, *where* should we do it? LAB produces more realistic, less noisy color than RGB or CMYK. It handles gross changes gracefully, but the delicacy needed to correct small color casts is unpleasantly absent.

The solution is to do the color twice. The first pass is not intended to produce compelling color—just color that is not known to be incorrect. Then comes the contrast maneuvering, and then the color enhancement—as opposed to color *correction*. It's a three-step, not a two-step: Color, Contrast, Color Again.

More accurately, there are three *mandatory* steps, steps that we will at least consider on every single image. These are covered in Chapters 3–6.

Additional steps that are used case by case get chapters of their own. There are also separate chapters on faces and skies, which don't follow the normal workflow rules; for this reason you won't see any portraits in the first five chapters.

Finally, the PPW advocates saving a conservative version of the file early on. The workflow confronts us with colors so intense that the screen can't display them properly. We then have to figure out how to bring them back within reason. It's the right way to do things but we risk desensitizing our eyes. We can be fooled into thinking that the garish is tasteful if, compared to the last thing we saw, it is. Hence, the conservative version lies in wait, just in case we feel like using it to weaken the PPW effect later.

All these maneuvers except the first step are accessible to ambitious beginners. On the other hand, some steps offer potential for even greater benefit through the use of masking techniques that beginners, ambitious and otherwise, usually aren't aware of.

Photoshop, Philosophy, and a Panel

As of this writing, no raw converter offers distinct separation of color and contrast, the basis of PPW's striking results. That means we do almost everything in Photoshop. This particular image arrives as a JPEG, but we must eventually consider how to treat raw images. That discussion is hereby put off until Chapter 14. For now, it's enough to say that the principles of PPW are effective no matter what is done first in the raw module—although some raw moves are more advisable than others.

This is supposed to be a quick workflow, so we automate where possible.

Actions, which have been a part of Photoshop since 1998, are a means of reducing tedium. We click the play icon in the Actions palette to perform a predetermined series of commands. We can write the actions ourselves, or borrow or steal them from others. Those used in the PPW can be downloaded for free. We also provide, at the same price, something far more valuable.

Shortly after releasing CS4 in 2008 Adobe introduced a separate module called Configurator. It lets us organize commands and actions into a single panel, where they can be accessed with a single click. A scripting expert can also program in conditional steps to give the actions more power.

This structure is ideal for the PPW, which features some complicated actions that are used in almost every image. And we just happen to have a scripting expert available.

Some Italian friends and I have spent a lot of time developing and documenting a panel that implements all this. It's free, it's now in its third release, and it has become immensely powerful. You can certainly run PPW without the panel, but after working with it for nearly two years, I would need to be hospitalized for acute depression if forced to give it up.

The panel installer is plug and play. It includes every action referred to in this book, and extensive documentation of each. You don't need Configurator, but at present you do need either Photoshop CS5 or CS6. The actions and documentation are separately

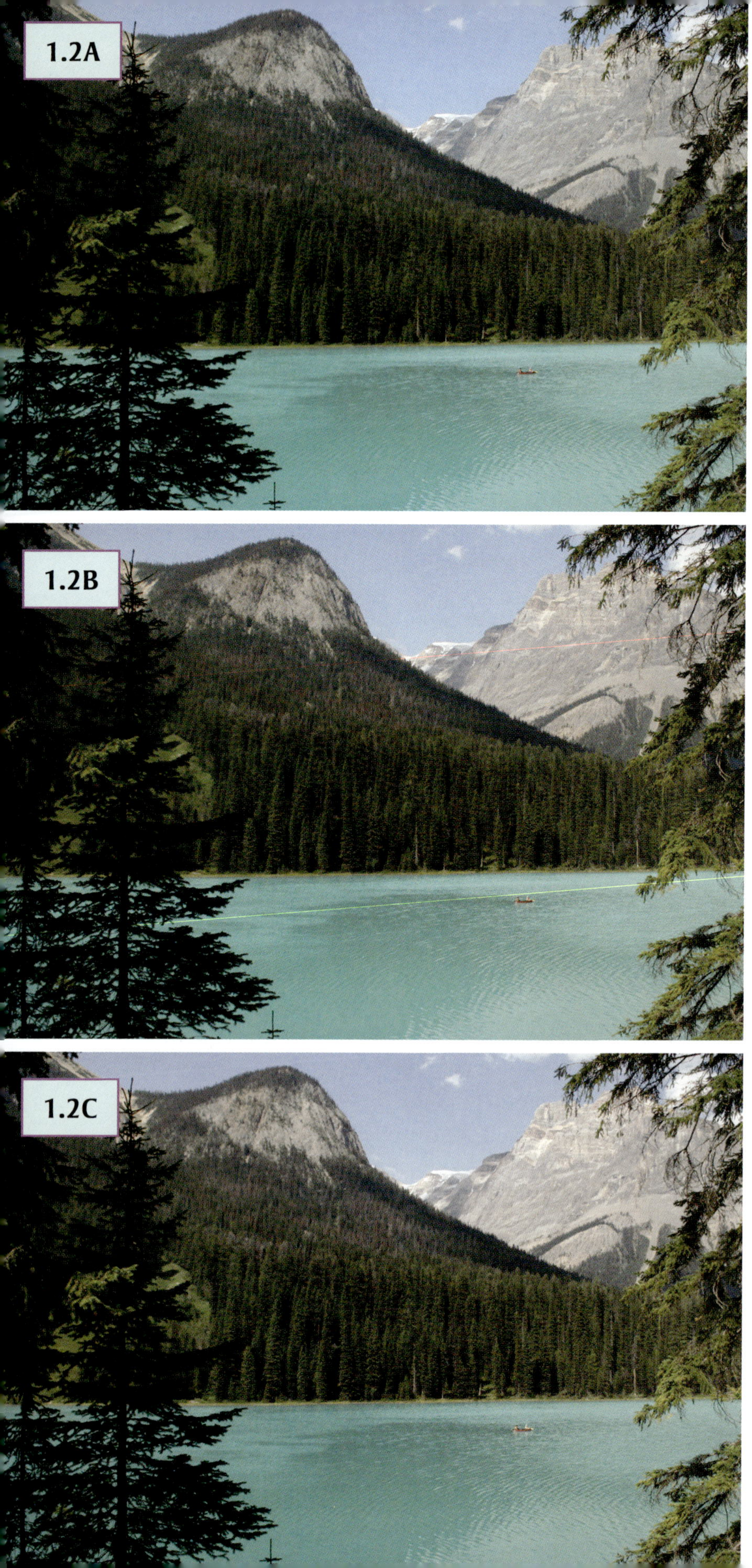

downloadable for those who don't qualify.

The current panel, complete with Big Brother scowling every time you screw up an image, is shown in Figure 1.2. Videos put the panel through its paces and give an idea of how much it adds to efficiency. Moreover, they explore the panel's most powerful feature, its ability to override certain action settings in favor of new ones. These options are also explained in the panel's documentation and in the workflow summary that starts on Page 439. Not here, though. Throughout this book the role of the panel is deliberately understated.

Why? First, we don't offer technical support. Second, actions historically don't require a specific version of Photoshop.

Figure 1.2 *Above, the original, downsized from Postcard 1.1. Middle, after a slight color adjustment. Bottom, after an adjustment of luminosity. Below, the PPW panel.*

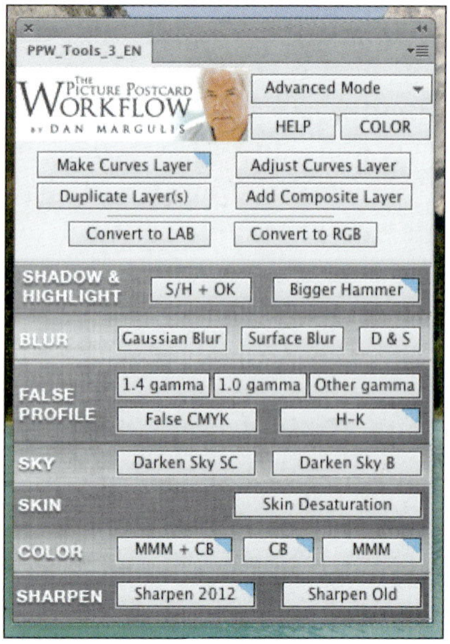

We have reports that our actions work in every Photoshop released in the last decade. Panels are not that way. One hopes that this will change; that panels from the current version (CS6, at this writing) will also work in future ones. And if not, one hopes that the same team will put together a new panel for the next Photoshop. But neither of these things can be guaranteed. If you work with something earlier than CS5, or some future version for which no PPW panel is available, you should still be able to use the actions.

Now, let's go start to finish with this Emerald Lake image. It will be done three times, each with different assumptions. First, I will show the normal PPW way. The budget is three to five minutes. Then I'll do it again, on the assumption that three minutes is too long, and that the job must be completed in one minute. Finally, I'll assume a very important image, where we'd be willing to spend as much time as needed to improve quality. You may find the recommended procedure for that contingency surprising.

To keep the average time down requires a buccaneering attitude and a slapdash approach. Some PPW steps involve choices for which the answer is not always clearcut. If you consider each step more carefully and experiment with different settings, I daresay you can get a slightly better result in fifteen minutes than in three.

The question is whether you would be better off with that single fifteen-minute version, or the ability to mix and match four very different slapdash versions that could have been produced in the same fifteen minutes. The answer: slapdash wins every time.

PPW From Start to Finish

• **1. Mandatory Step:** ***Check for and correct color defects.*** Covered in *Chapter 3.*

Mastery of this step is what has always distinguished the best retouchers from the tourists. It requires deciding whether we know roughly what the color values of certain objects ought to be. If we do, and the initial file doesn't match our expectations, we act; otherwise we move on.

The lake happens to be the most important thing in the scene. Concentrating on it at this point, however, would be a mistake. Unless you've been there you can't know much about its color. Its very name, in fact, suggests something unusual, unexpected. So you can't just assume that the water's current appearance is wrong. Instead, focus on things, however unimportant, that you *know the color of.* Those tiny clouds at top right mean nothing to the composition but a lot in correcting it, because very light clouds are reliably white, neutral.

The picture offers two other known, or at least semi-known, colors: the sky and the trees on the far shore. Each has a range of acceptable values, although much broader than for the light clouds.

Figure 1.2A is another copy of the original, downsized for convenience. My measurements found somewhat blue clouds. The sky and the trees were within recommended ranges, but barely.

We should agree that the clouds are wrong, if only slightly. The experienced, who know that all trees are not alike, would be suspicious here. Evergreens are bluer than most deciduous species. My measurements instead find these to be on the yellow side, not the blue one, of the recommendations given in Chapter 3.

According to those same recommendations, the original sky measures ever so slightly too green. If that were the only issue with the color it might not be enough to bother with. However, another way of saying that a blue sky is too green is that it has an outsize yellow component. That confirms my suspicions that the trees are too yellow. Also, a marginally green sky might compete with the lake. I would prefer something less green.

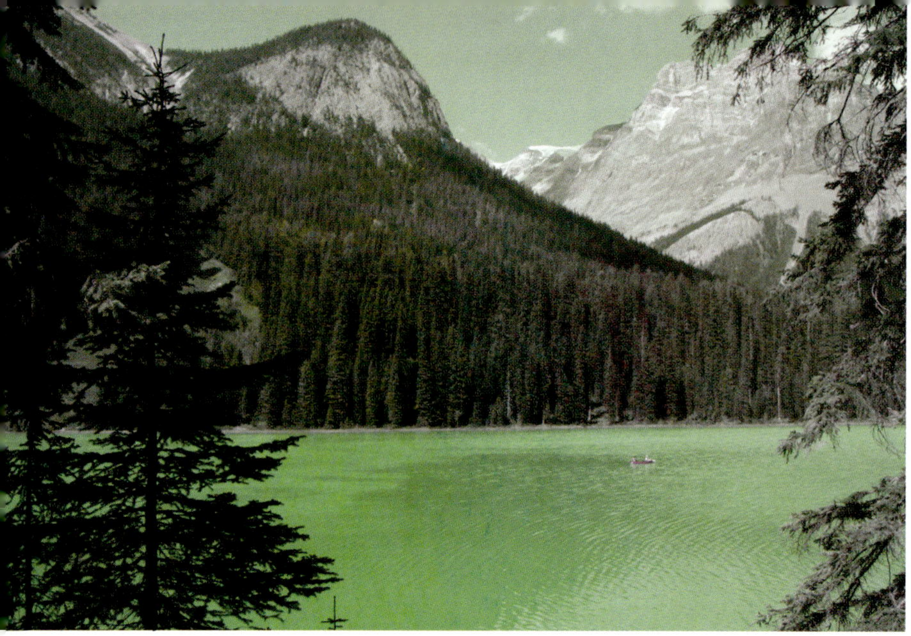

Figure 1.3 The color version of the file that provided the luminosity for Figure 1.2C. This color was discarded and replaced by that of Figure 1.2B.

It's now smart to save a copy. It may come in handy later.

• **2. Mandatory Step:** ***Better contrast.*** *Chapter 4.*

The previous step is supposed to ensure that we have acceptable, if not exciting, color. The only objective of the one I'm about to discuss is better contrast, or if you prefer, better detail, lightness, or luminosity.

The method calls for making a duplicate layer, in which detail will be improved in the green and red channels. If we can engineer a big improvement into the blue channel in five seconds or less, we'll do it, but the blue carries little weight in this operation.

We can replace one channel with a better one, or blend one into another to make a hybrid. Then, we consider curves to emphasize detail further, never worrying about what any of these moves do to the color.

This image offered few opportunities for such improvements. The blue was so poor that I replaced it with a copy of the red. I also applied a contrast-enhancing curve to the green, accounting for the appalling green cast in Figure 1.3.

Traditional workflows disapprove of things that make the picture look appalling, temporarily or otherwise. Ours has no compunction about doing so. Here, I don't plan to use the color at all, so it doesn't matter how bad it is. The layer only needs to be good for detail.

I therefore changed Figure 1.3's layer from Normal to Luminosity mode, allowing it to retain the color of the bottom layer, Figure 1.2B. Luminosity and Color modes are complementary. Each picks up color from one layer and detail from another. We use Color mode when we don't want to affect detail,

To use different wording with the same meaning, I would like the sky, and the background hills for that matter, more purple.

Figure 1.2B is where things stood after I applied curves on an adjustment layer to correct for the above. When finished, as always, I changed the layer mode from Normal to Color. In principle, doing this prevents any change in contrast, while retaining the new color. I would let you compare the results of Color and Normal modes here, but it would be a waste of space: the curves were so modest that you wouldn't be able to tell the two apart.

Even the difference between Figures 1.2A and 1.2B isn't huge, which occasions a reminder that this is the most difficult, frustrating step of the whole process. About a third of the pictures I work with need no color adjustment at all. Your number could be even higher if your files come from studio photographs. Furthermore, in many of the remaining files the adjustment is minor and probably won't affect the final result much if you omit it. I'd count this image as one of those. You'll get to see whether I'm right later in the chapter.

Lamentably, around a quarter of your images will fail if this initial color adjustment is overlooked or screwed up. You will see a tragic example in the next chapter.

and Luminosity mode when we don't want to affect color.

This step often gives dramatic results, but not here. Figure 1.2C strikes me as marginally better than Figure 1.2A. The trees and water are better defined. But it doesn't impress, at least not just yet. That's discouraging, because two of the three fundamental steps are already finished.

- **3. Optional:** ***Shadows/Highlights.*** *Chapter 7.*

Here's the easiest step of all. Would it be nice to add detail to the lightest and/or darkest areas? I see no need for more detail in these clouds. However, extra definition in the dark trees would be welcome. I therefore applied Image: Adjustments>Shadows/Highlights, at PPW standard settings. Figure 1.4 shows the modest improvement, before and after.

- **4. Optional:** ***The Bigger Hammer.*** *Chapter 10.*

This is the least commonly used option. Certain pictures live or die by what happens in the highlights. Waterfalls, white animals, interesting cloud patterns: for these, an application of Shadows/Highlights is nice, but we need something more powerful. This is the first of the more complex actions that we sometimes use.

Happily, this picture doesn't have the problem, so we can skip this sack of complications.

- **5. Optional:** ***Bringing two halves together.*** *Chapter 12.*

Photos shot in a mixture of sun and shade look too harsh. We humans adjust subconsciously to such conditions in a way that a camera can't. Evolution has equipped us with good perception regardless of lighting. It's not as if we see the sun and shade halves as equal, taken under uniform lighting, but we see them as a lot closer to that ideal than the camera does.

Proper practice has always been, therefore, to try to bring the two halves closer. But it turns out that this principle is true for just about any picture that can be described as having two halves—not just for obvious sun and shade.

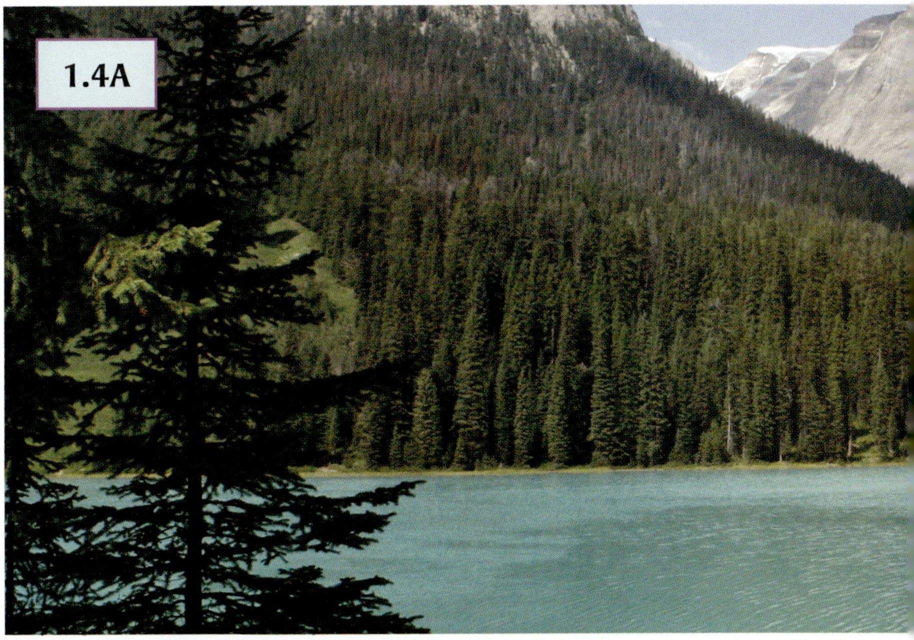

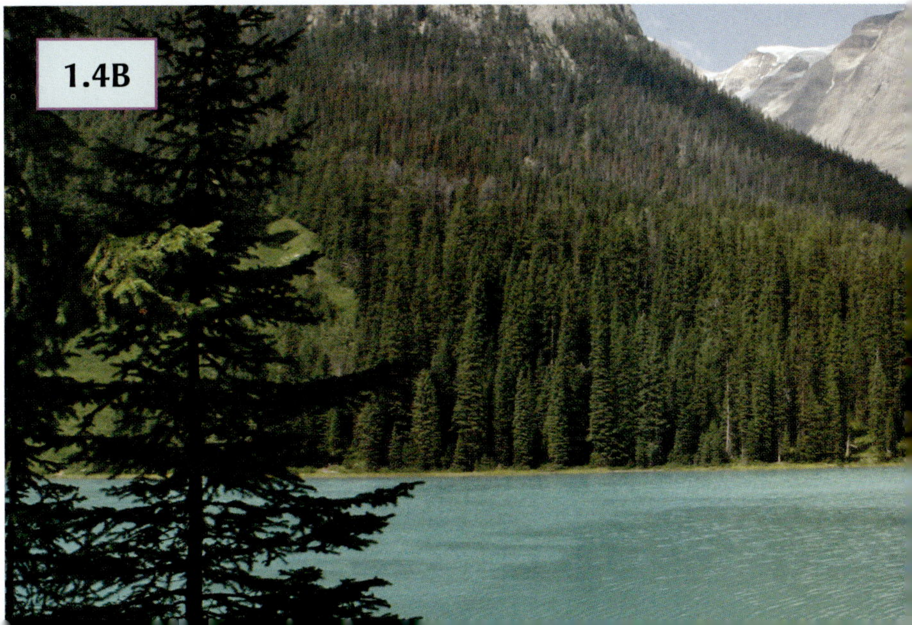

***Figure 1.4** Before and after application of the Shadows/Highlights command. The effect is minimal.*

This Emerald Lake picture is a close call. It can certainly be seen as two halves, but part of its appeal is that the brilliant lake is so light. So I vote to forgo this step.

- **6. Optional:** ***Alteration of neutrals to emphasize brighter colors.*** *Chapter 13.*

Scenes often look more three-dimensional if relatively neutral colors are darkened. It can also pay to make these near-neutrals grayer still, because it may help emphasize more vivid colors during the next step. I didn't think that either of these factors applied to this particular photo, and so did nothing here.

- **7a. Mandatory Step:** ***The Modern Man from Mars.*** *Chapter 6.*

Believable color requires not just brilliance but *variation*. The original photo has detail in the water, but next to no color variation. The background trees are likewise boring.

To deal with such situations, in 2005 I introduced something called the Man from Mars Method. It still has its uses, although they aren't documented in this book. Its replacement is usually better, always quicker and easier. It can be used more frequently because it has safeguards against certain common problems. Unless you've seen it before, you've never seen anything *like it* before, because it involves a false selection. It is the Modern Man from Mars, MMM for short.

The required selection is supposed to represent the most important area(s). It can be as rough as you like. My choice is shown in Figure 1.5. Apply the action or click the PPW panel button, and presto, Figure 1.6A.

This picture is primarily about the lake, but the trees also play a role. My selection conveyed this news to Photoshop, which proceeded to emphasize both contrast and color variation in anything looking like the selected area. It did so at the expense of the sky, the mountains, and anything else that, according to the selection, wasn't important.

Photoshop treats the selection as New Jersey drivers do red traffic lights: advisory only. It is used to formulate strategy, then discarded. So we see no evidence that it ever existed, no selection line or anything else.

This complex action delivers a layered file, separated, in keeping with our theme, into color and contrast components. Figure 1.6A is the default result; Figure 1.6B is after some adjusting.

Note: this action works hand in hand with the next one. Experienced PPW users usually prefer having both in a single larger action, called MMM + Color Boost. But the two are also supplied separately, if you are more comfortable splitting them.

- **7b. Mandatory Step:** ***The Color Boost.*** *Chapter 5.*

How much color is too much? Well, Figure 1.7A is a candidate. The PPW *always* goes for such color overkill, and cleans up the mess later.

This step again uses an action, albeit a much simpler one than MMM. It returns one layer that boosts the color beyond all reason, and a second that does nothing, but is there in case

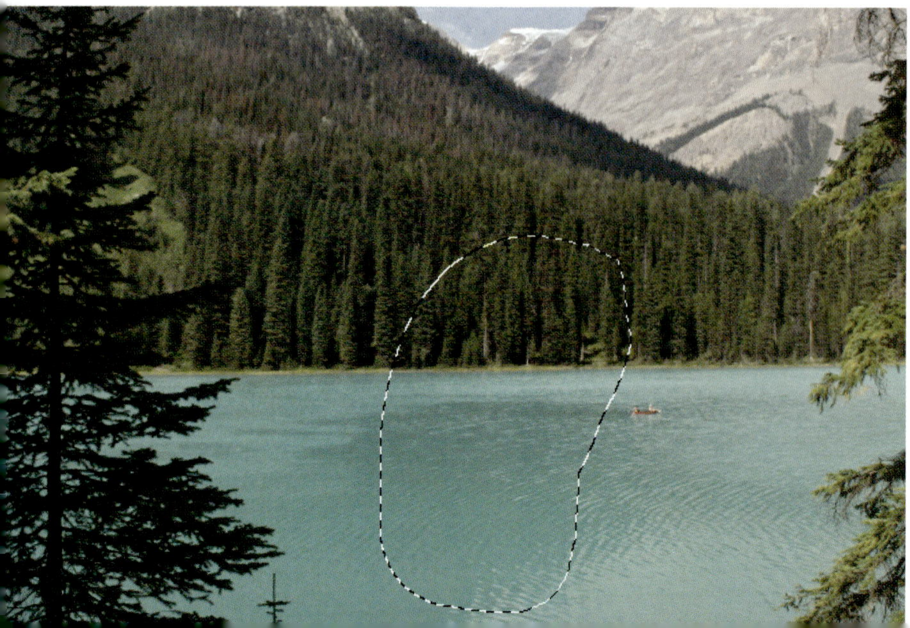

Figure 1.5 *The Modern Man From Mars action requires a loose selection to indicate the most important zone(s).*

we want to set endpoints or change overall image weight.

The client is always saying, give me bright, vivid, happy colors, but not *too much.* This type of unhelpful instruction should make us wonder what specific items, if any, constitute *too much.* It's easier to make this decision when looking at something indisputably too colorful than at a bland picture.

In Figure 1.7A, I say that *everything* is too much. I find the sky, the trees, and the water equally objectionable. And so my adjustment was the simplest possible: I reduced the opacity of the Color Boost layer.

It's more normal, in my experience, for only certain elements of the overly colorful version to cause the sensation of too much. And in that case we find a way to reduce the color in an unbalanced way that penalizes the offending areas more than the others.

For example, back in Figure 1.6A. I thought the color excessive. It wasn't because of the lake or the trees, though. The selection in Figure 1.5 had called for emphasizing them. As both key objects happen to be green, Photoshop made the rest of the picture more red, because the presence of reds makes greens seem more intense.

If there were no sky in the background I might have gotten away with it. The rocky hills in the background don't look bad. The pinkish clouds are another story. Therefore, to produce Figure 1.6B, I did *not* reduce opacity of the Color Boost layer, in fact I increased it. But I loaded a layer mask that favored the retention of green things and suppressed magenta ones. Aficionados of LAB will know where that mask came from.

But, back to Figure 1.7A. I noted that the lightest and darkest significant points of the picture weren't quite where they should be. The Color Boost action conveniently attaches an unused curves adjustment layer for exactly such contingencies. I used it to set appropriate light and dark points, in addition to my existing move on the color layer. Figure 1.7B is the result.

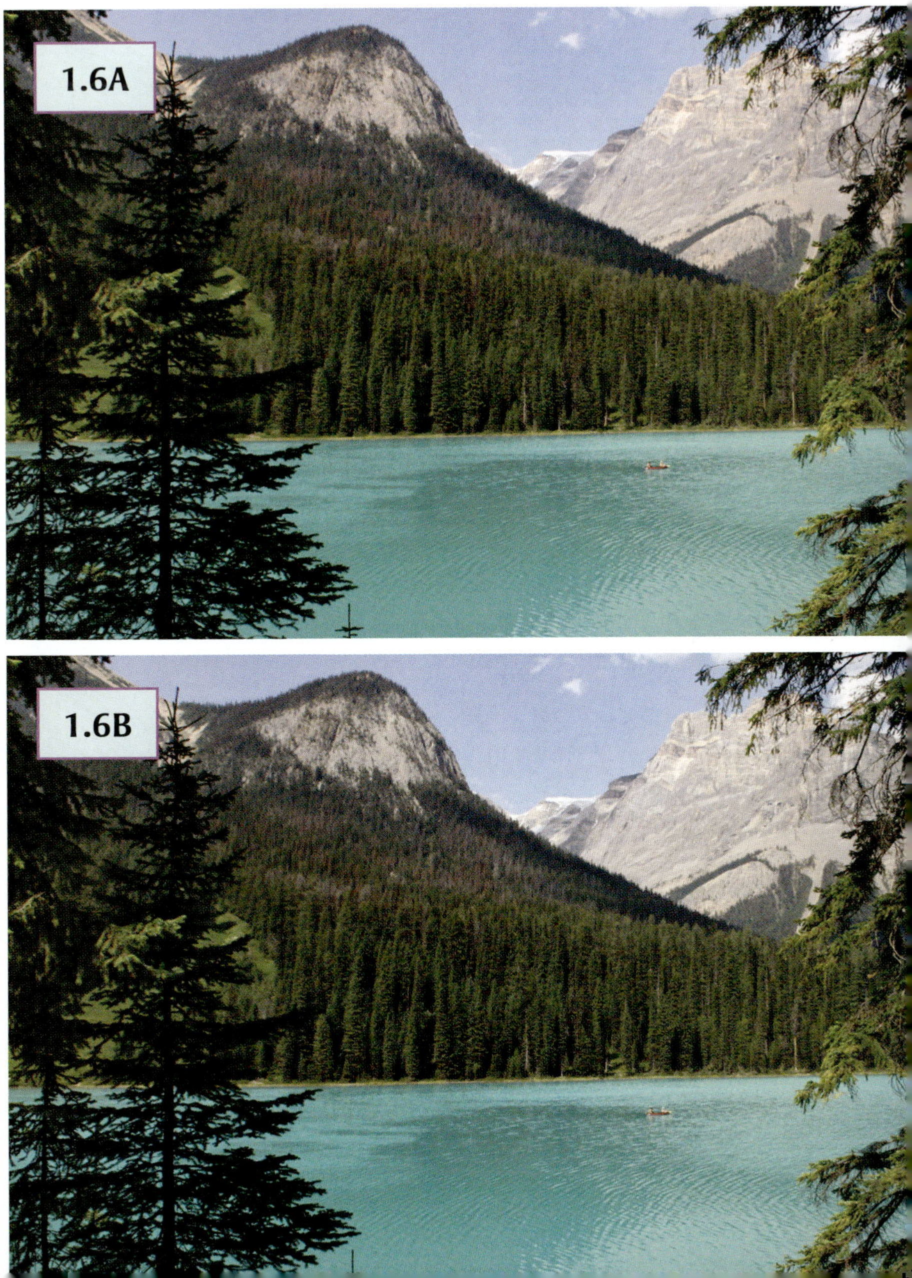

***Figure 1.6** Top, the default result of the MMM action. Bottom, after some further adjustments.*

- **8. My Method or Yours?** *The Sharpen action. Chapter 15.*

Every photo requires some form of sharpening. It should take place at or near the end of the process, which means right now.

The steps so far depend on one another, Sharpening is an independent. Ditch my method if you like and substitute your own.

The PPW Sharpen action is complex, offering many powerful variations. The default settings, though, usually give a reasonable result. To go from Figure 1.8A to 1.8B required only a single click in the PPW panel. Note that these samples, although cropped, are displayed at the same size as the opening Postcard 1.1 so that you can better evaluate what the action has done.

- **9. The Insurance Policy:** ***Compare to a Conservative Version.***

Figure 1.7A as printed here is deceptive. The actual file was so brilliant that many of its colors were out of the CMYK gamut, so what you see is seriously toned down. On the screen, it's almost blindingly colorful.

A wildly colored start point has a downside. Compared to the eyepopping screen version of Figure 1.7A, just about anything looks tasteful. With our eyes in that dazzled state, we are prone to approve something that we and others will later consider too loud.

Frederick Yocum, a beta reader who has suffered through two three-day classes with me, offers this rueful concurrence.

"I remember one of the most frightening things about the advanced class was discovering howlingly unnatural colors when the maestro ran an eyedropper over the image you just spent twenty minutes sweating over and thought was God's gift to veracity."

I therefore recommend that, after making what you think is the correct color decision, you compare it to something conservative. That's why long ago, after the very first step of correcting a modest blue cast, I had saved a separate copy, Figure 1.2B. I now reopened it

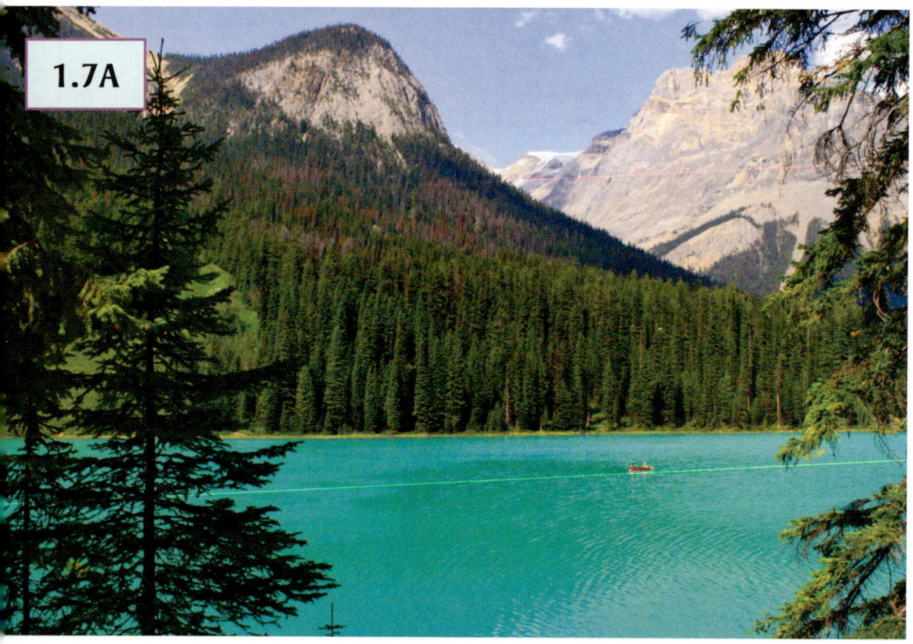

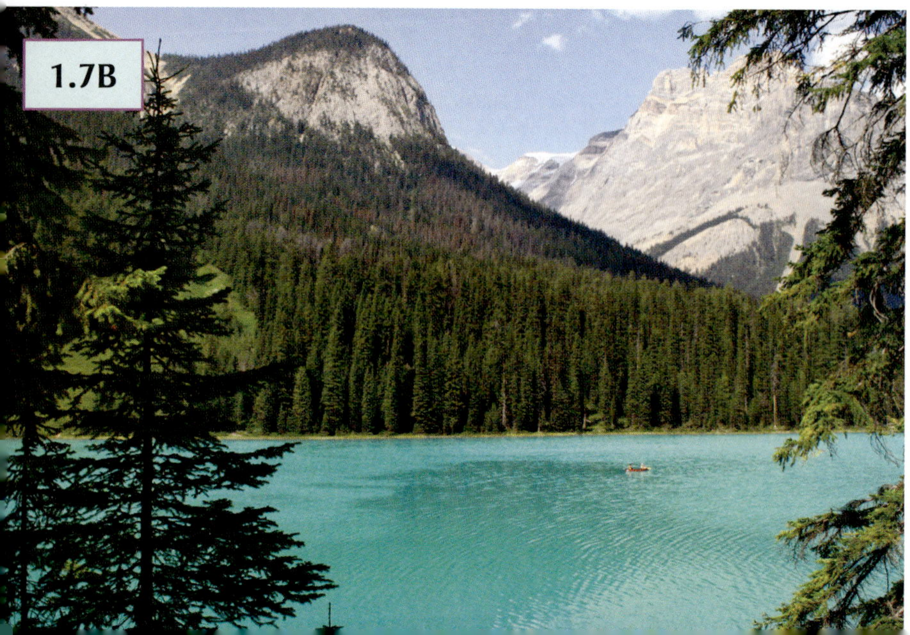

***Figure 1.7** Top, the default result of the Color Boost action. Bottom, after some further adjustments.*

to see whether I still thought that Figure 1.8B, which I had assumed was my final version, was worthy of that honor.

Figure 1.8B's trees and lake were better, in my opinion. However, I again noticed the slight pinkness in the sky that I complained about back in Figure 1.6A. So I decided to unite the two images in a way that introduced the lightest parts of the conservative Figure 1.2B while maintaining the vivid greens. The merged version will be shown shortly as Figure 1.10A. In principle, that's the end of the three-minute PPW, but now we have to discuss time and its relation to quality.

Tempus Fugit

After all these pages describing the correction of a single image using unfamiliar tools, one might assume that this procedure is convoluted enough to require hours per image. In reality, the steps are so repetitive, and so amenable to being automated, that with practice they become quick.

The *with practice* is a key phrase. For example, I mentioned that I cut down the pinkish areas of Figure 1.6A by using a layer mask that permitted greens but restricted magentas. If you've never tried it before it might take you a while to think of using an inverted copy of the A channel of LAB as the start of a layer mask. But having seen a plethora of previous provocations of this pinkness problem, I had that mask in position and finalized in less time than it took me to write this paragraph.

Before starting this chapter, I did a time test on a hundred images like this one. The average was two minutes, 45 seconds.

How long did it take to do *this* image? Well, several hours, obviously. After each step I had to save a copy and make notes on what I was thinking and what I had done. How could I write the chapter otherwise?

I did want to know how long it might take in real life. So, weeks later I redid the exercise from scratch with the stopwatch running.

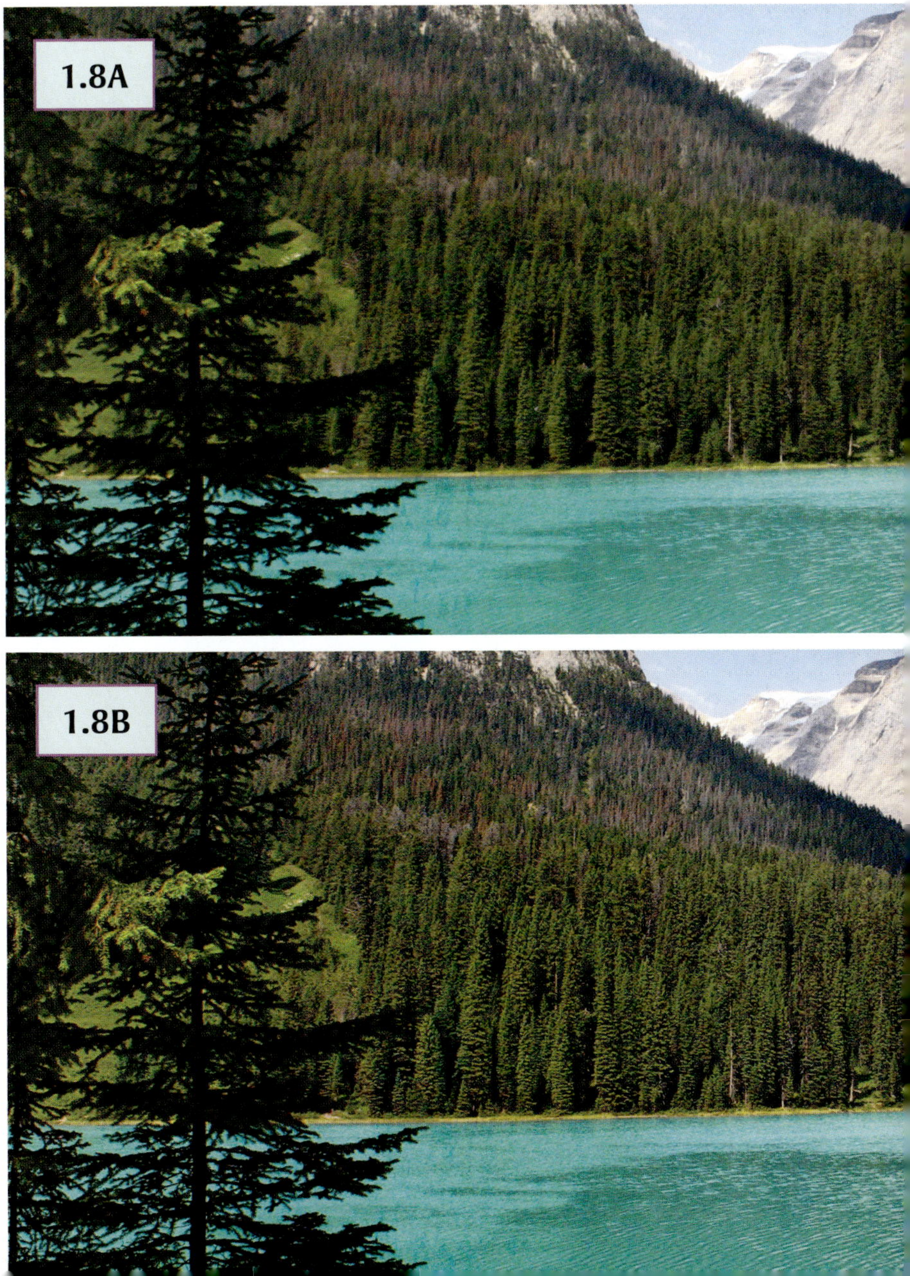

***Figure 1.8** Top, Figure 1.7B at actual size. Bottom, after application of a sharpening action.*

The time was 3:15, a little slower than average. I will show the result of this second try shortly. First, as mentioned at the top of the chapter, we need to discuss two alternate scenarios. We have been working on the assumption that spending three minutes on the image is satisfactory and that we are willing to do it if there's a quality gain.

Three minutes is a reasonable time for many applications—though for a different perspective, check out what one of the beta readers says in the box on this page.

Certain people simply cannot afford to spend more than a minute per image. And others, who I suspect constitute the majority of readers, would be willing to spend *more* than three minutes. How do we maximize quality for each group?

Limiting the time to three minutes required accepting certain shortcuts. As an example, for the application of the Shadows/Highlights command in Step 3 and the Sharpen action of Step 8, I advocated a one-size-fits-all approach, instead of trying to tailor the settings to the individual image. In Steps 7a and 7b, the MMM and Color Boost, I had to adjust the layer opacity sliders to create something that looked good to me. I forget what values I used and would not be able to duplicate them, because the approach was just to drag each slider to the left and drop it when it looked approximately correct. If that wound up being an opacity of 47% so be it. No time to investigate whether 42% or 52% would be marginally better, not if I want to keep within three minutes an image.

In short, we discard any step that doesn't make a significant difference. We want to be able to see the impact of the move immediately. We are not interested in improvements that can only be detected if we toggle back and forth five times.

Almost every step in the Emerald Lake exercise meets this criterion. The Shadows/Highlights move of Figure 1.4 does not, but it only takes a couple of seconds. Possibly the first color move, which created Figure 1.2B out of 1.2A, doesn't either. That one is more important than it looks, however, because subsequent steps magnify any color imperfections that are left in.

It goes without saying that we don't spend time on backups and things that let us go back to previous states. In the three-minute

Three Minutes? Perhaps

I average three minutes an image. So do many of my students. Beta reader James Gray, who calls himself a serious amateur photographer but not a Photoshop expert, and who doesn't know me, is one of those uncomfortable with such speed. Here's his view:

"I still cannot get my time to use the PPW down to a three-minute average. This is important because I think there is a market for the new book among people more like me. We really do not want people like me to get discouraged from using the PPW just because they find that they cannot get the time down to three minutes. Even if it takes 15 minutes it is still much faster than the 'old' way for most serious amateurs. So I think that I would like to see a sentence something like, 'Even if you cannot get your average time to be very close to three minutes per image you will still find that this workflow is much faster than the traditional work flow and better too.'

"In the colortheory group you told me that the way to get my time was 'practice, practice, practice'. Frankly I do not care if it takes me a lot longer to follow the PPW than it does for professionals who spend more than 20 hours per week using Photoshop. It is still a lot better than the traditional way and faster. As an aside I will say a few words about why I think I am slower besides not practicing enough yet. First, I usually only use the PPW on high value images and I have not yet gotten to the place where I am comfortable just creating new versions from scratch. Second, I am usually having so much fun playing with different masks and features of the PPW panel that I just do not hurry. It is more fun than crossword puzzles. Third, I have very little incentive, being retired, to speed up my workflow more than I already have using your techniques."

workflow, we flatten after every step. If, after looking at the final result, we want to go back to some intermediate step and resume from there, we hope the History palette will help us. Otherwise, we're out of luck.

The One-Minute Workflow

Reducing the average time spent to a minute involves even more compromises and shortcuts. There is no room for the final step of comparing the result to a conservative version. Whatever the workflow produces will have to be good enough.

We also give up the ability to adjust sharpening. Whatever the action gives us by default will have to do. If we are trying to process scores of files, we'll set up a hot folder that automatically applies the action to everything dumped into it, and saves the result.

What do we definitely retain? The two parts of Step 7, the Modern Man from Mars and the Color Boost, which are conveniently both contained in one action. These offer the most spectacular payback for the least investment of time.

With three minutes to play with, we'd take a look at some other steps to see whether they were helpful. With less, what we've got is good enough. If the picture starts with a terrible cast, for example, we'll have to fix it. That may drive the correction time for certain files above one minute, but if we don't do it often then the average time will still be acceptable.

Maybe we will consider using Shadows/Highlights, which can be applied in no time flat. But that's going to be about all.

How big of a price do we have to pay for all these omitted steps? We're about to see, but first we should discuss the opposite scenario. Instead of what to do when we must compress a three-minute workflow into one minute, let's ask what to do if we are willing to spend *more* than three minutes in the interest of quality.

When More Time Is Available

The question is how to spend the extra time, and the answer seems obvious. Eliminate compromises. Make backups. Consider all alternatives.

Obvious, perhaps, but wrong nevertheless. Starting over and doing a second version is a much better investment of time. If you're willing to go further, make a third version from scratch and maybe a fourth, too. After that, if you've still got time to kill, by all means do a version as carefully as you can.

Do the work multiple times, and you'll never choose exactly the same settings, particularly if you don't do the second version immediately but delay it long enough to forget what you did in your first effort.

Suppose that you do only one version. If you have made a poor fundamental decision anywhere along the line, all the care in the world in executing it won't save the plan; you'll see proof of this in the next chapter. The result will fool you, though, because it will still look much better than the original. Only a second, better version will convince you of your error the first time.

More commonly, neither version will be better in every way. Instead, each will have different strong and weak points.

This disparity between separately prepared versions did not exist in traditional workflows, which were more straightforward. Consider how I just did this image, and how it might differ if it were done again. There were ten listed steps, counting the one labeled 7 as two separate steps.

- Step 1, the initial color correction, and Step 8, sharpening, would likely be done almost identically if I reworked the image.
- Steps 2, the luminosity enhancement, 7a, the Man from Mars, and 7b, the Color Boost, all call for aesthetic decisions. Even if you don't think your taste varies from day to day, you will never be able to remember what choices you made the first time. And MMM

requires a selection; you saw mine in Figure 1.5. What are the odds I would duplicate it? Sure, the second effort would be similar, but it would produce a slightly different result, maybe better, maybe worse.

- Now consider Step 3, Shadows/Highlights; Step 4, the Bigger Hammer; Step 5, bringing two halves together; Step 6, the neutrality action; and Step 9, the blending with a previous version. Here the question is not what setting to choose but whether to use the technique at all. I don't recommend agonizing over these close calls. And it certainly would not be surprising if you made different decisions about whether to use one or more of them the second time around. Doing so might have a considerable impact.

In short, a second, third, or subsequent try will be different, possibly significantly so. It may be clearly superior; it may be garbage. More likely, it will be nicer in some respects and not in others. Furthermore, if you know you have already made one fairly good version, you can adopt a riskier policy the second time around. If the result seems better in certain ways, great, and if it gets thrown away it's no big loss.

And that is why it makes more sense to do alternate versions and blend them than it does to worry a single version to death.

The Final Faceoff

Figure 1.9A is another copy of the original for easy comparison. Figure 1.9B is the one-minute version I referred to a while ago: start with the original, then nothing but the color moves and a sharpen. Figure 1.10A is the final of the version I've been working on all chapter. It's the blend of Figures 1.8B and 1.2B.

Figure 1.10B is what I got when I redid the correction with a stopwatch. And Figure 1.10C is a more recent version, to wit, yesterday. I wrote most of this chapter more than a year ago. I figured that a new version made from scratch might be in order. What do you make of these five contestants?

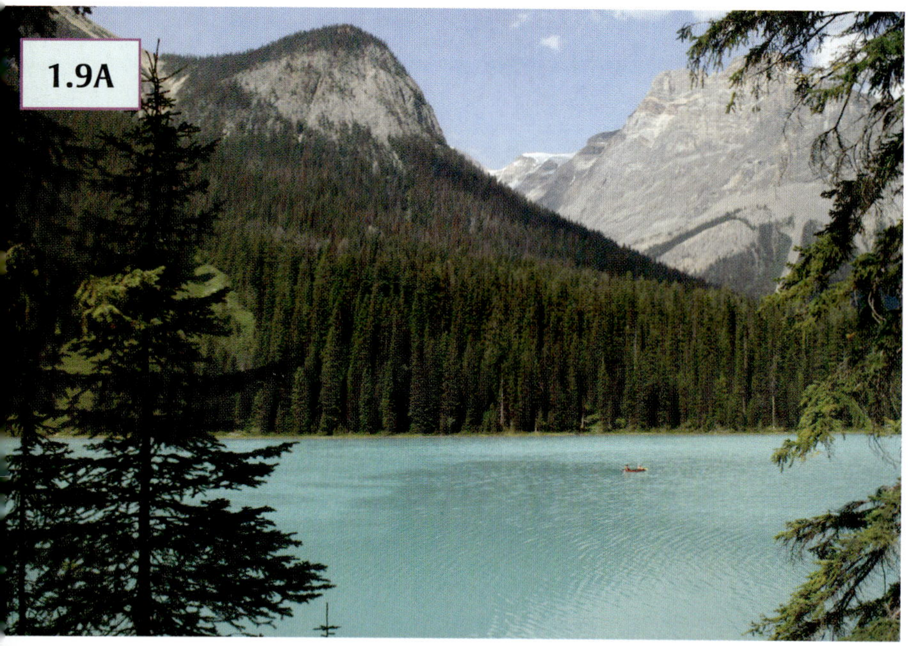

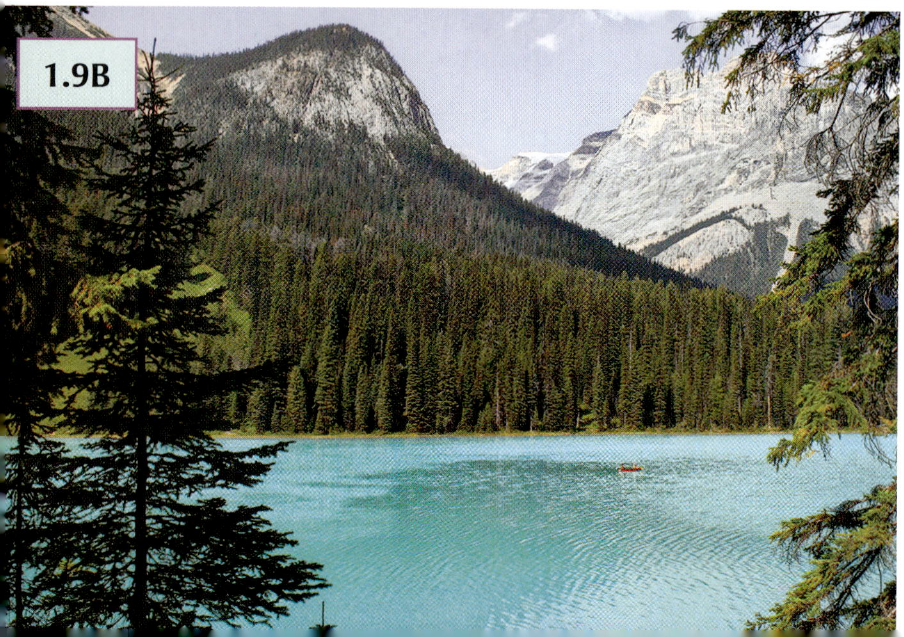

***Figure 1.9** Top, the original image repeated for comparison. Bottom, a version corrected using only the MMM + Color Boost action plus sharpening.*

The one-minute version, Figure 1.9B, demonstrates the power of the two actions it uses. It is not just better than Figure 1.9A, but it is also better, in my opinion, than anything that could have been done by traditional methods. The additional realism in the water makes up for certain deficiencies in color.

The one-minute result is not, however, competitive with any of the three versions of Figure 1.10, all of which are better for both color and contrast. If we have to choose one winner, I'll take Figure 1.10B.

But we don't have to do that. With these three available, we can choose the best of each. Or we can even go back to Figure 1.8B, another unblended version. Or Figure 1.2B, if we want more conservative color.

Figures 1.10A and 1.10B are similar; I prefer the water and the trees in the former but the background in the latter.

Figure 1.10C, on the other hand, is unlike the other two. Recall that at several points in the workflow I had to decide whether to apply a certain technique at all. I decided differently for four of these items between Figures 1.10A and 1.10C. (I don't recall how I did Figure 1.10B, because I was trying to go as fast as possible.)

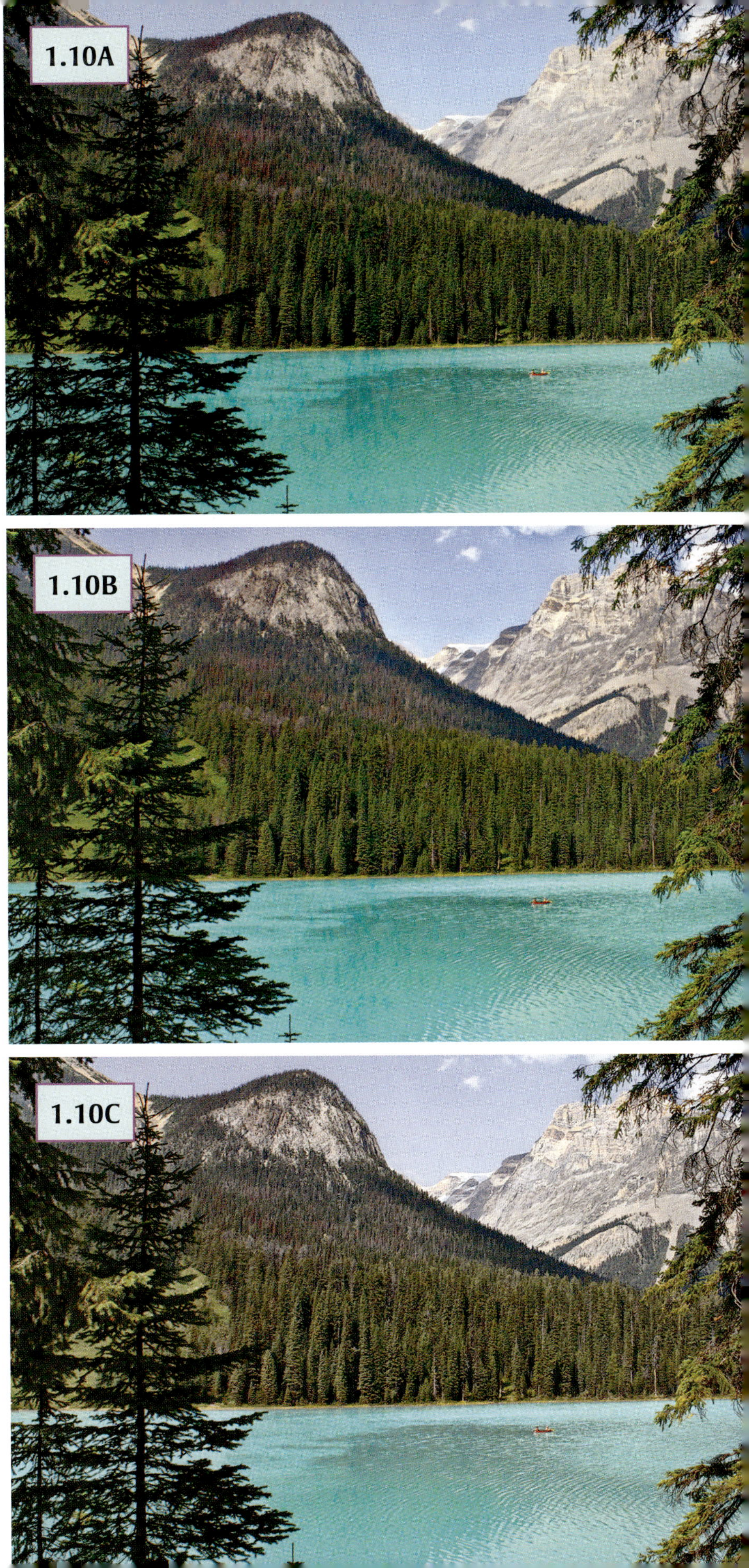

***Figure 1.10** Top, the continuation of this chapter's correction, combining Figures 1.8B and 1.2B. Middle and bottom, two subsequent versions, each prepared from scratch.*

Before concluding that my skills are fading because Figure 1.10C isn't as good as the ones I did more than a year previously, let me inform you that I would not have done it that way if it was going to be my only try. I didn't look at the two earlier versions before starting work, but I knew they existed. So in this third version, they were a safety net. I could afford to swing for the fences—to take risky actions that might or might not pay off.

Here I made use of the neutrality action discussed in Chapter 13. I darkened all semi-neutral colors. That was a good idea. But I also savagely desaturated them, thinking that it was conceivable that I could get back what I had lost with interest when I boosted colors later in the process.

As you can see, that concept did not work. Figure 1.10C's color is the worst of the three. But no need to worry—we don't have to use it. Meanwhile, its contrast, according to me, is the *best* of the three!

The next chapter discusses how to merge versions. The ways of doing so are infinite. Postcard 1.1 is in fact a composite of the three versions of Figure 1.10. Roughly it consists of 80% of the contrast of Figure 1.10C, with the rest, and all of the color, divided about equally between the other two versions. The resulting blend, in my view, looks considerably better than any of the three parents.

So that's a preview of how this image might be handled given only one minute, given three minutes, or given more.

Doing one version carefully will surely produce something better than doing it as fast as you can, but the difference could be slight. Making multiple versions and then discarding or uniting them is likely to make a *big* difference. In doing so, it will disprove that old saying about price, quality, and speed, along with several other misconceptions about how to create more attractive imagery.

The Bottom Line

This chapter introduces the Picture Postcard Workflow by taking one image from start to finish. We discuss what makes for an attractive picture, why realism and acceptability are not always the same thing, and the tradeoffs when time must be saved by shortening or omitting certain steps.

The workflow has some similarities to traditional methods but its strict treatment of color and contrast as separate entities causes peculiar-looking intermediate results. Also, its recommendation that we should shoot for color overkill and then reduce it seems counterintuitive.

The exact form of the workflow depends on the time allotted for the work. If time permits, you should make multiple versions of the same file and blend them, rather than trying to make one perfect version.

2

Five Lessons About Human Perception

The workflow isn't traditional. Neither are some of the traps new users can blunder into. This chapter explores the difficulties that one such user encountered—and how he could have avoided them. We close with an illustration of why fast is sometimes better than good.

In an age of instant gratification, it's only human to want to employ a tempting tool immediately. The spectacular color enhancements of Chapters 5 and 6 are easy to apply. In the enthusiasm to get going, however, one can overlook the fine points. If you do, be prepared to find out the hard way that volatile, unfamiliar workflows are dangerous if provoked.

One of the biggest problems in traditional workflows is getting the color bright enough, interesting enough. With the workflow we've just seen, the problem is the opposite—keeping the colors from getting completely out of hand.

It's worth spending a chapter to discuss this and other novelties before getting into nuts and bolts. We'll look at two pictures that changed my own views of what constitutes good taste in color and also good use of time in Photoshop. To add verisimilitude, we'll be studying not just how I did things, but how someone more representative of you did, and the problems he ran into along the way. We'll also see that the audiences who evaluated his work were fooled badly, and get my take on why.

Perception and Reality

Figure 2.1A hails from Italy. The professional photographer who shot it was studying the PPW based on fragmentary descriptions he had found online. He had never worked with me or seen others demonstrate it.

He produced Figure 2.1B and posted it for comment. His colleagues, unimpressed, pronounced it vulgar, too colorful.

Inquiries having been raised as to whether this proved that the PPW always yielded crass and tasteless results, I did my own version, Figure 2.1C.

The Italian audience liked it, saying that for an American I appeared to have good taste.

Please put yourself in their shoes. I assume you prefer my version because so far everyone has, and not just in Italy. But why? What factors cause you to perceive one version as more tasteful than the other?

* * *

Figure 2.1B is not all that terrible. Too loud, yes, but that's easily fixed. You may well ask, though, how a professional came to post such a monstrosity.

The answer is that the PPW can trick people. It always produces something excessively colorful (such as Figure 1.7A in the last chapter) and then asks you to tone it down creatively. It's a great policy, but a dangerous one because the wild color can desensitize our eyes. Compared to something enormously more colorful, Figure 2.1B must have looked good to this photographer. He should have compared it to the original instead.

◆ LESSON ONE ◆

◆ The last thing you looked at can seriously warp your judgment. If it was extremely colorful, it may con you into approving something that looks good by comparison but is itself too loud.

* * *

In the previous chapter I suggested the countermeasure of saving a conservative version early in the process.

No need here. The original, Figure 2.1A, has nothing obviously incorrect. *It* can be the conservative version. If you think that Figure 2.1B is too loud, then add a duplicate layer, replace it with Figure 2.1A, and reduce layer opacity to taste. It only takes seconds.

Figure 2.2 blends the two 50–50. See, Figure 2.1B isn't so bad after all!

Figure 2.1 *Below, the original. Opposite, two separate attempts to correct it.*

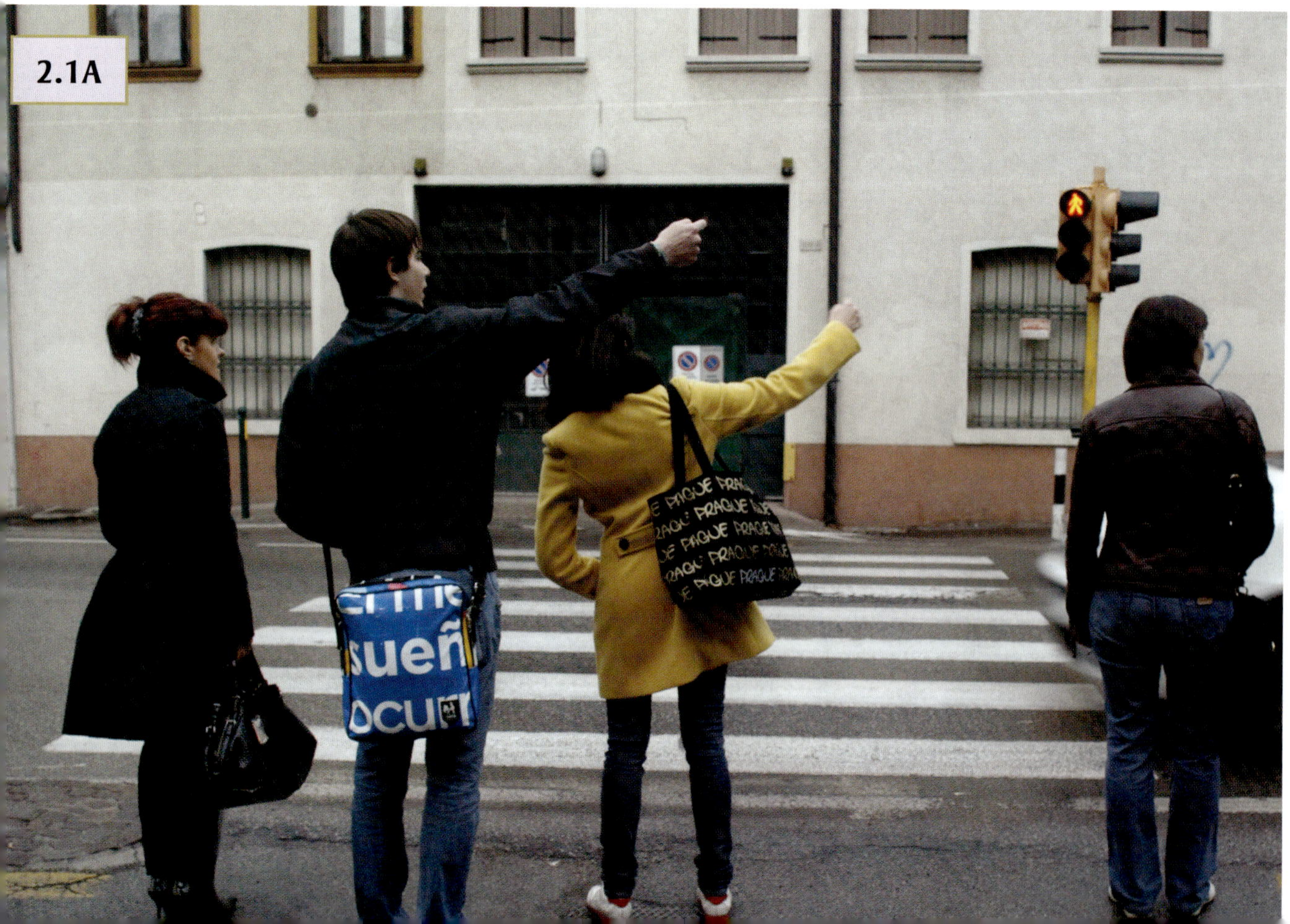

2.1B

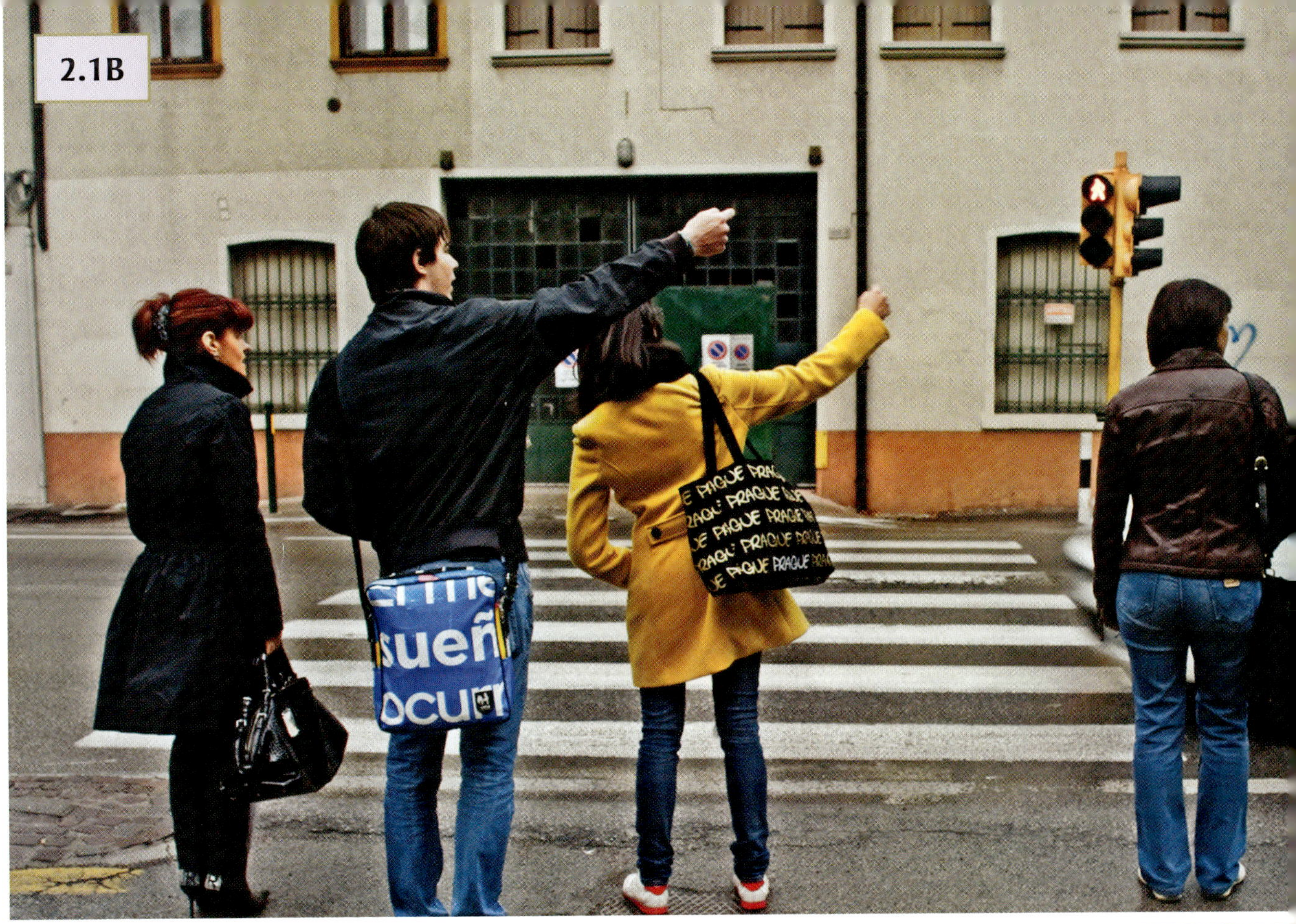

2.1C

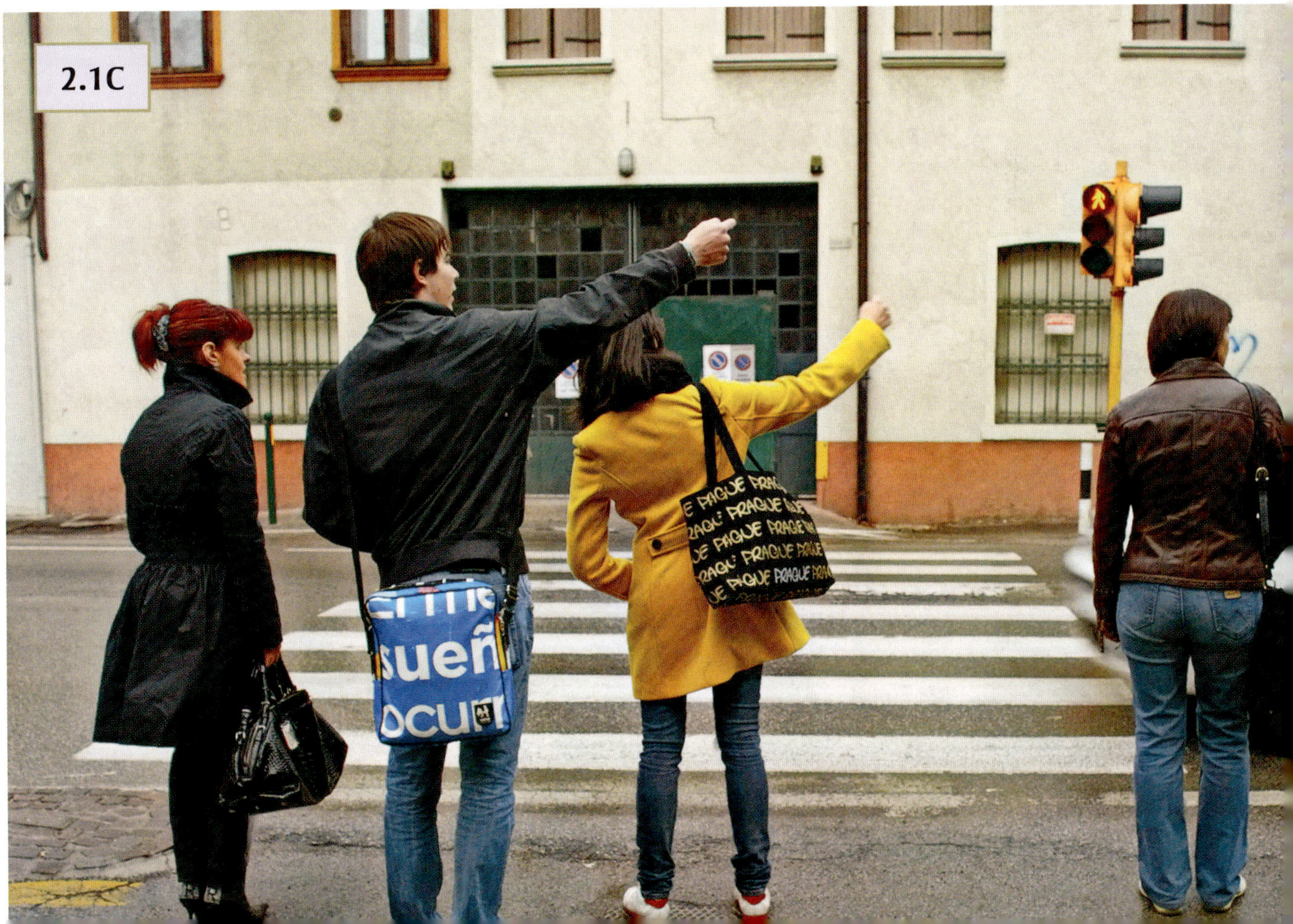

The main problem with Figure 2.1B is not its color choices. Hiraloam sharpening, which is described in Chapter 15, was misused. It has obliterated the orange of the Don't Walk signal, and inserted a nasty halo around the long black jacket of the woman at left.

The audience's assessment that Figure 2.1B is more colorful than Figure 2.1C is therefore a crock. Have a look at Figure 2.3, which compares three areas of each version. The red hair and face, the yellow jacket, and the pavement are all more strongly colored in my version, Figure 2.1C. Yet the audience emphatically says that my version is the less colorful one. How do you account for it?

One Rotten Apple Spoils the Barrel

You and I were not present when this picture was taken. We don't know the exact color of the hair, the face, the yellow jacket, or the pavement. Unless you're acquainted with these people or this location, either version could be closer to the original scene.

The picture contains, however, two elements we *do* know. First, the painted crosswalk and the letters on the blue bag should be white. The photographer and I both got that right.

The second is an item of Italian origin that was adapted by Americans, and exported back to Italy with outlandish markups. It uses fabric historically worn by sailors from the city of Genoa. In the early nineteenth century, some visiting American merchants thought they saw in it commercial possibilities beyond outfitting mariners. They asked their Italian hosts what the material was called. *Blu di Genova,* came the reply.

The Americans could not pronounce this, so it became *blue jeans.* Once another

***Figure 2.2** A 50–50 blend of Figures 2.1A and 2.1B.*

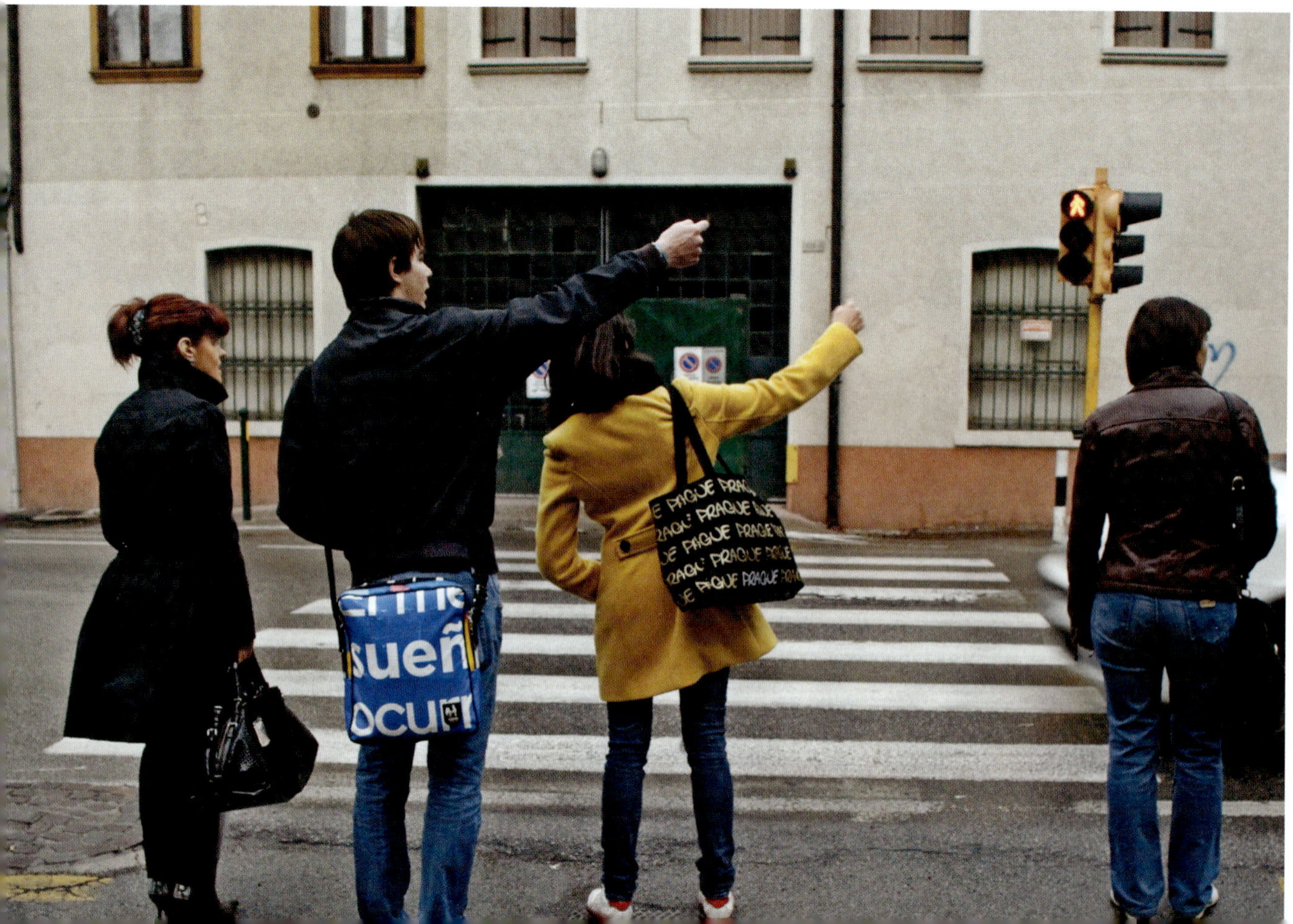

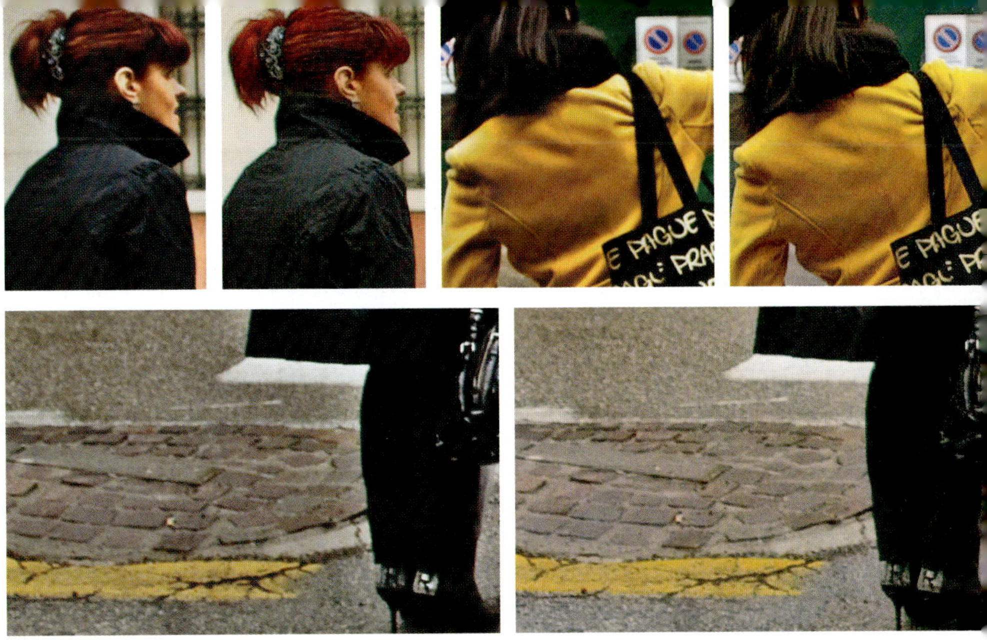

Figure 2.3 Comparison of three areas of Figures 2.1B (left versions) and 2.1C.

American merchant, Levi Strauss, invented and patented riveted pockets, a peculiarly American product was born. And, just as Americans pay ridiculous prices for the privilege of owning something "European", today's Europeans pay through the nose for Levi's. Purchasing a pair in Rome will set you back $100 or so, plus whatever outrageous Foreign Transaction Fee your credit card may impose. Even so does the world progress.

One benefit of our international culture is that everybody knows what blue jeans look like. And they know that my rendition (right halves of Figure 2.4) is closer than the photographer's.

Unless you can think of a better explanation, I have to believe that the jeans, and only the jeans, account for the audience's rejection of Figure 2.1B. Furthermore, I say that the presence of this one color that people know is too intense cons them into thinking that *everything* is that way. How else would you account for the near-unanimous, but incorrect, statement that the photographer's version is more colorful than mine?'

Beta reader Bevi Chagnon offered another factor: "Maybe it's because the detail was lost in Figure 2.1B, as in a printed piece that goes to mud because of too much ink. Your version opens up the shadow detail while keeping the color and saturation pretty much the same. Halos also contribute to that 'overcolored' appearance of Figure 2.1B. Personally, I can't stand looking at the yellow jacket because it seems so much like plastic."

Agreeing, John Pavel wrote, "The exaggerated highlights on the yellow coat (hiraloam) are what strikes me first. Contrast is excessive for such a dull day."

At some point during our work, the photographer and I each achieved wildly excessive color and had to decide how to cut back. The photographer apparently used the same approach I did in Chapter 1: he reduced the opacity of his color-boosting layer.

He therefore treated all colors as equally evil. In the Emerald Lake example in the preceding chapter, that was the right philosophy, but it's wrong here. When I did my version of this one, I concluded that the blues were a bigger problem than anything else, so my method of reducing color deemphasized them in particular.

◆ LESSON TWO ◆

◆ One rotten apple can fool the viewer into thinking the whole barrel is bad. Deciding how to reduce color makes the difference between a good and an excellent result.

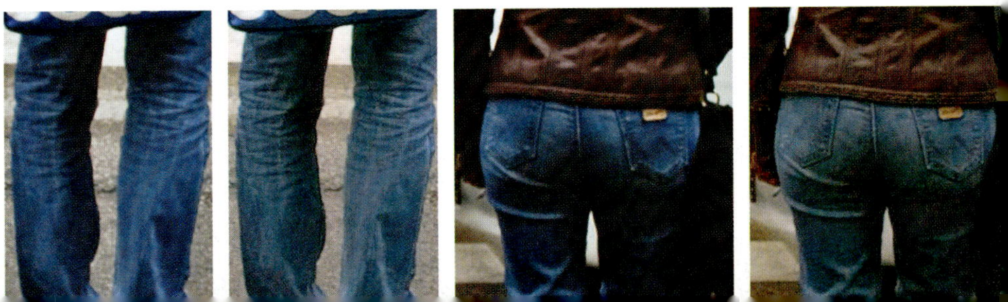

Figure 2.4 Unlike the three areas shown in Figure 2.3, the blue jeans of Figure 2.1C (right versions) are less colorful than those of Figure 2.1B.

Now that we have seen what happens when the final workflow step is fouled up, let's take a look at what happens when something bad occurs in the first step. Figure 2.5 shows a new original, and competing corrections by the same photographer and by me. How do you rate them?

Matters of Taste and Otherwise

Having spent the entirety of Chapter 1 creating a lake more brilliant than it is in real life, I am in no position to criticize the unrealistic greens of the photographer's version, Figure 2.5B. I've seen a lot of this type of greenness on sale in "fine art photography" galleries recently, so there's definitely a market for it. In fact, you'd have to download the image to see how green he has it. The galleries use fine inkjet printers with multiple inks, as well as high-quality paper. None of this was available for this book. So intense of a green is simply not reproducible here.

As to the merits of the two corrections, I know how you feel already, because, as with the earlier street scene, I've polled audiences. Nobody has yet voted for Figure 2.5B. What factor(s) do you think contribute?

Personally, I prefer color variation to monotony. My version, Figure 2.5C, has interesting yellows at the top and right, missing in Figure 2.5B. I haven't questioned audiences specifically about this, but I suspect they would feel the same way.

I'm more confident that they would prefer the added detail of Figure 2.5C. Color considerations aside, the water seems more active.

More than a thousand people have voted on two other questions, though. Unanimously, they say that the swan cannot be blue, as it is in Figure 2.5B. That flaw, by itself,

Figure 2.5 As in the earlier Figure 2.1, the original is below. On the facing page are two competing corrections.

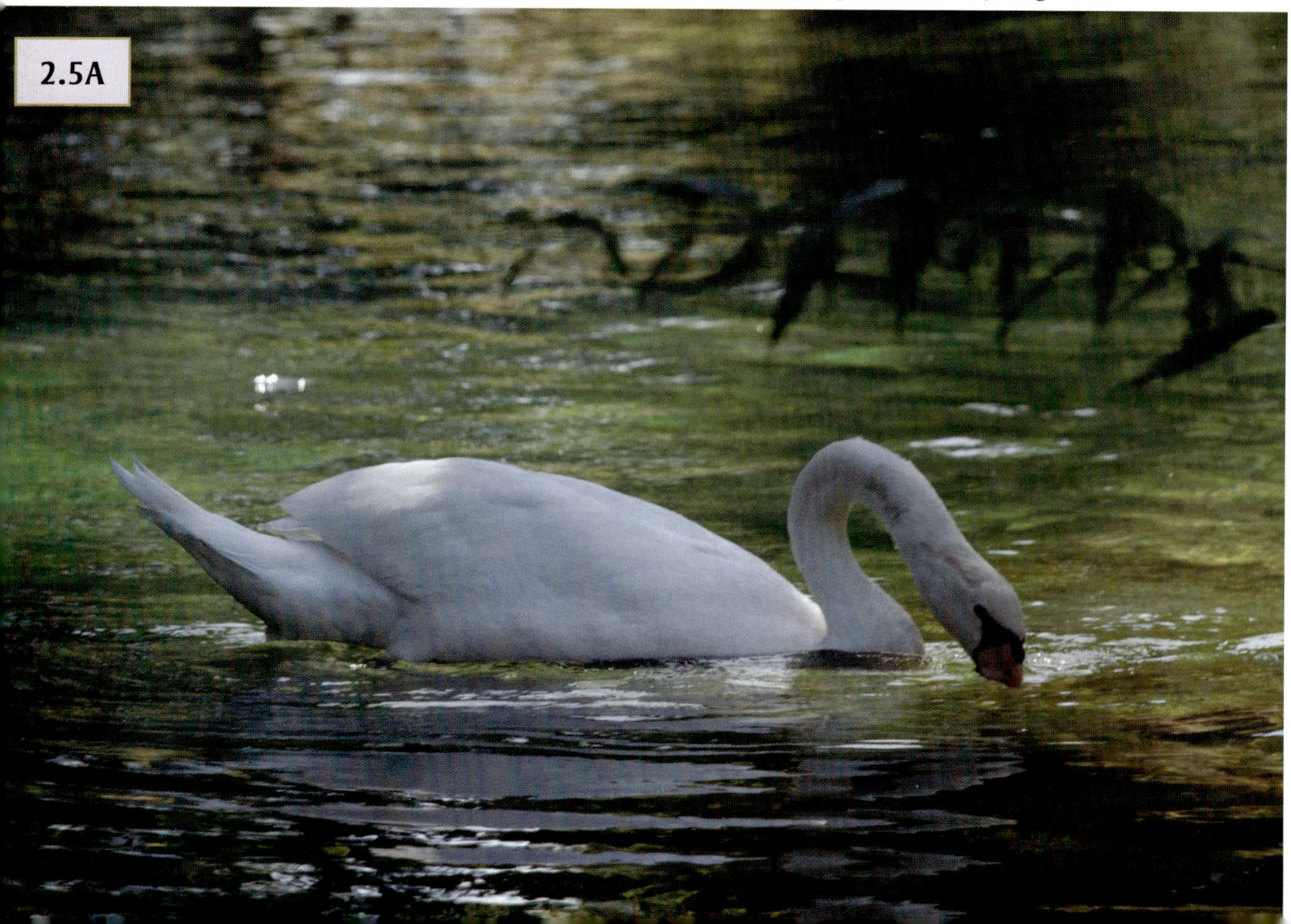

2.5B

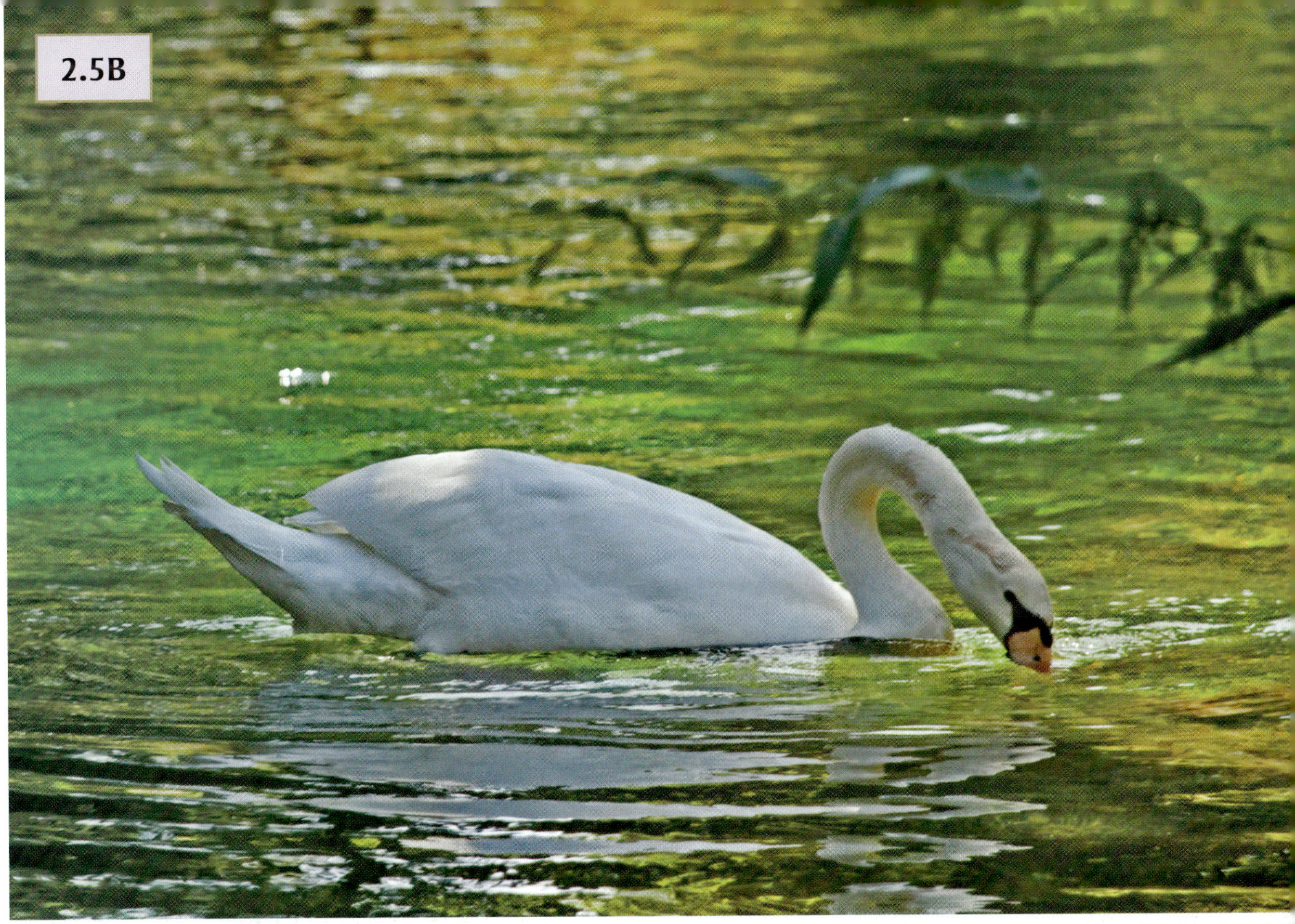

2.5C

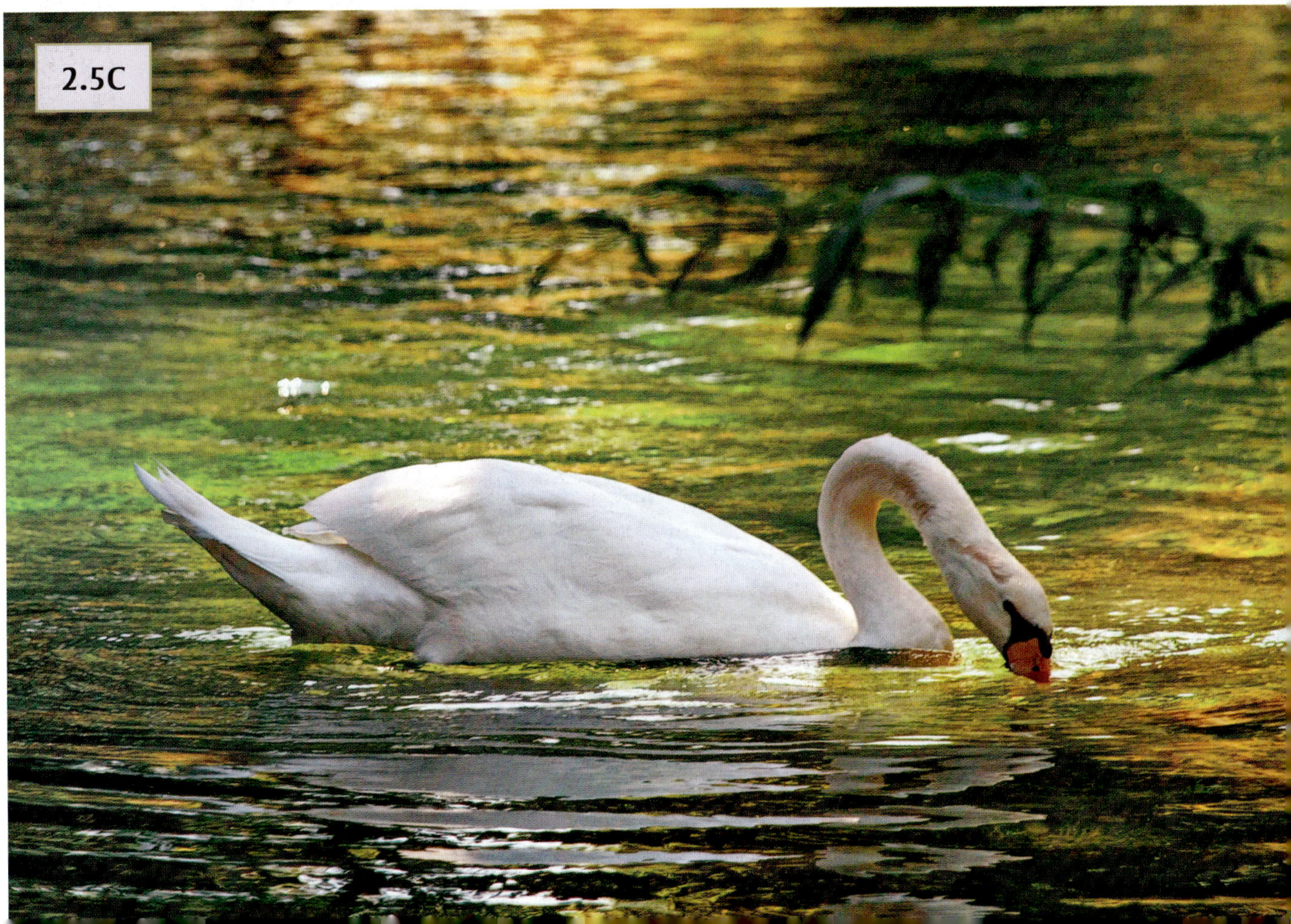

makes the version unacceptable, as indicated by the second unanimous vote, saying that 2.5C is superior.

The photographer's objectionable blueness came about because he omitted or mismanaged the very first step in the workflow.

That first step is to eliminate colors known to be incorrect, such as blue swans. Our next chapter, the most frustrating one in the book, will cover it. It's a difficult step, and most of the time is either unnecessary or unimportant. But then along comes a disaster waiting to happen.

The workflow makes all colors pop. Regrettably, it does not know whether the colors it's popping are right.

Small problems become huge ones if this step gets mangled. The original, Figure 2.5A, is so dark and moody that it's easy to overlook the slightly blue feathers. But nobody is going to overlook the blue bird of unhappiness in Figure 2.5B.

◆ **LESSON THREE** ◆

◆ The first color step can be ignored some of the time, but if you ignore it every time it will cook your goose, or swan, as the case may be.

* * *

This picture couldn't be much simpler from the point of view of the color detective. The background is a mystery. The water could be blue, for all we know. But we can say absolutely that swans are white.

The term *neutral* covers objects that are white, gray, or black, in other words, that lack color. Items of known neutrality are wonderful things, if you can find them. The easiest test of whether something that ought to be neutral really is: put the cursor over it and look at the Info palette. If the values of red, green, and blue are nearly equal, the object is neutral. An even faster way to tell, using equivalent values in LAB, can wait a chapter.

This first move is the most disciplined. Every other step in the workflow involves some flexibility, some creativity. Do the same image eight times, and you'll never get the same result twice unless you've made notes on what you did the last time.

I can vouch for this, because I happen to have *done* this particular image eight times. In the first half of 2010 I had to speak at several large conferences. The two exercises that form this chapter were featured. I didn't demonstrate how to do the street scene, preferring just to discuss the two corrected versions you saw in Figure 2.1. But I did this swan picture from scratch every time, to show the importance of the first step in the workflow.

An exercise like this in three minutes in public, with a projection system of questionable reliability while telling lame jokes in a foreign language and having to pivot 180 degrees every time you want to see the same screen that the audience does, is not as easy as it may sound. The eight results, in chronological order, constitute Figure 2.6.

Never the Same Way Twice

With only Figures 2.5A and 2.5B to compare to, any of these eight seem impressive—provided you don't compare them to each other. Even if you do, you have to be careful of what you're comparing.

My first reaction is that Figure 2.6A is the worst of the ballet. Its swan is technically neutral, but somehow there's a slight green flavor. And the background is boring.

Green casts are never right, even small ones. Figure 2.6C has the problem, too. If you're going to have a cast, make it a warm one. Figure 2.6E's swan varies toward purple and not green. For that reason, I'd hold my nose and vote for it over either Figure 2.6A or 2.6C.

Just as a rogue pair of jeans shouldn't convince us that a whole image is too colorful,

***Figure 2.6** Eight separate attempts to correct Figure 2.5A, mostly in front of live audiences.*

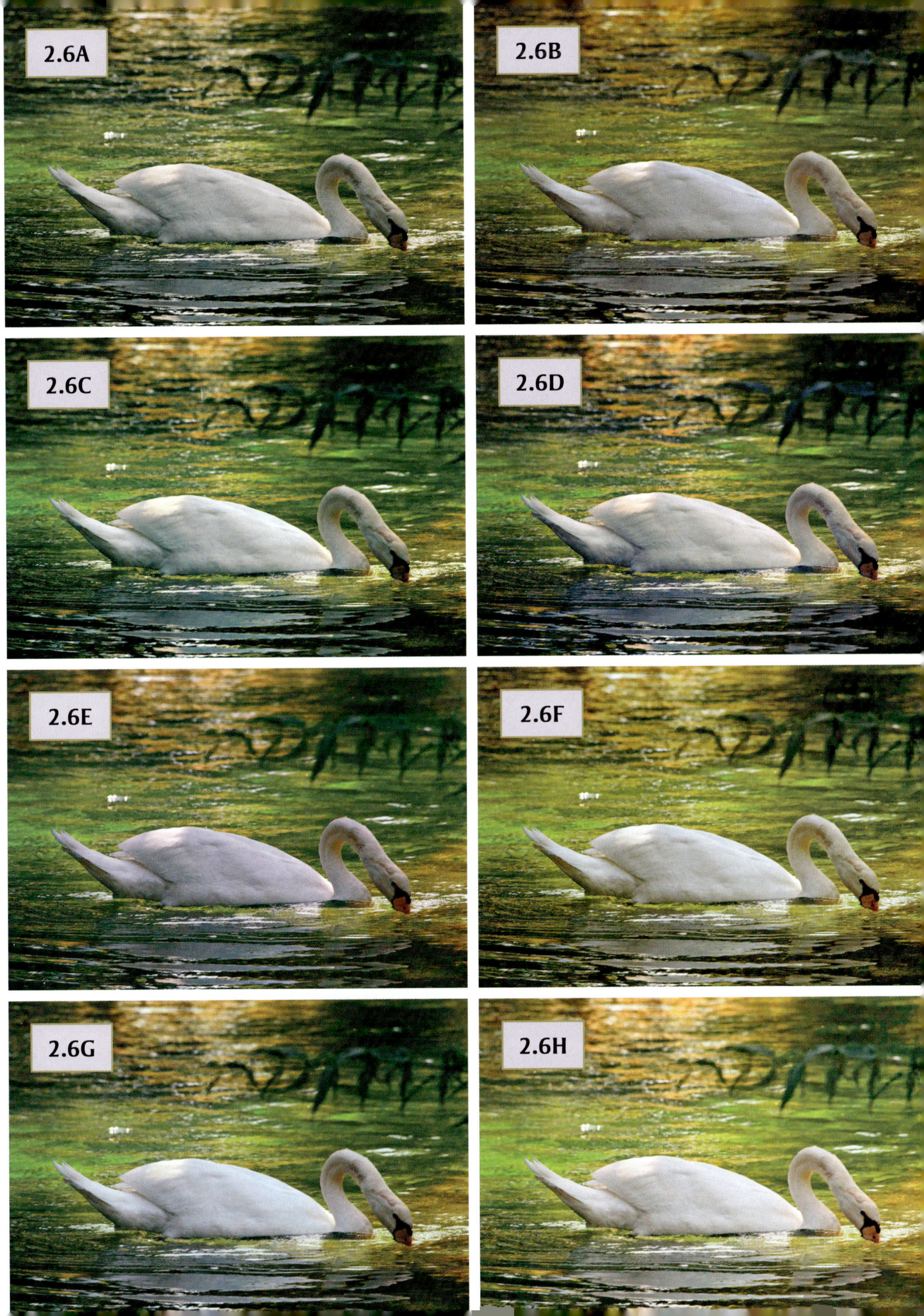

2.6A
2.6B
2.6C
2.6D
2.6E
2.6F
2.6G
2.6H

we shouldn't let a greenish swan talk us into trashing something perfectly usable.

Figure 2.6B's color is attractive. But its lake is not as dark as that of Figure 2.6A. The swan would be better defined if it were. A third version, using the color of one and the detail of the other, would therefore be better than either parent.

None of these eight versions is as good as the one that opened the discussion, Figure 2.5C. Not surprising: that one is a hybrid that uses pieces of seven of the variants.

I do not recommend making eight versions of any file. But I reiterate a standing recommendation: if extra time is available, making two or more quick versions from scratch and then combining them creatively is better than doing one version carefully.

How many versions should you make? It depends on how much time the photo is worth. If you're determined not to spend more than three minutes per image, then it's going to have to be one version and out. Some variants of Figure 2.6 are better than others but all beat the original handily.

It also depends on your level of comfort. The more you use PPW, the less apt you'll be to make some ugly error that destines the version for the trash.

With the luxury of extra time, try not to do one version right after completing the last one. That way, you won't remember exactly what you did the first time and your second version is more likely to be different.

In the current exercise I was lucky: days or even weeks separated each of my versions, so what I had done the previous time was long forgotten. On the other hand, all eight were done in *approximately* the same way. If this had been a real job and if I had taken leave of my senses and decided to do eight versions, they would definitely be more diverse than this group. I would try risky maneuvers on some, hoping to hit paydirt and being willing to rely on the other variants if I didn't. In this case, however, I was trying to impress people with the workflow and I could only create one version for them, so I wasn't going to chance doing the job some weird way.

Even so, these eight are different enough that if you compare one of them to another, you could find any of the following, among other possibilities.

- One version may have better color.
- One may have better detail.
- One version may be better in the lighter or darker areas.
- One may be better in light or dark areas, but only with respect to color or to detail.
- One may be better in certain colors but not others.
- One may be better, period.

If it's that last possibility, chuck the bad one. But this happens less frequently than you might think. If you persuade yourself, for example, that Figure 2.6B is clearly better than 2.6A, you've fallen into the same trap that the audience did in stating the street scene in Figure 2.1B was more colorful than 2.1C. It *was* more colorful, but only in certain respects, to wit, the blue jeans. Similarly, Figure 2.6A *is* worse than 2.6B, but only in certain respects, namely, its color. In terms of depth, detail, I'd say it's better.

◆ LESSON FOUR ◆

◆ Every corrected image has certain strengths and weaknesses. Making extra copies and combining them creatively can increase quality.

Demonstrations, Failed and Otherwise

These files can be merged to play up the strengths of each. It seemed to me that doing so might make a dynamite demonstration, one that would really make the point about why multiple versions are so valuable. And I gave that demo about a dozen times in 2011.

I stacked everything up into a single eight-layered file, earliest version on the bottom, with the top seven layers made invisible. The idea was to show the audience the second layer, compare it to the first, then decide whether to junk one or to combine the two, Whatever survived would get compared to the third version, for a possible further combination, and then to the fourth, and so on.

Unlike the correction itself, these merging steps were so obvious that there was little variation between performances. I started by joining the detail of Figure 2.6A and the color of Figure 2.6B. I was not a big fan of Figure 2.6C but I saw that its lighter half was better than what I had, so I merged it in through a layer mask that excluded the darker areas. And I limited the move to luminosity, because the color of Figure 2.6C is not that great.

Figure 2.6D had the opposite problem: good color, questionable contrast. So I always added about half of its color to the mix. And on and on, up until the seventh and final comparison, where I incorporated a certain percentage of Figure 2.6H's luminosity and a lesser one of its color.

The only time I made no merge was on the second-to-last comparison. There didn't seem to be a way to use Figure 2.6G to improve what I had after the first five merges. And this was peculiar, because before the exercise, I would ask the viewers to rate the eight variants. Every audience had at least a plurality and sometimes a majority in favor of Figure 2.6G.

In short, a convincing and very popular demonstration, so much so that I took it into my head that a full blow-by-blow description of the merging was in order here. You have just read a three-paragraph summary of what I did—can you imagine it fleshed out to six pages? In early drafts of this chapter, that's what it was.

The beta readers, some of whom had seen the live demonstration, pointed out that certain concepts don't translate well from stage to print, and this was one of them. They suggested that as written, it might be of interest to some but would be terribly tedious for others. I agree, so I have eliminated it, and recorded a video showing the whole procedure. Furthermore, just in case you want the full rundown, I saved the original draft that contains it, and have posted it as well.

Don't Believe What You See

Six of these eight originals come from live presentations in which the conditions may charitably be described as inadequate. The other two were done in my office as I practiced my spiel. These two had the benefit of a powerful computer, controlled lighting conditions, young monitor, you name it.

What was the impact of the vastly superior working conditions in my office? You guessed it. Figures 2.6A and 2.6E are the worst of the eight from the color standpoint.

I have an inadequate excuse for Figure 2.6E's purple swan. I had just started to play with the Modern Man from Mars action, which you'll see in Chapter 6.

All discoveries get overused and misused at first. I was under the impression that the new action was the answer to most Photoshop problems and possibly to global warming as well. And so I abused it.

Previously, only the first step of the workflow could alter gray balance. If the swan was neutral then, that's how it would stay.

The Bottom Line

People who say that a picture is "too colorful" are often deluded. A single offensive piece may convince them that the whole jigsaw puzzle is hopelessly loud. Our goal is to identify these obnoxious areas and cut them back more than the rest.

An effective way of doing so is to create multiple versions of the same picture. Each version usually has different strengths and weaknesses. They can be unified into a composite that offers the best of each parent, using layer masks, blending modes, and/or simple changes in opacity.

Being used to that insurance policy, I forgot that the MMM action had changed the rules. Since then, I've edited the action to avoid what happened and retain neutrality. At the time, however, in its zeal to distance everything from the greens that I had indicated were the most important color, MMM made the swan purple.

Why didn't I notice this? Probably for the same reason that the photographer didn't notice that he had a blue swan in Figure 2.5B. Human beings adjust quickly to whatever lighting they're confronted with. In a room with yellowish lighting we don't notice after a few moments that it isn't neutral. When staring at a screen showing a photo with an obvious cast, in short order it looks just fine to us.

◆ LESSON FIVE ◆

◆ When deciding if something that should be neutral is in fact neutral, don't trust your eyes. Trust the numbers.

Onward and Upward

This has been a chapter of extremes. We don't usually find such striking examples of a single color derailing an image as we did in the street scene of Figure 2.1. Failing to check the original color before the opening bell, which produced the blue swan of Figure 2.5B, is a grievous sin, but rarely is it punished so severely. And it is wildly uncommon to have eight versions to choose from.

On the other hand, the mistakes were real, unintentional, and were posted publicly. The eight versions of the swan are authentic and produced in front of bloodthirsty crowds.

Vivid colors are good things. Everybody likes them. Loudness is a bad thing. Nobody likes it. Sometimes a picture is in fact too intense overall. More frequently one or two parts are too intense, and they con the viewer into thinking that the whole picture is no good. Don't be hasty in deciding that everything needs to be cut back. Look for the specific areas that are offensive, and find a way to weaken their color.

Resist the curse of trying too hard. Decades of experience suggest that we should be careful at each step of the correction process. The decades of experience are wrong. Go fast, and then do the job again from scratch. None of the eight versions of Figure 2.6 took more than three minutes. If three minutes is all you have, any one of them is acceptable. If more time is available, some are better than others. The weaker ones were hampered by questionable decisions about color—the kind that all the time in the world wouldn't help. You've seen how much variation there is in my own work. In yours, there will probably be more. Protect yourself from bad decisions. Give yourself opportunities to take the best features from multiple versions.

We are about to enter the most frustrating and seemingly pointless part of the workflow, the first step, which checks for, and occasionally finds, color issues. Most of the time there isn't a serious problem, but we should remember Figure 2.5B's blue swan.

If that step is forgotten or ignored, now and then the picture for which you had such high hopes will instead offer another lesson in human perception.

3

Once for Color: Early Detective Work

The workflow commences with its most difficult step. Later moves will boost color substantially, which means that any minor imperfections may become major ones. A disciplined approach is needed to identify such color issues and eliminate them before they become fatal.

Exploits of the famous color theorist, Lieutenant Columbo of the LAPD, represent a non-traditional style known as the *inverted mystery.* Unlike the classical whodunit, the murderer's identity is known from the outset. The mystery is how Columbo, who already suspects the truth, will be able to prove it.

The end is an anticlimax. Columbo will find his proof, usually due to the perpetrator's own mistakes. In a final head-to-head scene, Columbo will, by fiendish logic, force the criminal to acknowledge defeat. In terms of drama, it's interesting, but to a true fan of mysteries, it's boring. The real work comes during the investigation, where all the clues come together into a harmonious whole.

The Picture Postcard Workflow is like that, too. We know perfectly well what the final scene is going to be like. Some kaleidoscope of wild colors will appear, and then, with approaches that are subtly different between images, we detectives will, by fiendishly clever logic, force the viewer to believe that an extremely colorful image is nothing of the kind. In terms of drama, it's interesting, as exciting colors always are, but to a true fan of color correction technique, it's boring. The real work comes earlier, where everything is prepared so that the final moment will go off without a hitch.

All good detective fiction serves up a lot of irrelevant information, such as Columbo's preference for chili. Otherwise the audience would know that every scene contains a vital clue.

It's the same way with this first step. We examine the picture for color flaws. Often enough there aren't any. In that case, we don't try to

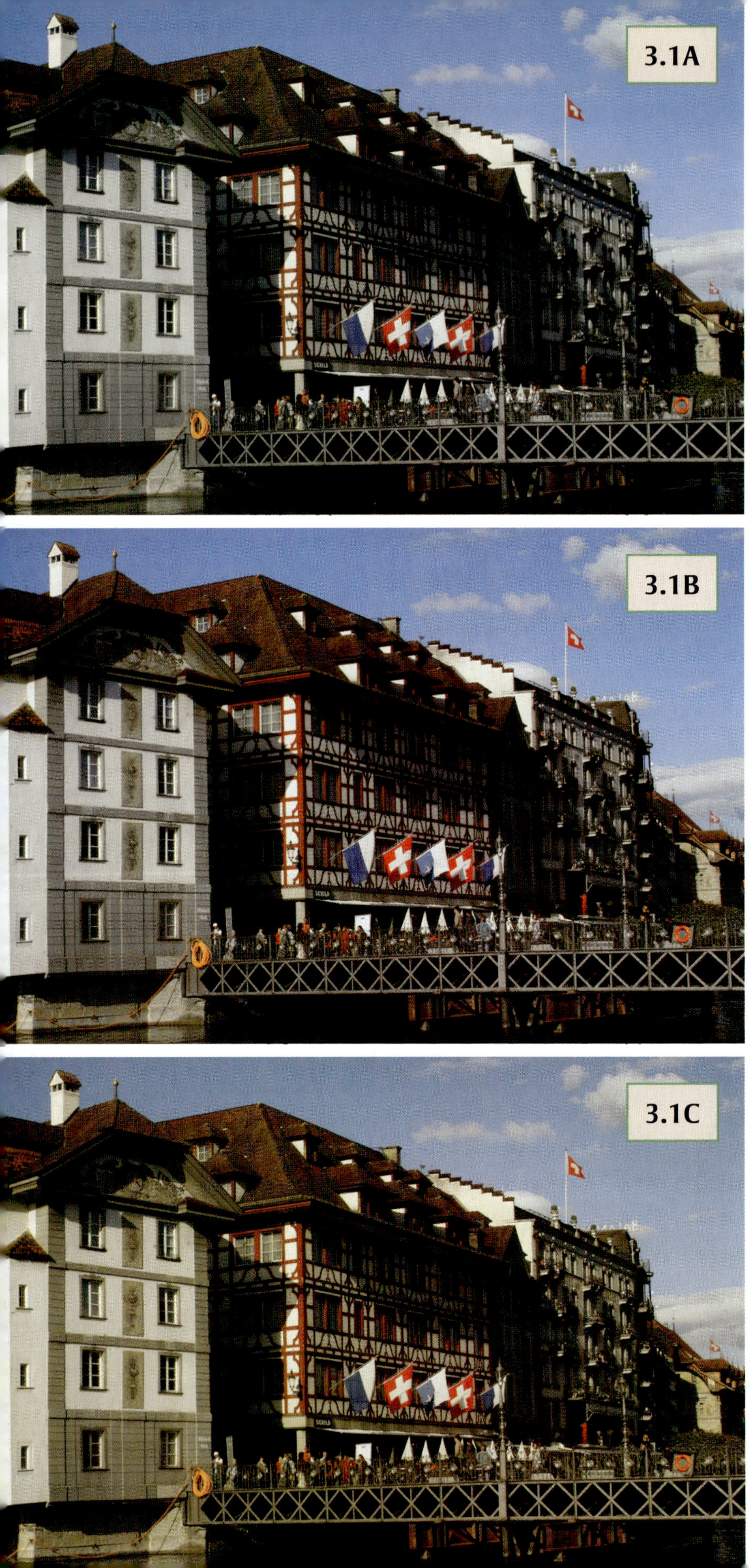

force something to happen. We simply say, as Columbo does, it's just standard procedure, sir, nothing to worry about.

Gathering the Clues

Perfect, or even attractive color, is not the goal of this chapter. Instead, we are trying for color that is *not wrong*—color that might cause a problem down the line. We have no interest at this time in changing detail, contrast, or *weight,* which is retoucherese for the overall feeling of lightness or darkness.

There needs to be an initial examination to see whether anything *is* wrong, because if there isn't we want to move briskly on to the contrast-enhancing moves described in the next chapter.

In traditional workflows this examination takes longer than it should. We want to keep it to ten seconds or less. If it turns out that something needs to be done, more time must be invested, but if not, onward.

Every picture in this chapter *does* have a color problem. Otherwise its inclusion would be pointless. I mention this so that you won't forget that usually there is either no issue or only a slight one. Subsequent chapters, which normally show the unvarnished original even when discussing some later

Figure 3.1 *Top, the original. Middle, a version corrected for color using techniques described in this chapter. Bottom, an alternate version created in seconds with a primitive tool.*

step, should give a better idea of how often we have to adjust color early.

Figure 3.1A, the original photo, is too dark. But this chapter, being interested only in color, snaps its fingers and snorts at darkness. Its only goal is to get to Figure 3.1B. Its methods take about a minute to achieve this.

Figure 3.1C is a more primitive alternative. It requires only seconds to execute and not too much brainpower. More about it later. For the time being, assume that Figure 3.1B is what we want.

You may be wondering whether it's really worth an entire chapter to discuss how to make changes as limited as between Figures 3.1A and 3.1B. Possibly it wouldn't be if we were planning to leave them as is. However, we intend to boost colors beyond belief late in the process, after which we will figure out an elegant way to cut back.

We now apply to Figures 3.1A and 3.1B the same Color Boost action we saw in the first chapter, Figure 1.7A. Lightening is still needed, and has been added equally to the two variants, producing Figures 3.2A and 3.2B. The two are intentionally much too colorful, par for the PPW course. Figure 3.2A exaggerates the deficiencies of its parent, Figure 3.1A. The background is distinctly cold. The clouds are blue, the roof's redness is suppressed, and the farthest building has a cyan tinge.

Picture postcards specialize in warmth, which we associate with sunlight and happiness. Yes, Figure 3.2B is too much of a good thing. Yes, it would be possible to continue the workflow from Figure 3.2A. Yes, it would still look better than the original. The coolness, however, would be a limitation that would preclude the best result.

It's easier to deal with excessively red areas than with an image that gives an overly cool impression, so we just choose Figure 3.2B, toning it down a little on the way to producing Postcard 3.3.

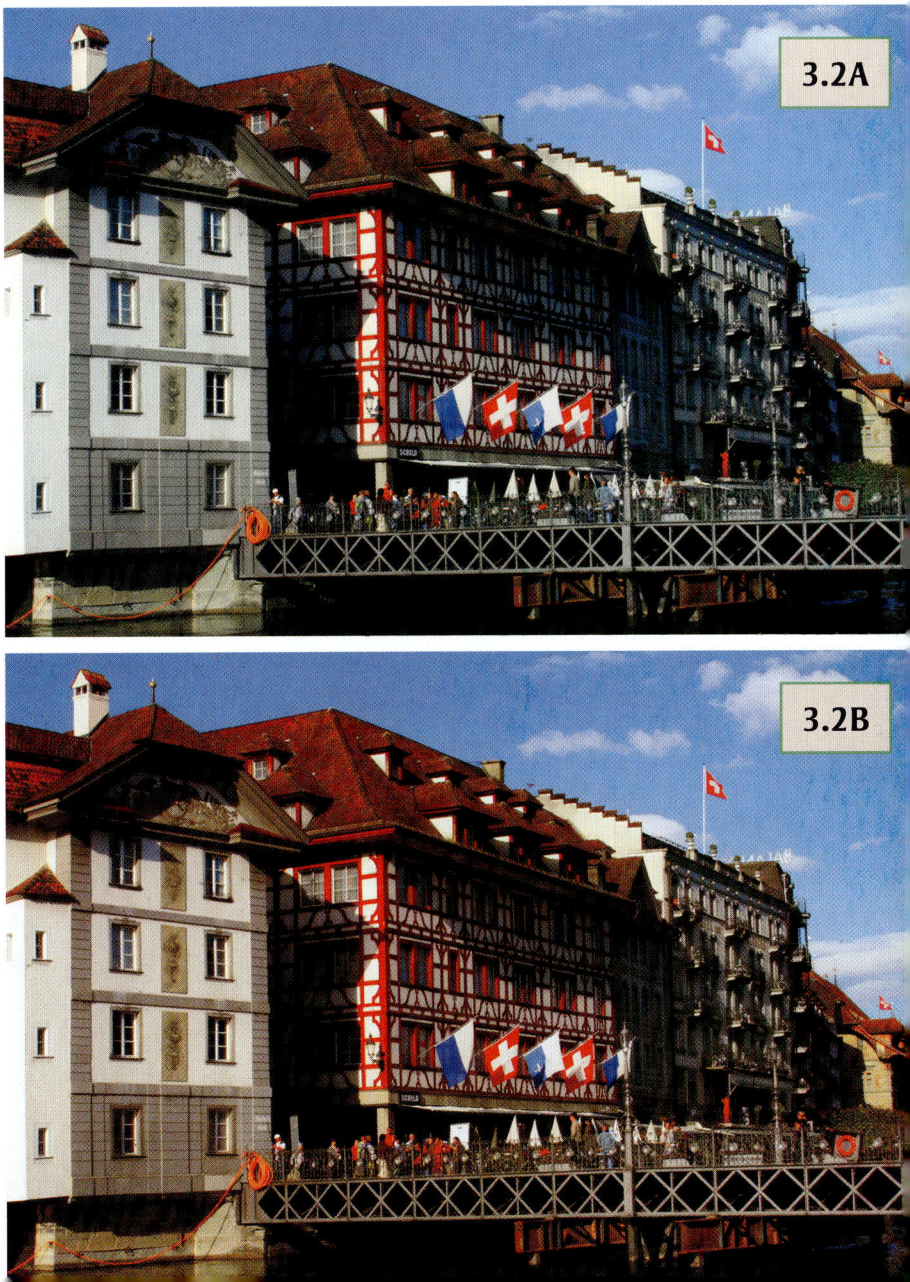

***Figure 3.2** Chapter 5's Color Boost action, plus equal lightening of both files, produces intentionally oversaturated renditions of Figure 3.1A, top, and 3.1B. Note the coolness of the top version.*

The Usual Known-Color Suspects

We intervene when we find convincing evidence that what we're looking at is wrong.

The most likely source of such evidence is being lucky enough to encounter objects that experience tells us must be *neutral*—white, gray, or black. Parts of the flags should surely be white; if we find that they aren't, the case is made for getting involved.

The second-likeliest source: things close to, but not necessarily truly neutral. Alternatives can often be ruled out. The light building at left might be white or gray, but we can't say for sure. However, based on extensive observation of similar buildings, it cannot be on the blue, green, or purple side of gray. If anything, it's a brownish gray, maybe with a tendency toward yellow.

In short, we don't know what it is, but we know many things that it is *not*. That we get it "right" isn't necessary. Any value that *could* be right is better than any that definitely isn't.

That same we-know-what's-wrong philosophy can be applied to three other common objects: trees and other green vegetation; faces, and skies. All three categories have broad ranges of what might be acceptable. But occasionally we find numbers that are outside them, indicating we need to step in.

Considering that this workflow is touted as an easier way, it must be disheartening to hear that the first of the three steps we are about to study is not only more difficult than the other two but also offers the least immediate gratification. Furthermore, it requires the most discipline, because the problems it addresses have right answers and wrong ones. Chapters 4 and 5 are more intuitive: the correct answers are the ones that look good to you.

As if that isn't frustrating enough, the techniques of the next three chapters are important in almost every image, but those found in this chapter are important in less than half.

Feedback from people who have adopted this workflow reinforces this statement. Uniformly they report difficulty in dealing with the more subtle cases. Some have even given up: they use the PPW anyway for the results they can get when the original color isn't off, and simply accept that a quarter or so of their images won't look very good.

Beta reader James Gray offers some encouragement. He notes my point that traditional professional workflows were even more demanding because they juggled contrast and color at the same time.

James writes, "Having a background in mathematics suggests to me that trying to adjust *two* variables at the same time is kind of nuts. When it is possible to separate variables and adjust them separately the process is much more logical.

"I might add some more about how to proceed if the reader finds this step too difficult at first. I did myself when I first tried the PPW. I found two alternatives. First I routinely adjust the color in Adobe Camera Raw. The other is a quick temporary step into LAB. I have used both techniques. Certainly adjusting color using a curves adjustment layer that is converted to Color mode is superior. You go into this later in the chapter. I can vouch for the fact that after some practice with the PPW first step it becomes easier."

* * *

If you're spinning your wheels in this chapter, you may wish to skip directly to the next one, planning to return later. After the first example, the rest is mostly drill. If you are interested in optimizing quality, you'll have to master these skills sooner or later, even if you decide not to use the rest of the workflow. However, there's no urgent need to get to that level right now.

***Postcard 3.3** Top, the original. Bottom, a corrected version using all facets of the PPW. Note the similarities with the color of Figure 3.2B.*

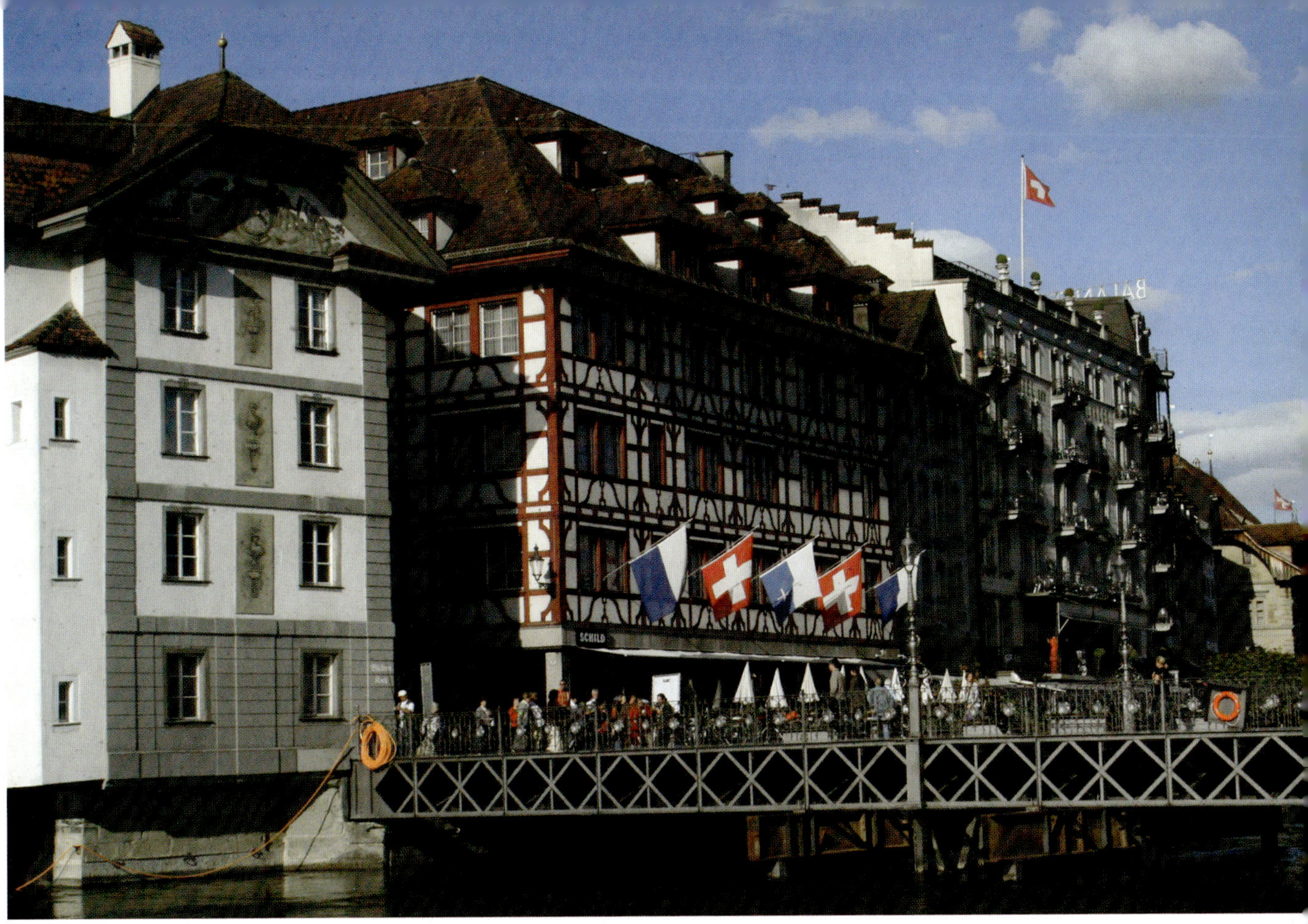
SCHILD

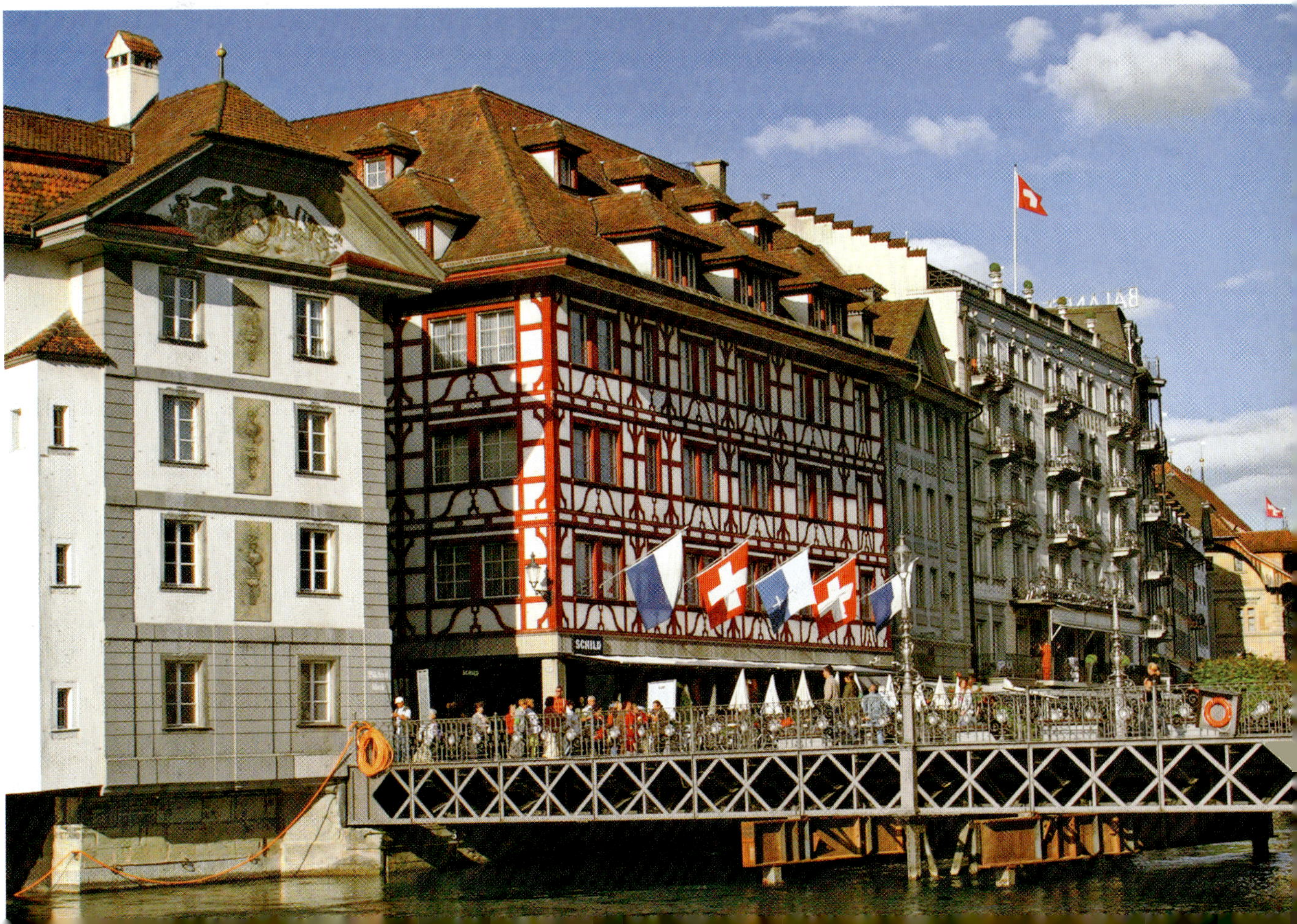
SCHILD

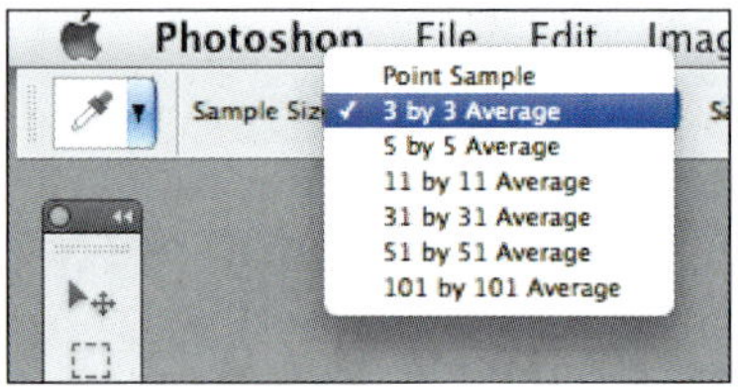

***Figure 3.4** Options for the eyedropper tool should be switched away from the default Point Sample.*

If you must have a simpler way, try this on Figure 3.1A.

- Make a duplicate layer.
- Image: Adjustments>Curves.
- Beneath the grid in the curves dialog reside three eyedroppers. Click the middle one. This informs Photoshop that you are about to tell it that a certain color should be neutral.
- Without closing the dialog, click the lightest area of the large cloud at top right.
- Click OK.
- Change the mode of the top layer from Normal to Color, indicating that you want to retain the detail of the original layer but use the color of the top layer.
- You have now produced Figure 3.1C. It looks too yellow. Lower the opacity of the top layer until you think things look better, maybe to 50% or 60%.

The only brainpower required is the decision that the cloud is probably too blue. The eyedropper maneuver turned it gray; your reduction of opacity split the difference. It's not as good as the method I'm about to describe, but it goes a long way toward solving the problem. No law prohibits correcting for color again after the entire workflow is completed if your first try didn't quite achieve its goals. But with no first try at all the later color problem may be so severe that it can no longer be corrected.

If still discouraged, perhaps you may take heart from knowing that in the old days we had it worse. We still had to adjust color this way but we also had to worry about screwing up detail. In the PPW, we don't.

Chapter Goals and Recap

This chapter strives to eliminate colors that can be proven incorrect. Its modest goal is not good color, not attractive color, but color that is *not clearly wrong*. Because the fireworks of Chapters 5 and 6 intensify color so much, problems that appear inconsequential now may become major later.

The work is done in RGB using a curves adjustment layer, occasionally more than one. The layer is set to Color mode, meaning that the original detail remains untouched. Therefore, this chapter ignores contrast issues altogether.

How Difficult Is It? This is the hardest chapter of all, and offers the least immediate rewards. It requires practice and is less intuitive than any other step. Particularly, PPW beginners often feel like they're doing something wrong if they can't locate a color problem worth correcting. In fact, the probable reason that they can't see one is that none exists.

How Often Is It Needed? Much depends on shooting conditions, but around a third of the originals I've tested don't have any color issue. In maybe another third, inaccuracies can be identified and corrected, but they're so minor that it's hard to tell the difference afterward. So, this chapter only has a significant impact on quality about a third of the time. Less, if most of your work is shot in a studio, where initial color issues are infrequent.

The Boys in the Lab

In detective work, there are times for subtlety in the investigation and times for more persuasive, or coercive methods. Our workflow has the same structure.

The spectacular color boosts, which we haven't looked at yet, will come in LAB, which delivers them easily, effectively, and attractively. But LAB, being rather a loose cannon, isn't good at making the types of subtle preliminary adjustments found in this chapter. Hence, if necessary, we solve the problems with RGB curves. And now we get into some serious irony.

LAB's potency in making bright but believable colors is well known, but it also has a reputation for not being easy to understand. Fortunately, when the time comes to put it through its paces, you don't have to *understand* LAB. All you have to do is decide when it's doing too much of a good thing.

Weirdly, the time to know how LAB works is right now—when we're still in RGB. The reasons are speed and ease of use. Everybody who's taken the trouble to learn the LAB evaluation procedure swears by it, even though they have very different ideas of what to do with the information.

Doubt the LAB advantage in color evaluation? Take a sky, any sky. No RGB or CMYK formula can define whether the color is acceptable. But in LAB, all you have to accept is that skies are usually blue, and an easy-to-check formula jumps out at you.

LAB, like the PPW itself, separates color and contrast. All detail lives in the L channel; all color in the A and B. Since the current step is concerned with color only, the L can be ignored for purposes of this chapter.

The A and B are opponent-color channels. The A runs from magenta to green. Remembering that these channels have no effect on literal darkness, light parts of the A are more magenta, darker ones more green, and midtones, neither. The B operates similarly from yellow (lightest) to blue (darkest).

The numbering system employs both positive and negative values. Negatives are cold (green or blue respectively) and positives warm (magenta or yellow). Values near zero are none of the above. If both channels are zero the object is neutral.

The further away from zero, the more intense the color. The limits are –128 and +127, but we never see anything even close in photographs. Plus or minus 50 is extremely colorful. Parentheses denote negatives, for reasons of typographic sanity.

Suppose that a sky measures $0^A(15)^B$. The negative B indicates a moderate blue. The 0^A says that the blue is pure, with no tendency toward magenta or green. This AB combination surely *might* be right for a sky. As this

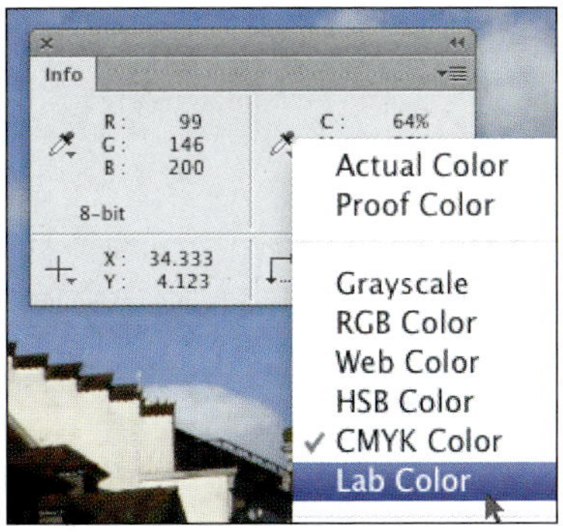

***Figure 3.5** Options for the right side of the Info palette should be switched away from the default CMYK in favor of reading values in LAB.*

chapter only concerns itself with the clearly incorrect, we'll have to leave this one alone.

How would we know that a sky is wrong, then? We already are ignoring the L. We may as well ignore the B, too. Skies are gray on overcast days—0^B, neither blue nor yellow. They can also be intensely blue—very negative. Or any point in between. So any non-positive value in the sky could be right.

The A is another story. Skies should not be magenta or green, at least not strongly so. It isn't necessary to have exactly 0^A, but it needs to be close. Purplish skies exist, but slightly greenish ones are more common.

Here, therefore, is the formula for evaluating skies. Ignore the L and also the B, unless it somehow winds up positive. Values of between $(5)^A$ and 3^A are reasonable. Anything else suggests a problem.

Testing the Evidence

Thinking in LAB while working in RGB necessitates changes in Photoshop defaults.

- Choose the eyedropper tool in the Toolbox. If the Options bar across the top of the

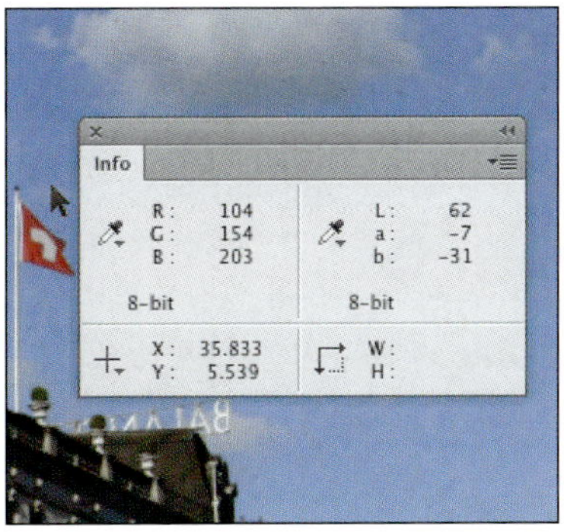

***Figure 3.6** Readings in the sky show that the value in the A channel is more negative than is recommended, suggesting that the sky could be too green.*

screen is not visible, double-click the tool to make it appear.

- Click and hold on Sample Size on the left of the bar. For more accurate readings, change the default Point Sample to 3 by 3 Average, as shown in Figure 3.4.
- Display the Info palette (Window: Info if it isn't open already). Observe that its top panel is divided into two halves. By default, the left half displays Actual Color—that is, values denominated in the file's own colorspace, RGB at present. The right half, by default, gives the closest CMYK equivalents based on the definition of CMYK found in your Edit: Color Settings dialog.
- Click the eyedropper next to the right half's values. Change it from CMYK to Lab color, as shown in Figure 3.5.
- Mouse over the sky and read the values in the right half of the Info palette (Figure 3.6). A reminder that the document itself is still in RGB, not LAB, but the Info palette is reporting equivalents.

Figure 3.6 indicates that the sky is at $62^L(7)^A(31)^B$. As noted earlier, the L and B values can be ignored, but the A is two points less than the minimum recommended value in the box on Page 51. In principle this suggests that the sky is too green; in practice it might mean blue-green. Remember, skies are *supposed* to be blue. We have no way of knowing whether this one is *too* blue.

Color concepts vary by culture. Mourners wear black in Western countries, but yellow in Egypt, red in parts of South Africa, and purple in Thailand. A North American can be *green* with envy, but the same emotion makes one *red* in South America. Someone who is *blue* is sad in the United States, but recovering from a hangover in Germany, and feeling romantic in Italy, where the equivalent of *Prince Charming* is *The Blue Prince.*

On the other hand, some meanings are universal. Spaniards say that optimists see everything bathed in rosy light; the French that they live the life in rose. American and Russian optimists look at the world through rose-colored glasses.

And so it is with *warm* and *cold,* at least with reference to color. Every culture says that any color redder than either a yellow or a purple is *warm,* and that anything bluer is *cold.* Furthermore, the emotional sense of these terms is the same the whole world over. Postcards, like coffee and biscuits, are best enjoyed warm.

Just a Few Loose Ends, Sir

A lot of bad skies pass our initial inspection because we can't prove them wrong. Known neutrals have less wiggle room. Looking for them should therefore be the first step in analyzing a file.

Perfect neutrals are 0^A0^B, neither magenta nor green, neither yellow nor blue. In practice, a slight variation can't be avoided. The flags, however, seem to be in sunshine. They have no excuse to be even slightly cold. So the desired target should be 0^A0^B, or something slightly positive in both A and B. Positive in only one of the two would create either magenta or yellow, rather than red or orange.

How about the things that are nearly neutral, but not necessarily perfectly so? We don't need to worry about the lighter areas of the left-hand building. They're almost the same darkness as the flags, so if the flags are right, the building will be also. But the grayish cement in the same building might need separate attention. Like the flags, if this cement is not neutral, it must be warm. At least in my opinion.

The opposite is true of the large cloud at top right. Very light clouds are predictably white. As they get darker, they can become more blue. Consequently, if not 0^B, the clouds need to be B–negative.

Finally, the darkest building, to the right of the one with the flags displayed, is in shadow. When a photo features sun and shade, these

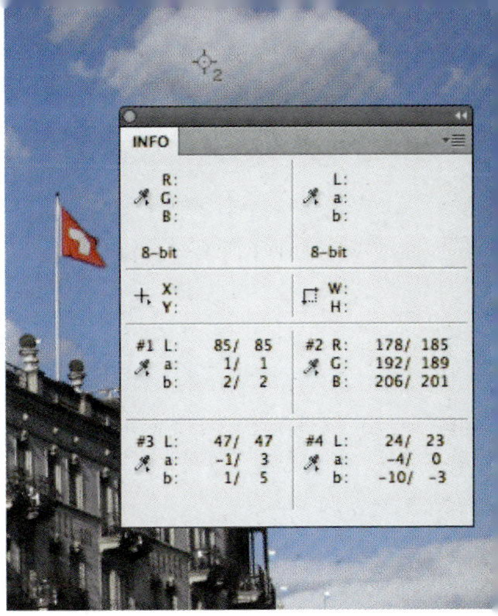

***Figure 3.7** The color sampler tool adds up to four fixed points to the Info palette. They have the same display options as in the main palette. When a curve or similar command is open, the slashes denote before-and-after values.*

shadowy areas usually come out cooler than a human would perceive them.

The last four paragraphs dumped on our heads a large number of items that require checking. To keep things straight, we wheel out the color sampler tool, which lives in the same toolbox location as its close relative, the eyedropper. If the eyedropper tool is already active, holding down the Shift key converts it temporarily into the color sampler.

Clicking with the color sampler active expands the Info palette with up to four reference points, each describing the current status of an area you clicked. A corresponding crosshairs, numbered from #1 to #4, stays in the image file for reference. For example, a crosshairs labeled #2 appears in the cloud above the Info palette of Figure 3.7.

To move one of these points, click and drag it with the color sampler active. To delete it, drag it out of the picture, or Option-click it.

The points are referred to only by number, which makes it hard to remember what they represent. To keep things straight, develop a pattern and stick to it. Mine is to start with the lightest and work down to the darkest. I clicked first, therefore, into the white area of the nearest flag. Next came the lightest portion of the cloud, third was the gray cement, and fourth the shadowy building.

The sky is so big and so uniform that sweeping the cursor over it and reading the changing values in the palette proper is easy. This is fortunate, because I had already reached the limit of four sampler points.

Each reference point has its own private eyedropper, so you can set some to read LAB while keeping others in Actual Color.

If a curve or any other dialog is open, slashes appear in each value box. To the left are current values, to the right those we get if we accept the curve (or whatever other adjustment is pending).

Figure 3.7 shows the state of the expanded Info palette while the curves that produced Figure 3.1B were still open. The mode of the curves layer had already been changed from Normal to Color. Before showing the curves, let's see what the original findings were and how the curves altered them.

Point #1, the white flag, was originally 1^A2^B, very slightly to the warm side of gray, just what we'd like. It doesn't change.

Point #2 reads RGB. I left it that way to show the LAB advantage. Yes, an experienced person can read that the blue value is highest and the green second-highest, meaning that the overall color is a greenish-blue. But it's hard for a non-expert to tell whether the values to the right of the slash are less colorful than those to the left, and even harder to know whether they represent a lighter or darker overall color.

If we switch its eyedropper to read LAB,

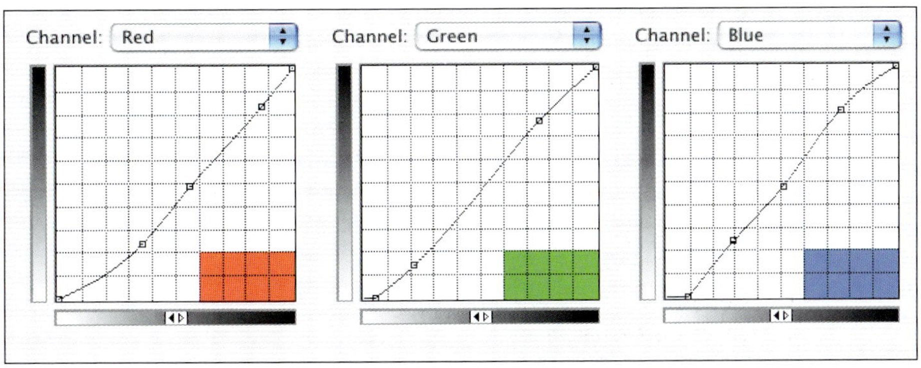

***Figure 3.8** The curves that transformed Figure 3.1A into Figure 3.1B.*

#2 shows $77^L(3)^A(9)^B$ before, $77^L0^A(7)^B$ after. Translation: it's still blue, but not as blue as it used to be. And the 0^A means that it's no longer green at all. That's a good thing. Nobody likes green clouds.

Also, the L values are identical, not just in this subpanel, but, within reason, in the other three. When the curves, which are shown in Figure 3.8, were first applied, this wasn't the case. The whole image got lighter. But changing the layer to Color mode restored, at least theoretically, the original darkness, while retaining the improved color. In traditional workflows, keeping the desired darkness is another worry added to an already troublesome step. With the PPW, we attend to the darkness issue in the next two chapters and ignore it here.

On to #3. The original cement was $(1)^A1^B$—slightly green-yellow. This is a poor choice, and is replaced by the warmer 3^A5^B. Why does color sampler point #3 move so much more than #1? Because the objectionable coolness gets worse as the picture gets darker. #4, the darkest of the four points, starts at a depressing $(4)^A(10)^B$, which needs a major move to get even close to neutrality. $0^A(3)^B$ is still blue, but at least it isn't that nasty green.

Curves and Opponent Colors

Writing these RGB curves becomes much easier with the realization that our ground rules turn RGB into a form of LAB—a pure opponent-color environment.

The A of LAB is divorced from darkness. It is pure color, green vs. magenta. If we "darken" the A the picture becomes greener (or, if you like, less magenta, it's the same thing) but not literally darker.

The green channel of RGB and its cousin, the magenta of CMYK, are in a sense similar. Darken either one and the picture becomes more magenta, which is less green. The difference from LAB is that the picture gets darker, too. That's why it's tougher to read RGB numbers; it's hard to understand to what extent they reflect color and to what extent darkness. That's also why traditional RGB curve corrections were so difficult.

The PPW jettisons this problem. Darkness is now irrelevant. The curves go on a layer that will eventually be set to Color mode. Darkening the green channel therefore darkens nothing. But it does subtract green/add magenta, reminiscent of the A of LAB.

Making the blue darker doesn't darken the picture, because Color mode prevents it. But it does make the picture less blue/more yellow. In this respect, it resembles the function of the B of LAB, except that to make something yellower, you lighten the B.

The red channel of RGB has no direct LAB relative. Instead, along with its CMYK cousin the cyan, it resembles working on both AB channels at once. Darkening makes the picture less red/more cyan.

It sounds, therefore, like we could fix up the color in any of the three colorspaces. CMYK, however, is not inviting. If we have to go to CMYK at all, it is normally done late in the process.

LAB is also inadequate. Its curves are more difficult to control, and any change would affect all darkness ranges equally. But in RGB, the curves are applied to a channel with variable color and darkness. So we can apply a curve that affects the color of darker areas, even though our use of Color mode means that the curve cannot change darkness itself.

The explanation makes it sound more complicated than it is. Let's give it a try.

Our picture is too cold. Click near the center of the red curve and move it down, toward lightness. (See box on curves orientation and shortcuts, facing page, for some warnings.) Lightening the red channel adds red/reduces cyan. Presto! Picture gets warmer.

The above may well get things close enough so that we can move on to the next step. However, it ignores what the boys in the

LAB found, which is that the coolness of the original is worse as the picture gets darker. So, let's be more sophisticated. Second try coming up.

Lightening the red channel with a point placed in the center lightens the mid-range more than the extremes. For better results, the point should be placed higher up, more toward the dark side.

To sum up: the curve as first applied makes the image lighter and redder. The effect is strongest in the darker parts and tails off as the image gets lighter. We then change the mode to Color, which eliminates the lightening effect but preserves the additional redness, which we have arranged to be most pronounced in the darker areas.

The third and final try is shown in Figure 3.8. The concept is the same: lighten the red channel, warm the picture. But points have been added to the other two channels to try to get closer to certain desired values. Nothing is sacred about these particular points. Once the red curve is lightened, diminishing returns set in. You could come up with slightly different curves that would be just as effective.

Just One More Thing, Sir

It may be easiest to start, as Columbo does, with the known result and work backwards. We know that the biggest problem is the coldness in the darkest part. So examine, please, the top quarter of each curve. To be precise, look at the 80% point: the intersection of the gridlines two down and two to the left from the top right. By default, a curve passes directly through that point. Do these three modified curves pass above or below it? And what do they accomplish?

Curves Orientation and Shortcuts

Richard Fariña's *Been Down So Long It Looks Like Up to Me,* a classic of the angry Sixties, speaks of the frustration of being a student. In today's world, where so many of us must work in both RGB and CMYK, not to mention LAB and grayscale, the truth of the title hits home.

Prior to Photoshop CS4, the most frustrating obstacle to learning curves was that Photoshop presents two contradictory default orientations. In CMYK or grayscale (including editing a mask) the default orientation is darkness to the right. Raising the curve darkens the picture, lowering it lightens. Unfortunately, in RGB and LAB, the default is the opposite. Darkness is to the left, so raising lightens, lowering darkens.

I have enough problems knowing which way is up in everyday life without Photoshop's help. It is inefficient, not to say mind-frying, to deal with two conflicting defaults, so I recommend that you choose one orientation and stick with it in all colorspaces. To do this, open the Curves dialog (not a curves adjustment layer), with Image: Adjustments > Curves. If necessary, click the arrow at the bottom next to Curve Display Options to expose what's underneath it. If you want darkness to the right—which is the way all curves in this book are shown—click Pigment/Ink %. Otherwise choose Light.

Implementing competing default orientations was a mistake that Photoshop made two decades ago. It wasn't nearly as bad as the mindless changes to curve adjustment layers in Photoshop CS4, which established competing curves dialogs! After 15 years of having the basic curve dialogs operate the same as curves adjustment dialogs, they now feature different shortcuts and different methods of measuring color. So, unless you take steps to resurrect the traditional dialog on adjustment layers, you are stuck with curves dialogs that behave differently at different times. The PPW panel accesses the traditional dialog.

It is unreasonable to subject readers to two sets of instructions on how the dialog works. Therefore, this book tries to avoid areas where the two dialogs differ, but where necessary, we use the traditional dialog. Although this book was prepared in CS5 and CS6, curve graphics are shown using the pre-CS3 interface. Today's interface puts the thin line of the curves themselves in the channel's color, which is hard to print and harder to read.

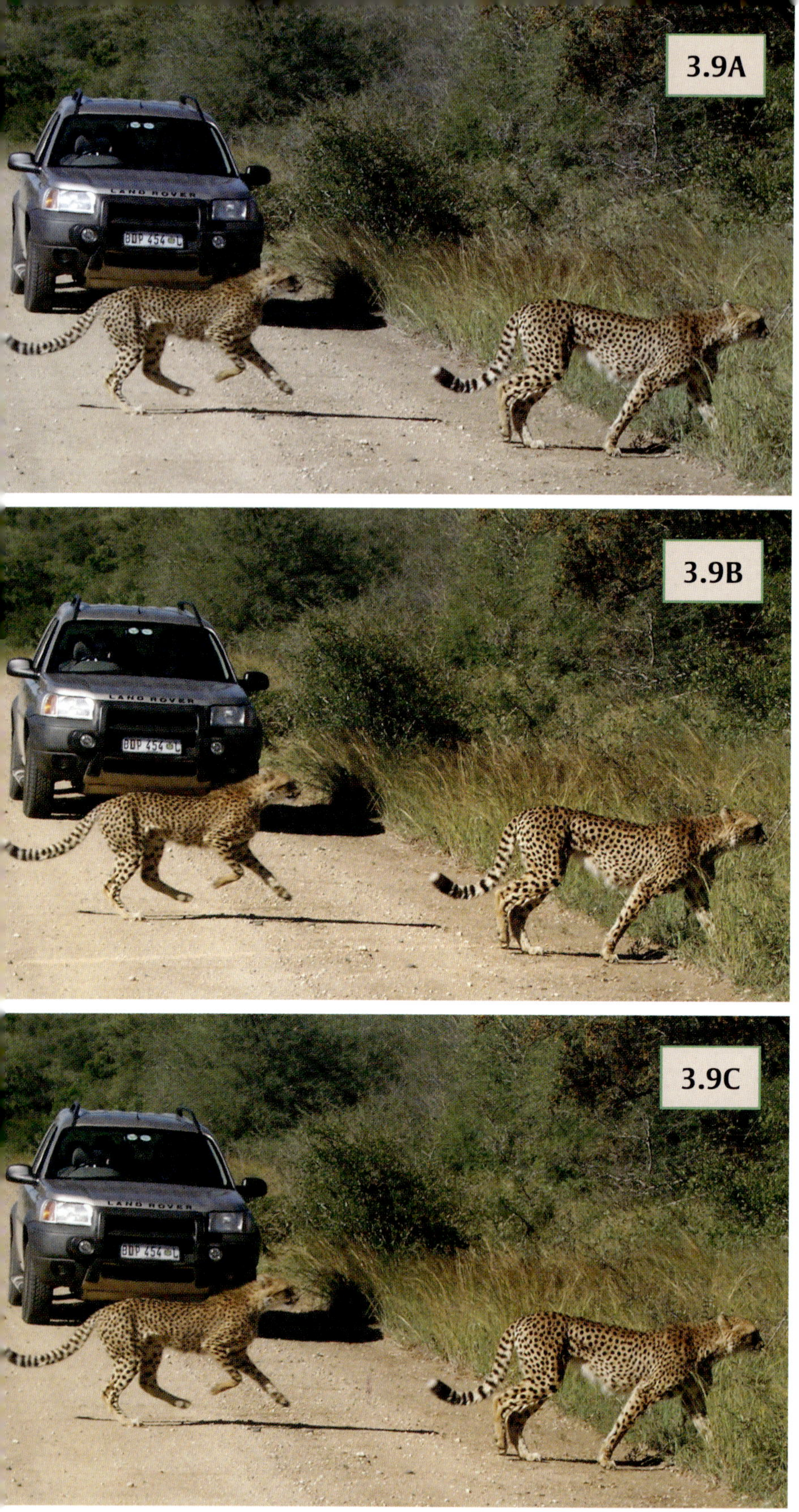

Figure 3.9 *Top, the original. Middle, after the curves shown in Figure 3.10 are applied, the image has become lighter. Bottom, setting the curves layer to Color mode restores the original darkness while retaining the new color.*

The red curve passes well below the control point. More red=less cyan (green-blue). The green curve is slightly above it. Less green=more magenta. The blue is even further above the point. Less blue=more yellow.

All three, therefore, try to add warmth. Why, then, use three curves? Wouldn't it be possible to do everything with the red?

Sure, but it would have to be a more extreme curve. That would make it harder to adjust other points lower down. Remember, this cast isn't as severe in lighter areas. A big curve to the red may make them *too* warm.

For example, note that the red curve gets drastically lighter at about the quartertone point. That's needed to fix the cloud, and secondarily the sky. An unintended consequence is that even lighter areas, such as the whites of the flags, are affected.

Those white areas, however, were already slightly red when we opened the file. I was willing to live with that slight warmth, but not to make them more red. To compensate, I lightened the green channel slightly and the blue greatly in the light zones.

After these curves comes one last step that is likely to be important later. If you've made significant changes to color, like I have here, save a copy of the file and set it aside. As we saw in Chapter 2, the final steps of the PPW can hoodwink users into thinking that loud colors are actually tasteful. When we work on a vivid picture for a few minutes, our eyes get desensitized. On reviewing the picture half an hour later, or even the next day, we can wonder what we were drinking when we produced it.

This file that we have just set aside can stop that depressing feeling. Its colors are conservative by definition, yet correct. So if, after going through the entire process, you find what you have is too loud, consider blending it with the conservative version.

So ends the first step of the workflow. We have created, and saved a copy of, Figure 3.1B. To get from there to the final version, Postcard 3.3B, requires things described in subsequent chapters. We've done what's needed for this one. You can download the original for future practice. You may find that you want to come back later and go through the whole process with this and/or other earlier examples.

For the record, the most important step here was the false-profile-plus-multiplication step to be shown in Chapter 12. That's what accounts for the recovery of detail in the dark half of the postcard.

The World's Fastest Animal

Given that we want a final picture in three to five minutes, how much time is reasonable for this first step? For curves as complicated as those shown just now in Figure 3.8, probably about a minute. Recall, though, that I talked about two other possible curves that weren't quite as good but took less time.

Losing a minute in a workflow this fast is undesirable. Fortunately, it's not usually necessary, because either there's nothing wrong with the original's color or because it is easy to fix. Reminder: finding out whether this is so should take less than ten seconds. Unless you can decide quickly which elements to check, though, it won't.

Our next opponent is Figure 3.9A. Quick! What numbers will find themselves under your magnifying glass?

No skies or faces are to be found here, at least not faces in normal lighting. There is greenery, however, behind the vehicle. Everything in front of it seems like it would naturally be yellow and not green.

Vegetation, being more green than magenta, is always negative in the A of LAB. It is also always considerably more yellow than blue, thus B–positive. In fact, the B must always be more positive than the A is negative, or as a math student would say, its absolute value has to be higher. My recommendation is to make the B 1.5 to 2.5 times further away from zero than the A is. Example: if you have $(10)^{A}$, its companion should fall between 15^{B} and 25^{B}. (Note: it came out during the beta-reading period that some instructors believe these numbers are too restrictive; they teach something like 1.2 to 3.0 times.)

The greens are definitely worth

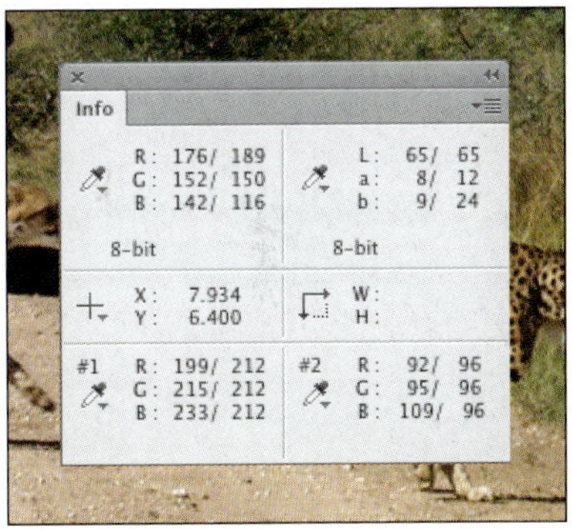

Figure 3.10 The Info palette, right, incorporates fixed reference points in the license plate and tire. When the curves dialog (below) is open, the reference points display before and after values, separated by a slash.

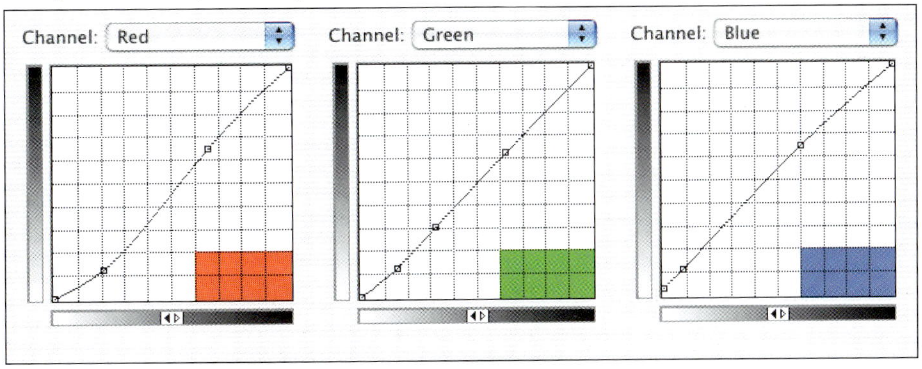

checking, but as we know, finding color issues starts with looking for areas that are known to be neutral, colorless, shades of gray. Not every original has them, but this one does. I'm not speaking of the vehicle, which may or may not be a silvery gray. I'm not speaking of nearly pure whites, such as the headlights, or pure blacks, like the grille. They're likely to be nearly correct even if the midrange of the image is messed up.

The license plate, however, must surely be neutral. And the tires, even if not black, must be a dark gray, or very close.

RGB can be used as conveniently as LAB in evaluating known grays, because the formula is simple: equal values in all three channels make a neutral.

Therefore, on measuring the license plate and the tires, we should encounter nearly equal RGB values. If not, we wheel out some curves to equalize them.

We mouse over the license and the near tire to get an idea of what their typical values are. When satisfied, we activate the color sampler tool and click one point into each.

What about the greenery, though? In the original, it measures $(3)^A2^B$. This isn't yellow enough, according to our recommendations. Why not worry about this one?

The answer is precision. We know that the original green is probably wrong but we'd have a gang of choices to choose from, each one possibly right. With the tires there is no such uncertainty. The sensible thing is to correct them (and the license) first, to see whether doing so happens to correct the greenery as well.

RGB uses a 0–255 scale. The higher the number, the lighter. #1 must be the license and #2 the tire, because $199^R215^G233^B$ is a much higher reading than $92^R95^G109^B$ and therefore describes a much lighter object.

Beta reader Frederick Yocum comments: "This paragraph helps people reorient themselves to the info points. You might want instead to remind them of your practice of going from light to dark. My own practice is #1 White point, #2 Dark point, #3 Neutral, #4 Flesh or some other point of importance.

"What pattern one chooses is not as important as choosing the same pattern each time." Very good advice.

We also now know that the tire starts out blue, not neutral. The red and green channels are almost equal but the blue channel is higher (lighter). The license is a more complex color: it's a blue because the blue channel reads higher than the other two, but it's a greenish blue, because the green is significantly higher than the red.

The heavy shadow to the right of the car indicates strong sunlight. So, if anything, I'd expect the tire to be somewhat warmer—slightly red or orange—if it isn't exactly gray.

Another reason to avoid blue tires was pointed out by beta readers Russ Brown and Marco Olivotto. This vehicle has been traveling through yellowish soil. Possibly some remains on the tire and imparts yellowness.

Some purists might say that the license plate falls in a shadow, which often imparts a bluish or cold cast, and therefore the greenish-blue current value is "accurate." There is indeed a case to be made for leaving it slightly blue—but not as blue as it is now. The human visual system hates cool color casts as much as impala hate these cheetahs.

Just to stay on course, let's assume that we've decided to obliterate the cast, not just reduce it, in both license and tire.

This is done with curves, normally on an adjustment layer. What follows isn't the only way to solve the problem of making the two areas neutral, but it's the simplest, and therefore perhaps the best.

New curve points can be clicked directly

***Postcard 3.11** (opposite) Top, the original. Bottom, a corrected version using all facets of the PPW. Note the similarities with the color of Figure 3.9C.*

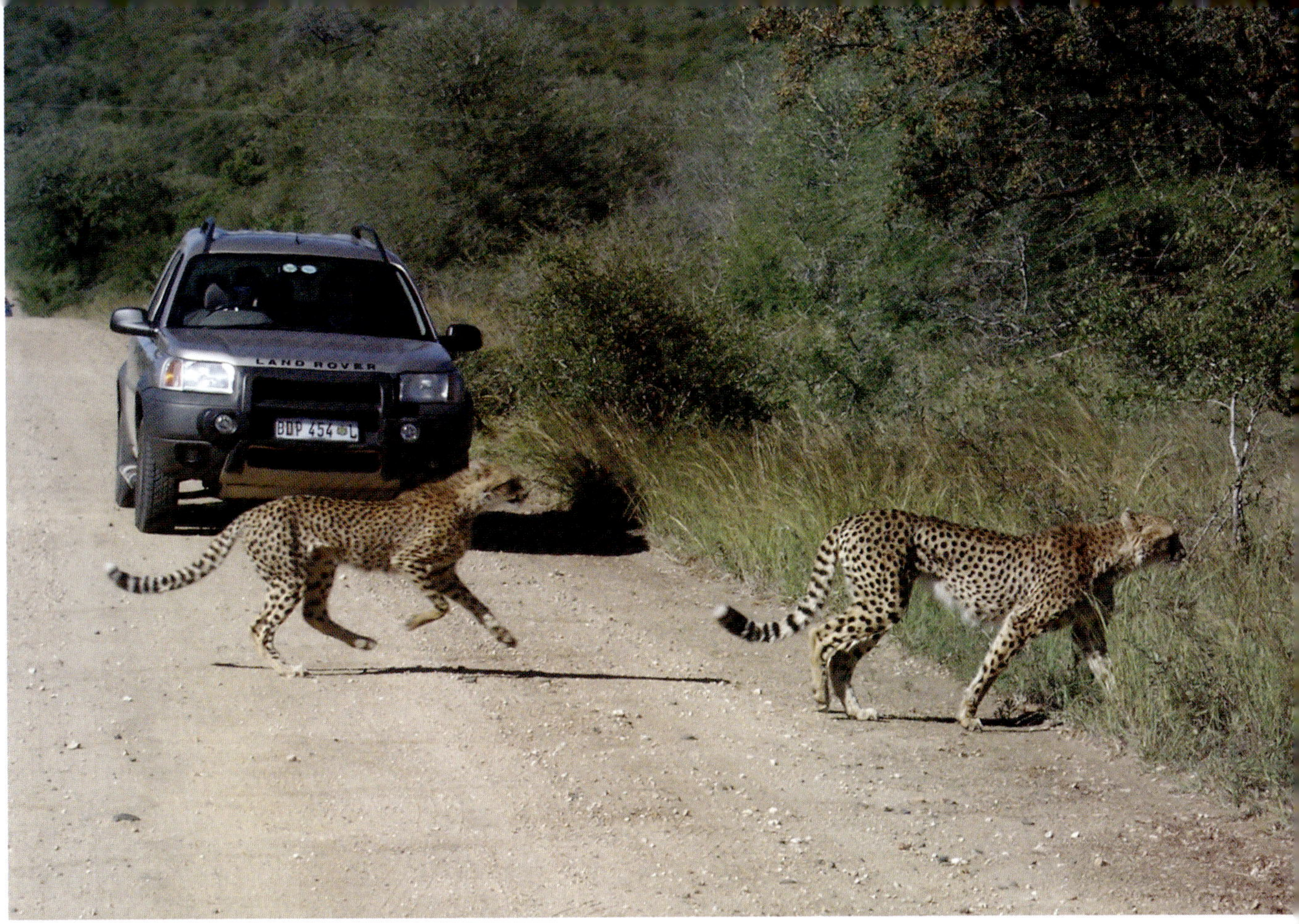
LAND ROVER

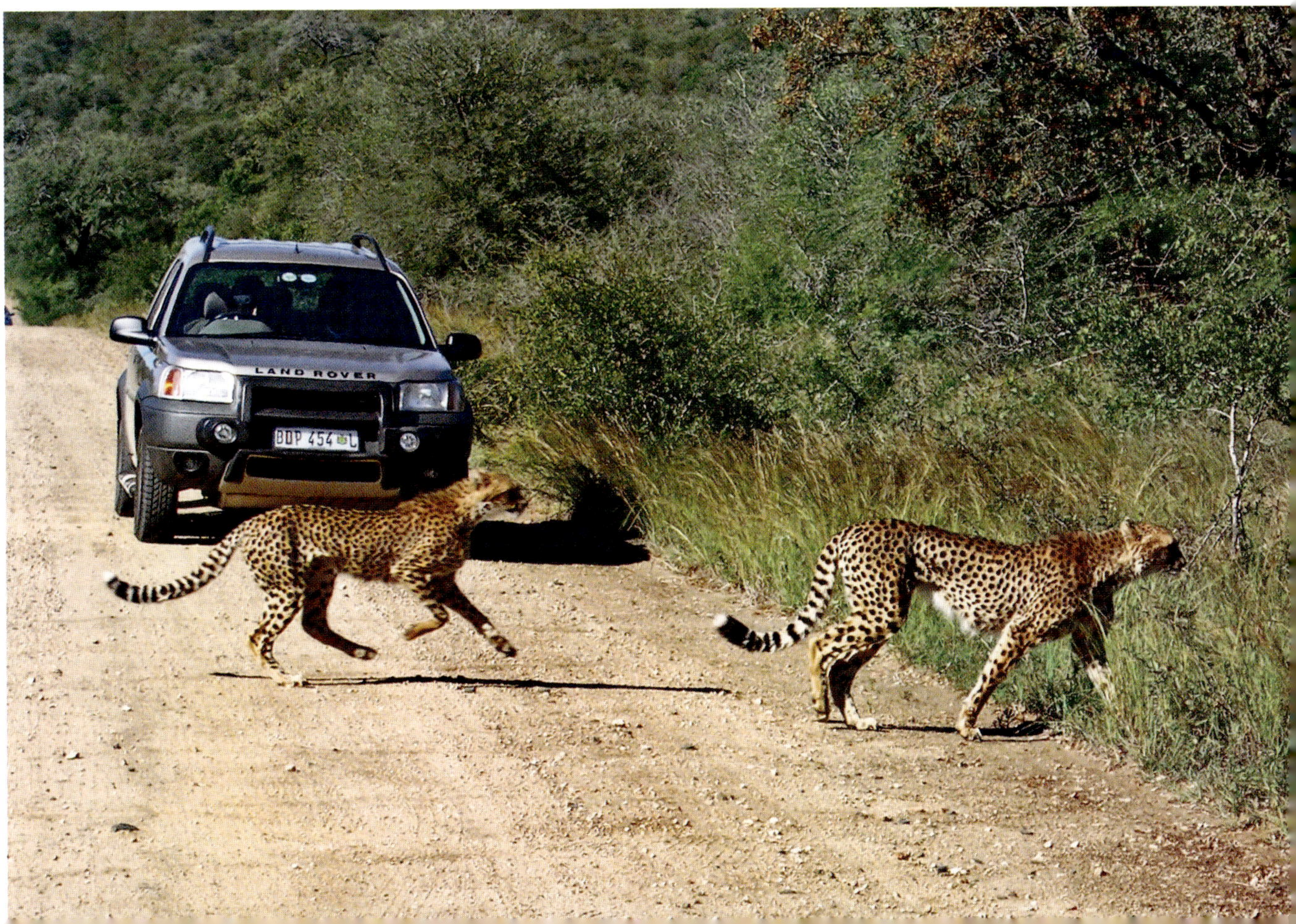
LAND ROVER

into the curves grid. The alternative is, with the curves dialog open to a certain channel, to Command-click somewhere in the image. This creates a point corresponding to the value of what's currently beneath the cursor. (Note: this procedure does not apply to curves adjustment layers from Photoshop CS4 on; the box on Page 43 explains. The procedure *does* apply if you are creating adjustment layers or editing existing ones by clicking inside the PPW panel, which accesses the traditional curves dialog.)

For this image, we'll show a third option. Moving the cursor to the reference point in the license plate, we Shift-Command-click. Doing so creates points in all three channel curves. (If you have the RGB master curve open, you won't see the points, but they'll be visible if you toggle to the individual curves.)

After repeating this procedure with the tire, each curve contains two points, one for the license and one for the tires. We now adjust until both reference points in the Info palette show approximately equal values in all three channels.

Radical curve shapes cause problems. The goal should be to equalize our two points at something like an average value for the three channels, instead of bringing the two lightest ones up to meet the darkest one, or the two darkest down to meet the lightest.

It's easy to do that for the tire. The original value is $92^R95^G109^B$. $100^R100^G100^B$, being a nice round number, seems a sensible target. So we drag the red and green curve points straight down, and the blue up, until the three numbers meet at 100.

That's an effective approach if the object is somewhere near the middle of all three channels—let's say nothing higher than 200 or lower than 50. When channels start out more extreme than that—and the license plate is $199^R215^G233^B$—caution is in order. One might think that, since the green value is right in the middle, we should leave it alone and force the other two to meet it. Lightening the red to 215^R would not be a problem. To darken the blue point as far as 215^B, however, would drastically steepen the light half of the curve, imparting a yellow cast to anything darker than the license.

Consequently, I decided to leave the blue curve alone. I checked to see whether the move to darken the tire had also darkened the license. It had not, so I brought the other two curves down to meet the new blue, at $231^R231^G231^B$. The final curves, and the modified Info palette, appear in Figure 3.10.

That the original of Figure 3.9A is slightly too cool should now be apparent. It is unclear that Figure 3.9B is any better. The curves have lightened too much, losing detail in the road and the animals' fur. In a traditional workflow, where curves are supposed to solve all problems at once, we'd have to start again.

But not in the PPW. As long as the curves address the color problems, we're home. Getting better detail is the job of Chapter 4.

To eliminate the contrast damage, if any, always change the layer's mode from Normal to Color. This mode tries to combine the color of the top layer with the detail of the bottom. The result is Figure 3.9C. The license that read $231^R231^G231^B$ in Figure 3.9B has been darkened to $212^R212^G212^B$. The tire is $96^R96^G96^B$.

Check out Postcard 3.11. The final version, which incorporates the multiplication described in Chapter 12 as well as the customary stuff covered in Chapters 4–6, owes much of its success to starting with the slightly corrected color of Figure 3.9B.

No Time Like the Present

Mild imbalances like those in the original cheetahs of Figure 3.9A are often harder to fix than gross casts, such as the one we're about to face off with.

The human visual system adjusts rapidly and unconsciously to strange conditions, such as the harsh lighting of a hockey rink. No measurements are required to detect the yellow cast in Figure 3.12. One need not be Sidney Crosby to know that the uniforms are supposed to be white and the pants and helmets black.

To make sure that we don't have half the uniform white and half some other color, we'll have to do a lot of cross-checking, and not of the kind that merits a two-minute penalty. But with so many points to choose from, the operation should be easy. There are only two obstacles: first, the four-sample limit in the Info palette, and second, the temptation to measure the player's face. I have recommendations for fleshtones, yes, but they don't necessarily apply to an athlete who's been exerting himself to the limit for 90 seconds or so in a cold environment.

These irritations aside, we will keep an eye on points of various darknesses within the uniforms, write curves to force them to be neutral or nearly so, and then change mode of the correction layer to Color so that we don't lose detail.

Because this is the easiest of the three shots that we've looked at in this chapter, I'll introduce the topic of setting highlight and shadow. Or, to use more precise language, choosing the lightest and darkest significant points of the image. Those experienced in color correction know that this difficult decision is critical, and even if you are not so experienced, you have probably read stuff that suggests it is true.

Nothing in the PPW repeals this commandment. Quality will suffer unless you establish the correct light and dark points. Unlike traditional workflows, however, there's no technical reason to do so immediately. This chapter, after all, is only about color. Light and dark points relate more to contrast.

On the other hand, you're going to have to adjust these points eventually. You have to identify them before you can adjust them. Even if you don't plan to act on the information right now, what better time to identify them than when you're already checking various points for color fidelity and placing samplers in the Info palette?

The Lightest *Significant* Point

At the end of the day, the lightest significant point has to be as light as possible, consistent with holding detail. The darkest significant point must be as dark as possible.

The word *significant* is not there just to add syllables. The literally lightest part of the picture is often something worthless. If so, it should be left to blow out, at $255^{R}255^{G}255^{B}$—no detail at all. If the white uniforms are left to blow out in the current exercise, and/or the black pants allowed to plug, the background and the face will gain contrast, albeit at a dreadful price. To get really first-rate images depends on knowing—eventually, that is—what parts, if any, you *can* blow out or plug.

Fortunately the choice of these points is obvious much of the time. Unfortunately, it doesn't happen to be so in this hockey picture.

The following discussion pertains only to the highlights. Finding shadows can safely be put off.

Consider Postcard 3.3, the Swiss lakefront scene. The three lightest objects are the

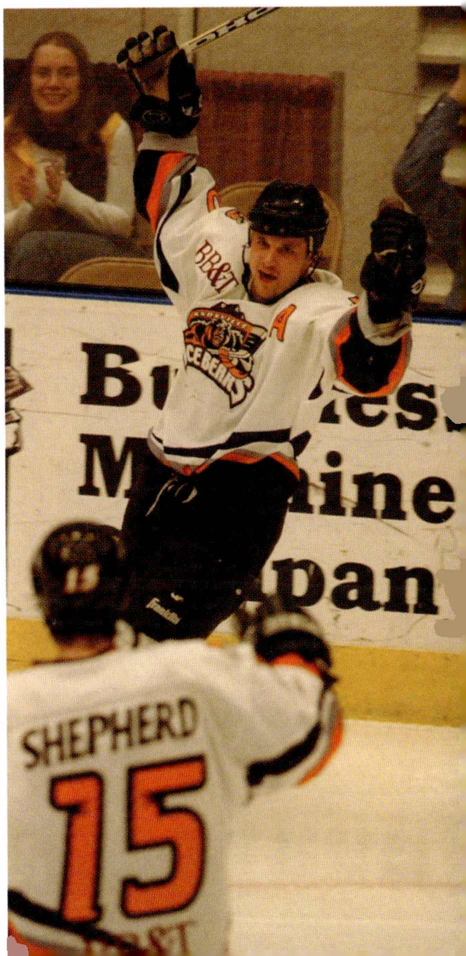

***Figure 3.12** The next opponent sports an obvious yellow cast.*

whitish building at left, the cloud at top right, and the white parts of the flags. Of these, the flags are certainly the lightest. The question is whether they are significant.

If this file were intended for newspaper reproduction, where contrast is at a premium and chicanery on the part of retouchers a necessary evil, I would declare those flags insignificant and let all their white parts vanish completely. For better printing conditions it may be too much of a sacrifice. These areas are small. I don't mind if some, but not all, blow out. So I found the relatively darker parts of these white areas, and noted it as the highlight for future use.

In Postcard 3.11, the cheetahs, the decision was already made for us. The original was as received from the photographer, no chance of going back to the raw capture. The left headlight was already blown out. The lightest surviving part of the image is the area immediately surrounding what's missing. Unless you're willing to lose more of the headlight, which I am not, that becomes the highlight.

In both previous images, therefore, we could rely on our eyes to tell us the proper highlight. But in Figure 3.12 we can't. Many candidates vie for lightest significant point in the two uniforms. We also can't rule out the possibility that the lightest significant

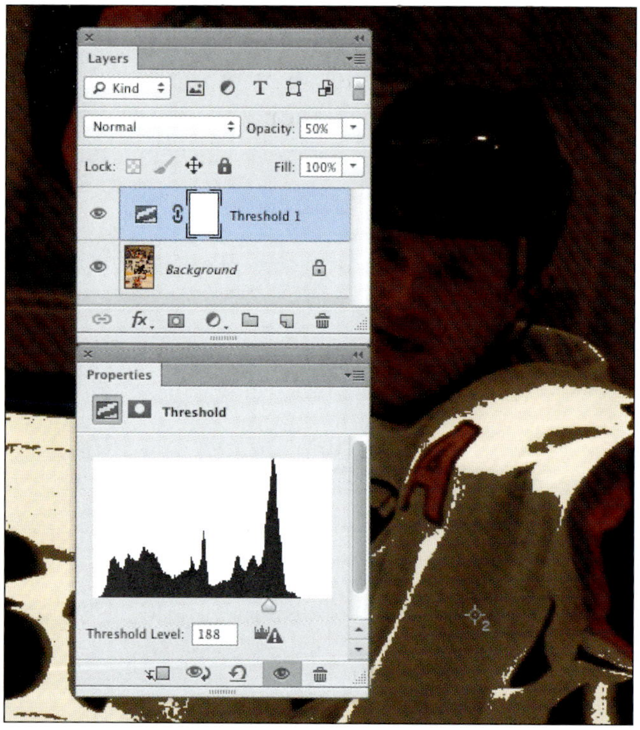

Figure 3.13 A threshold adjustment layer can identify the lightest areas. With the layer set to 50% opacity, the version at bottom left shows the default setting. In the other two, the slider has been moved to the right.

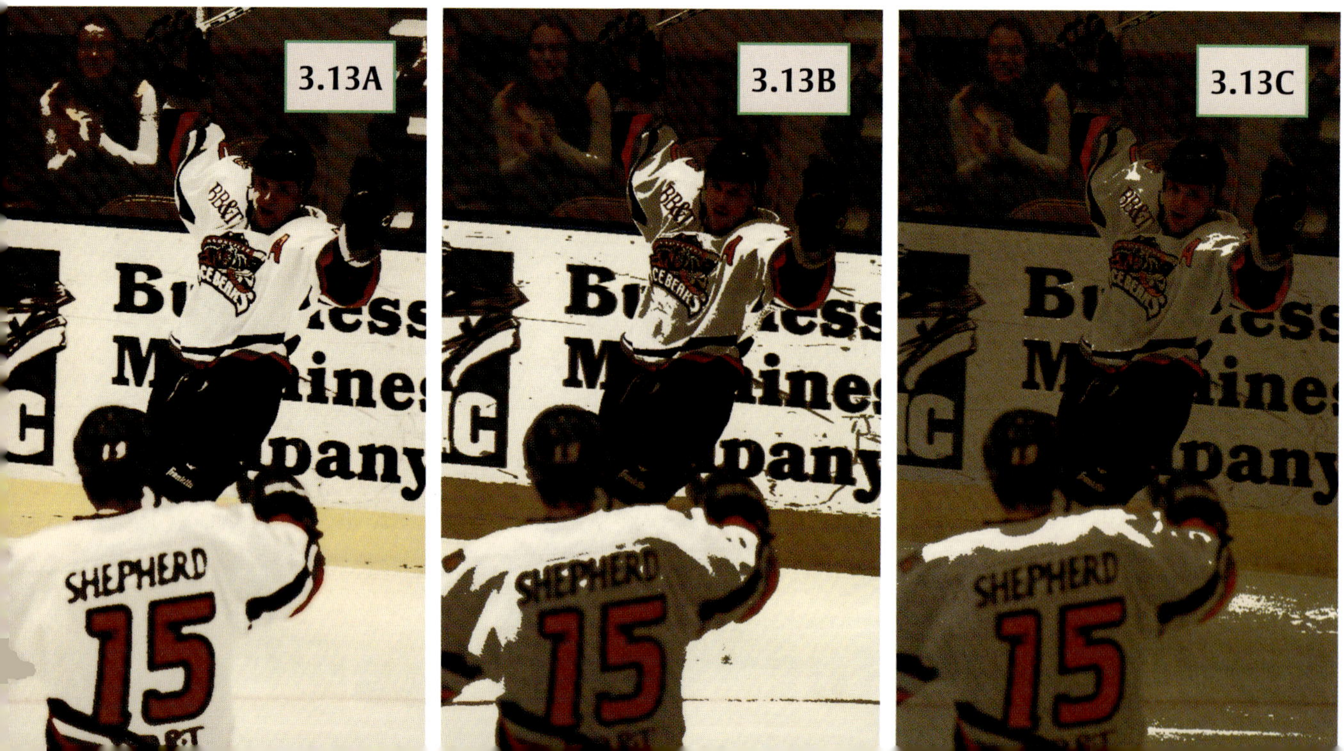

point is the ice. I emphasize again that this information is not important in terms of the current chapter, but it becomes critical later, and now is the logical time to investigate.

The Threshold Method

If you need assistance in finding a highlight or shadow, establish a threshold adjustment layer. The Threshold command divides the file into pure whites and pure blacks only. By default, anything darker than a midtone becomes black and anything lighter becomes white. We can, however, adjust a slider to make the break between white and black wherever we like.

Set the opacity of the threshold layer to 50%, allowing partial visibility of the base image, while making clear which parts the threshold is making black and which white. The default setting yields Figure 3.13A.

Now, in the Adjustments panel (Window: Adjustments) move the slider slowly to the right. More of the picture is now covered up. Figure 3.13B indicates that the white uniforms are generally darker than either the boards or the ice.

Going further, the boards have vanished in Figure 3.13C and so has almost all the ice, but scattered parts of the uniforms remain.

There is no need to discover the literally lightest point. I assume it must be somewhere in the top of the uniform of the player whose back is to us, because that's currently the biggest area of white. But I really don't care. The question is, which of the white areas of Figure 3.13C are vital?

"None" is a reasonable answer, although it isn't mine. I wouldn't like to lose the red line, but the tiny areas that Figure 3.13C shows might be lost in the ice are of no concern. Similarly, I am not losing sleep about the top of the uniform of the player with his back to us. The picture, in my view, is all about the other player, the one celebrating the goal. Detail in *his* uniform is important. I therefore clicked my first sample point into his near shoulder, and trashed the adjustment layer.

I wish Photoshop permitted more than four color sampler points. After the highlight, my other three choices all came from the uniforms: midway down the main player's ribs; the back of the other player's helmet; and the bottom of the first player's hockey pants,

Work in RGB, Think in LAB

The following areas can consistently be relied upon for clues about whether color is correct. If you set the Info palette to read LAB even though the file is RGB, you should be able to evaluate them quickly:

NEUTRALS. When fortunate enough to know that the desired color is a pure neutral, as in the hockey uniforms, we shoot for 0^A0^B. We understand that we won't find this exact reading wherever we click. Unless it's in sunlight, which suggests a bias toward warm colors, we should be just as likely to encounter slight greens as slight pinks or yellows.

Often, though, we can rule out certain possibilities. For example, in the cheetah image, I remarked that the tire was known to be neutral, but that if it varied, it must be in the direction of warmth (positive A and B) given that it was in strong sunlight.

FACES. Skin is always red—positive A and B. The B is usually higher. Small children and some Caucasian adults have higher A values. As a rule, though, a higher A should make you suspicious that the image is too purple.

GREENERY. Natural greens are A–negative, B–positive. The B is almost always further away from zero than the A is. Look at the ratio of the absolute values. If the B is less than 1.5 times the A, it suggests that the image may be too blue. If more than 2.5 times, it suggests excessive yellowness.

SKIES. Blue, of course. The B is always negative but there is no rule as to *how* negative. The A should be near zero. If not, it's more likely negative (greener, or better stated, more cyan) than positive (purple). Values lower than $(5)^A$ suggest excessive greenness; 3^A or higher implies that the image is too purple.

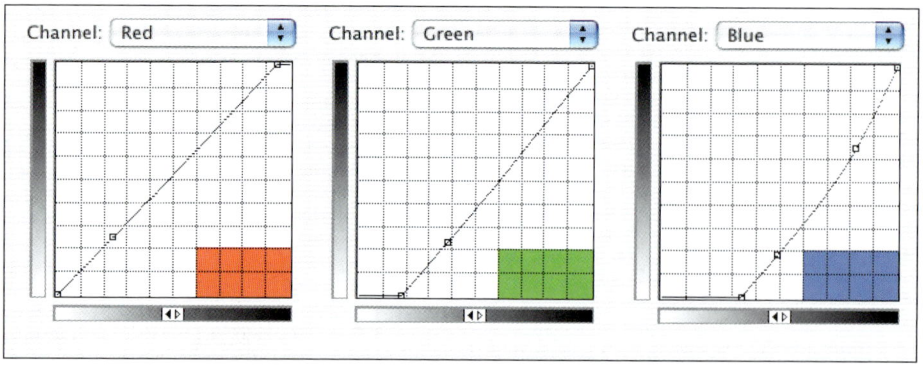

Figure 3.14 *These curves eliminate the yellow cast. Although four reference points have been chosen (see Info palette below), neutralizing the lightest one almost suffices to correct the image.*

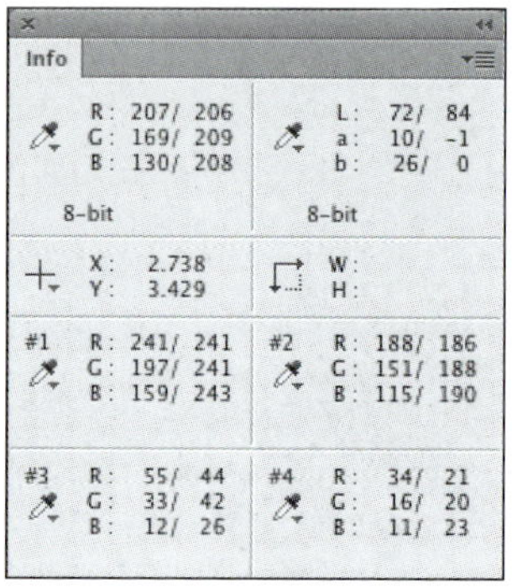

just below the logo. All were too yellow, as anticipated. I knew this because the blue channel, yellow's complement, has much lower values than the other two. The three numbers need to be equal if the area is to be neutral.

The cheetahs exercise suggested that we should now Shift-Command-click these four points into a curves layer. As far as I know, not having tried it, that ought to work. It would, however, be more tiresome than the third period of a one-sided hockey game.

The practical approach is to fix the lightest point and see what happens. Perhaps it will fix the other three points as well.

Accordingly, I moved the lower left points of the green and blue curves inward until each became equal to the red channel in the sampler point chosen in the shoulder. Then, I evaluated what the move had done to the other three points and discovered that it had gotten them fairly close.

And Sir, I Just About Forgot

The final curves and Info palette are in Figure 3.14. As you can see, I had to make a slight move in the green channel to neutralize the second lightest point, and a bigger one in the blue so the darkest points would not remain so yellow. (The third point, the helmet, is in strong yellow light and can't be neutralized totally with curves.)

Known neutrals, if there are any, are the easiest way to attack color imperfections. There are, however, three other common objects that can offer a clue that something is wrong. Each of the three exercises in this chapter has illustrated one. The Swiss scene had a *sky*. The cheetahs featured *natural greenery*. And now, we find some *faces*.

None of the three categories can give us the precision of a known neutral, because each has a broad range of acceptable possibilities. Nevertheless, the sky measured marginally too cyan, or green, in the Swiss shot. The greenery was slightly too blue, or not yellow enough, behind the cheetahs. And in the hockey original, it is almost as easy to predict that the faces will measure too yellow as it is to foresee that the Toronto Maple Leafs will not be winning the Stanley Cup in the near future.

Since all categories have now been introduced, it's appropriate to have a box summarizing the recommendations. You can find it on the preceding page. The guidelines for faces are vague, but here goes.

Skin is always red. It is therefore positive in both AB channels, more magenta than green and more yellow than blue.

Equal and positive AB is loosely referred to as *red*. In fact, it is better described as a reddish orange. This is a reasonable color for just about everyone except young Caucasian children. Lighter-skinned Caucasian adults usually have A>B. Darker-skinned people are usually the other way around. There are no set rules, but we should beware cases where the A and B are seriously different.

I pointed out earlier that the player's face may not follow normal guidelines because he has been exerting himself. The background woman is a better choice, in spite of being photographed through glass. In the original, she measures $28^{A}42^{B}$. As these two numbers are not close, we conclude that her skin is too yellow, as if this were a shocking discovery. For reference, the player starts out at $37^{A}46^{B}$.

After the curves of Figure 3.14, the woman measures $15^{A}22^{B}$, almost the same ratio as the original, suggesting she is still too yellow. The player is now $25^{A}28^{B}$. That's an acceptable value for the average Caucasian but is highly suspicious here. The player's face is apt to be much redder than the average Ice Bear. Having it on the yellow side of orange, however slightly, does not seem right.

I concluded, therefore, that the curves of Figure 3.14, although they do well with neutrals, need an adjustment for the fleshtones. Figure 3.15A is a straight application of the curves as shown. Figure 3.15B adds a tiny adjustment, making the green channel darker in the darker regions of the picture. Can you see the difference?

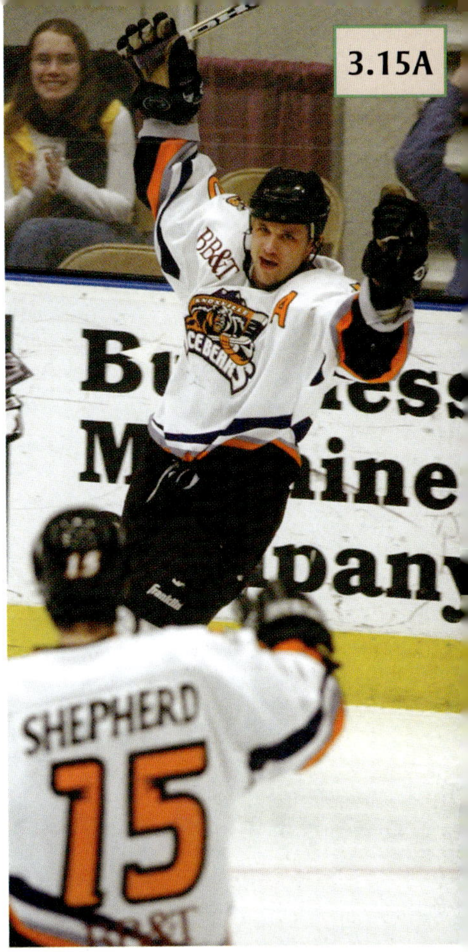

Resisting Temptation

Before leaving this picture, a few words about the virtuous life.

Back in the cheetahs exercise, the final step, Figure 3.9C, I set the curves layer to Color mode, restoring the original darkness while retaining the new color of Figure 3.9B. Figure 3.15C does the same thing to the current picture.

The two examples seem very different. The curves left the cheetahs image washed out, so the Color mode version was better than the one left in Normal mode. Here, however, the

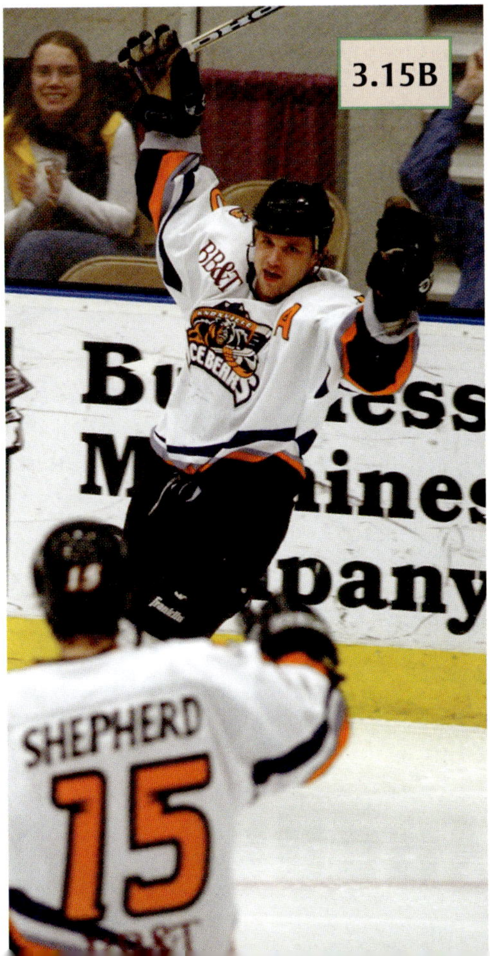

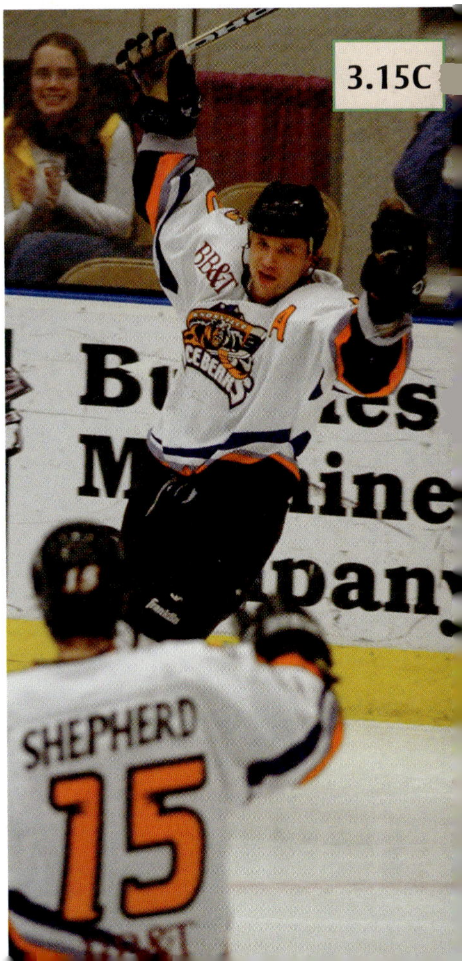

***Figure 3.15** Top, the result of applying the curves of Figure 3.14. Bottom left, with a further adjustment to make the faces less yellow. Bottom right, after the adjustment layer is changed from Normal to Color mode.*

opposite is true. The Color mode version, Figure 3.15C, is flat, too dark. So we ignore it and stick with Figure 3.15B, right?

Wrong. Moments like this are common in the Picture Postcard Workflow. Something that temporarily looks better gets rejected because a disciplined approach will permit something better yet, provided it isn't preempted by shortsighted actions now.

Figure 3.15B represents the traditional workflow, which became traditional because it was effective. What's not to like? One set of curves greatly improves both color and contrast, when compared to the original.

It's no coincidence. Setting highlight and shadow early in the process, which traditional workflows do, commonly improves color and contrast simultaneously.

I suggest that allowing color enhancement to be an inadvertent side effect is wrong. You should therefore take a deep breath, mutter to yourself something about how discipline wins hockey games and color correction contests, reject the siren call of Figure 3.15B, change layer mode to Color, and work with Figure 3.15C. Doing so offers better odds of eventually getting to Postcard 3.16. The big scorer in that process is the special highlight enhancement known as the Bigger Hammer, which is fleshed out in Chapter 10.

Having taught this workflow in small groups for several years, I'm able to say that experts—the experienced kind of retouchers who think the curve corrections of this chapter are easy—find it extremely difficult to develop the mindset that permits them to reject Figure 3.15B and its ilk. Once they overcome that obstacle, they're almost home free.

So are you home free, almost. You've now grasped the point of this first step. You understand that it can be difficult but that as long as you can make a reasonable improvement—to get, for example, into the neighborhood of Figure 3.15C—you'll be ready to move into the rest of the workflow.

Remember, also, that many of the images you will face require no adjustment at all at this point. You need to identify such situations quickly. It's time for a quiz to evaluate your skill as a color detective. Grab a piece of paper, please.

In Figure 3.17, I've rounded up eight images that we'll be working on in future chapters. Your challenge: for each of the eight, state what you would be looking for in terms of color.

Remember the objective. If something is wrong, then you have to fix it. If not, you want to know in ten seconds or less.

To make your life harder, these are the final, not the original files. Unless I've screwed up, any color issues they may have initially had should be gone now.

I recommend doing the exercise right now, before comparing your answers to mine.

Analyzing Figure 3.17

If you like, you can skip forward to see the uncorrected originals—the figure number is given for each.

- **Figure 3.17A:** this leopard, which is seen later as Figure 4.8, is one of my classroom exercises. It has chewed up and swallowed a whole gang of experienced retouchers who should have known better than to overlook what they did. The nose is certainly black and can be used as a reference point. The spots on the fur are a poorer choice because they could be a dark brown. Someone who's been on safari recently knows whether the fur around the animal's muzzle is reliably white. I haven't, and I don't. I do know, however, that it can't be blue or green, so negatives in either A or B are out.

The fur (forgetting the muzzle) is basically yellow, so we know that the B will be positive and the A near zero. But if the reading is something other than 0^A, then would you expect reddish yellow, or greenish yellow?

Again, not a hard decision. We run the

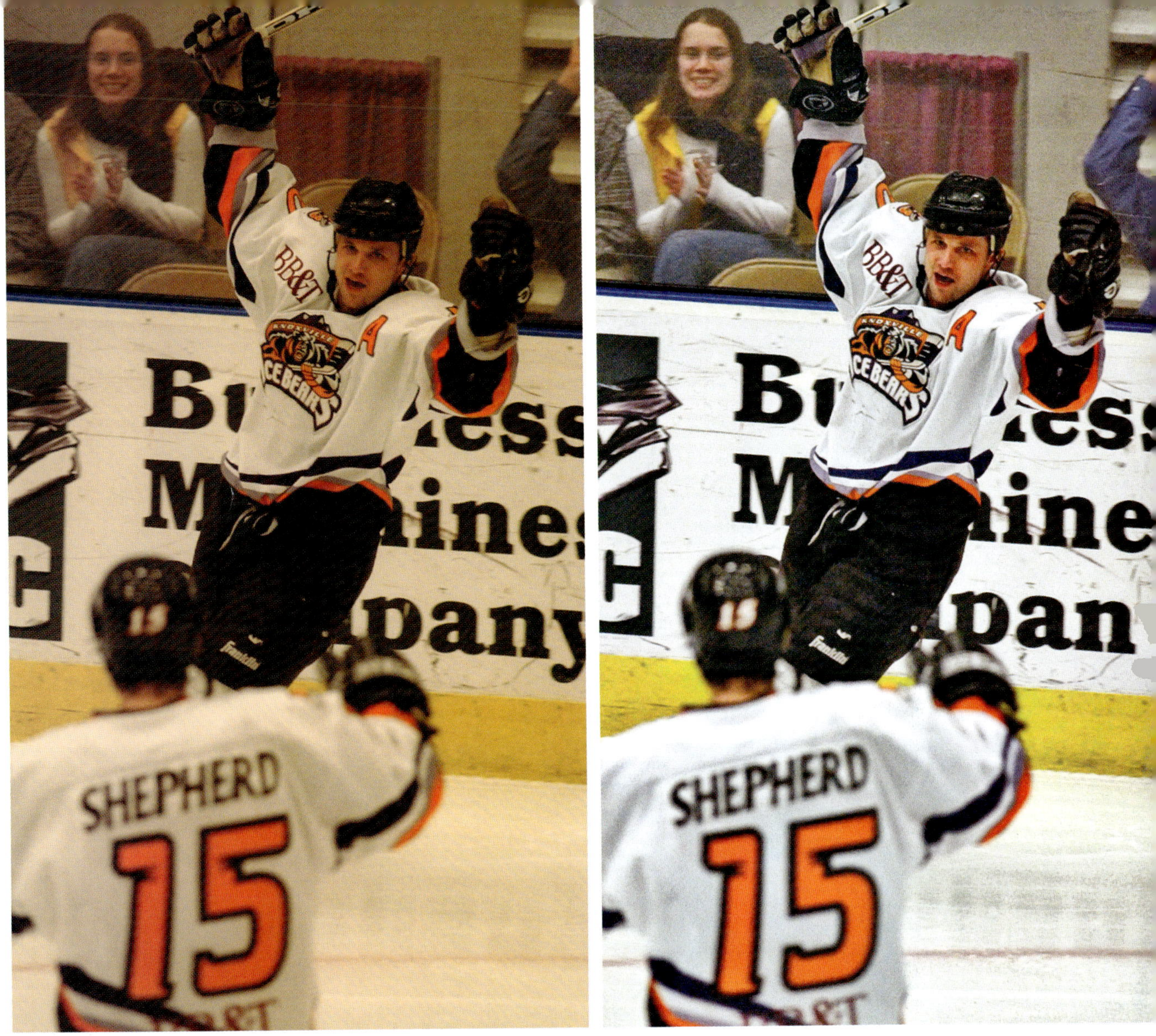

***Postcard 3.16** The original and the version based on Figure 3.15C, using all parts of the PPW.*

cursor over the animal and watch the changes in the A. If any negative values appear, we must intervene.

And what is the gotcha that has snared so many excellent retouchers? It's the defocused, detail-free area in the animal's haunches to the right of the picture. It sounds correct to say that this area is of zero significance. But if you say this, limit yourself to contrast. In terms of color, it's just as important as anything in the face. In the original, the area is slightly blue. Expert after expert has decided to ignore it, and paid the price. Columbo, of course, knows enough about investigation to adopt the right philosophy. He says, "I worry. I mean, little things bother me. I'm a worrier. I mean, little insignificant details—I lose my appetite. I can't eat. My wife, she says to me, 'you know, you can really be a pain.'"

Understanding the applicability to this chapter's own worries, beta reader Jacob Rus poses a pertinent query: "Is Columbo a worrier because he adopted that philosophy for the purposes of investigation, or is he a good investigator because his worrying is an innate part of his personality?"

I don't know. I analyze color, not character. I add, however, that more than at any other point in the workflow, right now is the time for worrying about little things.

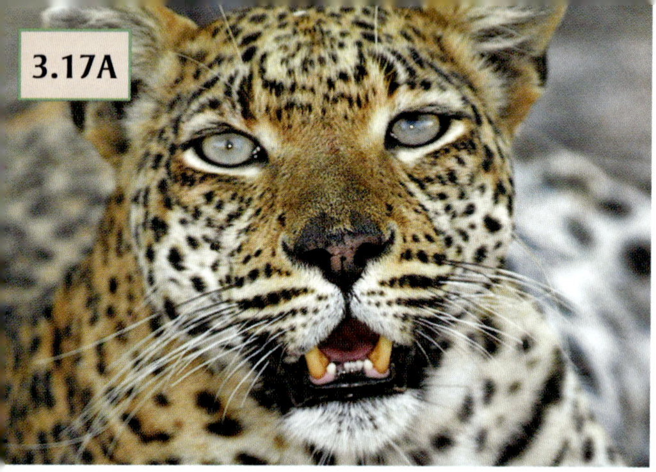
3.17A

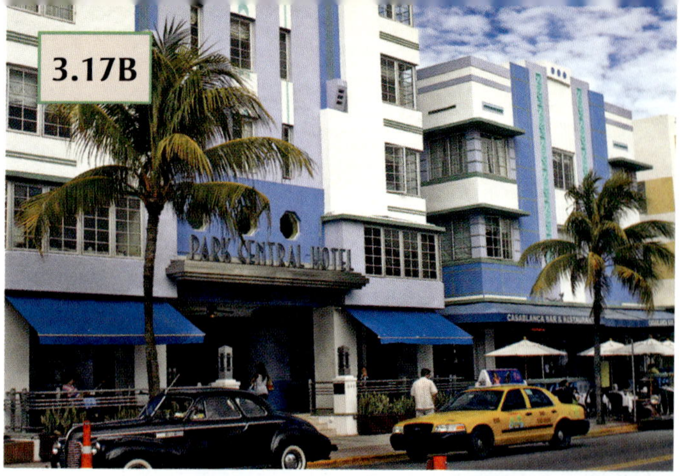

3.17B

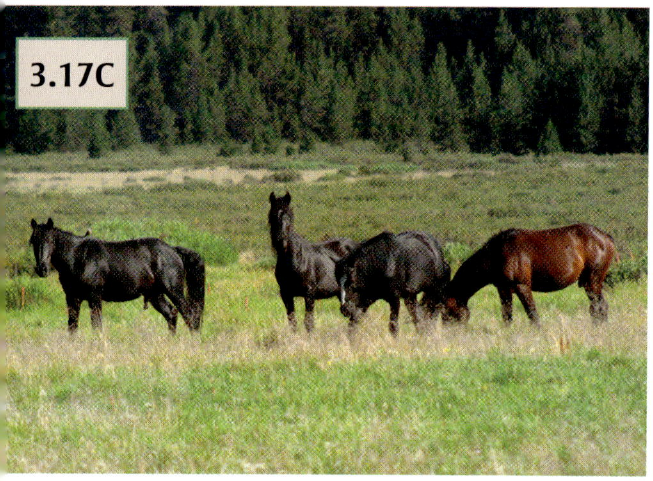
3.17C

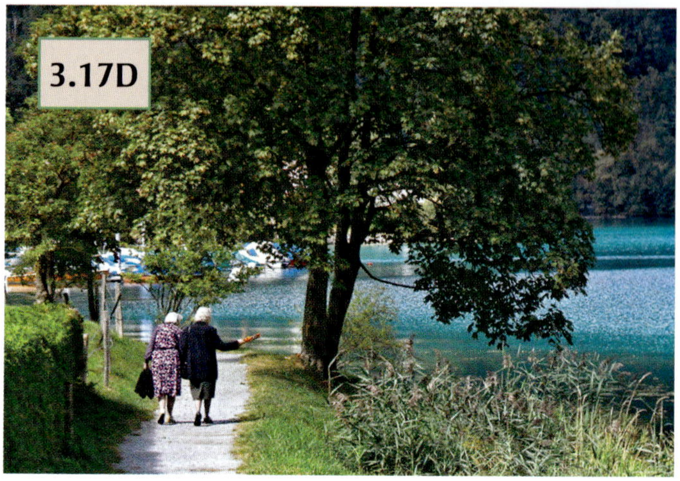
3.17D

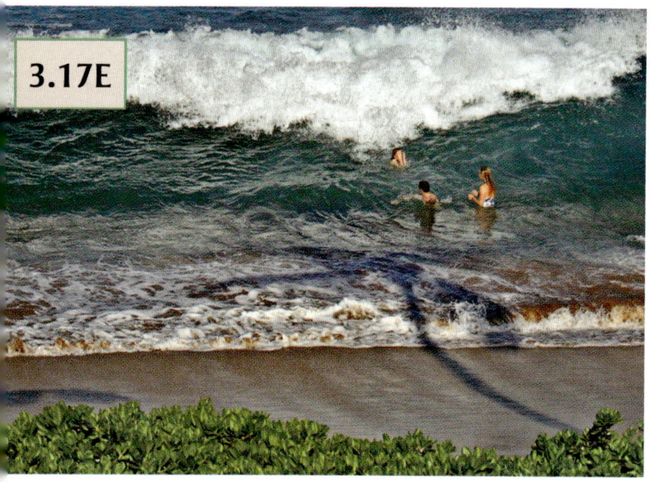
3.17E

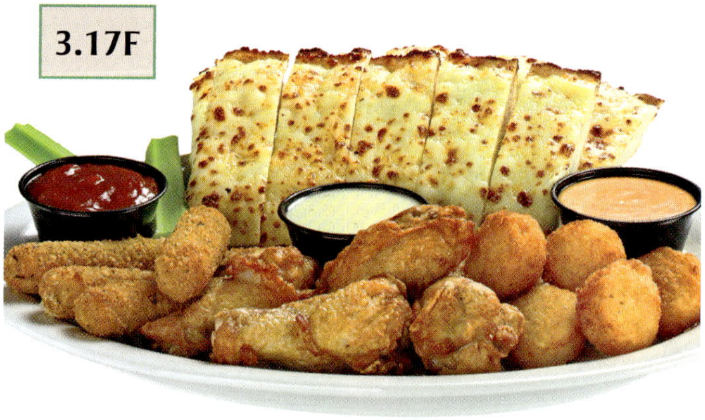
3.17F

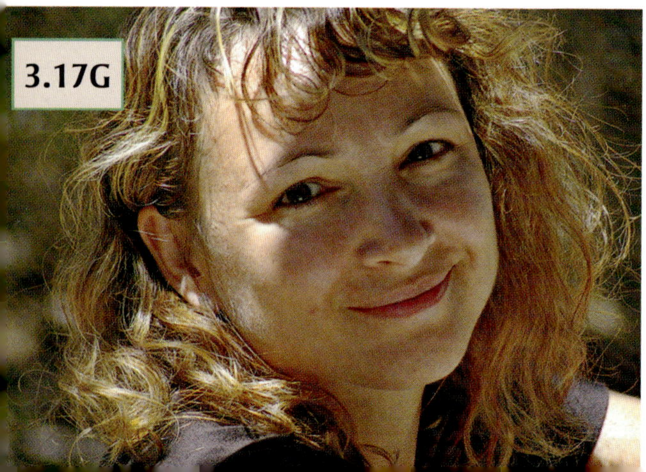
3.17G

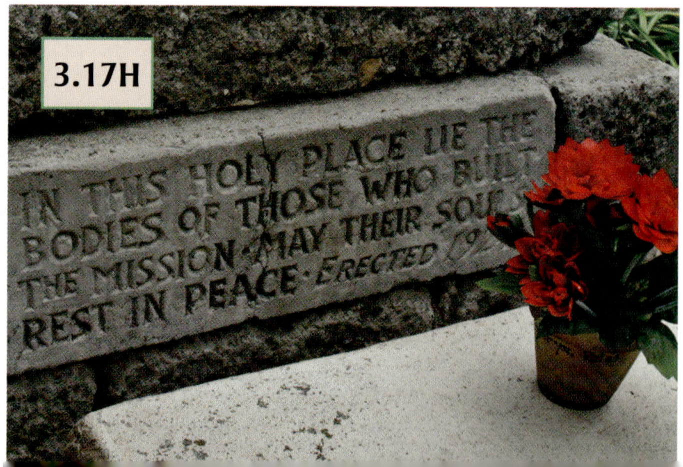

3.17H

* * *

- **Figure 3.17B:** South Beach, later Figure 8.5A, is noted for its Art Deco architecture, which features muted pastel colors. Anywhere else, we could surmise with confidence that the buildings are something other than light teal. Here we can't, but even in South Beach, light clouds have to be white and tires have to be dark gray. And, if it turns out that the tires have the same AB values as the car on the left, then that car must be black.

The palm trees appear to be in poor health, so it would not be surprising to find them yellower than usual.

In a tropical setting, near-neutrals such as the sidewalk or the marquee should not measure as cool. Warmth is pleasing, so probably a slight AB–positive would be preferred. This is as opposed to the light clouds, which are preferred neutral, and if not neutral, cool.

- **Figure 3.17C:** horses, later Figure 6.5C. This one is easy unless you decide that some of the yellowish vegetation is greenery. The three horses at left must be black and the right-hand one dark brown; no other combination makes sense.

A couple of fine points. Evergreens are bluer than other trees, so we expect to find those in the background near the bluest recommendation for greens, with the absolute A value perhaps two-thirds of the B. The grass in the foreground should have a bigger imbalance in favor of the B.

Also, the formula for browns varies with darkness. Brown is a species of red, therefore positive in both A and B. In dark, walnut browns, the two are roughly equal. Lighter browns are yellower, so the B becomes greater than the A. This horse is a dark brown, so we expect AB equal and positive. The other three should be roughly 0^A0^B, neutral.

Figure 3.17 These eight pictures appear in later chapters. They are the corrected versions, so you shouldn't be able to detect any color issues—but the originals may have had some. For each, decide which areas you would test for color accuracy. Remember the goal: ten seconds or less to decide whether there's a problem.

- **Figure 3.17D:** Swiss scene, later Figure 13.2A. This is the hardest one so far. We can measure the greens and the hair. The lake has an unusual hue, but it's in glacier country, so it could be right.

The truth sometimes lies in the subtle interplay of colors. The woman at right is wearing a navy jacket and a gray skirt. But before correction, for all we knew the correct jacket color could be black—it's certainly dark enough. The hint is how it relates with her other garments. The skirt measures decidedly less blue than the jacket, or, in LAB terms, more B–positive. If the jacket is blue, then the skirt is gray. If the jacket is neutral (gray or black) then the skirt must be some kind of yellow. Highly unlikely.

- **Figure 3.17E:** Hawaiian surf, later Figure 10.22B. Not much to work with beyond the foreground greens. The fleshtones are unreliable: in Hawaii, the skin could be rather yellow because of the strength of the sun, or alternatively rather red if the people have already spent more time in the aforementioned sun than their dermatologists would like.

The sand must be brown. As with the earlier horses, it is probably more yellow than magenta, hence a higher B than A, but little can be said for sure other than it isn't purple, so that the A can't be higher than the B. The dark water could be green, blue, or anything in between. The breaking surf should therefore either be white or cool, but the whitewater hitting the beach could be picking up brown from the sand underneath it. In short, there would have to be something seriously fouled up here before we'd have enough evidence to start correcting.

- **Figure 3.17F:** fast food, later Figure 13.12B. This advertising photo is another example of a picture with little to judge by. The plate needs to be fairly neutral, and the containers are certainly black. Just getting those two right may not be enough because the food, which is the focus of the image, is much darker than the plate and much lighter than the containers.

The fried food must be a yellowish brown, A significantly positive and B more positive still. This is a studio shot with carefully controlled lighting, so there's not much chance of the original falling outside an acceptable range. Trouble, however, lurks in the background pizza.

Yellow is B–positive. The A channel should be slightly positive, too, to add a slight warmth to the cheese. Having it negative courts disaster, because it imparts a tiny green cast that might become obtrusive later on. Along with green eggs and ham, advertisers don't like green cheese.

- **Figure 3.17G:** woman in shadow, later Figure 12.7B. Don't try to measure the fleshtone in the shadow, measure it in the sunlight. And be sure to take several samples, because she could be wearing blush, which would foul up the measurements.

The hair appears to have artificial color but it can hardly tend toward blue or green. Hence, we pass the cursor over the hair, where any negative A or B value tells us that we have to make a change.

We also should take a look at the shirt. Something that dark, like the jacket that the Swiss woman wears in Figure 3.17D, is almost certainly either black or navy. Anything else should arouse suspicion and start us looking for other hints of an overall cast. For example, if the shirt showed up as dark purple, we should revisit the face and ask ourselves whether it, too, might be too purple despite falling into the recommended range of color.

- **Figure 3.17H:** California mission, later Figure 10.4C. This one features some indirect reasoning. It is superficial to say that all this stone should be 0^A0^B, a perfect gray. The stone with the inscription seems to be much younger than the wall, so although the two are similarly colored they might not be identical. That also goes for a third object, the bench on which the flowers are sitting.

The bad news is that we don't have the advantage found in pictures of leopards, human hair, horses, and cheese. In all four of those previous examples cool readings—negative A and/or B—would have been unacceptable. Some rocks, however, have a bluish tinge, or even a slightly green one, so we can't be doctrinaire in rejecting slight negativity here.

On the other hand, we have at least three different "grays" here. If one of them measures slightly blue, fine. But if all have the same tendency, be it yellow, green, or whatever—that's too big a coincidence to buy.

We have greens to check for compliance with the recommendations. The flowers themselves are more difficult. They are surely much more magenta than they are green, and much more yellow than blue. So, we expect both A and B to be strongly positive.

An experienced person would surmise that the A should be the higher of the two. Equal AB in principle gives a red, but a rather orange one, reasonable for skintone and some flowers, but probably not these. When B is higher than A, the red is angrier, more fiery. When A is higher than B, the red is rosier, more peaceful. That color is more likely to be chosen for a memorial.

Just One Last Little Thing

Lieutenant Columbo always knows that something fishy has happened. We are worse off; our checking often finds nothing wrong.

When foul play is discovered, though, our strategy is much like his. The culprit is known, the question is how to bring him down. Columbo has his guile and we have our curves. Both, alas, require experience and discipline, which is why this is the hardest chapter in the book. Don't get discouraged now. Everything from here on relies more on your instincts than on formulas and memorization.

From now on, each chapter is broken in two. The second part is optional. In the first halves, the assumption is you know how to boot up Photoshop, create a layer or adjustment layer, change its opacity, and open various palettes, but that's about all.

These second halves assume you have no need of Photoshop's online help. Explanations of how commands work are cursory at best. Often these sections delve into theoretical matters or explanations of *why* things work as opposed to *how* they work.

This time, the second half of this chapter goes further in discussing the thought process that the successful color detective uses to determine whether an issue exists. It's not as technical as many of these second halves are. Nevertheless, you might want to skip it for the time being, returning after you've familiarized yourself with the rest of what the PPW has to offer. Because really you're ready to go now, as long as you don't make yourself crazy by looking for initial color problems that don't happen to exist. I do recommend, however, that before leaving the topic you test yourself with the quiz at the bottom of the Review and Exercises box below.

Remember that this chapter can safely be ignored in many images, probably in the majority for certain users. But, as Columbo so often reminds us, it's the little things that can trap us. Recall how the failure to execute properly here derailed the photographer who produced the eyepopping blue swan of Figure 2.5B. If that sort of thing starts happening to you, it's a good indication that you should stop blaming your monitor and that the time has come to revisit this chapter.

Remember also that speed comes with practice, and if you don't have the speed, this step becomes even more frustrating. If there's nothing wrong with the picture it should realistically take less than ten seconds to figure it out. And if you can do that, you can echo Columbo when he says, it's all a matter of routine, just routine, sir, that's all it is.

Review and Exercises

NOTE: Answers to this section, which appears in every chapter, are found in the Notes & Credits section of this book, commencing on Page 431.

✓How do you know that an object is neutral? Give the formula in both RGB and LAB.

✓How do you set up the Info palette to show LAB values even when the file is in RGB?

✓Define *highlight* and *shadow* in the sense normally used in color correction.

✓Which colors are denoted by positive and negative numbers in the A and B channels?

✓Refer to Figure 3.17. Match each item in the left column with its typical corresponding AB value.

1. The tip of the animal's tongue in Figure 3.17A.	A. 15^A71^B
2. The taxicab in Figure 3.17B.	B. 20^A50^B
3. The background trees in Figure 3.17C.	C. $(36)^A(15)^B$
4. The glacial lake in Figure 3.17D.	D. 30^A5^B
5. The dark seawater in Figure 3.17E.	E. $(1)^A2^B$
6. The fried chicken in Figure 3.17F.	F. 15^A20^B
7. The sunny side of the woman's forehead in Figure 3.17G.	G. $(15)^A20^B$
8. The stone marker in Figure 3.17H.	H. $(19)^A(7)^B$

A Closer Look

In color correction, as in love, trust is vital.

If we only knew exactly what values we were trying to achieve, the first half of this book would be simplicity itself. If you are told that at a certain point in the image, the red, green, and blue numbers should be equal, how hard is that?

The problem is we seldom encounter objects that justify insistence on absolute neutrality. Tires and hockey uniforms generally qualify.

The angels usually don't present us with such reliably gray things, which means we have to speculate. This is thought to be one reason that retouchers themselves go gray early.

Another reason may be that retouchers are vain, and don't like it when portraits of them are printed showing skintones appropriate for Martians. The gray hair, one may theorize, is a defense mechanism, the inclusion of a reliably neutral point for the benefit of whoever works on the picture later.

Scientific support for this surmise is as yet lacking, but photographers, who also know the importance of neutral reference points, often provide them in a less taxing manner.

Just to the right of the tombstone remnant in Figure 3.18, the photographer has placed a gray card—a commercially available aid, a known reference point. As soon as he exposes this image, he'll remove the card and shoot the scene again. His intention is to correct the image containing the gray card, and then transfer the curves to the cardless shot.

This valuable technique has been around for a long time. Traditionally, we'd use the known gray points as guidance while trying to establish full range. Doing this required care because of the possibility of messing up detail.

Today, we needn't worry about that. Our procedure is easy. On a new layer, drop sampler points into various gray areas of the card, Command-click them into the channel curves, adjust as needed to get R=G=B in all of them, and change the layer to Color mode, which in principle can't alter detail.

The gray card procedure is effective, too, provided you let it be your servant and not your master. The remainder of this chapter discusses grays, reliable and otherwise.

Using the Gray Card

One would have to be a perfectionist to complain that this gray card is by the side of the focus of attention, rather than on top of it, where it would certainly receive the same type of light as the stone. Having it so close to the side ought to be good enough, no?

We shall see. Figure 3.19 is the adjusted version, with the curves that got it there. The Info palette shows before-and-after values for four gray swatches. In the graphic above the curves, you can see the crosshairs denoting them. The values being displayed are prior to the adjustment layer being changed to Color mode.

When this screen grab was taken, the cursor was over the gravestone

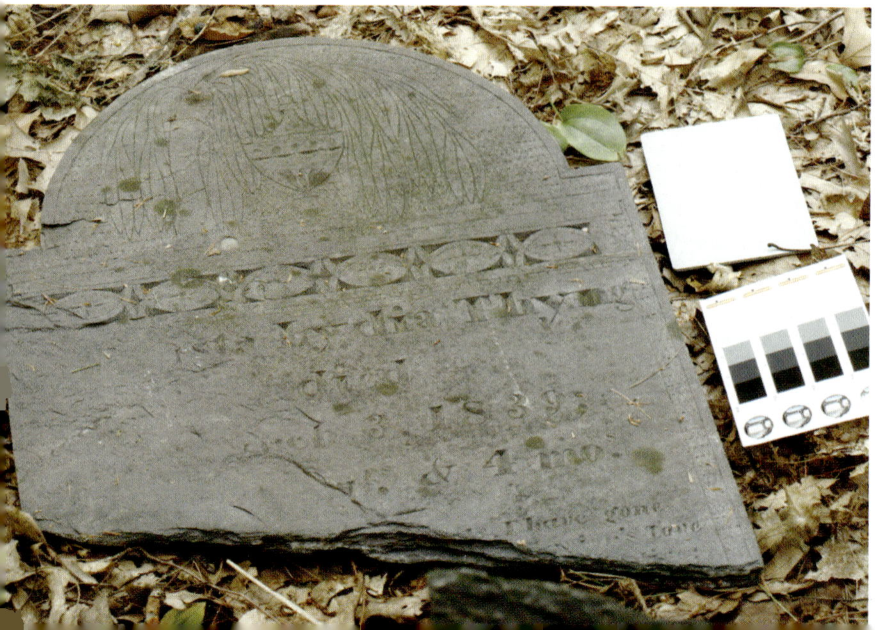

Figure 3.18 The photographer has placed a gray card in this scene.

itself, near the card. That, then, is a fifth point, shown at the top of the Info palette in both RGB and LAB. I left the other four points in RGB, as I intended to try to make them all more neutral with the simple formula R=G=B.

The pre-curve values for points #1 and #2, seen to the left of each slash, show the red channel is darkest and the other two are about equal. This combination produces cyan.

#3 is a transition. #4 is $43^R51^G37^B$. The green channel is lightest and the blue darkest. That combination makes it a greenish yellow, a color shared with none of the other three samples.

The curves respond by lightening the red, slightly darkening the green, and giving a customized treatment to the blue. The resulting numbers, the ones after the slashes in the Info palette, are about as close as a human can make them: a maximum of one point separates each member of a trio. So, as might be expected, the resulting picture, shown at the bottom of Figure 3.19, looks better than the original, Figure 3.18.

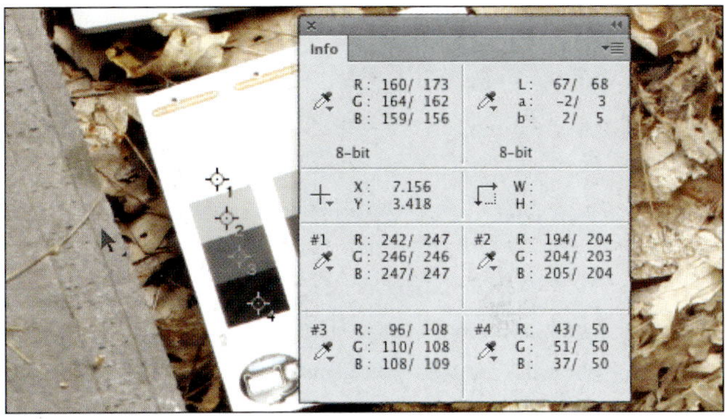

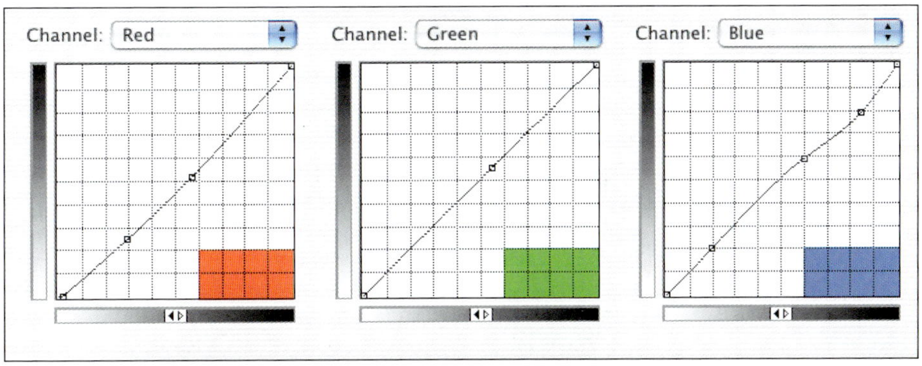

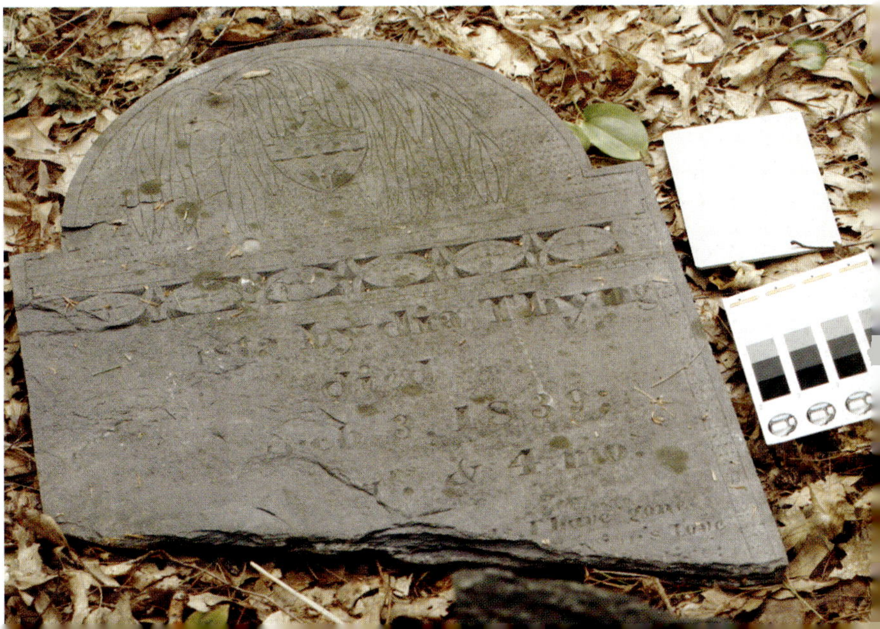

Figure 3.19 *An adjustment based on four values in the gray card. The Info palette shows values before and after application of the curves below. In the new version, bottom, the curves layer has been changed to Color mode.*

Ignoring the Gray Card

Let us now start over. Suppose that the gray card wasn't there. How would we approach this exercise? What colors can we be sure of? And what kind of penalty will we pay for ignoring the gray card?

The gravestone is not particularly colorful. It might even be 0^A0^B. If not, it should be somewhere in the neighborhood. This is trickier than dealing with the gray card, which we know should be very close indeed to 0^A0^B.

We can, however, rule out certain possibilities. The stone could be gray. It could be brown, which is a species of red. Granite can also be slightly blue. A purple tinge is much less likely. Yellow and cyan are, in my judgment, impossible, although some areas may be slightly green because algae or moss is present.

At the very bottom of the scene is a fragment

of the other half of the gravestone. It adds little to the scene except as a possible color reference, a substitute for a gray card, if you will.

The leaf on the right side of the top arch can also be evaluated for compliance with the recommendations for greenery.

I therefore placed four new sampler points as follows. One each on the left and right sides of the stone, just in case they don't agree with each other. One for the leaf, and one for the bottom fragment. The readings, the curves, and the results are shown in Figure 3.20. The four sampler points were set up to read LAB values rather than the RGB of Figure 3.19, because this time I wasn't trying for R=G=B.

Figure 3.20 An adjustment made without reference to the gray card. Samplers #1 and #2 are the left and right sides of the gravestone. #3 is the large leaf, and #4 is the darker fragment of the stone at the bottom of the image.

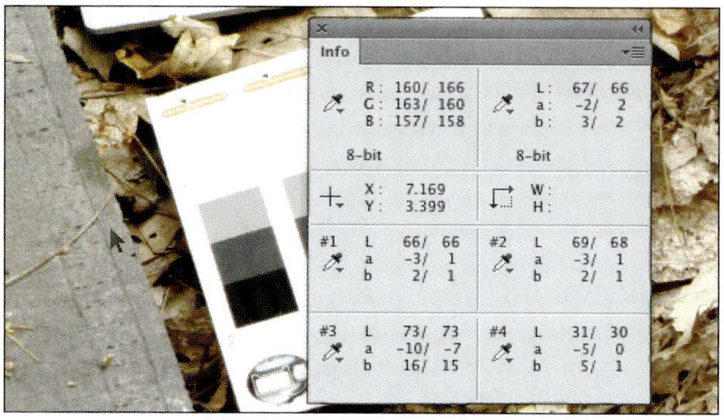

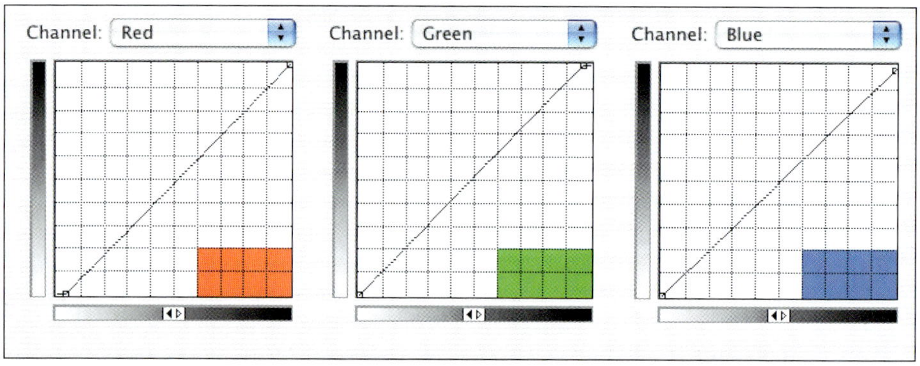

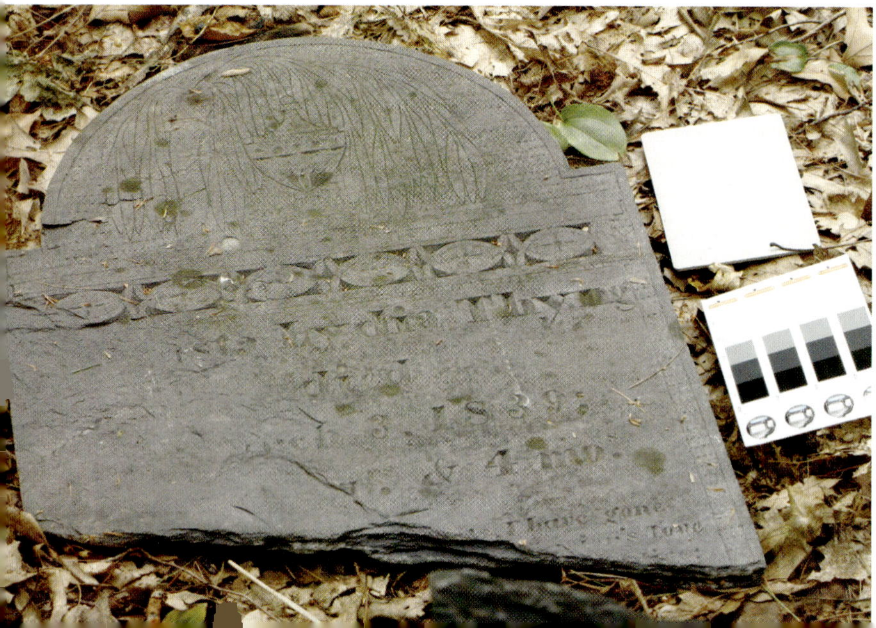

The process was simpler, in my view, than using the gray card. The two samplers in the main stone both read $(3)^A2^B$, more green than magenta and more yellow than blue. This color is not found in my list of possibilities. The dark half of the stone is around twice as bad, at $(5)^A5^B$. The leaf starts at $(10)^A16^B$. This barely complies with the recommendation that the absolute value of the B should be at least 1.5 times that of the A. I'm still dubious, because these values put it as one of the bluest acceptable greens, and my supposition is that in fact it should be fairly yellow.

The diagnosis is a lack of magenta in both stone fragments, or if you prefer, a weak A channel, or a green channel that's too light. All three phrases mean the same thing.

The cure might be to darken the green. The alternative would be to lighten both the red and blue. My choice was to start by lightening the red in the highlight. I therefore moved the lower left point of the red curve slightly to the right. Any of the following descriptions of the result is correct.

- The lightest parts are now less cyan than previously.
- They are more red.
- They are less green and less blue than they were.

- They are more magenta and more yellow.

That last description explains why I chose to play with the red channel rather than simply darkening the green. Moving this highlight point affects the leaf more than the darkest rock. I wanted to make that leaf warmer. Otherwise, a later attempt to make the dark stone less yellow might turn the leaf too blue.

This move in the red channel produced the following new values. Light stone: 0^A3^B. Leaf: $(8)^A17^B$. Dark stone: $(4)^A6^B$. I now turned my attention to the shadow point, the top right of the curves, and darkened the green and lightened the blue, producing Figure 3.20.

We now have two candidates: Figure 3.19, produced by reference to the gray card, and Figure 3.20, based on internal evidence only. The comparison does not favor Figure 3.19. The point shown at the top of its Info palette has gone to 3^A7^B, an orange. The defocused base of the tombstone has become slightly purple. The leaf to the right of the gravestone and to the left of the white card no longer complies with recommended values for greenery. It is $(5)^A17^B$, too yellow. The same spot in Figure 3.20 does comply, measuring $(7)^A15^B$.

Admittedly these peccadillos don't show up as major defects in Figure 3.19. However, the PPW often exaggerates all colors, including inaccurate ones. Let's try a torture

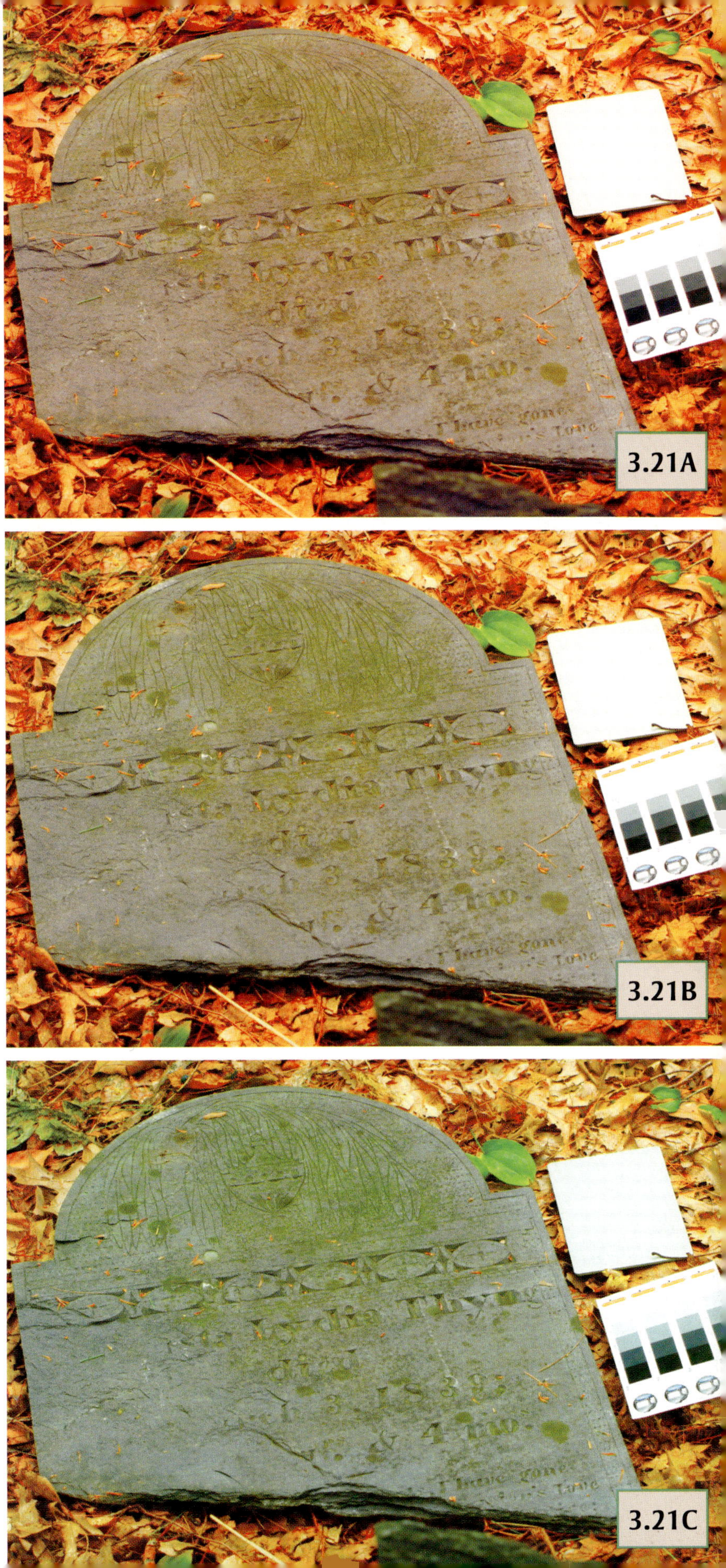

***Figure 3.21** Techniques shown in Chapter 5 drastically increase saturation in the versions seen so far. The same move has been applied to, top to bottom, Figures 3.19, 3.20, and 3.18.*

test to see just how accurate these initial adjustments were.

Figure 3.21A cranks up Figure 3.19's color beyond all reason. It uses a simple method shown in Chapter 5, the specifics of which are currently irrelevant.

The slight purple cast in the small portion of the base in the foreground has become quite evident. The dead leaves are the wrong hue, too rosy. The greens are too yellow. And the gravestone itself seems to have taken on a purple flavor, especially on the right side.

Identical moves applied to Figure 3.20 produce Figure 3.21B. And, for the sake of argument, when applied to the original, Figure 3.18, they produce Figure 3.21C. The first measurements revealed a cold cast and now it is obvious that they were correct. Everything in Figure 3.21C is distinctly cyan, which is why the leaves are so strangely muted.

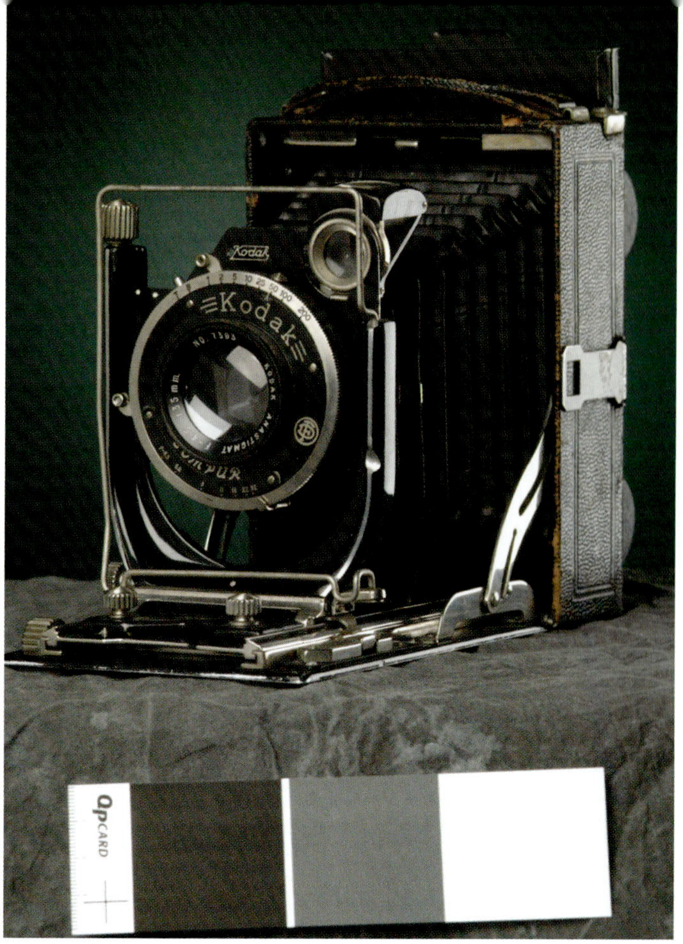

Figure 3.22 *The gray card is worthless in this original. The camera itself has enough known neutral areas.*

Advisory and Compulsory

The question is one of priorities, not trust. It isn't always possible, particularly in outdoor imagery, to eliminate every single color imbalance. We surely should try, but at some point we have to concede that certain target values can't be met, or that we simply don't know what those values should be.

Assuring color fidelity in objects that are about to be deleted, such as a gray card, is a low priority. Assuming you agree that the exaggerated colors of Figure 3.21B are superior to those of 3.21A, you have just decided that an inaccurate gray card is acceptable.

The Info palette of Figure 3.19 reported that Figure 3.19C's grays are as perfect as humans and commercial printers can obtain in the real world. The top of Figure 3.20's Info palette shows that the second-darkest gray swatch has been given a cool cast. In Figure 3.21B, that swatch looks distinctly blue. But one would presumably prefer that inaccuracy, if that's what you want to call it, over something involving the main gravestone.

All this is no knock on the use of gray cards. Few photos have as many internal clues as this one does. If they don't, a gray card can help. Even here, basing the correction on the gray card would do the trick if the curves were slightly modified to cater to the greens and the dark stone. So would reducing the opacity of the curve layer in Figure 3.19. Trouble lurks only when enough color is added later to call attention to inaccuracies. Graveyard scenes don't exactly cry out for vibrant colors. Nothing even close to the brilliance of Figure 3.21A is likely to be forthcoming.

* * *

Let's now consider one case where a gray card is actively counterproductive.

A gray card's purpose is to provide points of known neutrality. In Figure 3.22 we need the gray card about as much as a request from a

Nigerian banker for assistance in parking a few million dollars. It is a chimera, a will-o'-the-wisp, a useless temptation to go wrong.

We need no artificial neutrals because we're awash in the real thing. The camera is the subject. Unlike the gravestone, where we could only list things that we *didn't* want, this camera has a specific goal: 0^A0^B, pure neutrality. There is no shortage of places to check it.

Cameras of this traditional kind, being known neutral objects, are useful things to find in pictures. This picture is too easy to bother with further. Our final example features another camera, and a difficult double-cast problem.

Another Camera, Another Concept

For many years I have been preaching that the goal of color correction is to make the final product look like what a human would have seen, had the human been in the position of the camera at the time the picture was taken.

It's harder than it sounds. The following considerations are well known:

- Humans break neighboring colors apart, whereas cameras do not. This effect, *simultaneous contrast,* means that we perceive more variation than a camera does in forests, faces, and other large areas of a single color. The desire to put more variation in such scenes is an argument for using LAB in color correction.
- We adjust immediately to unbalanced lighting that's violent enough to provoke color casts in photographs. Because of this *chromatic adaptation,* pictures like the overly yellow hockey scene of Postcard 3.16 need to be corrected. In the rink itself, spectators would perceive the uniforms as white almost no matter how yellow the lighting.
- We are less disturbed by conditions that are slightly too light or too dark than the camera is. In response, we usually have to darken photographs that were taken in strong sunlight, and lighten those taken in unlighted rooms and similar dark conditions.
- The human visual system, incredibly, tries to compensate for as many lighting conditions as hit the eye, filtering different areas in different ways. This goes well beyond the capability of any camera. Photos shot with conflicting light sources are a big problem in today's professional world. Clients won't accept pictures that are yellow on one side and blue on the other, because they themselves would not have detected the imbalance that the camera did. Similarly, when confronted by strong light and strong shadow in the same picture, we adjust to both. A camera can only adjust to one, so the photograph looks unnatural.

In Search of Normalcy

Partial-light, partial-shadow pictures pose so many problems that the entire first half of Chapter 12 is devoted to them. Its methods won't work well unless we can eliminate a common color issue that bedevils this category.

Postcard 3.23 still has a shadow/sun distinction, but less than the original. It looks more natural. The idea that "sunny" areas—not highlights, not midtones—should often be darkened and made more vivid is, in fact, the quartertone quandary that this book will explore. For the time being, we only need to worry about color differences between the two areas, since we aren't yet considering lightness and darkness.

This image is littered with items known to be neutral. The camera and strap should be black. In isolation, the backpack might not be, but its measurements are almost the same as the strap and camera. So it must be black also.

Logic also says that the hair should be gray, that the watch should be a silvery neutral, and that the light stripes in the shirt are white. The greenery and the fleshtone can also be checked for compliance with standards.

The problem is that many of these objects fall simultaneously in sunlight, which the camera records as slightly yellow, and in shadow, which the camera sees as blue. Pumping more color into the existing file will create a crazy effect. The stripes will become bright blue and the

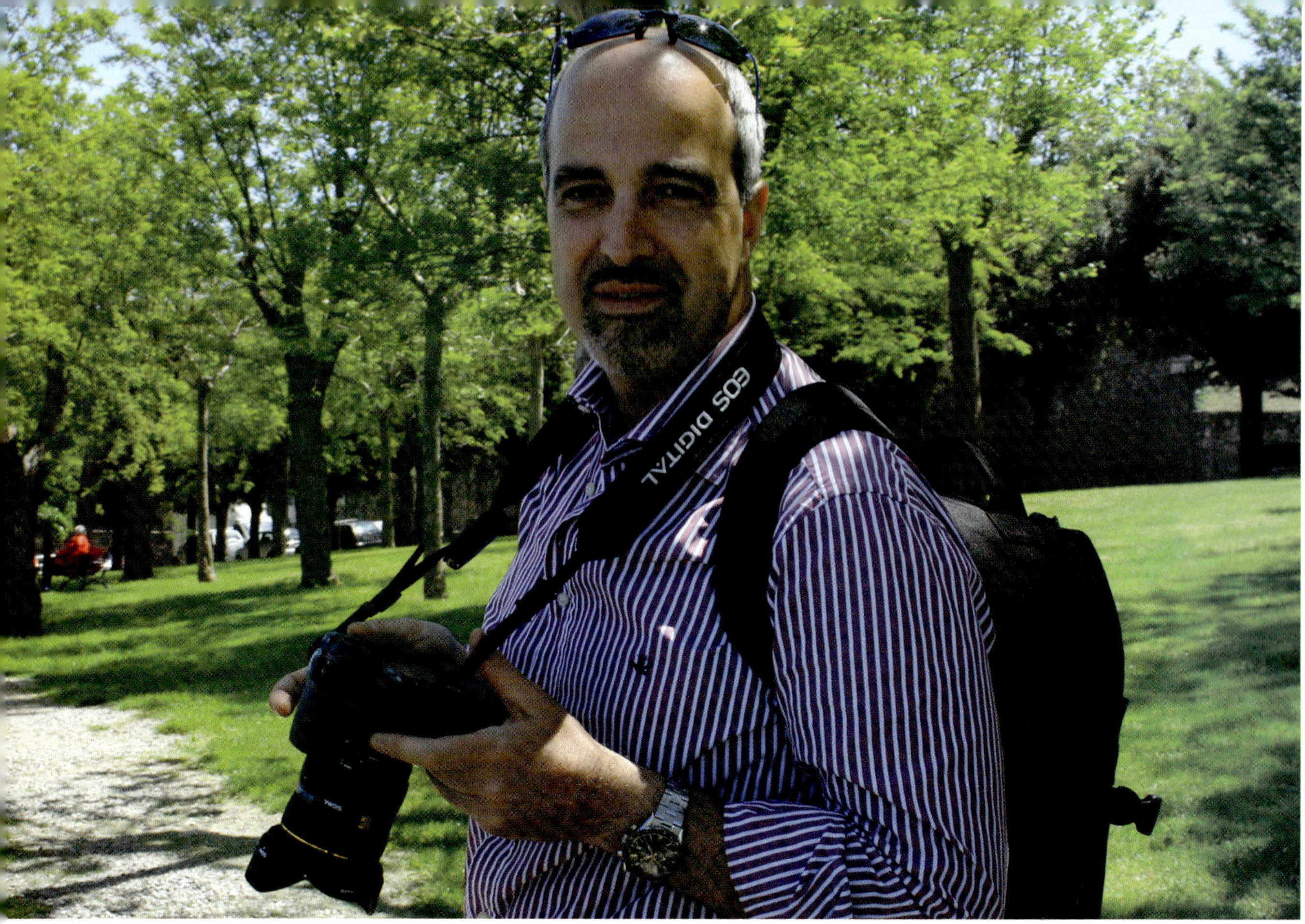
EOS DIGITAL

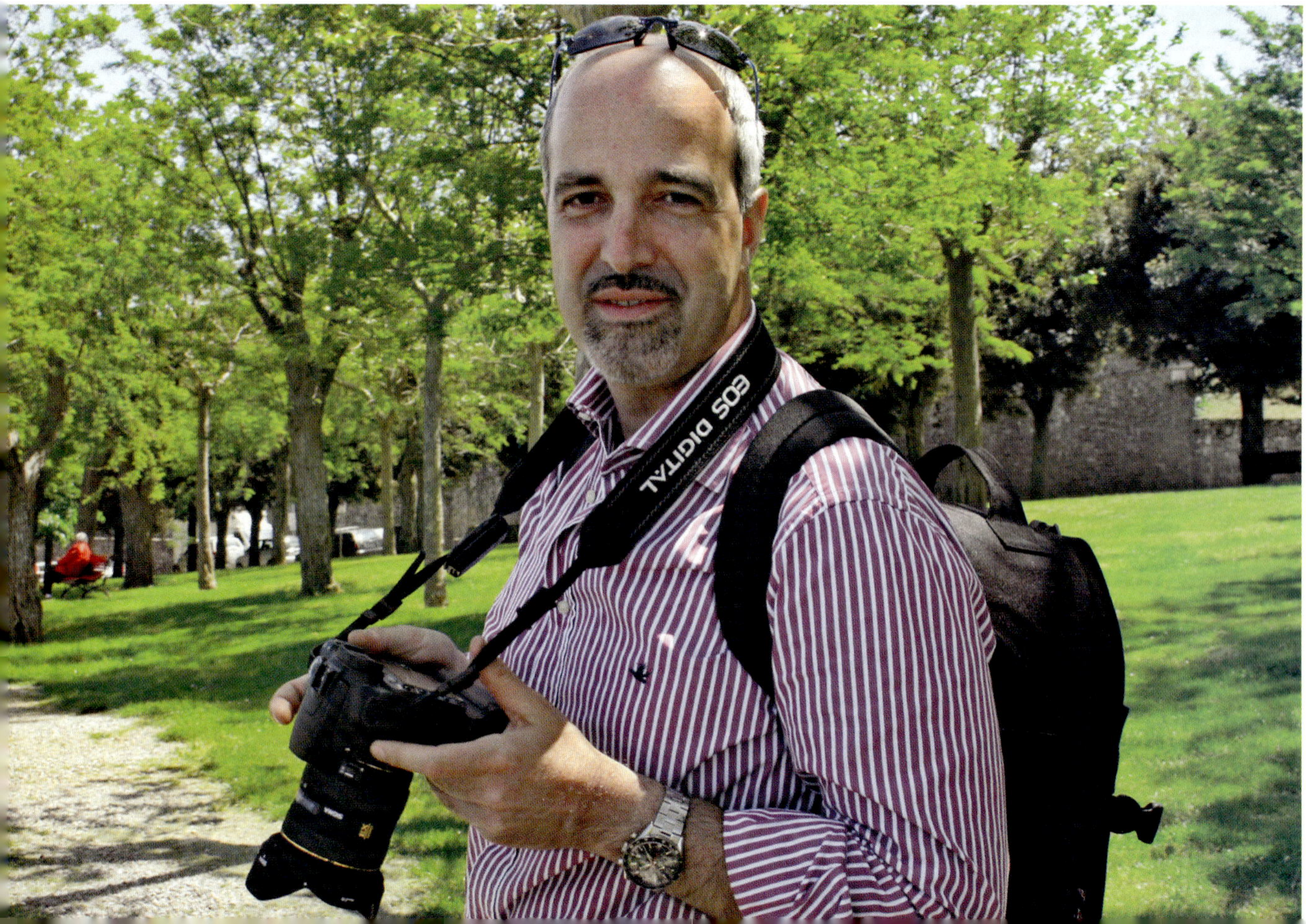
EOS DIGITAL

***Postcard 3.23** (opposite). More camera equipment for use as a neutral reference, this time with a complication. The original is partially in sunlight and partially in shadow, creating a color imbalance.*

fleshtone an unhealthy neutral when the setting is obviously bright and cheerful.

Typical sunlight-shadow pictures aren't this hard. Normally, sunlit areas are bright and shadows are dark. If so, it's easy enough to apply curves to make darker areas warmer and thus diminish their blueness.

Here, that easy lightness-darkness distinction isn't available, except in the deepest blacks. The stripes are in shadow and are therefore too blue, but the gravel path is the same darkness and falls in sunlight. Neutralize the stripes and the path will likely become bright yellow. Similarly, the watch, which falls in shadow, is almost as dark as the sunny top of the backpack.

First, the sunny areas. The hair starts out $242^R242^G242^B$, a perfect gray. The sunlit area on the top of the backpack is $132^R133^G137^B$, which is $0^A(2)^B$. A darker nearby area is $105^R108^G114^B$, which is $0^A(4)^B$. So at the outset the strap and background are slightly blue even though they are in sunlight. Conclusion: the hair probably should be slightly yellow, not gray. The two other areas also require the introduction of more yellow because they shouldn't have any blue tinge at all.

As for shaded areas, checking very dark blacks like the strap, the camera, and the bottom of the pack is likely to be misleading. Near the maximum darkness of $0^R0^G0^B$, (and these items are pretty close), the result always approaches neutrality even if the rest of the picture has a cast. For example, the top of the shoulder strap is $44^R54^G57^B$, or $(4)^A(3)^B$—cyan, but misleadingly close to neutral.

Instead, look for lighter neutral things within the shady area. We aren't always lucky enough to find them, but here two present themselves. The watch measures $91^R108^G133^B$, or $(2)^A(16)^B$, strongly blue with a tinge of green. Worse, one of the "white" stripes is $131^R158^G233^B$, or an eye-poppingly blue $5^A(42)^B$.

Careful curving can bring the two sides of this picture somewhat closer together for color selection. But with the sides this close in darkness and this far away in color balance it will not be possible to neutralize everything.

Given how conflicted the camera is, the logical solution is to have the sunny areas slightly warm and the watch slightly cool. They start out nearly neutral and very cool.

Of course, there's no telling how far we want

***Figure 3.24** Left, curves force the top of the backpack, which is in sun, to become neutral. Center, the curves are aimed at neutralizing the watch instead. Right, a 50–50 blend of the two.*

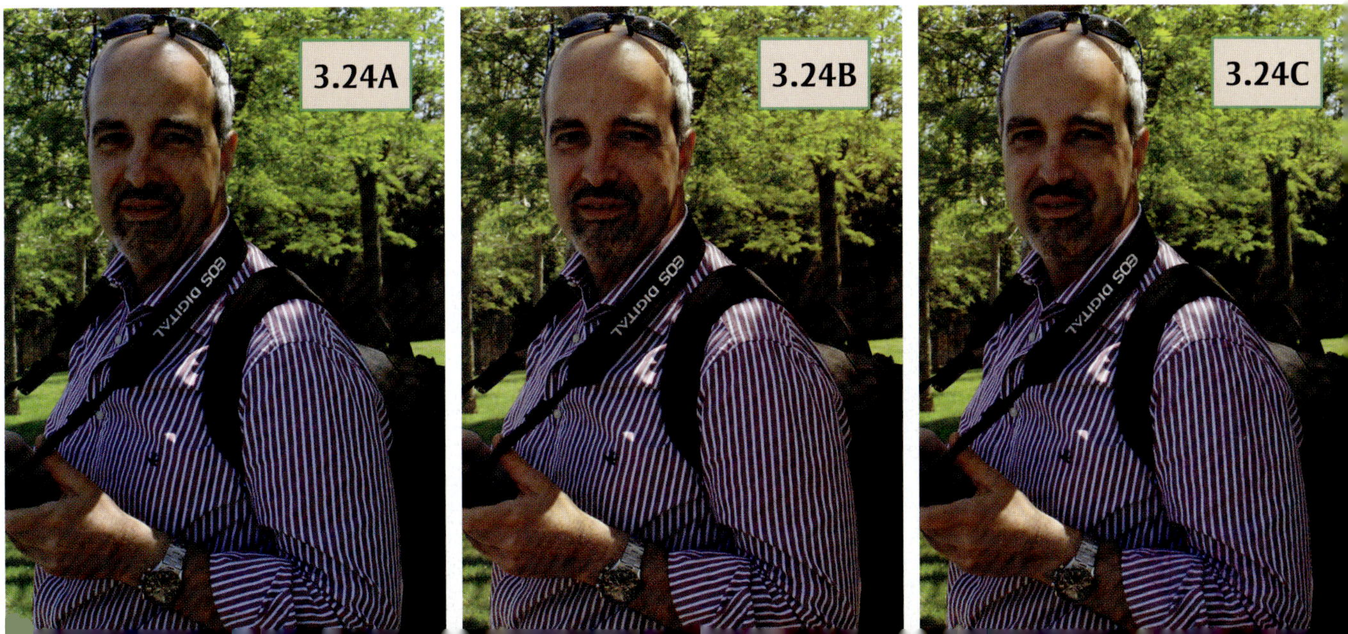

to go. Rather than juggle curves until they accidentally give us what we want, a more efficient way is to produce two extreme versions and split the difference.

Figure 3.24A is the first extreme. It's produced with curves that leave the hair gray and force the top of the backpack to neutrality. Notice how the face gets slightly redder. Figure 3.24B, a new copy, goes in the opposite direction. Its curves force the *watch* to be neutral, which makes the face redder still.

One cannot logically want anything cooler than Figure 3.24A, nor warmer than Figure 3.24B. Either one is plausible, but chances are that we prefer something between the two. So, we paste one as a layer on top of the other, and choose an opacity that suits us. I used 50% to make Figure 3.24C.

Keeping Things in Their Proper Order

To recap, I just advocated doing one color correction for the sunny areas and a different one for the shady ones, then finding a graceful way to merge them. The extra time to do it this way isn't extreme, which makes it possible for all but the most slapdash kind of work.

To end this chapter, I'd like to discuss some of the options for stubborn images like this one, in cases where the importance of the image permits the time for additional steps.

Here is another restatement of the Picture Postcard Workflow.

- Eliminate inadequate color, without concerning ourselves with matters of contrast.
- Optimize contrast, without heed to color.
- Intensify color.

The objective of this chapter is to take the first step: color that is not known to be incorrect.

How that goal is achieved is unimportant. My suggested workflow is just that, a suggestion. If departing from it gets the job done, go for it. Two beta readers, in fact, don't work in the way described in this chapter. Their first step is in LAB, using complicated masking to control the effect. Thereafter, they follow the PPW.

Now review the three basic steps above. Why is what we're doing in this chapter the *first* one? Its effects only become important when we reach the *third* step, not the second. Why not transpose the first two steps, doing contrast first and then knocking out bad color?

It's a deep question. The color step should come first as a general rule because changing color without changing contrast is unlikely to affect a subsequent contrast step. The converse is not true. For example, a typical sun-and-shadow picture, of which this is not one, has a blue cast in dark areas that doesn't exist in lighter ones. It's easy to repair that with curves, unless contrast has been reallocated so that previously dark things have become lighter.

Unfortunately for generalizations, one must also acknowledge that changing contrast might make the color move *easier.* It does so here, because any reasonable reallocation of contrast will produce a lighter watch while the backpack, camera, and strap remain dark. Subsequent curves can therefore target the watch with less collateral damage.

This changing of the order sounds like it might open up a large can of worms. It doesn't. Remember, many images arrive with no color problems at all, and most of the rest have only minor ones. A fraction of the remainder can't be solved by the techniques of this chapter, and many of those aren't worth the bother of doing something more complicated. So we are not talking about a common difficulty.

Nevertheless, any method that eliminates inaccurate color is a good one. Unless you're working in LAB like these beta readers, I recommend avoiding the use of masks and commands like Hue/Saturation until it has become clear that unmasked curves are not getting the desired result. At that point, anything goes. It is reasonable to combine Figures 3.24A and 3.24B with a mask based on darkness, for example.

Let's close with another last-resort method that sometimes works well with shadowy pictures like this one.

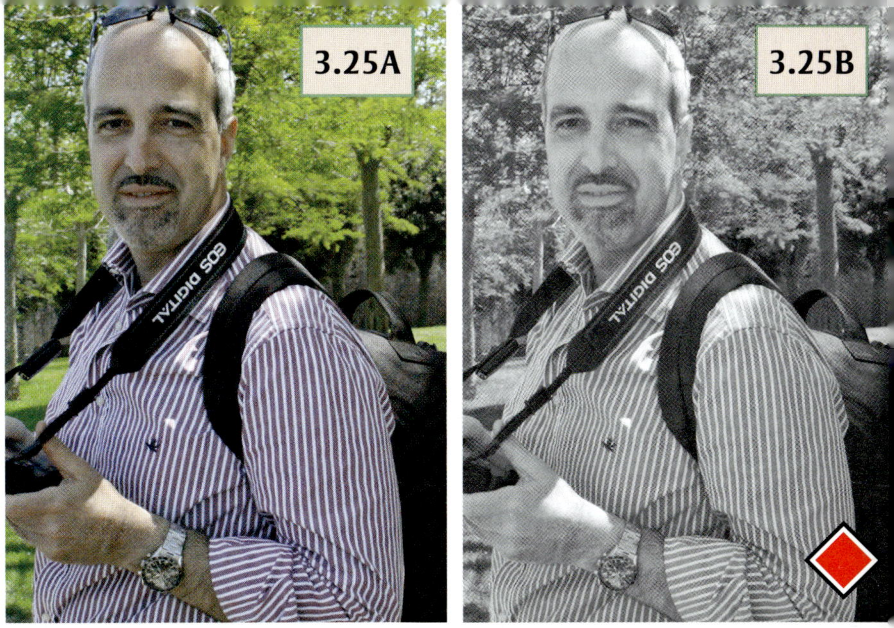

Figure 3.25 Top left, starting with Figure 3.24C, luminosity is corrected with the techniques of subsequent chapters. There has been no color adjustment. Top right, the resulting red channel. Middle left, the resulting blue. Middle center, on a duplicate layer, the red is replaced by a copy of the blue. Middle right, the blend mode is changed from Normal to Lighten. Bottom left, layer opacity is reduced and a similar slight blend applied to the green channel. Bottom center, curves are applied to adjust color. Bottom right, for comparison, the same curves applied to the pre-blend version at top left.

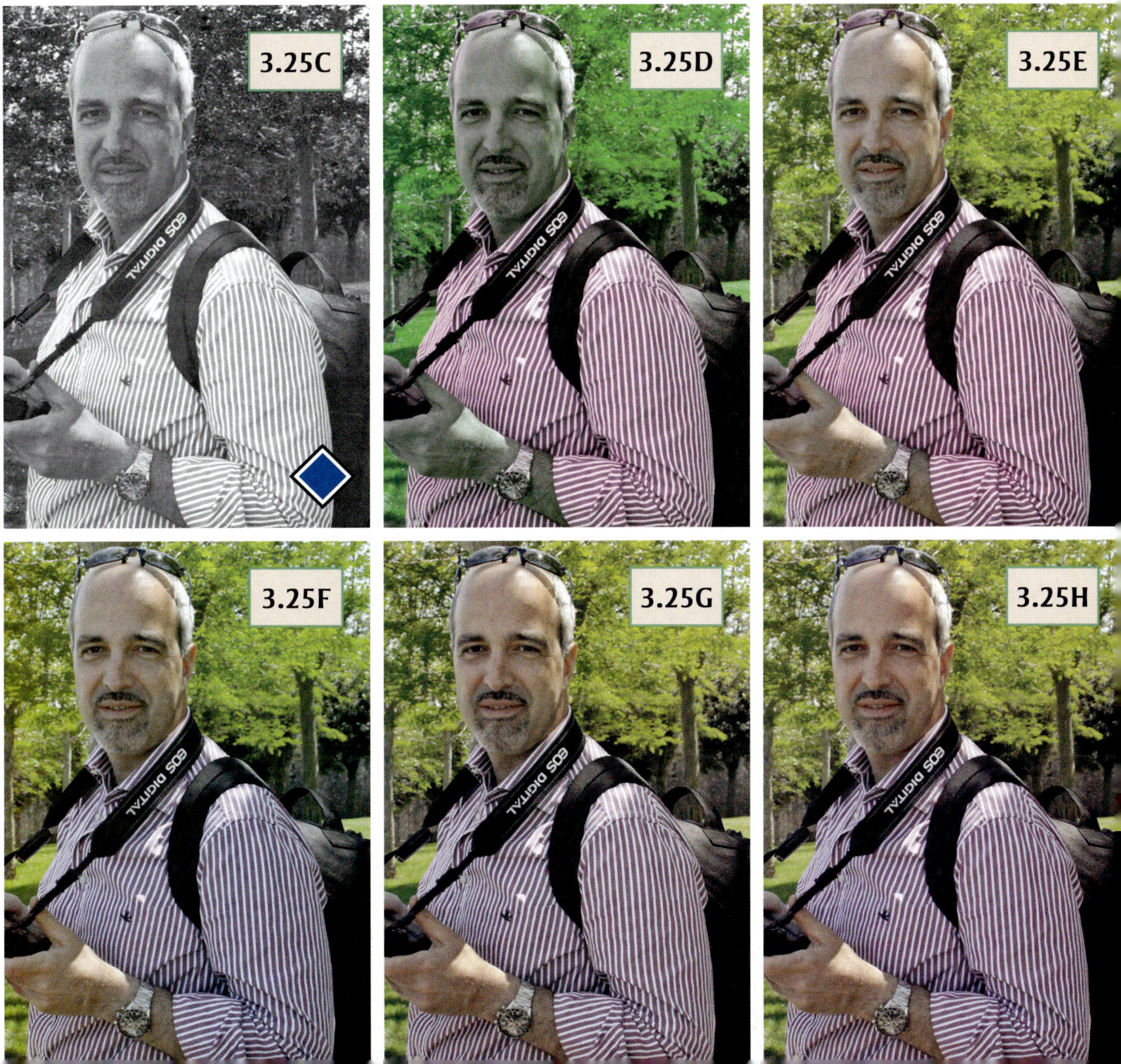

A Cure for the Blues

As noted earlier, I transposed the first two workflow steps. So, I followed procedures outlined in Chapters 4 and 12 to produce Figure 3.25A, which corrects weight problems but does nothing to improve the bluish watch and stripes.

The blue channel is usually the darkest of the three, except in areas that are themselves blue, like skies—or the problem areas seen here. The imbalance is mostly caused by an overly heavy red channel. So a careful blend of the blue into the red can be helpful. The blend needs to be in Lighten, rather than Normal, mode because the idea is to only alter the red in places where it is currently darker than the blue.

Figures 3.25B and 3.25C show the two channels; notice how much lighter the white stripes are in the blue, even though most of the rest of the scene is darker.

Figure 3.25D replaces the entire red channel with a copy of the blue, showing why not to use Normal mode. So, in Figure 3.25E, the blend is changed to Lighten mode. The stripes become pink rather than blue.

In Figure 3.25F, therefore, the opacity drops to 35%, and a similar slight blend of the blue to the green channel in Lighten mode reduces the pinkness. This pair of blends is unobtrusive, yet can enable a more effective correction. Figure 3.25G adds the curves. The resulting color is intensified in Postcard 3.23.

For reference, I include Figure 3.25H, which is the same thing without the channel blend. That is, the same curve attacks Figure 3.25A rather than 3.25F. The subtle extra blueness is in my opinion enough to derail any attempt to match the color of the final postcard.

* * *

We return to the questions of time and trust. Is it really worth it to spend the extra minutes to get to Figure 3.25F? Doubtless its color is better than that of Figure 3.24C, but then again 3.24C is a whole lot better than the original. The answer depends on how important the picture is to you.

As for trust, the key to success in this difficult chapter is to refuse to assume that something is wrong with the color unless you can prove it. Resist forcing something unknown to match a speculation rather than a certainty.

In the last two pictures, we can be very, very confident that the two cameras are supposed to be black, and not something close. It is one of life's little jokes that cameras are so much more trustworthy when they *appear* in the picture than when they take it.

The Bottom Line

This chapter discusses the most difficult, and least rewarding, aspect of the Picture Postcard Workflow. Chapters 5 and 6 show methods of introducing spectacular, yet believable color. They fail if the files being worked on have casts or other color imperfections. This chapter's role is to eliminate them. The goal is not to make attractive color, but color that isn't known to be wrong.

The procedure is to apply RGB curves on a layer, which will eventually be set to Color mode to avoid altering contrast. In the second half there is a discussion of exceptional cases, but it must be remembered that they are just that, exceptional.

4

Once for Contrast: a Whole Exceeds the Sum of Its Parts

Knowing that the color is at least adequate liberates us from needing to worry about it as we try to enhance contrast. Blend good channels into bad ones, apply curves to bring out detail, and ignore the resulting horrible color—just revert to that of the previous chapter.

Clichés about the Grand Canyon—breathtaking, indescribable, unbelievable—carry over to pictures of it. Nothing compares to seeing it in person, but Postcard 4.1 is a reasonable attempt, with a lot of apparent depth.

And now the hard part: what makes us say that?

* * *

To describe what's missing from the original, a layperson might use vague words like *snap* or *pop*. A professional would likely insist on more meaningful terms, such as *bite* or *guts*.

Precise words are hard to come by because we are used to evaluating the whole picture, rather than separating it into color and contrast components. Any discussion of the merits of the final version is likely to be derailed by an argument over whether we have hit the exact shade of orange-red we want.

In this chapter, that question is irrelevant. We deal here with contrast only—detail, definition. For present purposes the bottom version is better than the top because if we converted both to black and white, it would be clearly superior.

That, in a nutshell, is this chapter. It can almost be summarized as an attempt to make a better black and white, which will then be used, in Luminosity mode, to improve the contrast of a picture whose color is already adequate. Thus, we ignore color altogether, just as we ignored detail in Chapter 3. This chapter is the easier of the two in the sense that getting a strikingly better result isn't that difficult. It also can be harder if you become enamored of some of the more complex strategies that occasionally pay dividends. We'll come back to this Grand Canyon shot at the end of

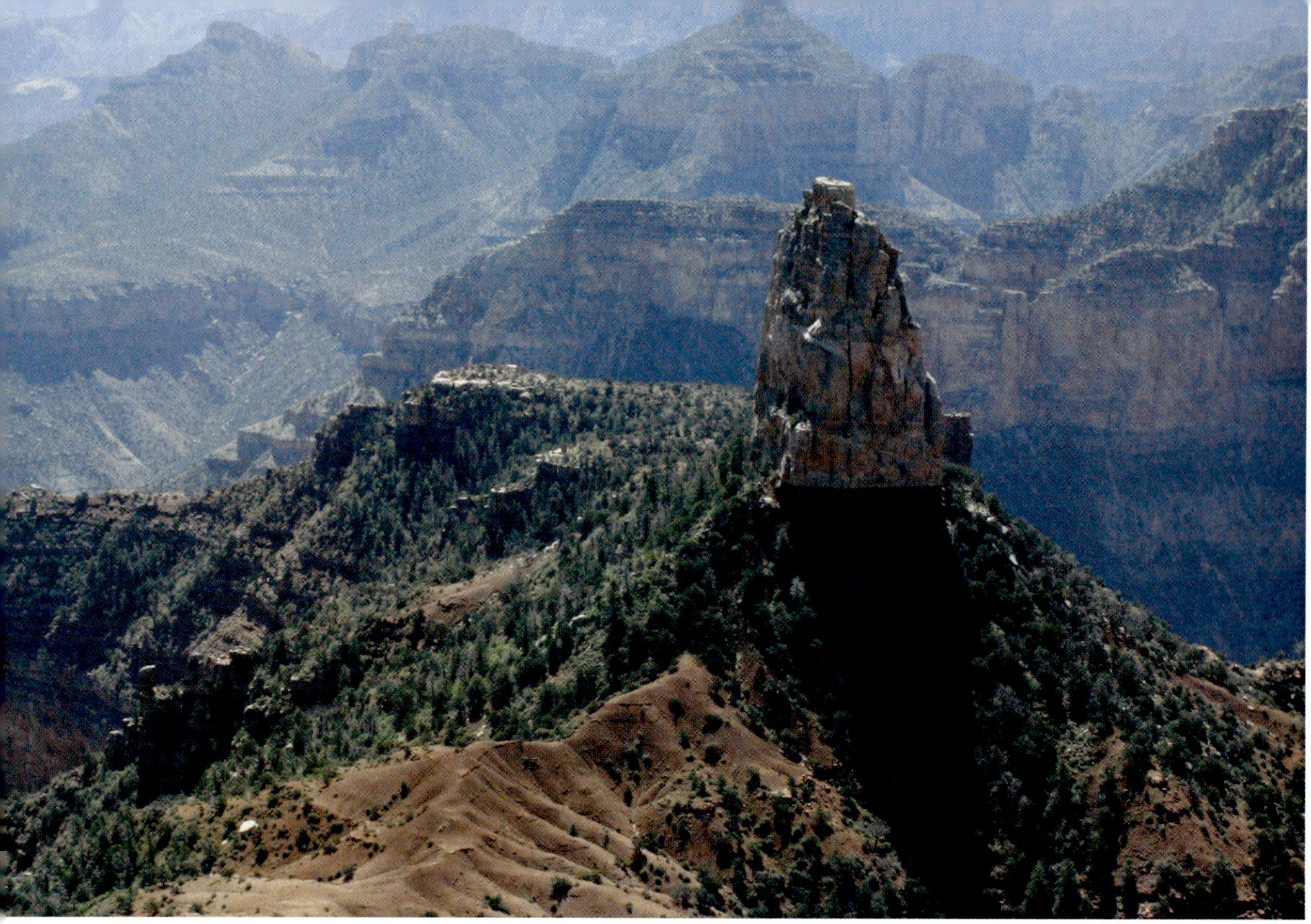

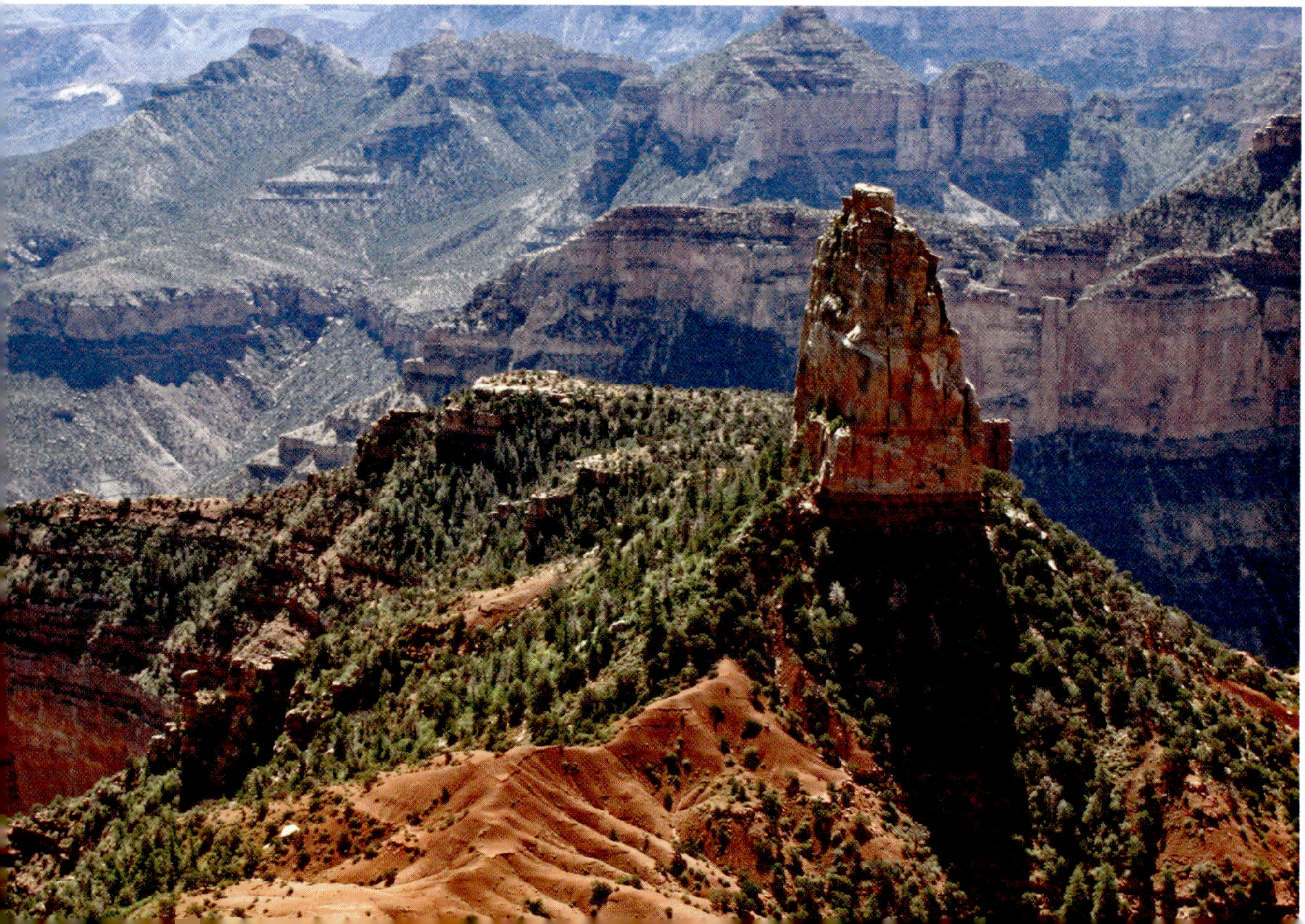

this first half of the chapter. Now, however, let's get a preview by analyzing the tools at our disposal.

A Quick Once-Over

The process begins with a duplicate layer, to which we do whatever possible to establish a feeling of depth. When finished, we change the layer's mode from Normal to Luminosity. This restores the base layer's color while retaining the contrast of what's on top.

Before that mode change, a slew of channel blending and curving possibilities offer themselves. Figure 4.2 illustrates the more common ones.

The original, Figure 4.2A, shows pink flowers on a background of tropical greenery. We first must attack color as in Chapter 3, but find out that there is no enemy. The greenery falls within the recommended range. The correct pink of this particular hibiscus is unknown, at least to me. Therefore, no move. In Chapter 3, I said that the decision that no change is needed should take less than ten seconds. Would you have met that deadline?

On to an examination of the channels. You can open the Channels palette (Window: Channels) and click each icon in turn. It can be done more quickly with keyboard shortcuts, and considering that you will probably be examining channels in every image you work on from now until the end of time, that's how you should probably go. Unfortunately, there's a hitch.

In Photoshop CS4 and later, Command–3 shows the first channel, red in our case, Command–4 the second (the green here) and so on. For the previous ten versions of Photoshop they had been Command–1, –2, and so on. Some have executed these "legacy" shortcuts well over a million times. Adobe said that the change was needed to make Photoshop's behavior match that of other Adobe products, and blandly suggested that we should just relearn.

In the first draft of this chapter, I made clear what I think should have been done to those responsible, as well as my general opinion of Photoshop CS4. The beta readers made me delete it all. I will point out that in Photoshop CS5 and later, the old shortcut behavior can be restored, more or less, in Edit: Keyboard Shortcuts by clicking Use Legacy Channel Shortcuts. The beta readers have also made me delete comments about what should have been done to the incompetent corporate bootlicker who approved releasing Photoshop CS4 without that obviously necessary change.

Now that you know or suspect what would happen to the unholy if I were dictator of the world, I point out that if you sit down at somebody else's computer the keyboard shortcuts could have been set either way. Also, somebody may have modified the default channel display preference by going to Photoshop: Preferences>Interface and checking Show Channels in Color. If so, change it back: you always want to view them in grayscale.

The changes about to be made go on a duplicate layer that will eventually be set to Luminosity mode. However, it should be set to Normal mode while you work. That's the only way to see the actual channel structure. Otherwise, you'd be looking at channels that have been revised to comport with your desire that the color not change.

Usually I prefer to blend first if the image is fairly good and curve first if it is flat. But either order works.

Many valid ways to blend channels exist. Without disparaging the others, I suggest Image: Apply Image because it is the most flexible. This command targets the active channel(s). The source of the blend can be any channel (including alpha channels),

Postcard 4.1 *The final version of this Grand Canyon shot shows more detail, particularly in the background, than is seen in the original.*

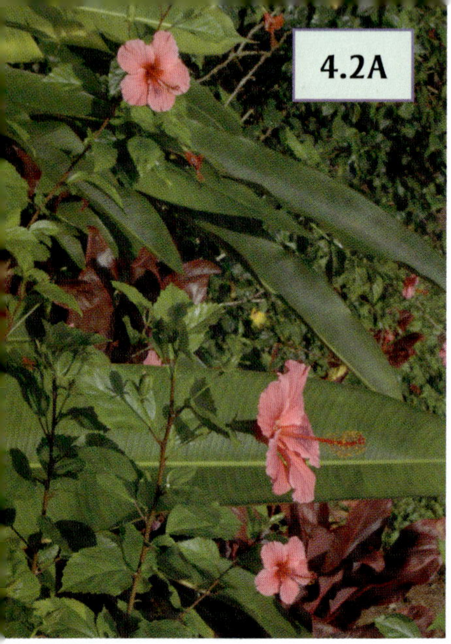

from any layer (including the merged composite), from the existing document or from any other document that is currently open and is the same size (usually a copy of the original). In Photoshop CS6 the command offers 23 different blending modes; fortunately only a few need concern us.

A blend modifies a channel to take on desirable characteristics of another. Less commonly, it can be the complete replacement of one by another. It can also be the complete or partial replacement of two channels by the third. That's what we'll look at first. And because the topic is confusing, after you hear my explanation, you'll get it rephrased by a beta reader. First, mine.

***Figure 4.2** Top, the original. Second row, using the red, green, and blue channels, respectively, as the luminosity layer. Bottom row, the original channels.*

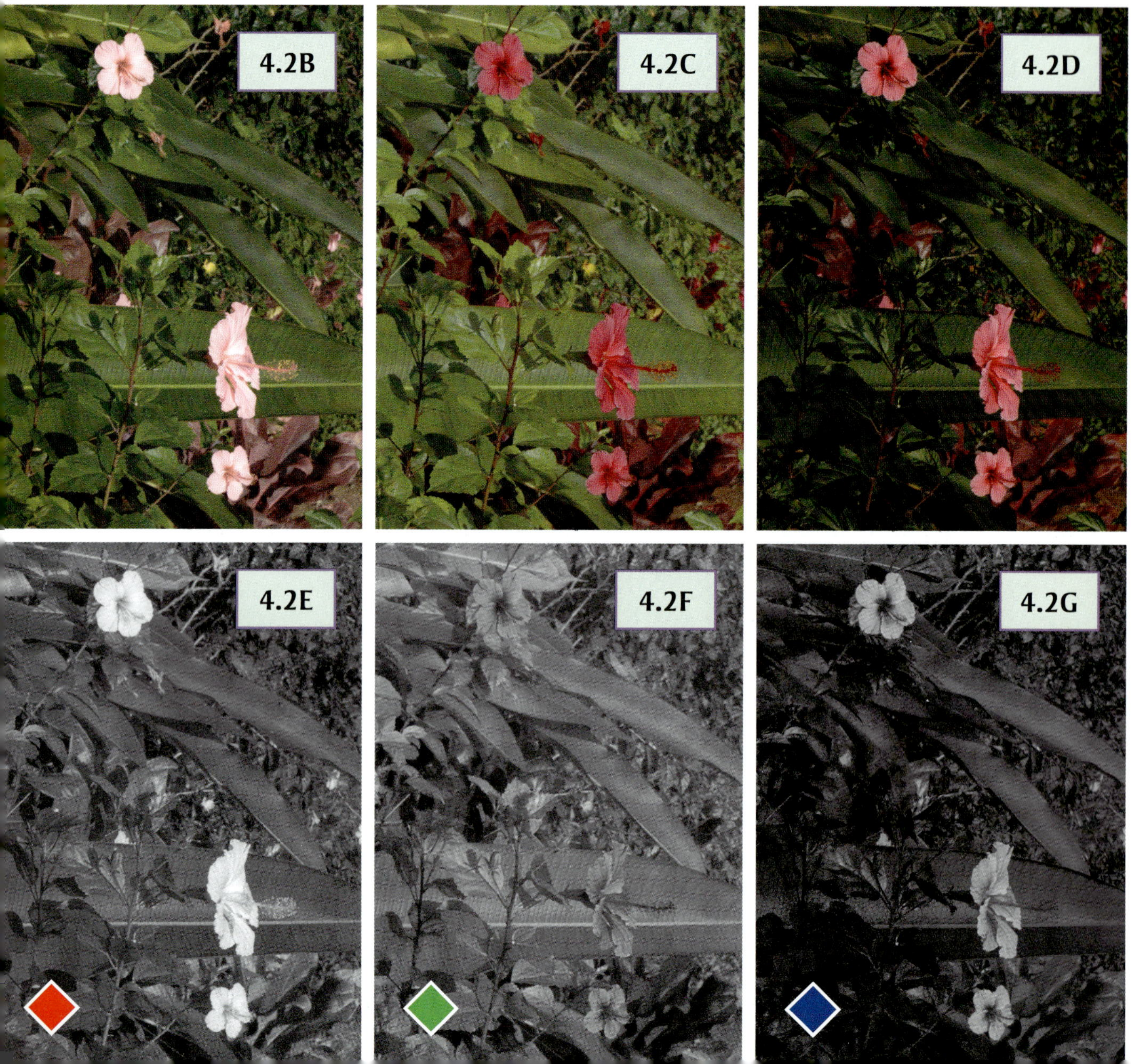

Let's try replacing the green and blue channels with copies of the red. To do so, the duplicate layer must be the active one.

The setup is shown in Figure 4.3. As Source, we specify the current image. We have no choice about the target: it's whatever is currently active. As all three RGB channels are open, all three will be affected by what's to come. Layer, for the moment, doesn't matter. For Channel, we choose Red. Blending must be set to Normal; watch out, because the Photoshop default Blending is Multiply.

And now, the same two paragraphs as explained by beta reader Bevi Chagnon:

"I'm missing a couple of steps and the explanation that Apply Image is done to a layer, not a channel. It's critical to clearly define early in the chapter how both layers and channels are used in this step. (I remember being very lost in your class when I first learned this basic procedure.)

"Maybe something like this:

"Let's replace the green and blue channels with a duplicate of the red channel. We're doing this to see if the red can be used to improve the contrast of the photo.

"Since the Apply Image command is applied to layers, we must first duplicate the photo's main layer (usually the Background layer) and make the duplicate active.

"Then, select Image: Apply Image. The setup is shown in Figure 4.3. As to source, we specify Red. As to target, we have no choice: it's whatever is currently active. Because all three RGB channels are active, etc."

Thanks, Bevi! I'll take it from here. The choice for Layer in Source usually is important but not in this particular case. The top layer is a duplicate of the bottom, so it matters not whether we specify top, bottom, or Merged. Blending should be set to Normal; Opacity to 100%. We now click OK, move to the Layers palette, and change the mode of the duplicate layer from Normal to Luminosity. Figure 4.2B is the unattractive result.

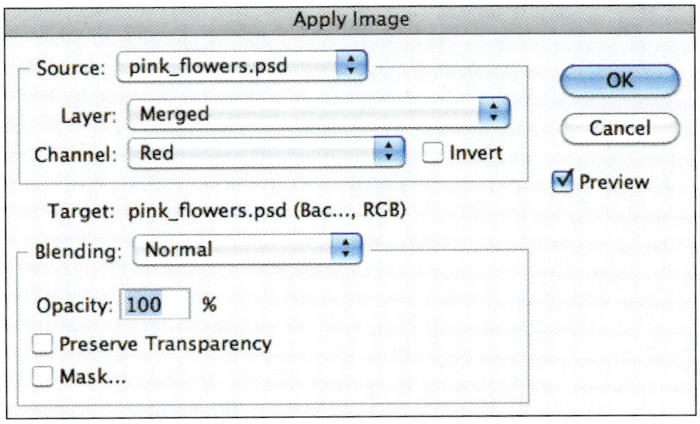

***Figure 4.3** The Apply Image command is the most flexible way to blend channels.*

And what did the file look like when the layer was still in Normal mode? Like Figure 4.2E, which is the original red channel. Since the green and the blue were duplicates of the red, R=G=B everywhere. As we know from the first chapter, R=G=B is the formula for neutrality. For the time being, then, the file looks like a black and white.

Since the red didn't exactly work, let's try using the green channel in the same way. If we were starting from scratch, we'd follow the same procedure. But we're starting from Figure 4.2B, where the red has already been used as a luminosity layer. Procedure, please?

Mastery of Apply Image

The three source layer choices in Apply Image are no longer identical. The green channel in the background layer is the original. In the top layer, it's a copy of the red. Choosing Merged as Layer produces a hybrid, based on that red but modified as needed to retain the color of the original.

More care with the Layer section of Apply Image is therefore required. To blend from the original green, use the settings of Figure 4.3, except change Layer to Background, and Channel to Green.

That yields Figure 4.2C. Doing a third version using the blue produces Figure 4.2D.

These three new versions are all worse than the original, in my opinion.

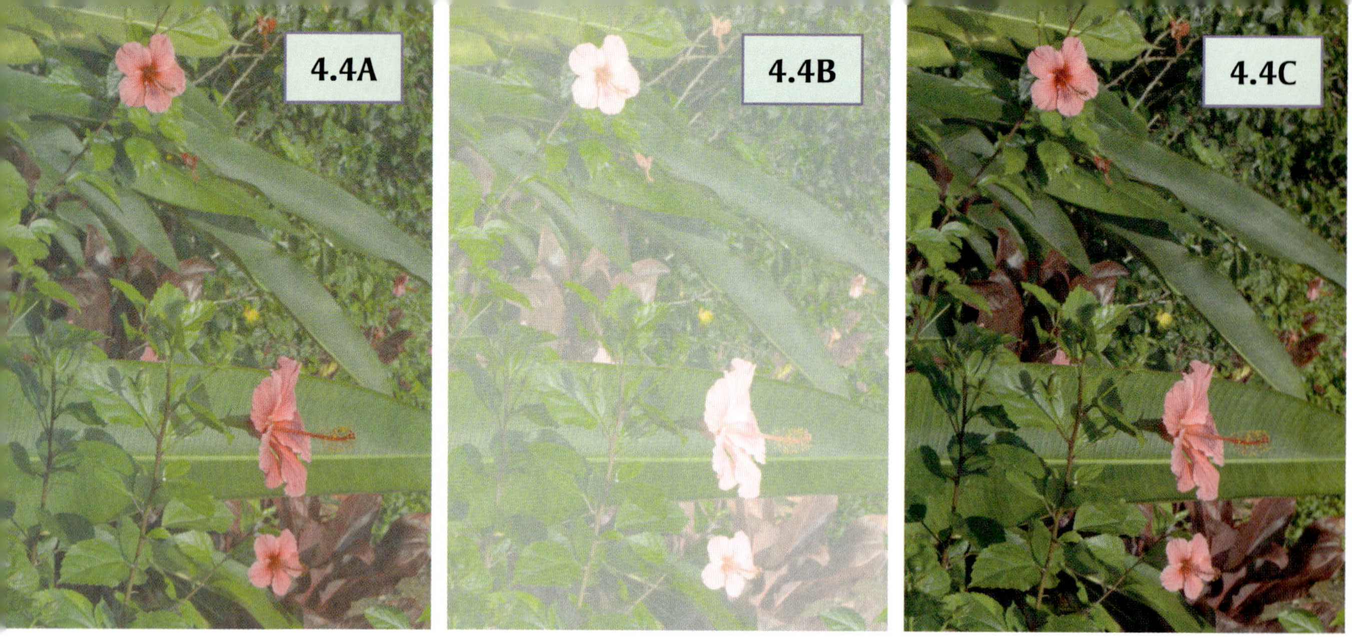

***Figure 4.4** The three channels don't contribute equally to image weight. In each of the above, one channel has been deleted on a layer that is afterward set to Luminosity mode. Left to right, the deletion of the red, green, and blue.*

They are, however, worse in different ways. Figure 4.2B has an excellent background but its flowers are a disaster area. Figure 4.2C is the reverse. Figure 4.2D has better contrast but its background is way too dark.

The flowers are more pronounced against a darker background. Split the difference between Figures 4.2C and 4.2D, or possibly between 4.2B and 4.2C, and the result should be better than anything shown. It's easy enough to combine two files, again with Apply Image. After flattening one and making sure that all three of its RGB channels are active, we apply the other to it at 50% opacity or whatever.

Before starting again with a different strategy, it must be pointed out that all channels are not created equal. Figure 4.4A shows the impact if the file has no red channel at all. That is, starting from the original, Figure 4.2A, I created a duplicate layer, in which I deleted (or filled with white, if you prefer) the red channel. This created a brilliantly red mess, which there is no need to look at. But after changing layer mode to Luminosity, the original color returns, minus the contrast contributed by the late lamented red.

Let's now try the same experiment with the green and blue channels. Deleting an entire channel sounds as if it would devastate the file. Figure 4.4C demonstrates that it isn't true—provided that the channel getting the ax is the blue.

Deleting the red had a much stronger effect. Note, however, that the flowers are no lighter in Figure 4.4A than in 4.4C. It shouldn't be a surprise. The original red, Figure 4.2E, is practically blank in the flowers, so deleting it doesn't damage them.

Figure 4.4B doesn't have much left after the deletion of the powerhouse green channel, which is worth roughly 60 percent of total luminosity. The red contributes half that, and the blue only about 10 percent.

If that's how it is, we shouldn't waste a lot of time improving the blue channel. If it can be done in less than ten seconds, fine. If not, we should confine ourselves to seeing whether the blue could make a useful blend source for the benefit of the *other* channels.

Figure 4.2F is the original green. Blending something else into it is dangerous because it might lighten the flowers too much. However, its unappealing flatness is in fact an advantage. Any curve that increases contrast in the foliage will have to boost it in the flowers, too, because in the green channel, and only in the green channel, they share the same tonal range.

The Steeper the Curve…

Chapter 1's curves could have eccentric shapes because their layer was set to Color mode, so contrast could not change. Now that we have moved into a color-free zone, where only contrast is important, we have to be more careful.

Enhancement of detail is governed by the catchy phrase *the steeper the curve, the more the contrast.* Locate the area you wish to improve and find where it falls on the curves grid. If you can make the curve steeper in that zone, you win. Unfortunately, steepening any part of a curve makes other parts flatter. Anything falling in those other zones loses contrast. Advanced retouching can be summarized as knowing how to write curves that increase contrast in important places while losing it in places that nobody cares about.

Careless curvewriting is costly. We're not very interested in the blue because it contributes so little to the contrast. But the green and the red do, especially the green. Turn back to Figures 4.2E and 4.2F. Which do you think will respond better to a curve?

Well, since the curve's purpose is to enhance contrast, it will have more of an impact in the one with poorer contrast, which is the green. I don't say, mind you, that the red is the better channel at present, or that the kind of contrast it has is good. But the flowers are light and the background is dark. Like it or not, that's contrast.

Figure 4.5 is an experiment. It shows an S-curve. It would resemble the eponymous letter a bit more if the point near the top right were raised, but that wouldn't be advisable because it would plug the shadows.

The new green, Figure 4.5A, is an improvement, which is what happens when everything falls in the steep part of the curve. Here, it's steepest in areas somewhat darker than a midtone, which describes pretty much the entirety of the original green.

As an example of what *not* to do, the same curve is applied to the red channel in Figure 4.5B. The flowers were originally light, so they fall into the pancake-flat portion of this curve, with herbicidal effects. What little detail they had is now gone. The green channel had no such problem because its flowers were much darker.

Notice, though, that the background greenery has gained definition. Losing the flowers is too high a price to pay for the improvement, but true contrast hounds lick their chops at what they see and try to think of a way to get at it.

While you ruminate on that possibility, think also about the curve shape. The idea is to get the third quarter steep, but this partial S-shape is not the only way to do it. I could have simply moved the lower left and upper right points inward, without

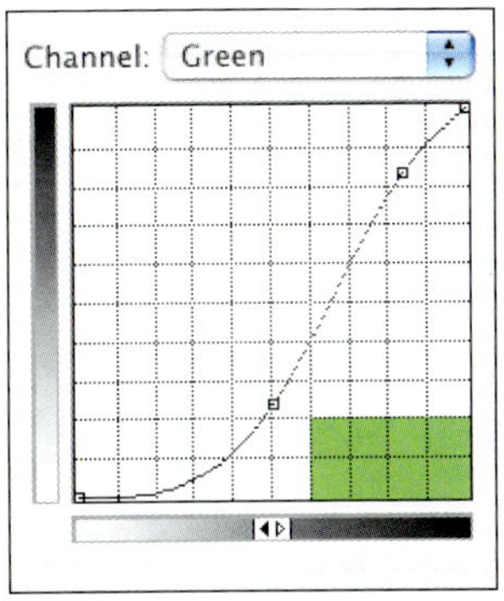

***Figure 4.5** This curve is applied to the green channel, left, where it adds detail, and to the red, right, where it blows out the flowers.*

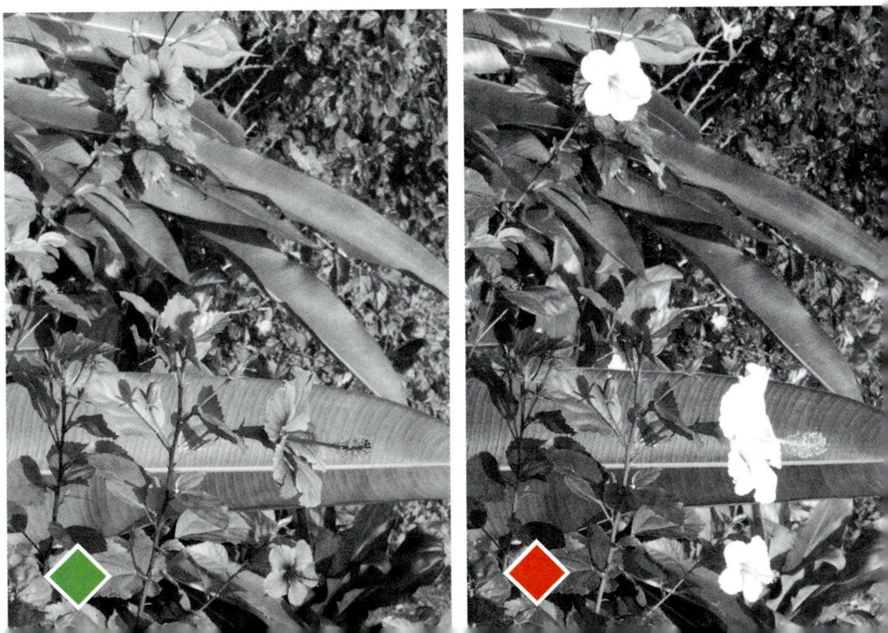

any points in between. That would have retained a straight line, rather than a curve.

Would it have done the job? Definitely. Would it have been slightly different than what's shown? Yes. *Better?* I'm not sure. Sometimes the structure of the picture makes the answer obvious, but not here.

Some beta readers understood what I just finished saying. Others saw it as inappropriate for the half of the chapter aimed at the less experienced, who presumably cannot be satisfied with a statement that another method might be better but that I have no interest in finding out.

I am sorry to seem uncooperative, but in my own work I do not have time to check every single promising possibility. I therefore cannot recommend the practice to others. The step being discussed in this chapter should take 20 to 30 seconds. There are usually several ways to execute it, more options than in the color moves of Chapter 3.

So there is no need to be apprehensive—just improve contrast in a logical way of your choosing, and then if time permits, do alternate versions of the entire image.

...The More the Contrast

With freedom comes frustration. Traditional workflows never had anything like the flexibility of this step, because in working on contrast, we always had to be careful lest the color go out the window. With PPW, we don't care if it does or if it makes a big splat when it lands. Once we accept that ghastly color is irrelevant, many pleasant possibilities present themselves.

What we've seen with this picture so far should convince us that there are more potential choices than we have time to test. And we haven't even explored some of the more advanced options, such as blending through a mask, or converting a copy of the image to some other colorspace and stealing a channel for use in the original.

Even if we set aside the three years needed to test every conceivable possibility, it might not do much good. Of all the steps in the workflow, this chapter's, contrast enhancement, leaves the most room for argument.

Consider, please, Figures 4.2B and 4.2C, versions where the entire picture is based on the contrast of the red and green channels respectively. You and I and the rest of the world would agree that the flowers are too light in one and too dark in the other. Suppose, though, that the final combination has to be some blend, with no mask or fancy blending mode, between the two. Should it be 50–50? If not, what percentage of each should we use? On this question responses would be all over the place.

Reasonable people might also quarrel over what to do with the background. My inclination is that the tropical greenery is important and that we should try to add contrast to it. Other people might feel that the flowers should be the center of attention and that a strongly detailed background would be a distraction.

Such aesthetic questions have no correct answers, and even if we thought they did and we knew them, we might change our minds once we started to work.

And that, gentle reader, is why we don't care whether the curve to the green should be a straight line or an S-curve. There are too many more important things to occupy us. Get the work done quickly, then do another one from scratch if you have time. You'll get a different result, which you can throw away, use instead of the first one, or blend with as you see fit.

Here are general guidelines for adjusting the contrast of any picture.

- Compare the red and blue channels. Usually some kind of blend suggests itself. Often this blend is in Darken mode, especially if it's the blue into the red.
- If you have blended the blue into the red,

look to enhance contrast further with a curve. If the other way around, don't bother, the blue has too little impact to make it worthwhile.

- The green channel is usually the flattest of the three and responds well to curving.
- I usually blend first and curve afterward, but there is no reason to avoid reversing the order. Also, it is permissible to have a second round of each, if desired.
- A bright color requires a very light channel somewhere. If a picture features several such colors it may be hard to do anything at all. In our example, the pink hibiscus blossoms are very light in the red channel, rendering it almost useless as a blend source or for curving. Fortunately, the green and blue have no such problem, but if other bright colors were hanging around, they might.

***Figure 4.6** The progression of the luminosity boost. Top left, the original. Top center, the blue is blended into the red at 70% opacity. Top right, a curve is applied to the resulting red. Bottom left, a curve is added to the green. Bottom center, the original green channel is blended into the current red, Darken mode, 30% opacity. Bottom right, the top layer is changed from Normal to Luminosity mode, restoring the original color.*

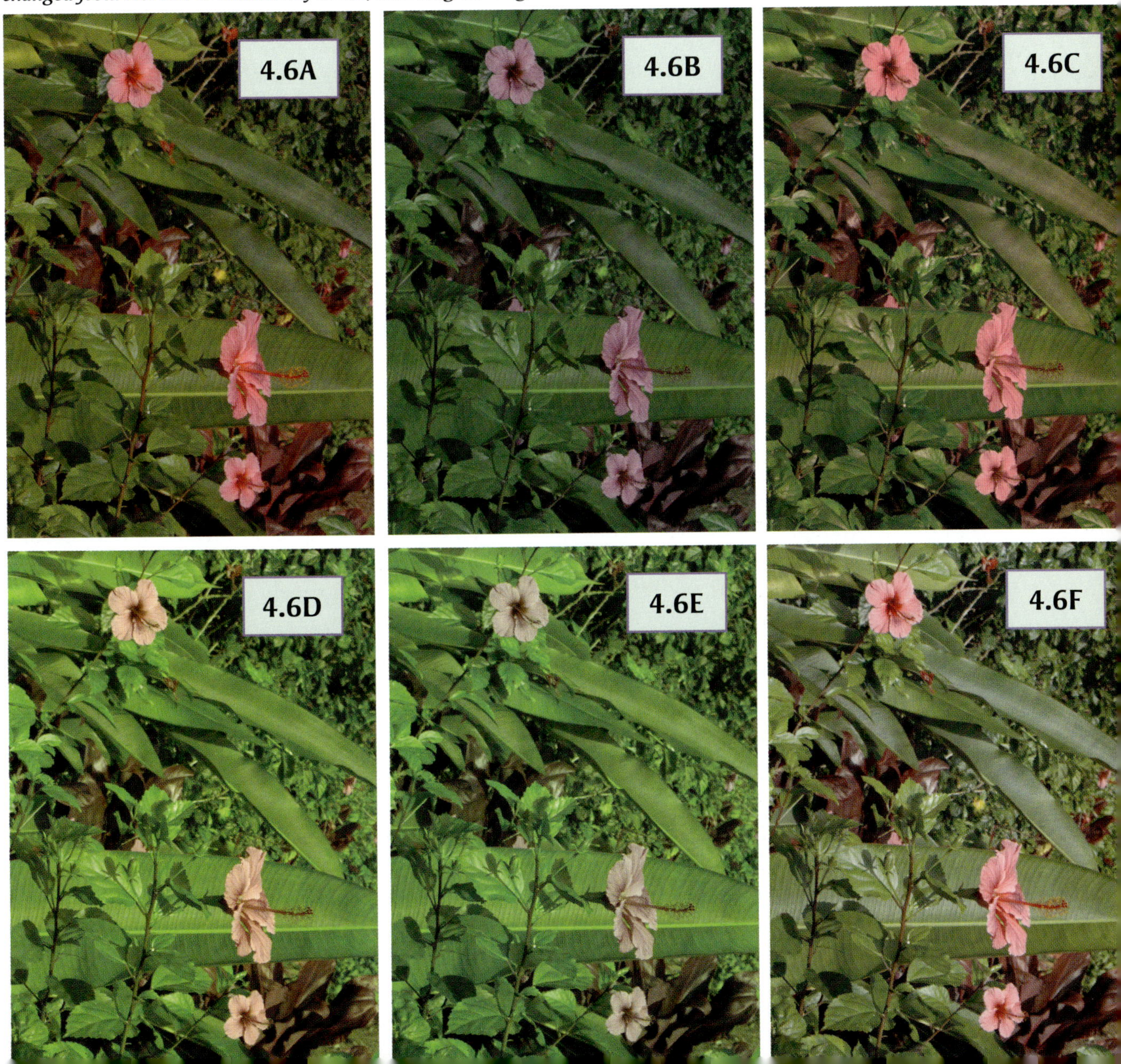

- You don't have to achieve perfection or even to finalize a shadow and highlight. We have one later step to make further adjustments if needed.
- The first few times you do this will likely go slowly, but speed picks up rapidly with practice. Here's a log of what I was thinking and what I did with this file in around 45 seconds. Questions you might be asking are interspersed in italics.

Step by Step for the Flowers

Starting from scratch with Figure 4.6A:

- Open the file and examine for color issues per instructions in Chapter 1. As pointed out earlier, none are to be found here.
- Make a duplicate layer, examine the three channels, and decide on a strategy.
- The green channel will respond well to a curve. I would like to apply a curve to the red, too, but at the moment I can't without blowing out the flowers, as we saw in Figure 4.5B. My solution is to darken them slightly by blending some of the blue into the red. Then, a curve that returns the flowers to near-white will increase contrast throughout the channel.
- The Apply Image command requires that the target channel(s) be the only one(s) open. Here, I must activate the red.
- Image: Apply Image. Layer=irrelevant; Channel (source)=Blue, Blending=Normal, Opacity=70%. Result=Figure 4.6B.

What's up with 70%?

It is what theoreticians refer to as SWAG—a Scientific Wild-Ass Guess. If it turns out later to be too low, I'll repeat the blend. If too high, I have a copy of the original red channel on the bottom layer and can blend it into this new one if needed. This, incidentally, is why I use Apply Image for blends and not Image: Adjustments>Channel Mixer, which can only make blends from the current layer.

Why not 100%?

It looks to me like there could be a loss of shadow detail in the blue channel, and if so I don't want to put that defect into the red.

Whaddaya mean "it looks to me like"? Why don't you check to make sure, like a normal author would?

I am on a time budget that doesn't permit investigations that are unlikely to serve much purpose. I can always blend again later if I feel like it.

- With this newly modified red channel still active, Image: Adjustments>Curves. Sweep the highlight point (the lower left one in my curves orientation) toward the center of the grid, until the very lightest part of the flowers blows out. This creates Figure 4.6C. Notice the extra detail in the leaves and flowers.

Yeah, and the color has gone to the dogs. I thought you were supposed to be doing this on a layer set to Luminosity mode!

All in good time. I can't use that mode just yet because the "real" channels would no longer be visible. I need to see them. Go back to Figure 4.4A, where I showed what happens when the red channel is deleted entirely. When the top layer is in Normal mode, the red channel is in fact blank, and the overall appearance of the file is bright red. Luminosity mode restores the original color while retaining the lighter look caused by the removal of an entire channel.

To accomplish this, detail has to be transplanted into the blank channel. So if you look at the red in Normal mode, it's blank, but in Luminosity mode there's something there—something theoretical only, a reconstructed channel that won't truly exist until the layers are flattened.

In the preceding step I was looking at the unreconstructed red only, and applying a curve until the very lightest part of the flower disappeared. I had to do this in Normal mode because otherwise that point would *never* disappear.

- Activate the green channel and apply the Figure 4.5 curve, producing Figure 4.6D.

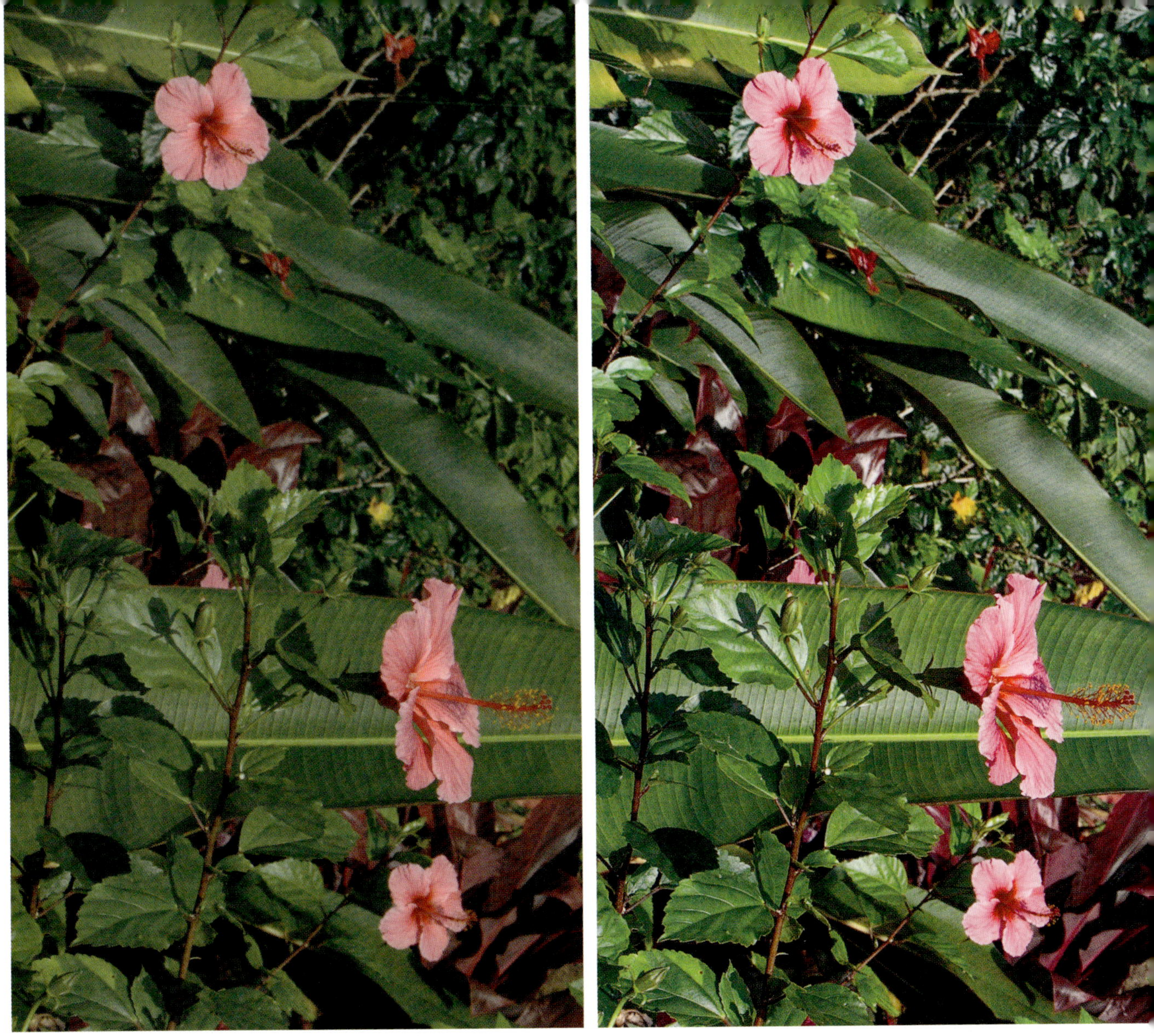

***Postcard 4.7** The biggest improvement in the final version is in the contrast areas addressed by this chapter.*

- The plan is now complete. Change layer mode to Luminosity and evaluate.

Further improvements are likely to be matters of aesthetics that not everyone would agree upon. For example, I felt that the flowers had gotten too light. Can you predict what I'm about to blend to darken the flowers and nothing else?

- Activate the red channel on the top layer. To it, Image: Apply Image. Layer=Background, Channel=Green, Blending=Darken, Opacity=30%. Result=Figure 4.6E, which has been kept in Normal mode for easy comparison with the other versions.

What is Darken mode?

It works exactly like Normal mode except that it does not permit any pixel in any channel to get lighter. A companion mode, Darker Color, does not permit any pixel to get lighter overall when all three channels are combined, but does allow lightening in one or two channels provided that the composite of all three channels remains darker.

Why the green as source?

Compare the original red and green. (Figures 4.2E and 4.2F.) The flowers are darker in the green but the background leaves are lighter. Since Darken mode permits nothing to get lighter, the leaves are excluded from the blend. The flowers get darker and almost nothing else changes. True, the red is no longer the same as in Figure 4.2E, but it didn't change enough to invalidate the blend.

Why the Background layer?

In principle the green from either layer would work. However, the top layer's green is much lighter than the bottom, owing to the drastic curve shown in Figure 4.5. To have the same impact, I'd need a higher opacity for the blend. I don't want to do that because the red channel, though light, is full of detail that I have no desire to erase. The 30% figure I used in the actual blend is, of course, a SWAG.

If this is such a hot blend, why not do it as the first step?

Starting by blending the blue into the red darkened the leaves as well as the flowers. If instead I had started by blending the green into the red, I would have lost the darkening effect in the leaves. What I *could* have done is blended into the green channel first and then the red, and if I have the time to do an alternate version maybe I'll try it that way. But for present purposes, I'm done. It's time to change layer mode to Luminosity, which produces Figure 4.6F and ends this chapter's contribution.

Postcard 4.7 adds all the color enhancements that we'll be studying in subsequent chapters. The maneuvers seen in this chapter, however, are the key to its success. Next most important is the Modern Man from Mars action described in Chapter 6. It added color variation, including shifting the flowers' hue. I could have prevented that easily if I had wanted to, in case you are wondering.

But whether you care for the final color or not, you must admit that the finished version has much more depth than the original, thanks to all this blending and curving.

What's Really Neutral?

Next up is the big cat of Figure 4.8. The improvement in detail found in Postcard 4.9 comes from the same techniques we just saw in the flower image. We again start from the original, shot as a JPEG by a specialist in wildlife photography.

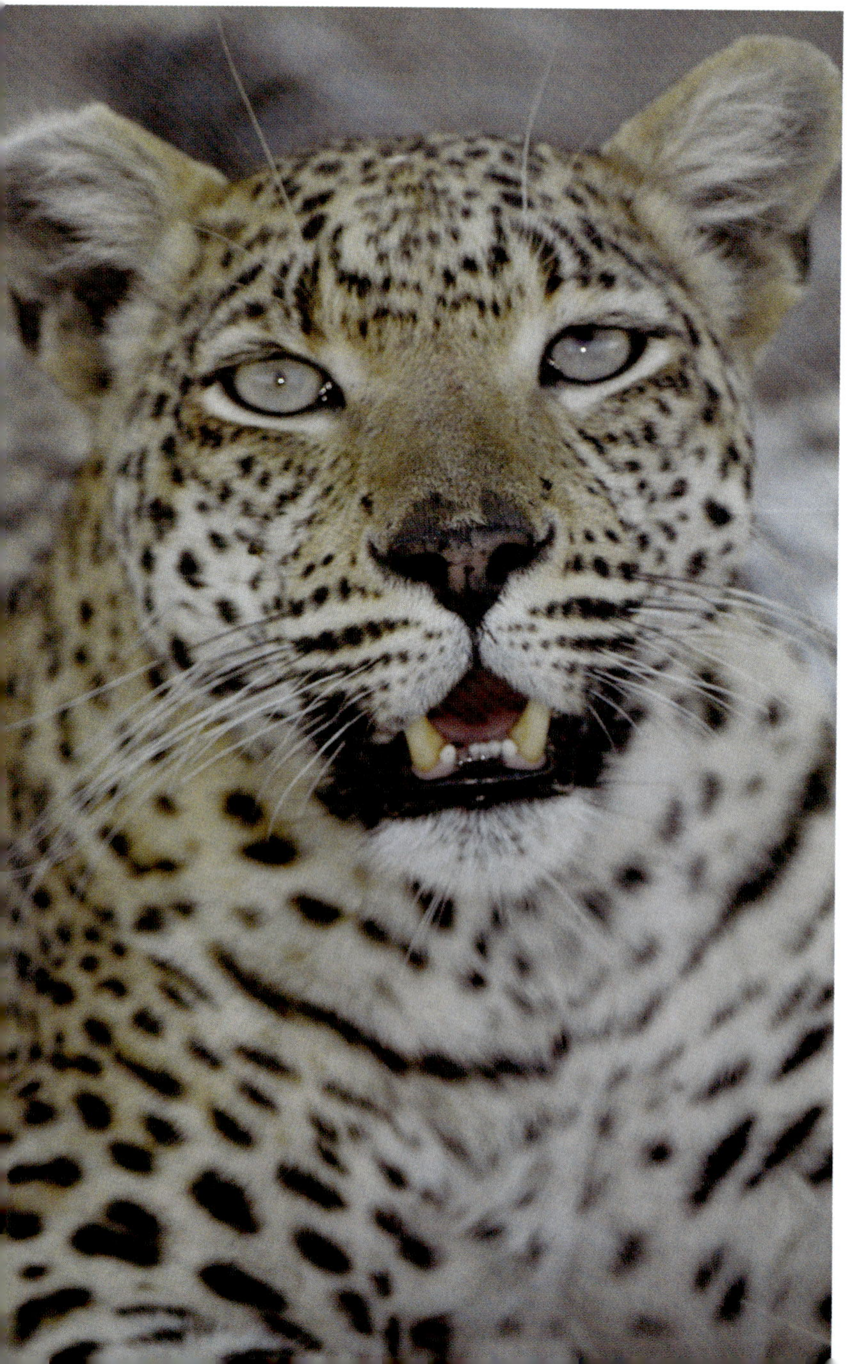

Figure 4.8 *The original color gives an unduly cool impression.*

- Open the file and examine for color issues per instructions in Chapter 1. What values would you look at? And where would you place the highlight?

The dark gums are reliably neutral, in my opinion. We should measure and hope to find 0^A0^B.

We can ignore the interior of the nostrils. It will measure black, because it can't be anything else. RGB doesn't support color in objects that dark. Meanwhile, the spots in the fur might be a dark brown and not a black.

The fur on the chin looks white, but it might not be. The rest of the animal's fur is best described as yellow, which means the B value is positive. The yellow tends toward brown. As brown is a form of red, the A channel should be positive, too, though not as much as the B. Surely it cannot be negative, which would add a greenish flavor. The chin fur, if not 0^A0^B, should follow the same pattern.

Negative numbers denote greens and blues, respectively. Maybe the eyes meet that description, but we should be able to mouse over any other part of the picture without encountering a minus sign.

A threshold adjustment layer showed that the literally lightest area is unimportant—in the haunches, to the right of the face. Next lightest is the whitish fur just beneath the nostrils. I dropped sampler points there, in the chin, and in the black skin.

In these three points, the initial values read $(1)^A(4)^B$, $(1)^A(7)^B$, and 0^A0^B. The black skin was correct as is, but both of the lighter areas were blue, especially the chin. They both also had a tinge of green. The blueness continued as I measured the slightly darker fur of the chest.

These findings suggest that the light fur should actually be white, not a shade of yellow. Otherwise one would have to believe that the bluish cast is much worse than it seems at first glance.

- Apply curves to correct any problems, ignoring the effect on contrast. Mine forced all three sample points to R=G=B.

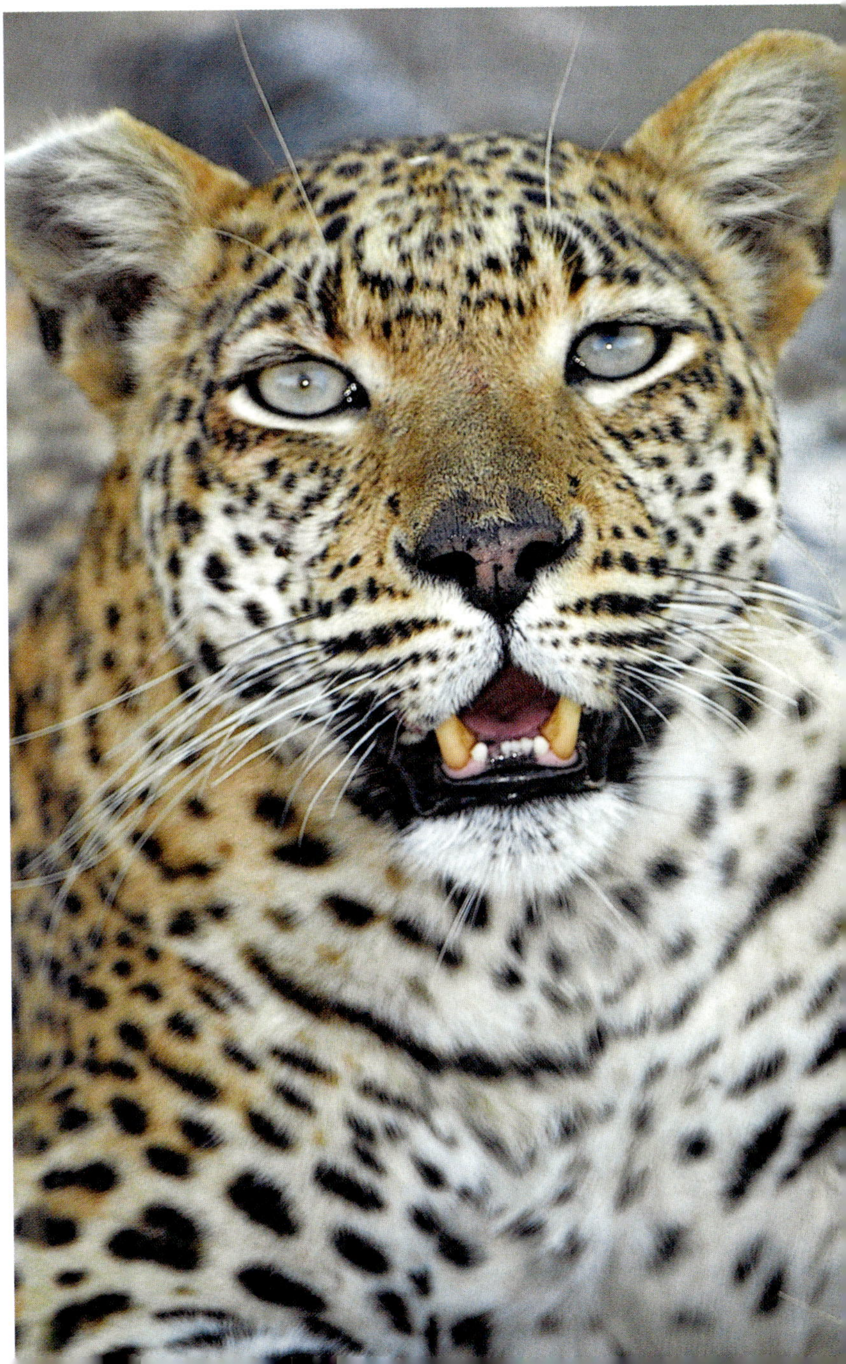

***Postcard 4.9** The increased depth in the final version derives from the steps described in this chapter.*

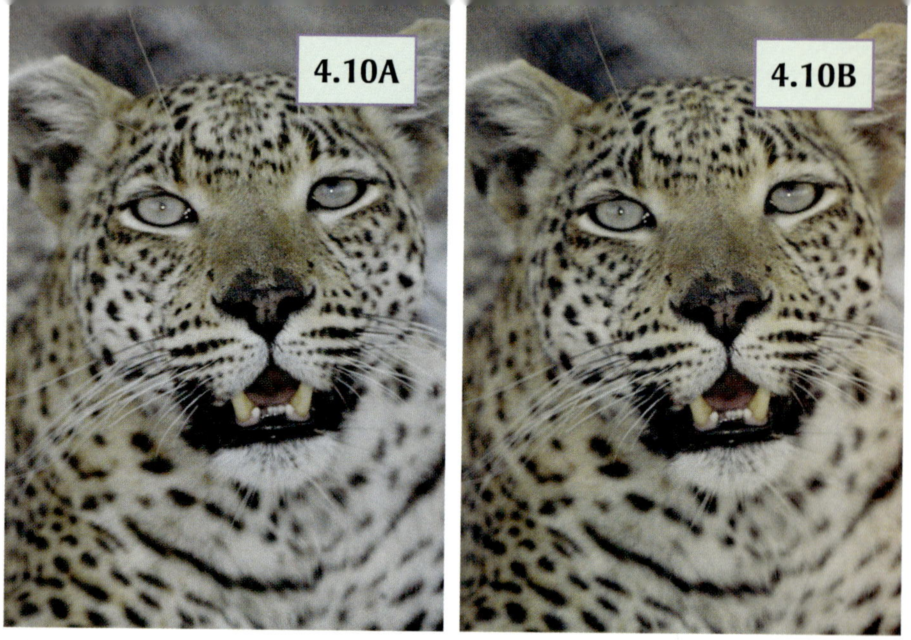

Figure 4.10 Left, the original. Right, after applying curves on a layer set to Color mode.

- Change mode of the curves layer to Color. This transformed the original, Figure 4.10A, into 4.10B and brought us back into the techniques of this chapter.
- Make a duplicate layer, examine the three channels of Figure 4.11, and choose a strategy.
- I will replace the red with the blue completely, none of this namby-pamby 70% stuff. Then, a straight-line curve, as earlier with the hybrid red channel in the hibiscus exercise, forcing the lightest part of the fur to near white.

Since you're trying to set the fur as a light point, wouldn't it make more sense to apply the curve first to the blue, and then replace the red with the result?

It would take no longer to do that, so any argument about the unimportance of the blue in the overall scheme of things is irrelevant. Nevertheless, I avoid it for a practical reason. Lightening the white fur may blow out the vague area to the right of the face. I don't care if this unimportant area shows real detail, but am hesitant about leaving something that large totally blank. (Much has been cropped out on the right; if the image is re-used at a different cropping the problem would seem bigger.) Leaving the blue channel as we found it guarantees *something,* however indistinct, will remain there, giving us what commercial printers refer to as a *scum dot,* rather than a lot of blank paper.

- I will then curve the green, just as in the hibiscus. The shape of this new curve will be entirely different, of course.

Figure 4.11 The red, green, and blue channels of Figure 4.10B.

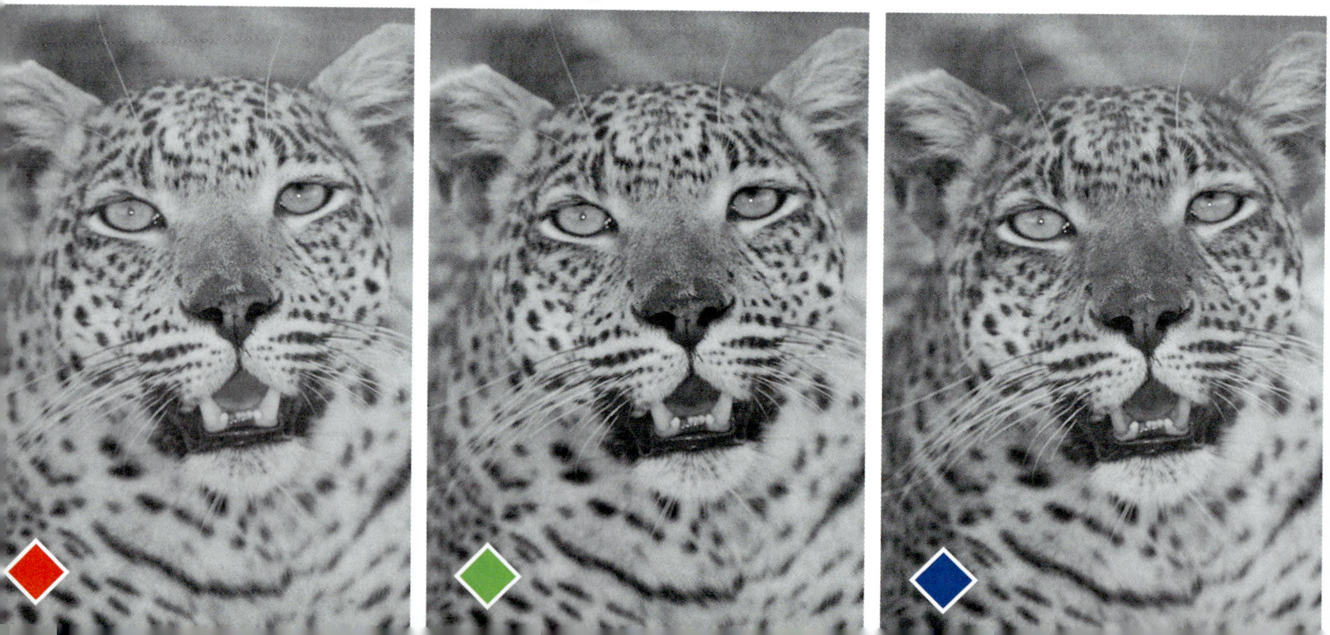

Why don't you just blend the blue into the green, as you did with the red? It seems to be the best of the three channels.

Beware of yellow objects when blending with a blue channel. Yellow is a light color, but it's dark in the blue. If that darkness gets transferred into the other two channels you can wind up with black daffodils or similar outrages.

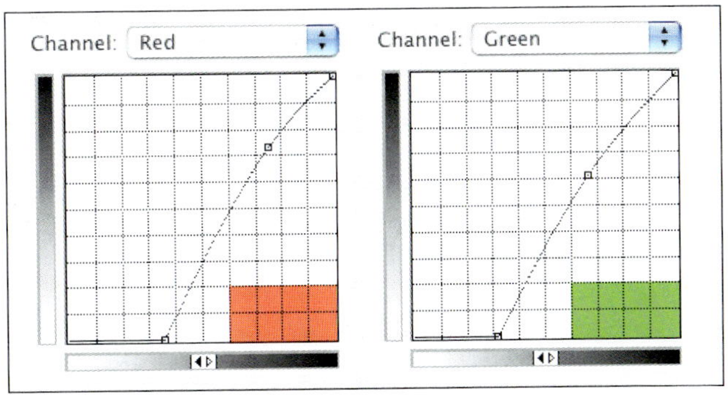

***Figure 4.12** After replacing the red channel with a copy of the blue, these curves are applied to the red and green. Top row below: the resulting channels. Bottom left, the resulting color. Bottom right, the layer is set to Luminosity mode.*

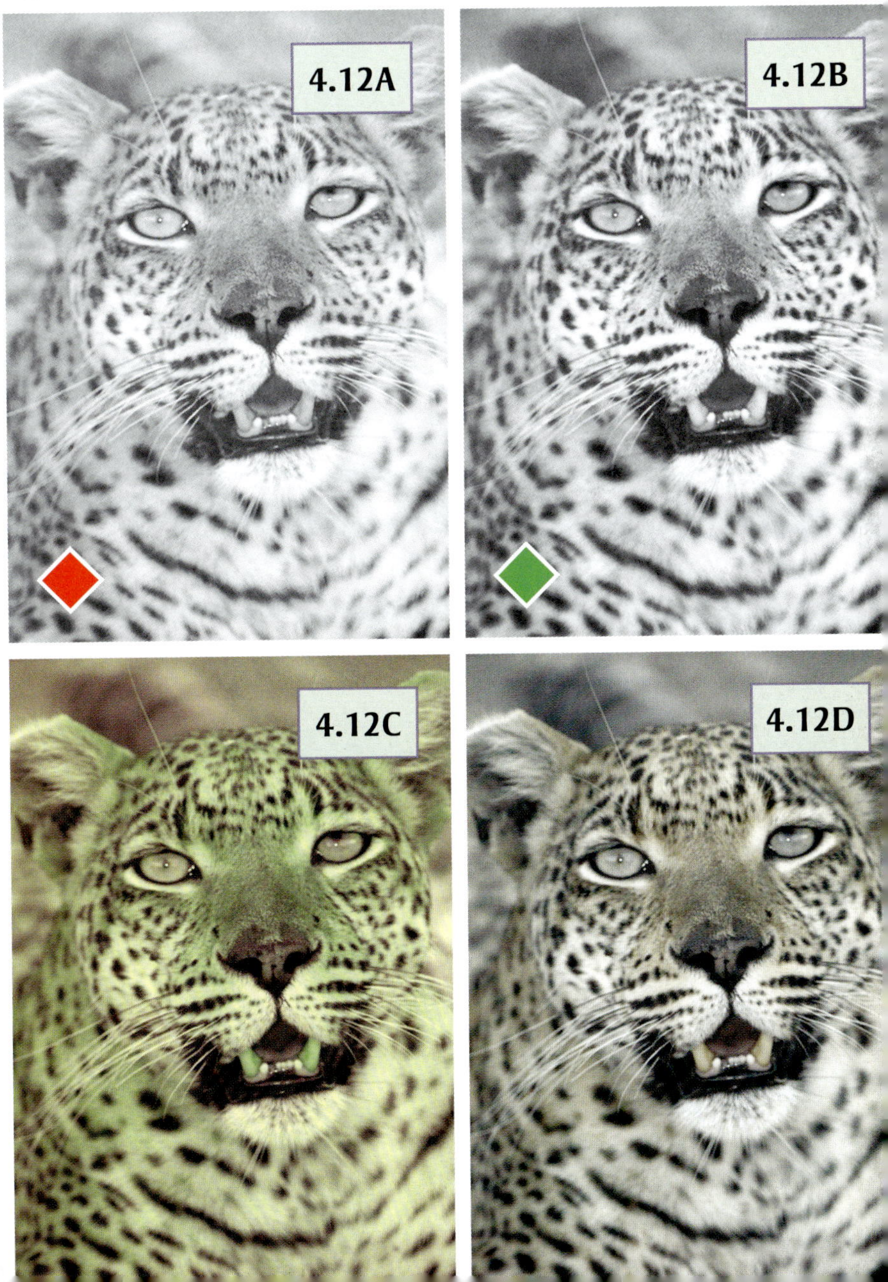

What Big Teeth You Have

The fur here is yellowish, but making it darker accords with our plan. What about the teeth, though? This cat has not been using Pepsodent. They are fairly dark in the blue, and I've just put that darkness into the red by blending. In Postcard 4.9, do you not agree that the teeth are darker than expected? If we also blend the blue into the more powerful green, the teeth will get *much* darker, unacceptably so.

Blending into the green should usually be avoided. That the green is more important than the other two channels put together is not lost on camera manufacturers. They devote more sensors and more processing to the green. As a result, the red and blue are noisier. A careless blend of one of them into the green can make the whole picture too grainy. I'm not saying don't ever do it; often enough it's the best choice, but check the source channel for noise before proceeding.

- Here we go, then. First, we will replace the inadequate red channel with a copy of the blue. Activate the red. Image: Apply Image. Layer=irrelevant; Channel=Blue, Blending=Normal, Opacity=100%.
- Now, to add contrast to the

two most important channels, apply the curves shown in Figure 4.12 to the new red and to the green. The new channels are Figures 4.12A and 4.12B. In partnership with the blue, which has never changed, they produce Figure 4.12C.

Why aren't you using a curves adjustment layer for this?

Chapter Goals and Recap

Color having been made acceptable, if not exciting, in Chapter 3, we switch to contrast.

The files stay in RGB. Work goes on a duplicate layer that eventually is set to Luminosity mode. This preserves color while allowing gains in detail.

We first consider replacing one or more channels with others, or some more subtle blend. Then, we look to improve the contrast of green and/or red channels, using curves targeted to the most important areas.

How Difficult Is It? With practice, the steps shown in the first half of this chapter come more easily than those of Chapter 3 did. On the other hand, enhancing contrast becomes addictive. Ways of going even further in adding contrast, such as using an artificial black channel, are discussed in the second half.

How Often Is It Needed? In my experience, most images benefit from some kind of channel blend. Around 90 percent gain from a contrast-enhancing curve. So, just about every image needs *something* found in this chapter.

The PPW Takes Shape

COLOR

- Kill incorrect color with RGB curves (Chapter 3).
- Identify highlight (Chapters 3–4).

CONTRAST

- Channel blends on luminosity layer (this chapter).
- Contrast-enhancing curves (this chapter).

COLOR AGAIN

SHARPEN

FINALIZE

- Consider blend with another version (Chapter 2).
- Convert to final output space, if needed.

It's awkward for a couple of reasons. First, the layer beneath the adjustment still must be in Normal mode for the curves to function correctly, but our plan calls for that layer to be set to Luminosity mode later. Second, one can't blend into an adjustment layer. I'm happy with the leopard as is, but recall that in the hibiscus image, I thought another blend was needed after the curves.

- Change the top layer to Luminosity mode. Figure 4.12D is the end result of this chapter's techniques. From there to the final version, Postcard 4.9, requires little more than the color boost described in the next chapter.
- If you have decided that you need a curves adjustment layer *in addition to* what's on your luminosity layer, stick with the previously recommended approach. Finalize your curves while the adjustment layer is in Normal mode, then switch it to Luminosity.

The last two exercises suggest why the PPW needs that color boost. An agreeable side effect of traditional workflows is that when they add range by finalizing highlight and shadow, color becomes more intense. That doesn't happen at this stage of the PPW because our use of Luminosity mode prevents it. Consequently, the two images as they stand after this chapter's work—Figures 4.6F and 4.12D—are both rather tepid. Nothing is particularly wrong; their color is just not as intense as we would hope.

To fix that, we will bring in the big color-adjustment moves of Chapter 5 and Chapter 6. But to use those powerful methods, we need the step described in Chapter 3. Imagine what would have happened if the animal had been left blue, as in Figure 4.8, and then the big color boost of Figure 4.9 had stretched out its claws!

The workflow steps thus far are interlocking. It seems like there are more of them than in a traditional workflow, but in fact they go faster because we don't have to be as careful with each one. Without having to worry about color, this chapter's moves go rapidly. Without worrying about contrast, the same goes for the techniques of the two chapters that sandwich it.

Efficiency is one thing; effectiveness another. This leopard image is part of the basic curriculum of my three-day, small-group course, Applied Color Theory. Students work independently on each exercise using whatever methods they like and the results are compared. Time is no factor; they usually take around 20 minutes per image, because they know their work will be evaluated by classmates' critical eyes and caustic tongues.

We saw that kind of comparison in Chapter 2, but every other correction in the book so far was executed without the benefit of seeing somebody else's work. Consequently, there's no guarantee that Postcards 4.1 and 4.7 are the best possible results.

This one is different. I've seen more than a hundred people who know what they're doing try to make something good out of this relatively flat original. Half a dozen of these are competitive with Postcard 4.9. Every one used some variant of blending with the blue channel as source. Traditional workflows produced cat food.

The Grandest Canyon in All the World

Back to the iconic postcard scene, the Grand Canyon shown at the outset in Postcard 4.1. An extraordinary amount of detail has emerged from the background. It's hazy and blurry in the original, crisp and well-defined in the final. A glance at Figure 4.13 should tell you how it got that way.

This exercise isn't just about the added detail. It's a showpiece for the three basic steps of the workflow. The objective is always to make the viewer feel a part of the scene. We want to *be* at Point Imperial. We are humans, not cameras. In adjusting the file, we must compensate for how humans see things.

- Human vision is self-calibrating. We

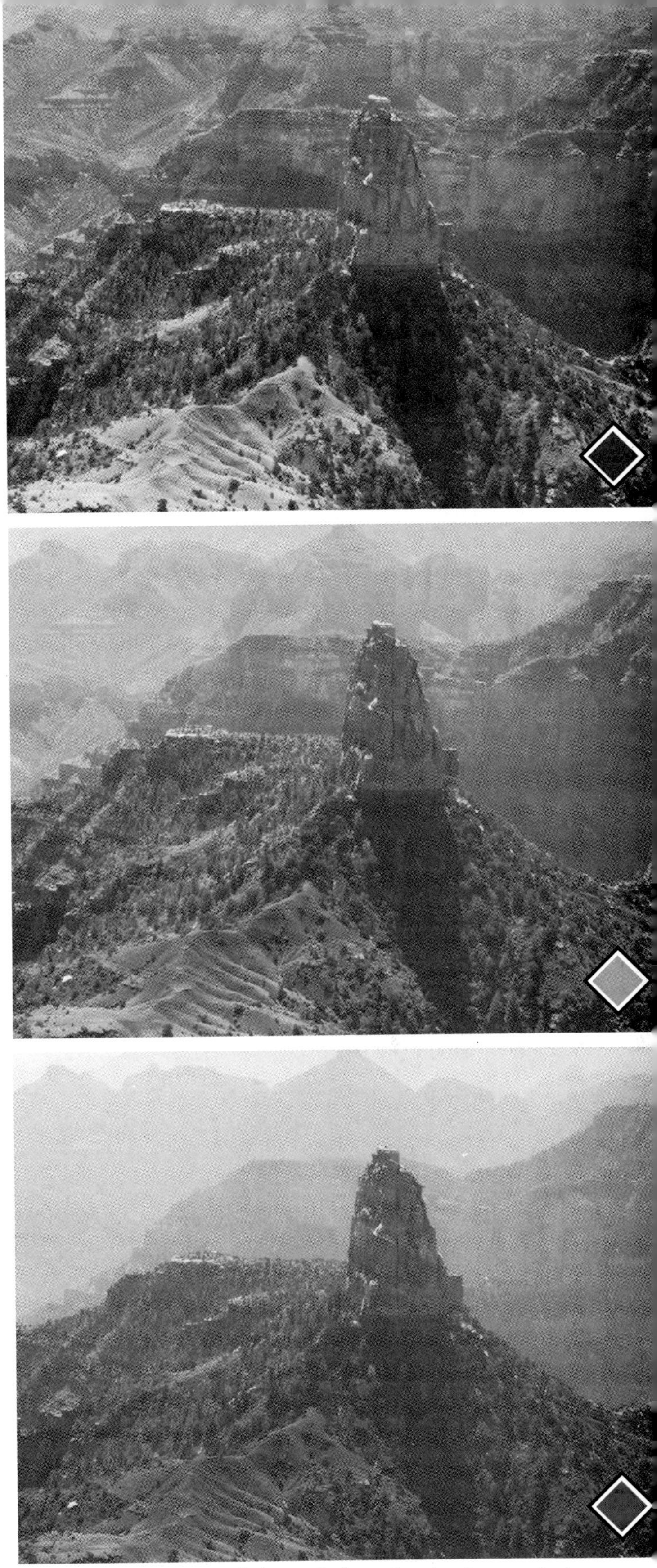

***Figure 4.13** The original channels from the chapter-opening photo of the Grand Canyon, Postcard 4.1.*

ignore most color imbalances; cameras convert them into ugly casts. We can adjust to multiple casts in the same scene; cameras can't. Catering to this phenomenon, *chromatic adaptation*, is the purpose of Chapter 3. The original of Postcard 4.1 has a bluish haze over the background. If there ourselves, we'd see some blueness, but not nearly as much as the camera did.

- We focus at multiple depths better than cameras can. To be sure, we concentrate on the foreground at the expense of the background, but the camera loses more of the background than we would. The job of this chapter is to add definition in the areas in which we wish to perceive it.
- The phenomenon of *simultaneous contrast* causes us to perceive more variation in adjacent colors than instruments do. So we see more diversity in the greens and reds of this image than a camera does. Recovering that variation is the job of Chapter 6, with a big assist from Chapter 5. You can see the added variation in the final version.

We start, as always, by looking for color defects. The problem is plain, but the solution is not. The haze is distinctly blue in the background. If ignored, the standard PPW color boost will make it *brilliant* blue.

On the other hand, if viewing the scene in person we would still perceive a certain blueness in the background, even granted our evolutionary propensity to adapt to and neutralize what we see. So it's probably wrong to force the haze to be completely gray.

It sounds like another SWAG is in the offing. That's true to some extent, but not as completely as you might think.

Like many with a prepress background, I used to be absolutist about color casts. Any areas that I knew a human would perceive as neutral were to be made so, period. Otherwise, the color imbalance would affect the rest of the image, and not just the grays. This, I thought, made for an unnatural look.

Perhaps so, but it can be an *attractive* unnatural look, at least to some people—it seems to be a matter of taste how strong a cast is tolerable. I'm still more conservative than most, but I have realized that there is a logical inconsistency in advocating unnaturally bright colors and deprecating unnatural casts, with one glaring exception.

An orange cast can create the illusion of sunlight. Redder casts add warmth. The Grand Canyon is noted for its purplish rocks, so I would not rule out a slight purple cast. Deliberate blue casts are much less common but occasionally useful. I sometimes accept these types of cast even though I know they aren't "natural". Votes in seminars indicate that the general public is more apt to accept them than I am.

Green casts, on the other hand, are disgusting. People universally feel that they make a picture look sickly and unattractive. We often force certain objects to be greener, as we did in Chapter 1, but never an entire picture.

This haze we're working with measures blue, but a *greenish* blue. As always, although the file is in RGB, the Info palette is set to read LAB equivalents. The literally lightest point, in the upper left, measures $(7)^A(26)^B$. Negatives are green in the A and blue in the B, so the light point is a greenish blue and the dark point more of a pure cyan (blue-green combination). Meanwhile, the trees are in the range of acceptable greens defined in Chapter 3. We don't know what shade of red the soil should be and so can't form any conclusions, especially because parts are in strong sunlight, which may drive it toward orange.

It's unclear how far we should push the haze toward gray. If we don't quite get there, the B value must be negative. How negative it should be can be described as fine artistic judgment or a SWAG at your discretion.

The negative A, however, should not be suffered to survive. My curves darkened the green channel and lightened the red to

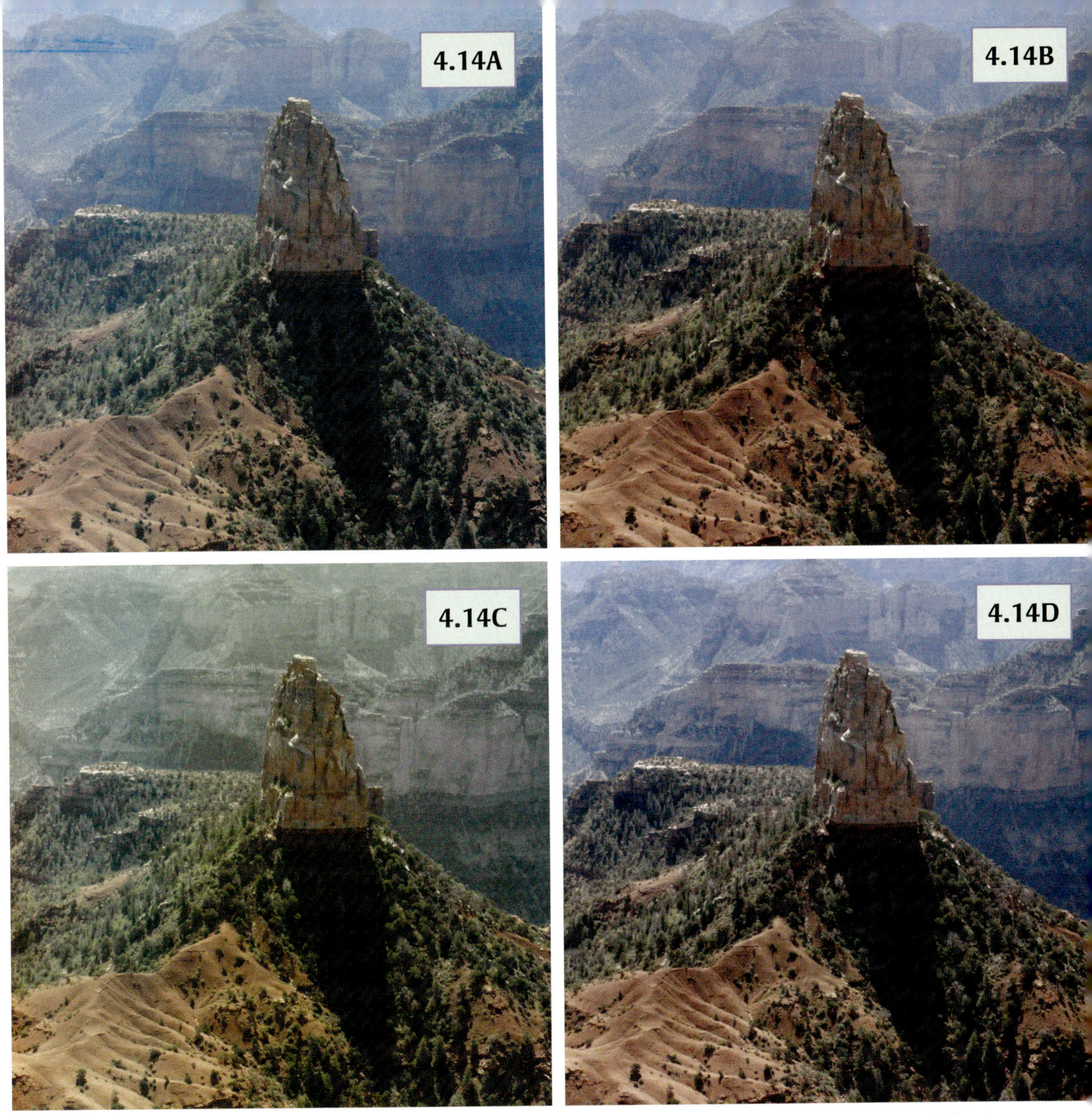

***Figure 4.14** Top left, the original; top right, after application of curves in Color mode, bottom left, after channel blending and curves to increase contrast on a duplicate layer; bottom right, the layer mode is changed to Luminosity.*

counter the cyan flavor. After the curves layer was set to Color mode, the original, repeated as Figure 4.14A, turned into Figure 4.14B. The point that was $(7)^A(26)^B$ had now become $0^A(22)^B$, indicating a move away from green and toward magenta, and away from blue and toward yellow. Note how the background seems purpler, less cyan.

The acceptable color puts us back into this chapter, with its focus on contrast. One can envision several options. All, however, give a more prominent role to the red channel, with its rich background detail.

I took a straightforward approach. I replaced the atrocious blue shown in Figure 4.13 with a copy of the red. And I used Apply Image, Normal mode, at 35% opacity to put some of the red into the green.

Moving on to curving, the lightest significant point, in the upper left, isn't all that light, except in the original blue channel, which no longer exists. Dragging the lower left curve point to the right lightens it, steepens the rest of the curve and thus adds contrast everywhere. Since we don't have to worry about color in this chapter, should we lighten all three channels, or just one or two? And should the lightening curve(s) be straight line(s), or some other shape(s)?

Well, how much lighter should the reddish soil in the foreground be than the greenery surrounding the spire? In the red channel, these two are quite distinct. In the green, they are about the same darkness.

To drive the two apart, you should work on the red, using an S-curve to lighten the soil while darkening the trees. If you just want to add detail to both without making the soil much lighter, work on the green. That's what I did. I first tried a straight-line curve, moving the lower left point inward until the lightest area reached 255^G, which is as far as one can go. This blew out the most extreme highlights in the green channel, but I did not care, as they were still present in the red and blue.

Before clicking OK, it seemed to me that things were slightly too light. This calls for a curve similar to the one applied to the green in Figure 4.12, bulging upward (toward darkness, given my curve orientation) in the center while lightening the light point. The questions are how far up the curve to insert the darkening point, and then how far to raise (darken) it. The second is strictly personal preference. The first depends on what we are trying to emphasize.

The curve is steeper to the left of the inserted point (lighter objects), and flatter to the right (darker ones). The rules of curving say that anything lighter than the point gains detail; anything darker loses. Very light areas (the background, and the red soil in the foreground) are helped. Very dark ones (some trees, plus the shadow that the spire is casting) lose detail. Anything in the middle, such as the spire itself, is hard to predict.

Since the curve applied to the green tends to plug darker areas, I suggest using a straight line in the red, lightening everything, and gaining contrast as well.

In real life these steps take, with practice, 45 seconds, the length of the written explanation notwithstanding. To summarize, starting with the color-adjusted Figure 4.14B,

Review and Exercises

- ✓What is the relative importance of each of the three RGB channels in terms of luminosity?
- ✓Why are the techniques shown here less impressive when applied to an image featuring several different colors?
- ✓Why do we keep the "luminosity" layer in Normal mode throughout blending and curving, and only change to Luminosity mode afterward?
- ✓Why should we be cautious about blending the red or blue into the green?
- ✓Figure 4.14D has a layer set to Luminosity mode with Figure 4.14B beneath it. Theoretically, this retains the color. But the color looks substantially richer in Figure 4.14B. Why is this?
- ✓Why do you suppose we have not yet seen a picture involving a person's face?

- Establish a duplicate layer.
- Replace the blue with the red.
- Blend 35% of the red into the green.
- Curve the new green more or less as shown in Figure 4.12.
- Apply a straight-line curve to lighten the red channel.
- Change layer mode to Luminosity.

Before changing mode at the end, the file is Figure 4.14C; afterward, it's Figure 4.14D, which is the final point for present purposes.

The final point for *all* purposes is Postcard 4.1, which illustrates how the workflow hangs together. The blue cast was minimized by the methods of Chapter 3, the greater depth was introduced by the methods of this chapter, a correction for the sun-and-shadow nature of this picture is found in Chapter 12, near-neutrals were suppressed by a trick found in Chapter 13, and the increase in both color and variation is from the next two chapters.

The Last Word Is Not the Last Word

This Grand Canyon image solidifies a suspicion that I hope you have been developing throughout the chapter. There's kind of a basic recipe for doing this, but it has many, many variants. The way I just showed is a sensible way to get better contrast in less than a minute. If the picture justifies more time than that, you can start to think of alternate ways, a fine sport if you don't care for crossword puzzles.

For example, if there's time to try another method, how's this?

- Discarding the duplicate layer and starting afresh with a new one, lighten the blue channel by moving the lower left curve point inward until the background nearly vanishes. This adds contrast to everything else.
- Apply this new blue channel to the red, in Darken mode, at I don't know what percentage. Nothing happens to the background. The main change is in the foreground soil, which gets darker.
- This last blend nullifies my previous objection to applying further curves to the red channel, when I thought doing so might make that soil too light. So, I now apply the lightening curve to the red rather than the green, blend the result into the green at some percentage, change layer mode to Luminosity, and take stock.

Would that work better? Haven't tried it, don't know. It's time for you to experiment on your own pictures.

Every subsequent move depends on the moves in this chapter. As we broaden our exercises to include color changes, we'll still discuss how to handle this step, though not in as much depth.

If you want more on this topic, with more explanations and new tricks, read on. If you're dying to get better color right away, Chapter 5 will set you up, and it's easier than this one, too.

A Closer Look

It is an oversimplification, but not by much, to say that the first half explained how best to convert color to grayscale, then pop it on top of the color and change mode to Luminosity.

If it were really the objective to get the best possible grayscale, the approach to each image would have been very close to what was shown. The differences:

- **Gross luminosity variations not as important**. Recall that in the last example, the Grand Canyon image, I decided against adding contrast to the red channel because I was afraid that the reddish foreground soil would become too light. If the objective were grayscale I'd have had to do it anyway, as otherwise the soil might become indistinguishable from the darker greenery behind it. But if one is green and the other red, the problem doesn't exist.
- **Lackadaisical approach to highlight and shadow**. In all forms of color correction, choice of and exact assignment of values to the lightest and darkest significant points is essential. The PPW is no exception, but we don't need to worry just yet. To be sure, many of the curves shown in this chapter come close to finalizing the two endpoints, but it's not a priority. In the canyon image, I knew that, when layer mode went to Luminosity, the curve I had applied to the green would put me in the neighborhood of a proper highlight in all channels. When I create high-quality grayscales, I make sure the highlight is more than just "in the neighborhood."

Detail from one channel can be transferred to another in many ways. For example, I have not mentioned Channel Mixer as an option, because Apply Image can do almost everything Channel Mixer can, whereas the reverse is not true. But if you're comfortable with it, you could start the Grand Canyon correction by swapping the red and green channels on a Channel Mixer layer, emphasizing the better background of the red by putting it in a channel that carries more weight in the luminosity calculation.

In the rest of the chapter, we'll look at less obvious sources for blends, review past images, discuss philosophy, visualize channels before actually seeing them, avoid snares caused by bright colors, and generally demonstrate why channel blending is a fiendish form of puzzle, if not quite as addictive as Sudoku.

The Case for Channel Blending

Channel blending to improve contrast is appropriate primarily in three cases.

- **One channel is clearly better than another.** In the Grand Canyon channels shown in Figure 4.13, both the red and green are incontestably superior to the blue. Granted that the blue doesn't contribute all that much, there's no sense in keeping it when something else is clearly better in all respects. Nice, isn't it, that we don't have to worry about color?

Occasionally one channel is clearly better than *both* others. In faces, for instance, the green channel is often better in every respect than the other two. When this occurs, we think about applying the good channel to the RGB composite, which copies it to both others simultaneously. (Warning: doing this increases apparent detail, which the subject may not appreciate, as it brings out facial imperfections.)

- **As a defense against later damage from a curve.** In red or orange objects, the red channel is often so light that a contrast-enhancing curve blows it out. A common countermeasure is to apply some of the blue channel, which is almost always the darkest, at a low opacity in Darken mode. Doing so prevents loss of detail when the red is adjusted.
- **To simulate a drastic change in lighting.** This effect is easier to demonstrate than describe. It occurred, sort of, in the Grand Canyon image, where the background became far more pronounced in the corrected version than in the

***Postcard 4.15** (opposite) The final version reverses the relative darknesses of the water and greenery.*

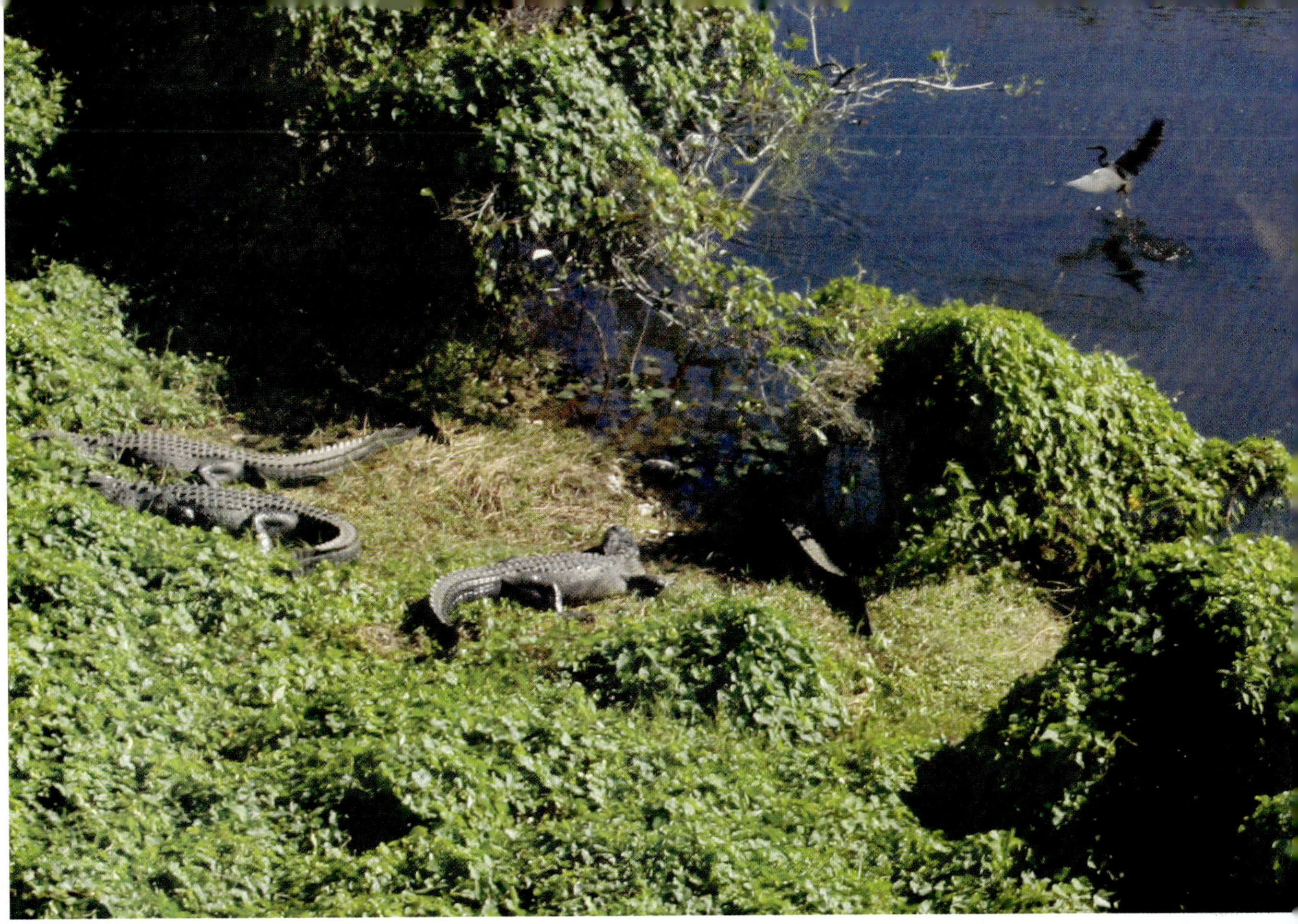

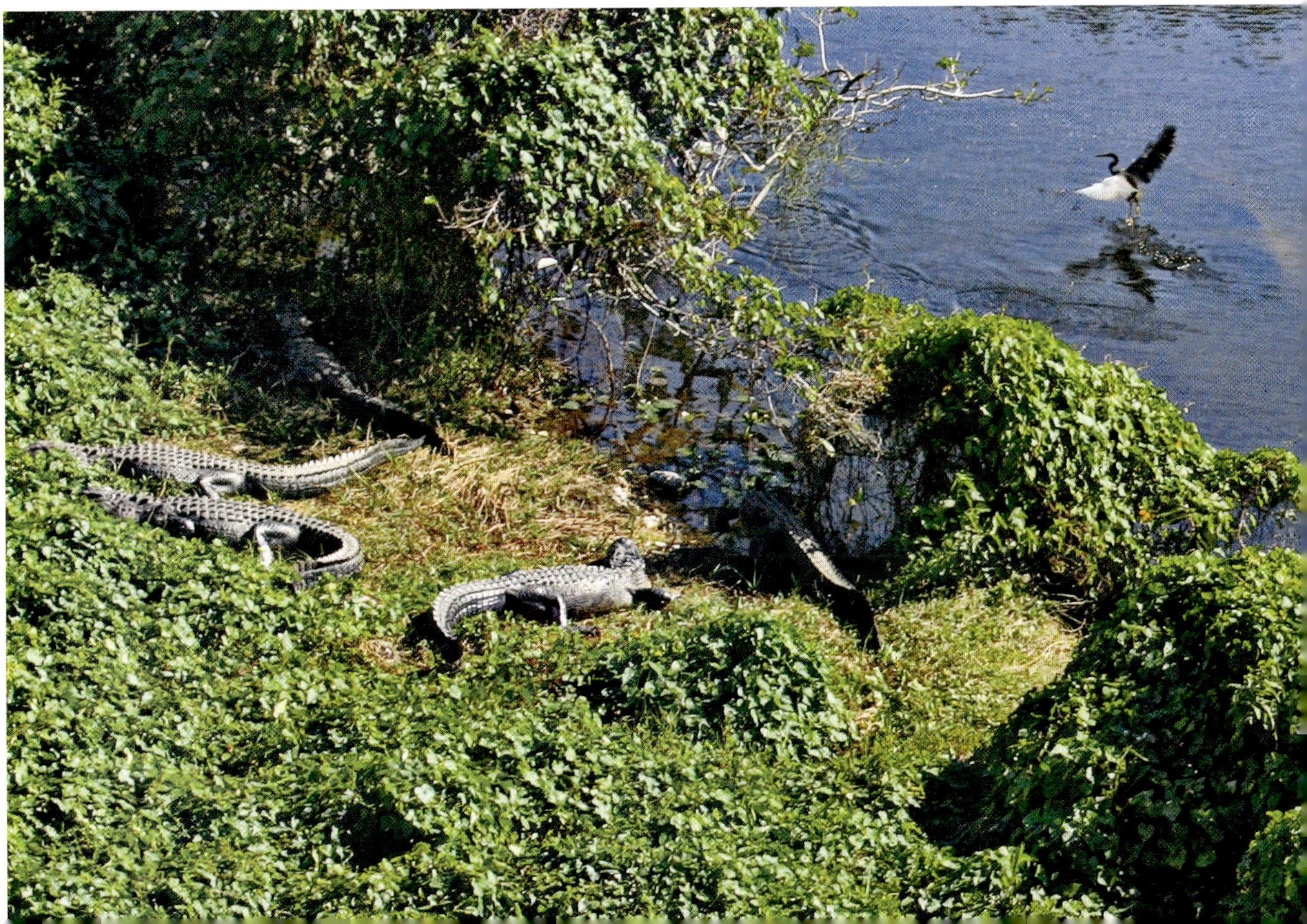

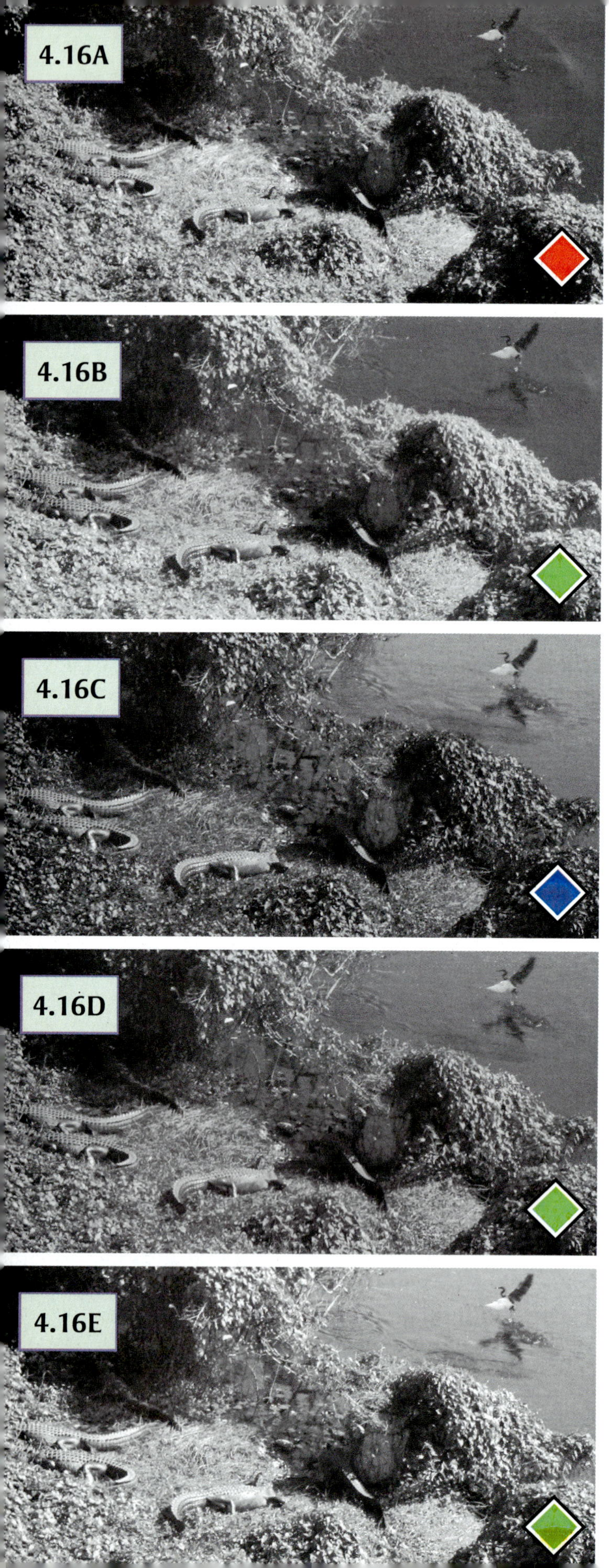

original. For a swampier example, let's head to Everglades National Park.

The color evaluation of Postcard 4.15 is brief. The gators are slightly warm, which makes sense because they are in sunlight. The water and greenery are also plausible. So much for Chapter 3. We now look at the channels, shown in Figures 4.16A, 4.16B, and 4.16C.

This picture has two halves. The lower left half—the greenery and the gators—is lighter than the water in the red and green channels. But in the blue, it's the darker half. Which concept do you think does better justice to the scene?

The gators are best defined in the blue. To emphasize them by blending, on a duplicate layer, Image: Apply Image. As no specific channel is active, the target is all three. Source is the blue channel, mode Normal. The opacity can't be 100%, or the greenery would become blackery. Instead, I chose 55%.

Unlike most of the blending percentages so far, this one is no SWAG. When I was applying the blue, although all channels were active, I had set up the Channels palette to make only the green visible. And I chose the opacity that made the two halves of the picture as nearly equal as possible, giving me Figure 4.16D. Equalizing the two sides creates the greatest flexibility in curving, since what helps detail on one side must also help the other.

The color now was Figure 4.17B; the original is reshown above it as Figure 4.17A. The lightest significant point was not obvious, so I used a threshold adjustment layer to investigate. I found a lot of light stuff in the greenery, but nothing large enough to measure, and hence too small to worry about.

The lightest *significant* element is the side of the nearest gator. Back on the duplicate layer, I went to the green channel curve and forced that point to 255^G (recall a similar move in the Grand Canyon image). I experimented with different

***Figure 4.16** Top to bottom: the red, green, and blue channels; the green after applying 55% blue; the final green after a contrast-enhancing curve.*

curve shapes but could find nothing better than a straight line. The green channel now was Figure 4.16E.

Finally, I went to the red curve and tried something similar, but I did not go all the way to 255^R, preferring not to risk blowing out the highlights.

The composite color now was Figure 4.17C. Changing layer mode to Luminosity produced Figure 4.17D, ending this chapter's work. From there to the final postcard required pieces of Chapters 5, 6, 7, 13, and 15. They all played a role, but the biggest benefit came from the luminosity moves just shown.

The Fourth Blending Channel

As if red, green, and blue did not provide enough rope with which to hang ourselves, the rest of the chapter discusses the use of other channels for blending. We commence with a truly horrible original. In Chapter 14 we will discuss how the aforesaid horribleness came about and how it should have been avoided. But for now, we have what we have. If this is the worst original you are ever confronted with, you lead a charmed life.

I would ordinarily try to show the channels on the same spread as the originals, but for Postcard 4.18 you should be able to say what they look like sight unseen. Most of the picture is a brilliant red, therefore the red channel is extremely light and the other two extremely dark. Further, because the subject is as lacking in detail as Siberia is in hippopotami, the red channel must be just about blank and the other two just about solid.

Correcting this lamentable state of affairs is likely to be easier said than done. If no channel has serious detail then the blends we've seen so far are useless, and curves are not much better.

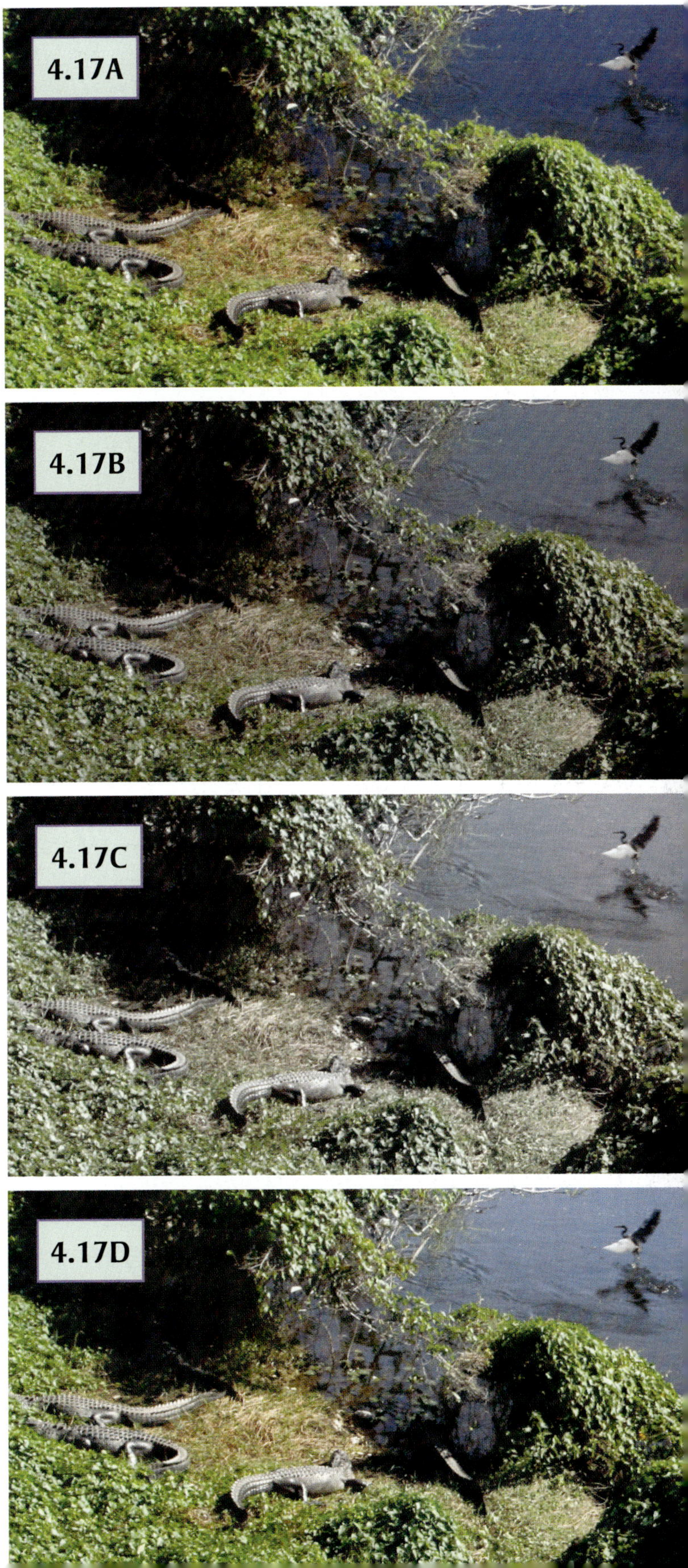

***Figure 4.17** Top to bottom: the original; the blue channel is blended into the RGB on a duplicate layer at 55% opacity; contrast-enhancing curves are added to the red and green; layer mode is set to Luminosity.*

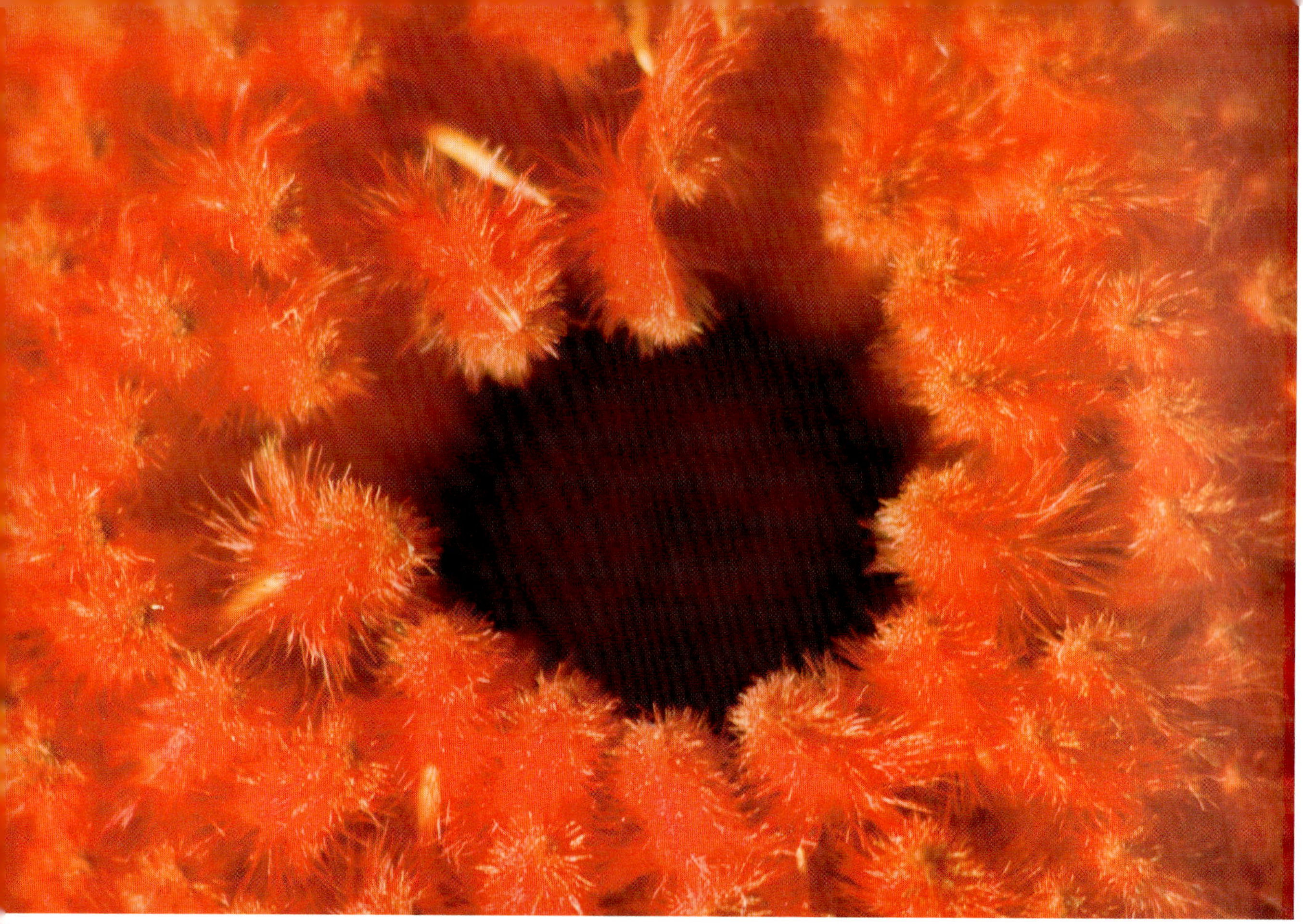

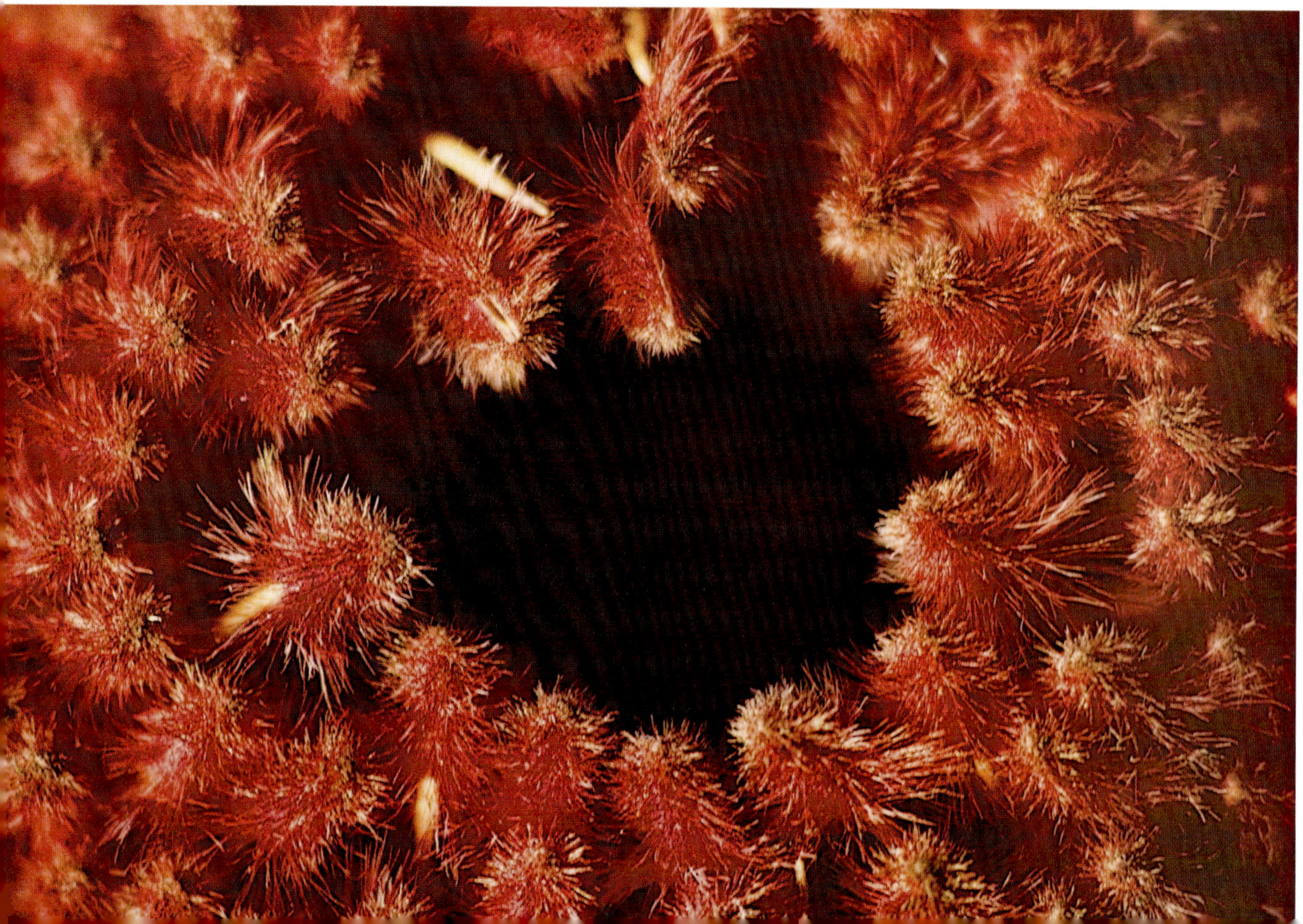

The solution is found in a channel we haven't yet spoken about.

The Apply Image command offers as a source any channel of any layer (or the merged layers) of any open document that's the same size as this one. But it doesn't offer only the red, green, and blue. Alpha channels, if any, are available too. Also, if the source document is in fact RGB, then "RGB" is itself a choice.

Applying RGB to a single channel asks Photoshop to convert the RGB file to grayscale, and apply that to the target.

This is roughly, although not exactly, equivalent to making a copy of the document, converting it to LAB, and applying the L to the targeted RGB channel. In fact, what I show might not be exactly equivalent to you doing it on your own system. Photoshop looks at the definition of grayscale in Edit: Color Settings to decide what to apply. If your setting there isn't the same as mine (and there's no reason it should be) we won't get precisely the same results.

Unless you have a strange setup, these differences are minor. And even though the resulting grayscale looks as detail-free as the green channel in this picture, it's much lighter. A curve will make parts of it even lighter and others darker, retaining the original weight, more or less. A curve to the existing green channel could only lighten it, which could throw off the balance, maybe even producing a washed-out look.

Certain blends can be repeated several times, gaining power with each repetition. Watch:

- The left side of Figure 4.19 shows the four original channels, including the RGB composite (grayscale), Figure 4.19D, with which I replaced the red, Figure 4.19A.
- I followed up with a contrast-enhancing curve to the new red, producing Figure 4.19E.
- The overall picture is now Figure 4.19F, which is dramatically different from the original. Consequently, a grayscale conversion of this image would be dramatically different, too. In fact, it's Figure 4.19G, which is clearly better than the first grayscale, Figure 4.19D.

Postcard 4.18 *(opposite) The original lacks detail. Repeated blends using the RGB composite as a source inserts it.*

Now we restart the merry-go-round by using this new improved grayscale in the same way as the old ratty-looking one. Of course, it gets applied to the modified image, not the original.

- I blended this new grayscale into the green of Figure 4.19F at an opacity of 35%. Figure 4.19H is the resulting green, and Figure 4.19J is the resulting color. Figure 4.19K is the grayscale that it produces, the third of our series, better than Figure 4.19G, which in turn was better than Figure 4.19D.
- I then discarded the red channel that I had been at such pains to make in Figure 4.19E, replacing it with the new grayscale of Figure 4.19K. Then, another curve to boost contrast even more. The new red was Figure 4.19L and the new color 4.19M. Changing the layer mode to Luminosity yielded Figure 4.19N.

We could make an infinite loop out of this, continually generating better grayscales and reincorporating them into the base file, but we get to a point of diminishing returns, and I think it's just been reached.

Bright reds pop up regularly. Before moving on to yet another possible blend source, here are a couple of tips on how to deal with them.

- When everything is red, nothing is red. Once done with this luminosity step, we would like to be able to enhance color, and especially to create some color variation. It will be hard to do that if the entire red area is close to the edge of our printable gamut. It is therefore often useful to rein in the color at this point.

The obvious way to do so is by using an earlier version. At the end of the process I had Figure 4.19M as a layer on top of the original. I then changed mode to Luminosity, producing Figure 4.19N, which, according to me, is too red. The solution is to duplicate the luminosity layer, change its mode to Color, and drastically reduce opacity, maybe to around 15%. This tones things down while retaining a strong red feeling.

No danger lurks in this procedure. If you think my final postcard is not red enough you can always blend a percentage of the extremely red original into it in Color mode. And if you think I built in too much detail you can use a blend from the original to soften it.

- A luminosity layer on top of something with brilliant colors runs the risk of calling for something out of the RGB gamut, which often obliterates detail. The solution is to convert the file to LAB, or possibly even CMYK, without flattening. The luminosity calculation isn't the same in all

Figure 4.19 *This page, top row, the original red, green, and blue channels. Bottom left, the RGB (grayscale) channel. Bottom center, the red is replaced by the grayscale and a contrast-enhancing curve applied. Bottom right, the resulting color. Opposite, top left, the new color produces a new grayscale version. Top center, 35% of the new grayscale is blended into the green. Top right, the resulting color. Middle left, the new color produces yet another new grayscale. Middle center, the red channel is replaced by the new grayscale and a further curve applied. Middle right, the resulting color, which now resides on a layer above the original. This file is used to generate the next three variants. Bottom row, luminosity layers have different results depending upon colorspace. Left to right, these files were flattened in RGB, CMYK, and LAB.*

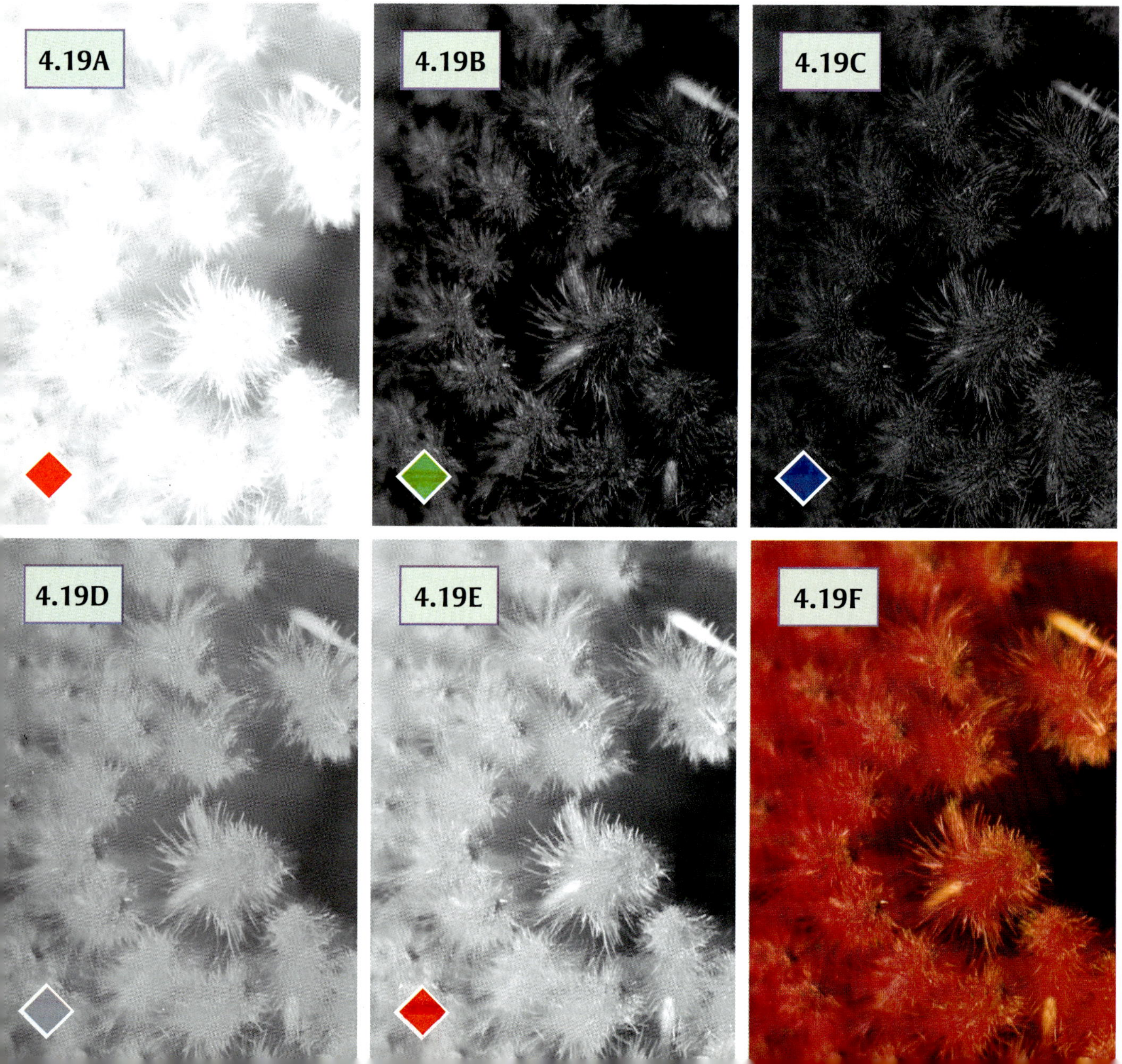

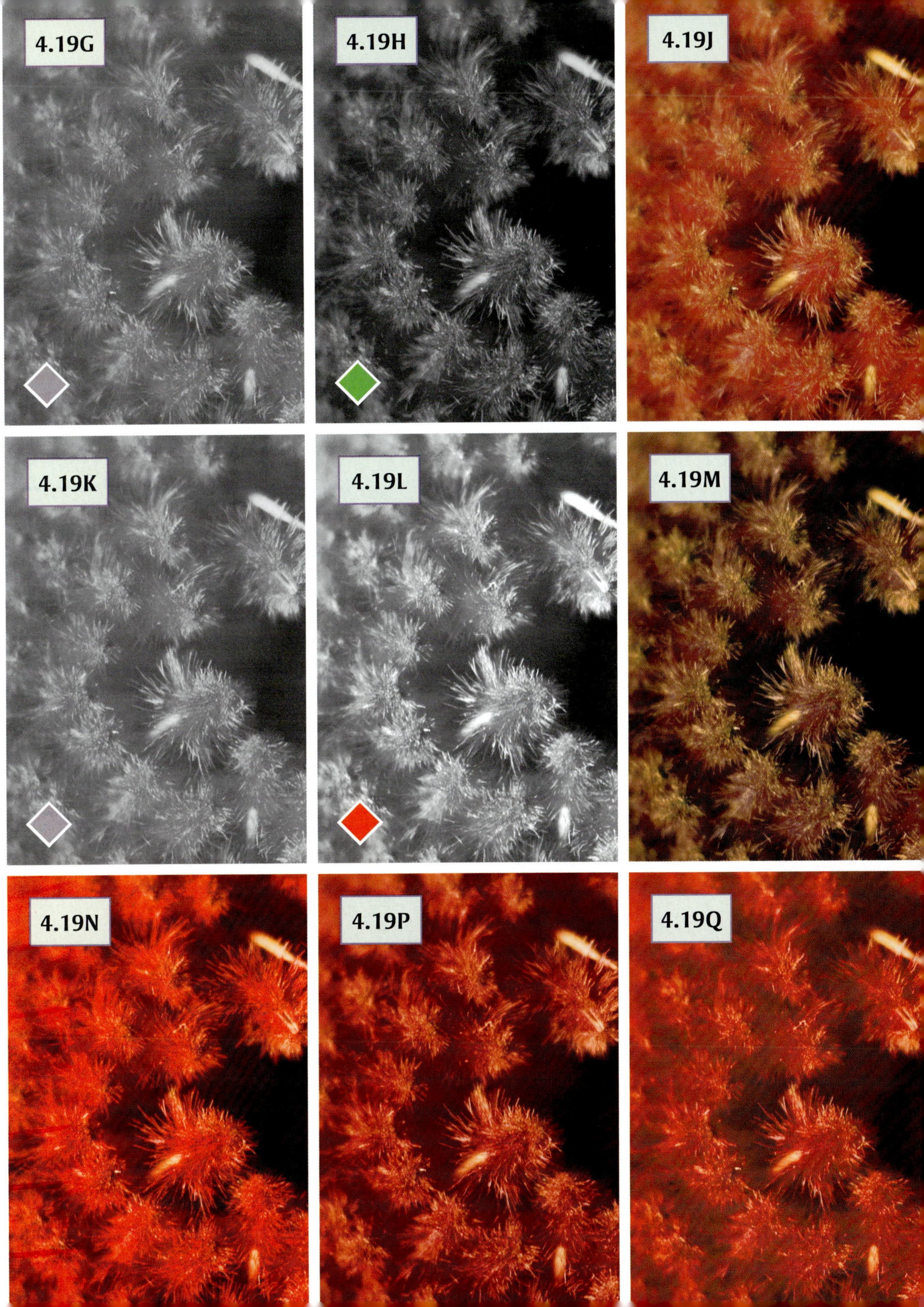
4.19G
4.19H
4.19J
4.19K
4.19L
4.19M
4.19N
4.19P
4.19Q

colorspaces, so the results often vary considerably. The luminosity layer calls for parts of these flowers to be almost as dark as a black. The bottom layer calls for them to be bright red. The request is impossible in RGB, because something that dark can't possibly be a brilliant red. Figure 4.19N shows that when the file gets flattened in RGB those areas become ugly black blotches.

In Figure 4.19P, the file was converted to CMYK and flattened there. This worked somewhat better, because the reds on the bottom layer were brought into the CMYK gamut before the luminosity layer was taken into account.

You're likely to get a more usable result in LAB, which can specify "colors" that no monitor can display nor any printer reproduce. Figure 4.19Q, then, is Photoshop's idea of how to represent a brilliantly red black.

The Least Common Denominator

Of course, you could mix and match these three versions, just as you could blend between the start and end versions of Postcard 4.18. In Chapter 14, we will learn why this original was so featureless as to require all these shenanigans to correct it, and how to avoid them in similar cases.

The final two exercises won't get all the way to a postcard. Instead they will offer some further options and cautions.

The problem channel in Figure 4.20 is obvious. The red and blue are reasonable already, but we have already seen how the green is more important than both of them put together, and this green is way flat. The question is what to do about it.

The first half of the chapter would suggest improving it with a curve and/or a blend from the red or blue. We just added the possibility of using

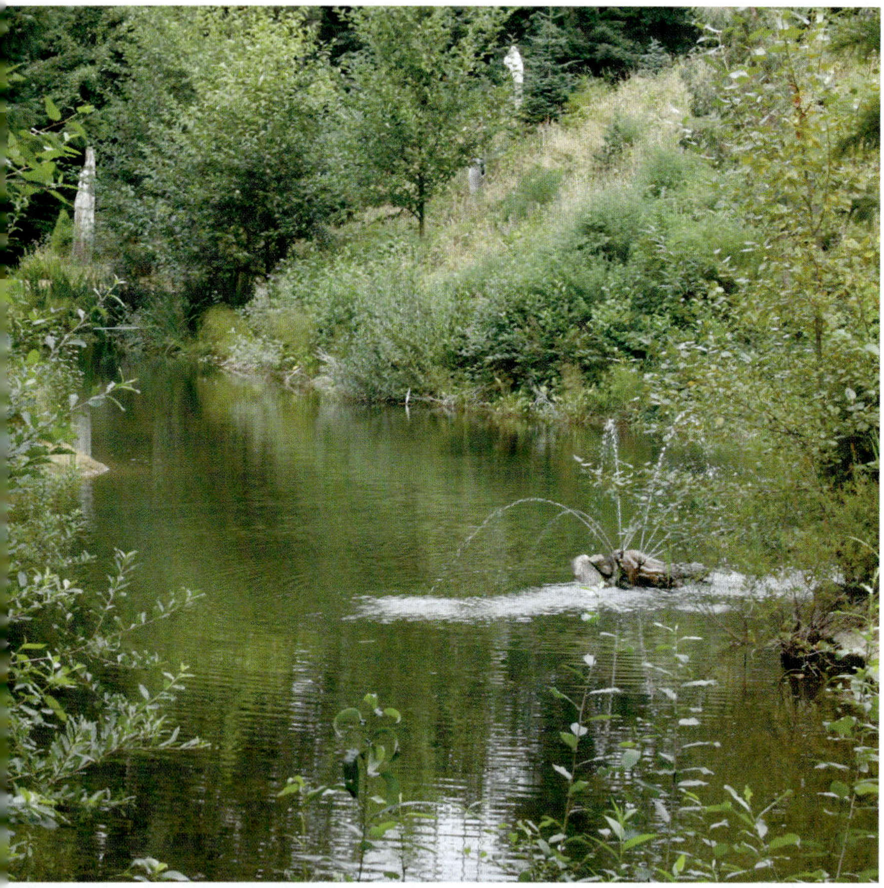

Figure 4.20 The original and its three channels. The green is clearly too flat and must be improved by one or more of the methods discussed in this chapter.

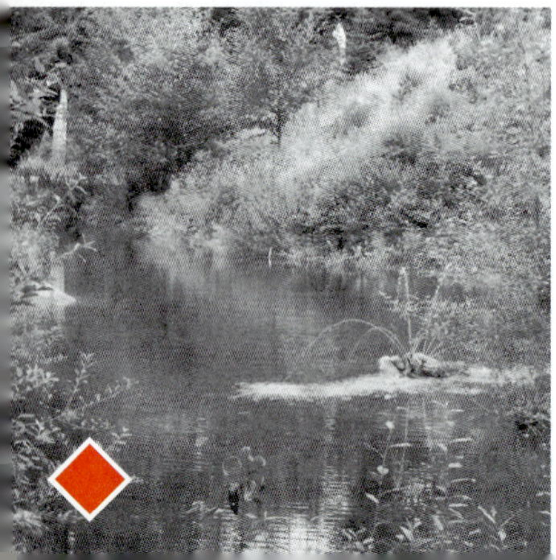

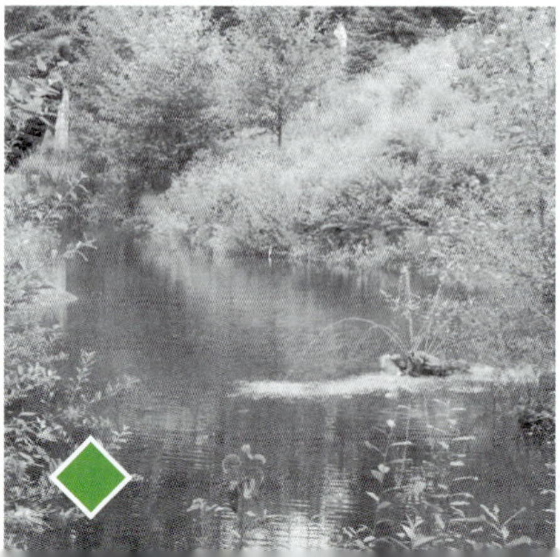

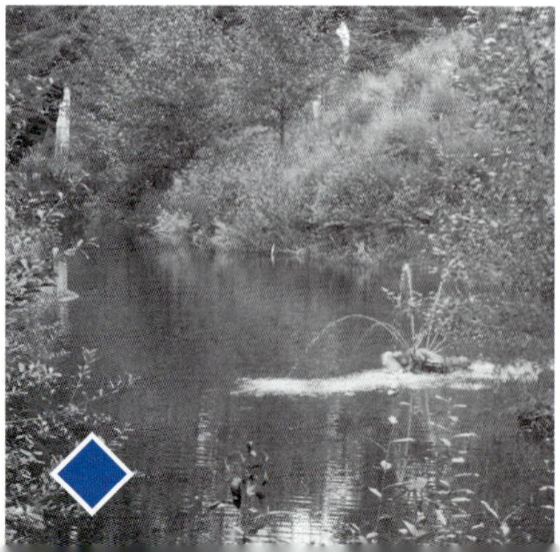

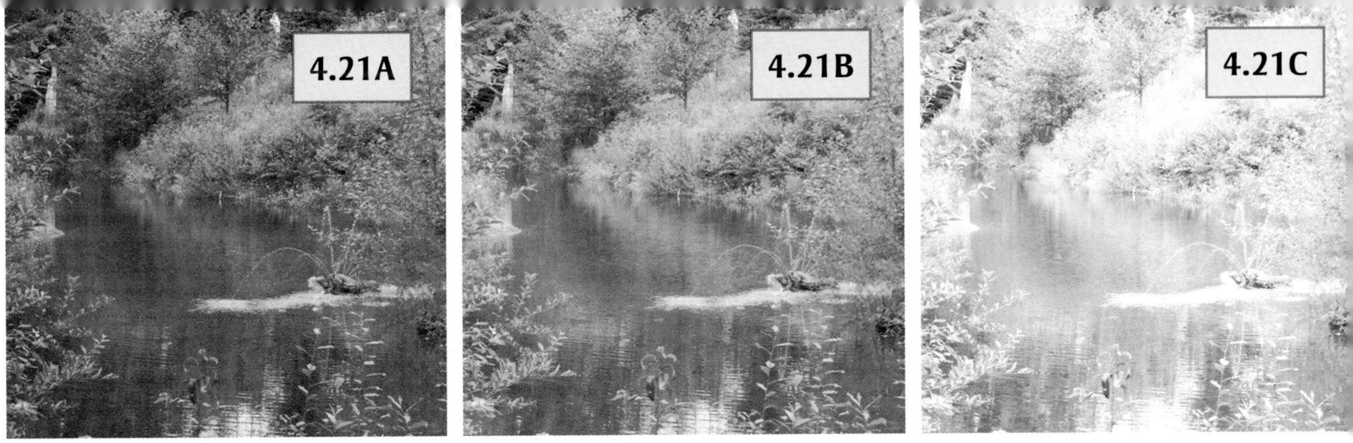

***Figure 4.21** Other candidates for blending use. Left, a grayscale of the RGB file as used in the previous example. Center, the L channel from a copy of the image that has been converted to LAB. Right, screening the red, green, and blue channels into one another to emulate a CMYK black.*

a fourth channel, a grayscale version of the RGB. Now it's time for a fifth option, to wit, using a modified version of a CMYK black channel. We don't blend with it in Normal mode; instead we will use Multiply.

Understanding why it works requires knowing how CMYK is constructed. The cyan, magenta, and yellow channels are close relatives of, respectively, the red, green, and blue, slightly varied from their cousins because of considerations of ink impurity and dot gain. The big difference, however, is that a certain amount of detail is subtracted from the CMY channels and used to construct a black. Black can only exist where there would otherwise be significant weight in all three CMY channels. Since the RGB channels are similar to what the CMY would be if there were no black, we can rephrase that last statement in a more decisive way:

The black is nowhere darker than the lightest RGB channel.

The black is thus a least common denominator. It is heaviest in neutral areas. It never appears in strongly colored areas. In the red flowers image, Figure 4.19A showed that the red of RGB is very light. Therefore the cyan of CMYK must also be very light, hence no black.

The cyan, magenta, and yellow channels are worthless for blending. They have yielded a certain amount of natural detail to the black. So blending from, say, the cyan would never make sense because its RGB cognate, the red, would always be better.

For our purposes, then, we can trash the CMY channels if we feel like saving disk space. It's not like we're trying to print out of this CMYK file, after all—it's a bogus separation, solely useful as the source of a blend. That's convenient. It means that we don't need a black constructed with the limitations of commercial printing in mind. Instead, we can configure Photoshop to spit out a black that's good for channel blending and not necessarily anything else. You will be pleased to know that a supplied action will do this for you automatically; you can read about it in Chapter 13.

Then again, there's more than one type of black. The heaviest conceivable black would replace CMY everywhere possible. This can be translated in two ways; they don't sound alike, but when you think about it, they mean the same thing. The first translation: the black replaces so much that every pixel becomes blank in one CMY channel; the only time no black is generated is when one channel was already blank. The second translation: the heaviest conceivable black appears everywhere except in areas that were originally brilliantly colored.

And the lightest black conceivable? In theory, a completely blank channel. In practice, if the CMYK file is intended to be printed, a blank black wouldn't work because CMY inks alone don't generate a dark enough shadow. So the minimum reasonable black would be one generated solely to heavy up the shadow. It would appear only in dark neutrals.

Any point between the two extremes could work, for an almost infinite number of possible

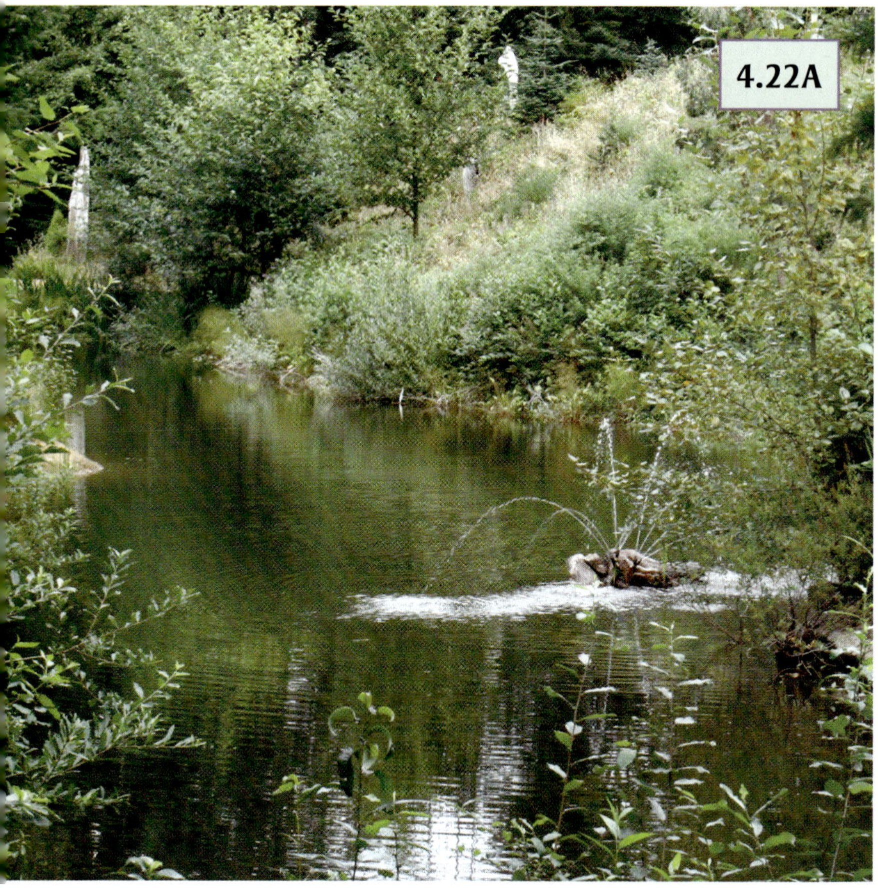

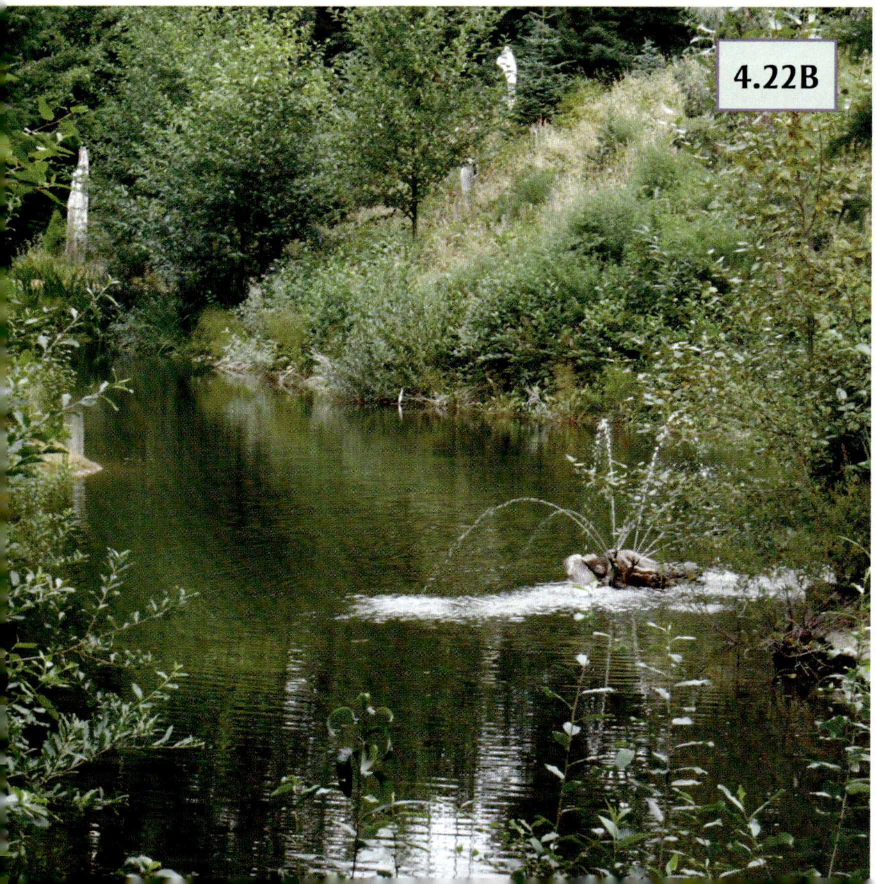

blacks. Experiment if you like, but to keep this discussion at less than the length of a Russian novel, we'll discuss only one style. We will now revert to exploring the strategy of improving the green channel of the current exercise. I offer three possible assistants: Figure 4.21A is a grayscale version, which is what would be used if we applied RGB to the green. Figure 4.21B is a close relative, the L of LAB. And Figure 4.21C is the black, or rather the bogus black. I got it by screening the three RGB channels into each other. An explanation of why this works is found in the second half of Chapter 13.

More Choices Than Time

We have already discussed more ways to improve the green channel than we have time to test. They fall into four different categories:

- A curve similar to the one shown for the green back in Figure 4.12.
- Applying the blue channel to the green at something less than 100% opacity. It doesn't look like the red is a good source candidate.
- Replacing the green either with the grayscale or the L channel, possibly followed by a curve to adjust overall weight.
- Multiplying the bogus black into the green, possibly using a mask so nothing gets too dark.

Testing every one of these options is lunacy. Any will yield better results than a traditional workflow. We have identified and targeted the weakness of the picture—a bad green channel.

***Figure 4.22** Top, a curve to the green channel. Bottom, starting from scratch, applying the blue to the green at 75% opacity. Both are on luminosity layers.*

Only a workflow that allows us to attack it without fear of other consequences can get an optimal result.

If you're in a hurry, choose one of the above options quickly and hope for the best. Otherwise, do two or more quick versions from scratch, including the color adjustments of future chapters. Then combine the one with the best color with the one with the best luminosity.

But if you have to pick one method in advance, which one? We'll compare the four basic approaches. In each case, the final stage is to adjust the lightest point in the water to a fixed value, so that the four contestants have the same tonal range and thus differ only in the way that contrast is allocated.

Figure 4.22A applies something similar to the Figure 4.12 curve to the green. Figure 4.22B instead applies the blue to the green at 75% opacity. Both corrections have been put on layers set to Luminosity mode. How big a difference do you see?

Moving on, Figure 4.23A replaces the green with the grayscale of Figure 4.21A. In other words, it applies the grayscale to the green at 100% opacity. In Figure 4.23B, the bogus black of Figure 4.21C has been multiplied into the green at 75% opacity.

Which Do You Prefer?

You get the deciding vote, but mine goes to Figure 4.23B by a whisker over 4.22A. I say the worst of the group is Figure 4.22B, but all four versions are substantially better than the

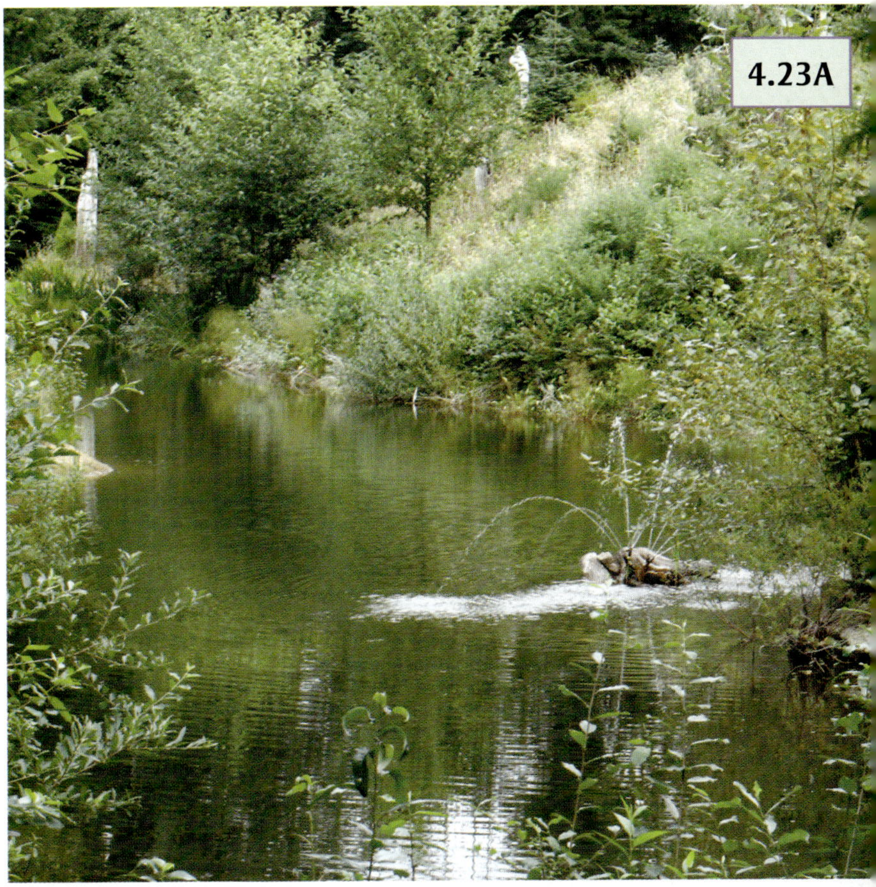

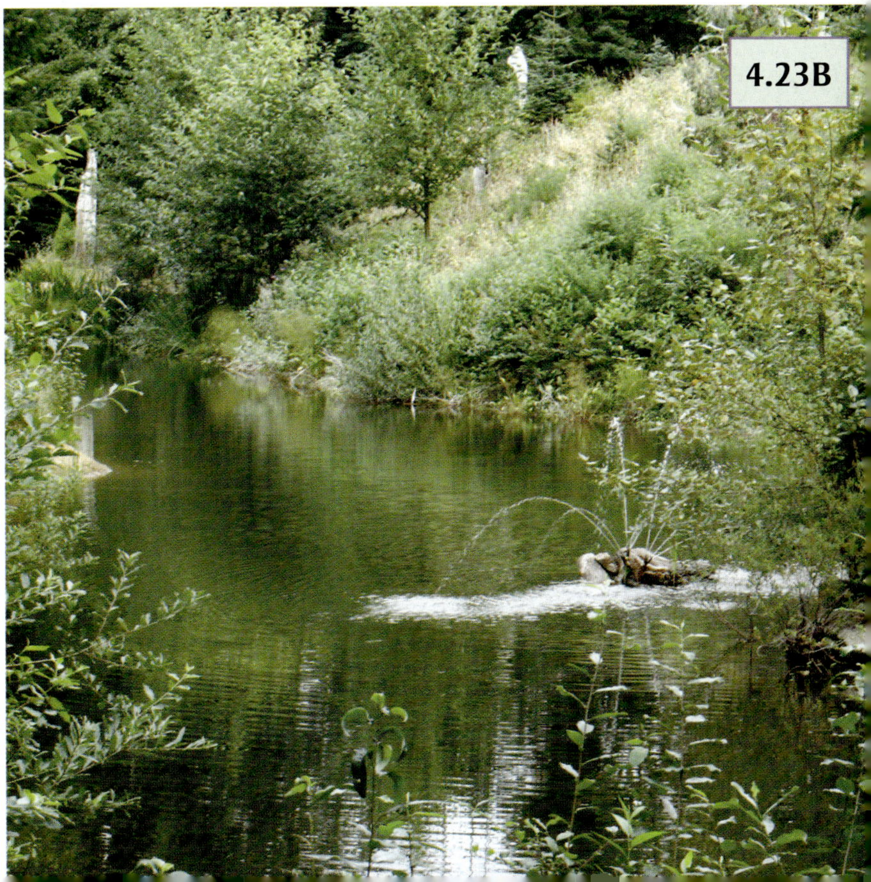

***Figure 4.23** Top, a new version prepared by replacing the green with Figure 4.21A. Bottom, instead, multiplying Figure 4.21C into the green at 75% opacity.*

original and would be difficult to achieve with traditional methods.

These four all darken colorful areas less than neutral ones. Note the difference in Figure 4.23B. The yellowish shrubbery at top center, and many of the lighter greens, started out more colorful than the rest of the picture. They therefore are darkened less than the background, producing better separation between the two. Perhaps more evident, the top left of the water carries a (literal, not graphic arts) shadow. Originally this shadow was less colorful than the rest of the water. It therefore gets darker faster, and is more pronounced against the greener water than it is in any of the other three versions.

Should Neutrals Be Darker?

The last chapter mentioned several instances of how human perception differs from that of a camera. Some are well understood; simultaneous contrast, for example, has been theorized for 500 years and was fully explained in the 1830s. Many of these theories involve color and have little to do with the subject of this chapter, which is lightness.

One exception: the German polymath Hermann von Helmholtz (1821–1894) demonstrated that humans perceive neutrals as being somewhat darker than artificial devices such as cameras do. This finding, known as the Helmholtz-Kohlrausch Effect, really has only been proven by comparisons of strong colors against grays and near-grays. However, it is a reasonable guess that it can be extended to say that the more colorful an object is, the lighter it seems to us, although not to a camera.

Whether this supposition is true has not affected color correction until recent years because it would have been too computer-intensive to come up with a way of emulating it. From time to time people did things along the same lines by using the black channel of CMYK for blending purposes.

Today, computers are fast enough to emulate the Helmholtz-Kohlrausch Effect on the fly, although nobody knows whether it should be done as a general rule. Certainly it works well in some images.

Chapter 13 introduces an action that does darken neutrals and near-neutrals. I mention it here because it goes hand in hand with the techniques of this chapter, in reallocating contrast in a more realistic way.

Rather than an interminable discussion of how we could create even more alternate versions by combining some of these steps, let's cut our losses right here and move on to the next exercise, not bothering to complete this one with the rest of the workflow. Then again, you might prefer the interminable discussion, because a tough quiz is coming up.

A Quiz: Name the Colors

Fixing luminosity can be very fast. The process takes a long time to describe, because I'm showing and describing each channel. But in real life, I completed each of these luminosity changes in a minute or less, with the possible exception of the alligators of Postcard 4.15.

If you wish to be that fast, though, you need to be able to visualize channels quickly. In most cases you may scarcely even need to glance at them, because you will know, for example, that the blue is dark in greenery, and the red in skies.

It follows that you should also be able to do the converse. That is, given the channels, you should be able to visualize the color. And that, gentle reader, is our next exercise.

Figure 4.24 shows the three channels along with the grayscale. They are in a random order. The grayscale conversion was into a 2.2 gamma, which should give it a comparable weight to the RGB channels. Warning: this isn't the Photoshop default for a conversion into B/W. If you try this on one of your own images without changing the aforementioned default, you'll get a grayscale version that's darker. Not hideously so, but enough to throw off your comparisons.

You don't get to see the color version yet, because you shouldn't need it. Assume, however, that there's nothing grossly wrong. Before extracting these channels, I had examined the file for color along the lines suggested in Chapter 3, and fixed what needed correcting.

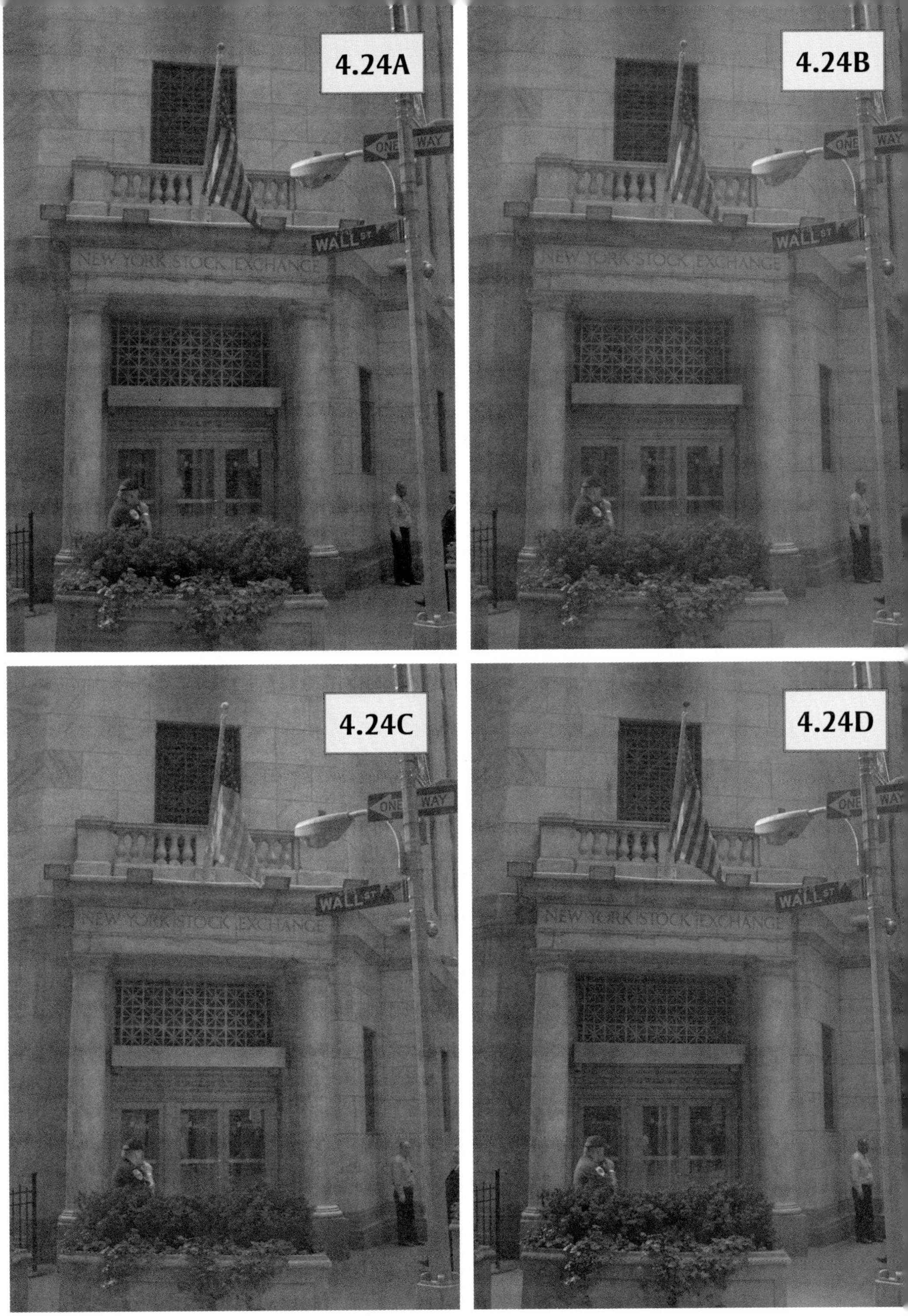

***Figure 4.24** In a random order are the red, green, blue, and grayscale channels of a picture that has not yet been seen. You are given that these RGB channels taken together produce acceptable color. Which channel is which?*

So, here's the quiz.

- Which channel is which?
- What color is the uniform of the man standing in front of the door?
- What color is the building itself?
- What can you say about image quality?
- Would an artificial black channel like the one in the previous example be helpful?
- What is the strategy for improving the contrast in this picture, given that the color is currently acceptable if not exciting?

It's true that you can find out the answers to the first three questions by turning the page. However, if you do, the angels will weep for you. Besides, seeing the color won't help you answer those final two questions. Understanding how channels work *will.*

And the Answers

- *Which channel is which?* In RGB, the lighter the channel, the more color is contributed. Conveniently, an object known to be deep red presents itself, namely the stripes of the flag. Whichever channel is lightest there must be the red; whichever is second-lightest is the grayscale. The blue and green may not be distinguishable with respect to the stripes, but the green must be darker in the blue area of the flag. And anyway, the blue channel is almost always the overall darkest of the three channels.

So far, it's easy. Figure 4.24C has the lightest stripes and therefore is the red. Figure 4.24B has the lightest stripes of the remaining three, so it has to be the grayscale. Distinguishing the green from the blue is tougher because the stripes are about the same darkness in each and the scene doesn't seem to have any other brilliant colors.

The usual rule that the blue is much darker overall than the other two doesn't seem to apply. This suggests that the building must be close to, if not exactly, neutral.

There are, however, two, and possibly three, areas where subtle differences could be expected. First, the canton of the flag is a dark blue, a desaturated blue, but a blue nevertheless, which means its blue channel must be slightly lighter than the green.

Second, the foreground plants must be a dull green, so their green channel has to be slightly lighter than the blue.

Third, these look like metal doors. The finish could be silvery, in which case the blue and green would be equal. But if they are not equal, then the doors either favor yellow or favor purple. Of these two possibilities, a brass finish isn't uncommon, whereas a purple door is about as likely as a 5,000-point gain in the Dow.

For all three of these reasons (the doors are not, in fact, equal) Figure 4.24A can only be the green, and Figure 4.24D the blue.

Having deciphered the identities, the next three answers are obvious.

- *What color is the uniform of the man in front of the door?* Dark blue, because its channels match the blue of the flag.
- *What color is the building itself?* Close to gray, because all three channels are nearly equal, which is the formula for neutrality in RGB.
- *What can you say about overall image quality?* It's extremely flat. The lightest point is the top of the street light but everything else is crammed into the midtone and up. Our experience shows that when a picture is this flat it's always rather gray as well.
- *Would an artificial black channel like the one used in the previous example be helpful?* Conceivably it might enhance the words *New York Stock Exchange.* On the other hand it might darken the flag too much, even if I tried to control the effect with curves.

Lies, Damn Lies, and Highlights

The most difficult decision, that of choosing a strategy to boost contrast, has been saved for last. First, however, I must clarify a statement about the previous exercise, the picture of the green lake.

The original, Figure 4.20, wasn't as flat as the stock exchange picture, but it wasn't full-range, either. Back then, I chose a light point in some reflections in the water, and decided to almost, but not quite, blow it out, leaving just a wisp of detail. I claimed to have done this entirely in the green channel, on a layer that was later set to Luminosity mode.

That statement contained, how shall I put this, a certain slight inaccuracy in the interest of not frightening half the readers off. There were *two* luminosity layers. It isn't possible to get that image light enough by manipulating only one channel on one layer.

Consider Figure 4.23A, where I blended the grayscale into the green. At that moment, my chosen point in the water became $217^R215^G246^B$ which, lamentably, is purple. When mode went to Luminosity, it came back to its original blue, at $211^R218^G240^B$. I had darkened the green, but Photoshop had to cancel some of the darkening to maintain the color.

At this point I wanted to lighten the image, but only using the green. As previously noted, a better green was going to be the key to good contrast because it could be improved more than the others. So I set up a curves adjustment layer, and dragged the green light point in until it reached 254^G. By not hitting the maximum of 255^G, I made sure that no detail would be lost.

But that value could not be held. When I changed the layer mode to Luminosity, Photoshop recomputed the point as $236^R240^G254^B$.

Much better than without the curve, but still not light enough.

Following through with my obdurate insistence on altering the green only, I set up a second curves layer, and did the same thing, resetting the green to 254^{G} in Normal mode. When I set this second curves layer to Luminosity, the new value was $247^{R}248^{G}255^{B}$, which I decided to live with.

If you don't get why I needed a second curves layer instead of just forcing a lighter green into the first one, go back to the explanation and reread the part about luminosity recomputation, as otherwise what follows will make no sense.

The first curve is being applied to a "real" green channel—*not* to one that has been reconstructed by Luminosity mode. Yes, it can be made lighter, but all detail will vanish in the light areas. The way I did it, the green continues to add detail throughout.

Repetition of steps to the point of diminishing returns is a common PPW tactic. We saw a version of it with blends in the red flower image of Figure 4.19. And indeed, we could have tried other repetitive blends in the lake example, too. But the most common use of repetition is what we just saw: where contrast in the green is at a premium, set the endpoints, convert to Luminosity, reset the endpoints, reconvert, and so on until satisfied.

One could spend weeks without exhausting every possibility of enhancing this stock exchange shot. In real life, we pick the approach that seems most promising, and go back and try others only if time permits. What's your choice?

I'll show four options. For fairness, I have picked out highlight and shadow points and made sure that all four contestants match each other there. That way, it's all about allocation and not about overall tonal range.

Showdown on Wall Street

The first strategy was just described: repeatedly lighten the green channel with luminosity curves until the desired lightness is reached. This requires four curves adjustment layers instead of the two in the lake image. We can now look at the original, which will explain why. It is the horrifyingly flat Figure 4.25A. The four layers of green curves, all in Luminosity mode of course, produce Figure 4.25B.

Now. Why is the original so flat, since the shadows indicate it was taken on a sunny day?

Well, it was shot in raw format. I opened it in 2011, in the then-current version of Camera Raw, with all values set to zero except the original White Balance.

Settings that conservative guarantee this type of dull result, so the conventional wisdom does not approve. It would advocate using a raw module, Camera Raw or an equivalent to create Figure 4.25C or something similar as a starting point. The file unquestionably looks better—at least for the time being.

Better-looking for the time being is a concept for which the PPW has little use. In subsequent chapters we will see example after example where making a picture better looking now precludes even bigger improvements later. Making premature moves in a raw module looks tempting, but is often damaging, and as a rule I recommend against it, for reasons stated in Chapter 14.

Subsequent chapters will also make clear, if it is not already, that neither the PPW nor any other workflow eliminates the need for thinking and for evaluating what kind of image you're working on. Any reasonable workflow is going to work better on certain images than others. In the Introduction, I showed several examples where PPW got results that are spectacularly better than those of traditional methods, including raw manipulation. However, I also showed Figure I-5, which was a spectacular result, too, impressing many of the beta readers. I pointed out, though, that other methods could have come very close to it.

Accordingly, guard against thinking that PPW will provide an incredibly better result every time. It's not going to happen.

The luminosity step described in this chapter exploits the differences between channels to make areas of definite color more interesting This photo is one of the minority in which the concept is ineffective. It is so dominated by neutrals that it won't matter what we use to correct it. The PPW, Camera Raw old or new, traditional methods, and even hitting Figure 4.25A with Image: Auto Tone all yield similar results.

Comparing Figures 4.25B and 4.25C is unfair. Forcing a light and a dark point where none exists in the original, as all pre-PPW methods do, intensifies color. Light channels get lighter, dark ones darker. The impact is usually desirable.

In our description of the PPW the necessary color boost hasn't shown up yet. It comes in the next chapter. So it's to be expected that Figure 4.25B will look tired next to 4.25C.

One should be skeptical of bright colors created by accident, as they are in Figure 4.25C. It doesn't mean they're ugly or unusable. There's no reason to avoid using them as a backup or supplement to the PPW's own color version. Here, to make the comparison more valid, I steal Figure 4.25C's color by placing Figure 4.25B on a luminosity layer above it. This produces Figure 4.25D. The repeated tweaks to the highlight end of the curve have produced something lighter overall, with more detail in the building. I find it slightly better everywhere except the flag, whose stripes are too dark. That's to be expected when the correction emphasizes the role of the green channel, in which deep reds are dark.

If you are a lunatic, you can try the same trick using the red channel rather than the green. It takes twice as long—eight successive curves

***Figure 4.25** Below left, the original. Below right, a succession of four curves applied to the green channel, followed in each case by a reversion to luminosity. Facing page, top left, a more palatable version created in Camera Raw. Top right, the color of C wed to the luminosity of B. Bottom left, starting from scratch, eight successive luminosity layers lighten the red channel rather than the green, with the color again picked up from C. Bottom right, an entirely different approach.*

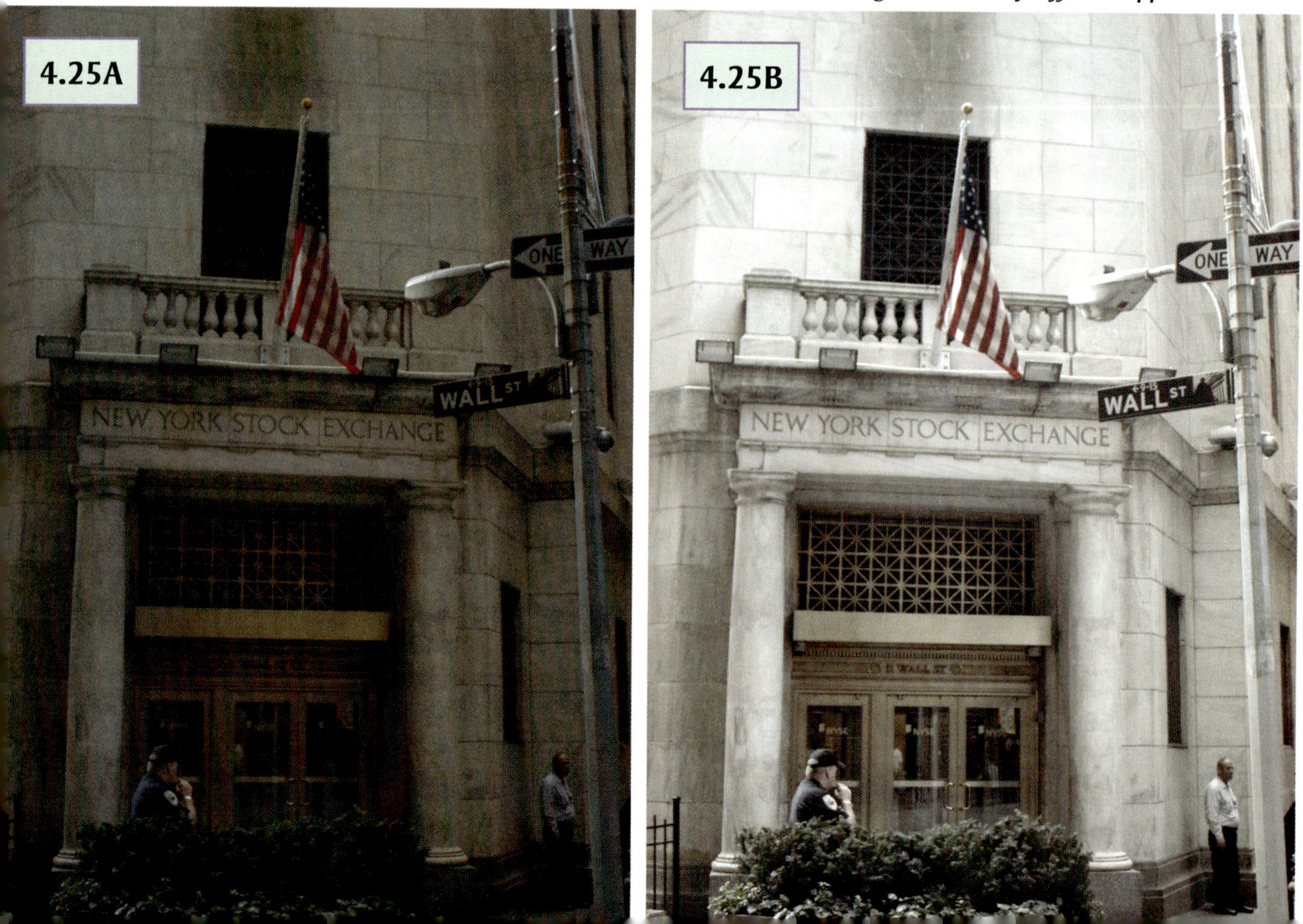

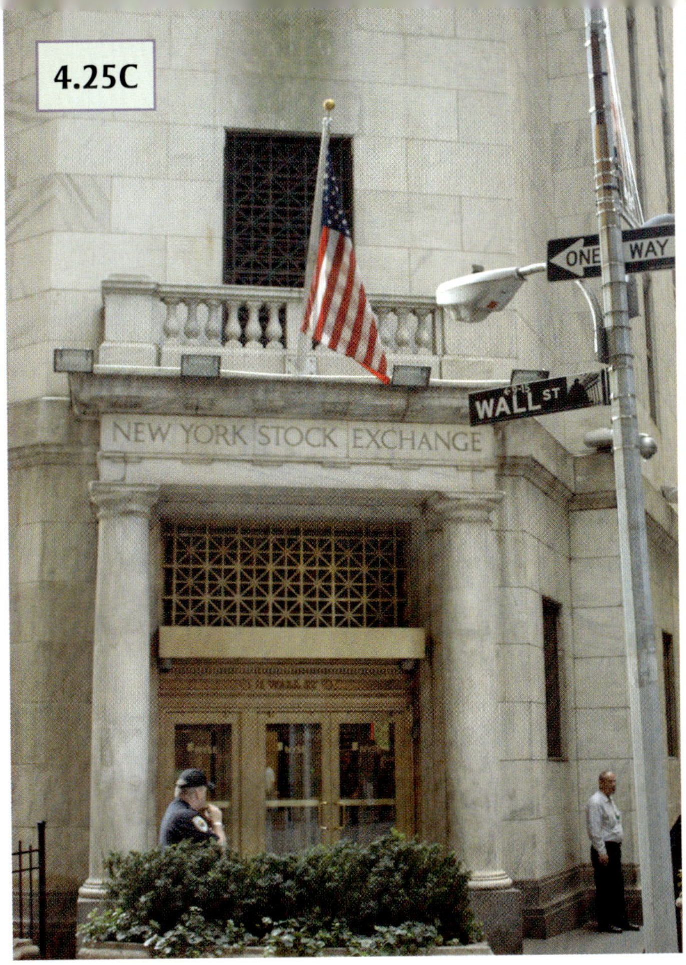

4.25C

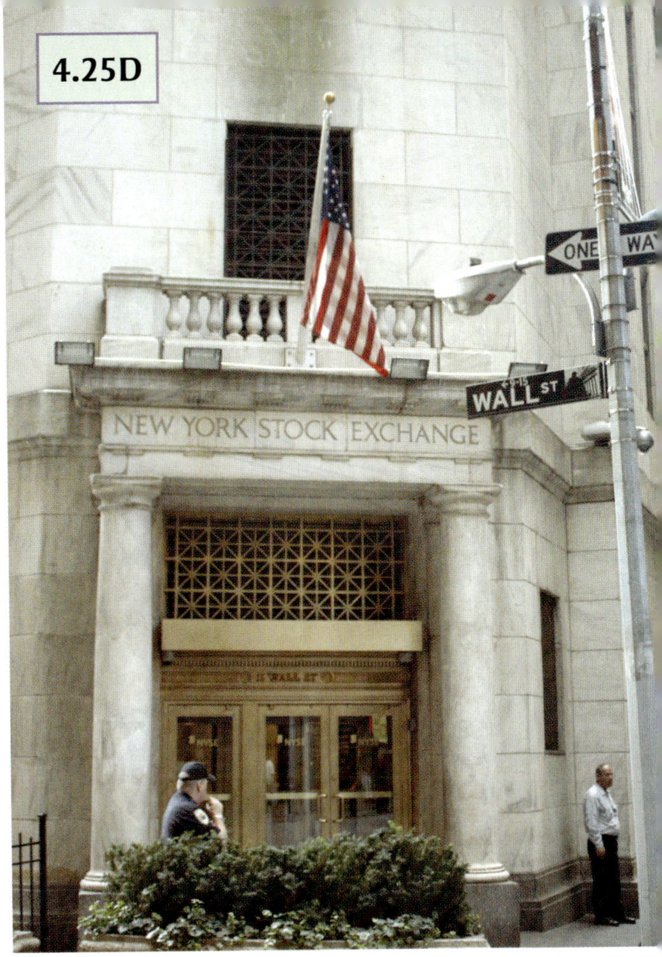

4.25D

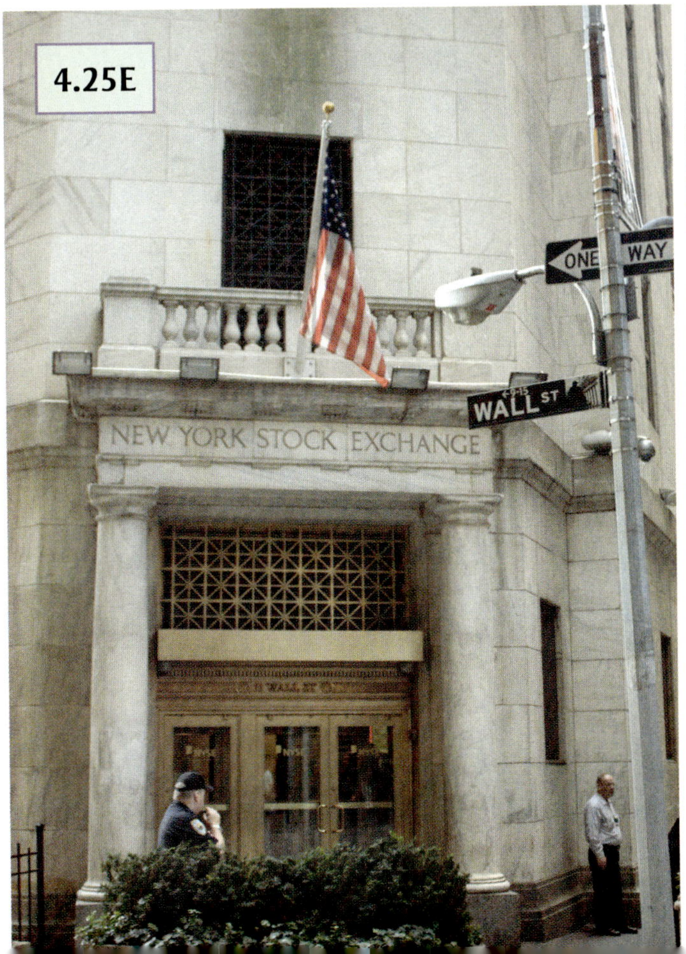

4.25E

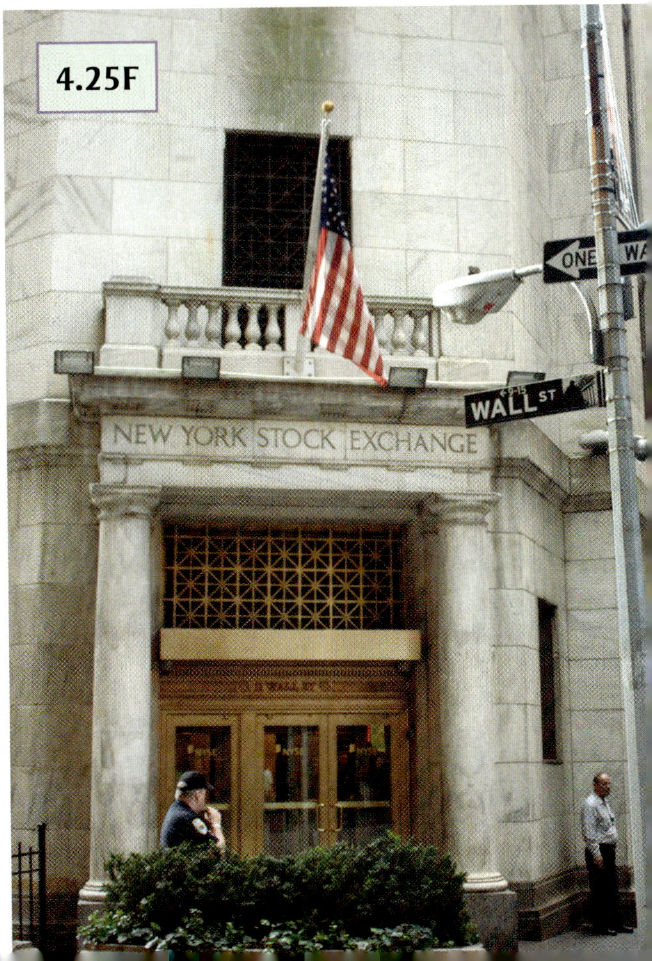

4.25F

to the red, to be precise—and the result, Figure 4.25E, is just as dubious. Now the stripes are too light, just as they are if you consider the original red channel, Figure 4.24C, as a black and white.

We can at this point (remember, we are talking about lunacy here) blend Figures 4.25D and 4.25E 50–50. Since the two are similar in the building, the main impact is to make the stripes similar to those found in Figure 4.25C. But before doing that, take a deep breath and then ask yourself what the devil you think you're trying to accomplish.

Doing things this way by my count involves sixteen different layers, of which thirteen contain curves and all of which require a mode change. Beta reader Jacob Rus pointed out, "I gotta say, trying to keep track of what's going on reading this whole description is definitely selling me on the 'wow this method is too complex' story."

True enough—in this particular case. PPW is not complex unless you force it to be that way. Occasionally there are reasons to do it. Trying to extract blood from this stone is not one of them. PPW is a disciplined and effective approach. It should not be turned into the greatest time-waster since the invention of YouTube.

The Bottom Line

Having dealt with color imperfections in the previous chapter, we now turn to contrast. Analyzing channels offers opportunities for blending, curving, or both. There are many more options than in traditional workflows, which have to worry about maintaining color. In fact, there are so many worthwhile options that it would be impractical to test them all. Instead, choose one, and then if time permits, try another version from scratch.

Everything is done on layers that are eventually set to Luminosity mode. The results are often much snappier than in traditional workflows. On the other hand, the color is typically bland at this point, necessitating the moves of the next two chapters.

The Opportunity That Doesn't Knock

We've seen that getting the darkness of the red stripes right is important. But do you care about whether they have strong detail? What about the yellowish parts of the door? (Not the letters, they're neutral.) How about the people? The plants at the bottom? None of these areas cry out for the type of dramatic contrast enhancement seen elsewhere in the chapter. The only thing that really needs enhancing is the building, and the building is neutral.

Here, then, is a one-sentence summary:

This picture is basically a black and white with color thrown in for decoration.

I mentioned on the first page of this chapter that the objective is to try to produce the best possible black and white out of a color original, and then use that for luminosity. But here, the original already *is* black and white, for all intents and purposes. So it's not surprising that all reasonable methods get more or less the same result. Don't be discouraged: in the large majority of pictures the PPW contrast method works better than alternative approaches. And the same can be said of the color method we are about to study.

How *should* this original be handled? I say that once we recognize that it's the exception that proves the rule, skip everything in this chapter and move on to the next one, which, with a single action, moves the file into LAB, boosts color, and incidentally offers a second opportunity to attack contrast through use of the L channel. All I did to make Figure 4.25F was to run that action and set the white point to match the others, accepting the action's default for the color boost. The whole thing took less than ten seconds, quite competitive with Auto Tone and faster than doing it in Camera Raw.

Note that these colors are crisper and cleaner. That's what happens when we treat the addition of color as something more than a pleasant side effect of setting range.

5

Once More for Color: How Much Is Too Much?

The easiest step in the workflow so far is also the most spectacular—and maybe the most counterintuitive. Throw in way too much color, and then figure out the most graceful method of backing off.

It's been a struggle, but we've reached the fun part. No more fancy strategies, no alternate methods unless you are ambitious, and few right or wrong answers.

At this point in the workflow, we should have excellent contrast, thanks to the techniques shown in Chapter 4. The color, however, is drab next to what a traditional workflow would produce. In this chapter, we make amends. The formula is simple:

- Introduce brilliant color, often to the point of absurdity.
- Figure out how to cut back to what looks good.
- Make any final changes to luminosity, such as setting highlight and shadow, or adjusting overall image weight.

The execution is even simpler. To save time, we reduce it to an action that takes care of all the tedious repetitive steps and leaves us with only a couple of things to do. It's called Color Boost, and is the first of many actions we'll be using. If you are working with the downloadable PPW panel, it's usually run in conjunction with an action to be shown in the next chapter. But the two can also run independently. In this chapter we'll take the easier path and assume that the Color Boost action, which is the simpler of the two, stands alone. I'll illustrate with one picture taken on an overcast day and only muted colors in the scene, then another taken in sunlight with vivid colors present. The book opened with a picture of Emerald Lake; these two come from the Emerald Isle.

I'll explain all the steps fully in the second example. For the first one it is enough to assume that when you play the action, a leprechaun inside your computer strokes your file with a shamrock and produces a layer with shimmering color.

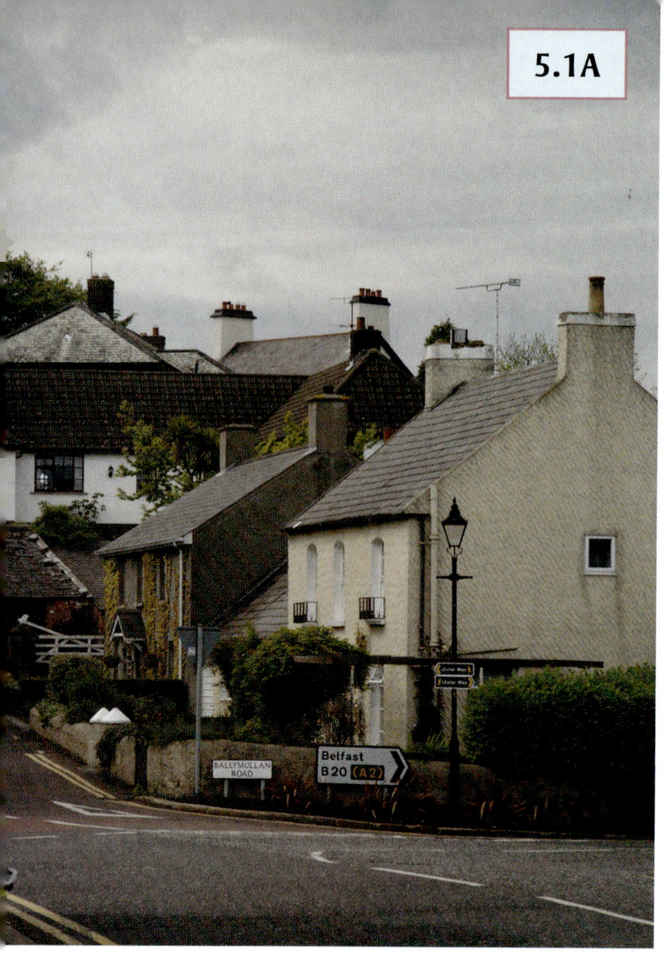
5.1A
BALLYMULLAN ROAD
Belfast
B20 (A2)

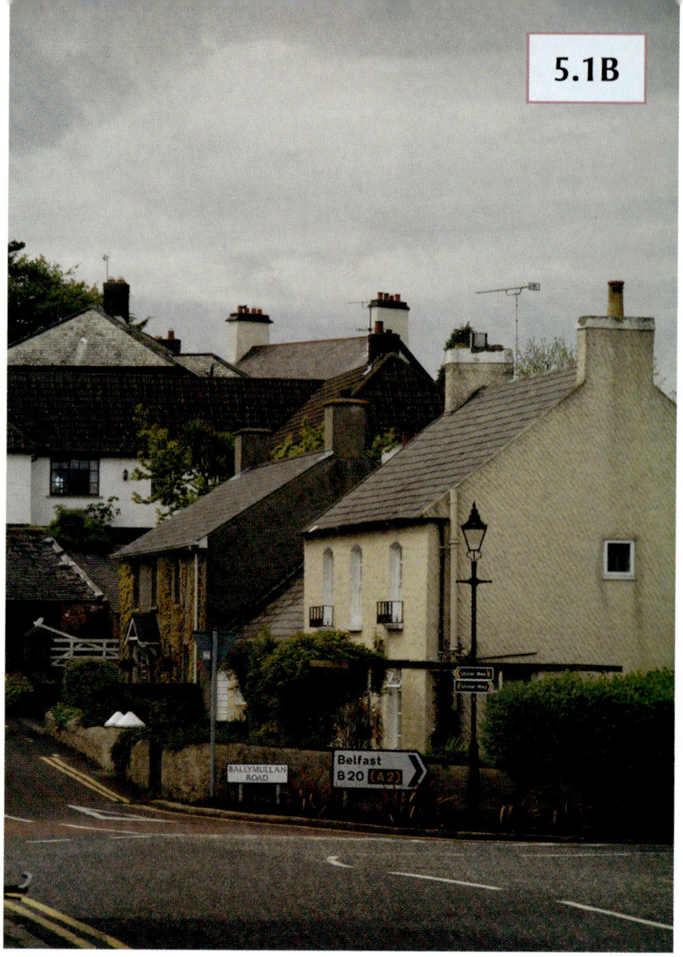
5.1B
BALLYMULLAN ROAD
Belfast
B20 (A2)

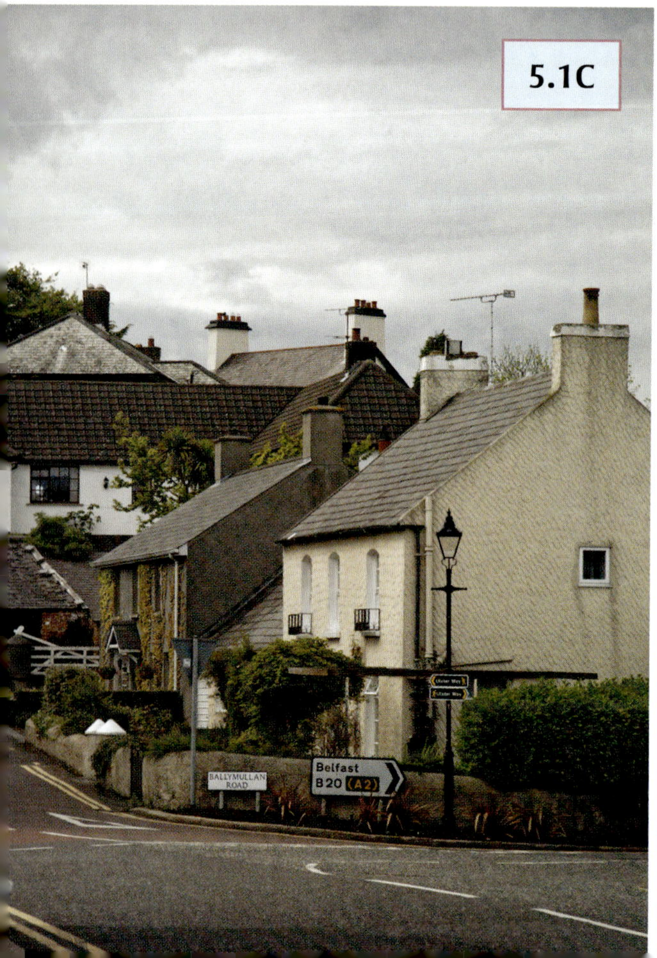
5.1C
BALLYMULLAN ROAD
Belfast
B20 (A2)

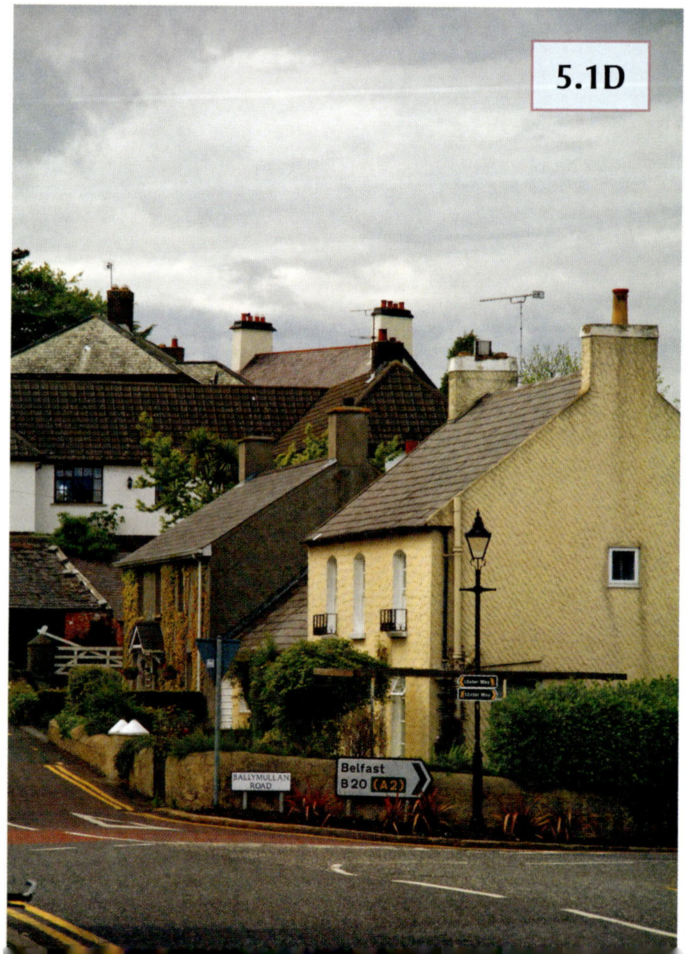
5.1D
BALLYMULLAN ROAD
Belfast
B20 (A2)

As Much Color As You Want

Chapter 3 says to look for known colors and adjust as necessary if they are wrong. Following this advice in the village scene of Figure 5.1A produces Figure 5.1B. The contrast-enhancing steps of Chapter 4 turn it into Figure 5.1C. Now we play the Color Boost action, and begorra, without further intervention, Figure 5.1D.

This scene is so bland that the action's default setting, which is very strong, actually gets us close to where we want to be. With more normal originals, it produces something distinctly too colorful. Usually, then, we'd reduce the layer's opacity. But it can also be increased. If there is any doubt that this method can produce wildly excessive color, Figure 5.1E, which doubles the effect by playing the action twice, ought to resolve it.

The rest is up to you. I'm sure you won't accept either Figure 5.1C or 5.1E, but rather will want something in between the two. The layer opacity slider lets you experiment.

Before making a final decision, however, a caution. Looking too hard at Figure 5.1E or its equivalent is pernicious. Next to something that colorful, *anything* looks tasteful. Just having it on the facing page is apt to make us think that Figure 5.1D is too bland.

On the monitor, the effect is even worse. This action is a color boost in the sense that Irish whiskey is a beverage—the statement is accurate but doesn't call attention to the kick. "Colors" too brilliant to be displayed on a monitor, let alone in print, arise frequently with this action. On screen, the reds in Figure 5.1E are like lasers. As Chapter 2 indicated, many of those starting out with this workflow choose their final percentage by toggling back and forth with an extremely colorful picture. Do that, and you're likely to be desensitized enough to approve something that tomorrow you will consider too loud. Instead, choose what you think looks good, then look away, or look at a different picture, and then come back and adjust your live file without further reference to anything more brilliant.

Why bother to have a ludicrously brilliant version at all, then? Wouldn't it be better to just try to cram color into the blander image until satisfied, as was done in the good old days?

No. The overkill version is useful because it highlights problems in a way that blander versions don't. As far as I'm concerned, all parts of Figure 5.1E are equally offensive, so a simple reduction of layer opacity works well. But more often, the added colors are

***Figure 5.1** Opposite, top left, the original. Top right, adjusted to remove a slight blue cast. Bottom left, the contrast of the color-corrected version is improved with blending and curves. Bottom right, the Color Boost action is played at default settings. This page, the color boost is doubled.*

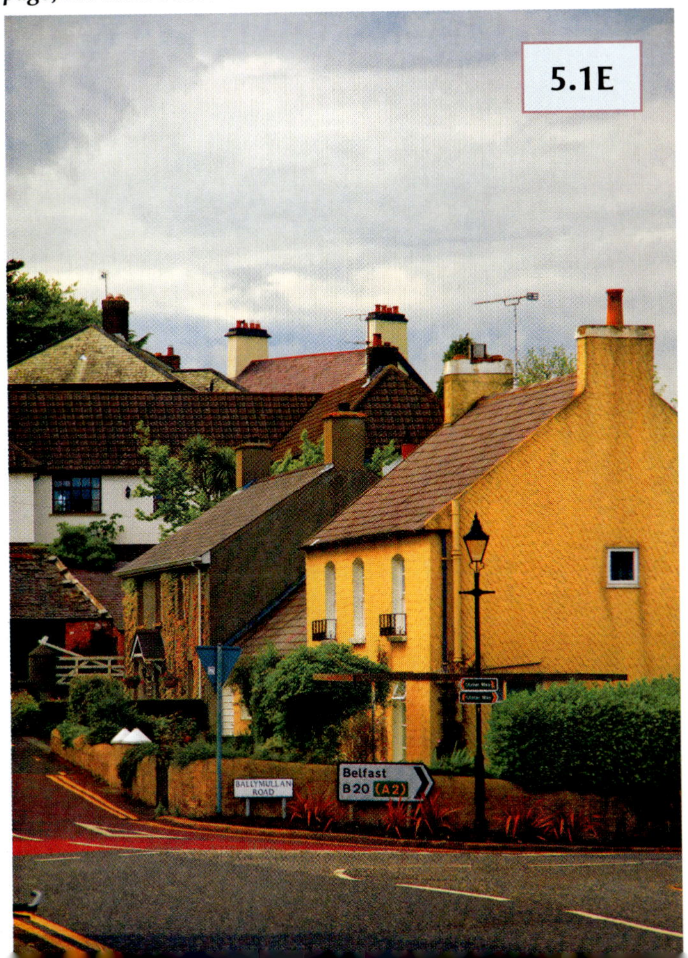

not equally bad, and in that case we choose an option that doesn't reduce them uniformly. I don't favor a really blue sky in this picture but some people probably do. If you want to tone down Figure 5.1E's sky less than the rest, that can be arranged. More on this later. But first, if you happen to have a glass of the aforementioned Irish whiskey handy, let's raise it to toast a disciplined workflow that depends on adjusting to the foibles of each picture. Then, we'll discuss how to manage this one.

- **Open and examine.** We are favored here with at least two objects known to be white, namely the lightest clouds and the road signs. The first reads as correctly neutral, the second starts out blue.
- **Locate the highlight.** No measurement is needed to see that the literally lightest object is in somebody's front yard to the left of the road signs. Unless you have a clue about what that thing is, and I don't, it can't be significant enough to worry about. Instead, choose the lightest cloud. It's not obvious where that is, so I'd go for the threshold adjustment layer trick described way back in Figure 3.13. It shows the lightest important area is slightly northeast of the leftmost chimney.

As you know, we can place up to four color sampler points to assist us when curving. I needed them all here: one for the highlight, one for a slightly darker cloud, one for the larger sign, and finally one for the road. That last is tricky: we don't know precisely what color the road should be, although it must be nearly gray. It cannot, however, be yellow, or even strongly warm. We have to watch out that this doesn't accidentally happen when we remove blueness from the sign.

- **Apply curves for color,** and set their layer mode to Color so that contrast doesn't change. So much for the first step. Figure 5.1A has become 5.1B.
- **Look for blending and curving opportunities to add contrast.** This picture has several possible solutions plus one trap lying in wait.

Skies are always best defined in the red channel. The same red is always weak in light yellowish browns,

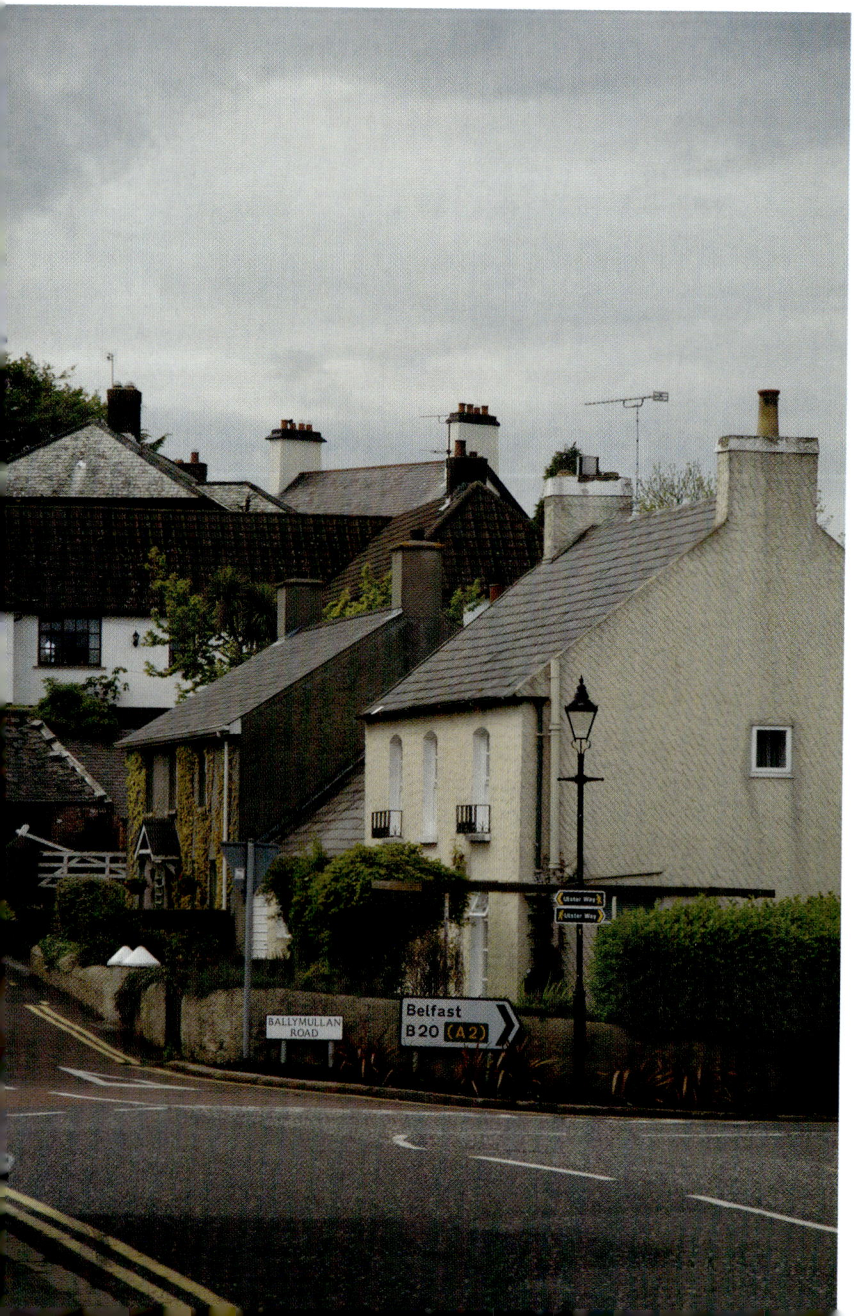

***Figure 5.2** The colors of the original photograph are bland, with a bluish cast.*

such as the foreground house. The red and green need to be lightened for the highlight in the clouds. When this happens, the house is apt to disappear in the red.

These common ailments are treated as follows: on a layer that will eventually be set to Luminosity mode, blend the red into the RGB, Darken mode. This darkens the sky a lot, the greenery a little, and the rest not at all.

Then, blend the blue into the red, Darken mode again, to strengthen the building without lightening the sky. Finally, apply straight-line curves to the red and green to lighten the clouds.

That last blend is a fine concept, but do you remember why it backfires here?

Light yellows like the foreground house present no problem. But if intense yellows are present, don't horse around with the blue channel. In such places it is much darker than the other two. The double lines in the road are bright yellow, as is part of the sign.

Blending the blue into the red will turn those objects dark brown, Luminosity mode notwithstanding. It is therefore better to substitute a blend from the green into the red. After that blend and subsequent curves, we have Figure 5.1C.

- **Apply the Color Boost action** (Figure 5.1D) and decide how to cut back the color. As discussed, I made only a small adjustment to the opacity of the Color Boost layer.
- **Adjust the endpoints** if needed. A proper highlight, or light point, is essential to quality reproduction. Traditional workflows, comprehending this, set it right away. The PPW dawdles, but the time has now come. Recall that right at the start I put a color sampler point in the lightest clouds. Now it needs to be checked. Usually the luminosity moves get it pretty close to where it's supposed to be, as they do here. Figure 5.2 repeats the original for ease of comparison; Postcard 5.3 is the final. Can you see that its clouds are slightly lighter than in Figure 5.1D?

Two steps came between what's described above and the final result—steps not specific to the PPW.

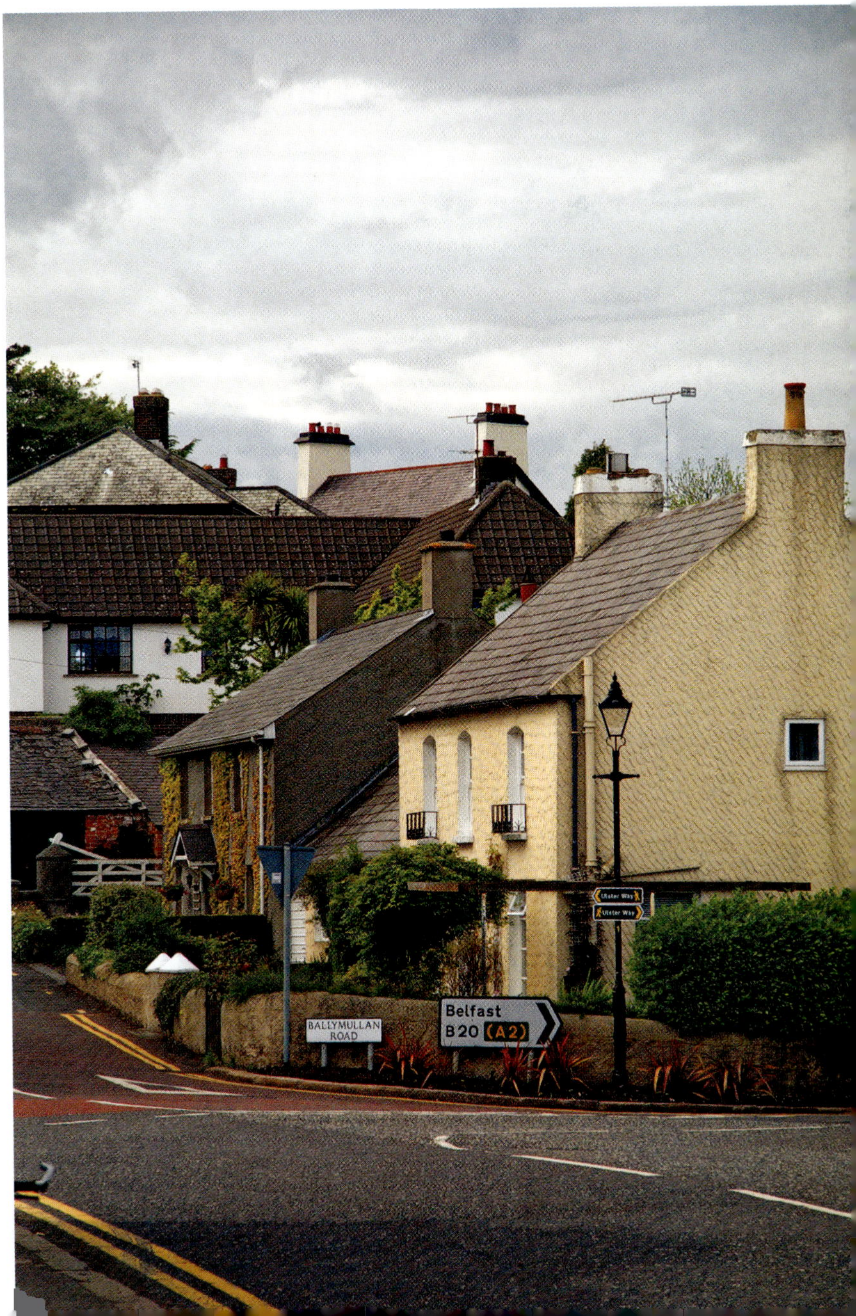

***Postcard 5.3** The final version is substantially more colorful—and it could have been made even more so.*

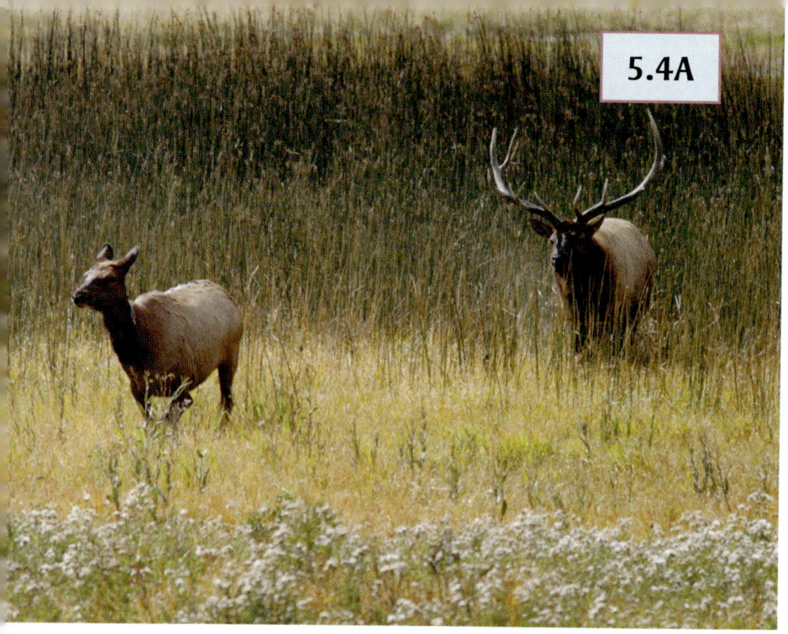

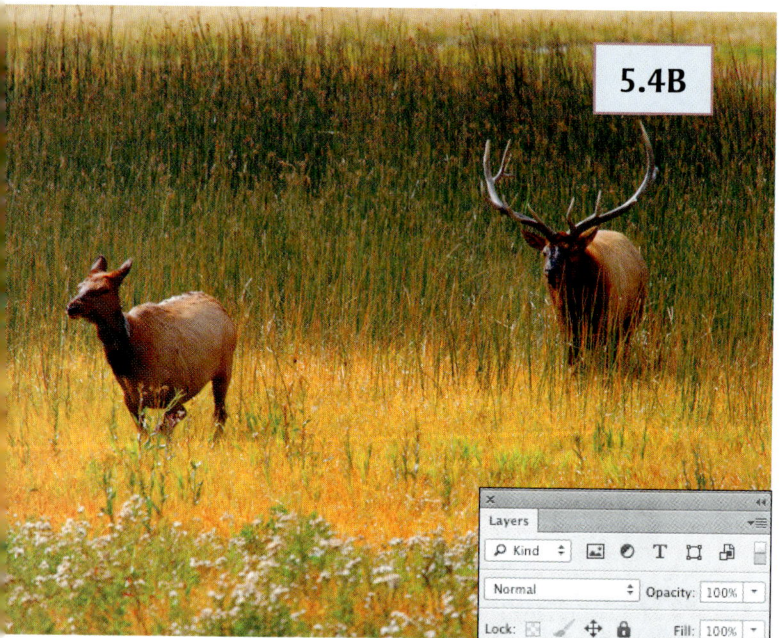

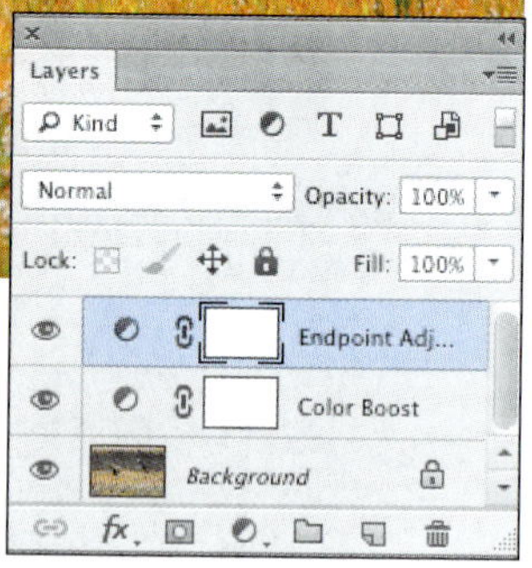

Figure 5.4 Top, the original. Bottom, the action uses the curves below on the Color Boost layer. The Endpoint Adjustment layer's default curves don't change anything.

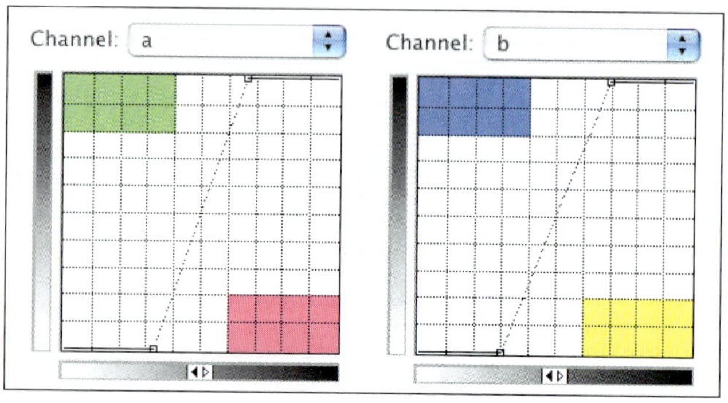

- **Sharpening.** Almost all images benefit from some kind of sharpening. Everybody has different opinions of how best to do it. Mine appear in Chapter 15, but there is no reason not to use your own if you prefer.
- **Prepare for output.** This chapter will leave us in the LAB colorspace. When finished, presumably we will have to either return to RGB or move on to CMYK, as I had to for this book.

Of all these steps, you will probably agree that the quickest and easiest was the one that's the subject of this chapter. This correction took maybe two and a half minutes from start to finish. The opening color curves were more difficult than usual, so allot more than a minute for them. The luminosity step is also about a minute. But this last color boost should take five seconds.

It takes longer if you decide to cut back on color more selectively, often with layer masks. We will now explore what they are, and what goes on behind the scenes in the Color Boost action.

The Color Boost Action at Work

If you aren't familiar with how to write actions, it's worth a look. I will kill two birds with one stone by having you rewrite the Color Boost action, thus saving me the trouble of having to explain what's in it. A reminder: this action is supplied, so the following exercise is for practice only. To get started, a file must be open.

- **Window: Actions** to bring up the Actions palette. In its flyout, choose New Action. You will be prompted for a name and asked in which action set to put it. If you want a new action set, that's in the flyout, too. Anyway, when finished, click Record. Photoshop will now keep track of all your steps.
- **Image: Mode>Lab color.** LAB is the favored way to enhance color, usually producing a more attractive result than RGB.

- **Add a curves adjustment layer** and name it Color Boost. Apply the curves shown to the A and B channels. Note: if this were being done for real, you would have to be very, very careful with this step. Any imperfection will ruin the action. Fortunately the curves in the supplied action have been properly tested!
- **Change layer opacity to 75%**, more than enough for the average picture.
- **Add a second curves adjustment layer** and name it Endpoint Adjustment. When the curves dialog opens, just click OK. Thus, for the time being, this layer does nothing.
- **Click back into the Color Boost layer** to make it the active one.
- **Click the square Stop playing/recording** icon at the bottom of the Actions palette.

And you're done. These steps can now be repeated automatically on other files. Just highlight your action, and click the triangular Play Selection icon.

* * *

The following example shows what layer masking is all about. Please assume that somebody has given you a copy of the Color Boost action, which you propose to test. You don't get a guinea pig, but rather the pair of elk in Figure 5.4A. You play the action, getting Figure 5.4B for your pains.

LAB, like the PPW itself, keeps color and contrast separate. You were introduced to LAB's strange numbering system back in Chapter 3. A brief review won't hurt.

The A and B are opponent-color channels containing no information about lightness. Where the A is light, it contributes magenta, where dark, green. If the A is a 50% gray it contributes no color. The further away from 50% gray, the more intense the color. So, the strongly magenta flowers back in Figure 4.2 were very light in the A. The elk in Figure 5.4A are somewhat light, because they are only slightly more magenta than green. And the fields are somewhat darker than 50%, being a bit more green than magenta.

The B is the same idea. Light parts of the channel represent yellow, dark ones blue. 50% gray is neither. All of Figure 5.4A is lighter than 50% gray in the B because every part of the picture is more yellow than it is blue.

As you recall, the numbering system uses a zero rather than the awkward *50% gray.*

Chapter Goals and Recap

This chapter boosts color. Also, there is a final opportunity to adjust contrast, if needed.

The method applies an action intended to produce excessive color. We then make an intelligent decision on how to cut back. We can simply reduce the opacity of the Color Boost layer, or load a layer mask.

How Difficult Is It? Easy, because the decision is one of personal taste. The first half of the chapter shows only two ways to reduce the color. It gets modestly more complex in the second half as we consider obscure possibilities for the layer mask.

How Often Is It Needed? In this workflow almost every image needs some kind of color boost. A second layer that finalizes contrast is often used to adjust endpoints, but not on every file.

Note: experienced PPW panel users prefer Color Boost as a combined action that adds the Modern Man from Mars method shown in the next chapter. However, each action can also play individually.

The PPW Takes Shape

COLOR

- Kill incorrect color with RGB curves (Chapter 3).
- Identify highlight (Chapters 3–4).

CONTRAST

- Channel blending on luminosity layer (Chapter 4).
- Contrast-enhancing curves (Chapter 4).

COLOR AGAIN

- Apply Color Boost (this chapter).
- Finalize contrast, including endpoints.
- Reduce color by masking or opacity adjustment.

SHARPEN

FINALIZE

- Consider blend with another version (Chapter 2).
- Convert to final output space, if needed.

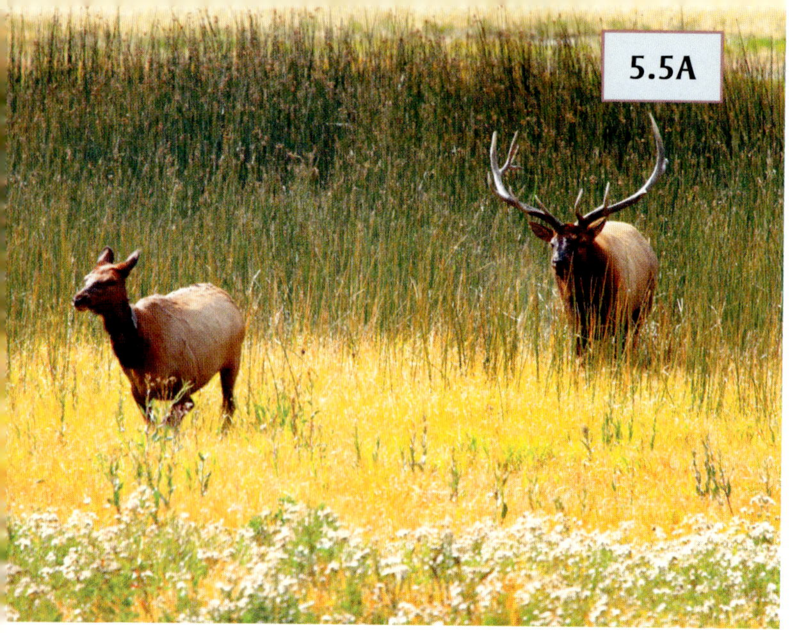

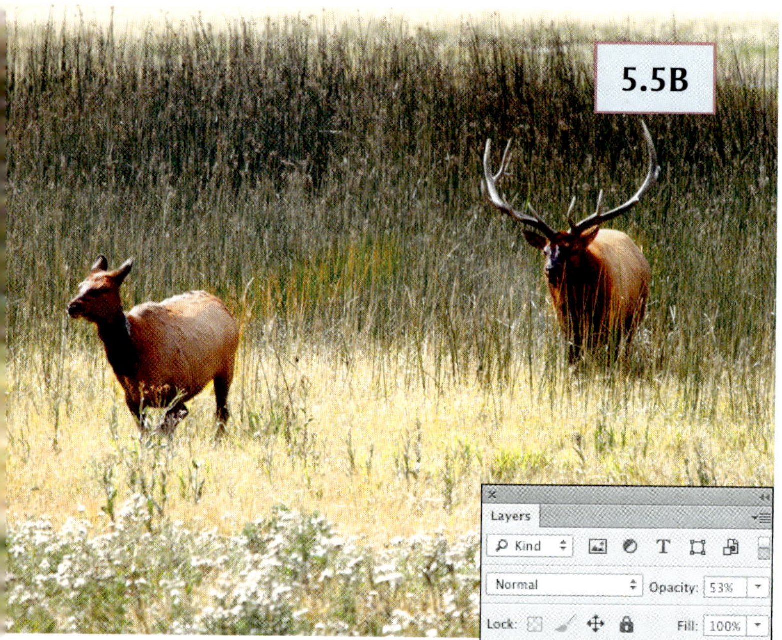

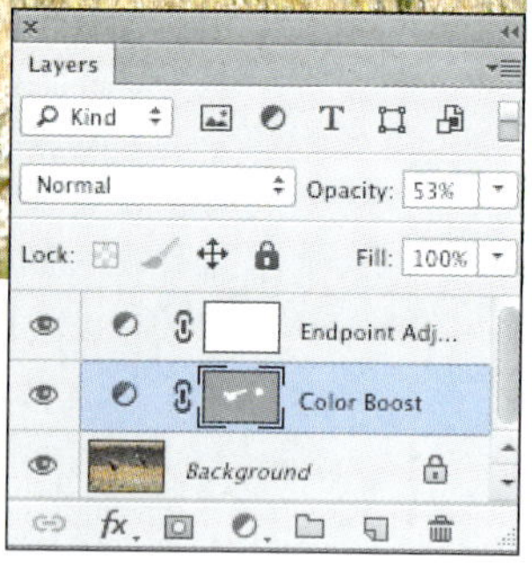

***Figure 5.5** Top, the first curve below is applied to the L. Bottom, the layer mask is inverted and the elk painted in. The second curve is then applied to the layer mask.*

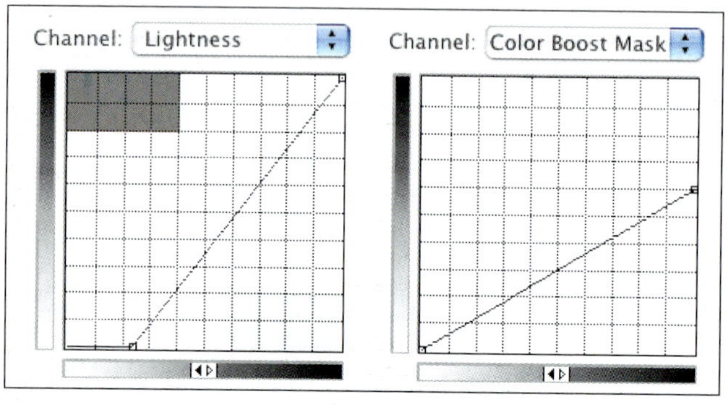

So, something perfectly neutral is 0^A0^B. Positive AB numbers represent the warm colors, magenta and yellow; negatives the cooler green and blue.

The curves of Figure 5.4 work because they pass directly through the center (zero) point, meaning that anything neutral stays that way. Meanwhile, everything else gets more intense, but the way LAB works emphasizes objects that already have pronounced color.

In the current picture, this means that the yellow ground cover changes more than the animals do. The general rule that more colorful things should intensify faster is a good one, but perhaps not in this image. Suppose, therefore, that we want the elk to gain color faster than the rest. In other words, we are not satisfied with simply reducing the opacity of the Color Boost layer.

Note the two different angles of the curves in Figure 5.4. This contradicts my 2005 book *Photoshop LAB Color,* which recommended equality. I have recanted, and now believe that the A curve needs to be steeper. The PPW panel reflects my current bias. You can override this preference for a single file, or permanently.

Painting the Color In

The L channel, which we haven't yet discussed, is much more intuitive than the AB. Think of it as a black and white. It's actually slightly lighter than a default grayscale conversion, but that should be inconsequential. If you want to see the difference, such as it is, turn back to Figures 4.21A and 4.21B.

The action's Endpoint Adjustment layer is reserved for maneuvers with the L. Usually it's just a matter of adjusting the light and dark points, if needed. The overall contrast should already be pretty good, thanks to the luminosity steps advocated in Chapter 4.

This time, however, those steps were never taken, because for purposes of demonstration we said this one was going to start and finish with the Color Boost action. Proper light and dark points happen to be present, but the overall impression seems too heavy to me.

Accordingly, I click into the top layer, and apply the lightening curve shown below Figure 5.5. (Remember, all curves throughout this book show lightness to the left, darkness to the right.) The result is Figure 5.5A.

Since the color is obviously excessive, why not just reduce the opacity of the Color Boost layer?

For one thing, we wouldn't know what to reduce it to. We might come up with something that looked good while the picture was dark and not so good afterward, and then we'd have to change it again.

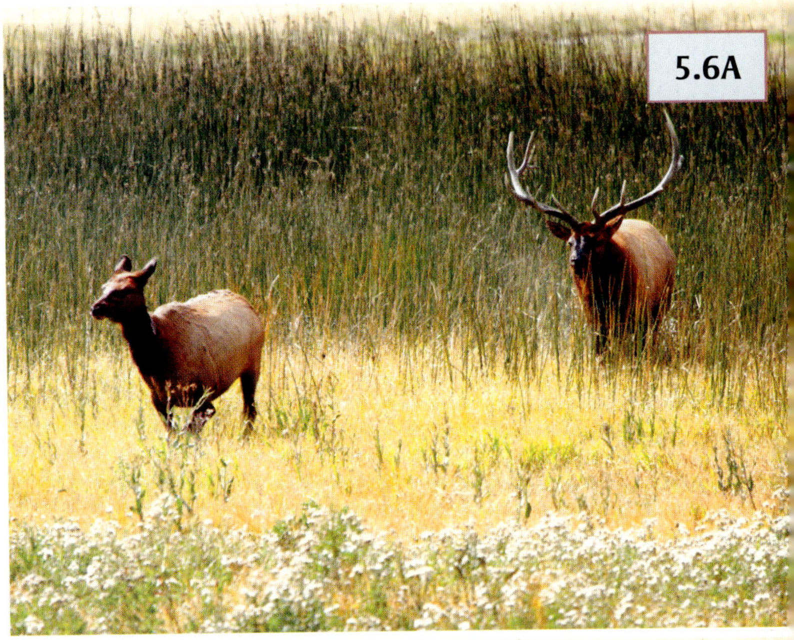

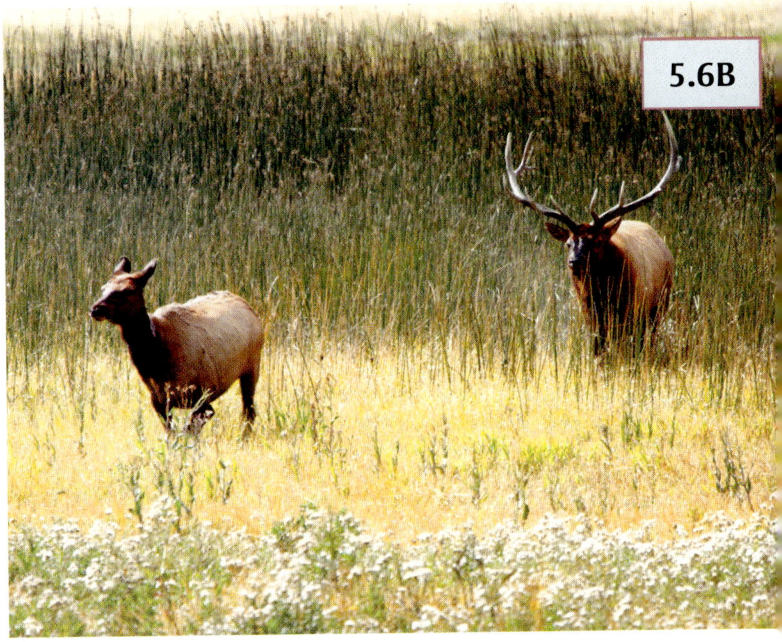

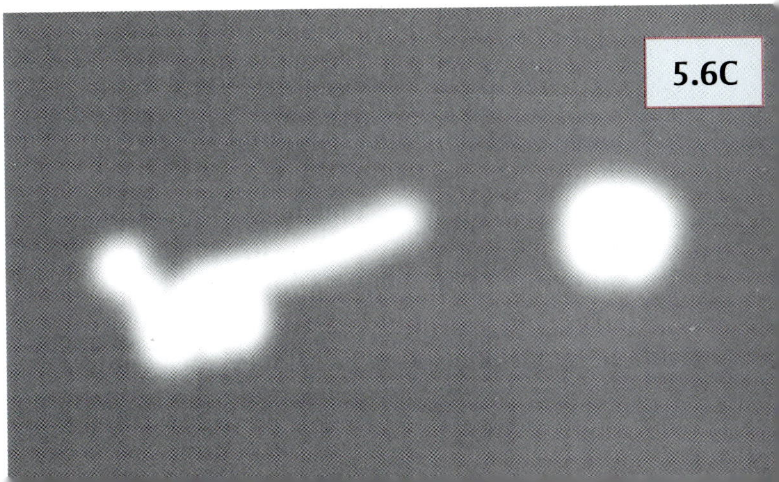

***Figure 5.6** Top, the second curve shown in Figure 5.5 is applied to lighten the layer mask, thus adding color to the background. Middle, layer opacity is reduced. Bottom, the final layer mask. Note the intentional "error" of having the light part of the mask extend into the background behind the female. Below: a more interactive way to lighten the mask: the Properties panel.*

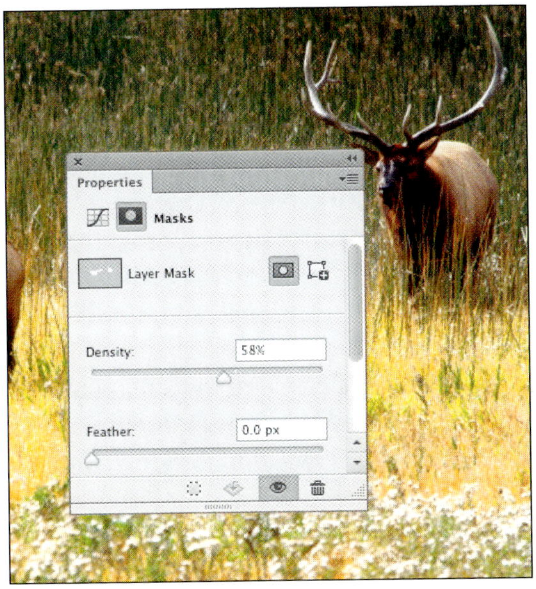

Actions and Automation

The PPW largely consists of steps repeated in image after image. You would not guess this from the last two chapters, both of which promoted methods that depend too much on the character of the challenge for them to be automated.

The steps in this chapter, on the other hand, will be applied to virtually every image we work on from now until the end of time. That is an awful lot of repetition. To prevent death by ennui, we automate. A brief review of what actions are and how to deploy them is therefore in order.

Almost any series of steps can be recorded as an action and then played with a single click. The actions live in action sets, which in turn reside in Photoshop's Actions palette. Editing the actions and/or moving them into different sets isn't difficult. You can record your own, or download the fourteen PPW actions. They can be as simple as opening a command and clicking OK (two steps, as in Chapter 7) or as complex as the one in Chapter 15, which involves some 110 steps.

Those who process large volumes of similar pictures, especially if speed trumps quality, use actions to create droplets—hot folders upon which scads of images can be dropped for processing during the dinner hour.

Scrolling through a bloated Actions palette to find the right one to click gets old rapidly. Adobe's free Configurator module lets us construct panels with buttons for frequently used actions and commands. It can also be scripted to do much more. An action doesn't add functionality by itself—it just speeds up the process. But with scripting, which must be done outside of Photoshop proper, all kinds of conditions can be added.

The free downloadable PPW panel installs all the actions automatically, and adds extensive documentation of each, accessible from within the panel itself. It needs no copy of Configurator, but runs only in Photoshop CS5 or later. Its extensive scripting adds great functionality. For example, it sees all actions as single history states that can easily be reversed, and it allows previewing different ways of applying the actions.

Automation is not a substitute for thinking, and actions are no substitute for analysis. But if you like the results that the PPW gets, it doesn't take much thinking or analyzing to conclude that automation has an important place in producing them.

But the main reason is that the next move is easier if we have blinding color to look at.

Adjustment layers, of which there are two in this document, carry layer masks by default. You can see their icons in the Layers palette of Figure 5.4, to the right of the curves icons. The blue highlighting shows that the Color Boost layer is active. And within the layer, the border around the layer mask icon indicates that *it* is active.

A layer mask can be understood as a window through which its layer is projected on whatever is underneath. If the window is clean—blank—we see the layer in its entirety. If it's dirty, we see a combination, and the dirtier the window gets, the less important the top layer becomes.

We could, for example, halve the boost by filling the layer mask with 50% gray. That would be stupid, as lowering layer opacity to 50% would do the same thing in less time.

Instead, we use the layer mask to massage certain areas. Here, we want it light for the animals, but dark elsewhere.

We have just produced Figure 5.5A. The Endpoint Adjustment layer is active.

- **Click back into the Color Boost layer.** Make sure that the layer mask icon is bordered, indicating that it's active and that whatever you're about to do will alter the mask and not the image proper.
- **Image: Adjustments>Invert** turns the layer mask black, which has the same effect as reducing layer opacity to 0%.
- **Set foreground color to white,** if necessary, at the bottom of the Toolbox. You can also type *dx*. The keyboard shortcut *d* changes the *background* color to white. *x* exchanges foreground and background colors.
- **Activate the paintbrush tool.** Choose a soft-edged brush of convenient size. In the Options bar, verify that Mode=Normal, Opacity=100%.
- **Quickly paint over the two animals.** Figure 5.5B's elk are the same as in Figure 5.5A,

because the layer mask has been painted white, allowing the color boost to take effect. Everything else is the original color, since the layer mask is black.

This is incredibly sloppy. Why don't you make a nice selection of the elk with the pen tool, like a normal retoucher would?

Doing it that way would take several minutes. Doing it as I did took several seconds. The point about sloppiness is correct; in fact it's emphasized with a deliberate error. Right behind the female, I've painted quite a ways into the background. The area of "error" is almost as large as the animal herself, and is evident in Figure 5.5B, even if you couldn't see the mask itself in Figure 5.6C.

It looks like these animals were cut out of some other picture and pasted into this one.

So it does. Temporarily. On the other hand, mistakes that are obvious here may be overlooked later. To continue:

- **Lighten the layer mask** with the second curve of Figure 5.5 or something similar. As long as the layer mask is active, curves work on it only and don't affect the base image. The white parts of this mask can't be lightened further. The curves turn the rest of the mask into a dark gray rather than a black. Figure 5.5B allowed nothing in the background and everything in the animals. Figure 5.6A allows some of the color boost to apply to the background as well.

If you need a more interactive way to lighten the mask, choose Window: Properties (Photoshop CS6) or Window: Masks (CS4/CS5; not available in earlier versions) to bring up the dialog shown in Figure 5.6. Adjusting the Density slider has the same impact of lightening the dark parts of the mask, and can be changed later if you like.

- **Reduce layer opacity to taste.** To get to Figure 5.6B, I chose 53%. The point of the layer mask, shown in Figure 5.6C, is now apparent. Without it, we'd be reducing the opacity of Figure 5.5A overall. Its yellows are so distracting that we would need a much lower opacity. The animals would return to their previous dull state.

The opacity doesn't have to be reduced so much because the layer mask is keeping most of the attention on the animals.

And one last point. The appalling "error" in Figure 5.5B, where my selection went well into the background behind the female, was never corrected. It's barely visible in Figure 5.6B. The question is, if you didn't know it was there, would you notice it?

The One-Minute Workflow

In moving from the original, Figure 5.4A, to Figure 5.6B, we bypassed the normal first two PPW steps—the initial correction for color and the luminosity layer. Consequently the whole procedure took less than a minute.

For a one-minute correction this isn't too bad. In fact, it's the answer for those unfortunates who don't have the three to five minutes per image that the rest of the book assumes. If you must average a minute apiece, then we've just seen a potential workflow. Open the file, apply the Color Boost action, adjust for color, adjust for contrast, save. Here's a better one: read the next chapter, and adopt the combined MMM + Color Boost action that it advocates. It won't add much time.

What's the price for passing up the other steps? That, of course, depends on the picture. If the original has a color problem, you may be out of luck. Most don't. This elk image doesn't. The color in Figure 5.4A may be bland but it isn't wrong.

The impact of skipping the luminosity move will range from enormous in something like the Grand Canyon of Postcard 4.1 to nil in basically neutral images like the New York Stock Exchange of Figure 4.25. The elk exercise falls in between. A pass of curves and blending in luminosity mode would have produced a snappier image. But if time is at a premium, one can live without it. For further

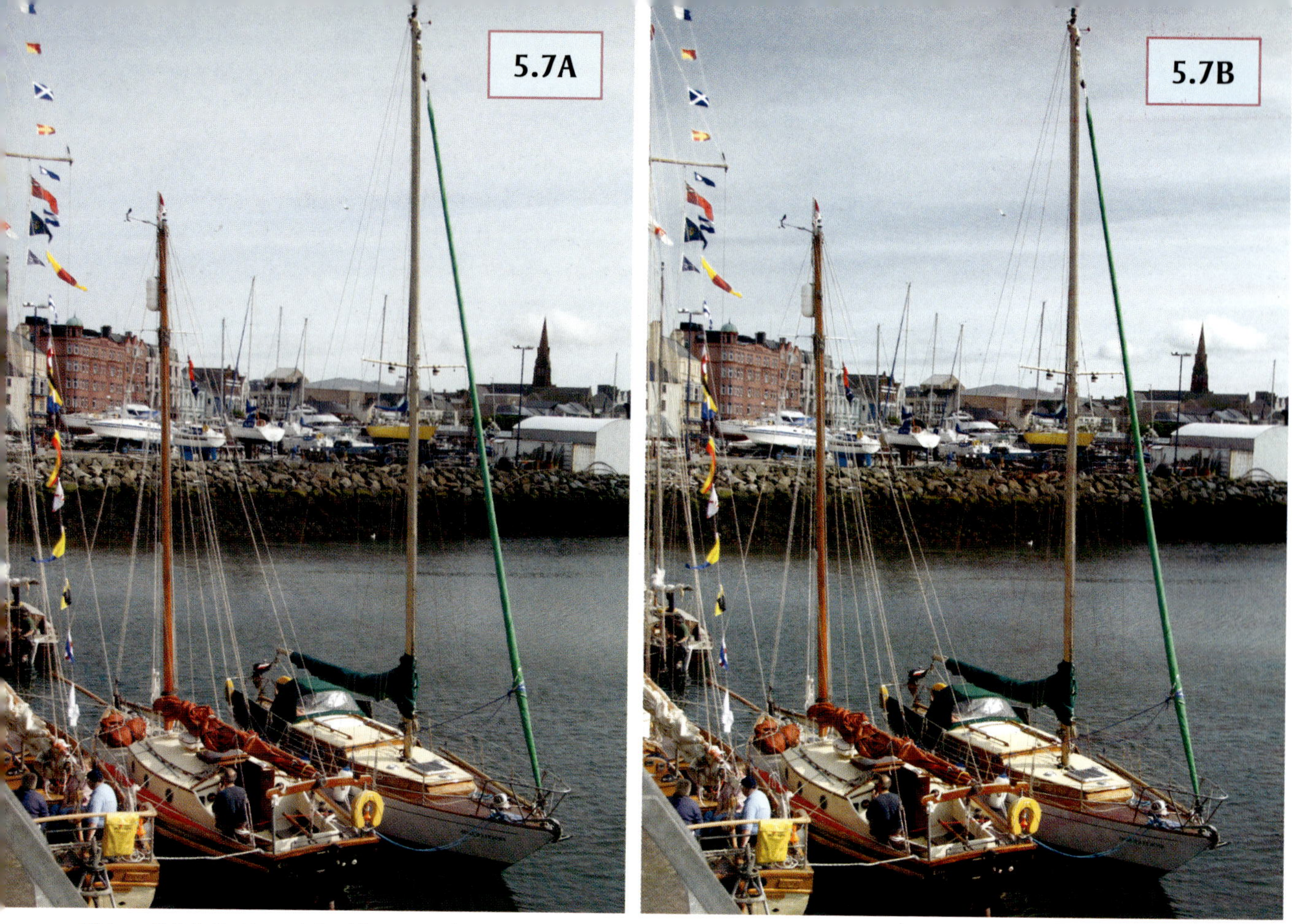

Figure 5.7 *Left, the original has no color issues. Right, luminosity blends and curves add depth to the sky.*

discussion, refer back to Figure 1.9, where a simplified correction of the Emerald Lake picture of that chapter is compared to ones using the full workflow.

In each image from now on, we expect to confront the equivalent of Figures 5.1E or 5.5A: something wildly colorful. We've just seen a good example of why it's helpful. In the elk image, can anyone really look at the bland original and tell that the most offensive colors are going to be the yellows?

Anyway, we've got the grossly colorful version. The mission now is to decide what is the ugliest part, and find a way to tone it down more than the others. If nothing stands out, we reduce color uniformly by reducing opacity. Painting a layer mask, as in the elk exercise, can work once in a while but should not be the first line of defense.

Suppose that somebody forces you to make a choice sight unseen. That is, you will apply Color Boost to the next image, and must specify how you will reduce its impact without seeing the picture. You might think that reducing the opacity is the default answer. It's not. I choose a straight opacity reduction only about a third of the time.

The added color is likely more objectionable in darker areas than in lighter ones. If so, we need to create a layer mask that is dark where the picture itself is. While several options suggest themselves, since the action takes place in LAB, the fastest is to use a copy of the L channel as the layer mask. To do this, activate the mask, and Image: Apply Image, choosing Lightness (or Lab; the two are the same in this context) as Source.

It may not always be the perfect solution, but it's a good one. If you want to read about more esoteric methods, the second half of the chapter awaits. But if you're just trying to get a hang of how all this works, and are dreading the introduction of even more tools in subsequent chapters, then you've learned enough options to do a very creditable job with this step right now. If you are planning to just graft this color boost onto an existing workflow without doing the Chapter 4 luminosity stuff, you may need a strong L curve like the one shown in Figure 5.5. But if you have tried to improve luminosity previously, the L adjustments should be simple.

And speaking of simple, it's now time to summarize what this chapter would have you do, assuming that you've followed the procedures of Chapters 3 and 4 to get here.

- **Play the Color Boost action.**
- **Decide whether to load the L as a layer mask.** Either way, jiggle the opacity to taste.
- **Adjust the endpoints,** if needed.

It's hard to get simpler than that. Now, back to Northern Ireland for a final example.

The Highlight Adjustment

Figure 5.7A emerges from the raw module in good shape. The day may not have been terrific, but it wasn't overcast either. The tonal range seems acceptable. The overall color is probably pretty accurate, albeit not suitable for a postcard.

- **The initial examination** finds nothing obviously wrong. The objects known to be white, such as the lightest cloud, are correct. So, no immediate color move.
- **Finding the highlight** doesn't require a threshold layer. It's obviously the cloud at lower right. There are lighter objects in various places but none of them are important and I do not care if they blow out. So, a

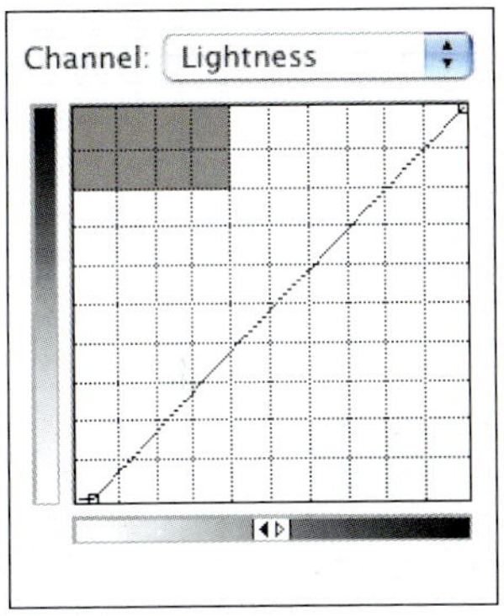

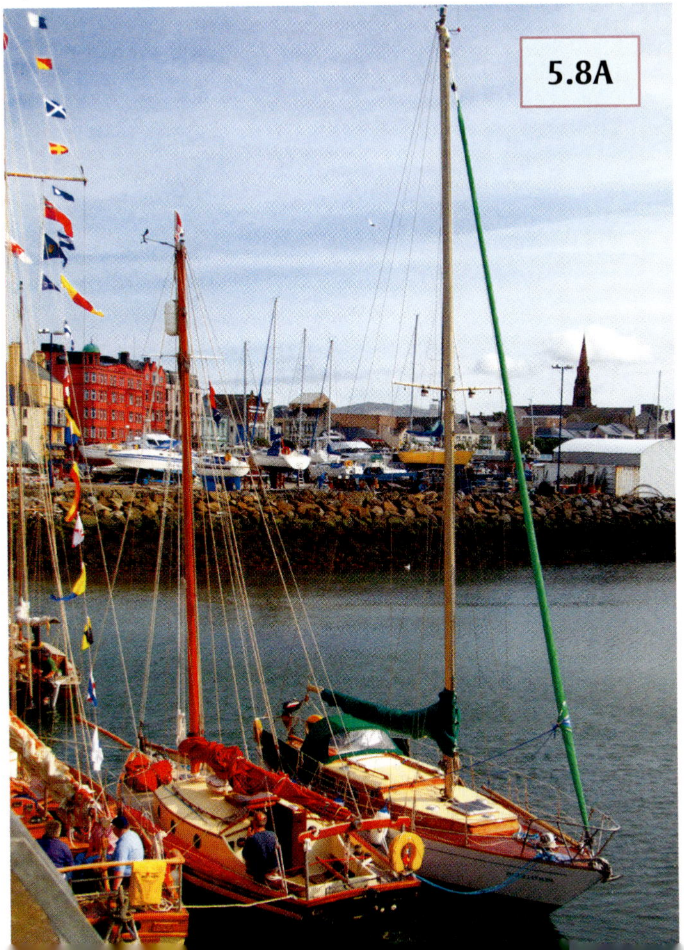

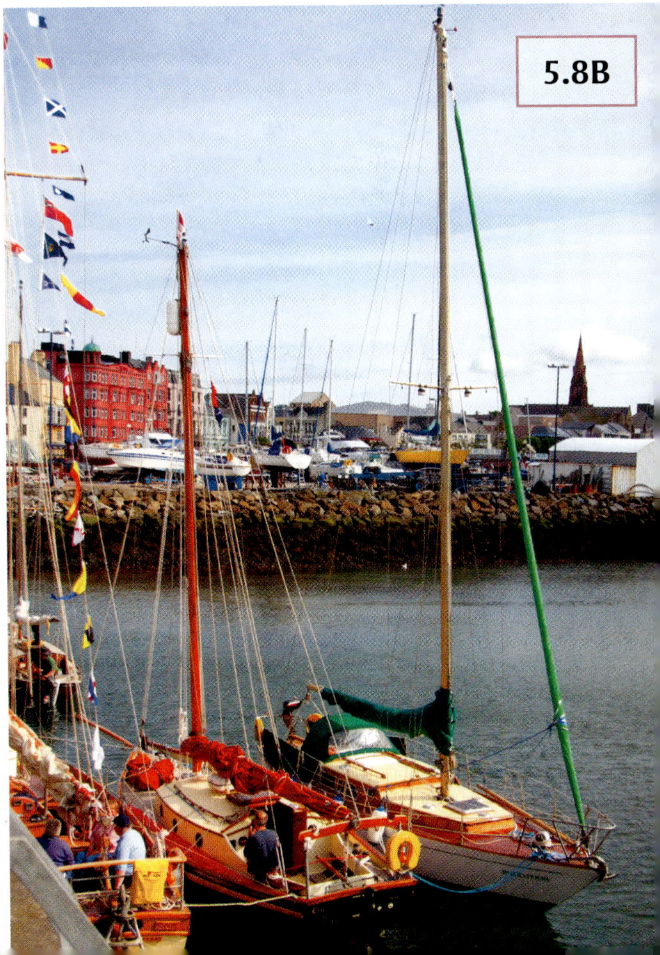

***Figure 5.8** Left, the Color Boost action is played on Figure 5.7B. Right, the curve shown adjusts the highlight.*

color sampler point is clicked into the cloud, for permanent placement in the Info palette.

- **The luminosity maneuvering** is nothing worth discussing. Figure 5.7B is not an impressive result, but it has a better sky, and more highlight detail.
- **Play the action**. The result can't be printed accurately because so much of it falls outside the CMYK gamut, but Figure 5.8A gives an idea.
- **Layer mask, or no?** Would you say that all colors are equally offensive here, or are the darker ones worse?

According to me, the latter. I have no issues with the bluer sky or the yellows, and am not terribly upset with the green. The red building on the shore is probably brick and if so it's way out of whack. The red rigging and mast have gone overboard, as it were.

If I'm right, we should load the L as a layer mask. We'll test that against two other approaches. Meanwhile, we'll move on to finalizing the highlight, using the Endpoint Adjustment layer.

In the LAB numbering system, the L has a hundred-point scale. 0^L is absolutely black and 100^L absolutely white. Some beta readers point out that the foregoing statement is imprecise because LAB can specify imaginary colors that are just as light as white or as dark as black. If I were you, I would lose no sleep over this. Instead, remember to use these absolutes only when you absolutely do not care about the objects they pertain to. I previously decided that the lightest object I do care about is the cloud in the lower right of the sky. That point should be set to 99^L. Not 100^L, which would leave the spot blank.

Similarly, we always look for a significant dark point (the *shadow*). It should be set to 5^L or darker, unless you're planning to take the file into CMYK (see box, this page).

The sampler points in the Info palette are reported in the current colorspace unless you have mandated otherwise. In Figure 5.7B, which was in RGB before being converted to CMYK for printing, the chosen highlight point read $246^R242^G242^B$. On conversion to LAB it read $96^L1^A1^B$.

When CMYK Is the Destination

LAB's amazing affinity for intensifying color comes at a price. It can create colors that are unprintably vivid, or that can't be displayed correctly even by today's best monitors.

If the final goal is an RGB file, this is not such a big deal. A monitor's gamut is not the same as that of a printer that requires RGB input, but it isn't all that different either. If the LAB file calls for colors too intense for either, what you see on the screen may not match the LAB values but it could be close to what a good inkjet printer might get.

When talking about offset printing, however, big differences are possible. Monitors can display a slew of colors that a commercial printer has no chance of matching. When this occurs, the solution is not to try to pump more and more color into the LAB file. Instead, don't ask for the impossible. Tone down the color boost until the file is limited to things that CMYK can reproduce.

The easiest way to approximate how CMYK will react to an LAB file is to View: Proof Colors. It's not perfect, but if your Color Settings are correct, it gives a reasonable idea of what will happen on press.

Colors that won't convert well into CMYK fall into three broad categories. First, mostly due to lousy cyan inks, brilliant blues are impossible. Second, pastels—light, but very pure colors—can't be duplicated unless the paper is a brilliant white. Third, vivid colors that are also dark often can't be achieved. The common example in outdoor scenery comes in darker trees. The monitor can display an intense dark green that a press can't match.

In exchange for these defects, CMYK offers the advantage of having all deep shadow information isolated in its black channel. Manipulating it to enhance shadow detail is more effective than any corresponding move in LAB or RGB.

For this reason, if the shadow value is too light when you play the Color Boost action, don't try to fix it if your final destination is CMYK. Instead, after the conversion, darken the black.

The color is just slightly to the warm side of neutral, which is fine—we should be more upset if it were to the cool side. 96^L is quite close to what's wanted for highlight. To finalize it requires only the slight curve shown, which converts Figure 5.8A into 5.8B. Do you see the difference?

Was It Worth It?

So much for the Endpoint Adjustment layer. We now click back into the Color Boost layer. The layer mask icon must be shown as active, as in the Layers palette of Figure 5.5.

Image: Apply Image. The layer mask, being active, is the target. The source should be Layer=Merged, Channel=Lab (or Lightness), Mode=Normal, Opacity=100%.

Let's now compare three ways of correcting this

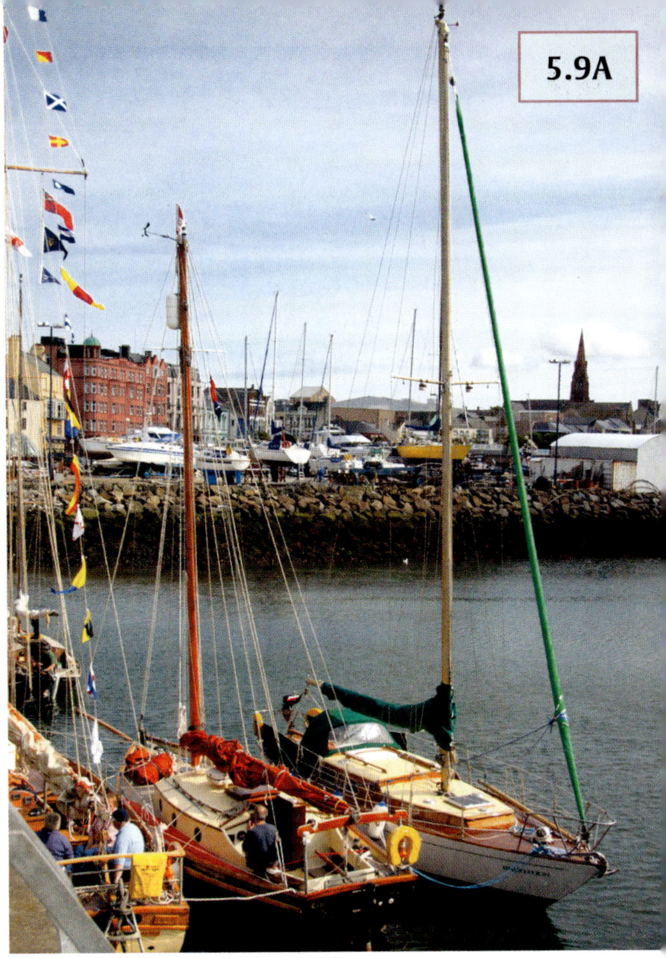

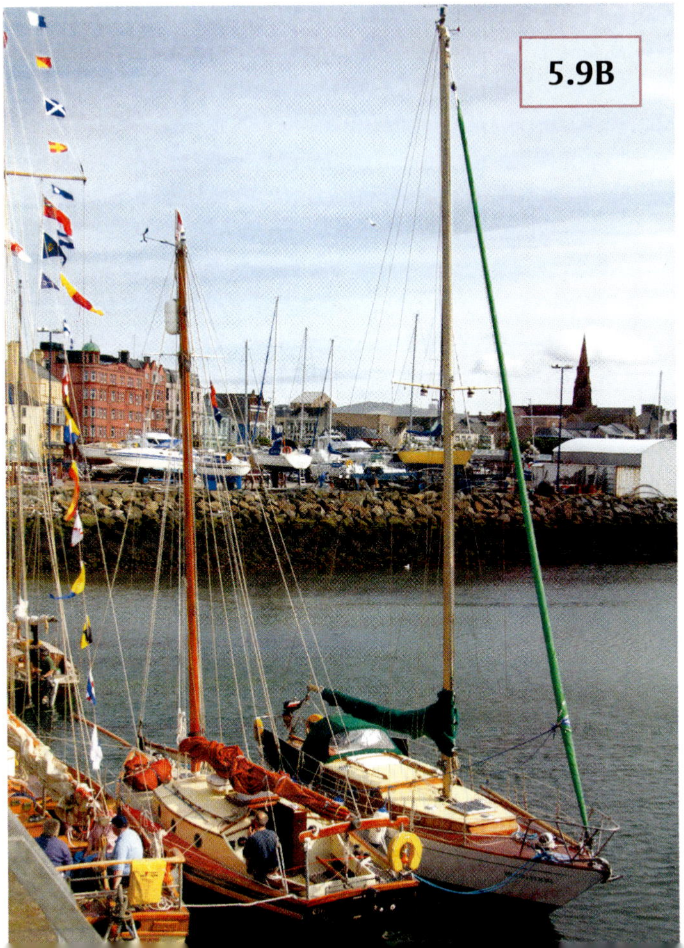

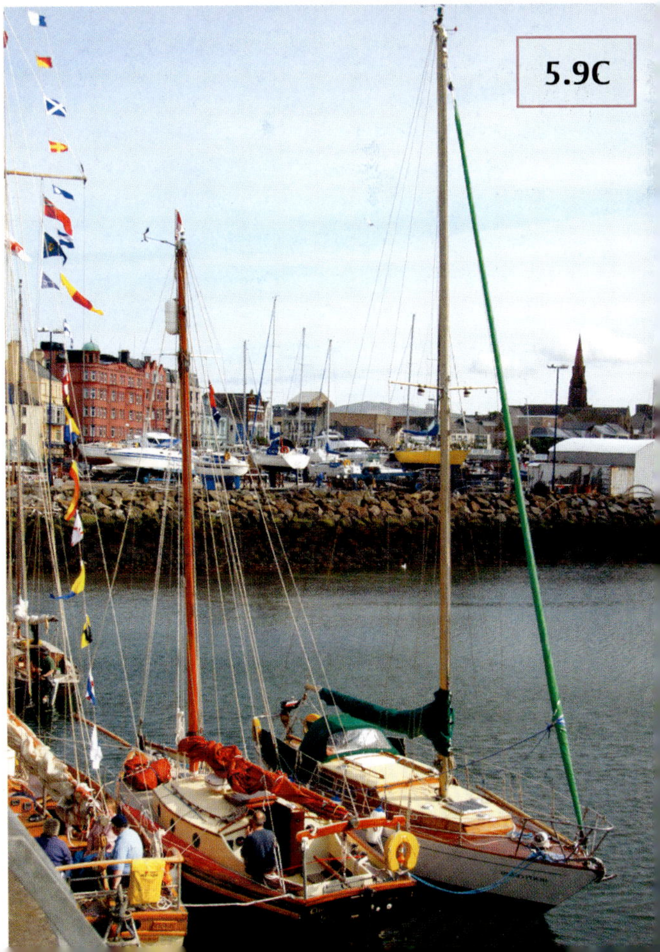

Figure 5.9 *Left, Top, starting with Figure 5.8B, the L channel is applied as a layer mask to the Color Boost layer, and opacity is increased to 83%. Bottom left, the layer mask is discarded and layer opacity reduced to 45%. Bottom right, a version prepared without the use of the luminosity-corrected Figure 5.7B.*

picture. It's hard to make the competition a fair one because the two likely methods require different opacities, but you should get the idea.

Masking the Color Boost layer tones down the color, just as lowering opacity does. In fact, if you load a mask you may need to *increase* opacity from the default 75%.

Figure 5.9A is Figure 5.8B, plus the layer mask and layer opacity increased to 83%. Its principal opponent is Figure 5.9B, which has no layer mask. Trying to match the reds between the two, I lowered its opacity to 45%.

Figure 5.9A, then, emphasizes lighter colors more. Do you think it is effective? Or do you prefer the better-defined dark colors of Figure 5.9B? Me, I vote for the bluer sky.

Figure 5.9C is the ringer. It's the one-minute workflow version, with no preliminary steps to adjust color or contrast. The Color Boost action therefore was applied not to Figure 5.7B, but to 5.7A, the original. The curve to the Endpoint Adjustment layer has to be a bit more extreme to achieve 99^L in the highlight. But I chose the same 45% opacity for the Color Boost layer as in Figure 5.9B. True, one would prefer the sky from one of the others. But it may be worth forgoing it if time is an issue.

It should be pointed out that this image is an ideal candidate for the one-minute workflow because it had no original color issues, and few opportunities to add contrast by blending channels.

The Fun Part Begins

You have now seen all necessary elements of the Picture Postcard Workflow. Some of the results have been great; others, like this one, are somewhat better than those of traditional workflows but not enormously so.

As we add options, the PPW advantage will become more decisive. The next chapter introduces a powerful and hitherto unknown method that can magnify the gains of the color boost we've just seen. Beginner or expert, you may well be better off skipping the second half of this chapter so as to get the immediate benefit of the next one.

So far, we've experimented with only two options for cutting back color: a reduction in opacity, or a layer mask based on the L. The second half discusses more complex masks. When those masks are right, they can make a big difference. Sooner or later, therefore, you should read that second half. But the first two options are strong ones, and should be sufficient for now if you care to move on.

Review and Exercises

- ✓Under what circumstances would you load a copy of the Lightness channel as a layer mask on the Color Boost layer, instead of just reducing that layer's opacity?
- ✓Assuming that you have decided to load the L channel, how would you do it?
- ✓If you wish to adjust a layer mask with a curve, how do you know whether the mask is active?
- ✓What are good final L values for highlight and shadow? In what common kind of work is it undesirable to finalize shadow in LAB?
- ✓The Color Boost action can easily produce colors far more intense than they were in the actual scene. Sometimes this is desirable and sometimes not. Put together a dozen or so of your typical images. Which ones, in your opinion, would benefit from such unnaturally vivid colors?

A Closer Look

Manipulating the Color Boost layer is an inverse beauty pageant, where the judges must choose the least ugly.

So far, the two obvious choices for color reduction have served us well. Most of the time they will continue to do so. But every so often we can do better, sometimes much better.

Fortunately, since we are working in color only, we can forget a lot of preconceptions about layer masks. They can look as bizarre as you like, and no one will be the wiser. We can apply drastic curves, superimpose one channel onto another, apply channels at less than 100% opacity, or paint directly into the mask.

Figure 5.10 shows the layer mask to be used in the next exercise. It's hard to believe that something so hideous could be effective. But as we saw earlier, when only color is being altered, masks need not be particularly accurate nor do they have to show good contrast. Something this weird could never be used for any type of maneuver involving detail.

The same warning applies here as in the second half of Chapter 4. There are more options available than would fit in the rest of the book, let alone one chapter. As always, you should decide what course seems the most promising for cutting back color. If you have more time, rather than wasting a whole day experimenting, do a second version of the picture from scratch, choosing a different method of color reduction.

We will now take a look at four different scenarios—the last three of which involve the use of the powerful AB channels of LAB. The first example, however, should be more routine.

Figure 5.11A is the original. The initial color step is familiar. The lightest clouds must be white. Evidently the pants should be neutral. The grass needs to fall within our guidelines for natural greenery. Investigation shows a slight blue cast, easy to correct with curves in Color mode. Caution, however: the pose indicates that it's a cold day. Yes, it's sunny too, but we don't want to go overboard with the initial correction.

The luminosity step is also familiar. The highlight is obviously the lightest cloud, at top center. The green and red channels will be lightened there to add contrast. This could cause the brownish rocky area to disappear in the red channel. To prevent this, we first blend the blue into the red. We must remember to use Darken mode, so that the sky doesn't lighten as the rocks get darker. Then the layer on which the blend was done is changed to Luminosity mode, and we get Figure 5.11B. It's an improvement, but as usual the colors are somewhat weak.

Not *horribly* weak, however. Applying the Color Boost action unleashes Figure 5.11C.

According to the instructions at the end of the first half of the chapter, we now check the highlight to see if it is acceptable, and it is. We are also supposed to decide whether to reduce the opacity of the Color Boost layer or to load a copy of the L as a layer mask, thus reducing the impact on darker colors.

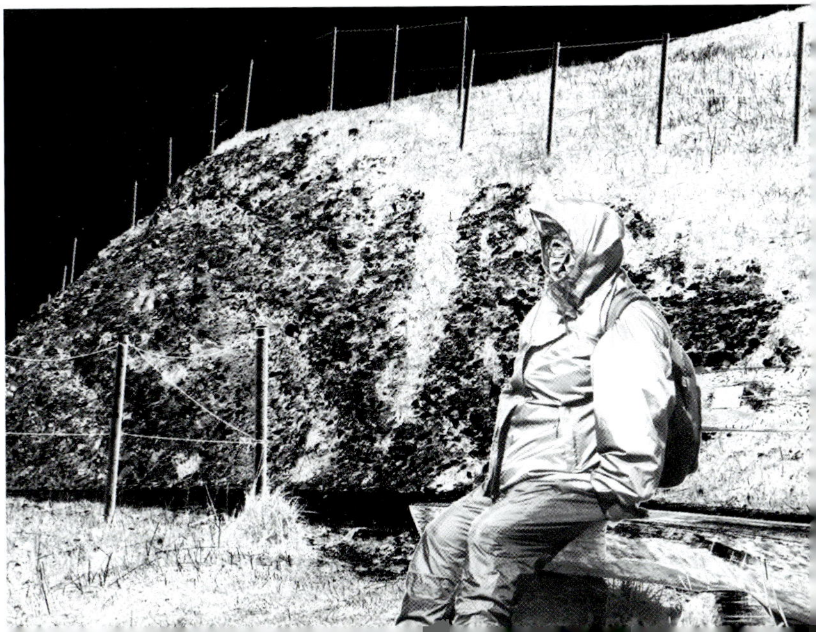

Figure 5.10 *This weird image is the layer mask that will reduce the effect of the Color Boost layer in the next example. Unusual masks cause no problems on layers that affect color only.*

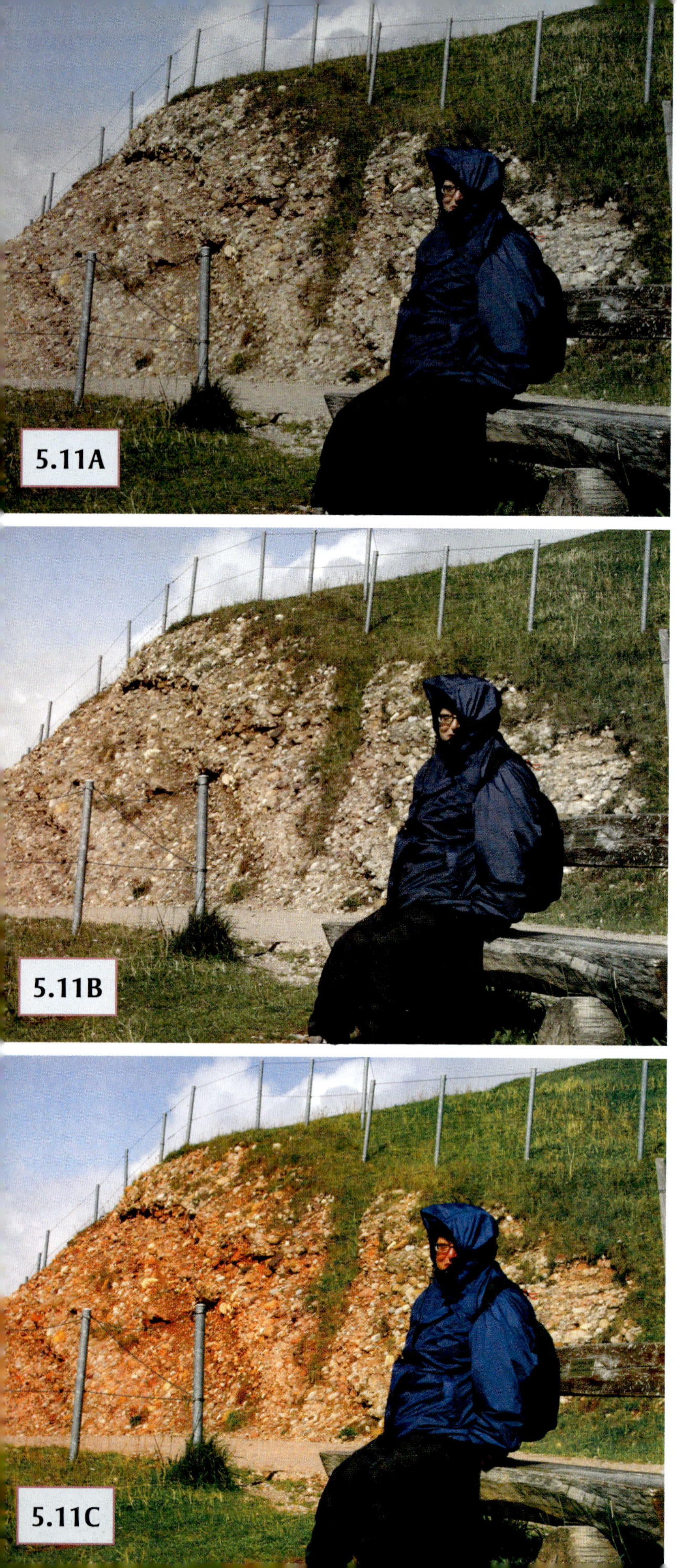

If those are the only two choices then the first clearly wins. The problem is not the darker colors; if anything it's the opposite. Figure 5.12A is my idea of the correct maskless opacity, 25%.

But we are allowed more than these two unsatisfactory options. We ask ourselves, what is the ugliest part of Figure 5.11C? My answer is that it's the brownish rocky area. I chose 25% opacity because that was the maximum I could live with in this area. Unfortunately, with so low an opacity, I couldn't get as much color into the jacket and the greenery as I wanted.

The Shape of the Mask Curve

Once a layer mask is loaded, curves can emphasize or de-emphasize whatever you like. Even a mask that lives on an adjustment layer can be altered just like any other channel. Curves to any mask employ the traditional Photoshop dialog that is shown elsewhere in the book.

With the dialog open, Command-click the significant area(s), placing point(s) in the curve. If a point gets pulled down, the mask gets lighter and the color more intense. If it goes up, the mask darkens and the color diminishes. There are, however, many ways to lighten or darken. All get slightly different results.

- **Lightening the midpoint** makes a vivid picture but most of the color is added in the midrange. It's not the same look as increasing layer opacity.
- **Lightening the quartertone point** is a quandary, likely to work either well or badly. We're very sensitive in this range. In this picture lightening the quartertone would emphasize the brown area, which is already objectionable.
- **Moving the highlight** toward the

***Figure 5.11** Top, the original. Middle, corrected for color accuracy and for luminosity. Bottom, the Color Boost action is added.*

center, thus retaining a straight line, favors the lightest colors because they fall in a steeper part of the curve: everything will gain contrast, but lighter areas will gain more than darker ones.

- **Lightening the shadow** by moving the dark endpoint vertically, thus retaining a straight line, favors the darkest colors.
- **Moving both highlight and shadow** to retain the same angle while moving toward lightness creates almost the same effect as increasing layer opacity.

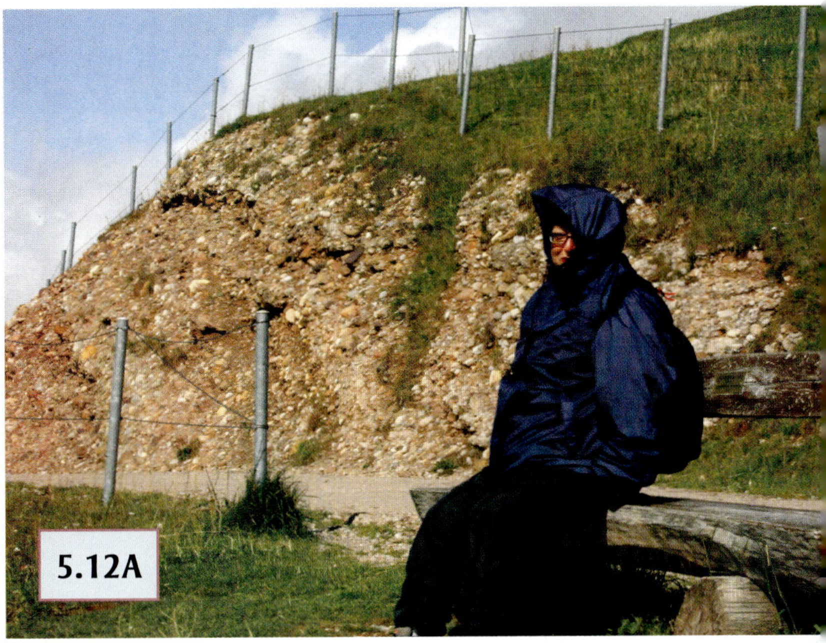

5.12A

Targeting the Color Zone

The most common curve in standard retouching approximates the shape of the letter S. A layer mask for color enhancement is more likely to be shaped like the letter U.

Looking at Figure 5.11C from lightest to darkest, I see sky, brown hillside, face, grass, jacket, pants. From ugliest to most acceptable, I see brown hillside, face, jacket, greens. I am indifferent about the sky and the pants.

Therefore, I load a copy of the L as a layer mask, and apply the curve shown, reaching what we saw earlier as Figure 5.10. The curve emphasizes color in the three-quartertone, which allows little enhancement of lighter things like the brown hillside.

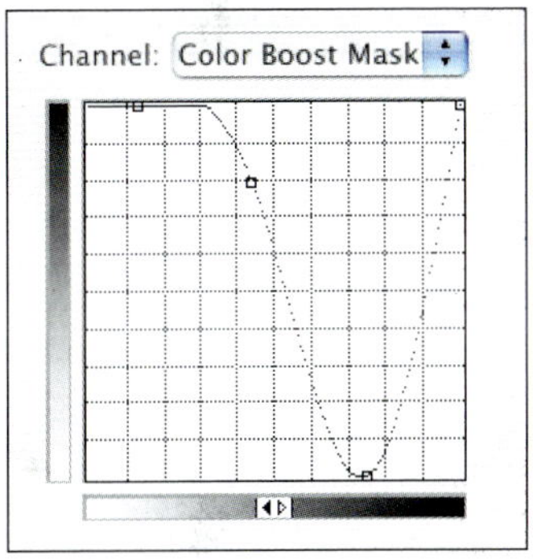

With that mask attached to the Color Boost layer of Figure 5.11C, and opacity reduced to 50%, we get Figure 5.12B, which must be considered an improvement over Figure 5.12A.

Figure 5.12 *Top, layer opacity is reduced to 25%. Bottom, the L channel is loaded as a layer mask on the Color Boost layer. Then, the U-shaped curve shown above is applied to the mask. Finally, layer opacity is set to 50%.*

Distinguishing between desirability and ugliness on the basis of darkness worked here, but it's more common to be able to distinguish by color. That brings the AB channels of LAB into the mix. We may not even need a mask.

Figure 5.13A features the subtleties of the desert in bloom. The drill is routine by now.

- Initial examination of the color reveals nothing wrong. A threshold adjustment layer finds the highlight in the water at center.
- The background rocks are weak in the red and green channels. The solution is to

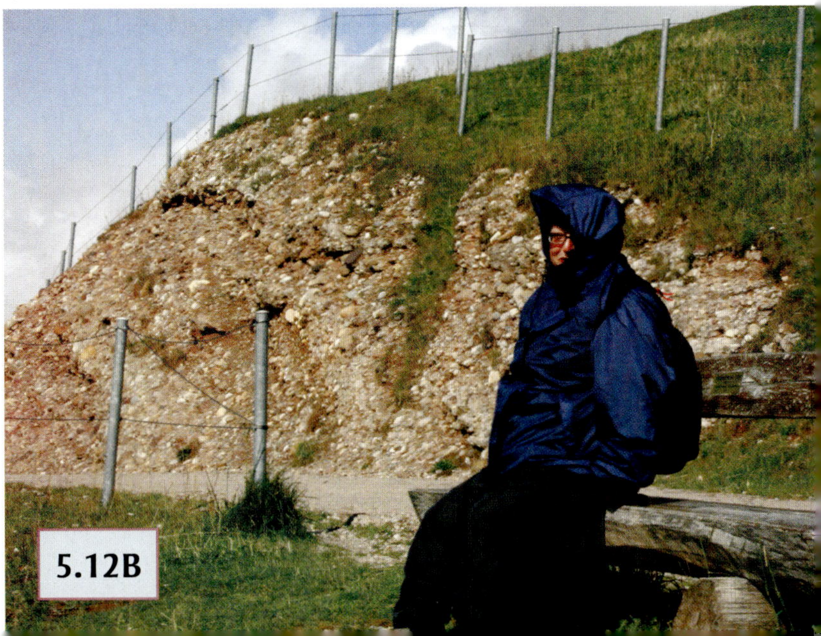

5.12B

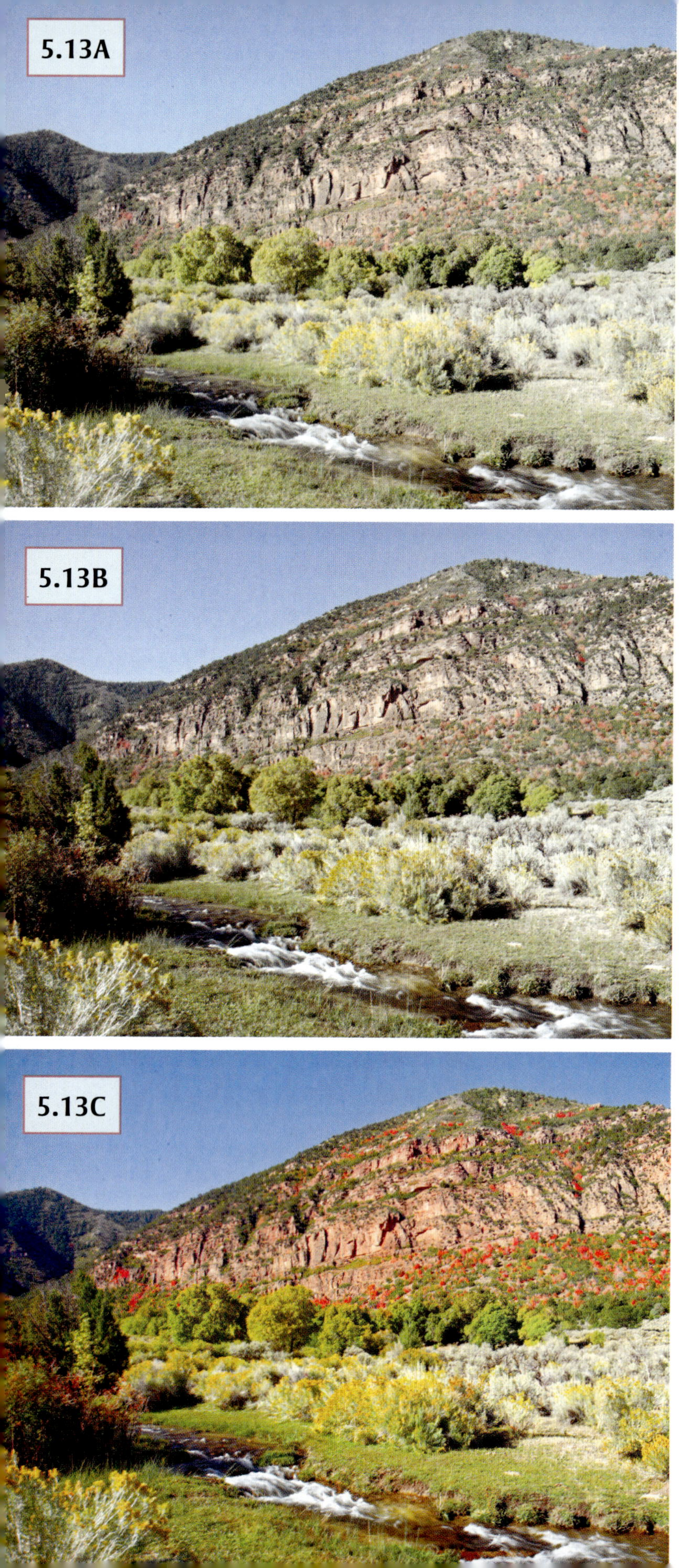

blend the blue into both, using Darken mode to avoid lightening the sky. I kept opacity to 35% for fear of making yellows too dark. Then, I applied contrast-enhancing curves to the red and green, producing Figure 5.13B.

- The default Color Boost action produces Figure 5.13C, and brings up the key question: what's ugliest about it?

The blotchy red flowers seem most offensive to me, followed by the darker greens. Once again, a simple reduction of opacity isn't adequate, as it would tone down useful light colors. Instead, this is a classic case for loading the L as a layer mask. Doing so makes Figure 5.14A, which has a hidden problem.

The SWAG Factor Rears Its Head

Jacking up color in LAB runs the risk of going outside, often far outside, the gamut of what can be printed. That's what's happening to the flowers in Figure 5.13C. The file, while in LAB, calls for flowers vastly redder than can be printed. Photoshop responds by generating a CMYK file that makes the whole area as red as possible, with no detail at all, making it seem as if somebody spilled droplets of red ink on the picture.

No big deal. Loading a layer mask fixes it painlessly. It's harder to see that the sky, too, is far out of gamut, and has lost all detail. Of course, it never had any detail to begin with, so we don't notice the loss.

If you'd like to see how big a color change it is, open up the Color Picker, and drop a swatch to represent a point I've chosen in the center of the sky. The original LAB file specifies the incredibly blue $64^{L}(3)^{A}(67)^{B}$.

You don't see that color, because no

***Figure 5.13** Top, the original. Middle, corrected for luminosity. Bottom, the Color Boost action is added.*

monitor can display such brilliance. Instead, your screen is likely to show you something like $63^L(9)^A(57)^B$, which is what you get if you convert these LAB values into sRGB.

Convert the LAB file into CMYK, with its notorious inability to make vivid blues, and the shift is even bigger. The profile I'm using generates $67^C35^M1^Y$. According to the Color Picker, this equates to $59^L(7)^A(36)^B$.

Compare the skies in Figures 5.13B and 5.14A, where the same point measures $64^L(2)^A(39)^B$. They're supposed to be of the same darkness, but 5.14A is darker, 5^L darker to be precise. They're also supposed to be the same hue, but 5.14A is $(7)^A$ greener. And Figure 5.14A is supposed to be roughly twice as blue as 5.13B. It is obviously not, but that's about as blue as it can get in CMYK.

Most methods of color management can cope with converting things that are slightly out of gamut. But when they are enormously out, when you're asking Photoshop to do something utterly impossible, you can't blame it for indulging in what was described earlier as a SWAG—a Scientific Wild Ass Guess. Photoshop's SWAG about what to do with the red flowers was a poor one. What it did with the blue sky is more acceptable, but a SWAG nevertheless. I don't loathe and despise Figure 5.14A but I think the sky is more effective, more complementary to the rest of the picture, in Figure 5.14B.

I might feel more strongly if this file were being output by a good inkjet printer on top-quality paper. Such a device can get a more brilliant blue than can be had in the pages of a book. Trying to do so wouldn't be a good idea. This picture is about the foreground. A dazzlingly blue sky would be a distraction.

A long discussion to get to a five-second move, but we'll see similar situations again and again. The B channel of LAB represents blueness vs. yellowness. Our world is a yellow one. All reds and all natural greens are more yellow than blue. The sky is often the only element more blue than yellow. If that's the case, we can isolate it easily and without a mask, using the Blend If section of layer Blending Options.

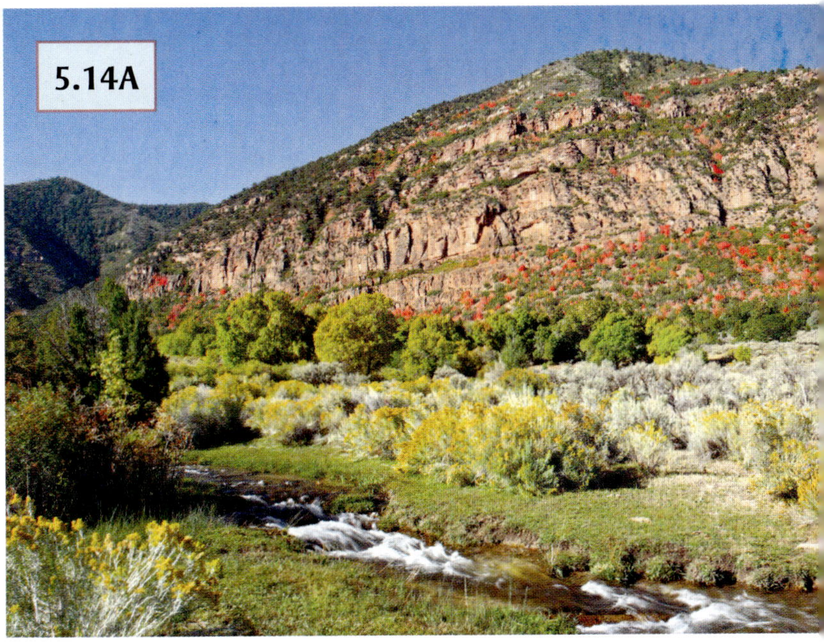

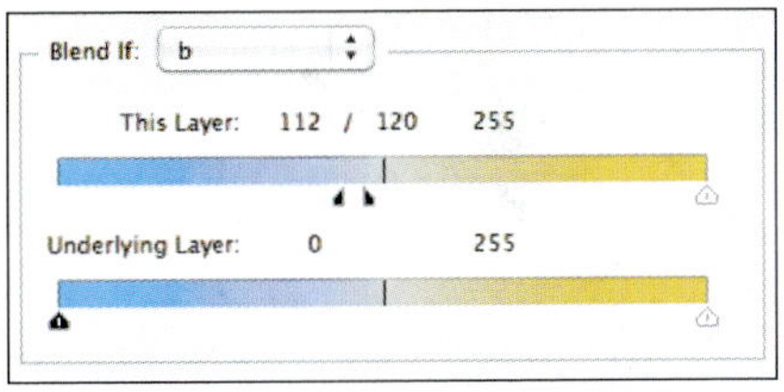

***Figure 5.14** Top, the L channel is loaded as a layer mask on the Color Boost layer of Figure 5.13C. Bottom, Blend If restores the sky to what it was in Figure 5.13B.*

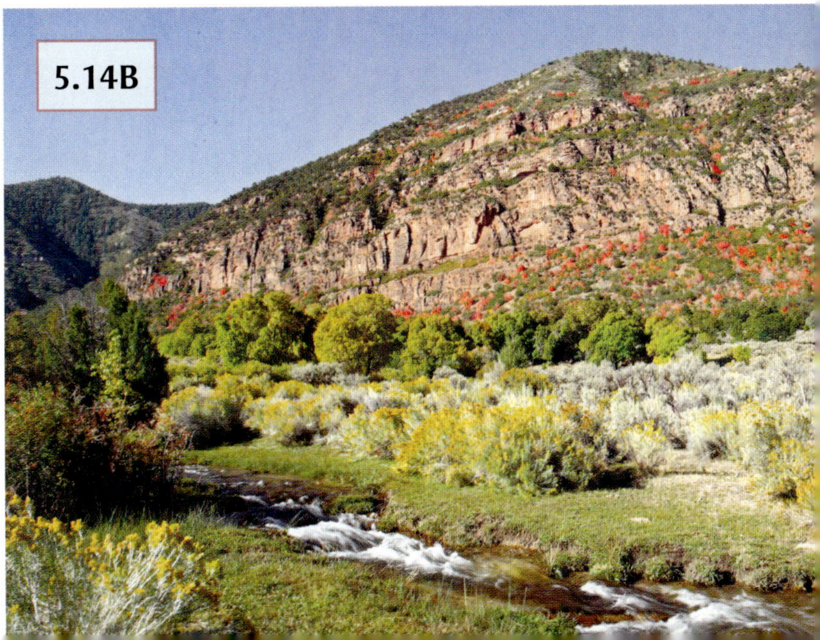

The Uses of Blend If in a Sky

In Figure 5.14A, I would like to cancel the color boost in the sky. To do this, double-click the Color Boost layer or use the flyouts in the Layers palette to bring up the Blending Options dialog.

Blend If resides at the bottom. It allows us to exclude content based on where it falls in any channel, on either the current layer or whatever is underneath. Here, we wish to exclude anything that's negative in the B channel, in other words anything more blue than it is yellow. Only the sky fits that description.

When the colors we want to exclude can be distinguished using either layer, it's better to base Blend If on the more colorful of the two. This makes slider placement less difficult. In the current example, correct practice is to choose This Layer, although the sky's color is so different from anything else in the image that either choice would work.

The method of exclusion is to move the B slider to the right, as shown in Figure 5.14. But note also that the left-hand slider is in two pieces. To split, Option-click-drag the slider. That avoids an edge where one layer is excluded. The split zone is a transition area with some characteristics of both layers. In a case like this where the distinction between sky and non-sky is screamingly obvious, there's little chance of getting it wrong with or without the split, but you might be surprised how easy it is to ruin a picture by overlooking a bad transition and not discovering it until much later in the process. For that reason, I always split the slider, no matter how unnecessary it may seem.

Working with Blend If can become addictive. It is sometimes useful to find out exactly what it affects. Beta reader Marco Olivotto, who teaches color correction and the PPW in Italy, has an ingenious solution. It has no direct application to this chapter, so I've detailed his procedure in the Notes & Credits section at the end of the book.

* * *

Figure 5.13C aroused the ire of a second Italian beta reader. Alessandro Bernardi wrote, "It looks too magenta in the rocks to me. If you think this is the right color, then you should point it out to prevent similar comments from the reader."

I don't think that this is such a horrible defect considering that we're only in Chapter 5, but in point of fact we're going to revisit this very same picture in Chapter 15, to show a different and unexpected color enhancement alternative, namely an unorthodox type of sharpening.

You may find you like that color, or parts of it, better. The concept of the workflow is simple, the ways of executing it are many.

Full Steam Ahead

Blend If is one of many simple ways to select the blue part of a sky. We will see more in the next chapter, and even more in Chapter 8. Masking by color content often requires more flexibility.

Cameras don't see through fog or smoke as well as humans do. Figure 5.15A presents a similar obstacle: steam. In Yellowstone National Park, swimmers are not welcome, unless they desire to be cooked medium rare.

Such thermal pools are often intensely blue or blue-green, but we can't tell through the steam. The foreground has no such obstacle. In short, the image is divided into a flat half and a half where the lighting is normal. As flat pictures usually lack color, chances are that when Color Boost is applied the foreground will be too intense. Using a lightness-based layer mask to restrict things won't work.

There isn't much color to check. The steam can't be either red or green, so the A channel must be no further from zero than the B is. It isn't, so we move on.

The luminosity step of Chapter 4 is unlikely to work here because the original is so neutral. The channels are too alike, just as they were in the stock exchange image of Figure 4.24.

That means that this picture should be correctable in less than a minute. The Color Boost action is played, and the top layer activated. A curve emphasizes the midtones as opposed to the highlights and shadows. Figure 5.15B shows the impact on contrast.

The Color Boost layer, however, has been turned off. I point this out not just to indicate its importance, but to illustrate a trap that awaits the unwary.

The default 75% opacity on the Color Boost layer is usually more than enough, but not here. Figure 5.15C raises it to 100%. In principle the picture retains the same detail as in Figure 5.15B.

In the lower right corner, this is not so. Something funky is occurring on the bank. Also, the deep blue water seems to have lost detail. Its darker areas in Figure 5.15B now seem to blend into the light water. Considering that the Color Boost layer is supposed to affect color only, and not contrast, why is this happening?

Gamut and Detail Loss

When working in an ultra-wide gamut colorspace, of which LAB is one, it's easy to create colors too intense for reproduction. It's also dangerous, because areas that are far out of gamut lose detail.

CMYK notoriously can't make good blues, so the most intense areas of water may pose a problem. It is less obvious that what's happening on the bank is also a gamut issue. The LAB file asks for a brilliantly yellow black, which no output device can reproduce because no such color happens to exist. Hence, a formless blob.

What's the strategy, then, for dealing with Figure 5.15C?

Our normal rule is to choose between a simple opacity reduction and one that uses a layer mask to emphasize color in the lighter areas. Neither approach works here, if you agree with my assessment of what's wrong with Figure 5.15C. I say that

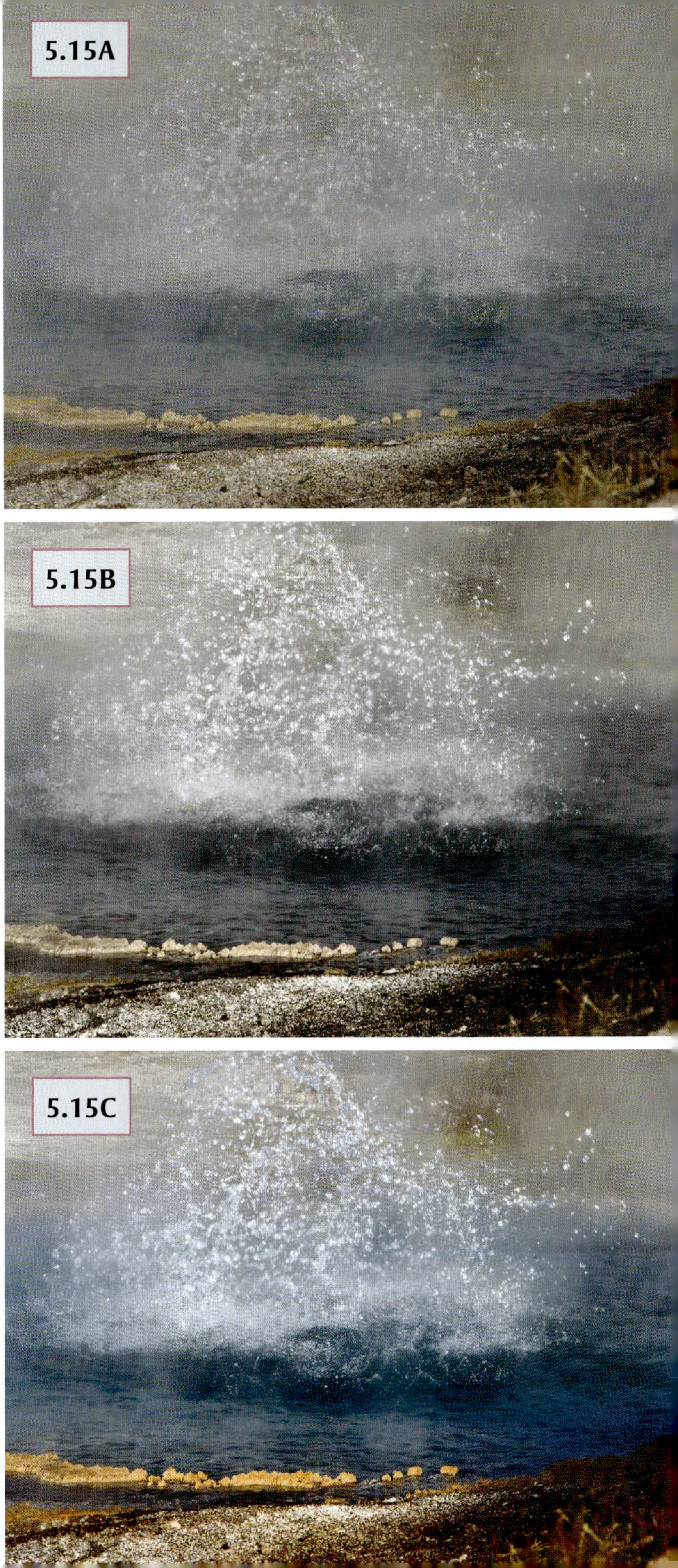

Figure 5.15 *Top, the original. Middle, corrected in the L channel only. Bottom, the Color Boost curves at 100% opacity.*

the blue is more or less acceptable but that the yellow areas have become too vivid.

That's no shock: the blues are partially obscured by steam and the yellows aren't. Reducing opacity to make the yellows acceptable will damage the blues.

The usual alternative, loading a copy of the L as a layer mask, makes matters worse. As Figure 5.16A shows, it's darker in the blues, and so would hurt them even more than the yellows. And if you're thinking about inverting the layer mask to favor darker areas, that won't work either. It would emphasize the parts of the water that are currently out of gamut.

The same applies to Blend If. The issue is one of yellow vs. blue, so the B channel suggests itself, as it did in the sky example of Figure 5.14. Blend If could exclude the yellow boost, for sure, but there are too many shades of blue. The sliders aren't subtle enough to be able to discriminate against the most brilliant ones.

The solution is to base a mask on the B channel itself. Some modification will be necessary. First of all, the B, Figure 5.16B, looks too flat. It's that way because anything lighter or darker would create colors far too intense to display on a screen, let alone print.

Second, it needs to be inverted. Its dark areas represent blues and its light ones yellows; we need the opposite to mask out the yellows and permit the blues. And third, the B is always noisy. It needs to be blurred.

These problems have all been taken care of in Figure 5.16C. I copied the B to an alpha

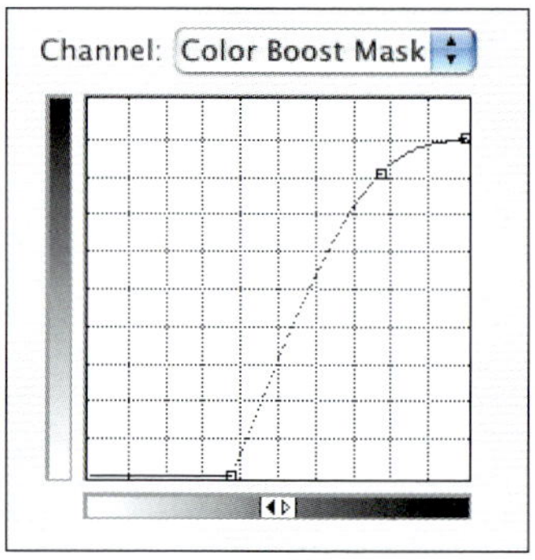

Figure 5.16 *Top, the L and B channels of Figure 5.15C. Bottom left, the curve shown is applied to an inverted copy of the B, which has been saved as an alpha channel. Bottom right, an inverted copy of the L is applied to the result in Darken mode.*

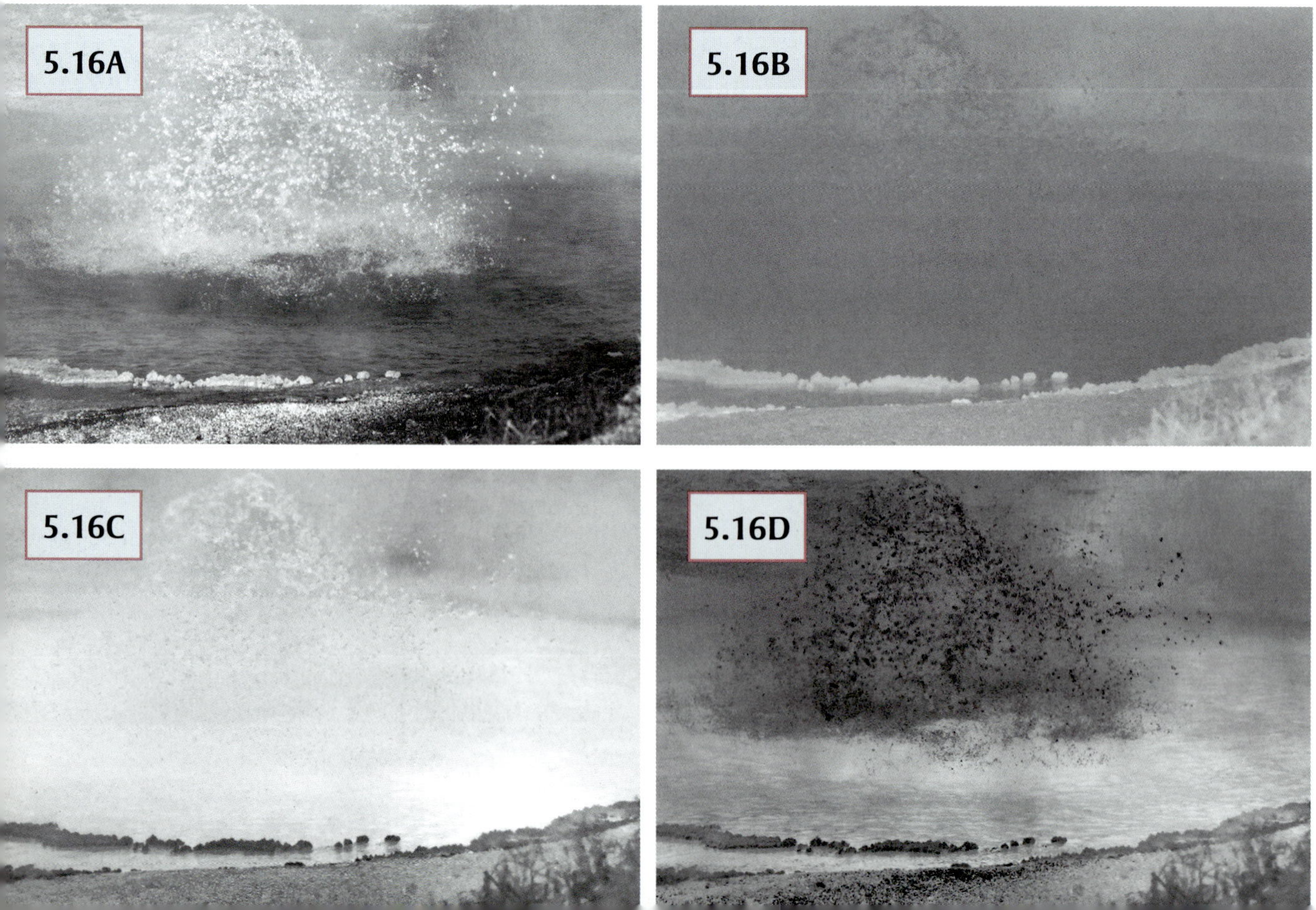

channel, inverted it, applied the curve shown to add contrast to the blues, and used the Surface Blur filter to cut the noise. I then loaded the alpha channel as a mask to the Color Boost layer, transforming Figure 5.15C into 5.17A.

Finding Flatness Is Fun

The mask curve tails off in its darkest areas. It prevents any part of the mask from becoming completely black.

This precaution is needed because the picture won't look natural if the yellows stay as bland as they currently are. It's one thing to downplay the yellow boost, another to eliminate it entirely.

According to me, Figure 5.17A is a step in the right direction, but it isn't blue enough yet. Since the opacity of the Color Boost layer is already 100%, the only way to get more blue is to lighten the corresponding areas of the layer mask (Figure 5.16C), which are already almost as light as they can be.

I therefore added a second layer that boosted color even more. It didn't have to be at a high opacity because what I had already wasn't that bad. So for want of a better idea, I duplicated the Color Boost layer together with its mask.

Figure 5.17 *Top, Figure 5.16C is used as a layer mask on 5.15C. Middle, the Color Boost layer, along with its mask, is duplicated at 35% opacity. Bottom, a similar version prepared with Figure 5.16D masking both layers.*

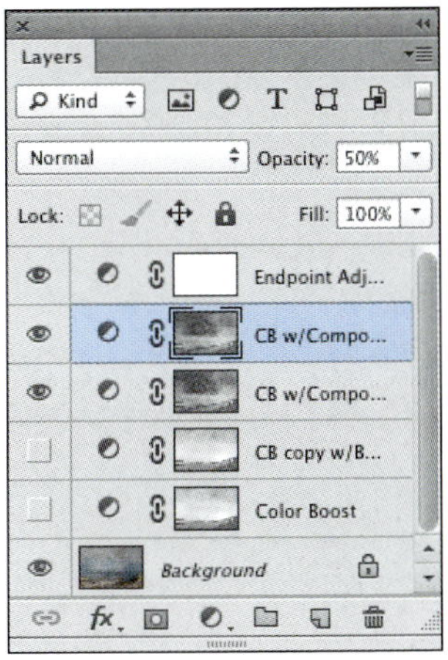

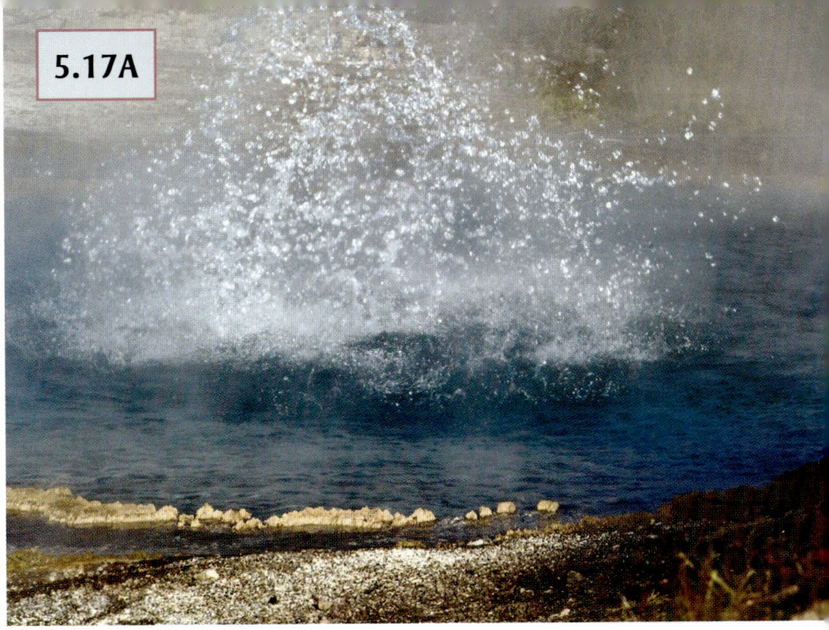

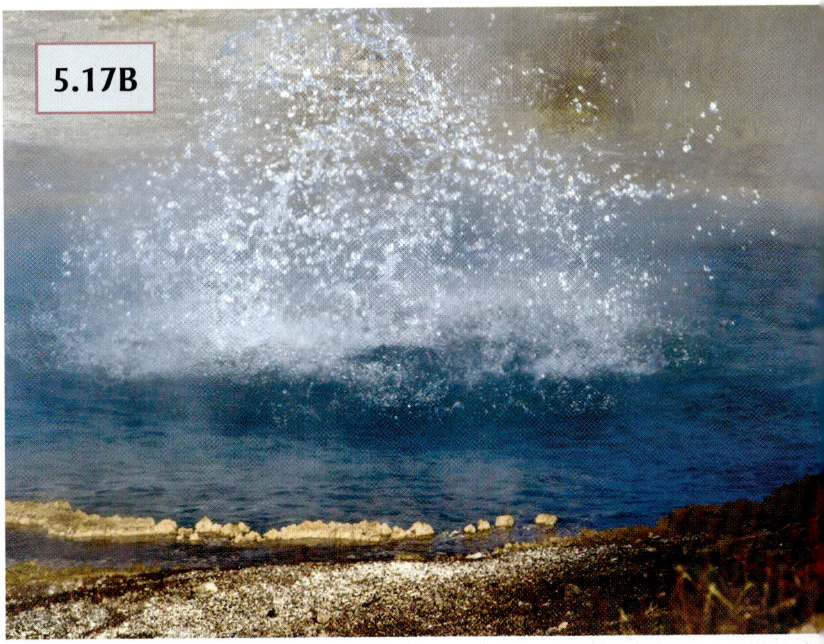

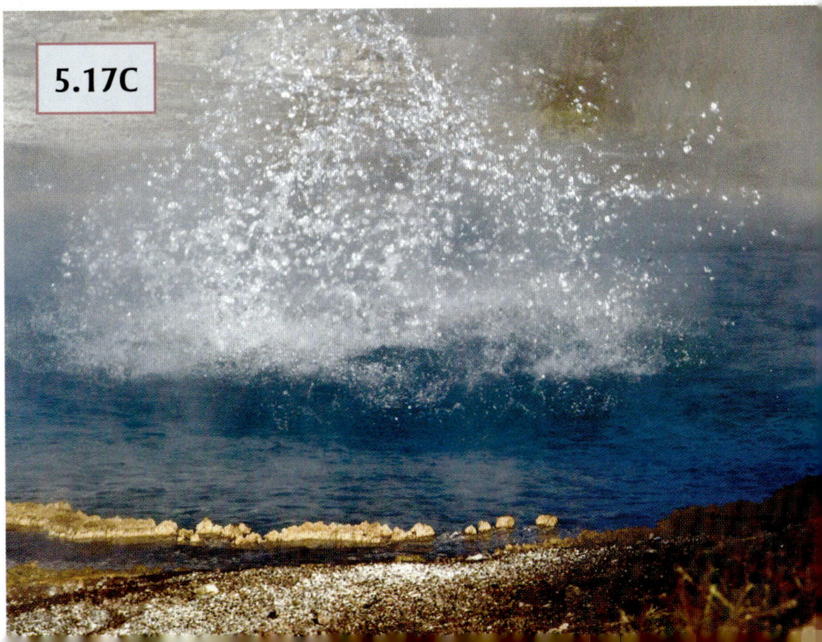

We could also duplicate it with a different mask, or no mask at all. Or we could produce a layer that boosted color by using another method entirely, such as with Hue/Saturation, or something done in RGB and saved as an optional layer, or the Man from Mars method discussed in the next chapter.

Any of these options yields two layers that enhance color in different ways. Some combination is likely the most pleasing. We may want to play up the new layer, in which case we lower the opacity of the original Color Boost layer.

The good news is that it should only take about 90 seconds to get from Figure 5.15A to the vastly better 5.17A. The bad news is that if we test every conceivable extra layer, it will take a week.

If you don't have a week, go as fast as you like. The Color Boost layer is ordinarily more than sufficient, *far* more than sufficient, without a second layer. If it isn't, any further boost you wish to make can be small. That being the case, it won't much matter what you put on the second layer. Duplicating the existing Color Boost layer is merely the easiest option.

I can't show you what happens with two Color Boost layers set at 100% opacity because the result would be so far out of gamut that I might be reported to the American Academy of Ophthalmology as a menace to society. Instead, Figure 5.17B sets the copy of the Color Boost layer, including its mask, to 35% opacity.

We could stop right there, or try some other option. What's there now, it seems to me, has a nice blue for the water. The steam, though, should be more neutral. Certain parts already are, because they started out that way and the Color Boost curves don't change them. But they intensify anything with even a hint of blue. So the transition between the lightest steam and the water gets bluer faster than I would like.

To compensate, I'd like the new layer to use a mask that is darker where the steam is. The A and B channels are no good because they have neutrals as their midpoint. I have a couple of actions that generate saturation masks; loading up one of them ought to work. But again: how much time is your picture worth? Because there's another easy option: using an inverted copy of the L channel that was shown earlier in Figure 5.16A. I mentioned this possibility previously, rejecting it because of potential problems with the blues.

But that was considering using it as the primary mask. Now we're talking about using it as a mask on a second layer, which is a different story with a different ending.

There's an even safer possibility. Start the second layer out with the existing mask, Figure 5.16C. Instead of replacing it with the inverted L, apply the inverted L to it in Darken mode. That gives Figure 5.16D.

There is no guarantee that our experiments with different masks on the second layer will improve Figure 5.17.B. If either of these proposed new masks *does* make a significant improvement, I'd consider it unlikely that further trials with the other would prove worthwhile. The two masks are just too similar. If you absolutely must throw more time at the picture, you'd be better off trying something more radical.

Enough philosophy. I now had one Color Boost layer using Figure 5.16C as a mask and another using 5.16D. With both at 100% opacity, the color was excessive. So I experimented with various combinations. The more settings I tried the less I liked what the first mask was doing. So, after about 45 seconds of playing around, I turned off the original Color Boost layer and duplicated the new one.

The color of Figure 5.17C is therefore produced by two layers, each using the same curves and Figure 5.16D as a layer mask. One layer is at 100% opacity and the other at 65%. That's higher than was used in Figure 5.17B, which is understandable because the masks are darker, hiding more of the color boost. I prefer Figure 5.17C to 5.17B because its bubbling water is more neutral, setting off the bluer water that surrounds it.

How Green Is My River

Creative color boosting can be as complex as you like. Our final exercise foreshadows what we'll be doing in the next chapter with another interesting point about vivid colors.

The Bow River, meandering through the Canadian Rockies, is in the same geological area as Emerald Lake, which we visited in Chapter 1. The river, like the lake, is fed by melting snow and glaciers. In common with Yellowstone, therefore, its temperature is rather uninviting for swimming, albeit for an entirely different reason. The mineral-rich glacial waters impart an unusual iridescent color, in some places more green than blue.

Starting with this chapter, I'll suggest rules to govern which colors should be made vivid and which should not. Here's one: where the color is unusual, emphasize it. And another: where the color is disagreeable, or suggests something disagreeable, try not to strengthen it.

Before applying these principles, we need to adjust color, if necessary, and luminosity. Figure 5.18A is the original. Nothing is obviously wrong with the color. The luminosity moves are straightforward and will be shown and discussed in a few moments. Figure 5.18B adds the default Color Boost action. And Figure 5.18C is my take on cutting back the excessive color.

As always, the key is to scrutinize the overly colorful version to decide what's most objectionable. I have no problem with the color of the water in Figure 5.18B. It's known to be both unusual and pleasing, but that message won't come across if the color is portrayed as dull.

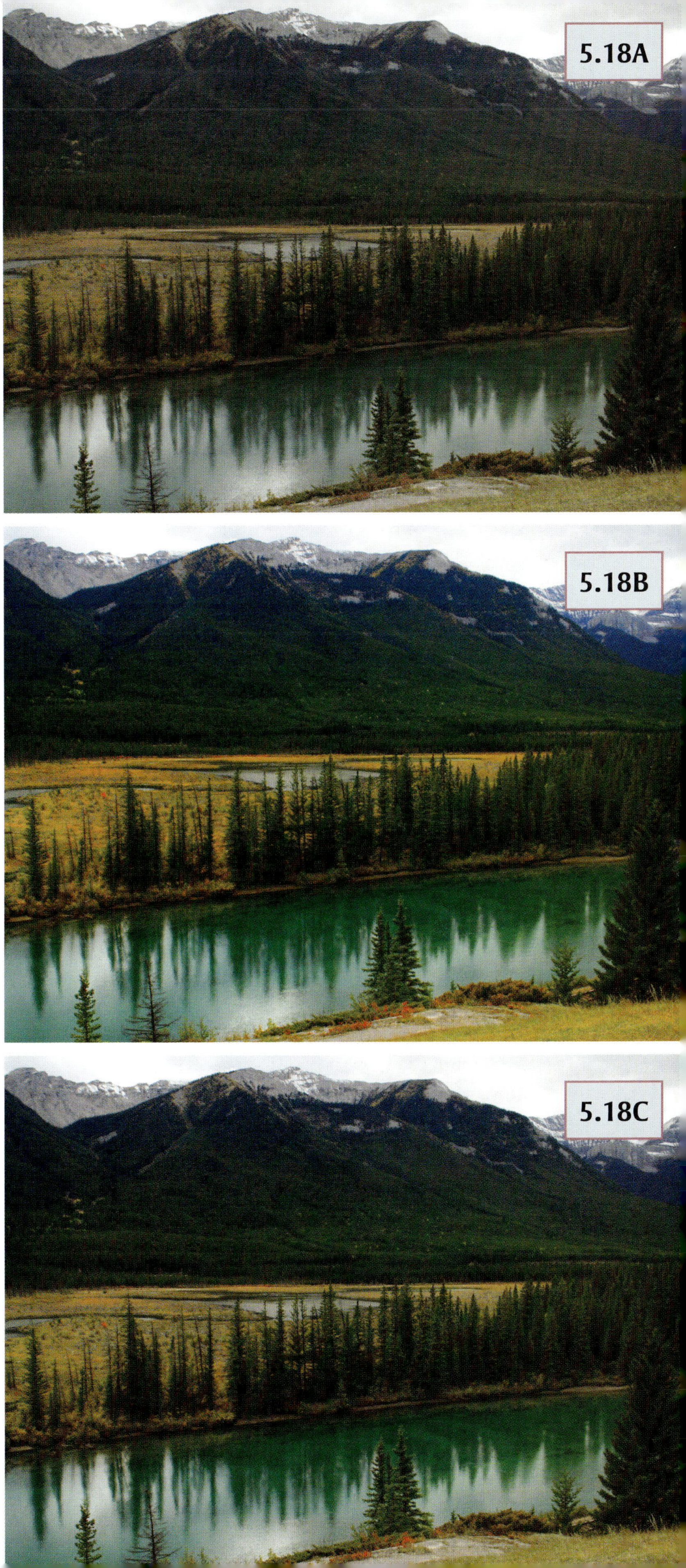

Figure 5.18 *Top, the original. Center, after luminosity moves and a default application of the Color Boost action. Bottom, the Color Boost layer is adjusted to favor greens.*

***Figure 5.19** Top, an inverted A channel is loaded as a layer mask to Figure 5.18B. Middle left, contrast is added to the mask, emphasizing greens. Middle right, the curve turns dark areas of the mask light. Bottom, magnified, the results in color of using the masks in the middle row. Red flowers to the right of the near bank show why the curve was needed.*

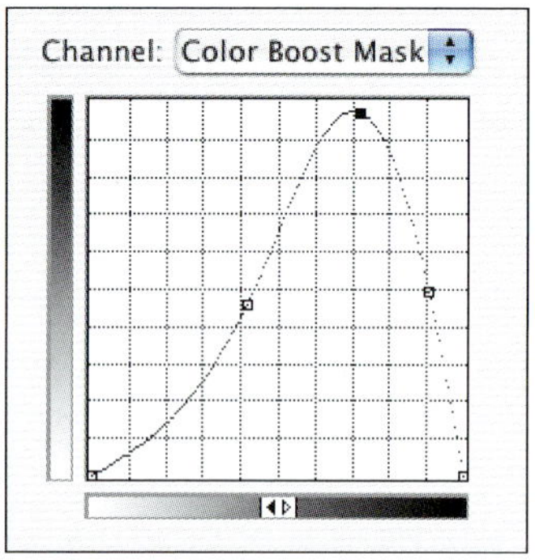

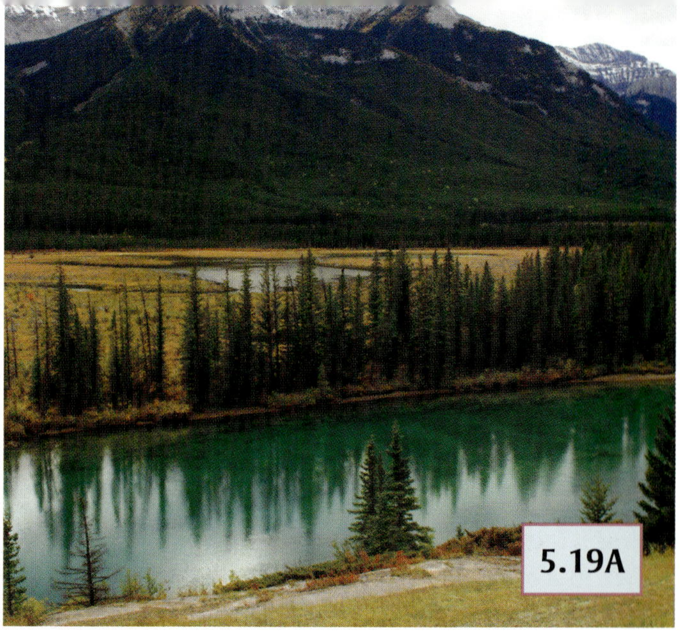

5.19A

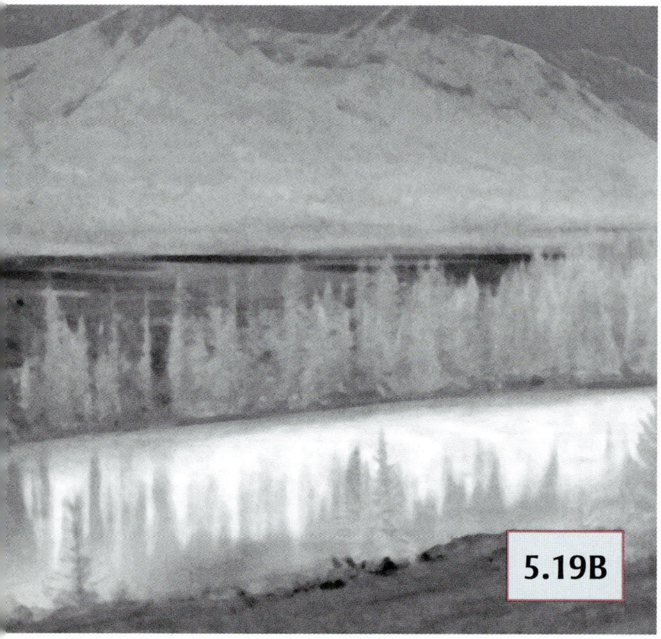

5.19B

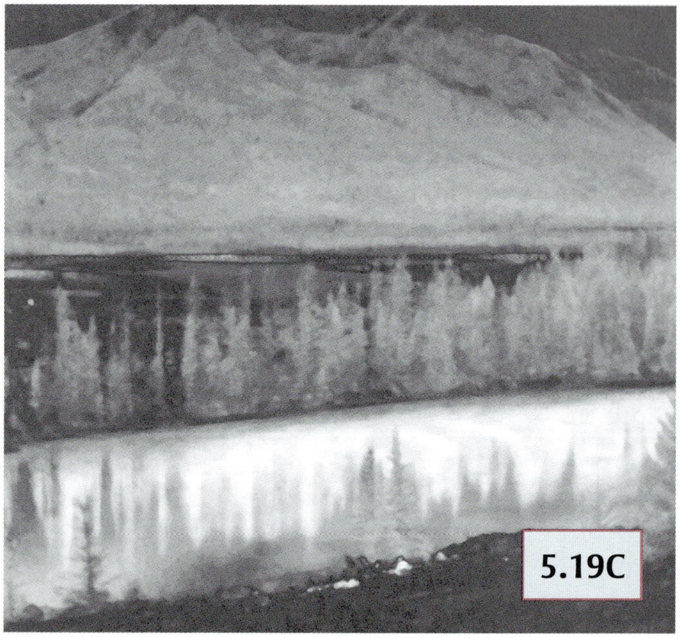

5.19C

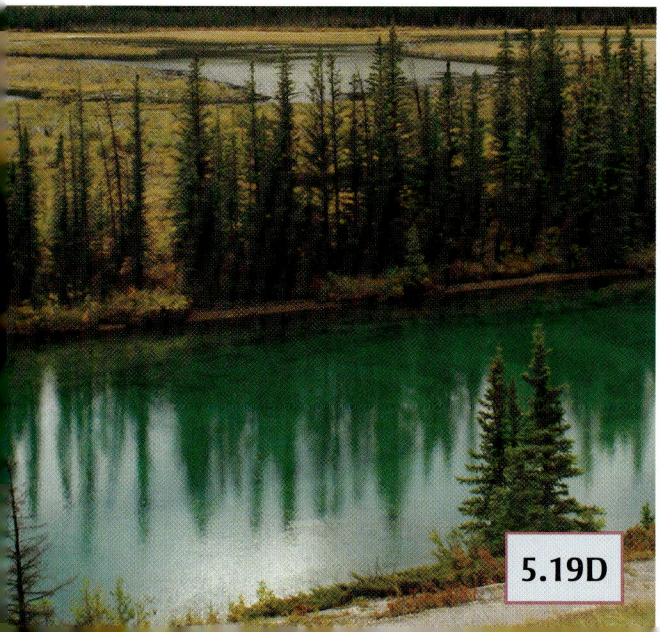

5.19D

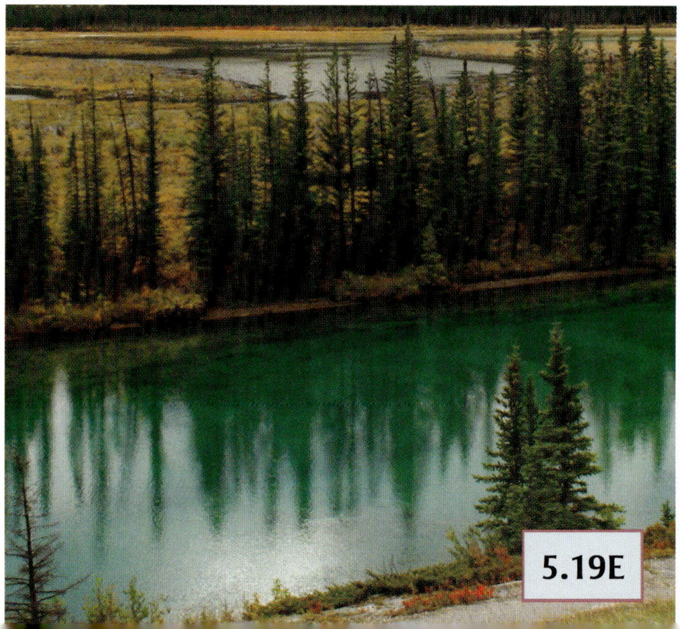

5.19E

I also lose little sleep over the thought that the trees have become slightly greener than they are in nature.

These objects might be described as the romantic parts of the picture. Yellow, burnt-out fields, on the other hand, don't merit that description. I say the yellows in Figure 5.18B are excessive.

So, the strategy is to keep the water about where it is, to reduce the color in the background green slightly, and in the yellows a lot. Do you agree? And if so, how would you do it?

More Masking Strategy

Simply reducing opacity is out. We only do that when all colors are equally offensive, which they aren't here. Unfortunately, the usual alternative, loading the L channel as a layer mask, doesn't work either. The idea of that move is to allow lighter colors to get more intense. Here, unhappily, that would be the yellows.

Inverting the mask wouldn't help. That would favor the darkest mountains, not the river.

When all else fails, look to the AB channels. Should we use the yellow-versus-blue B, as in the Yellowstone exercise, or is the magenta-versus-green A the better option?

An LAB novice might assume that, because yellow is such an area of concern, we'd choose the B. It's not so easy. Anyone would describe the river and the trees as *green,* not yellow. Both, however, are more yellow than they are blue. In the B channel, therefore, they are hard to distinguish from the "real" yellows.

In the A, they *can* be distinguished. The river and trees are both more green than magenta. The yellows are neither green nor magenta.

Warm colors (magenta and yellow) are portrayed as light in the AB. Cool ones (green and blue) are dark, and neutrals gray. The mask we seek for the Color Boost layer has to be light where greens are. So the copy of the A that we use for the mask has to be inverted. Then it needs to be blurred slightly, because the A and B channels are usually noisy.

The A and B are too flat to be effective masks unless their range is increased. Figure 5.19A uses an unmodified inverted A as the layer mask. One has to look really hard to see that more color is being retained in the greens than the yellows. To me, it looks like a straight reduction in opacity, even though I know it is not.

Figure 5.19B is the response. Contrast has been enhanced, in this case by applying Image: Auto Tone to the inverted, blurred mask. Then, the peculiarly shaped curve transforms it into Figure 5.19C.

The effects of these two masks are shown, respectively, in Figures 5.19D and 5.19E. Do you see why the curved version was necessary?

Before applying one of these torments as a mask, think of its structure. In an inverted A, green things are light. The yellow stuff, being neither magenta nor green, is darker. For that matter, so is the sky.

So far, so good. Darkest of all would be anything definitely more magenta than green. At first glance, it doesn't seem like any such objects are hanging around.

But some are. The bank hosts small red flowers, which have a powerful magenta component. In Figure 5.19B they are therefore even darker than the yellows. In Figure 5.19D they nearly vanish, because the layer mask refuses to allow them to gain color.

Hence, the inverted U shape of the curve, making dark parts of the mask light while darkening the semi-dark zones. In Figure 5.19E, the flowers are back.

Incidentally, I exaggerated a few paragraphs back when I suggested we couldn't use the B for a mask. I stated correctly that the greens sport a yellow component. However, with a careful curve they could be differentiated from the fields, which have a *strong* yellow component.

The true problem was those flowers. They're much more magenta than green, yes, but also much more yellow than blue. In the B channel, therefore, they can't be distinguished from the yellow grass.

Recapping the PPW, rev 1.0

This chapter and the two that precede it set out the basics of the Picture Postcard Workflow. The simple exercise we just completed shows both its attractions and its snares. If I were to dictate each step to you, the whole correction would take you a minute or less.

But I'm not usually available to dictate steps. Finishing in a minute depends on taking only five to ten seconds to decide whether anything is wrong with the original color. Worse, it also depends on understanding, after applying the Color Boost action, not just that the A channel inverted is the best choice for a mask but why the B inverted would be a bad one.

Learning to make these two judgments quickly takes more practice than, say, adjusting luminosity. So you have to decide for yourself whether you work on enough images to make the investment of time worthwhile.

But in principle, we're finished. Going from Figure 5.18A to Figure 5.18C/5.19E quickly is quite an achievement. If that result is good enough for you, close the book, donate it to your favorite charity, and start practicing.

You may have observed, however, that the book is only a third completed. The basic workflow isn't going to change. Every image will still see the three basic steps of color, contrast, and color again. But a lot of hitherto unmentioned options will strive for our favor. The color work of this chapter goes hand in hand with the powerful technique that will be introduced in the next one. A preview of what will be coming is in order. We go for a new beginning, starting from scratch with Figure 5.18A.

* * *

A small area of sky in the upper right is the lightest point of this scene. I wouldn't criticize anybody for choosing that as the highlight, but I wouldn't do so myself. If the lightest point were in some well-defined cloud against a darker sky, it would be a different story. But the entirety of the sky here, although not quite blank, doesn't offer much to work with.

As with most skies, if not satisfied with what's there, it's easy to replace it without being detected. We'll be discussing how in Chapter 8, which is all about skies.

I would ignore the sky and instead designate one of the light areas of the water as the highlight. I chose the nearest patch, and the nearest large green areas in the trees as the shadow.

Although it isn't being used as a highlight, measuring the sky makes sense. It seems as though it should be gray or white. In fact, that's what it is in the original, 0^A0^B. A useful piece of information, indeed, because we have so little else to go on. The foreground trees have the absolute B value around half again that of the A. The background mountains are even bluer (less yellow), with the B sometimes falling to 0^B.

The trees already are so blue (deficient in yellow) that they are almost, but not quite, outside of the recommended range for natural greenery. If they measured bluer still, it would indicate we should either lighten the red channel, darken the blue, or some combination.

I surmise, though, that the situation is like that of the Grand Canyon back in Postcard 4.1—a bluish haze in the background. There, the cast was so pronounced that I recommended cutting it about in half. Here, the blueness is so slight that I'm reluctant to attack it for fear it might make the fields too yellow. Therefore, I say that there should be no initial color adjustment.

So far, no change from our first attempt.

No change in the next step, either. Our hopes shouldn't be high for an enormous boost in contrast. The original has a full range, with delicate detail in both highlight and shadow. Curves will therefore have to be used cautiously if at all. Furthermore, the original is rather neutral. There won't be huge differences between channels, so blending opportunities will be limited.

Some gains are nevertheless possible, and we don't even need to see the channels to know what they are. The Grand Canyon exercise suggested that hazy backgrounds are best defined in the red channel and worst in the blue. That's true here as well, so, on a duplicate layer, I replaced one with the other.

Also, I lightened the midtone of the green channel slightly, hoping to pick up more contrast in the river and the background mountains.

Changing layer mode to Luminosity produced Figure 5.20A. This was the intermediate version that was not shown between Figures 5.18A, the original, and 5.18B, which applied the Color Boost action. It's better placed here, so we can compare it to what comes next.

First, though, compare it to Figure 5.18A. We should be able to agree that Figure 5.20A is a worthwhile, if not spectacular, improvement. To make it better yet, let's preview a couple of techniques that will be seen in subsequent chapters.

Introducing the PPW, rev 1.1

The moves we are about to see acknowledge two of the many ways in which human perception differs from that of a camera. First, we adjust to harsh lighting better than cameras do. The original has too much contrast between the strongly lit and darker areas.

Figure 5.20B is the PPW response to such a sun-and-shade condition. The idea is to open the shadows while darkening the quartertone, hopefully without losing too much midtone contrast. With Figure 5.20A as a base, I applied a false profile and then multiplied through a blurred layer mask. This method and its variations are fully explained in Chapters 11 and 12. The result is Figure 5.20B.

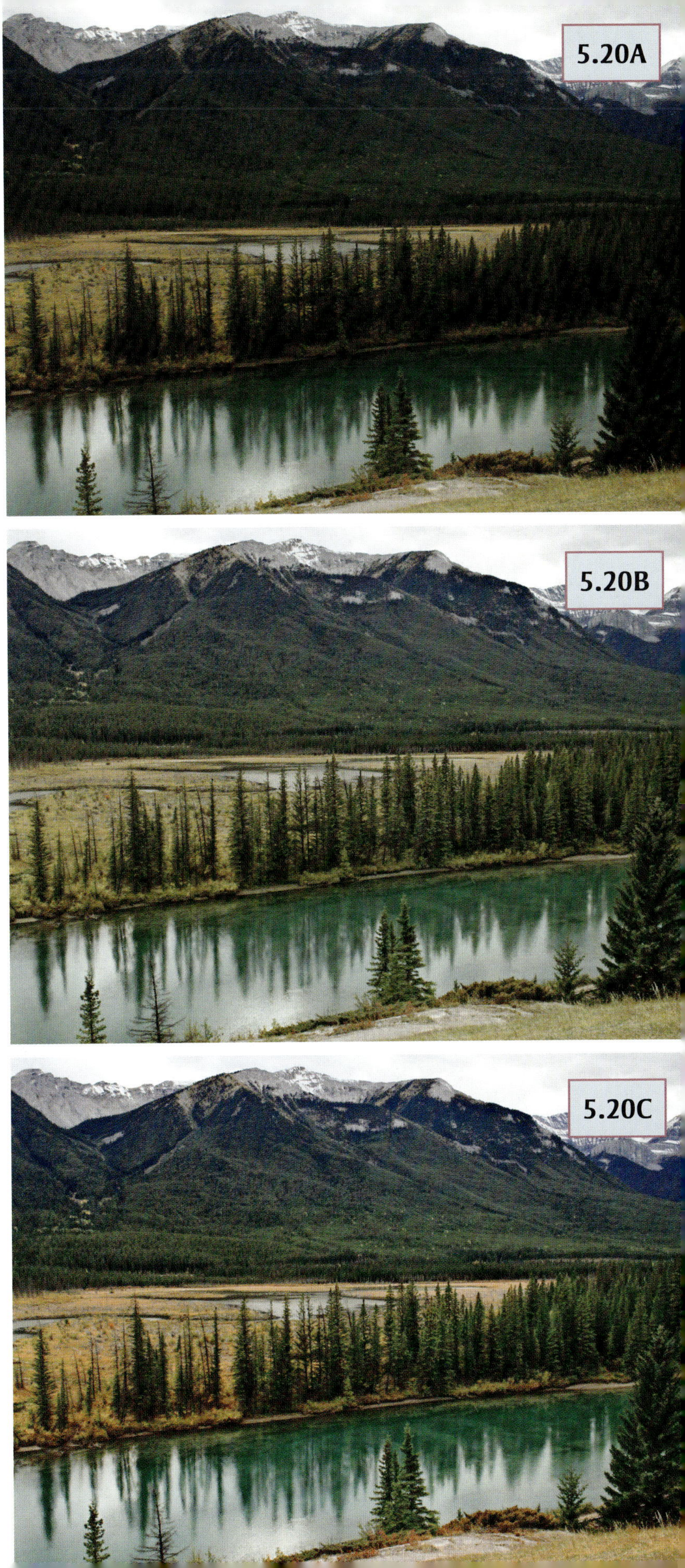

***Figure 5.20** Top, the luminosity maneuver that came between Figure 5.18A and 5.18B. Center, starting from scratch, a different luminosity version based on techniques developed in Chapter 12. Bottom, a further correction based on the Modern Man from Mars action shown in Chapter 6.*

Simultaneous contrast is the human propensity to perceive colors as different from their neighbors. The trees in background are mostly of the same species. The camera records this boring information faithfully. In print, we find the color dull and the lack of variation monotonous. If we were there, we'd see much more color variation, because that's how our visual system works. Furthermore, after returning home we'd remember the trees as being significantly greener than we perceived them at the time the photo was taken.

Figure 5.20C is the PPW way of creating color variation, an update of the Man from Mars Method that I introduced in magazine articles around a decade ago. The idea is to create not brighter color but color *variation* in the area(s) of most importance, here the greens. The next chapter discusses the ramifications of this method, which is reduced to a complicated action and hence is applied quickly. Figure 5.20C shows its default settings. Like Figure 5.18B, which used the Color Boost action's defaults, no judgment on my part was required.

Before you get all exercised and start thinking about junking the Color Boost action and just using this one, take a closer look. It is true that in some ways Figure 5.20C is better than a suitably toned-down version of Figure 5.18B, but in other ways it is worse. The fields have gotten rather orange. The water lacks punch. So it's not better. It's *different*—just as the multiple versions of the swan picture that I used to create a single strong variant in Chapter 2 were different.

The flexibility of the overall workflow is making itself apparent. Creating the new luminosity version, Figure 5.20B, might take as much as a minute. But the color versions, Figures 5.18B

Postcard 5.21 *This page, the original. Opposite top, the Color Boost methodology that produced Figure 5.18C is applied instead to Figure 5.20B. Opposite bottom, certain parts of Figure 5.20C have been added.*

5.21A

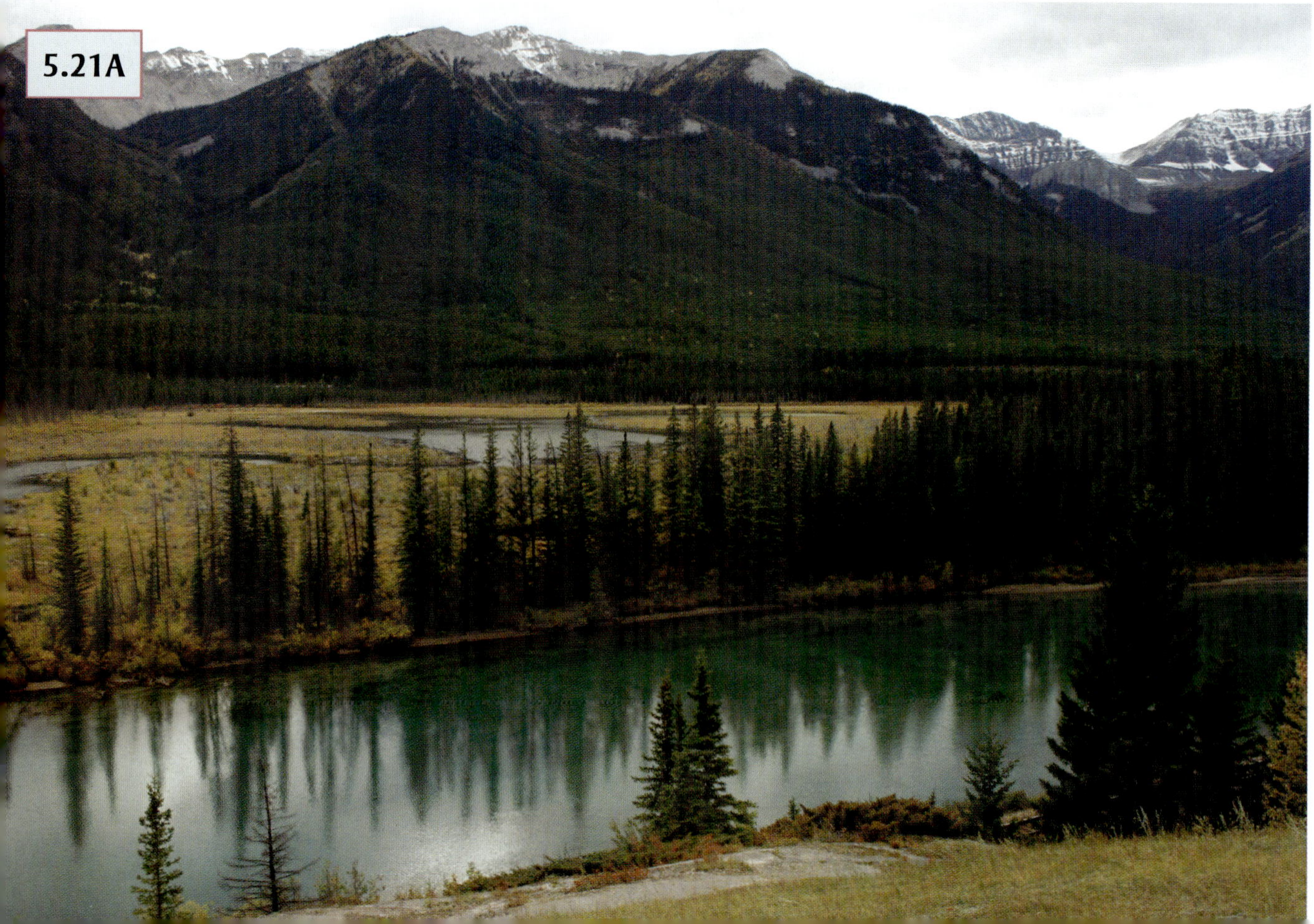

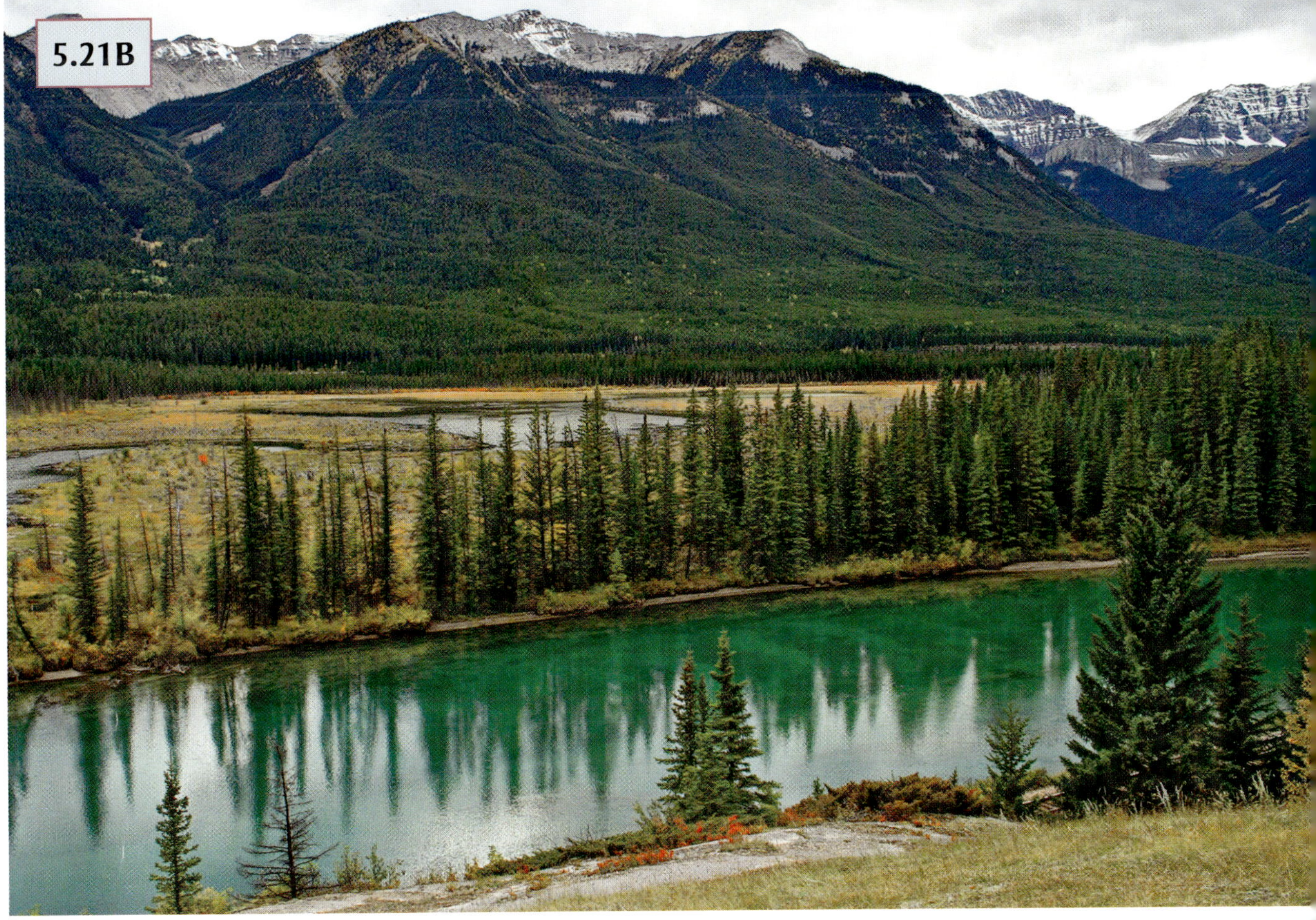
5.21B

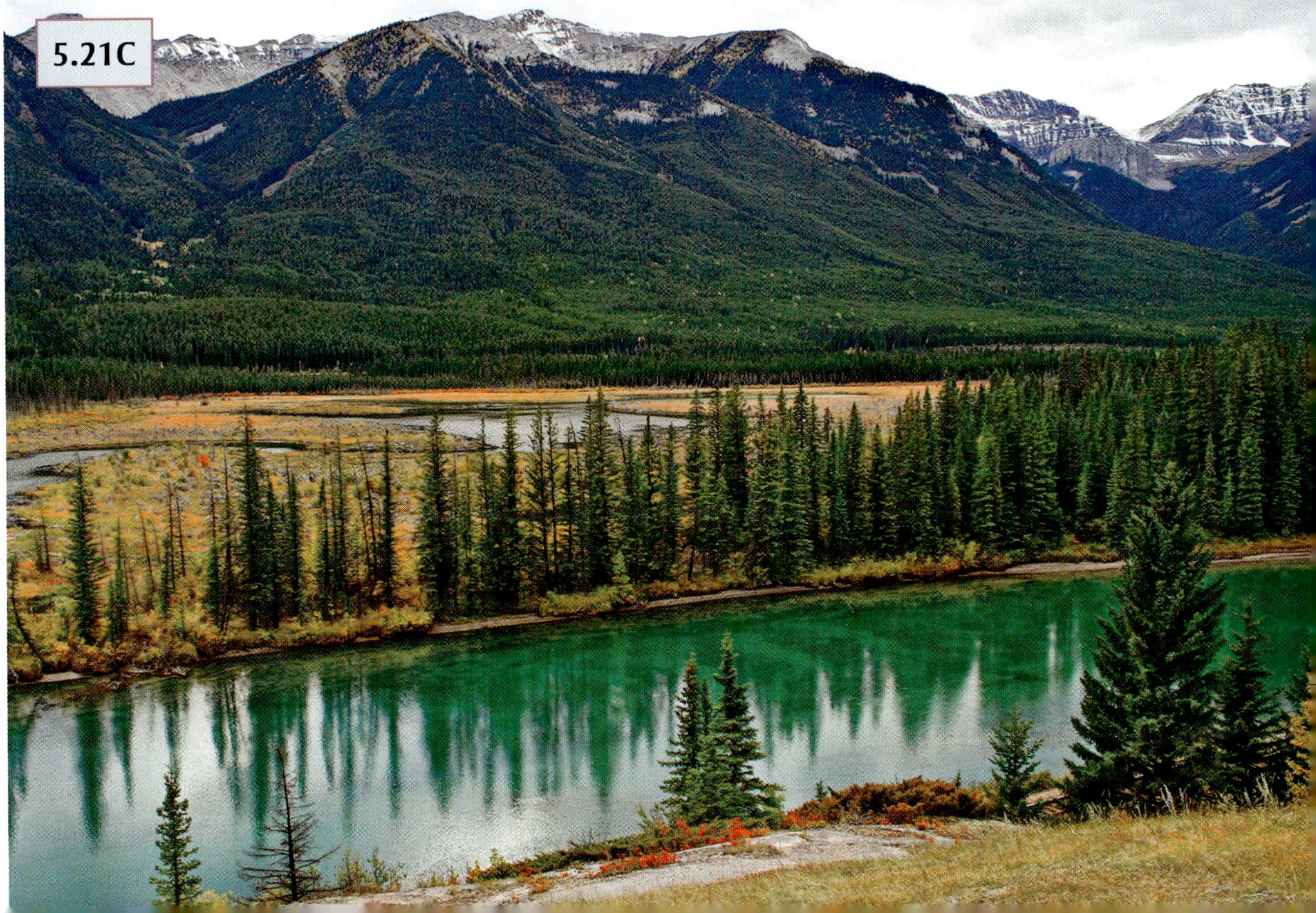
5.21C

and 5.20C, were made by straight actions that require no time at all.

Chapter 2 showed the power of having extra versions to play with. The candidates, though, have to be plausible, and not too alike. These two color versions pass both tests.

Introducing the Joint Action

The Color Boost and the Modern Man from Mars actions are partners. Both are needed in most images but how they relate to one another and how much of each to use is a hard, if enjoyable, decision. Once you are comfortable with them, I think you will want to use them interactively. For that reason, you are supplied a third action, MMM + Color Boost, that combines them.

The Bottom Line

The fun part of the workflow starts with a file not known to be incorrect, yet not colorful enough to be pleasing. This chapter shows how to intensify the color effect. Since everybody has their own opinion on how much to put in, there are no right or wrong answers—it's what looks good to your eye.

The method departs from past practice. Every file is treated with the same action, intended to produce excessive color. Upon seeing it, we decide how to back off. Sometimes we reduce all color uniformly; more frequently we use a layer mask to emphasize some colors more than others.

This step also offers a final opportunity to adjust highlight and shadow and/or adjust overall weight.

This chapter's action usually joins the one shown in the next chapter into a single action whose components can be adjusted independently. They are shown as separate actions in the two chapters for simplicity's sake.

That joint action is rather difficult to comprehend at first glance. I prefer to introduce its components separately, the Color Boost here and the MMM in the next chapter. I expect that sooner or later you will want to use the combined action, but playing them as separate actions works, too.

Sticking to two actions for the time being, I would sandwich the Man from Mars version, Figure 5.20C, between the good luminosity version, Figure 5.20B, and the Color Boost curve layers. Inasmuch as color has already been augmented in Figure 5.20C, adding the Color Boost action creates something far too intense to display, let alone print.

Happily, there is no longer a question of right or wrong. We juggle the opacities (and the masks, perhaps) of the two color layers until we find a combination that suits us. If we don't think that a certain layer is adding anything we delete it. If we come up with something that we later think is too loud we can always blend some of the original, duller color back in.

With the reminder that you need not agree with my choice, here are two options for a final product. Postcard 5.21A is the original. Either of the others constitutes an immense improvement. Postcard 5.21B is prepared without the benefit of the Man from Mars version. I just took the good luminosity of Figure 5.20B, applied the Color Boost action and the mask shown in Figure 5.19C, and adjusted opacity to taste.

To my way of thinking, Postcard 5.21C is more convincing because of the extra variation in the green hills.

But you can come up with your own version. It's time now to look more deeply at how to create desirable variation.

6

The Modern Man From Mars

Vivid color is attractive—in moderation. To make it lifelike and convincing, it has to vary, becoming less intense in certain zones and more in others. A new action produces that variation automatically—provided we're able to explain what the key areas are.

As a citizen of the world, I often find myself exploring unfamiliar regions. Until recently, it wasn't easy to access the web while in the car, so I became a connoisseur of guidebooks. The one I use for the island of Maui is truly excellent. I trust what it says. So when I read about the following suggested detour, I was on the hook.

> If you think the road to Hana looked lush and beautiful, wait till you see Nahiku. When plants go to heaven, Nahiku must be their destination. Everything green seems so happy and healthy, you can almost hear them giggling. Life bursts from every corner at the bottom half of the road. The whole setting is ensconced in an area packed with more shades of green than you ever knew existed.

This is quite some recommendation. The Highway to Hana that the author refers to is one of the great drives of the world. Around every hairpin curve, across every one-lane bridge, are waterfalls, rainforests, and drop-dead ocean views. Even on Maui, which is noted for its postcard scenes, this drive is special. If he says that it's small potatoes next to this Nahiku detour, I'm on my way.

Regretting at every pothole that I had consumed so much ahi poke at lunchtime, I left the highway and made my way down to the coast to see all the shades of green that had so smitten the scribe.

The verdict: New Jersey has better. Our forests are greener. They have more variation in color, too, because of a greater diversity of species.

Granted, this guy is not a color expert as far as I know. That should be a point in his favor. Those evaluating our work are mostly laypeople, too.

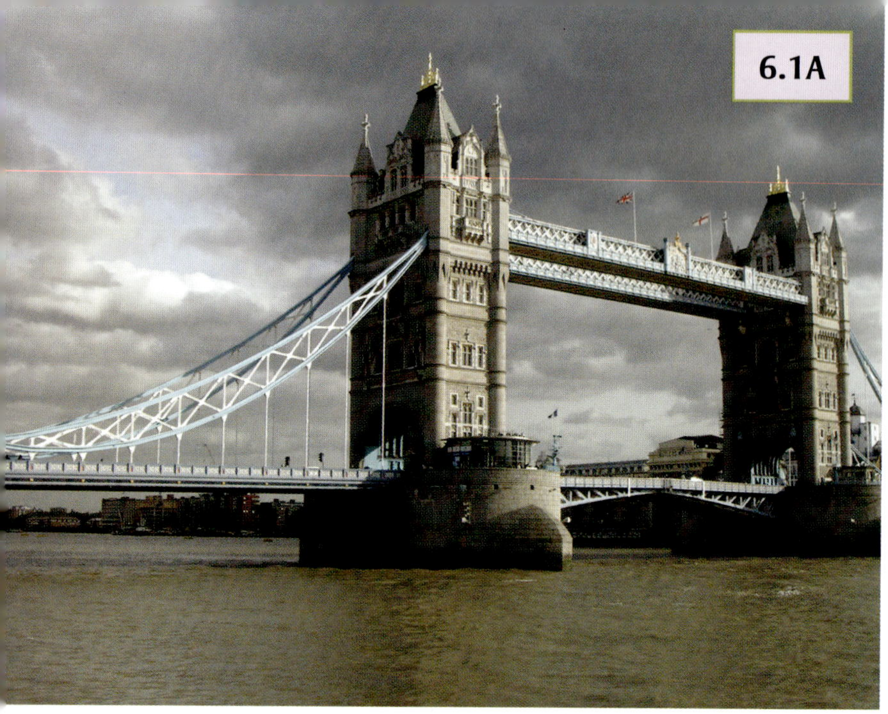

Understanding how they think can be key to having our own work properly appreciated.

And granted, the guy is probably crazy. Otherwise, why would he be an author? But still, how can he be remembering all these shades of green that don't exist? If you get hired to process his pictures, you can be sure that he's going to crumple any effort that doesn't reflect his memories into a little ball and fire it into your face.

Part of what he saw was simultaneous contrast, which we've already mentioned a few times in other chapters. Evolution has programmed us to see variation when confronted by a slew of similarity. He was probably also influenced by the smell, by the lushness of the growth, by the soothing sound of the wind, and the blessed relief the forest canopy offered from the tropical sun. Giuliana Abbiati and I are trying to develop actions and scripts to get these factors into the PPW panel, but no luck so far.

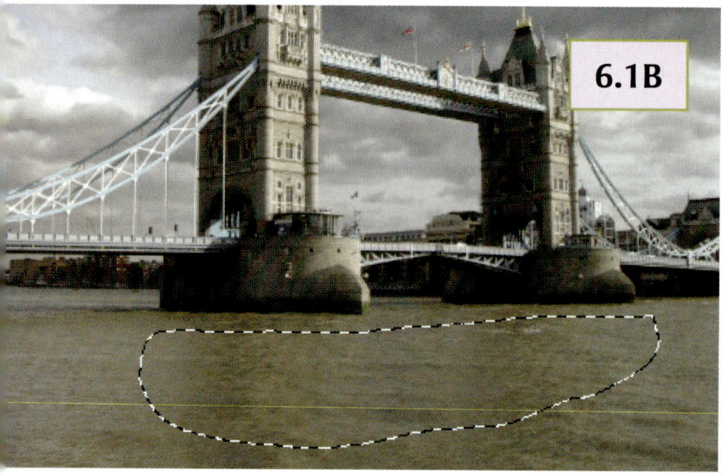

This chapter is about how to incorporate the variation that people think they saw but that the camera did not record.

A First Look at the Action

Instead of showing a picture of Nahiku, I refer you to the final example of the previous chapter. The picture had a similar problem, lack of variation in dark greens. Everything was moving along smoothly until Figure 5.20C showed up. I explained that it showed the default result of a certain action that would be introduced in the next chapter, to wit, this one. Indeed,

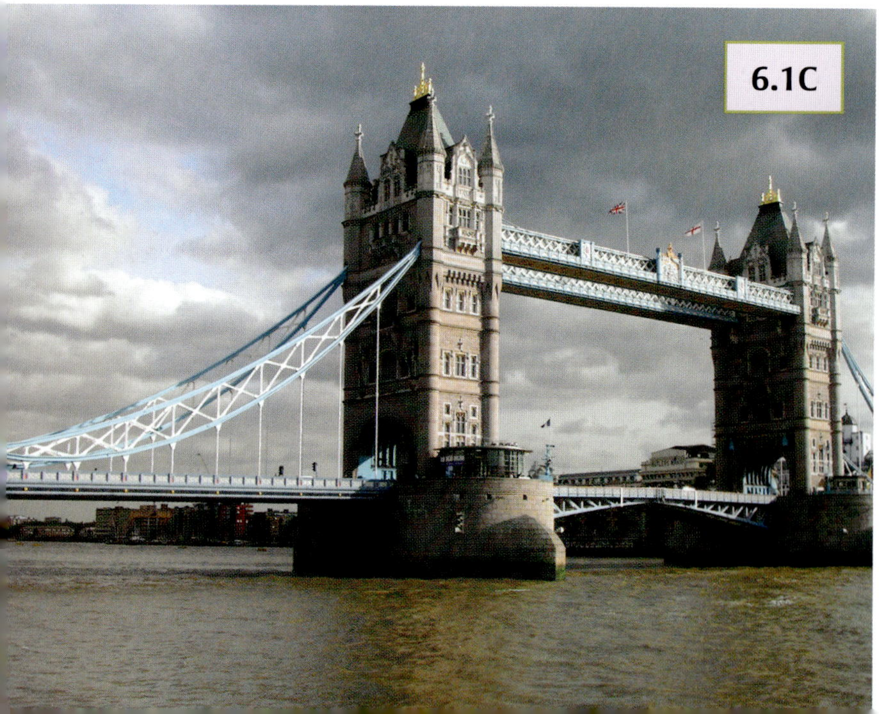

***Figure 6.1** Top, the original. Middle, a rough selection indicates typical water. Bottom, the MMM action played at its defaults.*

the unknown action created an interesting variation in the greens. Used in careful conjunction with the Color Boost action, it produced a more convincing result in Postcard 5.21C than Color Boost alone could in 5.21B.

Its use is easy, as is understanding when it's needed. How it works beneath the hood is another matter. You don't need to know this information to reap the action's benefits. Therefore, that explanation is hereby postponed until the second half of the chapter.

The action is called MMM; I'll explain why later. As MMM should be seen as a kind of bridge to Color Boost, it's appropriate to start out with a bridge, albeit larger and more iconic than any of the one-laners on the Highway to Hana.

The last example featured a river of an unusual color. Figure 6.1A shows another, though hardly the pellucid green of the Bow River. This one's name comes from the pre-Celtic *Tamas*, meaning, you guessed it, dark river. If you need further evidence, Robert Louis Stevenson wrote,

> Dark brown is the river,
> Golden is the sand.
> It flows along for ever,
> With trees on either hand.

Under these circumstances we are likely to prefer more variation to brighter colors, but we shall see. Here's the procedure.

- Make a loose selection, using any tool or method you like, of a typical area you're hoping to improve. Note the extreme precision and elegance that characterizes my use of the lasso tool in Figure 6.1B.
- Play the action. Result: Figure 6.1C.

The photograph dates from 2004. I don't think professionals of that time would have been able to equal Figure 6.1C no matter how much time they took. For us to achieve it by lassoing an area of water and clicking a button seems as shocking as a reasonably priced hotel room in London.

It looks like the action is a form of artificial intelligence, but there's only so far Photoshop can go without knowing whether it's a picture of Tower Bridge or Anne Boleyn. Not every file responds well to this treatment. And even in those that do, the effect may be too strong. In that case, we tweak some sliders. Let's do that now, and then discuss the action and its role in more depth.

Options Before and After Applying

Unlike the Color Boost action of Chapter 5, which only involves half a dozen steps, this action requires sixty. It is out of the question to do all this by hand; you need the action.

For efficiency, you should eventually use the combined action, which is called MMM + Color Boost. The two actions are also supplied separately, because many people have said that they're easier to learn that way.

Remember also that MMM requires a selection. It can be a selection of multiple areas, or a feathered selection, or even a selection of the entire image. If you haven't made one, and are using the PPW panel, you will get an invitation to use Select: Select All. If you are running from the Actions palette, you will get an error message and will have to click Stop.

The Layers palette of Figure 6.2 appears when the action runs successfully. The changes in color and in luminosity are adjustable separately. If the file had other layers previously, they're gone now. And the file is in LAB. Remember, the panel sees the entire action as a single history state, so Command-Z will reverse it. If you're using actions out

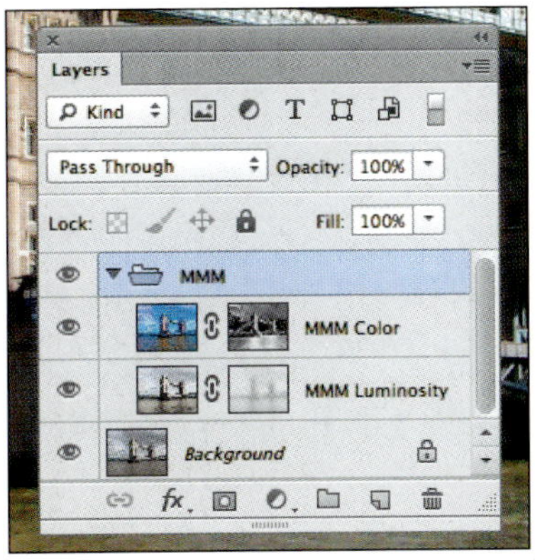

***Figure 6.2** The MMM action requires a selection. Right, the Layers palette immediately after the action has been played.*

of the palette, this isn't true: MMM is so complex that it fills up your whole image history.

Like the Color Boost of the previous chapter (and most other PPW actions, including MMM + Color Boost) all layers are grouped; note the folder icon at the top of the stack in Figure 6.2. You can toggle back to see what the file looked like before the action by clicking its eyeball icon, or you can reduce the group opacity to cut the MMM effect if you don't feel like adjusting individual layers.

Both the MMM Color and MMM Luminosity layers are set at 30% opacity, offering room for maneuver. Using these defaults, Figure 6.3A shows the effect of the MMM Color layer only, and Figure 6.3B MMM Luminosity only.

Remember that MMM is not the end of the process. The plan still is to run Color Boost. For reference, Figure 6.3C shows that action's defaults, without assistance from MMM.

If there's further time for investigation of MMM, try yanking the opacity sliders way up. In creating the variation in certain colors and tones, the action distorts others. Figures 6.3D and 6.3E show MMM Color and then MMM Luminosity jacked up to 70%, each without benefit of the other. This test should give you a clue as to what to look out for if you start to get frisky with the opacities.

No City of London bylaw requires that we use equal settings on these layers. Figure 6.3F employs 40% opacity on MMM Color

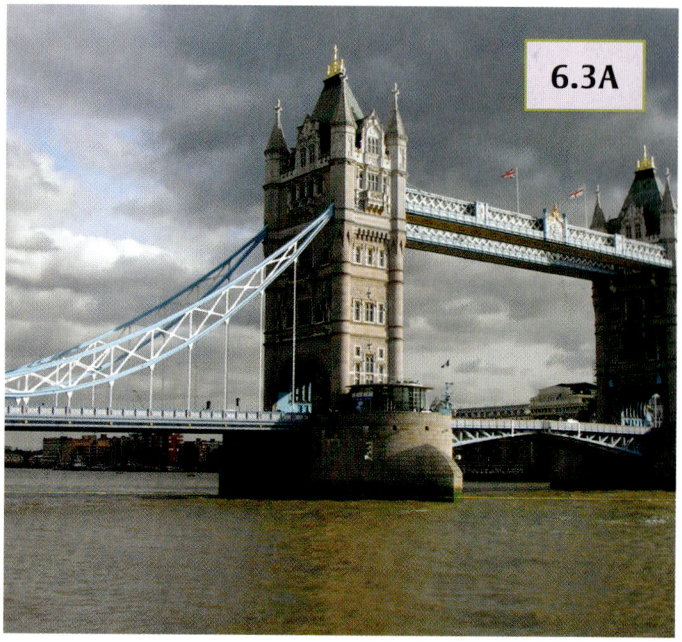

***Figure 6.3** Variations on Figure 6.1C. Right, only the MMM Color layer is active. Bottom left, only the MMM Luminosity layer. Bottom right, the default Color Boost action of Chapter 3, without MMM. Opposite, top left, MMM Color layer at 70% with no MMM Luminosity or Color Boost. Top right, luminosity only at 70%. Middle left, color at 40%, luminosity 20%, and no Color Boost. Middle right, 20%, 40%, 0%. Bottom left, 30%, 30%, 25%. Bottom right, 20%, 20%, 45%.*

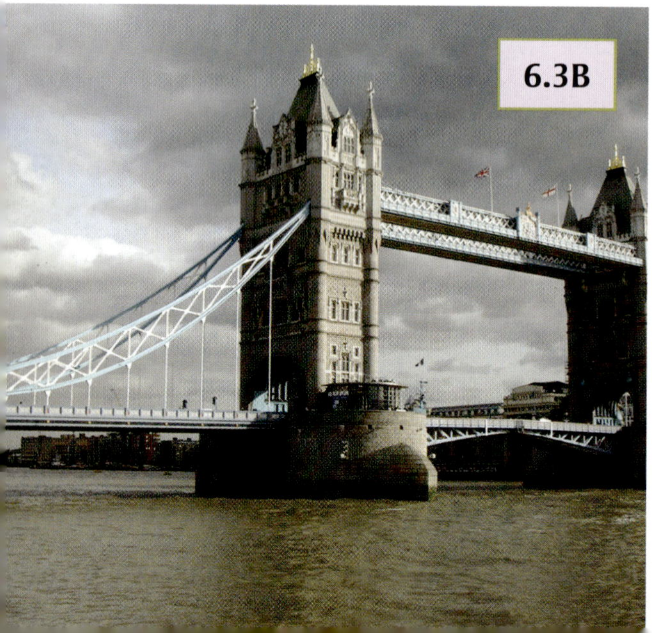

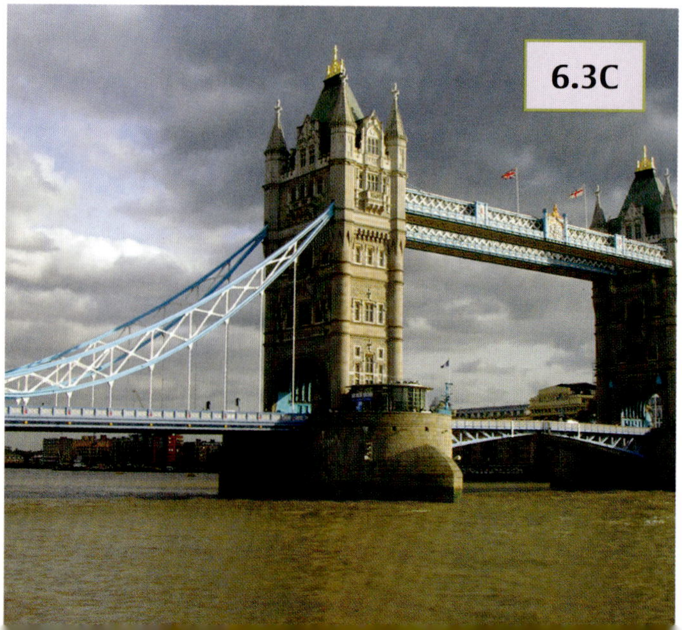

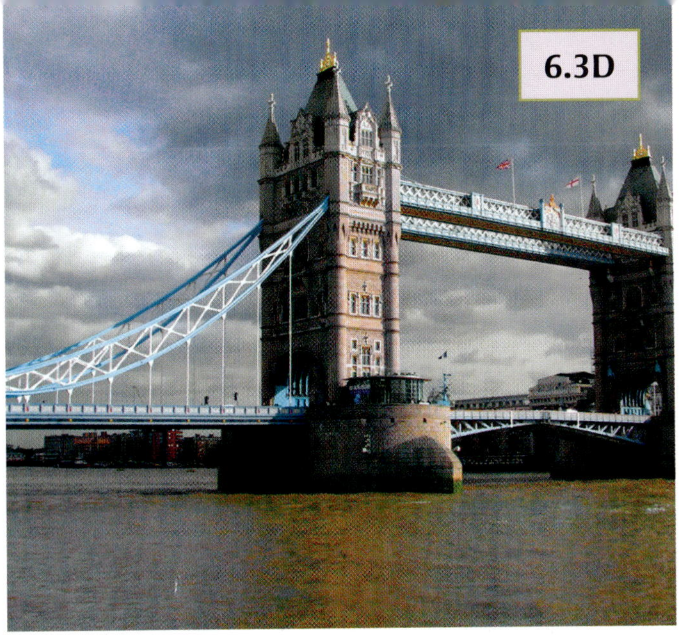
6.3D

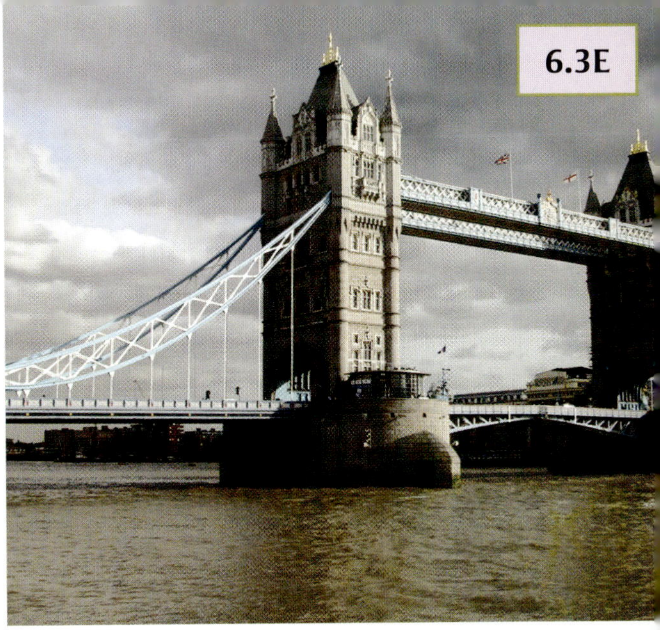
6.3E

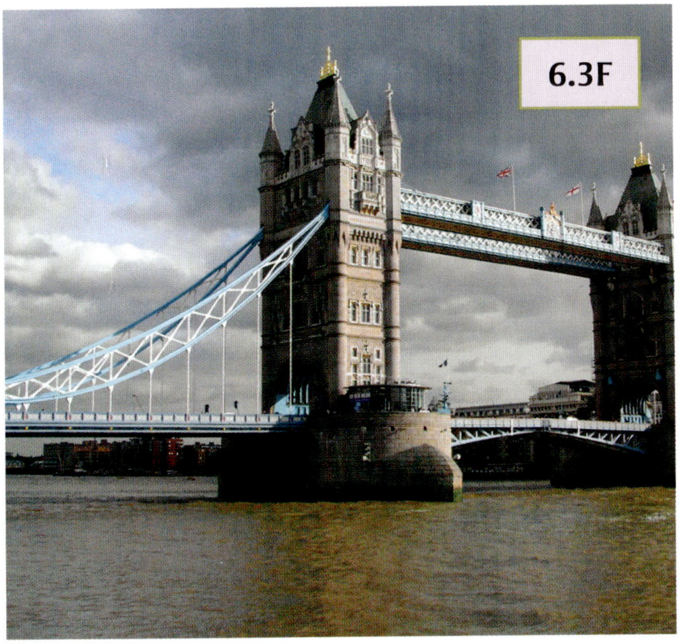
6.3F

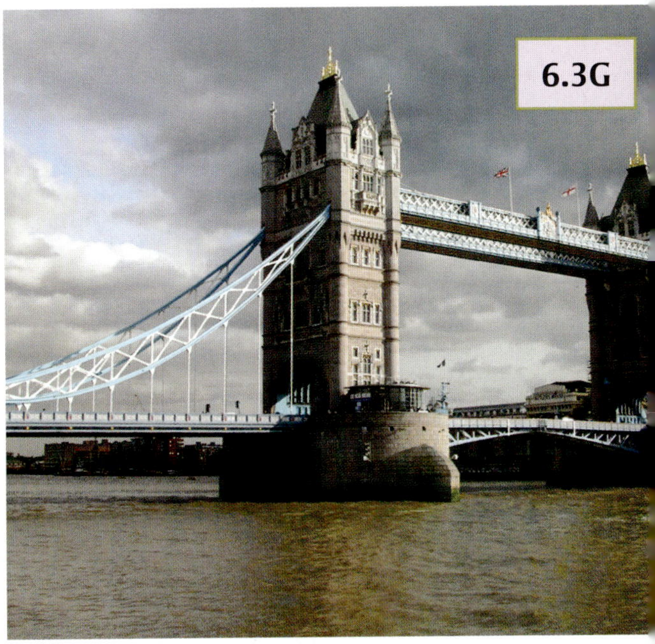
6.3G

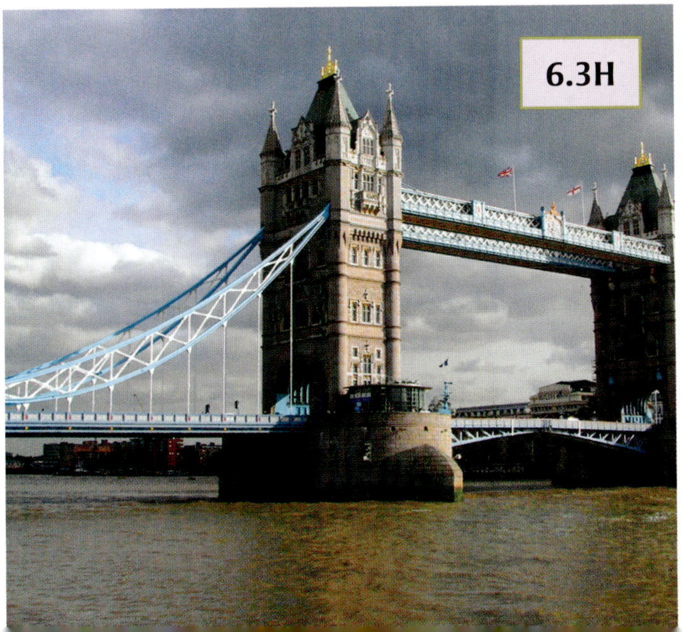
6.3H

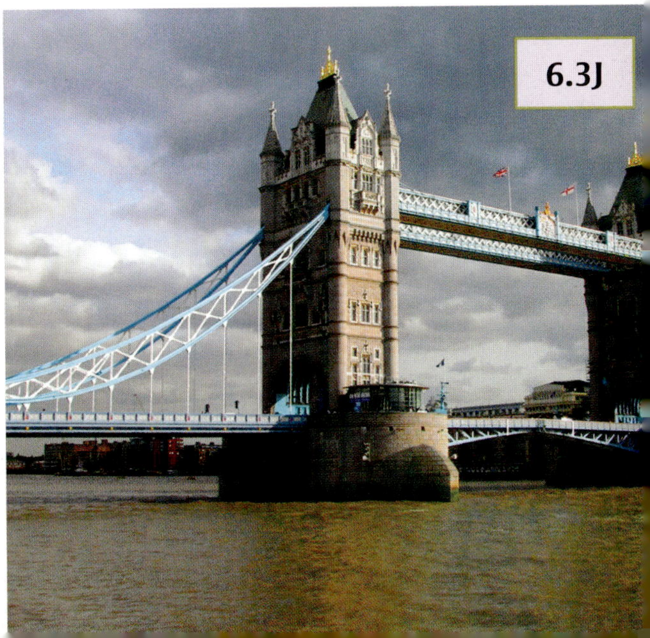
6.3J

and 20% on MMM Luminosity. Figure 6.3G reverses these numbers.

Finally, we may wish to consider how well these two layers work and play with the Color Boost action. Warning: the MMM action makes certain colors more vivid, so it must be expected that the Color Boost will have to be ramped down. Figures 6.3H and 6.3J show different combinations of the two actions.

We'll discuss the aesthetics of these alternate versions in the course of disposing of some of the issues that trouble people when they first start using this tempting but explosive technique.

FAQ About the MMM

- *What does "variation" mean, anyway? Isn't it just another form of color boost?*

Not necessarily. We have identified the parts we are interested in. The MMM Color layer expands their range, So, indeed, some areas receive a color boost. However, others become duller. The same thing happens in the separate MMM Luminosity layer: some parts of the important areas become darker and others lighter.

In a portrait, color variation is critical to believability. On the other hand, we usually don't want to make the face redder, which is what the Color Boost action would do. It is, however, acceptable for some parts, such as the lips and cheeks, to become redder provided that other parts become less red, thus preserving the illusion that the overall color hasn't changed much.

On the other hand, variation in luminosity often isn't a good thing in faces: it brings out more apparent detail, which may not be desirable. In Figure 6.3B, which excludes the color move, we can see that the luminosity adjustment was helpful because it created more contrast in the river. But a face and a river are not the same thing. More contrast accentuates wrinkles, imperfections, and other things that the subject would prefer remain unemphasized. If this picture were a portrait, we'd probably want to delete the MMM Luminosity layer.

- *What types of picture benefit the most from this procedure?*

Those with a large and significant area with limited color variability. In the picture we just worked on, the sky is large, but not particularly significant. The walkway between the two towers is significant, but it isn't large. The two towers themselves are large and significant, but they already have a lot of variation and detail. The river, on the other hand, covers more than a quarter of the picture, it's an important component, and it's monotonous. The action attacks this problem. Note how the reflection of the towers is better pronounced in all the versions that make use of the MMM Color layer.

Scenic shots are often dominated by a single color and respond well to MMM. The Grand Canyon shot that opened Chapter 4 is a study in purple. The Bow River scene that ended Chapter 5 is dominated by greens.

Faces are also an important target for MMM—if they're large enough. The same goes for commercial product photography.

- *What does MMM stand for?*

That these image types desperately need color variation is not a new idea. In 2004 I introduced a solution. My first demonstration put so much color variation in a face that my wife commented that the subject looked like a man from Mars. I was in need of a title, and *Man from Mars Method* it became.

It was one of the most popular and effective tricks I'd ever come up with—provided the image was right for it. Some non-experts used it but they had to be ambitious, because it was explosive and also required great care in choosing something called the pivot point, which need not be discussed further.

If you want details of the original MMM, pick up one of my post-2004 books—but this new action is better, safer, more flexible, and easier to use. Thus, the Modern Man from Mars. The initials stay the same, the application is different.

- *What, specifically, does this action do?*

It evaluates the area you have selected and comes up with a strategy for optimizing it. Then it discards the selection and applies the strategy to the entire image. The second half of this chapter goes into more depth.

- *What problems can it cause?*

In expanding the zones of interest it has to contract everything else. The MMM Luminosity layer can cause an undesirable contrast loss in areas that don't match the selection. If you notice this, delete the layer or reduce its opacity.

The color issue is more insidious. Unlike the Color Boost action, which just deepens existing colors, MMM changes hue. Suppose the selected object is a face, and we play MMM. The reddest parts get purpler; the least red parts, greener or more cyan.

Since the changes aren't limited to the face itself, anything more vivid than the reddest part of the face will get even more colorful. That may not be so horrid. Anything less red than the face, however, moves toward coolness, which could be a problem.

Compare Figure 6.3D, which has the color change jacked up beyond reason, to Figure 6.3E, which uses the original color. Notice how much bluer the sky is, and also the darker cloud. But nobody selected those things—it was the river that was selected.

The river is a dull yellow—about the same yellow as the towers, according to measurements in the B channel, which, you will recall, is yellow vs. blue. The only yellower things are the gilded top ornaments. The action turns them *seriously* yellow, but that's agreeable, at least to me. Everything else is less yellow than the water, so it gets pushed toward blue.

- *Then why didn't the clouds in the lower left of the sky get blue, too? They're white, which is certainly less yellow than the water.*

Chapter Goals and Recap

The Modern Man from Mars action works hand in hand with the Color Boost action of Chapter 5. You can run the two actions separately, but with practice you will want to run MMM + Color Boost, which combines the two interactively.

MMM's goal is variation in the most important areas. You guide it with a selection representing what you wish to improve. The selection is discarded before anything changes. Any selection method is acceptable, including multiple selections or Select All.

The action returns both a color and a luminosity layer. We can adjust their strength or discard either.

In seeking variation, MMM makes some parts more colorful and others less. This is an advantage over Color Boost, which can only intensify. MMM's disadvantage is that hue can shift noticeably.

How Difficult Is It? Not very, *unless* you are trying to make the absolutely best selection instead of a fairly good one. This topic is covered in the second half of the chapter. Also, working with the combined MMM + Color Boost action can be intimidating at first.

How Often Is It Needed? I use MMM + Color Boost on every image. About a third of the time I junk the MMM Luminosity layer. In a somewhat smaller percentage I either discard the MMM Color layer or reduce its opacity to almost nothing.

The PPW Takes Shape

COLOR

- Kill incorrect color with RGB curves (Chapter 3).
- Identify highlight (Chapters 3, 4).

CONTRAST

- Channel blending on luminosity layer (Chapter 4).
- Contrast-enhancing curves (Chapters 4).

COLOR AGAIN

- Apply MMM action (this chapter).
- Apply Color Boost action (Chapter 5).
- Finalize contrast, including endpoints.
- Reduce color by masking or opacity adjustment.

SHARPEN

FINALIZE

- Consider blending with a conservative version.
- Convert to final output space, if needed.

Because it would be offensive if they did. We are more disposed to accept a color change in something non-neutral, like the darker clouds or the blue sky. Unwanted shifts in neutrals limited the utility of the original Man from Mars Method. In the early versions of the present action I got tired of having to reprocess shots of green landscapes because white clouds had become pink. You may recall that because the issue had not yet been corrected, I wound up with an unexpected purple swan back in Figure 2.6E.

Accordingly, the current action incorporates a mask that keeps near-neutrals from changing. That's one reason why it's 60 steps. And speaking of pink:

The MMM action operates in LAB, channel by channel. We've already discussed the yellow vs. blue B channel. In the A, which is magenta vs. green, another problem develops. The water is nearly 0^A, neutral. The towers are a bit more positive, more magenta. The action obediently makes them more magenta still. As the opacity of the color layer goes up, the towers become distinctly pink. One need not be a yeoman warder to realize that this is not an appropriate color.

The question is, though, how much pinkness in the tower, how much blueness in the sky, will you tolerate? The more you're willing to accept, the more variation you can have in the water. Considering that the Color Boost action is yet to come, conservatism is in order. I prefer Figure 6.3J, which uses more Color Boost, less MMM, to 6.3H.

- *Where does this fit into the workflow?*

Hand in hand with the Color Boost action of Chapter 5. This last exercise shows why neither is adequate without the other. Color Boost alone works fine much of the time, but an image like this one lacks the needed variation. MMM by itself can't achieve strong enough colors without distorting them.

I've experimented with MMM at different times in the workflow with inconclusive findings. The logical place is right between the luminosity step of Chapter 4 and the Color Boost. Therefore, in the combined action, the two Color Boost layers are on top of the two generated by MMM.

Two Actions to Choose From

The usual tradeoff between speed and flexibility is present. The blunderbuss approach is to say that the workflow without MMM works fine. If MMM can make a contribution so much the better. So I will run MMM, choose something conservative, flatten the file, and run Color Boost.

The more meticulous play the combined action, MMM + Color Boost. Now four layers interact instead of two. Remember that Color Boost, unlike MMM, consists of curves. Even at the lower opacities of the combined action, they magnify whatever mischief MMM is up to. One can also delete one or both MMM layers and be none the worse for it. It takes some getting used to but I now have adopted the combined action for all of my own work.

Figure 6.3D convinces me, for

Figure 6.4 *When, as in this image, it isn't obvious what to select before running the MMM action, consider the Select All command.*

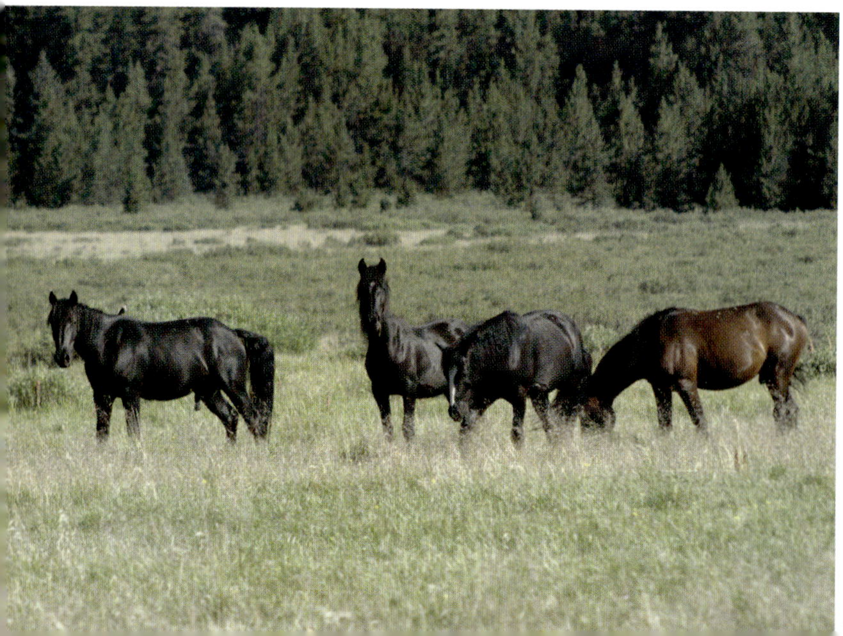

example, that my tolerance for the bridge going pink is going to be the limiting factor in my use of MMM. I want to apply as much MMM Color as I can get away with, because it does such a good job with the river. But it also causes the pinkness. It's tough to know when this becomes unacceptable without seeing the impact of the Color Boost curves.

- *When should I not bother with MMM at all?*

I believe that it should be tried on every image. All we need do is make a rough selection and play an action. We can probably do that faster than trying to figure out whether MMM is likely to work.

Remember, this is an adjunct to what has come before, not a mandatory step. Sometimes it adds little or nothing. In that case we trash it or reduce it to negligible opacity, at a cost of very little time.

- *How come I don't see a line of transition where the selection was made?*

The selection is advisory only. It's dumped before any changes are made to the file. Beta reader John Pavel reiterates the point: "it is only used to drive the action. It is not used to specify where the action will be applied (as you might expect with a selection in other contexts). The action applies to the whole picture."

- *Can I make multiple selections?*

Yes. Any Photoshop selection method works—including noncontiguous selections.

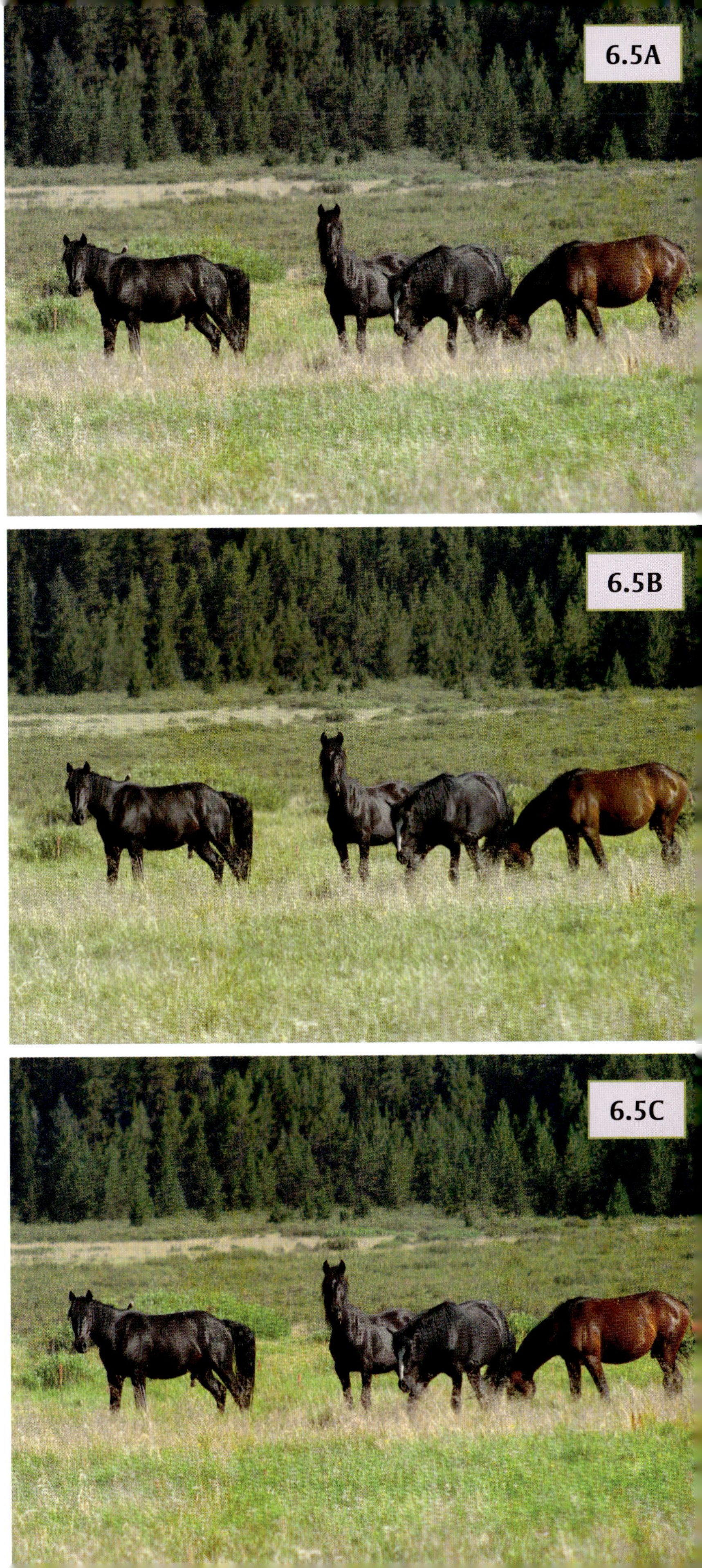

***Figure 6.5** Top, default MMM color after a Select All. Middle, an attempt to match its color intensity using the Color Boost action only. Bottom, a combined MMM + Color Boost version.*

- *How can I avoid selecting garbage that's hard to exclude from what I'm really after?*

Photoshop's calculations favor whatever is heavily represented in the selection. Unless the size of these areas of garbage is significant when compared to the overall selection, there's nothing to worry about.

- *What if I can't figure out what to select?*

Try doing Select: Select All. If you can't identify what's important, then maybe *everything's* important.

Figure 6.4's horses are too small and neutral to benefit from MMM. Everything else is green and could use variation. But which of the several flavors of green to select?

The answer is Select All. The original has nothing red, blue, or bright green. That gives MMM a lot of real estate to work with in expanding the range that the greens currently cover. Figure 6.5A is the default, at least for color, using Select All for the selection. I did not care for the MMM Luminosity layer's impact, so I trashed it.

Figure 6.5B reemphasizes the difference between Color Boost and MMM. It's Color Boost only. I tried to match the overall intensity of Figure 6.5A.

The variation that's missing when MMM is omitted is evident. Before dissing Color Boost, know that Figure 6.5B is better than anything one can do in RGB with curves or the Vibrance or Hue/Saturation commands.

That would be even more true if I were trying to incorporate more intense color, rather than just matching that of Figure 6.5B. But, just as Color Boost's limitation is that it doesn't make anything less intense, MMM's is that it can't push colors too far. We can crank up the layer opacity for more vivid greens, but the brownish areas will go pink. That's too high a price.

The solution is to mix the two. Apply the Color Boost curves before flattening the MMM layers, or use the combined action mentioned earlier. That's what I did to produce Figure 6.5C—it's the combined action's color defaults, using Select All as the selection. As in Figure 6.5A, I deleted the MMM Luminosity layer, which wasn't helping.

The two exercises so far show nothing more than MMM and Color Boost. To make up for the omission, we'll finish this half of the chapter with a start-to-finish postcard, followed by some pointers about what areas to select before invoking MMM.

Of Cream and Cragginess

Before going through the steps that produced Postcard 6.6, it should be remarked that this type of shot is tougher than it looks. If you don't believe it, there's no shortage of photos of this famous formation in Capitol Reef National Park, many by landscape photographers to whom you would think quality would be important.

Just take a moment, though, to visit images.google.com or almost any stock photo site. The search term is "Navajo Dome" and what it returns might be enough to cause one to consider jumping off the top of it. Even at thumbnail sizes, almost every version has horrible color, or next to no detail in the dome, or both.

The National Park Service describes the dome as "creamy white". You would never know this from the bright oranges and reds in the search results, but I've been to the park several times and can vouch for its accuracy.

As always, the first step is checking for color problems. The sky averaged about $(2)^A(23)^B$. Those values agree with my recommendation of between $(5)^A$ and 2^A, with the B an unknowable negative number.

The bottom right greenery is typically $(8)^A15^B$, in accord with the recommendation that the absolute value of the B should be 1.5 to 2.5 times that of the A.

***Postcard 6.6** (opposite) Navajo Dome, Capitol Reef National Park.*

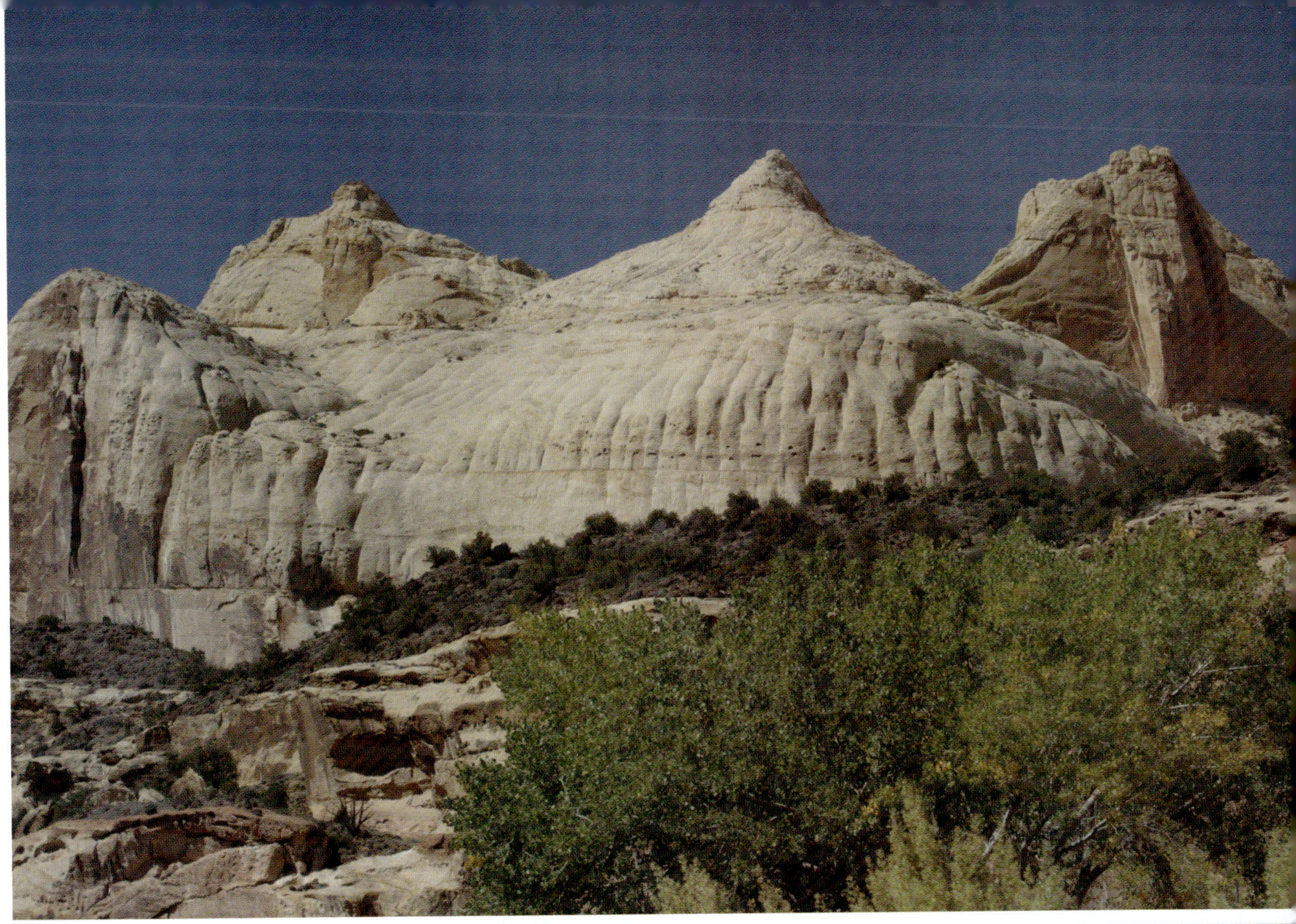

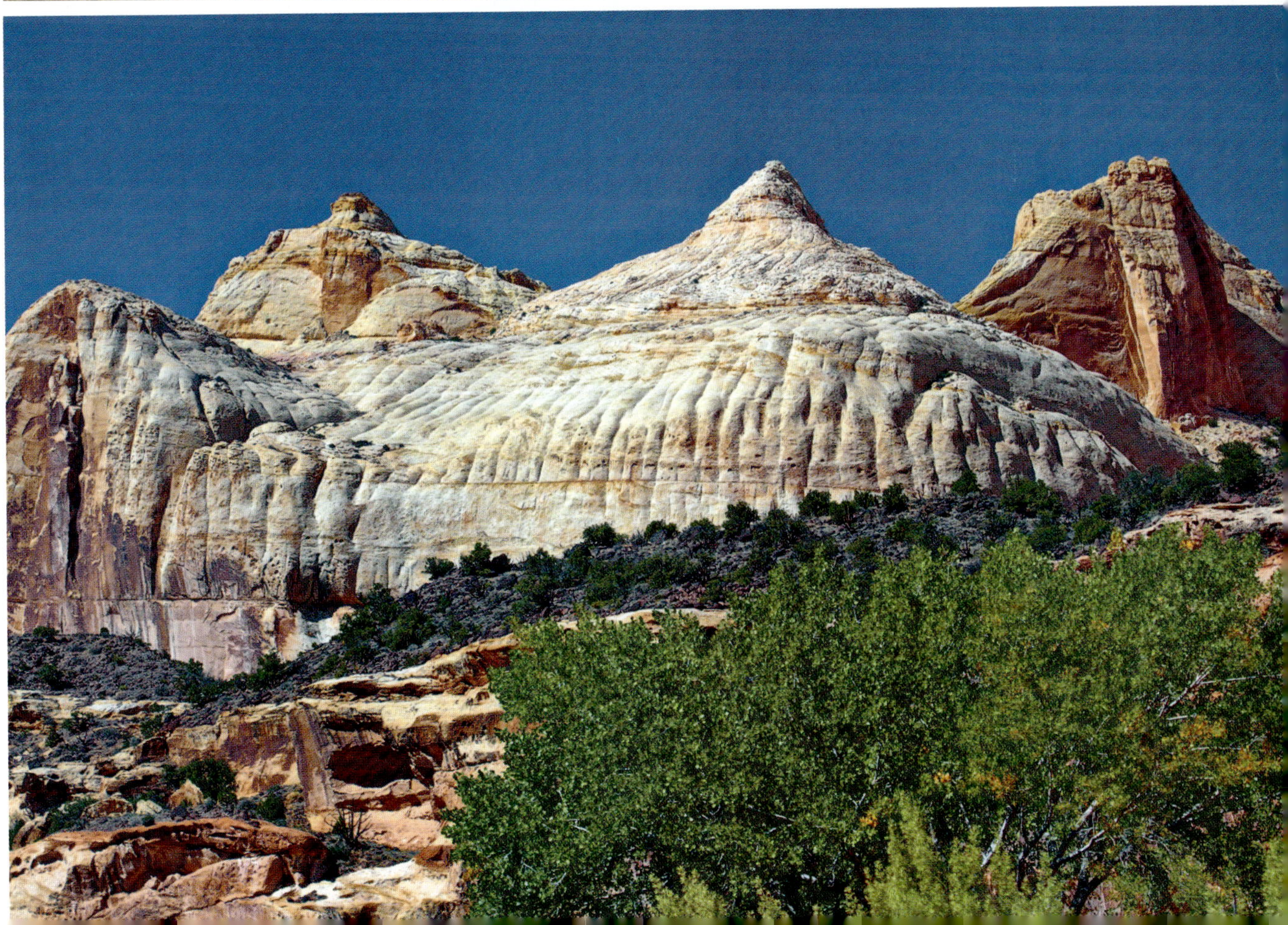

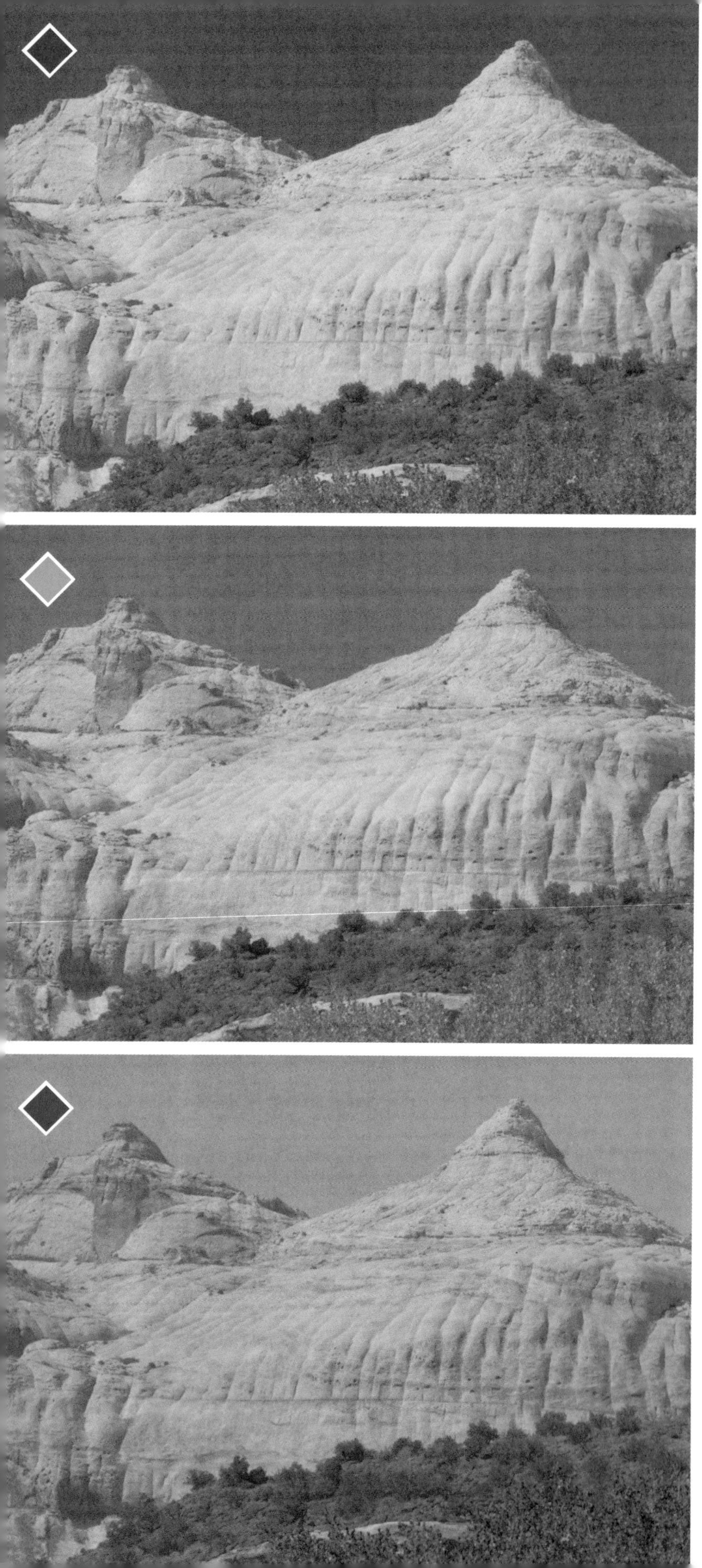

The highlight should certainly be somewhere in the dome but it wasn't clear where. I used a threshold adjustment layer to find out that the lightest parts were in the center. The point I chose read $220^R214^G206^B$, which, given my own color settings, corresponds to 1^A5^B. That's not bad for a cream color, which we would expect to be somewhat yellow (B–positive) with only a skosh of magenta (A–positive) for warmth.

In the slightly darker areas just above the tree line, however, I found stuff like 4^A8^B. On the left side, I found 6^A9^B. When the AB are nearly equal like this, they make more of an orange-red than a yellow. I confess to not being able to detect that in the original. The dome, however, is so lacking in variation that we know MMM is going to be used in a big way, followed by Color Boost. So even a slight pink cast is as dangerous as hiking in this vicinity without sufficient water.

The measurements indicate that the original dome is too magenta. As green is the direct opponent of magenta, the solution is to lighten the green channel where it is approximately the same darkness as the rocks of the dome. While I was at it, I made a similar adjustment to the blue, to reduce yellowness. Yes, a creamy white is slightly yellow, but my guess was that the original had too much.

From force of habit, I changed layer mode to Color, preventing any loss of detail that these modest curves might theoretically have caused but almost certainly didn't.

***Figure 6.7** The original red, green, and blue channels.*

Of Channels and Curves

Time now to flatten and duplicate the layer, in preparation for enhancing contrast. Pertinent parts of the channels are shown in Figure 6.7, which reveals that the red has little to offer in the dome.

The chosen highlight is heavier than it should be, which leaves a lot of room for maneuver. The red and green channels should be lightened considerably. The blue, remember, carries so little weight that it can be ignored—except as a source for a blend. It looks like just the thing to beef up the red.

An aesthetic question: do you think the sky is too dark? If you do, the blue should be blended into the red in Normal mode. If you don't, it should be in Darken mode, which prevents the sky and anything else from lightening. My choice was a little of both. First I blended at 40% opacity, Normal mode, which simultaneously darkened the dome and lightened the sky. Then, I blended again into the result, this time at 40%, Darken mode, protecting what was left of the sky.

With the red now redolent, as it were, with detail in the dome, it was time to lighten the red and green channels. The two curves were similar: lighten the highlight point while darkening the midtone. They were therefore steepest in the light half of the picture, assigning more contrast to the rocks and less to the greenery. Figure 6.8 shows the new red and green channels.

Back to the overall picture. Figure 6.9A shows the impact of the slight curves that reduced the reddish tinge. Can you see how it differs from the original in Postcard 6.6?

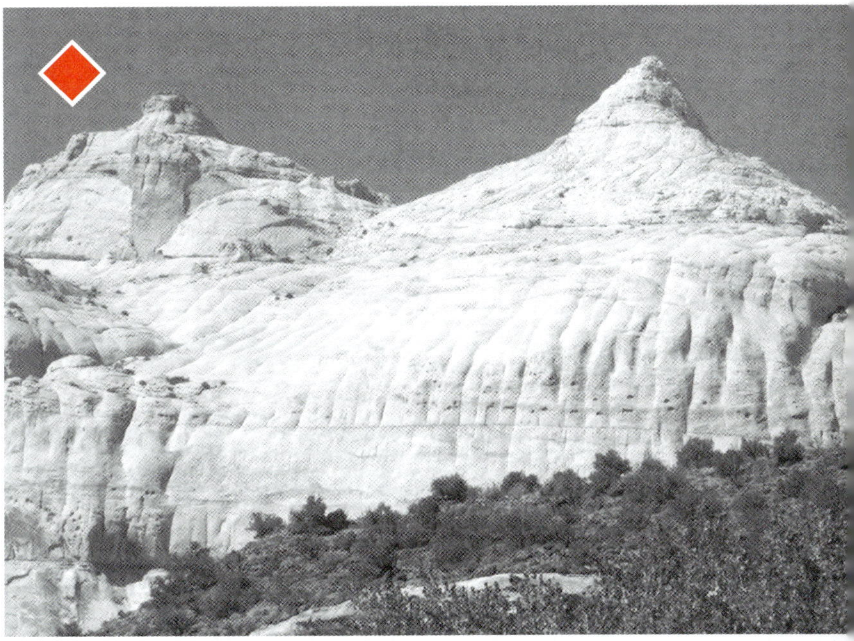

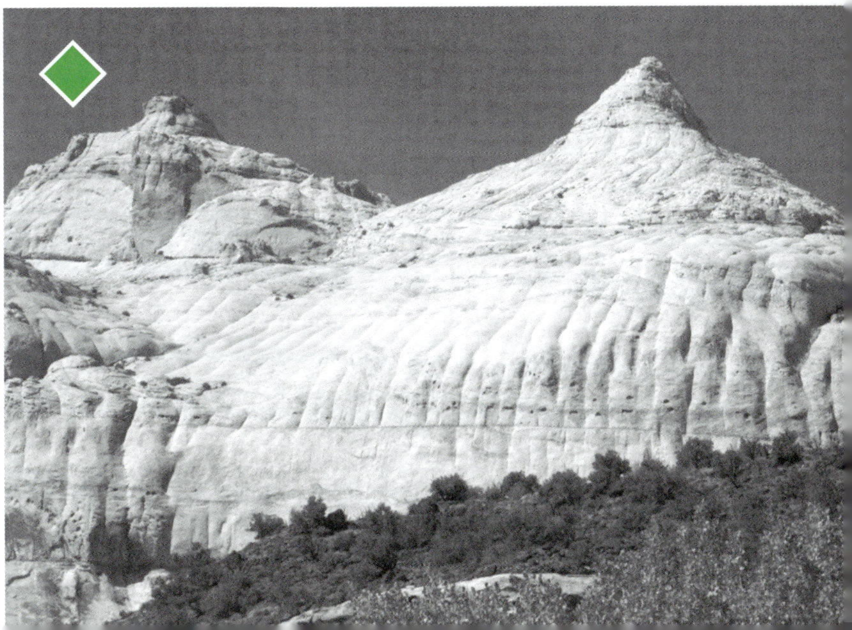

***Figure 6.8** The red and green channels prior to converting the layer to Luminosity mode.*

The next steps are familiar. The modifications to the red and green channels shown in Figure 6.8 produce Figure 6.9B. Upon conversion of the layer to Luminosity mode, we get Figure 6.9C.

Of Variation and Villainy

That brings us to the MMM, and with it, the important question is what to select. First, though, a warning from frustrated beta readers. Any selection other than a totally knuckleheaded one will get you the benefits described in this chapter, which is enough

6.9A

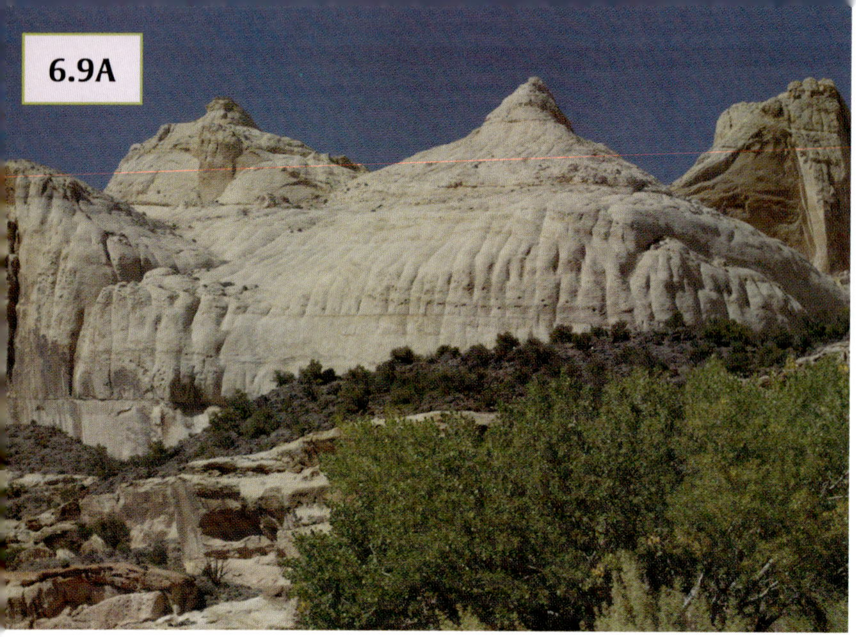

6.9B

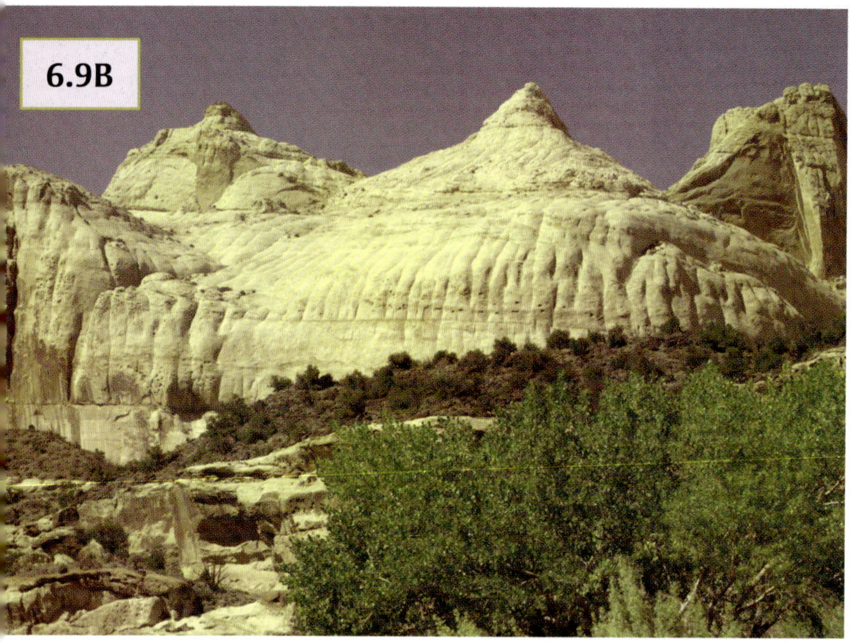

6.9C

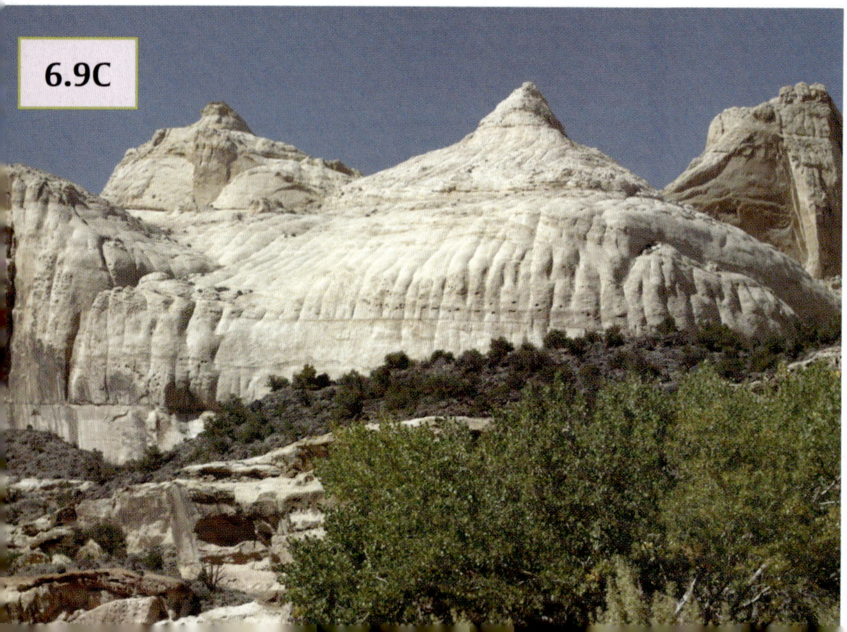

for most people. But some insist upon knowing how to find not just a reasonable selection but the best one possible. That part is hard. If you choose to make that extra effort, the second half of the chapter is for you. If not, I reiterate that any common-sense selection is a good one.

Here, the sky and the dark trees at the dome's base are not significant. The trees in the lower right foreground, however, are. Certainly we want to lasso an area of the dome. But should we then Shift-lasso (which adds to the existing selection) and grab some of those trees as well?

While you ponder whether that might be better, I will proceed with the more straightforward approach of lassoing the dome only, as shown in Figure 6.10A. With it, the default MMM produces Figure 6.10B.

The new color is surely useful to one extent or another, but what of the luminosity? To find out, click off the MMM Color layer's icon. That leaves Figure 6.10C, which should be compared to Figure 6.9C. Is it better, or should we trash the layer?

My vote is to keep it. Note, however, that the highlight point I chose has never been set properly. That gets done in the Color Boost action, which, as you should suspect, is the next move. (For this exercise you need access to all four layers, two from each action. It doesn't matter whether you achieve this by using

***Figure 6.9** Top, after the application of curves in Color mode to correct a slight imbalance toward red. Middle, on a duplicate layer, the red and green channels are changed to those shown in Figure 6.8. Bottom, the duplicate layer is changed to Luminosity mode.*

the combined MMM + Color Boost action, or by playing MMM first and leaving it unflattened before adding Color Boost.)

Figure 6.11A makes the change in highlight value on the Endpoint Adjustment layer. The Color Boost layer itself has been set to a high enough opacity for our goal, which is to have something distinctly too colorful. Once there, we can decide which, if any, parts are more offensive than others.

What happens now depends on personal taste. Either we cut opacity and reduce the color uniformly, or we discriminate by loading a layer mask, most often a copy of the L channel to favor lighter colors and suppress darker ones. We could also apply it to the blank layer mask at, say, 50% opacity to cut the effect in half, and so on.

I'd probably do something like that with Figure 6.11A, and would anticipate a first-rate result. But I think there's an even better way to exploit MMM—which is still active on its own two layers.

Back when we were working on the Tower Bridge shot, I pointed out in Figure 6.3D that MMM was shifting colors all over the place, except a group of white clouds. I explained that the action uses a mask that tries to prevent neutrals from changing. Nine out of ten times, that's the correct approach: we have more tolerance for change in colored objects than in neutrals.

One wonders, though, whether this might not be the one out of ten, given that the important part of the image is itself rather neutral. We can find out by Shift-clicking the layer

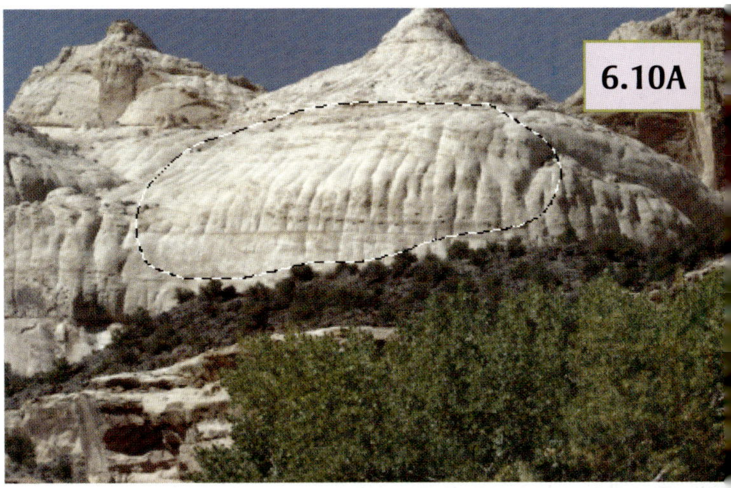

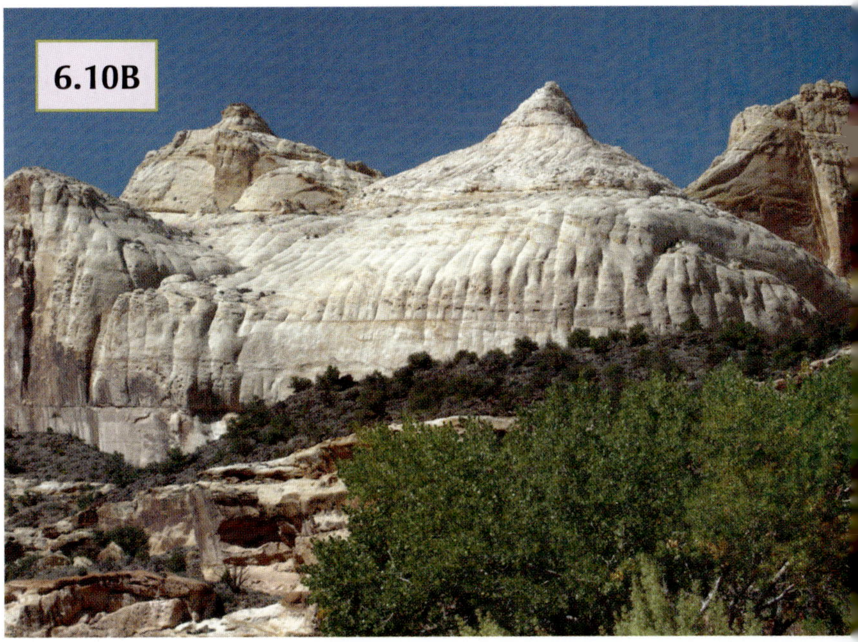

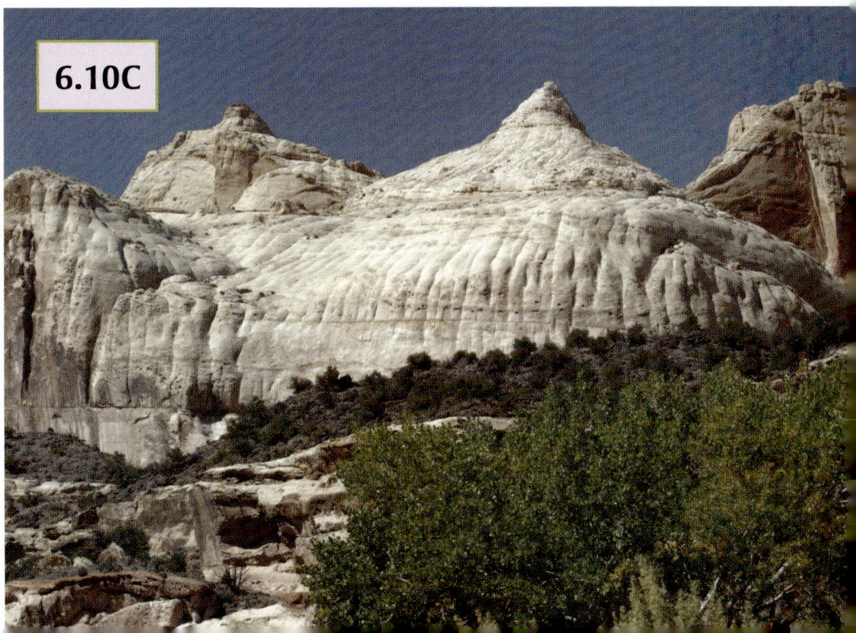

***Figure 6.10** Top, a lasso selection of the dome. Middle, the selection is used to produce a default MMM version. Bottom, the MMM Color layer is clicked off to evaluate the change in luminosity only.*

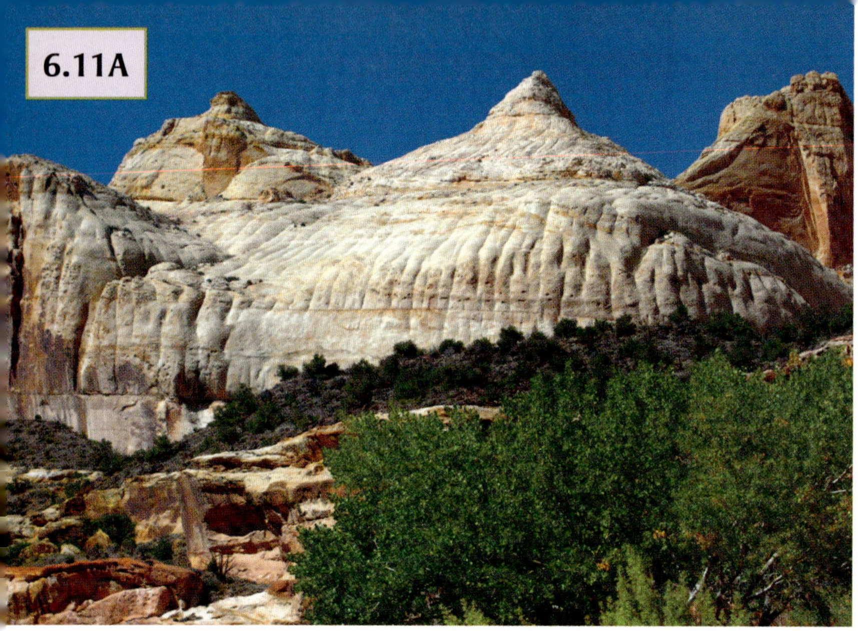

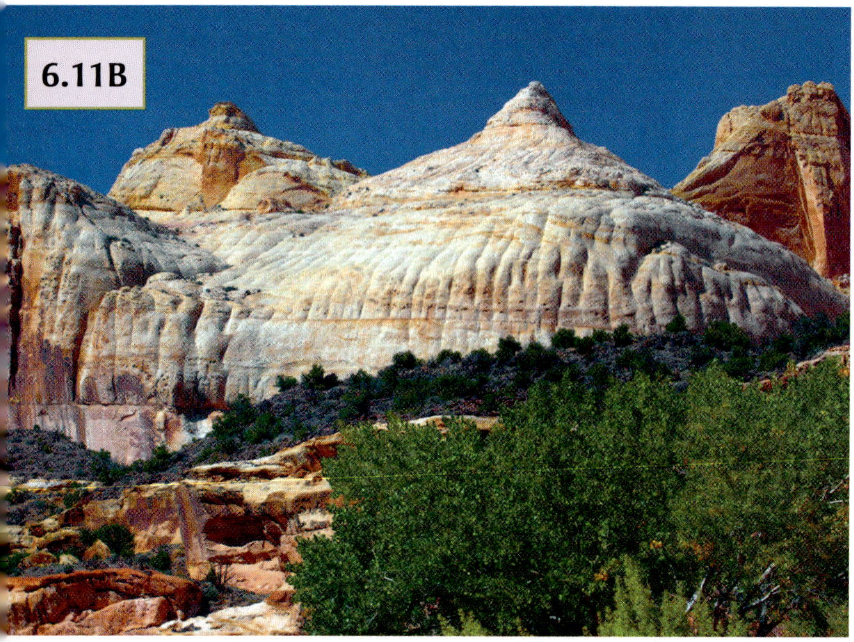

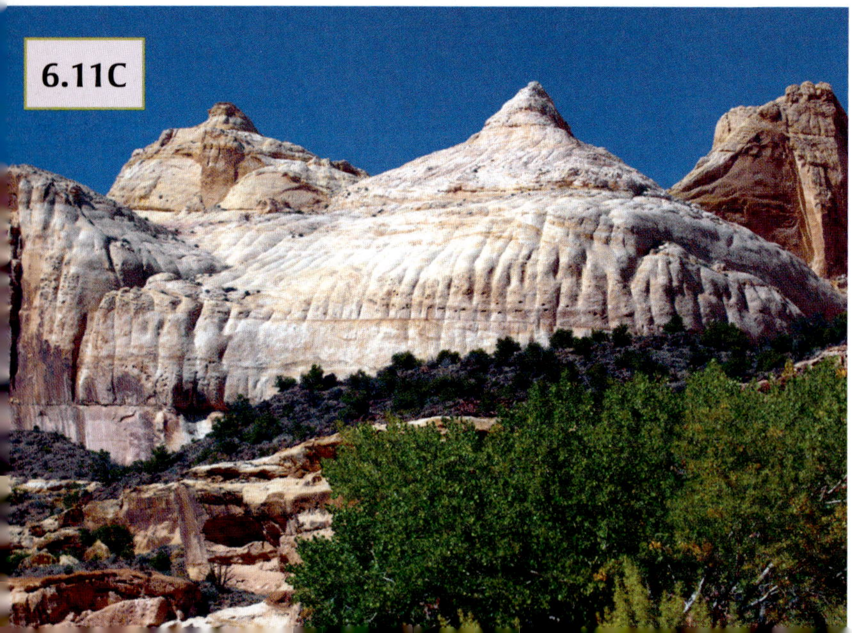

mask icon on the MMM Color layer. This disables the mask (note the red X in the Layers palette of Figure 6.12), and now we have Figure 6.11B.

This is more like what I had in mind for color variation. It's excessive, of course, but to get from here to Postcard 6.6 all I did was reduce opacity and sharpen.

And what of Figure 6.11C? Well, that's the answer to the question of whether to include the greenery in the selection that guides MMM. Using the luminosity-corrected file, Figure 6.9C, as a starting point, I did a second version. Instead of selecting only the dome (Figure 6.10A) before running MMM, I did a double selection (Figure 6.12) to include much of the greenery as well. I couldn't follow the subsequent steps precisely because the MMM Luminosity layer was so different. But in making Figure 6.11C I tried to match the intensity of Figure 6.11A.

As always, you get the final vote, but I say Figure 6.11C is too pink. MMM tried to establish more elbowroom for greens. That implies a shift towards purple.

Choosing the MMM Selection

Success with MMM depends on getting a representative selection of the important area. Don't make the mistake of selecting only the most intense part. And, if you are picking something fairly colorful, you should also consider the possibility of adding something more neutral.

***Figure 6.11** Top, Color Boost layers are added to the MMM effect of Figure 6.10B. Middle, the mask on the MMM Color layer is disabled. Bottom, a completely separate version, prepared using a different selection for the MMM action.*

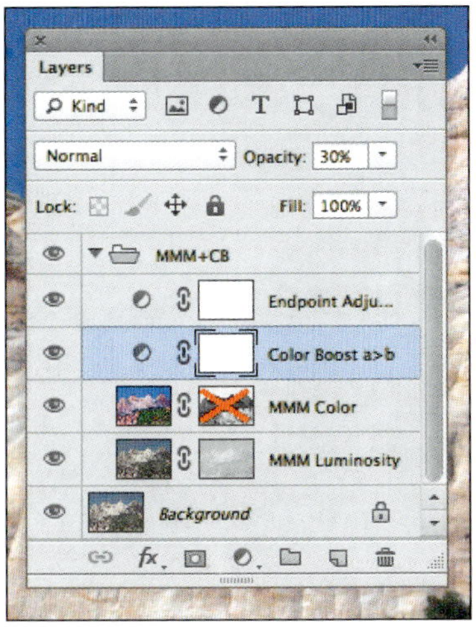

***Figure 6.12** Left, the Layers palette for Figure 6.11B shows that the mask for the MMM Color layer is disabled. Right, the selection of greenery in addition to the white rocks caused MMM to create a pink shift in Figure 6.11C.*

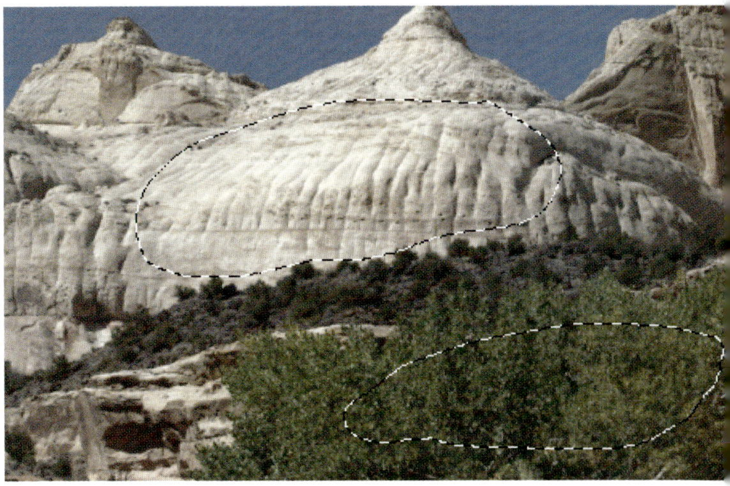

When one large object dominates the picture, adding color variation is advisable. That goes for geological formations, meadows, bodies of water—and faces. Studio photographers apply heavy makeup to their subjects to accentuate the variation between the cheeks and lips and the rest of the face. They do so because they recognize that without it the face looks dull and lifeless.

Alas, not all photos are taken in a studio and not all subjects wear makeup. MMM can come to the rescue, at least if the selected area is well chosen. For the original of Figure 6.13, I propose three options: the lips, the face (notice that one need not be too careful in making an MMM selection), and Select All. Before turning the page, which do you expect to do the best job, and which the worst?

* * *

The three versions are all MMM defaults, based on the selections shown in Figure 6.13. I hope you knew that the one based on the lips, Figure 6.14A, would be the worst. Everything else in the picture is less red than the lips, so it all shifts toward green. Admittedly the name of the action is Man from Mars and admittedly, Martians have been occasionally referred to as little green men, but it is difficult to explain the concept to clients.

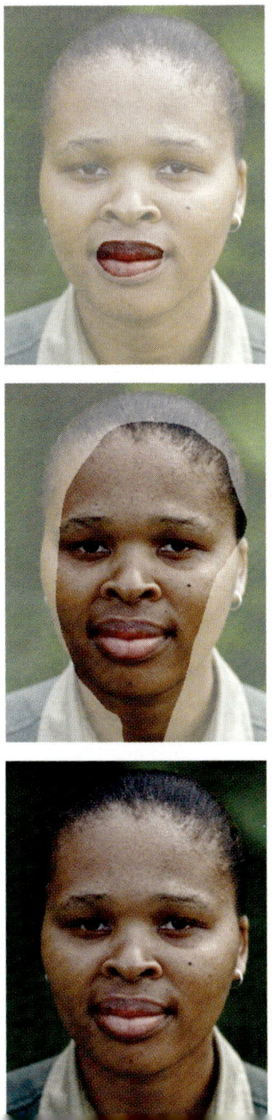

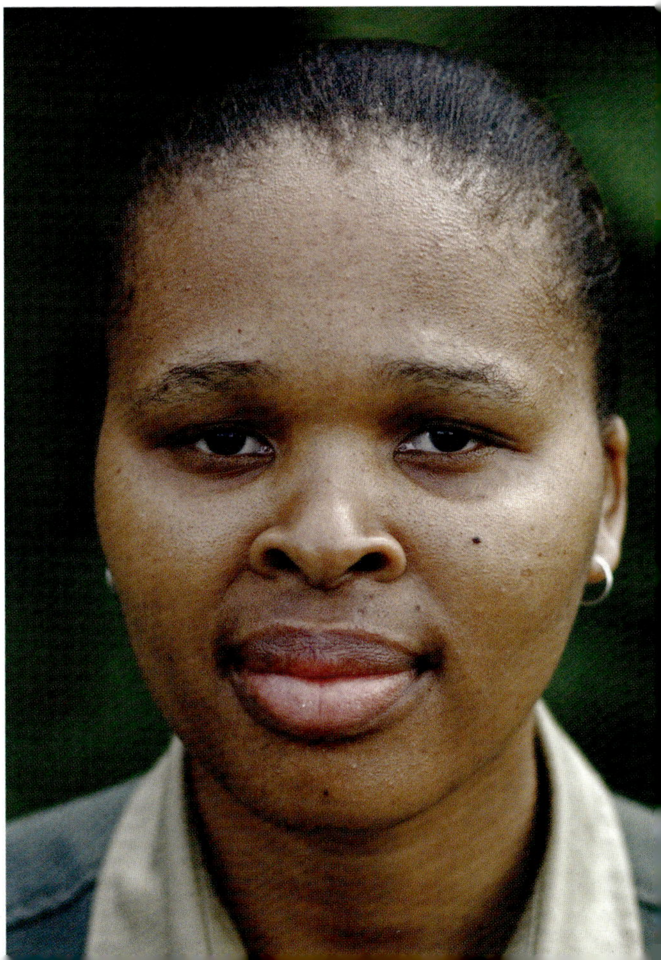

***Figure 6.13** Faces are always candidates for the MMM action. With this original, what will be the ramifications of each of the three selections shown? Turn the page to see the results.*

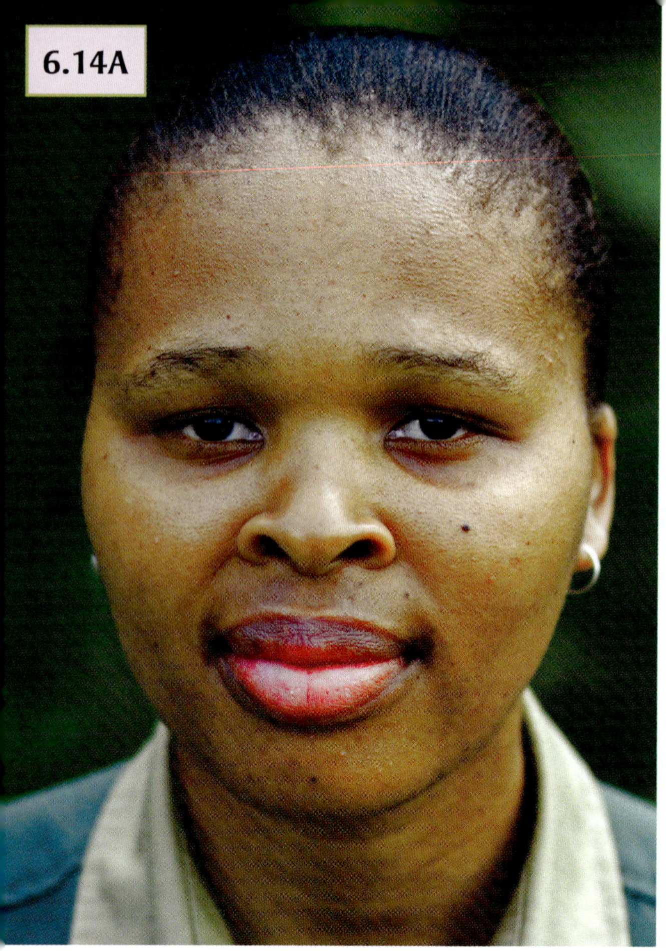

The best ought to be Figure 6.14B, the one based on the face. And it is, once we agree that the default MMM result goes overboard, as is commonly the case with faces. Cut this effect in half and it will be a big improvement over the original.

The Select All version, Figure 6.14C, is already a big improvement. It doesn't have the snap of Figure 6.14B. Some, however, might prefer its color. The lips in Figure 6.14B are redder because so much variation has been introduced, but overall I would say Figure 6.14C is the redder of the two.

That extra redness happens because Select All, as opposed to considering just the face, adds green areas to the selection. The picture has to shift to red to compensate. This face happens to have been cropped from a much larger photo, which had ten times as much green background. If I had processed the uncropped version with a Select All, it would have made the face *really* red.

***Figure 6.14** Default applications of the Modern Man from Mars action based on different selections. Top, the lips. Bottom left, the face. Bottom right, Select All.*

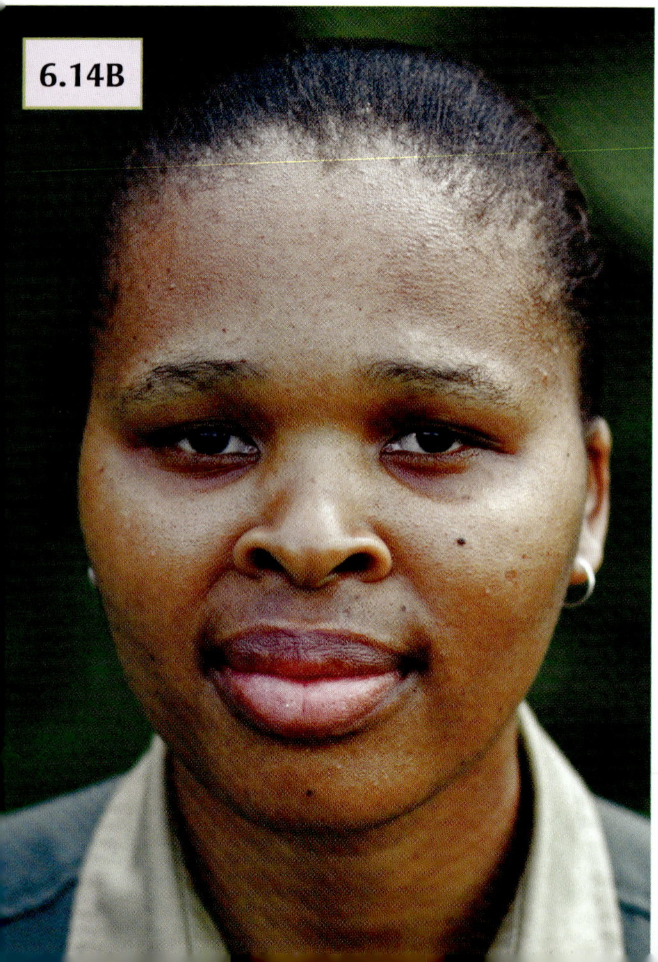

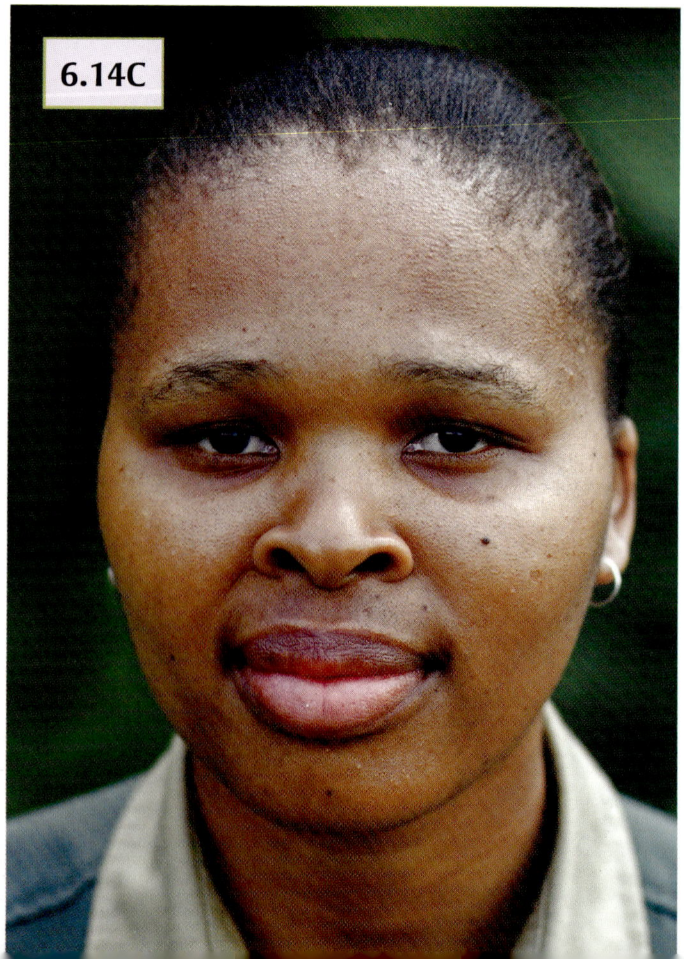

If you like the variation in Figure 6.14B but wish it were slightly redder overall, the fix is easy. Make the layer group invisible, restoring the pre-MMM look. Reselect the face, but this time also lasso the green area above the ear. And run MMM again. It eliminates the layers underneath and gives you what you want. At the end of the second half of this chapter, I'll discuss an even faster and more flexible method.

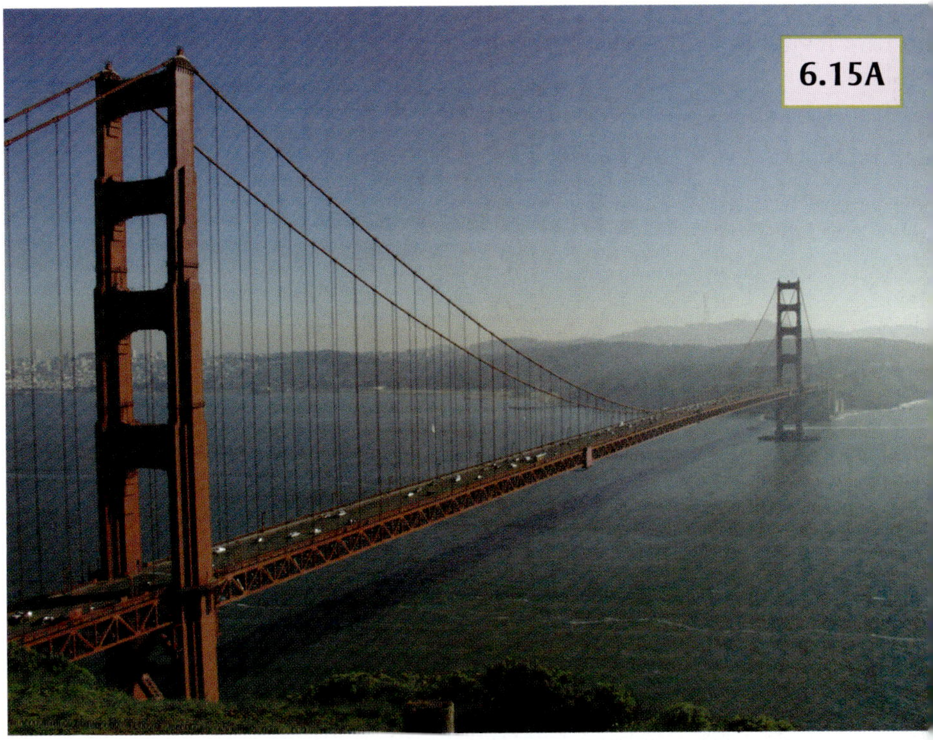

A Bridge Too Far

Here's another iconic bridge to match the one that opened the chapter. Same photographer, same general subject, same method of selection, but this time a disappointment. Figure 6.15A is the start point, 6.15B the standard selection, 6.15C the melancholy result. The sky turns a foul purple. So does the bridge's shadow.

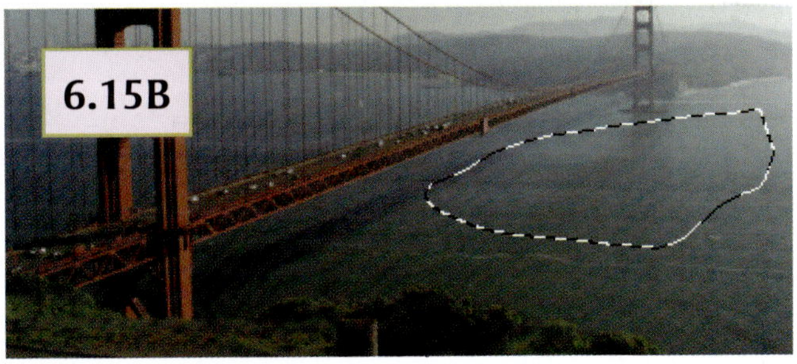

Can we discuss why this happened? Certainly, but why bother? The point is a simple one. *It didn't work,* at least not for color. It's not like Figure 6.14B, where a simple reduction in opacity will give a good result. This one's color can only be used if we put substantial effort into fixing it.

Doing that defeats the purpose. The MMM can be extraordinarily effective, as we've seen previously. And as we now see, it can be ineffective, too. What do you expect from a silly

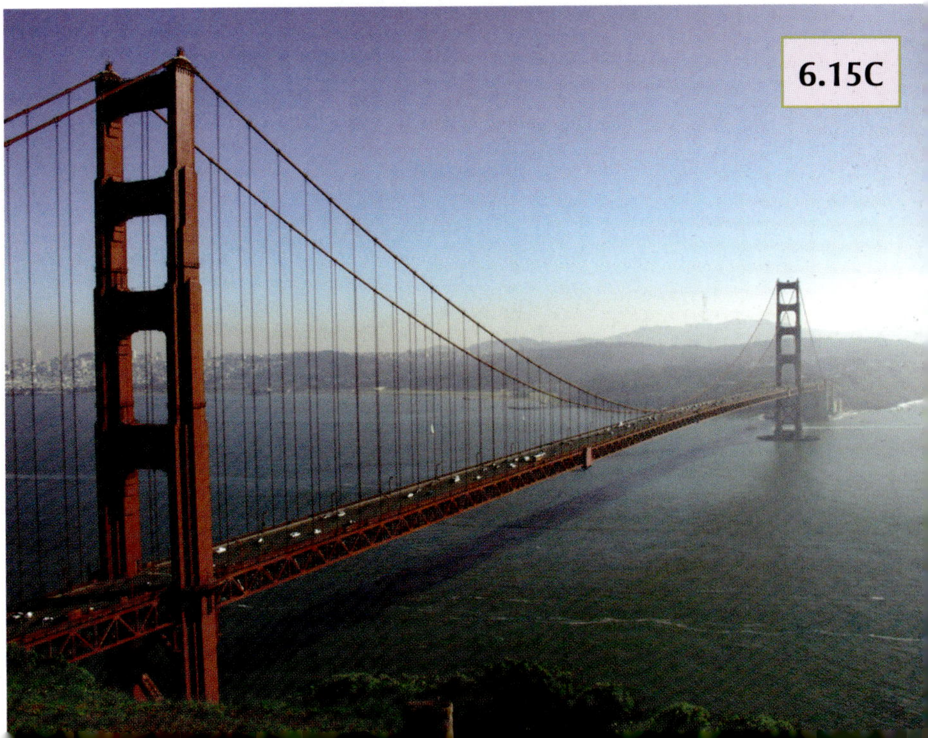

***Figure 6.15** Although the theme is similar to the Tower Bridge example at the start of the chapter, applying the MMM action based on a selection of the water is not successful, at least not in terms of color.*

algorithm that doesn't know what kind of picture it's working on?

It only took ten seconds or so to find out that Figure 6.15C was a step in the wrong direction. Considering the potential benefit if it had been more successful, it was an excellent investment of time all the same. Besides, the MMM Luminosity layer is probably useful.

MMM should be a part of your workflow because when successful it accomplishes things that no previously known method could. In the more technical half of this chapter, I'll offer a bit more about what goes on under MMM's hood. We'll start off with a which-selection-produced-which-version quiz, continue with a fleshtone exercise, and end with a discussion of novel improvements that developed from user feedback.

If that sounds interesting, go for it, but it's tough going and contains nothing essential. If you wish, move on to the next chapter, the easiest in the whole book.

Review and Exercises

✓There are two action choices. One is MMM only, the other a combination of MMM and the Color Boost that was introduced in Chapter 5. In the long run it's faster to use MMM + Color Boost, but it may seem daunting at first. So review your decision on which to use in a month or so.

✓Go back to the swan comparison in Chapter 2. Figure 2.6E was prepared using an early version of the MMM action. Why did the swan turn pink? Why wouldn't you get the same result today?

✓Forget the color for a moment. Explain why, in the different versions of the Zulu woman, Figure 6.14C came out so much lighter than Figure 6.14A.

✓If you play any of these actions from the PPW panel, you can cancel everything with an immediate Command-Z. This safety net is not available if you're working without the panel, because MMM completely fills your image history, flushing records of what you did previously.

✓Take a dozen of your own images of different subjects. Run MMM on them as quickly as you can. Are you able to generalize as to which categories it does best on, both for color and luminosity?

A Closer Look

The MMM action is a novelty, introduced in 2010. Yet it is based on an ancient command, one that has been neglected as useless for nearly two decades.

Those familiar with my writings know of my contempt for the use of the histogram in color correction. It is my belief that histograms are an invention of the devil for the purpose of tormenting the faithful. I am convinced that, in view of all the misunderstandings they have caused, that we would all have been far better off if no bleeping histograms had ever been included in Photoshop in the first place.

Nevertheless, it is sometimes possible to turn the devil's tools against him. If it turns out that we have stupidly not been doing so for twenty years, blaming Photoshop doesn't help.

Before launching into what a histogram has to do with something as seat-of-the-pants as MMM, it's time for a quiz. You should be able to predict now what effect a certain selection will have on the action's workings. So, let's head to California's Anderson Valley, home of fine Pinot Noirs and Figure 6.16. The four thumbnails show likely MMM selection choices. There's a typical red, a typical yellow, red plus yellow, and the whole shebang via Select All. The four results are in a jumbled order. To make differences more obvious, all MMM layers have been increased to 50% opacity rather than the default 30%. Can you pick out which version pertains to which selection? (Warning: the beta readers say you will not find this quiz too easy.)

An Equal Rights Act for Pixels

We'll get back to the quiz in a few pages. Meanwhile, "The Equalize command," according to Photoshop documentation, "redistributes the brightness values of the pixels in an image so that they more evenly represent the entire range of brightness levels."

This is like saying that burning a house down redistributes its structure in such a way as to make it less susceptible to an infestation of termites. Both assertions are true, but understate the disadvantages.

Equalize dates from the time of the Russian Revolution. I don't know who thought it up, but it was part of Photoshop and several competitors in the early 1990s. Some competitors called it Equalize, too. Others, more accurately, named it Equalize Histogram.

After so many years of railing about the worthlessness of histograms, I am not about to defile my book with a picture of one. Let us just say that a histogram is a graphic that shows approximately the distribution of pixel values in a certain channel, or overall, or in one of several contexts. There appears to be something in the histogram graphic format that hornswoggles the credulous into believing that it is more accurate in predicting image quality than would be, say, a table of tides in the Bay of Fundy.

Unless and until the histogram can learn what pixels represent significant objects, and can distinguish noise from real detail, it will remain an inadequate alternative to opening your eyes and looking at the screen.

I am not against using histograms in the absence of something decent to look at. A camera's tiny display cannot tell us whether we are blowing out important information. A histogram can't, either, but it can tell us that we are blowing *something* out. So, we take its word for it, reserving the final decision until we get a look at it on a monitor. From that point on, however, I am about as fond of the histogram as the Alternative Minimum Tax, if so much.

Everybody knows that the most fundamental step in color correction is establishing proper light and dark points. If the image doesn't have these it will almost invariably be improved when they are incorporated. Top retouchers achieve them with channel curves. Photoshop's Auto Tone and Auto Contrast commands are less sophisticated, but setting light and dark

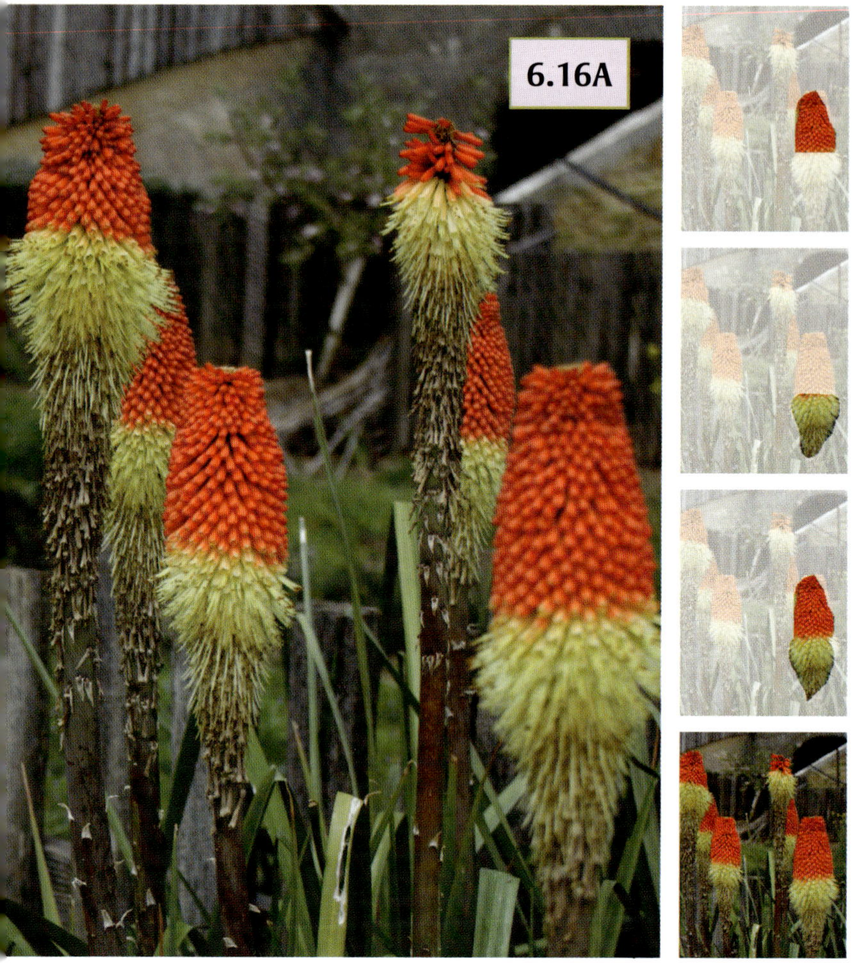

Figure 6.16 *An original and four prospective MMM selections. Opposite, the results, in a random order.*

points is what they do, often effectively. And every camera manufacturer incorporates some such routine when they produce JPEGs, as otherwise people would say that their product was junk because it produced such flat files.

These automated moves could, in a manner of speaking, be tied to equalizing the histogram. Somebody could say, the histogram is empty in its lightest zone, therefore the data must be stretched to fill it in.

And speaking of stretches, that's how I would characterize such an explanation. Equalize, though, is a histogram-worshipper's dream. Its philosophy is not just that the histogram should fill the entire available space. Rather, it wants pixels to be distributed evenly throughout the histogram. As many quartertones as midtones, as many highlights as three-quartertones, as many values ten percent in from the white point as forty percent in from the shadow.

This is a surpassingly stupid idea. No reason at all exists to suppose that leveling the histogram is desirable. It forces contrast not into the most important part, but into whatever occupies the largest area, which is often a worthless background. Apply Equalize to Figure 6.17A and behold 6.17B.

This horrifying apparition is begotten because about three-quarters of this picture is white—the background and the shirts. Everything else—the faces, pants, and hair, is not just much darker but also much more important to image quality. The whites have a short range, probably not even a quarter of the possible tones.

Any sentient being would reason that in a picture so full of whites, three-quarters of pixels might well live happily in one quarter of the histogram without causing any calamity. But in the egalitarian nightmare world of Equalize, the

Worksheet for Figure 6.16

Figure 6.16A is the original. Opposite, randomly ordered, are applications of MMM, with both layers set to 50% opacity. For each, please state which of the following selections was in place. (Answers, Page 171.)

1. The reds.
2. The yellows.
3. Both reds and yellows.
4. Everything (Select All).

Version	Selection
6.16B	
6.16C	
6.16D	
6.16E	

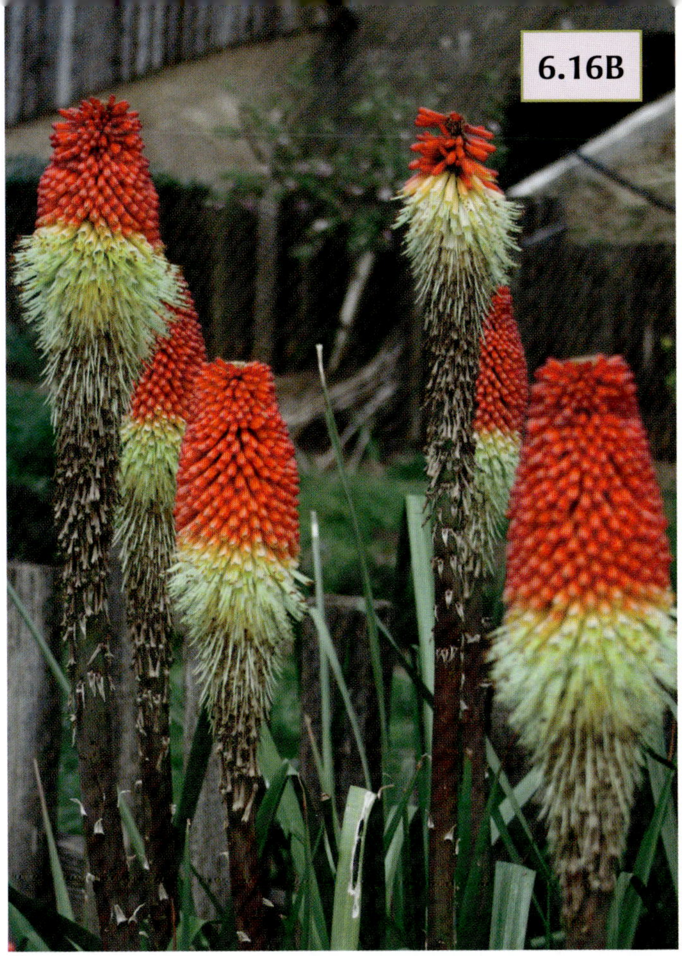

6.16B

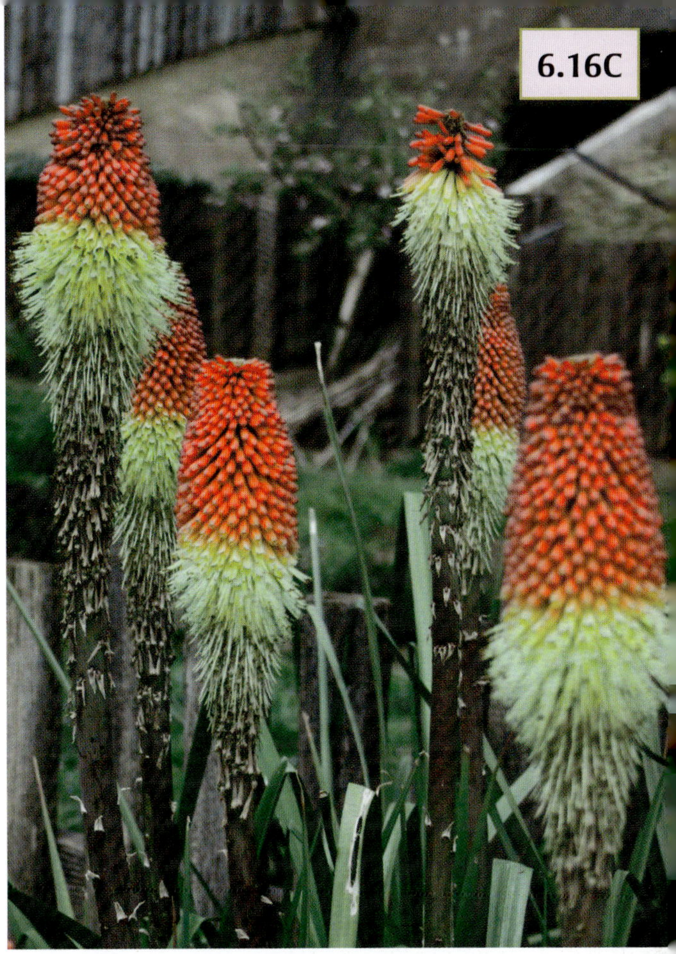

6.16C

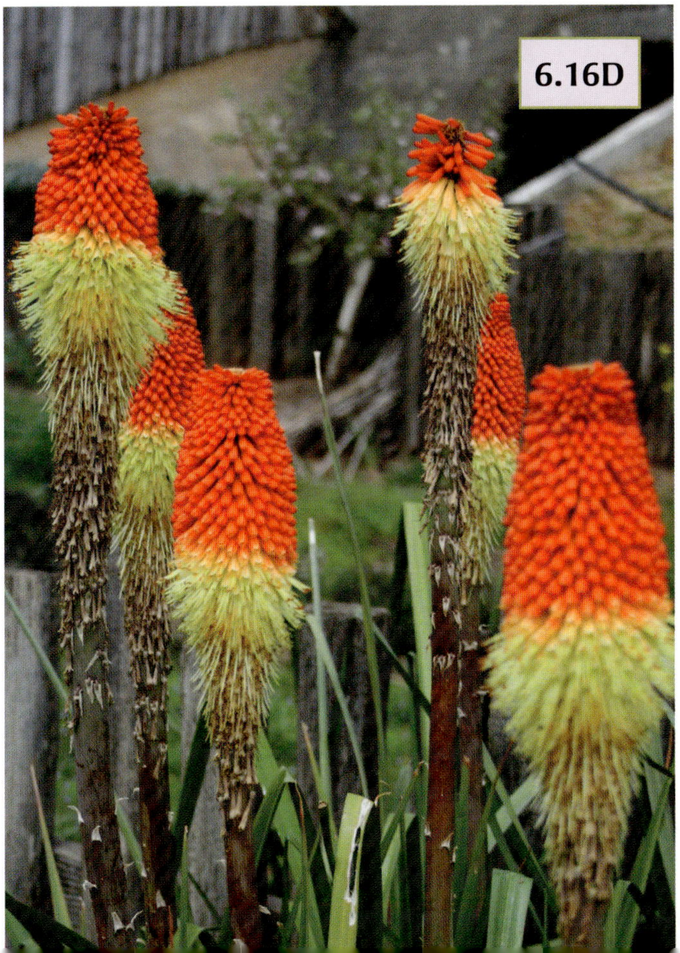

6.16D

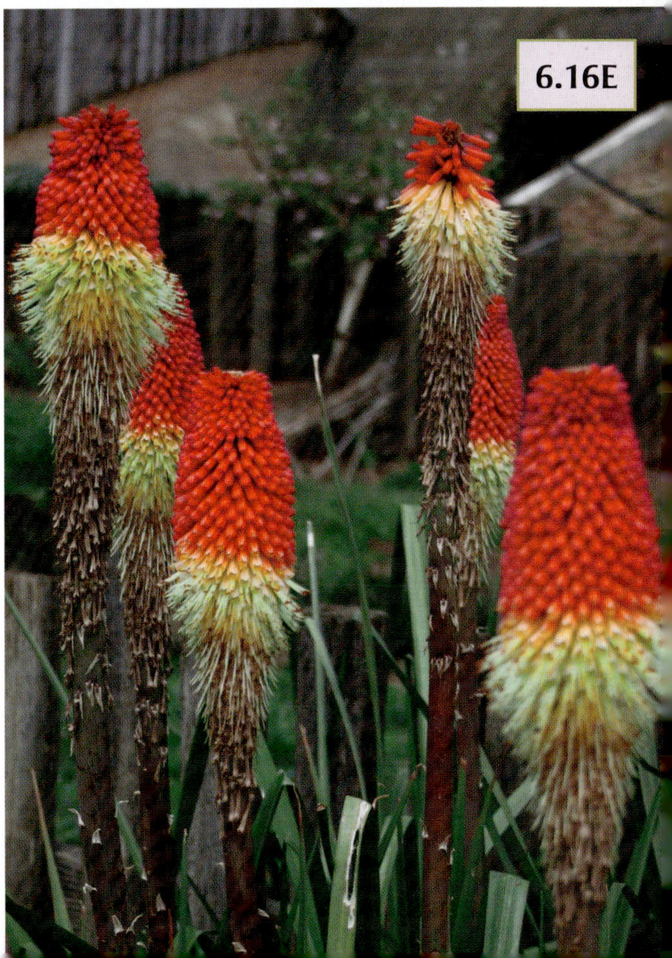

6.16E

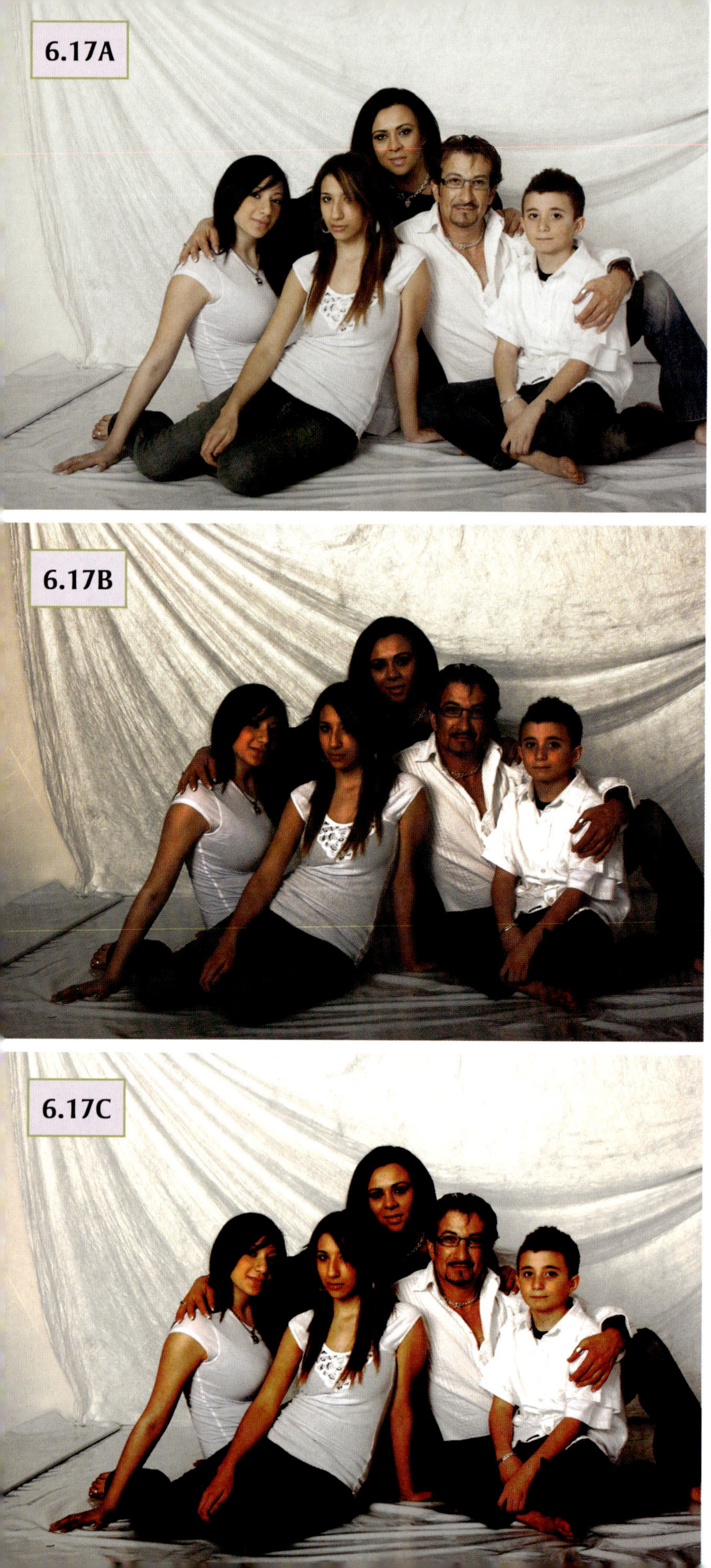

lightest three-quarters of the picture must fill the lightest three-quarters of the histogram. It does not care that this savages everything important by jamming it into the darkest quarter of possible tones.

Even in the early 1990s, when nobody knew much about image adjustments, stuff like Figure 6.17B was enough to convince people that Equalize was a good way to make pictures look worse, sometimes a lot worse. And so it went into history's ash can.

I have a large library of Photoshop books that I have mooched off various publishers. For sport, I just took about 15 of them off the shelf and checked their indices for any mention of Equalize. Result: zero mention in any of the books aimed at image quality. Two that are more general introductions to the program, one for Photoshop 7 and one for CS5, devoted a couple of paragraphs to it for form's sake. Neither author explained it correctly.

Why, then, should I squander so much venom trashing an antique that nobody, including me, has paid attention to for nearly twenty years?

The Equation Changes

Equalize has an option, illustrated in Figure 6.18, unshared by Auto Tone or other automated commands. I have selected the woman's forehead. When I now Equalize, up pops a dialog asking if I want the change to affect only the selected area, or the whole scene. The latter choice produces Figure 6.17C. Let's analyze it.

The instruction is to equalize the histogram within the forehead but

Figure 6.17 *Top, the original. Middle, an application of Equalize. Bottom, starting from the original, an application of Equalize using the woman's forehead as a selection.*

to apply the adjustment to everything. When complete, some pixels in the forehead are pure white and an equal number pure black, and an equal number halfway between, and so on.

Even in the original, you can see a reflection in an area right above the woman's nose and eyebrows. Evidently some of the pixels there must have been extremely light—lighter even than the girls' blouses. After equalizing, we know that some pixels in the forehead are not just light but blank, pure white. Yet the blouses hold detail. The boy's shirt does not. It is blown out completely, indicating that it was originally lighter than the lightest part of the forehead, which in turn was lighter than the blouses.

On the shadow side, no part of the selected area was originally as dark as anyone's hair. Since Equalize requires turning part of the forehead into pure black, the hair must get that way too. It is detail-free in Figure 6.17C.

Back in the early 1990s, the conventional wisdom that Equalize was worthless was correct. Photoshop did not have layers, and blending was horrendously slow. If you have to take Figure 6.17C or leave it the choice is easy.

But today, we do have layers, and actions, and computers that can run them in seconds instead of the hour or so that would have been required back then. With a little imagination, we can foresee that the effect of Figure 6.17C might possibly be useful if it were cut back by 95 percent or so.

It's not quite that easy, but that's the basic idea. Figure 6.19 uses the same selection and today's MMM action, the steps of which are as follows.

- Convert the file to LAB and flatten. The action could not work in RGB, because Equalize tries to suppress color changes. It has to be applied channel by channel, which works in LAB but would be a disaster elsewhere.
- On a duplicate layer, apply Equalize to each channel in turn, using the user-defined selection as the base and choosing to apply it to the entire channel rather than just the selected area.
- Immediately after each one, Edit: Fade to drastically reduce the impact. In keeping with my current views, the A is faded less than the B.
- Name the layer MMM Color and change it to Color mode, at a low opacity so that the effect can be increased if needed.
- Duplicate the MMM Color, rename it, and change its mode to Luminosity.
- Group the two layers to provide a convenient way of toggling back to the pre-action appearance.
- Add a mask to the MMM Luminosity layer to shield highlights and shadows against damage when the action increases tonal range.

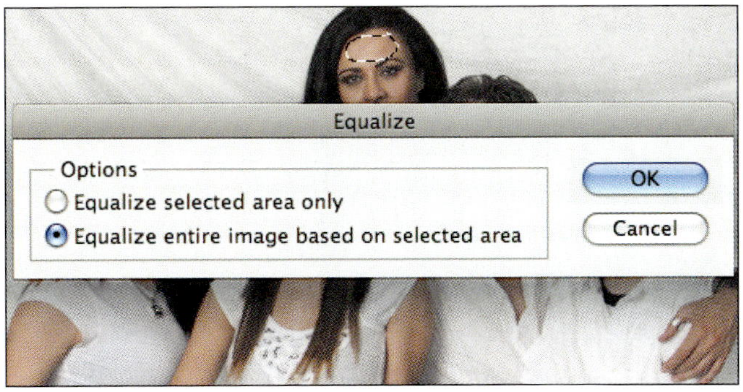

Figure 6.18 *Unlike other commands, Equalize can use a selection as the basis for a global correction.*

Figure 6.19 *A version using only MMM, which is based on Equalize in the LAB channels. It shares the initial selection with Figures 6.17C and 6.18.*

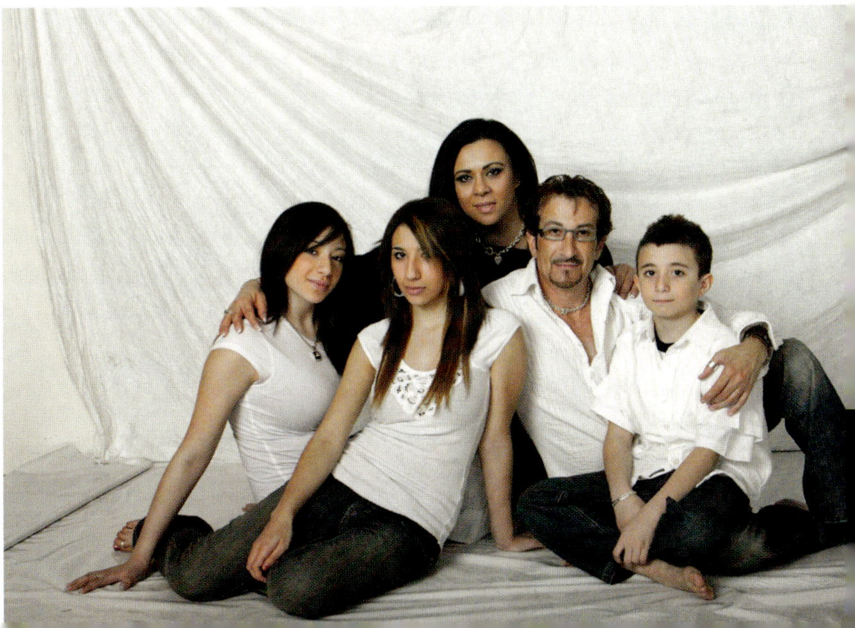

- Add a mask to the MMM Color layer to minimize changes in near-neutrals. Reminder: we tolerate unexpected changes in colorful things more than in gray ones.

Let us now return to the quiz. Figure 6.16A is the original. You have to identify the selections that produced the other four variants. The choices are the reds; the yellows; the reds and yellows together, and Select All. If you're having difficulties deciding, ask yourself the following:

- Which one(s) will show a color shift?
- Which will be the lightest?
- Which will have the least intense reds?
- In principle, what is the AB formula to produce these reds, yellows, and greens?
- What do you think the average AB value of the original as a whole is likely to be?

And the Answers

Reds are strongly AB–positive. Yellows are strongly B–positive but close to 0^A. Natural greens are strongly B–positive and somewhat A–negative.

All three are strongly B–positive. So, therefore, is the file's average B value, because these colors cover almost the entire picture. The average A is probably close to 0^A, because the green objects cancel out the reds.

Hue shifts occur only when the AB ratio changes. Just making a color more intense isn't likely to be seen as a mistake.

None of the four potential selections should cause much of a shift in the B. Whatever happens to the reds in that yellow-vs.-blue channel will also happen to the greens and yellows. Everything else in the picture will, in principle, be driven toward blue as the yellowest part of the B channel expands. But how would you know? If there were some purple flowers hanging around, then we could see the shift. But there aren't. The neutral background theoretically gets bluer, but it's hidden by the mask that prevents neutrals from shifting.

The magenta-vs.-green A channel is another story. If we choose either the yellows or Select All, both of which are A–neutral, everything else gets more intense, but there is little hue change. If we select the greens, it shifts everything toward magenta. But selecting the greens isn't one of the options. If we select the red, which *is* one of the options and is heavily magenta, everything else moves toward green.

Making greens greener may not be discernible. But making *yellows* greener almost certainly is. Two versions use reds as part or all of the selection. Figures 6.16B and 6.16C exhibit the telltale green shift in the yellows.

Basing the selection on red must produce a more drastic move. Equalize forces the dullest red to a bright green and the brightest one to an even more brilliant red. If instead the selection is both reds and yellows, then the brightest red will still go to the most brilliant red possible. But it will be the yellows that move to brilliant green. The dullest red will become gray, or possibly blue-gray.

After all the fading and masking, we won't think of the reds having turned either green or gray. Nevertheless, the dullest reds will become much duller if the selection is of reds only rather than reds and yellows. There will be more variation, which you may find more interesting. But the overall impression is not as brilliant. Figure 6.16C has the dullest reds overall and slightly greener yellows. These factors identify it as having used reds as the base selection. Figure 6.16B must have used reds and yellows.

We shouldn't see much color difference between the other two, because the two selections have similar AB values. Select All is roughly 0^A and somewhat B–positive. The yellows are also roughly 0^A and more strongly B–positive. The main difference in color is that Select All will force the yellows to be brighter whereas selecting the yellows will give them more variation. That should be enough for us to choose the other two, but there's an even stronger clue.

Yellows are always light; dark yellow is an oxymoron. The average yellow is much lighter than the average of the whole picture. Our two remaining versions, therefore, compare the use of a light selection to a dark one. The perverted mind of Equalize tries to compensate by pushing the non-selected area away.

Figure 6.16D is distinctly the lighter of the two remaining. It must therefore have been based on the darker of the two selections, to wit, Select All. Figure 6.16E was based on the yellows.

* * *

Certain beta readers found this quiz highly informative. If you didn't, Russ Brown's comments may console you.

"Sorry, but this whole exercise confused me. Trying to understand the application of Equalize to MMM had my head spinning and by the time I got halfway through "And the Answers', I was losing the will to live. I know this is the more difficult part of the chapter but it sounds like a geek describing the merits and differences between a Pentium and a Celeron processor.

"The flower photo looks like the antithesis of what you would use MMM to improve. There are no large areas of dull color and any increase in saturation will send them way out of gamut. I think I understand that the strong colors help to illustrate the way the process works, but ...is it really necessary to know in such detail how it works, if everyone is simply using the action? Sure, give a rundown of what's under the hood, but if someone wants to examine it in this depth, I'm sure they'll figure it out for themselves."

I am basically sympathetic to the above. Also it must be remembered that Russ's comments pertained to an earlier draft that was not quite as lucid as this one. I agree that most users don't need this information. Then again, they don't really need *anything* in this "Closer Look" half of the chapter, which is why the first half of each chapter starts with an invitation for people to skip the second half.

There's a Dance in the Old Dame Yet

I have repeatedly described Equalize as stupid, and, just now, perverted. Why not, then, use a custom curve, or even Auto Tone?

Auto Tone doesn't have Equalize's convenient option of applying an effect to the entire image based on the contents of a selection. With some effort, we could script our way around that difficulty and construct an automated clone that used Auto Tone in exactly the same way that MMM uses Equalize.

Unfortunately, it wouldn't work as well. Making an appropriate selection would prove an obstacle. Recall Figure 6.18, where I lassoed a dark-haired woman's forehead. Equalize and Auto Tone would not get identical results on that small selection but by the time we were done fading them they would be hard to tell apart.

Suppose, though, that my lasso technique had not been so impeccable, and I had picked up a smidgen of hair. Auto Tone requires that some pixels become extremely dark. The hair sample, tiny as it is, will satisfy that requirement, but the skin probably will stay lighter than a midtone.

Equalize would get something radically different, and for our purposes, better. It wants the darkest ten percent of tones to be occupied by ten percent of the picture's area. That rule forces some skin to be very dark, whether a tiny amount of black hair is selected or not.

There is no denying that slipshod lasso technique is one of my shortcomings, but it's not an issue here. What if there's a strand of hair in the middle of the forehead, too small for us to see at this size but not small enough for Auto Tone to ignore? What if the forehead contains

Answers to MMM Quiz

(Page 166)

Figure 6.16A is the original. The other four are MMM versions. Opacities of all color and luminosity layers were set to 50%.

The action used the following base selections:

6.16B: Both reds and yellows.
6.16C: Reds only.
6.16D: Select All.
6.16E: Yellows only.

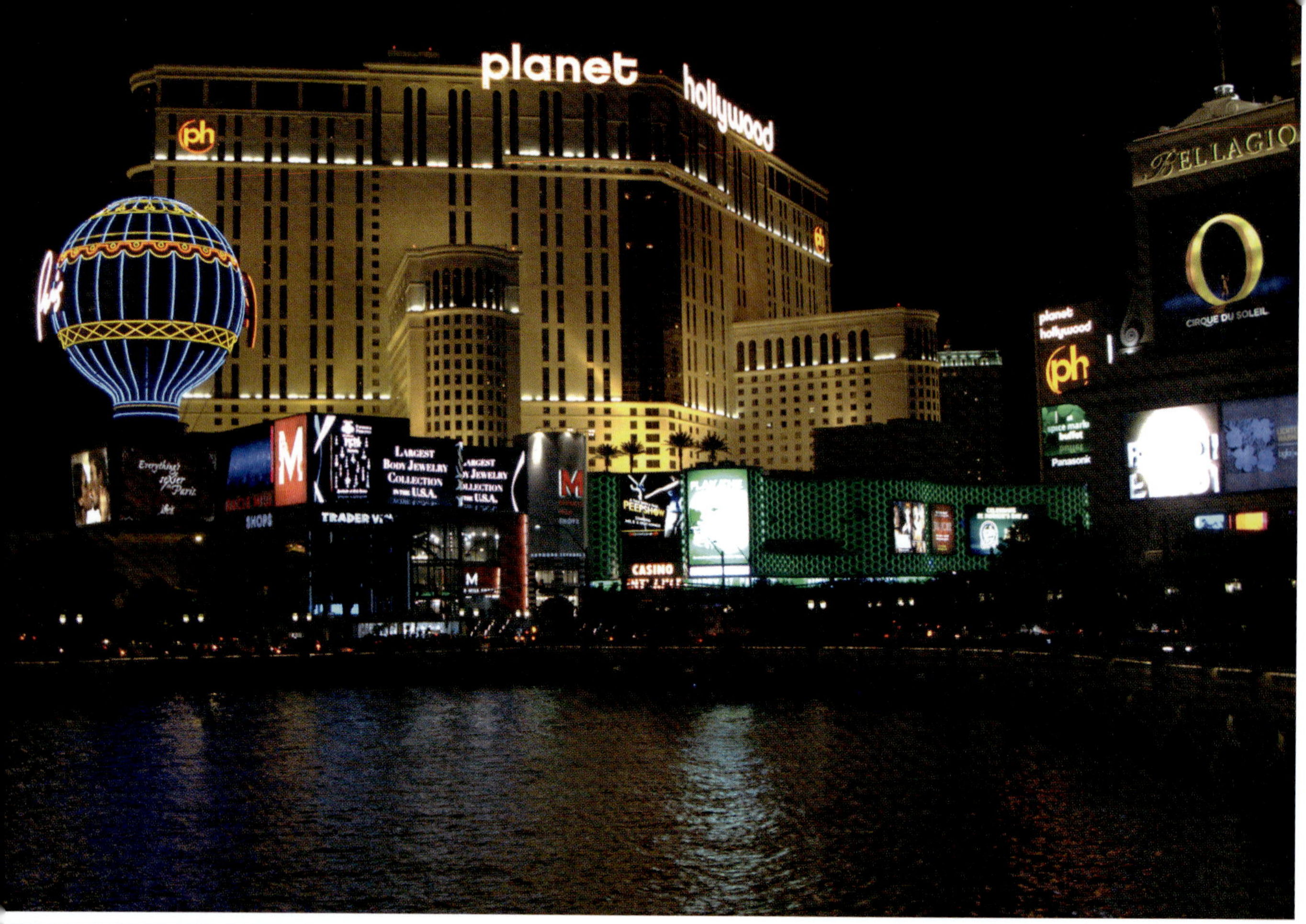
planet
hollywood
BELLAGIO
O
CIRQUE DU SOLEIL
planet
hollywood
Largest
Body Jewelry
Collection
in the U.S.A.
TRADER VIC
SHOPS
PEEPSHOW
CASINO
Panasonic
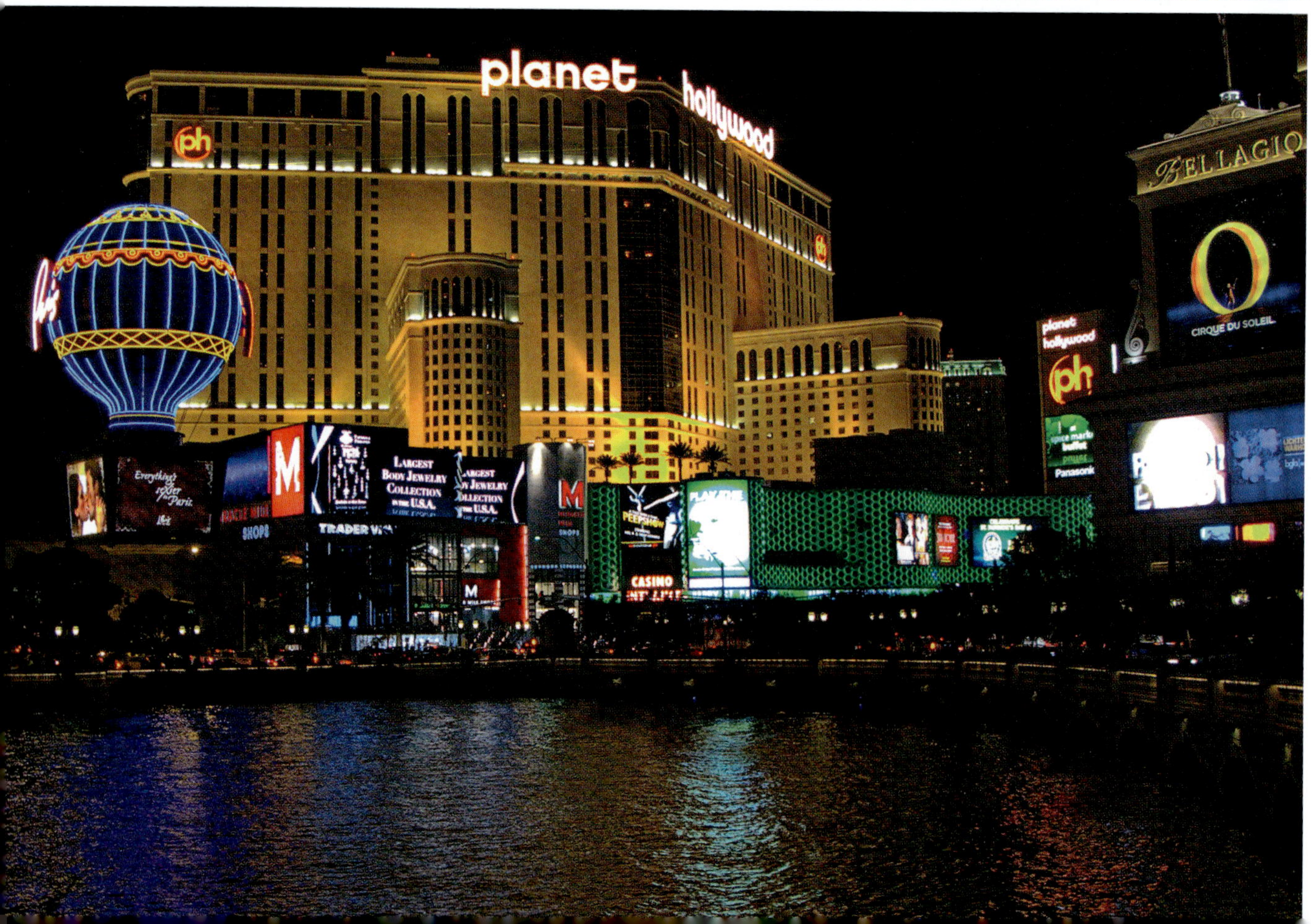
planet
hollywood
BELLAGIO
O
CIRQUE DU SOLEIL
planet
hollywood
Largest
Body Jewelry
Collection
in the U.S.A.
TRADER VIC
SHOPS
PEEPSHOW
CASINO
Panasonic

dark noise? Or better yet, go back to the flowers of Figure 6.16A. The "flowers" are made up of tiny blooms that almost obscure a much darker background. How could you select representative reds without picking up some of the background? Lassoing for Equalize is fast and worry-free, as long as you're sure that most of what you're getting is red.

As for a custom curve for each image, in principle it would be better but nobody would be able to tell the difference. Adding variation has an outsize effect on apparent quality but the actual moves are rather small. The curves advantage would be invisible.

Using a custom curve for every image would also be prohibitively time-consuming. So Equalize it is. It's ironic to revivify this fossil just in time to solve a very modern problem.

Workflow in the Age of Facebook

Photoshop's interface looks the same worldwide, but the program comes in many different languages. I released the MMM action in 2010 and updated it several times as errors and improvements were discovered. None of the early versions worked in foreign-language versions of Photoshop. In 2011, I put out a major revision that was supposed to correct this issue.

I own Photoshop only in English, so I could not by myself find out for sure that the problem was solved. I had to co-opt a European friend to run several tests before releasing anything so that I could tell people that as far as is known these actions run in all languages.

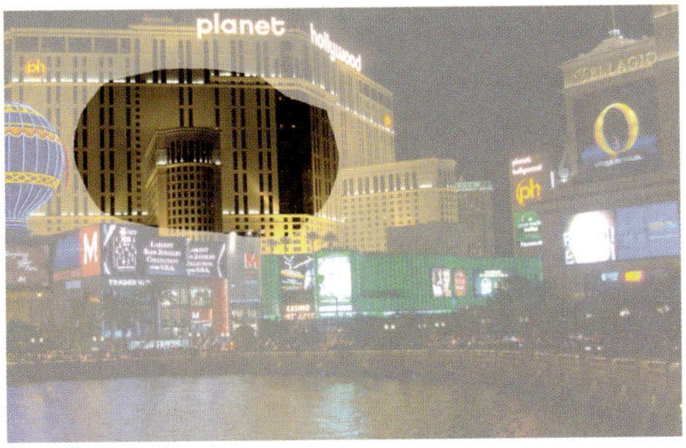

***Postcard 6.20** (opposite) The selection shown above and the defaults of the MMM + Color Boost action created this postcard in seconds, not minutes.*

They *did* run, and they arrived on a day when my friend was preparing a gang of galleries for posting on Facebook. That kind of work was rare five years ago but many of us are deluged with it today. In the days of print advertising the number of pictures in the final product was severely limited by cost. Even before most people had broadband access we had to be reluctant to post multiple images, particularly if of high resolution.

Today, however, if it's worth showing a single picture, it may well be worth showing twenty. And often enough, these pictures aren't going to have a long shelf life.

This book's workflow can be executed in three minutes on average. Sometimes, however, we don't have three minutes to spare. And today, it happens a lot more than sometimes. Furthermore, it's often happening with substandard photos, perhaps shot on a cell phone.

Postcard 6.20 came from a serious camera, but hand-held, which in principle disqualifies the photo for advertising use. Certainly, though, it's the kind of shot that might be posted in an online gallery. To make this postcard, I lassoed the area shown, played the combined MMM + Color Boost action, played the sharpening action to be described in Chapter 15, converted into CMYK for printing, and headed for the casino. I did not change the default settings of either action.

I estimate the time involved as five seconds to decide what to select, one second to operate the lasso tool, and two seconds apiece to click on the actions.

For ten seconds of actual human intervention, this isn't bad. You can now appreciate why my friend was deliriously happy to receive the action when it happened that he was preparing a scad of pictures for Facebook. Like me, he's an imaging professional. When his pictures don't look good, the average viewer wonders why, because the average viewer doesn't have a good grasp of how much time is involved.

The shimmering reflections are improved because MMM holds the neutrality of the rest of the water better than Color Boost does alone. Also, the hotel has a bit more variation, and the neon colors are marginally more pleasing due to better variation. Still, most of the success should be credited to Color Boost and not MMM.

The Color Boost action is fairly new, but the technique of steepening the AB curves to enhance color has been around for a while. Without the action it would have taken longer and some manual retouching might have been necessary, but we could have gotten something nearly as good.

In many cases, though, the techniques of years past could not have done as well, as we're about to see.

In the Wonder-Working Days of Old

Concepts change slowly, methods more rapidly. In 2002, I wrote, "The usual problem with faces is not so much a lack of color as a lack of color variation. Cheeks and lips should be redder than the rest of the face even in men, and particularly so in women."

The original Man from Mars Method was introduced later, but as the quote indicates, the need for it was certainly understood. Without it or an equivalent, something is missing.

Figure 6.21A is the original that the foregoing quote referred to. Figure 6.21B is as corrected in *Professional Photoshop Fourth Edition.*

Considering it was 2002, I have no apologies to make for the correction. This studio portrait is by a professional who specializes in this type of work. We expect the original to be good, so we don't anticipate an enormous improvement. The corrected version was state-of-the-art in its day. Detailing is better, but the choices at that time were only to make the faces paler or redder, not a little of both. Consequently it cannot compete with today's version, Figure 6.21C, which happens to be our first full correction of a face.

I've avoided this critical category not because the PPW can't handle it, but because more caution is required than with landscapes. We'll go into that more in Chapter 9, but this exercise can be a preview with an MMM emphasis.

In the Las Vegas nightscape we just looked at, nobody cares what color the neon is, as long as it's bright and varied. That gives us flexibility that is missing when the subject is a person.

The quiz that opened this discussion wasn't chosen by accident. We don't have a green background in the current picture, but otherwise the featured colors are reds and yellows, just as in the flowers of Figure 6.16A.

Forgetting detail for a moment, two of the Figure 6.16 variants make the red flowers redder. Few tears need be shed over this development. But how would you feel if I made the *faces* of Figure 6.21 redder?

Similarly, two or three of the Figure 6.16 variants add a green tinge to the yellowish flowers. I can live with that also, but how would you feel if the blond women's *hair* went green?

And the Figure 6.16 contestants all add detail to various areas of importance. But how do you think these women would feel about having their pores and wrinkles emphasized?

In sum, we have to be careful to avoid three effects that viewers and models have little tolerance for: beet-red fleshtones, green-haired blonds, and contrast that ages the skin.

Avoiding the contrast gain is as easy as eliminating the MMM Luminosity layer. The color issues need more attention.

- The original measures a bit pink. Reading Chapter 3 literally, it should be corrected—but not if we're afraid of green hair.
- The MMM and Color Boost are so likely to strengthen color that a standard PPW countermeasure is to desaturate skintones first. More about that in Chapter 9.
- The two subjects have such different complexions that we need to make selections of each so that neither will be short-changed. Recall, though, the lessons of Figures 6.16B and 6.16C. The faces are red and definitely must be selected. The best way to prevent that selection

from turning yellows green is to lasso a largish quantity of blond hair.

All these things were duly done this time, but not in 2002. The rest of the exercise was similar.

- In neither case did I alter the initial color.
- I had introduced channel blending on luminosity layers in the mid-1990s, although it was called *plate blending* back then. By 2002 the technique was well established. It wasn't considered for every image, as the PPW now recommends. But I was saying then, as I do today, that in fleshtone images it's often wise to blend the green channel into the others. In 2002 I went so far as to replace the red and blue entirely, and then applied a false profile to lighten the result. This time, I blended the green at a lower percentage, followed by curves. This produced a lighter look without gross reflections.

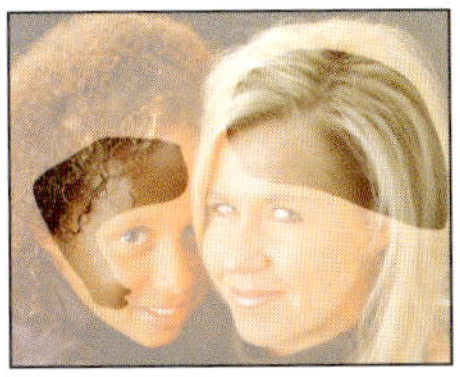

***Figure 6.21** Right, the original studio portrait. Below left, a correction published in 2002. Below right, today's correction using Modern Man from Mars for skintone variation. The selection is seen at left.*

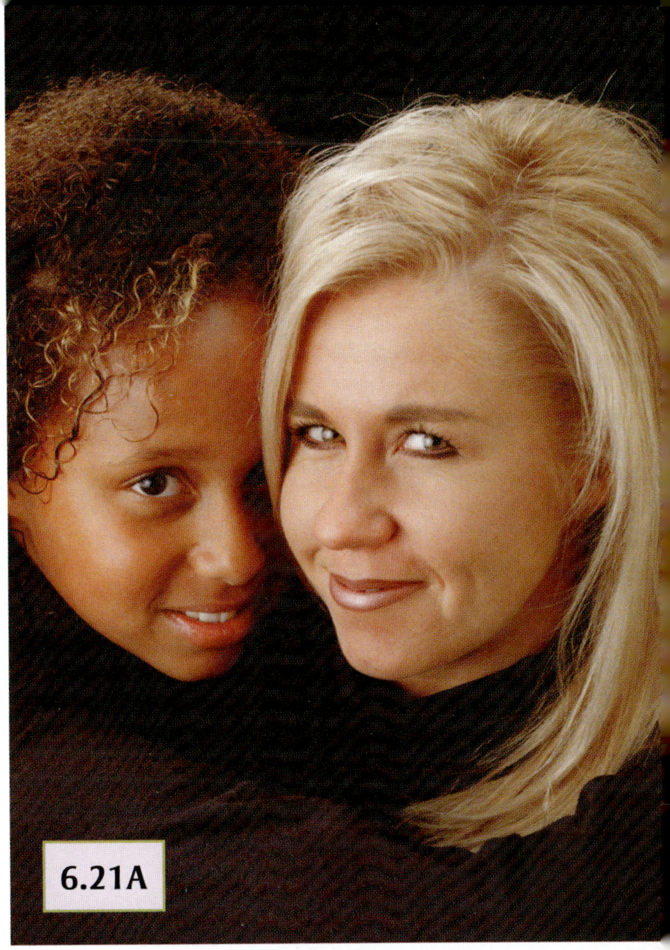

6.21A

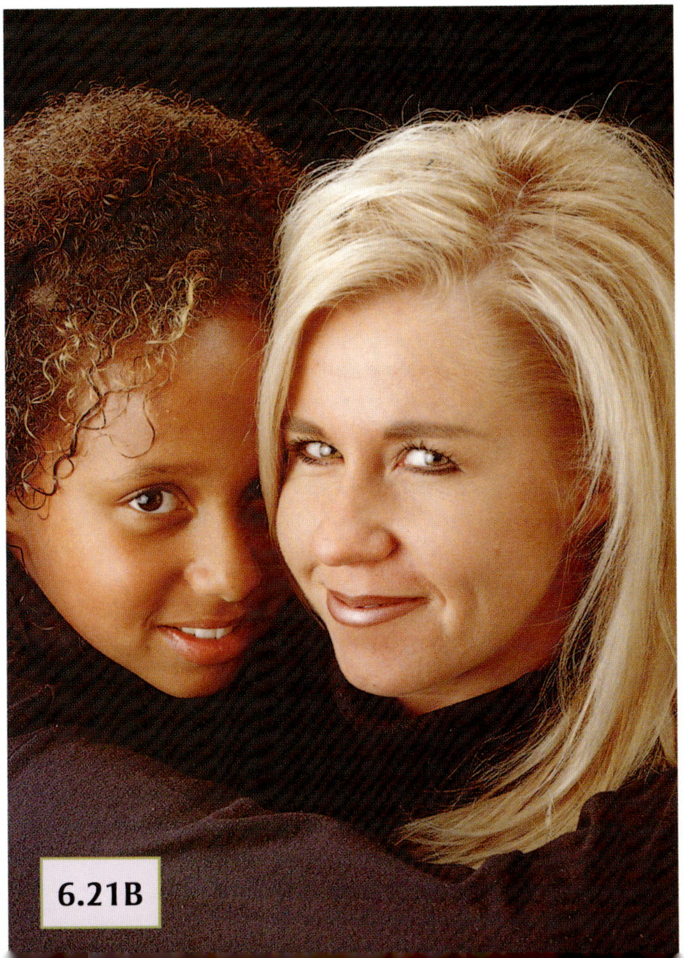

6.21B

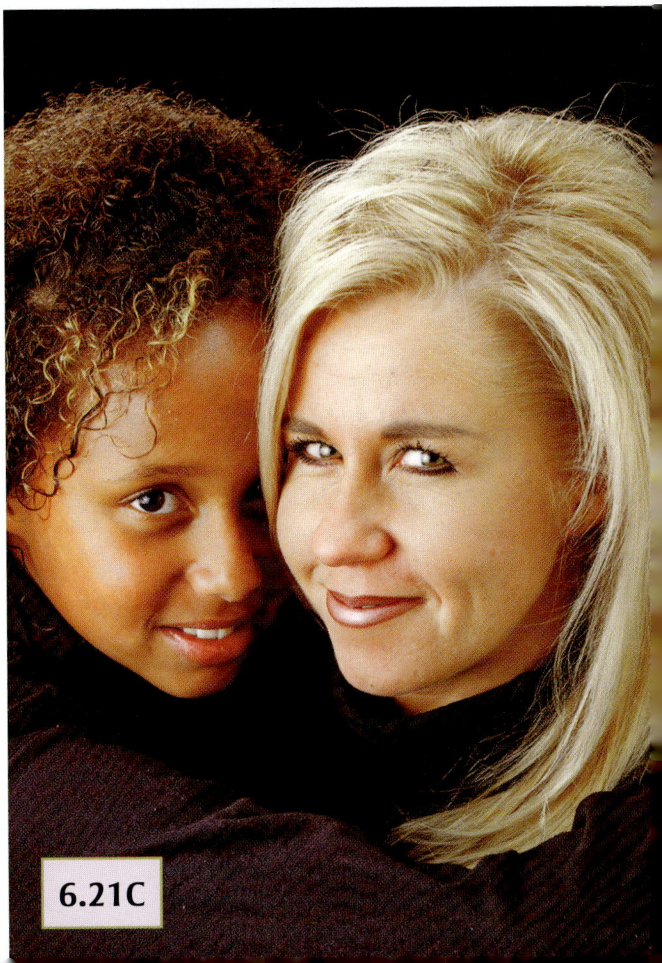

6.21C

- In the next chapter, we'll explore the Shadows/Highlights command, which I applied here to get better detail in the dark hair. I couldn't in 2002 because the command did not exist and I was too naive to think up a substitute.
- The commands *did* exist to apply something along the lines of the Color Boost action, and I used them gently on both occasions. The big color move this time, however, is MMM, the tools for which were available in 2002, but not, alas, the knowledge of how to deploy them.
- The 2002 version used the best sharpening methods known at the time, getting more detail in the hair and eyes without roughening the skin. We can do better today, although it should be conceded that today's sharpening action would have taken about half an hour to run on a 2002-vintage computer.

When Everyone Is Somebody

The development of this action has continued even as this book was being written. Two important features were added, both in response to beta reader comments. Both are advanced enough that there was no point in mentioning them earlier; the appropriate time is now.

First, the action is so powerful that it can be frustrating. It's no use explaining, as I did in the first half, that it's far easier than the original Man from Mars and that it's capable of extraordinary results. It isn't hard to make a selection that will produce something useful. As you saw earlier, though, figuring out whether another selection might do better yet is no picnic, which gets people irritated. Trying a different selection, let alone several, is quite cumbersome, or at least it used to be.

The version of the PPW panel being released with this book's publication permits easy comparison of the results of up to four selections. Option-click the action, and up pops a dialog allowing you to choose your selection tool, make new selections, and then toggle between previews. The original selection is never lost; you can revert to it whenever you think necessary.

We have posted a video by Alessandro Bernardi showing how this works as a creative tool in the preparation of fashion advertising, his speciality. Clients often don't know exactly what effect they are after. Having the ability to test various selections opens many possibilities.

This improvement requires use of the panel; the second one does not. It was suggested by beta reader Adriano Esteves, who uses the MMM action extensively and had already developed the technique for his own work.

The MMM Color layer causes hues to shift. Depending upon the image, this can be attractive, debatable, or outright wrong. Adriano suggests avoiding the risk by changing the layer mode from Color to Saturation. Do this to a tomato, and certain parts will become more red or less red, which is a good variation. Nothing, however, will move toward orange. Here's what R.W.G. Hunt, one of the greatest authorities on color, has to say about this situation.

> A pale red tomato...is more acceptable in a reproduction than an orange or a magenta one. Correctness of hue would, therefore, seem to be more important than correctness of saturation. Moreover, the variations in saturation which occur in natural colours are generally similar to those produced by adding white light uniformly over the whole field of view. Hence, if, in a reproduction, all colours are desaturated by about the same amount, one would expect the result to look more natural than if colours of different hues and saturations were desaturated to different extents, so that some colours shone out like signal lights, while others were grossly desaturated.

A grossly pale tomato is indeed probably better than one with grossly incorrect color, but if limited to the sort of moves we'd make with MMM, the above statement is dead wrong. The comments about uniformity of saturation are also incorrect. I know, because I've asked more than a thousand people to evaluate alternate versions in similar cases, and the results are decisive. Adriano should be happy, because his suggestion about how to alter saturation runs counter to Hunt's advice.

Who's correct? Judge for yourself. This section was a late addition to the chapter. After writing it, I said to myself that what this book really needs is a picture of tomatoes. So I pulled one of the exercises out of Chapter 13 and substituted Figure 13.4, which speaks to the very point we've been discussing.

Hue shifts are often good things. The blond hair in Figure 6.21C looks better than in 6.21B because it is less similar to the flesh. This wouldn't happen with Adriano's idea. However, his suggestion yields a more conservative result and can be used in combination with MMM Color. Figure 6.22A shows how, when pushed too far, the MMM Color layer produces green-tinged hair.

Figure 6.22 *The PPW panel offers the option of adding an MMM Saturation layer, giving us three ways to alter color. Top, starting with an original corrected for luminosity only, a version produced only with the MMM Color layer, at an extreme opacity. Bottom left, a similar version produced with MMM Saturation. Bottom right, a version using only Color Boost.*

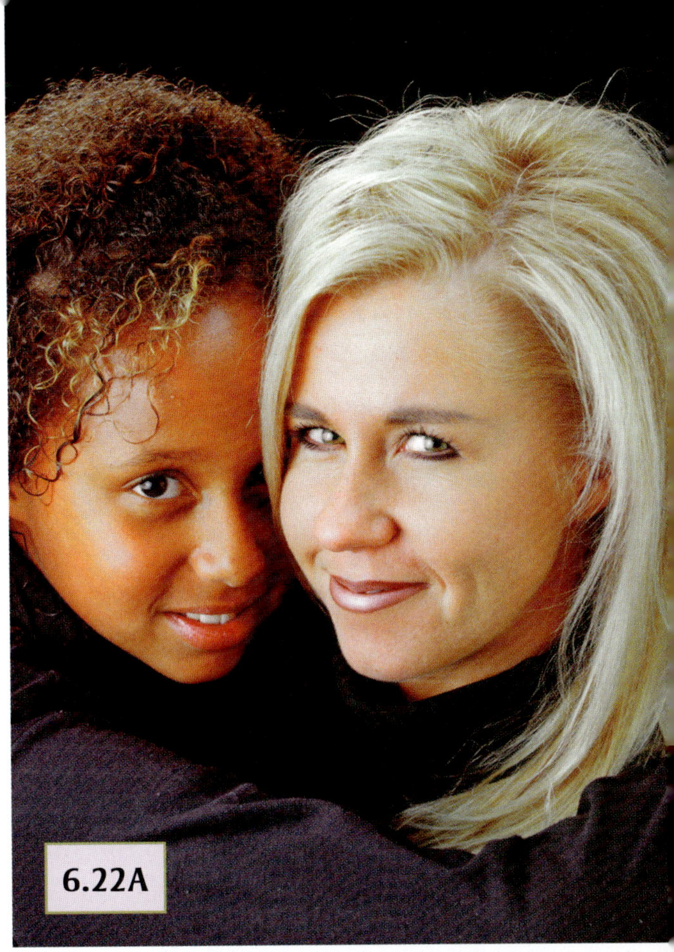

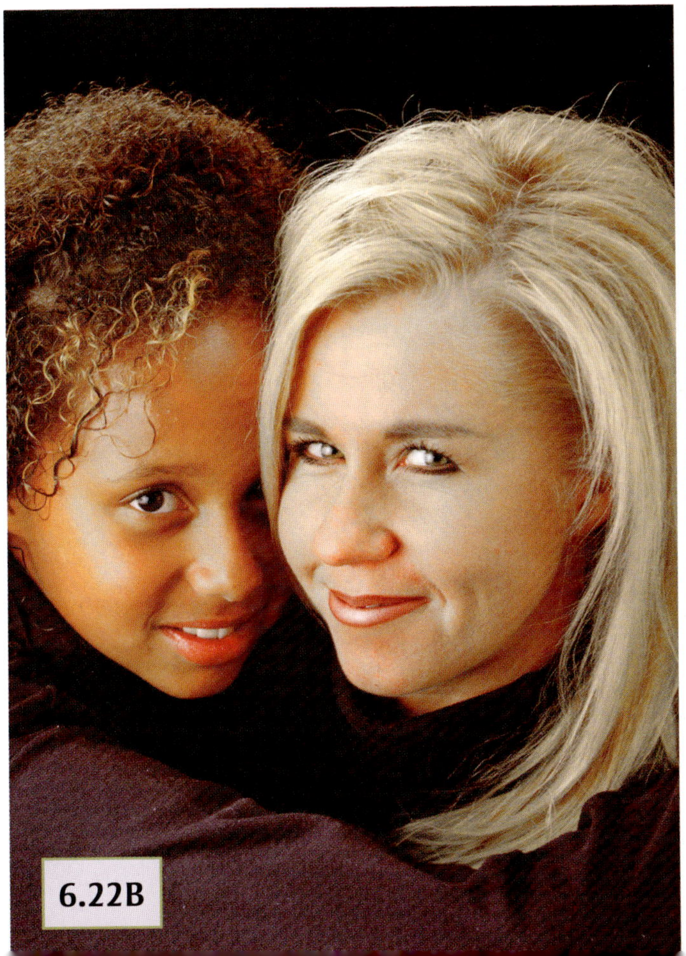

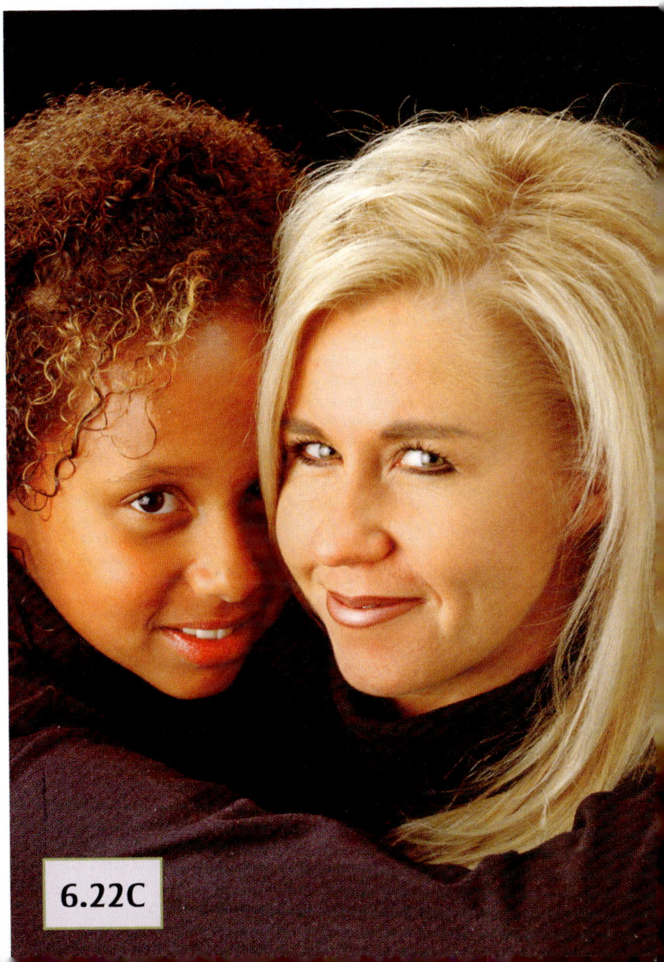

For this reason, the new PPW panel offers the option of adding an MMM Saturation layer, either by default or one file only. I have activated the default for my own work and am very glad I did; it certainly helped in this image. Figure 6.22B shows its impact, again with a heavy hand on the opacity slider, Figure 6.22C completes the trio with Color Boost only. The final step is some kind of blend between some or all of these three, and possibly with the file as it existed just prior to the action.

Even so does knowledge progress. Just to make it up to Hunt, I'll quote him again. The following is more or less the theme song of the PPW. When speaking at conferences, I have it up on the screen as the audience files in.

> It is only on rather special occasions that the reproduction and the original are seen side by side; more usually the reproduction is seen at a different place or time, and the time interval may vary from a few hours to several weeks or even months or years. The human memory therefore plays an important part. It might be thought, then, that the process involved in appraising colours in a reproduction consists of making mental comparisons between the sensation produced in the mind by the reproduction, and a recollection from the memory of the colour sensation produced by the original object at the time when the picture was taken, It is, however, a fact that the average person generally feels competent to appraise the colours in pictures taken by people other than himself, of objects which he has never seen, at times when he was not present.

The Bottom Line

The Modern Man from Mars action operates in an unprecedented way. The operator indicates a typical zone of importance with a selection; the action then applies changes to the picture as a whole.

The purpose is to enhance color and/or contrast variation in important areas. MMM works hand in hand with the Color Boost action of the previous chapter; each has different strengths and weaknesses.

Getting used to MMM takes time, so it is supplied both as a standalone action and a combination MMM + Color Boost that allows interactivity between the two effects.

And All Shall Equal Be

The history of digital imaging is littered with corpses of snake-oil salesmen and their mysterious, magical plug-ins that purported to work miracles, accompanied by demonstrations of the one or two files in the universe on which the plug-in actually produced good results.

I would not like to join them, so let me remind you that I made the PPW panel and these actions free long before this book was published, and that there's nothing secret about what they contain. MMM comes in the form of an action because it has too many steps for any reasonable person to want to apply without one.

Understanding what each step does is not strictly speaking necessary. If color is your career or your passion it's probably worth knowing. MMM is revolutionary but it isn't the last word. Today we have ideas that leave the corrections of 2002 in the dust, and machines that can implement them rapidly enough to be practical. In ten years someone will have invented something that outperforms the PPW. Maybe that person will be you.

If you aspire to that, it might be well to ask why it took so long to get this far. And you will find that it was neither the fault of Photoshop nor of an imperfect understanding of what was needed. Rather, it was because every expert had dismissed as primitive and useless the command that had been lying in wait for us for nearly two decades, lurking and laughing at our failure to understand that it was the key to the variation we sought.

7

Shadows/Highlights

The terminology is confusing, but the execution is simple. The easiest part of the PPW is just a matter of deciding whether the lightest and/or darkest areas of the picture could use more detail.

Traditional graphic arts terminology divides images into five ill-defined zones. From lightest to darkest, they are *highlight, quartertone, midtone, three-quartertone* and *shadow.* The three terms describing the intermediate zones flaunt no alternate meanings to confuse us. We are not so fortunate with the two bookends.

An object in sunlight often casts a *shadow.* Everybody who speaks English uses the word in that context. Imaging professionals, however, also use *shadow* to denote something heavier and unrelated, namely the darkest areas of the picture. Furthermore, we sometimes refer to *the* shadow, by which is meant the darkest significant point. *Highlight* is similarly ambiguous.

The good news is that keeping the meanings straight is the hardest part of this chapter. The rest requires little thought and less technical skill.

We hereby add an optional step between the introduction of better luminosity (Chapter 4) and the color enhancement steps of the two subsequent chapters. We ask ourselves whether we would like to see better detail in highlights and shadows—and I am using the graphic arts definition of those words, the lightest and darkest zones. The three possible answers depend on the image. They are:

1. No. It is unimportant or possibly counterproductive.
2. Yes. It would be nice to add detail to at least one of these two zones.
3. Yes. It is absolutely critical to inject more detail into at least one of these two zones. Otherwise the picture is a failure.

If the picture happens to fall in Category 1, we skip what's discussed here and move right on into color enhancement as though this chapter never existed. If, however, it falls into Category 2 or 3, we will take action. First, we need a settings change.

Open Image: Adjustments>Shadows/Highlights, known as Shadow/Highlight in versions CS-CS3. Click Show More Options if needed to display the entire dialog. Enter the values shown in Figure 7.1, and click Save As Defaults. (Note: if you're using the PPW panel, you need not do this, as the panel has these values locked in; still I think making your defaults match the panel's is a good idea.)

This preliminary step is needed because Photoshop's defaults for this command are too strong. Originally they were even harsher. They were ratcheted downward, but still not

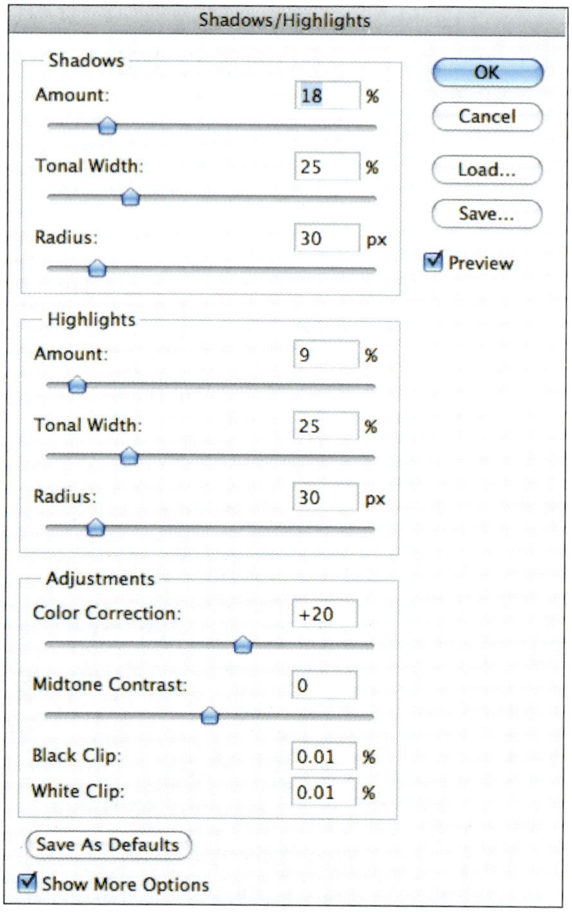

***Figure 7.1** Photoshop's defaults for the Shadows/Highlights command are too extreme. Instead, enter these settings and click Save as Defaults at the bottom of the dialog.*

***Figure 7.2** (opposite) The impact of applying the S/H commands on three images of different character. The values are those of Figure 7.1.*

enough, in CS5. We want something strong enough to have impact, but weak enough to avoid damage. The plan, you see, is never to change these settings at all. (Note: a specific exception is pointed out in the second, more technical half of this chapter, but for the time being it can be ignored.)

The procedure is simplicity itself.

- Assuming you have decided that the picture falls into either Category 2 or 3, open the S/H dialog.
- Click OK.

Renouncing the ability to tweak these settings means we don't have much to discuss. First, a quiz. Go back to the chapter we just finished, which contains nine original images. For each, write down whether you think S/H is appropriate. If you answer Yes, please specify whether it is because you want better highlights, shadows, or both.

We'll start with a quick before-and-after look at what the command does. Then we'll discuss why, in a dialog full of options, I recommend you not change them. Finally, I'll give my own answers to the quiz so we can see whether we agree.

Highlighting the Issue

Figure 7.2 shows the impact, at full size, of applying these new S/H defaults to three disparate images that I would say all belong to Category 2. That is, increased detail in highlights and/or shadows would be welcome, but is not critical. The results are mixed.

S/H is helpful for dark hair. In the first example, the hair has picked up a bit of detail. For my money, though, the most important thing is that the eye has been opened.

The church is the least impressive of the three. I wouldn't cancel the change, but I see only a tiny gain in the shadowy areas of the stone. The clouds are slightly darker.

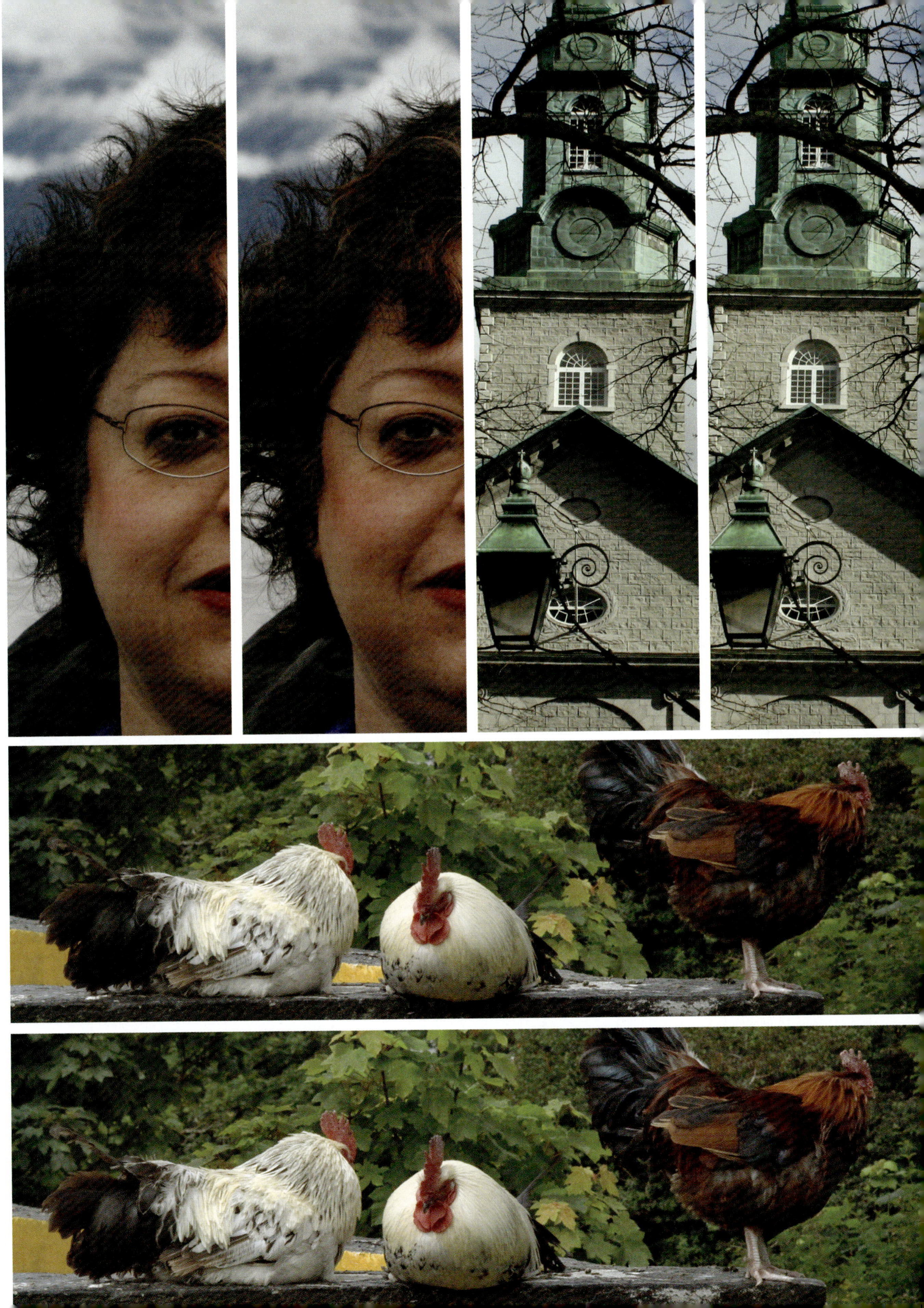

The chickens image shows the biggest improvement, which isn't saying much. The rightmost bird has gained detail, as has the background greenery.

The Picture Postcard Workflow is built for speed. We concentrate on methods that will produce the biggest benefits in the time we have to spend on them. I classify the Figure 7.2 results as benefits, but not big ones—hardly ones of the magnitude seen in previous chapters. This should explain why I recommend one-size-fits-all settings.

Chapter Goals and Recap

A light application of the Shadows/Highlights command is appropriate for many files. The recommended time is between the luminosity steps of Chapter 4 and the color boosting of Chapters 5 and 6.

The improvement, while noticeable, is not nearly as big as those of other chapters. Don't spend time adjusting the S/H settings. Instead, go with a one-size-fits-all approach. If more time is available, use it to experiment with color enhancement, not S/H.

How Difficult Is It? Piece of cake.

How Often Is It Needed? Probably a majority of all pictures, but not much more.

The PPW Takes Shape

COLOR

- Kill incorrect color with RGB curves (Chapter 3).
- Identify highlight (Chapters 3–4).

CONTRAST

- Channel blending on luminosity layer (Chapter 4).
- Contrast-enhancing curves (Chapter 4)
    - Consider S/H command (this chapter)

COLOR AGAIN

- Apply MMM + Color Boost action (Chapters 5–6).
- Finalize contrast, including endpoints.
- Reduce color by masking or opacity adjustment.

SHARPEN

FINALIZE

- Consider blending with another version.
- Convert to final output space, if needed.

Then why bother to do it at all?

To open S/H manually and click OK requires ten seconds at most. Using the PPW panel to click an action that does the same probably cuts the time down to two seconds.

The benefit is admittedly modest, but it's worth two seconds, or maybe even ten.

When we encounter a picture in Category 3—highlights and/or shadows critical to image success—we use a supplementary enhancement action. Look ahead to Chapter 10 for the type of image that qualifies: waterfalls, snowy winter scenes, light animals, cloud formations, and the like.

We haven't encountered any of these yet because I've withheld them. The more powerful, if time-consuming, Chapter 10 method will do the heavy lifting in such images.

That leaves Category 2, photos where the extra detail is nice but not essential, like those shown in Figure 7.2. Fooling around further with them scarcely seems like a good use of time. If you want to experiment, do it later in the process with the color enhancements.

Quiz Answers: The Pictures of Chapter 6

These delicate settings won't cause much damage even if applied to an inappropriate picture. You can even use them more than once during the process.

The problem, if any, is likely to be artistic. You can improve detail in an insignificant area, and thereby distract from something more important. It is appropriate to use S/H most of the time, but before applying it you should be sure that there's something worth improving.

I asked you to review the originals of Chapter 6 and decide whether you would use S/H, and if so, why. My own answers follow.

- *Tower Bridge* (Figure 6.1) **Yes**. The parts of the bridge that are in shadow carry detail. The lighter parts are too small to be helped, but the background clouds will benefit. So, a case for S/H in both highlights and shadows.

- *Horses* (Figure 6.4) **Conditionally Yes**. Nothing in the highlights, but the dark manes will surely benefit from S/H. The problem, if you think it is one, is that the background trees may gain so much detail as to distract from the horses.
- *Navajo Dome* (Figure 6.6) **Yes**, definitely. This might even be a Category 3 picture because the light areas of the dome are so important. The dark trees at the bottom of the dome will also be helped.
- *Zulu woman* (Figure 6.13) **Yes**. The highlights aren't important, but the hair is a tempting S/H target.
- *Golden Gate Bridge* (Figure 6.15) **No**. Nothing of interest is found in the highlights. Some parts of the bridge are dark but lack detail. We shouldn't try to bring out stuff that isn't there.
- *Red and yellow flowers* (Figure 6.16) **No**. Applying S/H would bring out detail in the background. That might strike you as technically correct, but I think it would distract attention from the flowers and is therefore an error. This is a more extreme case of the horses image of Figure 6.4. The decision of whether to accept extra detail in the background is more a matter of taste there.
- *Seated family* (Figure 6.17) **Yes**. Everybody is wearing white shirts and has dark hair. The need for S/H is obvious.
- *Las Vegas nightscape* (Postcard 6.20) **Who knows**? The composition is so weird that we almost have to try it and cancel if it doesn't work. Chances are that S/H will bring out a passel of noise in the night sky. There might be a benefit in the lights, though.
- *Two women* (Figure 6.21) **Yes**. We compared a PPW correction with one done in 2002, before S/H existed. As pointed out then, the dark hair was improved. I don't see any other benefit.

The summary: I expect no disagreement that Shadows/Highlights should be applied to five of these nine. Two more are debatable, and two others, in my opinion, shouldn't be touched. Of the five definites, one is a candidate for being treated as Category 3, highlights critically important.

These pictures weren't chosen with proving anything about S/H in mind, but the ratios happen to be representative of what you'd get with a larger sample.

All six of the ones to which I answered Yes sport shadow detail as a target, but only three have interesting highlight detail. This is also typical. Category 3 pictures are almost always dominated by highlights, but Category 2 usually finds more benefit from S/H in the shadows.

* * *

The easy concepts of this half-chapter don't merit either a postcard example or a review section. The second half is difficult and offers little immediate sustenance. S/H can be seen as foreshadowing a topic that becomes crucial later in the book: the importance of large blurs to masks. We will cover that, explain the clipping options that are occasionally useful, and discuss why results are different in RGB and LAB. We will end with a hypothetical exercise that may be of use to a few readers: how to create an ersatz S/H command if Photoshop didn't have one.

None of this makes much of a difference unless you're seriously interested in the topic. If you decide to skip ahead, the next two chapters will discuss two common subjects that don't really follow the PPW rules as discussed so far.

A Closer Look

The operation of the Shadows/Highlights command depends upon the use of an unseen blur. I've advertised Chapter 10 as being a stronger method of enhancing highlights and shadows. As you might expect, it uses a hidden blur, too. Moreover, the powerful multiply tricks to be shown in Chapters 11 and 12 depend on blurs. Sharpening, too, which we'll be talking about in Chapter 15, is little more than a blur in reverse.

In fact, a large part of the progress in image correction over the last decade is in exploiting these hidden blurs. If you decide to study the topic, so much the better. But it isn't necessary if you just want to improve your results quickly. All the methods just described work. Fortunately, most people don't need to know why. At least, not most of the time.

S/H is a sophisticated command, perhaps the best feature introduced in Photoshop in a decade. But I found that teaching the theoretically correct way to use it caused students to burn up a great deal of learning time for very little gain. Hence, the simplified recommendation found in the first half of this chapter: use S/H with our predefined settings right after the luminosity step and before MMM + Color Boost.

The *optimal* time to apply it, if you care, is somewhat different.

- Moving S/H earlier and applying it before, not after, the luminosity step, can get better results, provided that the original isn't flat. That is, only do this if highlight and shadow values are already in the right neighborhood. And if you have decided to use the methods of Chapter 10 because you have a Category 3 image (critical detail in highlights and/or shadows), then make a change, to be described in a moment, in the usual S/H values.
- If the original *is* flat and Category 3, apply S/H after luminosity while still in RGB, and make the same change.
- If none of the above, then convert the file to LAB after the luminosity step and apply S/H there rather than in RGB. As the next steps, the color actions, work in LAB, just leave the file in that colorspace afterward.

Again: following these complicated rules will not gain you a whole lot over doing it the simple way. But let's look at why they are nevertheless correct, at least in theory.

Keeping the Options Straight

Some of the command's options, shown back in Figure 7.1, are easy to understand, others less so. The higher the Amount, the stronger the effect—but the range on which it acts doesn't change. The higher the Tonal Width, the more liberal S/H is in its definition of shadow and highlight. The 25% in my suggested defaults means, approximately, that the shadows half of the command won't lighten anything lighter than a three-quartertone. The Photoshop default, 50%, would allow midtones to be lightened somewhat. And the highlights half works the same way.

The Radius and Color Correction fields will be discussed later. Midtone Contrast should be avoided as there are always better alternatives.

That leaves the two Clips. My defaults are the same as Photoshop's. Both automatically blow out a tiny percentage of the highlight and make the same tiny percentage of the shadow pure black. Everything between gets reallocated.

If the file is in reasonable shape before applying S/H, this is a good rule. That certain parts of the highlight have gotten lighter and certain parts of the shadow darker will not be obvious.

If, however, the file is a flat one then S/H may make a huge change, because it sets a highlight and shadow where none previously was to be found. Worse, it can fool the unwary into thinking it's a good thing. Proper highlights and shadows always make a picture look better, so it is no surprise that a flat original, like Figure 7.3A, looks vastly better after an application of S/H, Figure 7.3B.

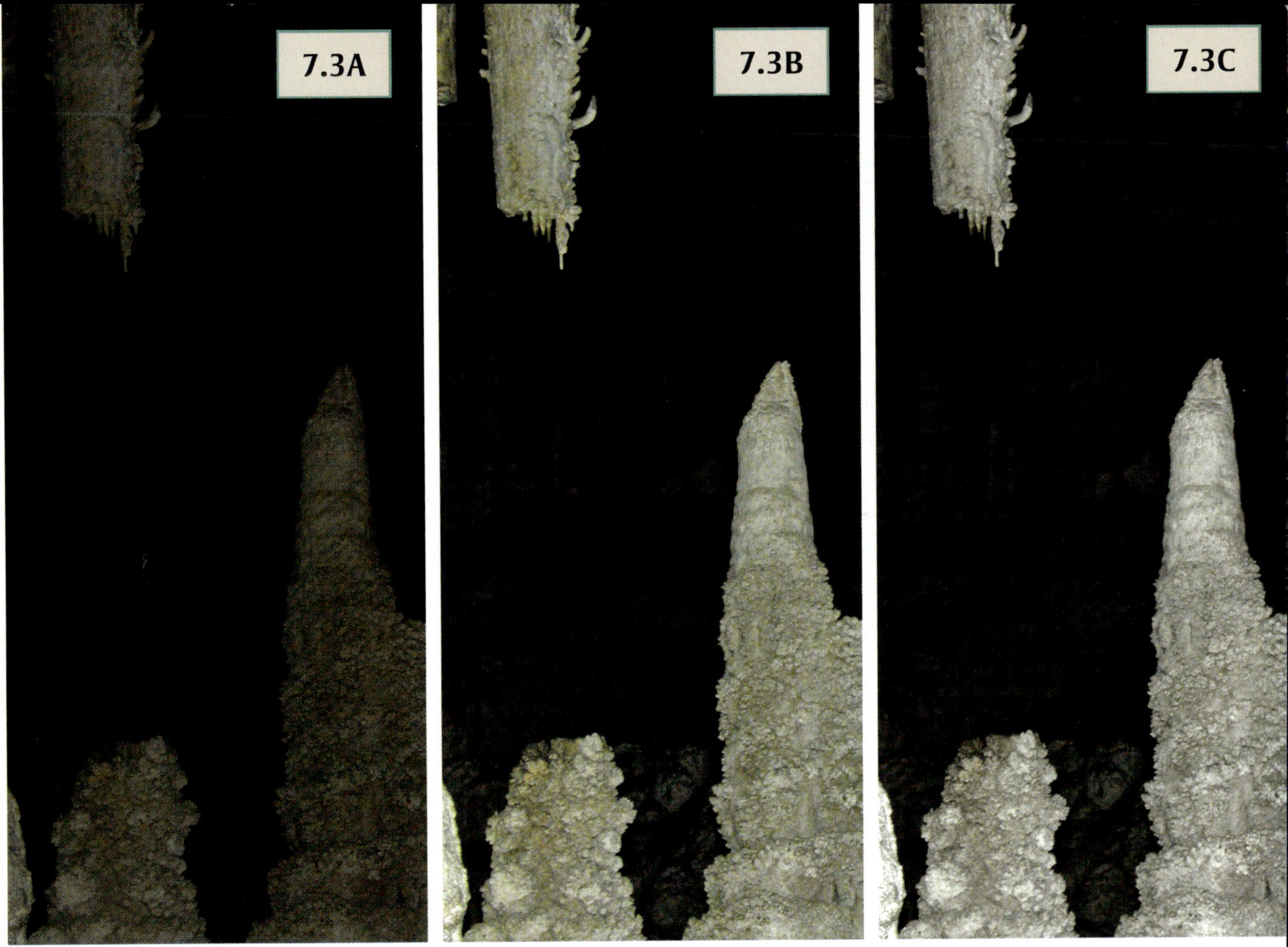

***Figure 7.3** It's tempting, but unwise, to apply S/H to flat pictures. Left, the underground original. Center, S/H is applied with this chapter's defaults. Right, doing Auto Tone first and then S/H results in more detail and better color.*

The problem is that this is the wrong way to do things, and likely pre-empts doing it the right way later. Figure 7.3C, a primitive alternative, applies Auto Tone first (on a luminosity layer to prevent color shift) and *then* S/H to a flattened file. Detail is markedly better.

Despite the protection of the luminosity layer, we observe some disagreeable developments in Figure 7.3B. The default +20 in S/H's Color Correction field has boosted color inappropriately in certain areas.

Photoshop's +20 is a good default for shadows and a poor one for highlights. Unfortunately, we have to choose one value for both. I would say that +20 is the least evil alternative. It doesn't work well here, though. Setting it to 0 would eliminate the problem, but a better solution is not to apply S/H until the picture has close to a correct tonal range.

If we set the Clips to 0, no highlights will be made lighter, no shadows darker. We can also restrict the effect to one side by zeroing out only one Clip. Again, however, I prefer positive values as a default—with one exception.

If you think this is a Category 3 picture, you should zero out the Clips regardless of when you apply S/H. When shadow or highlight is that important, the decision of what to clip, if anything, should be made by us, not some algorithm.

The matter is not one of great import. Nevertheless, a beta reader submitted, and we have posted, a tech note partially disputing the above. Details are in the Notes & Credits section.

Amount, Tonal Width, and LAB

Assisting us with our conquest of the Shadows/Highlights command and alternatives will be a conquistador. I am not a big fan of Francisco

Pizarro González, but his hometown of Trujillo (the one in Spain, not the one in the country he sacked and despoiled in the process of wiping out a culture superior to his own) thought he was worth a bronze equestrian statue, sculpted by an American, ironically enough. The fierce Extremadura sun causes problems with overly dark shadows in most photos of this scene.

To avoid confusion, please note that in all the following examples I have disabled everything having to do with highlights, Clip included. So the only thing that is changing is the treatment of shadows.

Figure 7.4A is the original. Figure 7.4B is our default S/H, limited to the shadows. Can you see the difference in the face?

If not, Figure 7.4C should show it. Amount is changed from 18% to 100%, but otherwise the settings are the same.

In both versions the correction is limited to the darkest areas. In Figure 7.4D Tonal Width is increased from 25% to 50% to go along with the 100% Amount. The correction moves well down into the midtone.

That move was done in RGB. Figure 7.4E was converted to LAB first. The settings are the same, but the appearance is not.

Nobody is planning to use either of these last two versions. We have been talking about something subtle, like Figure 7.4B. If those are the settings, nobody is going to know or care whether we did the work in LAB. But it's worth knowing why LAB is different. It may not pay off in this context but it does in several others. The key question: which of these last two versions is the darker? And why?

To save you the trouble of opening the images and toggling back and forth, I'll give you the first answer. The LAB version, Figure 7.4E, has a lighter sky. But the statue is darker. Can you explain that?

The Tonal Width setting calls for the lightening effect to cut off at 50%—that is, only in the darkest half of the picture. But *half* has a different meaning in different colorspaces.

Warning: the explanation of this point and its significance is so mind-numbingly dense that when I tried to present it in early drafts of this chapter, some beta readers actually said that it put me in Pizarro's league for sheer cruelty. I will therefore compress it greatly here.

The most commonly used RGB workspaces these days are Adobe RGB and sRGB. If you have an identical-looking document in each, the channels won't look the same, but this is because their color is defined differently. Considering only the overall lightness of the channels, the two match closely.

Contrary to what you might expect, all three individual RGB channels usually look darker than the L channel of an identical document converted to LAB. We noted this briefly back in our discussion of Figure 4.21. The L channel has to be lighter, because in figuring how to display or print the composite color, Photoshop *interprets* the L as being darker than it does RGB.

Let me repeat that mouthful in different words. The L channel has to be light because it is going to be interpreted as being dark.

One more time: if the two files are intended to match one another, a 50% gray in RGB has to convert to something lighter than a 50% gray in the L channel, as otherwise Photoshop will interpret it as being too dark.

Hoping that three repetitions have clarified the situation, let me advise that a 50% gray in sRGB or Adobe RGB is equivalent to a 46% gray in the L, and state the ramifications.

- Half of these two RGBs is devoted to tones darker than this one, but 54% of the L is.
- Half of these RGBs is also devoted to lighter tones, but only 46% of the L is.
- Therefore, the L channel reserves more of its resources for portraying dark things, and less for portraying light ones, than RGB does.
- Consequently, if identical corrections are applied to identical-looking RGB and LAB files, the results will *not* be identical. The changes in the LAB file will be subtler in dark areas and harsher in light ones.

We are more sensitive to color variation in lighter tones, more sensitive to contrast in darker ones. Because the L handles darks more delicately, LAB is the colorspace of choice for many operations. Its noise control is significantly better. I reiterate that at settings as mild as those in this chapter you won't see a difference. But in some other contexts, you will. For example, if you skip ahead to our final example, at the (inappropriately) high settings that produced Figure 7.7B out of an RGB file, doing it in LAB substantially

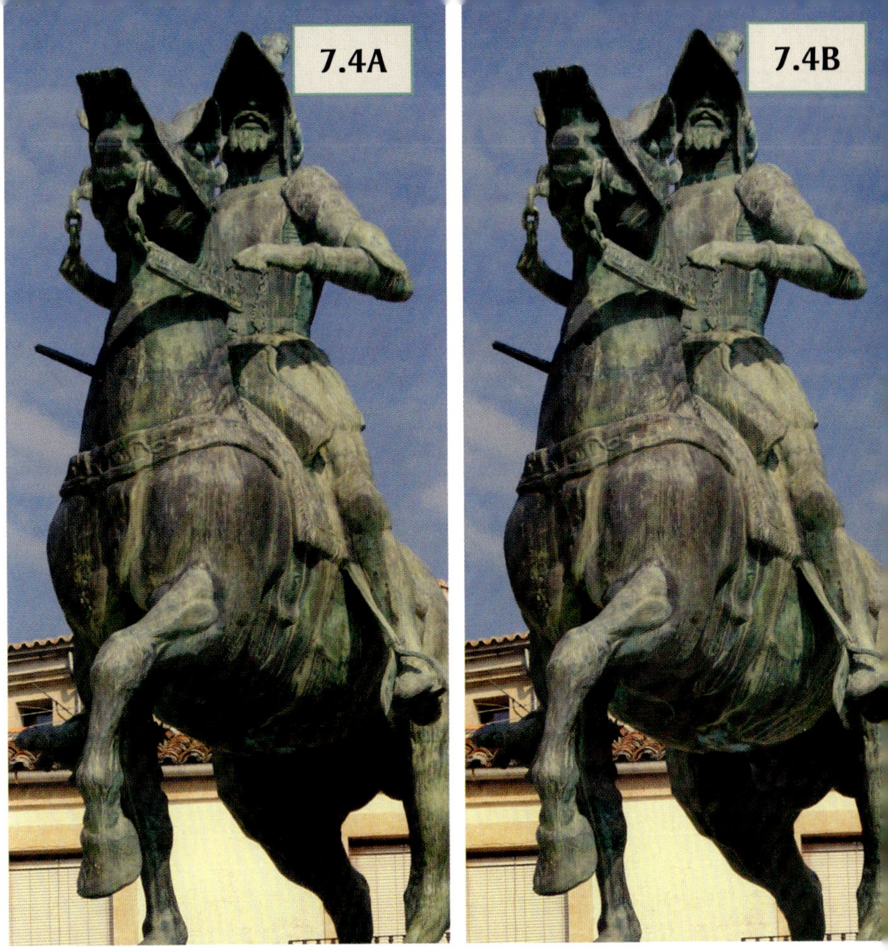

Figure 7.4 *Top left, the original. Top right, this chapter's default S/H settings, limited to shadows only. Bottom left, Amount is increased to 100%. Bottom center, 100% Amount and 50% Tonal Width. Bottom right, the same settings, but applied in LAB rather than RGB.*

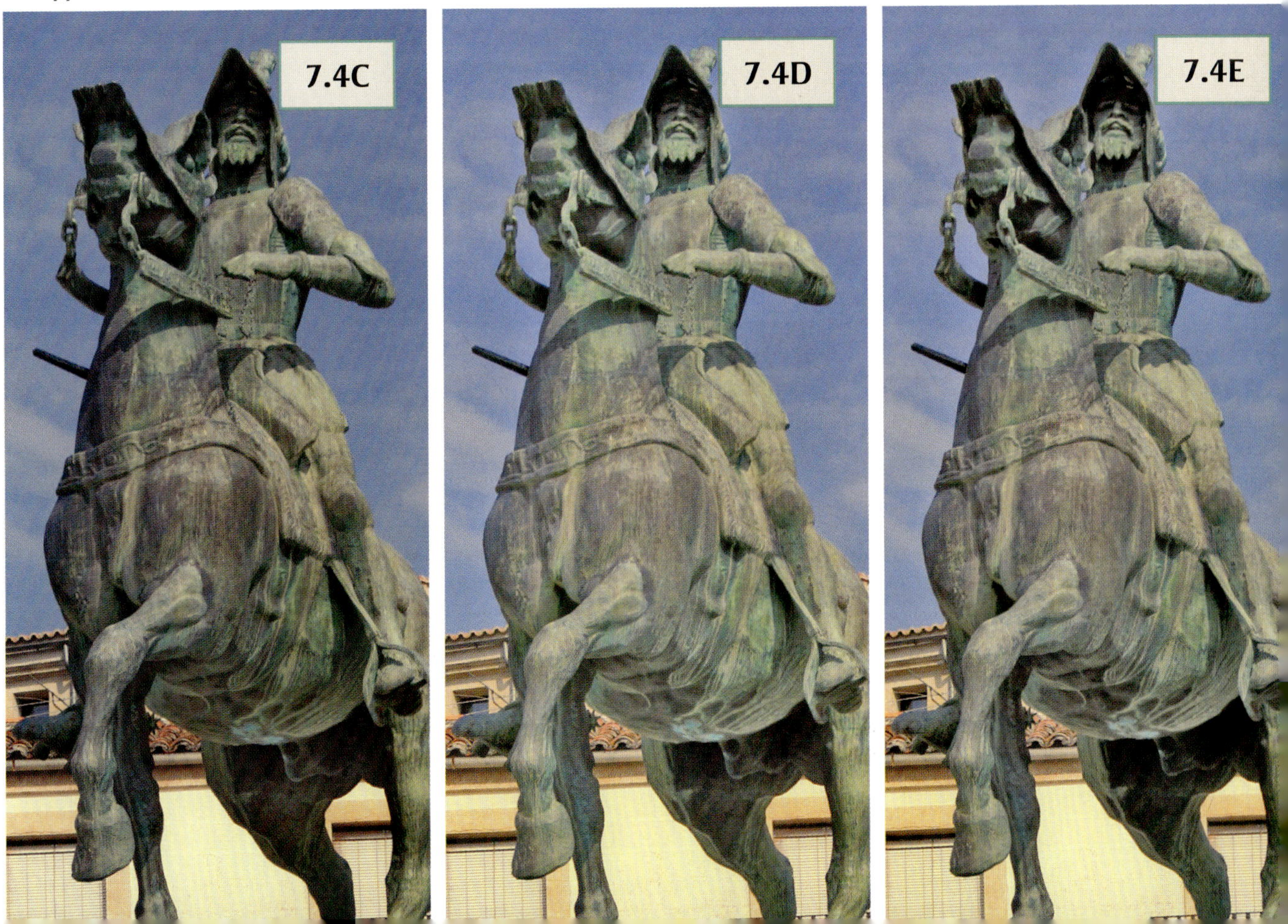

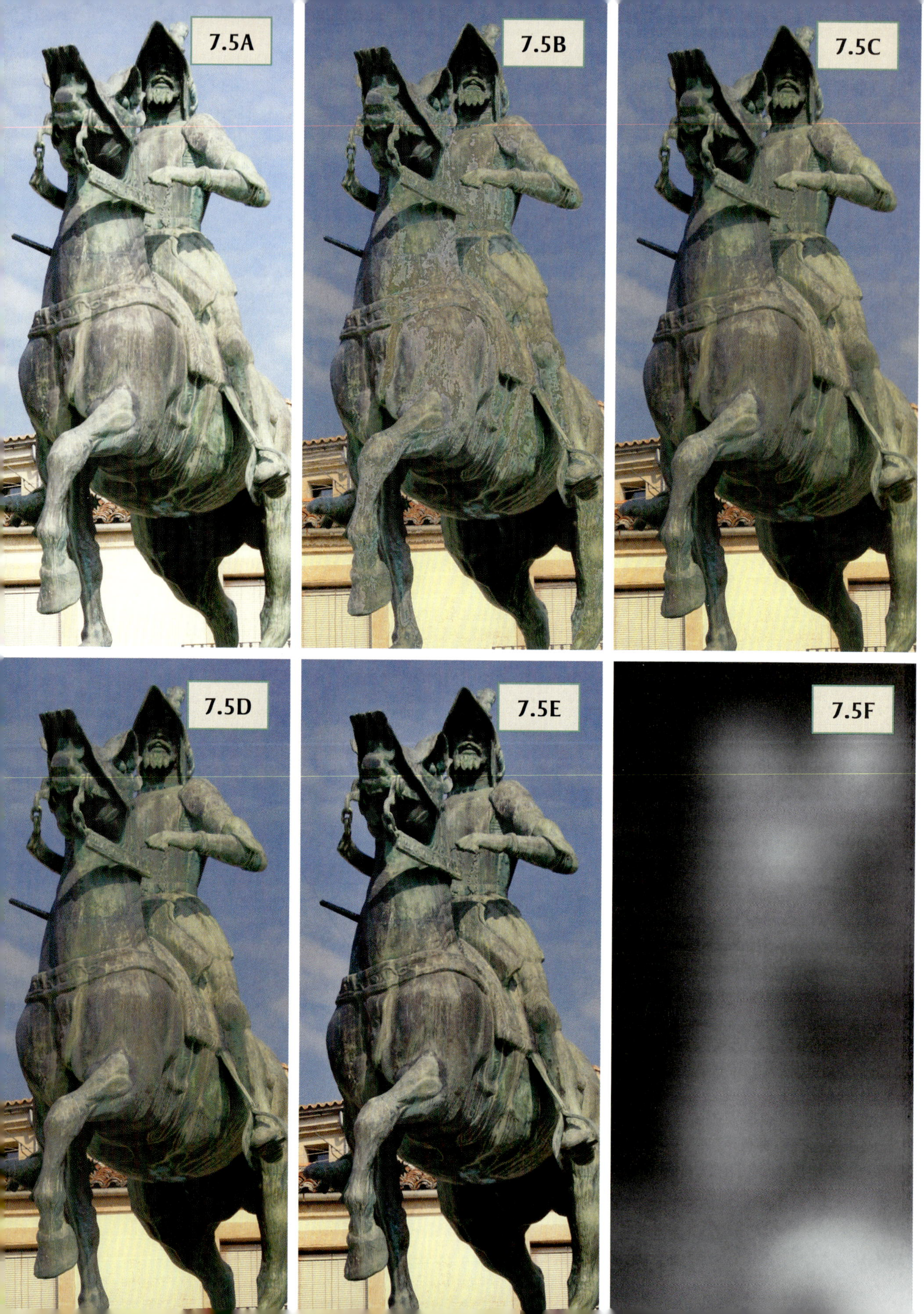
7.5A
7.5B
7.5C
7.5D
7.5E
7.5F

reduces noise. It's not worth showing, but you can grab the file and experiment with it.

They didn't have Photoshop back in Pizarro's sixteenth century, but we can surely go back to the twentieth. The Shadows/Highlights command did not exist, but the need for it did. Let's cobble together a substitute.

Some readers wanted to know the point of a complex technique that takes twenty times as long as what we can already do with a single click. The question has a certain logic.

First, many people are interested in the vague concept known by the misleading initials HDR. If you're one of them, you may discover that you suddenly understand its basic concepts after you go through the following exercise.

More importantly, a lot of the PPW's power is contained in Chapter 12. If you have any difficulty in understanding how it works, and a lot of people do, this exercise will help.

Am I telling you to use the following technique? Of course not. Just use S/H. What I am saying is that knowing how to make this substitute S/H is good for the soul.

How to Make an Ersatz S/H

The task is to increase detail in the shadows, using only commands available in the mid-1990s. For simplicity, I'll emulate a Tonal Width of about 30%, work in RGB, and not do anything that depends on the specifics of this image.

Forcing more detail into the shadows is easy. We merely apply a curve that drastically lightens the midtones, arriving at Figure 7.5A. It has gained shadow detail at the rather high price of blowing out most of the light half of the picture, which shouldn't be changing at all.

Figure 7.5 *(opposite) A quick attempt to emulate the Shadows/Highlights command. Top left, a curve is applied to the entire picture, washing out the lighter areas. Top center, simply replacing light areas is gross. Top right, using a layer mask based on an inverted channel. Bottom left, apparent sharpness is gained by blurring the layer mask (Gaussian blur, 15 pixel Radius). Bottom center, the mask is blurred instead at 45 pixel Radius. Bottom right, this second mask.*

Just restoring the light half to its original state, as I did with Blend If to produce Figure 7.5B, is too simplistic. Pizarro's horse has a better chance of flying than this version does in a professional environment.

This attempt to merge two pictures of radically different darknesses failed because the transition is nonexistent. Big blotches appear where the two halves meet.

The alternative is Figure 7.5C. With the light version on the top layer and the original on the bottom, I loaded a copy of the RGB composite from the original layer as a layer mask. It had to be inverted to allow more impact from the top layer where the picture is dark. Then I applied a curve to turn the darkest two-thirds of the layer mask black.

That last move prevented anything originally relatively light from changing, but avoided the harsh transitions of Figure 7.5B. Lightening is strongest in the face and other dark areas, lessening as the original lightens, and disappearing altogether at a certain point.

This effort does not measure up to Figure 7.4C. The settings in that earlier version were stronger, true. Yet the face in Figure 7.5C is somewhat competitive. The horse is not; it seems to lack detail, almost as if someone had blurred it.

To see why, look at the shadow that the reins throw onto the animal's neck. Figure 7.5B isn't good for much, but it does show that the shadow itself is dark enough to be affected by our primitive attempt at S/H. The sunny part of the neck is not. The contrast between the two areas is less in Figure 7.5C than in 7.4C. The same appears to be true for several other areas where the horse changes darkness. For example, the reflection in the horse's near shoulder is not as well defined in Figure 7.5C.

The overall impression is unnatural because the contrast loss isn't uniform. The light part of the image is fine, as are the deep shadows. But the difference between something that was fairly dark and something *really* dark has diminished. The solution is to fool the mask by blurring it.

Beta reader Frederick Yocum responds: "I kind of conceptually understand what is happening. You create a mask that bisects the image so the transitions from one version to the other are along the landmarks of image detail. Blurring the mask allows the transitions to become more extreme. Even as I type this I don't understand what I am trying to say. But, 'the solution is to fool the mask by blurring it.' is a bit like saying 'abracadabra'."

Back to me. I am not talking about a namby-pamby little mincing Milquetoast of a blur, the kind that one might use to eliminate noise. I mean a *really big blur.* Figure 7.5D has a Gaussian blur, 15 pixel Radius, to the layer mask.

And now you know the secret of the Radius field in Shadows/Highlights.

Figure 7.5E uses 7.5F as a mask. The Radius is 45, rather than 15. The best Radius is image-specific: here, the reflections are so large that a big one is in order. The best channel for the layer mask is also image-specific. I used an inverted RGB composite for simplicity. An inverted copy of the blue channel would have been a better choice, as the blue is always the darkest channel in green objects. Using it as the mask would have allowed more impact in the important areas as opposed to the background.

For that matter, the type of blur is image-specific, too. Gaussian blur isn't the only choice. And we haven't even considered some kind of composite mask based on more than one blur or more than one channel.

With things as violent as what's shown here, all this image-specific stuff makes a difference. The explosive moves shown in Chapters 10, 11, and 12 are subject to the same layer masking considerations.

***Figure 7.6** Left, an application of S/H at 100% Amount, 30% Tonal Width, 45 pixel Radius. Center, a similar version produced using the methods of Chapter 10. Right, a version produced using only limited shadow enhancement, but all steps of the PPW except for sharpening.*

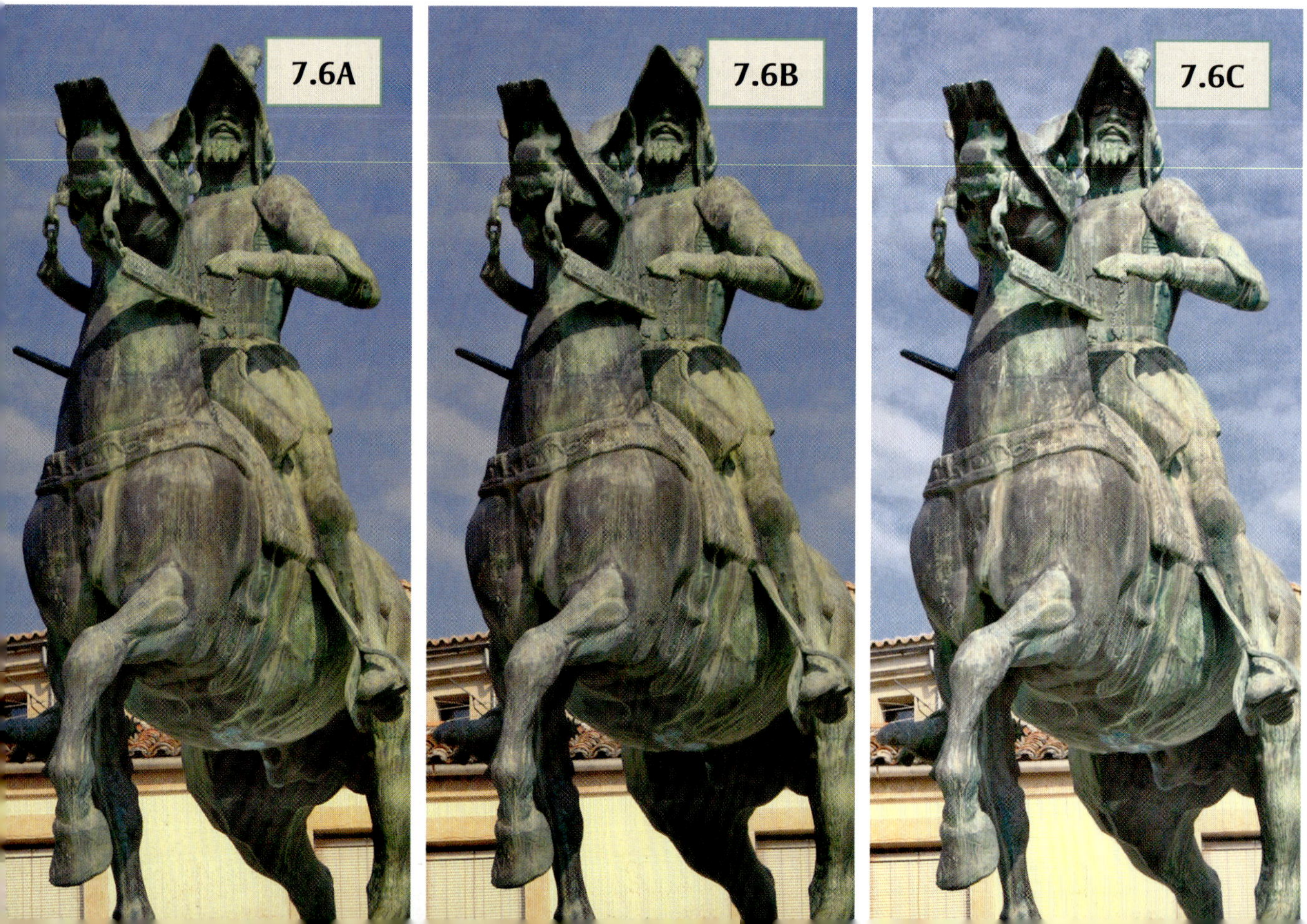

Figure 7.6A is S/H, still limited to shadows, with a 45 pixel Radius, 100% Amount, and 30% Tonal Width. These values, much stronger than the ones I recommend, were chosen as being most directly comparable to the competition we're about to look at.

The S/H method in effect applies its correction through a mask, just as I did in Figures 7.5C, 7.5D, and 7.5E. Where the mask is light the correction will be more intense and where dark less so. When the mask is fuzzy and defocused, few people can detect signs of chicanery. The S/H Radius field takes care of that defocusing.

An alternate way, instead of correcting *through* the blurred mask, is to use the mask itself as the correction. Applying the mask to the image in Soft Light mode produces Figure 7.6B. Chapter 10 is based on this technique. I wouldn't recommend it here, because this is not an image of Category 3. It delivers shape rather than fine detail, which is normally an advantage in the shadows. We'll see an example in a moment of how S/H can augment noise, which is one of the reasons I advocate much lighter applications of S/H than those shown here.

Another reason is that such huge moves aren't needed. Figure 7.6C runs through the entire PPW, sharpening excepted. It uses the multiplication methods shown in Chapter 12. It employs only the subtle S/H settings shown in Figure 7.1. Why should anything stronger be necessary, especially when there could be a downside?

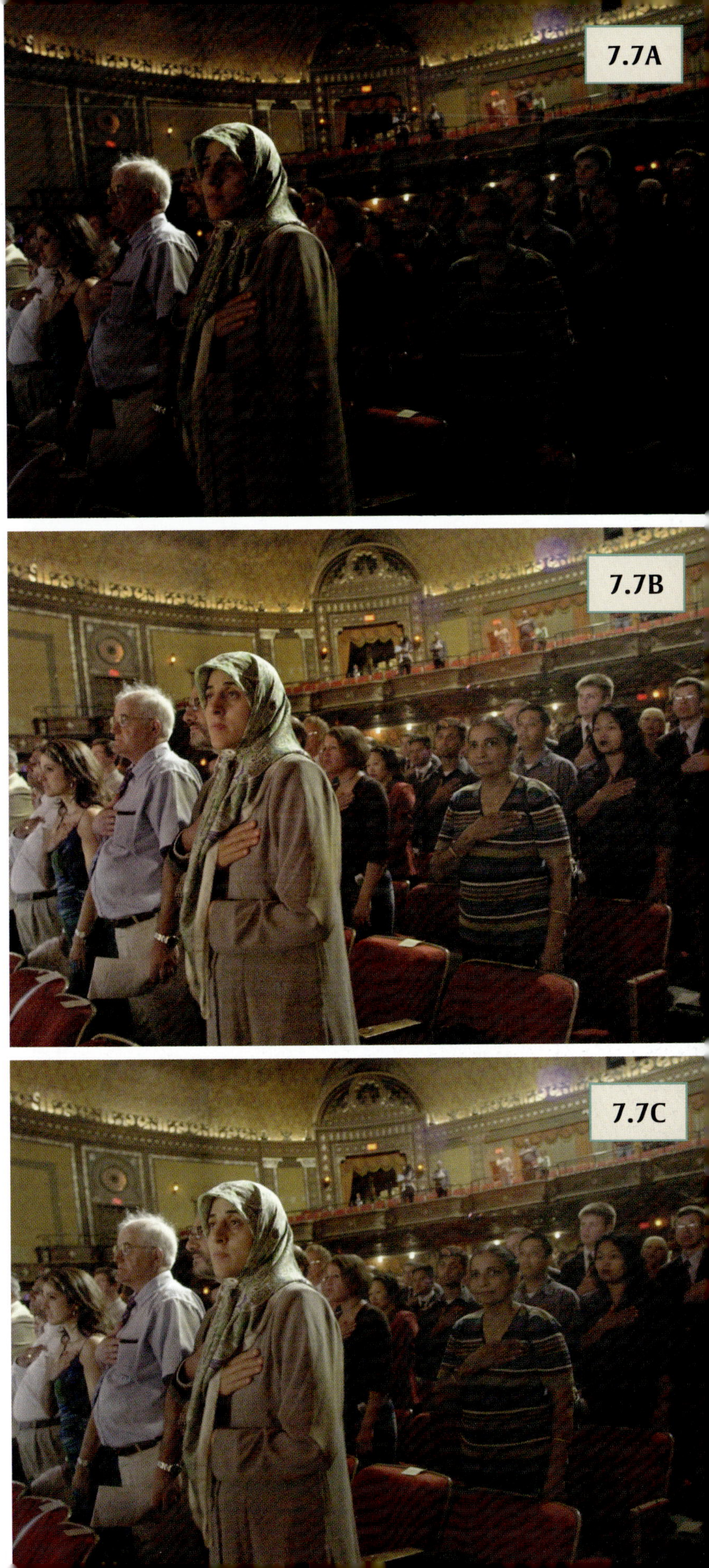

***Figure 7.7** Top, the underexposed original. Middle, the pre-CS5 defaults of S/H are applied. Bottom, starting from scratch, a gamma correction with the Exposure command, followed by a darkening curve.*

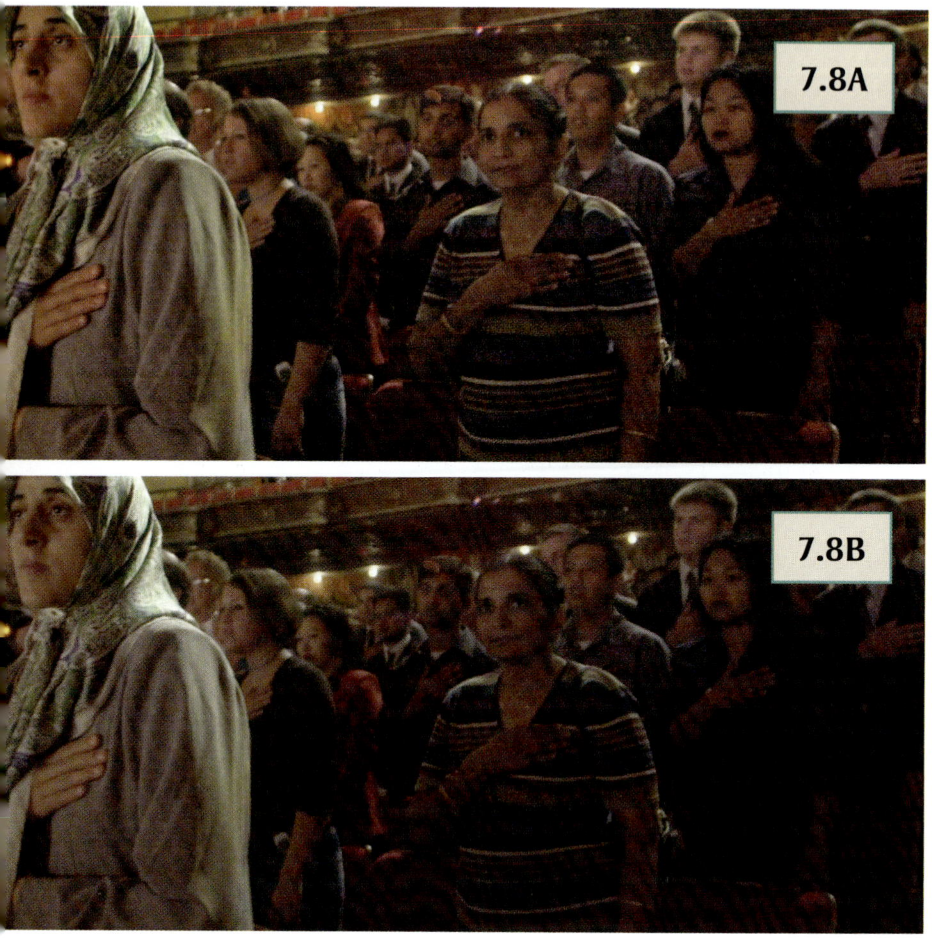

Figure 7.8 *Upsized sections show more noise in Figure 7.7B, above, than in Figure 7.7C.*

Where Is Your Allegiance?

A disciplined workflow is virtuous enough to avoid being seduced by moves that make the picture look better temporarily but hurt quality in the long run. Here's an example.

S/H was originally seen as a way to rescue seriously underexposed photos like Figure 7.7A. Pre-CS5 defaults produce Figure 7.7B.

It makes a good demo that doesn't stand scrutiny. Scores of other ways of lightening the picture would do better. Figure 7.7C was produced via Image: Adjustments>Exposure>Gamma Correction>2.0, followed by curves to darken the shadow.

Underexposed images are often noisy, especially in the shadows. The Pizarro image didn't have that problem and S/H brought out appealing facial detail. This time, though, in exaggerating what it thinks is detail, S/H emphasizes noise. Check out the differences in Figure 7.8.

Such is the case for using S/H quickly and in moderation. The picture we ended with is perhaps an appropriate one. These are new citizens swearing their allegiance to the United States. This momentous decision requires most of them to renounce allegiance to their former nations.

Although theirs is far more consequential than any we'll ever make in Photoshop, it is essentially the same decision we face in adopting and changing workflows. We consider the possibilities, evaluate alternatives, choose the one we think has the most potential. We give due respect to history but we refuse to be slaves to it.

History suggests that most of these people are making the right choice. It was certainly the right one for two of my grandparents. We all hope it turns out to be so for these new citizens as well.

History also suggests that those in our profession succeed when they are open to studying new ideas. I hope and expect that this will continue to be true, too.

The Bottom Line

A light application of Shadows/Highlights is often helpful. Fine-tuning the settings is not worthwhile.

Studying how the command works is a useful prelude to discussion of masking and of sharpening, but does not directly affect the simple way in which the command is used in this workflow.

8

The Sky's No Limit

Skies—or at least their blue parts—don't behave like other objects. Added detail is unwelcome, because it probably also adds noise. Added color is unwelcome, because it probably produces something out of gamut. Fortunately, skies are so easy to select that powerful automated solutions can be developed. You just have to say the word—but it's a word that doesn't seem to exist in any language.

Professional digital image manipulation has only been around for a quarter century. For most of that time computers were too slow to allow much experimentation. It cannot be surprising that our understanding continues to improve. The previous chapter pointed out how shadow technique has improved since 2002, for example. The tools were always there; the knowledge was not.

On the other hand, professionals have tried to make pleasing pictures for better than half a millennium. Figuring out how to get proper perspective and lighting into paintings took well over a century. Earlier efforts were less realistic because the painters, like early Photoshop users, didn't have the technique to match the power of their tools. They did, however, know what they *wanted* to achieve. Do we? This chapter will discuss a word that does not exist, and a technique that takes more liberties with the truth than any tried heretofore.

We begin two thousand years ago, less than a century into the Christian era. The Roman emperor Domitian felt the need to erect a marble arch in memory of his older brother Titus, identified as *Tito* in the third line of the inscription. The massive structure became the model for similar arches throughout the world.

The arch survives. So do the first words of its inscription, *Senatus Populusque Romanus* (the Senate and people of Rome) in the form of their acronym SPQR, now, as then, a source of civic pride to Romans. Italians living in other areas of the country, not knowing Latin, believe that SPQR stands for *Sono Pazzi Questi Romani* (they are madmen, these Romans). The acronym shrugs off the insult and still decorates most government

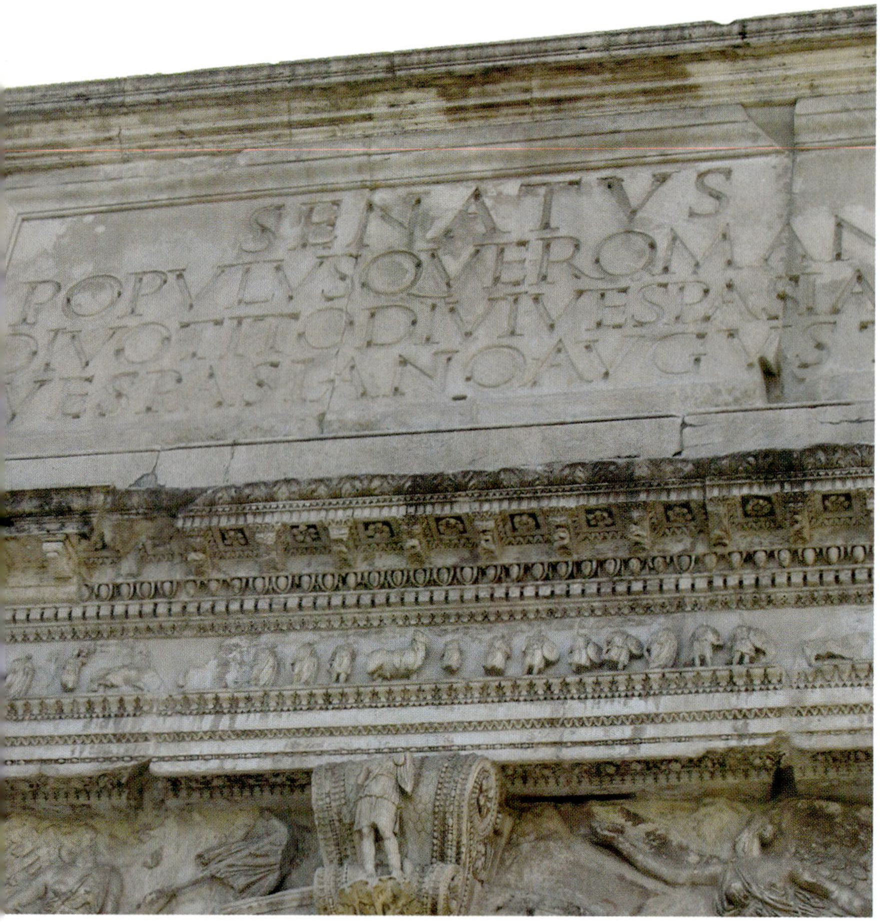

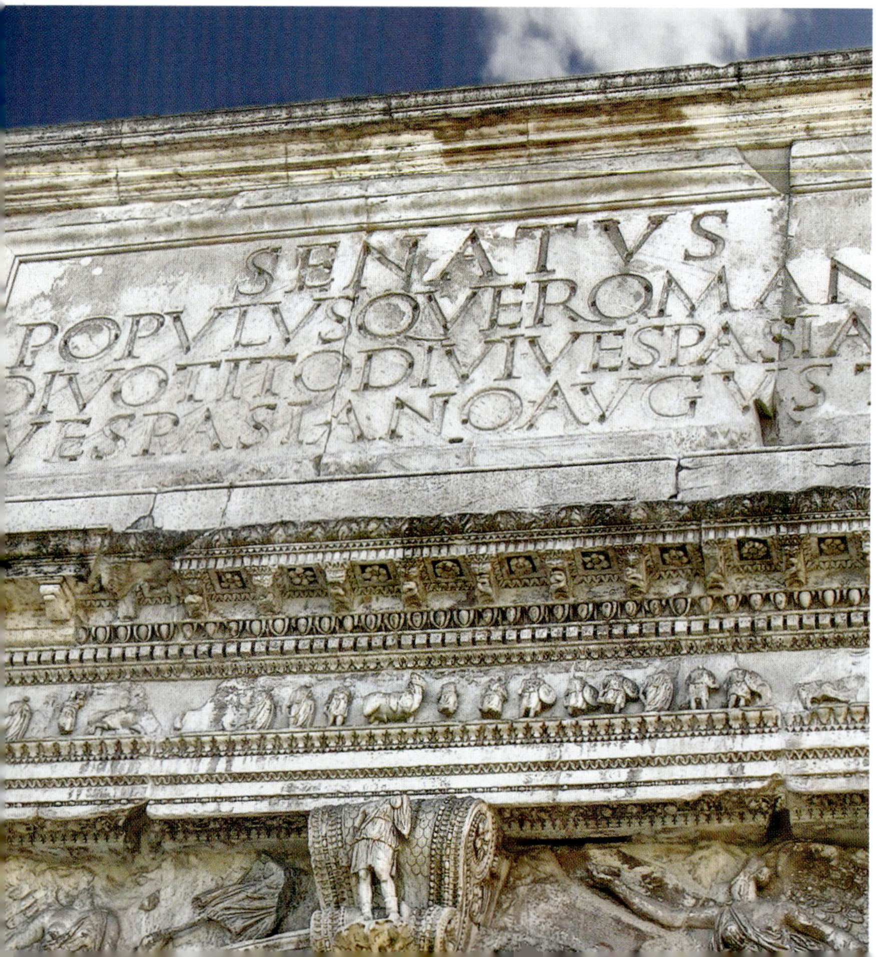

works in Rome, right down to its manhole covers.

SPQR is not quite as ubiquitous today as the shapes of the letters in which it is inscribed. The Arch of Titus stands near the Palatine Hill. If you have ever wondered how today's most popular serif typeface, Times Roman excepted, got its name, compare the designs of these capital letters to those of Hermann Zapf's Palatino.

So distinguished a structure deserves a better reproduction than the original of Postcard 8.1.

The marble is an off-white. As with similar scenes, we would like more color variation—but perhaps not so much as in our next postcard, which also hails from ancient times. This one is from a different continent, and a better photographer. The subject is, in a manner of speaking, the same: it's Arches National Park.

The browns in the original of Postcard 8.2 are monotonous, easy prey for the Modern Man from Mars action of Chapter 6. So the Picture Postcard Workflow correction is probably even more effective here than it was with Titus's Arch. Indeed, this photo has been used as a class exercise, with about fifty students trying to improve the original and then voting on the results. The preferred versions all resemble what you see here.

Both final postcards have extra snap and lots of color variation. Do you see, though, the big lie that they share?

***Postcard 8.1** The Arch of Titus, Rome.*

Friends, Romans, Countrymen

The skies aren't the only attractive parts, but it's hard to think these postcards would be as successful without them. No sky existed in the original Roman image; the one you see in the corrected version was imported from California. The sky in the Utah exercise exists deep within the original photograph, but it has to be tortured out of it with the action that is the focus of this chapter.

Proper sky can make a big difference in outdoor shots. Skies shouldn't, however, be forced into the PPW structure as seen so far. You can get away with it sometimes, but often it produces a dazzling blue that detracts from everything else, or something full of noise, or with illogical-looking transitions. Plus, we as yet have no solution to the problem illustrated in the Utah original: a sky that the camera captures, but is nevertheless too weak for our purposes.

These first two postcards show that solutions are available. In this chapter, I'll show them. In the next one, I'll suggest that a face is like a sky—it doesn't fit neatly into the PPW as described thus far, and needs special handling. Indeed there are similarities, but a sky offers more flexibility than a face, for two reasons.

First, viewers are more gullible about skies than any other object. The two postcards take some liberties with their foregrounds but nothing compared to the distortions going on in the skies. It's hard

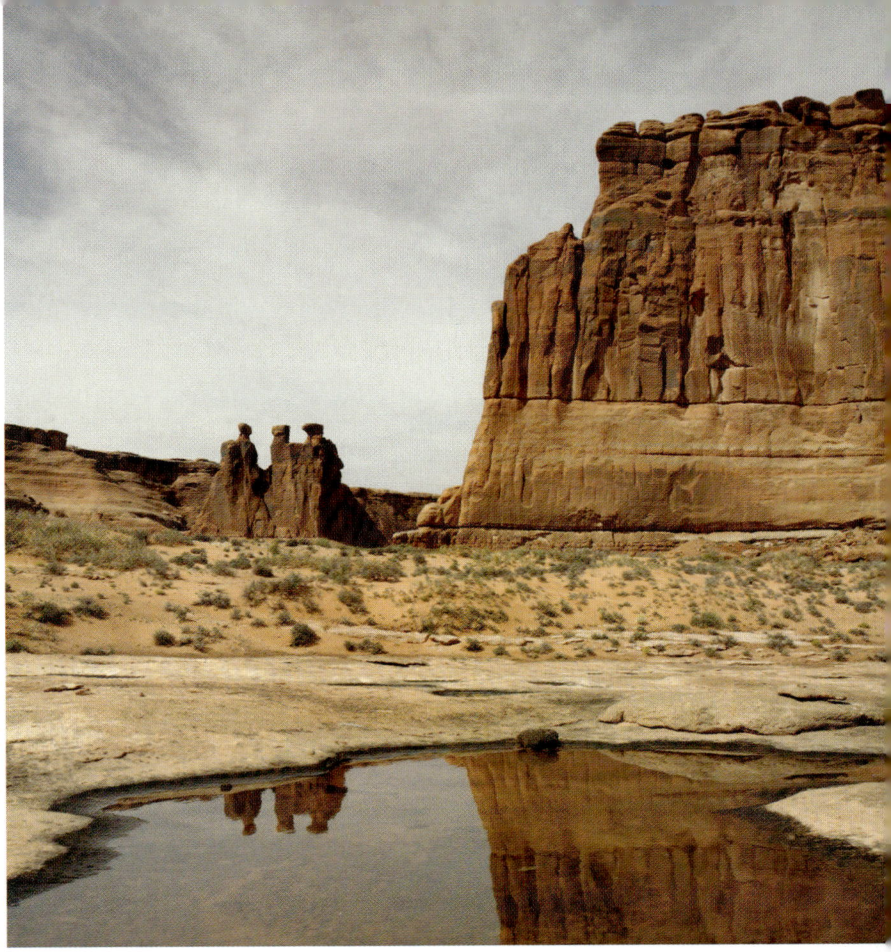

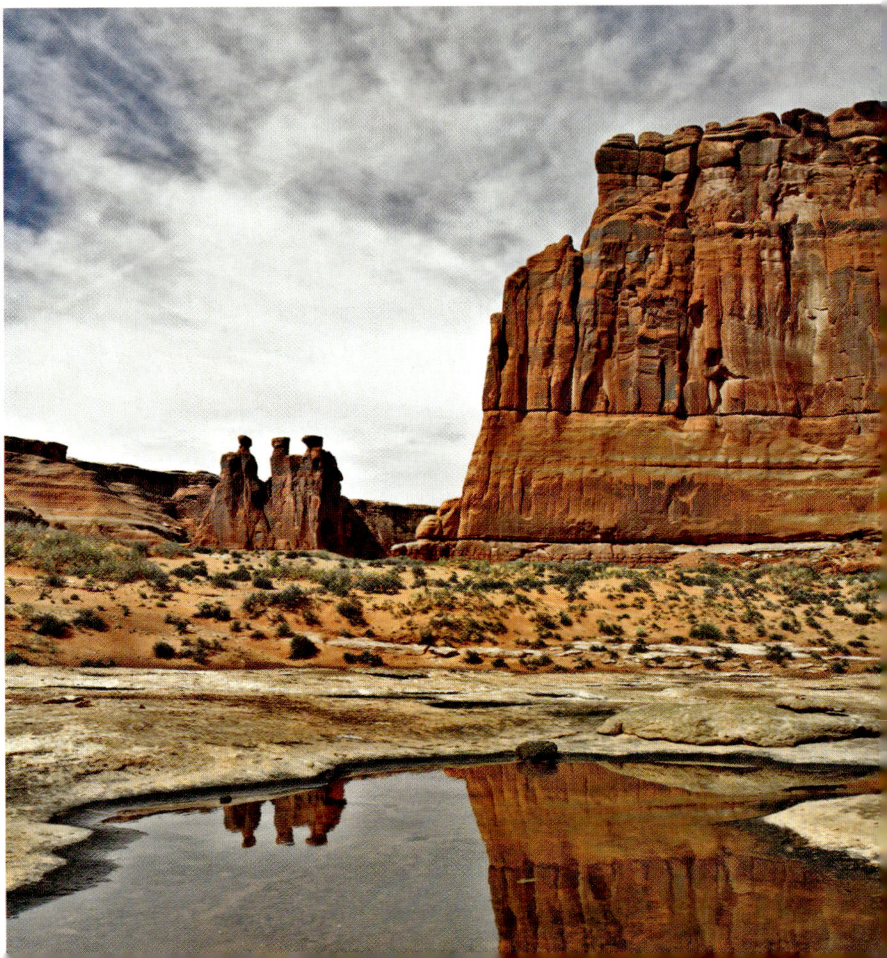

***Postcard 8.2** Arches National Park, Utah.*

to make a believable merge of one person's face into another picture. Nobody notices, however, when a sky is stolen from one file and pasted into another. I have a whole folder full of nice skies, ready to join my Praetorian Guard at a moment's notice.

Second, skies are ridiculously easy to identify, even by an algorithm. They can usually be selected by an action, and even if the selection isn't perfect it's easy to clean up.

The Word That Isn't There

These first postcards illustrate the two common problems. First, the sky or large parts of it can be worthless or missing altogether, In that case, we have to substitute another.

Second, we may find that the blue part of sky is present, but seems too weak. Unfortunately, the word *sky* includes clouds. On the colortheory list, which is heavily international, I asked whether anyone's language had a specific word for the blue areas of skies, and nobody knew of one. The closest anyone came was *azure*. For a footnote, consult the Notes & Credits section.

Which of these two scenarios is more common depends on the type of work. Professional photographers with good equipment rarely confront the first issue. Amateurs with cheap cameras see it all the time, as do people who process images shot by others.

All outdoor photographers, however, encounter the second problem regularly. It's therefore the more important case, but it's also the harder one, at least for the inexperienced. So we will set it aside for the moment and solve the first problem instead.

Therefore, we have a Picture A that, like our first original, needs to have its sky replaced. That implies that we have a Picture B hanging around, unrelated to Picture A but containing a suitable sky and resolution. There are many ways to do what comes next; here's mine.

- Pop into Picture B. With the lasso, marquee, or whatever other tool you fancy, quickly select more than enough sky to cover the problem area in Picture A.
- Edit: Copy it to the clipboard.
- Over to Picture A. Edit: Paste. The substitute sky now covers a lot of things that it shouldn't be covering. It does, however, live on its own layer.
- With that layer active, use the move tool to nudge the new sky into an attractive position, being sure that it completely covers everything you wish to replace.
- Hide the new sky layer by clicking off its eye icon in the Layers palette. Click into the background layer.
- Make a selection of the original sky or lack thereof. Usually that's easy. In Postcard 8.1 you could even do it with the quick selection or the magic wand tools.
- Activate the top layer and click its eye icon to make it visible again.

* * *

We will now complete this in two ways: a quick and dirty one, and then a preview of how we'll handle the second problem. Quick and dirty first.

- With your selection still active, Layer: Layer Mask>Reveal Selection. Or, quicker, click the layer mask icon at the bottom of the Layers palette; Reveal Selection is its default.

You now have a layer mask that is white where you had made a selection, namely, the original sky, and black everywhere else. Blackness blocks the top layer; whiteness allows it to show. Since it is white only over the original sky, in theory we are done now. The new sky replaces it. In practice, however, we get a nasty edge where the two layers meet. Therefore,

- Being sure that the layer mask is active (look for the border around its icon in the Layers palette), soften the edge by running Filter: Blur>Gaussian Blur at a Radius of 3 or 4 pixels.
- Without doing anything else first (because if you do, this command won't be available)

Edit: Fade Gaussian Blur>Opacity=100%, Mode=Lighten. If you don't, the edge of the new sky will take on a light halo.

* * *

The slower, more flexible way picks up with the new sky on a top layer, which is active, and with the old sky having been selected.

- Select: Save Selection. The ensuing dialog suggests saving a new channel in the current document, and asks for a name. "Sky Mask" should do. Click OK.
- Select: Deselect. The previous step saved a channel that we can reload as a selection whenever we like. It isn't needed right now.
- In the Channels palette, click the Sky Mask. Run through the same Gaussian blur plus Fade routine described above.
- Click RGB in the Channels palette to make the composite color visible.
- Layer: Layer Mask>Reveal All, or click the icon at the bottom of the Layers palette.
- Unlike the first time we did this, the layer mask is blank because no selection has been made. So, with the layer mask active, Image: Apply Image. Channel=Sky Mask; Mode=Normal; Opacity=100%; click OK.

The two methods produce identical results. The second, however, leaves us with an extra channel containing the sky selection.

This non-printing channel, which experts snootily refer to as an *alpha channel,* can be used again and again, in return for the an increased file size and the inability to save a JPEG that contains it.

For example, suppose our client is happy that we have provided a sky in Postcard 8.1, but feels that it is too dark. We don't have to agree, but we probably do have to comply. So we Select: Load Selection, and in response to the prompt, load Sky Mask. Now the new sky is selected and we make the change. This is highly handy if we happen to have forgotten exactly how we blurred the mask channel.

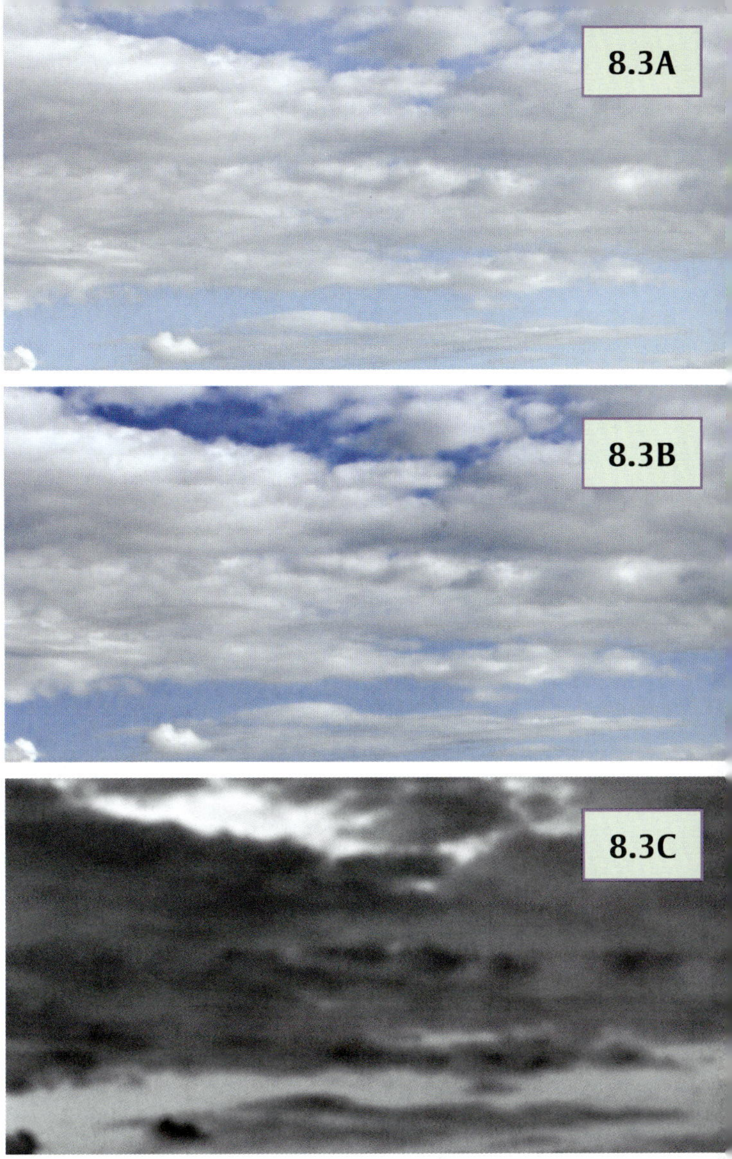

***Figure 8.3** Top, the original. Middle, default results of the Darken Sky SC action. Bottom, the alpha channel that the action generates.*

Beta reader Marco Olivotto has a different view. He writes, "I suggest that the layer mask should be blurred, not the alpha channel. When the layer mask is created, a new alpha channel appears: modify that, and you modify the mask. The original selection should remain untouched in the Sky Mask channel so that different blurs can be performed if needed. Blurring first yields two identical channels (Sky Mask and the layer mask); at that point it would be better to have two different channels. In complex selections this has saved me many times."

This makes perfect sense to me. The question is whether it makes sense to you. If, instead, it makes your eyes glaze over, then I can't agree with Marco. We are about to study an action that features an alpha channel, which the action then blurs and uses as a layer mask. It's quick and foolproof. It is correct that an expert who has seen the image can make a better blurring decision than the action's rigid rules can. Hmm. Maybe in the next revision.

The Action in Action

The objective is that of Postcard 8.2—to darken the word that's not in any language, the blue part of the sky, without affecting the clouds too strongly. The method is the Sky Boost SC action, which finds the blues in an image and generates a smooth mask. The second half of this chapter discusses how, and also explains a second and similar action called Sky Boost B. For the time being, it's enough to say that the two compute their mask differently. Chances are that Sky Boost SC does a better job, except that in complex skies with a lot of interaction between clouds and blue the other is sometimes better. For now, we'll simply assume that the SC version is the right one. There is, of course, no reason to avoid trying both ways, if the importance of the image justifies the time.

* * *

Figure 8.3A is an original sky. Figure 8.3B is the default result of playing Sky Boost SC.

***Figure 8.4** The Layers and Channels palettes immediately after the Darken Sky SC action runs.*

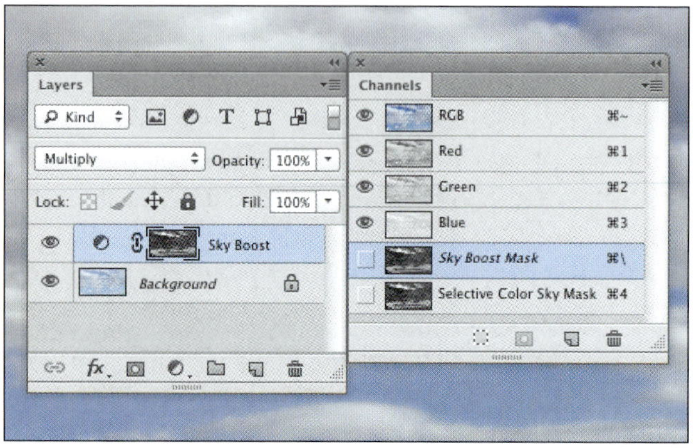

Figure 8.3C is the alpha channel, which you rarely need to look at. Notice, though, its smooth transitions. It's unlikely that anyone will be able to detect selection lines.

Figure 8.4 shows the Layers and Channels palettes immediately after running the action. On top is a curves adjustment layer in which the curves change nothing. The layer is set to Multiply mode, seriously darkening the picture. But the alpha channel has been loaded as the layer mask, so only blue things get darker. The result is identical to duplicating the background layer and applying the same mask; the advantage of the adjustment layer is that it creates a smaller file.

Note that the Channels palette shows not four channels but five. (I am not counting the RGB composite as a separate channel.) The layer mask counts as a fifth channel. For the moment it and the alpha channel are identical. But if you start horsing around with either, they won't remain that way, and you'll have to decide whether that's advisable.

If you think this action is needed, I recommend applying it after the luminosity steps of Chapter 4 and the optional application of Shadows/Highlights. Occasionally it makes such a dramatic difference that the whole picture comes to life. More often, it is a pleasant improvement but nothing worth invading Carthage over.

My experience suggests 50% opacity is usually about right for the multiplying layer.

How Does It Know What's a Sky?

This action has no clue as to what's a sky and what isn't. It does, however, know how to identify what's blue.

Fortunately, the sky is usually the only blue thing of any significance. It was that way in Postcard 8.2 and also in Figure 8.3. Otherwise further action is required. In planning this chapter, I wanted to run a full postcard exercise right here, showing an original that had the extra-object-that's-light-blue problem.

It was not easy to find such an image, especially because I wanted one where other light blues aren't distant enough from the sky to make them easy to select.

I have about a thousand files that could benefit from a Darken Sky action, but only a handful that meet the above criteria. I was looking for something Roman, or even Italian, and came up empty. I wound up in someplace nearly as decadent as ancient Rome, with an original that would get thumbs down from any emperor worth his purple.

Figure 8.5A is so flat that it's not obvious that darkening the sky is worthwhile. What *is* obvious is that getting the color right will be challenging.

Mercifully, identifying the highlight is easy. It's in the lowest clouds, which should certainly be white. Unmercifully, the location, South Beach, is noted for its art deco architecture, which features use of subtle pastels. Making assumptions about the color of buildings here is as dangerous as some of the cocktails along Ocean Drive.

The darker clouds and the whitewall tires are not white in reality: dark clouds take on some of the blueness of the sky, and white tires are somewhat yellow. But I would like to keep these things fairly *near* white.

Also, I kept an eye on the palms, which must be green, on the street, which could be almost anything but green, and on the coupe that context says must be black.

Juggling all these priorities is awkward with a picture this flat. The white tires and the dark clouds are nearly the same darkness, which makes accurate curving hard. I therefore decided to look at luminosity first.

Channel blending seemed like a bad idea. The red was too dark in the buildings. The taxi was too dark in the blue. The green, happily, had everything of interest clustered together. So the strategy was to open range using only curves to the green channel.

I found that it had to be done in installments. The chosen highlight point started at $150^R159^G167^B$. On an adjustment layer, I moved the green to 250^G. Going any further would have cost detail.

Changing this adjustment layer to Luminosity mode produced Figure 8.5B. The highlight was now at $198^R207^G215^B$. To retain color, Photoshop had darkened my new green channel (and lightened the other two).

Chapter Goals and Recap

Skies often don't have as much punch as we would like. This chapter introduces a pair of actions that darken blue areas to differentiate them from clouds and other neutrals.

The actions work by creating an alpha channel that selects blues. It is loaded as a layer mask on a multiplying layer. Usually the sky is the only blue area in the picture. If not, edit the layer mask to prevent the other blues from darkening.

How Difficult Is It? In basic form it's simple, although having the alpha channel available opens some complicated options. Make sure that there is no blue cast in the original, or clouds will darken too rapidly.

How Often Is It Needed? Depends on how often you encounter this type of sky.

The PPW Takes Shape

COLOR

- Kill incorrect color with RGB curves (Chapter 3).
- Identify highlight (Chapters 3–4).

CONTRAST

- Channel blending on luminosity layer (Chapter 4).
- Contrast-enhancing curves (Chapter 4).
    - Consider S/H command (Chapter 7).
    - Consider boost to sky (this chapter).

COLOR AGAIN

- Apply MMM + Color Boost action (Chapters 5–6).
- Finalize contrast, including endpoints.
- Reduce color by masking or opacity adjustment.

SHARPEN

FINALIZE

- Consider blend with another version (Chapter 2).
- Convert to final output space, if needed.

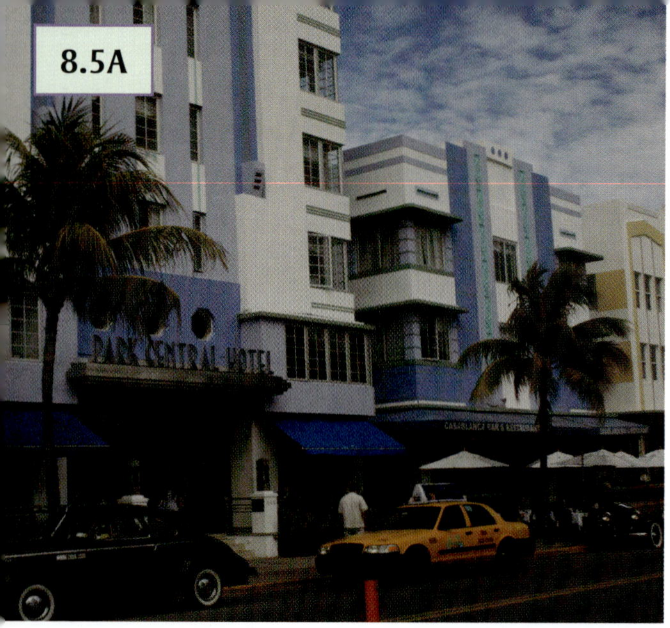

8.5A

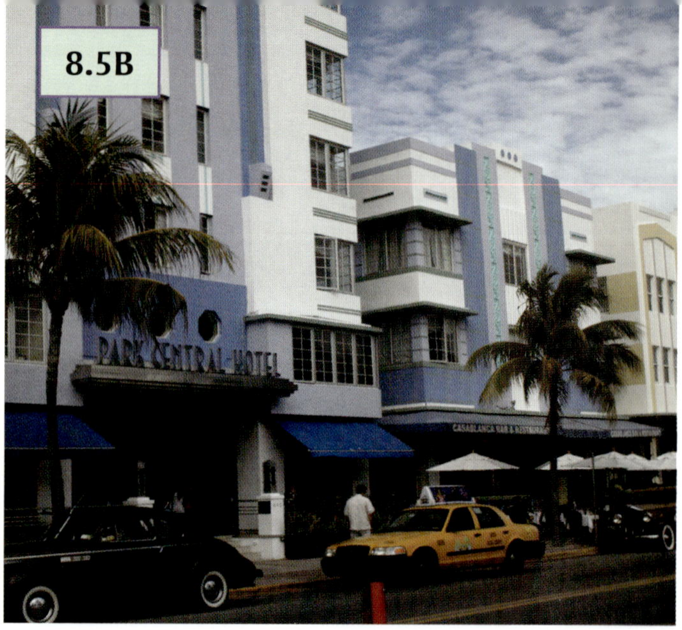

8.5B

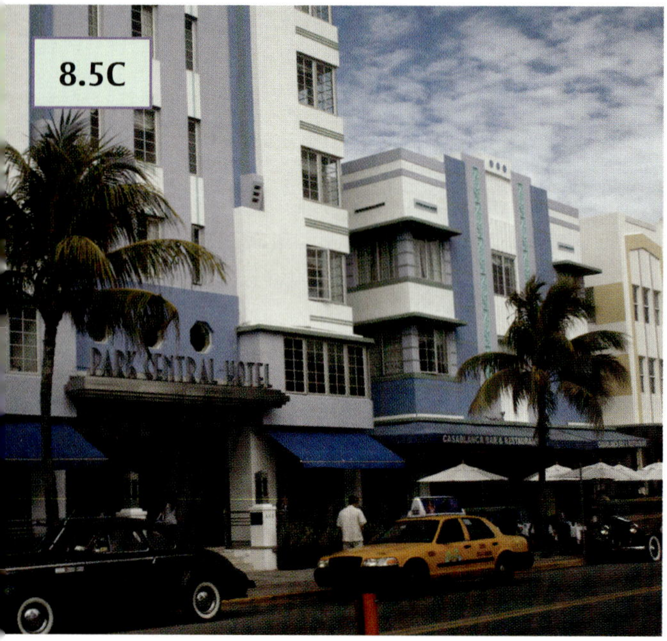

8.5C

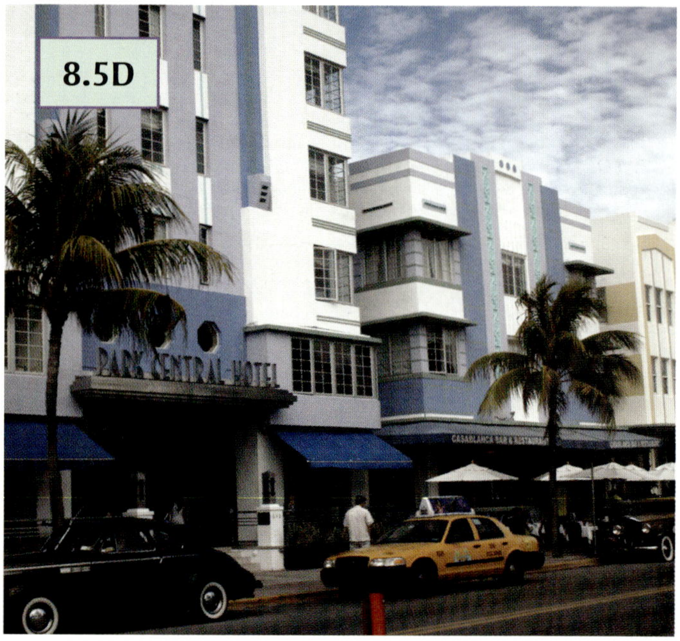

8.5D

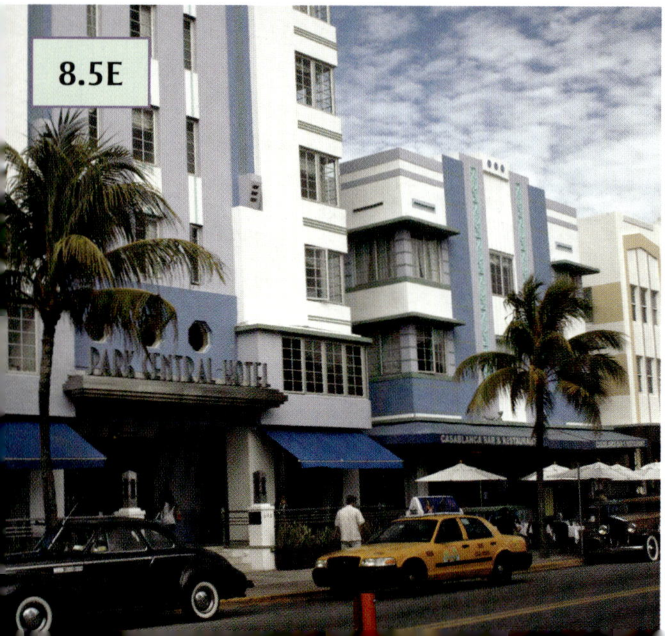

8.5E

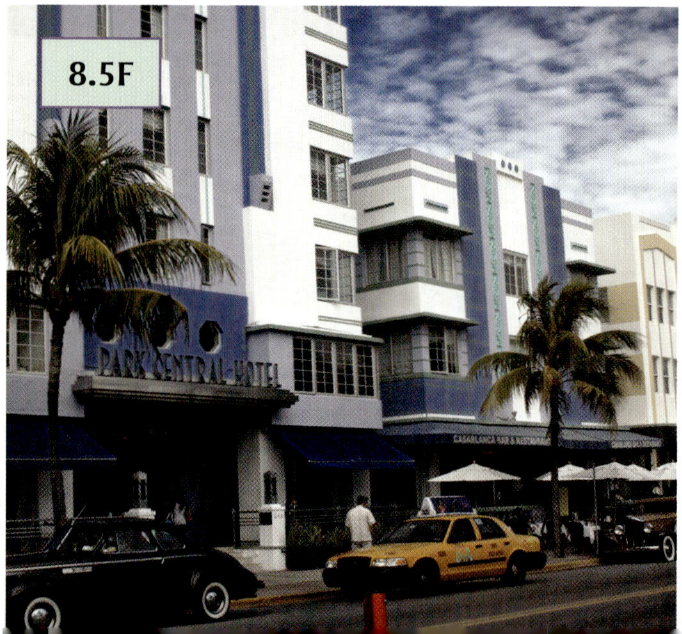

8.5F

Because the image's contrast was now about halfway to where it should be, I could trot out the color curves that would have been too difficult earlier. After applying them on an adjustment layer and then changing layer mode to Color, I had Figure 8.5C. It's now clear that the original had a cold cast. This is a bad thing to have in a tropical climate, especially with the Color Boost action lying in wait.

Next came the second installment of the green curve. On a third curves adjustment layer, the green was set once again to 250^{G}. When the layer went to Luminosity mode, I had Figure 8.5D—and that's the last step that requires a brain in this correction.

Chapter 7 says that, with the luminosity step out of the way, we should decide whether applying Shadows/Highlights is appropriate, which it surely is in view of how the cars are being lost in the shadows. One click in the PPW panel produced Figure 8.5E.

Before this chapter, the next step would have been Modern Man from Mars and Color Boost. But now we should consider the Darken Sky SC action. Applying it produces Figure 8.5F and the problem I have been referring to. Since the action assumes that everything blue is a sky, which doesn't happen to be so here, the blue parts of the buildings have gotten hammered.

Adjusting the Layer Mask

The blues get darker by the grace of the layer mask, which is at least somewhat light in all blue areas, black everywhere else. Our job is to make the mask black everywhere except the sky.

Figure 8.5 *(opposite). Top left, the original. Top right, a highlight is established in the green channel and the layer changed to Luminosity mode. Middle left, a curves adjustment layer eliminates a slight blue cast. Middle right, the highlight is again established in the green channel on a luminosity layer. Bottom left, after flattening, the Shadows/Highlights command is run. Bottom right, the Darken Sky SC action darkens more than just the sky.*

If the left-hand building were the only one in the picture, adjusting the layer mask would be a piece of cake, because none of its blue areas touch the sky and are therefore easily selected by lassoing. But the next building has blue areas right on the skyline.

One strategy is to select the sky, then invert the selection and fill the layer mask with black. That selection is tougher than it looks, because some of the sky is peeking through the windows at its left.

Instead, I would take the three seconds necessary to make the type of lasso selection shown in Figure 8.6A. Now, with the layer mask active, Edit: Fill>Use=Black. This produces Figure 8.6B. Note the erroneous darker blues at the top of the middle building, where I could not be accurate with the lasso.

No problem, because I have already filled almost the entire mask with black, guaranteeing that this tiny problem area is the only one remaining. I used the quick selection tool to grab it in Figure 8.6C. Edit: Fill again and the darkening, as desired, was limited to the blue parts of the sky.

Before finalizing color, a housekeeping matter of some importance. As Figure 8.4 reminds us, the document currently has five channels: the three RGB, the layer mask, and the alpha channel. After these latest shenanigans the layer mask and the alpha channel are no longer identical. Adjustment layers don't survive the conversion into LAB, so we have to flatten the image before converting. When we do, the layer mask will disappear forever. We should therefore ask whether we might need it.

The answer is an emphatic yes. We have decided, by using the Darken Sky action, to jazz up the sky. Figure 8.6B suggests that this was a good idea. But is the execution perfect? Should it be slightly lighter, more cyan, more purple? It's hard to know before we see the

***Figure 8.6** The process of excluding the blue areas of the buildings from the layer mask. Top right, a rough lasso selection of everything other than the sky plus a small area that will have to be selected more carefully. Bottom left, after filling the selection with black on the layer mask, almost all blues have been restored. Bottom right, a more accurate selection of the remaining area.*

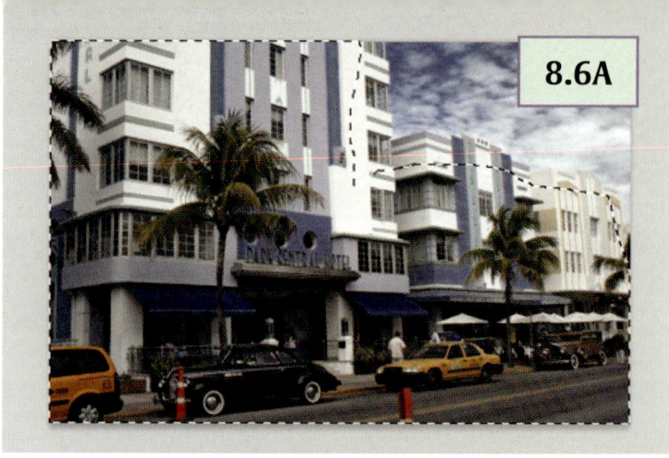

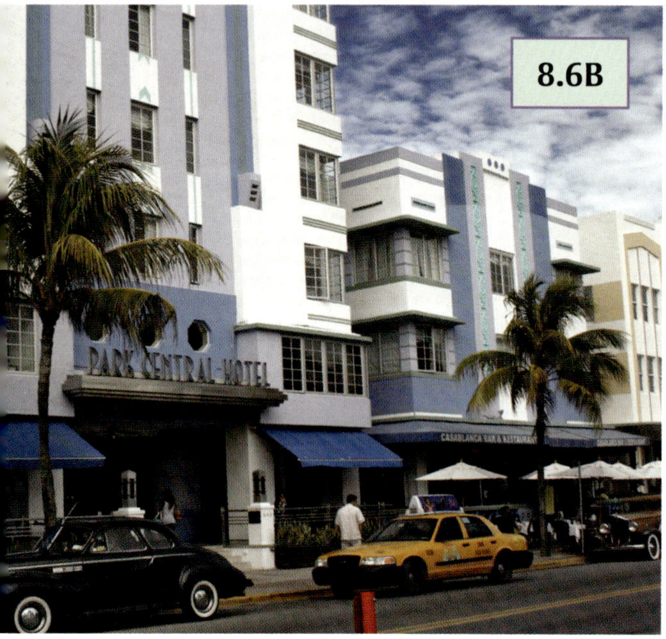

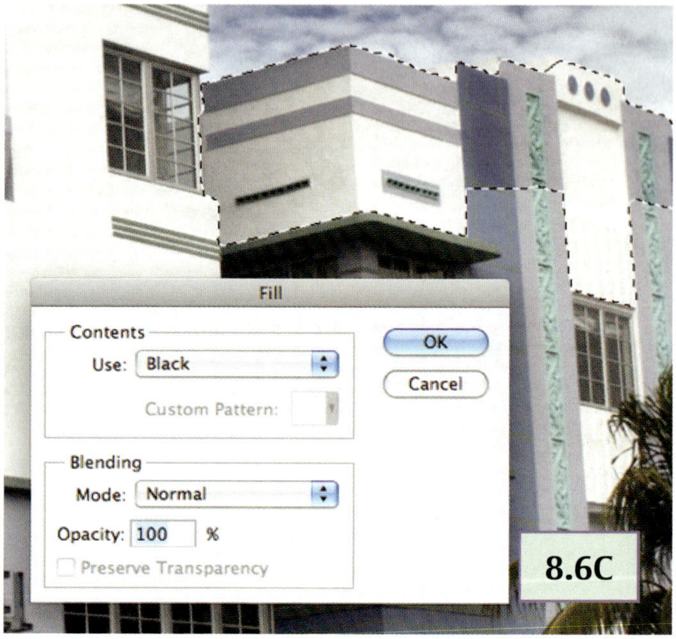

final color, which will happen after the conversion. If, at that time, we decide to change the sky again—well, then we may regret discarding the current layer mask.

Therefore we move to the Channels palette, which should show the layer mask as active; if not, click its icon. From the flyout at the right of the palette, choose Duplicate Channel and assign a new name, such as Edited Alpha. Now it won't matter when the layer mask vanishes later. If, after whatever we do in LAB, we want to change the sky, we Select: Load Selection and a nice option called Edited Alpha presents itself. (Meanwhile, to avoid clutter, drag the original Sky Mask alpha to the palette's trash icon; why take up space with a useless channel, now that you have a properly edited version?)

Behold Postcard 8.7. What happened in LAB was routine, not nearly as difficult as the original color moves of Figure 8.5. I made a rough lasso selection of the buildings, similar to that shown in Figure 8.6A, and ran the combined MMM + Color Boost action described in Chapter 6.

I had no great expectation for the MMM part. I wasn't sure what kind of variation it was going to insert. It turned out to be unattractive, so I discarded the two layers. This failed experiment cost perhaps fifteen seconds. I consider it time well spent, just as I would have considered the experiment of darkening the sky worthwhile, even if I decided after seeing it that it was ugly.

***Postcard 8.7** (opposite). Ocean Drive, Miami Beach.*

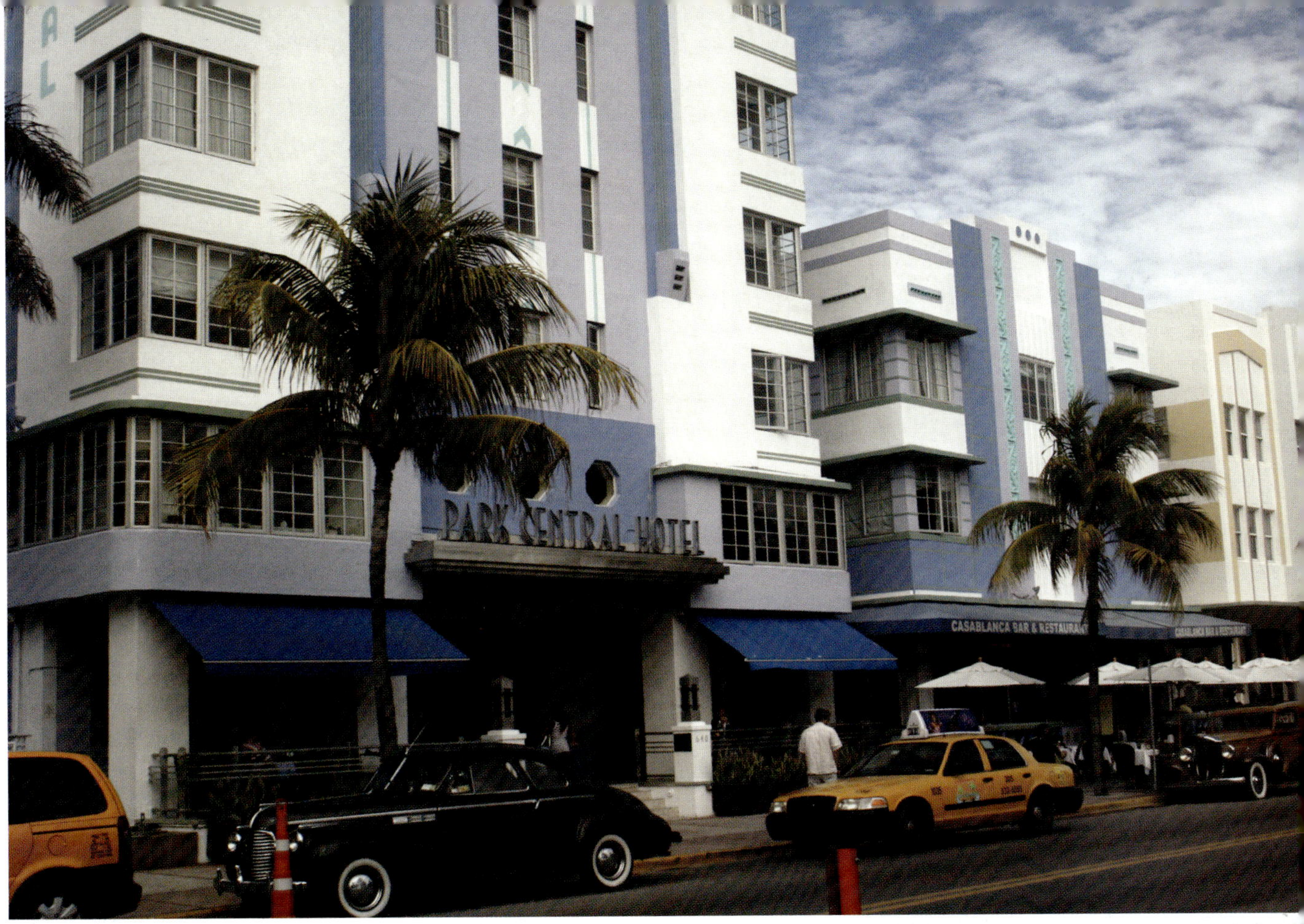
PARK CENTRAL HOTEL
CASABLANCA BAR & RESTAURANT
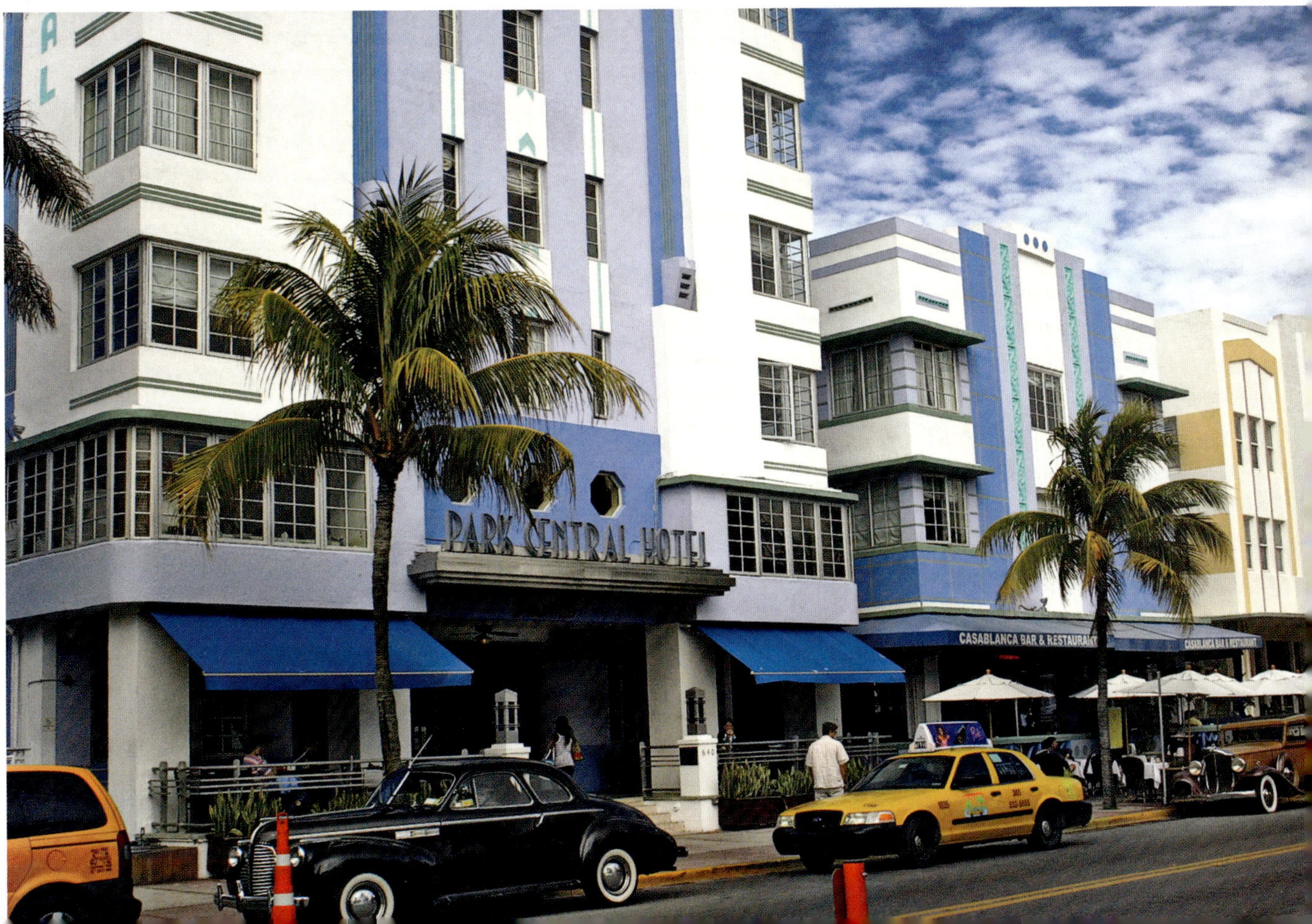
PARK CENTRAL HOTEL
CASABLANCA BAR & RESTAURANT

So, Color Boost only. I did not think any part of the picture was more offensive than any other, so I just reduced opacity of the Color Boost layer to taste, and finalized the highlight in the Endpoint Adjustment layer.

It turned out that I did need that copy of the edited sky mask. Skies are frequently noisy, particularly in an underexposed original like this one. So after the color moves, I flattened the file, loaded that channel as a selection and did some blurring.

Some people may have just decided that this section isn't as boring as it seems. The need to reduce noise in skies is frequent. Maybe we should run this action on every picture that contains a sky, whether it needs darkening or not! You never can tell when that alpha channel will be useful!

It's an interesting idea, but unless you have this specific type of picture, featuring not just other blues but ones that can't be easily lassoed, there's no need. The mask already exists, if you know where to find it.

The second half of this chapter shows where. It's more difficult than what we've seen so far but it isn't a killer. After explaining how LAB usually allows us to isolate skies undetectably, we'll discuss some interesting new options. I'll also show how the action generates its alpha channel.

The break comes here because this chapter affects certain people more than others. If you don't work with many skies, you've seen enough at this point and should probably move on to Chapter 9. If your practice *does* involve a lot of skies, keep reading.

Meanwhile, if anybody admires your sky work and asks you to put into words what you did, reply that the proper words don't exist—or at least one of them doesn't.

Review and Exercises

✓State the differences between a selection, a mask, and an alpha channel.

✓What are the drawbacks of retaining an alpha channel in a file?

✓After the action runs, why does the Channels palette show five channels (other then the RGB composite) rather than four?

✓Can you think of other situations where a color-based alpha channel would be useful, e.g. a mask for yellows?

✓What happens to adjustment layers when a file is converted from RGB to LAB or CMYK?

✓Under what circumstances should you consider running the Darken Sky B action rather than the Darken Sky SC we've been discussing?

✓Why is it important to neutralize clouds before running either action?

A Closer Look

The explanation of the last Miami Beach exercise, which produced Postcard 8.7, omitted one step. Figures 8.5B and 8.5C show that the original had a mild blue cast. In correcting it, I wanted to err on the side of warmth.

As a result, the taxi came out slightly orange. This is another demonstration of the volatility of the PPW, because in Figure 8.6B, the last step before applying the color boost, I can't detect that this orangeness is about to develop.

I did not think that the rest of the picture looked bad. So, still in LAB right after the Color Boost, I drew loose lasso selections around the taxi and also part of another that appears in the final postcard but is cropped out of Figure 8.5. I then created another adjustment layer, this time Hue/Saturation rather than curves. Doing this automatically produces a layer mask that blocks everything unselected.

In the H/S dialog I chose Yellows, customized some settings, and shifted hue away from red.

At this point beta reader John Pavel asked: "Would a curve tweak to the AB channels have done the trick, with or without a selection?"

Part of the answer is easy. If the cabs have been selected their color can be changed in several ways, of which AB maneuvering is one. My use of H/S is no better from a quality standpoint, but it saved effort. Changing color with a curve requires a perfect selection of the cabs, which may take time. I didn't have to be careful with mine because it was clear that nothing close to the cab would be affected by H/S set to Yellows. Without the selection, the buildings, which are slightly yellow, might change. Whether they *would* or not is irrelevant; using my loose selection as a mask preempts any problem.

The deep part of the question, though, is whether to use a selection at all. I should have made clear why I was doing it.

In other chapters we've often corrected through masks based on channels. The change is subtle enough not to throw off overall balance. A completely artificial selection, like the one I just made of the cabs, is a different story. They are generally to be shunned. Even if the viewer can't detect a selection line, the selected object may look out of place because its color no longer matches that of its surroundings.

John was therefore quite correct in suggesting that a global approach might be better. If the color of a certain object is wrong, it suggests that the rest of the picture is, too. Accordingly, three things should be true before altering color through an artificial selection.

- You have finished all basic color correction and are still dissatisfied with a certain object.
- Either the object's color is so well known that a viewer will detect inaccuracy, or else it is irrelevant to the rest of the picture, and any attractive color will do.
- You are completely certain that the rest of the image is satisfactory and does not reflect the same problem that the object does.

The taxis meet these conditions. Viewers know what their true color should be. Correcting away from orange is dangerous in a tropical scene like this. The last thing we need is a cold cast. So I would say that if the rest of the picture is slightly too orange we should go with it.

The conditions are also met for the sky. Its color has little to do with the rest of the image. We have great flexibility to change it to something we like better. And, as with the cabs, skies are easy to select, at least if we use H/S. There usually aren't other blue or cyan objects; if there are, they can normally be lassoed out in seconds. Only something like the Miami Beach picture, with other blues that aren't a snap to select, presents an issue.

Hue/Saturation is one of the few commands that can tell one color from another. What if we have to use one that can't, like a blurring filter of some kind? Photoshop ought to have one that's restricted to skylike colors, but it doesn't, so we have to improvise.

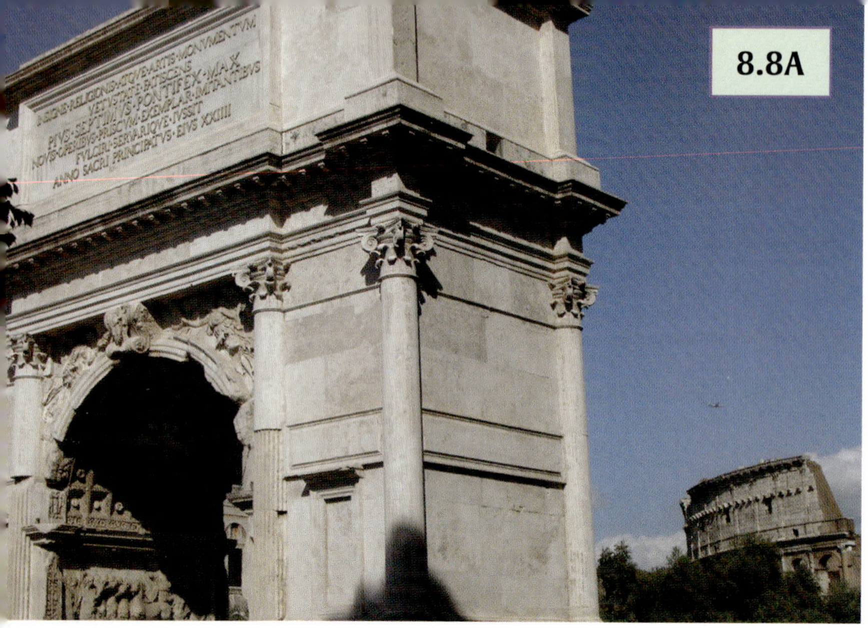

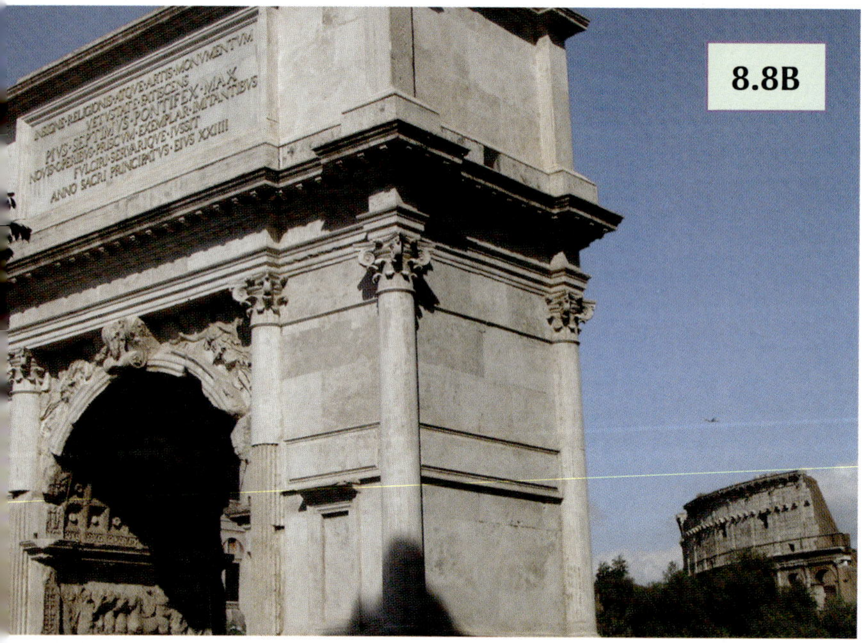

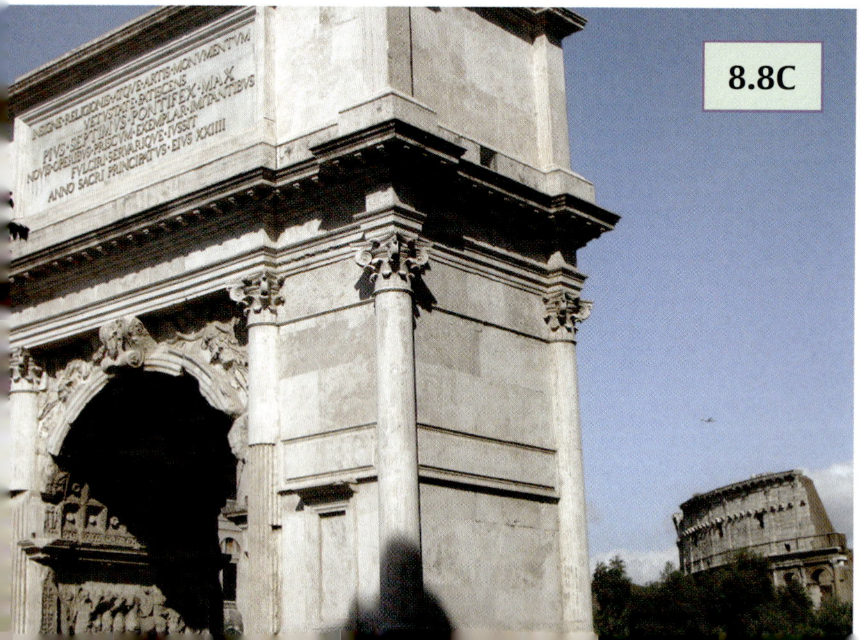

All Roads Lead to Rome

Back we go to the Roman empire for a variation on an earlier theme. It's another arch, this one of the triumphal persuasion, the model for similar ones in London, Washington, and a slightly better-known one in Paris. But this is the Arch of Constantine, constructed in 315 AD, complete with view of the Colosseum in the background. Unlike Figure 8.1's Arch of Titus, it arrives with a sturdy, if boring sky.

The original photo, which isn't being shown yet, had the arch slightly purple, typically 3^A1^B or so. That really can't be right; if this marble is not neutral (and it doesn't seem to be, by context) then it must be some kind of brown. Brown is a red, therefore we expect B to be as least as high as A, with both positive. To fix this, I darkened the blue channel slightly in RGB. The difference is so small that I won't show the comparison. Figure 8.8A, then, has already been adjusted for color.

When objects are nearly neutral, as the arch is, there's little merit in blending channels, as a rule. But it can't hurt to look, and when I did, there was a surprise. The blue showed much better contrast in the lettering than the red did. So, on a separate layer, I replaced the red with the blue, changed mode to Luminosity, and had Figure 8.8B.

The inscription is now better, but the sky has gotten lighter. I care not so much as a quincunx for this. If we want it darker or a different color later, Hue/Saturation is available when we go to

***Figure 8.8** Top, after correcting the original's color. Middle, the blue channel replaces the red on a duplicate layer. Bottom, adjustment layer curves to the red and green. Layers for the middle and bottom versions have been changed to Luminosity mode.*

Figure 8.9 *Right, the MMM + Color Boost action produces better color but the sky is noisy (below left). Below center, the noise is removed. Below right, the move is restricted to blue areas with the Blend Ifs shown.*

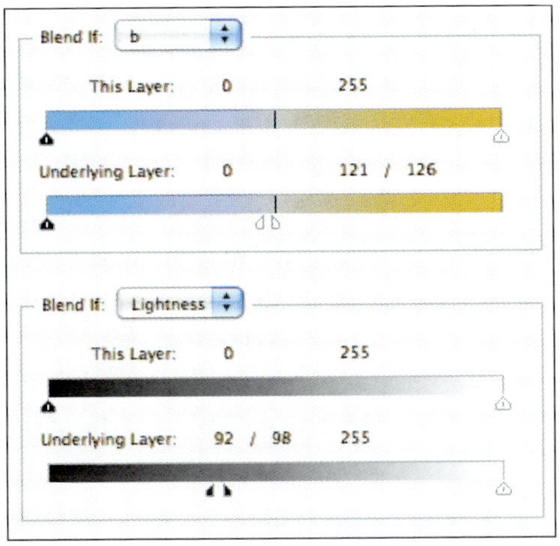

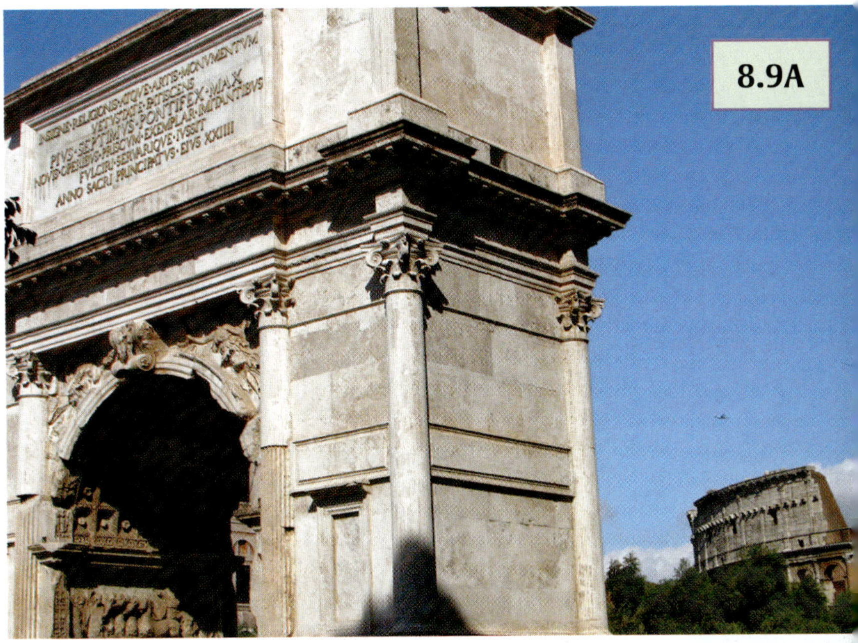

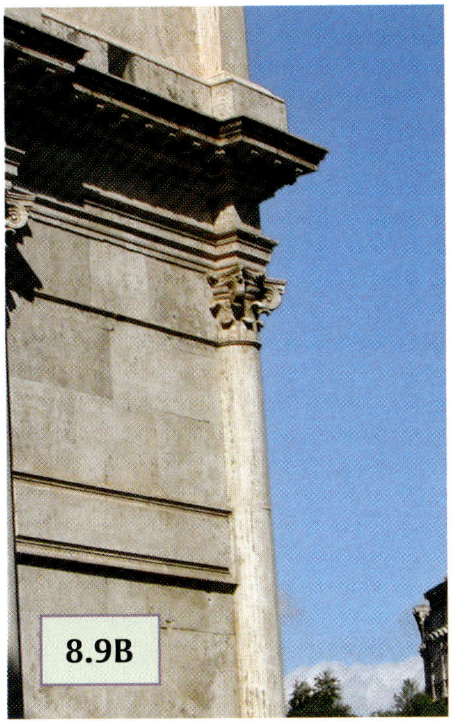

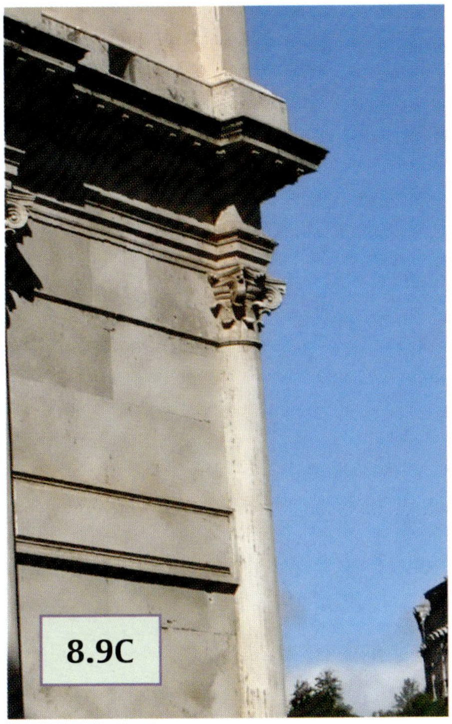

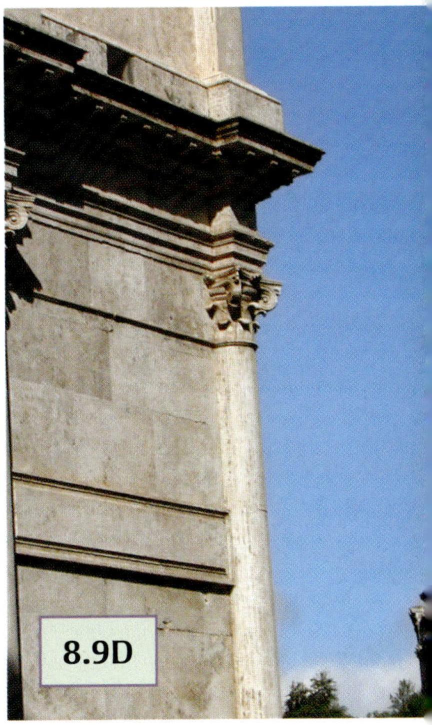

LAB. Nothing else will be affected if H/S is set up for either blues or cyans.

Moving right along, on a curves adjustment layer I lightened the red and green channels, then set mode to Luminosity. This produced Figure 8.8C.

Next came Shadows/Highlights, the result of which is not interesting enough to show, although it helped a little. That made it time to consider the Darken Sky action.

My conclusion was no. The purpose of the action is to strengthen the transition between sky and clouds, and almost no clouds are present.

So, on to the MMM + Color Boost action, with

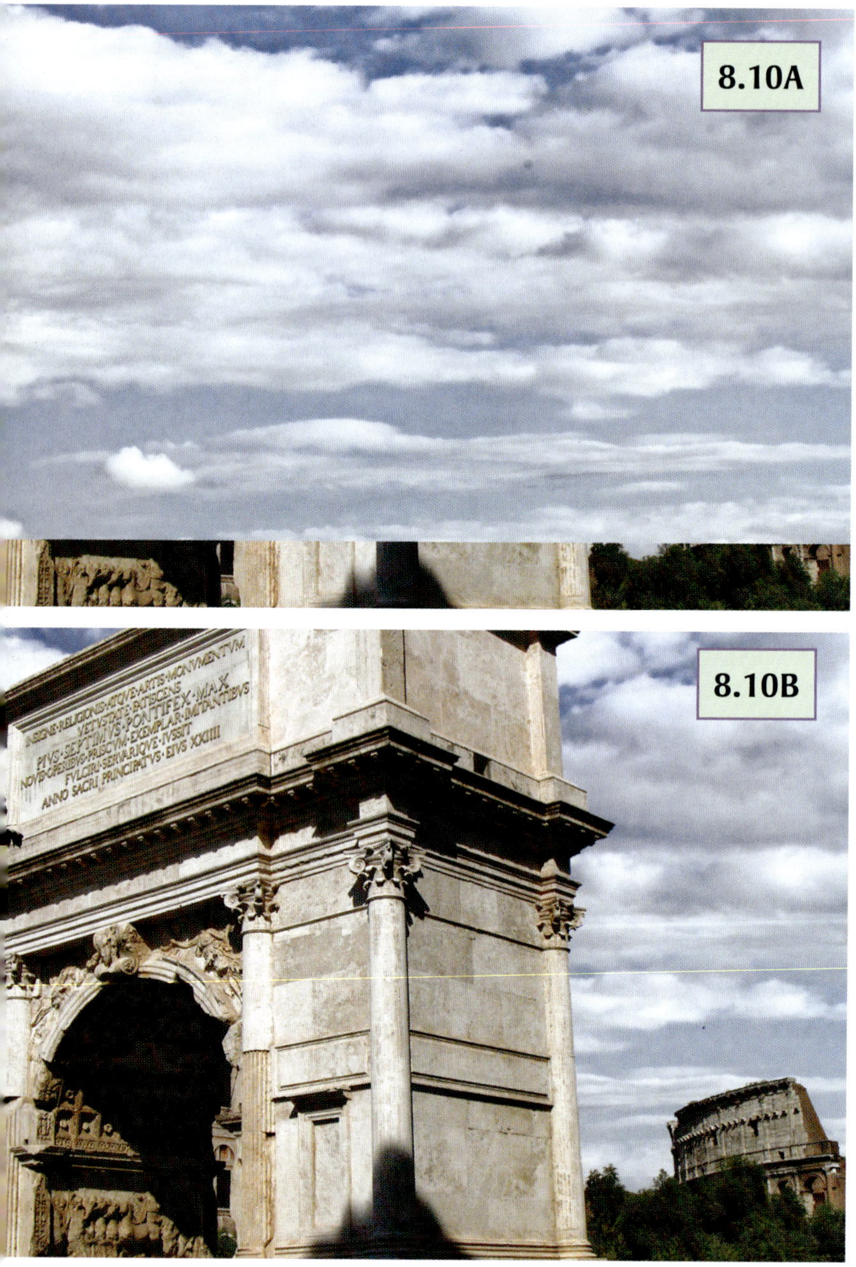

***Figure 8.10** Top, a prospective replacement for the sky is positioned on a new layer. Bottom, Figure 8.8's Blend If settings are applied.*

modifications to my taste. Figure 8.9A represents a typical, unremarkable use of the PPW: an early color adjustment to minimize a cast; channel blends and curves in Luminosity mode; Shadows/Highlights; and a color enhancement in LAB. Quick and effective, but Figure 8.9B, an enlarged section, reveals excessive noise.

Let's face it. The PPW takes a lot of the worry out of our lives, but it's stressful for the poor images. Emphasizing detail also emphasizes noise.

If you're willing to accept the dishwater-dull Figure 8.8C as a final result, you don't have to worry about noise. If you'd like to have an arch with the depth of Figure 8.9A, you do.

Noise reduction technique is beyond the scope of this book, but we can use aggressive settings to smooth noise on a duplicate layer, and later restrict the effect to sky areas.

I used the Surface Blur filter on a duplicate layer to produce Figure 8.9C. It's on a duplicate layer. The trick is to set up the layer structure to disallow the softening of the two structures and the greenery, as in Figure 8.9D.

The Blend If section of layer Blending Options is occasionally useful in RGB, but a powerhouse in LAB. It's easier to differentiate objects by their color than their darkness. Some parts of the sky are darker than most of the arch, but never the entire structure. But all parts of the sky are *bluer* than all parts of the arch.

The B channel of LAB (yellow vs. blue) can therefore distinguish the two. The setting shown disables the noise-free layer except where it is blue. The additional Lightness (L) control guards against the possibility that some of the shadows may also be blue.

Yon Cassius Has a Lean and Hungry Look

Blend If's applications are legion, at least in LAB. Skies are found everywhere in the world. The Arch of Constantine and the Colosseum are not. The Figure 8.8 skies are less distracting than the ones in Figure 8.9.

***Postcard 8.11** (opposite) The Arch of Constantine, Rome, with a sky from Arches National Park, Utah.*

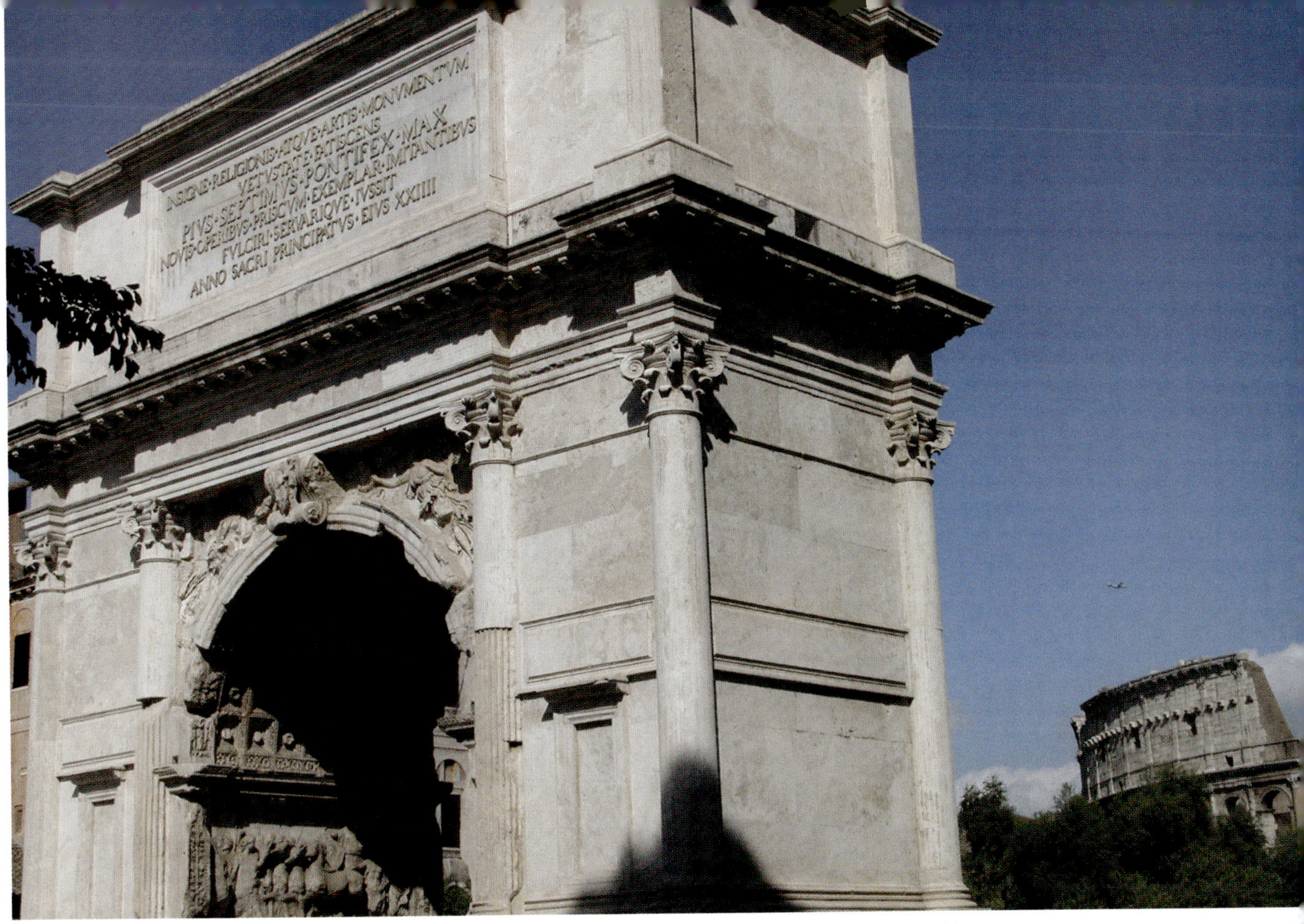
INSIGNE·RELIGIONIS·ATQVE·ARTIS·MONVMENTVM
VETVSTATE·FATISCENS
PIVS·SEPTIMVS·PONTIFEX·MAX
NOVIS·OPERIBVS·PRISCVM·EXEMPLAR·IMITANTIBVS
FVLCIRI·SERVARIQVE·IVSSIT
ANNO SACRI PRINCIPATVS·EIVS XXIIII

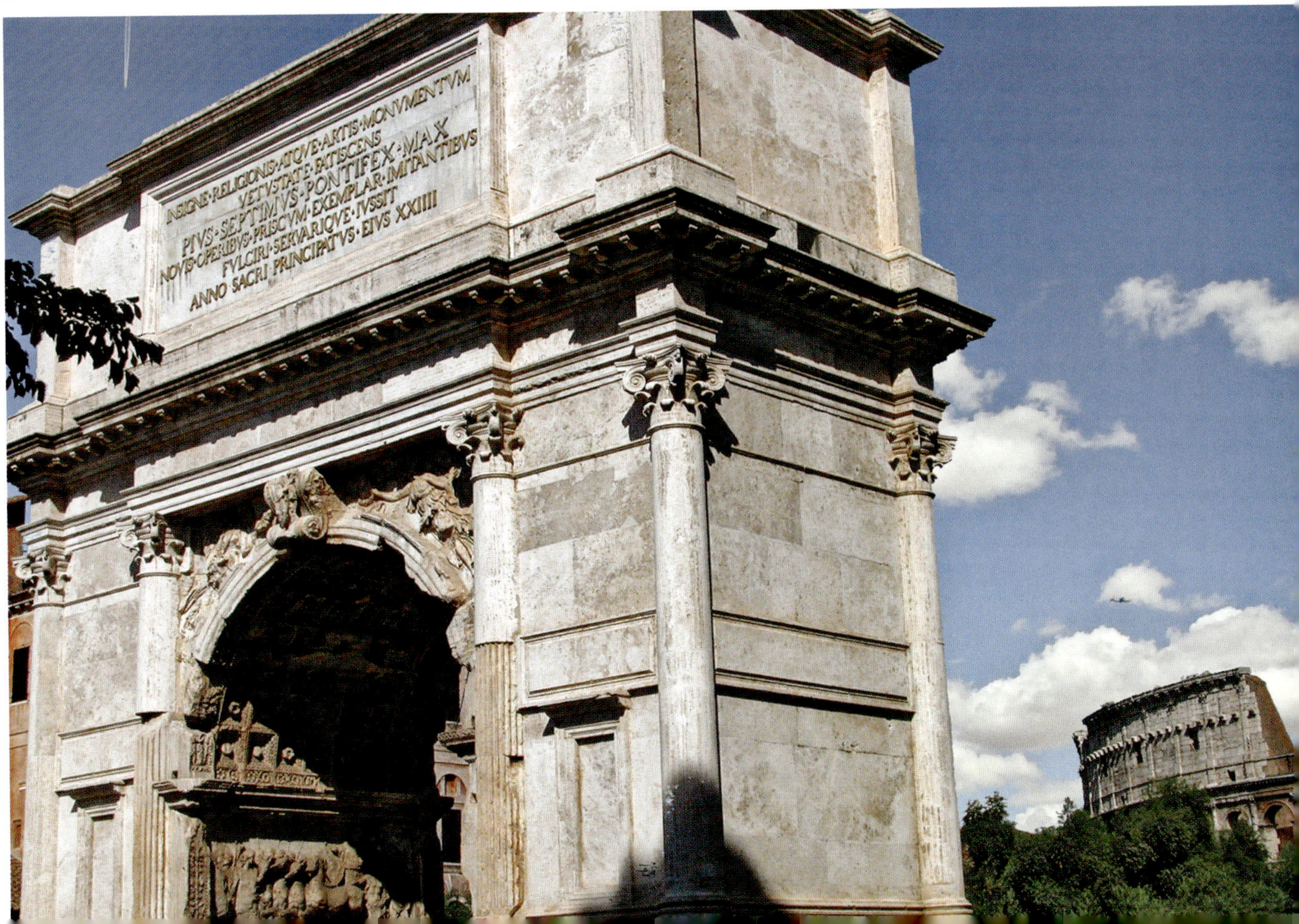
INSIGNE·RELIGIONIS·ATQVE·ARTIS·MONVMENTVM
VETVSTATE·FATISCENS
PIVS·SEPTIMVS·PONTIFEX·MAX
NOVIS·OPERIBVS·PRISCVM·EXEMPLAR·IMITANTIBVS
FVLCIRI·SERVARIQVE·IVSSIT
ANNO SACRI PRINCIPATVS·EIVS XXIIII

The MMM + Color Boost action has two layers that enhance color. Putting a Blend If on either may do what you want. All the action's components are also grouped into a layer set at the top of the layer stack. To restore the original sky, just activate the set and pop Figure 8.9's Blend If on it *in reverse,* disallowing blues.

But, as my late mother used to say, if you're going to be a pig, you may as well go whole hog. If the sky is too boring, and too colorful, and too noisy, why fix it? Find a superior sky, and swinishly sneak it in.

The sky with which I illustrated the action way back in Figure 8.3B was a lot more interesting than the one we have now. So, in Figure 8.10A, I paste it on top of Figure 8.9D. Notice the intentional mistake—I'm not quite covering the bottom of the sky between the Colosseum and the arch.

After applying a suitable Blend If, I had Figure 8.10B. Look hard, and you'll see the "mistake" where the two layers meet, but I doubt the average person would notice—another reminder of how much flexibility we have in enhancing, or even replacing, skies.

From a pure retouching standpoint the replacement is successful, yet Figure 8.10B is not persuasive. The strong shadows on the sides and underneath the arch announce the presence of abundant sunshine. The sky announces that the day is overcast. The casual viewer may not be able to put two and two together but still is likely to feel that there's something rotten in Rome.

Not to worry. I suggested earlier that you should maintain an arsenal of skies for just such contingencies. If this one doesn't satisfy, the file is set up so that others can be tested quickly.

Instead of the unconvincing sky we just saw, I would look for one with similar color and depth to the original. It should have some clouds for interest, but not enough to suggest something other than a sunny day. A dark background seems to help the arch. On the other hand, an itty-bitty nub of a runt of a cloud in the original seems to emphasize the Colosseum. I would add to the list of desiderata a more significant cloud, against which the Colosseum would be well defined.

I found a candidate in the same place as the earlier Postcard 8.2, a folder of professional images of Arches National Park, the hot, arid climate of which is somewhat like Rome's. Using the same Blend If settings, it merged seamlessly into the final version of Postcard 8.11.

The practice of replacing a sky to emphasize other important areas is difficult to condemn on grounds of ethics and impossible on grounds of technical difficulty. I still always prefer to start with the actual sky as recorded by the camera, as fewer things can go wrong. In our final exercise we'll do that, in the course of demonstrating how the sky actions derive their masks.

A Colosseum for Our Time

The final exercise should really be the Colosseum itself, but I don't happen to own a photo of it with the desired characteristics. We'll substitute a stadium that is accompanied by the requisite clouds. In honor of our ancient theme, this image comes from a prehistoric era: the age of scanned film.

As many files from that era do, this one starts with foul color and a noisy sky. But those can be handled routinely. One look at Postcard 8.12 tells us that deepening the sky is the key to adding drama. The whole original, except the flags and the top of the tower, is light and monotonous. There's a limit to how much the stadium can be darkened. But when azure areas are deepened, nobody is the wiser.

The first PPW step, to check and correct for known colors, particularly neutrals, is familiar. Using the color sampler tool, I popped three fixed sampler points into the Info palette. I took the lightest and darkest area of the cloud at top right, and also the top center of the angled tower, which is a dark gray.

***Postcard 8.12** (opposite) Olympic Stadium, Montreal.*

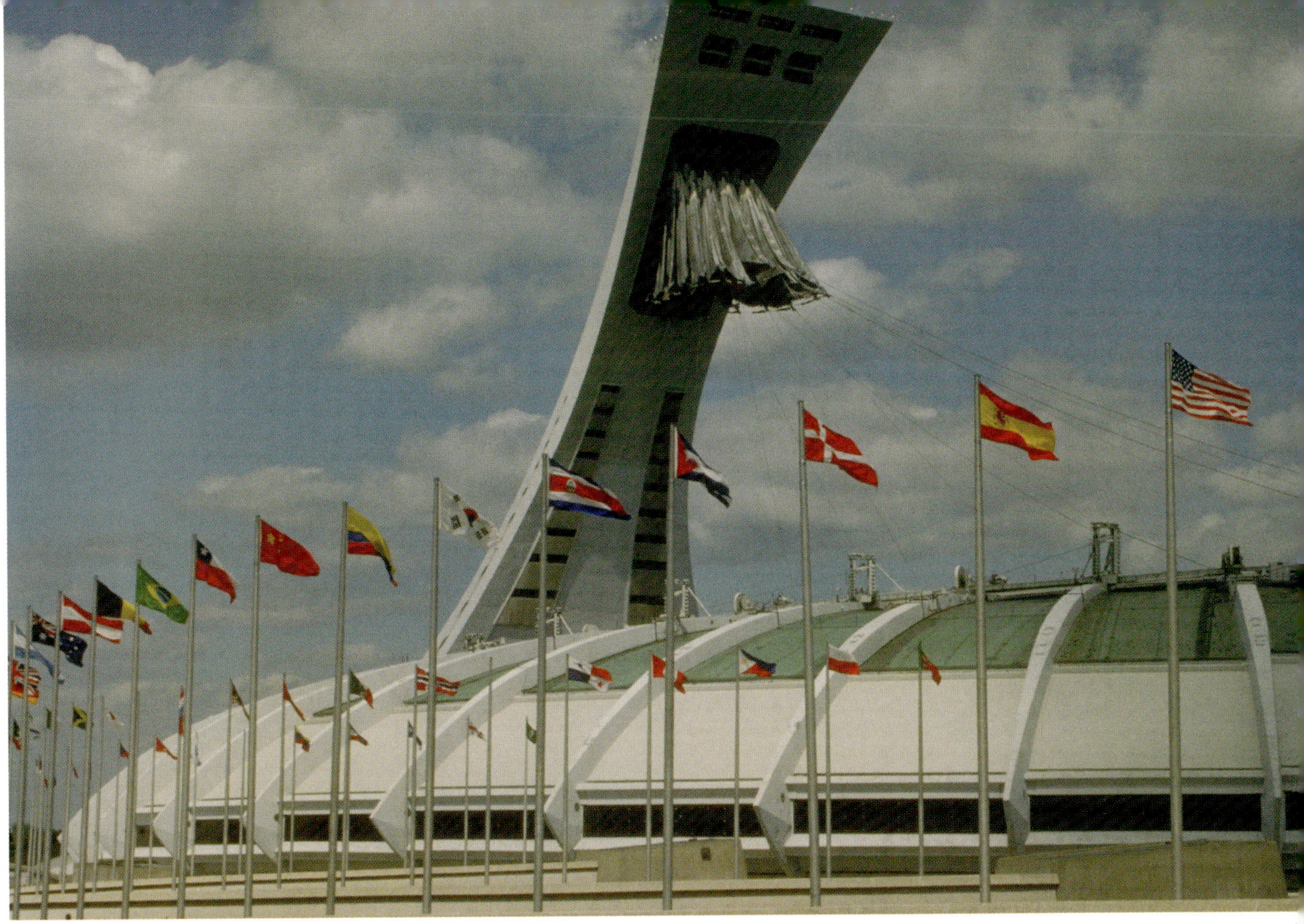

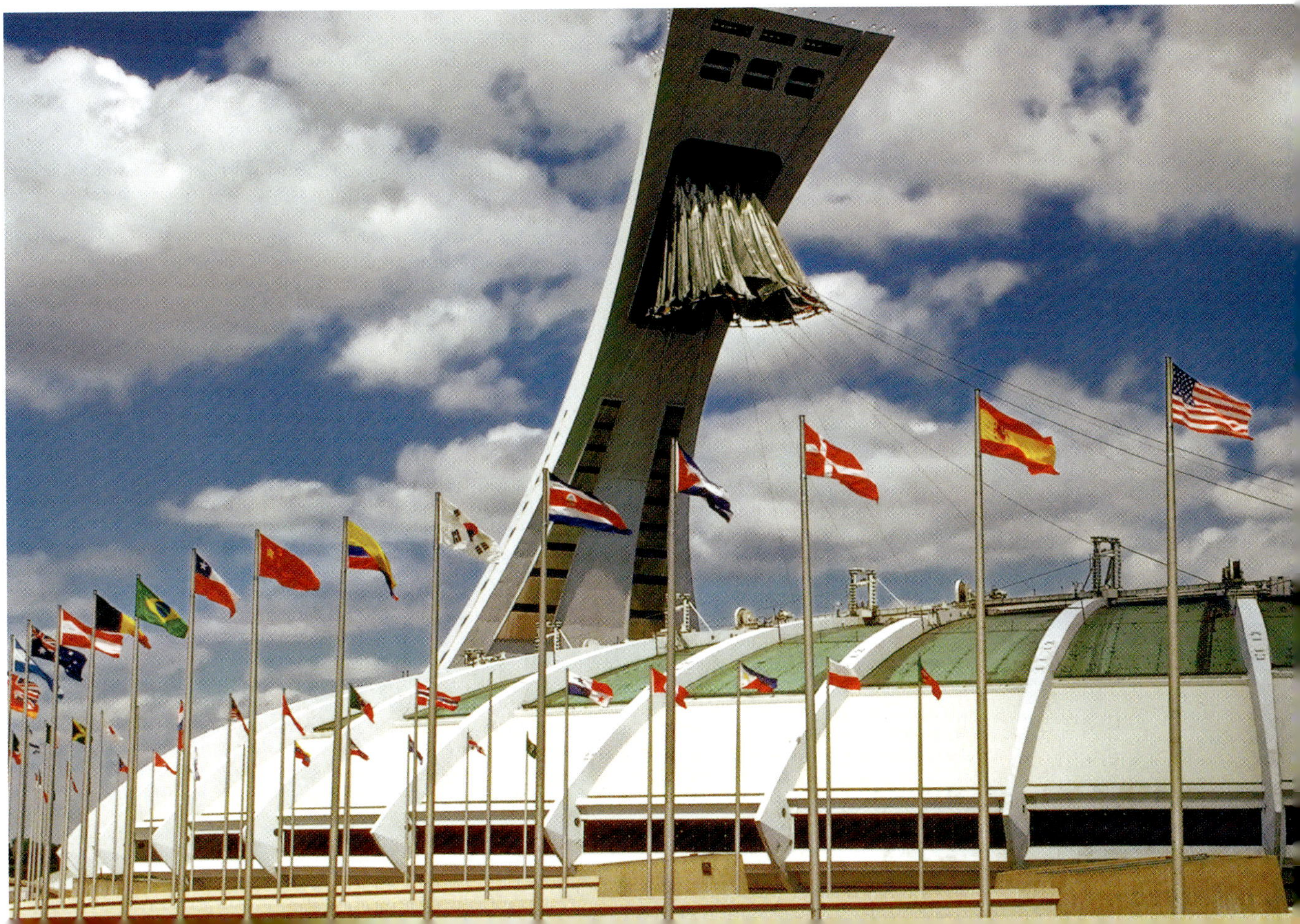

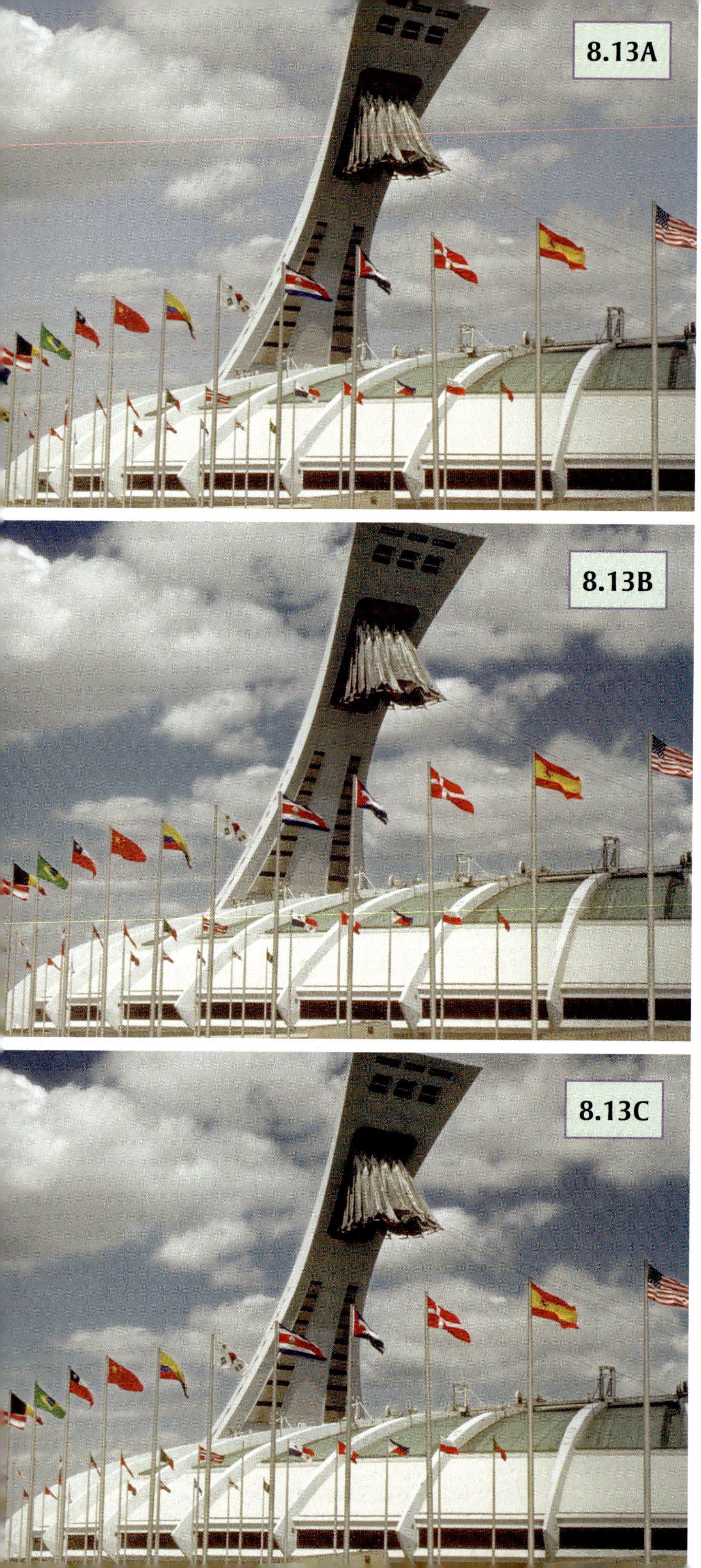

After correcting this with curves on a layer set to Color mode, I turned to contrast. With so many bright colors, channel blending would be difficult. As for curves, we don't want extra detail in either the azure sky or the flags. That leaves the stadium and the clouds. Since both are neutral, it won't matter which channel(s) we curve. But the red is always noisiest in a sky. So, best to establish highlight in the green only, on a luminosity layer.

Surely these two light objects can benefit from Shadows/Highlights. Applying it produced Figure 8.13A.

If this chapter's moves didn't exist, the next step would then be color enhancement. This would be one of the rare cases where I wouldn't even bother glancing at MMM. The idea of that action is color variation, but the flags have already given us all we need. And color variation in the sky and stadium is probably unwelcome.

So it would be the Color Boost action alone, in its simplest form. Figure 8.13A could use more color generally, but I wouldn't favor any one part over another. I would just play with the opacity slider until content, rather than messing around with layer masks.

This scenario, in short, is basic PPW: curves to correct a color problem; another curve to the green to add shape; click S/H, and a simple color boost. I make it a two-minute correction but more than half of it is the first curves.

Now, let's darken the sky.

***Figure 8.13** Top, after the original has been corrected for color, luminosity, and Shadows/Highlights. Middle, a default application of the Darken Sky SC action. Bottom, the Darken Sky B action is applied instead, with opacity adjusted to get closer to the middle version.*

How Does It Identify Blues?

Figure 8.13A is the start point. Figure 8.13B applies the Darken Sky SC action at its default settings. Figure 8.13C uses Darken Sky B instead. At its defaults the blues were significantly lighter than in Figure 8.13B, so I duplicated the multiply layer at a low opacity to try to get them closer.

The two aren't identical. Figure 8.13C's sky is more dramatic because of a darkness change from the left to the right side. Some might like that and others might not. I remarked earlier that this action usually produces more noise, but this time, the opposite is true: the sky is noisier in Figure 8.13B.

Surprises like these are to be expected. Both methods look for blues, but they do so in different ways. I thought I was going to be able to offer advice here on when to use each one. When I ran tests both ways on a large number of eligible pictures, however, all that could be said was that the results were unpredictable, although I can make two generalizations:

- In a simple sky like those of Postcards 8.1 and 8.11, with only a few clouds, stick with the quicker SC action. Testing the B action is a waste of time.
- The B action is more prone to give lightness variation across the sky, as it just did in Figure 8.13C.

If the sky is complex, I think you should make an extra copy of the file, run one action on each, and discard the one that looks worse.

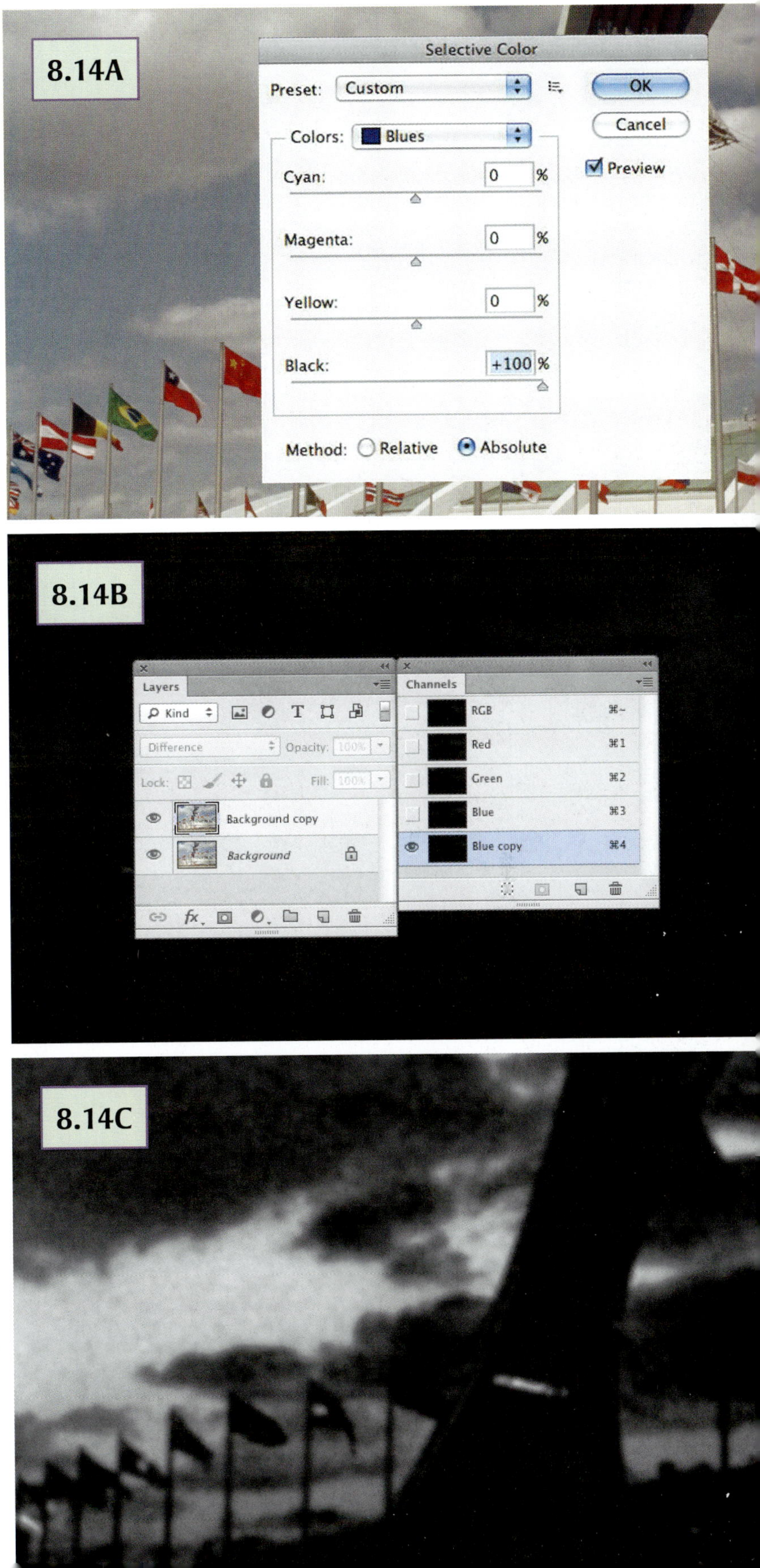

Figure 8.14 The initial steps of the Darken Sky SC action. Top, on a duplicate layer, Selective Color is applied to Figure 8.13A in Cyans and Blues. Middle, the layer mode is set to Difference, and the blue channel is shown and copied. Bottom, the final alpha channel after contrast enhancement and blurring.

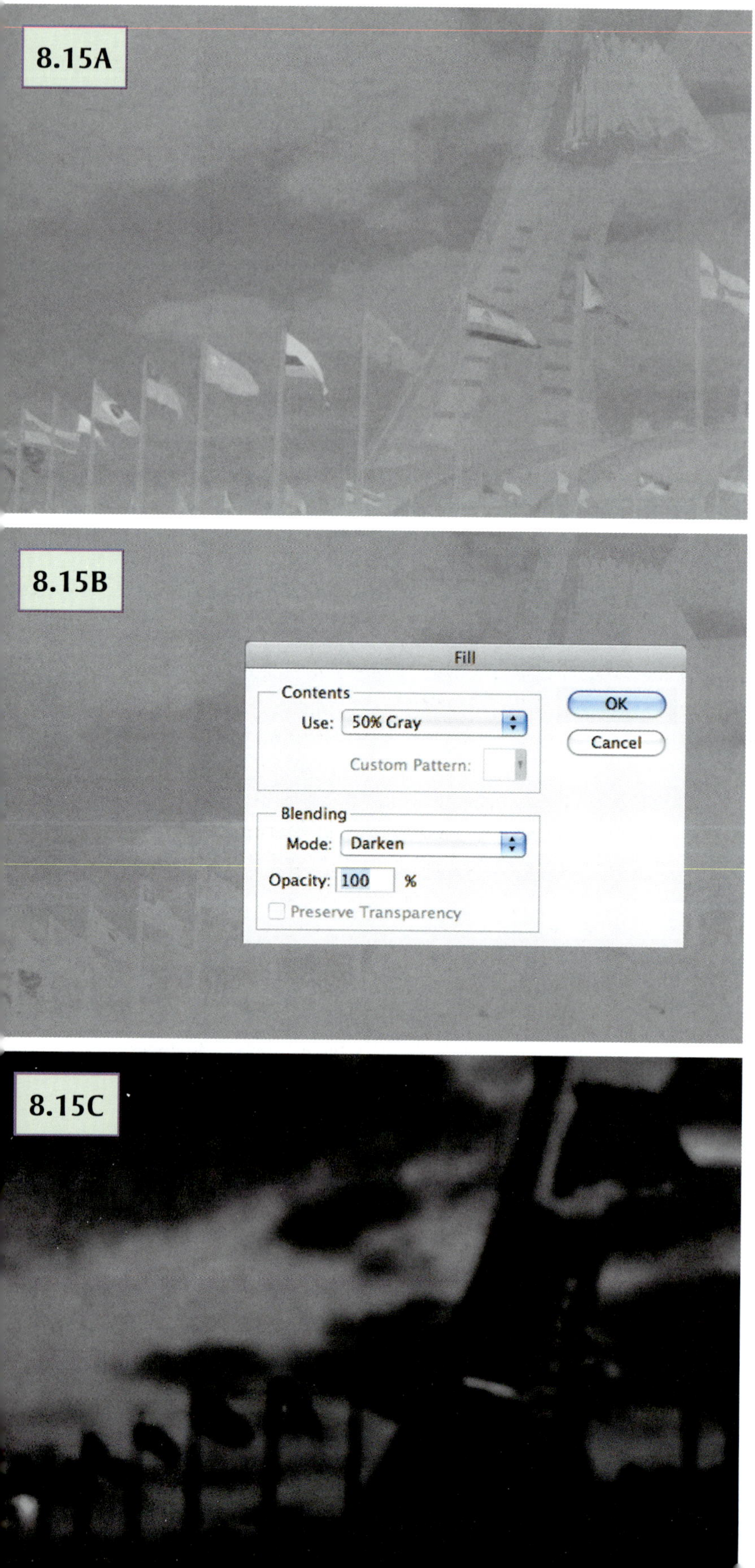

How can this be reconciled with the recommendation that we forgo exactly this kind of experimentation when applying the Shadows/Highlights command in the previous chapter? It's a question of how much benefit we might get from the experiment, and how important it would be. The very fact that we've decided to apply a sky action at all indicates that we find it an important element. In the discussion of S/H in the previous chapter this was not so.

The SC action produces its alpha channel as follows. Remember, please, that these steps are just a way of finding blues.

- On a duplicate layer, open Image: Adjustments>Selective Color. Choose Cyans, and change Black to +100%, Method=Absolute.
- Before closing the dialog, change Blues as in Figure 8.14A. The azure sky has become darker, but too neutral.
- Change layer mode to Difference. This mode produces black where the two layers are identical, something else where they aren't. The bigger the difference, the lighter the result. At first glance you might think that the whole picture had turned black, because there is no difference except in blue areas, and most of the original picture isn't blue. But a closer look would clarify.
- Enter the Channels palette. Select and duplicate the blue, which is the highest-contrast channel at the moment (Figure 8.14B).

Figure 8.15 *The initial steps of the Darken Sky B action. Top, the B channel when Figure 8.13A is converted to LAB. Middle, a fill in Darken mode eliminates yellows while retaining blues. Bottom, the final alpha channel after contrast enhancement, inversion, and blurring.*

- Discard the difference layer, now that the alpha channel has been saved.
- Open the alpha channel and Image: Auto Tone to add contrast. Blur it to minimize noise. Figure 8.14C is the final mask. As you can see, it's noisy.

The Alternate Mask in B

The AB channels of LAB are difficult for newcomers. They are, however, highly useful for masking because they represent color only and are unaffected by changes in darkness.

A sky mask must be based on the B, which is yellow vs. blue. The yellow half, naturally, is irrelevant. Unlike the first action, we don't have to worry about cyans, because cyan is more blue than yellow. And this mask may contain some purples not found in the Darken Sky SC action, as all purples are more blue than yellow.

Dark blues, which are present in the flags, provoke different behavior from the two actions. In Figure 8.14A, the Selective Color command tries to darken them, but there's only so far it can go. The B channel action has no such limitation. It may well affect the flags more strongly than the sky. The steps to make its alpha channel are:

- Duplicate the file and convert it to LAB.
- Show the B channel (Figure 8.15A). Lighter grays denote objects more yellow than blue; darker ones more blue than yellow.
- As shown in Figure 8.15B, Edit: Fill=50% Gray, Mode=Darken. This doesn't affect items that are more blue than yellow, because they are already darker than 50% Gray. But everything more yellow than blue is now lumped together, all changed to 50% Gray.
- Apply Auto Tone and blur, as was done to make the SC mask earlier. This channel, however, has to be inverted as well, because the sky needs to be light.
- Return to the RGB file, create a new channel, and use Apply Image to replace it with the B channel from the LAB file.
- Discard the LAB file.

The final alpha channel is Figure 8.15C. It has a lot in common with the SC mask of Figure 8.14C, but seems more subdued because it has identified a small Australian flag in the lower left as by far the bluest object in the picture.

I happened to use the B action to make Postcard 8.12, and I didn't do anything to protect the Australian flag. So, with the alpha channel being as light as it is there, why didn't the flag become eyepoppingly unnatural?

The action tries to make the flag much darker and bluer. But it can't. The flag is very dark already, and about as blue as it can get.

In theory this was worth worrying about, but in practice it was a phantom problem. It's hard to predict that in advance.

I therefore close by suggesting that when in doubt, try both and choose one, or even blend the two alpha channels.

Skies don't often make or break a picture. But sometimes they do. And sometimes, if we don't protect them, they can become a distraction. In either case the lessons of this chapter are valuable. In color correction, the sky is not the limit unless you permit it to become one.

The Bottom Line

Pictures with prominent skies have been avoided so far because they can easily be made too colorful or too noisy. It's a phantom problem. Skies can easily be selected and altered, or even replaced entirely, and no one will be the wiser. In this respect skies are unlike almost any other object.

The chapter also introduces a pair of actions that combat the common problem of the blue areas of a sky seeming too weak. Each darkens blues while hardly affecting clouds.

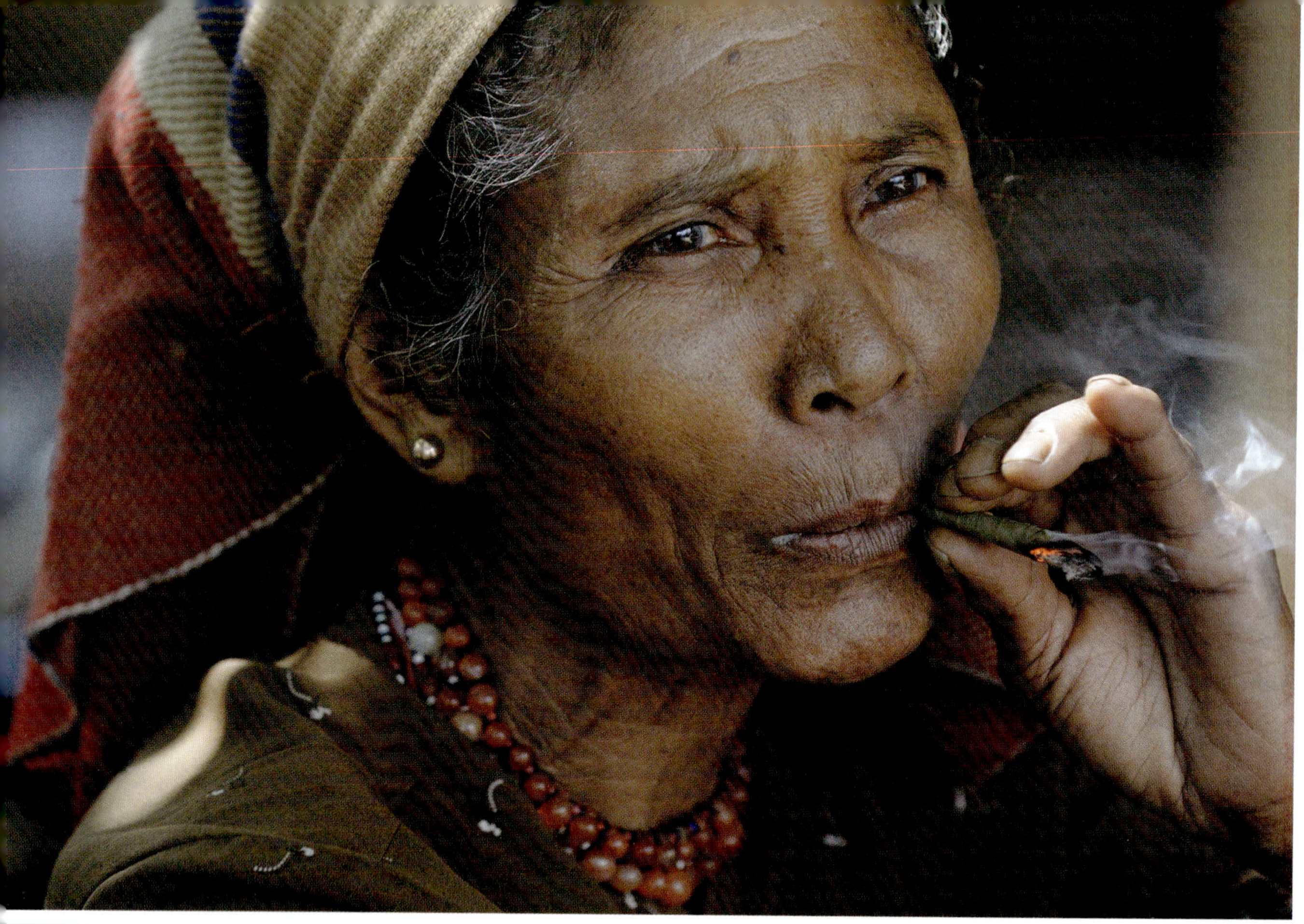

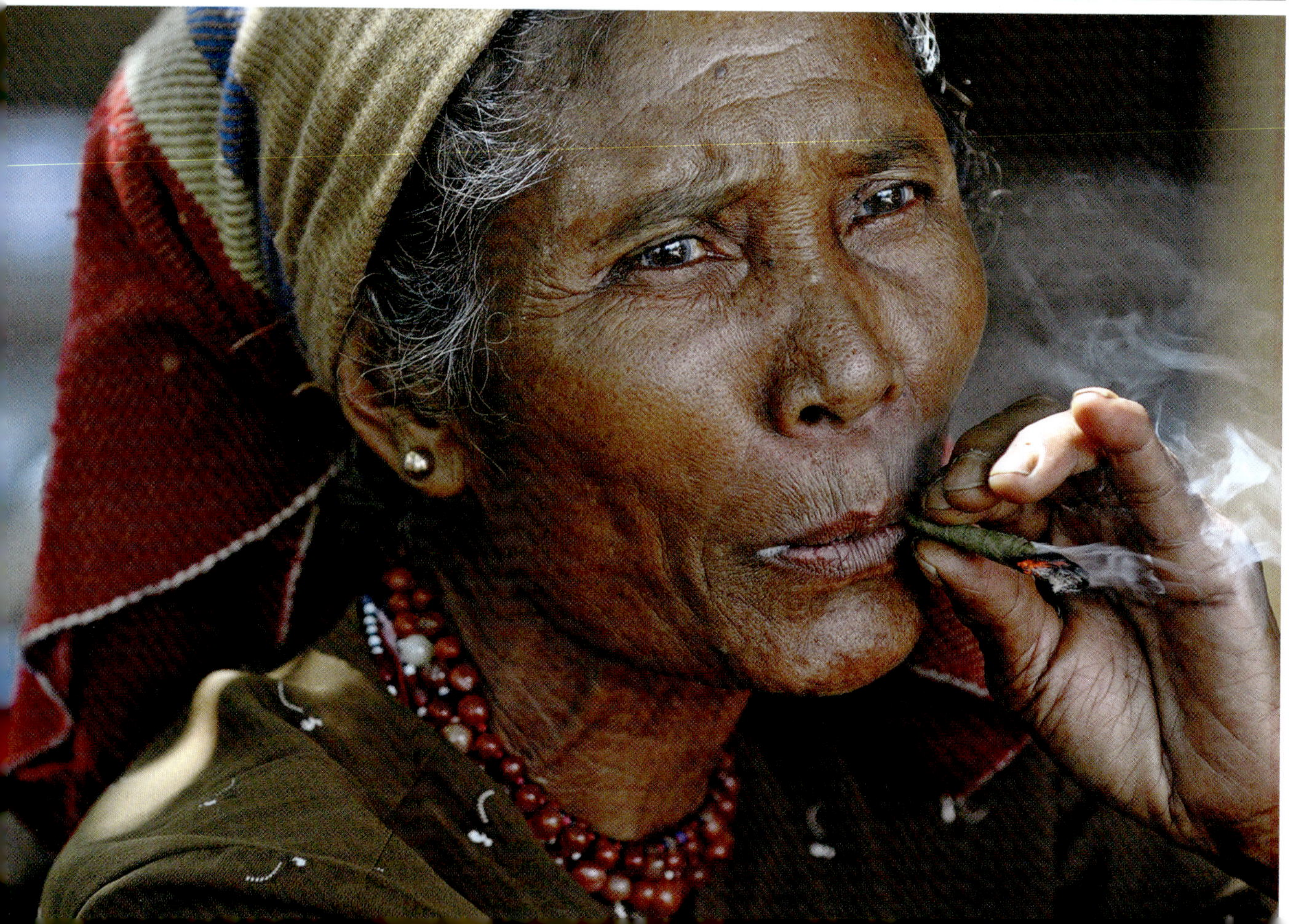

9

A Face Is Like a Sky

Faces don't fit neatly into prepackaged workflows. We don't like them too colorful, because it suggests anger. We don't like them too detailed, because it suggests age. These statements are true of no other objects we commonly work with. Since the end of the workflow is designed to add spectacular color, we take pre-emptive steps to protect skin.

The Picture Postcard Workflow caters to those who like vivid, happy colors. It deliberately forces in too much color and then has several strategies for keeping the most appealing areas while toning down the rest.

The strategy succeeds because people accept and even prefer colors more intense in print than in nature. This is particularly so in landscape photography, where greenery seems too dull without our intervention.

The glaring exception is in portrayal of human skin. We have almost no tolerance for adding redness beyond what nature put there.

In the workflow's first three years I opined that a face should be treated like anything else: if making it colorful is too obnoxious, figure out how to make a layer mask to tone it down.

That position was too doctrinaire. I should have said that skintone needs to be toned down as a matter of course so that the rest of the workflow doesn't make it too red.

Skin is therefore an exception to our previous rules, just as skies are. Two examples should make the issues clearer. Both are fine originals from top professionals. Postcard 9.1 comes from Vietnam.

I have always wondered how good photographers can coax poses like this out of their nonprofessional models, because I can't. It is high time something was done about this injustice, but we don't have to worry about it for the next exercise, which uses a professional model.

Anti-postcard 9.2 hails from an advertisement for a company that

***Postcard 9.1** (opposite) Portrait of woman smoking, Vietnam.*

makes nail products. Again, the PPW brings out a spectacular amount of detail. Note, also, the lifelike variation in the skin color.

There's only one problem. Show this "correction" to an art director and you are likely to find yourself on the receiving end of a barrage of obscenities, perhaps accompanied by an iPhone being thrown at your head.

This could be preferable to showing the proof to the model. Those nails look like lethal weapons.

Why Skin Is Different: Contrast

The anti-postcard uses the same workflow seen in previous chapters. The initial color appeared OK, so no need for immediate

Anti-postcard 9.2 *An advertisement for nail products, "corrected" as if it were a landscape.*

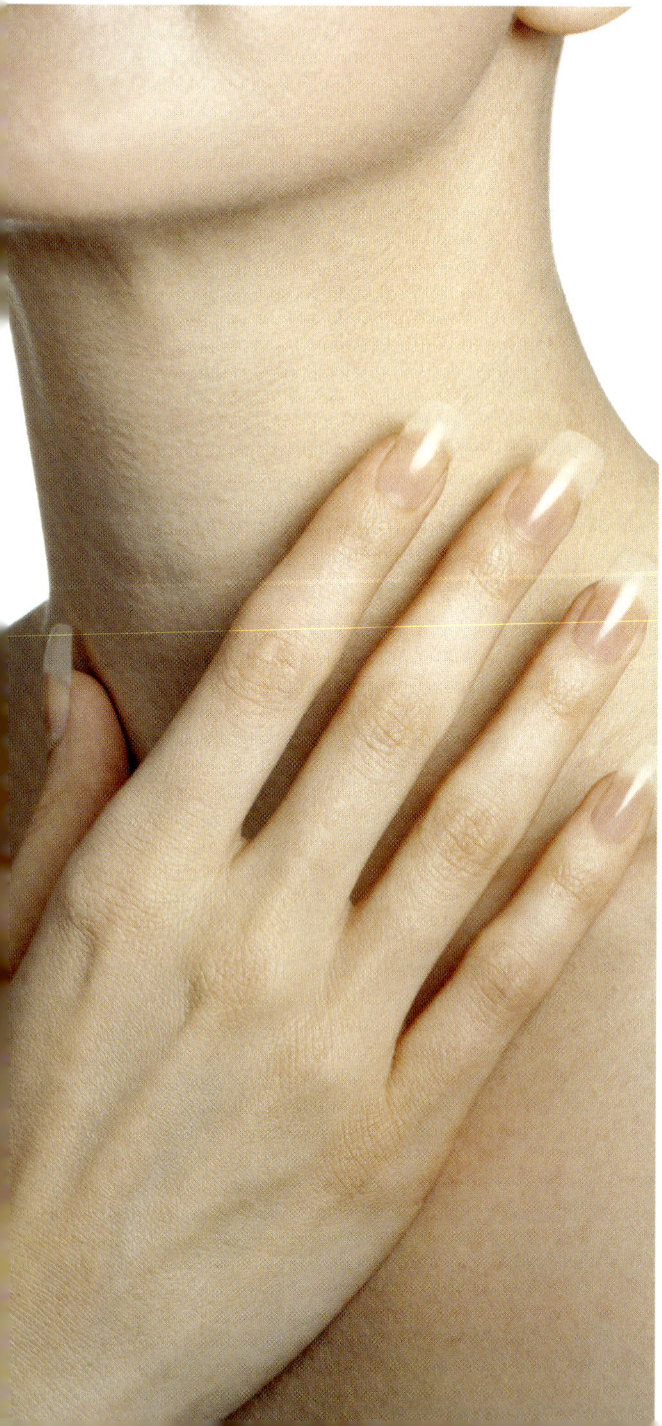

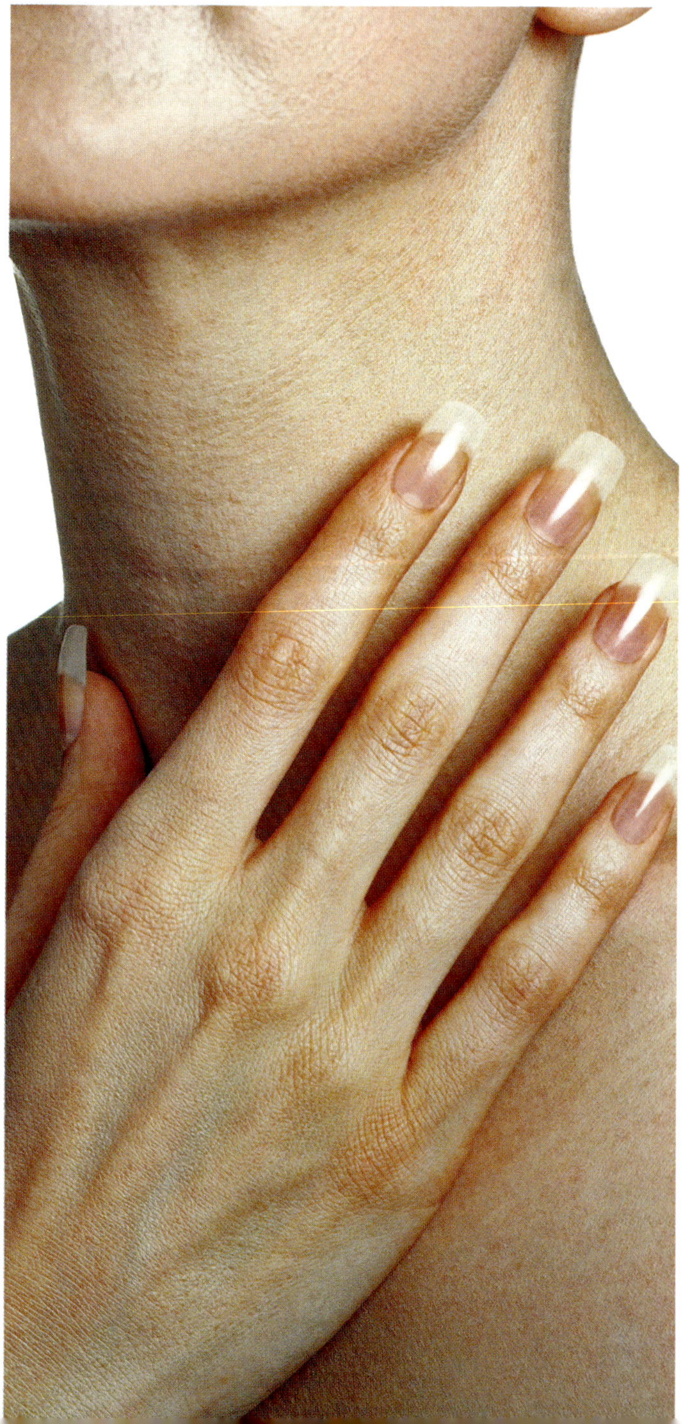

curves. Detail in the red channel was poor, so it was replaced with a mix of blue and green. Curves were applied for further contrast and layer mode switched to Luminosity. I judged there was no need for Shadows/Highlights. I selected the nails before running the MMM action; look how much redder they have become than the rest of the skin. A light color boost, a slight change to the L channel, a sharpen, and done. Nothing out of the ordinary, no moves greater than would be used, for example, in a landscape.

Yet this picture is a disaster.

The reason is aesthetic, not technical. It isn't like a bunch of artifacts got introduced. The detail is all real. We just don't like it.

Skin and skies are the only two things that behave like that. We don't add contrast to the blue areas of skies because any detail found there is probably noise. (In Chapter 8, we were darkening those areas, not adding contrast.) Wrinkles and pores are natural detail, but they make the skin look older, so we avoid adding contrast—sometimes.

The beta readers weighed in here. Alessandro Bernardi, who does fashion work in Italy, states that the trend is moving away from soft-looking female skin. He says that blemishes and wrinkles are removed but that the plastic look is passé.

Clarence Maslowski proposes adding automobiles to the list of things that are like skin and sky. I agree that getting a lot of detail into car bodies is not necessarily good, but I don't think that it's ever suppressed artificially. Color accuracy is only important if the car is the subject of an ad. Otherwise, we have much more flexibility than with either skin or sky. So, no sale for me.

A third reader accused me of sabotaging the anti-postcard with deliberately excessive moves. Not true; they are similar in magnitude to those used in Postcard 1.1.

We have to appreciate that there are two kinds of portraits. In the older woman of Postcard 9.1, the extra contrast is good, in my opinion. It adds a gritty realism and enhances the emotional impact of the composition.

But in Anti-postcard 9.2, it's not good at all. This is unfortunate, because two major steps are aimed at getting this contrast: the blending and curving of Chapter 4, and the luminosity aspect of the Modern Man from Mars of Chapter 6. These two steps usually make changes for the better, and in Postcard 9.1, they did. In the anti-postcard, they changed things for the worse. Set aside the color for a second. If we are just speaking of detail I would not split the difference between the two versions; I would want no contrast gain at all. In fact, it is common professional practice in pictures like this to soften the skin by blurring or some other expedient. Some would even say the original itself is too detailed.

So the crucial step in working on a portrait or other image in which skin is critical is deciding whether it belongs to the first category, where detail is good, or the second, where it isn't. The second category seems like it happens a lot, but that's deceptive because it is much more common in advertising. Sure, if it's a wedding shot of a bride, or an image of a baby, it has to be treated as Anti-postcard 9.2 should have been. Be very conservative with the luminosity moves of Chapter 4. I noted in Chapter 6 that the MMM Luminosity layer of the MMM action should be turned off as a matter of course in portraits. That goes double for when a soft look is desired.

But the first category is more common—Often the face isn't even large enough for the extra contrast to be annoying.

No matter how large, though, and no matter how old or tough-looking the subject, we don't want the skin to become too red.

Why Skin Is Different: Color

Back to the anti-postcard. What is it about the original, if anything, that makes us think it needs improvement?

We've already decided not to "improve" its detail in the conventional sense. The lack of color variation is more troubling.

Putting the anti-postcard on a layer above the original, set to Color mode, seems like it might work. When I tried it, I had to reduce the layer opacity to 20% because anything more created reddish areas that suggested a skin disease and yellowish ones indicating liver failure. It was an improvement at 20%, don't get me wrong, but such a small one that I won't even bother to show it.

The veins in the anti-postcard have turned a noisome green. This was not the limiting factor. Viewers tolerate added coolness in fleshtone much more than added warmth. Even though more of the picture is getting cooler than warmer, the enhanced reds and yellows are the limiting factor. The second half of the chapter shows a better example.

The expression of the problem may sound confusing, but the solution is simple. Every time an image features skintones, desaturate them (make them less colorful) before applying the MMM and/or Color Boost actions.

By now the phrase *every time* should suggest automation. Just as Chapter 8 showed an action that tries to identify and darken skies, this chapter introduces one that attempts to identify and desaturate skin. The sky action requires some thinking. It isn't always appropriate, and has two variants. The Skin Desaturation action is easier: it is to run in every image that showcases flesh.

Beta reader Frederick Yocum, dissenting: "In the kind of pictures I deal with, most people are not light-skinned. I think when we look at someone who is ebony, almost black, we need increasing variation. One way to get more variation is to lighten the skintones, the other is to boost the color…because of this, I have a problem with the words *every time*."

Omitting the action in such circumstances is reasonable. Remember, though, our two color-enhancing actions are quite potent. I used the Skin Desaturation action for the dark-skinned woman in Postcard 9.1 and it still has plenty of color and variation.

Chapter Goals and Recap

Portraits and other skin-critical images have two unusual features. First, extra detail is sometimes welcome and sometimes not. Second, we have almost no tolerance for faces getting too red.

Solving the first problem requires nothing more than recognizing when softness is desired. If it is, avoid contrast-enhancing moves. The second problem is always present. To defeat it, a simple action desaturates skintones before going to the color enhancement moves of Chapters 5 and 6.

How Difficult Is It? Portrait handling has traditionally differentiated the really skilled person from the amateur. This is still true to some extent. The action, however, is simple.

How Often Is It Needed? The action is recommended for every image that involves skintone and is headed for color enhancement.

The PPW Takes Shape

COLOR

- Kill incorrect color with RGB curves (Chapter 3).
- Identify highlight (Chapters 3–4).

CONTRAST

- Channel blending on luminosity layer (Chapter 4).
- Contrast-enhancing curves (Chapter 4).
    - Consider S/H command (Chapter 7).
    - Consider boost to sky (Chapter 8).

COLOR AGAIN

- Desaturate skintone, if any (this chapter).
- Apply MMM + Color Boost action (Chapters 5–6).
- Finalize contrast, including endpoints.
- Reduce color by masking or opacity adjustment.

SHARPEN

FINALIZE

- Consider blend with another version (Chapter 2).
- Convert to final output space, if needed.

Postcard 9.3 *(opposite) Tourists breakfasting near Barberino Val d'Elsa, Tuscany, Italy.*

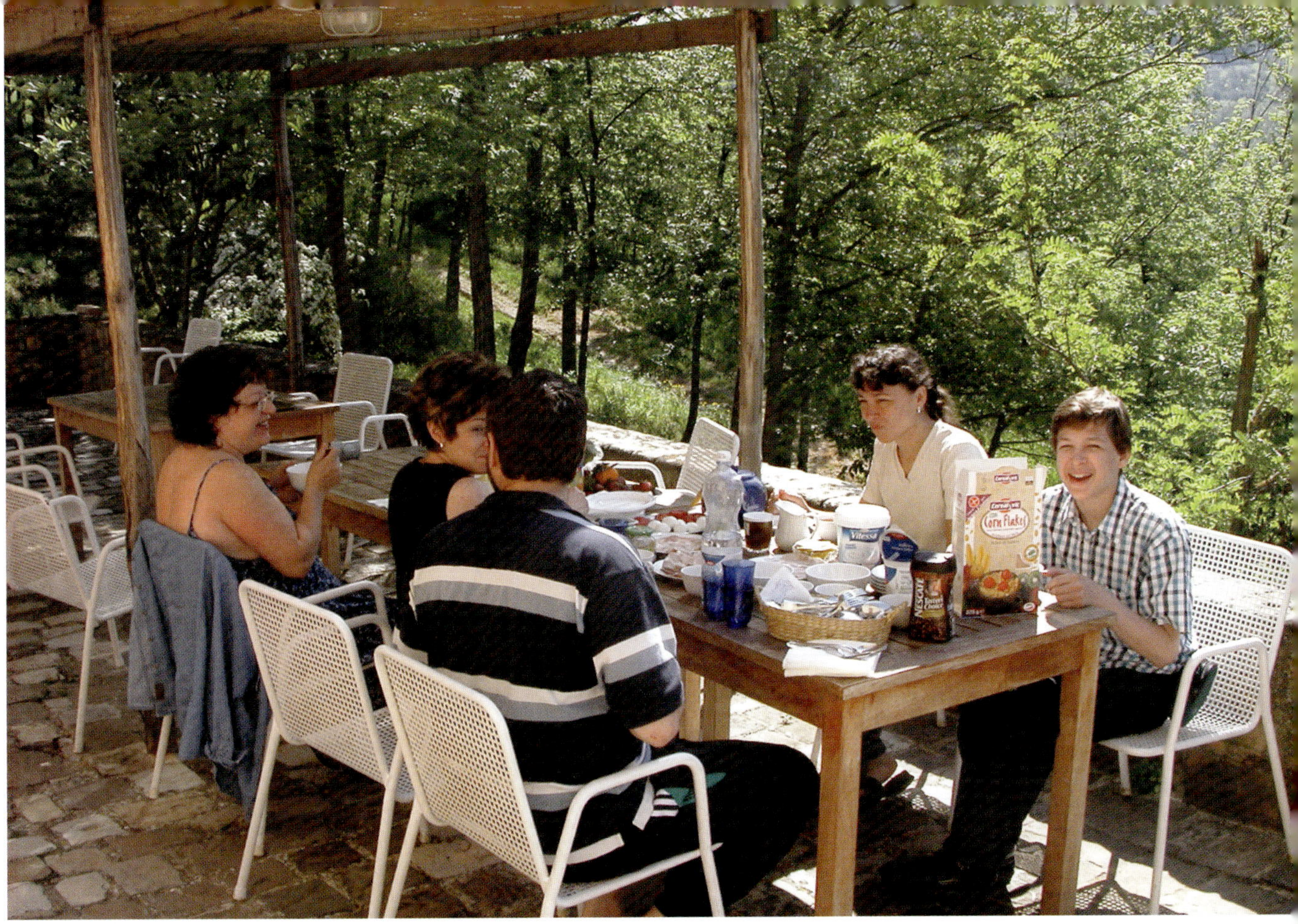
Corn Flakes
Vitessa

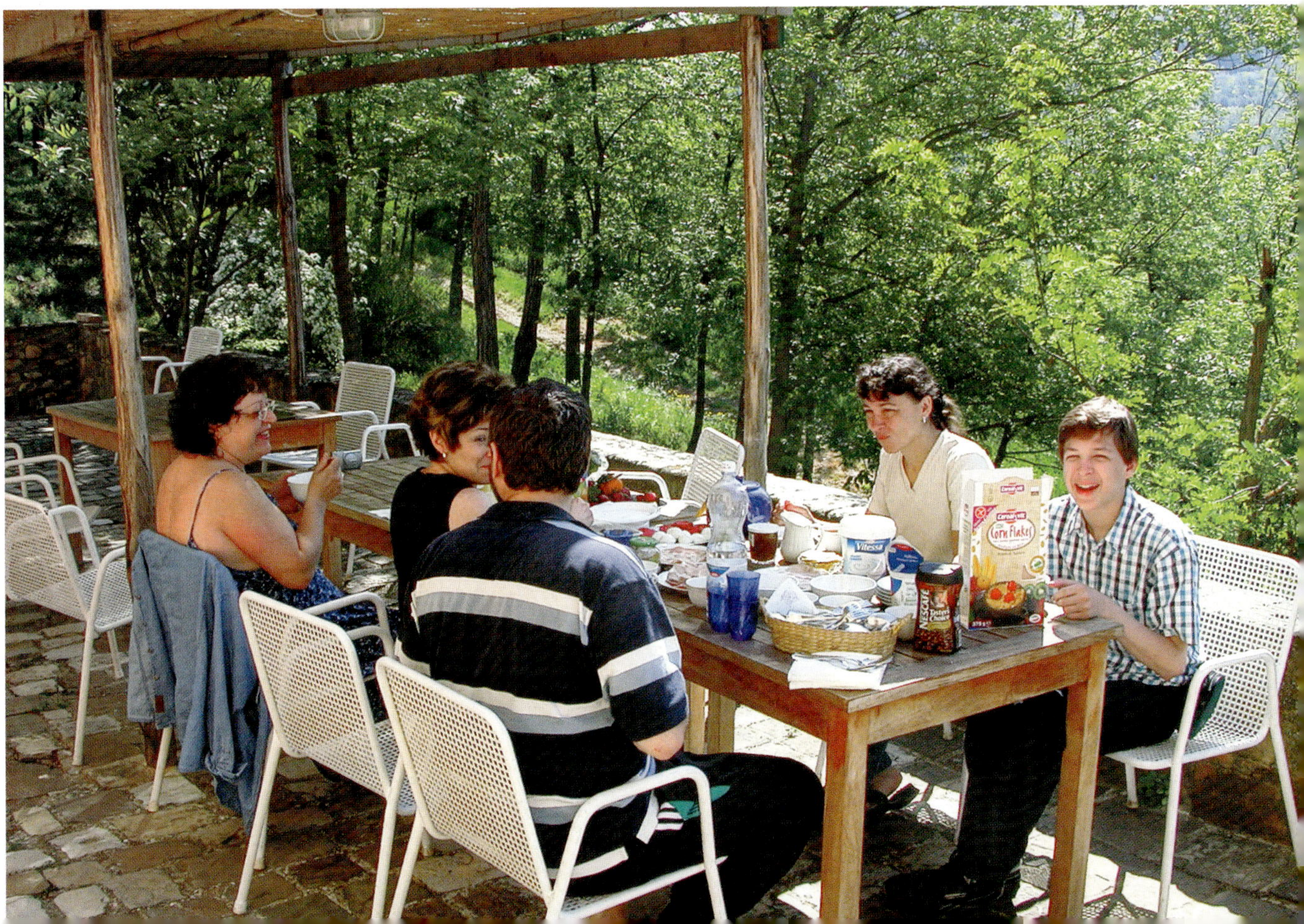
Corn Flakes
Vitessa

Under the Tuscan Sun

Tuscany is always described as being a lush, romantic green. The reality is somewhat different. Romance requires us to make the background more vivid—but we can't make the faces beet red.

If this were a portrait of the boy or of the woman facing us, we'd have to decide whether to omit the luminosity step, as suggested in Anti-postcard 9.2. But here, the faces are so small that if we bring out wrinkles nobody will notice. So we treat the faces just like any other object for contrast.

Setting the original color can be tricky enough even without skintones. This shot is kind enough to provide several sample points. The man's shirt has white areas; the chairs are probably white, and so are some items on the table.

All these areas currently measure AB–positive, not the 0^A0^B that makes a neutral. A slight warmth is probably not bad, but the overall look seems somewhat purple, as the rock flooring measures higher in the A.

Sunlight, a good thing to suggest in a Tuscan image, is always more yellow than purple. So I would say that a color correction is needed, but a careful one. It would not do for this scene to leave a chilly impression. So, on an adjustment layer, I darkened the blue channel slightly, which makes things less blue = more yellow. Also, I slightly darkened the red, making things less red = more cyan. This is less risky than playing with the green channel and chancing a cast even deadlier than a cyan one. After converting the layer to Color mode, I had Figure 9.4.

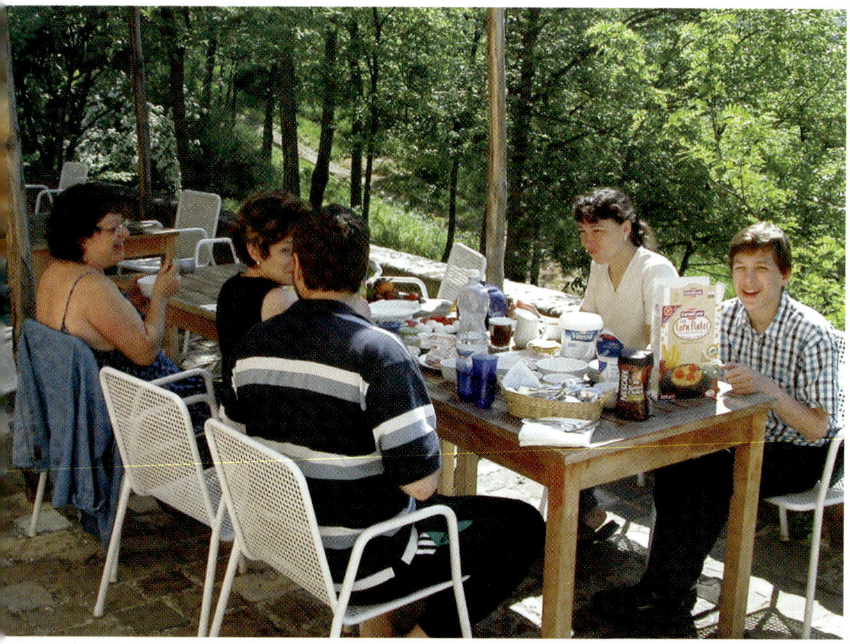

Figure 9.4 *Curves in Color mode reduce the red cast. Below, the resulting red, green, and blue channels.*

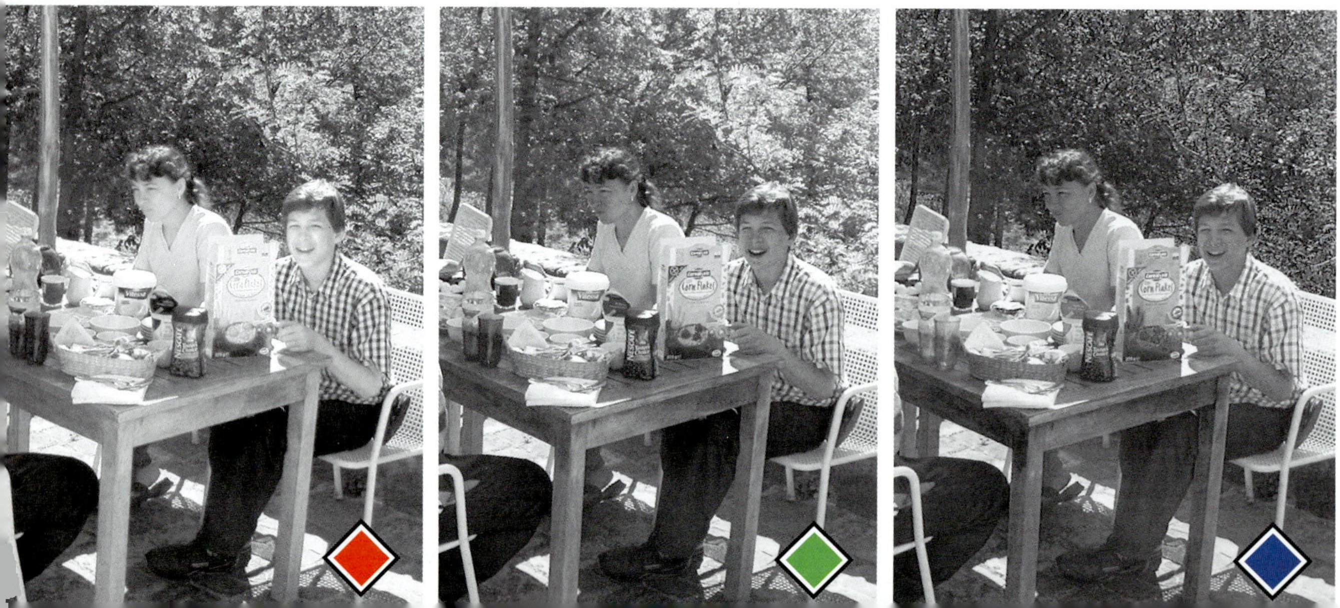

The Green Channel for Contrast

All channels seem to have full range already, without any obvious target for improvement. Curves are therefore unlikely to help. But channel blending will.

Faces usually show the best contrast in the green channel and the worst in the red. Figure 9.4 displays the expected red deficiency, but it isn't clear whether to blend the green into it, or the blue. Either will darken and add depth to the faces. The question is whether we want to add depth to the greenery as well. The more we want dark greenery the bigger use we make of the blue in blending.

The decision is not an easy one, as I found out. I made a duplicate layer, blended the green into the red at 50% opacity, and then the blue into the resulting red, again at 50% opacity. Finally, I applied a slight curve to the green to enhance midtone contrast. After changing the layer mode to Luminosity, I had Figure 9.5A.

I knew I had another correction of this original, done more than a year previously. It is a bad policy to poison one's mind by referring to such an alternate before starting from scratch. But the time had now come for the confrontation. On comparing the two I thought I had done worse this time around, and that the culprit was overly light greenery. So I tried again. This time, I blended 20% of the blue into the *green*. As the green has the most direct impact on

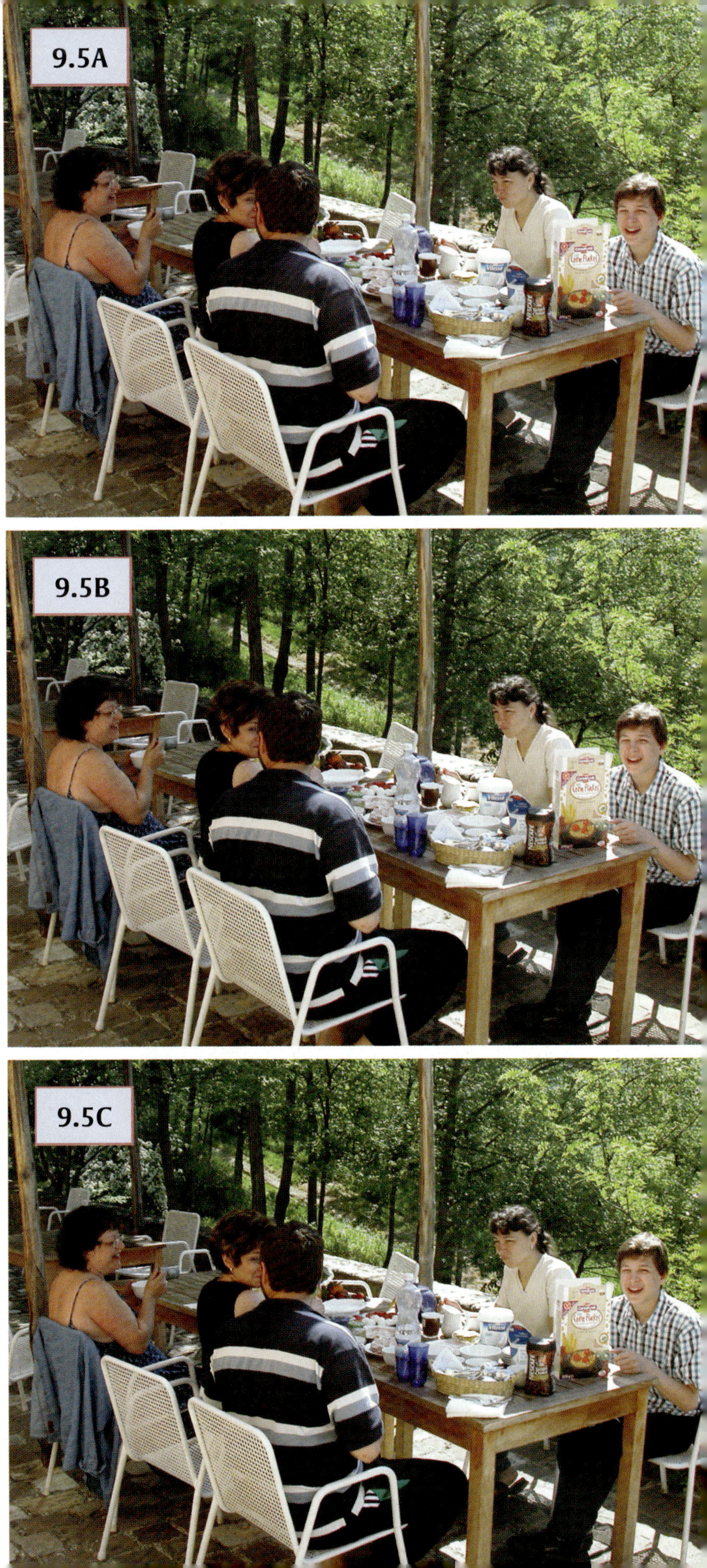

***Figure 9.5** Top, a new luminosity version featuring a blend of the green of Figure 9.4 into the red. Middle, instead, the blue channel is used to blend into the green, creating darker background leaves. Bottom, the Skin Desaturation action is applied to the middle version.*

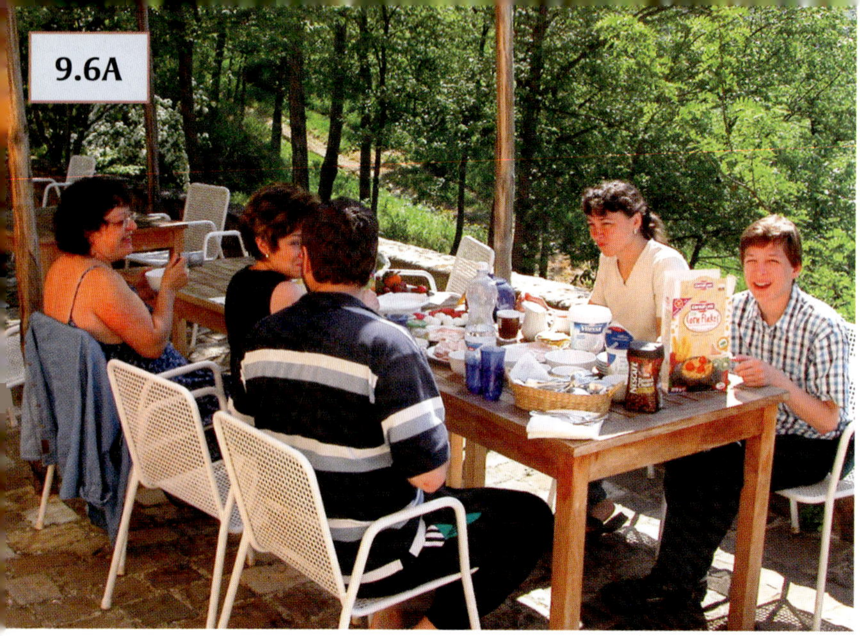

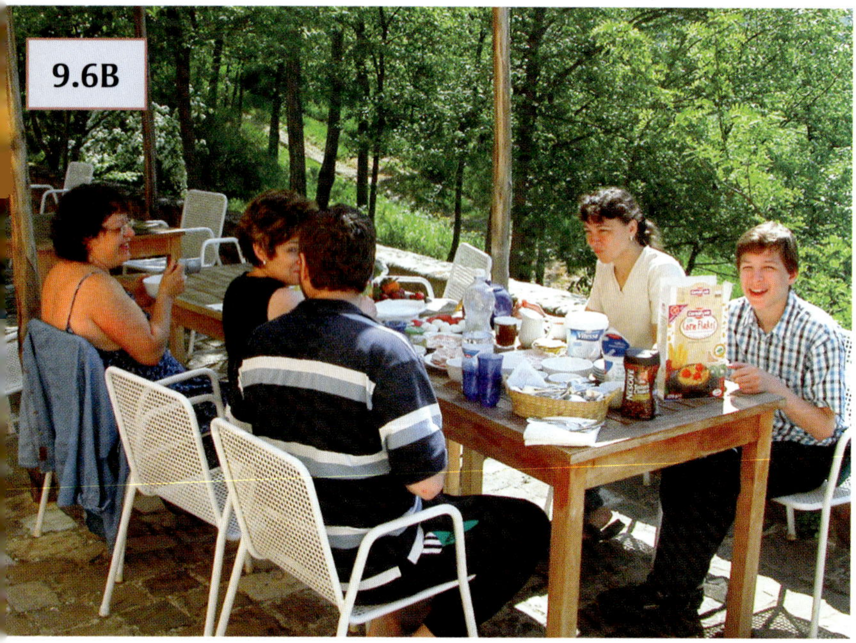

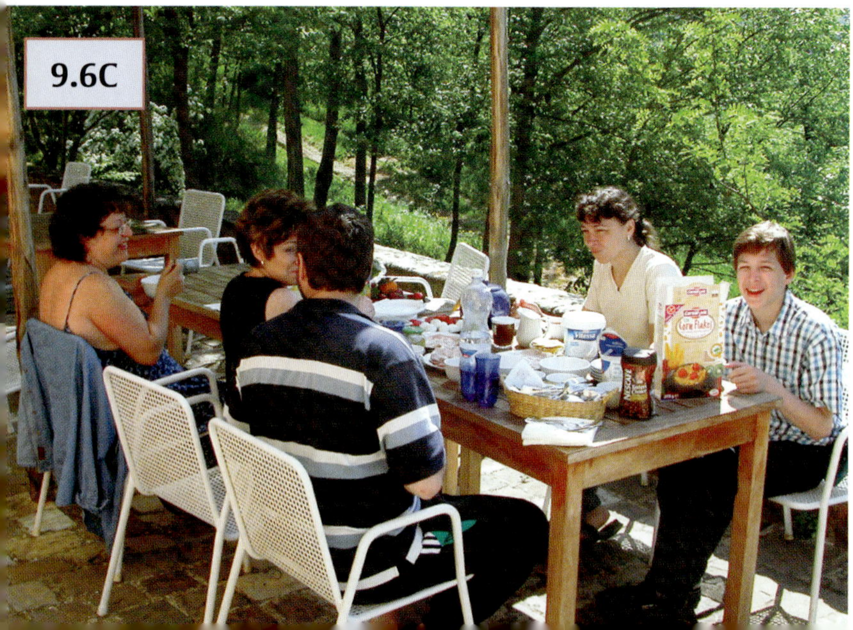

luminosity, this move had a big effect. The new result was Figure 9.5B, and 9.5A got the Command-Delete treatment.

The next query was whether to run Shadows/Highlights as per Chapter 7. Another toughie! There is plenty of dark hair and clothing, and a lot of light things on the table, but in my view they all would distract attention from the people if we enhanced their detail. So, my decision was no S/H.

The next step required no such thinking—only the admission that the file contains important skintones. Since it does, it calls for the Skin Desaturation action, which produced Figure 9.5C. As with the Shadows/Highlights command, I don't recommend taking the time to investigate using settings other than the default.

You may not see much difference between Figures 9.5B and 9.5C. Once we go into color enhancement, however, there is one, and it becomes important.

Skin desaturation may remind you of the very first step of the PPW, where we examine for incipient color issues and repair them with RGB curves if necessary. Often the change is not apparent. Those beginning with the workflow often think it isn't important. A reminder of why we do it will be coming right up.

After desaturating the skin, we move on to color enhancement: a

***Figure 9.6** All three versions were produced using the luminosity of Figure 9.5B and the same MMM + Color Boost settings. Top, the color correction that produced Figure 9.4 is omitted, as is the Skin Desaturation action. Middle, the color correction is there, but the Skin Desaturation action is not. Bottom, both are present.*

rough selection of the people, the MMM + Color Boost action, and adjustments to taste. I saved my settings and selection so that I could repeat them on two extra versions.

Figure 9.6A, then, has no initial color adjustments and no skin desaturation. That is, it uses the original color and not that of Figure 9.4. It does, however, share the luminosity of Figure 9.5B.

Next, Figure 9.6B applies the same enhancements to 9.5B: the original color correction that produced Figure 9.4 is included, but the skin desaturation is not.

Finally, Figure 9.6C includes everything. I hope you agree that the faces in Figure 9.6B are too red. And the red cast in Figure 9.6A—which was hard to see in the original file—is now obtrusive.

Without the skin desaturation it would be difficult to boost color enough to make the background greens as vivid as we'd like.

A Collection of Adjectives

This chapter's innovation, automatic skin desaturation, is easy to apply. Unfortunately, the rest of the process of dealing with faces is not. Retouchers who specialize in skintone have traditionally made more money than anybody else in the graphic arts, for good reason. Clients are more particular about this type of work than any other. The methods of dealing with problems can be complicated.

One of the biggest issues is the one we saw in the first two examples. The woman in Postcard 9.1 needs as much detail in the skin as possible, at least in my opinion. Obviously the skin advertisement of Anti-Postcard 9.2 calls for as little as possible. But most portraits are more ambiguous. How do you propose to correct a portrait, say, of a man over 40?

Here are two sets of adjectives:

Set One: Strong. Older. Tougher. Decisive. Meaner. More natural. Harsher. Bolder. Determined. Fierce. Weathered. Two-fisted.

Set Two: Soft. Friendly. Family-oriented. Well-meaning. Scatter-brained. Gentler. Confused. Approachable. Flabby. Avuncular.

Set One articulates some of the likelier reactions if we decide to emphasize detail. Set Two's terms might be used if we go for a softer look. In each set some words are positive, some are negative, and some may depend on an individual's point of view.

Probably we will choose something between the two extremes. But how far to go? If we know the man it may bias us in one direction, but it might not be the direction he would choose himself.

If the job absolutely must be done in three minutes, then we have no choice but to make a decision and stick with it. We run the PPW as usual, with the addition of the Skin Desaturation action before the final color enhancement.

We likely won't be under such time constraints. If we aren't, the recommendation, as always, is to do two versions and investigate blending them. But there's a skintone-specific twist: I recommend, if time permits, doing one version for strong facial detail and another on the assumption that such detail is bad.

A Sad Tale of Skintone

In the first draft of this chapter there was, right here, a seven-page demonstration of the above concept. However, as you know, this book was carefully vetted by a conscientious group. The atmosphere was one of calm professionalism, understated language, and mutual respect.

For example, beta reader Russ Brown wrote of the seven-page exercise, "This demonstration is a disaster...truly hideous...it convinces me only that the PPW is unsuitable in all but the mildest of applications for virtually any pictures where the primary subject is a face."

Others weren't quite as diplomatic, but you

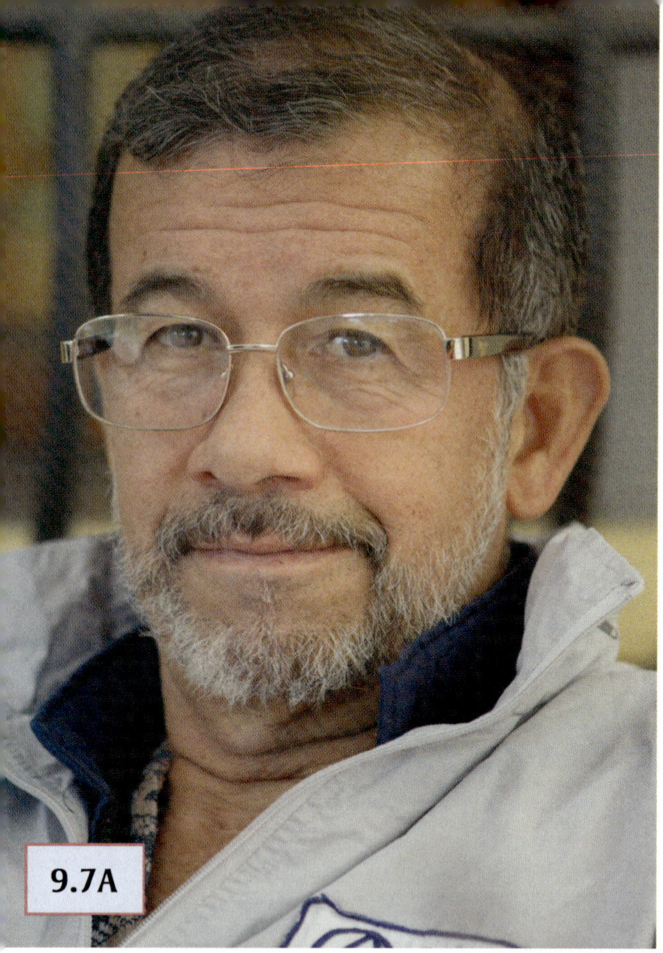

get the idea. Then again, still others thought it was a valuable exercise, and just about everybody bought into the basic concept.

Some readers submitted their own version of the portrait, showing that indeed mine was inadequate. This is why so many examples throughout the book are from classes, where I've seen scores of people's results on the same image. When all you have to compare to is the original, it's easy to overestimate the quality of your correction. I daresay I do this less than other people, but I still do it occasionally, as this sad experience reminds me. I'm not going to get discouraged by it and I recommend that you don't either, when, as is inevitable, it happens to you.

As a substitute exercise, I offer Figure 9.7A, which has been vetted, too. This is one of the chapters so heavily revised that the group had to read it twice. Figure 9.7B is my correction. You'll find how I did it in the second half of the chapter.

***Figure 9.7** Top, the original. Bottom, two corrected versions, each created by a method to be described in the second half of the chapter.*

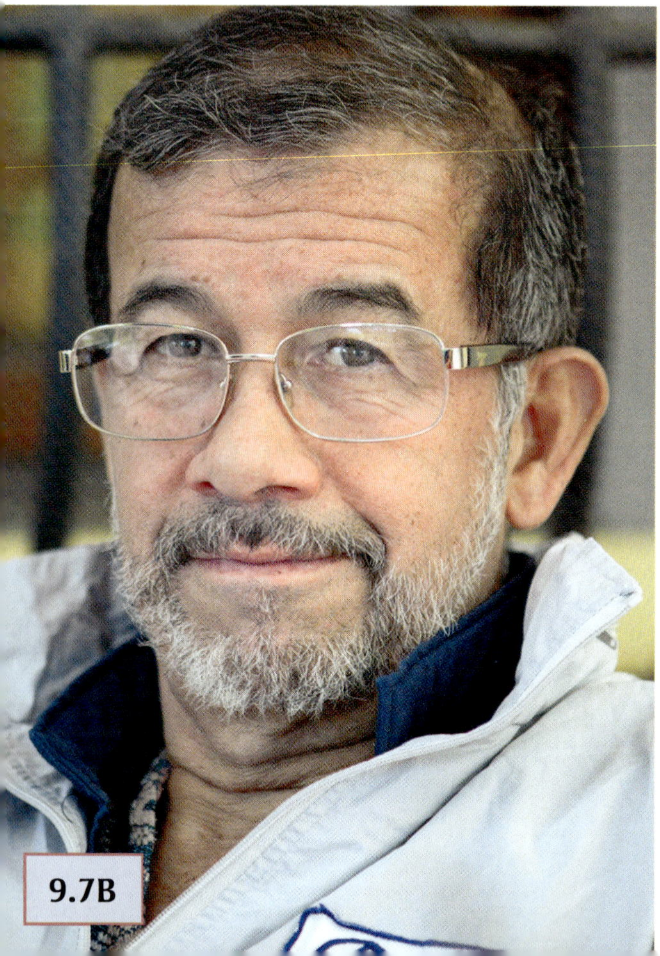

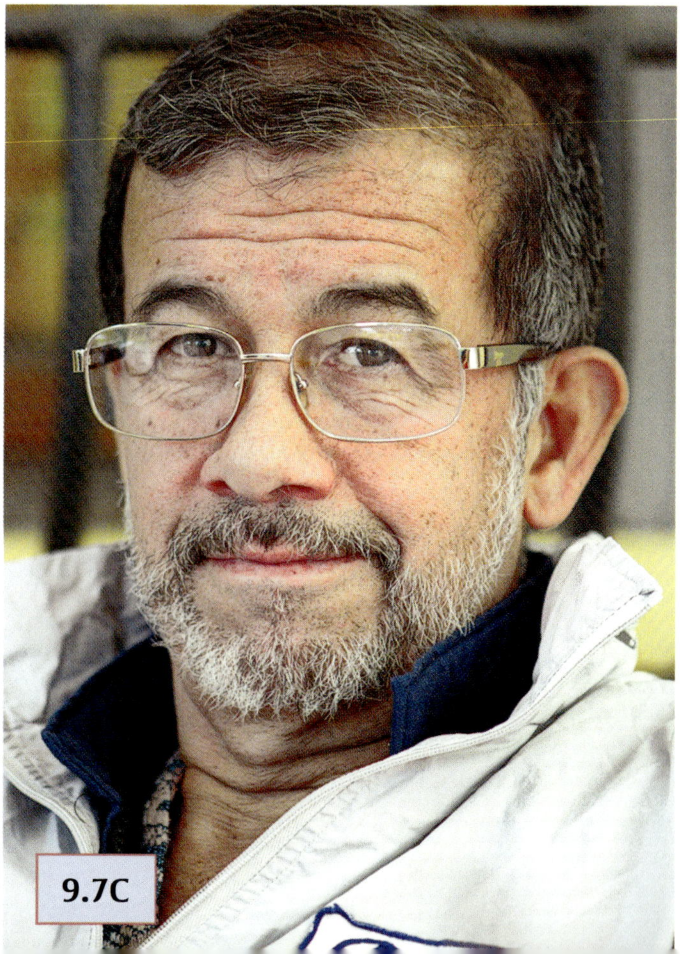

Some readers came up with their own corrected versions of this shot, of which Figure 9.7C is one. Both it and Figure 9.7B were put together in the style described: one harsh, strong version, one soft one, blended together creatively. Both beat the single-version finals from other people—but you'll find another version that's better than either near the end of the chapter.

* * *

The treatment of portraits is notoriously subject to personal preference. As we have seen, there is also less tolerance for "creative" color moves than there would be in, say, landscapes. This chapter demonstrates how the PPW is modified when important skintones are present. The modifications themselves are simple: an action that requires no thinking, and an early decision about contrast. You should not delude yourself, however, into thinking that the basics of fleshtone work are easy. Your good taste is at the same premium it would be in a traditional workflow.

The second half of this chapter, in addition to the fleshing out of Postcard 9.7, discusses the technical details of the action, a bit more about why reds are so offensive, and offers broad numerical guidelines about skintone. If these topics interest you, read on; if not, move on to Chapter 10 to learn about the action that's the bigger brother of the Shadows/ Highlights command.

Review and Exercises

✓The second step of the workflow (luminosity layers, Chapter 4) is intended to increase contrast. What other step(s) in the PPW also can increase contrast?

✓How would you reduce facial contrast during the second step, if you wanted to do that?

✓Faces, along with the blue areas of skies, are the only common objects in which added detail is unwelcome—sometimes. What rules would you follow in deciding which types of skin can take more detail and which should not?

✓This chapter suggests desaturating skintones before applying color enhancements for fear that otherwise parts of the skin will become too red. Find three of your own landscape images that feature plenty of greenery. See whether you think the same thing is true. Should you desaturate the greens before applying the MMM and Color Boost actions?

A Closer Look

Considering how long people have been working professionally with digital color it is surprising to find disagreement on fundamental items. A couple of years back I posed a hypothetical question to my appliedcolortheory list, which is populated largely by high-end users. I asked them to predict, for a series of unseen images, whether they would accept more intense color than was found in the actual scene. And I listed a dozen or so common objects for discussion.

You would think that there might be a consensus on such a simple matter as whether it is logical to portray flowers as more brilliant than they are in nature. But there was no such agreement on flowers, or wood, or buildings, or clothing, or half a dozen other things. In fact, there were only three areas of unanimity.

The first had to do with postcard-type images. Everyone agreed that it is not just permissible but desirable to boost certain natural greens.

The second was the topic of the previous chapter: the blue areas of skies. Here the basic idea was right but its expression was not. Almost everybody said they would often be willing to make the sky more intensely blue. They meant to say that they would often make it *darker.*

The third was this chapter's focus. Everyone said that faces shouldn't get more colorful. Some agreed with my proposed exception, which is that people with unusually light or unusually dark skin are often helped by additional color but everyone in the middle is hurt.

One way or another, the consensus is that blue skies and faces don't conform to the same rules as other objects. Actions to select each of them seem in order. Which of the two do you think is harder to implement?

Back When the Sky Was Young

It is harder to design an algorithm to isolate fleshtones than skies. When the sky was young, it did not have to worry about large predators coming along and taking a bite out of it. It could therefore afford to adopt a pleasing and unique color. Meanwhile, our prehistoric ancestors, living alongside large carnivores with larger appetites, wisely chose a color shared with many other things in nature.

It stands to reason that we find more objects similar in color to fleshtones than to skies. It's therefore more likely that an algorithm would incorrectly identify a non-fleshtone as being one. Images like Figure 9.5C, where the Skin Desaturation action also desaturated the wood of the breakfast table, are more common than ones like Figure 8.5F, where the Darken Sky SC action mistakenly darkened parts of buildings, too.

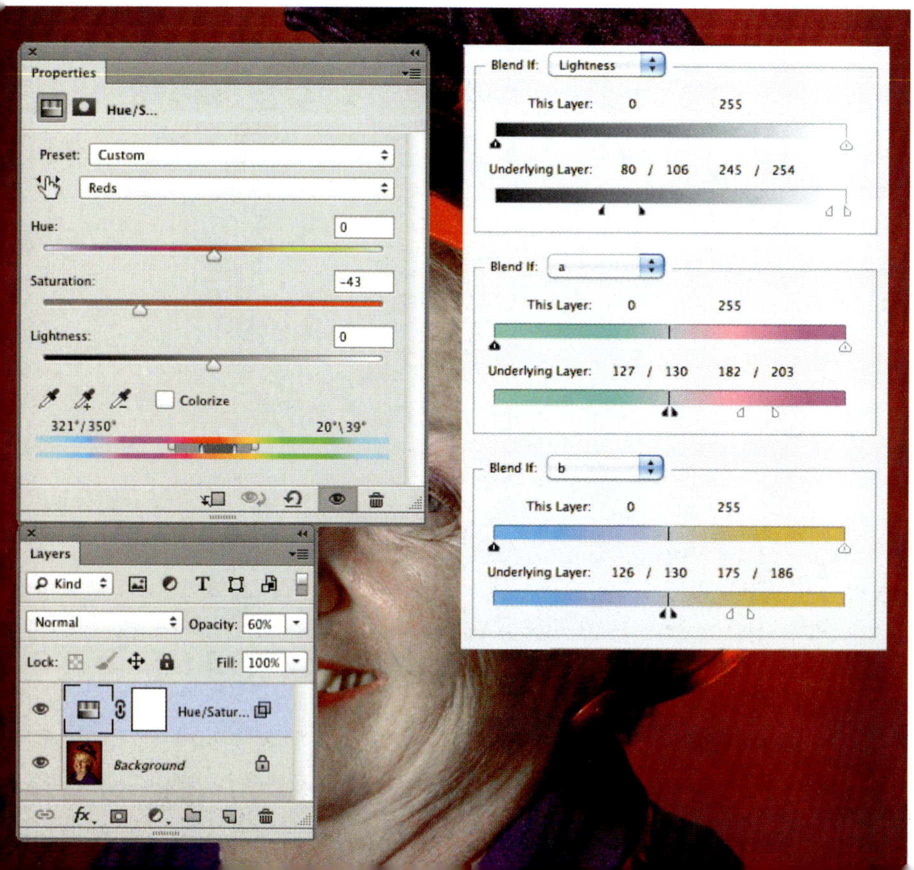

Figure 9.8 The structure of the Skin Desaturation action.

The Skin Desaturation action adds a Hue/Saturation adjustment layer in LAB. The definition of Reds is customized to favor pinker tones and that color is then desaturated. There are also Blend If alterations to the A and B channels to exclude objects that are too strongly or too weakly red or yellow to be likely fleshtones. The layer arrives with a default opacity of 60%, so there is room to maneuver without having to open the H/S dialog. Figure 9.8 summarizes these moves.

Figure 9.9A is the original; 9.9B is the action's default. Figure 9.9C changes opacity to 100% and then duplicates the layer, showing how far the action can be pushed and what it is identifying as flesh.

Skin, being red, must measure positive in both the A and B channels. That lets us exclude the purple clothing, which is A–positive but B–negative, more blue than yellow. The hat, the beads, and the background, however, all are red. The action nevertheless does not believe

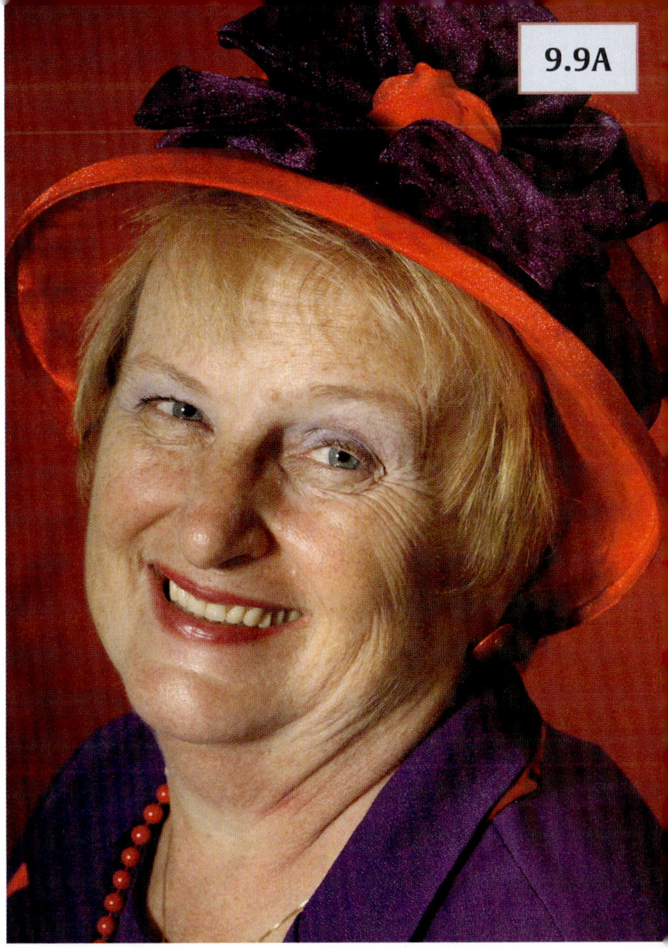

***Figure 9.9** Top, an original. Bottom left, after the default Skin Desaturation action. Bottom right, the desaturation layer is duplicated and opacity is set to 100% on each.*

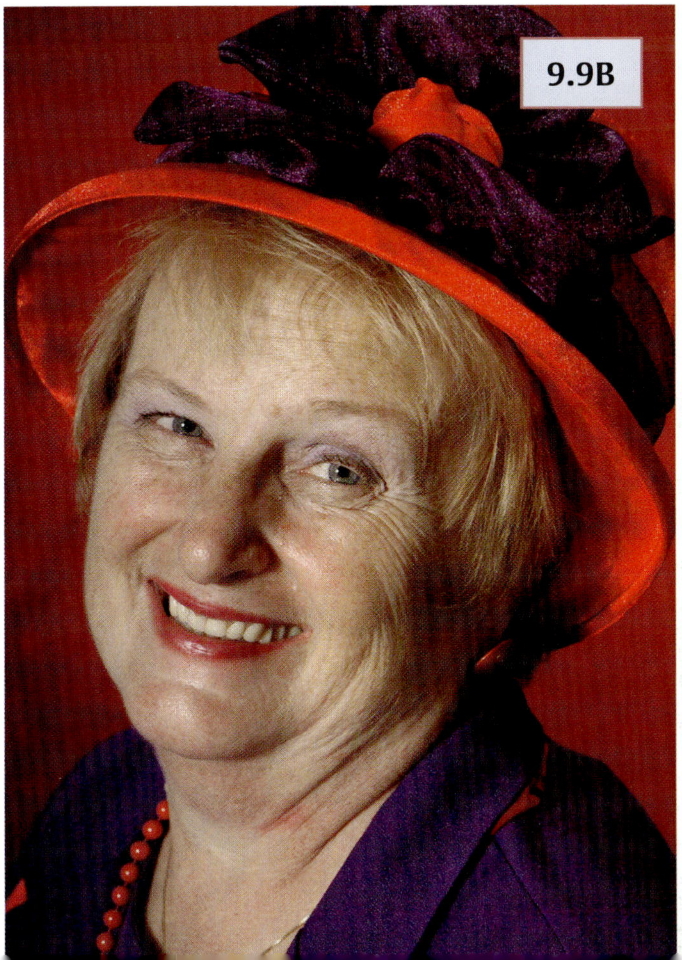

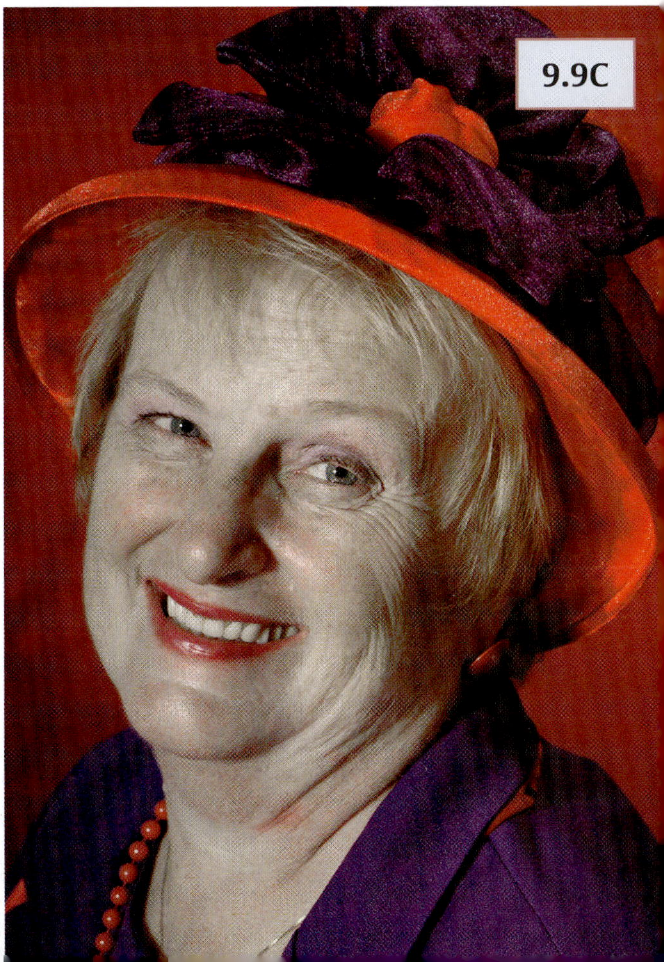

they are fleshtones, because they are either too dark, too colorful, or both. Unsurprisingly (and in my view, correctly) the lipstick is also excluded. The biggest problem is that the hair is included for desaturation. It would be impossible, in my view, for an automated routine to get that right, because the hair and the cheeks sport almost identical color.

The long and the short is that the action shouldn't cause problems unless the portrait is of extreme importance, in which case a certain amount of local retouching will be necessary, as it always has been.

The Case for Desaturation

Consider Figure 9.10A which, like Figure 9.9A, is professional studio photography. One expects the initial color to be reasonable, and it is in both cases. But we always look to improve it.

Figure 9.10B applies the full fury of the PPW color arsenal. The Modern Man from Mars action is run at maximum opacity without masks, together with the Color Boost action, also at maximum opacity.

This version is done to prove a point, and in fact it proves two. The first is that although it seems counterintuitive to desaturate, there is no disadvantage in doing so. The PPW is capable of producing vastly more color than anyone would ever want. It laughs off any desaturation; it's still possible to make the image much too colorful.

The second is simply to reinforce the idea that redness is bad in fleshtones. Figure 9.10B introduces color variation, which is ordinarily a very good thing in faces. Admittedly we don't want this much of it; we will reduce the effect drastically. But try to imagine how it will look when we do. Would you guess that the added redness will seem more offensive than the move toward blue in the forehead?

I certainly would. In real life the decision would be even more one-sided, because here I had deleted the MMM action's masks. It happens that those masks suppress blue more than red in this image. I would therefore trash Figure 9.10B and run the Skin Desaturation action on the original, producing Figure 9.10C. From that, we can get to Figure 9.10D using the same techniques, albeit at much lower settings and with a different MMM selection.

I find Figure 9.10D more realistic. It makes 9.10A look flat. However, it is already on the verge of going too red, in my opinion. And remember, the move was applied not to Figure 9.10A but to the grayer Figure 9.10C. Without that desaturation step, we might still have been able to produce some attractive variation but nothing like what is shown in Figure 9.10D.

Before moving on to a discussion of appropriate fleshtone values, would you care to speculate on why adding redness to fleshtones is so offensive? After all, Figure 9.10B doesn't really change the average value of Figure 9.10A's face. Some parts get warmer and others get colder. Why should either effect be worse than the other? Why should we have to desaturate the whole face first? And why are we so upset about the reds, considering that we know they represent makeup, which is not necessarily the same color as human skin?

An average person has an easy answer. We don't like the red because it looks ugly.

No doubt, but if you really want to be successful with faces it is probably useful to understand why. Nobody really knows, but I will shortly offer a suggestion, one we will revisit in subsequent chapters, particularly when we get to sharpening.

The Rose in Her Cheeks

Some would favor a more pronounced effect and some a subtler one, but anyone who works on portraits would agree that Figure 9.10A has to move in the direction of 9.10D. The standard explanation, of which I may be the originator, is

***Figure 9.10** Top left, an original. Top right, with a robust application of the MMM + Color Boost actions. Bottom left, the Skin Desaturation action is applied to the original. Bottom right, moderate MMM + Color Boost is applied to the desaturated version.*

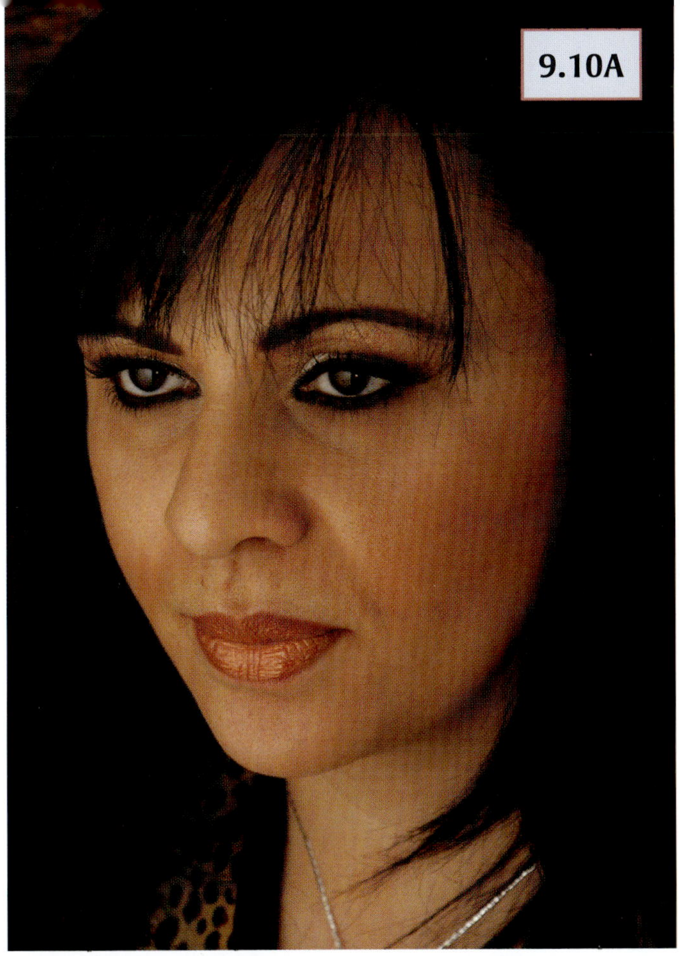

9.10A

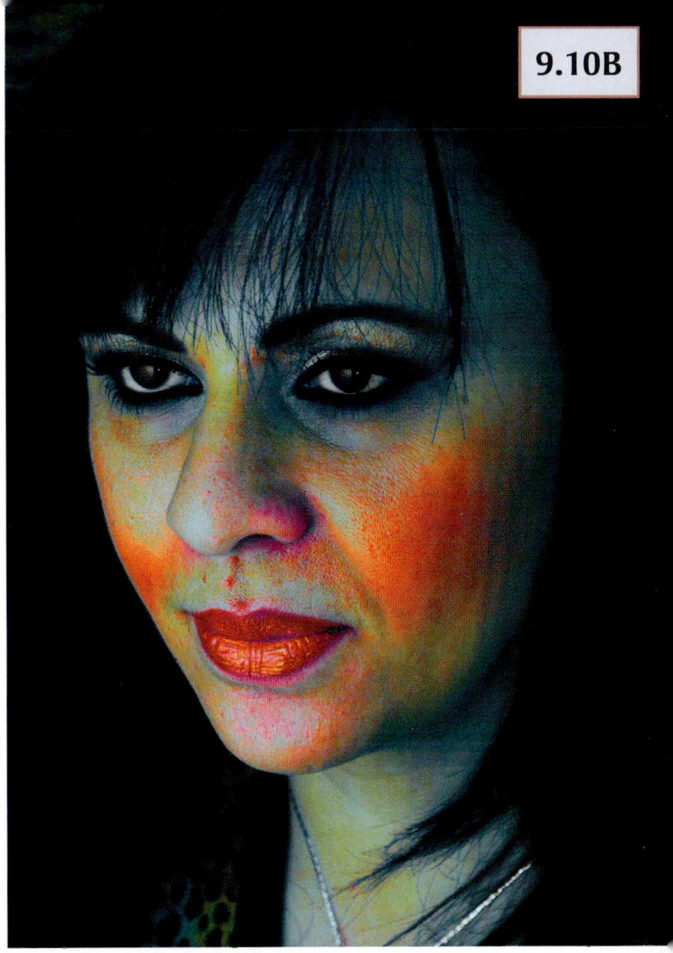

9.10B

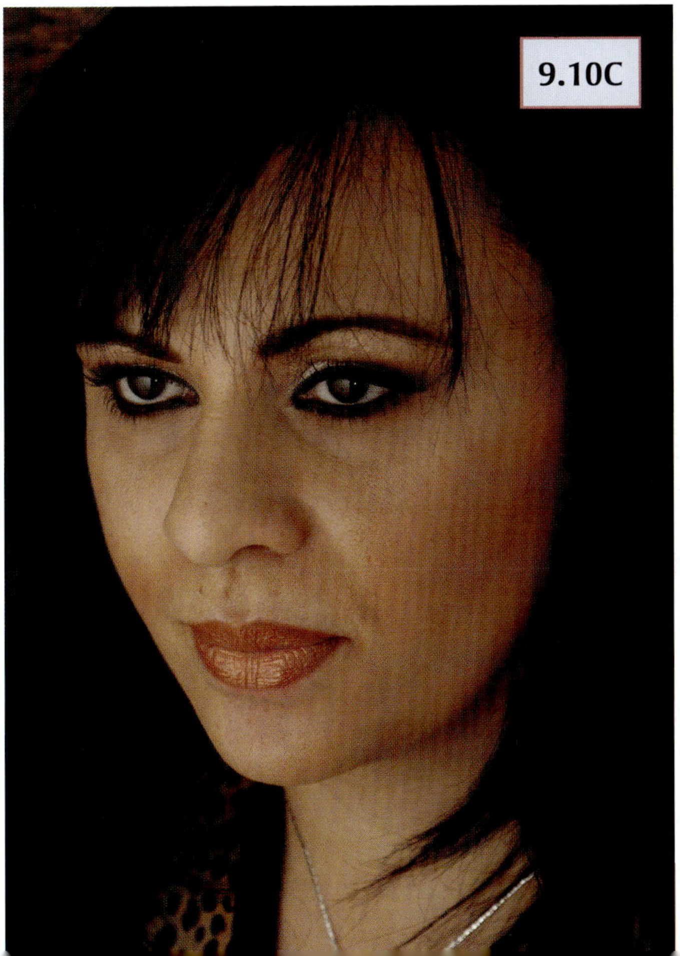

9.10C

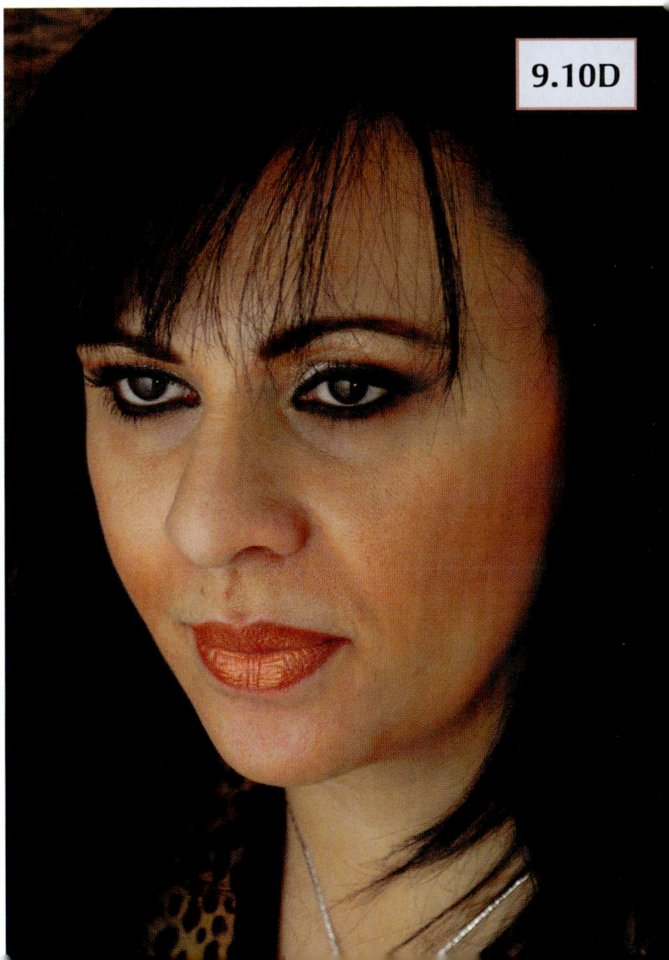

9.10D

that the corrected version caters to the human sense of simultaneous contrast—our propensity to see variation when confronted with large areas of similar color. In real life, we would concentrate on the face to the exclusion of other items; therefore we would break the colors apart to some extent. The effect is impossible in print because we can't avoid being distracted by the rest of the page. So, an uncorrected photograph of this nature is boring, unnatural.

A similar argument governs the elimination of casts. Chromatic adaptation prevents us from detecting overall color imbalances that a camera finds apparent. If our entire environment is slightly green we adjust; but a printed photograph doesn't permit this adjustment. Therefore, we ax the imbalance, again making the picture look more like what we would see in real life.

This line of examples can be taken further. Beginning with Chapter 11 we will see why it is desirable to reduce variation caused by different lighting, such as in a picture having both sunlight and shade.

All these human adjustments are consistent with an evolutionary imperative. Humans do a poor job of running the earth, but the fact is that we do run it, having become the dominant species on the planet. Scientists have had a hard time explaining how this happened. The eminent color theorist, Friedrich Engels, wrote,

> Man's early development, at least in part, was as a tree-dwelling race. Otherwise, one cannot explain its survival among the huge beasts of prey who shared its habitat of tropical or subtropical forests.

This all sounds as convincing as many of Engels' other theories about family development, but it turns out to be just as wrong. For more than a century researchers have known that our Neanderthal relatives were no better at climbing or living in trees than we are. Furthermore, recent anthropological findings have suggested that more species, birds of prey included, dined on our ancestors than had previously been supposed. Which leaves Engels' assertion unanswered.

The conventional wisdom, which becomes more dubious day by day, is that man is smarter than other animals. When attacked by a saber-toothed tiger, it is not obvious that this purported intelligence did our ancestors much good.

Since they could not out-run or out-fight their enemies, and since they could not smell them from afar, it must have been critical to our ancestors' survival as a species to identify threats instantaneously, perhaps before the threat had identified *them.*

All the visual factors identified above help do this. We reference all scenes to neutrality, so that familiar objects don't take on unfamiliar colors. We spread out the fleshtones to be sure we are identifying a human face and not one of a threatening apelike species.

Any potential animal threat presents itself as fairly neutral, as predators do not care to advertise their presence. All are a warmish color, at least on land. And almost all, except night predators, fall in the quartertone range.

Is it any wonder that we are more sensitive to color issues in this type of image?

Beta reader James Gray, who studies these matters, gets to the same conclusion through different logic. He doesn't think that our ancestors were as defenseless as Engels and I make out, commenting "I do not think it would be a cakewalk for a leopard to attack a troupe of chimpanzees. Likewise I doubt attacking a band of any hominids would have been a safe thing for a leopard and most other predators. Also the conventional wisdom that humans are really bad runners needs to be taken with a grain of salt. Many species are much better sprinters than we are. However, recent research points out that humans have much better stamina for distance running than most other species. One other physical skill that humans have is throwing ability. Throwing rocks would have been a very good predator defense. None of this invalidates your comments about our visual system...I do think it makes more sense for us to see more contrast in the warm-neutral quartertones."

As to why incorrectness-too-red is worse than incorrectness-too-cold, here's my position, accept it at your own risk. If I were designing a visual system to rapidly identify threats, I would immediately set brightly colored objects to one side. Roses do not threaten us and neither does anything else of that intensity. We do not need to perceive detail in flowers, at least not instantaneously; far better to focus our attention on the warmish-neutral quartertones that could represent danger.

Anyhow, that's my explanation for why the reds are so much more offensive than the blue-grays in Figure 9.10B: they send us mixed signals, provoking the subconscious feeling that we are looking at a flower and not a woman.

Two Theories, One Quiz

If you don't like that explanation, James offers another: once again, different reasoning, same conclusion. He writes, "I think it far more likely that the primary issue is with species recognition of faces. In other words it is more about recognizing human faces than recognizing predators. A lot of research indicates that humans are remarkably good at discriminating small variations in facial characteristics."

Either theory implies that we evaluate faces far differently than a camera does, and that nobody understands exactly how nor are they ever likely to. We have a much better grasp of what we are looking for in a landscape shot than in a portrait, because the phenomena of simultaneous contrast and chromatic adaptation are better understood than what happens in faces.

Therefore, we work with the slight handicap of not knowing what we're trying to do. The two examples that started this chapter (the Vietnamese woman and the hand model) were exceptions, where the desired treatment is clear. Most portraits are more ambiguous, such as the man in Figure 9.7A, whom I promised to correct in this half of the chapter.

First, however, a quiz about skin color. Can you guess the LAB equivalents for some of the images in this chapter?

Several of the files we've been studying were measured for average skintone, in the forehead where possible. Otherwise, the values were taken in the neck. Where two versions of the same photo appear the measurements were taken at the same points. The files were already in CMYK for printing; the LAB equivalents were computed using the profile I think best for this printing condition.

The L channel measures darkness, the lower the darker. Our samples range from 82^L to 43^L.

The A is magenta vs. green and the B is yellow vs. blue. Skin is always red, which is a combination of magenta and yellow; therefore the values are always positive in both channels. The more positive, the more colorful. As a rule, the AB are about equal, but if one is slightly higher it's more likely to be the B. One of the six samples has the two equal and one other has the

Skintone Quiz Worksheet

Here, from lightest to darkest, are typical skin values of six illustrations in this chapter. Can you match each to the figure with which it corresponds? (Answers, Page 242; if you want less of a challenge, skip ahead to Figure 9.13, where they're arranged side by side.)

1. 82L,8A,19B
2. 66L,23A,25B
3. 58L,22A,20B
4. 58L,20A,26B
5. 54L,8A,8B
6. 54L,22A,26B

Figure	Skin Value
9.1B (woman smoking, final)	
9.2A (hand advertisement, original)	
9.7A (man, original)	
9.9A (woman in red hat, original)	
9.10A (black-haired woman, original)	
9.10D (black-haired woman, final)	

imbalance at $82^L8^A19^B$. Is it a coincidence that this is also the lightest sample?

You have two choices on how to proceed. The more challenging way is to write down the Figure numbers from the worksheet on the preceding page, and go back to look at each individually. Looking at them side by side makes for an easier comparison. If you'd prefer to do that, skip ahead to Figure 9.13; it's hidden there so that those who elect the hard way won't be distracted.

We'll go over the results at the end of the chapter. Now, back to the exercise.

A Tough Guy and a Sweetheart

If you must be finished in three minutes, then treat a portrait as any other PPW exercise, except for the need to be more careful with exuberant color. Make a guess as to how much contrast to build in, and live with it.

If the portrait is worth more time, though, I suggest catering to its ambiguity by doing two versions, each with different goals. In one, go for strong detail, in the other for softness. In short, one tough guy, one sweetheart. When both are complete, consider how to blend them.

This is a liberating philosophy. If you know a second version is available, you don't have to back off anything for fear of being tasteless. Go for strong effects, and weaken them later with the other copy.

The two have to be treated differently for color. A strongly-featured face is apt to be more suntanned, more of a golden color. The softer face should be lighter and pinker, or the overall look will be unrealistic.

The initial inspection is valid for both versions. Figure 9.7A is the original. I used a threshold adjustment layer to learn that the lightest point is in the white logo at the bottom of the jacket. I wasn't sure, but thought that I might wish to blow that area out, particularly in the tough guy version. So I looked for an alternate. The next lightest point is in the left side of the jacket collar.

Now for color issues. The logo area measures $202^R205^G207^B$, indicating a flat image. It should be much lighter. Moreover, that value is $(1)^A(1)^B$, slightly cyan. The second point, on the left side of the jacket collar, is even more cyan, at $(2)^A(3)^B$. On the other side, a similar point is $(2)^A0^B$, slightly green rather than cyan.

All these values are cool, which makes little sense in a picture taken in sunlight. And it is irritating that the cast seems to get stronger going from right to left.

To further confound matters, it also seems to change as the picture gets darker. I won't give the fleshtone value because it's part of the quiz, but parts are suspiciously pink given a person of this fairly dark complexion. The dark hair, however, measures 1^A8^B, rather yellow. This can't be right, because the hair is much too dark for him to be a blond. But what color should the hair be? If we have to guess, black. Fortunately, we don't have to guess.

If there were no background, dark brown hair would be a possibility. But there *is* a background, and it provides some confirming evidence. The windows behind him are barred and the bars are dark. They are almost certainly black. Their AB values match those of the hair. I might believe that one of these two objects is dark brown, but two is too much of a coincidence to buy. I say they are both black. That doesn't mean that they'll be black in both my versions. Remember, a more golden look is desirable in the tough guy variant, the preparation of which starts now.

The Beginnings of the Tough Guy

The color situation, we've just seen, is complicated: a cool cast in the light parts and a yellow one in dark areas. Plus, the cast also moves from right to left.

Compensating for all these factors with curves is challenging enough that I reversed the normal order of things. Rather than attempting to correct the flat original for color, I took steps to open its range first. The theory was and is a good one: the farther away strategic points are from each other, the easier it will be for a curve to affect some without ruining others. So,

- On a curves adjustment layer, I adjusted the highlight in the green channel only, setting the white logo area to 255^G. I chose the green because it is key to contrast in faces, and in this version I am presupposing facial contrast to be a good thing.
- I now changed layer mode to Luminosity, producing Figure 9.11A.
- On a separate curves adjustment layer, I went to work on the color. I pushed the light half of the picture away from any coolness; I added yellow to the face and reduced it in the dark hair, without eliminating the yellowness entirely. When finished, I changed layer mode to Color, and had Figure 9.11B.

I will thank you to hold your insults about this "correction". Yes, it is well understood that the process of aging yellows the corneas, slightly desensitizing one to yellow casts. While I am not exempt from this effect, things are not yet so bad that I can't see that Figure 9.11B is too yellow. If this were my only correction pass, no way would I accept it.

But it isn't. The plan has always been to produce a second, softer version. For the one I'm currently showing, a suntanned face is a priority. That has happened; the problem is that the rest of the picture has gotten too much of what I was trying to get into the skin only. But when the second, non-yellow version becomes available, I can blend it into this one, using a layer mask to limit the impact to areas lighter than the face. Or at least, that will be one of the options, which is all it can be since I haven't gotten around to making the second version yet.

Proving again that there is more than one way to skin a cast, beta reader Marco Olivotto suggests, "You complained that the original hair was too yellow, yet it is yellower in Figure 9.11B than 9.11A. You could at least keep its original yellowness with a mask. Hair and skin live in different ranges in the B channel. Blending the softer version (as you write above) makes sense, but a B channel mask sounds like a simpler solution to me."

- I flattened the image and made a duplicate layer in preparation for luminosity moves.

The bottom of Figure 9.11 shows the three channels that were available for this task. They verify what I said earlier about the critical role of the green in faces. Ignore the darkness issue, and note how much more detail the face has in the green than in the red.

- I applied an S-shaped curve to the green to gain further facial detail. The curve could not be very strong, as otherwise it would lose too much of the jacket and the hair.
- On to the red. Blending a percentage of the newly modified green into it seems like it would work, possibly as well as the alternative I chose. I drastically lightened the midtone of the blue channel, increasing facial detail at the cost of lighter things. Doing this has little impact on overall contrast, because the blue is so much less important than the red, and vastly less than the green. However, this modified blue looked like an excellent blend source into the red. I applied it to the red at 45% opacity, using Darken mode so that the jacket, eyes, and dark collar would not lighten.
- I adjusted the light point of the resulting red, because the blend from the blue, although adding detail, had made the channel too dark. Applying a straight-line curve that simply resets the light point retained that contrast.
- Changing layer mode to Luminosity created Figure 9.12A.
- I wasn't sure whether applying the Shadows/Highlights command would help. I tried it, and it didn't. So, no change.
- And now for something you haven't seen yet. Chapter 13 introduces an interesting action known as H-K. A description is unnecessary here, but in Chapter 13 there is a recommendation not to use a certain part of it on fleshtone images, because it exaggerates wrinkles—as you can see in Figure 9.12B.

This completes the series of steps aimed at

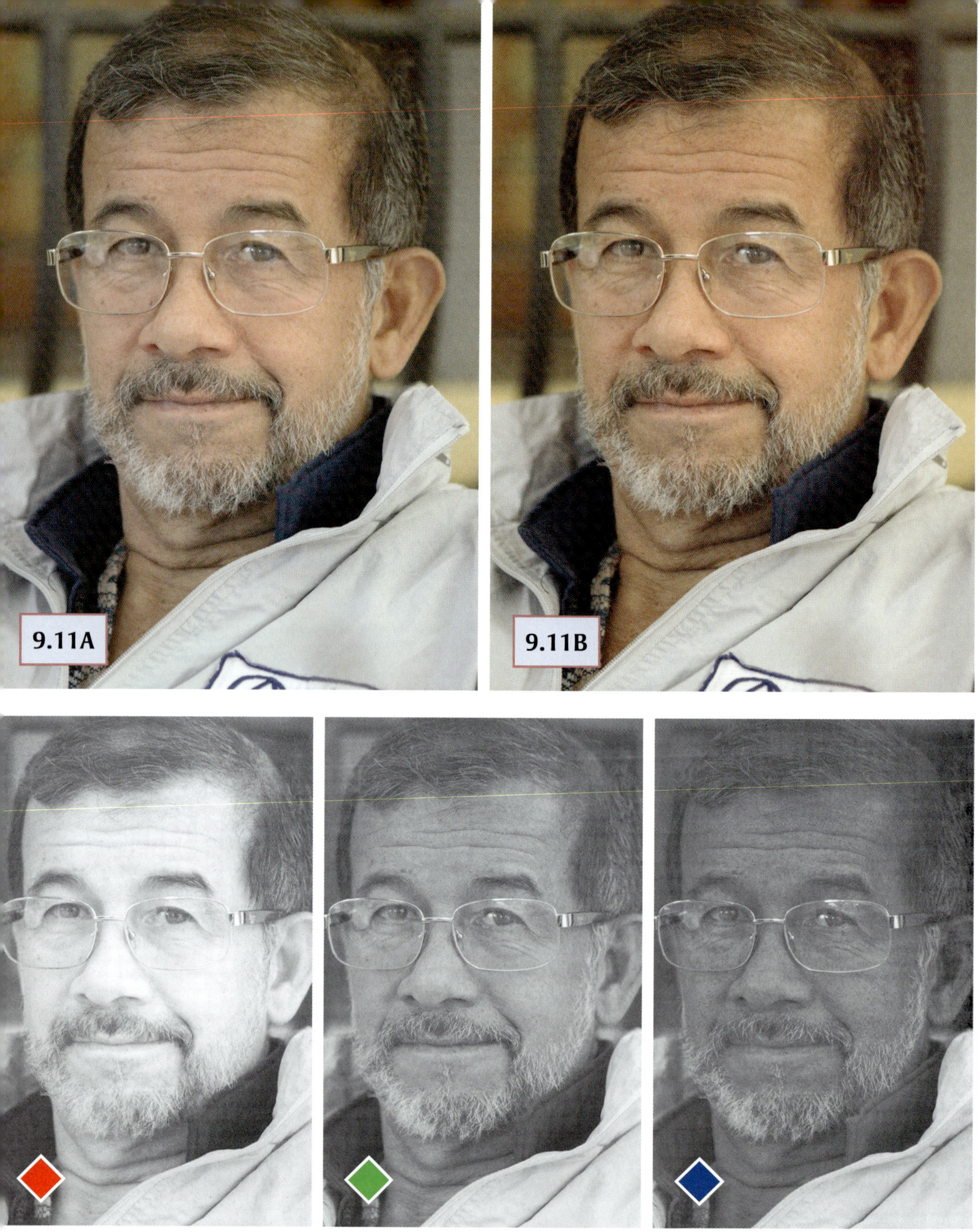

Figure 9.11 *Top left, starting with the original of Figure 9.7, a curve to the green channel on an adjustment layer lightens the highlight; the layer has been changed to Luminosity mode. Top right, a color adjustment, deliberately trying for an extreme yellowish, suntanned look. Bottom row, the channels of the top right version.*

gaining facial detail. If it seems like it was all too complex and time-consuming, it wasn't. Remember, it was understood that this run-through will not yield a final product, but rather something that will be heavily modified with a later blend. That means we don't have to be very careful, as there is much more tolerance for error. For example, I just faced a choice of channel. I wanted to blend into the red, and could have done so either with the green or the blue. If I were being careful I would try both. But with this current strategy it isn't worth the time. Either blend works, so just choose one and live with it.

Finishing this version required nothing unusual. The Skin Desaturation action was clearly necessary because even Figure 9.12B is arguably too colorful in the face. I then made a rough selection of the face only, not the hair, and ran the MMM + Color Boost action. Recall the recommendation that when running this action with faces, the MMM Luminosity layer should be disabled, for fear of exaggerating wrinkles. Naturally, I ignored this advice. I will show the final result after finishing the softer variant.

First, a brief interruption for Figure 9.13, which is a hint for the quiz you were given on Page 233. Since some people prefer not to look at it before solving the quiz, I needed to bury it someplace later in the chapter, and here is where it fell.

A Novel Way to Beat a Cast

Back to the original, Figure 9.7A, for another fast version, this time with emphasis on softness.

In principle the initial color issues are the same, except that in the last version I was looking for yellower skin and here I would like something pinker. I could certainly pick up the

***Figure 9.12** Left, channel blending and curve adjustments, reverted to Luminosity mode, add detail to Figure 9.11B. Right, the H-K action to be described in Chapter 13 adds even more depth.*

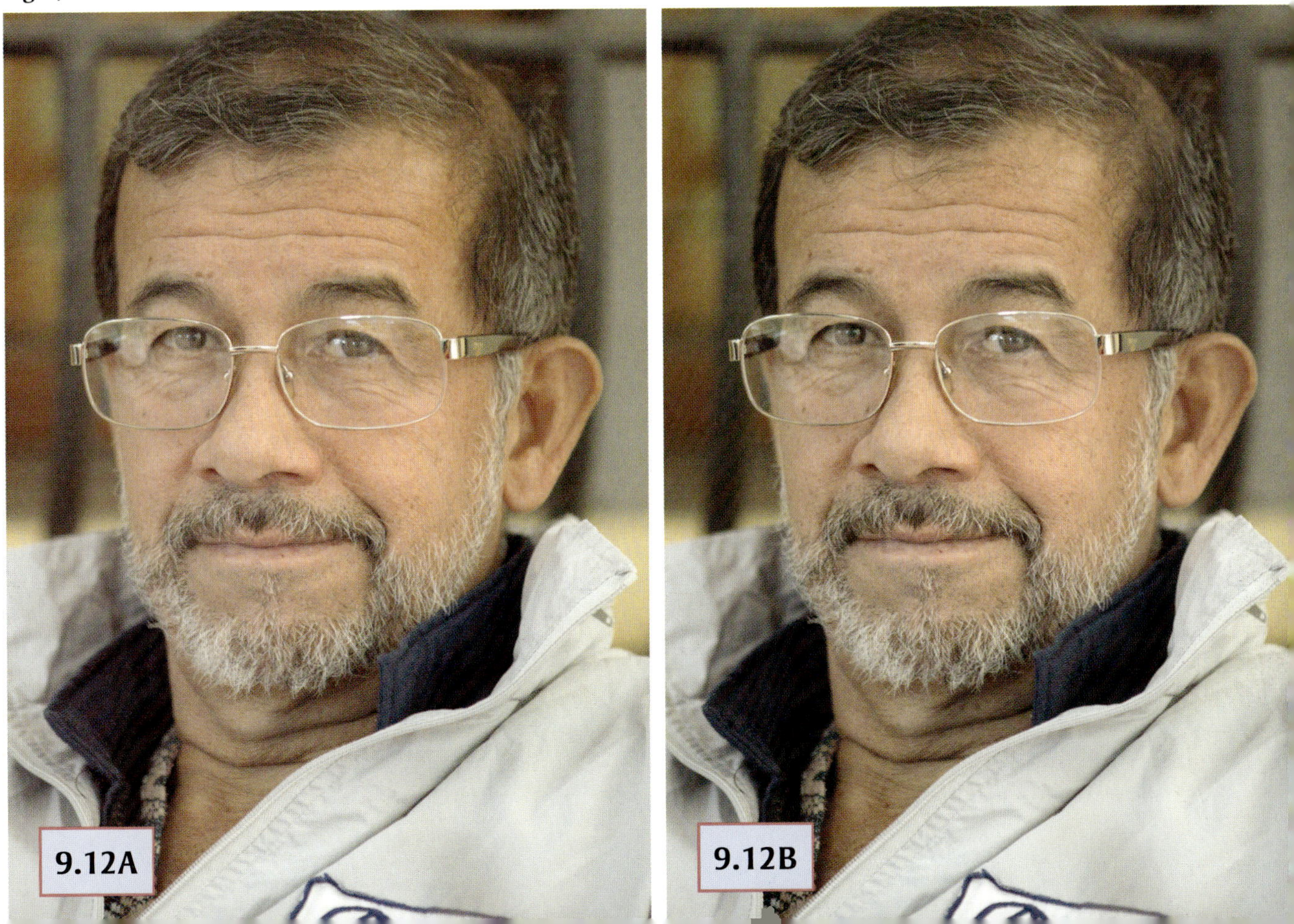

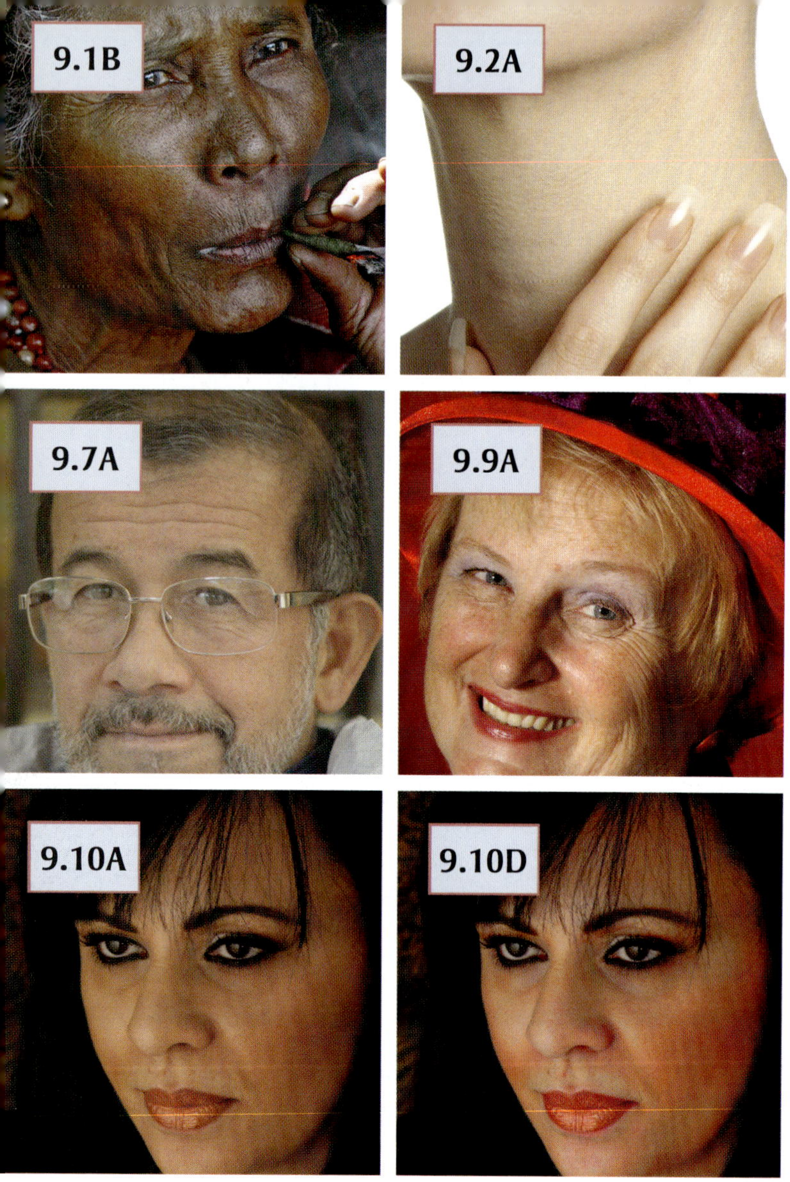

Figure 9.13 The six originals for the quiz on Page 233.

curves from the last go-round and modify them to accomplish that.

When two versions are intended from the outset, though, it pays to vary the approach. A different method, even a technically inferior one, will improve the picture if properly used, and will do so in a way that won't match the result from curves. But the two corrected versions will share certain features. What they share is presumably good. Where they differ, it's more likely to be because of an eccentricity or error. So if the two versions are blended, the result turns out better than either parent with astonishing regularity.

If you're motivated to kill a cast in a way other than with RGB curves, sensible options are to enter LAB and correct in that colorspace through a mask, or open the file in Camera Raw and use the White Balance sliders.

The method I'm about to show is a third option. It was developed for images with severe casts, of which this is not one. For portraits shot indoors in bad lighting it is extraordinarily effective. Because I can't as yet explain why that is, I was reluctant to put it in this book. But since I now have to keep the beta readers' attention as they go through the chapter a second time (see my explanation for this at Figure 9.7), I hope that this will pique their interest.

This photo is actually horizontal, cropped to fit the layout. If you download it, the following will be easier because there is a much yellower background wall to work with.

The method requires finding an area of background that shows the cast; quartertones are best, and walls are convenient places to find them. As mentioned earlier, the following technique works really well with violent casts. This one isn't, but I still have the feeling of a warm cast in spite of the cool values measured in the light areas.

- With the eyedropper tool, click the representative area of background to establish a new Foreground Color.
- Add a new or duplicate layer. Edit: Fill>Foreground Color.
- Image: Adjustments>Invert. The layer is now filled with a dark blue, rather than yellow.
- Change layer mode to Color. The result is Figure 9.14A.
- Establish a layer mask, and apply the composite RGB to it, producing Figure 9.14B.

Let's step back. The top layer is filled with a blue. It poisons the background more effectively than any other area, because this particular blue is the direct opponent of that yellow background and only an indirect opponent of, say, the face. Once layer opacity is reduced to something tolerable, the background gets more neutral, shifting it away from the face.

- In Figure 9.14C, layer opacity drops to 25%.
- Now, in principle, curves to get rid of any remaining color problems. My opinion, however, was that this color was good enough for present purposes, so I did nothing further.

So much for the initial color. The PPW normally now tries for better contrast. But the point of this version is to avoid contrast in the face, so the fancy blending of the previous try is inappropriate. Fine; that makes life easier, but we still have to establish a proper light point, because Figure 9.14C is too flat and too dark.

- I chose to lighten this file with Image: Adjustments>Exposure. I did so because it creates a slightly different result from doing it with curves. Ordinarily this is a terrible way of doing things, because Exposure applies the same correction to all channels, like a master RGB curve. Doing this torpedoes contrast in the lightest channel, here the red. Good retouchers avoid this because they don't like losing detail. Here, of course, I was pleased that the face didn't get all the shape it could in Figure 9.14D.
- Last time around, Shadows/Highlights didn't work. This time, I expected that it would, because it establishes light and dark points but

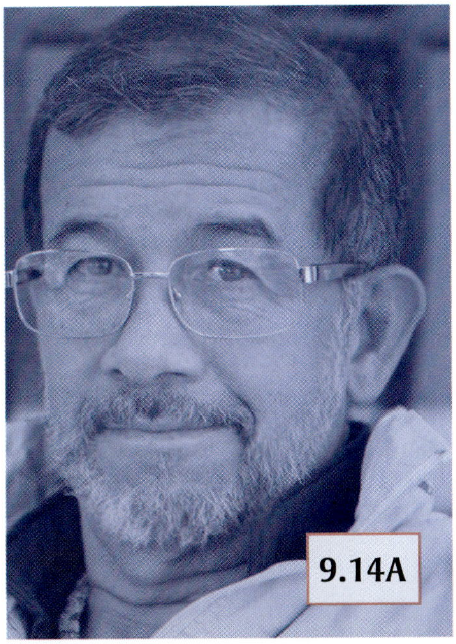

Figure 9.14 *Top left, starting with the original of Figure 9.7A, a new layer is filled with blue and set to Color mode. Top right, the RGB composite is loaded as a layer mask. Bottom left, layer opacity is reduced to 25%. Bottom center, the Exposure command lightens the file. Bottom right, the Shadows/Highlights command establishes endpoints. The original blue tint (above) is the inverse of a yellow sampled from the background (below).*

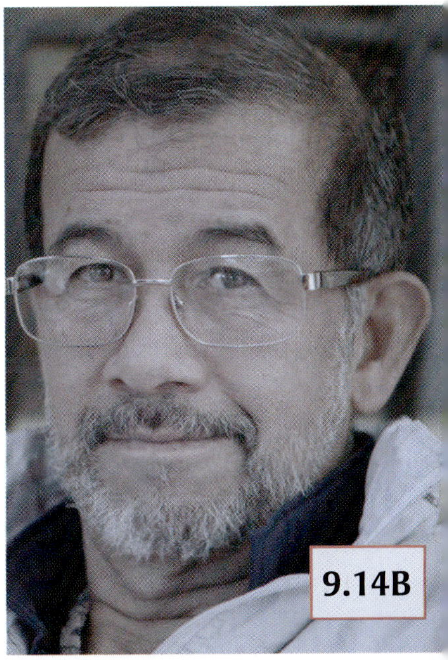

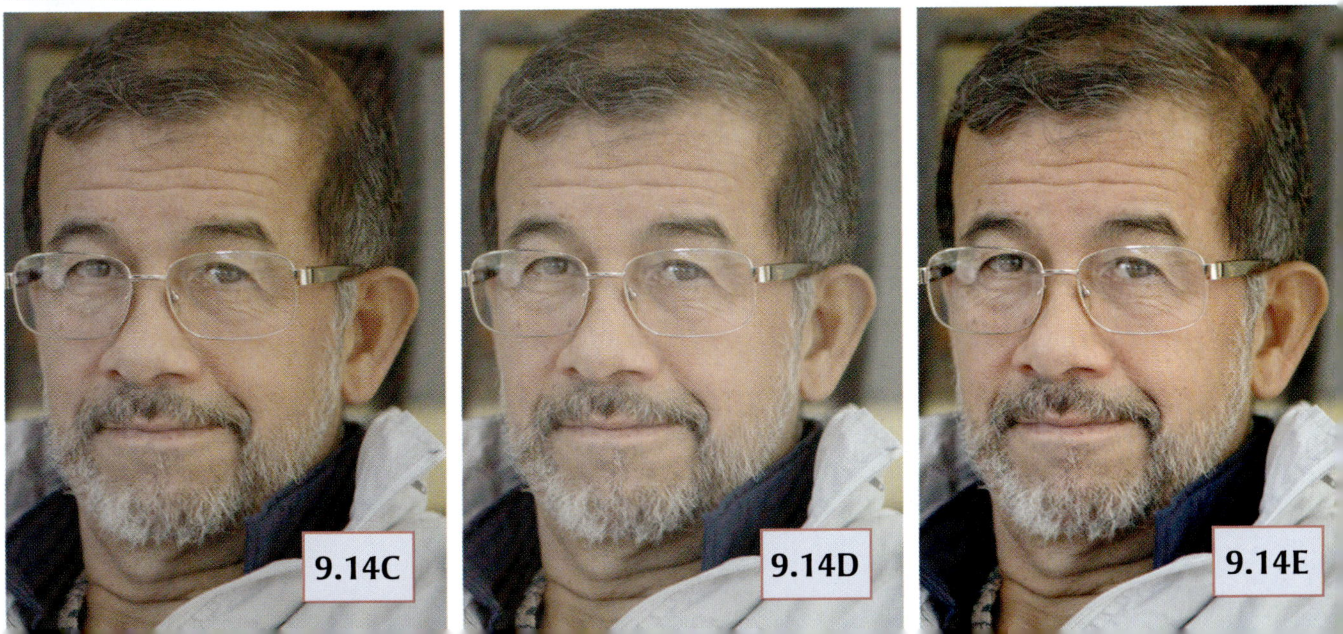

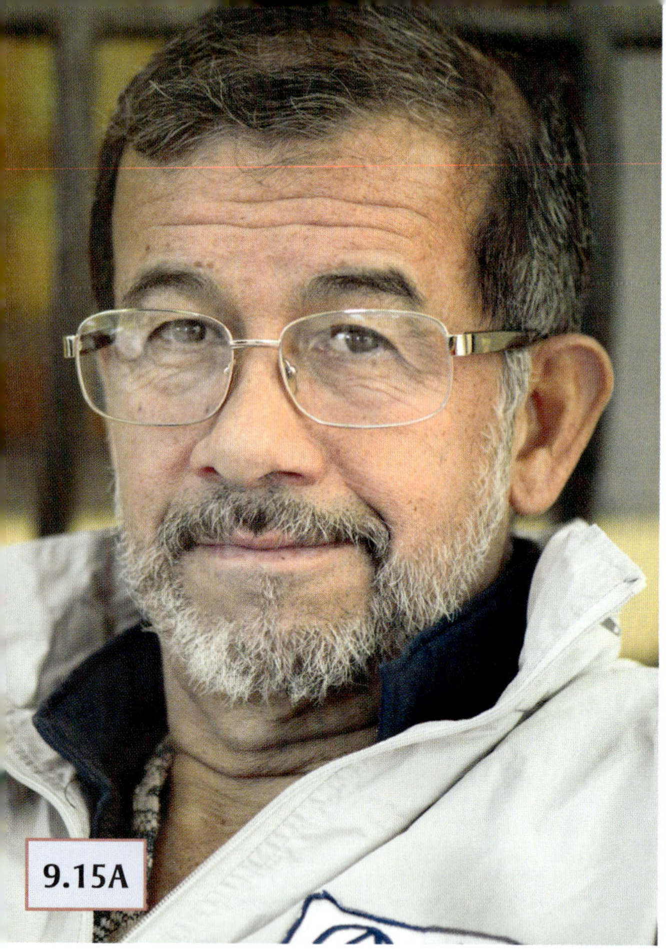

9.15A

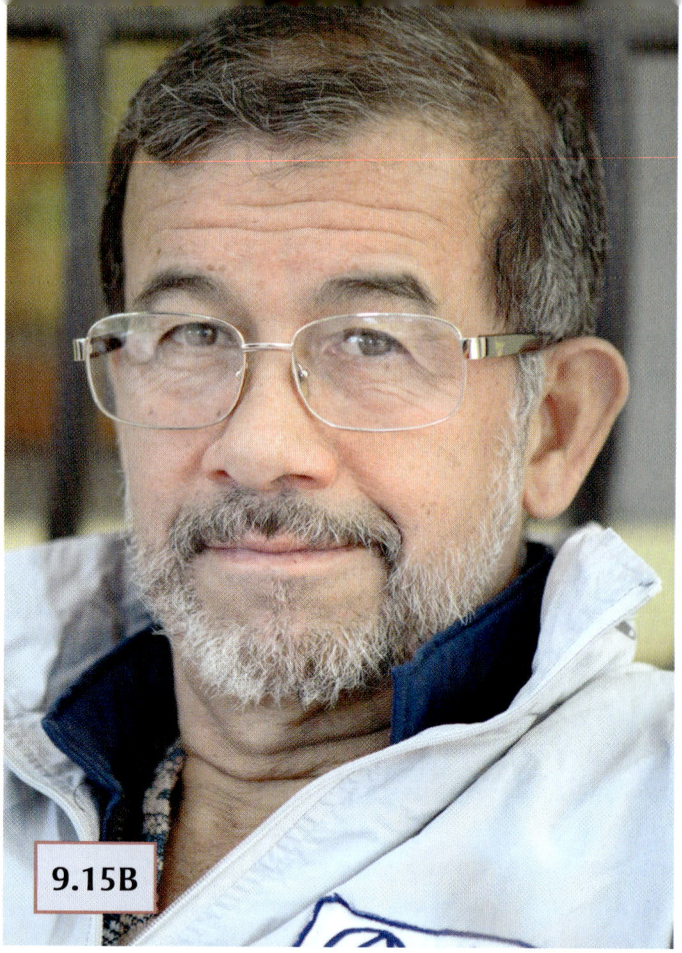

9.15B

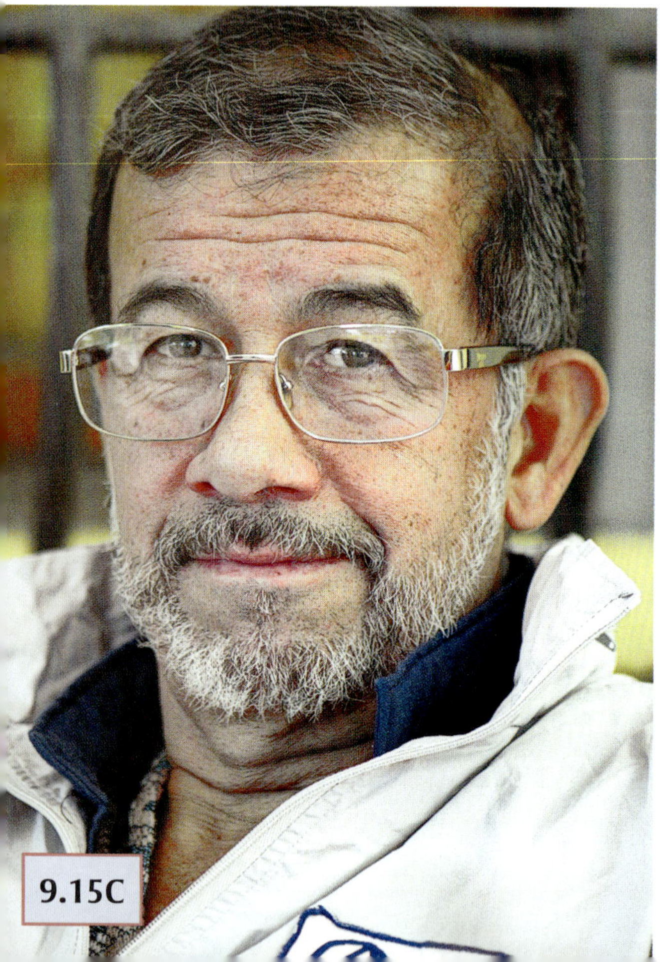

9.15C

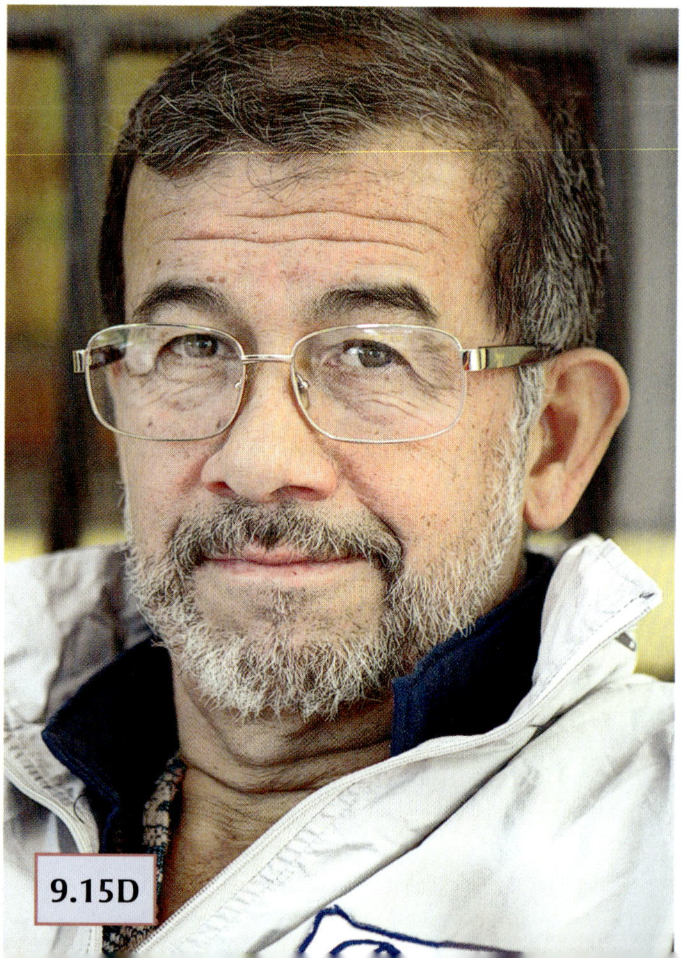

9.15D

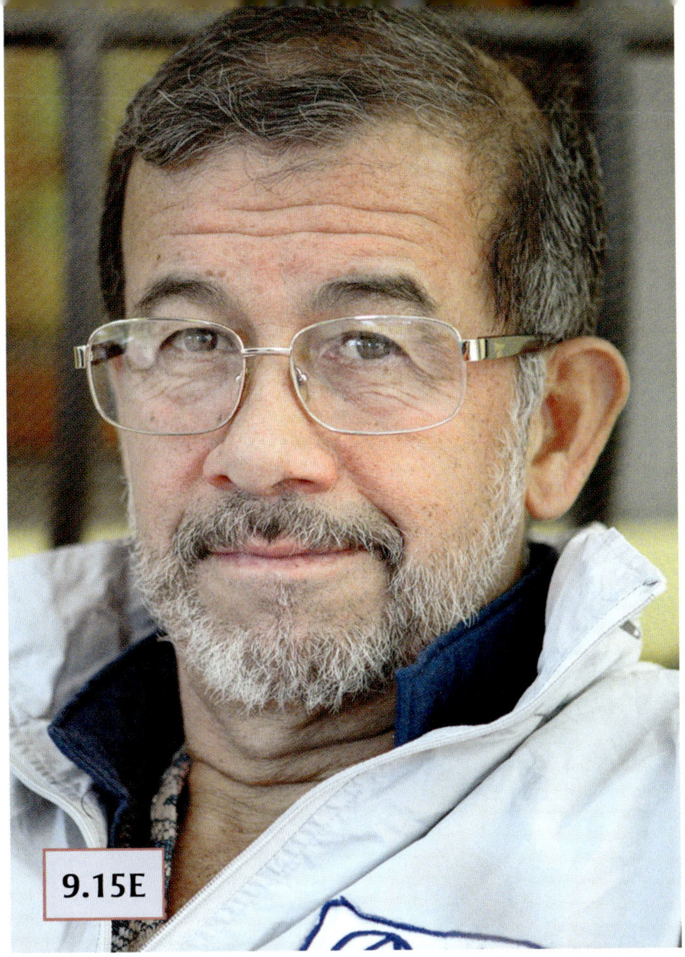

Figure 9.15 *Opposite, top row, final versions of the two corrections being discussed. Bottom row, two others prepared by a beta reader, using the same approach of one harsh and one soft image. Above, a 75–25 blend between Figures 9.15B and 9.15C.*

puts most of its impact in areas other than the face. Figure 9.14E is the PPW default result.

- With no desire to add further detail, there wasn't much left to do except run the Skin Desaturation action and do the usual things in MMM + Color Boost, remembering to turn MMM Luminosity off this time. So much for the grunt work. The two files are ready to merge.

The Best of Two Extremes

Figure 9.15A is the final, color-added version of the tough guy image we last saw in Figure 9.12B. Its counterpart, the softer version with color enhancement added, is Figure 9.15B. To round things out are two versions submitted by one of the beta readers. I don't know what methods he used, but the idea was the same. Figure 9.15C is his tough guy, 9.15D his softer version.

In evaluating these we cannot be deluded by first impressions. Figure 9.15C is hideous, but for its purpose, it's better than my Figure 9.15A. It features interesting color variation and a boatload of facial detail, mostly objectionable. It is extreme, but that just means it will be blended at a lower opacity.

On the other hand, his soft version is poor. Age spots are highlighted and wrinkles are more exaggerated than in my Figure 9.15B, which appears to portray a younger man.

When I united my two versions, I split the contrast 50–50 between them. For color, though, I understandably went 75–25 in favor of Figure 9.15B. The result of these blends has already been shown in Figure 9.7B.

The beta reader didn't provide a combined version, so I had to be his proxy. The blend was nasty because of the excessive detail in the softer version, Figure 9.15D, which I used for a base. I held my nose and added Figure 9.15C on a luminosity layer at 35% opacity. Then I copied Figure 9.15C to a third layer and changed mode to Color. I was not able to use a big opacity because the lips were getting too red. So I added a layer mask, applied the RGB composite to it to prevent darker areas from getting too colorful, and set opacity to 50%. The result was shown earlier as Figure 9.7C.

The Bottom Line

Fleshtone images are suitable for the PPW but two issues must be kept in mind. First, we have almost no tolerance for additional red. To avoid this, an action desaturates fleshtones.

Second, extra detail can make people look older or possibly even less healthy, but it can also make them look stronger or more distinguished. Before starting any portrait, decide whether you want that strong look. If you don't, avoid channel blending and curves that would enhance contrast in the skin.

As noted earlier, Figures 9.7B and 9.7C both beat out competition from people who used one-pass workflows. Yet we can do better. I offer Figure 9.15E as another vote for doing multiple versions. It's a simple 75–25 split between my Figure 9.15B and the reader's Figure 9.15C.

Answers to the Quiz

You were asked to choose values for six illustrations featuring five individuals.

I would try to narrow things down. I notice that the lightest choice (remember, in LAB, the greater the L, the lighter) is a full 16^L away from its closest rival. That's huge, considering that it's more than the difference between the second lightest and the very darkest of the six (14^L). Apparently one of our six contestants is much lighter than the other five. Without a doubt, it's the original hand picture, Figure 9.2A.

On the other side, a layperson would surely say that the corrected Vietnamese woman of Postcard 9.1 is by far the darkest of the six. But, confound it, the quiz box alleges that one other is just as dark, at 54^L.

Even if you believe that it's a typo, there is no problem. Of the remaining images, the uncorrected woman of Figure 9.10A is definitely darkest. Her skin is red, much more colorful than the brown of the other. Her AB values must be much higher, further away from 0^A0^B, more saturated.

Answers to Skintone Quiz
(Page 233)

Following are the matchups of figure numbers in this chapter with their typical skintone values. The numbers in parentheses are those of the worksheet.

9.1B: 54L,8A,8B (5)	9.9A: 66L,23A,25B (2)
9.2A: 82L,8A,19B (1)	9.10A: 54L,22A,26B (6)
9.7A: 58L,22A,20B (3)	9.10D: 58L,20A,26B (4)

No sweat is needed to deduce that the Vietnamese woman is $54^L8^A8^B$ and the other woman $54^L22^A26^B$. If you would like to know why the Info palette defies logic by saying the two are of equal darkness, there are three reasons.

First, one woman has extremely black hair, far darker than her skin. Simultaneous contrast causes us to perceive the skin as lighter, differentiating it from the hair.

Second, in Chapter 13 we will discuss a phenomenon known as the Helmholtz-Kohlrausch Effect, which causes us to perceive colored objects as lighter than more neutral ones that an instrument thinks are of the same darkness.

And third, one version is corrected while the other is flat. We do a little highlight-setting in our own minds and again perceive the flesh as being lighter than the Info palette does.

Anyway, we're down to three, the corrected version of the black-haired woman (Figure 9.10D), and the originals of the seated man (9.7A) and the woman in the red hat (9.9A). The remaining values are $66^L23^A25^B$, $58^L22^A20^B$, and $58^L20^A26^B$. Several approaches would solve the puzzle. I would point out that the B usually is higher than the A in skin. In one of these, the opposite is true. That one should seem significantly more pink than the other two. I say it's the man. And since the black-haired woman is surely darker-skinned than the woman in the red hat, there is no difficulty with the final two choices.

One last point about variation. Almost any layperson would call the corrected woman, Figure 9.10D, more colorful than the original, Figure 9.10A. The numbers say she is slightly *less* so. Color variation into a face cons the viewer into perceiving more color overall. This is one reason for the Skin Desaturation action.

The quiz wasn't difficult. Working with fleshtones is. It also offers no end of rewards.

10

The Bigger Hammer

Exceptional images demand exceptional techniques. The Shadows/Highlights command is a convenient solution for enhancing detail in the lightest and darkest parts of the image. But for some pictures the need is more critical, and a more powerful tool is required.

There was once a plumber who announced that he needed to add only two tools to make his chest complete: a bigger hammer, and a bigger wrench.

I have often felt the same way about color correction. Postcard 10.1 displays many of the improvements that are typical of the PPW. Depth has been added, as has color variation in the critical parts. The tree is slightly greener.

The biggest difference between the original and the corrected version, though, is in the water, which has dramatically better detail.

This is the type of image that was referred to menacingly as Category Three in Chapter 7. I said then that more than half of all pictures benefit from added detail in shadows and highlights, hence the recommendation to apply the eponymous Photoshop command. But I suggested doing so at fixed settings, because the benefit was so small that it doesn't justify a lot of time.

Every now and then, though, something like Postcard 10.1 comes along. If the focus is interesting cloud formation, or smoke, or a snowy landscape, or a white animal, the methods of Chapter 7 no longer suffice. Instead of an area where correction is of only minor interest, we get something so crucial that the whole effort can be regarded as a failure if it isn't enhanced adequately. Shadows/Highlights, even at very strong settings, isn't up to this kind of challenge. A bigger hammer is needed.

As with most PPW techniques, this one can be automated. The action provided is no walk in the park but it's more comprehensible than, say, MMM. We only apply it to a minority of images, but when we do it can be spectacularly successful. We'll take a quick look at its fundamentals, along

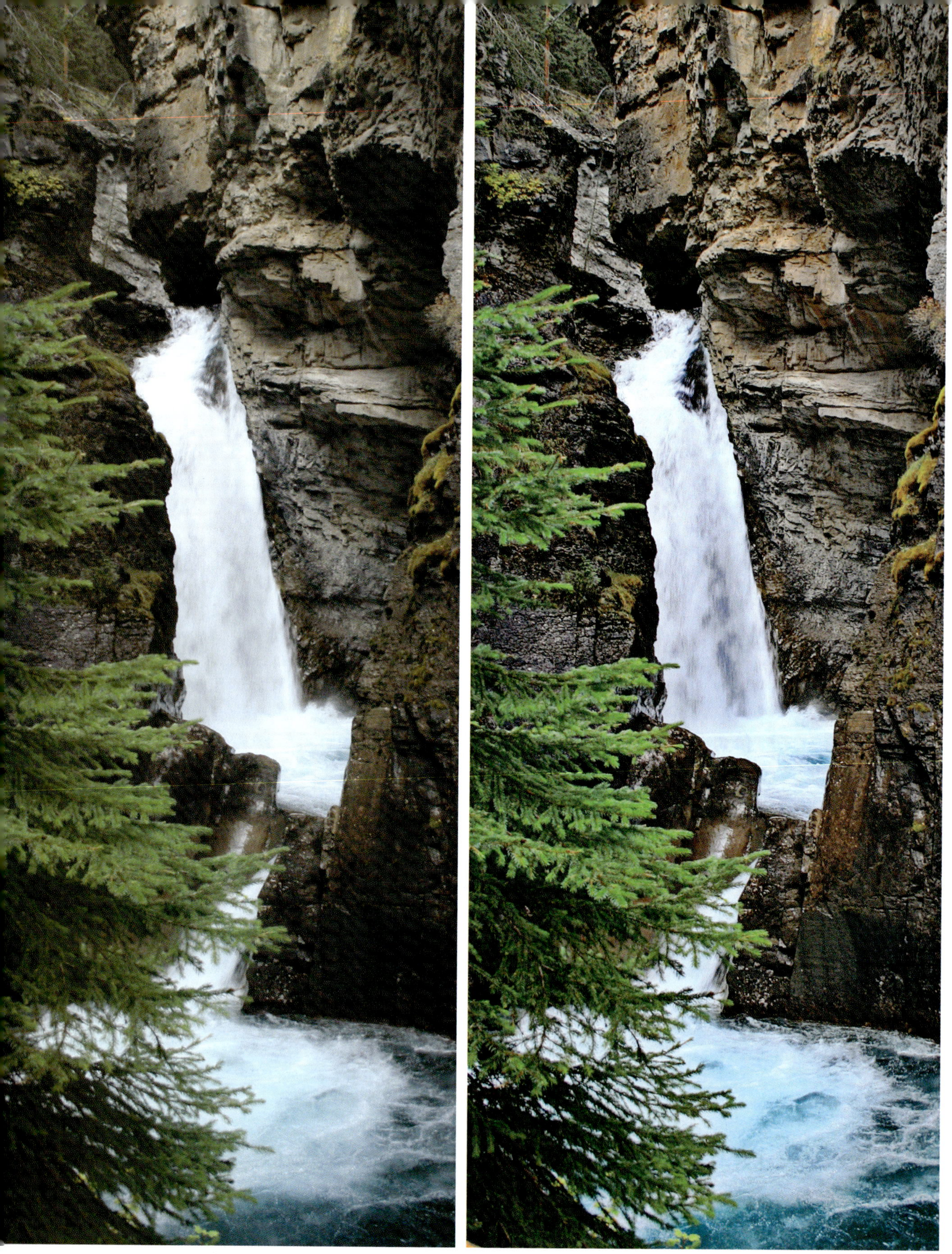

Postcard 10.1 *Sunwapta Falls, Alberta, Canada. The Bigger Hammer action creates strong detail in the water.*

with the two basic ways of modifying the action. As usual, we'll go into more depth in the second half.

Footprints in the Sand

If you agree that the sand is too light and needs greatly enhanced detail, Figure 10.2A is a picture that might need a Bigger Hammer. We will dip toes in the water first with a hypothetical method, and then jump in with the real thing.

Figure 10.2B is a negative version, Image, Adjustments>Invert, which seems a silly way to begin. It goes on a layer with the uninverted original underneath.

We now change the mode of the aforementioned inverted layer from Normal to Overlay. In this mode, if the top layer is light, it lightens what's underneath. If dark, it darkens, and if neither it does nothing.

In the inverted layer the beach is dark, therefore it darkens that part of the picture. The foreground tree, inverted, is light, therefore it lightens. The result, Figure 10.2C, is encouraging, but not particularly good.

When merging two layers of radically different darknesses, which these two, being opposites, surely are, a massive blur is needed somewhere. Here, I just applied Filter: Blur> Gaussian Blur with a big Radius to the inverted file, still on its overlay layer.

Figure 10.2D, the result, is an improvement but has two flaws. First, although it shows more detail, the color is too dull. Second, while the beach now looks nice, the effect in the shadows seems exaggerated.

So much for hypothetical. We will now start from scratch and do things properly.

The color problem occurs because the inverted overlay darkens everything that's light and lightens everything dark, and does so channel by channel. That is all well and good in the waterfall, which is light in every channel. But the lightest parts of the trees are light in the green channel and dark in the red and blue. The overlay darkens the green and lightens the red and blue. In other words, it moves the three closer to equality. As we know, R=G=B makes a gray. These greens haven't become exactly gray, but they are grayer than they were originally.

The problem is evaded by neutralizing the overlay itself. That way, it either lightens all channels or darkens them all. Colors that change will become either darker and richer, or lighter and cleaner. Either alternative is usually better than grayer.

There are two basic approaches to making the overlay neutral. We could proceed as previously, with an inverted copy of the RGB file, to which we would apply Image: Adjustments>Desaturate, a conversion of the RGB to grayscale, or one of many substantially equivalent commands. Second, we could use an inverted copy of a single channel.

If you choose the second approach, any channel could be the best. If you have to take a guess without seeing the picture, then the best guess is to use an inverted copy of the red channel. That's what the action uses by default, although if you have the PPW panel you can change it.

The Steps of the Action

If you have decided that the picture warrants the Bigger Hammer, the recommended time to apply is right after Shadows/Highlights and before entering LAB. If you would like to emulate the action, do the following, starting with a flattened RGB file.

- Make three duplicate layers in addition to the background. From the top, the layers are named Unblurred, Darkening Layer, Overlay Layer_Red (if you are using the panel and choose a different channel as the inverted overlay, the name of this layer changes accordingly), and Background.
- Activate the Overlay Layer. Image: Apply Image, Layer=irrelevant, Channel=Red, Blending=Normal, Opacity=100%, Invert checked.

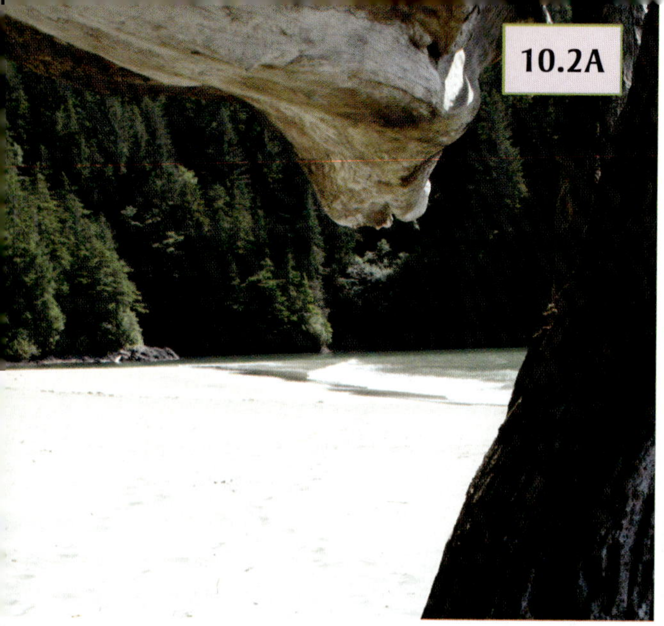
10.2A

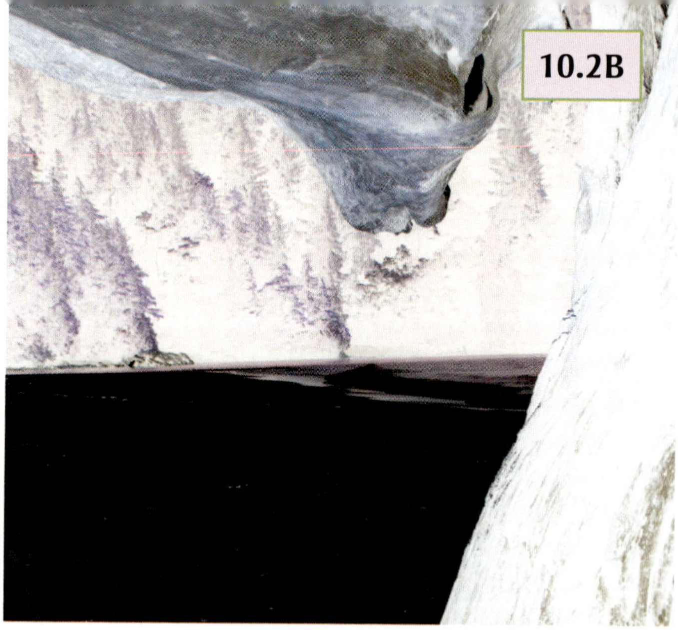
10.2B

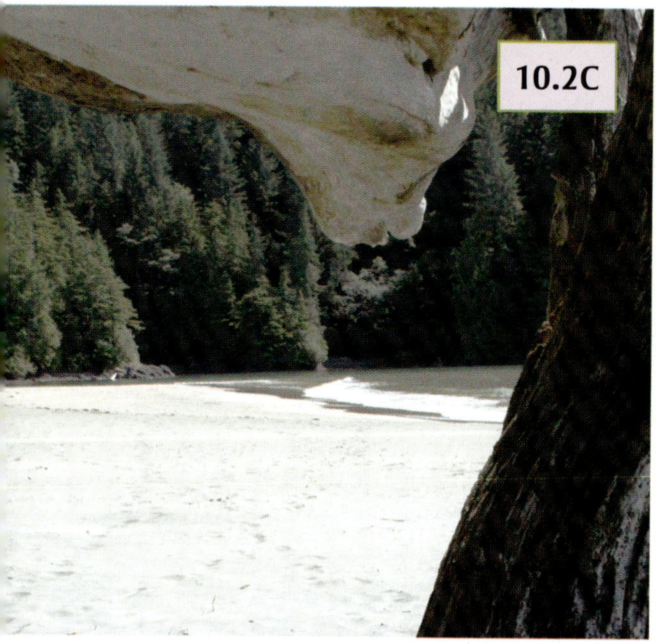
10.2C

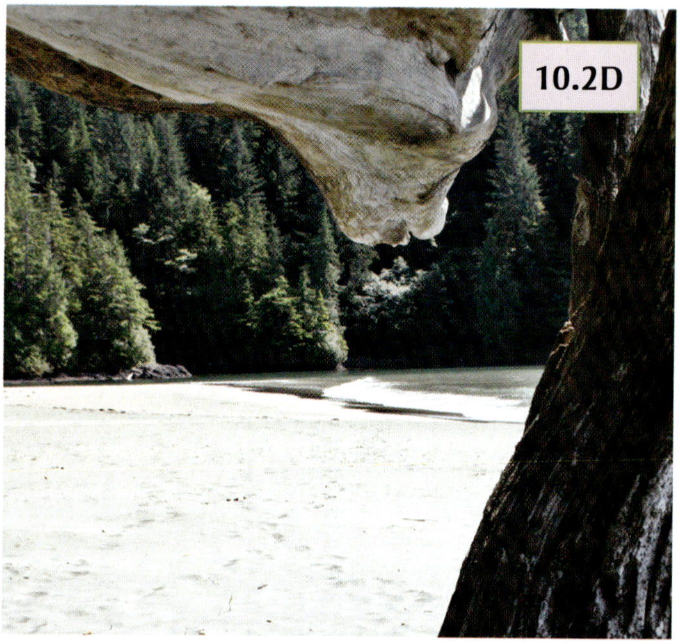
10.2D

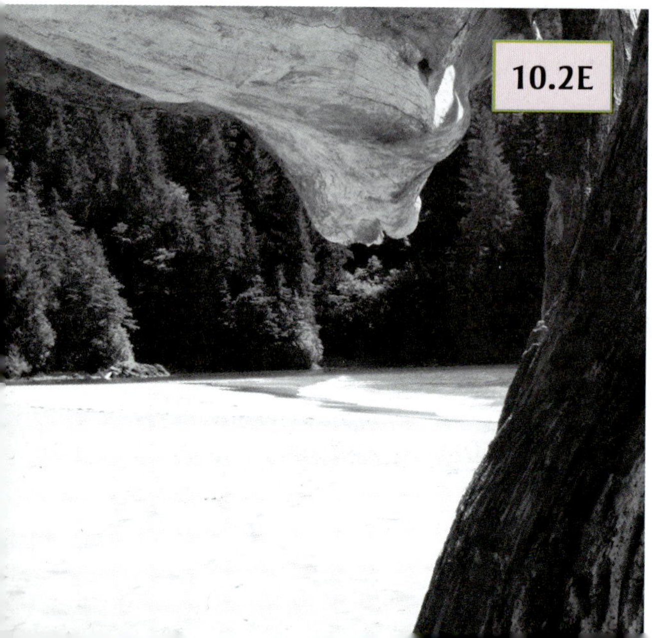
10.2E

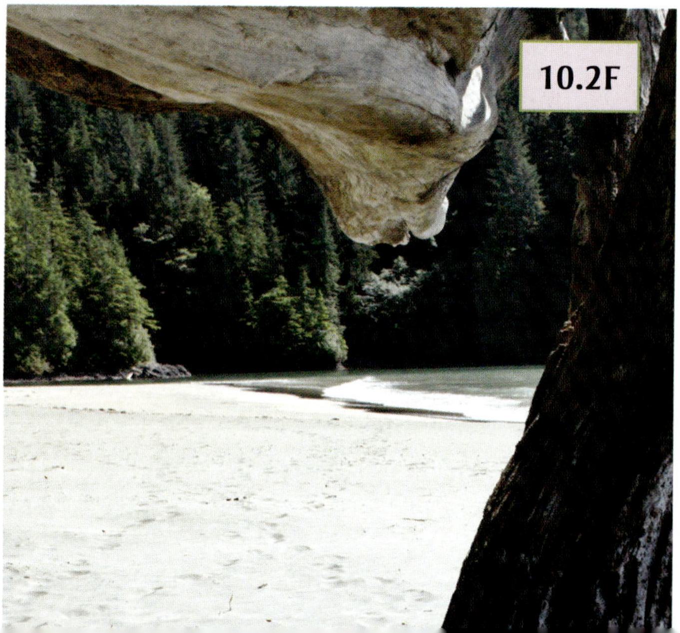
10.2F

- Change layer mode to Overlay.
- Activate the Darkening layer. Change mode to Darker Color (Photoshop CS3 and higher; with earlier versions, substitute Darken) and opacity to 50%.
- Activate the Unblurred layer, but make it invisible by clicking off the eye icon.
- To it, Image: Apply Image, Layer=Merged, Channel=RGB, Blending=Normal, Opacity=100%, Invert unchecked.
- Return to the overlay layer. Filter: Blur: Gaussian Blur, Radius=35.0 pixels.

Figure 10.2E shows the red channel of Figure 10.2A, the original. Figure 10.2F is the result of running the action. It's similar to Figure 10.2D, but better because of the added color and weight in the background trees.

* * *

The particulars of the foregoing steps were chosen because I think them the most likely to be correct sight unseen. Naturally, they sometimes aren't optimal. But if you wish to do better, the image has to be important enough to justify experimentation. Therefore, exploration of the following questions is hereby put off until the second half.

- When is an inverted red channel the wrong choice for the overlay?
- What happens if we alter the Radius value, or use a different filter altogether?
- What is the point of the invisible fourth unblurred layer?

* * *

Excluding the above still leaves a couple of easy options in the form of the opacity sliders on the middle two layers.

- The darkening layer reacts to the reality that the shadow enhancement is usually (but not always) too strong in relation to the highlight move, So by default, it moves the shadows halfway back to the original. If set to 100% opacity, it eliminates all lightening while allowing the beach or waterfall or whatever to darken all it likes. This usually

***Figure 10.2** (opposite). Top left, the original. Top right, a copy inverted while still in RGB. Middle left, the inverted copy is applied to the original in Overlay mode. Middle right, instead, the inverted copy is heavily blurred before being applied. Bottom left, the red channel of the original. Bottom right, the default result of the Bigger Hammer action.*

Chapter Goals and Recap

The Bigger Hammer method is for cases where highlight and/or shadow detail is critical. It supplements the work of the Shadows/Highlights command.

The method places an inverted, heavily blurred channel on a layer set to Overlay mode. Doing so greatly increases detail in the lightest and darkest regions of the photo.

An action is supplied whose defaults usually work well. The second half of the chapter discusses how to fine-tune them, if necessary.

How Difficult Is It? Moderately if you stick to the basics. This kind of enhancement is often so important, however, that you may wish to investigate some of the more complex variants in the second half.

How Often Is It Needed? Less frequently than any other workflow step.

The PPW Takes Shape

COLOR

- Kill incorrect color with RGB curves (Chapter 3).
- Identify highlight (Chapters 3–4).

CONTRAST

- Channel blending on luminosity layer (Chapter 4).
- Contrast-enhancing curves (Chapter 4).
    - Consider S/H command (Chapter 7).
    - Consider the Bigger Hammer (this chapter).
    - Consider boost to sky (Chapter 8).

COLOR AGAIN

- Desaturate skintone, if any (Chapter 9).
- Apply MMM + Color Boost action (Chapters 5–6).
- Finalize contrast, including endpoints.
- Reduce color by masking or opacity adjustment.

SHARPEN

FINALIZE

- Consider blend with another version (Chapter 2).
- Convert to final output space, if needed.

looks artificial, but setting opacity to 0% is often just as bad because it can put so much detail into dark areas that they start to look eerie. The default is therefore 50%—but it's easy to try other settings.

- Without the overlay layer the Bigger Hammer action does nothing. The darkening layer is a copy of the original, and the unblurred layer is invisible. Deactivate the overlay layer and you're back at square one. Similarly, if you like the effect but think it's too much, reduce the overlay layer opacity.

Some Things Are Written in Stone

The instant the waterfall of Postcard 10.1 opens we should be thinking of the Bigger Hammer. Figure 10.2, the beach, might take a second or two longer for the realization to sink in.

If you save the Bigger Hammer for obvious situations like these, however, you're missing opportunities.

The stone memorial of Figure 10.3 isn't as clear a candidate as the other two. It does, however, have important shadow and, to a lesser extent, highlight detail. So I would give the Bigger Hammer a try.

The default result, Figure 10.4A, is encouraging. The inscription is more legible. I would be willing to accept the improvement as is and move on, but it might be worth investigating other possibilities.

The Darkening layer has been disabled in Figure 10.4B by changing its opacity from the default 50% to 0%. I'd split the difference, as I consider Figure 10.4A too dark and 10.4B too light.

I have another objection, though. The foreground bench is the cognate of the waterfall of Postcard 10.1 and the beach of Figure 10.2. Each is the lightest significant part of the image. The difference is that the waterfall and the beach were also the most important objects in their respective pictures.

This bench is not. The focus of this picture should be the memorial and, secondarily, the flowers. Bench detail is a distraction. My solution is Figure 10.4C. The Darkening layer remains off but the overlay layer goes from 100% to 50% opacity. This cuts the highlight gain in half and produces a softer bench.

The decision is image-specific, even if we limit the discussion to stone memorials. Figure 10.5A's uses material of roughly the same texture and darkness. But this time the added pop in the highlights is welcome. It makes the text more readable in Figure 10.5B, the Bigger Hammer's defaults.

Having an action makes it easy to test doubtful cases: if it doesn't work, cancel it. In moving from Figure 10.5C to 10.5D, the Bigger Hammer brings out detail in the sunny areas and also in the dark greenery. Between Figures 10.5E and 10.5F the girl's clothing has picked up some useful weight in its lighter areas and in the sky.

Figure 10.5 therefore shows originals of three distinct categories. The question now is what to do with each, understanding that we still haven't hit the color enhancement

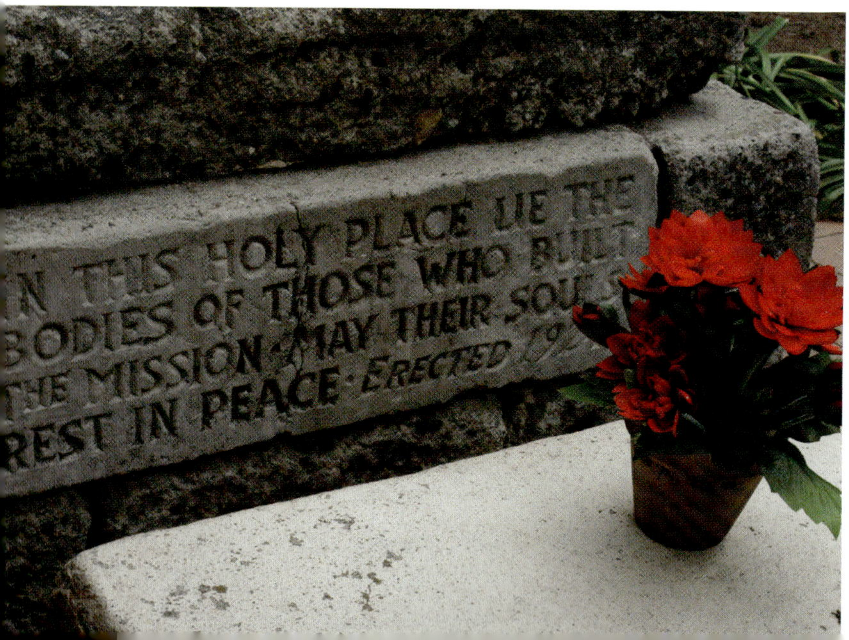

***Figure 10.3** A memorial in Mission San Juan Capistrano, California.*

step. Personally, I would probably leave Figure 10.5B alone. The light stone in Figure 10.5D seems overdone but I like what is happening to the greenery. I would probably use the move shown in Figure 10.4C, eliminating the Darkening Layer while reducing opacity of the Overlay Layer. And in Figure 10.5F I would reduce overlay opacity only.

These decisions are matters of taste. However, I trust we agree that the Bigger Hammer was beneficial in all three cases. The question is, how do we identify such pictures? The waterfall that dominates Postcard 10.1 screams out for the Bigger Hammer regardless of the rest of the scene. But do you see what all the other photos have in common?

Sun, Shade, and the Camera

The five pictures that start with Figure 10.2 all were taken on sunny days. Strong shadows (literal, not graphic arts definition) are being cast in each.

Cameras and humans perceive

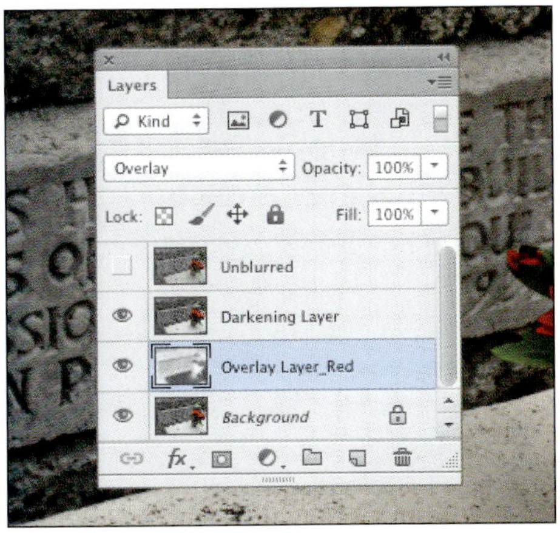

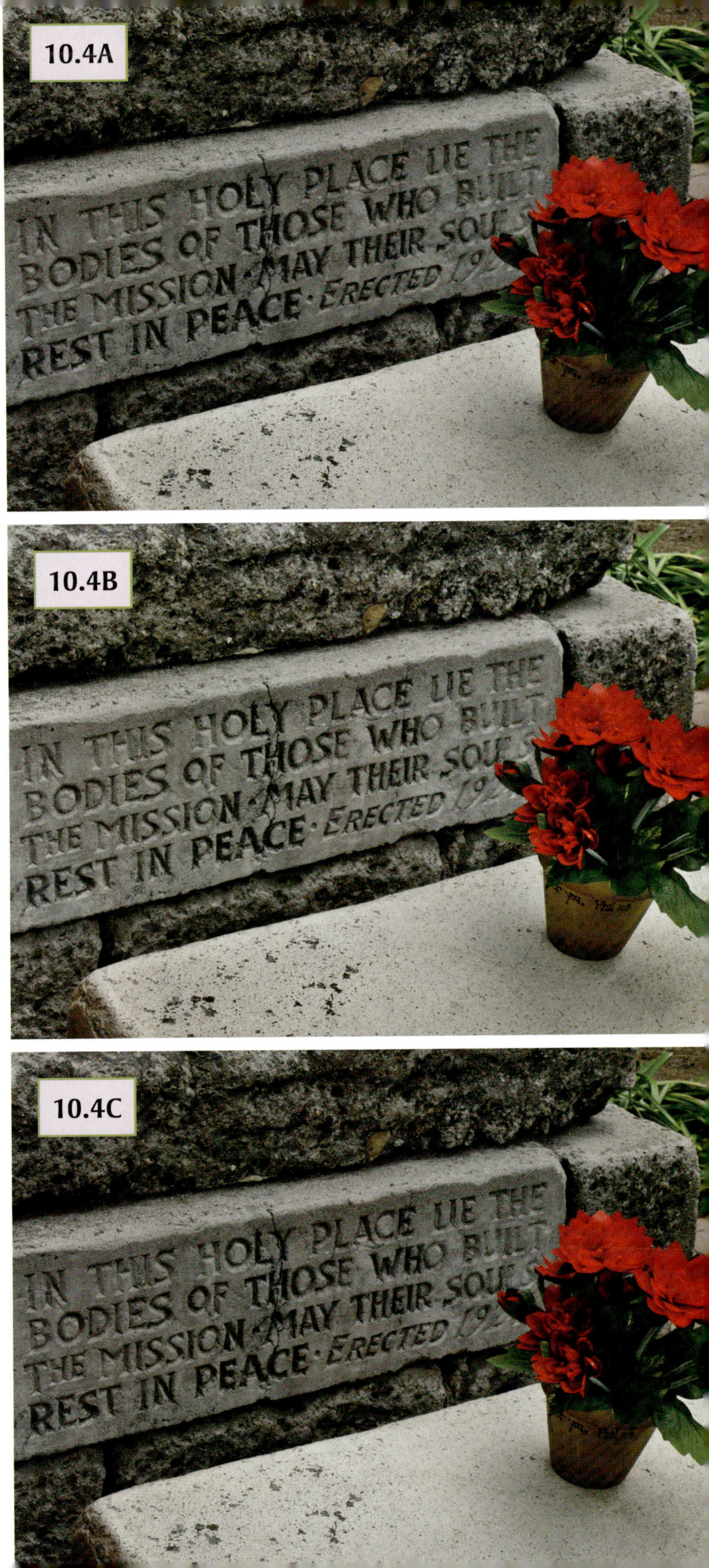

Figure 10.4 Top, a default application of the Bigger Hammer action. Middle, the Darkening Layer is disabled. Bottom, with the Darkening Layer still off, opacity of the Overlay Layer is reduced to 50%.

such scenes differently. Members of our species don't like to be blinded by reflected light, so we have a filtering mechanism that causes us to perceive such areas as darker—as quartertones, usually. We don't trust objects that are hidden by darkness, so we devote extra resources to resolving them, resources that are not clearly understood and that a camera does not possess.

Look again at the three photos of Figure 10.5. In each case, the two halves—sun and shade—have been brought closer together. The lighting seems more uniform.

The concept of reducing the difference between two halves of an image is not limited to sun and shade, although that's the most obvious case. Our next three chapters study ways of improving such situations; the Bigger Hammer is but a small part.

Much of the fascination of color correction comes from the feeling that just when we know what it's all about, some new complication rears its head. It's time to close out this half of the chapter with the most difficult correction in the book so far. What is your strategy for dealing with Figure 10.6?

Happy and Unhappy Times

This raging fire is to appear in a daily newspaper. My earlier statement that it is difficult is no mere speculation. The image has been a required exercise in my advanced courses since 2006. I have seen nearly a hundred versions of it, many prepared by some of the best retouchers in the world. The rules prohibit use of selections and local retouching. Class evaluations rate it as one of the half-dozen or so most valuable experiences in the entire

***Figure 10.5** None of these three originals is an obvious candidate for the Bigger Hammer, but all seem to benefit to some degree. The right-hand versions of each show default Bigger Hammer settings.*

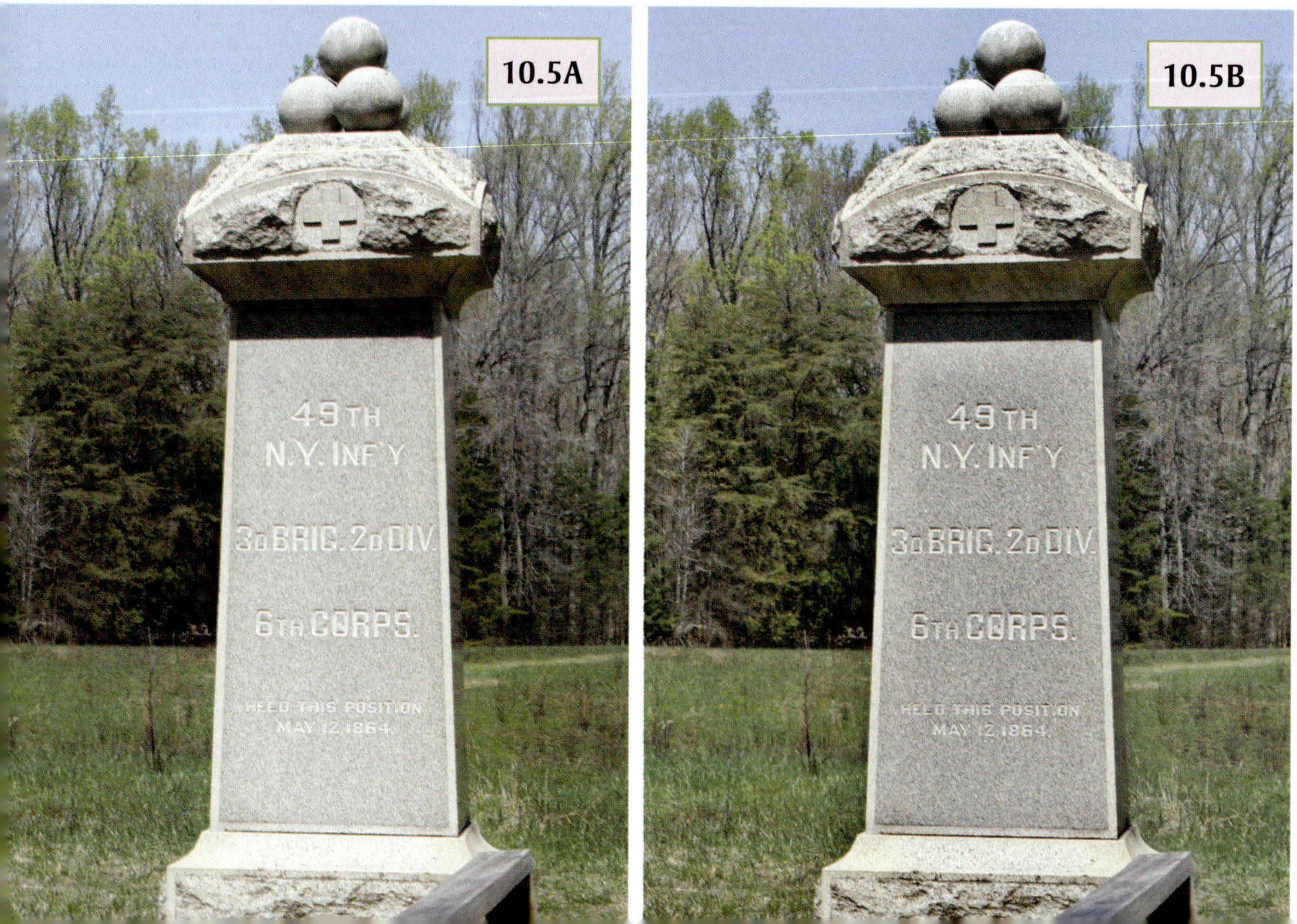

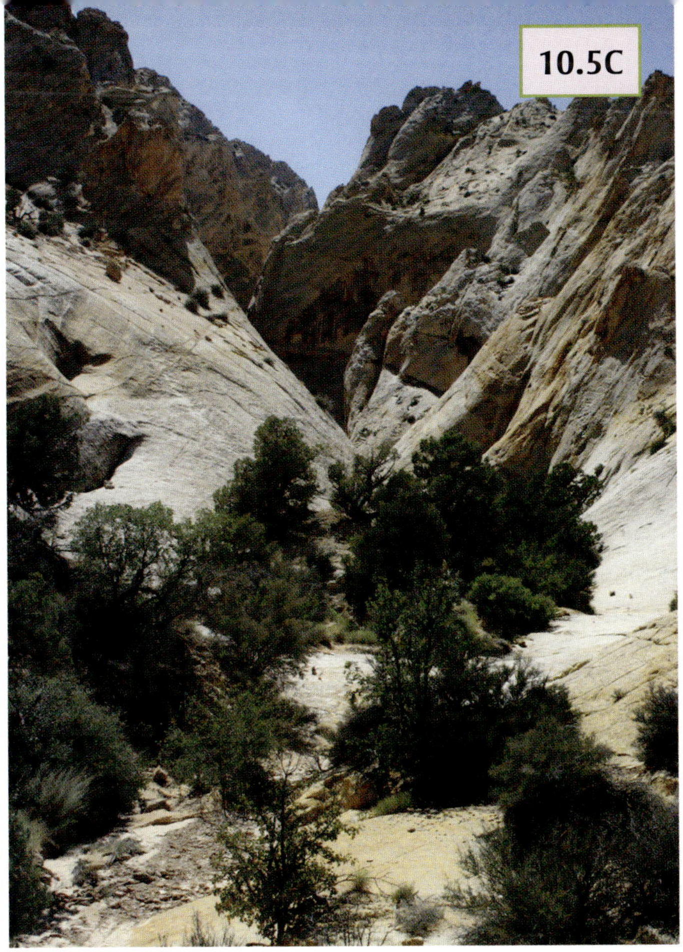

10.5C

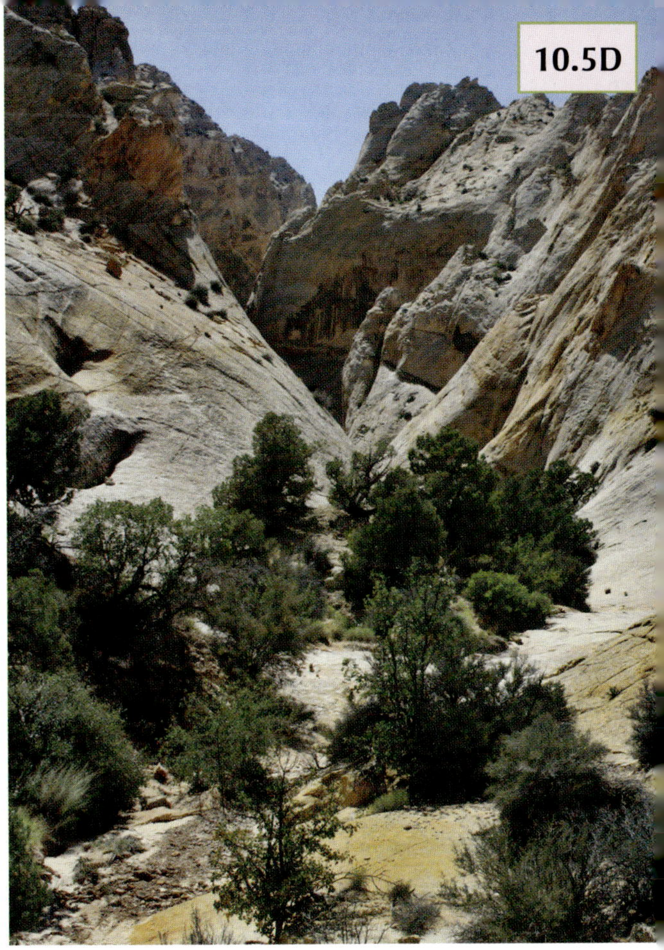

10.5D

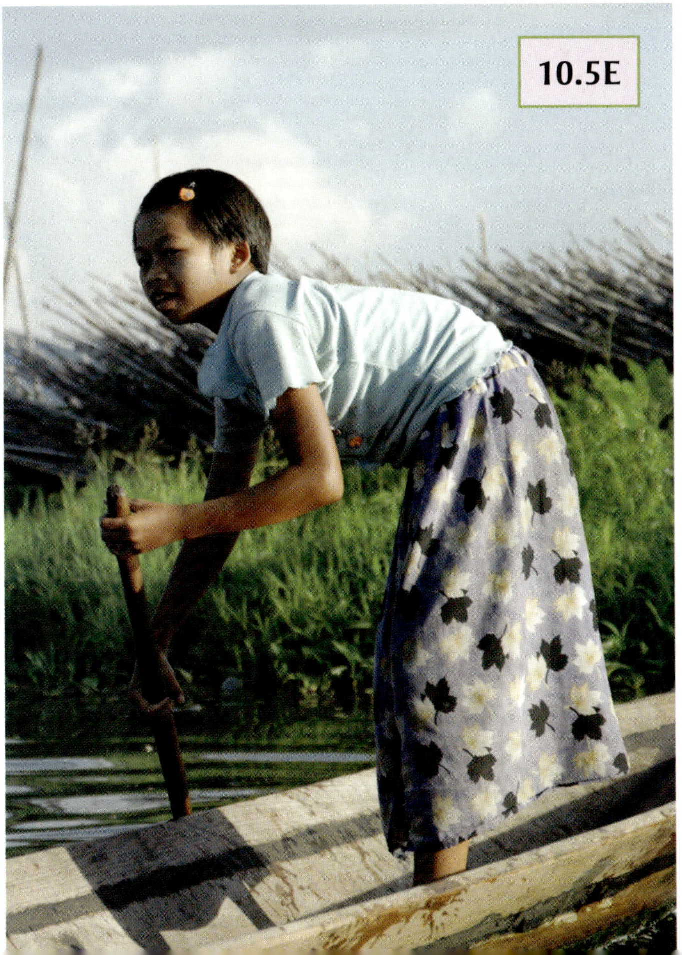

10.5E

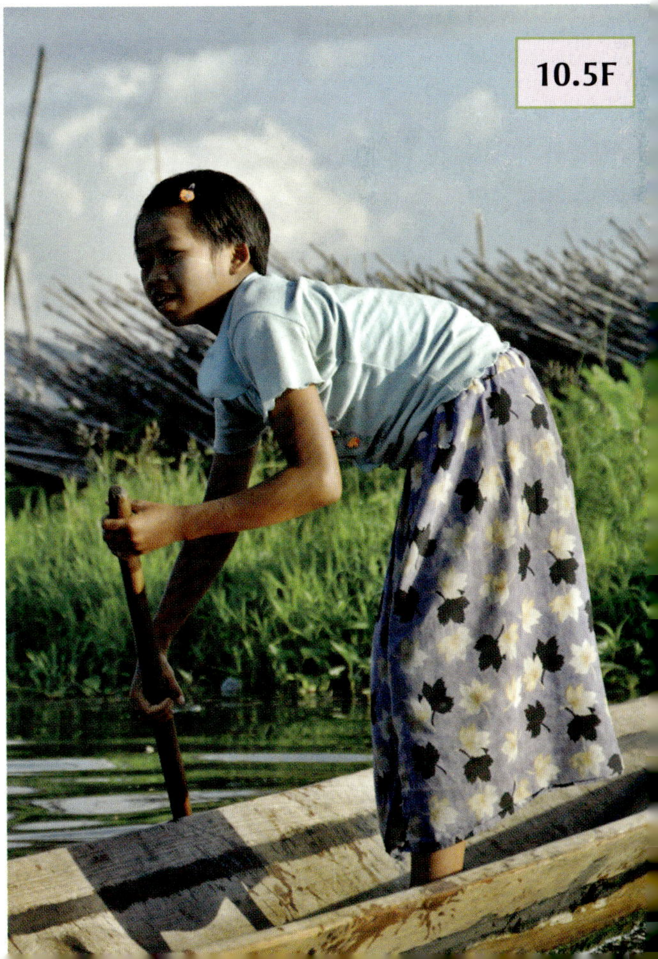

10.5F

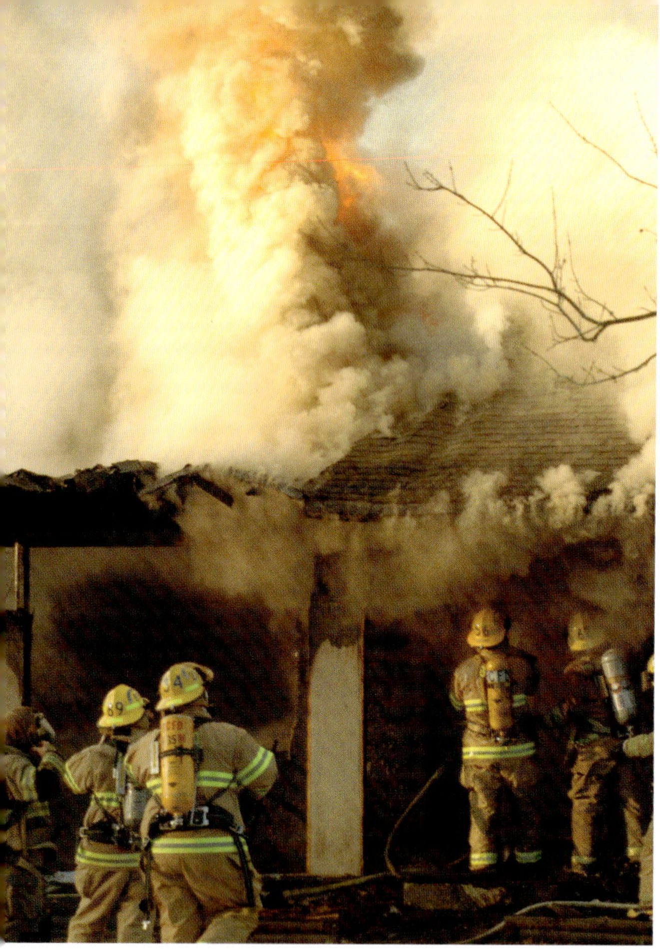

curriculum. The exercise calls for careful thought about objectives.

Our procedure is called the Picture Postcard Workflow—yet nobody would think of putting *this* scene on a picture postcard.

We have just looked at a somewhat similar example. Figure 10.5A commemorates the Battle of Spotsylvania Courthouse. Its background greenery is similar to that found in exercises in many other chapters. But those postcards all shared a positive context—the viewer was supposed to feel good about the scene, and possibly to wish to visit such a beautiful place.

Accordingly, we introduced bright, vivid, happy colors. This would be less than tasteful in portraying the site of some of the most appalling slaughter in a chillingly bloody civil war. A more subdued approach is needed to retain the dignity of the setting.

Figure 10.6 *The fierce light of the fire creates a yellow cast. Meanwhile, the need for detail in the smoke suggests the Bigger Hammer. Below, the original RGB channels. Note how the red channel is blank in the strongly yellow areas.*

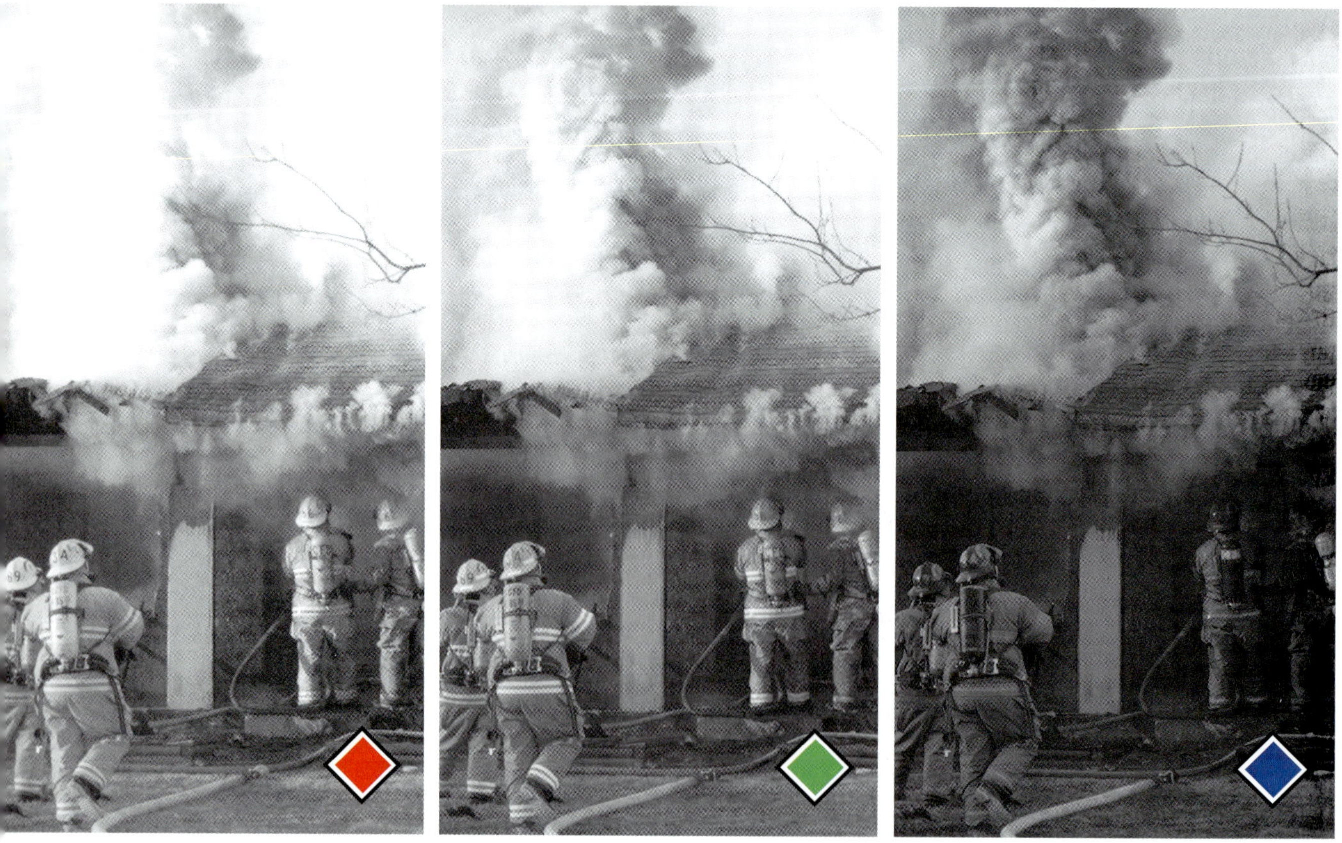

The current fire exercise also portrays unhappiness, not to mention physical danger. We don't want to fill it with joy and delight. On the other hand, no other picture we've worked on has featured colors as necessarily brilliant as the roaring flames behind the smoke, and the reflective striping that the firefighters wear. If we were actually at that scene the flames would be blinding. We can hardly tone them down just because the photo happens to depict something sad.

We're about to spend a lot of time with this image. The first halves of these chapters are intended to be accessible to non-experts. As noted, though, this particular picture has proven itself too difficult for many highly skilled people. So proceed at your own risk—but don't be frustrated. If it seems to have suddenly gotten much harder than the rest of the chapter—well, it has.

Where There's Smoke, Is There Fire?

Maintaining strong yellow-oranges in the flames will be a chore. Their fierce light has caused the camera to record a huge cast that human observers would adapt to and ignore. Eliminating that yellowness without dephlogisticating the flames is tough. Also, with a fire this powerful it stands to reason that the picture must have at least a slight warm or yellow cast, but how much? And should the lightest smoke, in the center of the pillar of fire, be yellower than the puffs on the right? If left *somewhat* yellow, won't the light smoke become *ridiculously* so once it gets to the Color Boost action?

The first step, the reduction of the cast in RGB, will be a nuisance because, as shown in Figure 10.6, the red channel starts out blank. It might be wise to force detail in by blending with another channel before embarking on a curves adventure. Offhand I can think of at least eight ways to shoehorn some shape into this red, but without trying them all I can't tell you which is best.

If and when we are able to establish decent color, the next step, getting a reasonable luminosity layer, will be no barrel of joy either. We can't do much curving for contrast in the smoke without making the bottom half of the picture too heavy. The blue channel has excellent smoke detail but can't easily be used as a blend source because its yellow objects are almost solid. We can hardly afford to have the stripes become black.

And eventually we will suffer even more headaches in the color enhancement phase. The rest of the picture may compete with the flames if we jack the color up too much. We probably will have to conjure up an unusual layer mask to make it all work.

In short, every step of this process, bar one, is of the type that might lead us to consider another line of work. The one exception, is the subject of this chapter. This original screams out for the Bigger Hammer just as much as the waterfall of Postcard 10.1 did. The lightest part of the smoke is critical to image quality and must have a drastic improvement if the result is to be considered successful.

At the end of the description of the steps we'll see a gallery (Figure 10.9) of the best classroom versions. It's there not just to point out that many interpretations are possible, but to provoke the realization that if these are the best, it can't say much for the other 95 percent. Which is just another reminder that of all the photos we've worked on so far, one has to be the hardest. This happens to be it.

Preparing the Fuel: Seven Variations

Producing inadequate images irritates me more than perhaps it should. Not having been satisfied with how I did in the aforementioned classes, I tried to improve this time as I prepared it for the book. I found, as has almost every other professional, that the biggest problem was the initial step of getting reasonable color.

Many originals have no color issues, and when they do, a set of RGB curves is almost always sufficient to cure them, as we saw in Chapter 3. Occasionally, though, we get a mess, usually photographed in abnormal lighting, as this one was.

As always, we look for areas of known neutrality. The puffs of smoke at roof level on the right side might be close. So might the dark area at left above the firefighters' heads. Both start out grossly yellow. They probably should retain a certain amount of warmth and not be forced into grayness.

Meanwhile, we locate, presumably using a threshold adjustment layer, the lightest significant point in the smoke. This, too, starts out grossly yellow; it needs to be made somewhat less so, but nobody knows how much. We have to make sure that killing all this yellow doesn't snuff out the flames as well.

RGB curves can't handle such massive adjustments, at least not in one step. On the other hand, methods that make gross changes to color, of which I'm about to name several, are imprecise. The best solution, in my view, is a combination approach. Do something that reduces the cast, but don't try for perfection. Then, once the cast is more manageable, wheel out the RGB curves.

I can think of seven reasonable ways to do this. Or, more accurately, in preparing this demonstration I tried out seven different methods. In my next life perhaps I will show a hundred pages of step-by-step to indicate how each one turned out. Here, instead, I'll talk about the one that you already know about, and later demonstrate fully the one that I actually used. As for the other five, I will name them, but declare that a full explanation is beyond the scope of this book.

In listing these seven, remember that everything is eventually changed to Color mode to preserve the detail. Remember, too, that other approaches exist and I don't necessarily condemn them, I just don't list them.

The first possibility is based on Chapter 3.

- As usual, choose color sampler points, such as the small puffs of smoke. Apply slight curves that move tentatively in the direction of neutrality, then change mode to Color. This forces a recalculation of everything. There still won't be much in the red channel highlight, but it won't be blank, either. Now, add a second curves adjustment layer and again move gently toward where you wish to go. Change again to Color mode and add a third, and perhaps a fourth, curves adjustment layer. Hopefully this will subject the cast to death by a thousand cuts.

The above procedure avoids a drastic curve shape that could make the whole scene look bizarre. On the other hand it is not for the curves novice. It might be better to try one of the following options, which are listed more or less from easiest to most difficult. None can solve all the problems but any might get you close enough that standard RGB curves could finish the job. Please forgive the sketchy descriptions.

- Open a curves adjustment layer. Click the neutral eyedropper tool, which is the middle one of the three below the curves grid. Then click one of the small puffs of smoke, forcing it to be a pure gray. You'll have to set a low layer opacity, and it's a really blunt instrument, but it might get you close enough.
- Or, establish a photo filter adjustment layer. Choose something on the purple side of blue (the opponent of the greenish-yellow cast in this original) as your filter. Change the layer mode to Color. Reduce opacity to taste. If you want something similar but more sophisticated, go back to the last chapter and look at the procedure that transformed Figure 9.7A into 9.14C.
- Or along the same lines: open a copy of the file in Camera Raw (JPEG and TIFF are currently the only two formats permitted.) Under White Balance, move Temperature toward blue and Tint toward

magenta. Place the copy as a layer on top of the original file, and change layer mode to Color.

These last two approaches each have strongest effects in lightest areas. Although there is no simple way to control how far into the dark areas they go, they won't hurt the flames as much as the lighter yellows.

- LAB connoisseurs might try either of the above in their favored colorspace; the results would be different. Alternatively, they could put the file into LAB and apply curves in the shape of an inverted S to the AB channels. This shape emphasizes strong colors and neutralizes weaker ones, just what we want.
- Another LAB alternative: make a duplicate layer, invert it, and change its mode to Color. The top layer now sports a blue-purple cast that is the direct opponent of the green-yellow one. Changing the top layer to 50% opacity would create a grayscale image, because the color of the top would cancel that of the bottom. Instead, load an inverted copy of the original B channel as a layer mask. That mask is darker where the yellow is strongest, so it tries to prevent the flames from being contaminated by the top (blue) layer. With curves to the mask and a good opacity decision one can subdue the raging cast in the lesser yellows while holding the impact of the flames.

When I tried all six methods the last two got the best results, for what it's worth. The seventh method, the one I'm about to demonstrate, was just as good, and furthermore is a useful segue into the next three chapters because of its use of blurred layer masks.

The Many Uses of One Channel

All six methods discussed above depend upon finding a way to exclude rich yellows while desaturating lighter ones. The two LAB maneuvers worked well because these two regions are strongly differentiated in the B channel. That differentiation can be exploited in various ways, including using the B channel itself as a mask.

The fact is, however, that a comparable channel already exists in RGB. Do you know to which one I refer? If not, go back to Figure 10.6 and ask yourself which of the three shows the most contrast between the lightest area and the orange flame.

With such a channel available, the strategy should be about the same as the one just described in LAB. On a top layer, grayscale. On the bottom, the original. To merge them, a layer mask, which needs to be light for the light smoke, dark for the fire to prevent the grayscale image from contaminating the bottom. According to me, the original blue channel meets that description. Therefore:

- Starting with the original, make a duplicate layer.
- Do something to turn the new layer gray. I used Edit: Fill>50% Gray, but it can be done many other ways, such as Image: Adjustments>Desaturate.
- Add a layer mask to the gray layer. To it, Image: Apply Image, Layer=Background, Channel=Blue, Blending=Normal, Opacity=100%.
- Change layer mode from Normal to Color, producing Figure 10.7A. It is almost a black and white, except areas that were originally bright yellow.
- In addition to its usefulness as a layer mask, the blue channel has the best overall contrast. To exploit it, add a third layer. It can be a new layer or a duplicate of whatever you like, because it is about to be completely replaced. With all channels open, use Apply Image to apply the same blue channel from the background layer.
- This third layer, which now has copies of the blue in all three channels, gets changed to Luminosity mode. The result is impossibly dark. In Figure 10.7B the opacity has been cranked down all the way to 35% and still things are unhappy. The light areas

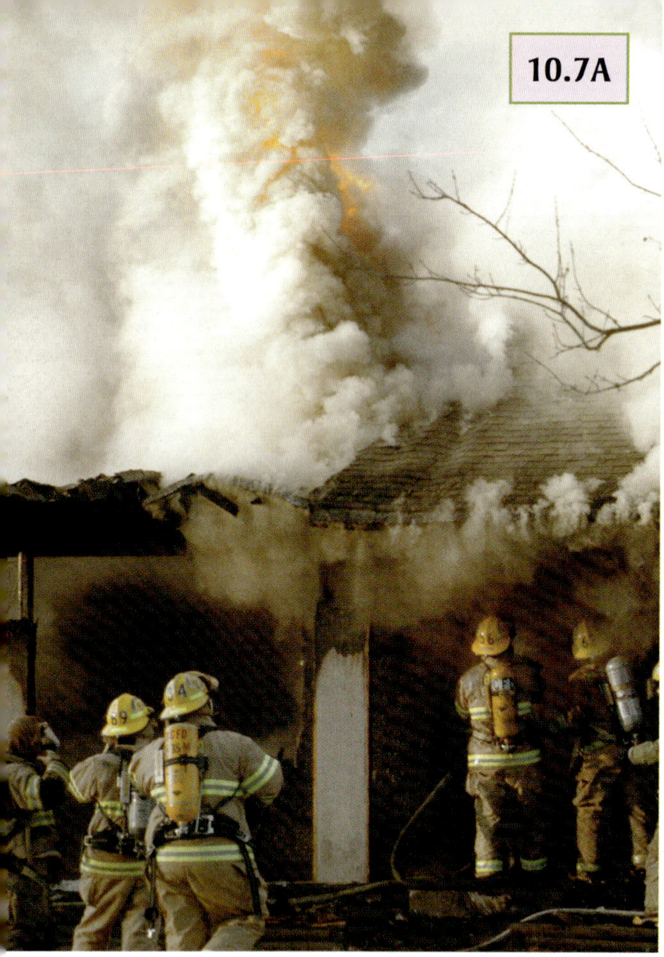
10.7A

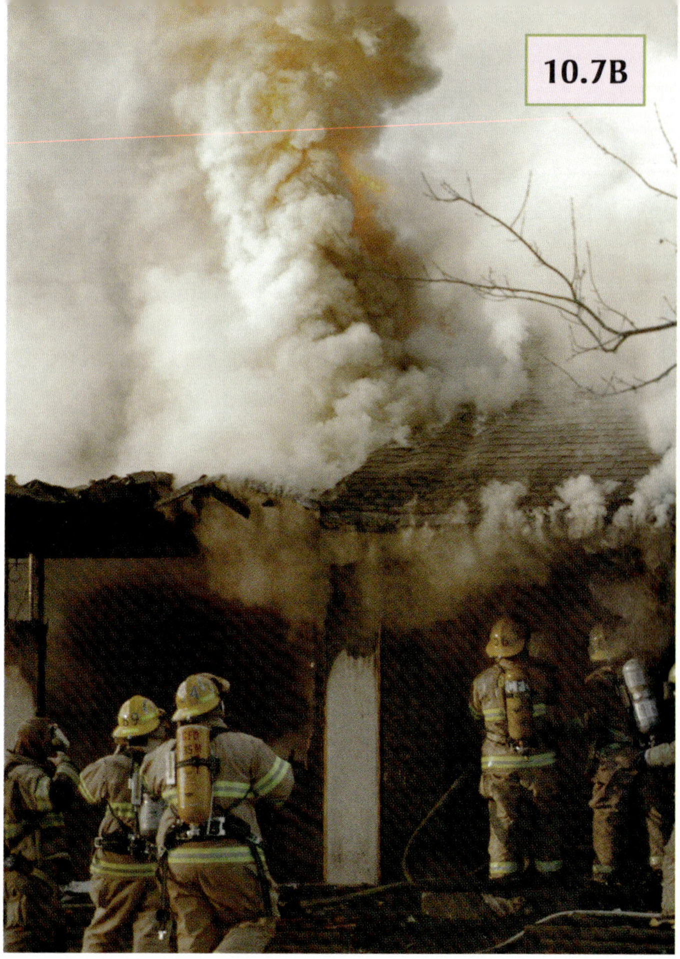
10.7B

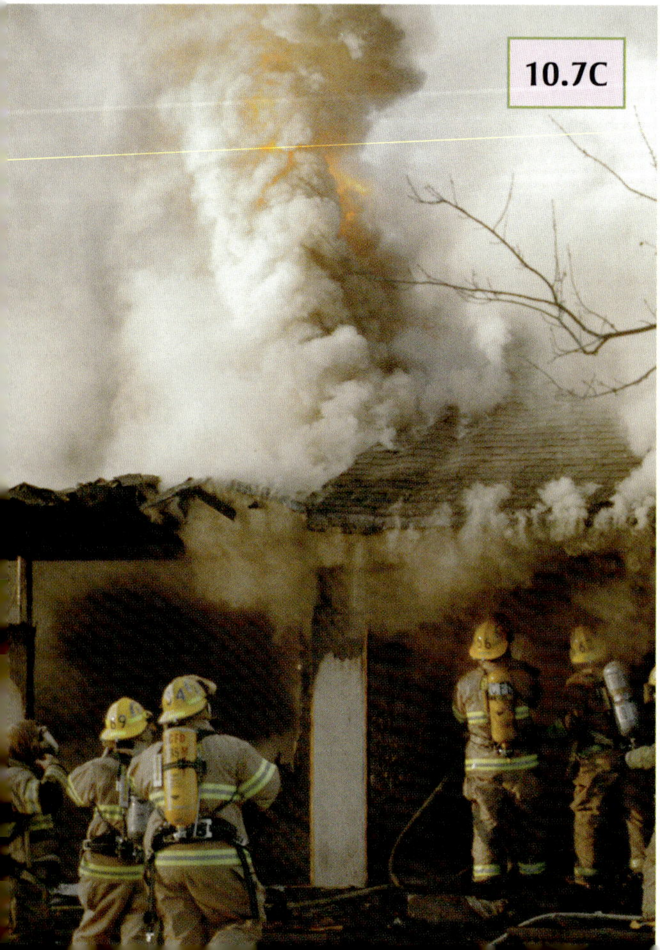
10.7C

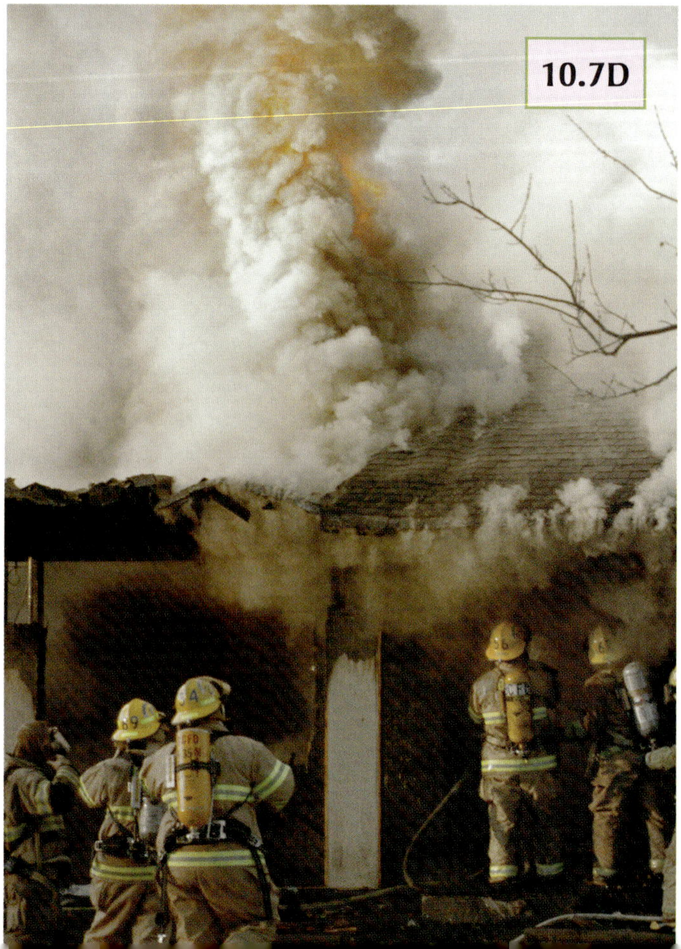
10.7D

aren't bad, but regrettably the flames have gotten too dark to be credible.

• The solution is another layer mask, yet another copy of the original blue, loaded in the same way it was on the second layer. The opacity of this newly masked layer goes up to 50% to make Figure 10.7C.

The file is now blessed with six copies of the original blue channel: the base blue, the red, green, and blue on the top layer, and two layer masks. This is about to be cut to five.

When Masks Need the Big Blur

Figure 10.7C is better than 10.7B, but unimpressive. It just seems that the smoke has gotten darker. Figure 10.7D adds detail by hitting the top layer mask with a big blur.

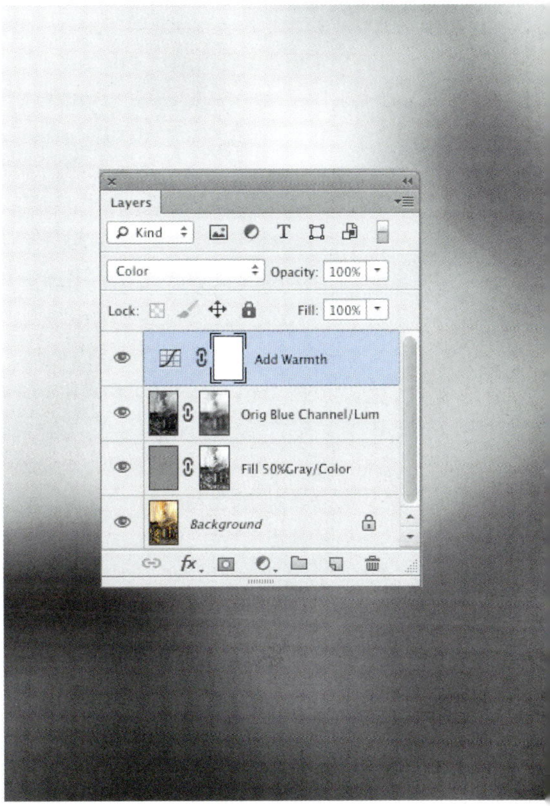

***Figure 10.7** Opposite, top left, on a layer set to Color mode, a completely gray top layer is merged with Figure 10.6, using the original blue channel as a layer mask. Top right, another copy of the blue channel is added as a luminosity layer, 35% opacity. Bottom left, the opacity is increased to 50% but yet another copy of the blue channel is added as a layer mask. Bottom right, the layer mask is blurred heavily. This page: top, the mask itself. Bottom left, a slight curve to the entire image in Color mode corrects a greenish cast. Bottom right, a new luminosity layer is added.*

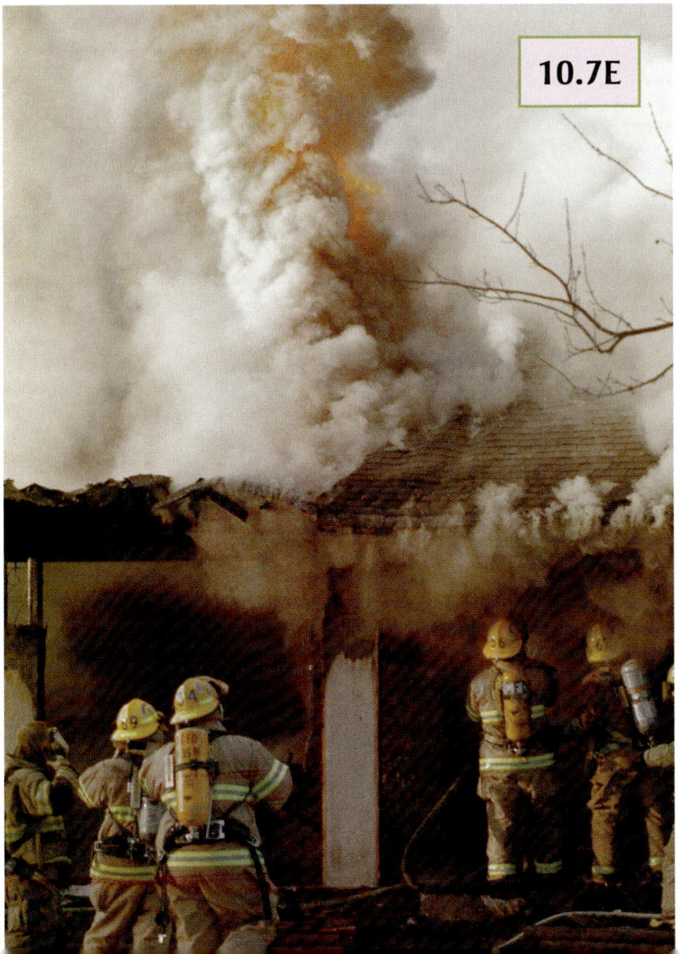

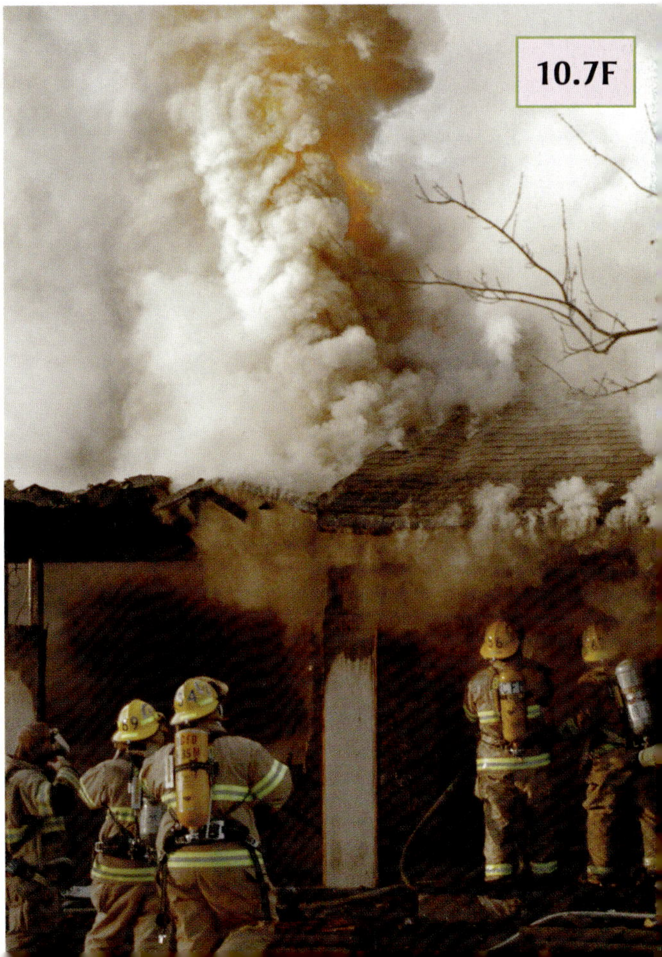

We've seen this idea before. The middle layer of the Bigger Hammer action is heavily blurred, too. But the layer mask on our current middle layer, the one that produces Figure 10.7A, is not.

Here's the rule, which, by insistence of the beta readers, is put in boldface: **when merging a layer with a big difference in weight compared to what's underneath, a major blur of the layer mask is in order.**

Here, the middle layer's mask is exempt from blurring because the layer is set to Color mode, rendering weight irrelevant.

The same rule applies to the Bigger Hammer itself. The Overlay layer, being inverted, is as different from the Background layer as possible, so it must be blurred. Why have we not run across more such blurs in the past?

Some of the new files that I created with eight versions of the same picture in Chapter 2 were straight blends—no mask, no overlay, therefore no blur. Others did use layer masks, but always it was to make modest improvements in similar-looking pictures. There wasn't the gross difference in weight that we see between the original and its blue channel in Figure 10.6.

Before any wheels start spinning and you decide you have just understood how HDR works, a gentle reminder that what has been done here is only a preliminary step. Figure 10.7D is so vastly better than the original that it's easy to say that the color issue is solved. It is not. Extreme methods like this masked blending for color get results that look nice at first glance but aren't quite accurate enough for later color enhancement. We have to take it as a starting point only.

Treating Figure 10.7D as the original, I would look at three sample points: the lightest smoke, some medium smoke at right, and a medium part of the dark house interior on the left side. Their values are $(1)^{A}2^{B}$, $2^{A}11^{B}$, and $7^{A}18^{B}$. We don't realize how bad these are because we compare them to the disastrous Figure 10.6, where they are $(7)^{A}29^{B}$, $10^{A}39^{B}$, and $8^{A}20^{B}$. The negative A in the light point shows that the smoke is still slightly green. We can't accept that. Also, the other two points show up as yellow, rather than the desired orange-red.

- Add a curves adjustment layer. Use it to darken the green channel, thus moving the image toward magenta. Set mode to Color. This produces Figure 10.7E. At this point we can flatten the layer structure shown inset into the blurred mask, and see if anything further can be done with luminosity.
- On a duplicate layer, replace the red channel with a copy of the green, which is a slightly darker channel. Apply curves to both to create a lighter highlight. Set layer mode to Luminosity, producing Figure 10.7F, a minor improvement over 10.7E.

Automation Clicks In

The rest goes very fast, particularly if you are using the PPW panel. The following sequence assumes that you have it, but there should be no difficulty figuring out the equivalent ways of doing it without the panel.

- Click the S/H action.
- Click the Bigger Hammer. Figure 10.8A shows its importance in a picture of this type. The PPW panel offers flexible preview options that can add to this step's value.
- Make a loose lasso selection of the upper half of the picture. Click the MMM + Color Boost action, producing Figure 10.8B.

Further adjustments are personal. The MMM Luminosity layer's effort to improve contrast was ineffective, so I turned it off. I altered the Endpoint Adjustment curves to establish better highlights and shadows. I tried to get slightly stronger flames and a less saturated bottom half by using the B channel as a layer mask for the Color Boost layer, but could scarcely see the difference afterward.

It's now time to have a look at some alternate interpretations. Figure 10.9 presents five of the best classroom results as determined by student vote, plus the final version of the one we just finished. Which is your favorite? (Note: the classroom versions were prepared for a larger size, so their sharpening is suspect and may leave them slightly soft.)

Two things differentiate these successful versions from the hundred unsuccessful ones that space does not permit showing. First, everyone set the lightest smoke to give a full range while retaining detail. This is harder than it looks: note that Figure 10.9C is blown out in this area.

Second, everybody used the Bigger Hammer or a predecessor. The voters would not accept a less prominent pillar of smoke than what is seen here.

Two versions are very colorful, three much more conservative. I dislike the ostinato yellow of Figure 10.9D; if you want a lot of color I would go with 10.9G. In fact, I *did* go with it: it's my version from the actual class, which took place almost two years before I prepared a version for this book. As you can see, my tastes have changed.

Among the conservative versions, the experts preferred Figure 10.9E. They hadn't seen my Figure 10.9B, but I have, and I still like their choice.

I wonder, though, how much being an expert biases ones judgment. Experts know that the lack of highlight detail in Figure 10.9C, and the subdued flames in Figure 10.9F, are defects. Non-experts might not appreciate this and conceivably would cut these two entrants more of a break.

One last point. Compare my final version, Figure 10.9B, with the last version of it you saw, Figure 10.8B. You can certainly see that I've increased contrast by setting

***Figure 10.8** Left, default Shadows/Highlights, followed by the Bigger Hammer, are applied to Figure 10.7E. Right, the MMM + Color Boost action is added.*

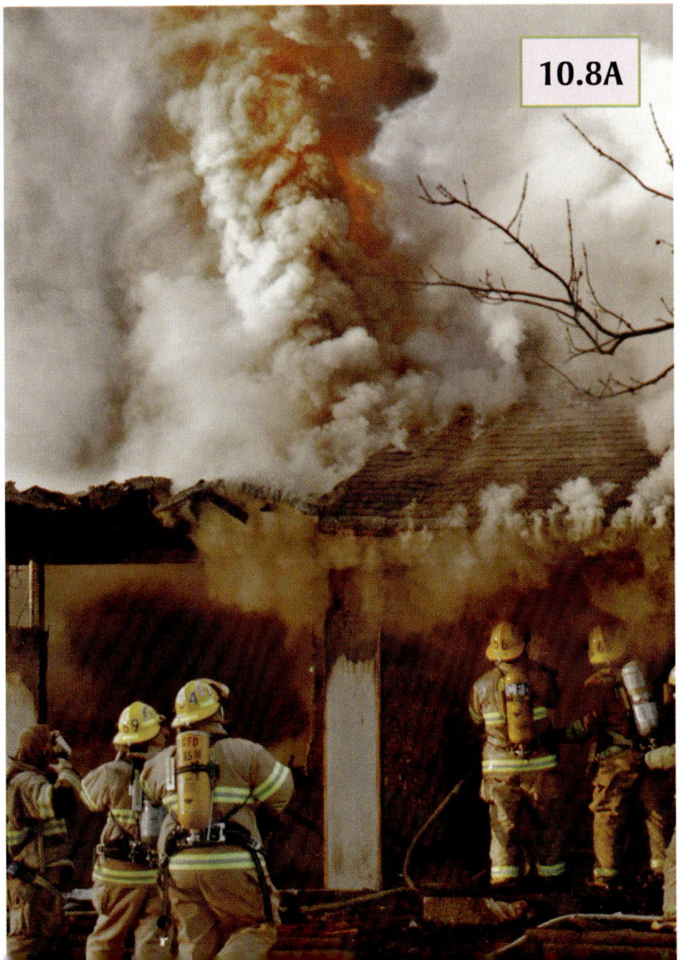

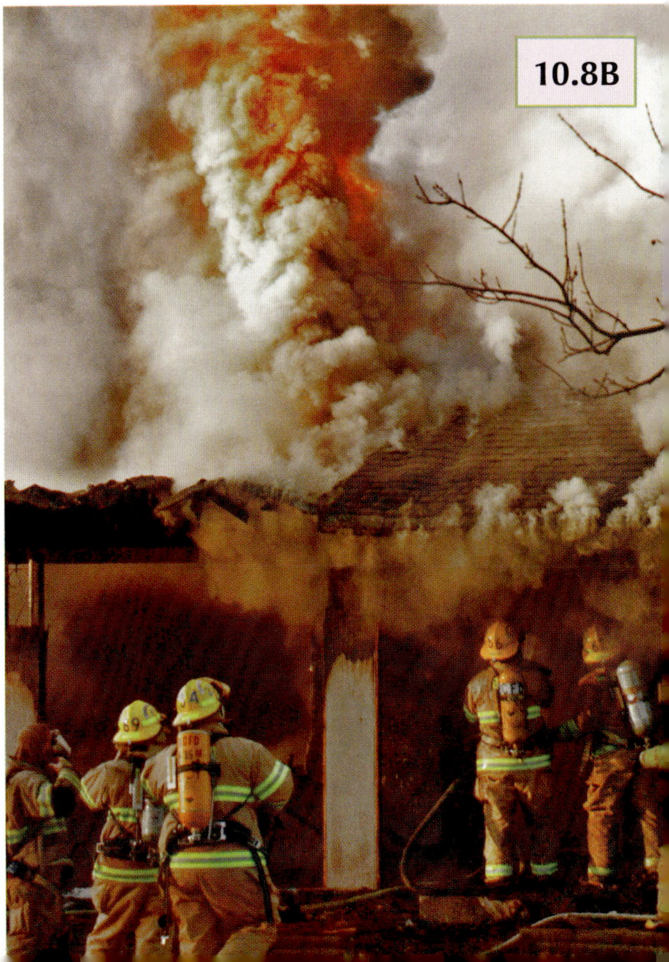

better endpoints, but do you see the extra warmth? When I looked at the other versions, I decided that Figure 10.8B was too vanilla-looking. I toggled it with my previous entrant, the extremely colorful Figure 10.9G. I decided that my new version was better for contrast but that I wanted a hint of the extra color. So I blended the old version in, Color mode, 20% opacity.

This again makes the point that it is better to make multiple versions of a picture than to try to love one of them to death. I wasn't deliberately making the file I was working on too bland, I just didn't realize that I had done so until I saw another option.

Nevertheless, the Bigger Hammer

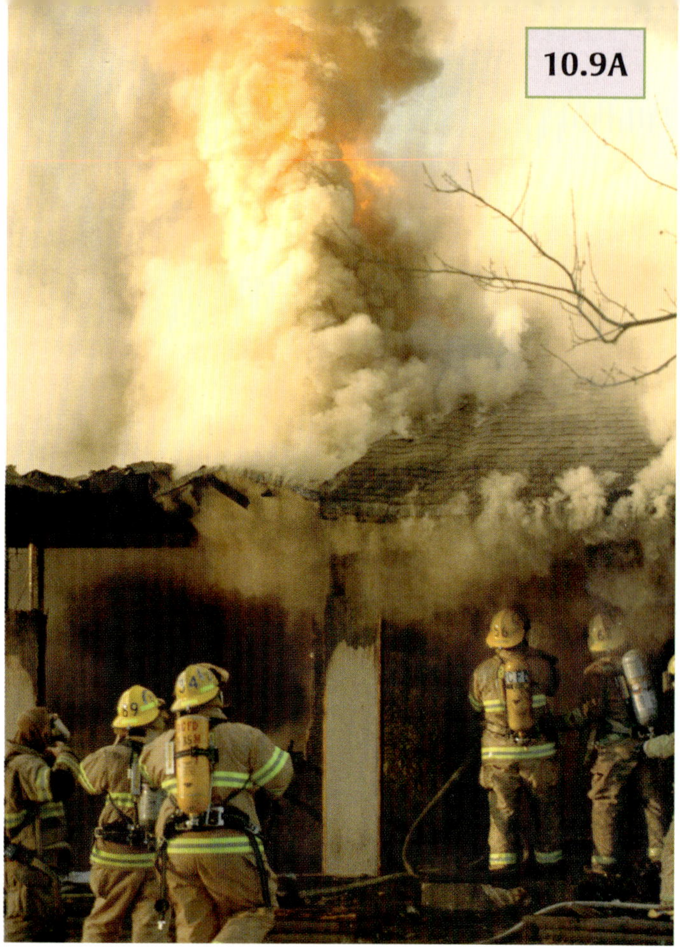

***Figure 10.9** Top, the original of Figure 10.6 repeated for convenience. Bottom left, the version prepared during this chapter. The other five represent the best versions from nearly a hundred top retouchers.*

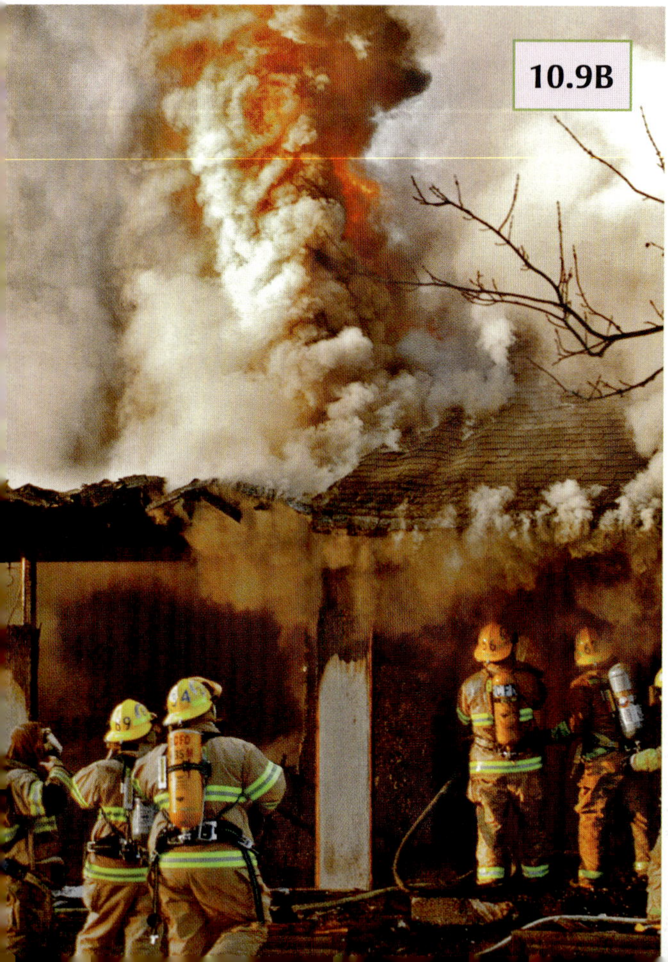

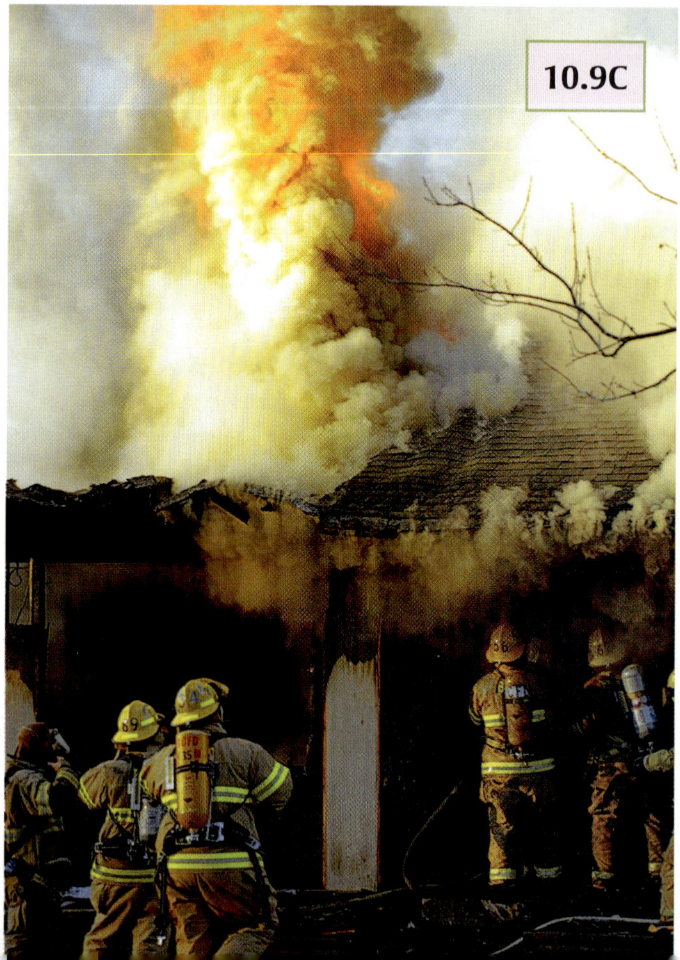

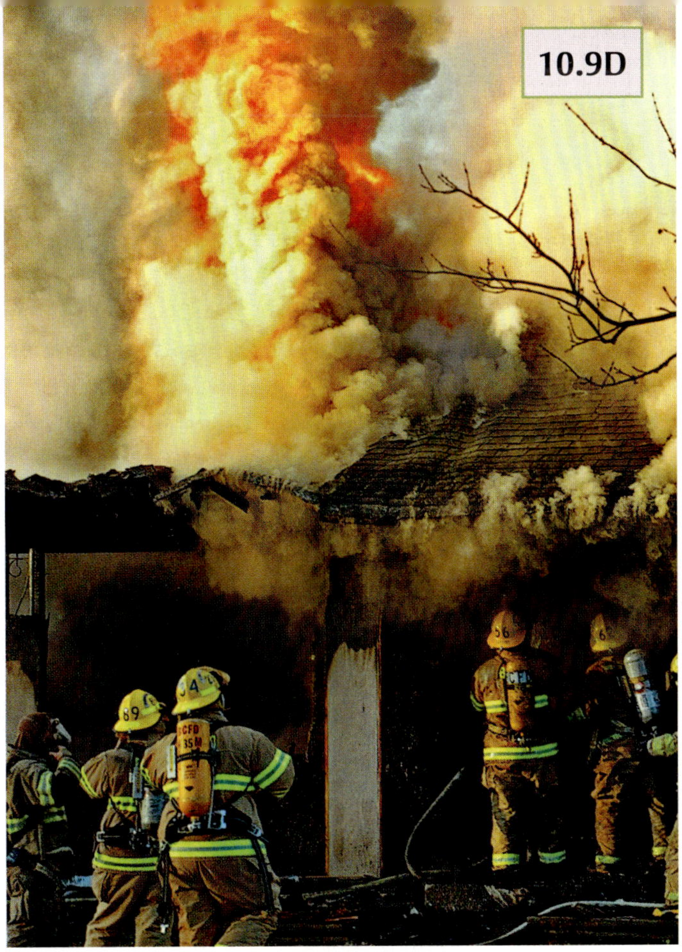
10.9D

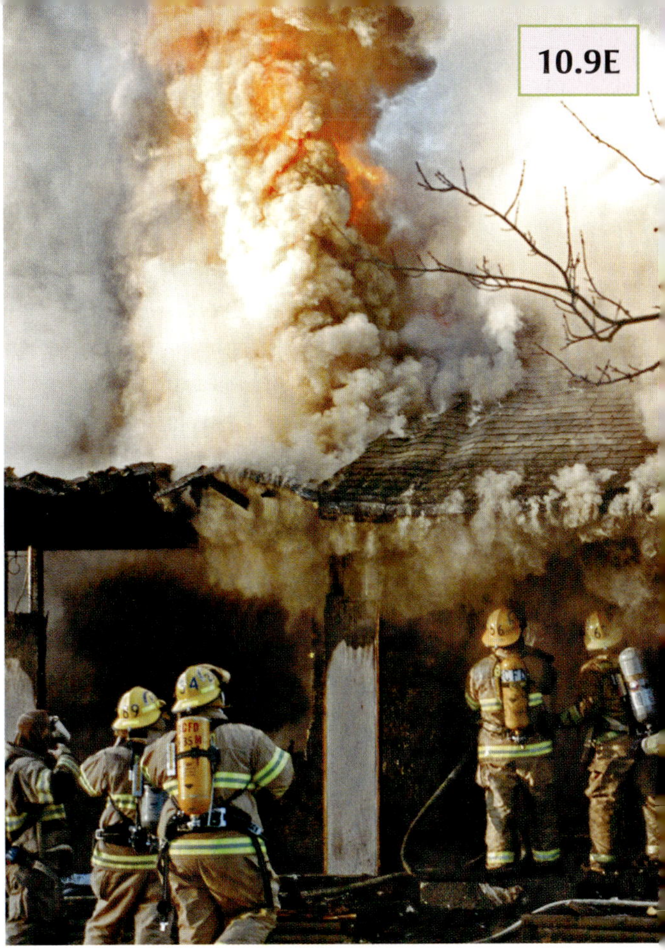
10.9E

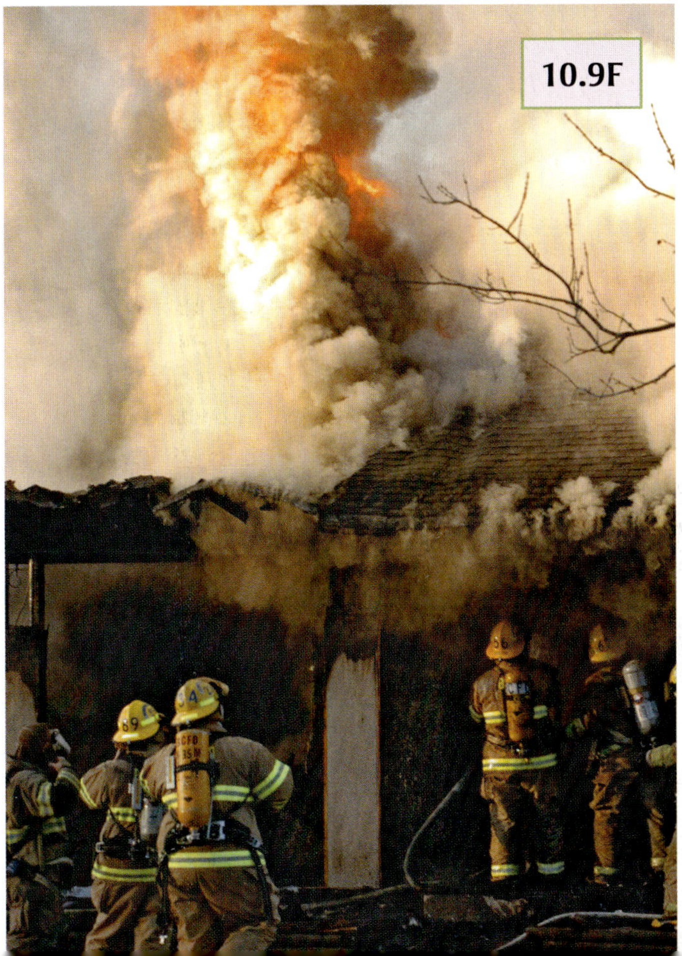
10.9F

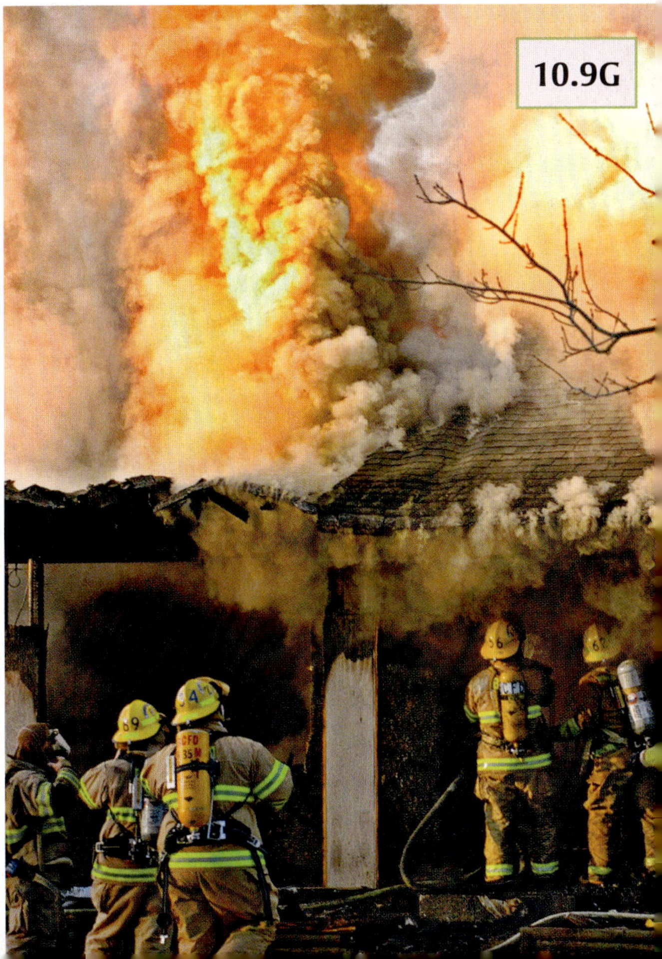
10.9G

can benefit from extra time, perhaps more than any other tool. And because it is of critical importance to a small percentage of images, it's worth spending the second half of this chapter in a discussion of some of the options. It is long, involved, and technical, worse even than the exercise we just went through. Most readers can safely skip it and move on to a two-chapter study of multiplication. I recommend plowing through the second half now only for those who frequently run into this type of highlights-are-critical scenario, or who are interested in sharpening theory.

Review and Exercises

✓How can you quickly toggle between the pre- and post-Bigger Hammer versions?

✓If, after running the action, you conclude that what it is doing to the highlights is good, but that the shadows are either too strongly affected or not strongly enough, what do you do?

✓Gather several pictures of people, taken under various lighting conditions. Run the Bigger Hammer action on them. This is sure to create an unpleasant effect, but what if you reduce the opacity of the Overlay layer to 20%? Are any of the pictures improved?

✓The second half will discuss under what circumstances it pays to use a channel other than the red for the blurred inverted overlay. What is your prediction as to when it is appropriate? Is there a certain category of image for which the red is probably a poor choice?

A Closer Look

The options shown in the first half consisted of changing the opacities of the overlay and the darkening layers. We now will consider several others, to wit:

- A blending mode other than Overlay.
- An overlay channel other than the action's default red.
- A method of controlling color shifts.
- A blur radius other than the action's default 35 pixels.
- A filter other than Gaussian Blur.
- Methods of dealing with haloing.

You have read the warning at the end of the first half about the difficulty of what is to come. You know that the Bigger Hammer isn't for most images. Yet you have decided to read on. The punishment begins with a quiz. Figure 10.10A is an original that might qualify for the Bigger Hammer because of the need for greater detail in the light yellows. One of the remaining five variants is the result of the default action, which uses the inverted red channel as the overlay. The other four, in a random order, use the green, the blue, the RGB, and the RGB desaturated, which is what you would get by converting the file to grayscale. All overlays have been inverted and blurred at the same settings as the default. Your job is to match the five versions with the overlay channels that produced them.

While you mull it over, let's move on to the first topic. Overlay is one of several modes that operate in approximately the same way, but with slightly different results. If you're curious, you can find the formula for computing an overlay in the Notes & Credits section.

Many of Overlay's relatives, notably Linear Light, are useful in other contexts. As far as I know, however, the only two that work well in the Bigger Hammer are Overlay and Soft Light, which I use under the following circumstances.

In Chapter 7, the discussion of Shadows/Highlights, most of the benefit came in the shadows, although a few files were helped by its highlight settings. With the Bigger Hammer, it is just the opposite. The criterion for its use is absolutely critical detail either in the highlights or in the shadows. In the first half of the chapter we looked at seven originals. The memorial of Figure 10.3 is hard to classify. Our motivation in all six of the others—the waterfall of Postcard 10.1, the beach of Figure 10.2A, the memorial of Figure 10.5A, the golden valley of Figure 10.5C, the woman's light shirt of Figure 10.5E, the light smoke of Figure 10.6—was to enhance the highlights. Shadows were definitely secondary.

That's how it plays out in real life, too. Images with the opposite problem do exist, just not nearly as frequently. Occasionally we find something like Figure 10.11A. It would be nice to get better detail in its clouds, but even nicer to get something more out of the dark foreground.

The rule is: when you find a picture of this unusual type, use Soft Light for the blending mode of the inverted layer rather than Overlay. It provides softer transitions in the shadows and doesn't exaggerate the highlights as drastically. Also, consider changing the third layer from Darker Color to Lighter Color, after which it may be necessary to reduce the opacity of the Overlay—er, Soft Light—layer.

Figure 10.11B, then, shows the Bigger Hammer default. In Figure 10.11C, the mode of the middle layer has been changed from Overlay to Soft Light. Note the more realistic clouds. Figure 10.11D keeps that layer in Soft Light mode, but changes the third layer from Darker Color to Lighter Color. Obviously you can split the difference any way you like, or use some of the other options we're about to discuss.

Let's dispose of the quiz. If you need a hint, ask yourself why I chose the lily picture for Figure 10.10A, rather than simply continuing discussion of the Icelandic scene of Figure 10.11, where the need for the Bigger Hammer is clearer.

Want another hint? Suppose the quiz has the same format, but spotlights a different picture, a

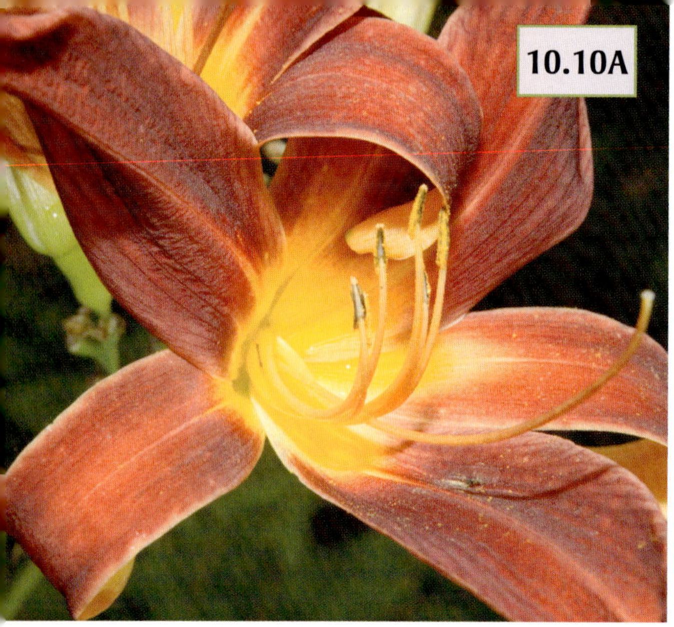
10.10A

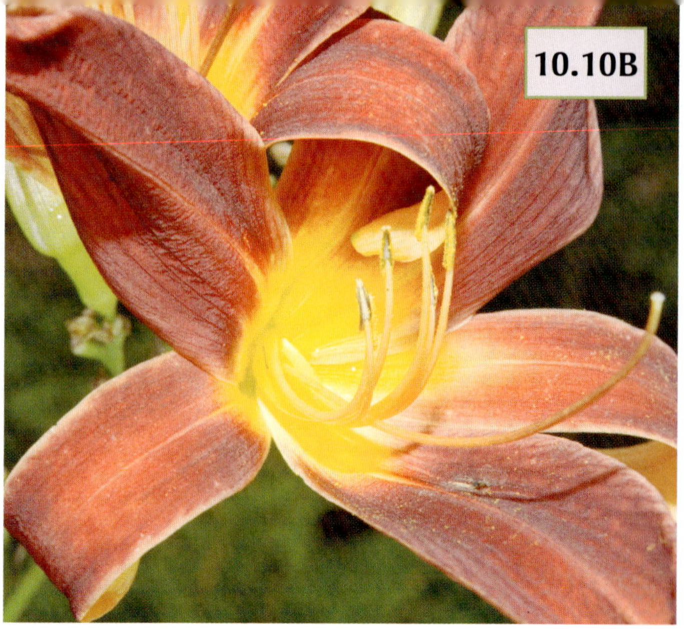
10.10B

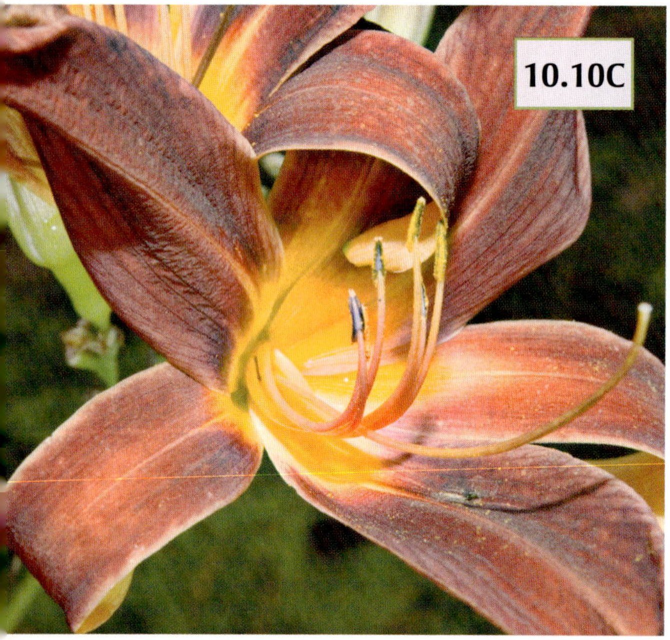
10.10C

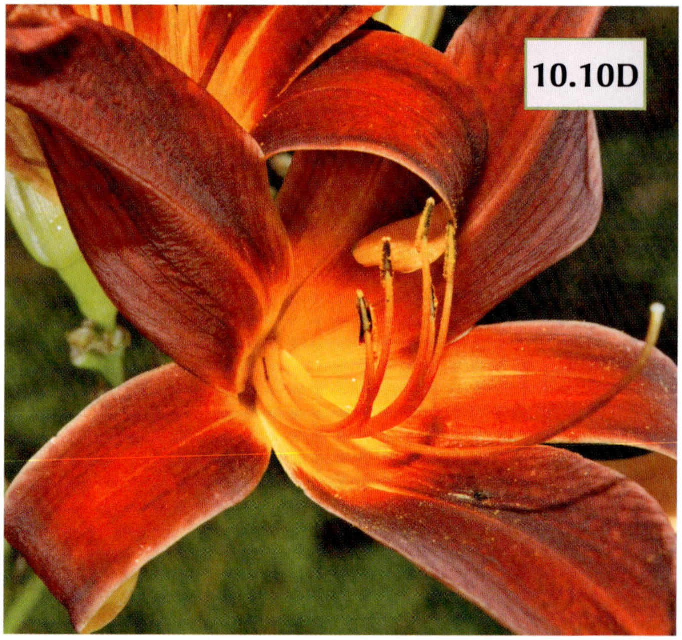
10.10D

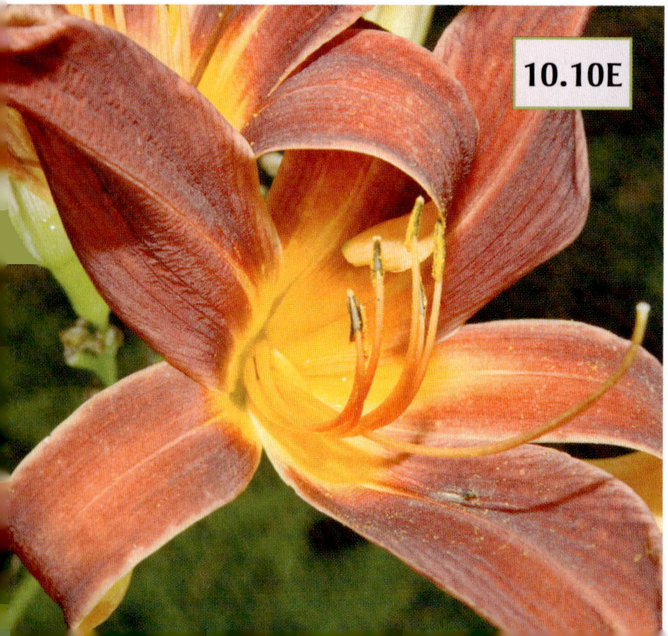
10.10E

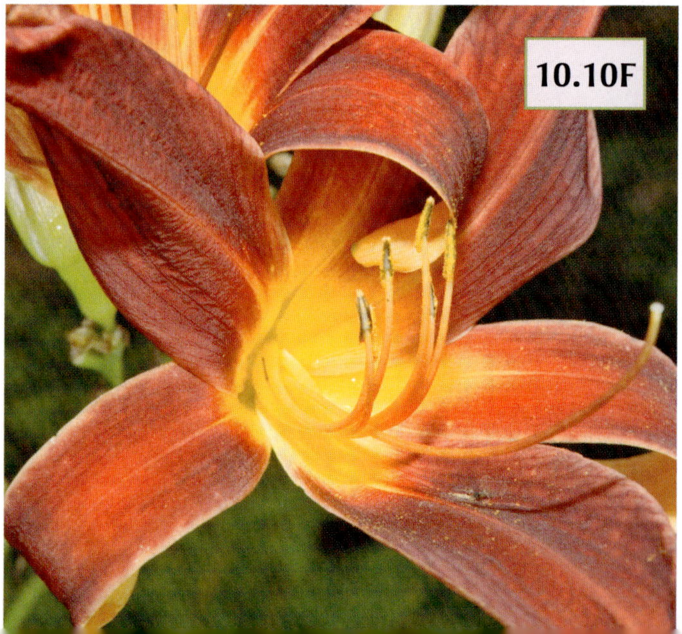
10.10F

hypothetical one that you're not allowed to see yet. Which two of the five quiz overlays would you think are likeliest to be the hardest to tell apart? And another, again assuming a picture that you're not allowed to see yet: which overlay would you think will be the easiest to identify?

The Brighter, the Lighter

To know which overlay is which is much easier when there are bright colors and more difficult when neutrals dominate. The clouds in Figure 10.11A wind up the same no matter which channel we use for the overlay, because being neutral, all their channels are the same. Ditto for almost the entire foreground.

The overlay that would usually be the easiest to identify, if we've never seen the image, is the RGB composite. It produces the most subdued colors, because it is the only overlay of the five that darkens light channels and lightens dark ones. But in this Icelandic shot, we might not be able to see any difference in the blue sky, the only significant colored area.

If Figure 10.11A were the quiz image, we would, however, be able to identify the inverted blue overlay. The blue channel is surely the lightest in this sky, so it would create the darkest sky of any of the five.

For similar reasons, we could identify the red, which would produce a slightly lighter sky than any of the others.

I doubt that anyone would be able to distinguish the green from the RGB desaturated. This pair is the one that's always the toughest to tell apart. Recall from Chapter 4 that the formula for averaging the channels to construct a grayscale image (or a desaturated RGB, if you prefer) is roughly 3–6–1. So more than half of the desaturated RGB is a copy of the green channel. Naturally, the two are always quite similar. The only time the difference is significant is in strongly colored objects, which the Icelandic picture doesn't feature. By strange coincidence, the quiz picture we're about to analyze happens to have some.

* * *

The first half's originals were not as colorful as the flower of Figure 10.10A. The presence of such strong color is an argument against the Bigger Hammer. Here the original could be the best of the six versions on the page.

In spite of these gloomy results, the Bigger Hammer is in fact useful with originals like this; it can bring out detail in the center of the bloom if handled properly. We'll get to that in due course, but right now we have to identify these variants whether they are beautiful or as ugly as American politics.

Normally the easy pick would be the RGB composite, which suppresses color. This time another variant is even more obvious. The day lily showcases reds and yellows. The red areas are dark in the green and blue channels, light in the red. The yellows are dark in the blue, light in the red and green. The greenish background is

***Figure 10.10** (opposite) Top, the original. The other five, in a random order, show Bigger Hammer defaults using five different overlay channels.*

Choosing the Proper Overlay

Figure 10.10A is the original. The other five, in a random order, use the Bigger Hammer action at its default settings, except that different inverted channels are used as the overlay. Identify which of the following channels correspond to which version. (Answers, Page 267.)

1. Red.
2. Green.
3. Blue.
4. RGB (color).
5. RGB (desaturated).

Figure	Channel(s)
10.10B	
10.10C	
10.10D	
10.10E	
10.10F	

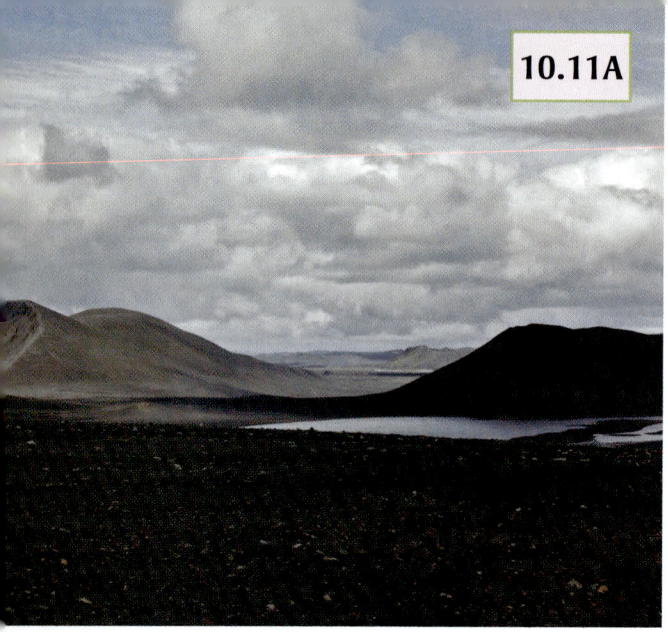

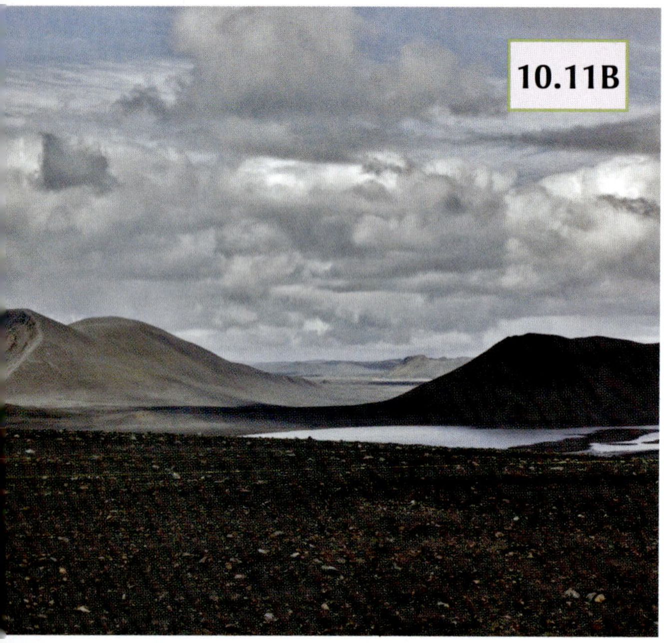

so neutral that the choice of overlay channel may not make an obvious difference.

In the flower, however, it does. Whether yellow or red, it's light in the red channel. That statement cannot be made about the green, the blue, or the RGB whether desaturated or not. Consequently, if the red channel is used for the overlay the center of the flower must wind up much darker than the other four. Presto! Figure 10.10D has been identified.

Next easiest is the straight RGB. Reminder: it suppresses colors because only it can move channels in different directions, and always toward more equality. We're likeliest to notice its reduced color in reds, because the yellow areas are so extreme in each channel that the overlay won't have much effect. The suppression of reds reveals Figure 10.10C for what it is.

When the overlay is gray—as it is in the remaining overlays—all channels move in the same direction. The blue channel must be very dark in the strongly yellow areas. Inverting it flips it to light. Using the inverted copy as an overlay causes all yellows to become lighter. That will smash detail in the red and green channels, both of which already were quite light in yellow areas. (The blue, being so dark to begin with, is little affected.)

To find the one based on the inverted blue overlay, therefore, look for the one with the worst detail in the yellow center of the flower. That's Figure 10.10B.

***Figure 10.11** Top, the original. Middle, the Bigger Hammer defaults. Bottom left, the Overlay layer's mode is changed to Soft Light. Bottom right, the Overlay layer is still in Soft Light but the Darkening layer is changed to Lighter Color mode.*

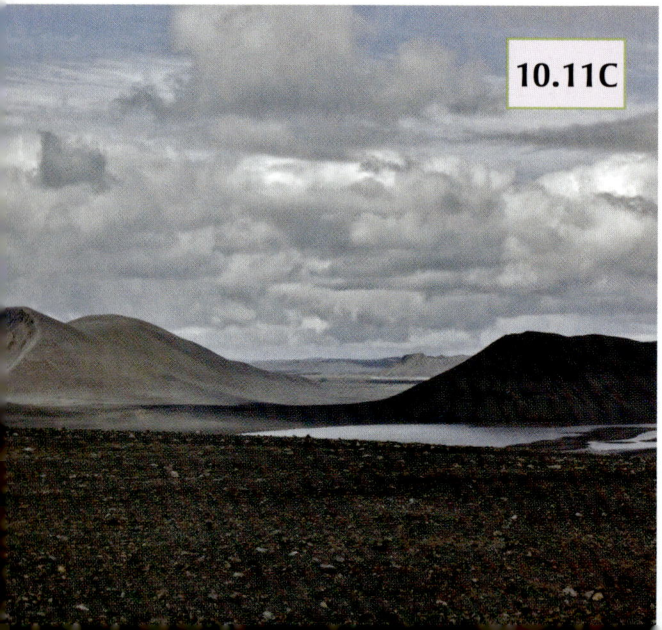

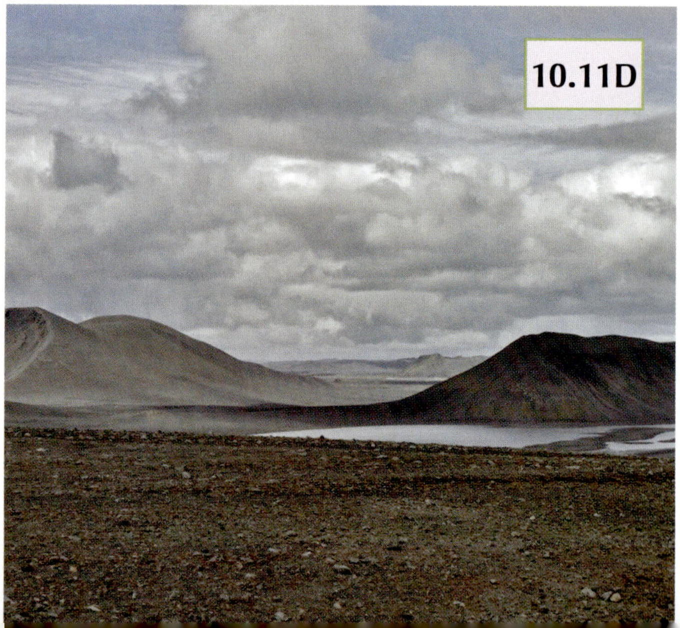

Now to the hard part, distinguishing Figures 10.10E and 10.10F. Since, as noted before, the RGB desaturated is based around 60 percent on the green, these two are always similar, and nasty to tell apart.

Here, the green channel, before being inverted, must be quite dark in the reds and quite light in the yellows. The desaturated RGB cannot be quite so extreme, because it averages the very light red channel into reds and the very dark blue into yellows.

Remembering that these channels are both inverted before being overlaid, the result must be that the yellows are slightly darker and the reds slightly lighter when the green is the overlay. That makes it Figure 10.10E, while the desaturated RGB is Figure 10.10F.

Switching Channels in Theory

If that quiz helps you to visualize channels rapidly, it was worth the pain. Many steps in color correction require that kind of quick evaluation.

When, then, might it make sense to substitute a new overlay channel? First, if we wish to make a big alteration to the darkness of certain area(s). That wasn't the case in the flower we've just been working on. Second, if we have some reason to fear damage from using the red channel. That did happen in Figure 10.10D and would also happen in most portraits, as faces are red, too. Third, we may feel that only a certain overlay will bring out the detail we want.

The first two concepts are easier than the last, but even so there are exceptions. For example, the red-channel default improved Figure 10.5F, a shot of a girl piloting a rivercraft. If we had substituted the blue channel instead it would have produced a darker sky and blue clothing, and a lighter face. Would it have been better overall? The only way to know would be to try it.

It gets worse if the third consideration is the big one. Let's pretend we are correcting the flower instead of dealing with a quiz about it. What should we try, and how much time should we allot for it?

Well, it isn't a classic example of something that would obviously benefit from the Bigger Hammer. Still, the yellow center of the flower could use extra detail, and the Bigger Hammer might provide it. So I would say that running the action as a trial is certainly worth it regardless of how big a hurry we're in.

Doing so produces Figure 10.10D, with better yellows and worse reds. In principle, we now have the following options, at least, in order of increasing time:

- Conclude that the move is worthless and cancel it. Time lost: less than five seconds.
- Try to pick up some of the extra detail without making the reds look silly by lowering opacity of the overlay layer to 15% or whatever. Total time: maybe fifteen seconds.
- Instead, realizing that the good and bad parts of Figure 10.10D can be separated, load a copy of the original green channel as a layer mask on the overlay layer. Some reduction in opacity may still be needed, but the mask will retain the yellows but disfavor the darkening of the reds. Total time: perhaps thirty seconds.
- Look for some better option for the overlay channel. This will take much longer—or at least it will without the PPW panel.

Are any of these last moves worth the effort? It depends on the importance of the file. For the sake of argument, say that this one merits

Answers to Bigger Hammer Quiz

(Page 265)

Figure 10.10A is the original. The other five use the default settings of the Bigger Hammer action, except that they all use different channels for the Overlay layer. All overlays were taken from the base layer, and have been inverted and blurred.

10.10B: Blue.
10.10C: RGB.
10.10D: Red.
10.10E: Green.
10.10F: RGB, desaturated

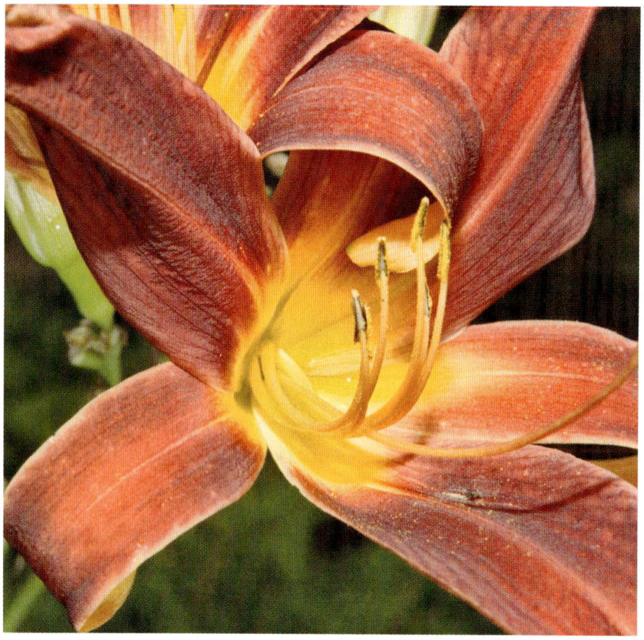

***Figure 10.12** The original (Figure 10.10A) is applied to the RGB overlay version (Figure 10.10C) in Color mode.*

a look at the last option. We know that the red channel is a poor choice. Figure 10.10B shows that the blue obliterates detail in the yellow areas, but you should know that without needing a trial. That leaves three. Is it worth the time to test all of them?

To make the answer to that question more palatable, the PPW panel added interactive previews in 2012. Option-click the Bigger Hammer, and instead of simply running the action the panel asks which channel to use for the overlay, how big a blur to use, whether to emphasize shadows, and whether to retain the original color. RGB and RGB/Desaturated are both options for the overlay. Full details are in the documentation that can be accessed from within the panel.

The same panel dialog gives the ability to change the action's defaults. My recommendations would be: if you usually work on files less than 10 megabytes, lower the Radius setting to 25 pixels. If you commonly work on files greater than 30 MB, up it to 50 pixels. And if you commonly work on portraits, change the default channel from red to RGB desaturated.

The Red, and Other Exceptions

Understanding how the overlay works, and how changing source channels affects it, can be baffling. You have to take the inversion into account. Objects that are light on the bottom layer become dark on the overlay. And dark parts of overlays darken whatever is underneath. So an inverted overlay darkens light things, thus adding detail to them. The same thing happens in reverse to dark areas. Objects that can't be described as either light or dark aren't impacted as much.

If that sounds like gobbledygook, there is a pleasant catch. You hardly have to worry about it unless the object is red.

Don't believe it? The first half of the chapter shows seven originals, but only one color vivid enough for this topic to be significant: the flowers of Figure 10.3. Coincidentally, they're red. The rest of the images tend to involve greens, like those of Postcard 10.1 and Figure 10.2. Those greens are rather dull. Their green channels are always slightly lighter than the other two but generally all three are somewhere in the middle. The impact of using one as opposed to another for the overlay is small.

The red and green channels are, however, *grossly* different in the flowers of both Figures 10.3 and 10.10. The red is very light and the green very dark.

Colors that are both brilliant and in need of detail are almost always red. If you are about to call me an idiot because the yellows of the day lily constitute exactly such a case, my response is, yes, they do. And now, flip through the pages of this long book and see if you can find another example of strongly detailed, yet brilliant, yellows. Good luck. I can tell you that, along the way, you'll encounter a lot of such reds.

Back to work. Let's recap the structure of the three RGB channels to see what their impact would be as an overlay.

- The red starts out light in both the reds and yellows. Applying it as an inverted overlay creates much worse reds, but good yellows.

- The green is dark in reds, light in yellows. It creates reds that are improved somewhat, and good yellows.
- The blue is dark in both. It creates somewhat better reds, and much worse yellows.

The green is the best choice of the three, being the only one that improves both reds and yellows. However, note that it only improves the reds *somewhat.* Red objects are light in the red channel, dark in the green. Overlaying an inverted green channel onto itself is good for red things, because it lightens them and thus extends their range. But applying the same green overlay to the red channel is bad, because it lightens areas that are already light, shortening their range and damaging detail.

The gain in the green channel outweighs the loss in the less powerful red. However, a greedy person would want a loss in *neither.*

Therefore, a greedy person would think of an inverted RGB rather than a single channel. That way, each channel is applied to itself as an inverted overlay. All light areas in each channel get darker, all dark ones lighter. Detailing in the reds is, in theory, better in all channels, not just the green.

We've already tried this, and uncorked Figure 10.10C. Its color is the worst on the page, but has the best detail overall.

The crummy color is easily corrected. Take a copy of the original and paste it on top of Figure 10.10C in Color mode, producing Figure 10.12. I deliberately force you to turn pages to compare it to the other variants. It's definitely better than any of them, in my opinion, but how obvious is the improvement? Enough to justify the extra time involved? Only you can make that call.

Switching Channels in Practice

Why, then, shouldn't the above procedure—using an inverted RGB as the overlay, followed by restoration of color—be the default? Its detail should theoretically be better because it would never alter a channel inappropriately.

Just because something is theoretically better doesn't mean that it *is* better in real life. Even superficially similar files, like our next exercise, the red flowers of Figures 10.13A and 10.14A, can behave differently. Use of the red channel also has a specific advantage in avoiding haloing issues with skies, as we will see shortly.

Figures 10.13B and 10.14B apply the Bigger Hammer defaults, meaning the inverted red channel overlay, to their respective originals. Figures 10.13C and 10.14C instead use the inverted RGB. All overlays were blurred equally. All darkening layers are identical. No effort was made to enhance the color of any version along the lines of Figure 10.12.

Thus we have two originals of similar subjects. In each case two variants are generated using the same procedures. In each case I would say that one of the variants is better than the original and one arguably worse. Logically one would assume that the same variant would get the same result—but they don't.

I say that the clunky red flowers make Figure 10.13B worse than the original, Figure 10.13A. The RGB overlay version, Figure 10.13C, is better than either. We can attend to the subdued colors in LAB, but we need the additional contrast in the deep reds.

The next picture's red flowers tell an entirely different story. In Figure 10.14B they are full and convincing. Figure 10.14C has picked up and emphasized reflections, harming detail. Also, forgetting color issues, which could be fixed later, its water is too dark.

Without the PPW panel's ability to preview different options rapidly, this exercise would be frustrating. When the quality gain is more dramatic, the solution is usually clearer.

In the next example we'll study the Radius setting. But we must also decide which channel to use for the overlay. You haven't seen the photo yet, but based on the following description, which do you think would be best?

The scene is one of gloomy weather in the countryside. The sky is gray, with little detail. Several large, low-lying and interesting clouds,

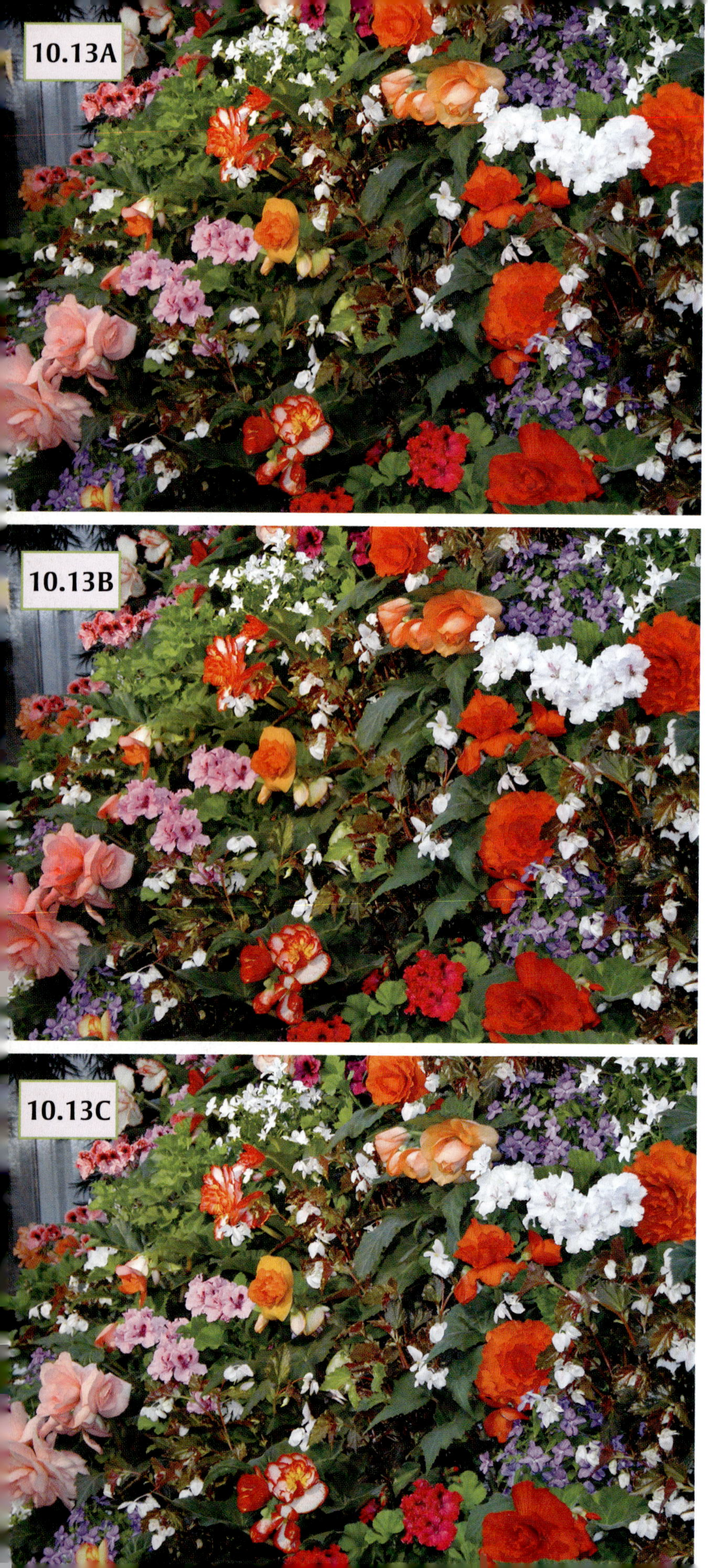

however, have settled into the background forest and hill, almost at ground level. The trees are very dark in view of the poor lighting, scarcely green at all. In the foreground is a greenhouse. Small parts have red roofing; they are the only areas of the picture that are not dark green or gray.

It sounds like this will be a better candidate for the Bigger Hammer than any of the flowers we've just been looking at. The large clouds, which are highlights, are the focus of attention. A blurred inverted overlay will improve their shape. Meanwhile, anything that lightens the forest is good, and the Bigger Hammer does that, too.

So, what should the overlay be? When you've got an answer, turn the page and check out the original of Postcard 10.15.

Channels in Greenery

Natural greens occur so frequently that knowing the channel structure should become instinctive. Red is medium dark, green medium light, and blue dark. In red objects such as the recent flowers or the roofing, red is light and green and blue are dark. Clouds and this gray sky are both neutral. Neither is affected by our choice of overlay. Instead, we ask ourselves about places where the channels aren't equal, meaning areas of color, the more pronounced the better.

We see the same kinds of trees here as in Postcard 10.1 and Figure 10.2, but these are much darker, offensively so. The blue channel, being darkest in natural greens, will lighten them the most if used as an inverted overlay.

***Figure 10.13** Top, the original. Middle, the default Bigger Hammer action is applied. Bottom, a blurred, inverted copy of the original RGB is substituted as the Overlay layer.*

The red roofing isn't as important as the trees, but to the extent that we care, it should probably get lighter rather than darker. This is again a vote for the blue rather than the red.

Making the correct choice here is key to the success of Postcard 10.15. There was no initial color or luminosity move of the types discussed in Chapters 3 and 4. A big use of Color Boost is inappropriate for a scene this gloomy. The only things after the overlay were MMM, the establishment of a lighter sky, and sharpening.

The result indicates the importance of this step, in the right kind of picture, of which this is one. If I were in a huge hurry I suppose I would just run the Bigger Hammer defaults and say it was good enough, but it would have to be a *really* huge hurry.

In real life, I would just use the panel to invoke the blue overlay. For teaching purposes, however, I did it from scratch, assuming no action, no panel.

I added two duplicate layers to the original. To the middle layer, I applied the blue, inverted; I set the top layer to Darker Color mode, 50% opacity. So far, the differences between this and Bigger Hammer defaults are the use of the blue channel rather than the red, and the lack of a blur.

There is no point wasting space by showing this state of the image. It was clear that the trees remained too dark. After fooling around with its opacity, I decided to delete the Darkening Layer altogether. Doing so produced Figure 10.16A, which looks silly because the overlay hadn't yet been blurred.

Blur size has a major impact on amorphous shapes like clouds.

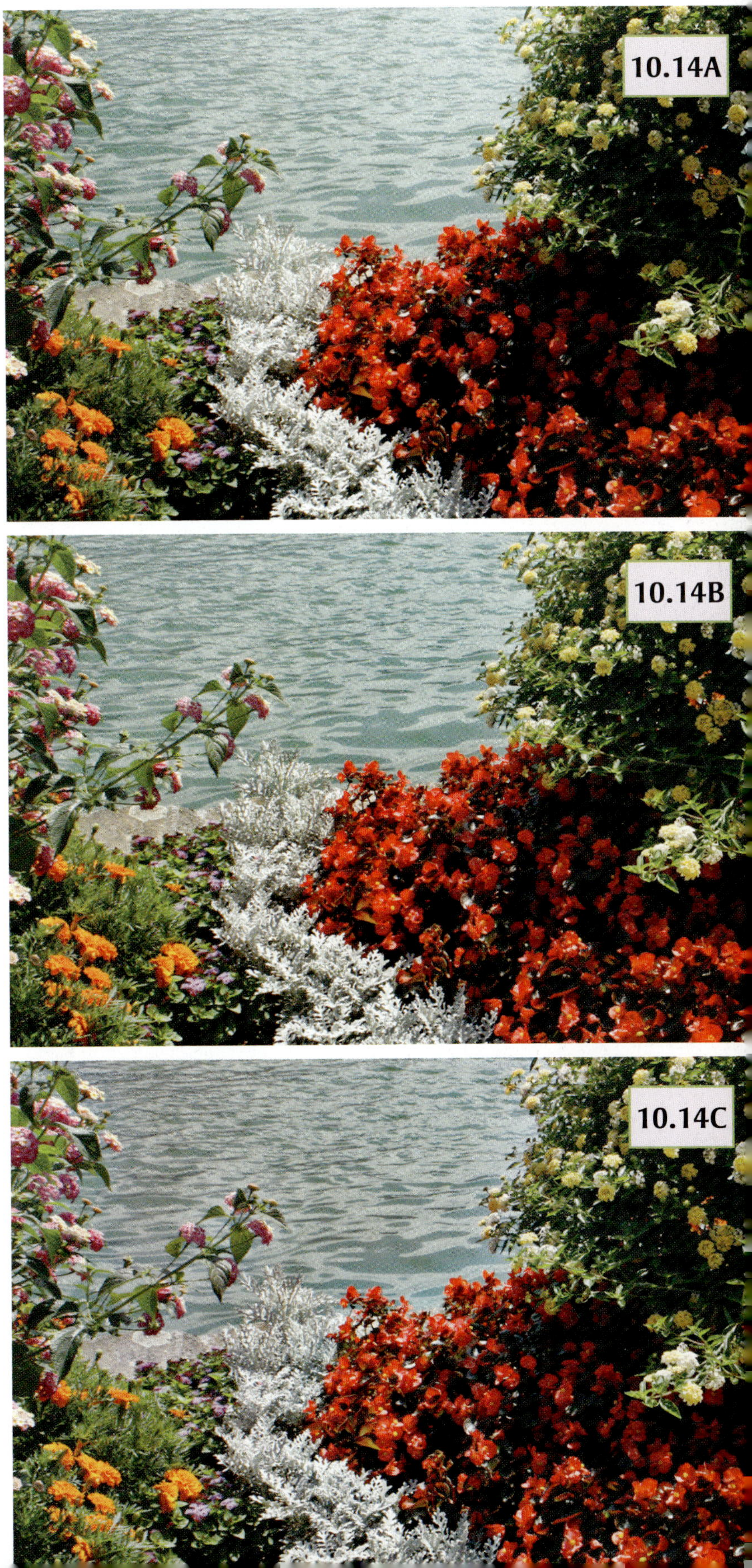

***Figure 10.14** Top, a new, but similar original. The middle and bottom versions are produced exactly as in Figure 10.13.*

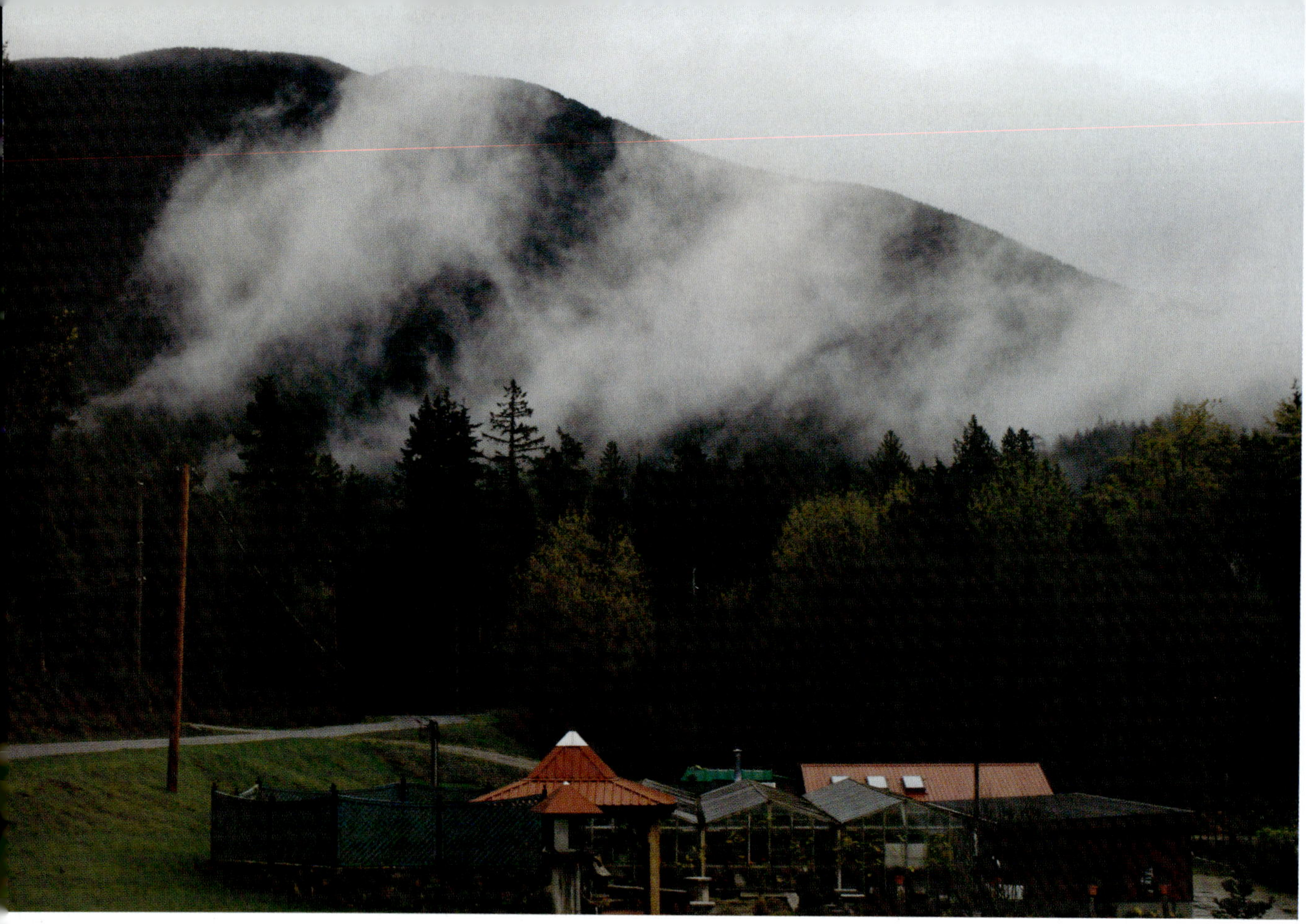

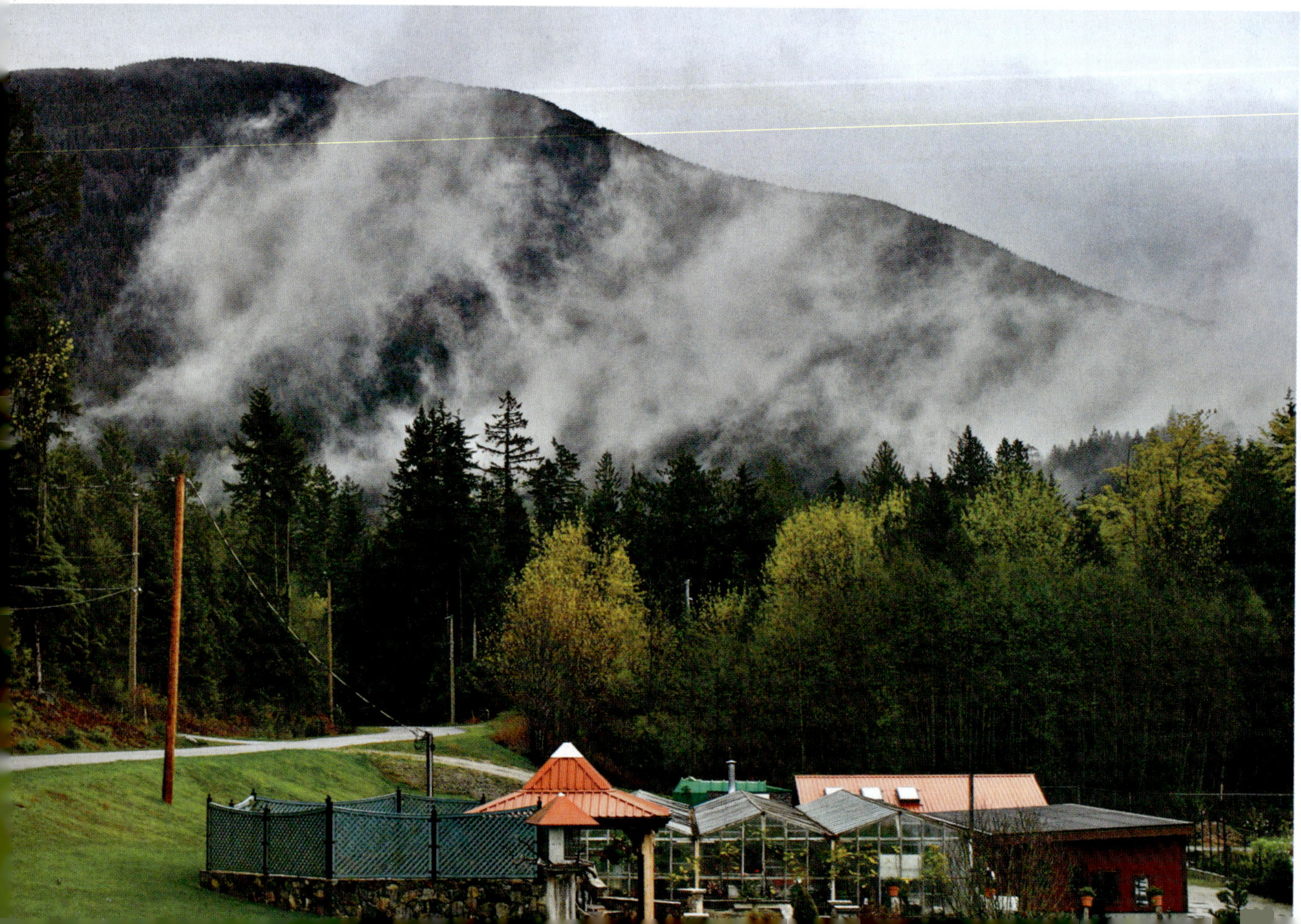

Postcard 10.15 *(opposite) A typical day scene, according to my experience, in the inaptly named Sunshine Coast of British Columbia, Canada.*

So can the type of blur. In the second half of Chapter 11 we'll discuss other options, but for now we'll look at Gaussian blur only, applied to the inverted blue overlay. Figures 10.16B, 10.16C, and 10.16D show the impact of Radii of 25, 40, and 55 pixels, respectively. (To put these numbers in context, the printable width in Postcard 10.15 is slightly less than 2000 pixels; larger files require larger Radii to achieve the same effect.)

The decision of which of the three is best is hereby left to you. It doesn't take long to preview different blurs, once you've decided to experiment, even if you aren't using the panel.

The Role of the Blur

Professional color correction favors the aggressive. Nobody I know has gotten rich in the field by overestimating the taste of typical clients. If you don't know your audience's taste, you should go for bright colors and heavy sharpening. I've had this debate elsewhere and don't intend to pursue it here, but one point about our current techniques is somewhat new.

The rules for viewer acceptance of our work are as simple as they are stupid and meaningless. Bright colors are always right, except when they are too much. Added contrast is highly preferred, as long

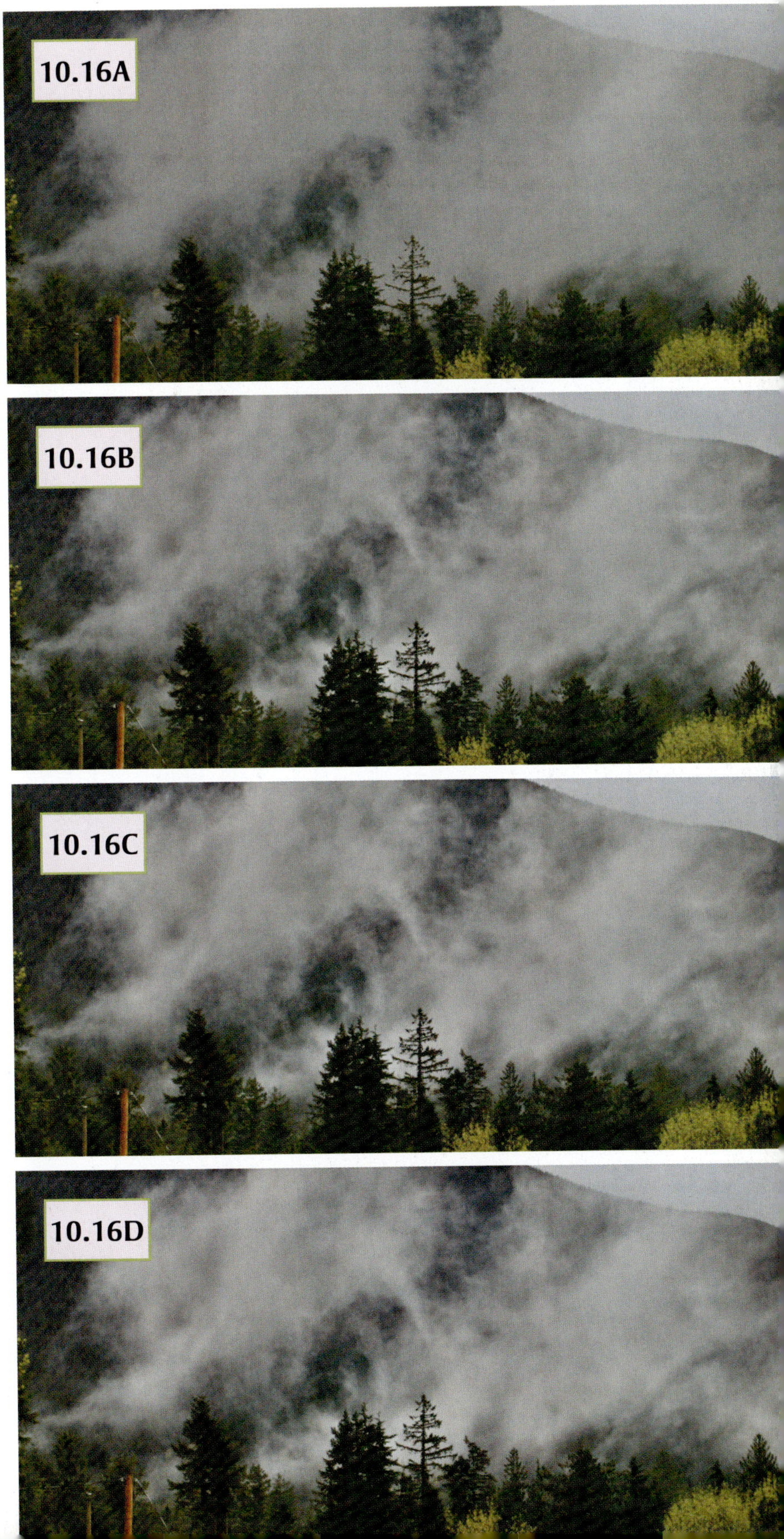

Figure 10.16 *Top, an inverted copy of the blue channel is overlaid onto the original. The remaining three versions blur it. Radius increases each time.*

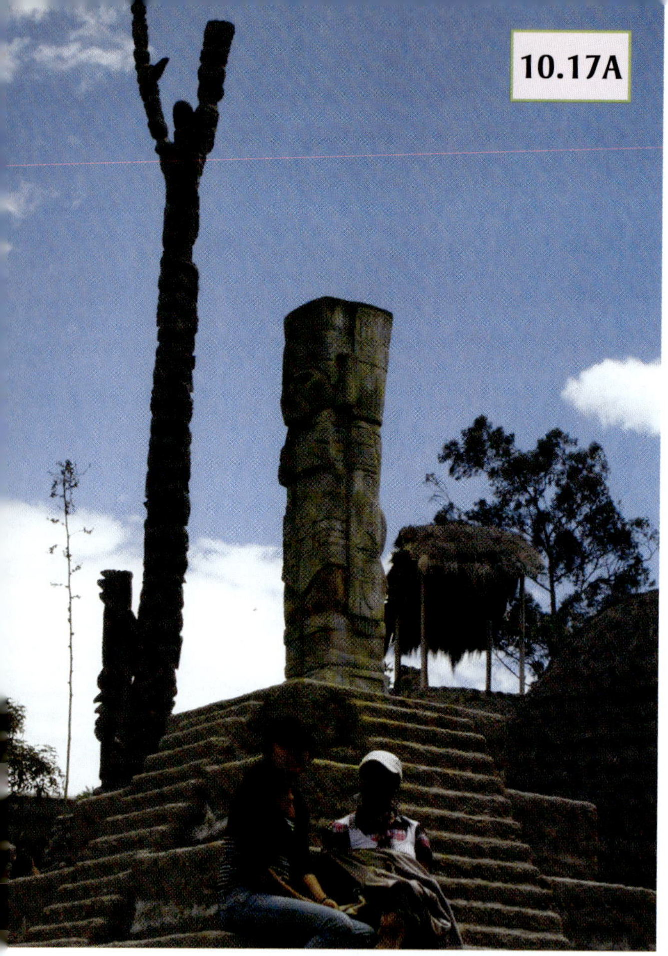

as it doesn't go too far. Strong sharpening is also a great idea, as long as it isn't too heavy. Now all we have to do is guess what *too much* and/or *too far* and/or *too heavy* mean to people we don't know.

Your judgment as to whether the color is too vivid is apt to be warped if you insist on evaluating it next to some of the impossibly loud products of the Color Boost action. Avoid that error, though, and you're looking at the same thing another viewer would. I don't believe that your awareness that the MMM action was used to produce the color would skew your opinion.

The same is also true of luminosity blends and curves. When you evaluate them on screen, you perceive, more or less, what the viewer will.

Starting with this chapter and continuing through four others, however, a nasty complication introduces itself. We are using large blurs as masks to alter the perception of contrast and depth. This is related to what is

Figure 10.17 *Top left, the original. Bottom left, a default application of the Bigger Hammer action. Bottom right, using the blue channel rather than the red for the overlay produces haloing in the sky.*

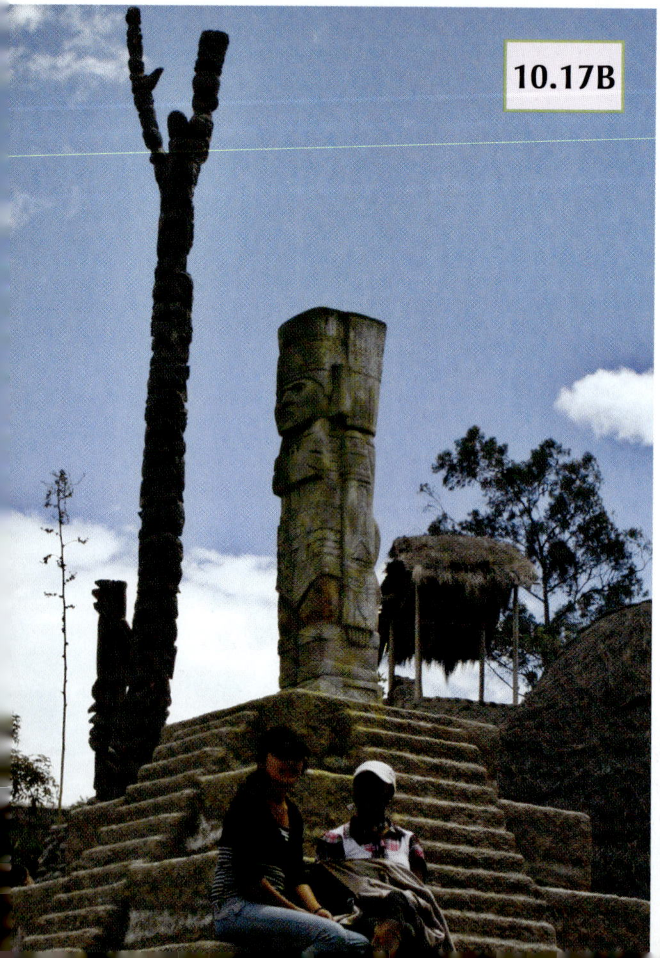

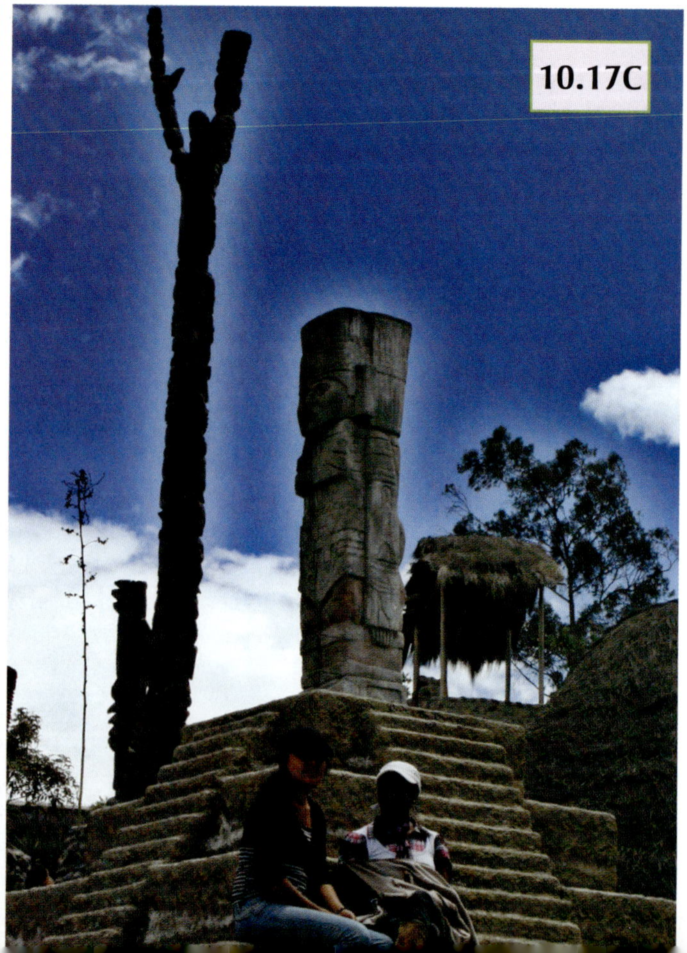

known generically as unsharp masking, but traditional USM uses much smaller blurs, because bigger ones were impossible technically at the time the methods were developed. Today there is no such limitation; we use a nontraditional form of USM known as hiraloam. We also use something closely related in the blurred multiplication masks shown in the next three chapters. The Bigger Hammer is a more distant relative, and the Shadows/Highlights command even farther removed.

This is the first of five chapters that are thus seriously concerned with the impact of blurring in contrast enhancement. If you want to count the Chapter 7 discussion of S/H, that means six full chapters are devoted to this broad topic. I believe you will agree later that lavishing such space on the technique was worth it. There is, however, a problem in evaluating its effects.

All these blurring methods alter the picture in ways that do not correspond to any feature of the human visual system. They introduce artifacts, intelligent ones hopefully, that fool the viewer into perceiving stronger transitions.

The trick, as ever, is not to go too far. The good news is that the tiresome words *too far* are more specific this time than usual. They mean that the artificiality has to be strong enough to intrude upon the viewer by drawing attention to itself.

The bad news is that you and I are terrible judges of whether this is happening, irretrievably biased by our own knowledge of what shenanigans have taken place. The people who evaluate our work know deedle-de-bop about Bigger Hammers or inverted blurs or the Helmholtz-Kohlrausch effect and will probably die of boredom if we start discussing them. They are unlikely to detect the telltale signs of our technique, because they don't know what to look for.

This chapter's examples all show evidence of skulduggery that we can see but would be invisible to the public at large. Worse artifacting should be fixed. On the other hand, trying to erase every last hint of the trickery does no good other than wasting time that might otherwise be spent on Facebook.

Serious problems with artifacting, often termed *haloing,* are more common with the techniques of the next three chapters than with the Bigger Hammer. In fact, finding a suitable example was so difficult as to require chicanery. I could locate files where I personally would be inclined to intervene to reduce some minor defect, but this wasn't enough. I wanted something where the action leaves a clear, obvious, unmistakable, and undeniably ugly artifact. In showing this, it's not fair to just jack up the values beyond any recognition. Doing that in the discussion of color actions made sense. Applying the MMM and Color Boost at wildly excessive settings helped us understand what those two actions do. Such an example here would not be helpful, and would demonstrate only what everybody knows, that almost any maneuver can look stupid given stupid enough settings.

So I looked for something that would come out drastically wrong without the use of intentionally incorrect settings. The closest I can come has no sabotage, but it requires two steps that cannot be recommended.

Halos for the Unholy

The opponent is Figure 10.17A. It is likely better handled with the techniques of Chapters 12 and 13, but trying out the Bigger Hammer can't be faulted. The default result is Figure 10.17B. So far, so good. Now, the two missteps.

- The motivation for using the Bigger Hammer is usually to improve light areas. Not here. In the Icelandic scene of Figure 10.11, we learned that when shadows are more important than highlights, we should switch the overlay layer's mode to Soft Light. But for this demonstration we have to pretend that we didn't pay attention. Overlay mode it is.
- We often want to darken the blue parts of skies. I don't know whether that's wise here, but for the sake of argument, let's say it is. If so, we

ought to use the Darken Sky actions laid out in Chapter 8. But if this demonstration is going to work we have to pretend we didn't read that part, either.

Instead, we will try to rejigger the action by substituting the blue channel for the red. Since blue things are always much lighter in the blue than the red, they will become darker if the channel is inverted. Thus, substituting the inverted blue for the inverted red will force a darker sky. So, we apply the blue channel from the Background layer, inverted, to the Overlay Layer. And to make things fair, we blur at the same radius used by the action.

These shoddy moves give us what we deserve, Figure 10.17C. The question is how to fix the haloing around the vertical objects. My answer is to drag the Overlay Layer to the trash and start over without the two stupid misconceptions. We'll talk shortly about more normal options for repairing such damage, but first we need to consider what caused it and why it doesn't occur more often.

None of the ingredients for halo stew is unusual, but so many are required to be used simultaneously that a really bad result like Figure 10.17C is rare. Here's what's needed:

- High-contrast transitions in the overlay layer. We have that in the blue-channel overlay of Figure 10.17C: the vertical elements are very dark and the sky is very light. In Figure 10.17B that artifact-friendly contrast is missing because in the copy of the red channel it uses for the overlay, the sky is almost a midtone.
- Although the overlay must be high-contrast, the base layer can't be. If the original sky were slightly lighter, let alone as light as the blue channel, the halo would have nothing to sink its teeth into.
- The edge where the two objects meet has to be lengthy, as otherwise the halo won't be obtrusive enough.
- The halo-provoking object also has to be wide, as otherwise the big blur will obliterate it. The large tree at the right of Figure 10.17C creates a halo. The more slender vertical stalk at left is too narrow to do so.
- The area of possible effect has to be uniform or almost so, as detail interferes with our ability to perceive the halo.
- For every light halo there's a dark one, but as a practical matter only the light halo is important. The dark halos usually fall in objects that are themselves too dark to show them. Also, dark objects generally have a texture.

Queries for the Saintly

That is quite a flurry of factors that have to be in play before haloing becomes an issue. Consider what common picture elements might meet all these requirements at once. You will conclude, correctly, that most offensive halos come where a cloudless sky butts a dark background. Skies are smooth enough and dark enough to show the halo. The background is often big enough to provoke it.

Five remedies suggest themselves. The first is already incorporated into the Bigger Hammer action: the red channel is the default inverted overlay. The reason should now be clear: it's the best insurance against haloing in skies.

Second, as was discussed in Chapter 8, skies are easy to select in LAB. Solving a problem like this one can be as simple as Blend If. We'll take a look at an example in the second half of the next chapter.

Third, we could use a larger blurring radius. It wouldn't cure what ails Figure 10.17C, but in less extreme cases a more diffuse halo is harder to detect.

Fourth, we could employ something other than Gaussian Blur to defocus the overlay, or even use some combination of filters. We will postpone pulling the pin on that grenade until the next chapter, too.

Fifth, the old prepress remedy: when in doubt, use force. An invisible unblurred layer is there for those preferring to paint through masks.

We turn first to a quiz. Please cover the bottom half of Figure 10.18 while you answer.

Our new original, Figure 10.18A, is an interesting study in how halos develop. As with the last picture, it's questionable that we should be using the Bigger Hammer on it at all. My inability to find a more convincing example is another indication that the problem may be overstated. Be that as it may, we're about to run the action, with the Darkening Layer disabled so that we can get a better feel for what the overlay is doing. Where, if at all, do you expect problems with haloing?

For a hint, uncover the bottom half. Figure 10.18B is what will be described in Chapter 15 as a *halo map.* It shows where a blurred overlay version is *lighter* than one produced without blurring. Figure 10.18C is the opposite; it shows the way in which the blurring *darkened* the final result. Contrast has been enhanced in each to make the halos more prominent.

Remembering that we are talking only about the blur and not the overlay, here are your quiz questions, from easy to hard:

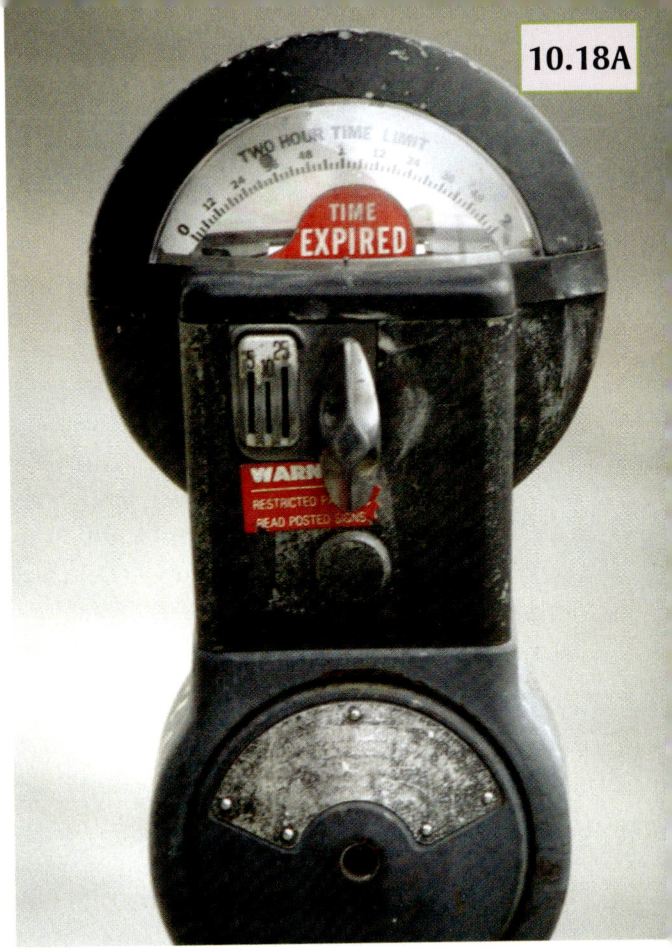

***Figure 10.18** Top right, an original to which an inverted overlay will be applied. Bottom left shows the light halos produced when the overlay is blurred. Bottom right, the dark halos.*

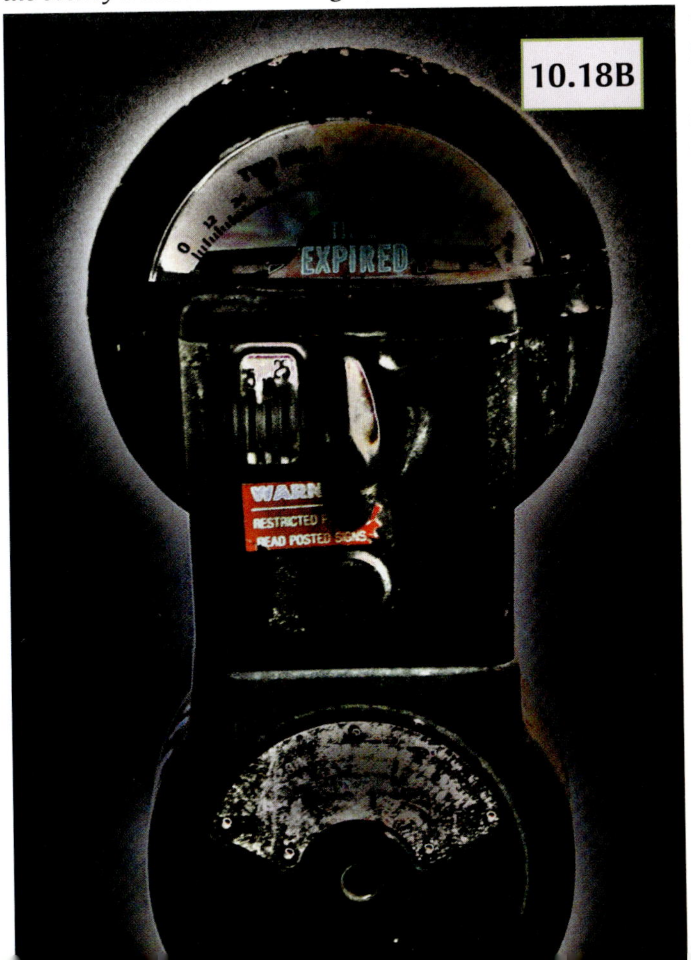

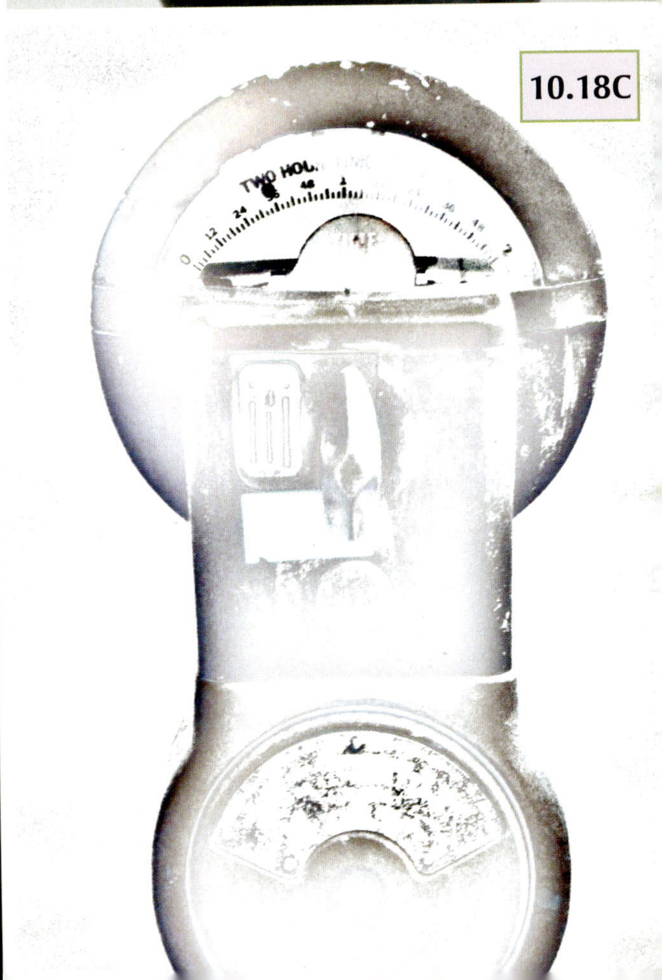

- Explain why a light halo surrounds the meter while a darker one is found just inside its edge.
- Why is the light halo outside of the top circular part of the meter so much more pronounced on the left side than on the right?
- Moving down the left of the meter, to the narrow point below the red warning sticker, why is there almost no outside light halo, especially compared to what's happening at the top?
- Why is the halo darkest on the inside top edge of the meter, where it meets the glass just right of center? Why shouldn't it be darker on the outside, where it meets the background?
- The black type and time scale seem to be dark halos themselves. No doubt they will look better that way, but why is it happening?

Time now to find out how it all shakes out. Figure 10.19A uses an inverted red channel for the overlay. Figure 10.19B blurs it by 35 pixels. We would now be at Bigger Hammer defaults, except that this version has no darkening layer.

Another way of looking at it: Figure 10.19B is what you would get if you started with Figure 10.19A and applied Figure 10.18A to it in Screen mode, followed by Figure 10.18B in Multiply mode, thus establishing the light and dark halos. (Reminder: contrast in the halo maps has been enhanced, so the screening and multiplying would have to be done beforehand.) You should recall this method when we discuss sharpening in Chapter 15. The action advocated there makes use of something quite similar.

Before discussing the merits of the parking meter image, I repeat the disclaimers attached to the previous exercise: this is not a classic case for Bigger Hammer (although I could certainly see using it if you want to show how beat-up

Figure 10.19 *Left, an inverted copy of the red channel is applied to a duplicate layer set to Overlay mode. Right, the layer is blurred at a Radius of 35 pixels.*

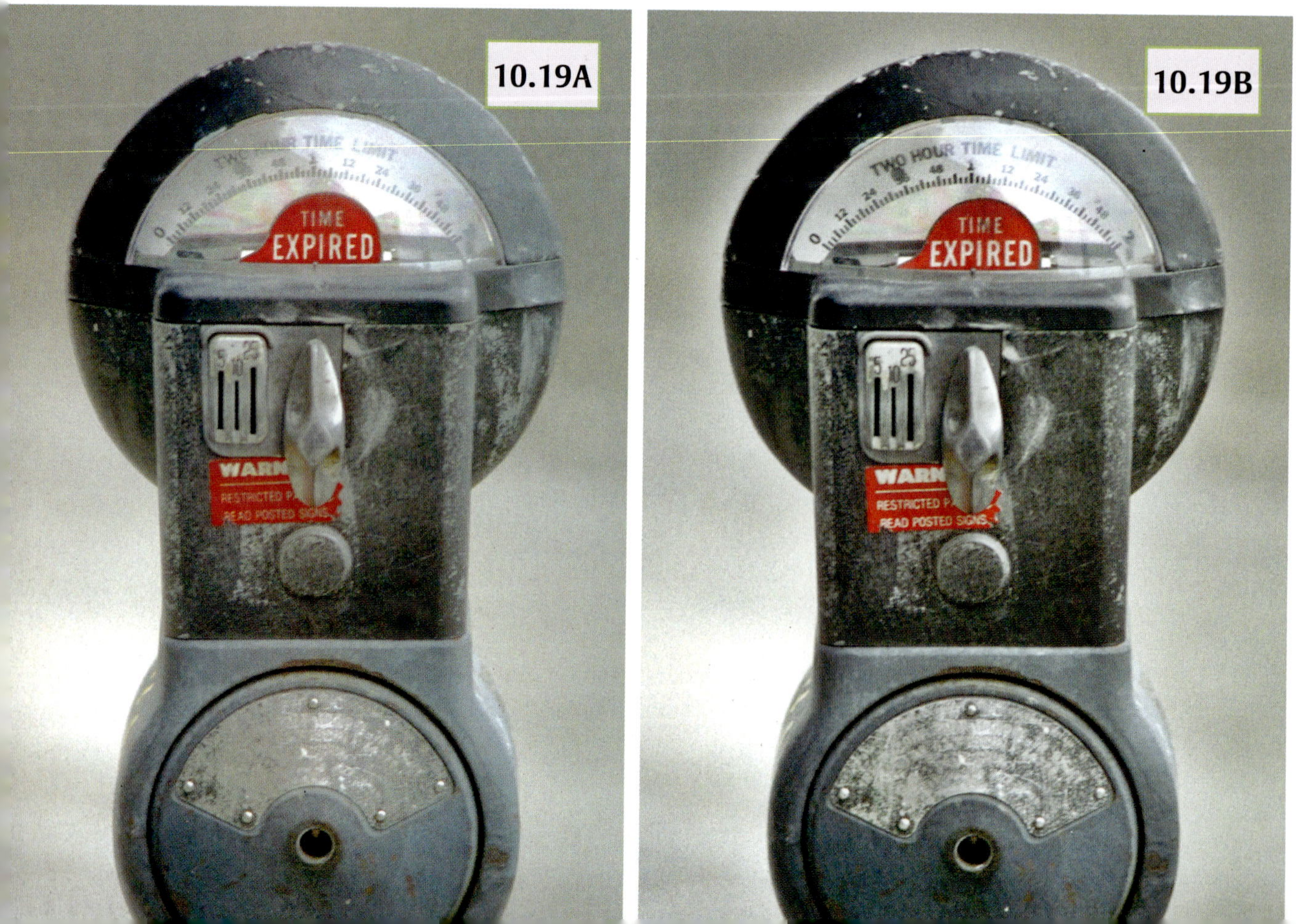

this meter is); the blurring radius is specific to the size of my file, which is a bit over 900 pixels wide as you see it; there is usually a darkening layer in place; and when, as here, the shadows are more important than the highlights, we use Soft Light mode and not Overlay. In short, this version is to study artifacting, not how to use the Bigger Hammer properly.

As far as I'm concerned the dark halos are very effective at giving shape to the meter. I can't believe that any non-expert would recognize them as artificial.

The light halos are more of an issue, as they are in every form of sharpening. Lessening them is one reason for the default darkening layer that's missing here. Admittedly these light halos are not as disastrous as those in the sky of Figure 10.17C. But this background is as smooth as a sky, so it does a poor job of hiding halos.

I can see light halos everywhere around the meter and you probably can, too. However, someone who doesn't know our secrets might not. The one exception, I would say, is the area around the meter at upper left. A nonexpert viewer might find fault with it, so my personal decision would be to intervene there, but not necessarily in other areas. If, that is, for the sake of argument, I liked the meter itself.

Before discussing how to diminish the halo, here are the quiz answers.

How Many Halos Can Dance on a Pin

- Where a dark object like the meter meets something light like the background, this inverted overlay always produces light halos in the light one and vice versa. The overlay layer is inverted, so the meter is light and the background dark. Blurring it inserts a large area

Figure 10.20 *Left, the blur is doubled to 70 pixels, with the mode still Overlay. Right, back to 35 pixels, but layer mode is now Soft Light.*

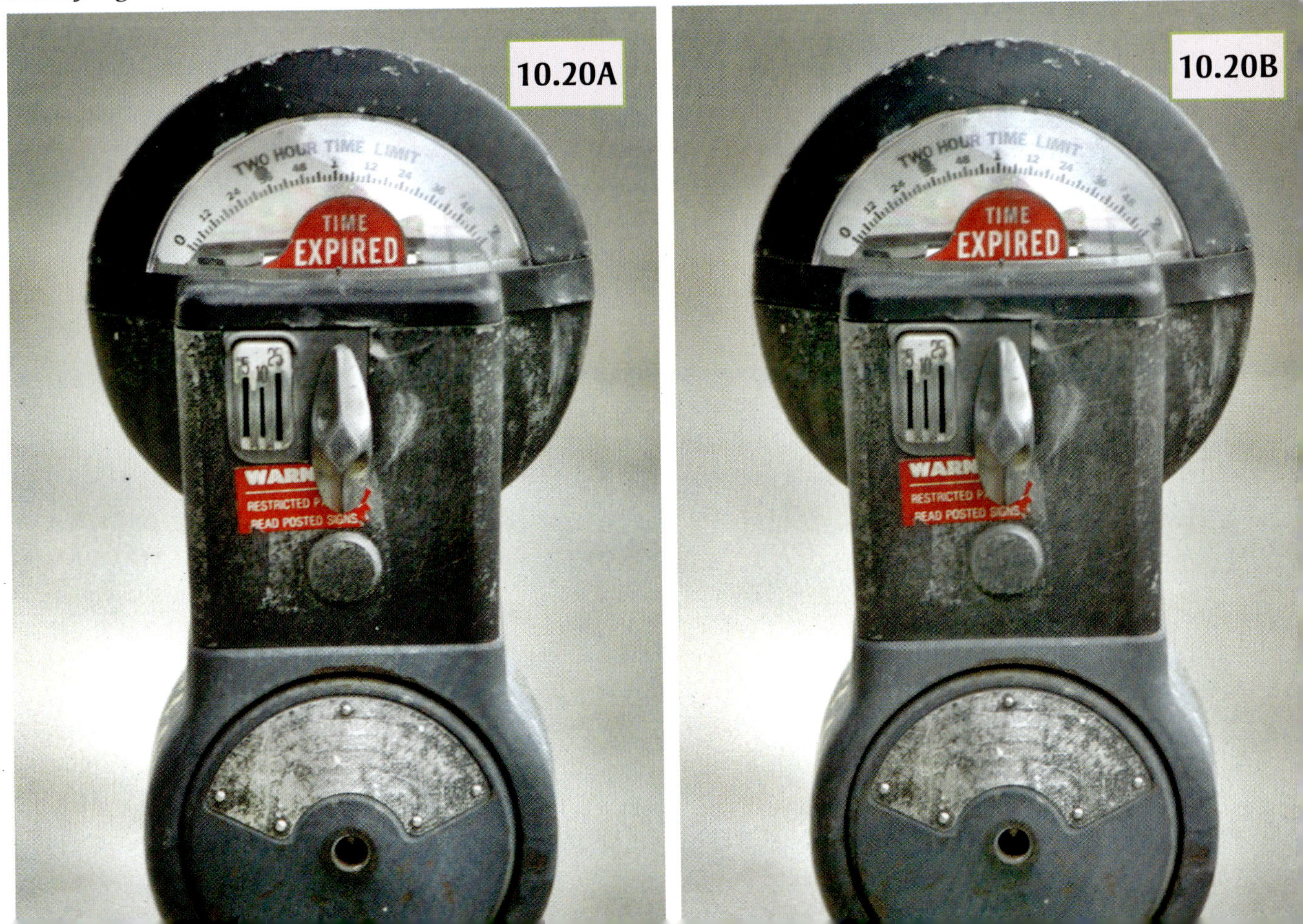

of gray between the two. Therefore the background is generally dark, but becomes lighter as it approaches the edge. The overlay doesn't lighten the background near the edge as much as it does areas further away. This is what creates the halo. Similarly, the meter is light when inverted, but gets gray near the edge when blurred. The overlay lightens its interior more than the edges.

- The background varies little at the top of the picture. The meter, however, is darker at top left than top right. In other words, there is more contrast between the two objects on the left side, resulting in a more pronounced blur and, therefore, a more discernible halo.
- Even more contrast occurs halfway down on the left side, in the narrowest area of the meter. The background is now lighter than it was at top but the meter is the same. Therefore in principle the blur's effect is even stronger and the resulting halo more prominent. But there's no place to put this theoretical halo. How do you lighten something so nearly blank? Instead, the background practically vanishes.
- The dark halo at top where the metal meets the glass is stronger on the right side. The metal is equally dark on both sides but the glass is not; a reflection causes the right side to be lighter, thus more contrast with the metal and a more obvious blurring effect.
- Changing the overlay layer to Normal mode would reveal a blurry mess. The object, however, could still be identified as a parking meter. But the type and time scale would be gone, wiped out by the blur. The overlay therefore causes the entire area to darken whether it was originally white or black. This emphasizes the type, which is a good thing. Notice how in the unblurred Figure 10.19A, the type has actually moved in the opposite direction—it's gotten lighter.

A Season in Purgatory

Getting rid of offending halos can be as easy or as difficult as you make it. Let's run down some of the choices.

- Remember that we have left out a customary step that might solve the problem by itself. Recognizing that light halos are more offensive than dark ones, the Bigger Hammer action includes a layer that by default cuts all lightening, including the halos, by half. That layer was omitted here. Reducing the intensity of the light halos that much would probably make them acceptable; the question is whether the meter then would seem too dark.
- The overlay could be redone with a larger blur radius. Figure 10.20A doubles it. The halos are more diffuse than those of Figure 10.19B, which makes them more tolerable.
- Figure 10.20B follows the Bigger Hammer recommendation for the somewhat uncommon photos where detail is more critical in shadows than in highlights. The overlay layer is identical to that of Figure 10.19B, but the layer mode has been changed from Overlay to Soft Light, with favorable impact on the haloing.

Setting esoteric blurring methods aside until the next chapter, the remaining option is the brute-force one. The action saves (as an invisible layer) a copy of the overlaid version before the blur has been applied. In other words, it provides the equivalent of Figure 10.19A, for use in combatting whatever depredation the blurring process may have introduced.

Using it is pain-free. Not much is needed, as the defects it tries to correct are fragile. If done properly the merge is not detectable. And if you don't need it the layer will vanish the next time you flatten the image.

The idea is to use as little of the unblurred layer as possible, consistent with solving whatever problems are being targeted. The obvious way of doing so is also the best. Make the unblurred layer visible, but hide it again by adding a black layer mask. Then, with a brush set to low opacity, paint lightness into the mask in the areas you wish to alter.

No great precision is needed. If you're trying

***Postcard 10.21** The west coast of Maui, Hawaii.*

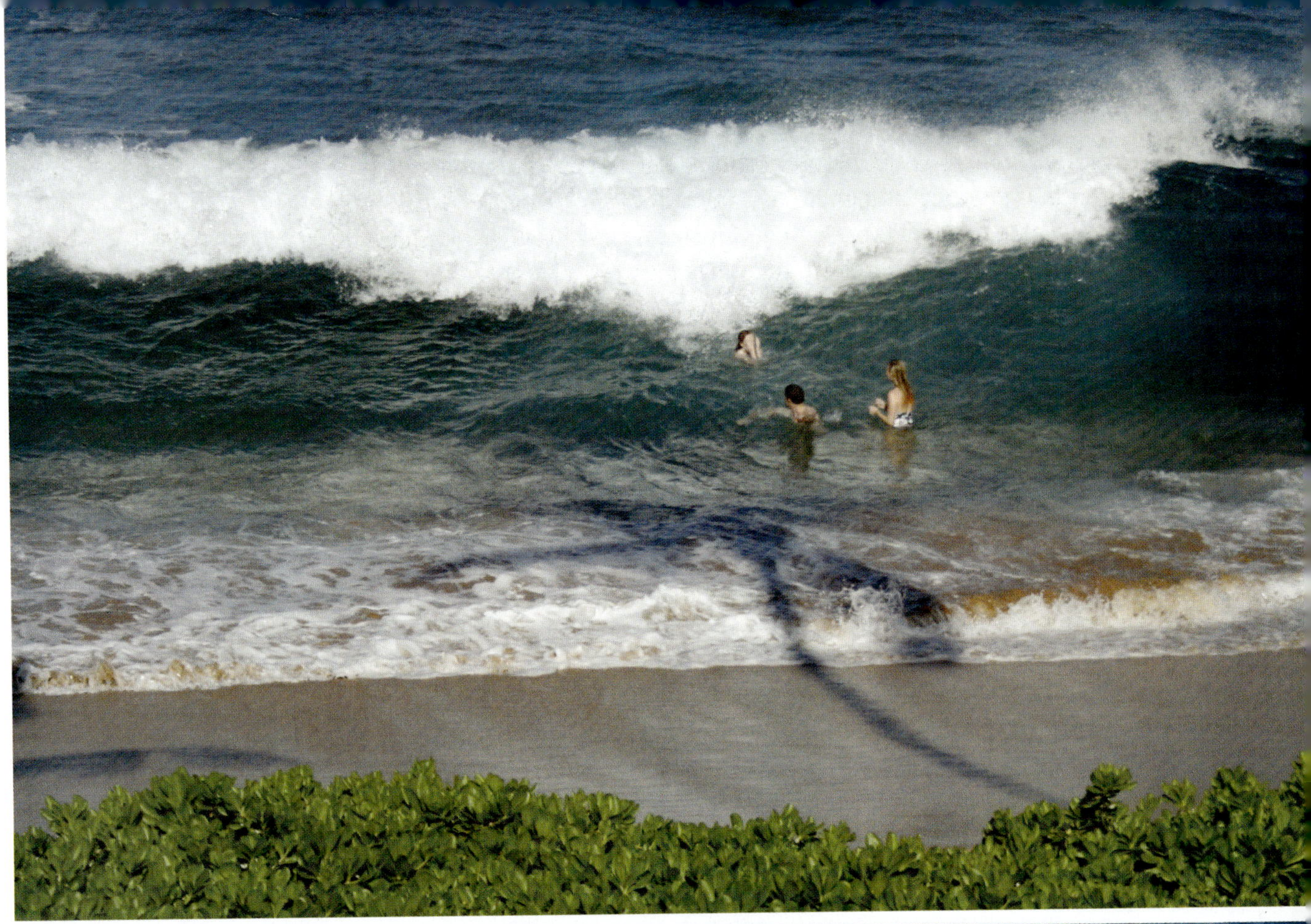

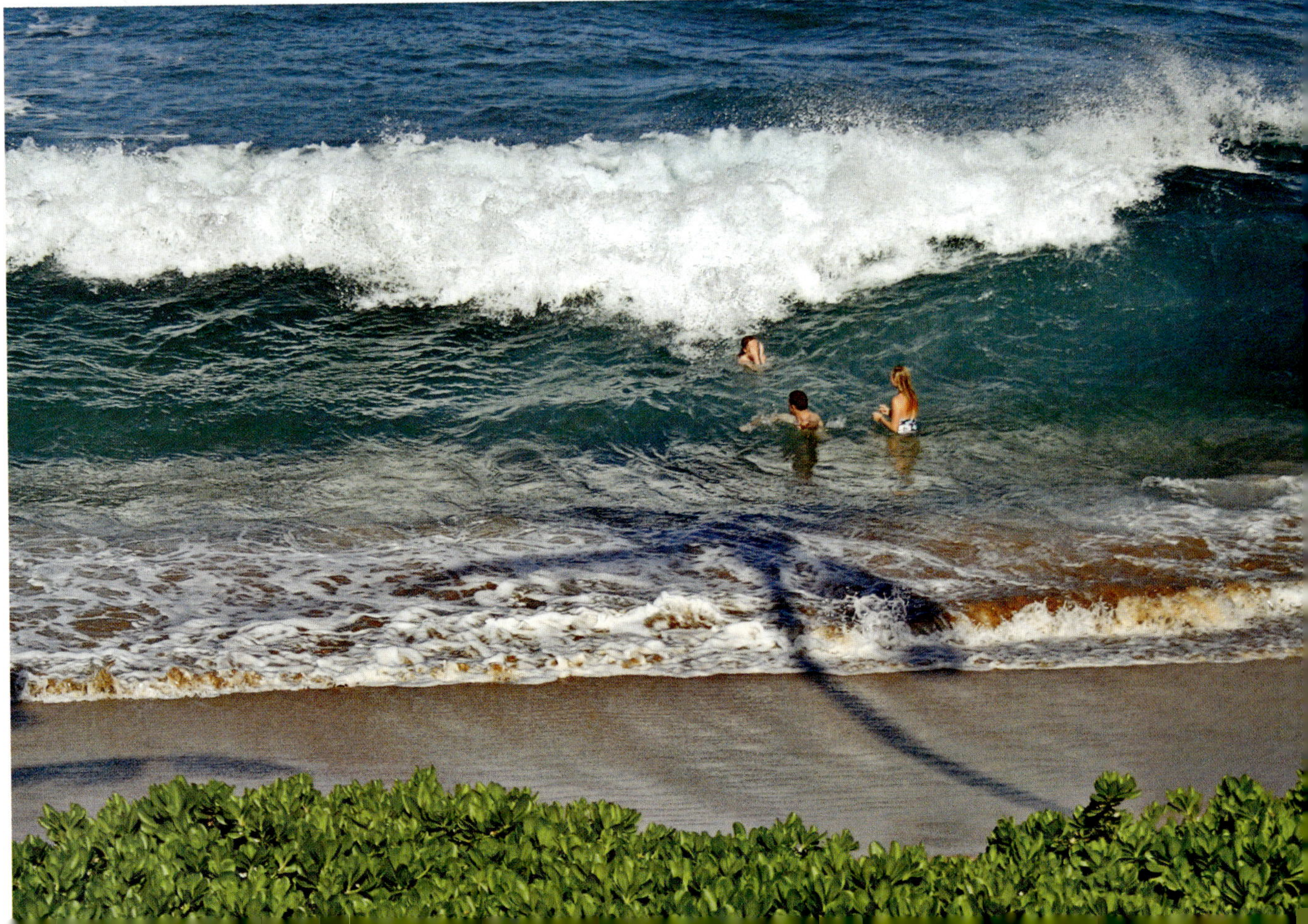

to knock out the halo in the upper left of Figure 10.19A, painting over the entire area will do the trick but moving the brush in a zigzag fashion would also work. Breaking the halo into pieces prevents people from perceiving it just as well as eliminating it entirely.

If the objective is to reduce all the halos slightly, even the ones that are not prominent, you could still brush into the mask manually, or you might make a rough feathered lasso selection of the affected areas and apply a slight lightening curve to the mask.

Figure 10.22 *Top left, minor corrections for color and luminosity to the original of Postcard 10.21. Top right, Shadows/Highlights is applied. Bottom left, the default Bigger Hammer action is added. Bottom right, the invisible unblurred layer.*

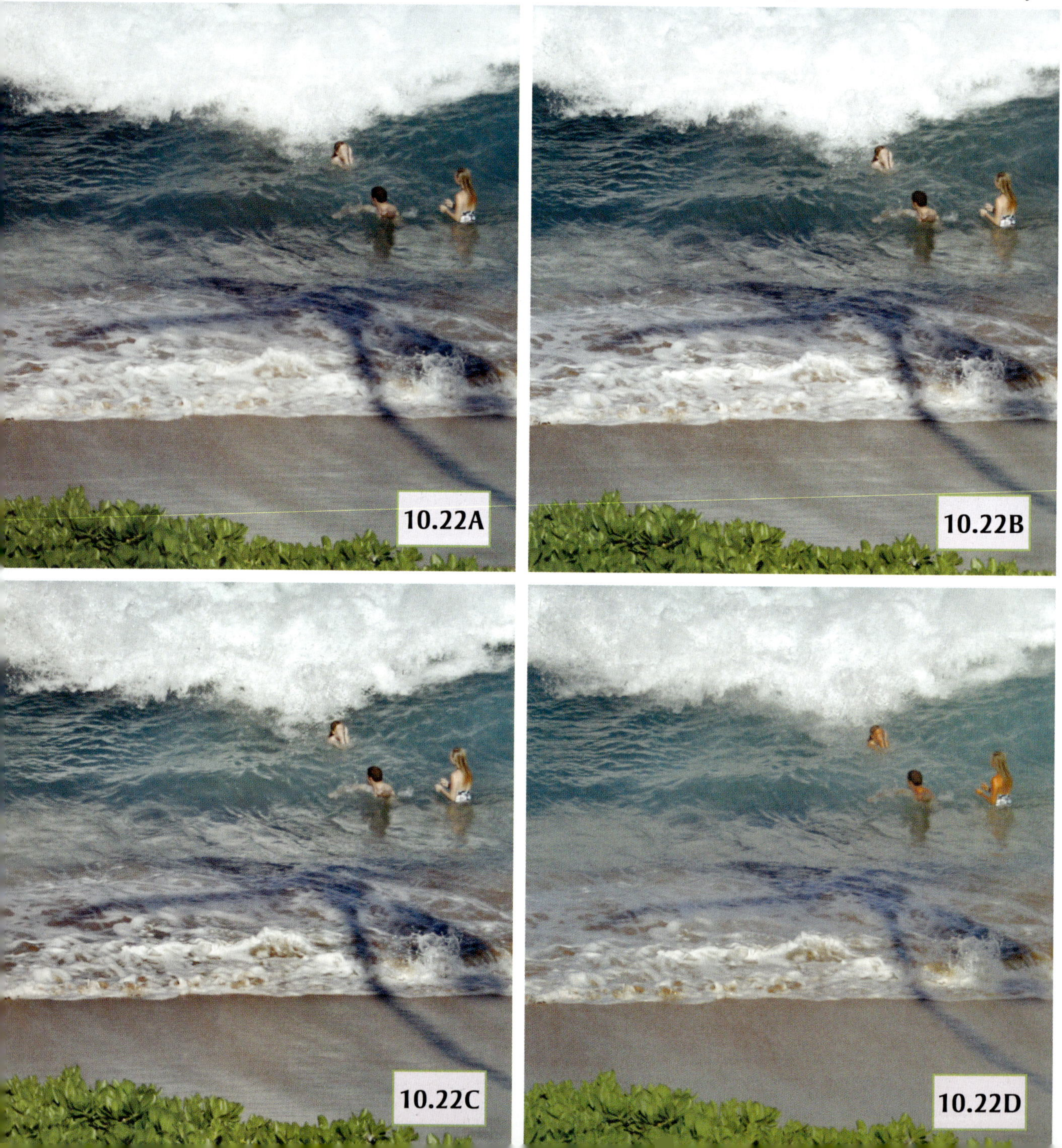

Another variant: texture is the enemy of any artifact. Introducing some into the layer mask often defeats halos. It can be as simple as adding noise, or as complicated as painting something in and then applying an artistic filter.

Our guardian angel is that the blurred and unblurred versions aren't as different as Figure 10.19 suggests. They have so much in common that most merges are undetectable. This suggests another trick, and in honor of the Time Expired flag in the meter, it will be the last one for this chapter.

The moment we see Postcard 10.21, we should know that the Bigger Hammer is going to play a role in the correction. Detail in the surf may make or break this scene.

You might think haloing would be a problem. The leading and rear edges of the breaker butt water that is much darker. There is just as much contrast on each side of the edge as there was in the sky debacle of Figure 10.17C. But this picture has so much texture everywhere that we don't perceive the halos that logic says must be in the water. The only place haloing is visible is where the greenery at bottom butts the smooth-textured sand. I would say removing it is optional.

In the unblurred parking meter of Figure 10.19A, we saw that the overlay was trying to lighten the black type of the time scale. Blurring actually reversed this, so that the type became darker than it was originally. As it happened, this looked good, so we ignored it.

Now we will look at the opposite, where the overlay wants to make something darker, the blur causes it to become lighter instead, and this time it *doesn't* look good.

The Land Beyond the Halo

I started the correction of Postcard 10.21 with two very mild moves. The original had a slight blue cast in the shadows, which I fixed with curves. Then I did some slight luminosity blending using the green channel as a base. After these two steps I had Figure 10.22A. The gain over the original is there, but it's small.

I am ordinarily about as inclined to go skydiving without a parachute as to let software choose my highlight. An algorithm can't tell what is significant, only what is lightest, and usually I can figure that out for myself.

Not in this case, though. The lightest point is certainly somewhere in the breaker; each point there is as significant as any other, and I will be sent to a place where halos are not permitted if I can tell you which one is lightest, even with the aid of a threshold layer.

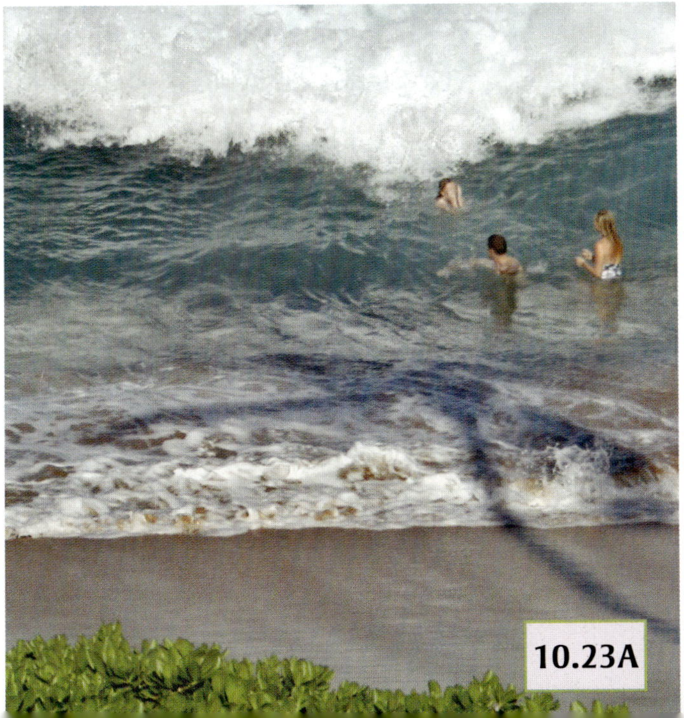

Figure 10.23 *Left, Figure 10.22C adjusted with a heavier Darkening layer and with the Unblurred layer exposed through a layer mask. Right, the layer mask, with what it is exposing superimposed.*

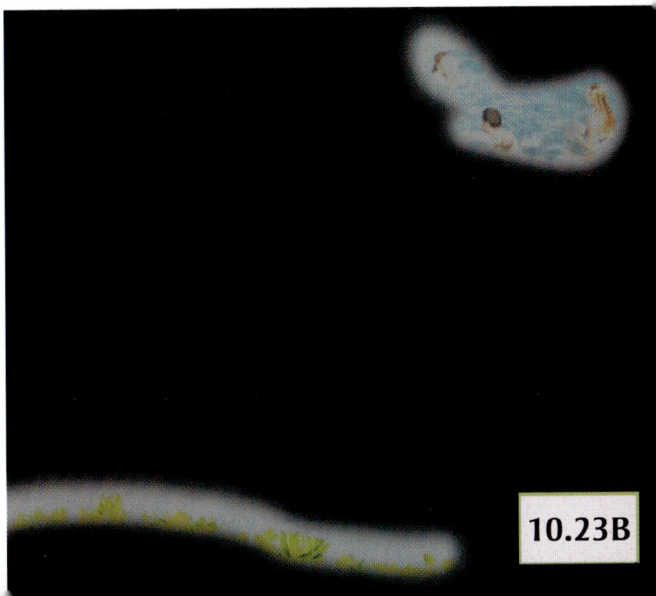

The Shadows/Highlights command comes to the rescue, producing Figure 10.22B. As explained in Chapter 7, its defaults blow out a tiny percentage of the lightest pixels. That rigid mathematical approach works well here, because the very lightest pixels are of no importance..

Enter the Bigger Hammer. Figure 10.22C is the default; 10.22D the unseen unblurred layer. It brings up the question of whether to stick with the default inverted red for the overlay. Using the blue instead would create a lighter beach and darker water. The green would do these things also, but not as strongly.

I thought that people's views on this might vary, so I assigned this as an exercise in advanced correction classes. I expected a repeat of the interesting divergence seen earlier in another class effort, the house fire of Figure 10.9.

Nothing of the kind happened. The opinions were so uniform that I pulled the exercise out after three classes. Only the people who used the Bigger Hammer or something similar got acceptable whitewater, but those who did always tried to get something comparable to Figure 10.23A, which is a revised version of 10.22C. So the comparisons were not interesting.

When doing it myself, I felt that the water was a bit too light in Figure 10.22C, so I increased opacity of the darkening layer to 75%. I then turned to what I perceived as a problem with the people. Skin is light in the red channel. Using an inverted copy as an overlay darkens the flesh strongly, as Figure 10.22D indicates.

But that's before the big blur. The faces are treated as if they were part of the water, which the overlay is forcing lighter. Consequently in Figure 10.22C, the people look unhealthy. They shouldn't be as dark as in the unblurred version, but it's easy to split the difference.

I therefore activated the Unblurred layer and loaded a black layer mask. Then, I painted lightness into the appropriate area. While I was at it, I partially erased a small halo on the shore where the greenery meets the sand.

Figure 10.23B shows my painting technique to be slovenly at best. Surely the mask could have been restricted to the people only, without risking darkening the water between them!

But can you see any indication of this peccadillo in the final postcard? If not, it's another indication of how forgiving this method of merging versions is.

Options, options. So ends our look at most, but not all, of the ways to customize this powerful tool. Please remember that only a small percentage of photos benefit from the Bigger Hammer. And the action produces decent results on most of them, without any extra shenanigans.

When highlight detail is critical, the Bigger Hammer need not be quite so blunt an instrument as its name suggests.

The Bottom Line

Some photos have a critical need for extra detail in the highlights (and, occasionally, the shadows). This chapter introduces a powerful method of bringing it out using an inverted, blurred overlay layer.

The basic technique has been reduced to an action that works well enough in most cases. The second half of this chapter discusses several custom options to maximize the method's effectiveness, always assuming that the job is important enough to justify the extra time.

11

Of Bridges and Blurs

Images shot in a combination of sun and shade often look unrealistic. Multiplying the file into itself through a blurred layer mask can make the two halves interact more harmoniously.

Building bridges was harder two thousand years ago than it is today, so the Romans chose the narrowest part of the Arno. Their effort no longer stands. The replacement, which the locals for some reason call the "Old Bridge", is less than half that age, but it's still only 100 meters long. Walking it takes longer than you'd think because of the pedestrian traffic. Cars, of course, are out of the question.

The three arches are pretty enough, but the overall structure hardly compares for architectural merit and elegance with London's Tower Bridge, which we corrected way back in Figure 6.1. And surely, as an engineering marvel, it is not even on the same planet, let alone the same continent, as the Golden Gate Bridge we worked over in Figure 6.15, not to mention being about a billionth of the size.

In terms of historical and cultural significance, however, Florence's Ponte Vecchio (Old Bridge) equals if not eclipses its two rivals. It would take a long chapter to flesh that statement out and a lengthy book to cover the contributions made by Florence to the development of our understanding of art in general and our work in particular.

Suffice it to say that the Ponte Vecchio labors under a disadvantage. In the midst of the city with the greatest artistic stimuli in the world, with the most breathtaking architecture and sculpture, the city where Michelangelo, Ghiberti, Donatello, and Brunelleschi plied their trade, the city that launched an artistic reformation greater even than anything in our own time—in the midst of all this, the Ponte Vecchio is an unimpressive sight, unless somebody tells you what it is and why it is important. The same cannot be said for, say, the Duomo or the David.

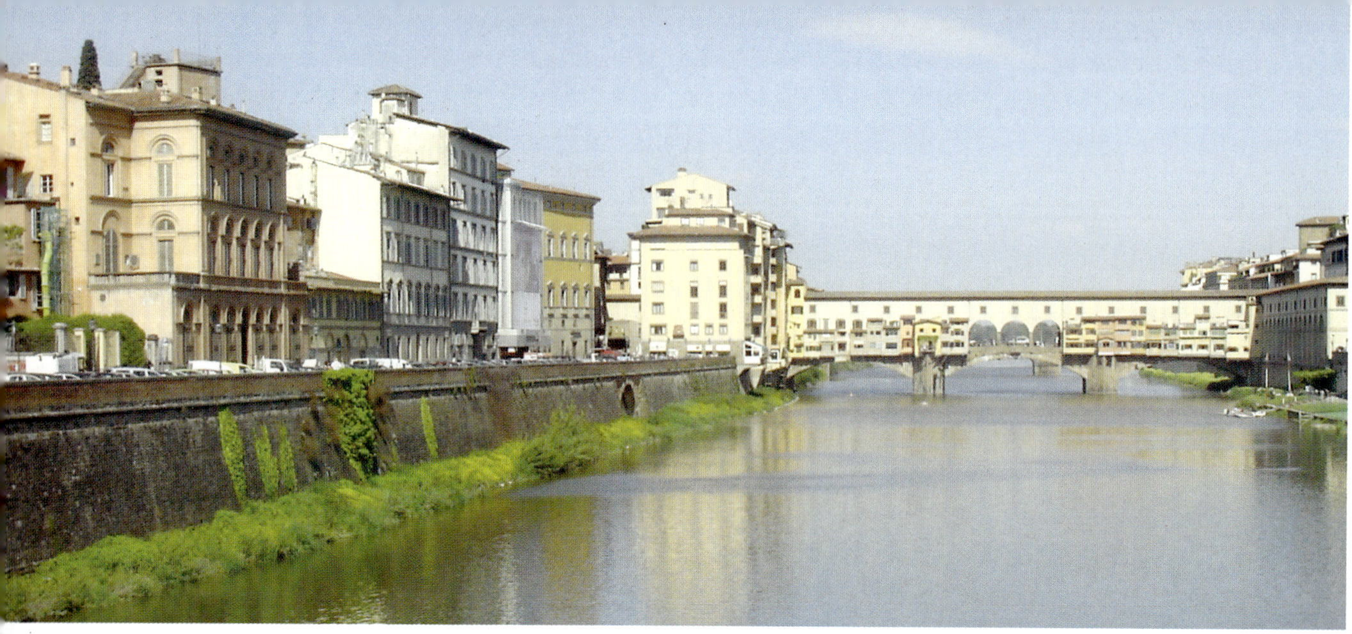

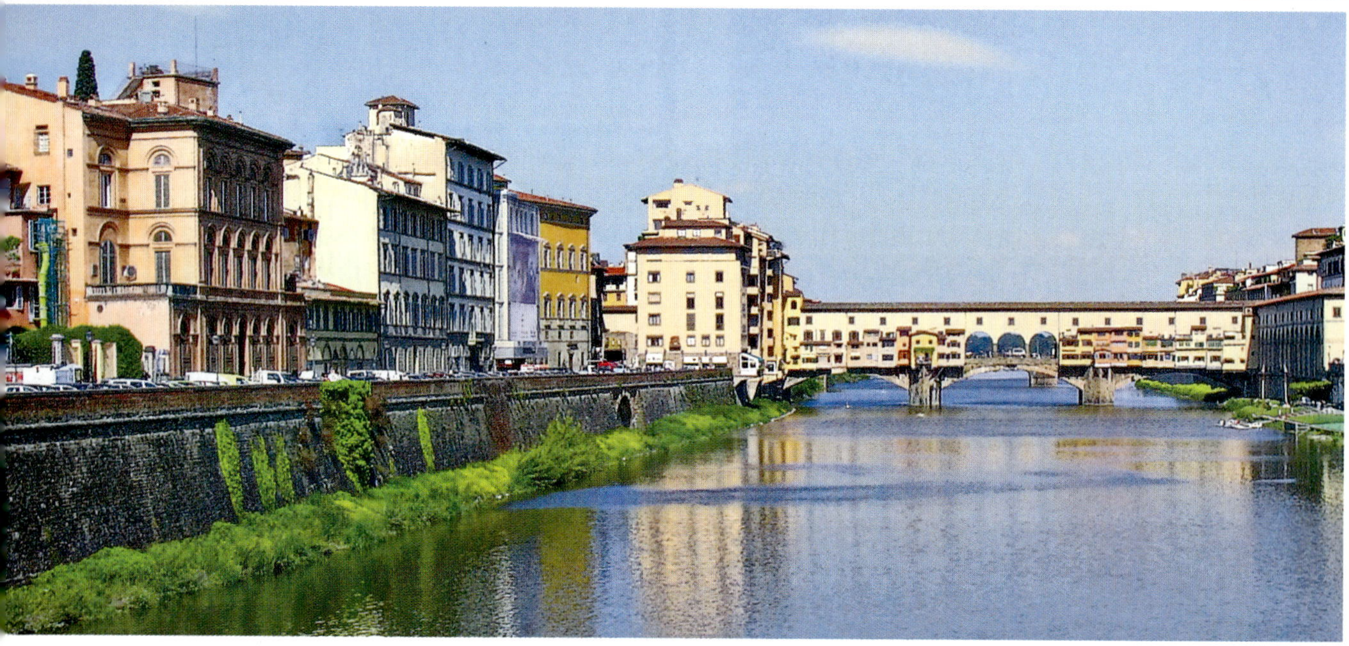

***Postcard 11.1** The Ponte Vecchio and Arno River, Florence.*

A simple photo, by a simple tourist with a simple camera, of a simple-looking bridge, is what we have to work with. This chapter is a kind of bridge itself, if you will, to what comes next. This exercise involves an original whose dubious quality, one would hope, is not typical of what you normally encounter. Ditto for both example images in the second half.

The next chapter will unleash the hidden power of the technique we're about to examine, and then we will look at good originals. Don't start trying to apply this stuff seriously until you've read it.

Of Sun and Shade

Shimmering reflections always make a good start to a postcard. Usually, though, either the beauty of nature is the point of the image, as it was in the shot of Emerald Lake in Postcard 1.1, or there is something spectacular on the shoreline, such as the Las Vegas neon in Figure 6.20. Neither applies here.

Postcard 11.1 is effective nevertheless. Clearly it has benefited from the Modern Man from Mars action of Chapter 6; one would be hard put to account for the color variation otherwise. No doubt the Color

Boost of Chapter 5 also livened things up. It seems that the original had a yellowish cast that has been corrected. But these three factors all pertain to color. What explains the sensation of greater depth?

The three originals in this chapter, besides being amateur work of questionable merit, share one other factor. This one comes from Italy. The two in the second half hail from Hawaii. The sun is strong in both locales.

Scenes featuring both sun and shade are problematic for cameras. Those of our prehistoric ancestors who were blinded by sunny areas and/or could not discern what was in shadowy ones became victims of Darwin's theories. Natural selection has provided us with a visual system that can adjust to darkness at the same time as brilliance elsewhere in the scene, just as we can adjust to a scene that has a color cast on one side but not the other. Cameras, on the other hand, take an inflexible view of incoming light that often yields overly dark, featureless shadows or overly light sunny areas, or both.

I propose that we should correct for this, and not just when the cause is sunlight. My preferred procedure is to multiply through a blurred layer mask. Let's do the postcard step by step, which is not a big chore because most other PPW steps aren't appropriate for it.

Cruising the Amusing Ponte Vecchio

The file arrives as a JPEG from an old, inexpensive digicam. This doesn't affect the subsequent procedure, at least not in principle.

- We begin by looking for impossible colors. As always, although the file is in RGB, we think in LAB. The sky, measured at top center, is $(3)^A(22)^B$. The greenery on the left bank seems to average around $(20)^A45^B$. Both objects fall within the ranges recommended in Chapter 3. The concrete banks vary, but are always a yellowish or warmish gray, which makes sense in sunlight.

Exact building colors are unknown, but the light center of the bridge measures 0^A21^B. To its left the A actually goes negative. These numbers describe a yellow bridge, possibly even a greenish yellow. That's impossible. Stone that old has to be some kind of brown. A yellowish brown, surely, but nevertheless brown, not yellow. This requires a positive A, meaning that the bridge gets pushed toward magenta and away from green. Since it already has a strong B–positive (yellow) component, adding magenta moves the bridge toward red.

Things now get dicey because the cloud above the bridge starts at $1^A(8)^B$—blue, tending toward purple. Adding magenta carelessly to the lighter areas may put a cast into the sky. This is, in fact, one of the trickiest initial color corrections in the book. Now, back to the workflow, as we currently understand it from the "PPW Takes Shape" box in Chapter 10.

- Luminosity moves are usually available, but not here. The blue isn't helpful for blends because its buildings are so dark. The setting is so neutral that the red and green look almost alike. And, because the original is already full-range—the light and dark points are correct—there aren't good curving opportunities either. So, I pass.
- Whether to apply Shadows/Highlights is debatable. The light bridge areas and the reflections in the water are the center of attention, but they don't really contain any detail, except in relation to much darker objects. Using S/H would bring out some definition in the buildings that are in shadow. I'm not persuaded that's a good idea; it might be a distraction. Again I move on without change.
- If we see no purpose in using Shadows/Highlights then there likely isn't any reason for the Bigger Hammer.
- We now consider whether to use one of the sky-darkening actions of Chapter 8. I say this sky is OK as is.
- The question of desaturating fleshtones does not arise, as this picture has none.

* * *

So far the only change to the original has been a color adjustment that produced Figure 11.2A. Now comes the novelty.

- We note the division of the photo into light and dark halves, and desire to bring them closer together. Before doing so, we decide that it is not simply a matter of forcing more detail into the highlights and shadows, because that would suggest the Bigger Hammer approach.
- Add a curves adjustment layer, without altering the default curves. Overall appearance therefore doesn't change.
- Change the adjustment layer's mode from Normal to Multiply. Doing so produces Figure 11.2B, which can almost be described as a night scene. The weight of the lighter

***Figure 11.2** The progression of Postcard 11.1. This page, top, a yellowish cast is corrected with curves in Color mode. Bottom, an adjustment layer is added and set to Multiply mode. Opposite, top, the RGB composite is loaded as a layer mask on the multiplying layer. Middle, the layer mask is blurred with a Radius of 50 pixels. Bottom, the MMM + Color Boost action is added and adjusted to taste.*

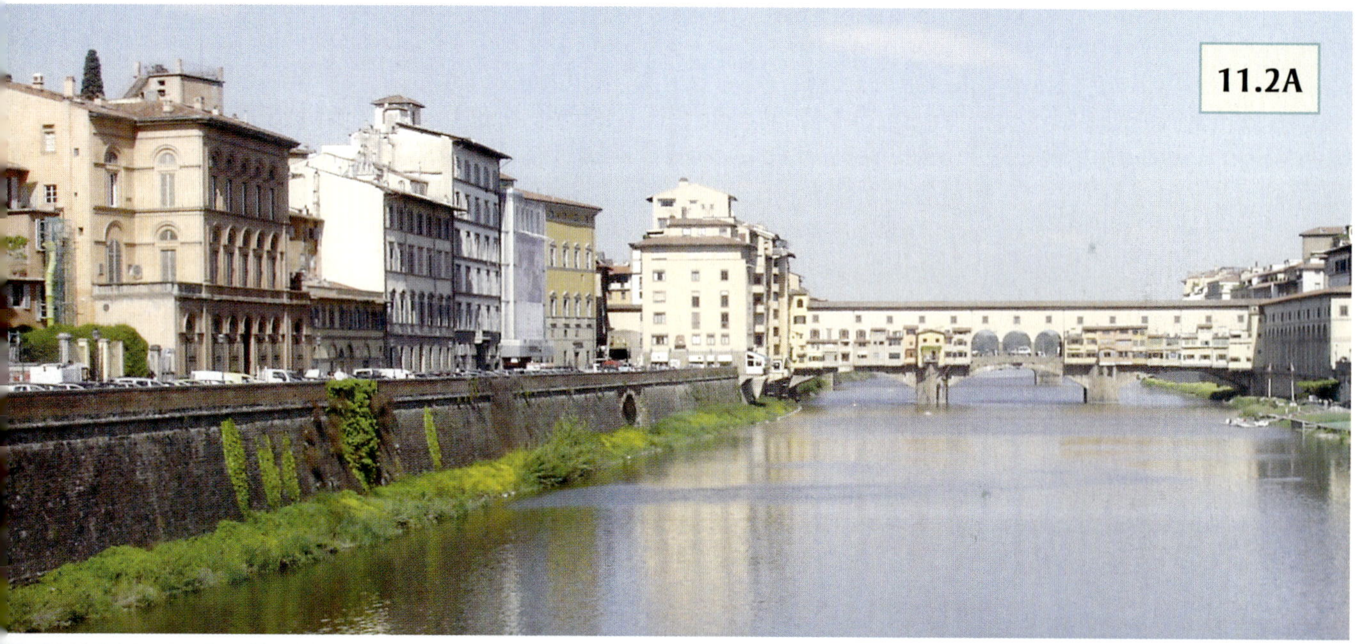

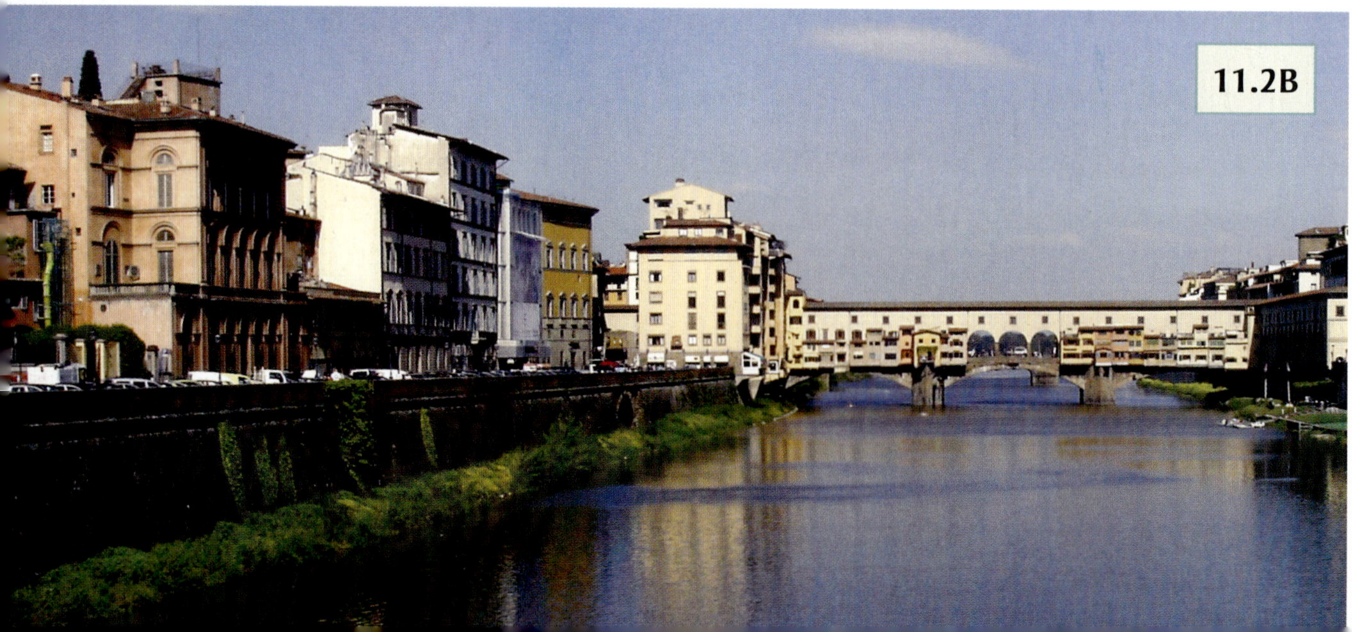

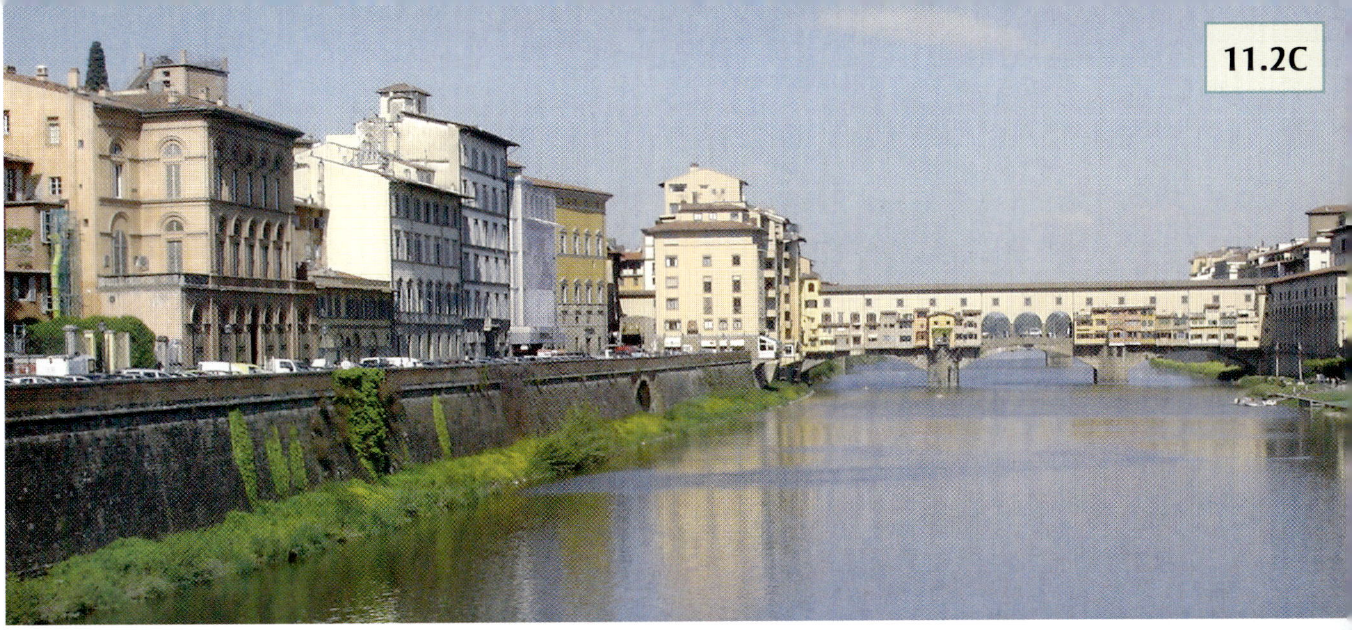
11.2C

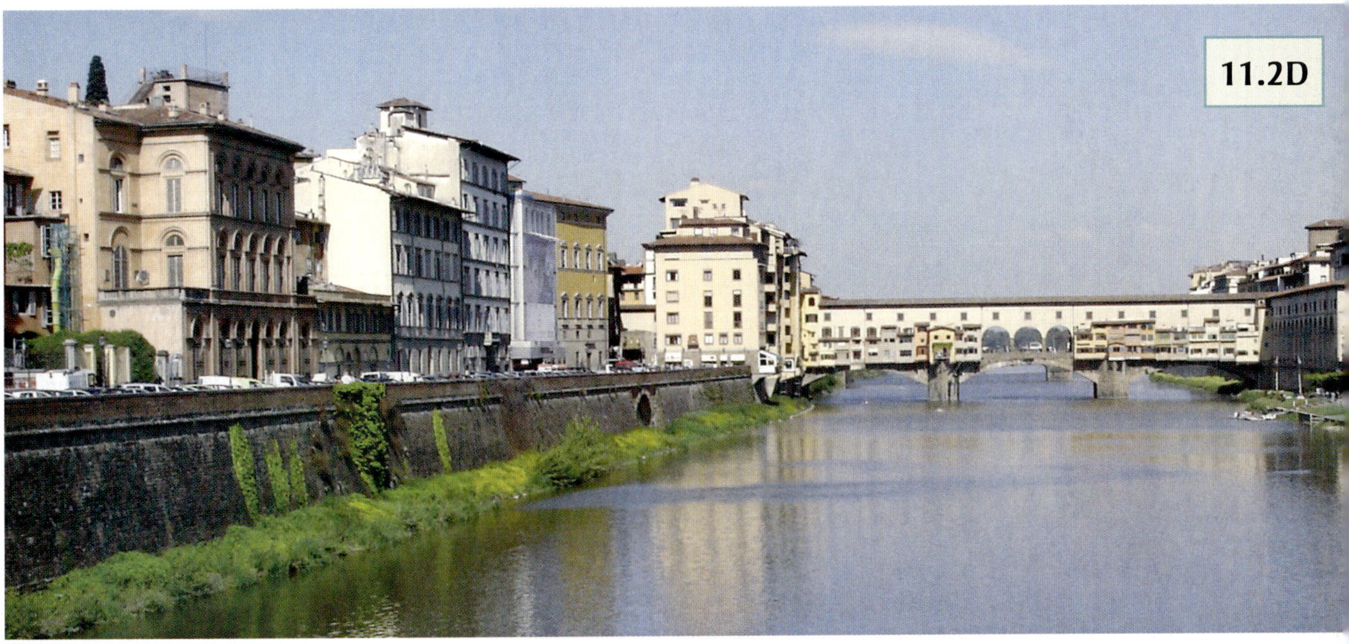
11.2D

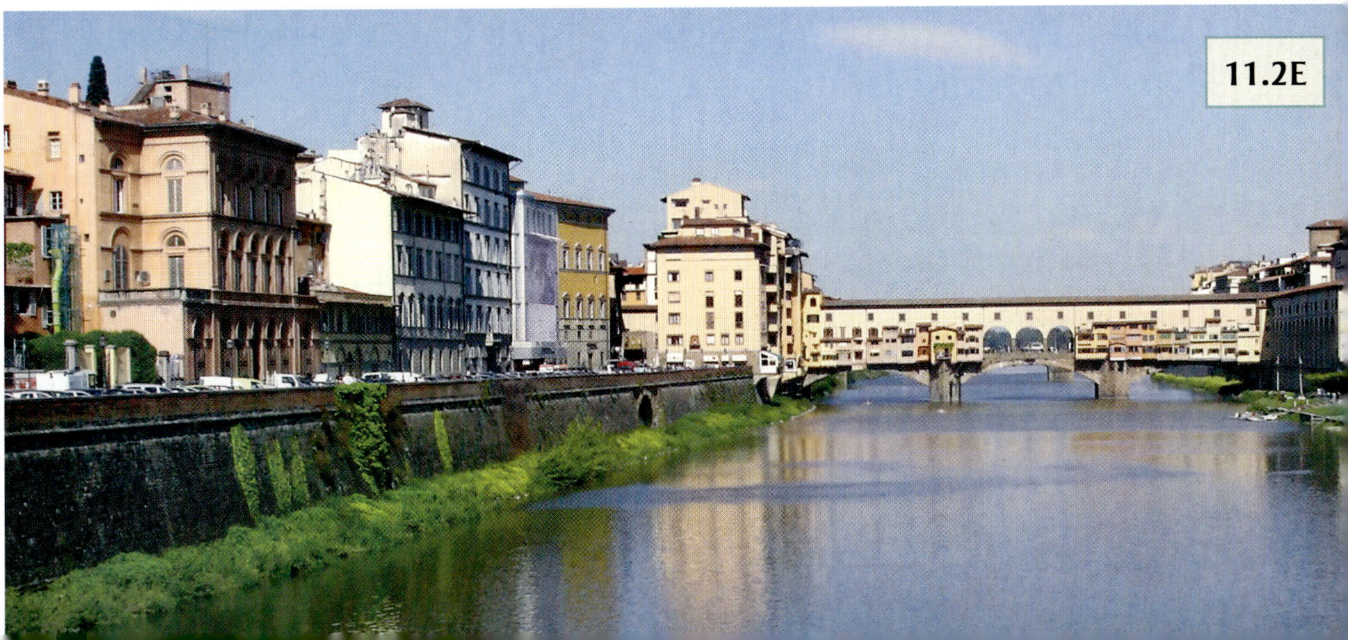
11.2E

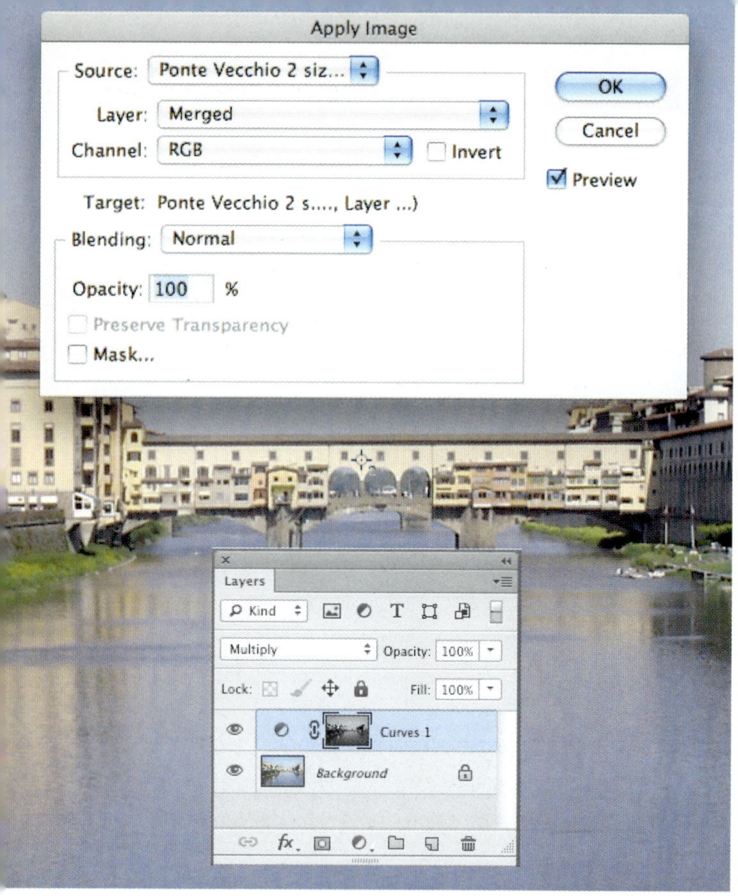

***Figure 11.3** Setting up the multiply layer. The RGB composite of the merged file is being applied as a layer mask. Note the border around the layer mask's icon in the Layers palette, indicating that it is active.*

parts is reasonable, but the plugged shadows are unacceptable.

To restore something close to the original shadows while retaining the added weight in the quartertones, a layer mask is required. It needs to be dark where the image itself is dark, as that will cause Photoshop to favor the bottom, lighter layer when merging the two. A copy of any existing channel will therefore make a good layer mask, though some are doubtless better than others.

- The layer mask is there automatically when the adjustment layer is created, unless you've changed some settings. By default it is white, meaning that it doesn't obstruct the layer's impact at all. Now, first verifying that the mask icon in the Layers palette is bordered, indicating that it is active, choose Image: Apply Image. Dialog, palette, and bridge are all shown in Figure 11.3.

The layer mask is a single channel and cannot contain color. Nevertheless, we can specify "RGB" as the source of the blend. Doing so causes action behind the curtain. Photoshop converts a copy of the file to grayscale, and loads that as the layer mask. Or, we could substitute the red, green, or blue channels. The four possibilities each have two suboptions. The default is Layer=Merged (that is, the whole picture as we currently see it), but can be changed to Layer=Background. The first, in effect, takes the channel from Figure 11.2B, the second from the drastically lighter Figure 11.2A. So, there are eight immediate choices. In the second half, we'll discuss how to evaluate them. For now, the default—RGB, Merged—is a good one.

- OK the Apply Image settings shown in Figure 11.3, producing Figure 11.2C.
- Chapter 10 taught that when merging two layers of significantly different darkness, any layer mask should be blurred heavily. Figures 11.2A and 11.2B, which are being merged here, surely qualify. Therefore, being sure that the layer mask is still active, as the Layers palette in Figure 11.3 indicates, apply Filter: Blur>Gaussian Blur. To make Figure 11.2D, I used a Radius of 50 pixels.

So much for the multiplication technique. The image is now ready for MMM and Color

Chapter Goals and Recap

Scenes with both sunny and shady areas need our intervention, because humans perceive the two as being more similar than a camera does.

This introductory chapter suggests that multiplying through a blurred layer mask is the most effective method of getting realism. The examples are instructional only and not typical of real work.

Chapters 12 adds the missing pieces and extends the concept to any scene that can be broken into light and dark halves, even if they are not specifically sun and shade.

Boost. Those settings are personal preference. Figure 11.2E works for me, but not for beta reader Alessandro Bernardi, who remarks that any Italian would know that the muddy Arno will be this blue and this reflective on the same day that the church beatifies Silvio Berlusconi. To that, I retort that Italians must not be as romantic as they are cracked up to be, if they don't see the use of a small fib in a good cause.

The steps just shown were effective but would not be with most sun-and-shade cases. Every pixel of the final version is darker than it was originally. The shadowy areas on the buildings and elsewhere are therefore compressed into a smaller tonal range and exhibit less contrast. In this particular image there is no crisis, as these areas are unimportant and perhaps even distracting. But in most similar images loss of shadow detail would be undesirable.

The solution is as simple as it is counterintuitive. The color-adjusted original, Figure 11.2A, would strike most as being too light. In spite of that, it should be made lighter. That will make the later multiplication work ever so much better, provided we don't tell anybody that we took such a crazy-sounding preliminary step.

That preliminary lightening will be fleshed out in the next chapter, whereupon this method will suddenly become more important and far-reaching than what you have read so far may suggest. You are welcome to proceed there now. If you care to stay here, though, the second half of this chapter isn't nearly as dense as the previous one. It deals with choice of layer mask, varied methods of blurring it, how to use the Properties panel to alter it if desired, and options for dealing with the artifacts that the methods described here occasionally cause.

Review and Exercises

✓You are getting ready to load a copy of a certain channel into a layer mask that is currently blank. You open Apply Image and designate the source channel. How do you know whether you are applying the channel to the layer mask, or to the image itself?

✓Under what circumstances must a layer mask be blurred heavily?

✓Explain when you would use the techniques described here in preference to the Bigger Hammer of Chapter 10, and vice versa.

✓Find some of your own images that involve sun and shade. Use the technique shown here, and afterward click on the layer mask and open the curves dialog. Click a point into the curve at roughly the quartertone—that is, about a quarter of the distance between the white and dark endpoints. See what the impact is when you move this point up or down, thus darkening or lightening the layer mask.

A Closer Look

Photoshop often lets us do the same thing in different ways. For example, I suggested using adjustment layers for multiplication in the first half, although duplicate layers work just as well. The reason was pragmatic. If you want to save an intermediate copy of the file, adding a duplicate layer doubles its size, whereas an adjustment layer's effect is negligible.

Pragmatic reasons also explain the recommendation for a layer that multiplies and does nothing else. Applying curves to darken an adjustment layer set to Normal mode would be more flexible. Multiplying is faster, however, and offers equivalent quality if we are willing to make simple edits to the layer mask later.

The bigger problem is finding a good layer mask. The opponent is Figure 11.4A, in which the foreground is good and the background washed out. Multiplying it as shown in the first half makes Figure 11.4B, which doesn't go as far in improving the background as we might like.

No law prohibits taking seconds. So, we duplicate the multiplying layer. And again. Figure 11.4C, then, has been multiplied three times.

The file now has four layers. For convenience, we merge the top three, leaving only the original and a triple-multiplied version. We wind up with Figure 11.4C on top, 11.4A beneath it, and 11.4B defunct.

All we need to do now is merge the background of the top layer with the foreground of the bottom—and do it convincingly.

To do so, load a certain channel as a layer mask and blur it a certain amount. To make life easier, we restrict the discussion to six possible masks: the red, green, and blue channels, each from either the top or bottom layer.

- Describe in words what you would like the layer mask to look like.
- Before deciding which channel to use, which layer do you intend to take the mask from? Remember, the top layer, being multiplied, is much darker than the bottom.
- Which choice for the mask source—top or bottom layer—makes the subsequent choice of channel more important?
- If you are forced to take a mask from the bottom layer, which channel would you predict is the best choice?
- If you are forced instead to use the top layer, would your predicted channel be the same?

You should now be ready for a quiz, in which I show the six possible results in a random order, and you identify the masks for each. That was the original plan, intended to make a point in a painful way. I expected the differences to be so slight that you would be deterred from spending too much time in searching for masks when pictures aren't very colorful.

I always take every quiz in each of my books, once enough time has passed for me to forget the answers. Inasmuch as I didn't happen to get a perfect score on this one, it seems a poor idea to subject you to it. So you get off easier, perhaps, than you deserve. No quiz, at least not right now. Instead, I'll offer another suggestion on mask sources, right after giving my own answers to the five questions above.

What the Mask Ought to Do

- The ideal mask for this particular file should be light in the canyon, dark in the foreground.
- I am unsure whether to take the mask from the top or bottom layer, but I suspect the bottom, the lightness of which will produce a fuller background. The problem, if it exists, is that it may make the foreground greenery too dark.
- The more colorful the picture, the more varied the channels. The top layer, Figure 11.4C, is colorful. Therefore, its channels have more individual character and a correct choice will be more important than if we take from the more neutral bottom layer, Figure 11.4A.
- Because the bottom layer is so colorless it is hard to say which will be the best choice. The question will be decided by the contrast on the

left side between the large tree and the red cliffs. Green objects are darkest in the blue channel, red ones lightest in the red. Either might be slightly better than the other. I do know that the green channel is the worst choice of the three.

- If we instead are taking from the top the answer is definite. The multiplication has turned the foreground greenery black, making it equal in all three channels rather than darkest in the blue. Consequently, the best mask from this layer is the channel that is lightest in red areas, namely the red.

The question that I blew that caused me to cancel the quiz was in distinguishing the result of using the lower blue as opposed to the lower red as a mask. One resulting version had slightly lighter background greens. I incorrectly identified this as being the one with the mask based on the blue channel, because it's almost always darker in green objects than the red is. I did not appreciate that this original has a blue cast in the background that is particularly pronounced in the shadows.

To be truthful the differences between the channels on the lower layer are so small as to be of no consequence to the final result after the rest of the workflow has had its say. Whatever, we move on. Figure 11.5A uses the red of Figure 11.4A, the lighter layer, as the layer mask.

It's hard to call the result worse than the original, but the transition between foreground and background is funky. The rules say that when the two layers are greatly different in darkness, the mask must be blurred heavily. Figure 11.5B, which has had a 45-pixel Gaussian blur applied to the mask, proves the point.

Would the red from the darker layer work better? See for yourself in Figure 11.5C, which uses the same blur.

So far, the time involved is negligible. Assuming you are using Apply Image to put the channel into the mask, the preview lets you get a quick view of all possibilities. So if the question of whether the blue or red is more suitable disturbs you, finding out the answer for sure takes seconds.

It's time to summarize and to look at more advanced (and time-consuming) options.

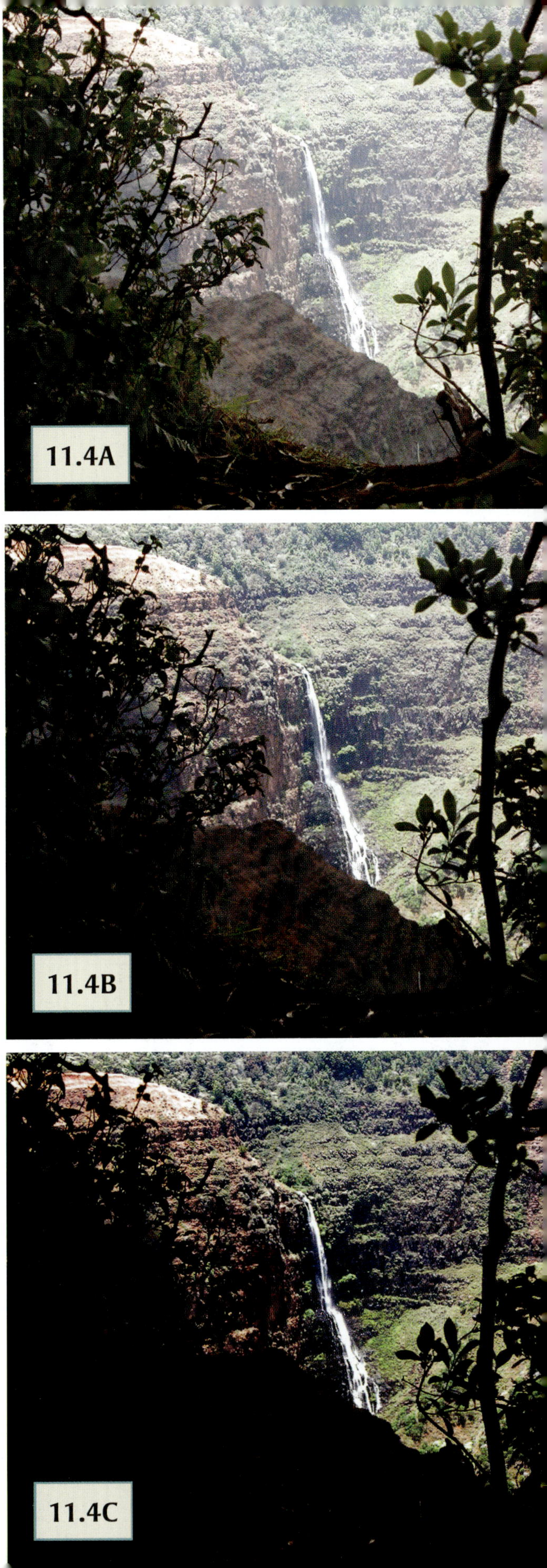

***Figure 11.4** Top, the original. Middle, with a duplicate layer set to Multiply mode. Bottom, with two additional copies of the layer—in effect, a triple multiplication.*

How to Create an Alternate Mask

The technique as shown works well in this admittedly unusual kind of picture. Going from Figure 11.4A to 11.5B should take less than a minute and the quality gain is huge. A working knowledge of channel structure is extremely helpful as a rule, and I strongly recommend you acquire it. In this picture, however, it isn't needed. The quality difference between the best and the worst choice here is trivial.

So far, then, there is no reason to be terribly worried about not being able to visualize channels. The rest of the chapter explores how to go further, if justified.

There are two subtopics. One is the choice of mask; the other the method and strength of blurring. We'll look at that in the next example. Here, we will assume that the 45-pixel Gaussian blur of Figure 11.5 is optimal, and examine only how a better blend might be obtained.

Figure 11.5 *Top left, Figures 11.4A and 11.4C are merged, using the red channel of 11.4A as a layer mask. Top right, the layer mask is blurred at a Radius setting of 45 pixels. Bottom left, a similarly blurred copy of the red channel of Figure 11.4C is substituted as the layer mask. Bottom right, a similarly blurred copy of Figure 11.6B is used as the mask.*

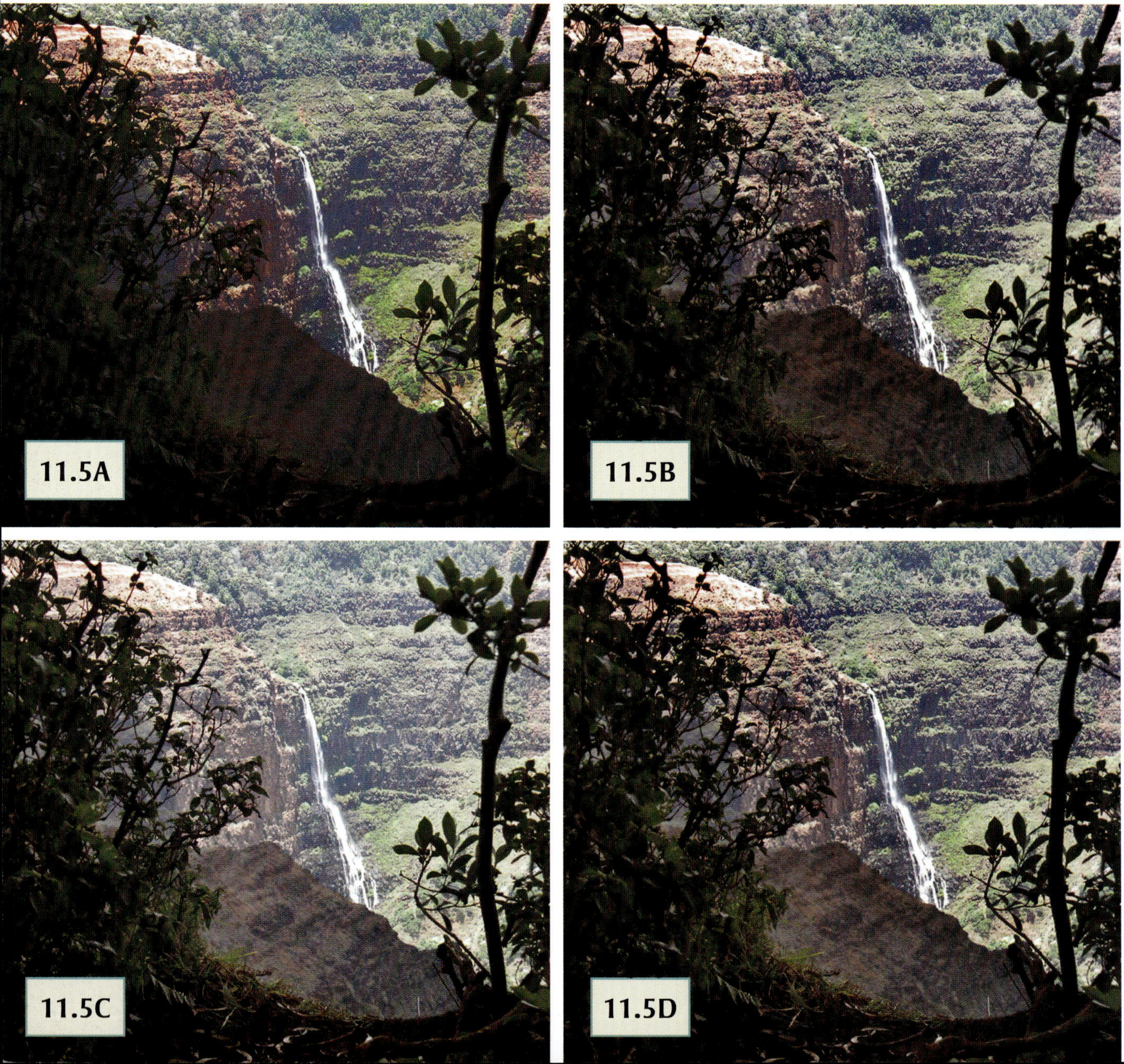

We always face the choice of which layer to use for the layer mask, as well as which channel. Sometimes we wish that there could be an intermediate result. Suppose we feel that the background in Figure 11.5B is too dark but that of Figure 11.5C is too light. We could make two copies of the file, mask each differently, and then blend them.

That procedure ends up with the same thing as if we had made an alpha channel in which the two original reds were blended, and then loaded as a layer mask.

It's faster to blend directly into the mask. Starting with a blank mask, apply the red channel, Source=Merged. Then apply the red channel, Source=Background layer, at 50% opacity or whatever.

- The same approach can produce a mask that is, say, a mix of the red and blue channels.
- The existing layer mask can be edited to emphasize certain areas and not others. We have already gone through this in Chapter 5, where the objective was to tone down offensive colors being introduced by the Color Boost action. Some people paint into the mask to alter it. Others, including me, think that curves give a more natural-looking result. An example was shown back in Figure 5.12.
- You can experiment with lightening the mask or blurring it. The Properties panel explained way back in Figure 5.6 can help. (Note: Properties did not exist until Photoshop CS4, when it was introduced as the Masks palette. The name was changed, and some functionality was added, in Photoshop CS6.)
- You can forget about altering the mask and just set the multiplying layer to less than 100% opacity.
- If your multiplying layer is, as suggested, a curves adjustment layer, you can manipulate the curves while leaving the layer mask alone.
- So far we have only mentioned red, green, and blue as possible channels for the mask. As was pointed out in Chapter 4, in the discussion surrounding Postcard 4.18, the RGB composite is often a good option—and there are others, notably an artificial black, which you can read about in Chapter 13.

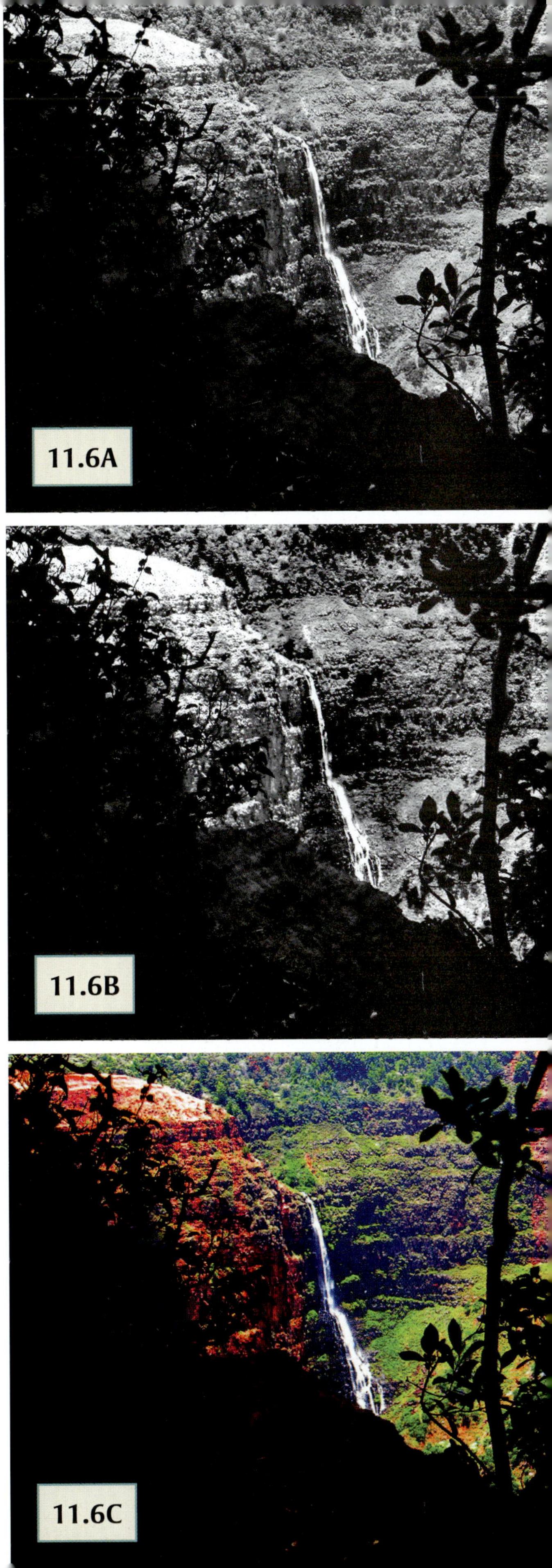

***Figure 11.6** Top, the red channel of Figure 11.4C. Middle, the source of the layer mask (later blurred) used to produce Figure 11.5D. Bottom, the source of the mask is a copy of Figure 11.4C that has been made much more colorful.*

- Finally, you can duplicate and alter the file to produce a different type of channel, which you can then steal for the original file. Figure 11.5D was so created.

If you choose to enter this last dark alley, the usual exit is to brighten all colors. After all, the more colorful a picture, the more its channels vary, so the more likely we are to find one that does what we want.

The "more colorful" part is simple. Make a copy of the picture, apply the Color Boost action to it, and set the Color Boost layer to 100% opacity. Then reconvert the file to RGB. Its ridiculous color is inconsequential because the file will only be used for its channels. Return to the original file, and check out the possibilities. Apply Image permits us to apply channels from any open document that's the same size as the current one. Therefore, we can target the layer mask, designate the copy as the source, and toggle through the channel possibilities.

Figure 11.6A is the red channel of Figure 11.4C, which is three multiplications, no layer mask. Figure 11.6B is the red channel of Figure 11.6C, the extremely colorful alternative just discussed, which is on its way to the trash just as soon as we steal this channel.

Figure 11.6B is somewhat lighter in the reddish areas than Figure 11.6A is. This is good, because it gives more contrast with the dark foreground trees.

Figure 11.5D started with this new red channel, appropriately blurred, as a layer mask. I then made two duplicates of the multiplying layer, mask included. The background now approaches the darkness of Figure 11.5B, its closest competitor. In my opinion, it is better because the trees stand out more. But it's up to you to say whether it was worth the extra effort.

One final tip. When on a channel-mining expedition you make a colorful duplicate file in LAB, convert it to sRGB afterward even if your normal choice is Adobe RGB or something else. sRGB has more pronounced differences in channels. Since the duplicate will be trashed shortly, there is no downside.

Four Styles of Blurring, in Theory

The last chapter's discussion of how to avoid obvious haloing announced that different methods of blurring would be discussed here. The topic is geeky and before beginning I remind you that I also said there was an easy automated way to get rid of most haloing. Feel free to skim over the next couple of pages to get to the recommendation. But if you are game for some theory (and a quiz that I *did* get right), here we go.

In the previous chapter it became obvious that something drastic needed to be done to defocus the Bigger Hammer action's Overlay layer. Here, disfiguring the layer mask of a multiply layer has been shown to be necessary, too. What *isn't* obvious is how to do it. I have presented Gaussian blur, which isn't the only option. Let's look at others, starting with a computer-generated graphic and then moving on to a photograph.

Figure 11.7A is the hypothetical original. We would like to blur to eliminate its noise, but with a careful eye on anything that could cause

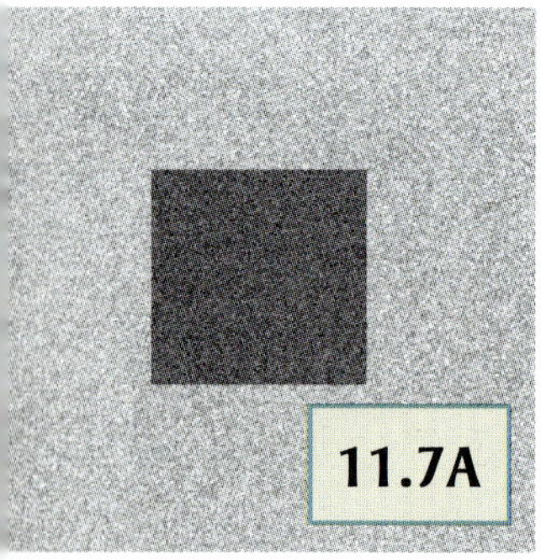

Figure 11.7 *Top, a hypothetical original. Bottom row, four different ways of blurring it, all using the same Radius. Left to right, they are Gaussian Blur, Surface Blur, Median, and Motion Blur.*

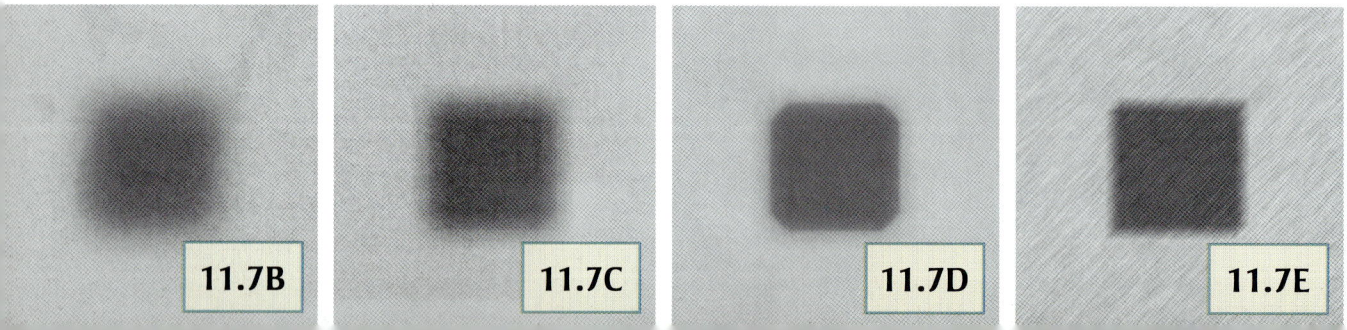

haloing if it gets used as a mask. I discuss five alternate routines, and show four of them, each of which happens to use the same Radius setting. Let's say that it's 20.

All these methods change each pixel depending upon what its neighbors are. You might assume that this refers to its neighbors within 20 pixels. That's 20 pixels in each of four directions, a total of 1,600 pixels to consider. In practice some blurs do this and others don't, but for the time being let's accept the slight inaccuracy.

How, then, to blur?

- The simplest way would be to replace each pixel with the average (or, if you must have the precise term, the mean) value of its 1,600 neighbors. This way isn't shown because it would always be worse than any of the four alternates.
- A Gaussian blur, at least in Photoshop's implementation, reaches out much further, evaluating pixels as far away as triple the Radius. But the further away the neighbor is, the less it counts for in the average. In Figure 11.7B,

Figure 11.8 *A real picture (seen in Figure 11.9) blurred in the four different ways shown in Figure 11.7. The order is the same: Gaussian Blur, Surface Blur, Median, and Motion Blur. Radius is always the same, 50 pixels.*

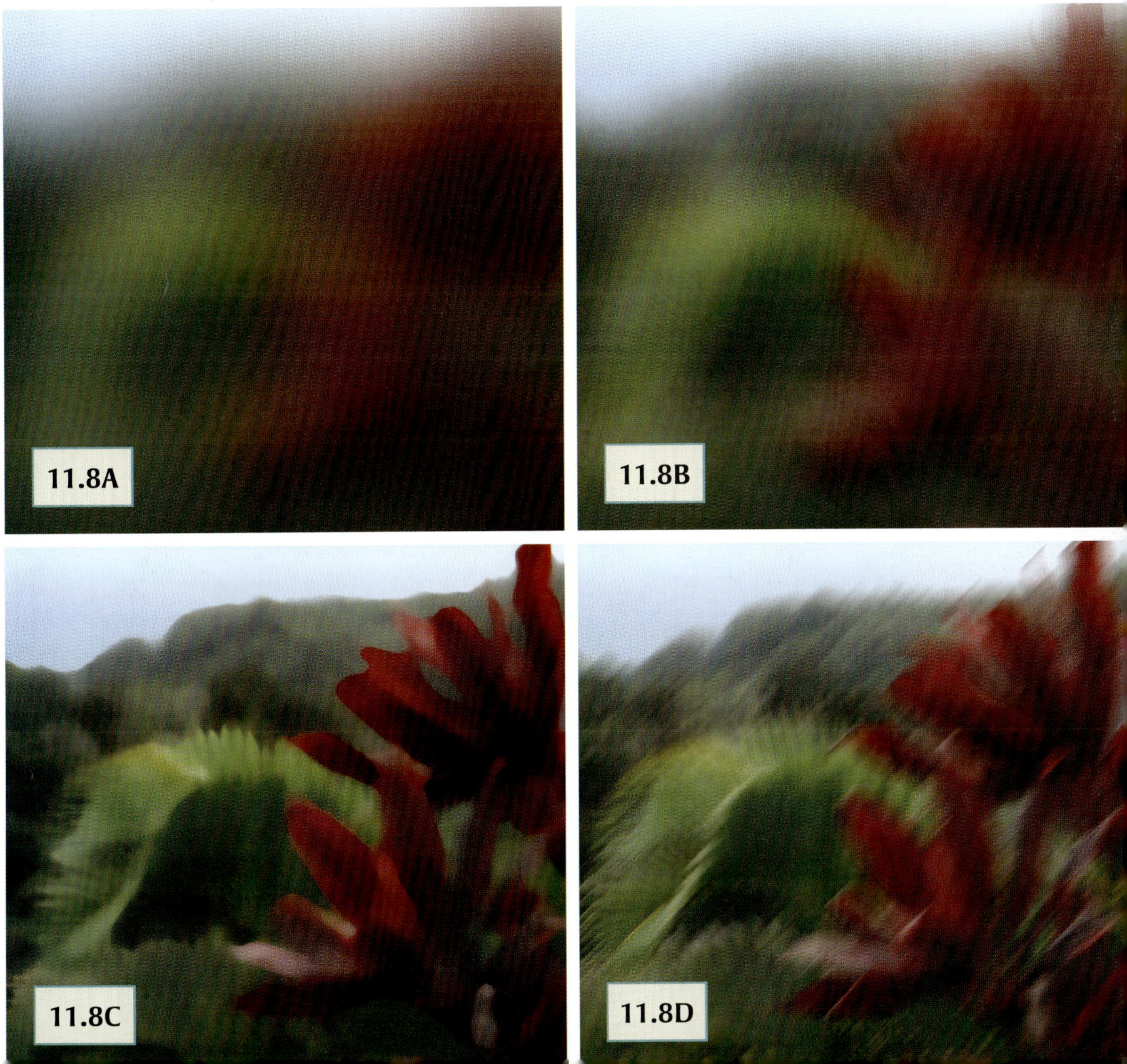

the blurry shadow of the dark square doesn't extend nearly as far as it would have in the first, unseen method.

- It extends less still in Figure 11.7C, the Surface Blur filter. This is an even more sophisticated algorithm, which is not to say a better one for these purposes. It is a Gaussian blur, too, in the sense that it discounts relatively distant pixels. But it also applies a second fudge factor, discounting pixels that are very different from the one being changed. The blurred shadow therefore tails off more quickly, because it is not only distant from parts of the lighter area but also different. For this example the Threshold field in the Surface Blur filter was set to its maximum 255.
- Figure 11.7D is the ancient Filter: Noise> Median command. Annoyingly, the result is in many ways superior to the more modern filters. The noise is gone and there is no haloing to speak of. There is only one problem. It's a big one. The dark square has lost its corners.

The algorithm is the culprit. It replaces each pixel with whatever value would put it in the middle of its 1,600 neighbors, with the proviso that it must match at least one other pixel in the aforesaid neighborhood.

By in the middle, I do not mean the mean, if you know what I mean. I mean equal numbers of lighter and darker pixels in the surrounding area. So, if we were looking at only three neighboring pixels, and they were 200, 199, and 1, the Median filter would return 199, because there are just as many greater values in the

Which Blur Made the Mask?

Figure 11.9A is the original file and Figure 11.9B a multiplied layer on top. The other five, in a random order, merge the two via a layer mask based on a certain channel, blurred at a fixed Radius. One mask comes from the original and is therefore unblurred; the other four come from Figure 11.8. First, please name the masking channel. Then, identify which blur goes with which version. (Answers, Page 302.)

1. No blur
2. Gaussian Blur
3. Surface Blur
4. Median
5. Motion Blur

Figure	Blur Type
11.10A	
11.10B	
11.10C	
11.10D	
11.10E	

Figure 11.9 *Left, the original. Right, a double multiply similar to the triple multiply of Figure 11.4C.*

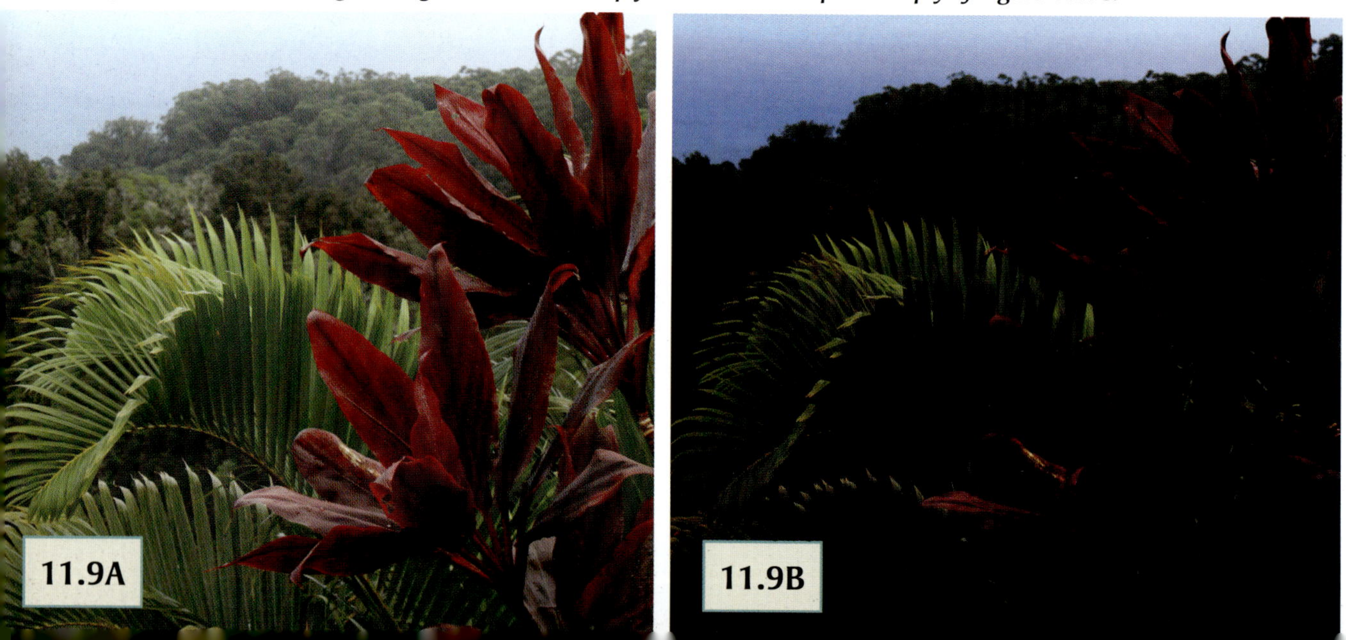

sample as lesser ones. In fact, 200, 200, and 1 would return 200, since there are just as many greater *or equal* values than lesser ones.

This filter wipes out the noise, which is surrounded by large areas of contrasting darkness and so assumes the character of what surrounds it. Now let's look at a more complicated case.

***Figure 11.10** These five, in a random order, are versions of the multiplied file to which a certain channel, the same one each time, has been added. Four use the appropriate channel from the versions of Figure 11.8. One takes it from the unblurred original, Figure 11.9A. Can you name the channel being used throughout, and the specific blur for each mask?*

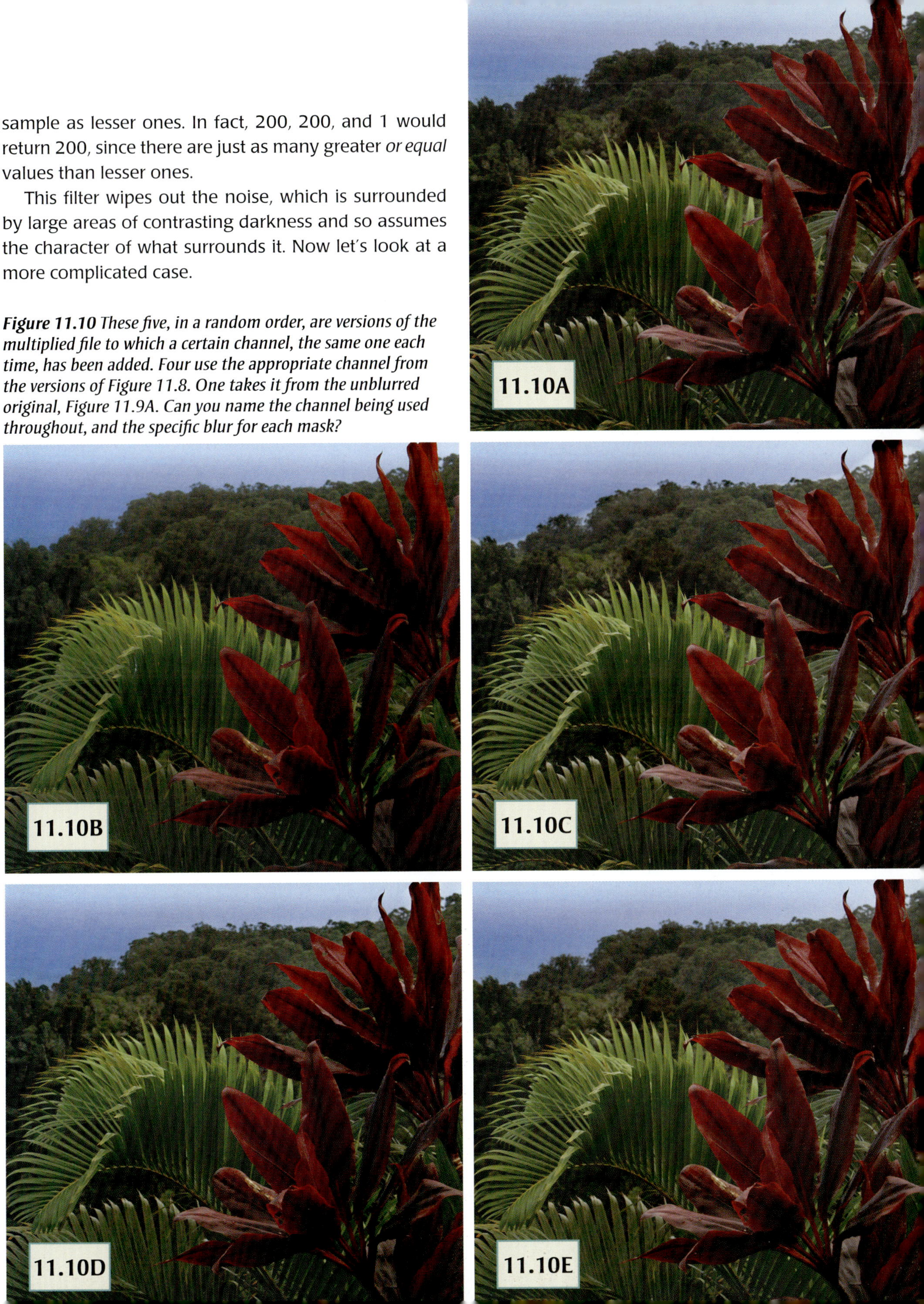

Consider a pixel just outside the left border of the dark gray box. To its left are basically only pixels that are just as light as it is (the noise being uncommon enough to be insignificant) and to its right only dark ones. However, looking up and down finds only lightness. So the majority of its neighbors are light, and the pixel we're talking about doesn't change. For the same reason, a pixel just inside the box will remain dark. The edge is respected, the noise eliminated, and in principle everyone is happy.

The difficulty comes at the corners, which are surrounded by more light gray than the middle edges are, and therefore change. Rats.

- Finally, Figure 11.7E shows Motion Blur, at an angle of 45 degrees. This filter does some blurring but its signature is that a faint copy moves in the indicated angle. Unlike the others, it does not wipe out the noise. It does, however, change it into streaks rather than dots. Since the point of blurring a mask is to obliterate detail, this might work, you never know.

Four Styles of Blurring, in Practice

The same four blur methods are shown in Figure 11.8, this time with a real photo that we will later use as a mask source. Flip back to Figure 11.9A if you'd like to see the unblurred original.

The four blurs come in the same order as in Figure 11.7. Radius is now 50 pixels in each. Nevertheless, the Gaussian Blur of Figure 11.8A seems more drastic than the Surface Blur of Figure 11.8B. The Median filter of Figure 11.8C shows its characteristic imprecision where the foreground meets the background. And the Motion Blur of Figure 11.8D is a law unto itself.

Now comes the quiz. Figure 11.9A, again, is the unblurred original. Figure 11.9B, on a layer above it, is a double multiplication along the lines of the triple multiplication shown in Figure 11.4C. A layer mask is now needed to unite the two and to save time I will tell you that it should come from the bottom layer.

The preliminary question: if you are limited to the red, green, or blue from the bottom layer, which of the three would do the best job?

Now, the quiz itself. The channel that I hope you just picked is used as a layer mask throughout Figure 11.10, but it is blurred in different ways. In fact, each is taken directly from the four blurred versions of Figure 11.8. A fifth version has no blur at all, which is to say that it is the appropriate channel of the original, Figure 11.9A. The five variants of Figure 11.10 are in a random order. Your job is to decide which mask is in use for each. Please do so before resuming reading. As a side question, which of the five do you think is the most convincing?

Answers to the Quiz...

My first reaction to these five quiz variants is that there is a solution for everyone, regardless of taste. If none of the seven seems perfect, there will always be an easy blend to get whatever effect we want.

Your first reaction should be that investigating the fine points of layer masking is a bottomless pit into which unlimited quantities of time can be poured. I have found it so myself, and again suggest that sometimes the easy, inelegant way is better than the fancy intellectually correct one. Nearly foolproof ways of creating beautiful masks exist and can be reduced to actions, but at present such actions take an unacceptably long time to run. The *at present* should be stressed because many actions shown in this book would have been unacceptably slow on computers of five to ten years ago. For the same

The Bottom Line

This chapter should be seen as a preliminary to the next one rather than showing a ready-to-go method. It introduces the concept of balancing a picture by multiplying through a heavily blurred mask.

As presented here the method rarely works because darker areas become too heavy. The next chapter shows the solution and changes the topic from a curiosity to a method of enormous utility.

reason, we must anticipate that better ways than those suggested here will be available in the not-too-distant future. On to the quiz.

First, the preliminary question. The appropriate mask for merging Figures 11.9A and 11.9B is the blue from the bottom layer—it's lightest in the blue areas, darkest in the greens, and close to the darkest in the reds. So there is good contrast between foreground and background. The lower blue is therefore the channel being used in all five masked variants.

Now, the individual answers. Figure 11.10B is the one with the unblurred mask, because it lacks the detail of the others.

If you have read the previous discussion it should be equally clear that Figure 11.10C's layer mask was blurred with the Median filter. The clue is the inaccuracy at the shoreline. You and I can see white halos where the filter misinterprets the shape of the trees.

The question is, however, what would we think of this picture if we were members of the 99.9999 percent of the population that doesn't have a clue about the Median filter? Put yourself in that position, and I suspect you will agree that they won't know. They will think that these white lines represent real detail, surf, rather than some kind of digital defect. Yet another lesson in how forgiving this process is.

Distinguishing the other three is harder. I'd go by the darkest areas in the greenery, and possibly in the red plant as well. The darker these are, the more intense the blur must have been. The Radii of all three remaining blurs were the same, but Figure 11.8 shows that some seem stronger than others. The order of most to least apparently blurry follows the order of Figure 11.8: Gaussian, Surface, Motion. In our quiz, they appear to correspond to Figures 11.10A, 11.10E, and 11.10D.

...And What They Show

Three areas determine which variant is best: the foreground plant life, the blue background, and where the two intersect.

The foreground seems acceptable in all but the unblurred Figure 11.10B. The background is little affected by blur method because there's not much detail to enhance. The intersection of the two areas can be a problem.

Heavy blurring, whether on an overlay layer or a layer mask, risks objectionable artifacts. In the current picture, offensive halos may occur in the same places they would if we were using the inverted overlay method, the Bigger Hammer of the previous chapter.

The discussion there of the disastrous haloing in Figure 10.18 set out what's needed to provoke the problem. Two objects must share a lengthy border, there must be great contrast between them, the lighter one cannot be so light that it can't support a halo, and the light object must be so smooth that nothing will disguise the halo. This is a lengthy list of prerequisites. A sky hitting a dark horizon is not the only thing in the world that meets them, but nine times out of ten it's the culprit. Granted, we have water here and not a sky, but it might as well be one—it's just as blue and almost as smooth.

You may, therefore, object to any or all of the variants as having a problem in the transition. If you do, there are easy and hard ways of fixing it. The hard way, though more elegant, is still the hard way: it is to construct a better mask. I recommend either of two easier ways.

First, we could, prior to blurring the layer mask, copy what we have, which is Figure 11.9B, onto a single new layer. The PPW panel lets you create this with a single click. Add a black layer mask so that this new composite layer becomes invisible. Return to the first layer mask and blur it. If you see obnoxious halos, return to the black layer mask on the top layer, and softly paint in a white or light gray where you see the halo.

The second easy way is a variation on what was discussed in the second half of Chapter 8, during the discussion of how to isolate skies.

As noted back then, blue things aren't as common as red or green ones. The B channel of LAB is yellow vs. blue. A sky is usually the only object that's more blue than yellow, as it is here. If not, whatever else that's blue is probably easily masked out. Hence, the following nearly foolproof procedure.

- If you suspect that sky haloing may be a problem, repeat the procedure previously described: before blurring the mask make a composite copy of the file for the top of the layer stack. It takes one click in the PPW panel.
- Make the new top layer invisible, return to the multiplying layer, and blur the mask. If it turns out that you were worrying about nothing, throw the top layer away.
- If nasty haloing occurs, Layer: Merge Visible. This preserves the invisible unblurred layer for future use.
- Convert to LAB, declining the invitation to flatten the file. That's the point of the previous step: multiply layers don't work the same way in LAB and RGB, and adjustment layers don't survive the conversion at all. So the document needs a single layer based on a blurred mask, with a second layer, based on an unblurred mask, above it. You now have two choices.
- First, you could make the top layer visible, and then make it invisible again by adding a black layer mask. Then, choose white as your foreground color, and an appropriately sized brush at around 70% opacity. Now, paint into the layer mask where the offensive halo is occurring. The technique is easier than it sounds. The results are definitely undetectable to a non-expert and likely not to an expert either.
- Alternatively, with the unblurred layer active and visible, double-click its row in the Layers palette to bring up the Blending Options dialog, the bottom of which is the invaluable (in LAB) Blend If. Choose the B channel and insert the values shown. Note the split slider on the left. To get it, Option-click-drag the slider, and presto, two halves. If you need an explanation of why this works, refer back to the discussion of Figure 8.9, which falls in the middle of an entire chapter about skies.

Answers to Layer Mask Quiz

(Page 298)

All five versions use the original blue channel as a layer mask, as this gives the best contrast between the foreground and background. Each version is blurred with the same Radius setting. The specific blurs are:

11.10A: Gaussian Blur
11.10B: No blur
11.10C: Median
11.10D: Motion Blur
11.10E: Surface Blur

...and Beyond

As noted at the outset, Photoshop offers many ways to do the same thing. We could also try altering the blurred mask, perhaps by fading it directly after the blur, or by changing its mode to Lighten, which discourages this type of haloing. We could hit the mask with a cocktail of different blurs and/or Radii. We could make two prospective masks, one based on red, one based on blue, and then blend them. And on and on.

Beta reader James Gray suggests yet another method: "If the blurring creates nasty halos, step back and undo it. Make a crude selection of the area in which the halo occurred, and feather it heavily. Invert the selection, and blur again. There is much less blur in the affected area and as a result there is much less halo. It takes longer to explain than to do."

Having spent a lot of time studying such options, I observe a similarity to online gaming: stimulating for a time, highly addictive, and ultimately not of much use.

The next chapter, however, presents what is truly a game-changer.

12

When the Story Has Two Sides

Our eyes adjust to multiple lighting conditions within the same scene. Cameras don't. Photos taken on sunny days often have blown-out highlights and/or muddy shadows. The solution is to lighten the file artificially, then establish a more correct look.

In late 1334, a son and heir was born to King Alfonso XI of Castile and his consort, a Portuguese princess. Upon the father's death, the boy became king at age sixteen. Although Alfonso had few scruples about murdering enemies, real and imagined, his son was worse. History therefore knows him as *Pedro the Cruel.* During his bloody and war-ravaged sixteen-year reign, he arranged the killing of, among others, his wife. He suffered the same fate himself in 1366 at the hands of an illegitimate half-brother, who took over the throne.

There is a small problem with the above tale. Many subsequent historians do not concur in the judgment commonly applied to this king. They call him *Pedro the Just.* How he could have been both things at the same time is an apt introduction to this chapter's topic.

* * *

Slightly over a century later, Pedro's crown was held by a pair of co-equal monarchs. American schoolchildren know them by the anglicized names of Ferdinand and Isabella. They were forward-thinking enough to risk sponsoring world exploration, and particularly a certain voyage in 1492. Teachers usually present Ferdinand and Isabella much more favorably than they would, say, Pedro the Cruel.

There is a small problem with this tale, too. In 1480 Ferdinand and Isabella established the Spanish Inquisition and saw to it that it was kept busy thereafter. Spain had previously been the most vibrantly multicultural nation in the world. Catholics, Jews, and Moslems lived in harmony, and left an inspiring artistic legacy, particularly in architecture.

Right around the time of Columbus's voyage, Ferdinand and Isabella decided to expel all non-Catholics from the country, first relieving them of as many possessions as practicable. Thousands tried to avoid this fate by "converting" to Catholicism. Many were brought before the Inquisition, which had methods of determining to its satisfaction whether the conversions were genuine.

There will be no descriptions here of what these methods were, or of the pitiful exodus of newly impoverished Jews and Moslems, fleeing Spain on donkeys or however else they could.

A century earlier, these same pathetic refugees had been valued members of society, treated equally with Catholics during the benevolent reign of the extraordinarily tolerant monarch known today as Pedro the Cruel.

Of Mood and Mudejar

Postcard 12.1 takes us to Pedro's palace. His taste for Moorish-inspired architecture is clear. The corrected version is not achievable by methods discussed in previous chapters. What is the key step?

Pedro the Cruel/the Just and the Ferdinand/Isabella team each did some admirable things. But each had a dark side. Neither can be properly understood without taking both sides into account.

It isn't too much of a stretch to repeat this warning phrase with respect to the original of Postcard 12.1, and for that matter for just about any other daylight picture of this site. Seville is in southern Spain and the perpetual sunlight is harsh. So nearly every picture taken outdoors there has a dark side, too.

To take it further: Pedro's reputation as the Cruel largely comes from historians who wrote during the reign of his murderer. These historians, shall we say, were not in a position that encouraged impartial commentary. They gave us a one-sided, distorted view that would be (and has been) rejected by more detached observers.

The equivalent of the biased historian in our work is the camera. Its inability to cope with multiple light sources is every bit as bad as the historian's reluctance to cheese off the current powers that be.

When we are in a dark area our eyes quickly adjust, just as they adapt to brilliant sunshine. A camera can operate in the same fashion if the photographer knows how to make it do so.

Unlike the camera, though, we can adjust to both conditions simultaneously. When we look at a serious sun-and-shade scene like Postcard 12.1 we certainly know that it contains shadowy areas, but we can perceive what's inside them fairly well. Cameras can't. They construct their reality with the assumption of a uniform source of light.

When the sun and shade effect is this strong the camera gives us our choice of poison. We can elect to get something like this palace shot where the shadows are seriously plugged, or we can expose so that the dark parts look good but the lighter ones blow out. An example of that effect is the previous exercise, Figure 11.9A, taken in Hawaii under even sunnier conditions than those of Spain. The foreground vegetation, the dark side of the scene, looked good. The hint of the light blue ocean in the background had almost vanished.

We do not, of course, wish to eliminate the sense of sun and shade altogether in either case. Nor should our maneuver eliminate setting the light and dark points as we normally would. A credible reproduction requires, though, that the two halves be brought closer together.

In the last chapter, we did this by multiplying through a layer mask. As pointed out then, however, the method *as stated* rarely works in real life. The reason is that it darkens both halves, although the light half is affected much more.

The three examples shown in Chapter 11

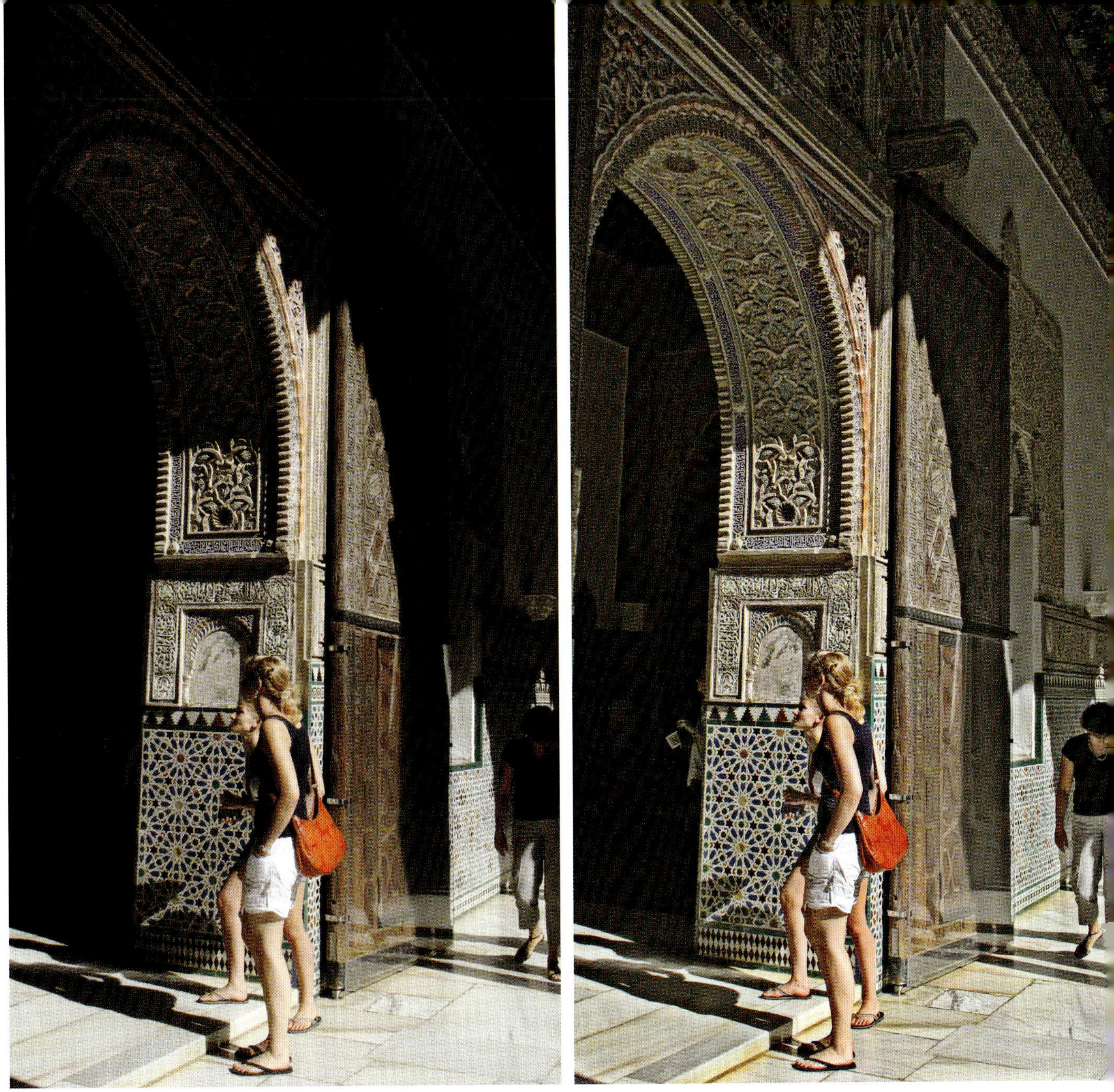

***Postcard 12.1** A fourteenth century palace in the Real Alcázar, Seville, Spain.*

all were relatively light in the dark half. Making the dark half darker wasn't desirable but it was no catastrophe. Usually that isn't the case. We can't possibly afford to make the dark half of the original palace picture any darker than it already is. Yet the basic idea of multiplying through a blurred mask seems like it would work well.

The solution is to first make the whole picture much lighter, whereupon the Chapter 11 method works.

How to Make the Scene Lighter

To make something lighter the usual approach is to apply curves. Unexpectedly, curves don't work as well as two other options: assigning a false profile, and the Image: Adjustments>Exposure>Gamma Correction command. Those two are equivalent in all but a small minority of cases; the exceptions will be discussed in the second half with the brevity the topic deserves.

Personally I use the false profile method.

The PPW panel offers two scripts, one called 1.4 gamma and a more extreme one named 1.0 gamma. Each lightens and adds a curves adjustment layer set to Multiply mode, with a blank layer mask activated. The lightening effect isn't permanent until you change colorspace, such as by moving into LAB.

We believe these panel scripts are foolproof, although possibly we haven't met sufficiently talented fools. The needed false profiles are installed automatically and the panel knows which to use, because it senses your own RGB workspace.

If you understand what that last sentence means, then you understand why we don't supply a separate action and you need to record your own if you're not using the panel. If you don't understand the meaning, relax, you don't need to if you're using the panel. And if you think I am being condescending by not explaining what it means, permit me to make it clear.

If the Spanish Inquisition had been able to force its victims to study RGB profiles and their ramifications, it would have had no need for the Iron Maiden.

* * *

If uncomfortable with the above, you can safely avoid all of it by using the Image: Adjustments>Exposure settings of Figure 12.2. These numbers closely match the panel's 1.4 gamma script for most users.

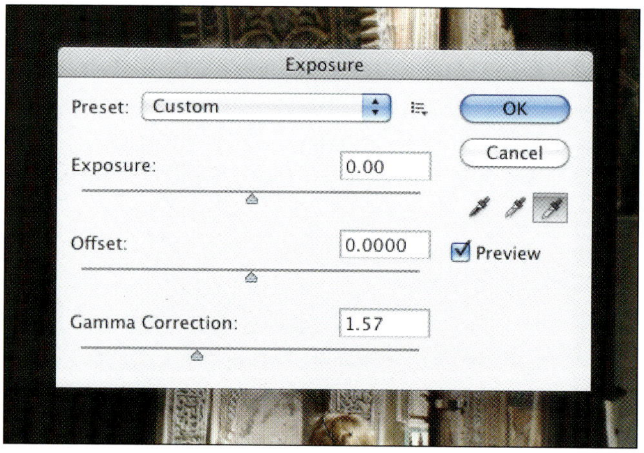

Beta reader John Pavel, who says he is not an expert user, inserts a question: "Why do you prefer an apparently more complicated method that is harder to tune?"

Clicking a button in the panel is not complicated. I feel that tuning is unnecessary. That's why the panel only has two such scripts, one for grossly dark images. Some serious users of the PPW, people whose views I respect, prefer more options. You can therefore download a patch that adds several more false profiles to the panel—or you can use the Exposure command.

I haven't been convinced of the need for any of that. None of the remaining four exercises in this half starts out grossly dark (there is one such example in the second half); therefore every exercise will be lightened using the panel's 1.4 gamma script.

And I use false profiles because I believe that in general they have an infinitesimal technical advantage, which you can read about in great detail in the PDF documentation for the panel. So use Exposure if you like, and let's leave the religious wars to Ferdinand and Isabella.

Black, White, and the Grave

The next example continues the theme of combined brilliance and darkness in politicians and photographs. And because it is almost a black and white picture, it rules out a lot of normal PPW maneuvering, allowing us to focus on this chapter's technique.

In the Spanish and Anglo-American traditions, tombs are solemn affairs to the point of being stuffy. Ostentation and artistic embellishment are frowned upon as tasteless.

The Russian tradition has no such limitation. Graveyards are full of whimsical, even humorous tributes. The monument's form can be a comment on the decedent's life.

***Figure 12.2** These settings are in use throughout the first half of the chapter as a preliminary to multiplying through a blurred layer mask.*

It is not difficult to divine the comment in the design of the tomb of Nikita Sergeyevich Khrushchev. The architect correctly suggests that, like Pedro the Cruel and like Ferdinand and Isabella, Khrushchev was an individual with many admirable traits who happened to have a serious dark side. The same problem of sun and shade that confronted us in the picture of Pedro's palace is also present here, although in a reduced form. The sun in Moscow, after all, isn't what it is in Seville.

The steps, including the addition of lightening that was missing in Chapter 11, follow those in the box on this page.

- Examine the original, Figure 12.3A, for color issues. I found none.
- Use a threshold adjustment layer to find the lightest and darkest points of the monument with any detail at all, and put sampler points there for later reference.
- The luminosity stage, which usually is one of the most potent steps in the workflow, is a washout. Everything of importance here is neutral, so all three channels are alike and blending is useless.
- Curves for contrast don't help either, because every channel is already full range.
- Application of the Shadows/Highlights command is inappropriate, in my opinion. The interest object here is the bust. Engineering extra detail into the lightest whites and darkest blacks will be a distraction.
- Since we don't even want the modest assistance of S/H we don't want the Bigger Hammer either.
- The blue sky seems dark enough, so no need to alter it with an action.

* * *

The first seven steps of the workflow have thus been completed. The file is unchanged from when it was first opened.

That's good, because it allows us to see the impact of the new method without the confounding factor of other improvements. To start, we ask ourselves, does this picture have two sides? Here the answer may not be as obvious as it was in Pedro's palace, but it's yes just the same.

If we agree that it does, the second question is, which side is more important in terms

Chapter Goals and Recap

When an image can be divided into a light and a dark half, photos taken in sun and shade offering the prime example, the two halves need to be brought closer together.

Chapter 11 showed how to do this by multiplying through a blurred layer mask. Unfortunately, doing so often leaves the dark side too dark.

This chapter's solution is to lighten everything before multiplying. It temporarily leaves the image too light, but the final result is what counts.

How Difficult Is It? The lightening is easy, the choice of layer mask only slightly harder.

How Often Is It Needed? It's more common than one might think. It is not limited to sun and shade, but applies generally to any image that can be divided into light and dark halves.

The PPW Takes Shape

COLOR

- Kill incorrect color with RGB curves (Chapter 3).
- Identify highlight (Chapters 3–4).

CONTRAST

- Channel blending on luminosity layer (Chapter 4).
- Contrast-enhancing curves (Chapter 4).
    - Consider S/H command (Chapter 7).
    - Consider the Bigger Hammer (Chapter 10).
    - Consider boost to sky (Chapter 8).
    - Consider lighten and multiply (this chapter).

COLOR AGAIN

- Desaturate skintone, if any (Chapter 9).
- Apply MMM + Color Boost action (Chapters 5–6).
- Finalize contrast, including endpoints.
- Reduce color by masking or opacity adjustment.

SHARPEN

FINALIZE

- Consider blend with another version (Chapter 2).
- Convert to final output space, if needed.

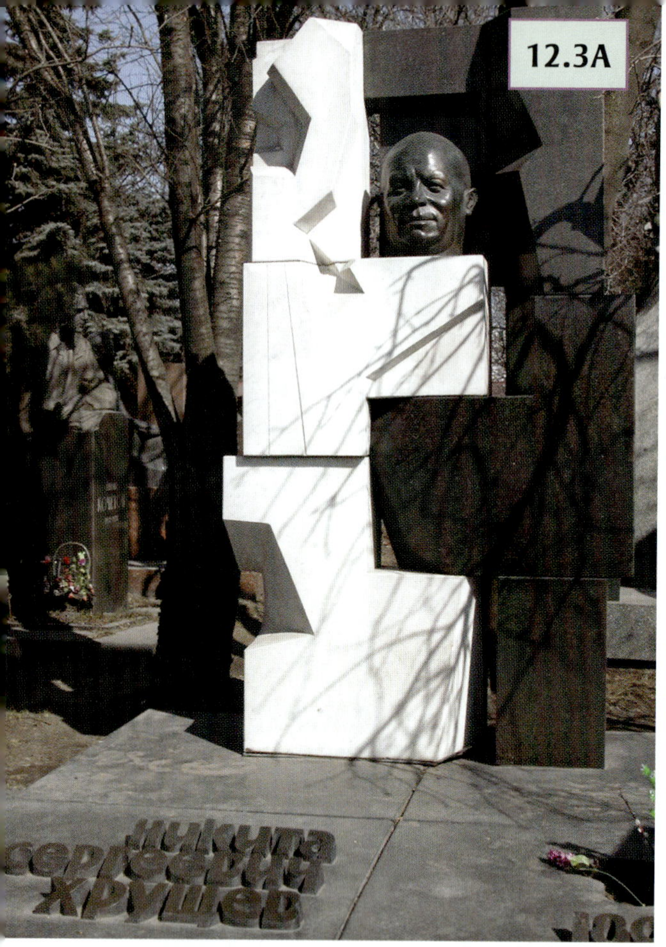
12.3A
никита
сергеевич
хрущев

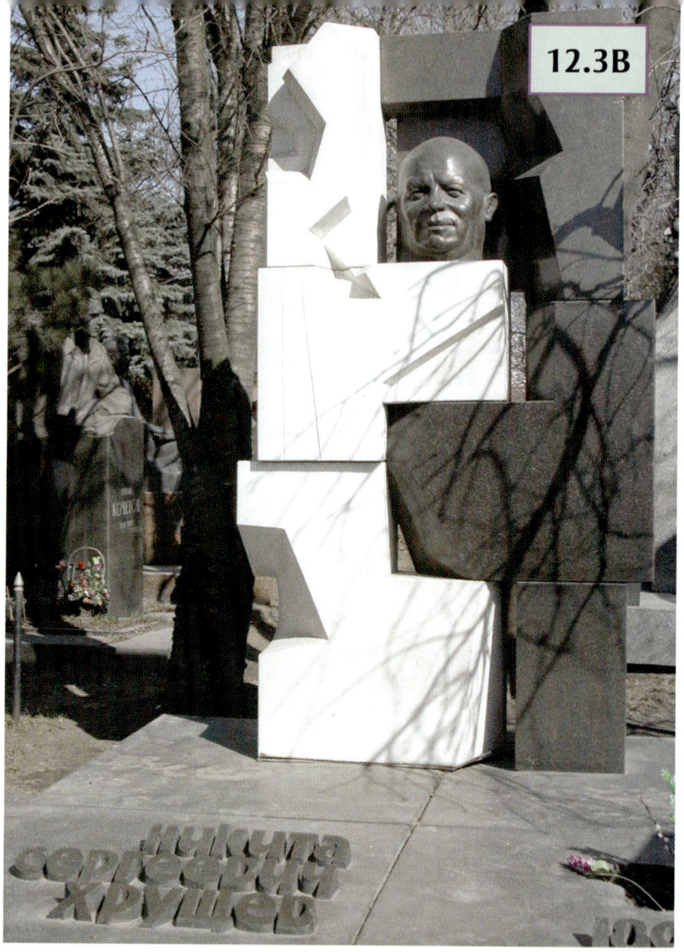
12.3B
никита
сергеевич
хрущев

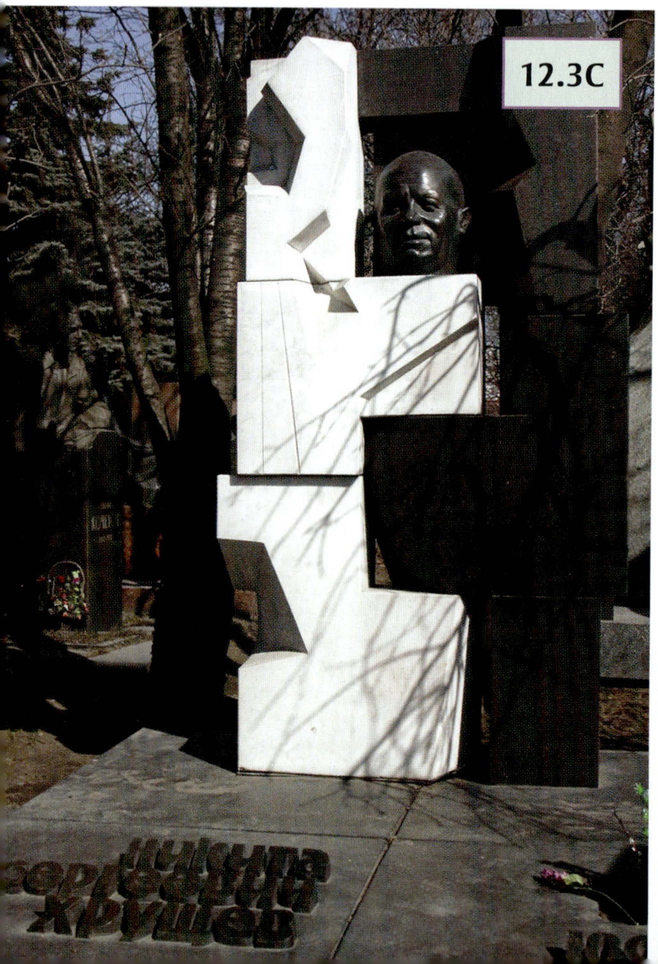
12.3C
никита
сергеевич
хрущев

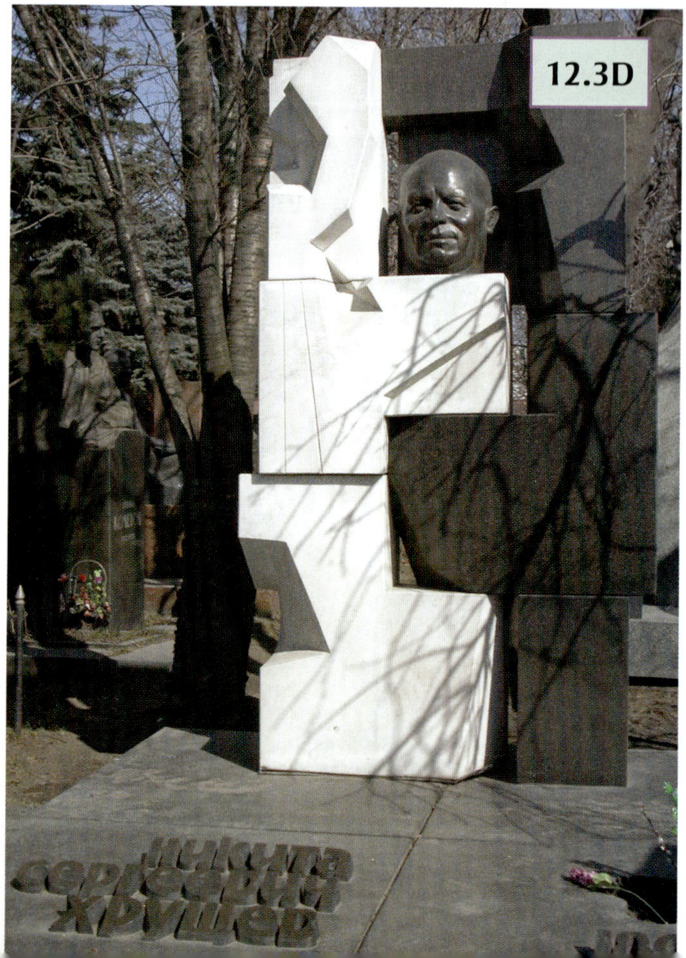
12.3D
никита
сергеевич
хрущев

of detail? I have three different answers for the last three exercises. In the Hawaiian ocean scene of Figure 11.9A, the dark side was more important. In Postcard 12.1, Pedro's palace, the light side was. And I would say that the two are of equal importance here in the Khrushchev tomb.

- Apply the PPW panel's 1.4 gamma script, or else Image: Adjustments>Exposure> Gamma Correction=1.57 as shown in Figure 12.2. Either creates Figure 12.3B.
- Add a curves adjustment layer, but don't change the default curves. Set the layer mode to Multiply, producing Figure 12.3C. (Note: if you're using the script, this step is already taken care of.)
- The adjustment layer carries a layer mask, which the script makes active. Check for the border around the mask's icon. Now, Image: Apply Image, and make a decision about the source of what you are about to apply. As you may recall from Chapter 4, you have at least eight options: red, green, blue, and RGB composite, each from either the merged file or the original bottom layer.

The choice of channel can sometimes be important, but to keep things simple you may wish to limit yourself to the RGB composite. I will do that for the rest of this half of the chapter. The choice of layer, however, makes a difference. My recommendation: if you have decided that the dark side is the more important of the two, use the merged. If you think the light side is more important or have no preference, use the background.

- Apply Image's defaults are Layer=Merged, Channel=RGB. We'd use those if the dark side wer more important, but that isn't the case

***Figure 12.3** Opposite, top left, the original. Top right, the Exposure command is applied at the settings of Figure 12.2. Bottom left, the document is multiplied. Bottom right, a layer mask is added. This page, left, the layer mask is blurred heavily. Right, a final version.*

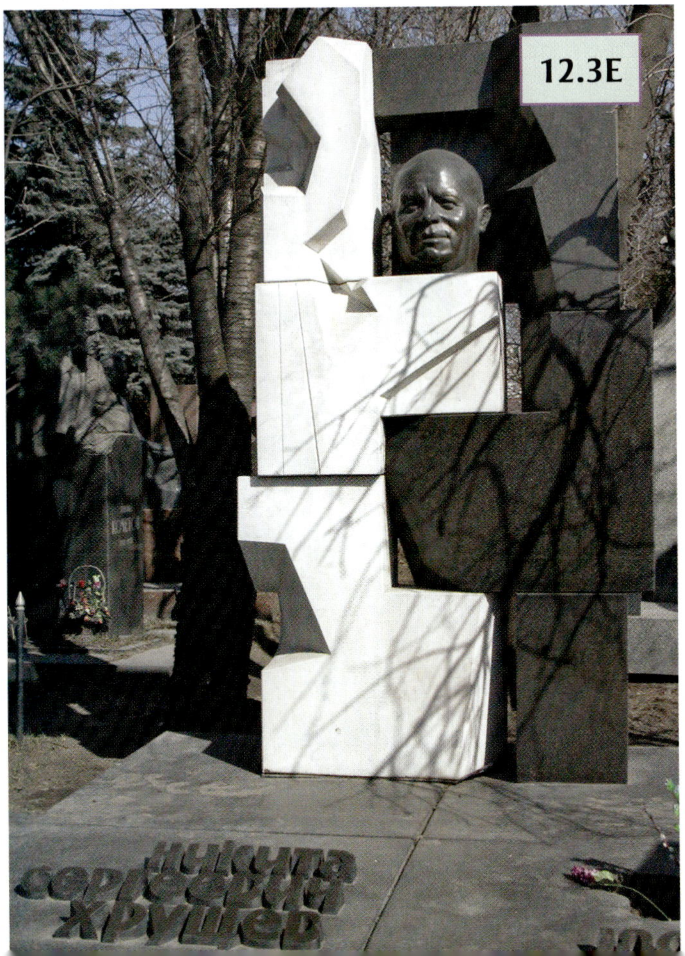

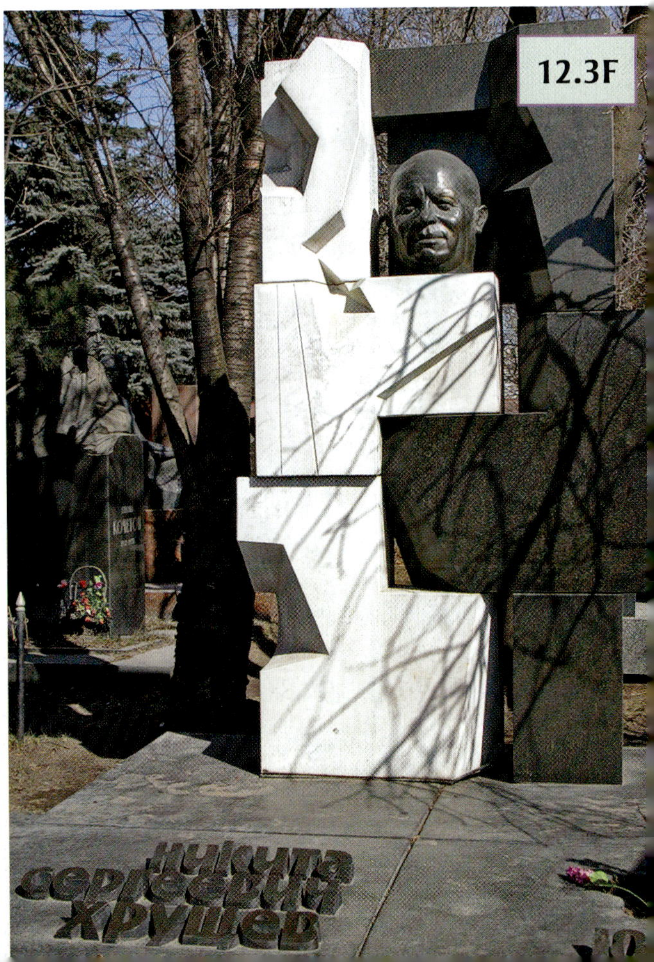

here, so we change the first setting to Layer=Background. The result is Figure 12.3D.

- Figure 12.3C is now, in effect, the top layer and 12.3B the bottom. The layer mask unifies them. We know that when layers differ greatly in darkness, and these certainly do, the mask has to be blurred heavily. I chose Filter: Blur>Gaussian Blur>Radius=45.0 pixels, changing Figure 12.3D into 12.3E and ending the maneuvers described in this chapter.
- Figure 12.3F, the final, is produced with a light application of the MMM + Color Boost action, followed by sharpening. If you find the effect too strong, blend it with the original, Figure 12.3A, until you have something more to your taste.

Of Politicians and Photographs

World leaders who are completely evil, with almost no redeeming bright side, are thankfully rare. Those who deserve sainthood because they almost completely lack the dark side are even rarer, although some have existed. Far more common are types like Pedro the Cruel, Ferdinand and Isabella, and Khrushchev, combinations of light and dark. That other political figures seldom have so spectacular a dark side as these shouldn't stop us from thinking about them in the same way.

Politics is again similar to the situation in our own field. In photography, the sun can create a two-sided image. Sometimes the effect is extreme, sometimes small, but always it should be taken into account, because this technique is made for it.

The analogy can be taken further. Anyone who supposes that this bright-and-dark-side business is limited to world leaders has a lot to learn about the human condition, particularly marriage. And anyone who supposes that the bright-and-dark-side issue is limited to when the brightness is caused by the sun will miss out on many opportunities.

In fact, the principle of bringing two halves closer to equality, even when the sun is not the cause, is so universal that this becomes one of the most important chapters of the book. Also, it completes the Picture Postcard Workflow: the four chapters to come are only embellishments, not fundamentals.

It's fitting to celebrate with some final postcards. The rest of this half will do three, all of which have the two-sides syndrome caused specifically by the sun. In the second half none of the examples are the fault of the sun, and we will discuss some exceptions and other options.

Let's look at Figure 12.4, which shows the three originals.

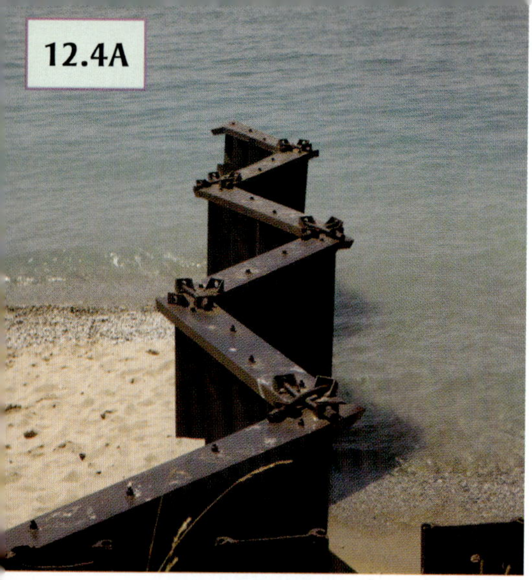

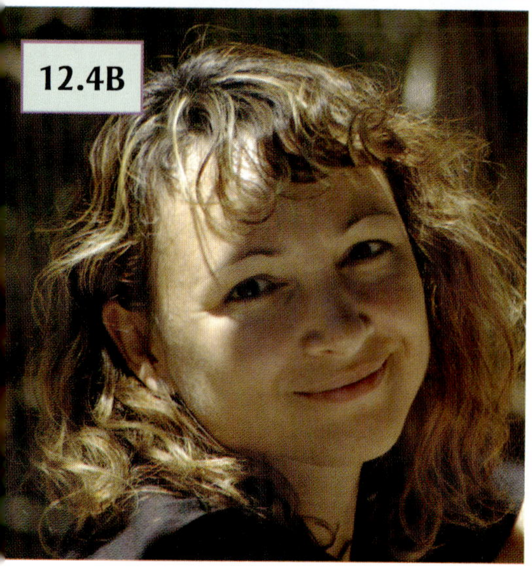

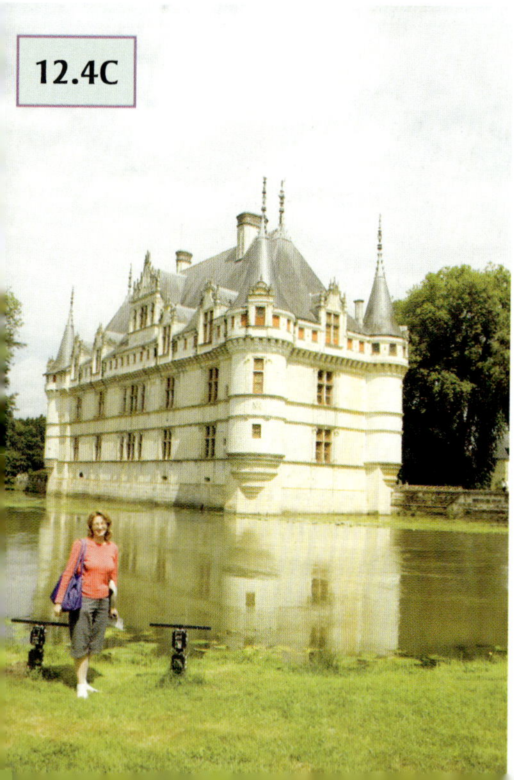

***Figure 12.4** The next three originals to be discussed.*

First, now that we have a complete workflow, which parts of it do you think will have the most impact on each of these images?

Second, do you agree that each merits the multiplication technique of this chapter?

Third, which parts of this workflow do you think will take longest?

Three Examples, Three Challenges

My answers are, first, I expect that the MMM action will create more interesting water in Figure 12.4A. It will also be important in the woman of Figure 12.4B but the real question will be how contrast is handled. The Bigger Hammer and possibly the Darken Sky actions should help make the top half of the chateau of Figure 12.4C less boring than it is now.

Second, the woman of Figure 12.4B is the most obvious example of a picture split into areas of sunlight and shade, but the other two also qualify. The right half of the water break in Figure 12.4A is surely in shadow. And, although the castle scene of Figure 12.4C is very light, the sun is leaving shadows.

Third, just before I wrote this paragraph I quickly corrected all three photos, with a stopwatch running. I didn't take notes or save intermediate versions, so I can't give you a precise summary of what went down.

Now that I have these corrected files as a backup, I'll start from scratch, and this time I *will* take notes. A reminder: this is the recommended way for dealing with important work: do two or more versions quickly rather than one version slowly, and blend as seems appropriate.

Anyhow, the times were a bit higher than average. Figure 12.4A presented no difficulties and I was done in 1:45. Figure 12.4B featured an initial color issue and some finagling with the color boost, since my first settings were producing bright red lips. Total time was 3:30. And I found Figure 12.4C the most time-consuming, 5:30, also largely due to troubles adjusting the color properly at the first step.

As we start over on each of the three, as with the previous exercise, we will follow the steps in the order of the box on Page 307. First up is the water scene. To save space, I'll show them in a smaller, heavily cropped format. Figure 12.5A is the first original.

* * *

- There are too many possibilities for the water and metal to make measuring worthwhile. The sand should be a yellowish brown, and brown is a type of red. All reds are AB–positive, which means we need a somewhat positive A and an even more positive B. The actual measurement was around $10^{A}20^{B}$. I concluded that nothing was known to be wrong, so no first color step was needed.
- Just about any dark point on the right side of the break could be chosen as a shadow. Whites in the water and on top of the metal are all too small to be significant. I couldn't tell by eye whether the sand was lighter than the pebbles. A threshold adjustment layer informed me that it was, so I put a sample point in the lightest sand, near the water just to the left of the break.
- That point in the sand read $220^{R}189^{G}165^{B}$. Lightening it would expand the whole picture into a longer tonal range, thus adding contrast. But a preliminary blend can enable an even more dramatic boost in detail.

Ask yourself which of the three original channels shown in Figures 12.5B through 12.5D is easiest to correct for contrast. The answer is the blue, because its sand and water fall in similar ranges. One curve could improve both. In both the red and the green a curve designed to improve the water might blow out the sand, which is much lighter.

The situation may remind you of the alligators image shown back in Postcard 4.15. The blend is different but the idea is the same: force two areas toward a more similar range, so that curves can be more effective.

- Therefore, with all three RGB channels open, I used Image: Apply Image, with the

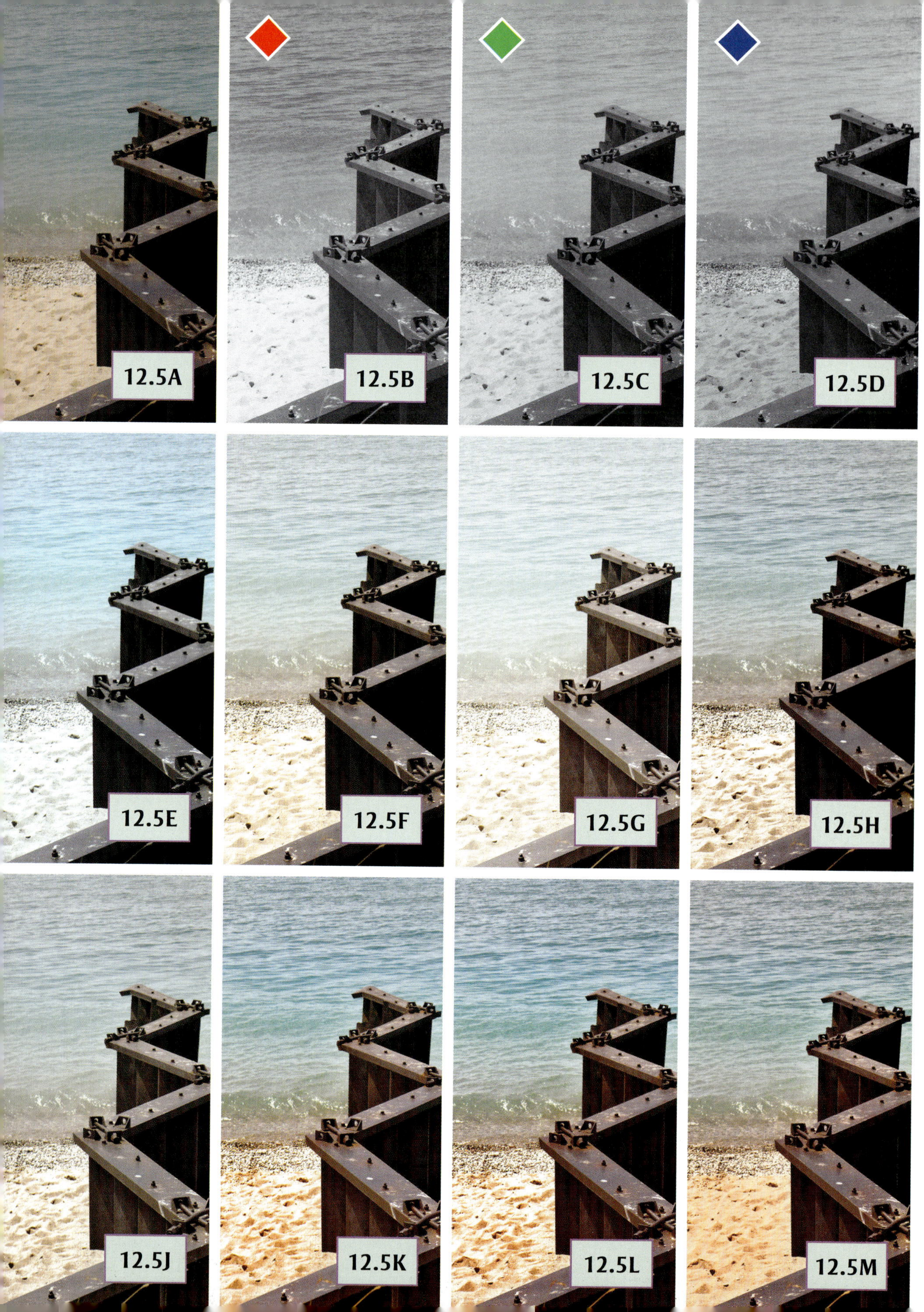
12.5A
12.5B
12.5C
12.5D
12.5E
12.5F
12.5G
12.5H
12.5J
12.5K
12.5L
12.5M

blue channel as source and an opacity of 50%. Unlike the earlier gators image, this time I went with Darken mode, for fear that otherwise the water would lighten excessively. The red and green were both changed for the better.

- Time for the curves. Still on the duplicate layer, I set the sand to $245^R245^G245^B$, using straight-line curves. The new color file is 12.5E. I now changed layer mode to Luminosity, restoring the original color and yielding Figure 12.5F.
- I applied the Shadows/Highlights command because I thought we could use detail in the darkest areas. It's not worth showing the slight improvement.

***Figure 12.5** Opposite, top row: the original and the three RGB channels, Middle row: the composite after channel blending and contrast-enhancing curves; the layer is changed to Luminosity mode, after which the file is flattened and Shadows/Highlights applied; a false profile of gamma 1.4 is assigned; the file is multiplied. Bottom row: a blurred layer mask is added; the MMM + Color Boost action is played at its default settings; the settings adjusted to taste; a version previously done from scratch. This page, left, the original, right, the final postcard.*

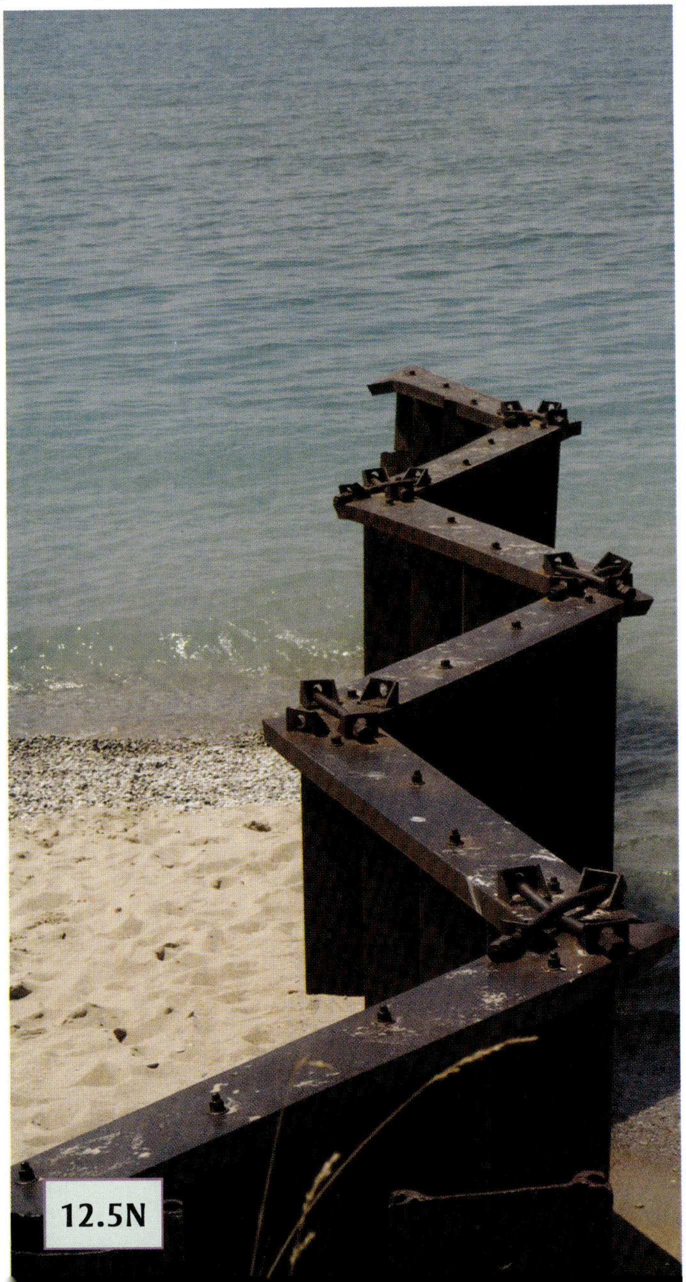

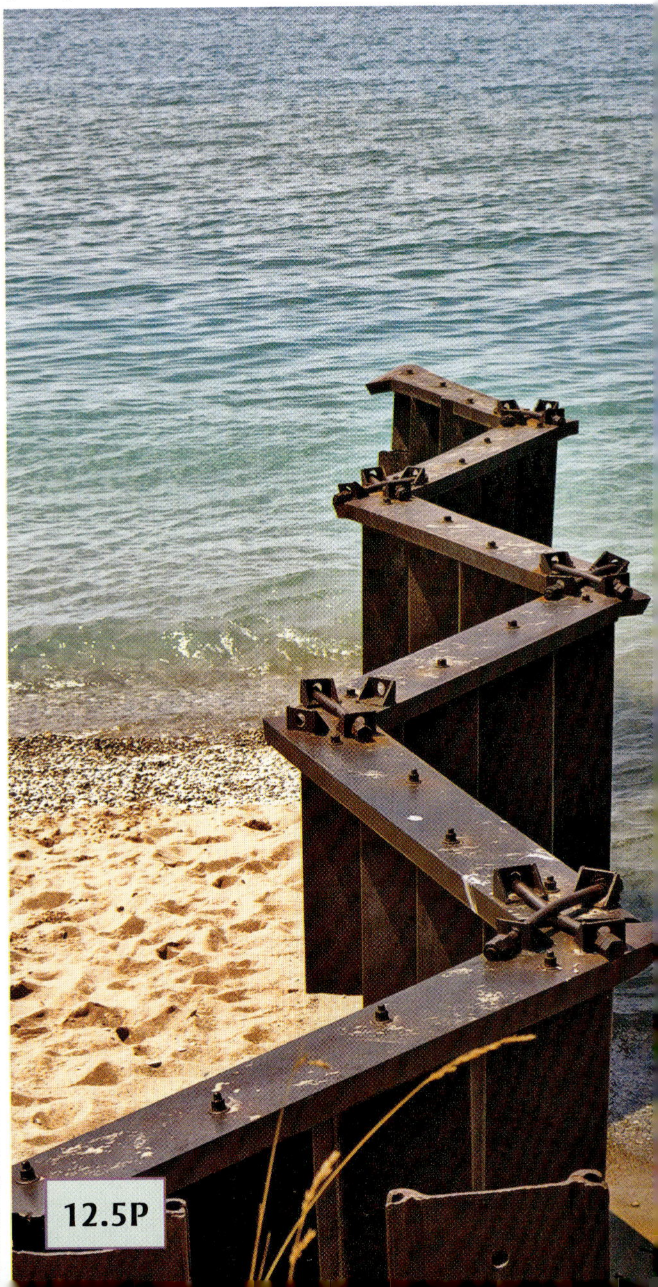

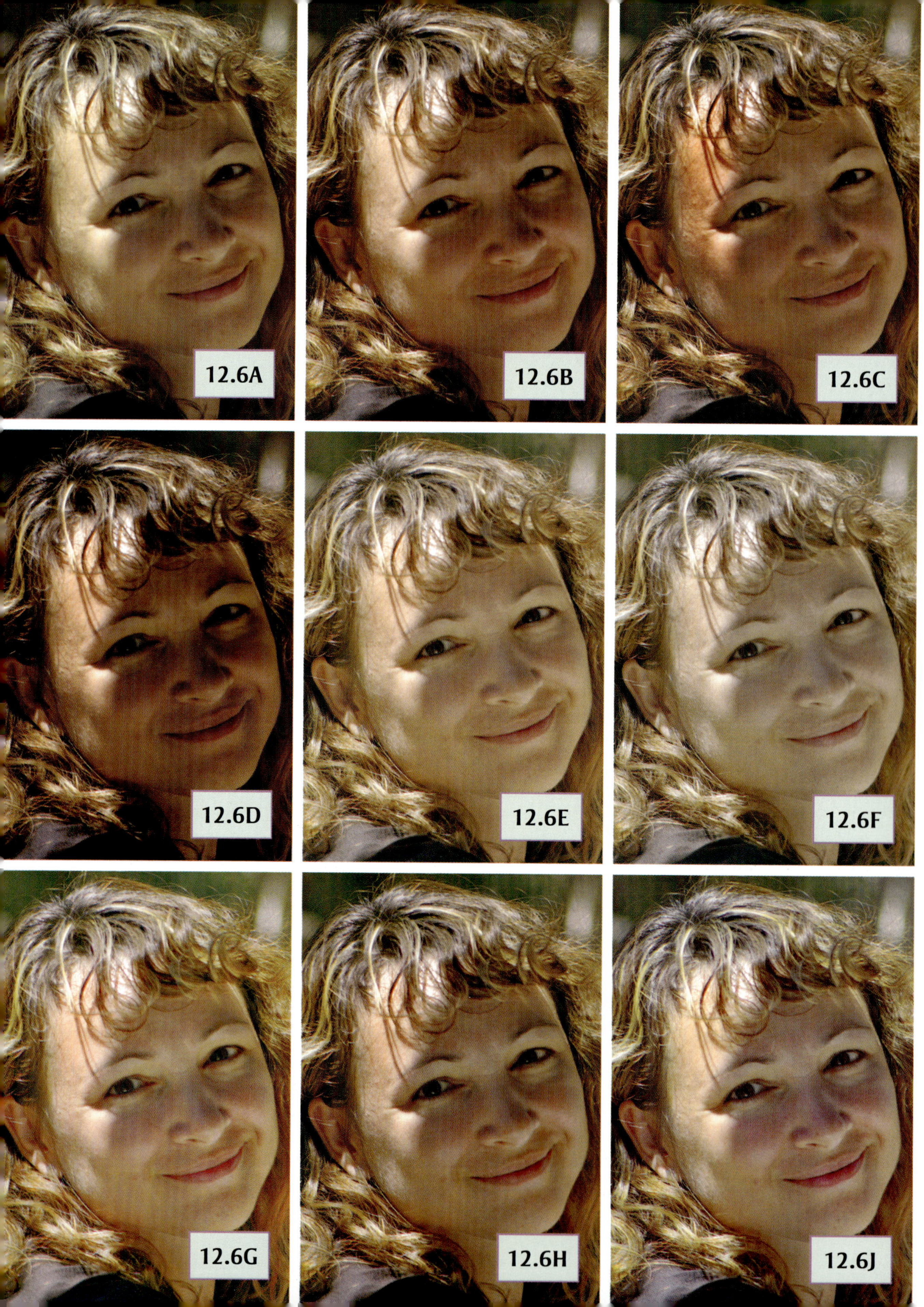
12.6A
12.6B
12.6C
12.6D
12.6E
12.6F
12.6G
12.6H
12.6J

- This added shadow detail was nice but not critical, so the Bigger Hammer action was not appropriate.
- No sky, so no Darken Sky action.
- The sun-shade issue calls for multiplication. First, the Exposure setting or the false profile discussed earlier produces Figure 12.5G. It seems like a brisk move in the wrong direction—so far, the original looks like the best of the bunch. Now, I added an adjustment layer that adjusted nothing, but was set to Multiply mode, yielding Figure 12.5H. The dark half of this picture is not more important than the light half, so my choice of layer mask was the RGB composite, Background layer. Then, a Gaussian blur at a 50-pixel radius produced Figure 12.5J.
- No fleshtones here, ergo no Skin Desaturation action.
- A quick selection of a typical area of water and sand, followed by the MMM + Color Boost action, solved the problem of not enough color. The default settings made Figure 12.5K.
- The adjustments to these settings, as we know, depend on personal taste. I came up with the slightly darker Figure 12.5L.
- Recall that before starting, I did another complete version to check timing. That version is Figure 12.5M. The water is hard to tell apart from 12.5L, although the sand is darker and seems less active. Usually when we do two versions there is more of a difference. This exercise, though, is so straightforward that there wasn't much room to vary the moves. I wasn't taking notes during the first effort, but it looks like I must have selected more of the water and less or none of the sand before running MMM.

__Figure 12.6__ (opposite) Top row: the original; after RGB curves to lessen a yellow cast; the Bigger Hammer action at its default settings. Middle row: after the Bigger Hammer has been reduced to 25% opacity, the file gets a false profile and is multiplied; a blurred layer mask is added; the Skin Desaturation action is applied. Bottom row: the MMM + Color Boost action defaults; the settings adjusted to taste; a version previously done from scratch.

In real life, if doing two versions, I would intentionally use different layer masks on the two versions. I might use a copy of the blue channel rather than the composite RGB, for example. In principle that would result in lighter sand and darker water. I don't know offhand whether that would look better, but if I were really doing two versions, I would find out by doing one each way.

Of the two I have to work with, I felt that Figure 12.5L is better for contrast and 12.5M for color. So, to get the best of both, I made a new layer on Figure 12.5M, applied Figure 12.5L to it, then changed the layer mode to Luminosity. A reminder that I could have done the same thing if the layer order was reversed by using Color mode.

After this blend and some sharpening, Figure 12.5P is the final. The original is shown next to it as Figure 12.5N. Now, on to our skintone exercise.

The Case of the Unknown Skintone

- Something seems to be wrong with the color of Figure 12.6A, but it's hard to pin down because of the lack of known values. I can't tell whether the shirt is supposed to be black or a dark blue. At present the part of it that's in sunlight measures 6^A0^B, a dark magenta that is unlikely to be right. It would be a very uncommon color for such a garment. Meanwhile, although skin has a broad range of possibilities, a reasonable starting point is AB values positive and roughly equal. I sample the light area on the left side of the face below the eye, and find 12^A24^B. A much darker area on the right side, below mouth level, gets the same reading. Having the B so much higher than the A suggests a yellow cast. However, the area below the eyes measures so much redder than the rest of the skin that I suspect she's wearing makeup there: on our left it's 18^A17^B and on the right 16^A17^B.

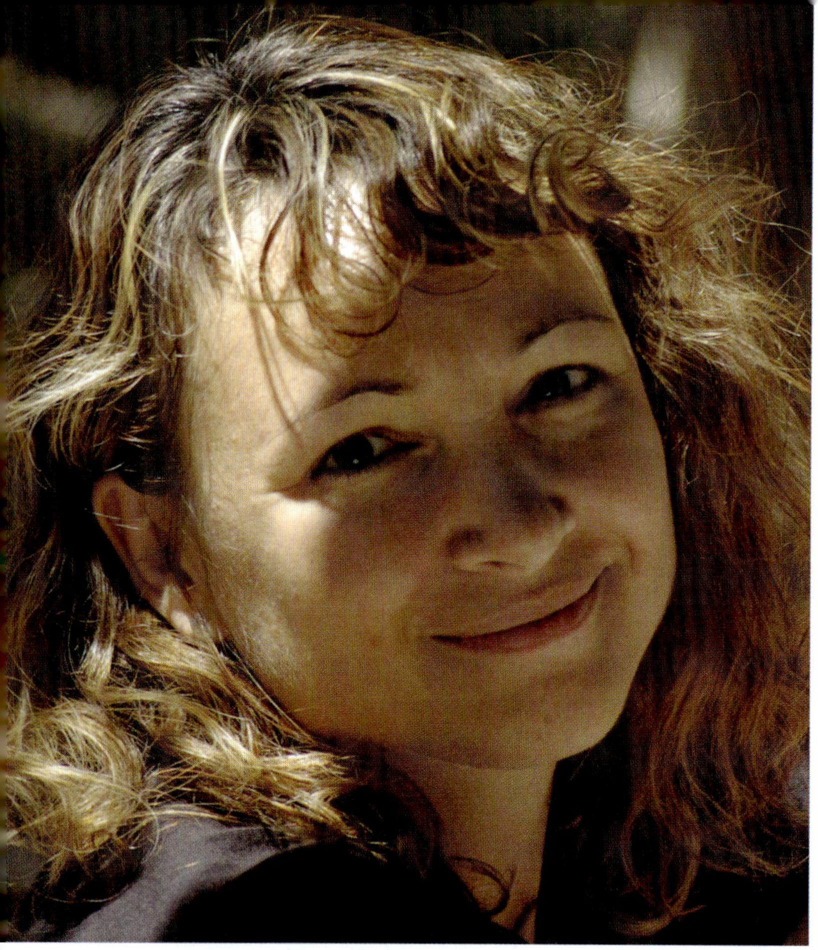

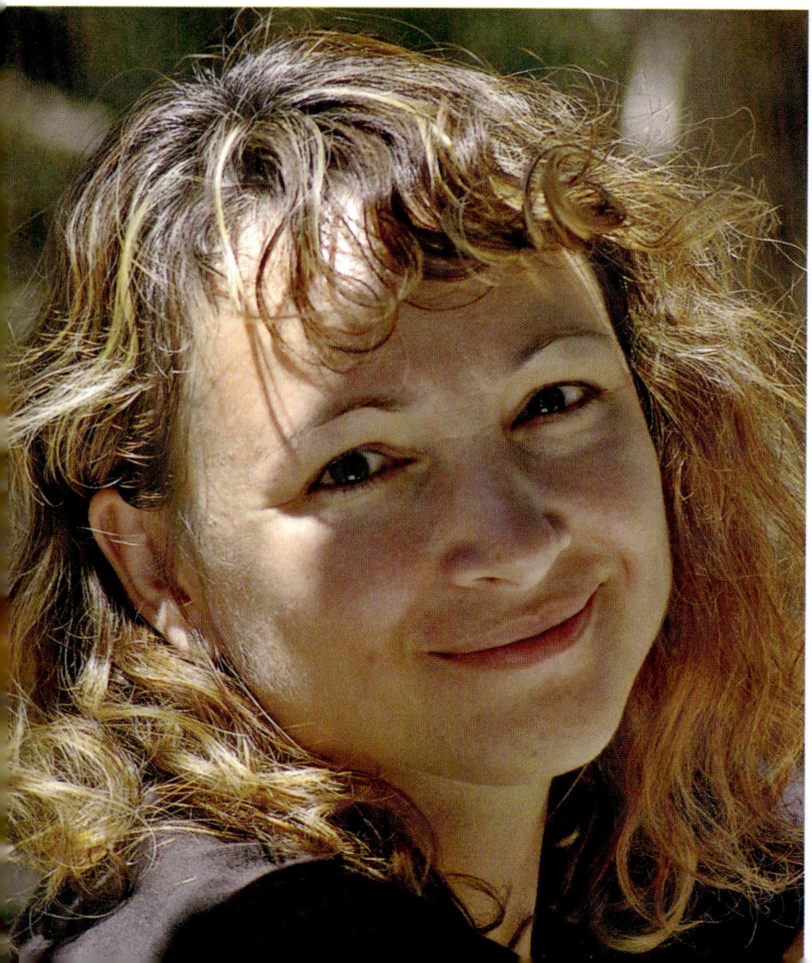

This will therefore be a tricky set of curves. The woman definitely needs to move toward red but we have to be careful not to overdo it or the area below the eyes will go crazy. I wound up with Figure 12.6B.

- Unlike the last example, identifying the highlight is no sweat. It's a nearly blown-out area near the top of the forehead. And there are several possibilities for the shadow.
- The green channel usually shows the best face and this file is no exception. However, as discussed in Chapter 9, faces are the exception to the general rule about always adding contrast. Blending with the green emphasizes texture and makes the skintone more realistic, but omitting it makes the subject look younger, as we see fewer imperfections. I gave it a try, but decided it wasn't attractive and cancelled it.
- Curves for contrast are also difficult. The highlight and shadow are already good for darkness, so there isn't any free lunch as in the previous example. I tried lightening the quartertone in the green channel. It made the darker half blotchy, so I abandoned this move as well.
- The Shadows/Highlights command would bring out detail in the hair, but I'm not convinced it's a good idea, and did not use it. Others might disagree, but I think we want to focus attention on the face.
- This isn't the classic image for Chapter 10's Bigger Hammer, but that action might help fill in the lighter area on the sunlit side of the face. It costs only a few seconds to try. At default settings the effect seems overdone, as seen in Figure 12.6C. I reduced the opacity of the overlay layer from 100% to 25%,

***Postcard 12.7** Control of shadow in a portrait.*

meaning that the new version, which isn't shown, is a mix of Figures 12.6B and 12.6C, with 12.6B being three times as important.

- No sky here, so no Darken Sky action.
- This picture is the most obviously affected by sun and shadow of the three current exercises. Unlike the others, the dark half is the more important because more of the face is in shadow than not. After applying the false profile or Exposure command to lighten, I put on a multiplication layer, creating Figure 12.6D, and used the RGB from Layer=Merged as the layer mask. After blurring, notice how light the shadow has become in Figure 12.6E. This is typical of the technique and has to be corrected at the Color Boost stage on the Endpoint Adjustments layer.
- As this image involves flesh, I ran the Skin Desaturation action, producing Figure 12.6F. This move toward blandness is yet another example of how the PPW often does things that temporarily make the picture look worse. But it's needed, because the next step is going to add a lot of color. People are willing to accept exaggerated color in a picture like the water scene in the previous exercise. They won't accept bright red skintones.
- I made a rough lasso selection of the entire face plus much of the hair, and ran the MMM + Color Boost action. The default settings made Figure 12.6G. A reminder about MMM with respect to faces: the MMM Luminosity layer should usually be discarded, as it can produce disagreeable contrast.
- With the luminosity adjustment gone, I darkened the hair, using a straight-line move on the Endpoint Adjustment layer. Then, I took a tip from the end of Chapter 6. You may recall that a beta reader suggested adding a second MMM Color layer, but setting the mode to Saturation and adjusting opacities to taste. It worked well here, because the original MMM Color layer was making awkward changes in hue, pushing the lightest part of the hair toward green, and making the area under the eyes rather pink. I ended with Figure 12.6H.
- Figure 12.6J is the version I did previously. There is much more difference between it and the version just finished than there was between the two corresponding versions in the water scene, Figures 12.5L and 12.5M. This difference illustrates why doing two quick versions is better than one careful one.

According to me, Figure 12.6H is still too yellow. On the other hand, Figure 12.6J is too pink. Because it was done before I knew the value of saturation layers, it has too much color variation for my taste. The two versions are closer for contrast than they are for color. Figure 12.6H has a slightly darker sunlit cheek, presumably because, as I recall, I didn't use the Bigger Hammer action in making Figure 12.6J.

A skeptic might ask why I didn't just do it right the first time. If only it were that easy! I was trying my best both times. The big difference came at the initial color adjustment. It was a difficult step with no clear targets. It can't be surprising that my two results varied so much. The only thing to compare them to was the original, Figure 12.6A. That comparison is extremely favorable for either of my versions. It's only when the two are seen together that their respective deficiencies become apparent.

Once having applied the curves that produced the initial color adjustment, Figure 12.6B, I was sunk. I do not know how to do it more carefully, and the color is technically acceptable. But it no longer matters how careful I am with the half-dozen subsequent steps. It's possible to get slightly better than Figure 12.6H, but not nearly as good as if Figure 12.6J is around to blend with.

Given disparate interpretations like this, I recommend putting two copies of one as layers on top of the other. Set one layer to Luminosity and the other to Color mode. Adjust opacities to taste. Postcard 12.7 shows,

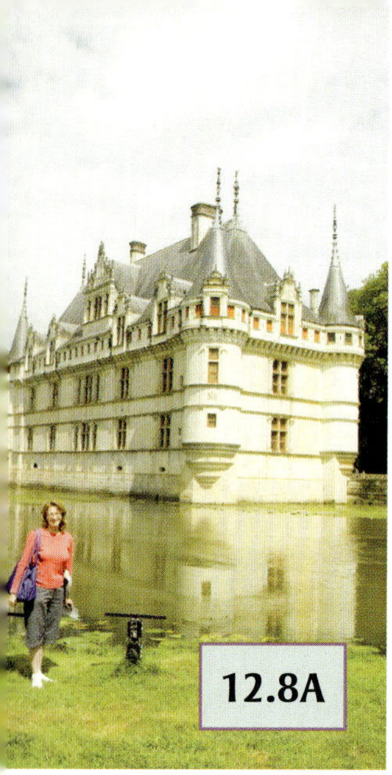
12.8A

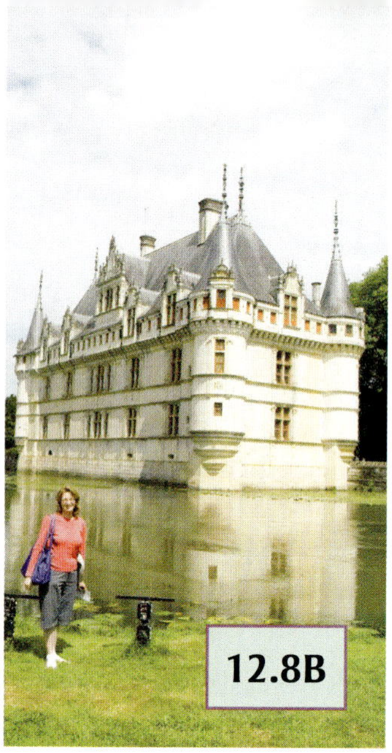
12.8B

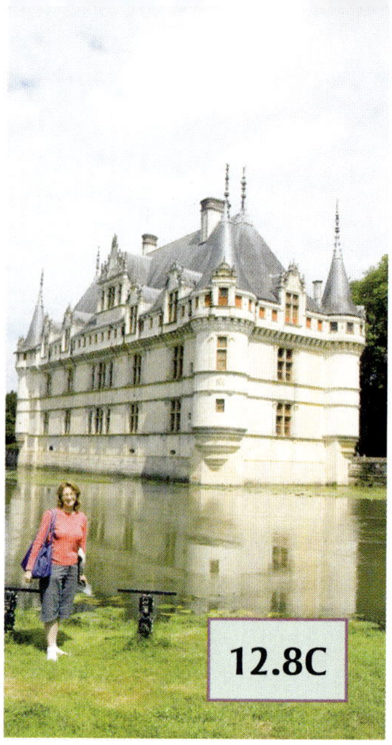
12.8C

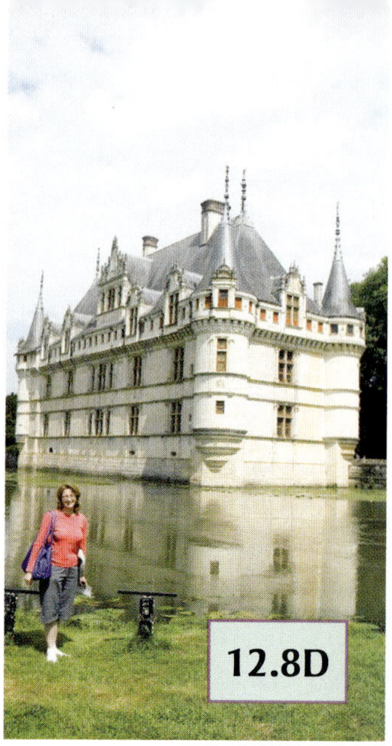
12.8D

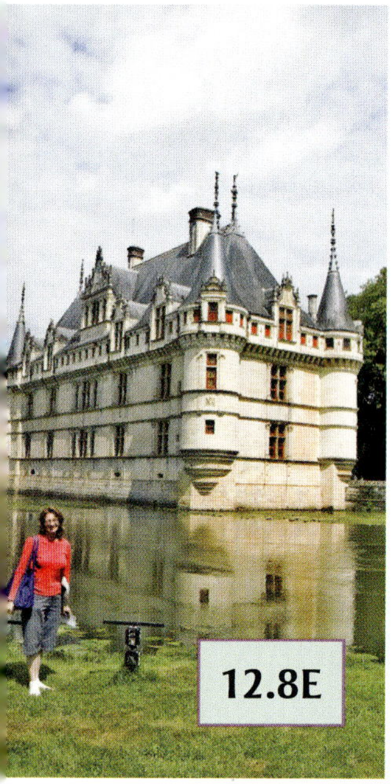
12.8E

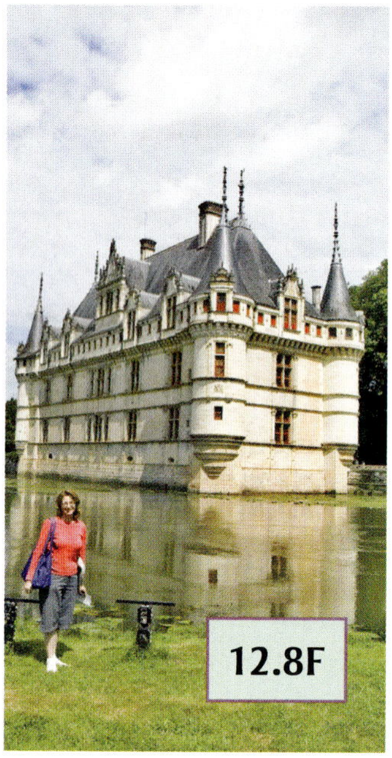
12.8F

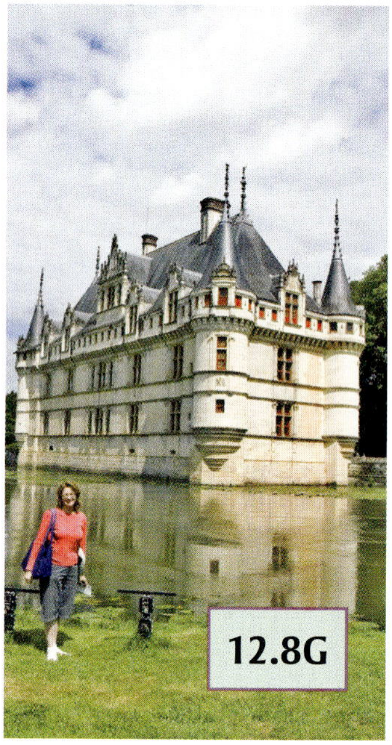
12.8G

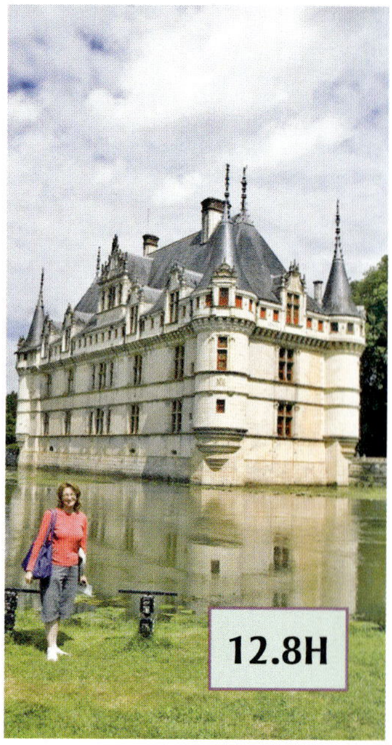
12.8H

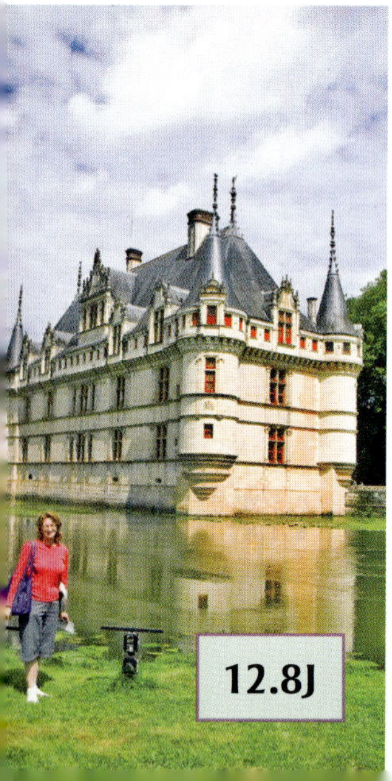
12.8J

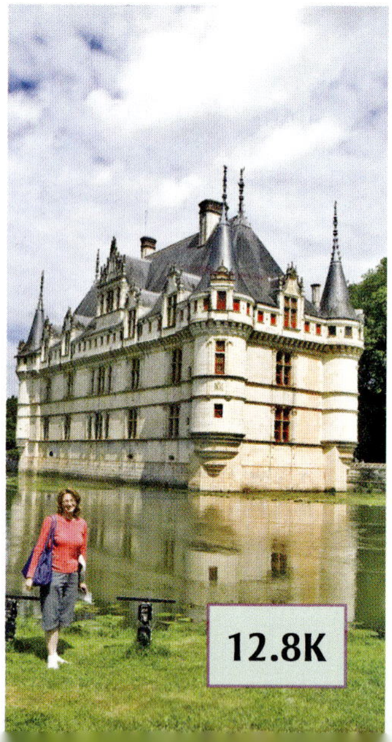
12.8K

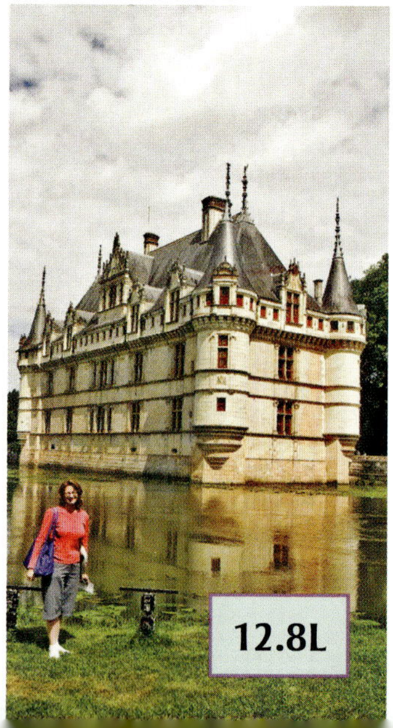
12.8L

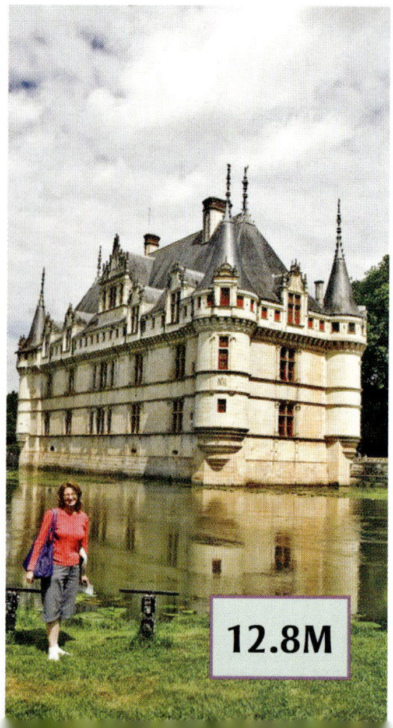
12.8M

at larger size, my final version. To get there, I took two-thirds of the color of Figure 12.6H and one-third 12.6J. The luminosity I judged to split 50–50.

On to the final exercise.

Another Castle, Another Cast

• The chapter started with a castle, so it's fitting to end with one, albeit of rather a different character. This scene, first shown as Figure 12.4C and now repeated as Figure 12.8A, has several points that offer reliable color guidance.

The sky is full of clouds that ought to be white, meaning 0^A0^B. Instead, they are consistently $(1)^A2^B$—slightly yellow and slightly green. The chateau itself measures $(1)^A12^B$, somewhat to the green side of yellow. Parts of the foreground should conceivably be yellow, but even the greenest part, just to the right of the woman's feet, is $(13)^A69^B$, which violates the recommendation that the absolute value of the B in greenery should be 1.5 to 2.5 times that of the A.

All three measurements suggest moving in the positive direction in the A, away from green and toward magenta, and in the negative in the B, away from yellow and toward blue. The chateau really can't be straight yellow, although it could be a yellowish brown like the sand in Figure 12.5P. And the grass is not just too yellow but too colorful. Adding a magenta component tones it down. I just have to be careful that the woman's shirt does not become too magenta.

***Figure 12.8** (opposite) Top row: the original; after RGB curves to lessen a yellow cast; after a second set of curves; various changes made in Luminosity mode. Middle row: the Bigger Hammer action, default settings; the same action using desaturated inverted RGB as the overlay layer; the Darken Sky B action is added at default settings; a false profile/multiply/blurred layer mask move. Bottom row: the MMM + Color Boost action defaults; the settings adjusted to taste; a version previously done from scratch; a version intended to combine the best of each.*

In principle all this means that the blue channel is too dark, the green too light, and the red probably too light in the grass and maybe elsewhere.

It is one thing to know the desired result, however, and another to get it. You may recall that I struggled with this the first time and wound up with the longest correction of any of the final three exercises. This time around, I got so frustrated that I found myself using two sets of curves. Figure 12.8A is the original, 12.8B the result of my first curves, which were, as always, on an adjustment layer set to Color mode. The foreground is still too yellow and so is the chateau. At least, though, it's more correct than the original. So, a second curves layer, Color mode again, produced Figure 12.8C. Meanwhile, note how the elimination of the yellow cast has helped the blueness of the sky.

That the first step is sometimes as difficult as it is here poses an obstacle to those just getting used to the PPW. Such people suspect that if they don't see the sorts of problems that afflict this particular image there must be something wrong. No. Always remember that for every picture as hard as this one there are five like the water scene of Figure 12.5 that don't need a first step at all.

• Rather than use a threshold adjustment layer I moused over the clouds and found the lightest significant area. The shadow is surely the dark area to the right of the chateau.

• The chateau is blown out in the red channel and only somewhat better in the green. The blue shows good detail but its vegetation is quite dark. In view of the weak detail in the light clouds and building, I was already foreseeing using the Bigger Hammer action. First, though, a cautious move. On a duplicate layer, I blended the blue, which had the best chateau, into the RGB (that is, into the red and green channels simultaneously) at 20% opacity. It was hard to see an overall difference after moving to Luminosity mode.

- In the green, everything of significance is in the light half. This isn't true of the other two channels, where the vegetation is darker. A curve that darkened the midtone of the green put everything of importance in a steeper area of the curve, gaining contrast. Figure 12.8D shows the result of the blue blend and the green curve after the layer mode has been changed to Luminosity.
- Nothing of great moment is happening in the shadows, but the highlights, in the clouds and perhaps in the chateau itself, are very important. In principle I should have used the Shadows/Highlights command right now to emphasize them. I was a little leery, for fear of blowing out something useful. I knew that the next two steps would add detail to the sky, so I decided to forgo S/H this time. My recollection is that on my first try, my decision was the opposite.
- That the Bigger Hammer action should be used was obvious. Detailing in the clouds and chateau is critical. The default result, Figure 12.8E, is impressive, but creates an overly dark shirt. The default uses an inverted red channel as the overlay, and the shirt is originally quite light in the red.

I could have tried to fix this with a mask, but instead, following a recommendation in the second half of Chapter 10, I replaced the overlay with an inverted, blurred, and desaturated copy of the RGB composite, producing Figure 12.8F. (This was, incidentally, before the latest version of the PPW panel. With that panel, we can now Option-click the action and quickly preview the results of many different overlays.)

- The patches of blue peeking out of the clouds should be augmented. Chapter 8 says that the more complex the clouds, the more we should be prone to use Darken Sky B. As this is a rather complex sky, I did so, obtaining Figure 12.8G. The extra depth in the sky is welcome, but what happened to the woman's bag is not. As explained in Chapter 8, the sky actions know only that skies are usually the only blue object in the whole picture. This time, that assumption doesn't work. The bag is strongly blue as well.

By toggling the visibility of the top layer, I learned that the action also impacted the pants and the leftmost reflection in the water, although not as much as the sky and the bag. I thought about leaving the darkened reflection in, but decided against it.

Getting rid of these undesired darker blues is easy because they are so distant from the sky. The sky actions use a multiplying adjustment layer. Its layer mask is black everywhere except areas that the action has identified as blue. It can easily be modified.

Making sure that this layer mask was active, I used the lasso tool to make a very rough selection of everything surrounding the woman, then Edit: Fill>Black. This prevented the layer from impacting the selected area. Meanwhile, no selection line is visible, because everything touching the selection was already black in the layer mask. The version going forward has the sky of Figure 12.8G, but everything else comes from Figure 12.8F.

- It's hard to accept that a picture this light needs to be lightened even further, but the presence of sun and shade says that it does. So, I applied a false profile, made a multiplying adjustment layer, loaded the RGB from the background layer into the layer mask, and blurred, yielding Figure 12.8H.
- Flesh is present, so in principle the Skin Desaturation action is called for. It wouldn't hurt, but the face is so small that it's hard to think it would help much, so I omitted it.
- Feeling that the sky had had enough attention already, and that the greenery is not particularly important, I made a quick lasso selection of the chateau, the water, and the woman. The MMM + Color Boost action defaults used it to produce Figure 12.8J.

Experiments with the four resulting correction layers should always commence, in

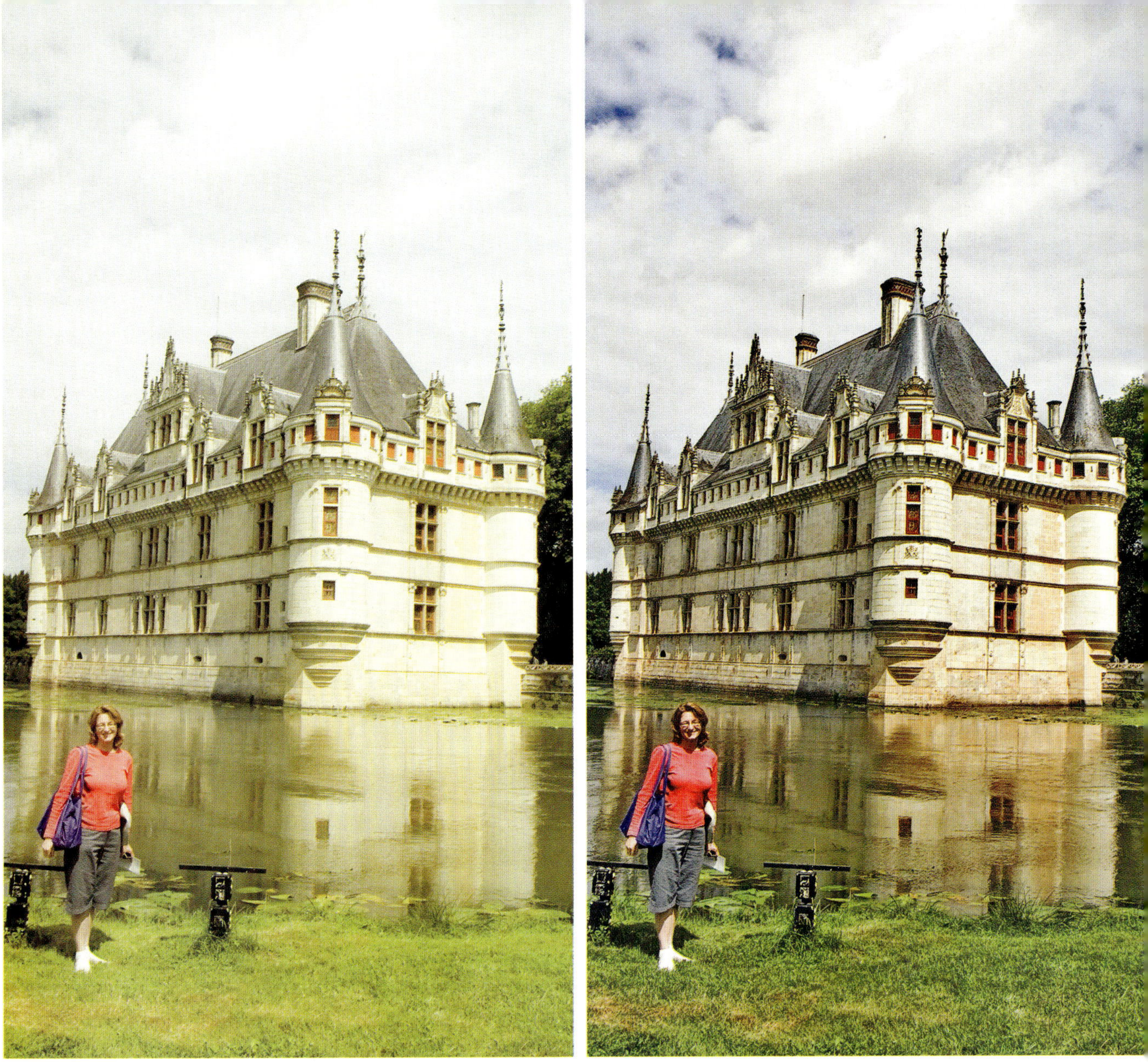

***Postcard 12.9** Château d'Azay-le-Rideauile, Loire Valley, France.*

my opinion, by turning off the MMM Luminosity to see what happens. This time, it did a good job, and I restored it. Next, I turned off the Color Boost layer. I found that the MMM Color layer, the only color adjustment now visible had altered the hue of the grass and the castle unduly, so I cut its opacity in half.

I always look at the Endpoint Adjustment layer before restoring the Color Boost. I don't think it's feasible to finalize color without seeing the true contrast. Here, I moved the endpoints of the L curve to make slight tweaks to highlight and shadow.

I now reactivated the Color Boost layer and took stock. The shirt was the most objectionable item. Reducing opacity enough to make it acceptable leaves the rest of the picture dull. A luminosity-based layer mask won't work because so many things share the shirt's tonal range. Here knowledge of LAB structure is useful. The A channel is magenta vs. green. The shirt is far more magenta than anything else in the picture. I therefore used Image: Apply Image to copy the A into the layer mask. I had to check the Invert box, because the natural state of the channel is that magenta things are light and green ones dark; the opposite is needed. After adjusting opacity to taste, I had Figure 12.8K.

Two Sides of the Story

Having thus finished a correction on which I took notes at every step, it's time to look at what happened when I didn't. Figure 12.8L is the one I prepared before writing this last section. This is the third such comparison in the chapter, and the one with the biggest variation between the contestants. The reasons are instructive.

Figures 12.8K and 12.8L each have strengths and weaknesses. Making the former involved two sets of color curves at the outset. In the latter I recall limiting myself to one set, meaning that I could not fully defeat the yellow cast. Now that I see the two final versions it seems that the truth lies somewhere in the middle. Once committing myself to two sets of curves in Figure 12.8K, I appear to have yielded to the mistake, common among monarchs and Margulises, of falling in love with one's own conception. Having decided to take such strong measures to defeat the yellow cast, I became fixated on definitive victory. My policy of unconditional surrender resulted in an overly cool look. The yellower feel of the earlier version, Figure 12.8L, is more attractive to me, but I'd like to split the difference somehow.

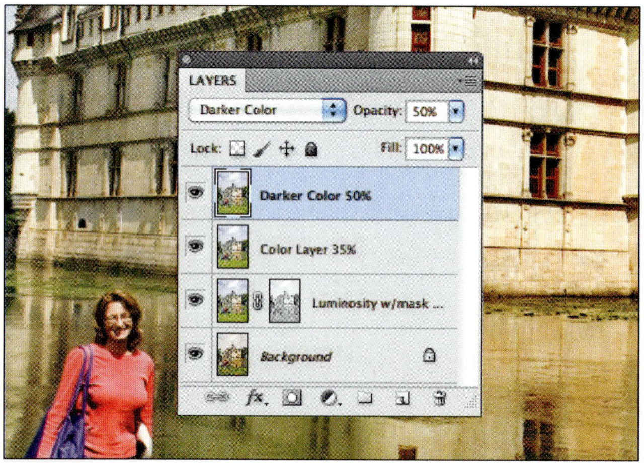

Figure 12.10 *The Layers palette for the final correction. The bottom layer is Figure 12.8L and the top three are all copies of Figure 12.8K.*

The contrast issue is more complicated. To my eye the yellower version is rather clunky in the sky and somewhat too dark overall, but with nicer reflections in the water and generally better darks.

- Consequently I merged the two. I copied the cooler version to a new layer on top of the warmer one, then duplicated it, setting the lower new layer to Luminosity and the upper one to Color. This structure gives great flexibility. I adjusted opacity of the color layer to my own taste, which turned out to be 35%. On the luminosity layer, however, I wanted a layer mask, because I think that the lighter half of the cooler version is better than the warmer one, but its darker half is worse. The choice of channel for the mask makes little difference. It need not be blurred because the bottom two layers are so similar in weight.

For the record, I loaded the composite RGB, Merged layer, as the layer mask. With the new mask restricting how much of the top layer shows through, I reduced layer opacity to 59%, begetting Figure 12.8M.

Final Thoughts on a Workflow

One last blend suggested itself. I felt that the sky of Figure 12.8K remained better even than in the composite version, Figure 12.8M. So, to my three-layered document I added a fourth, yet another copy of Figure 12.8K. This one was set to Darker Color mode (requires Photoshop CS3 and later) and again opacity was adjusted to my taste. The document now consisted of Figure 12.8L on bottom, and three copies of Figure 12.8K on top, set respectively to Darker Color, Color, and Luminosity modes, as shown in Figure 12.10. The opacities of these three layers are up to whoever is doing the work. My own choices produced Postcard 12.9.

This ends the preliminary discussion of

how to treat pictures that are divisible into two halves, and for that matter, it completes the Picture Postcard Workflow. The second half of this chapter, and the four chapters that follow, are add-ons that could apply to any workflow. So at this point you face certain decisions as to how to proceed.

You can go back to previous chapters to firm up your technique before proceeding. If you choose that route, you may still want to at least skim the second half of this chapter. Remember, the two-sided character of everything we've seen so far has been caused by strong sunlight. Three of the four examples in the second half have two sides for other reasons.

The second half also discusses how to avoid being fooled into using this multiply technique where it isn't appropriate, and how to deal with extremely dark originals. It offers a few comments about fleshtones, and talks about how false profile plus multiplication differs from the Bigger Hammer.

You may also wish to experiment with different types of files, different masks, and different types of blurs. This chapter only scratches the surface of the technique and its possible variations. Even experts have trouble grasping why such big blurs are needed.

James Gray, a beta reader who was having trouble with this very concept, offers help: "You have said a lot about blurring in this chapter and the previous two. It seems to me that one really important part of blurring hasn't been emphasized enough. In one place you mention almost in passing that blurring obliterates detail in the mask. This is really the point of the blurring. Using a layer mask with lots of texture/detail will tend to counteract whatever the layer is doing and will eliminate a lot of *its* texture/detail. You make note of this in your evaluation of how to figure out which images in Figure 11.10 do not have a blurred layer mask. The main way to tell is that texture detail seems obliterated or badly reduced."

* * *

In photographs and in politics, it often is obvious that somebody or something has two sides. A key to success in both disciplines is learning to identify the nonobvious cases, and to bring those two sides, the two sides that others may not perceive, into a harmonious whole.

Review and Exercises

✓ This chapter uses heavily blurred layer masks to unify the two parts. Why? What happens if the blur is omitted? On what types of merges is it unnecessary?

✓ Remember that both the false profile and Exposure methods lighten everything, including the shadow. You should assume that you will have to darken the shadow later, presumably but not necessarily with the Endpoint Adjustment layer of the Color Boost action.

✓ Go back to Chapter 7, and reconsider Figure 7.4A, the statue of Pizarro. In view of the sun and shade in the scene, can you get a better result on it now?

✓ There is nothing sacred about using Multiply mode as the means of darkening the top layer. Curves and other methods in Normal mode should work just as well.

A Closer Look

The pictures in the first half all featured strong sunlight coupled with some shadowy areas. This is the classic signal that the methods of this chapter are appropriate. Really, though, they should be considered for any photo that is easily divisible into light and dark portions. Using it in *every* such case is unwise; you will later see how I embarrassed myself publicly by not heeding this advice.

I've provided two actions that lighten and multiply, one stronger than the other. The actions use false profiles. The weaker one, which was in use throughout the first half exercises, assigns a gamma of 1.4 as opposed to the 2.2 that most of us use. This corresponds to an Exposure>Gamma Correction setting of 1.57. The stronger one, which was used without explanation in the palace image of Postcard 12.1, has a gamma of 1.0, which corresponds to Exposure>Gamma Correction 2.2. Note: these equivalents are only exact in Adobe RGB, sRGB, or other spaces that employ a 2.2 gamma. ColorMatch RGB and ProPhoto RGB do not.

The question of whether to use Exposure or a false profile has been studied in some depth by beta readers Alessandro Bernardi and Marco Olivotto, who were also on the development team for the PPW panel. Their findings are detailed in the documentation file for the false profile actions, which is found in the Help section of the panel. (If you don't have the panel, you can download the documentation separately.) The executive summary of that lengthy document is that the difference is inconsequential unless there is vital detail in the deep shadows. In that case the false profile method is more likely to be smoother, but there are some exceptions. My recommendation therefore is to stick with the false profiles in general, but in extremely important images that depend on good detail in dark areas, try both.

The false profile is a redefinition of RGB. It creates an immediate lighter appearance, but that appearance is not locked in until there has been a shift in colorspace. Since the PPW always winds up in LAB, that requirement is met. If you are using false profiles in some other context there can be a fatal ambiguity.

Some PPW advocates disagree that two false profiles are enough. If you become one of them, the panel has a prompt that allows you to expand it to contain more options.

If you decide to stick with two, the stronger one (1.0 gamma) should be reserved for cases where at least the dark half of the scene is grossly plugged, as it was in Postcard 12.1. The next exercise shows its impact and also has a comparison of what happens with and without the multiplication.

The Fire Next Time

Giant redwoods are not just among the largest life forms on earth, but among the longest-lived. They can reach ages of nearly 2,000 years, at least if man is not around. Enough groves have been protected so that extinction from logging is no longer probable, as it was once. The reason that loggers prized these beautiful trees also accounts for the long life: redwood is highly resistant to fire, a useful attribute in the construction of buildings and in forest survival.

Fire is therefore the redwood's friend. It wipes out ground cover that prevents its seeds from germinating, as well as more vulnerable trees that can interfere with its root system.

Of course, no wood is unaffected by a raging fire. A mature redwood can be 100 meters tall, well out of the reach of flames. A serious fire can, however, do quite a number on the lower trunk, sometimes hollowing it out almost completely.

Such is the scene in Figure 12.11A. The man is inside a giant redwood whose guts were burned away a long time ago. The tree itself ignored the damage and continued to thrive. It did not, however, generate an internal light source. The redness in the eye reveals that flash is serving as a substitute. Its effects are similar to sunlight, although not so pronounced. Both create lightness and shadow, so both suggest the multiplying technique.

As a formality, I have examined this file for initial color issues and found none, nor did I see anything that channel blending or Shadows/Highlights could help. So our first move should be that of this chapter.

This original can be classified as grossly too dark in spite of the flash, so I suggest the stronger lightening setting. The false profile actions deliver a multiply layer, but I have turned it off, so Figure 12.11B is a straight 1.0 gamma false profile.

If we decide to follow the recipe, we add a multiplying layer. As the dark background is not clearly more important than the light parts, we use the RGB composite from the background layer for the layer mask, and blur heavily, yielding Figure 12.11C. But now the question is whether we want it. In other words, should

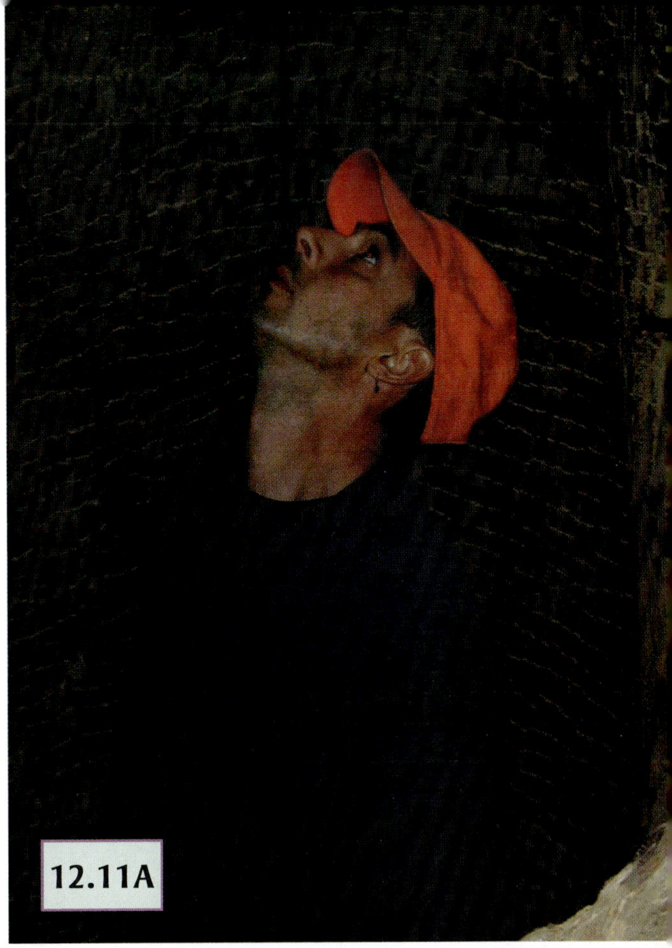

12.11A

***Figure 12.11** Top, the original. Bottom left, a false profile, gamma 1.0, is applied. Bottom right, a multiplication through a blurred layer mask as described in the first half of the chapter.*

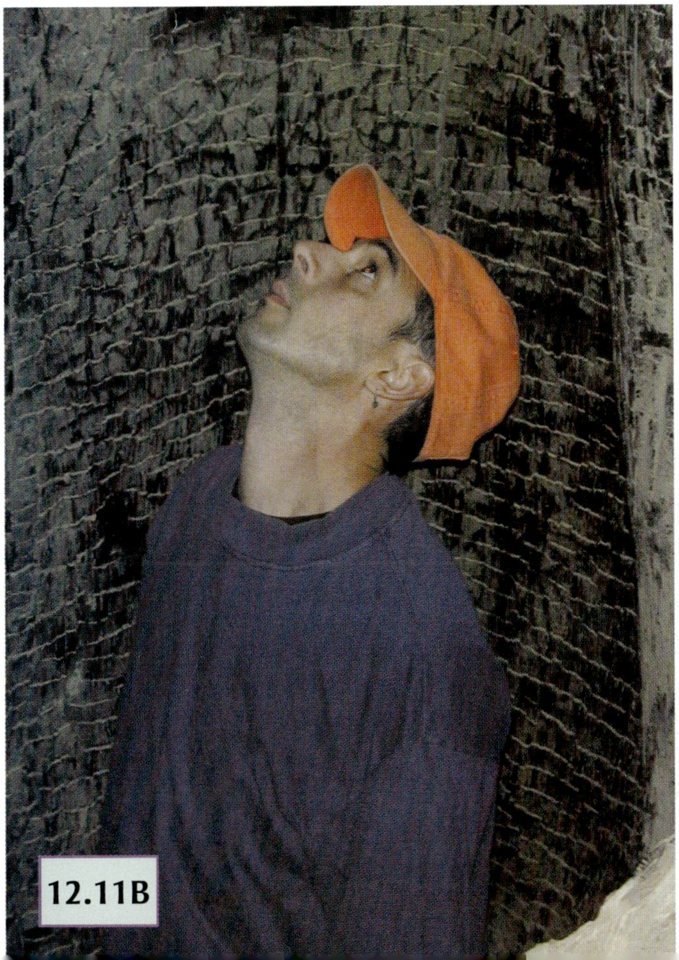

12.11B

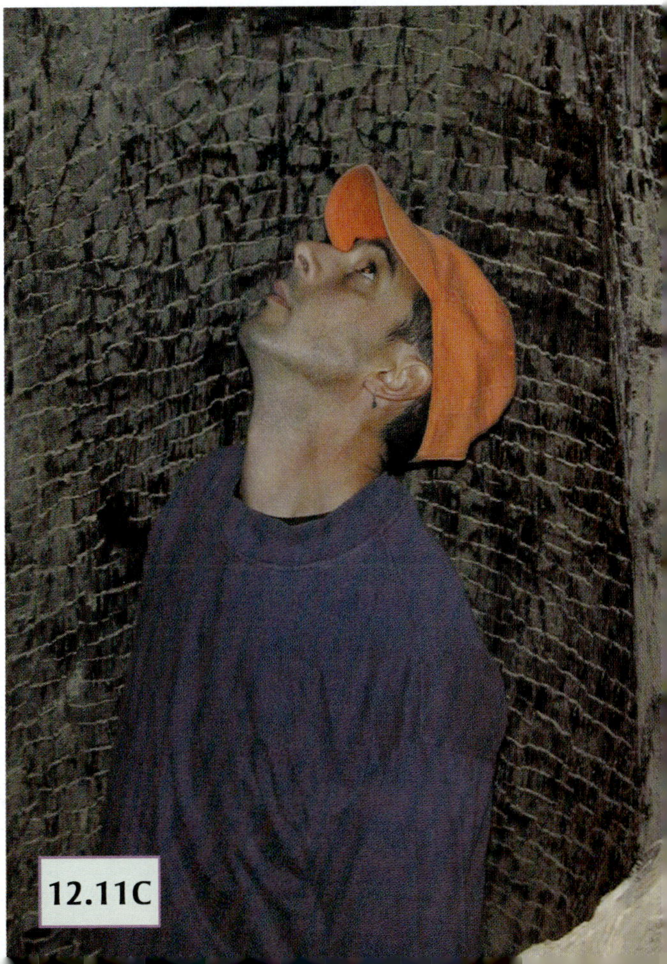

12.11C

we continue the workflow from Figure 12.11C, or trash it, abandon the multiplication idea, and forge ahead with Figure 12.11B?

Either way, the procedure should be about the same. We identify some kind of highlight in the lower right, and find a shadow in the darkest burnt area. It never hurts to try, but it's unlikely that the MMM action will be helpful, because this picture doesn't need much more color variation. What it does need is color vitality. We should be long past the point of being upset by how washed out things are at present. The Color Boost action will fix that, and will also give the opportunity to set the endpoints.

The picture features important fleshtones, so we will run the Skin Desaturation action before doing any of the above.

The highlight is too dark at the outset, and the false profile has made the shadow too light. These are most conveniently corrected with the Endpoint Adjustment curves of the Color Boost action, although you could try other methods. The three basic approaches are:

- Starting with Figure 12.11C, run Skin Desaturation, run MMM + Color Boost, presumably turning all the MMM stuff off, move the ends of the Endpoint Adjustment curve toward the center to fix the highlights and shadows, and adjust the Color Boost.
- Same as above, except start with Figure 12.11B, the unmultiplied version, instead.
- Same as above, still using Figure 12.11B, but this time with a curve like that shown in Figure 12.12, darkening the midtone with the idea of putting more shape in the face. The curve goes on the Endpoint Adjustment layer of the Color Boost action.

These techniques produce, respectively, Figures 12.13A, 12.13B, and 12.13C. Which of the three do you prefer?

Before responding, consider the purpose of the picture. How does your answer vary, if at all, in each of the following scenarios?

- The guy is on vacation and wants the photo as a souvenir.
- It's going in a magazine devoted to the ecology and etiology of supersized conifers.
- The subject is a young woman instead of a young man.

I don't know about you, but I get three different answers to these questions.

The Three Keys to Success

The idea of the multiplication is to bring two halves together, normally to simulate more uniform lighting. The two halves are most closely aligned, therefore, in Figure 12.13A. I would choose this one for an article about redwoods, because the scorched wood is more detailed here than in the other two.

Figure 12.13B omits the multiplication, so its two halves are more varied in darkness. Neither half has as much detail as in Figure 12.13A. If this were a picture of a young woman I would probably go for it nevertheless. Letting parts of the face become darker, as is happening in the other two, increases facial detail. Note the difference in the five o'clock shadow. Many find that sort of rugged effect attractive in men but not in women.

Now compare Figures 12.13B and 12.13C. The difference is the central point that darkens the midtone in Figure 12.12. It was omitted to produce Figure

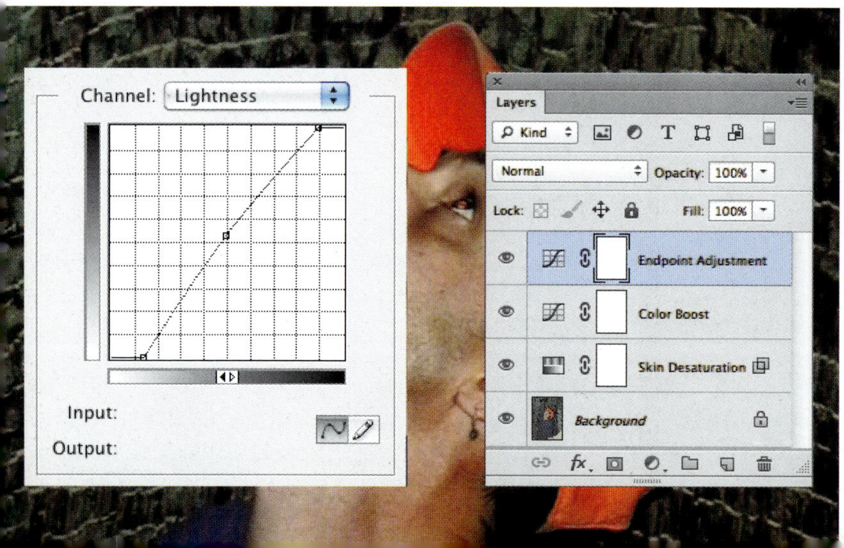

***Figure 12.12** A curve on the Endpoint Adjustment layer adds weight. Note the second layer, which desaturated the skin, as described in Chapter 9.*

12.13B. Having it in the curve assigns more range to the light half and less to the dark half. The face gains contrast at the expense of the wood. The man is now similar to the one in Figure 12.13A, but the wood has less detail.

Logically it would seem that we have to vote for Figure 12.13A, because it's at least as good in every respect and better in some than Figure 12.13C. But we have to ask ourselves what the picture is about. If the focus is the tree, or even the man and the tree, then Figure 12.13A is better. But if this is a picture about the man, with the tree a secondary consideration, then I would vote for Figure 12.13C. It has enough detail in the background to let us know where the man is standing. Any more is a distraction.

The three keys to using the multiply technique are:

- Identify the image as having two sides.
- Evaluate the relative importance of the two sides.

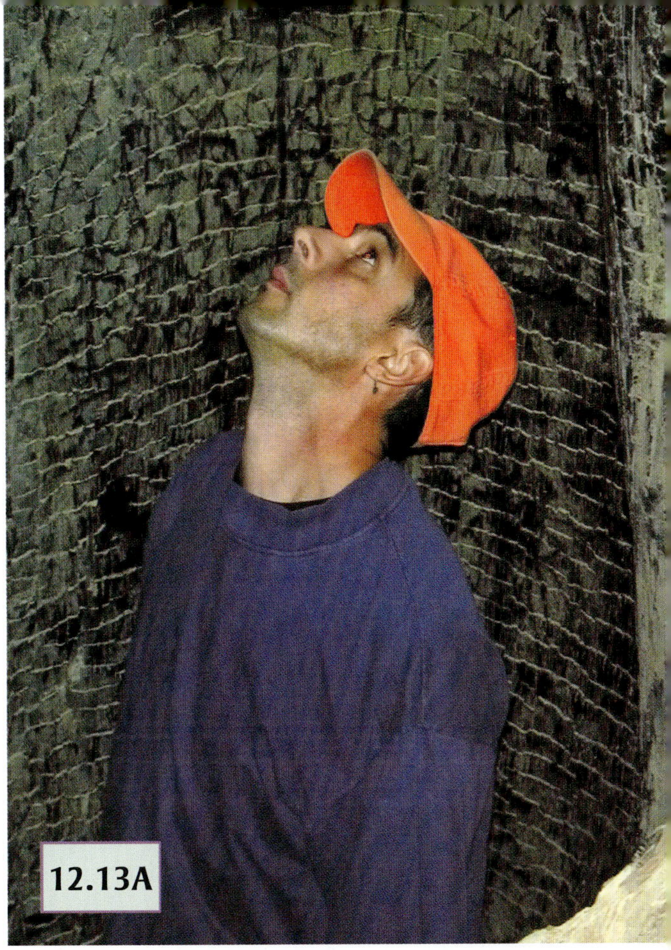

Figure 12.13 *Top, a version based on Figure 12.11C. Bottom left, the same moves applied to Figure 12.11B. Bottom right, also based on Figure 12.11B, incorporates the Lightness curve of Figure 12.12.*

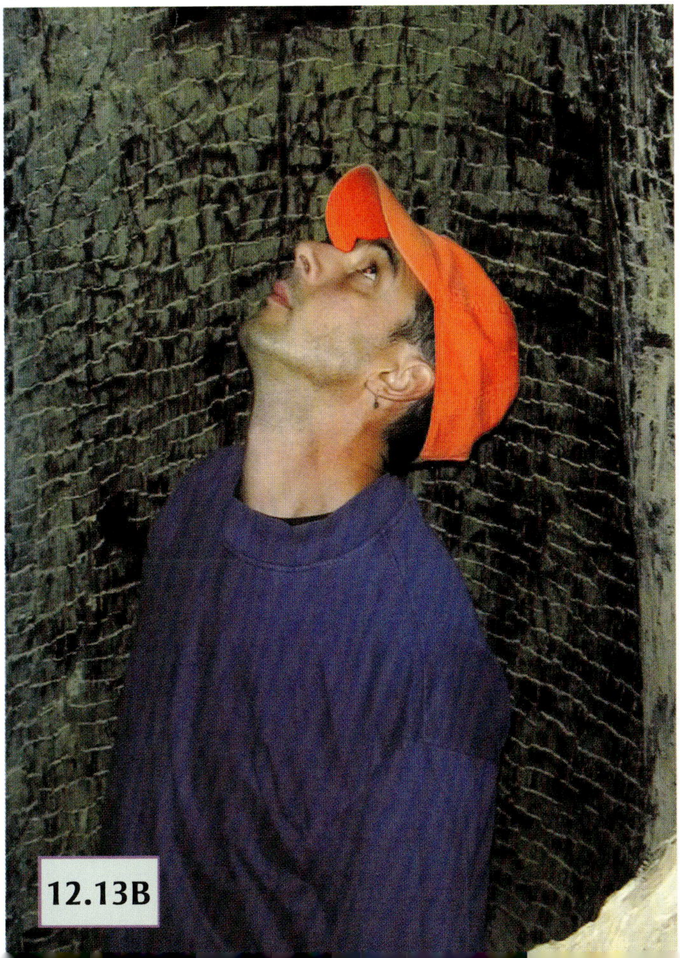

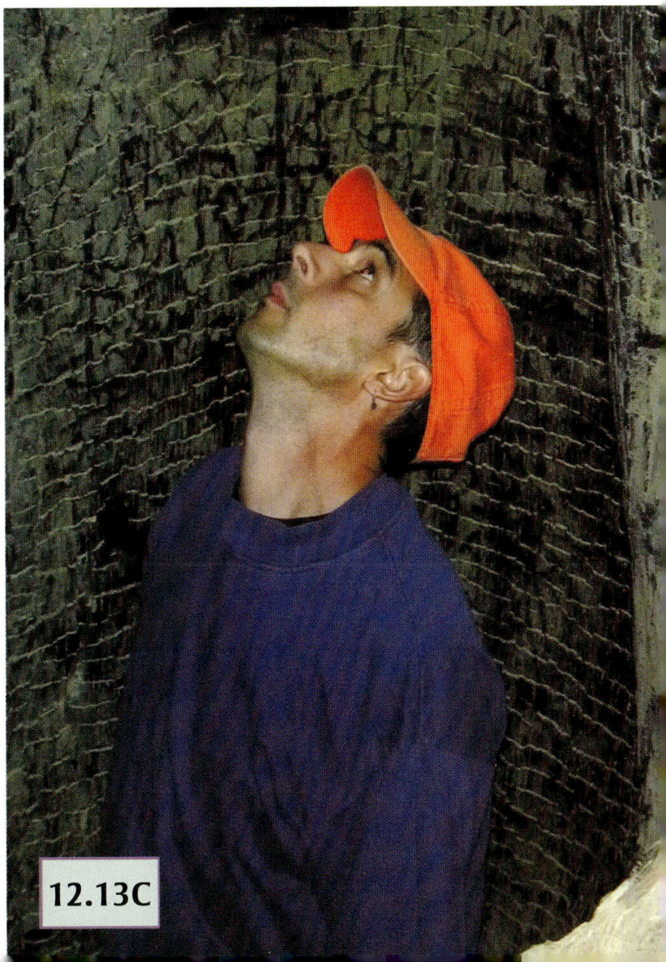

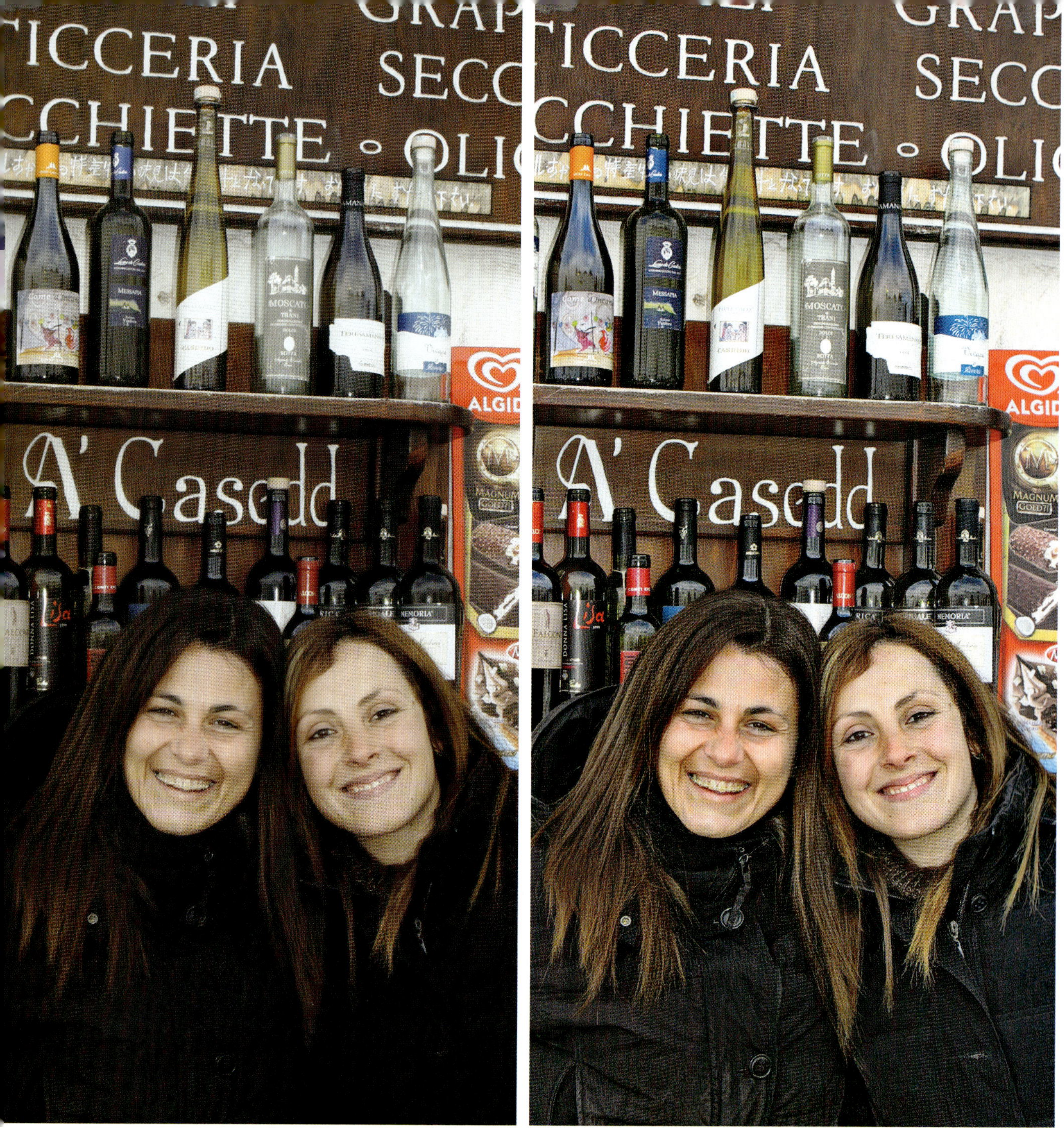

***Postcard 12.14** Women outside market in winter, Alberobello, Italy.*

- Decide whether the picture might be right for the Bigger Hammer instead.

The fact is that the two-sided character is more important than the light source. Postcard 12.14 has no sun to speak of, but the scene definitely breaks into distinct light and dark parts. One would think this isn't a good example for the PPW, because none of these objects will look good if they get more colorful. Also, the picture is so neutral that it's unlikely any sort of channel maneuvering will pay off.

The final version has more believable, more varied skintone, thanks to the Skin Desaturation followed by the Modern Man from Mars actions. But the big difference is the extra detail in the hair, jackets, and dark bottles. That comes from

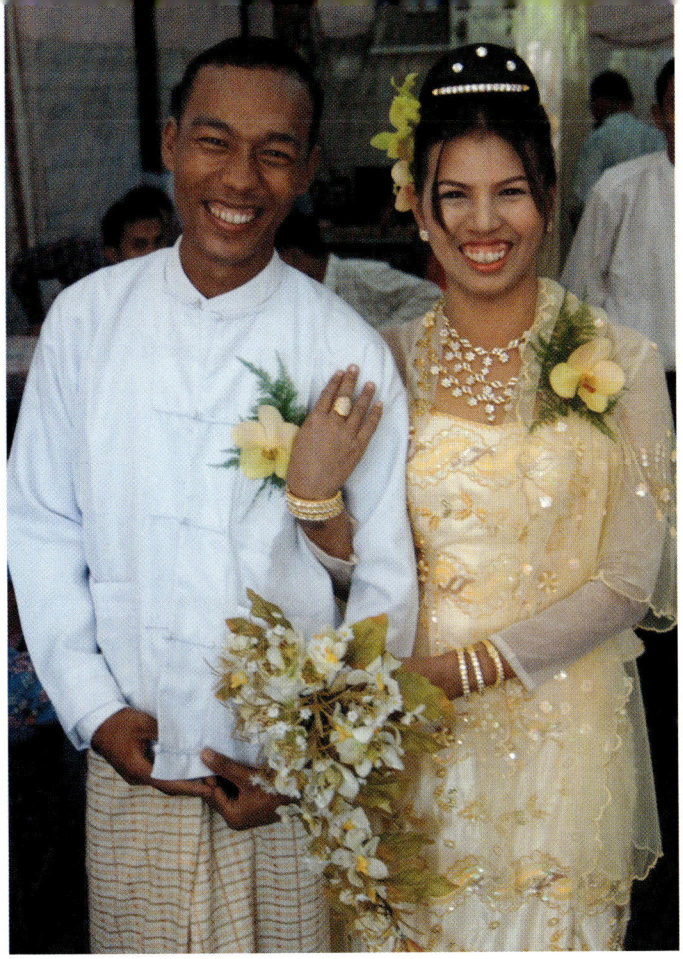

***Figure 12.15** The subject is somewhat similar to that of Postcard 12.14, with strong differences between light and dark areas and two people in the foreground. Do you see the subtle difference in content that would suggest doing this another way?*

the false profile/multiply/blurred mask strategy we've been studying, and is difficult to achieve in any other way.

Now comes the question of whether to use the Bigger Hammer action instead of, or possibly in addition to, this multiplication stuff. The truth is that the two methods often do about the same thing. The Bigger Hammer has a more potent effect in the lightest and darkest areas, if they happen to have small areas within them that already show contrast. In this postcard the labels, both black and white, would be more legible with the Bigger Hammer.

Unless you're a real Bigger Hammer expert, though, I'd be wary of using it on a skintone image. You have to be very careful in the choice of overlay channel. Also, the Bigger Hammer darkens things lighter than a midtone and lightens things darker, and does so channel by channel. In portraits, the green channel can fall on both sides, as can the blue. The Bigger Hammer may then darken half the skin and lighten the other half, with less than optimal results. Also, as we discussed in Chapter 9, we shy away from adding detail to a face, which the Bigger Hammer may do inadvertently. And as if that isn't enough, if the face is large enough, it may be smooth enough to show artifacts. Don't get me wrong, it can be a powerful tool in images of people, but you have to watch it like a hawk.

As we move from Italy to Burma, the objection to the Bigger Hammer seems to disappear in the wedding picture of Figure 12.15. In the blue channel at least, the faces are definitely darker than a midtone. Furthermore, I would be a lot more interested in adding detail to the bride's gown than to the labels in Postcard 12.14. I may have to use the multiply technique as well, because I think the picture is two-sided: the clothing is light, everything else, including the faces, is dark. So it seems they should be brought closer together.

I used these principles to prepare a correction of Figure 12.15 in competition with experts, and got slaughtered. You'll see their results, and mine, and my amended one, later. But now, can you see the flaw in my reasoning above?

The Bigger Hammer Compared

While that question hangs, we move on to a new exercise, one that compares three techniques. The original is Figure 12.16A. Left to their own devices, each of the three competing methods would yield slightly different color. For a fairer contest, I have made a command decision about what the final color should be, and have applied it to all three in Color mode, so that we are comparing contrast only.

Figure 12.16B is this chapter's default approach. With so neutral a subject no preliminary channel moves are possible, nor is there an initial color issue. The multiplication is therefore the first step, and also the last, being that I intend to assign the color from somewhere else. It's a rote repetition of the recipe: false profile of 1.4 gamma, or equivalent Exposure, use of the bottom layer RGB as a blurred layer mask, and endpoint adjustment. As advertised, the two sides have come closer together, and as usual, the effect is more noticeable in the shadow.

Figure 12.16C, the default Bigger Hammer, is more dramatic—if drama is what you're after. The background is darker and more detailed. The shadow is more abrupt. The procedure was more interested in lightening the background greenery than in getting more detail in the dark halves of the elephants.

I know people who like this kind of effect but I am not particularly interested in what is going on behind the waterhole, I think what's happening in front is more important and regard the elephants of Figure 12.16B as more natural.

One might wish to have the background approximately as dark as in Figure 12.16C, without all the added detail. If so, the solution would be to use the first approach but modify the adjustment layer that is doing the multiplying. Figure 12.16D is based on 12.16B, but instead of an adjustment layer with default curves unchanged, it employs the curve shown to the left of the caption. The adjustment layer is still set to Multiply mode, and the layer mask is still in place.

One could easily confuse this with the similar curve shown in Figure 12.12, which modified the man-in-tree picture. The difference is, that one suppressed shadow detail to a certain extent. We don't have to worry about that happening

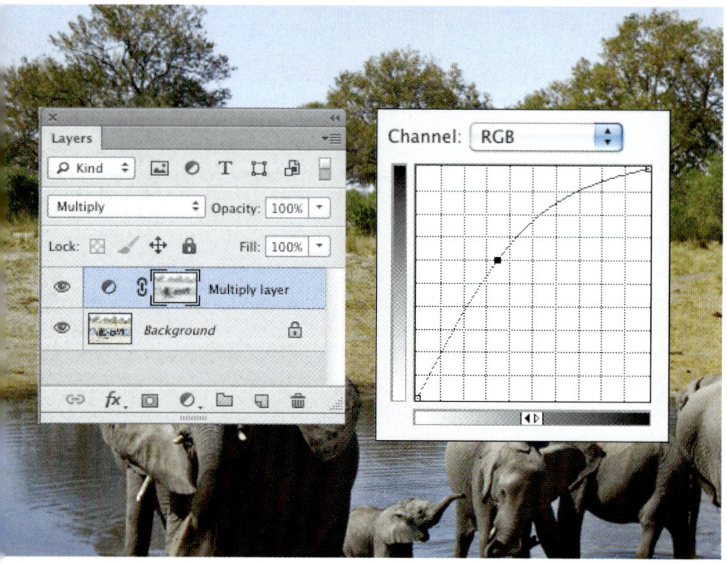

***Figure 12.16** This page, bottom, the original. Opposite, top, the normal false profile/multiply/blurred layer mask technique. Middle, the Bigger Hammer action's defaults are used instead. Bottom, again the multiply technique, but this time with the curve shown at left applied to the Multiply layer. For ease in comparison, all three versions on the opposite page have had the same color applied, so that they differ only in contrast.*

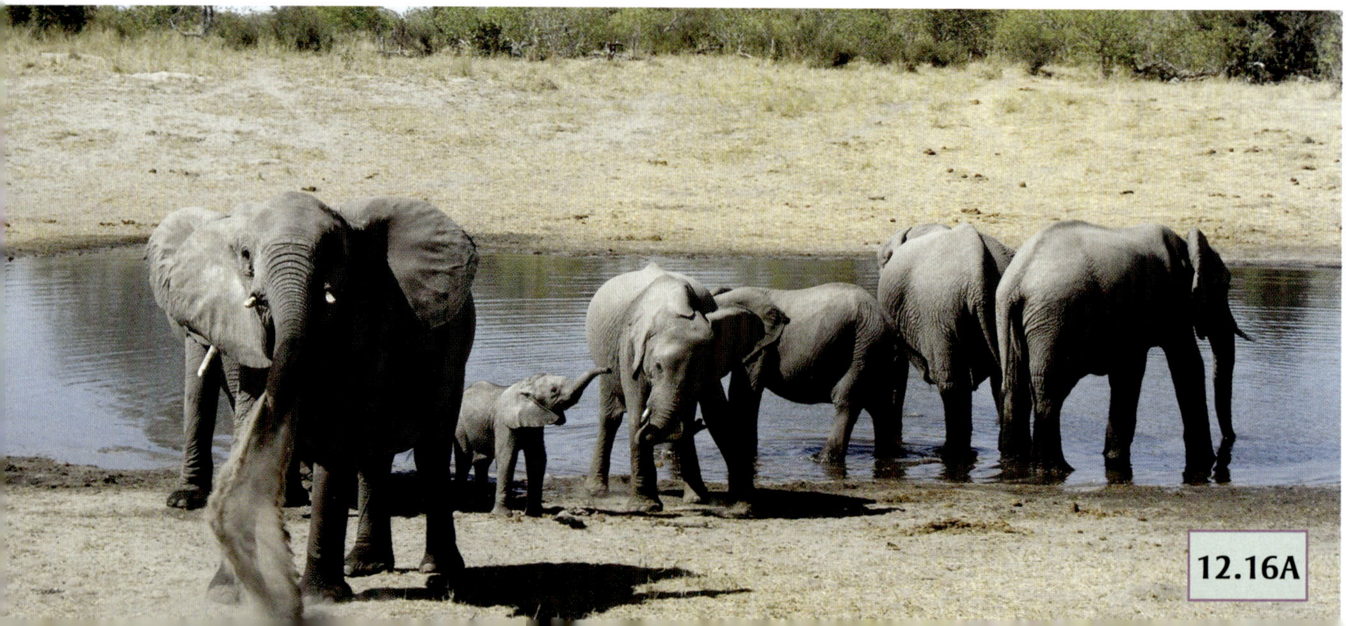

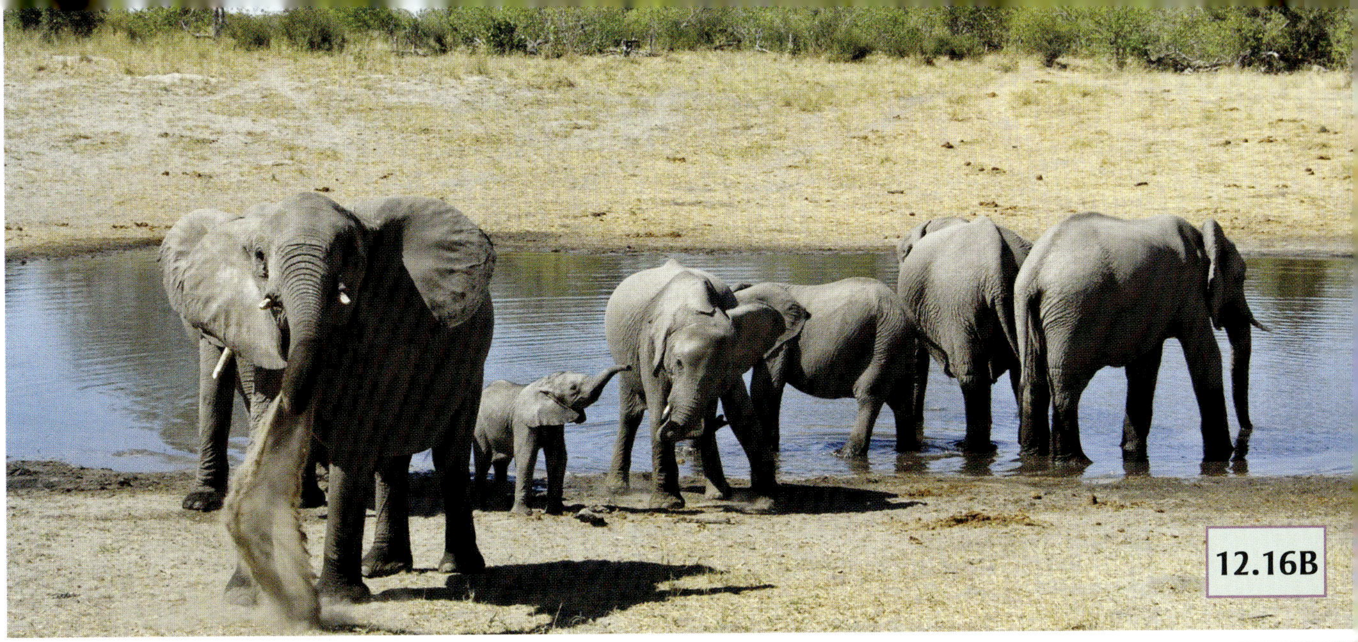
12.16B

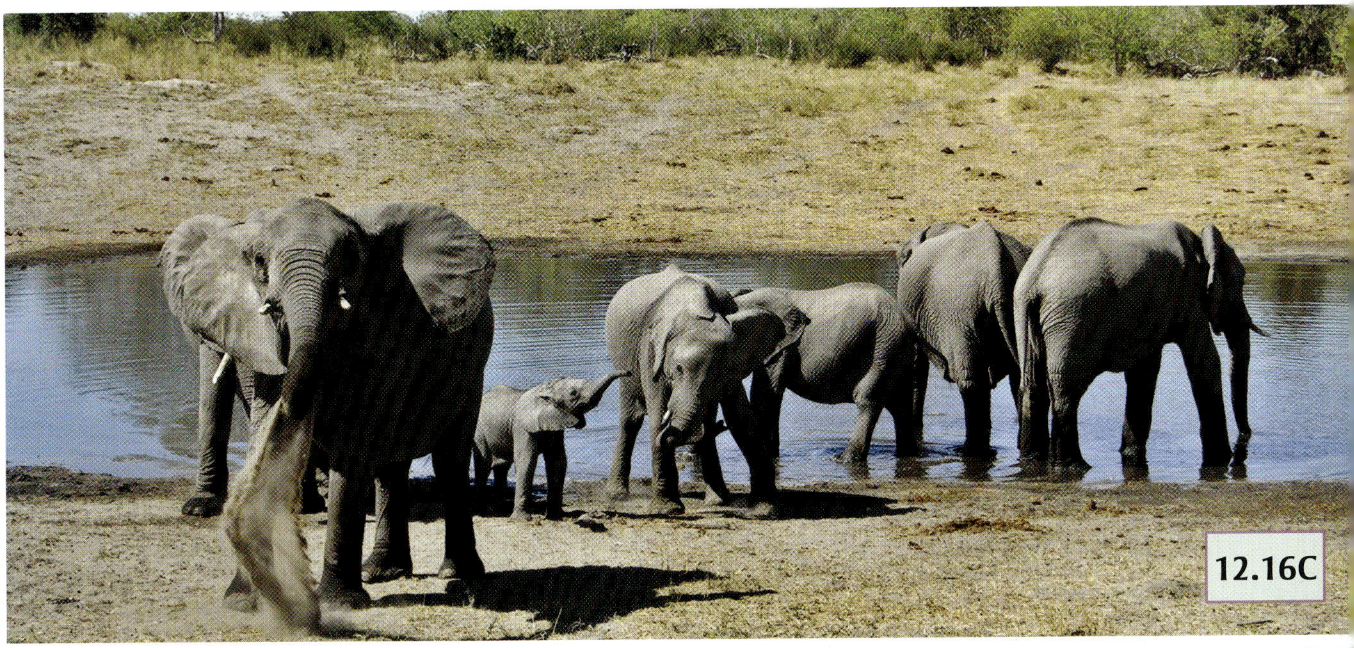
12.16C

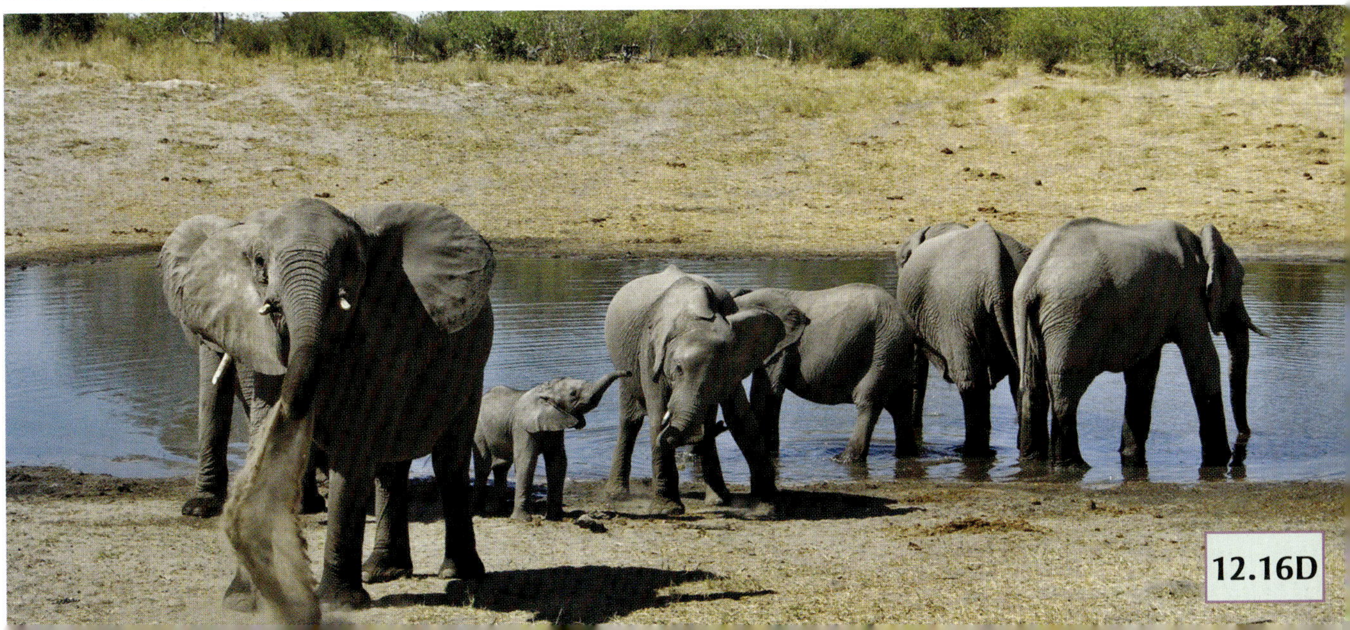
12.16D

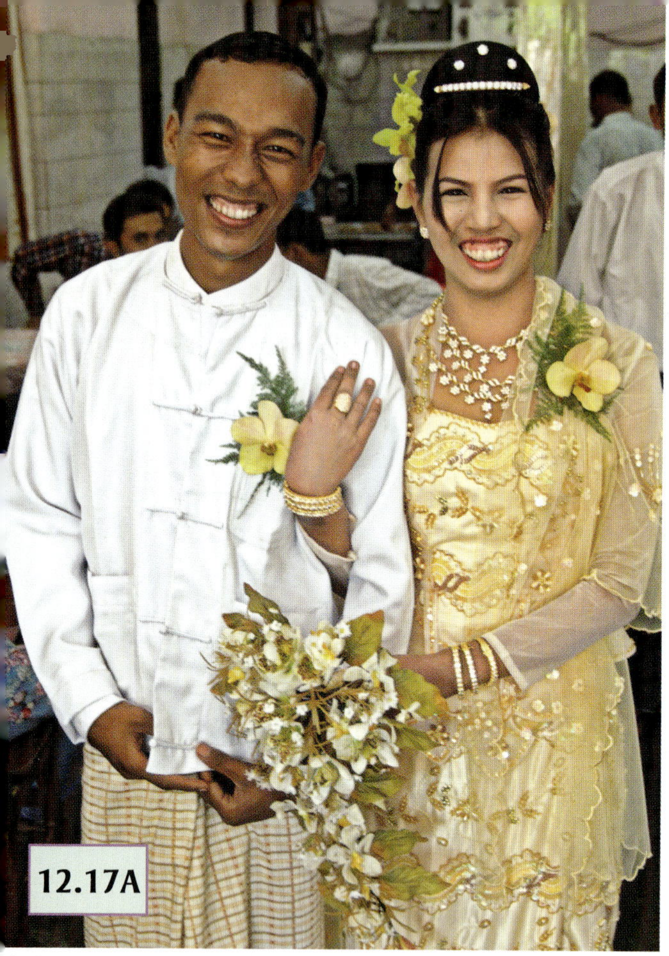

12.17A

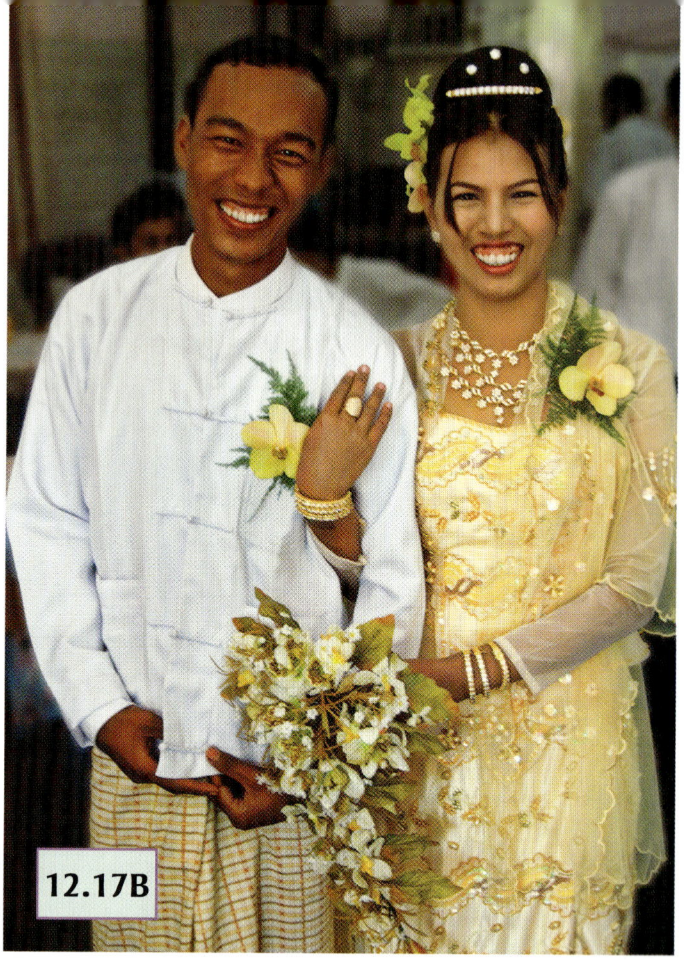

12.17B

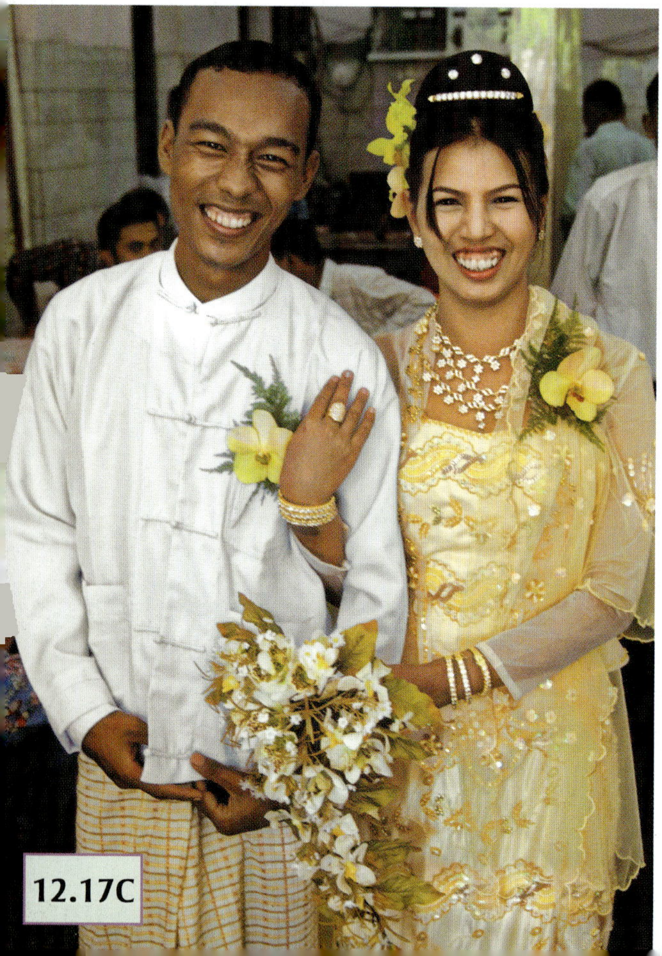

12.17C

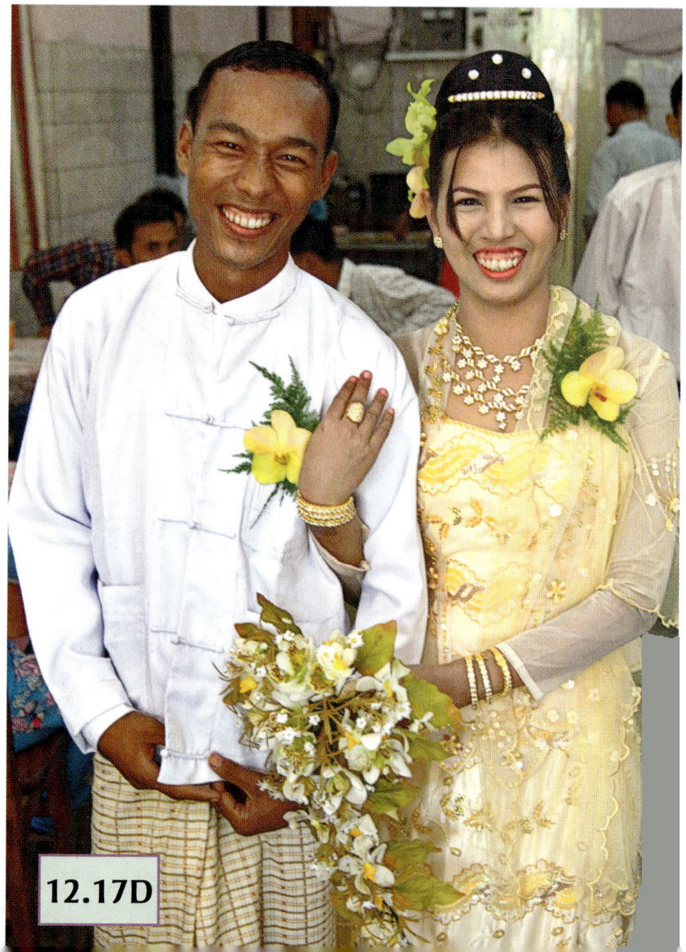

12.17D

here because this curve operates through a layer mask that prevents much from happening to the darker half no matter what kind of curve we apply. This one mostly darkens the yellowish background.

Which of these three is best? I suspect that if we put it to a jury we'd get a split decision. Since you don't have to please a jury, but only yourself, you can choose the one you want, and know which technique will give it to you.

Too Soon Old, Too Late Smart

I was proud of my 2009 version of the Burmese couple, Figure 12.17A. I was confident that nobody would get the same detail in the gown and that all competitors would be washed away in a tsunami of adulation for my own cleverness.

The first part of this supposition proved correct. The gown came out better than in any other version. When the votes were in, however, Figure 12.17A went the way of Walter Mondale, Kim Campbell, and Mikhail Gorbachev.

I had failed to appreciate the difference between this original and the earlier Postcard 12.15. In that one, the bottles and signs in the background were an important complement to the people, establishing the scene in an interesting way. But this wedding picture is about the couple only; the background serves only to distract from them.

The photographer who worked on Figure 12.17B, one of the winners, realized this. She selected the background and applied a blur. I think she did so too heavily, but this is likely sour grapes, having learned that I had gone to great trouble to enhance contrast in an area so unimportant that a more sensible person had blurred it.

Figure 12.17 *Five corrected versions of the original of Figure 12.15. Bottom right, the status of Figure 12.17D prior to boosting color in LAB.*

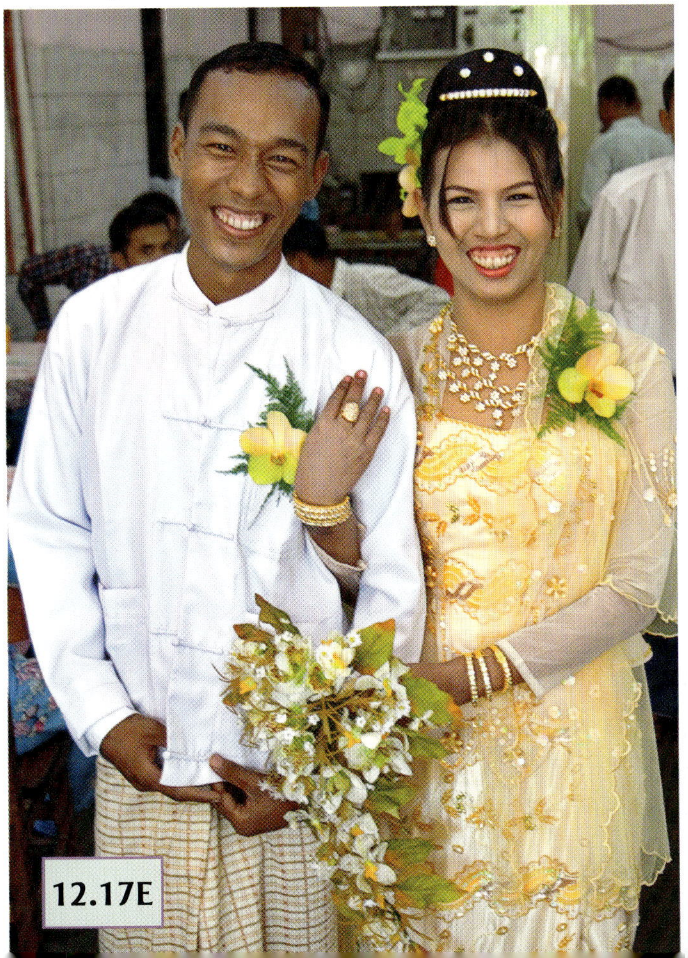

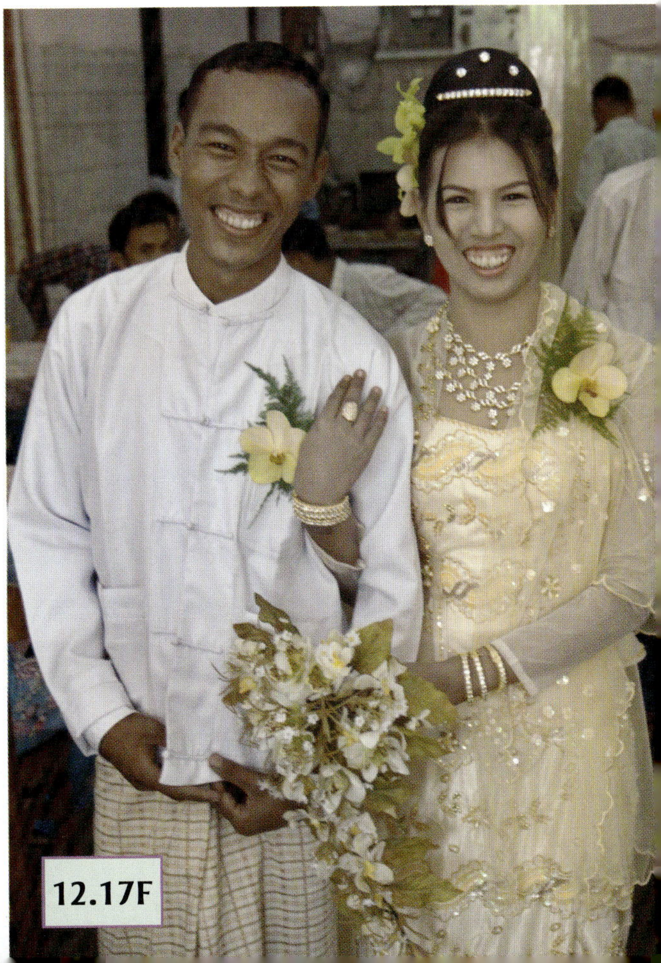

Figure 12.17C, another winner, was done by a well-known imaging author. It doesn't have the blur but does deemphasize the background by keeping the foreground distinctly lighter. I like the skintone better, too.

Figure 12.17D is a version I just did. I used the Bigger Hammer, but, fearing that I would overemphasize the background as I had in 2009, I set the darkening layer to 100% opacity rather than the default 50%. Then I used this chapter's multiply method, with the layer mask at a low opacity so that everything but the clothing and faces would darken more than usual.

This image was originally slated for another chapter. In preparation, I did Figure 12.17E. It's more similar to Figure 12.17D than two separate corrections usually are. Nevertheless, it isn't as good, in my opinion. Figure 12.17D has a certain extra something, a feeling not so much of greater depth but almost of more austerity, in a way that plays up the color of the gown and faces. That added something is a novelty that we will put through its paces in the next chapter.

Because the idea of color and contrast being treated as separate entities may still seem foreign, even this late in the book, have a look at Figure 12.17F, which looks almost like a grayscale image. It is what the picture looked like after I had run the Skin Desaturation action, and just before I used the MMM + Color Boost action to get to Figure 12.17D.

That should put us in the proper frame of mind. Remember, with this workflow there is no need to worry about not having enough color, the fear is about having too much. "Too much" contrast is unusual, Figure 12.17A being the unhappy exception. But excessive color can be a headache, and we will now study one final way of avoiding it.

Let's close with another reminder. Photos taken in strong sun are the most obvious candidates for the multiplication treatment, but they are not the only ones. Many studio photographs, particularly of commercial products, show two distinct sides and should be handled the same way. The determining factor is the character of the image, not the lighting that produced it.

That last statement is true for more than just this chapter, and it does *not* have two sides.

The Bottom Line

This chapter addresses photos that can be described as having two or more significant areas that are strongly separated in darkness. The typical example is a photo taken in strong sunlight, but many other categories qualify.

The method is to multiply the file through a heavily blurred layer mask, as shown in Chapter 11. However, that method was incomplete, because almost every picture to which it applies needs to be artificially lightened first. This chapter introduces actions that do so, based on false profiles. Using the Exposure command is generally equivalent.

13

The Black Art of Color Enhancement

Color alters our perception of darkness. A new action caters to this human foible by darkening more neutral areas. It also takes a novel approach to restricting the amount of brilliance that can be put in. The result can be deeper-looking pictures, with more room to add interesting variation later. The method is derived from CMYK.

Composers of classical music, like professional retouchers, often cross swords with the people who interpret their work. It is not enough to provide a bunch of notes without an explanation of how to play them, any more than it is for us to provide a file with no indication of what it's good for.

The composer has to give guidance for how fast the music is supposed to be played. Although the best composers of instrumental music throughout the last two centuries have spoken German or Russian, the convention is for these instructions to appear in the Italian language. *Lento* (slow), *Adagio* (at ease), and *Moderato* denote relatively sedate tempi. A more common choice, however, is *Allegro* (bright, cheerful).

Our own field is similar, which is unsurprising, since the art forms are closely related. If we must guess what to do with the next picture, sight unseen, *bright and cheerful* sounds right.

The word is no model of clarity in Italian any more than the phrase is in English, either in music or imaging. Composers often add some other Italian adjective. Allegro *agitato,* Allegro *assai,* Allegro *con brio,* Allegro *con fuoco,* Allegro *giocoso,* and Allegro *giusto* mean slightly different things, at least in principle. In practice a musician may interpret them as identical.

All six put together, however, aren't seen as often as a specification more annoying than the Missa Solemnis sung by a chorus of cats: Allegro *ma non troppo.* The last three words mean *but not too much.*

* * *

A more aggravating and less informative phrase would be hard to find. Two of the four movements of Beethoven's Ninth Symphony are marked *Allegro ma non troppo.* This instruction is so meaningful to conductors

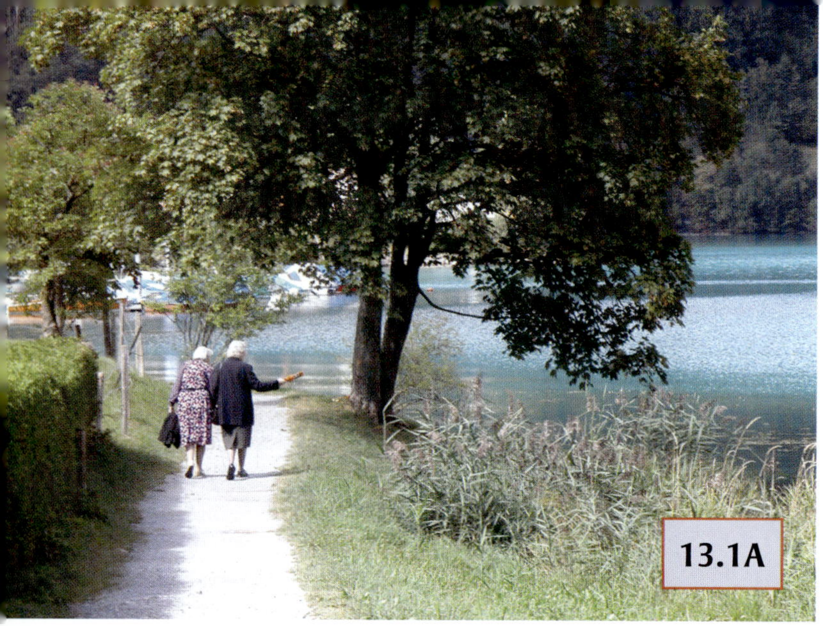

13.1A

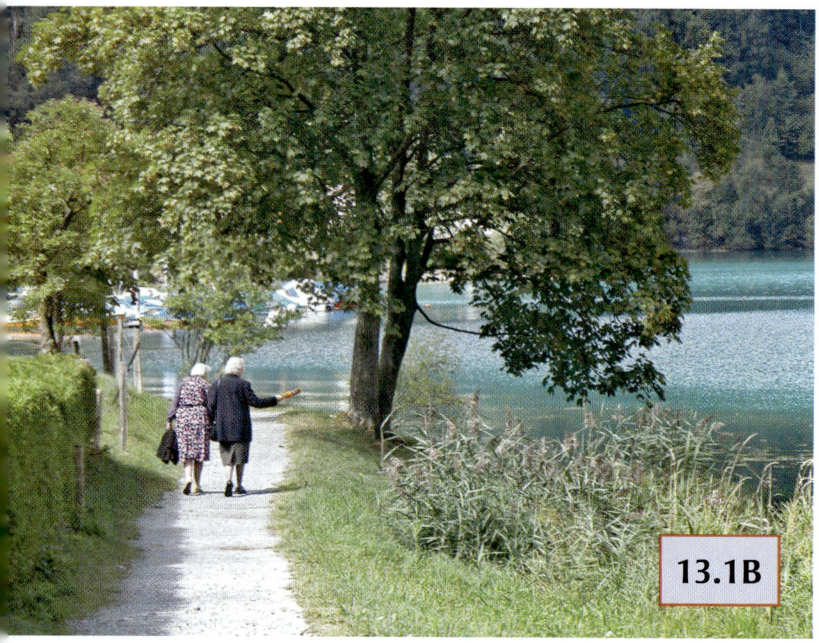

13.1B

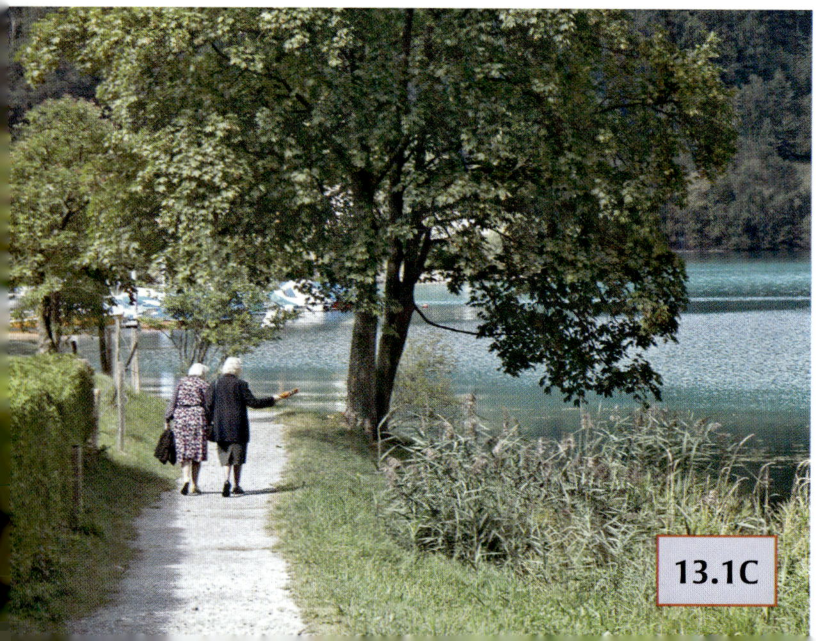

13.1C

that any two recorded performances of the symphony can vary in length by a quarter of an hour.

The phrase *but not too much* signifies even less, if possible, in imaging. No matter what you think *too much* means, the Color Boost and Man from Mars actions discussed in Chapters 5 and 6 provide it *molto presto*. Those chapters devoted a lot of time to reducing their impact gracefully, in tune with the meaning of the picture.

This chapter introduces another way of making sure that what we get is not too much. It is a moderately complex action known as H-K. Why it is called that is a long story. What it does is a longer one. It is much easier to show than to explain; if you need to know exactly what it's doing, the second half of the chapter will fill you in.

The action discriminates against duller colors in two ways that can be adjusted independently. A layer called H-K Effect makes them darker. Another named Color Only tones down all but the purest colors.

The first layer often makes the picture seem deeper. You will either like the look or you won't; no fine judgment is called for. The second is tougher to evaluate, because it makes the picture look worse, temporarily. The idea is to make it easier to boost color later. If it works, it can accent the most vivid objects with less risk of hearing our viewers speak the dreaded words *too much*.

Now, an example. Go back to the final exercise of the last chapter, the photo of the Burmese wedding couple. Figure 12.17D made use of H-K; the otherwise

***Figure 13.1** Top, the original. Middle, a version corrected using the normal workflow steps but not including color enhancement. Bottom, the H-K action is added.*

similar Figure 12.17E did not. Figure 12.17D's background is darker and less colorful, making it less likely to draw attention away from the faces.

Here's another example, in a more obviously postcard-like setting. Figure 13.1A is the original. A small purple cast, as measured in the A–positive, B–negative trail, is removed easily with RGB curves.

The green channel forms the basis of some luminosity moves. When done, I vote for Shadows/Highlights, but not the Bigger Hammer. Then, seeing sunlight and shadow, comes the multiplication technique of Chapter 12, lightening, multiplying, loading the lower layer's RGB as a layer mask, and blurring.

This familiar stuff gets us to a familiar spot in Figure 13.1B. The contrast is much better, the color acceptable but not exciting. Up until now, we would proceed briskly into LAB for some color development. But here comes the novelty. Playing H-K at its defaults produces Figure 13.1C. It's hard to describe the effect, other than that it doesn't look as nice as Figure 13.1B.

Six Cases for H-K

Fortunately, the final result is what counts. After H-K, I applied MMM + Color Boost to Figure 13.1C, adjusting the settings to obtain Figure 13.2A.

Then, for comparison, I applied the same action and the same selection to Figure 13.1B, the one that did not use H-K. Because the settings were optimized for the much less colorful Figure 13.1C, opacities needed to be cut to try to match Figure 13.2A more closely.

When I did so, however, I got Figure 13.2B. It's much better than the original, no question. But I prefer Figure 13.2A. Which of the two would you say is more colorful?

It's a split decision. Figure 13.2A is more colorful in the water, the top of the hedge, and the greenery ahead of the ladies. It is *less* colorful in the side of the hedge and the center of the tree. I think this arrangement of color is what makes it successful.

You might wish to think of H-K as being somewhat like the Bigger Hammer action of Chapter 10: not essential to the workflow, not

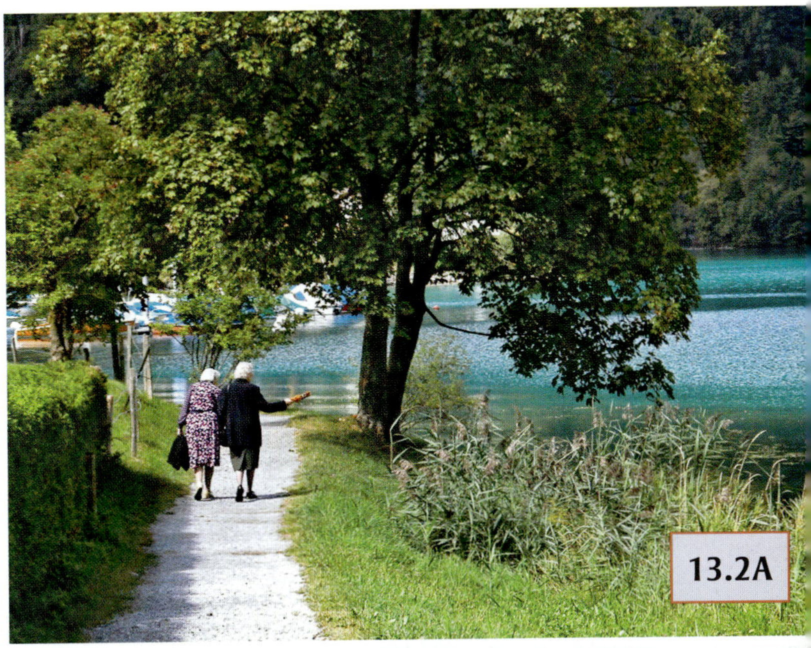

13.2A

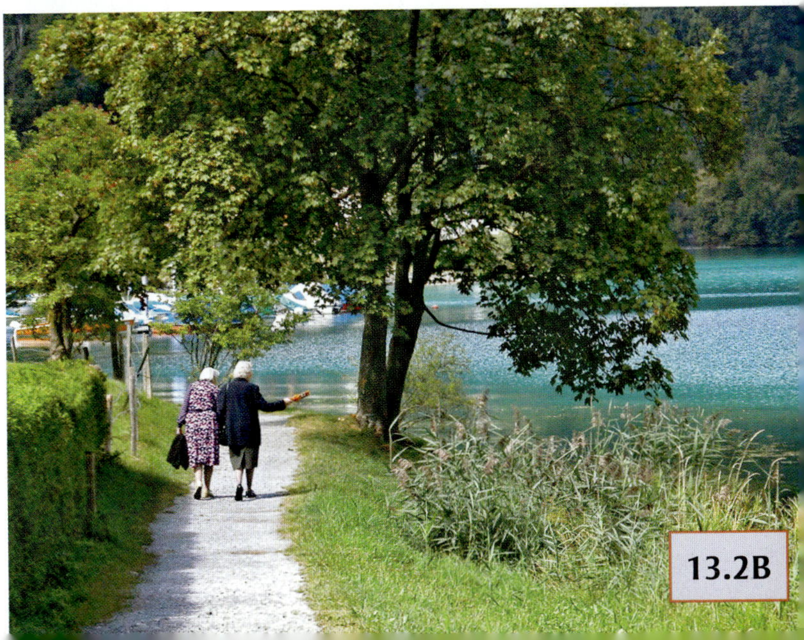

13.2B

***Figure 13.2** Top, the MMM + Color Boost action is applied to Figure 13.1C and adjusted to taste. Bottom, the same settings are applied instead to Figure 13.1B and further adjusted to try to come closer to the top version.*

useful in most pictures, but quite effective when it is. It's like the Bigger Hammer in that, being an action, you can give it a spin and if it doesn't look good, cancel. Taking a look costs only a few seconds.

It's a bit more forgiving than the Bigger Hammer. If you misuse H-K you may get an image that looks too conservative, but it's unlikely to be really objectionable.

Chapter Goals and Recap

De-emphasizing duller areas is often the way to emphasize brighter ones. This chapter introduces an action that does so in two independent ways. It darkens near-neutrals in the quarter- to midtone. It also muddies them, preventing them from getting too colorful later.

How Difficult Is It? The only difficult decision is how much to dirty the colors, if at all.

How Often Is It Needed? Depends on the type of images you work on. The chapter identifies six categories where the action is useful.

The PPW, Final Version

COLOR

- Kill incorrect color with RGB curves (Chapter 3).
- Identify highlight (Chapters 3–4).

CONTRAST

- Channel blending on luminosity layer (Chapter 4).
- Contrast-enhancing curves (Chapter 4).
    - Consider S/H command (Chapter 7).
    - Consider the Bigger Hammer (Chapter 10).
    - Consider boost to sky (Chapter 8).
    - Consider lighten and multiply (Chapter 12).

COLOR AGAIN

    - Consider the H-K action (This chapter).
- Desaturate skintone, if any (Chapter 9).
- Apply MMM + Color Boost action (Chapters 5–6).
- Finalize contrast, including endpoints.
- Reduce color by masking or opacity adjustment.

SHARPEN

FINALIZE

- Consider blend with another version (Chapter 2).
- Convert to final output space, if needed.

H-K is the newest addition to the PPW, the one with which I have the least experience and which hasn't been fully evaluated in competition. So it wouldn't be surprising if some of the following advice doesn't hold up over time.

At the moment I recommend using H-K in six image categories and will show examples of each throughout the chapter. I use the action, when appropriate, after all other contrast steps and before color enhancement. The six categories are:

- The picture is so full of semi-vivid color that enhancing it risks an overly intense look. Many nature shots are like this, as is the Swiss scene just shown. The path, the background, and the women's clothing don't threaten to get too colorful, but three-quarters of the picture's area consists of strong greens and cyans, which might.
- The picture showcases areas of intense color, stronger than in the Swiss scene. Exception: don't use it when less important areas complement the intense object. For example, a picture of a rose might qualify for the treatment if the background is neutral, but not if it's green.
- The composition is one of the rare kind in which cheerful colors are unwelcome.
- The scene contains really brilliant color.
- Everything is dominated by a single color, vivid or otherwise.
- Cheeriness is not objectionable as such, but there is limited flexibility to change color because the subject is something familiar, such as food or a product offered for sale.

The H-K Effect layer (the one that darkens neutrals) isn't recommended for portraits unless a somber or weathered look is desired. For an example, turn back to Figure 9.12B, where I was trying to make a man look older, which is not usually the objective.

The Color Only layer may be useful if you are concerned that the skin may get too colorful later. It can be used as a partial or total

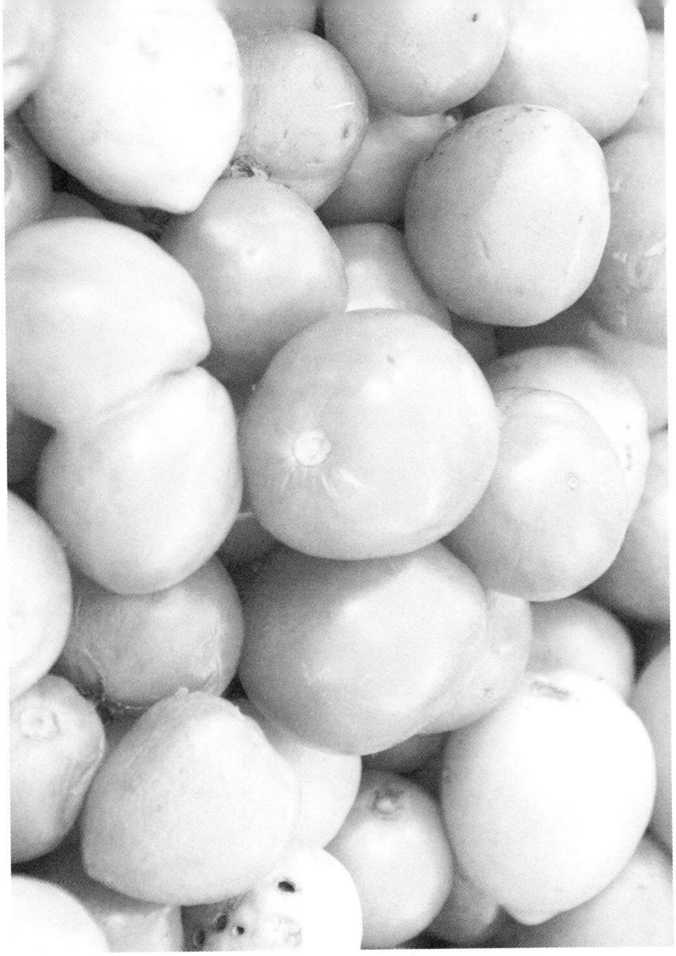

***Figure 13.3** The Ersatz Black channel emulates the traditional black channel used in commercial CMYK printing. It is light in colorful objects such as tomatoes.*

substitute for the Skin Desaturation action shown in Chapter 9.

* * *

The best music often is in debt to the past. The twentieth-century composers Shostakovich and Villa-Lobos each created works that, although sounding modern, were inspired by the style of Bach. The relation would be obvious even if the composers didn't freely admit it.

This action is like that, too. It's full of stuff that couldn't have been duplicated in an age with slower computers. But the principle dates from the dinosaur days of retouching, when the world worked in CMYK. The presence of a black channel that did not behave like the other three, or like any of the channels in the then little-known RGB, had a host of uses for those in the know.

The H-K action honors past practice by generating and exploiting an alpha channel by the name of Ersatz Black. By default you aren't even aware that it ever existed: the action discards the channel after use. If you use the PPW panel, you have the option of retaining it. The second half of the chapter discusses why and when you might want to do that.

The black magic is that such a thing is quite light in colored areas but almost as dark as an RGB channel in neutrals. At the end of Chapter 6, we discussed the views of color authority R.W.G. Hunt on the proper way of assuring credible color in tomatoes. It's time to follow up on that. Tomatoes, being strongly red, must be light in the Ersatz Black channel, which is shown in Figure 13.3.

This channel can, with some masking help, be used to darken everything but the reddest parts. It can also be used to poison color. Since the channel is almost blank in red areas, the damage will occur elsewhere.

And why would we want to damage *anything?* Because even sight unseen, we know that this picture falls into the second category described above: at least some of these tomatoes must be vividly colored, and there's no complementary background color.

Much Faster Than Possible

The wildly creative Robert Schumann occasionally bowed to convention. The first movement of his Second Symphony is marked with the ubiquitous *Allegro ma non troppo.*

To describe the speed at which the opening of his emotionally wrenching Second Piano Sonata should be played, however, Schumann evidently couldn't find the right Italian words. Reverting to his native German, he marked the first movement *So rasch wie möglich* (as fast as possible).

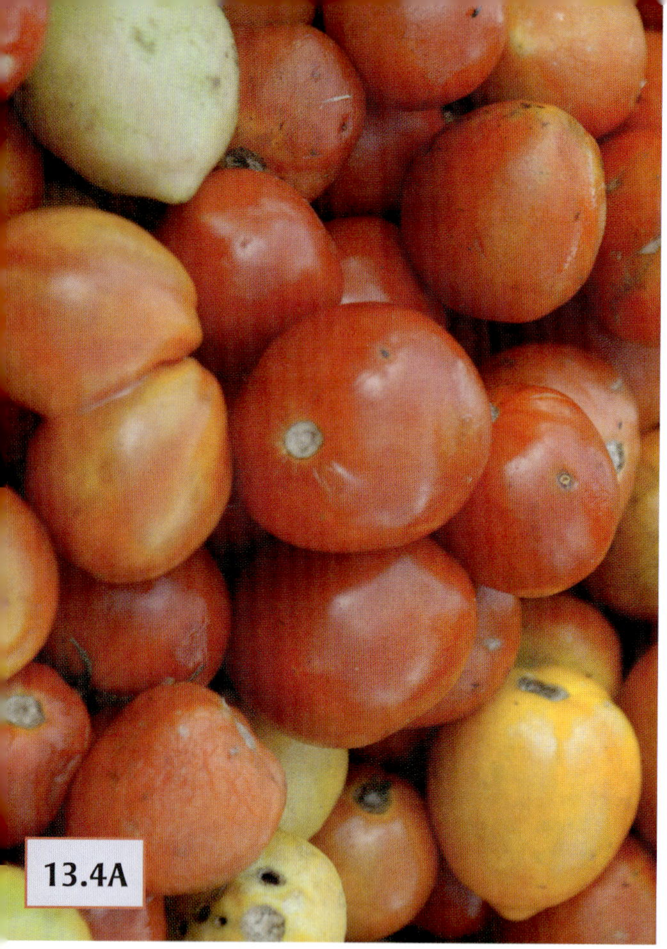
13.4A

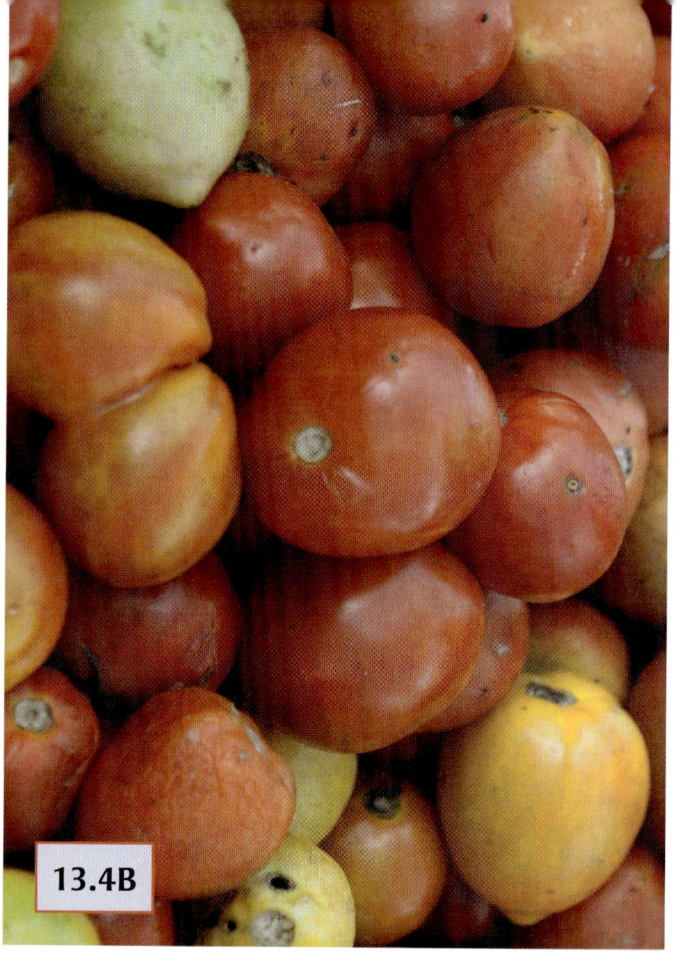
13.4B

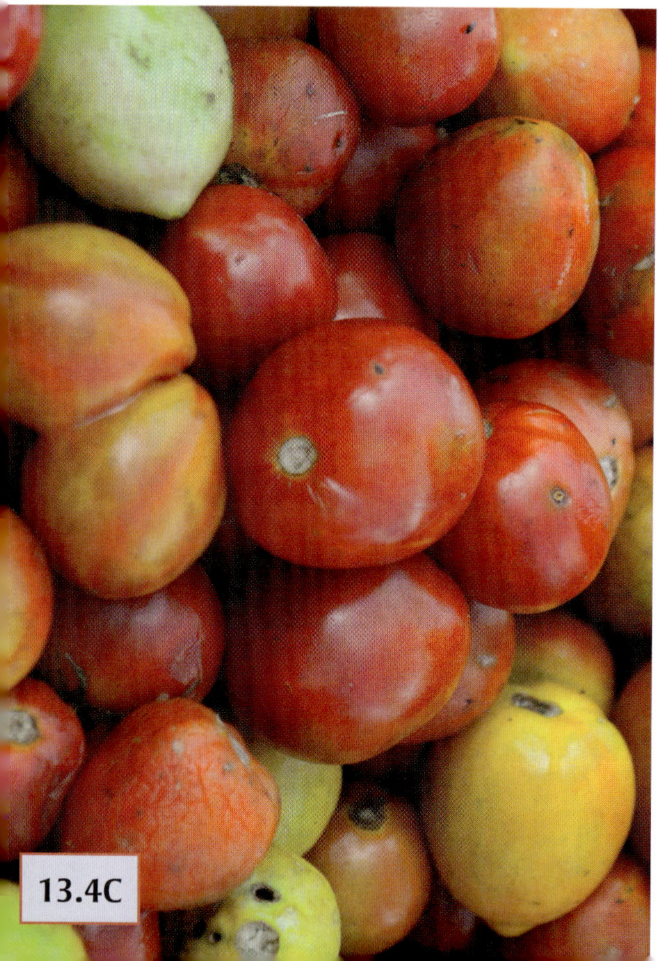
13.4C

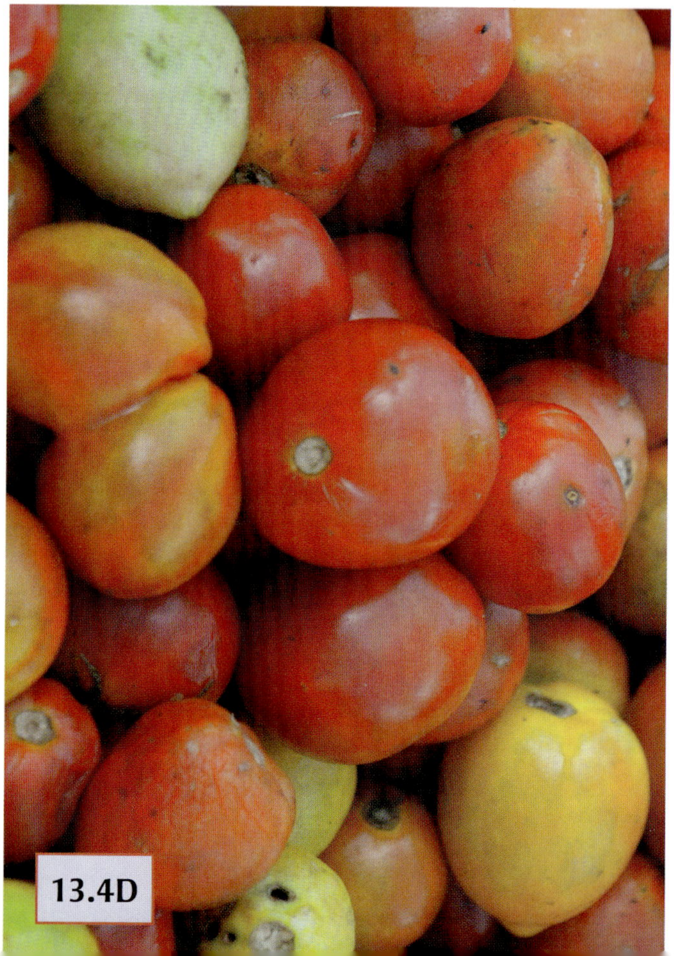
13.4D

At last, an unambiguous instruction, unlike the "but not too much" drivel that infests both music and imaging.

Complications arise, however, halfway through the movement, when the pianist is still supposed to be playing as fast as possible. Schumann now adds a new notation: *Schneller* (faster)! And shortly thereafter: *Noch schneller* (faster yet)!!

Schumann thus merits comparison with retouching clients. Here he is, with a straight face, demanding that his piece be played as fast as possible, then *faster* than possible, and finally much faster than possible.

Piano virtuosi, like retouchers, take a dim view of impossible instructions. Some think that Schumann must have been crazy (regrettably, this turned out to be true) and simply ignore them. Others don't actually start the movement as fast as possible, leaving room for them to speed up twice later. The majority view, as nearly as I can tell, is to start out as fast as possible and then surreptitiously slow down, so as to be able to pick up speed later.

The imaging analog is plain. Intense colors often fall outside of the printable gamut, meaning that the photographer would like us to print them much faster (er, much more colorfully) than possible. In that case, we have to follow the beat of the virtuosi, and slow down (er, diminish the color of) the rest of the picture, so that when we jack up the color as much as the process permits, the brightest parts will seem all the more brilliant.

* * *

The human visual system does not behave like a camera or any other artificial measuring device. Some differences, like chromatic adaptation (our self-calibrating vision, which ignores casts that a camera sees) and simultaneous contrast (our changing perception of color depending upon its neighbors) are well known. Adjusting digital images to compensate for them is standard practice.

Others haven't been explored as much. In the late nineteenth century, it was observed that we humans see strongly colored objects as being lighter than a machine would. That is, if we see a patch of strong red next to a patch of gray, and the Info palette says they both have the same L value and are therefore equally dark, we humans would nevertheless perceive the gray as darker.

This phenomenon is called, rather ponderously, the Helmholtz-Kohlrausch Effect, after the two scientists who documented it. Now you know where the H-K name comes from.

Nobody knows how far the effect extends. Are very subdued colors still seen as slightly lighter than pure grays? And should we compensate for it in color correcting?

The action's H-K Effect layer assumes that the answer is yes. It darkens near-neutral areas without changing their color.

The Color Only layer has more to do with Schumann than Helmholtz and Kohlrausch, because the idea is to emphasize bright colors indirectly, by suppressing dull ones.

The impact is largely in the quartertone to midtone range, which is the critical one in human perception. The layer is set to Color mode, at 45% opacity.

How much, if any, of either layer to use is up to you. Figure 13.4A is the original tomatoes image. I played the action and liked what the H-K Effect layer was doing. This is the easy part—we tend either to think that it's good or bad, so it's rarely necessary to adjust opacity.

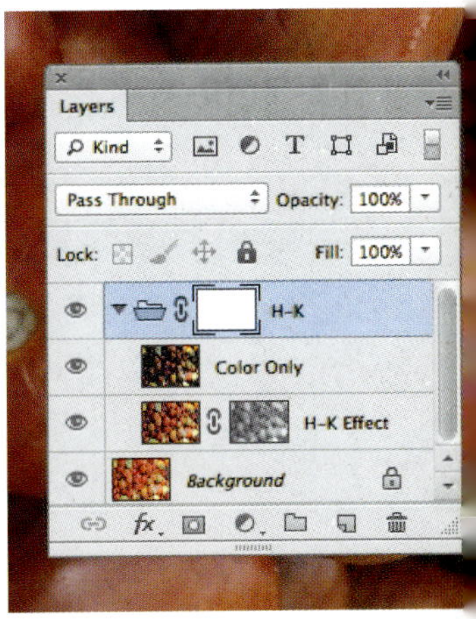

***Figure 13.4** Opposite, top left, the original. Top right, the H-K action is played. Bottom left, the MMM + Color Boost action is played on the result and adjusted to taste. Bottom right, an attempt to match the look, applying MMM + Color Boost to the original instead.*

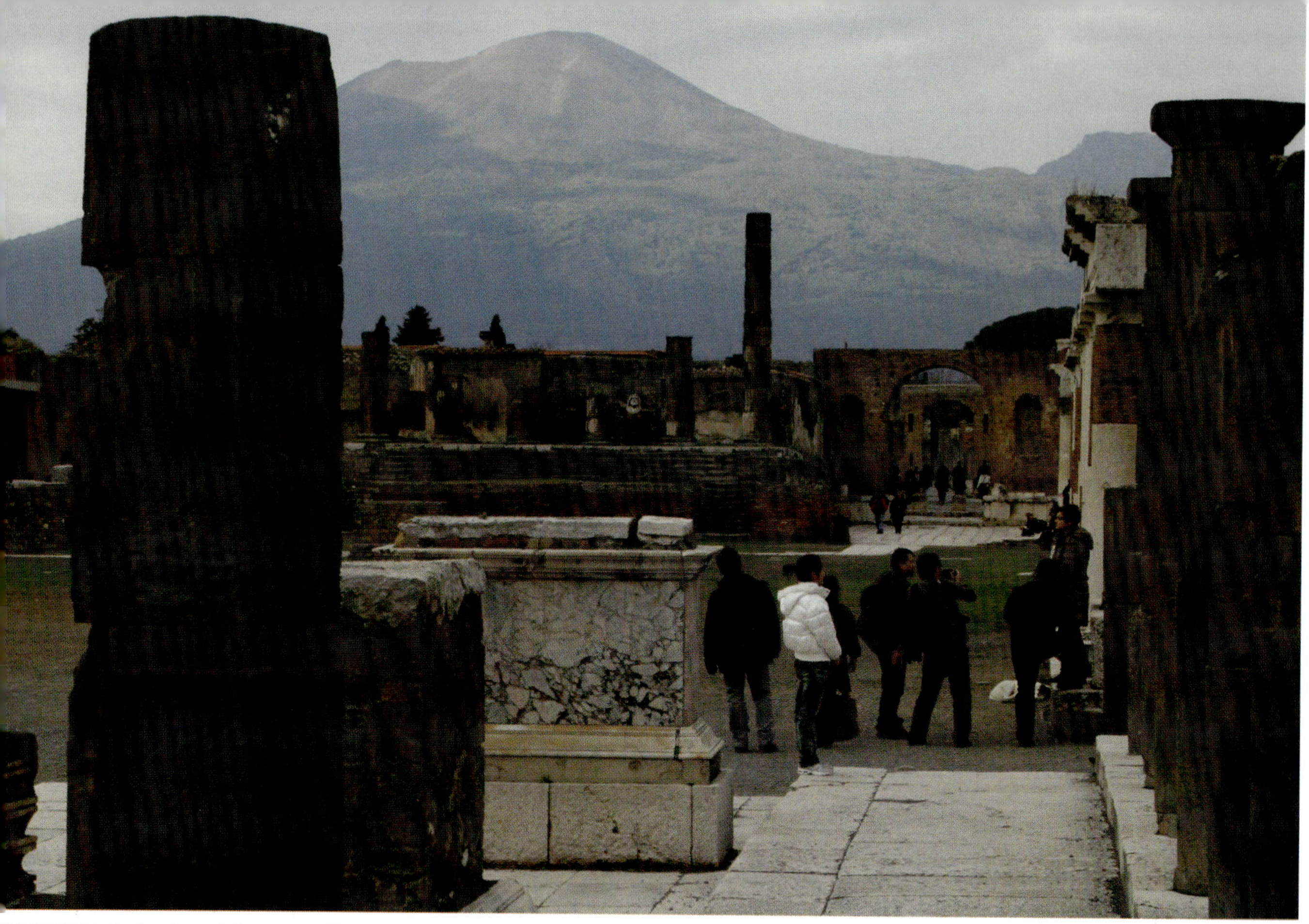

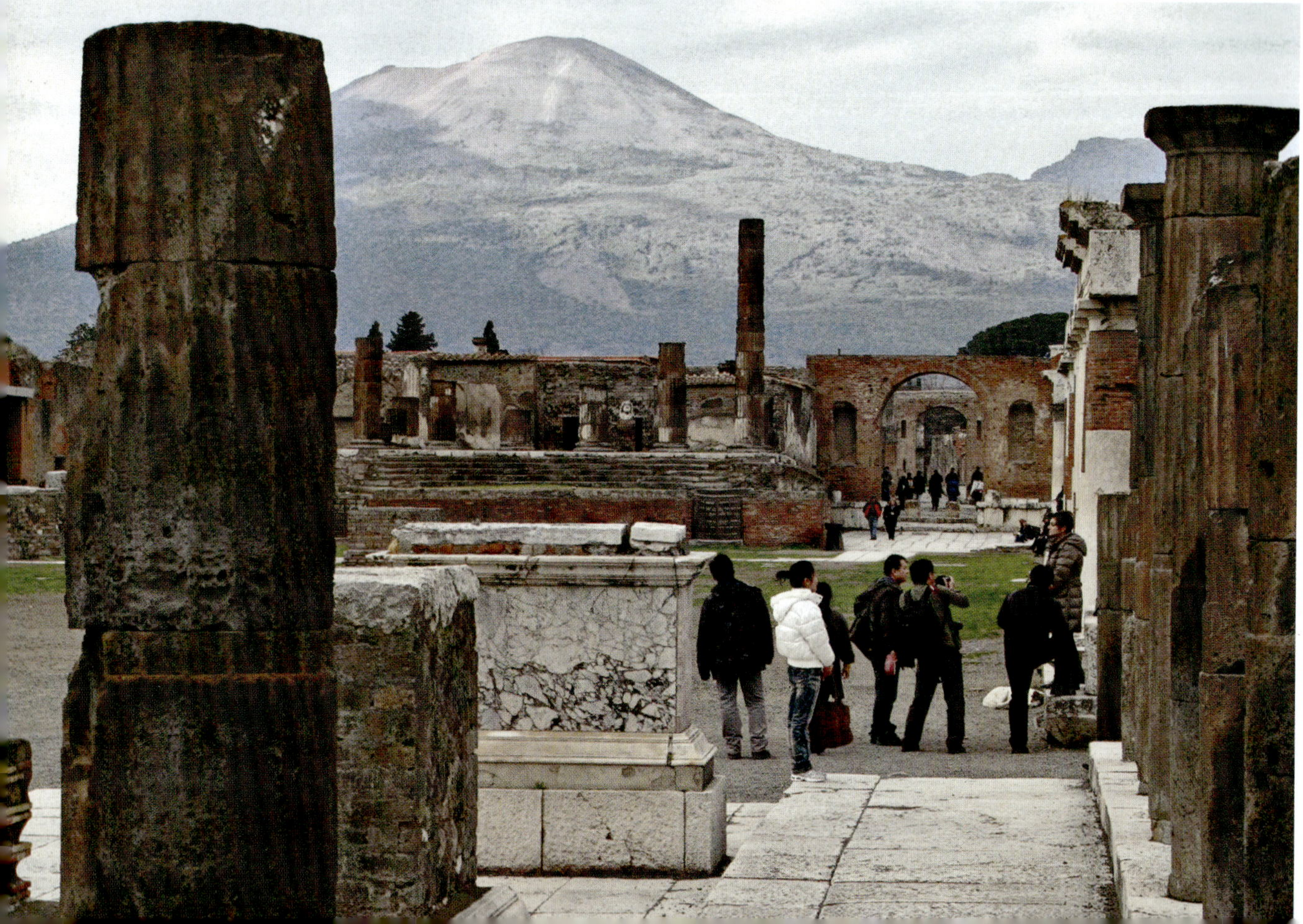

***Postcard 13.5** (opposite) Pompeii and Mount Vesuvius, which obliterated it in 79 AD.*

The Color Only layer is more of a guess. It should suppress duller colors enough to have an impact when everything is intensified later on, but not make things so gray that we can't tell what they are.

Here, the layer hurts duller reds more than it does the brighter parts of the tomatoes. My feeling was that the default setting was too high. So, for Figure 13.4B, I left the H-K Effect layer at its defaults, but reduced Color Only opacity to 25%.

Is the result worse than the original? Perhaps in the sense that tomatoes should not be as brown as these are. But they seem more three-dimensional. Once we have that, there's no difficulty restoring agreeable color. Figure 13.4C runs this duller version through the MMM + Color Boost action.

Its competition is Figure 13.4D, which runs the same action with the same selection on the original, Figure 13.4A. Again I tried to adjust settings to get the closest match to Figure 13.4C. It just isn't possible. The lighter half of the largest foreground tomato is about equal in both. But the dark half on top is more subdued in Figure 13.4C, more colorful in 13.4D. The extra color seems to bring this area closer to us, the opposite of what's needed. If we want to perceive a rounder fruit, the top must seem further away—in other words, duller.

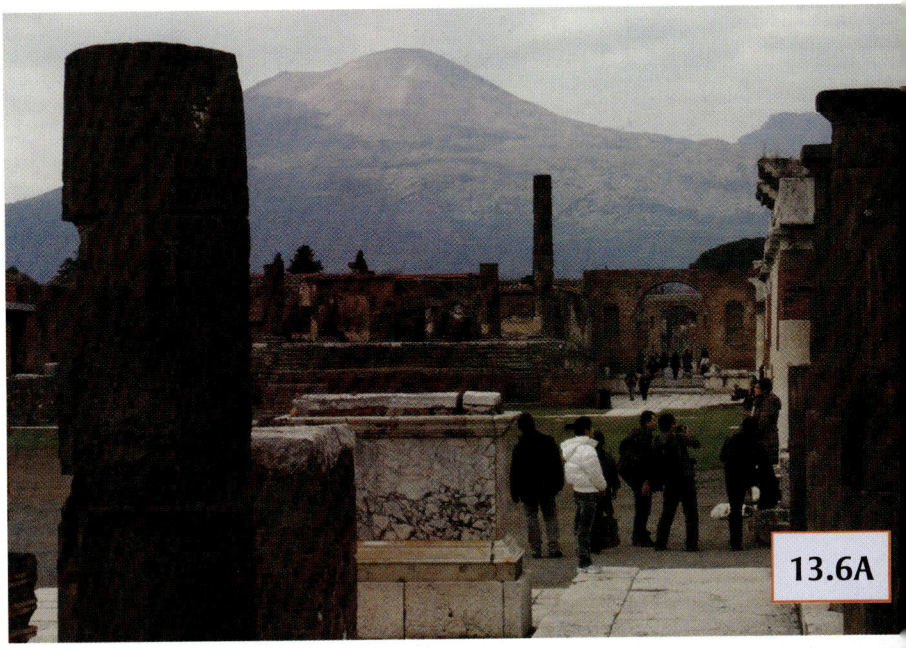

13.6A

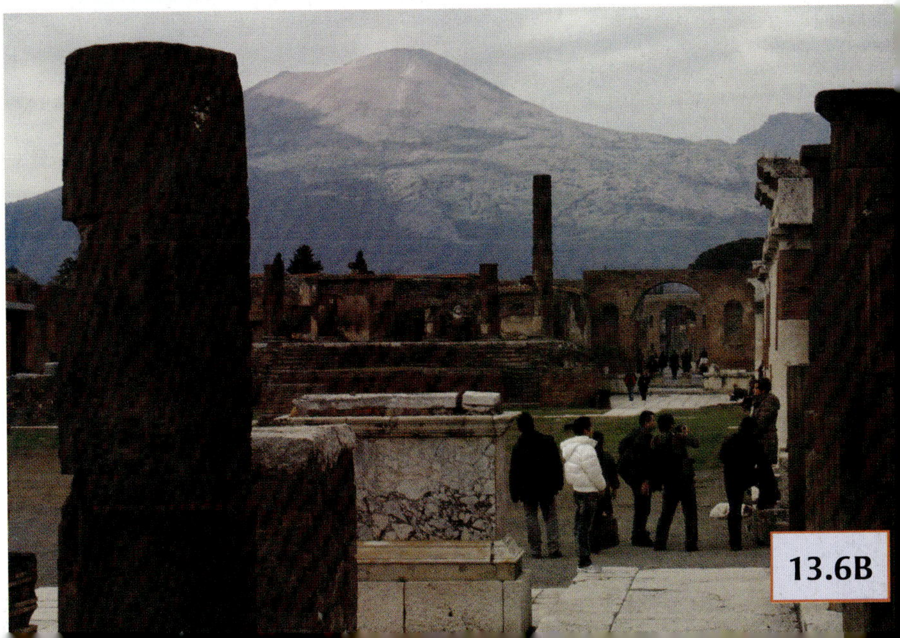

13.6B

***Figure 13.6** Top, a cool cast in the original is eliminated. Bottom, a luminosity move seems to bring the volcano closer. Is that desirable?*

One last thing, just in case you're getting tired of all the musical analogies. The eponymous Hermann von Helmholtz (1821–1894), was an extraordinary individual. His interests ranged from physics to physiology. He invented the opthalmoscope, the first method for physicians to look inside a patient's eye, and laid the groundwork for our present knowledge of how the eye is structured to receive color information.

As his career progressed he became a specialist in how humans perceive things but he declined to limit himself to vision. Although his book on human optics dominated the field for around half a century, his most lasting contribution to human culture was a book entitled *Lessons on the Sensation of Tone as a Physiological Groundwork for the Theory of Music.*

When All Is Smoke and Ashes

Late in the year 79 AD, the innocent-looking mountain in the background of Postcard 13.5 played its own interpretation of *Allegro con fuoco.* Within two days meters of pumice and ash had buried the city shown here, together with thousands of its inhabitants who had already died of thermal shock.

Eighteen centuries passed, and archaeologists began to excavate, finding a well-preserved Roman town to testify to the terrifying power of nature.

It offers an unparalleled snapshot of what life was like in the time of the Empire. And if that snapshot is not a postcard image, no such thing exists: more than two million tourists visit Pompeii annually. Yet the scene is as frightening and as tragic as it is impressive. How does it get portrayed in a Picture Postcard Workflow?

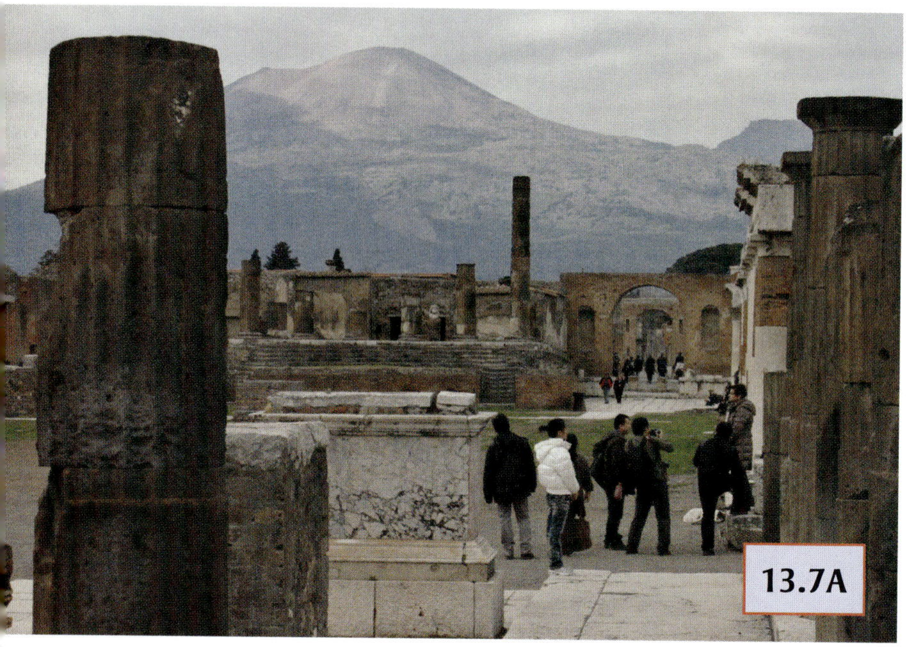

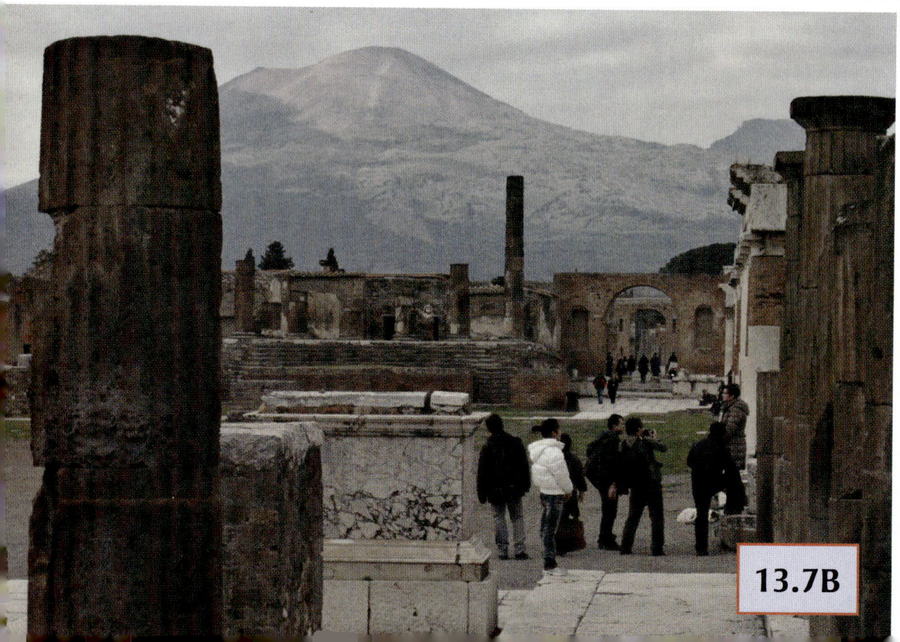

The answer is, in terms of contrast, no different from a photo of any other attraction. There should be just as much detail in these ancient structures as if they had been constructed in our own century.

As for color, though, many of these buildings antedate the Christian era and all have been buried in ash for two millennia. It is hardly sensible to give them the vividness that would be appropriate for a modern scene.

On the other hand, we don't want something that looks like a black and white. The tourists could have helped us out by wearing colorful clothing, but they have decided not to cooperate. The grass, however, has enough color to serve our purposes.

These considerations put the photo in the third category that suggests H-K, one where happy

***Figure 13.7** Top, after applying the Shadows/Highlights command, a false profile and multiplication through a blurred layer mask to Figure 13.6B. Bottom, the H-K action is added.*

colors are unwelcome. Earlier, I used the word *somber* to describe certain images.

If you would agree with *somber,* or disagree with *bright and cheerful,* then you should be thinking about H-K or something similar.

* * *

The original has a mild cool cast, measured by A–negative values in the marble. It is easily corrected in Figure 13.6A.

The next workflow step is luminosity. Bluish, hazy backgrounds like this are common in outdoor photography. The solution, from the contrast point of view, is to blend the red channel into the others, Darken mode, on a luminosity layer. We fleshed out that technique in a picture of the Grand Canyon, way back in Figure 4.14.

In Figure 13.6B, which repeats this method, Vesuvius seems closer, more ominous. One wonders, though, whether it's for the better.

As usual, it depends upon the use of the image. Vesuvius is currently the most dangerous volcano in the world. The most recent of its history of catastrophic explosions came in 1944. If motivated, Vesuvius could offer the city of Naples, population one million, the same treatment it meted out to Pompeii.

If I were writing an article about that theme I think Figure 13.6B would be a good start.

If, on the other hand, the article was about the tragic end of Pompeii, whose residents were going about their business, oblivious to the danger that would shortly annihilate them—well, the vaguer volcano in Figure 13.6A would seem more appropriate.

I went with Figure 13.6B. The Shadows/Highlights command now seemed appropriate, but not the Bigger Hammer. The foreground column, a critical element, is in deep shadow. This calls for the false profile/multiply action, or equivalent, from Chapter 12. I think that the dark half of this picture is more important than the light half, so I used the top layer's composite RGB as the layer mask

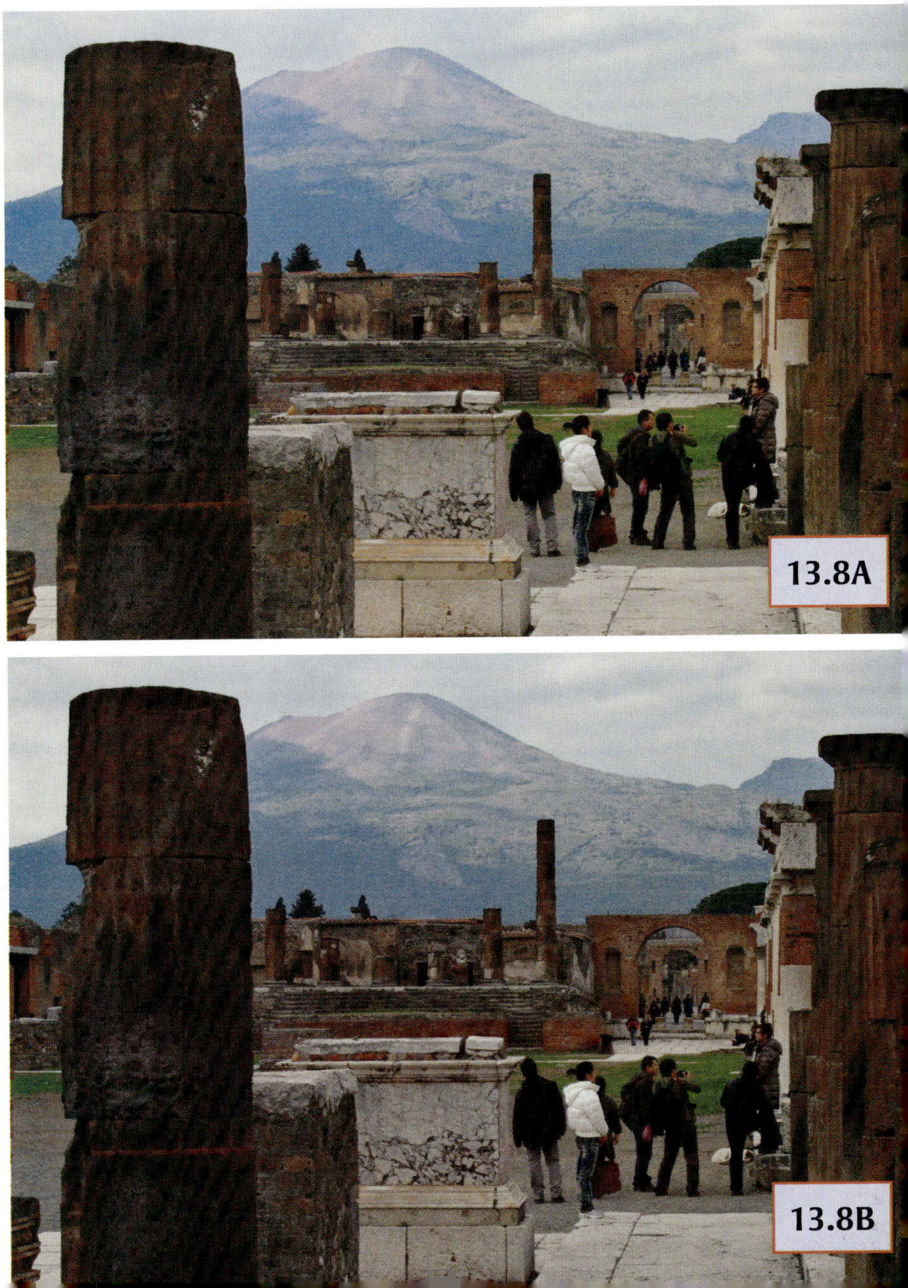

***Figure 13.8** Top, the Skin Desaturation action followed by MMM + Color Boost is played on Figure 13.7A. Bottom, the same procedure applied to Figure 13.7B.*

rather than taking it from the bottom layer as usual.

This produced Figure 13.7A, which isn't particularly colorful. Nevertheless, it needs H-K, which yields Figure 13.7B.

Don't think that this changes enough to warrant the trouble? Then watch what happens when we try to enhance the color. Even though the faces are small, we can't afford to have them too red, so the Skin Desaturation action is in order. Then, the MMM + Color Boost action.

Figure 13.8A does this to Figure 13.7A. Figure 13.8B repeats the same procedure with the H-K version, Figure 13.7B. Granted, these are both default settings that need to take further adjustments. Still, you can see that it's going to be preferable to work with Figure 13.8B. We don't have to worry about the blueness in the background or some of the weird color shifts in the ancient masonry. For the record, to get the final postcard, I did nothing more than turn off the MMM Color component in Figure 13.8B.

A Gift From Santa

Composers, like photographers, retouchers, and Photoshop authors, have to make a living in a world whose economy doesn't favor them. Certain compromises in terms of catering to the taste of the masses, must be made to keep the cash flowing.

***Figure 13.9** Left, the original. Right, after a color correction to eliminate a yellow cast, a luminosity move, Shadows/Highlights, and the Bigger Hammer.*

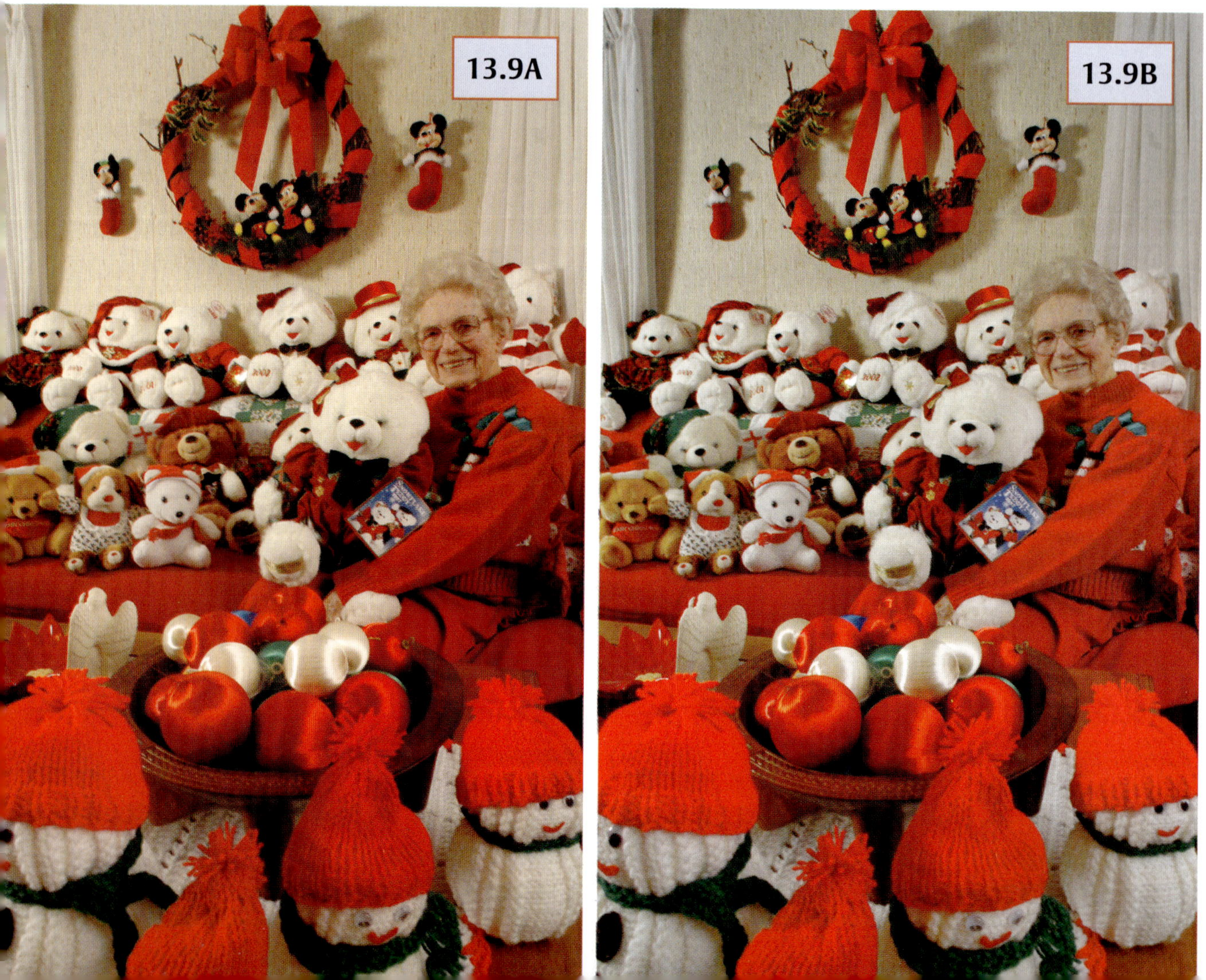

One of Beethoven's biggest money-makers was a potboiler entitled *Wellington's Victory.* Long on bombast and short on musical value, it played to the masses, who found it exhilarating. The critics did not. One of the leading such contemporaries, Gottfried Weber, lambasted the piece as being unworthy of the composer of the Fifth Symphony.

Beethoven himself admitted that the composition was a piece of junk, although that is not the exact word he used. Noted neither for modesty nor diplomatic language, the composer retorted, "You pathetic worm, *[was ich scheiße]* is better than anything you ever thought of." You will have to supply your own translation.

Manufacturers of digital cameras don't merit comparison to Beethoven. They do, however, pander to the masses just as he did. More potential buyers are clueless than competent. It is in the manufacturer's interest to set up the camera so that the clueless get good-looking photos more often than not. My thesis that we normally want bright, cheery colors is nothing new. The manufacturers, logically enough, build in a bias toward such colors.

This bias toward the brilliant accounts for atrocities like Figure 13.9A, a newspaper photo for an article about a woman who collects Christmas decorations, particularly teddy bears.

***Figure 13.10** Left, the H-K action is played on Figure 13.9B. Right, the result, after playing the Skin Desaturation action, goes through a color boost.*

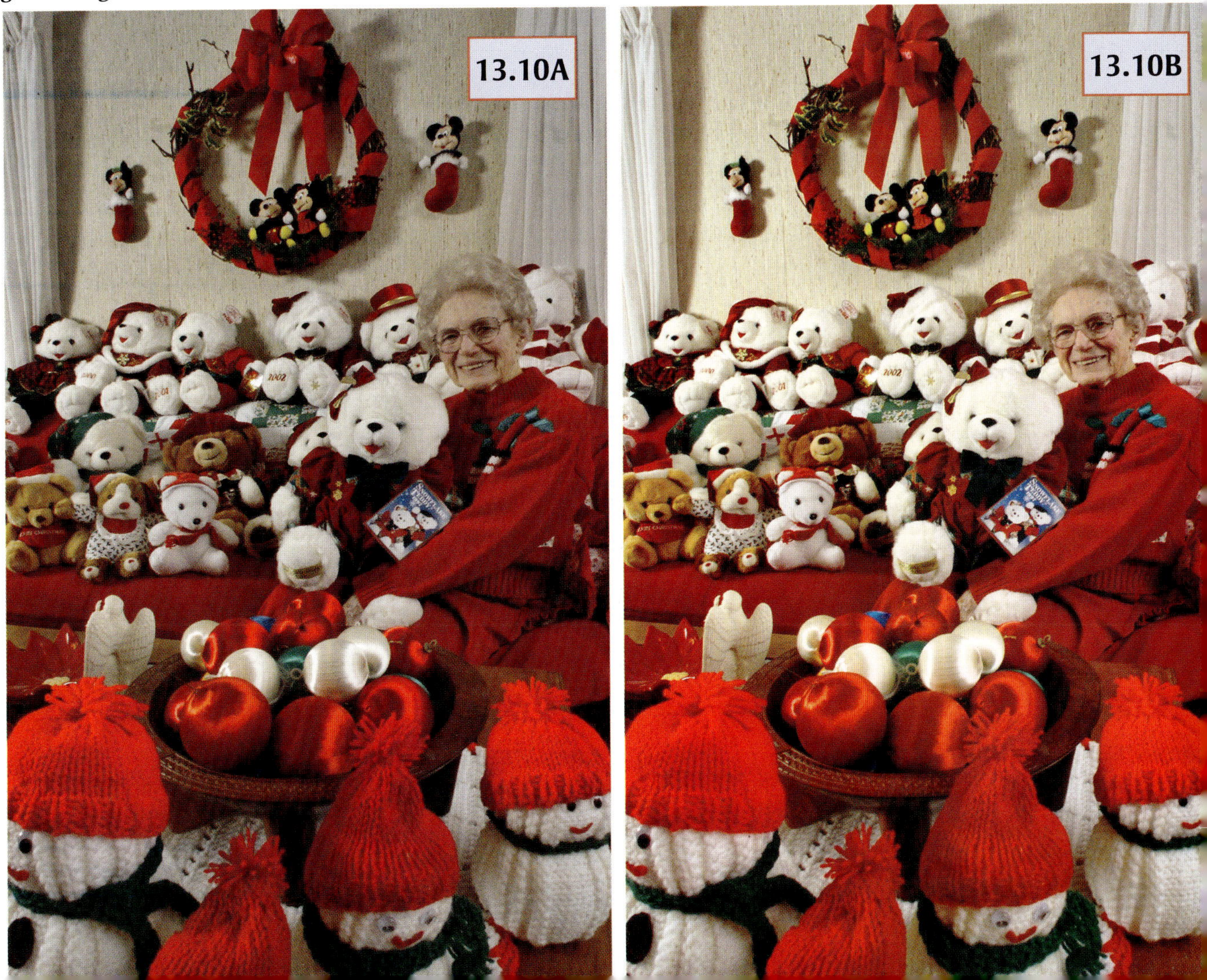

The camera thought that all reds should be bright ones. It therefore presented us with an overwhelming redness in which all reds are equal and almost detail-free.

If the reds weren't quite so intense this would be a clear case for the MMM action of Chapter 6. We would break the reds apart both in terms of color and intensity and that would be that.

Here it isn't so simple. The original RGB is already out of the printable gamut of this book, so any effort to make the file even redder is worse than useless.

Also, viewers have preconceptions of what "Christmas Red" is. We have less flexibility to alter the hue of this red than we do, say, the lake in Figure 13.2A.

The photo therefore qualifies for H-K under the fourth criterion, the presence of large brilliant areas, and to a certain extent under the sixth, the inability to make large changes therein. H-K can discriminate between brilliant reds and very brilliant ones. It can make the lesser reds more neutral and create the needed variation.

The procedure is straightforward. A yellowish cast needs to be minimized. Some detail in the reds can be incorporated by blending the RGB composite into the red and green channels on a layer that will later be set to Luminosity mode. The Shadows/Highlights command will help but not as much as the Bigger Hammer, needed here because detail in the white bears is critical. The default of using the red channel for the Bigger Hammer overlay won't work because it will make these reds too dark. I used a grayscale copy of the RGB as the overlay instead, yielding Figure 13.9B.

Next came H-K, Figure 13.10A. Note how the reds of the sweater and couch are differentiated from the foreground hats better than in Figure 13.9B. Now there is room to run MMM + Color Boost, which I did to produce Figure 13.10B.

In the Beginning, or at the End?

Music can be played loudly or softly, and so can color correction. I would class Bigger Hammer as a loud correction, and H-K as a soft one. By *soft,* I mean that its results are, though noticeable when toggled on and off, not very intrusive. Accordingly we have great flexibility as to when to apply it.

One of the hardest things for those learning the PPW to buy into is that so little color is needed before moving into the final phases. It does not make sense to them that acceptable results can emerge from something as colorless as the post-H-K Pompeii version of Figure 13.7B, or the nearly grayscale bridal intermediate of Figure 12.17F.

In a 480-page book there is no great rush to prove otherwise, but in a quick session at a trade show, there is. Two years ago, at one such event, I got the message across by demonstrating that, in about ten seconds, the mindbendingly monotonous Figure 13.11A could morph into something with more color than anybody would ever want, namely Figure 13.11B. Everything was done with a predecessor of the MMM + Color Boost action, including a robust curve to the L channel to establish more contrast.

This scene surely qualifies for the fifth category: a file with almost everything the same color. We're desperate for more variation. The MMM action will be helpful, limited, however, by how intense a red we dare produce. True, the audience would doubtless accept more variation from the original red than it would in the Christmas scene of Figure 13.9A. This cliff, however, isn't credible with reds as intense as on the left side of Figure 13.11B.

***Figure 13.11** (opposite) Top left, the original. Top right, an overly dramatic adjustment using an early equivalent of MMM + Color Boost. Bottom left, the H-K action is played on the corrected file, but only the H-K Effect layer is visible. Bottom right, the Color Only layer is added. This exercise reverses the normal procedure of running H-K before enhancing color.*

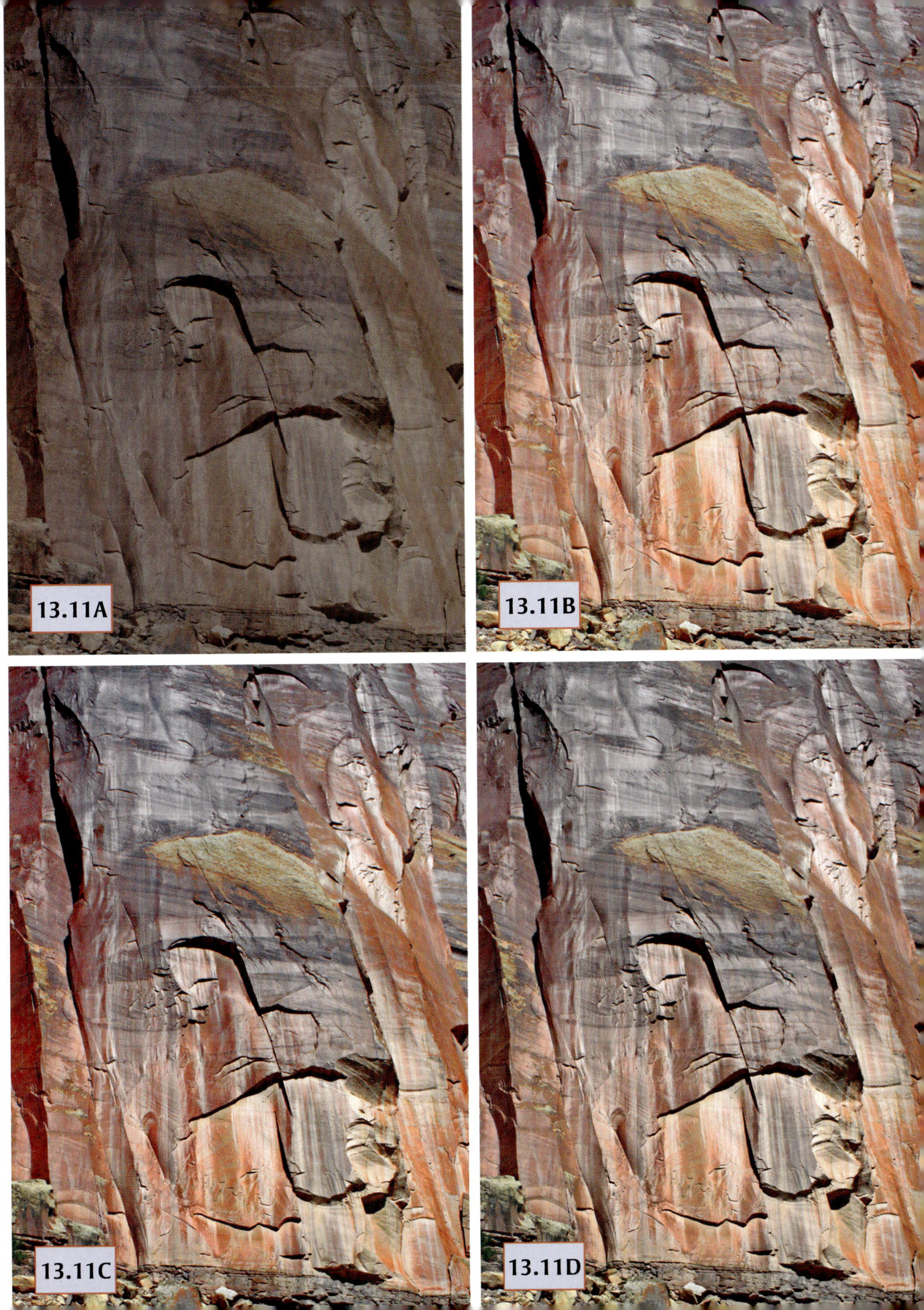
13.11A
13.11B
13.11C
13.11D

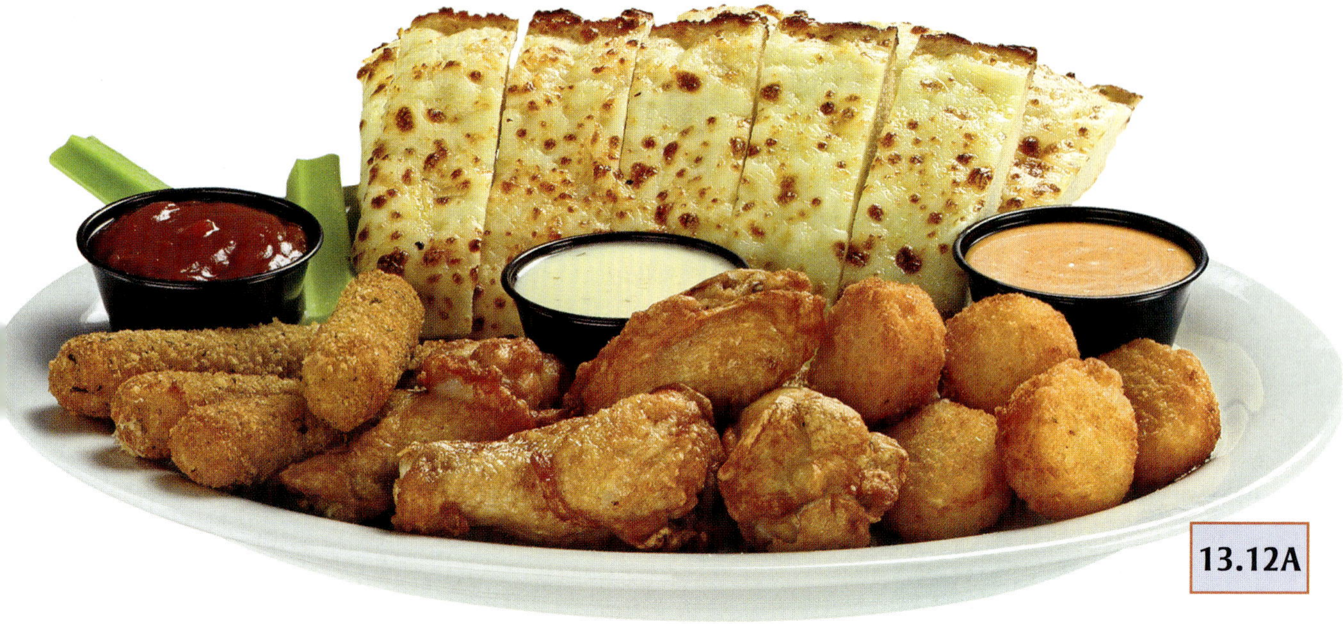

13.12A

Figure 13.12 Food photography, ordinarily shot in studio conditions, poses challenges because there is limited flexibility to alter the color without making the food seem unappetizing. Above, the original; below, a corrected version.

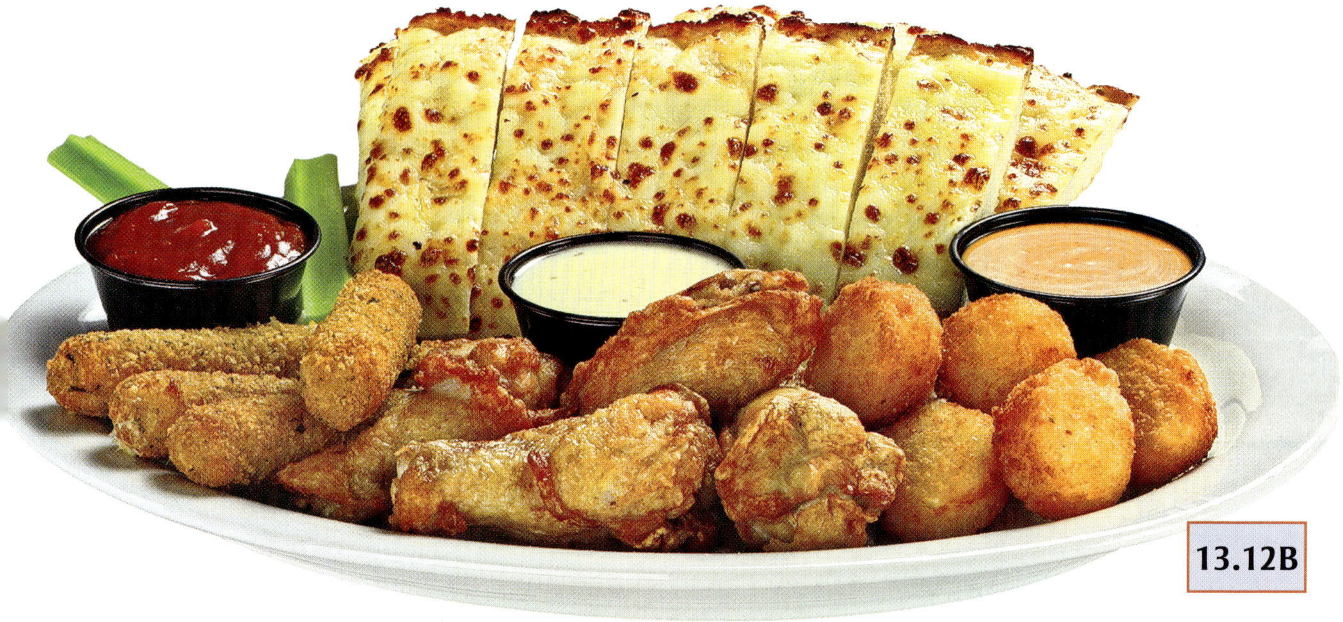

13.12B

I should have used H-K, I suppose, but I was hampered by the fact that it did not exist. So Figure 13.11B is what I have. Fortunately, nothing but orthodoxy stops us from applying H-K at the end of a workflow rather than sometime in the middle.

I converted Figure 13.11B to RGB, and played the action. Figure 13.11C shows the impact of the H-K Effect layer only; Figure 13.11D adds the Color Only layer.

I like both better. Color hasn't changed in Figure 13.11C, but the picture looks somehow deeper when its neutrals are darkened. Making them more neutral still in Figure 13.11D also seems to me to work. I would still say that the picture is too colorful, but that's easily fixed. Remember, the top layer of the action comes at an opacity of 45%. You can swing it out to a higher value for a stronger effect. Or you can just copy the original, Figure 13.11A, to a new layer, set mode to Color, and reduce opacity to taste. As usual at this stage, many options present themselves. The right one is the one that looks best to you.

Adding Spice to the Recipe

Although PPW was developed for outdoor pictures, it outperforms traditional methods in indoor commercial photography, too.

The original, Figure 13.12A, exemplifies the sixth and final category of images that benefit from H-K. It is not a sad picture in the sense of our earlier Pompeii shot; brightness and cheeriness are in fact welcome. However, we are limited in how far we can move the color without making the food unappetizing.

We have two big advantages, though. First, studio photos rarely have color issues that cause later problems. Second, time is no factor. A good deal of money is being spent to take this picture and much more on buying advertising space for it. Image quality is crucial to success. In the overall scheme of things it matters little whether it takes us three minutes or three hours to provide it; the budget covers it and more.

The old-fashioned way is to try to correct this picture very, very carefully, in view of its importance. Today's way, recognizing that slight misjudgments with powerful tools are severely punished, is to do multiple versions quickly. Yes, even an original this good can be significantly improved in three minutes—but there's no guarantee that a second try wouldn't be even better. Plus, we can consider blends, in case one version has better color, or contrast, or highlight or shadow detail, than another.

To maximize the potential of this strategy, intentionally use different methods each time. In fact, it's better if you don't do the versions consecutively, so that you will have forgotten the way you did it the last time.

According to me, the biggest problem in this image is compensating for simultaneous contrast. All three of the fried foods in the foreground are approximately the same brown. If we were looking at the actual meal and not a photo we would see more variation. The second problem is that the slices of pizza in the background seem slightly too light for the rest of the picture.

Saying for the sake of argument that you agree with the above diagnosis, what are the available cures? And what are their disagreeable side effects, if any?

A warning from the beta readers: this exercise is a difficult one. But if you stick around, they have words of encouragement for you. Mine would be: Figure 13.12B is just an average correction—in more ways than one.

Three Sets of Three

Let's take the fried products first. As always, we think of color and contrast separately.

Whatever contrast can be built into this food is welcome, provided the shadows don't plug. The three normal ways of proceeding may produce mixed results.

Channel blending is unlikely to work, because the food isn't colorful, so there can't be much difference between channels.

Curving, either at the luminosity stage or as part of the Color Boost action, can put more detail into the fried food. The cost will be a loss of detail outside its range. We would lose something in the black containers, about which we should lose no sleep, and possibly in the red sauce. The pizza, unfortunately, is much lighter than the fried food, so we could lose some of the realism in the cheese.

The H-K Effect layer (not the rest of the action) is the most likely to be painless. It should make the file more three-dimensional by deepening neutral parts.

For improving color there are three options as well, each of which has a drawback.

Both color layers in the MMM + Color Boost action create variation. The Color Boost layer makes the entire picture more colorful. Not much room for that here, maybe a little.

The Modern Man from Mars, which is about variation, will run into difficulty with the A channel. The pizza starts out neither magenta nor green, but the rest of the picture is A–positive, more magenta than green. The MMM's philosophy is to spread things apart, which it accomplishes by making the pizza greener and the fried food redder (which is what happens if it gains magenta). Neither concept is appealing. As with Color Boost, we can probably get away with a little of it—a very little.

The third tool is the Color Only layer of the H-K action. People usually don't object to added grayness provided it plays up the bright areas. This picture, though, is likely the exception. Gray food is just as unpleasant as overly colorful food, maybe worse. So again, limited at best.

So much for the fried stuff. Now, let's consider how to add weight to the pizza. We can start by eliminating curving, at least unless a layer mask is involved. Anything that adds enough weight to the pizza will likely make everything else too dark. That leaves, surprise, three possibilities.

Channel blending is more of an option with the pizza. The blue channel should be dark and the other two, especially the red, light. Strengthening the red with a blend may prove useful.

Second, the Bigger Hammer might work. There's no call for the type of massive increase in highlight detail shown back in Chapter 10, but if we cut back enough on the action's opacity, the effect might be pleasing.

Finally, we could treat the picture as containing two halves. The false profile and multiplying methodology of Chapter 12 would close the gap between them.

The Bitterness of Defeat

Nine potential methods thus compete. Many, like the Bigger Hammer and the color actions, can have a violent impact. Yet like a Bach fugue, a correction may consist of many voices. Any change in one of them could render one or more of the others offensive.

Diehard one-version types may advocate setting up an enormous file, with Smart Objects nested within Smart Objects. Perhaps in this way true interactivity between the nine methods is possible. This is fine in principle, but eats a prohibitive amount of time. Even granted an important image like this one, it is far more effective to move quickly and combine. Here's how I approached it.

- My first attempt was the simplest. I assumed that the studio color was correct. I made a luminosity layer, blended from the blue into the green and red to darken the cheese slightly, and decided not to run Shadows/Highlights in view of the unimportance of the detail in those zones. I played the H-K action at its defaults. Then I selected some of the pizza and some of the fried food, and played MMM + Color Boost, where I adjusted the endpoints and the color.

You don't get to see this version. I had failed to heed my earlier advice that MMM might turn the pizza green. My use of H-K's Color Only layer had made the picture quite gray, so I was forced to use a heavy hand when boosting color. When finished, the color was worse than the original. The luminosity was somewhat better, so I kept it around for a while as a potential source for blends. It turned out not to be so good for that either, so that file has been consigned to pixel heaven.

- Having learned my lesson, I started the next bout by making the cheese slightly redder. I passed up luminosity moves in favor of an application of the Bigger Hammer at an opacity of 35%. In view of the lack of success on my first try, this time when I applied the H-K action I lowered the opacity of its Color Only layer to 20% instead of the default 45%. Then on to the color boosting as before.

Another try, another failure. When I compared the two versions I discovered I had fallen victim to believing my perception. After staring at my Bigger Hammer version for long enough, I had adjusted to it and convinced myself that the pizza was the right weight, when in fact it was much too dark. The color was also nothing to write home about—too red.

My wife suggests that I should take my failings to a therapist and not inflict them on readers. Nevertheless, this discussion of how not to do things is no waste of space, as it offers an important lesson.

"I have to second that," wrote beta reader Russ Brown, speaking for a big consensus about the preceding paragraph. "I must admit that I feel not so bad after making some stupid mistake when I read that even you are prone to the same sorts of errors."

Adriano Esteves added, "This is *very i*mportant. When we struggle on how to blend and how to get there we can always remember that we fail several times before getting to something really better."

Since they're so adamant, I'll add my own cadenza: this book is about a workflow that can be highly automated. It has not been successful in automating good judgment and taste. Until it does, mistakes are inevitable, no matter your experience level. The goal

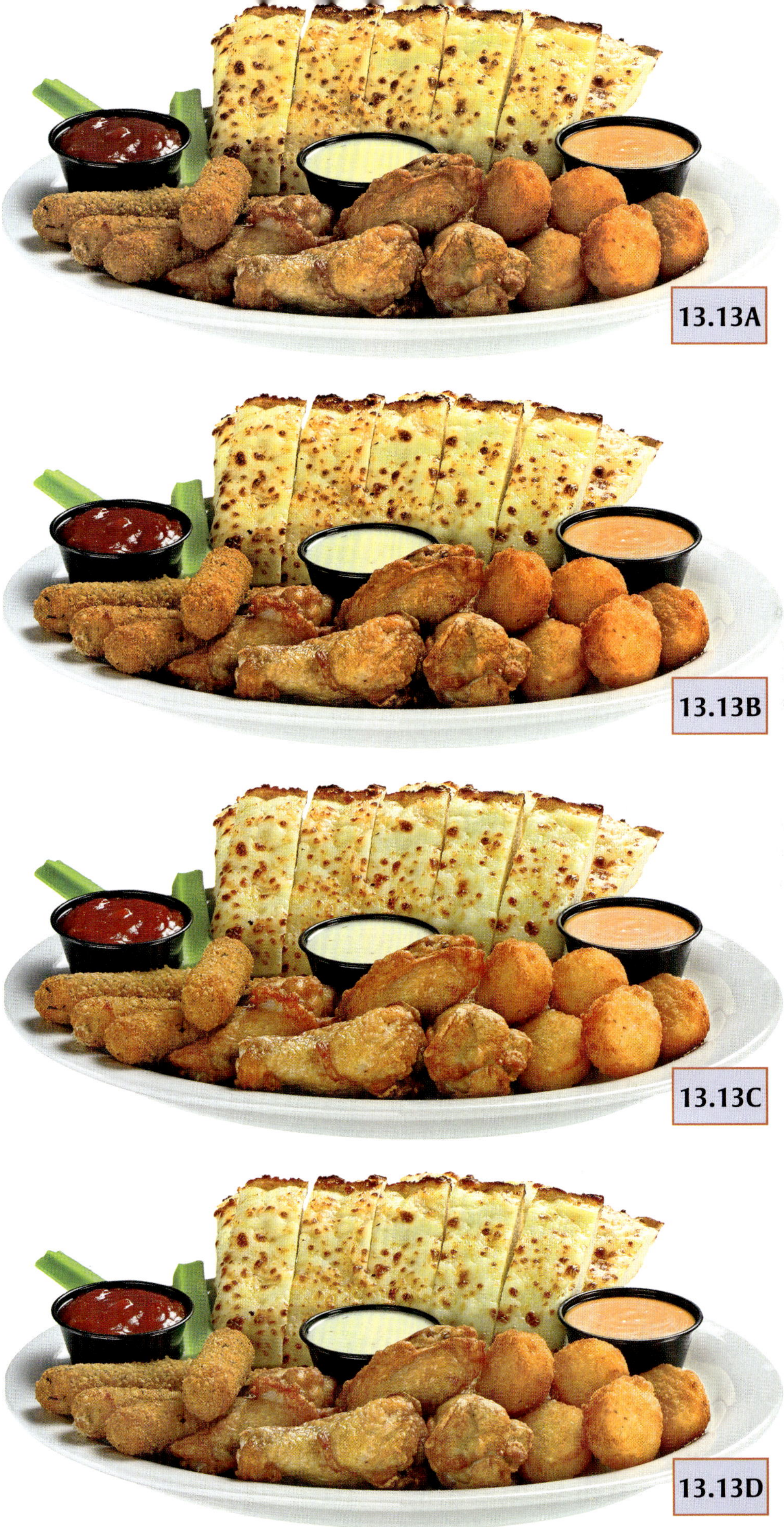

Figure 13.13 *When a picture is worth a lot of time, it pays to correct in a variety of styles, then consider whether they can be blended.*

is to reduce their frequency, not eliminate them altogether.

I have corrected many more images than the average bear, which means that I am more experienced than almost anybody at discovering that what I did is no good. When it happens, I use very bad language. I throw things. I occasionally resort to rum. But I never feel that I am too stupid to exist.

Wrecking a promising image always feels bad, and I'm sorry that I can't offer a cure. There is, however, a silver lining: when you make something beautiful and say to yourself that you could not have done it last year, it feels *really good.*

Four for the Road

The current picture is different from most in two ways. First, the original was taken by a professional under excellent conditions. Second, the subject is unforgiving. It's much easier to get disagreeable color in a food shot than a landscape.

On another image, our first two versions might be just as bad, *but there would be no way of knowing,* because they look good in comparison to the original. In fact, even these two losers would have their uses if nothing better were available: either could be blended 50–50 with the original to make an improvement. Of that approach, more anon.

- Before starting this picture, I would have thought that multiplication would work best. However, I wasn't going to give up on other options yet, feeling that my first two efforts didn't prove much. So I tried again, reusing the curve that gave me warmer cheese, this time with a combination of luminosity moves and a lighter touch of Bigger Hammer. I reverted to the default H-K color setting of 45% opacity before boosting color, and got Figure 13.13A. The gray mozzarella sticks convinced me that this part of the action is counterproductive, at least at such high opacities.
- The next version went the same way, except that I omitted all luminosity moves, used Bigger Hammer at a higher opacity, and reduced opacity of the H-K color layer to a modest 10%. This yielded Figure 13.13B, the first I was reasonably happy with.
- It was finally time to try the strategy I had the most hope for. I had already found out that the Color Only layer was not getting the job done. I now wanted to find out whether the H-K Effect layer might have any better luck, so I resolved to do two more versions. For the first of these, I followed the previous procedure with two exceptions. I omitted the Bigger Hammer in favor of the false profile action, and I eliminated the Color Only layer altogether. This produced Figure 13.13C. Note the difference in the relative weights of pizza and fried items between this version and Figure 13.13B.
- On to the test. Figure 13.13D was done the same way as 13.13C except that I turned the H-K Effect layer off completely; notice how much lighter the fried food became. Also, while I knew that the default 45% on the color layer gave a ridiculous result, I thought that 10% might give more of an opportunity for a boost later, so I tried it.

At this point we should have seen enough. Further versions are unlikely to do any better, although they can do no harm. Now that we have multiple versions, the question is whether they can be blended advantageously. Presumably you agree that Figure 13.13A has the worst color of the four discussed so far. That doesn't disqualify it from being used for its contrast. You can test it by making it a layer, set to Luminosity mode, over whichever of the other three you like best.

Personally, I favor Figure 13.13C, but would probably move it somewhat in the direction of Figure 13.13D. Your preference, of course, could be different. Before spending a lot of time testing blends, however, there's one last surprise, which perhaps should be played *fortissimo,* just like Haydn's.

The Power of Consensus

No intelligence was involved in creating Figure 13.12B, which I rated as the best of the bunch by a slim margin. It's nothing more than a mathematical blend of the four Figure 13.13 variants—each counting for a quarter. (Doing this is easy; combine the versions into a document with four layers; set the second layer to 50% opacity, the third to 33%, and the top to 25%.)

That it should be so good makes little sense. After all, it averages in a rather poor version (Figure 13.13A). However, I have done this kind of averaging with picture after picture, and have consistently gotten the same puzzling results. The averaged version is usually better than the work of any individual.

A simple statistical explanation suggests itself. If the versions of five experts share a certain characteristic and that of a sixth doesn't, it's probably because the sixth person has done something wrong. Averaging eliminates eccentricities, which are likely to be errors. We will hear more on this topic in the next chapter, which discusses methods of acquiring a file in raw format.

If you choose to continue with this chapter, we'll be discussing some of the specifics about how the H-K action works, some of the other options it offers, and a look at various uses of the Ersatz Black channel, should you decide to save it.

For further study, if desired, the lengthy in-panel documentation for this action was written by Marco Olivotto, not me. It therefore explains things from a different perspective, and possibly more understandably.

Meanwhile, I hope you will be able to use the H-K action, as well as the tricks in previous chapters, to compose visual music to the tempo that pleases you. We have seen how the methods work to establish mood, from somber to professional to cheerfully giddy, and how they can be adapted to any time constraint, from throwaway work that must be done quickly to advertising material where time is no object. May your results be ever colorful—but not too much.

Review and Exercises

✓Describe the two layers of the H-K action. Which do you think is more likely to be useful?

✓The action by default creates an artificial black channel and then deletes it. The deletion makes sense because such a channel prevents saving the document as a JPEG. However, there are many reasons to think about keeping it. They are discussed in the second half.

✓Making the buildings in the Pompeii exercise too colorful is clearly a bad idea. Why, then, should we not stick with Figure 13.7B and forget a subsequent color boost altogether?

✓This chapter describes several categories in which the action is known to be effective. Set up a collection of a dozen or so of your own images on different subjects. Try out the action, each layer alone, to see if you find more areas of utility.

✓The Color Only layer often makes the file look worse. Do not reject it on this account. It may enable a more pleasing color boost later.

A Closer Look

Back in the last century, a certain exercise always caused great wailing and gnashing of teeth in my advanced color correction courses. Most professionals in those days had grown up always being given CMYK files to correct, because that's what the drum scanners of the day delivered. Many of them therefore found RGB files to be slimy and malodorous and were not quite certain of what to do with them.

Hence, the following exercise. You are given a certain RGB file. To make it easy, it doesn't contain any really bright colors of the type that are difficult to reproduce in CMYK. You are also given a beautiful CMYK conversion of it, to prove that a near-perfect match is possible.

Before handing the two off to you, however, I do an Edit: Fill>White of the CMYK file and save it. So you now have a good RGB file and a blank CMYK one that matches it in size. Your mission is to recreate the good CMYK.

Sounds easy enough, until you hear the catch. *You are not allowed to convert anything to CMYK.* You have to construct your CMYK channels from scratch, using the RGB channels as a starting point. Really good retouchers found this fairly easy. Would you?

The Black Art of Separation

Getting a *beautiful* separation without a conversion involves some things that you don't need to know how to do, like compensating for ink impurities, the total ink limit, and dot gain. It is, however, very useful to consider how you would proceed if these tiresome factors did not exist. So let's consider the broad outlines. I'd suggest grabbing a couple of your own files and following along.

Starting with an RGB file, Select: Select All, Edit: Copy, File: New, Color Mode=CMYK Color, Background Contents=White, click OK. As the size of this new file matches that of the RGB file you copied to the clipboard, you now have, as desired, a blank CMYK file to work with.

Into the blank cyan channel, apply its close relative, the red of RGB. Similarly, replace the blank magenta with a copy of the green, and the blank yellow with a copy of the blue. Now take a look at the overall color of the CMYK file. No, it isn't a perfect match to the RGB, but it's a good deal closer than one might expect.

Before correcting to make it even closer, though, you need a black. Here's the rule to bear in mind: the black can nowhere be darker than the lightest corresponding area in any of the three RGB channels.

The crudest way to comply with this rule would be to copy any RGB channel, let's say the red, into the blank black. Now apply the green channel to the new black, Lighten mode. Follow by applying the blue in Lighten mode.

In practice this black would be too dark for quality printing and also, as far as I know, too dark for anything we might want to use it for in color correcting a photograph. You could lighten it with a curve. Simpler yet, you could use Screen mode rather than Lighten when blending the three RGB channels into each other. Some commercial printers would find even that too dark, and would lighten it further somehow.

No matter what kind of black you've produced, you can't just tack it on to the existing file. The CMY channels already produce approximately the right weight. To retain it, you have to find a way to subtract the impact of the new black from the CMY channels. How to do so is irrelevant to this book, but once you have figured out a way, all the requirements for a good separation are met.

H-K creates what we call Ersatz Black as described above, by screening the three RGB channels into each other. It discards Ersatz Black after using it, but the PPW panel can override that choice. The action never creates a CMYK file as such because there's no need for one. A second action, called False CMYK, *does* create a bogus separation.

The agenda for the rest of the chapter:

- Explain how the action uses its Ersatz Black channel to get what it wants without messing everything up.
- Offer a tantalizing look at other neat things that can be done with artificial black channels.
- Show how two images that were worked on by a gang of experts in past years can be done better today, one with the False CMYK action and the other with H-K.

Can't Tell a Book by Its Cover

What we are about to talk about is deep and little documented. Beta reader Frederick Yocum offers the following warning: "I found the book cover exercise [the one we are about to see] understandable and clever, but confusing because it flipped the action on its head. That has its uses in that it helps us think about principles, but readers might also find themselves going off on a tangent."

To set the stage, you have to imagine yourself as a professional retoucher, which means that you have to deal with art directors.

Running type on top of a picture is a common design element nowadays. Sometimes the type is placed over a light background that doesn't hamper legibility. Often, however, the picture needs to be ghosted. Here is a hypothetical, very hypothetical example.

Suppose that someone is given a title and assigned to design a cover for this book. A normal person might think that the pictures herein are probably adequate, and could locate one featuring an area light enough that type could be surprinted without difficulty.

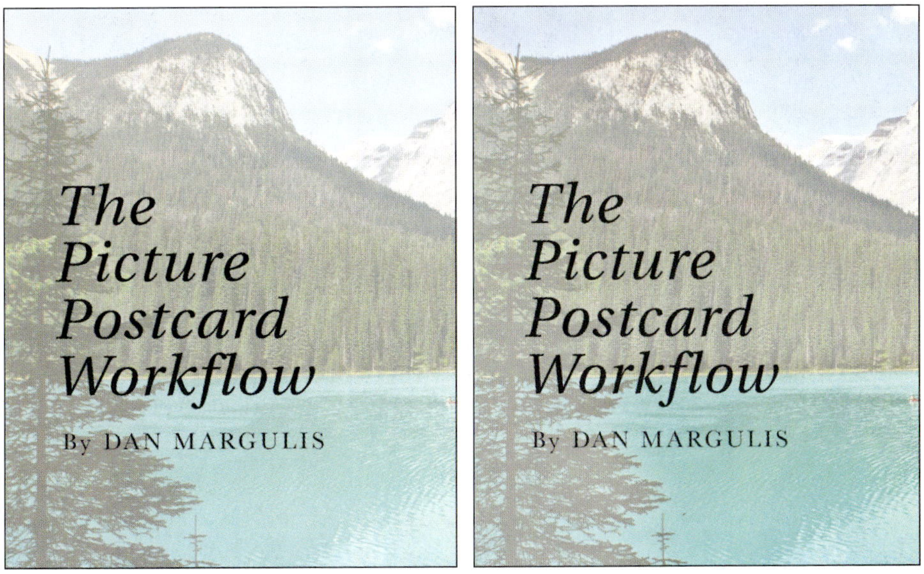

***Figure 13.14** "Ghosting" a picture is a common request in advertising. The picture must be lightened so that the text will be legible. Which of these hypothetical book covers would you choose?*

Art directors don't necessarily think so rationally, and might decide that logic requires that the cover feature the very first postcard from Chapter 1, and that no layout but that of Figure 13.14 will suffice.

Picking up Postcard 1.1 unaltered is out of the question. Nobody could read black type against such a dark background. So the picture must be lightened drastically. For verisimilitude, I have run the word *Workflow* across two objects of different darknesses, and also chosen a serif type with fine lines for the name, in the interest of irritating the pressman. These are typical examples of the thinking of certain art directors.

The type is legible in both versions of Figure 13.14. Which do you prefer?

If you're thinking that one version is darker than the other, you're mistaken; their average L values are equal. The traditional way of ghosting a picture is shown on the left, but the right-hand version is better. We sense that this is something called Emerald Lake, the postcard effect is more pronounced, and the type is easier to read.

The left-hand version shows more contrast in the background trees. Does it help? I say not. The exercise shows how we identify brighter objects by their color and not their detail. The extra

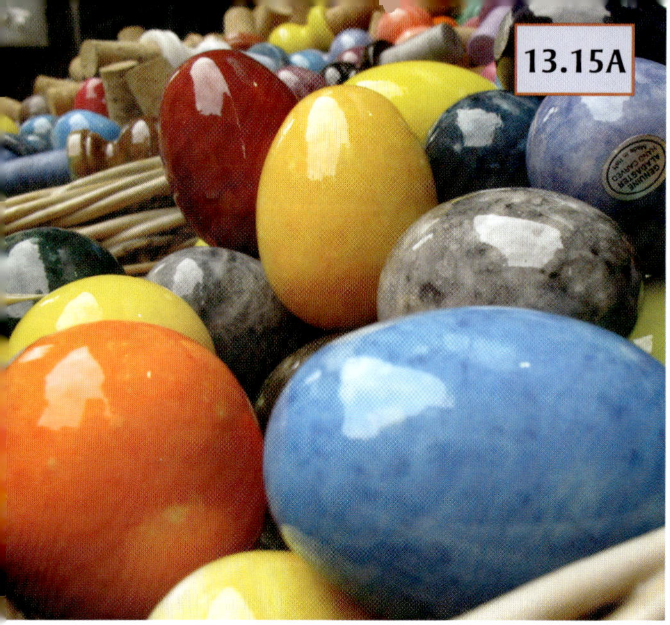

blueness in the sky and the extra greenness in the lake help us know these objects for what they are.

The success comes from the Helmholtz-Kohlrausch Effect in reverse, just as Frederick said. Instead of darkening relatively neutral things, this process lightened them. I made a blurred, inverted copy of the Ersatz Black channel from the H-K action, and used it to mask a lightening curve. This protected the more colorful areas (the lake and the sky) to some extent.

Figure 13.15 *Top, the colorful original. Middle left, the Ersatz Black channel. Middle right, the default H-K action result. Bottom left, without the Color Only layer. Bottom right, Color Only is restored and the H-K Effect layer removed.*

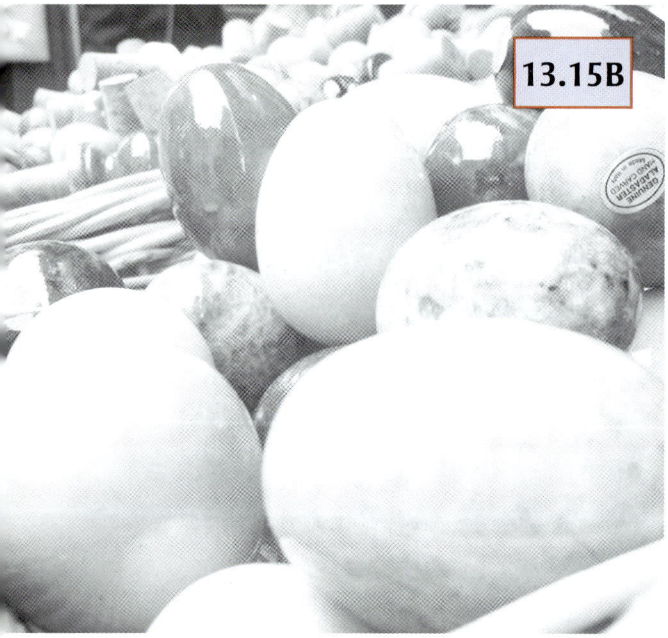

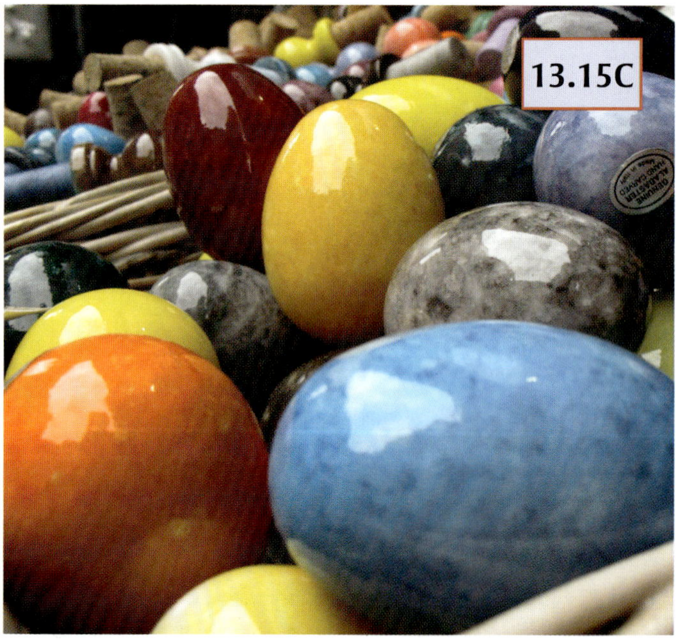

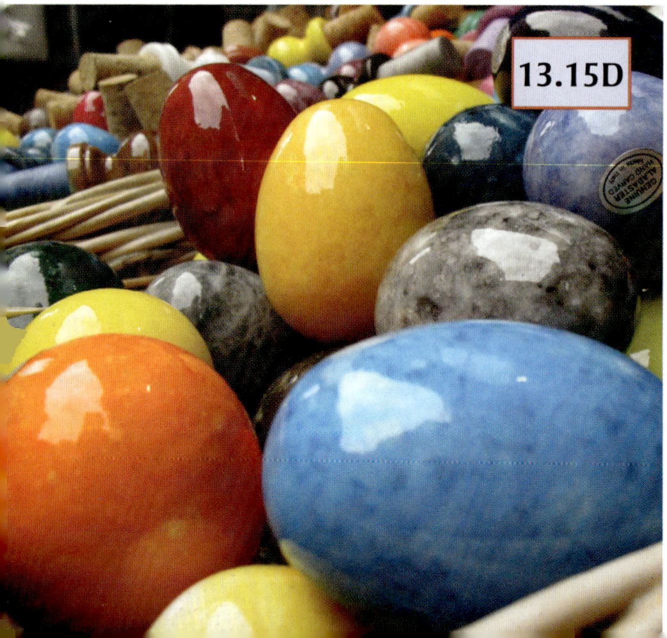

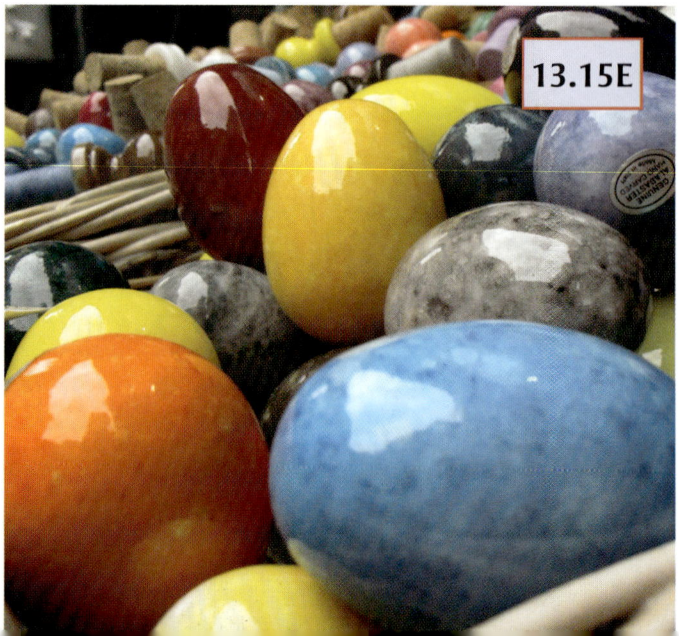

The H-K Action Revisited

Let's study the function of the two H-K layers in a very colorful file.

Figure 13.15A is the original. Figure 13.15B is the Ersatz Black, produced by screening the three RGB channels into each other. The H-K action uses it internally, but then throws it away. If you are working with the PPW panel, option-clicking H-K allows you to override that default and save the channel. You can also set that as your permanent default if you like.

Figure 13.15C is the action's result, untouched. It's broken into two subcomponents. Figure 13.15D has the H-K Effect layer on, the Color Only layer off. Figure 13.15E is the reverse.

Figures 13.15C and 13.15E look worse than the original, but this is nothing unusual in the PPW. The point here is the same as it was in the hypothetical book cover: to emphasize the most intense colors by playing down the rest.

Figure 13.15D tries to do this by darkening the less colorful objects. Often this gives a pleasing sense of depth but I don't think it's happening here. So I would turn the H-K Effect layer off.

The Color Only layer is another story. Remember, it is not just toning down all color. It discriminates, suppressing semi-neutrals more than brightly colored objects. The advantage is seen in Figure 13.16A, which subjects 13.15E to the MMM + Color Boost action.

Its competition is Figure 13.16B, which uses the same selection and the same action on the original, Figure 13.15A. I cut the Color Boost layer's opacity in half to try to get closer to its opponent, but I still get the impression of a lot of color with not enough shape. The less saturated blues and oranges in the two foreground objects give added depth in the version prepared with the help of the H-K action, Figure 13.16A. Having slightly dull colors when we enter the color enhancement phase is actually an advantage. This is a point to be kept in mind when studying raw acquisition in the next chapter.

So far in this exercise, you don't need to have seen the Ersatz Black channel, Figure 13.15B, or even know that it exists. The action has done everything and presented you with what you need. You should realize that everything in Figures 13.15 and 13.16 requires unseen intermediate steps. For example, how does the action unite the original, Figure 13.15A, with the Ersatz Black, Figure 13.15B, to create Figure 13.15D?

The color isn't supposed to change, which implies that things will be done on a layer that will later be set to Luminosity mode.

The simplest way to add depth on this layer

***Figure 13.16** Left, the MMM + Color Boost action is played to Figure 13.15E. Right, using the same selection, the action is played instead to the original, Figure 13.15A. The Color Boost was reduced, but nevertheless the result lacks depth.*

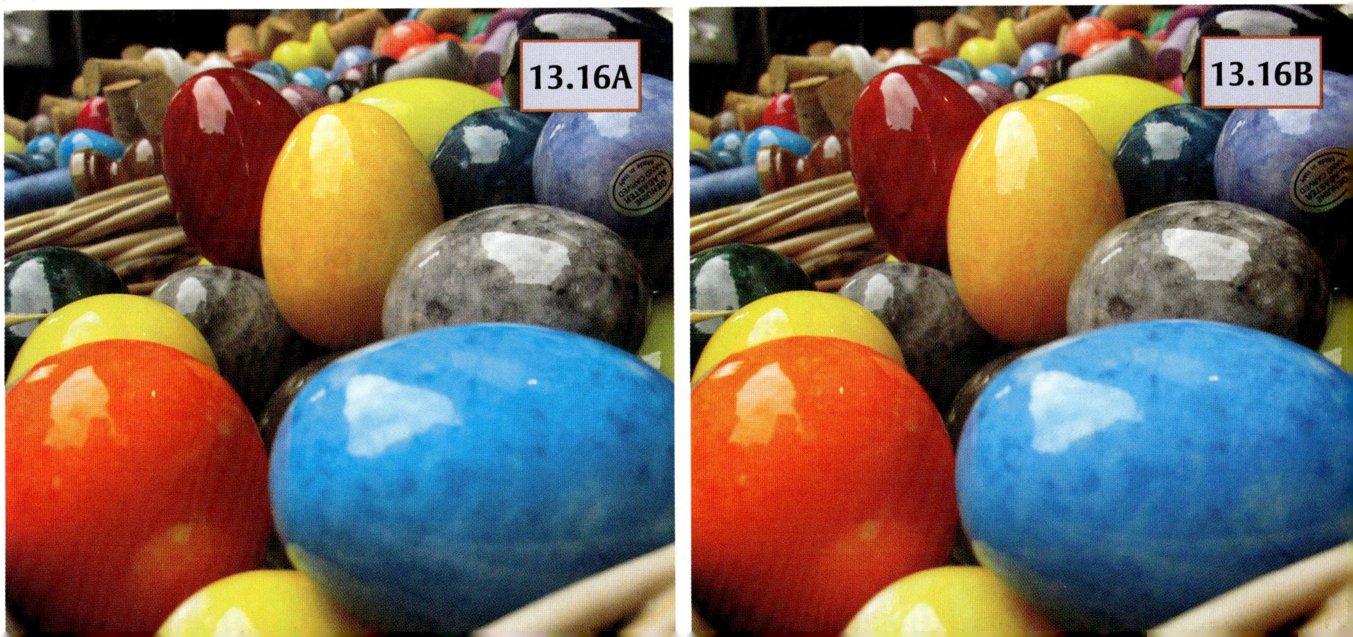

would be to multiply the Ersatz Black into the original. That won't work in the shadows, though. The top left corners of both Figures 13.15A and 13.15B are dark. Multiply the two and they become black. Worse, the same will happen with the dark neutral eggs. A straight multiplication will cost them all their detail.

Something needs to restrict the darkening to the midrange. The action uses the blurred mask shown in Figure 13.17A. Note how the upper left of this mask protects shadows.

The Color Only layer in principle is simpler. Blurring of masks is needed only when two layers differ greatly in contrast. Since this layer is going to be set to Color mode, contrast is irrelevant and the blur is unnecessary.

If we just multiply Figure 13.15A and 13.15B and put the result on a color layer, though, there's a catch. The layer will be completely black beyond a certain darkness point. Since blacks are neutral, the layer will neutralize whatever's beneath them. We could prevent total grayness by reducing its opacity, but still these dark areas would get grayer much faster than the rest of the picture, disturbingly so.

The action's solution is to apply a darkening curve so that even more of the layer becomes black, and then to use quite a low layer opacity. This emphasizes color shifts in the quarter- to midtone range, which is where we are most sensitive to color variation. Figure 13.17B is the intermediate result. As a layer over Figure 13.15A, set to Color mode at 45% opacity, it produces Figure 13.15E.

The next example will focus on focus.

Color, Neutrality, and Fast Recognition

Our visual system evolved in a time when immediate recognition of peril was critical to survival. At that time, we were not the threat to ourselves that we are today. Any other species that might threaten us was not at all colorful.

Brightly colored objects, like flowers, skies, butterflies, or these alabaster eggs, posed no threat to our ancestors. There was no point in devoting precious visual resources to resolve details in brilliant objects whose very color served as an identification tag.

In evaluating a scene containing both bright colors and near-neutrals, therefore, our system tries to find more defining characteristics in the near-neutrals. Color correction should cater to this effect. Unfortunately, there is no obvious way to do so in Photoshop, which is why we have an extended discussion of the issue not just here, but in two other chapters.

Chapter 15 introduces a novel tool called Hiraloam Color, whose purpose is to accentuate

Figure 13.17 *Left, the layer mask for the H-K Effect layer. Right, the Color Only layer, set to Normal mode, 100% opacity.*

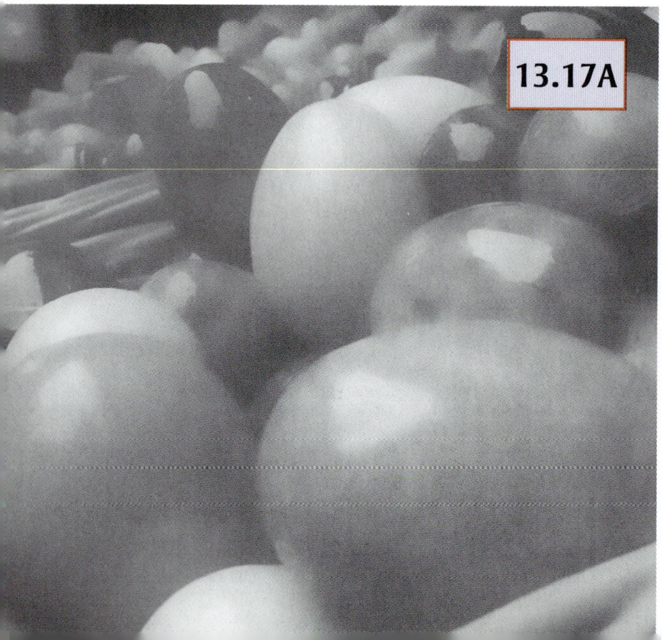

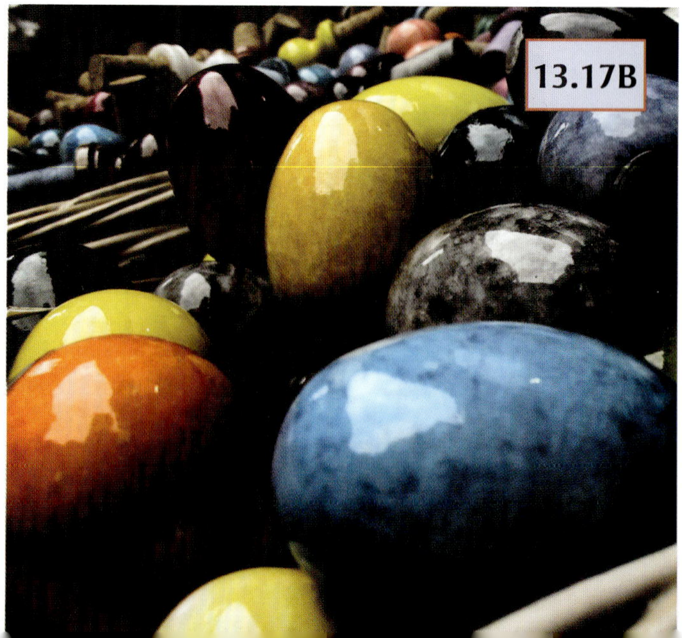

the brilliance of small objects that cannot be hazardous to our health, leaving us to concentrate on things that can be.

Chapter 9 emphasized that while we need color variation, we have to avoid sending confusing signals about whether an object falls into the non-threatening color category. We cannot, for example, let a face get so red that our instincts begin to tell us that it is a flower. Also, it suggested that we are programmed to devote more visual resources to resolving detail in the threatening range. Dangerous animals reside in the warm neutral quartertones—that's where we need to see best.

Unfortunately, our methods of adding contrast and sharpness don't understand this concept. They add definition everywhere, unless, of course, they operate through an inverted copy of Ersatz Black or something similar.

Think about it. The inverted copy is light in neutral areas, dark in colored ones. If we use it as a mask while we sharpen or add detail some other way the added snap will go just where we want it. And it will not confuse the issue by monkeying with strongly colored objects.

By coincidence, Chapter 15 happens to cover this very topic, optimizing sharpening, and this kind of mask is a prime feature. There is accordingly no need for a sharpening example here. Instead, I'll show the reverse.

The Blackness of the Bokeh Polka

In the first half of this chapter I complained about a foreign phrase that means whatever the listener wants it to. The target of my wrath then happened to be Italian; we now turn attention to Japanese.

The word in question is *bokeh.* Its precise meaning, as far as I can determine, is, "there's something wrong with this picture because certain irrelevant garbage is competing for attention with what I'm trying to portray and I would like to delete it or blur it or pour bleach on it or send an exploding cigar to the photographer, but sink me if I know how to do any of these things, so it's up to you, and if you can't do it to my satisfaction then I will condemn you to my colleagues for your lack of grasp of bokeh."

That's what it means today (and the beta readers emphatically concur), but I think it *used* to mean that many pictures look better with a somewhat blurry background. You may recall that I had some difficulty grasping this concept in one of my corrections shown in the last chapter, the abysmal Figure 12.17A.

Before the digital days this effect was photographic. If the depth of field was shallow and the background distant, the desired fuzziness would be there. The problem nowadays is how to emulate that effect when the photographer has already shot the background in focus.

The current picture is a candidate for this kind of treatment. The subject is the collection of brilliant alabaster eggs. Irrelevant stuff in the background competes with it. I would think about flexing some bokeh muscles here.

Adding such an effect is tricky no matter what you try, but an inverted Ersatz Black can make it easier. Again, our opinion of sharpness, focus, depends more on what we perceive in dull areas than in vivid ones. Blur the neutrals and the lack of focus seems natural. Blur things with strong colors and it just looks weird.

Photoshop has a couple of nice new blurs that attempt to emulate lens effects. For simplicity, though, I'll just use Gaussian blur here.

The start point is Figure 13.16A, with MMM + Color Boost already having been applied to a base file of Figure 13.15E.

- I now can produce a better Ersatz Black. If I previously saved the one shown in Figure 13.15B, I trash it. Because the current file is more colorful than the original was, running the action again will generate a more extreme Ersatz Black, with less weight in strongly colored areas. Obviously, I specify this time that the channel is to be saved. I ignore the rest of the action, turning off the H-K layer group and flattening the file. So the current state is Figure 13.16A, with an improved Ersatz Black channel in reserve.

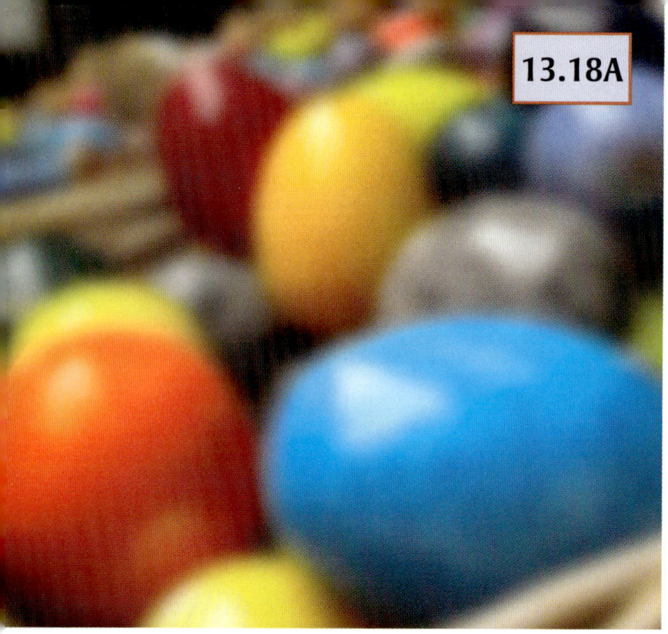

- I make a duplicate layer, to which I apply a robust Gaussian blur of 12 pixels, producing Figure 13.18A. Does it really seem like this is going anywhere?
- To prove a point, I now load the new Ersatz Black channel as a layer mask. Figure 13.18B, the result, is ridiculous because the color is being blurred heavily and the neutrals less so.

Figure 13.18 *Top, on a duplicate layer, Figure 13.16A is blurred heavily. Middle left, a newly produced Ersatz Black channel is loaded as a layer mask, making matters worse. Middle right, the layer mask is inverted, restricting the blur effect to more neutral areas. Bottom left, the layer mask is blurred. Bottom right, the original (Figure 13.15A) is repeated for convenience.*

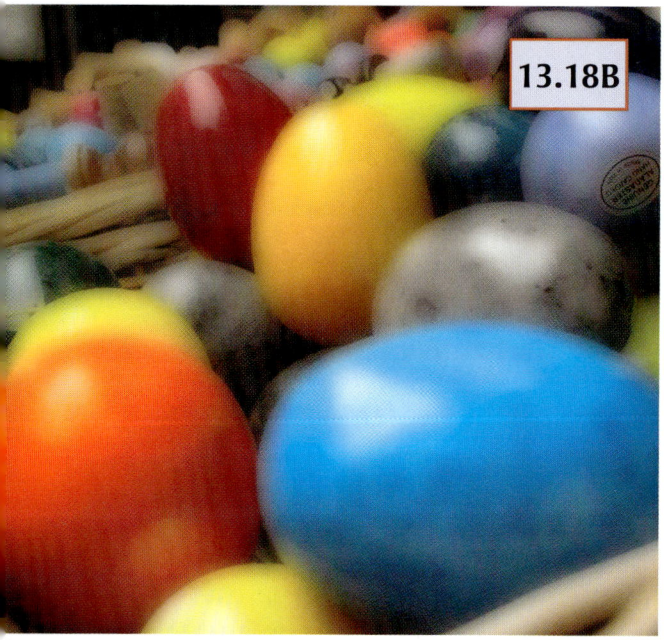

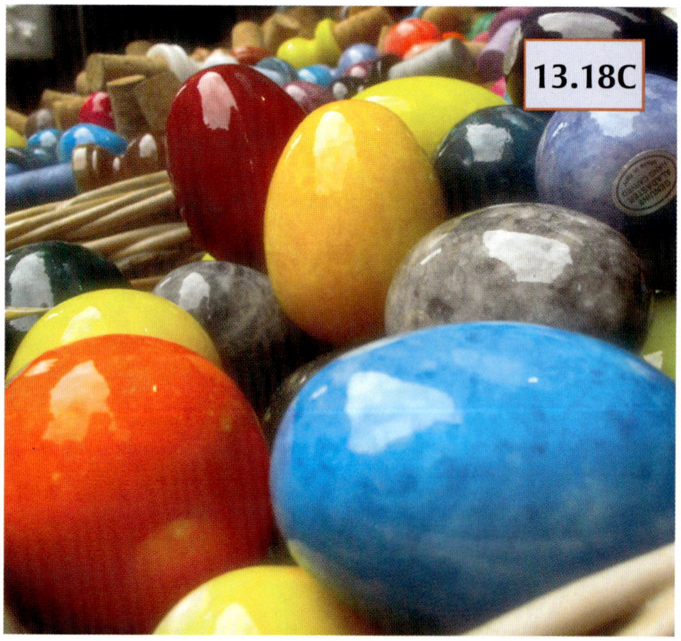

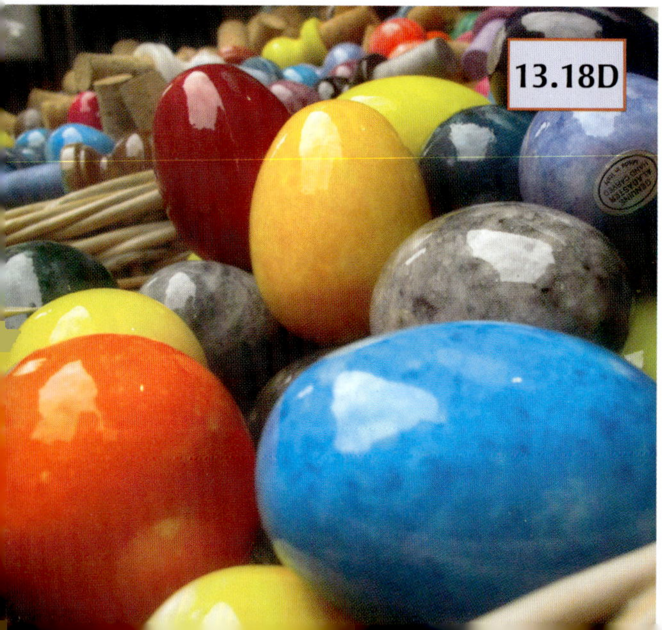

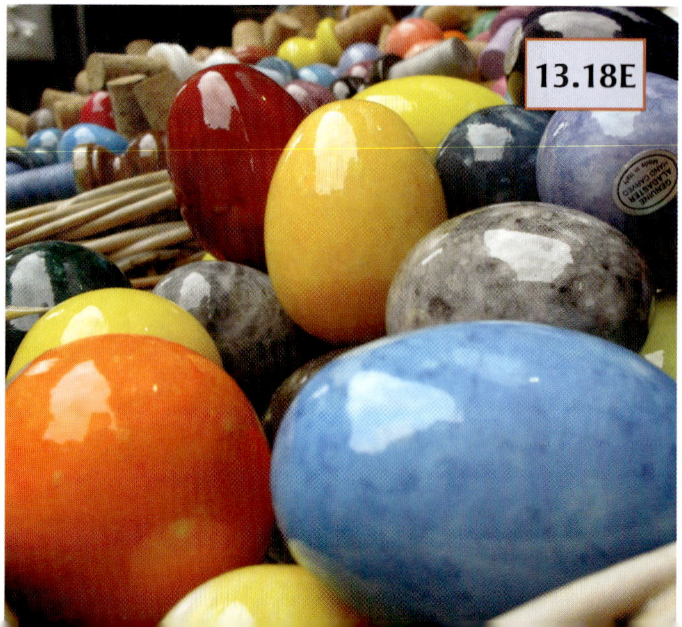

- With that nonsense out of the way, I invert the layer mask, producing Figure 13.18C, which is more like it.
- Reminder, though, that two layers so very different in contrast call for a big blur of the layer mask. I choose the same 12-pixel Gaussian blur as previously, and get Figure 13.18D.

I would say that these last moves have made the eggs more prominent and everything else less so. For ease in comparison, I now repeat the original, Figure 13.15A, as 13.18E. I hope you agree that (assuming the blur of the background to be a priority) Figure 13.18D is more successful. It took only three basic steps to create it: an H-K run using the Color Only layer, which enabled a more effective MMM + Color Boost layer, and the blurring business just discussed.

This exercise should pique your interest in the many uses of blacks, bogus and otherwise. As this is the last chapter that is uniquely PPW (the next two being related, but not essential, matters) it is time to examine again whether all these new techniques produce better results than the old ways. We have ways of checking.

Raise a Glass to a Better Way

Figure 13.19 is no postcard, and not a tourism photo, either. Instead, like the earlier Figure 13.12 it is a studio shot for advertising, this time in magazines. The product is the sparkling wine. The food is supposed to look appetizing, too, but it is not the focus of attention.

This kind of file used to be bread and butter for professional retouchers. A gang of money gets spent on the photography, the advertising agency, and the magazine insertions. Quarrels about how much time it takes to correct the color are uncommon.

Consequently, this exercise went into my book *Professional Photoshop Fifth Edition* (2006). The correction I offered then is reprinted here as Figure 13.19B. It does not measure up to Figure 13.19C, which I just did in less time that it took me in 2006, to judge by the description of the steps in that book.

I have no apology to make for Figure 13.19B, in view of its time frame. It received scads of reader compliments and the photographer's endorsement. Furthermore, this original has been one of the exercises in my advanced color correction classes for many years. It wasn't easy back in the old days. Figure 13.19B stood as the best effort by anybody until late 2008.

Classes today, however, have no trouble leaving it in the dust. The final four versions of Figure 13.19 were voted the best from my 2011-12 advanced classes. I dislike Figure 13.19F's color choice, and Figure 13.19D is heavy-handed in dark areas, particularly the sauce. Both, however, are competitive with, if not better, than Figure 13.19B. The remaining two are much better than that 2006 version. Figure 13.19G is my own favorite of the student-prepared files.

The components show the progression of technique. The wine, being yellowish, has most contrast in the blue channel. That can be blended slightly into the other two to make the bubbles more pronounced. People have known how to do such blending for a decade. So, looking only at the beverage, Figure 13.19B holds its own with the modern versions. The sparkle is well defined, much better than the original.

Color, alas, is another story. Early versions of Man from Mars did poorly in pictures featuring neutrals, as this one does. The color variation found in every other correction except Figure 13.19F separates the wine from the background. Putting any of the other four modern versions on top of Figure 13.19B and changing mode to Color would make a big-time improvement.

We know a bit more about color today than in 2011, but I can't claim color superiority for my Figure 13.19C over the four student versions. I do say it beats them in two respects. First, even if the food is not the most important thing, it still plays a role, and the food in Figure 13.19C is superior to any other. Second, awkward shadows fall on the foil. The riband (black logo strip), a critical element, is more legible in Figure 13.19C than in the others.

The Role of False CMYK

These two gains were provided by H-K and a similar action that we haven't discussed yet. It is called False CMYK. Heed that name. It is a temporary stop only, not for printing. Instead it is assumed that you will convert back to RGB or LAB once you have taken advantage of what this CMYK has to offer, which is a black channel designed for dramatic moves.

False CMYK is well documented within the PPW panel, so I will give only a brief summary. Its most common use is as an adjunct to Chapter 12's method, which applies a false profile to lighten the

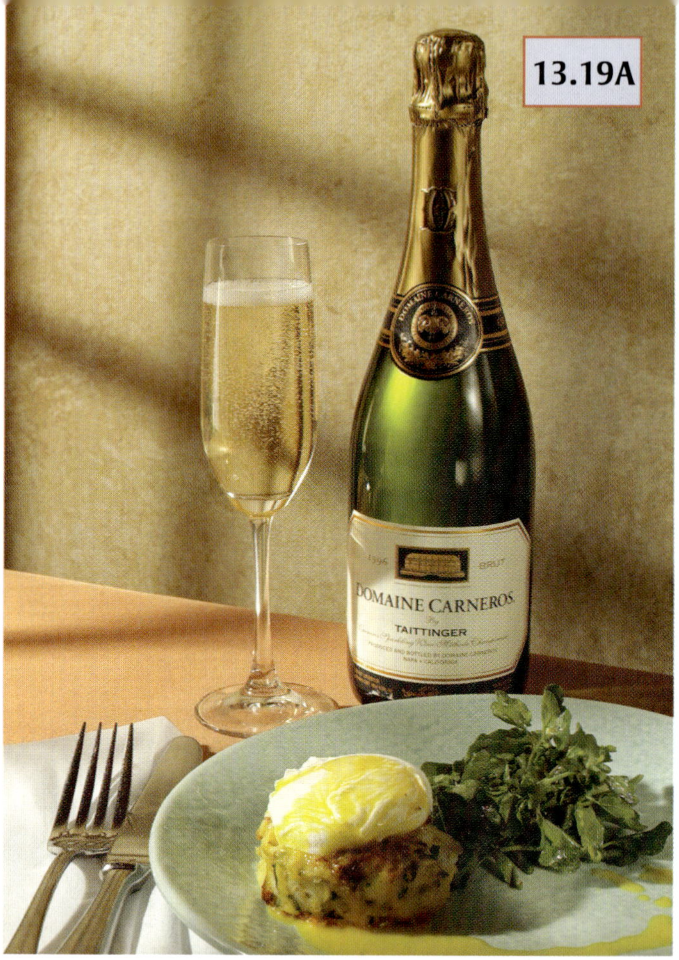

Figure 13.19 *Top, the original is for magazine advertising of the wine. Bottom left, as corrected in the 2006 book Professional Photoshop Fifth Edition. Bottom right, as corrected today. Opposite, advanced retouchers used this as a classroom exercise in 2011 and 2012. These are the four best results from about thirty entrants.*

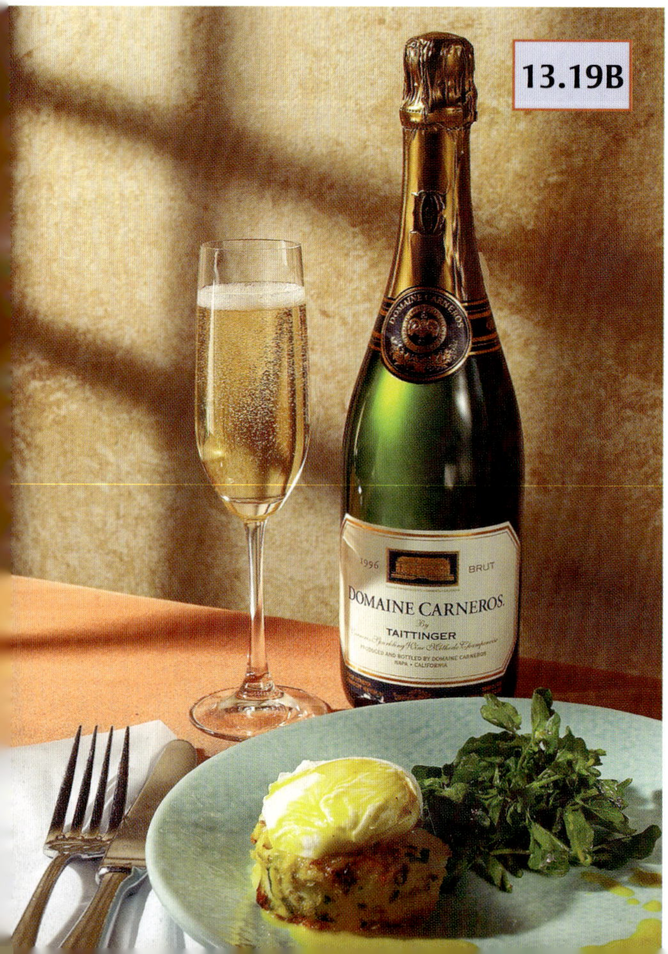

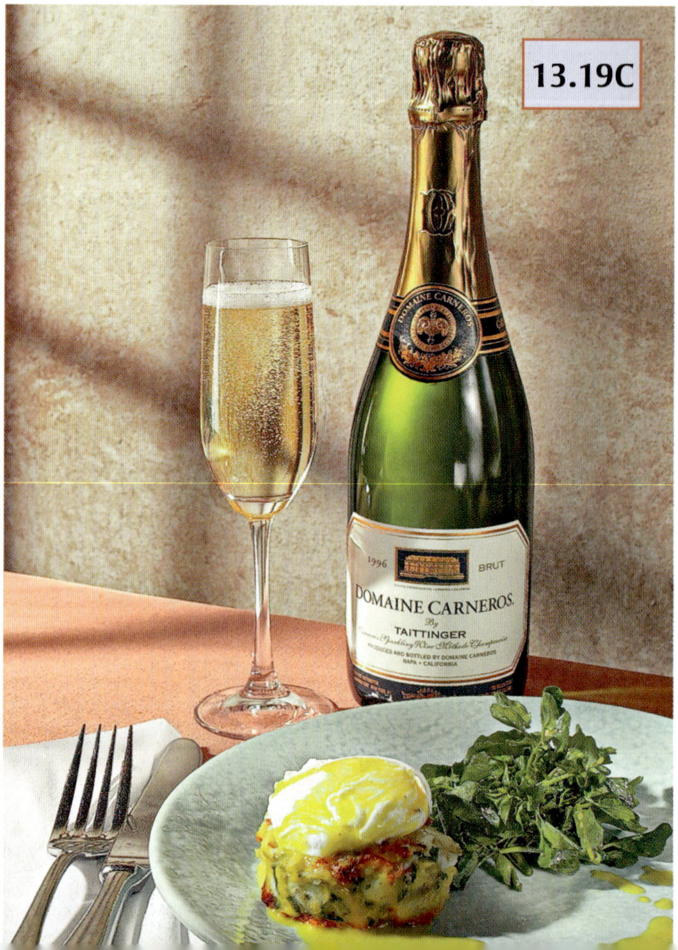

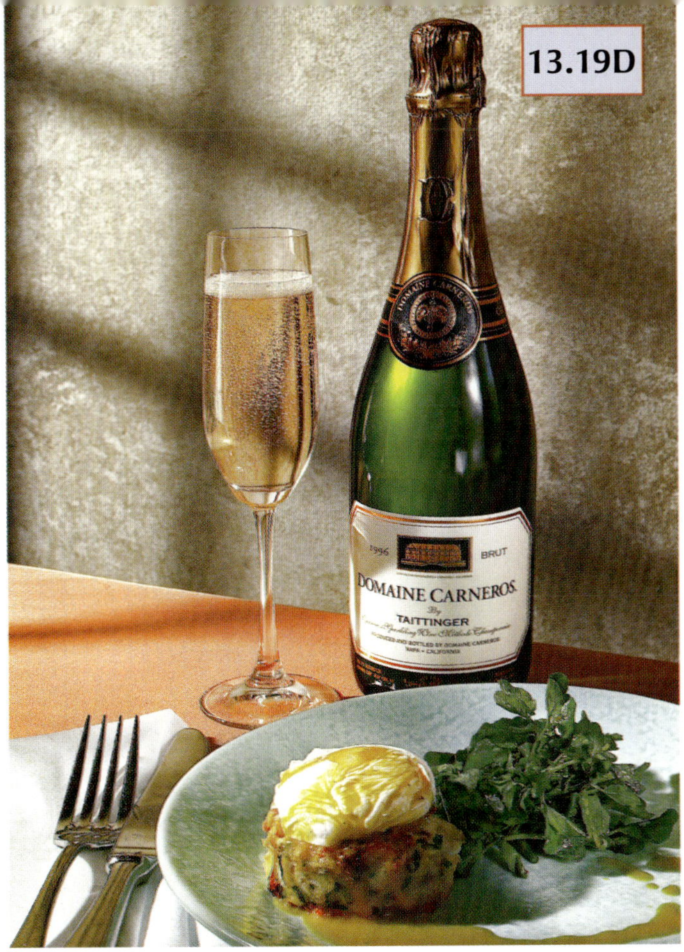

13.19D

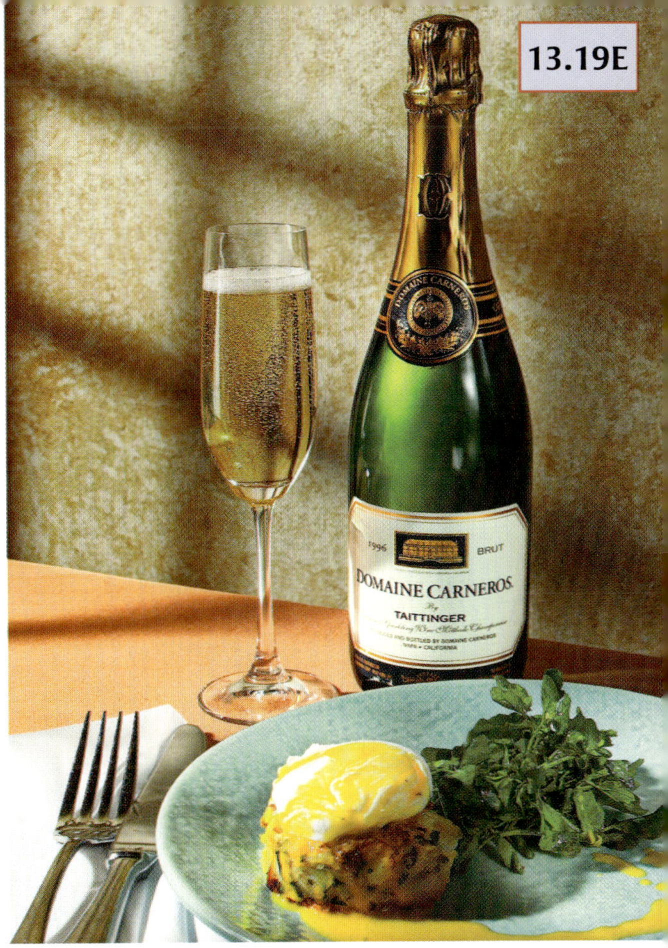

13.19E

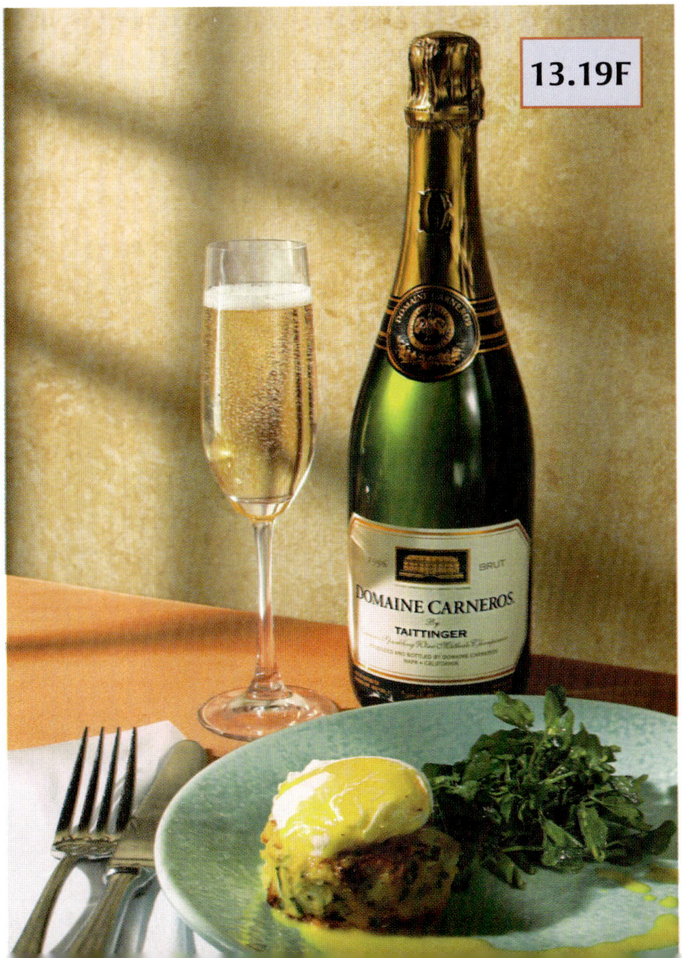

13.19F

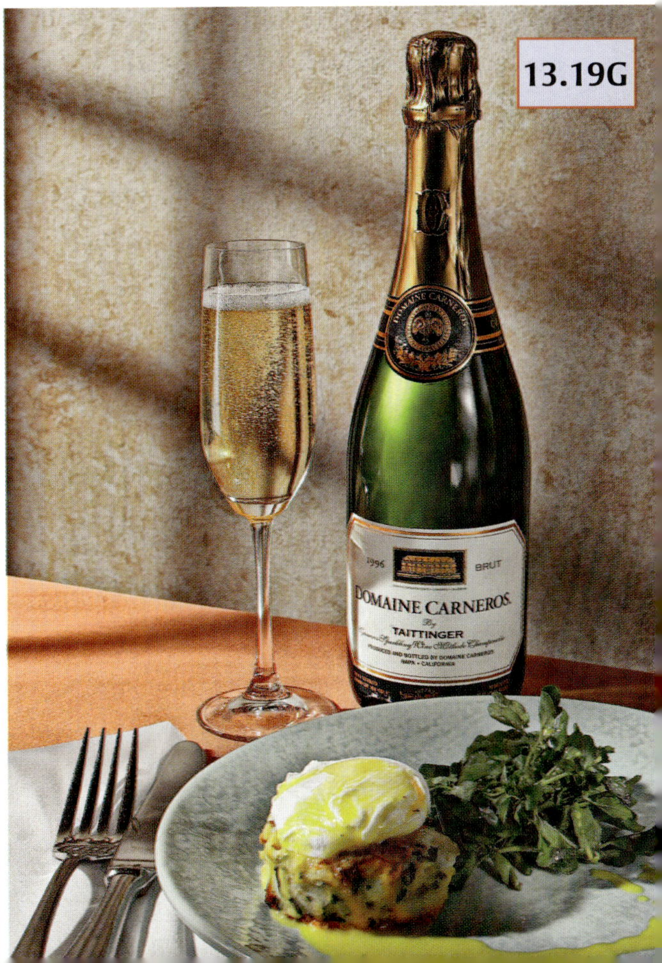

13.19G

picture, then multiplies through a blurred layer mask.

As explained in Chapter 12, the Exposure command can be used as a substitute for a false profile. And although you can access the false profile routines from within the PPW panel, they aren't part of the action set. The reason: to assign the proper false profile requires knowing what you have chosen for RGB workspace within Color Settings. The PPW panel has access to this information, but simple actions do not. Without the panel, you could only use an action I provided if your RGB workspace happens to match mine. It's no big deal: you can always write your own action, as only a few steps are involved.

To prepare an RGB file for False CMYK, either assign your own false profile or click one of the PPW scripts and discard the multiply layer. The result looks washed out, but nevertheless click the False CMYK button.

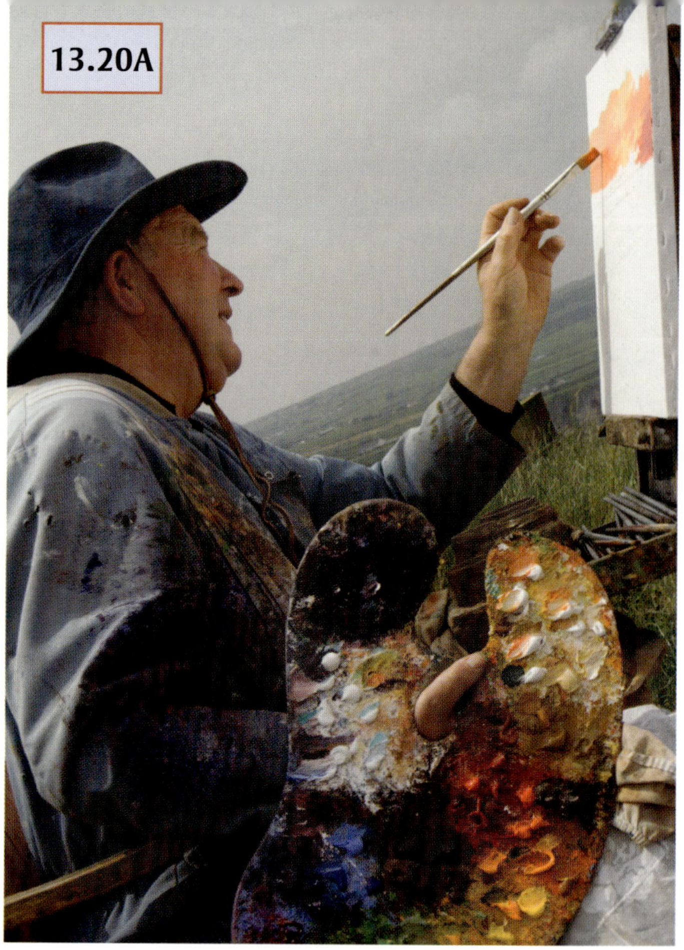

***Figure 13.20** Top, the original. Opposite top left, a correction that uses H-K to emphasize vivid paint colors. The other three versions are from an experts-only class in 2009.*

The darkest point of the resulting CMYK image remains much too light. To compensate, apply a steep curve to the black channel. This move enhances contrast more dramatically than H-K. It is good when shadow detail is critical.

The problem is that when we darken so drastically using only a black channel, the image looks thin even though its endpoints may be correct. So, normally we move back into RGB for a multiplication through a blurred layer mask.

I doubted that this would be a good approach for this subject. I was deathly afraid that the blacks might plug, and I knew I would have other ways to darken the image later. So I tried a combined strategy.

- Initial color moves to reduce yellowness and add redness.
- Blends to emphasize the beverage.
- Shadows/Highlights.
- The H-K action, retaining the Ersatz Black channel, but throwing away everything else. The file itself does not change.
- The strongest false profile, 1.0 gamma. The PPW panel's script inserts an automatic multiplying layer. To its layer mask, I apply not a standard channel but the Ersatz Black that I saved earlier. The result is a picture slightly lighter overall than the original but much lighter in the dark neutrals.
- And now, the False CMYK action, followed by a big curve boosting the black channel. This type of curve, shown on the final page of the chapter as Figure 13.21, is what accounts for the extra detail in the crabcake and the dark label. There is no need for multiplying afterward.
- MMM + Color Boost, sharpen, and Save.

All this took careful planning and a certain amount of time. Now let's show something much simpler, with the same result.

13.20B

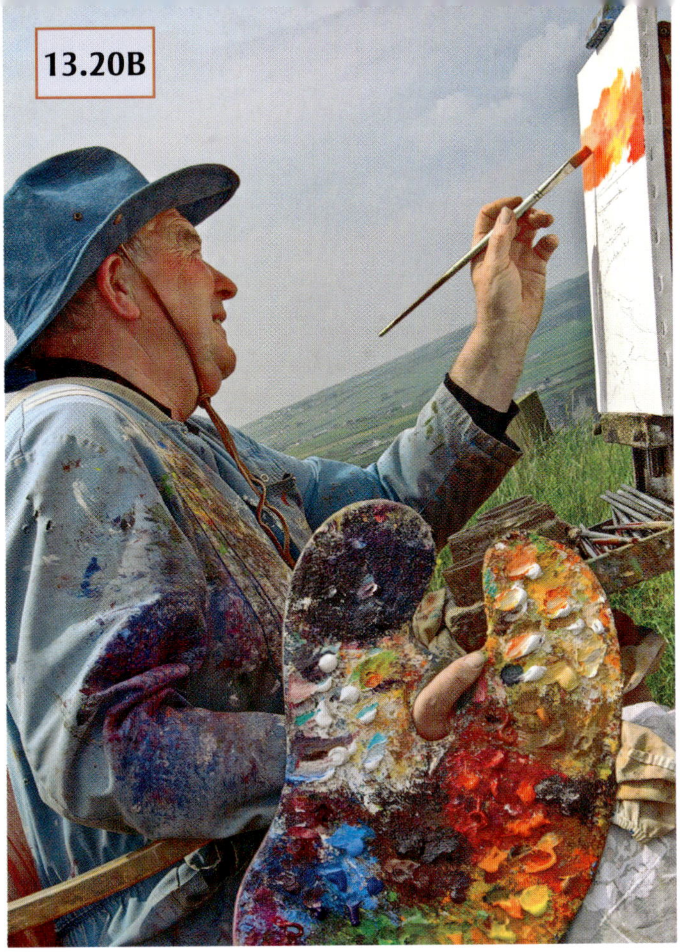

13.20C

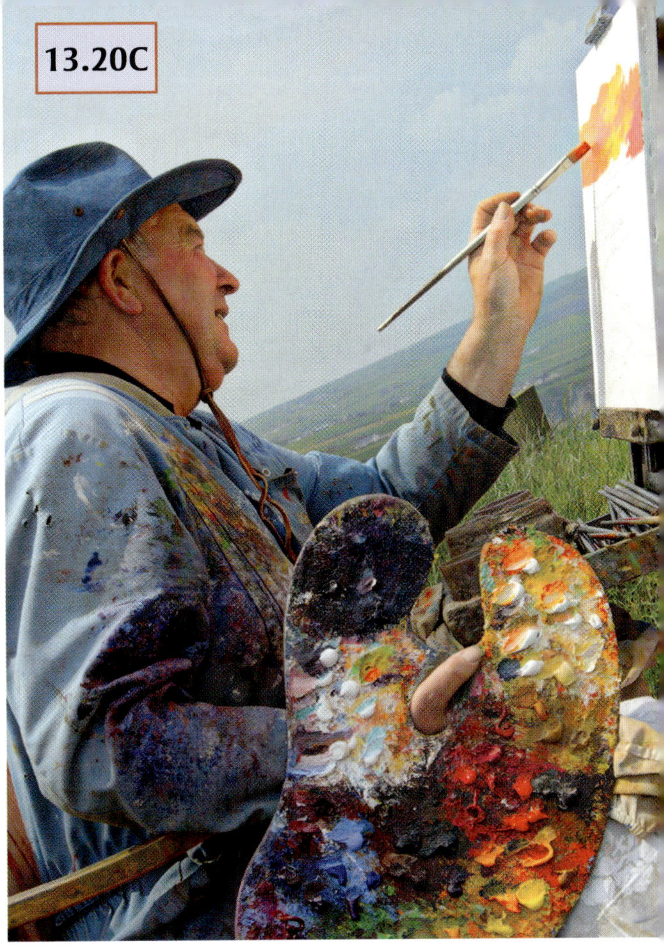

13.20D

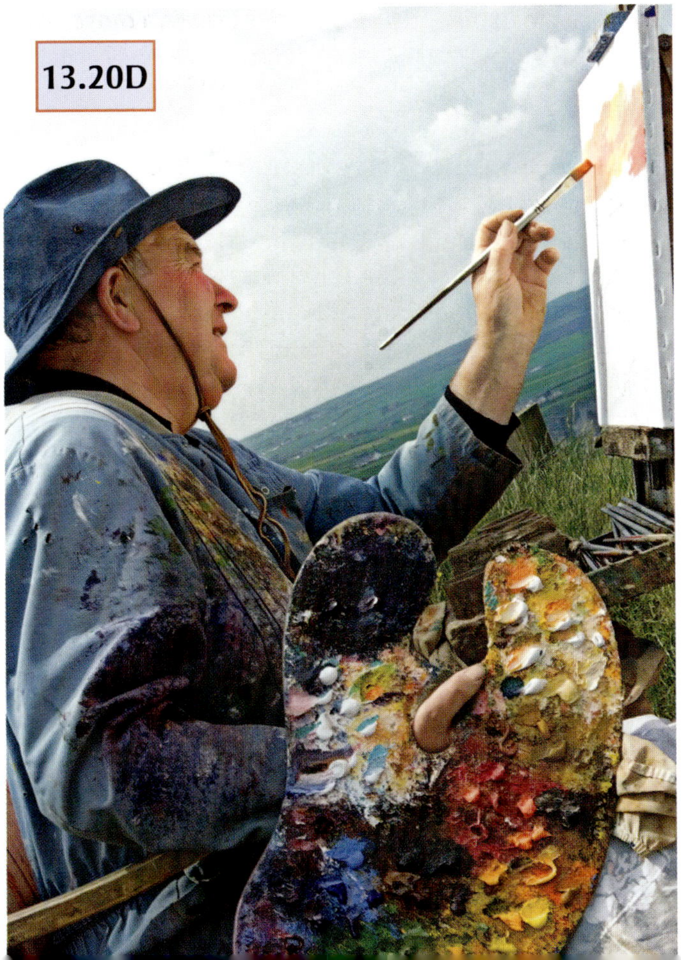

13.20E

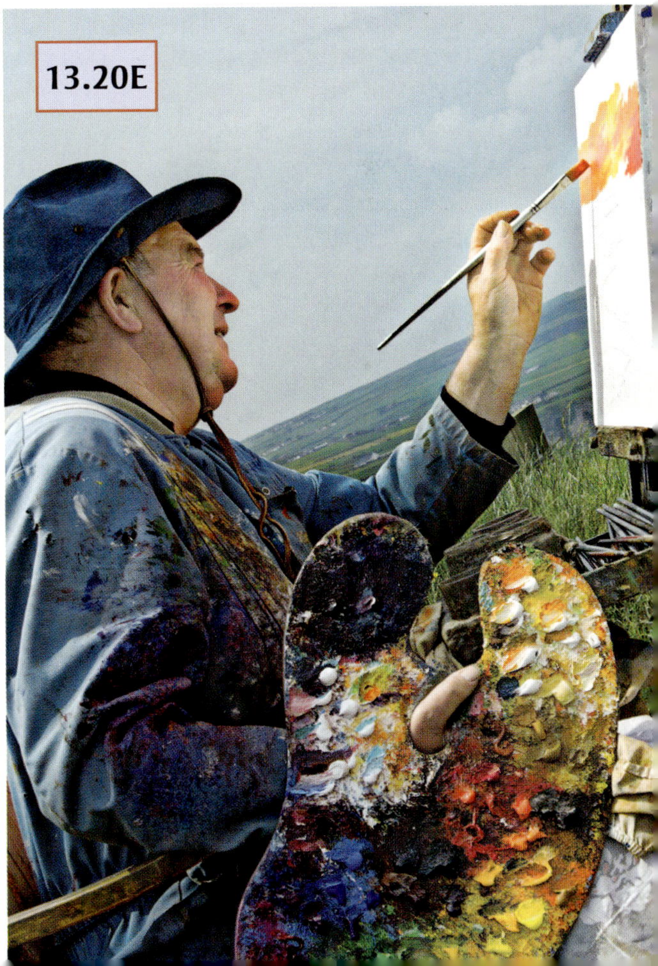

Of Painting and Pixels

Figure 13.20A is the start point for an exercise in the same 2009 superadvanced class that worked on the Burmese wedding image of Figure 12.17. Unlike that picture, I was a winner with this one, albeit with an entrant that falls short by today's standards.

Figure 13.20B is what I produced today (in 2012) in about a minute. Figure 13.20C took me twenty times that long in 2009, and it isn't as good. The other two were my competition back then. Figure 13.20D is a worthy opponent. Many attendees liked Figure 13.20E, but I don't, although I agree it is a huge improvement over the original.

Everybody came up with similar contrast although some of the channel blending caused differences in the weight of the sky and the face. The four corrections are not identical in their choice of overall color, but they are closer in that respect than were the variants of the wine image of Figure 13.19.

There is really only one problem in this picture, and it's a big one. All sorts of internal clues point to this man having an unusually red face. Figure 13.20E goes way overboard in trying to compensate, in my view. The other three seem to me more accurate for the skin.

It would not do to make him any redder, but unfortunately some of the paint is supposed to be brilliant. Any move to saturate it is likely to leave the face completely unacceptable, and maybe the smock, too.

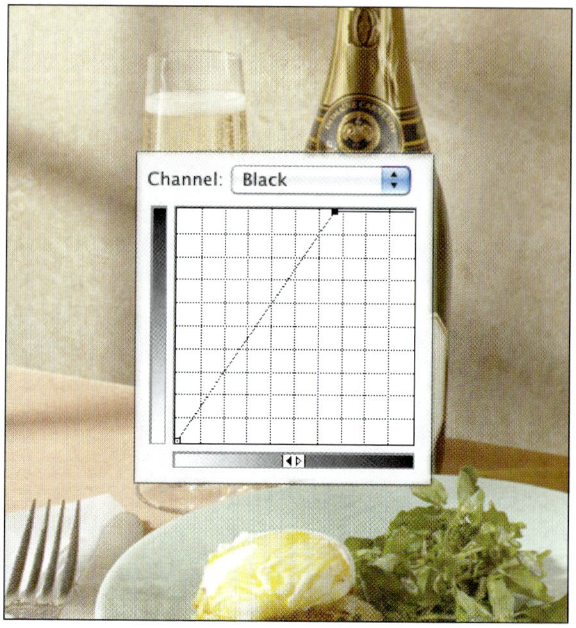

***Figure 13.21** The type of black curve generally applied after playing the False CMYK action.*

None of the three 2009 winners solved the problem. Their paint was too subdued. Only Figure 13.20B has bright paint and acceptable skin. (Because two beta readers challenged that last statement, I reiterate what I said a short time ago: examination of the original should persuade us that this man has much redder skin than the average Caucasian, and furthermore some blotchy areas that are even redder.)

The reasons for today's superiority are the H-K and Skin Desaturation actions, neither of which existed in 2009. Both suppress duller colors while leaving the paint alone. There was nothing remarkable about my workflow here, which is why it only took a minute. Both H-K and Skin Desaturation were applied at their defaults; I saw no need for further adjustments. Once they had done their work I was able to use much stronger settings in MMM + Color Boost.

The composer has his music, the painter his canvas. The tools develop, the artistic sensibility grows, and the result improves year by year, decade by decade. So let it be with us.

The Bottom Line

The H-K action described in this chapter emphasizes brighter areas by darkening and desaturating duller ones. Doing this is not always effective but it distinctly improves many pictures, particularly in combination with later color enhancement.

The action employs an alpha channel that is similar to the black of CMYK. Similar channels have many other uses in color correction. The second half of the chapter discusses some of them.

14

etaoin shrdlu And Its Progeny

The history of the graphic arts is one of new technologies displacing older ones. For each successful innovation, however, several dozen proposed ones failed, normally because they didn't improve on existing methods. Today's raw modules may fall in either camp.

Ottmar Mergenthaler's invention, the Linotype, was incredibly slow and tedious in comparison to, say, InDesign CS6, but thousands of times faster than the previous method of arranging letters by hand. It was therefore one of the most significant advances in our cultural history, for it made the modern newspaper possible.

Linotypes nevertheless required armies of operators to produce modest amounts of type. Working conditions were brutal. The technology was called *hot type* for a reason. Working in a room where lots of lead was being noisily melted down was physically challenging, and required lifting and moving heavy forms. It was an all-male field.

Accuracy was important. No Command–Z existed for an operator who hit the wrong key. The entire line had to be reset directly beneath it, and the proofreader manually removed the one with the error.

The operator tried to help the proofreader out by making his mistakes obvious. He would fill the rest of an errant line by running his finger down the leftmost and then the second leftmost line of keys. Those particular keys were lower-case only, and formed the iconic phrase *etaoin shrdlu.*

* * *

Linotype machines ruled typesetting for seventy unpleasant years, beginning in about 1890. As soon as an alternative became available, the industry jumped at it. That alternative was the computer, at a time when most people had no idea what a computer was. Typography developed into the first fully computerized industry, largely because it made only tiny demands on the impossibly slow computers of the 1960s. Consequently, it became possible to set type professionally, much faster than ever before, a quarter century before one could do the equivalent with images. There were growing pains, as always when a new technology takes over. How to design the keyboard was one big issue. Engineers at Harris-Intertype Corp., which marketed the first phototypesetting system, thought the answer was obvious. The current generation of typesetting professionals will be the likely operators of this new product; these professionals are all trained on Linotype keyboards. Therefore, we will use the etaoin shrdlu layout!

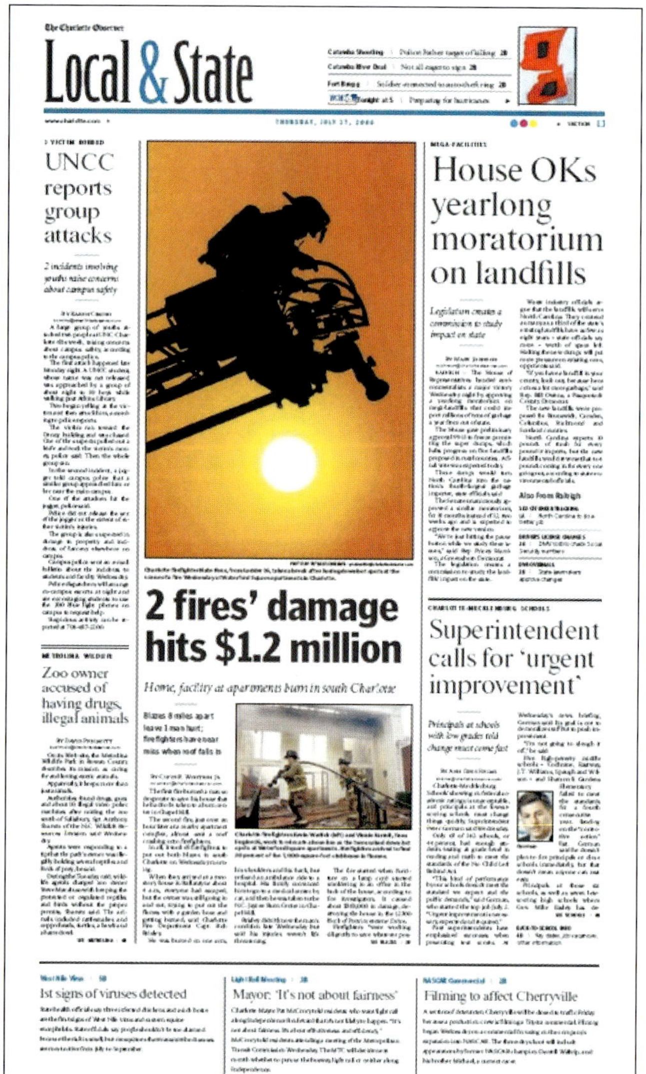

Local & State

UNCC reports group attacks

2 incidents involving youths raise concerns about campus safety

House OKs yearlong moratorium on landfills

Legislation creates a commission to study impact on state

2 fires' damage hits $1.2 million

Home, facility at apartments burn in south Charlotte

Zoo owner accused of having drugs, illegal animals

Superintendent calls for 'urgent improvement'

Principals at schools with low grades told change must come fast

1st signs of viruses detected

Mayor: 'It's not about fairness'

Filming to affect Cherryville

***Figure 14.1** Alleged overenthusiasm in correcting the sunset and firefighter image cost the photographer his job.*

This reasoning left something to be desired. Linotypes cast their type as the operator keyed it. If he typed even remotely as fast as we do today, he would outrun the machine and make it jam. Solution: slow him down by putting the most frequently used letters in the far corners. Hence, etaoin shrdlu.

It did not occur to these engineers that there was no longer any point in so handcuffing the operator; that their devices would soon be used mostly in settings that resembled offices rather than factories; that this would open up the field to tens of thousands of potential employees (and cheaper ones, to boot) who knew how to use a keyboard whose top line of letters starts with QWERTY but not one whose left side reads etaoin shrdlu.

etaoin shrdlu Rides Into a Sunset

Fast forward forty years, to 2006. The main photo on the page of Figure 14.1 was taken by a member of the newspaper's staff who specialized in fire images and had won prizes for some of his shots. Our previous chapter repeated a question that we've heard before: how much color is too much? Well, according to the newspaper, *this* much color is too much. So they fired the photographer!

This attack of etaoin shrdlu Syndrome came about when the photographer deliberately underexposed the shot, leaving it very dark. He was worried that he would lose the shape of the sun otherwise. He knew he could restore the color and brilliance later. He did not care that he would lose all detail in the firefighter, whom he had already decided would be a silhouette only.

Here's the newspaper's version, in an article informing readers of the firing.

> In the original photo, the sky in the photo was brownish-gray. Enhanced with photo-editing software, the sky became a deep red and the sun took on a more distinct halo.

> [The newspaper's] photo policy states: "No colors will be altered from the original scene photographed."
>
> [The photographer] said he did not intend to mislead readers, only to restore the actual color of the sky. He said the color was lost when he underexposed the photo to offset the glare of the sun.

The policy is ambiguous, so we don't know whether it tilts at windmills or is merely the stupidest journalistic move in 58 years. If it is to be read as not allowing variation from the original *photograph,* it's the latter. Newspaper photography is frequently shot under terrible lighting conditions. The Christmas decoration original of Figure 13.9A, also from a newspaper, is a good example. Published photos are often shot by reporters who would not know an f-stop from a lens cap. And even if a pro is shooting, a fire image is likely to start with a cast. Another newspaper fire shot showed that, back in Figure 10.9A. Failing to correct for the color imbalance would make the newspaper look ridiculous.

If, on the other hand, the policy means that the colors must match the original *scene,* not the photograph, it is no more enforceable than an edict that all days shall be sunny whenever a news event needs shooting. Who is to judge, since the scene can't be imported into the newsroom for inspection and comparison? Certainly these numbskull editors shouldn't be involved. Read their quote again: "the sky in the photo was brownish-gray."

You don't have to be a Helmholtz to understand that a sky featuring so strong a sun cannot possibly be brownish-gray. Plus, we have the photographer's statement that he intentionally shot the scene too dark with the intent of correcting back to something like this.

This firing produced a lot of online commentary from photographers. Incredibly, close to half of them thought that the newspaper's position was justifiable, though some found the punishment harsh.

Several argued that the standard should be whether the effect could have been achieved in a darkroom. If not, they said, it isn't the photographer's traditional role and at least he should have notified the newspaper before doing it.

Those saying this were etaoin shrdluists. But the real significance is that the shooter's strategy was an early example of a way of thinking that was uncommon back then but is a major part of the PPW today.

By underexposing, the photographer made the file look worse, in order to make it look better later. It was an unusual practice for the time, but no more. The techniques of the last two chapters—the false profile scripts and the H-K action—both make the file look worse temporarily but enable a final image that would be hard to achieve otherwise.

We're no longer in 2006, and we do have a professional newspaper photographer on the beta reading team. Russ Brown comments, "All well put! This is a subject close to home and I agree wholeheartedly with your assessment. In my view, the shooter did entirely the correct thing and what I would have done myself. It merely demonstrates that he knows his job!"

Ridiculing the editors is so easy that it can hide the complexity of two underlying issues. Both are critical to the topic of this chapter, which is how to use raw modules.

First, the photographer's philosophy, which Russ endorsed, cannot be limited to moves that actively make the picture look worse. More often, it requires us to decline what seems to be a tempting opportunity to make things better, so as not to pre-empt a more effective correction later.

Second, the editors' criticism was basically that the photographer departed excessively from the original. Today's problem: just what *is* that original?

Definitions and Objectives

Traditional cameras delivered film. Digitizing required a scanner.

Today each camera is its own scanner. It produces a digital file in a standard format, commonly JPEG.

The better cameras have another option, which is to deliver a file in a format today described as *raw.* Such files cannot be opened directly in Photoshop or similar programs; a separate module is required, one capable of decoding output from the specific camera. The most well-known is Adobe's Camera Raw, which is bundled with Photoshop.

Disadvantage: It takes extra time to deal with a raw file, since it almost invariably has to be worked on in Photoshop as well.

Advantages: Camera manufacturers want their JPEGs to look good right out of the box. Behind-the-scenes correcting therefore goes on. The JPEGs usually get delivered with a full tonal range even if the original exposure was flat. Often they also favor vivid colors. These tweaks usually work, but sometimes they don't. In that case, the damage can be difficult or impossible to repair. The raw file bypasses these automated corrections, allowing us to make sure that any idiocies in the handling of the image are our own and not those of a brainless algorithm.

* * *

Whether to shoot raw in the first place is beyond the ambit of the present work; we just need to know how to work with raw files when we get them. A comparison of raw converters is not going to be forthcoming, either. I have worked with many, and have tentative opinions of which are currently best, but the field is changing so rapidly that it would be a waste of space to discuss them.

Most specifics of Camera Raw will be put off until the second half. You should be aware, however, that it changed considerably with the 2012 release of Photoshop CS6.

Any raw file definitely must be opened inside the raw module, because Photoshop itself can't. The question is how many other features to use. The recommended answer is, not too many. The reason for the recommendation: etaoin shrdlu.

Changes in Camera Raw

The Camera Raw module was introduced in Photoshop 7, back in 2002. Its methods of color correction stayed basically the same for the next decade, although some new features were added.

With Photoshop CS6 the features that interest us were overhauled and improved. Channel curves were added. Some sliders remained the same, others were either removed or renamed because they no longer operate in the same way as before. The new Basic layout is more logical. All slider default values are now 0. Where possible, they work on a scale from −100 to +100. When sliders are moved to the right, the image lightens, when to the left, it darkens.

The changes are discussed in detail in the second half of the chapter. Meanwhile, when necessary we'll use CR-CS6 to indicate the new behavior, and CR-CS5 for the way it's been in previous versions.

The More Things Change...

Color correction technique has improved drastically in the last quarter-century, except the most basic thing of all. We still have to set a shadow and a highlight, just as we did in Photoshop 15 years ago, or with a drum scanner 25 years ago.

Or, for that matter, with a paintbrush 500 years ago. By that time, painters had learned that every picture, with rare exceptions, needs something approximately white (or an off-white of similar darkness) and something else approximately black. This practice carried over into the age of engravings and then halftone printing.

A painter, an engraver, a darkroom technician, a dot etcher, a scanner operator, and a digital retoucher all evaluate individual images and make decisions about highlight and shadow points based on experience and common sense. A camera, or at least its hardware component, doesn't. It must be prepared to record detail in excruciatingly light things and also excruciatingly dark ones. No scene is likely to exhibit both extremes at once; in fact it is unlikely to contain either. So, if the whitest whites and darkest blacks are reserved for the lightest and darkest things that cameras can distinguish, every picture is going to come out desperately flat.

This returns us to a question as thorny as it is simple, and as underdiscussed as it is thorny. *What is the original?*

I say the original is the file as delivered to us prior to any human intervention. This statement sounds more definitive than it actually is.

The camera transfers no color, no channels, no sharpness into the raw file, only a slew of data that needs to be decoded and assembled. Each raw converter does this slightly differently, so each one spits out a different file.

The camera *does* pass on information about any ambient color cast that it has detected. We normally call this *white balance*, an inaccurate but acceptable term. Raw modules try to use this information, so I consider the white balance to be part of the original. Any adjustment beyond that, however, is not. The light point of the actual file is presumably much darker than the hypothetically whitest point that could ever be recorded. Since that hypothetical white would have to be set to the whitest possible value, namely $255^R255^G255^B$, the "white" of the current file needs to be much darker. Leaving it that way, however, has the unfortunate side effect of making the image look like crap. And the same goes for the treatment of the darkest point. Without intervention, it will be much lighter than it should be, as the camera reserves darker tones for things that don't exist in the current scene.

Such a file looks worse than a camera-generated JPEG. It looks worse than a drum scan from the 1980s. In short, it looks worse than anything called an "original" at any time in the past. While you and I and good photographers everywhere perhaps understand that the past is the past and the present is tomorrow, the average viewer does not.

Beta reader James Gray: "I love your question 'What is the original?' If I tweak camera controls that are designed to 'improve' saturation, sharpness, and contrast, is that human intervention? If I create a script to apply the Auto correction in Camera Raw before I ever looked at the files, would that be human intervention? Suppose I did not automate it and just as a matter of habit applied the Auto setting to all my images without looking at them, would that be human intervention? I suspect we agree."

Figure 14.2A is a raw original, in the opinion of one of the converters. By historical standards it's horrible. A nonexpert viewer would conclude that the photographer, who is one of the most talented currently practicing, is seriously overrated.

Figure 14.2B demonstrates why setting the endpoints is mandatory. Sooner or later, that endpoint-setting has to be done. But before you start saying that there's no time like the present, two warnings.

- Drum scanner operators, in the days before the desktop revolution, had to set highlight and shadow immediately, because

Chapter Goals and Recap

Images shot in a raw format must be processed by a specialized module before they can be worked on in Photoshop. Camera Raw, which ships with Photoshop, is such a module.

The Picture Postcard Workflow is useful no matter how the file is acquired. However, it is more effective when the raw modules are used conservatively.

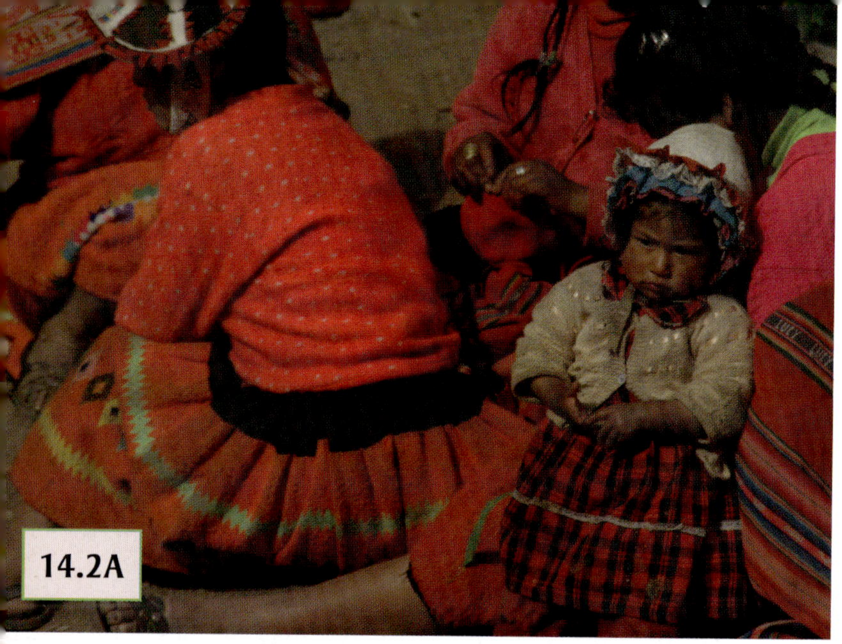

14.2A

if they didn't nobody else would later. We should therefore pay attention to the lesson of etaoin shrdlu: beware of doing things the way they've always been done, if there's never been an alternative to doing things that way.

- *Better* and *better-looking* are not synonyms. Figure 14.2B looks so superior to 14.2A as to provoke a misconception. That it is much better than a very bad thing does not prove that it is a very good thing. The truth is that Figure 14.2B is terrible, a common result when one tries to correct bright reds with a master curve. If you want a better file at the end of the day, start with Figure 14.2A.

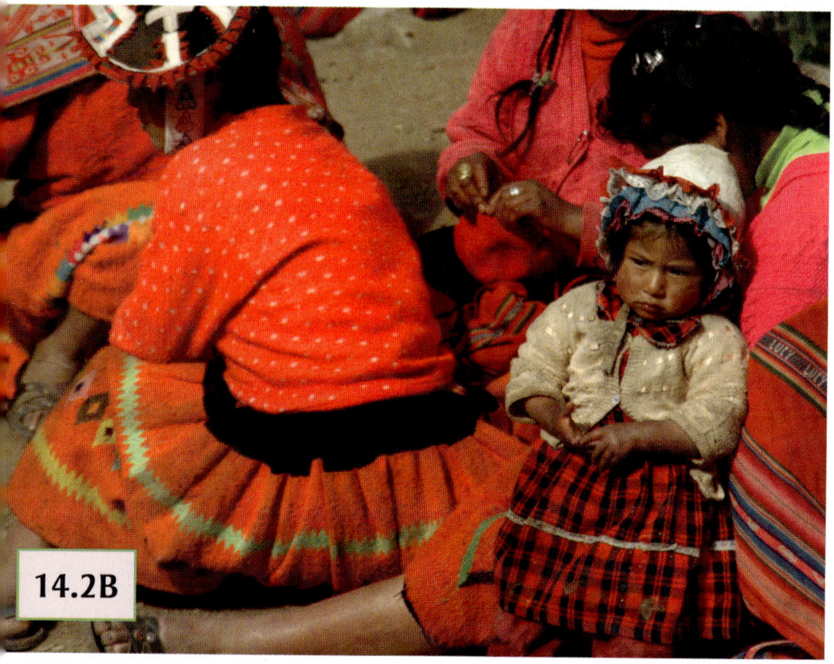

14.2B

A Solution That's Outdated

Building serious correction capabilities into raw modules is feasible, but at the moment all are etaoin shrdlu-ized, although some are at least looking at other alternatives.

Figure 14.2B isn't a perfect representation of past practice; master curves have never been a part of a serious workflow. Nevertheless it illustrates why the traditional way became the traditional way. One simple move produces what appears to be a major improvement.

The curve extends the range of every channel. This begets two happy consequences.

We expect to see better detail once light and dark points have been set. The girl's cap and jacket have become much lighter, increasing contrast.

The move also benefits color, though. As we know, equal values in the three RGB channels make a neutral. The further they get away from equality, the less neutral,

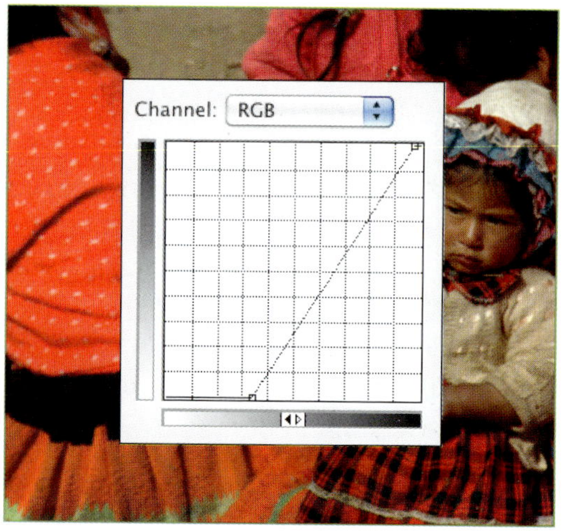

Figure 14.2 *Files acquired in a raw module are typically flat, above, unless correction controls within the module are activated. Below, the master curve shown establishes highlight and shadow, improving color and contrast simultaneously, but decreasing the chance that the final version will be a good one.*

the more colorful, things become. The bright reds and pinks of Figure 14.2B imply a very light red channel, which Figure 14.2A doesn't have. Forcing at least one channel to become very light and at least one other to become very dark seems a perfect solution. Better color, better contrast—what's not to like?

The questions are, do we really want this brighter color to happen by accident, or would we like to take control? Do we wish to handcuff ourselves by restricting contrast moves to those that don't damage color, or would we prefer to ignore color as we add detail?

* * *

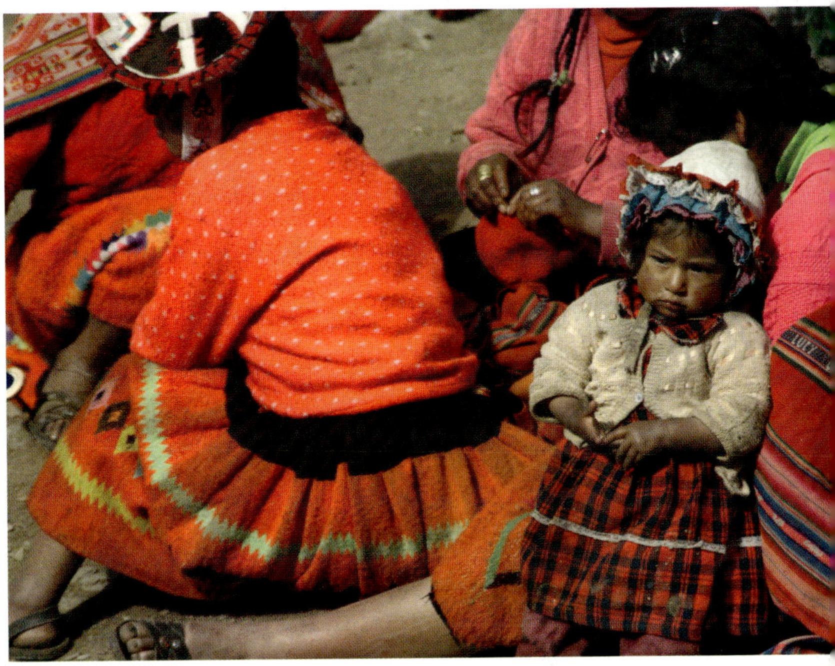

Figure 14.3 *Although the color of Figure 14.2B is good, there are better ways. Above, the MMM + Color Boost action is run on Figure 14.2A.*

The questions answer themselves, but even if they didn't Figure 14.3 would. It skips every intermediate PPW step and applies the MMM + Color Boost action, including manual color and endpoint adjustments, directly to Figure 14.2A. It wouldn't have been easy to get there had we fallen victim to the temptation to make things look better in the raw module. Our actions need room to operate. They're less effective when applied to something as colorful as Figure 14.2B.

Similar comments apply to contrast. Opening it up too early can pre-empt more powerful tools later.

Why Less Is Better

Today's raw modules can't get to Figure 14.3 because they don't separate color from contrast. Why not? Because it has never been done that way.

It has never been done that way because until recently it *couldn't* have been. My first book appeared in 1994, at the time of the introduction of Photoshop 3. Unless I've forgotten something, every single step to produce Figure 14.3B was feasible then, if anybody had known how to do it. There were no actions, so one would have had to do every step manually. There was no multiple undo or History palette, so backups would need to be made periodically to avoid losing the whole job in the event that an error wasn't noticed until it was too late to correct. Worst of all, today we are spoiled by having all our imaging whims fulfilled instantly, Back then, there would be a minute or two delay at each step while the tortoise computers of the epoch crunched the instructions.

I don't happen to have a 1994 computer at hand, or a copy of Photoshop 3, but I'd guess that getting to Figure 14.3 would have taken around three hours, rather than the thirty seconds it took me just now.

The techniques I advocated in 1994 were the best ones for that benighted time, and maybe for 2004 as well. But methods that were prohibitively time-consuming back then are reasonable today.

Now we just have to wait for the raw modules to catch up.

The Choice of Starting Point

The foregoing discussion does not imply refusal to adjust anything at all in a raw module. If we started with something, say, a quarter of the way between Figures 14.2A and 14.2B it's unlikely that it would hurt and it might actually make the correction easier.

Figure 14.4A is a camera-produced JPEG. Figure 14.4B is based on a raw file that this model produced simultaneously. It was opened using the color defaults of pre-CS6 versions of Camera Raw. Current defaults produce similar results on this particular file. For the rest of the chapter, we'll use the abbreviations CR-CS6 and CR-CS5 to indicate which version of Camera Raw was in use.

Figure 14.4C, obviously the flattest of the three, was also opened in CR-CS5, using the same settings as in the earlier Figure 14.2A. Notice how as the contrast increases in this trio, so does the color.

In Figure 14.4A, the JPEG, the algorithm couldn't find a likely highlight. So the light green areas aren't light enough. Figure 14.4B, the Camera Raw default, comes closer. It is therefore apparently the best of the three at the moment. If this were a final correction, it would still need work because it is not yet full range: the light areas could get lighter still without losing detail.

We could arrange for that to happen in Camera Raw or another module. I'll show such a version in a moment, but you should already know what it's going to look like. It will bear the same relation to Figure 14.4B as 14.4B does to 14.4A: higher contrast, better detail, and greener. Sounds good—until you think about it.

A picture like this, dominated by a single color, screams out for the Modern Man from Mars action described in Chapter 6. Even without that consideration, the Color Boost action of Chapter 5 almost always is superior to trying to enhance color in RGB.

We can try using those actions no matter what happens first in the raw module, but if the color is already attractive their utility is sharply lessened. Even Figure 14.4B approaches the kind of pleasing color to which further enhancement is dangerous. Note the intensity of the yellows in the melon at top left. The hypothetical (for now) version in which full range is set in the raw module would be even worse—although it temporarily may look better.

The flatter, the better is nevertheless not a good policy either. Here, I would choose to start work with Figure 14.4A, the JPEG, because its color as yet leaves a lot to be desired. That enables a major move with the PPW color actions, which would not be possible starting with the more colorful Figure 14.4B.

Not too long ago I would have recommended starting with the even duller Figure 14.4C. I'll explain the change of position, and also what to do if there isn't a convenient JPEG, right after we use this image to compare the results of PPW methodology to that of what a raw module can do.

Rules and Results

To make the test fair some PPW moves must be omitted. There can be no initial color adjustment, no Shadows/Highlights or Bigger Hammer, no multiplication through a mask, no H-K action. That leaves the luminosity maneuvering discussed in Chapter 4 and the color adjustments found in the MMM + Color Boost action of Chapters 5 and 6.

The channels of Figure 14.4B are shown in Figure 14.5. The blue is bad but this has little impact on luminosity. The other two would be improved by a curve like the one shown. It establishes light and dark points but also suppresses detail to some extent in the lightest and darkest areas, because of the slight flattening near each end of the curve. The literally darkest areas here are the shadows between the melons. We don't care if they lose detail. The literally lightest area is the front of the melon at top left. It's more important than the shadows but still, if it helps the other melons, we should be prepared to give up some detail.

The following may not be the best approach, but it addresses all the points above.

- On a duplicate layer, apply the curve shown to the green channel.
- Substitute the new green channel for the blue. As noted earlier, a better blue is not a big deal, but it does help, and this move takes seconds. I would not do it if it took longer.
- Set this new layer to Luminosity mode.
- Add a curves adjustment layer and apply a new S-shaped curve to the green, similar, but not as drastic, as the one previously shown. That first curve lightened the green channel dramatically, but a lot of that was reversed when the layer was changed to Luminosity mode.

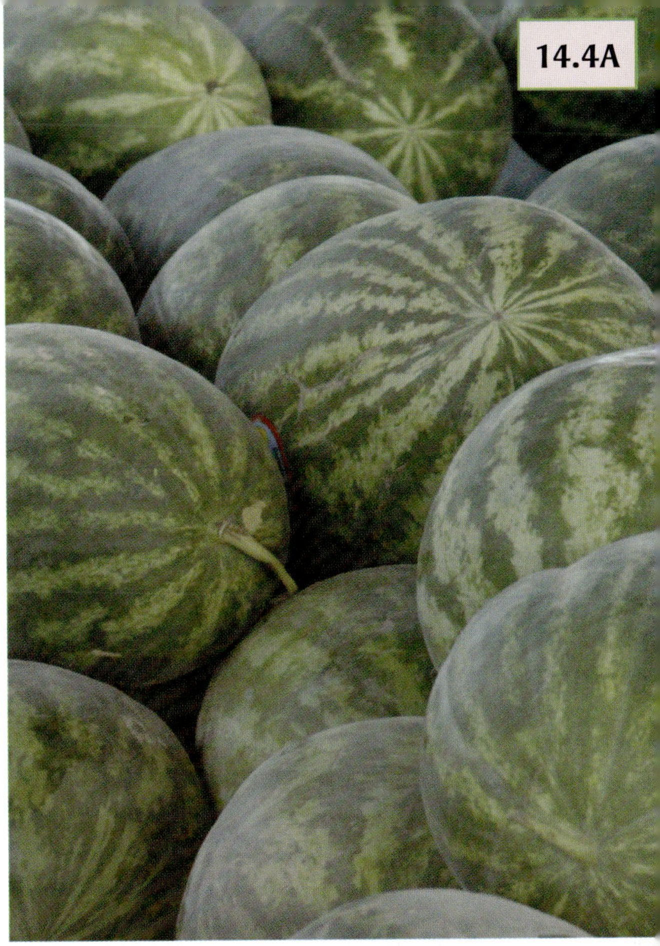

Figure 14.4 *This file was shot by a camera that delivers both a JPEG and a raw file. Top, the JPEG. Bottom left, a default open in CR-CS5. Bottom right, opened in CR-CS5 with all settings except White Balance zeroed out.*

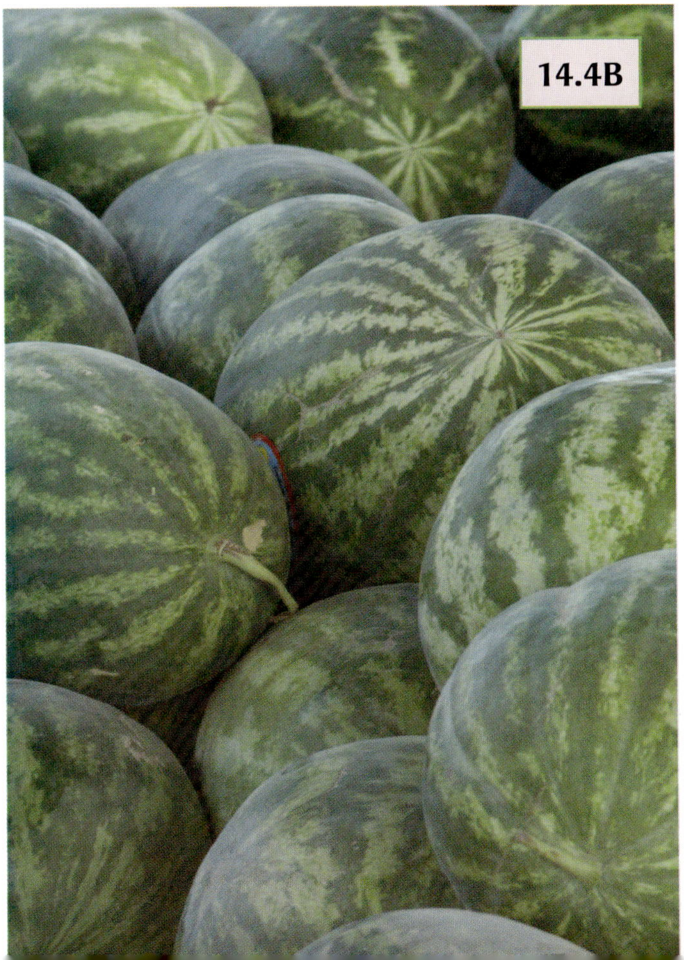

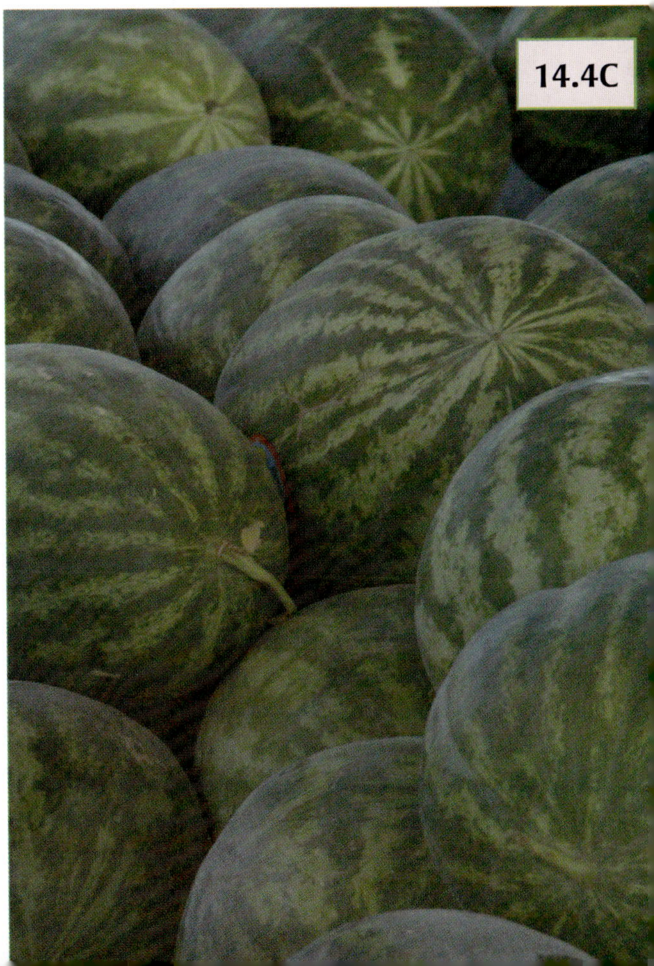

- Change this adjustment layer to Luminosity mode also. This yields Figure 14.5.

As far as I know no current raw converter does any of these things. Most, including CR-CS6 but not CR-CS5, can apply the first curve to the green, but can't set mode to Luminosity. One would have to acquire the image twice and merge the two in Photoshop. It would be quicker and just as effective to do it all in Photoshop in the first place. And no raw converter can blend channels, as I did here, or set up a second luminosity layer.

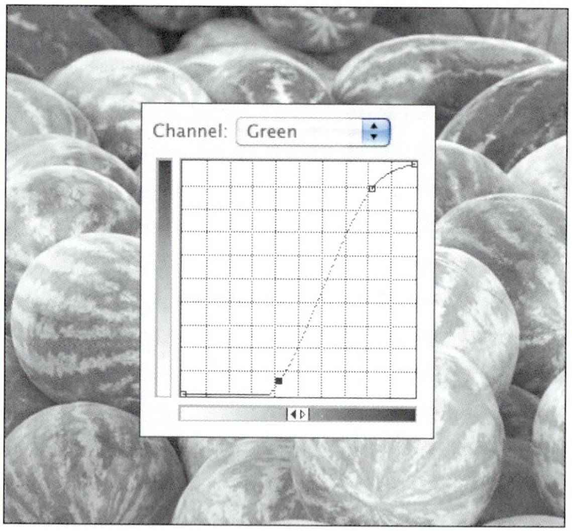

Note that we have gotten away from etaoin shrdlu methods already, in two respects.

- We haven't bothered to finalize highlight and shadow. The color enhancement provides a second chance.
- There has been no effort as yet to make the color attractive, so Figure 14.5 looks dull.

The Color Is Added

The rules require that we move directly to color enhancement. Therefore, starting with Figure 14.5, I lassoed a couple of melons and ran the MMM + Color Boost action.

I used the Endpoint Adjustment layer to finalize highlight and shadow, but left everything else alone. Before comparing the result

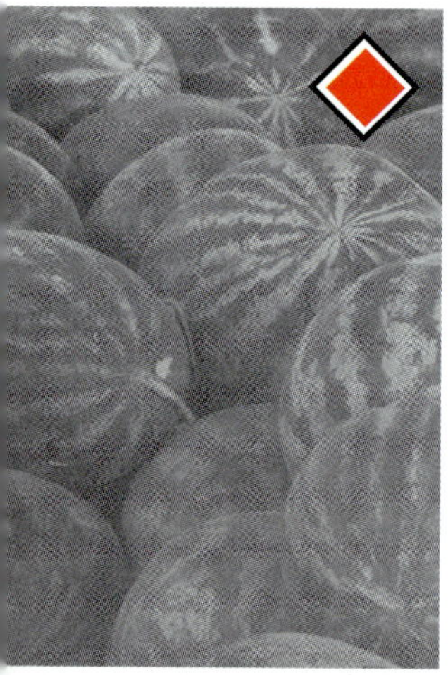

***Figure 14.5** Left, the three original RGB channels of Figure 14.4B. Above, the general shape of the curve needed to improve them. Right, after channel blending to replace the blue, and curves to the green on two different luminosity layers, the resulting file is flattened, and placed on a layer set to Luminosity mode above the JPEG shown in Figure 14.4A.*

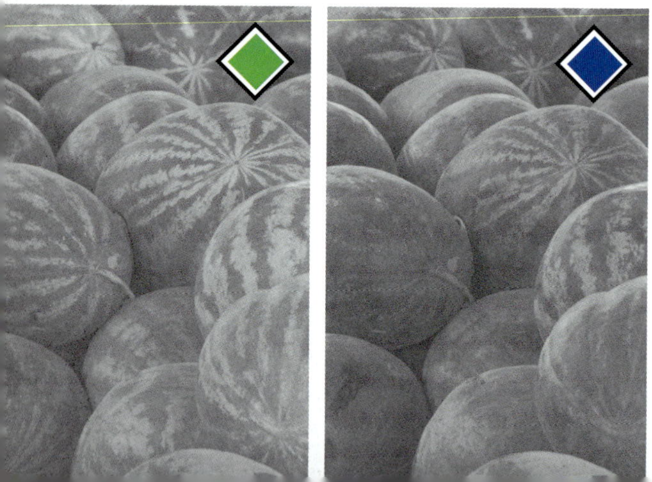

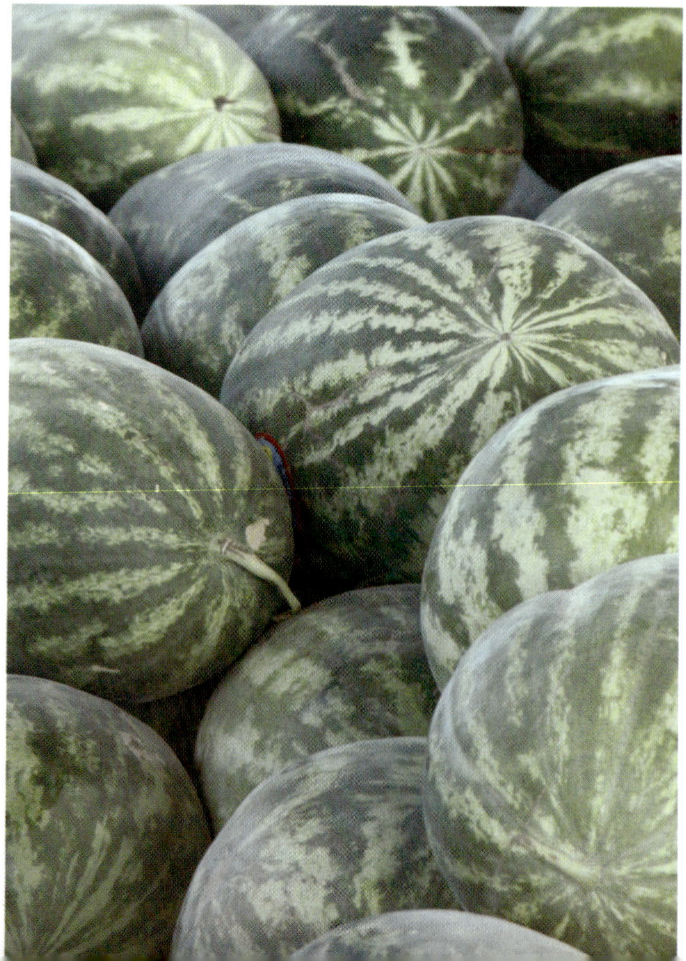

to an intelligent correction in the raw module, let's review what the action's components did.

Figure 14.6A shows the new luminosity and the old color. It's better than Figure 14.5 due not just to the corrected endpoints but because the MMM Luminosity layer found extra detail in the melons.

Figure 14.6B adds the MMM Color layer, producing more variation. Figure 14.6C shows what the Color Boost layer does without MMM Color.

* * *

Finally, the confrontation. Figure 14.7A is the Camera Raw entrant, with human intervention in the form of a curve that sets highlight and shadow to match the values in my PPW effort. This makes the result both snappier and more vivid.

Figure 14.7B is that partial PPW version, using only luminosity moves and one color action.

Figure 14.6 *Partial results of the MMM + Color Boost action applied to Figure 14.5. Top, further improvement in contrast from the MMM Luminosity and Endpoint Adjustment layers. Bottom left, the MMM Color layer is added. Bottom right, the Color Boost layer only, without MMM Color.*

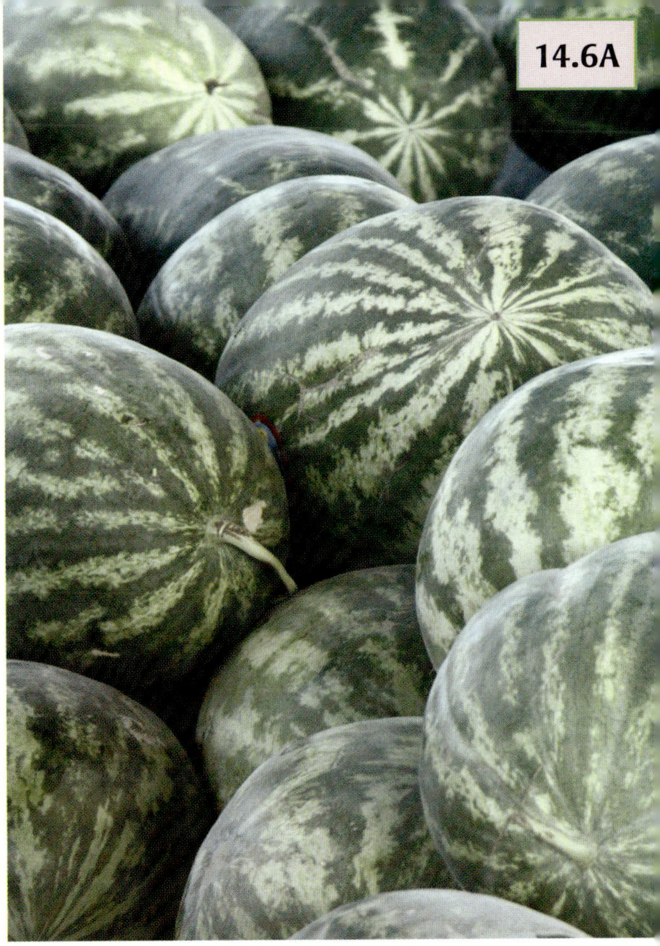

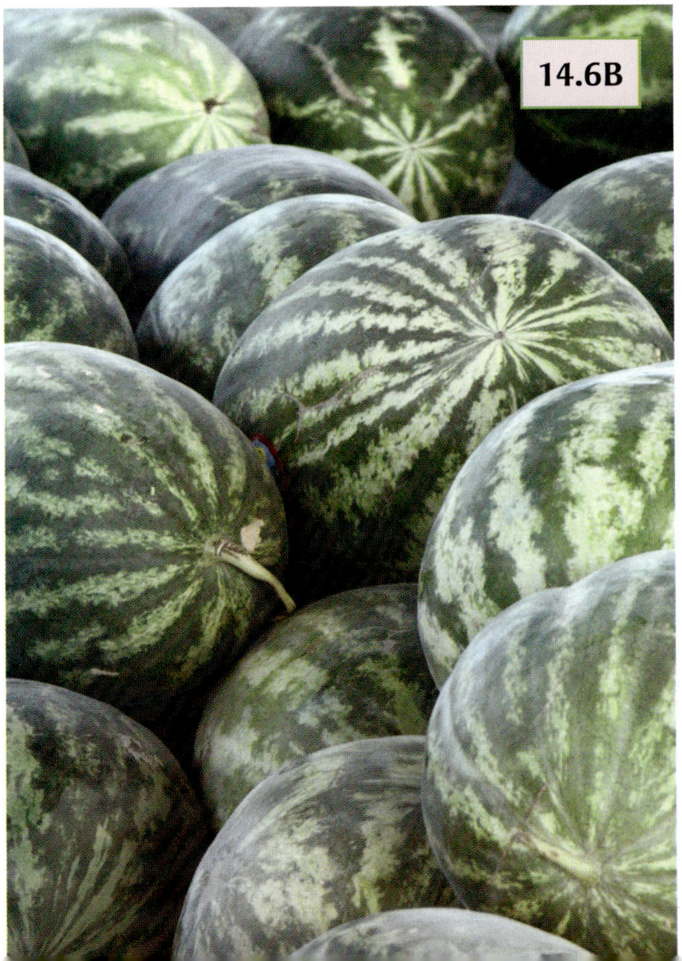

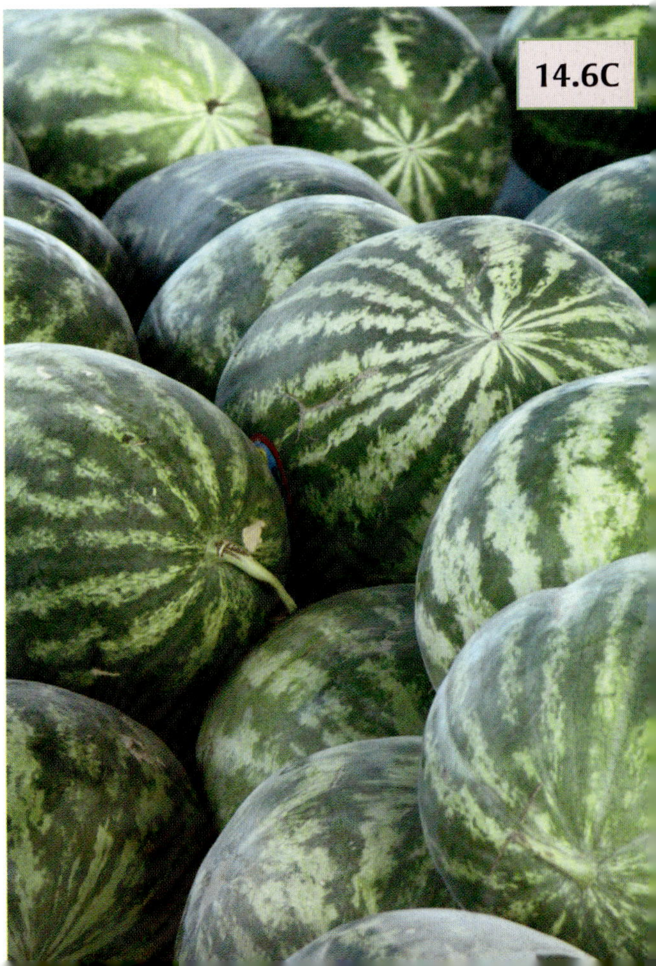

To get a better idea of the strengths and weaknesses of the pair, Figure 14.7C is the Camera Raw color coupled with the PPW contrast. Figure 14.7D is the opposite. What are your preferences?

All this leads up to a recommendation for how to use a raw module to maximize quality. You may have wondered why it hasn't been forthcoming so far. After all, normally the first half of the chapter states recommendations, and the second half says why.

Here, no general recommendation is possible. It depends on your camera. It depends on how much time you have to work on each image. It depends on whether you tend to work on one file at a time, or have to process many raw files. And it also depends on your skill level—as we're about to see.

The Experts Take Their Licks

The more colorful the picture, the worse the traditional workflow handles it. Raw modules all require that traditional workflow.

A nearly neutral picture, like that of the Stock Exchange back in Figure 4.25A, handles just as well in etaoin shurdluland as in the PPW. Something with a lot of bright color, like the Peruvian scene of Figure 14.2, favors a more modern approach. And something in the middle, like the melons we just worked on—well, it's hard to say. There may be channel blending opportunities. The Man from Mars routine may generate color variation that otherwise wouldn't be possible. We may be able to use the Bigger Hammer, or a multiplication, or the H-K action, none of which currently exist in raw modules.

Or not.

My own view of the comparison we just made: the PPW method seems clearly better in terms of contrast. I could have improved the Camera Raw entrant by using something other than a straight-line curve, but probably not enough. As for color, I'm not fully satisfied with the PPW version, but the Camera Raw version is too green and too monotonous in my view. So, probably I would want something between Figures 14.7B and 14.7C. I reiterate that it would probably not be possible to create that version working only with Figure 14.7A.

After about a year in which I did several hundred images in two different ways, and concluded that there was a considerable advantage to being conservative in acquiring, I acquired an opportunity to see whether this was true for people other than myself.

In March 2009, I put together a couple of superadvanced courses in San Diego, invitation only, to people who had already taken at least two three-day courses with me. Each student in my classes, as you've already seen a few times, works on the same image, trying to get the most attractive result, followed by a showdown.

This time, there was a new wrinkle. The classes worked on 26 images, in half of which everybody got the same original. The other half featured two different start points for the same photo. Sometimes half the class got the raw and the other a file derived from it in a way they could not control. More frequently, neither got the raw. Half got a flat-looking version and the other half an attractive one. The melons image wasn't part of the festivities, but if it had been, half the class would have started with something like Figure 14.4B and the rest with 14.4C. The groups were randomly assigned. Each person got to work on equal numbers of flat and open versions. The attendees did not know whether there was one original or two. Fifteen people participated, including myself.

***Figure 14.7** (opposite). Top left, a version created in Camera Raw establishing correct highlights and shadows. Top right, a version prepared using Figure 14.4A and using PPW techniques for luminosity and color. Bottom left, combining the color of the first version with the luminosity of the second. Bottom right, the reverse.*

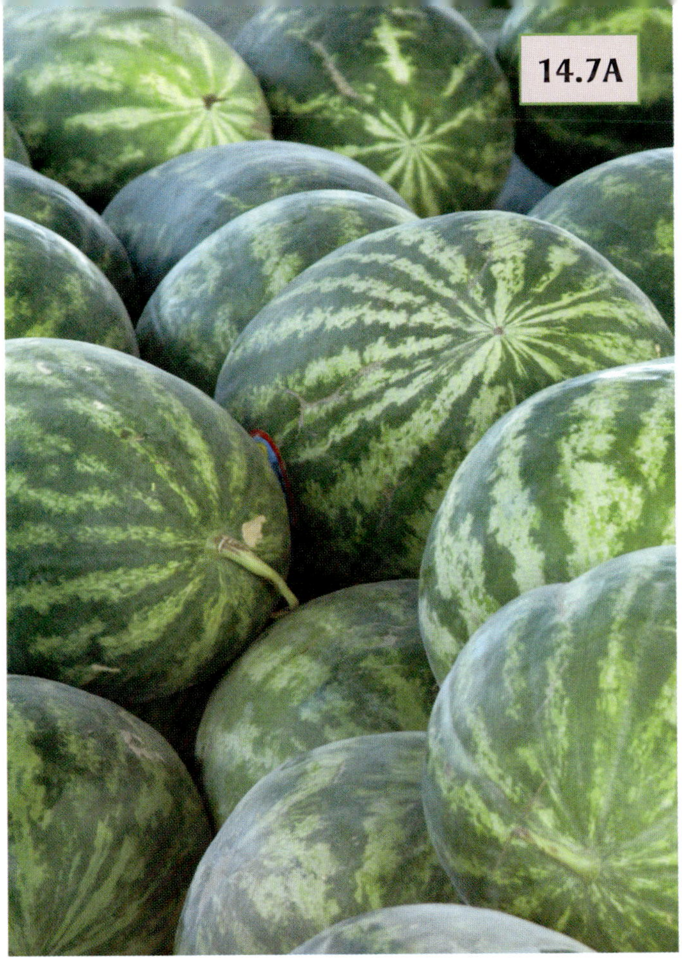
14.7A

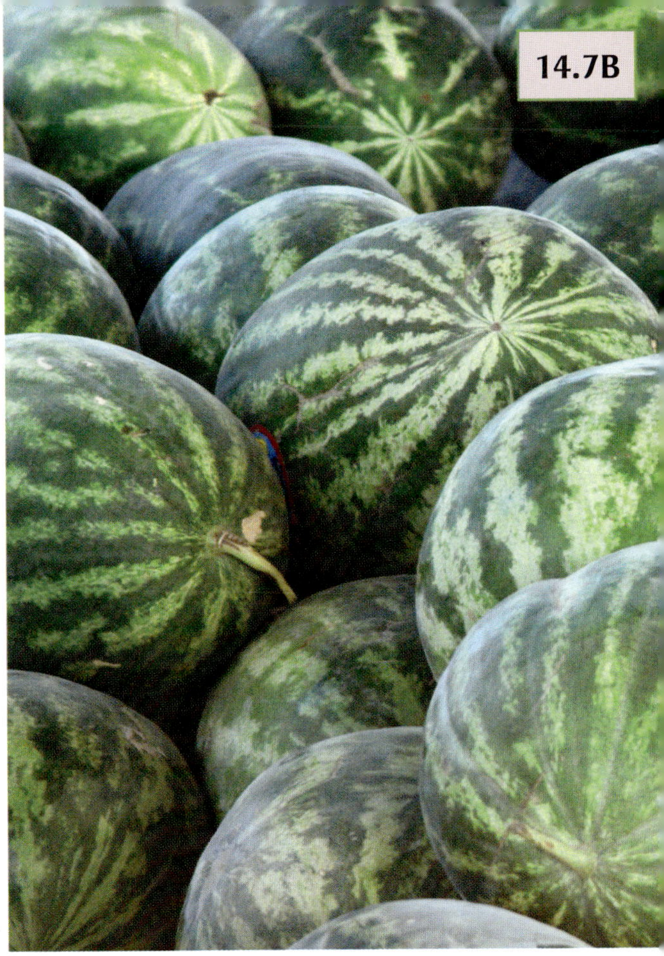
14.7B

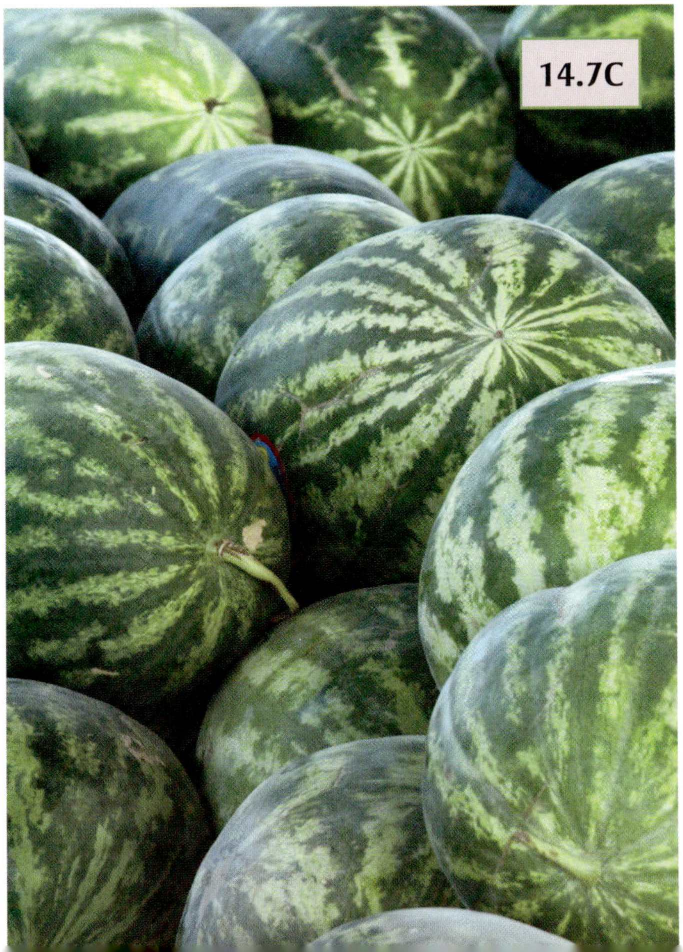
14.7C

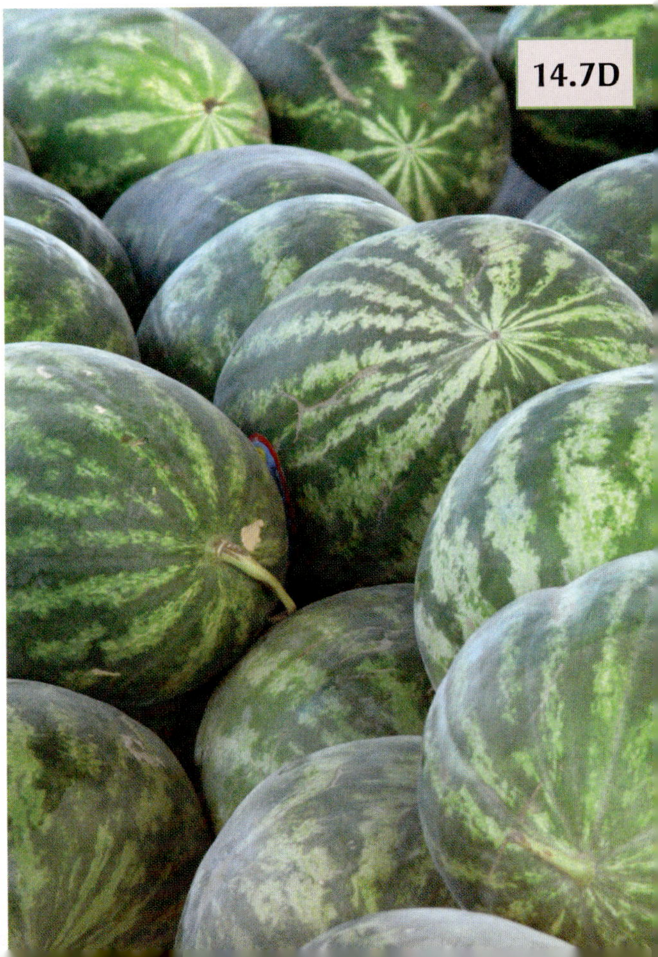
14.7D

Such a test would be meaningless with a non-expert group, because there would be too many errors that would confound the results. One of our exercises was shown back on Figure 12.15, a Burmese wedding. I happened to receive the open (attractive) version and turned it into garbage, as Figure 12.17A attested. My failure, however, had nothing to do with the method of acquisition and everything to do with a bonehead decision about how to treat the background. Everybody else made their share of errors, too, but at a much lower rate than a less-skilled group would, making it possible to draw conclusions.

The results were decisive, as confirmed by votes from the group members. On the whole the groups starting with flatter originals got superior results to those starting with better-looking ones. In certain pictures the advantage was greater than others. The painter image at the end of the last chapter produced what was evaluated as equal quality from both sides. If you're interested, Figure 13.20A was the good-looking original, and the two people who produced Figures 13.20D and 13.20E were working with it. My 2009 correction, Figure 13.20C, was based on a flatter original that isn't shown.

At the other extreme, every single person who started with the flowers of Figure 14.8A did worse than every single person who started with the uglier Figure 14.8B.

The Meaning of the Win

Having had time to try to work out what this means, I've altered my view somewhat, assisted by feedback from many people who are just learning the PPW.

The experts using flatter versions won resoundingly in terms of final contrast. Figure 14.8C, corrected in that class, has shape in the flowers. People starting with Figure 14.8A generally got colored blobs.

Anyone who studies Chapters 4, 10, and 12 should have little difficulty getting better contrast from conservative acquisitions. Color is another story. The experts got better color from the conservative versions, too, but the victory wasn't quite as pronounced. Also, they had some failures.

Meanwhile, feedback confirms that the final color moves are intuitive but that first getting the image to a point where they won't cause damage can be an issue. If the color is mildly drab, like the flowers of Figure 14.8B, our methods work well. If *seriously* drab, like the melons of Figure 14.4C, we'd better hope that there is absolutely no inaccuracy. If there is, the PPW will magnify it.

Doing *some* of the work in a raw module is unlikely to hurt, provided it still leaves room for our actions to bite—and it may be safer. At the time of the class, I thought that the best Camera Raw approach would be to zero everything out except the initial white balance, on the theory that everything can be done better with other methods. (Note: this is CR-CS5 language, which is what was in effect at the time. In CR-CS6, zeros are the defaults, and produce a full range, or nearly so, not the flat file that I wanted.)

After reconsideration I say that while PPW works no matter what you do in the raw module, it works better with a conservatively corrected original. In other words, the objective should be neither the extremely dull melons of Figure 14.4C nor the much brighter ones of Figure 14.4B. Instead, we should try to start with something in the middle, along the lines of Figure 14.4A.

How to do that depends on a lot of factors. So, let's consider the simplest case, with a big hypothetical in the middle of it.

Assume you are about to work on a single file currently in raw format. Now, the catch. You must state the values you will use to open it in Camera Raw, without knowing anything about the picture. In Photoshop, having seen it for the first time, you must have a complete correction finished in one to three minutes.

Therefore, whatever your settings are to open the file had best be good ones, because you simply do not have time to go back and open it a second time. *What Camera Raw values do you pick, sight unseen?*

The Educated Guess

Even the weakest digital cameras try to establish a shadow and highlight in their JPEGs. Some discriminate by color, guessing that greens should be made more vivid and fleshtones less so. Others even ask for user input as to the type of picture, such as whether it's a portrait.

A raw module's defaults are a different kind of educated guess as to what might present an unknown picture in its best light. Figure 14.9, on the other hand, is an educated guess as to what might make an unknown picture *easy to correct.*

There's merit in both approaches. For example, many of us have to decide whether a photo is promising enough for us to work on it at all. Say we have a record of a wedding. There could be hundreds of shots. Only a quarter may eventually be processed. It would be nice to quickly eliminate some

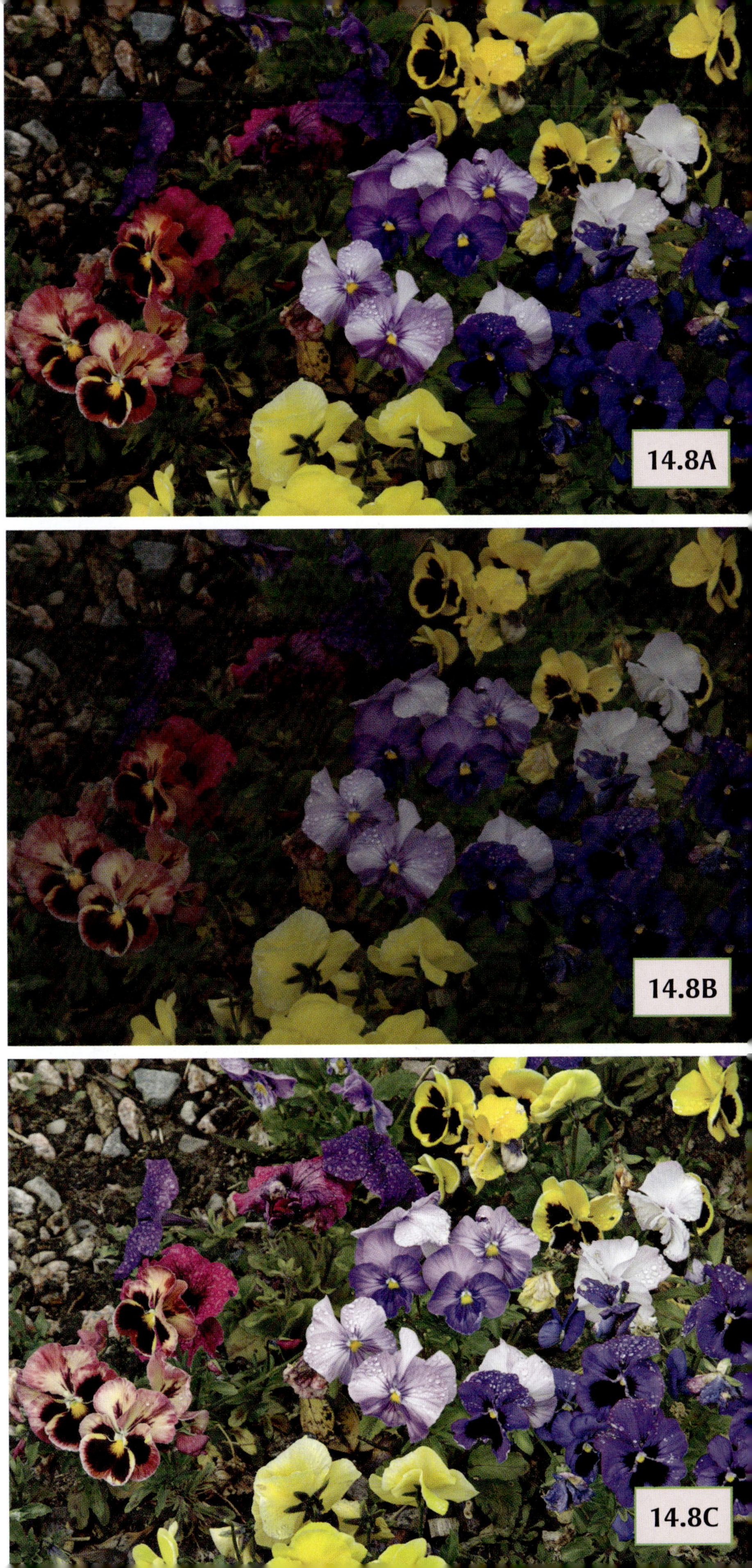

***Figure 14.8** A group of very experienced retouchers engaged in a color correction competition with this image. No one had access to the raw file. Half the contestants were given the top version and half the one in the middle. Guess which group scored a decisive victory? Bottom, a sample correction that voters found appealing.*

so as to have fewer to study later. How do we make the initial cut?

If the files are JPEGs, selection will be easy. We don't even have to open them, just have them in a folder. The Bridge module has been around since Photoshop CS2. Effective with CS5, clicking a thumbnail in Bridge and then hitting the space bar generates a full-screen preview of good enough quality for these purposes of cutting down the field.

Raws can be viewed that way in Bridge, too—through their current setting. And an open image like Figures 14.4B or 14.8A is easier to evaluate than their flatter counterparts, 14.4C and 14.8B. For this reason, although I could save the settings of Figure 14.9 as my own defaults rather than as a preset that has to be loaded each time, I keep the program defaults until I am ready to open the file as opposed to just examining it.

A picture that looks better at present, however, is not necessarily the one that will look better in the future. The question is how far to go in toning down what the raw module wants to do, without making it unduly difficult for ourselves later.

Here is a file that has been acquired five different ways, only three of which are worth showing. Figure 14.10A is a default open in CR-CS5. Figure 14.10B was also opened in CR-CS5, but with the settings recommended for that module in Figure 14.9. The final variant, Figure 14.10C, was opened in CR-CS6, using the Figure 14.9 settings that pertain to it.

Discussion of why the two recommended settings don't look the same is hereby put off until the second half. For now, Figures 14.10B and 14.10C are both good starting points for whatever you wish to do with this image.

The same cannot be said of Figure 14.10A. Everything on the bottom is manageable. We wouldn't be able to get color variation in the rocks but it isn't clear we want to; it might distract from the woman and the seal. The sweater and the face don't want to get much more colorful than they already are. About the only thing that might be difficult is a move to differentiate the face from the hair.

The sky is not quite blank in Figure 14.10A but it's pretty close. Some might feel that this is OK. If so, there's no problem. But others might want to see action there, maybe more even than in Figure 14.10B. This may not be possible starting with Figure 14.10A.

And now a word about the missing contenders. I have a default version opened in CR-CS6, and also a JPEG produced by the camera. They aren't shown because, at least at first glance, they're similar to Figure 14.10A.

Which is what you might expect. JPEG algorithms all assign a full range to the picture, but most also realize that important detail is more likely found in the quartertones and midtones than in the lights and darks. So they short-change the shadows and highlights. Often they deliberately jettison a specified small percentage of pixels at the extremes. The more drastic the suppression, the better the result usually, but the more likely it is to meet disaster when highlight and/or shadow detail happens to be critical.

This dilemma doesn't quite go all the way back to the days of etaoin shrdlu. Prepress folk, however, faced it before the days of Photoshop: how do we take a file from RGB into CMYK for printing? The choices were the same. Do we want a conservative approach, or one that gives better results on most images but has a higher rate of catastrophe?

As a prepress practitioner in the last century, I voted for the first option and still believe it was the correct choice. Clients by and large couldn't distinguish good from excellent work, but they did recognize garbage and would reject it when they saw it, often with the addition of a few obscenities.

If I were a camera manufacturer today, I'd vote the other way. Some potential buyers are knowledgeable, but twenty times as many aren't. If they get a good-looking photograph they're thrilled; if not, they assume it's their own fault.

The manufacturers have bought into this philosophy. This particular camera is aggressive. Its JPEG had no sky at all.

CR-CS6, on the other hand, preserves more highlights than its predecessor. Its version had enough substance in the sky to support something like the Bigger Hammer action, if one were inclined to try it.

Harder is one thing, hopeless another. If the sky is a blank, as it was in the JPEG, you are out of luck unless you steal a sky from some other picture, as we did back in Figure 8.11B.

A human scanner operator would have known better than to blow out the sky in this picture, but an algorithm that applies rigid formulae does not. Really bad premature decisions were therefore uncommon in the etaoin shrdlu era. The advent of digital cameras turned a minor problem into a serious headache, from which the raw module sometimes offers blessed relief.

This is another reason for conservatism. We can always suppress highlights and shadows later if we want to; if already suppressed by the time we start work they may be impossible to resuscitate.

Something Out of Nothing

At normal settings, a raw module occasionally delivers a file where highlights are completely blank. Most raw converters let us attempt to recover the missing information. Often it doesn't work. However, if the objective is to get detail into a currently blank area, we have to give it a try.

Why isn't that try made automatic in the settings of Figure 14.9?

Please remember the original rules for those settings. They are to be chosen without seeing the image, and no second chances at acquisition are allowed. Under these circumstances we do *not* want the settings to attempt to recover occult highlight detail. A big blank area cannot be made any worse than it already is. However, the rest of the picture *can*. If we leave room for hidden highlight detail that maybe exists in five in a hundred files, the other 95 may be damaged.

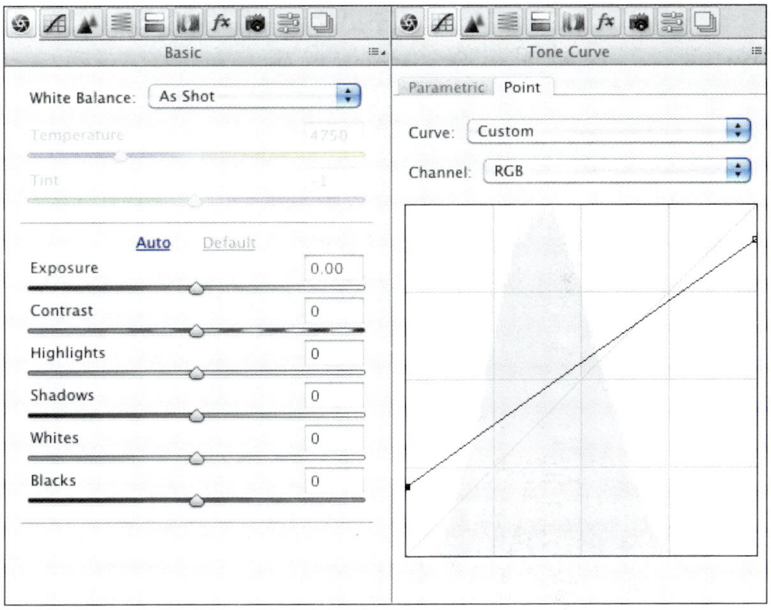

Figure 14.9 *Above, recommended presets in Camera Raw commencing with Photoshop CS6. Below, the recommendations for previous versions. Further recommendations are in the second half.*

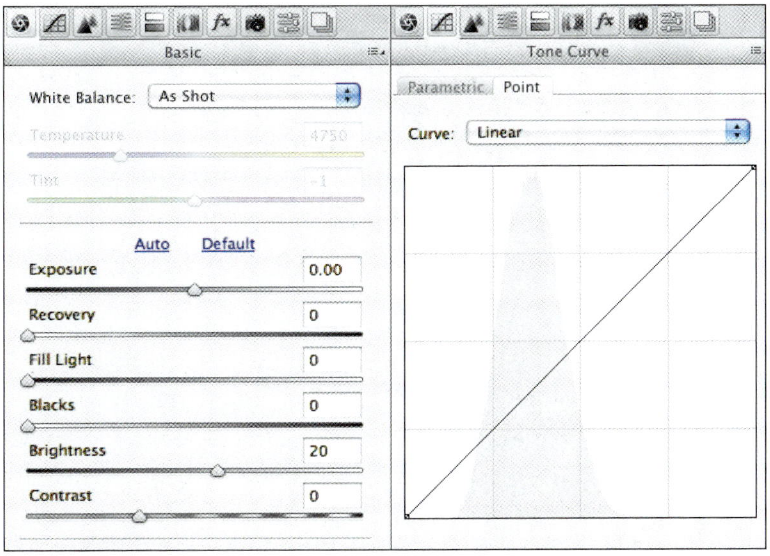

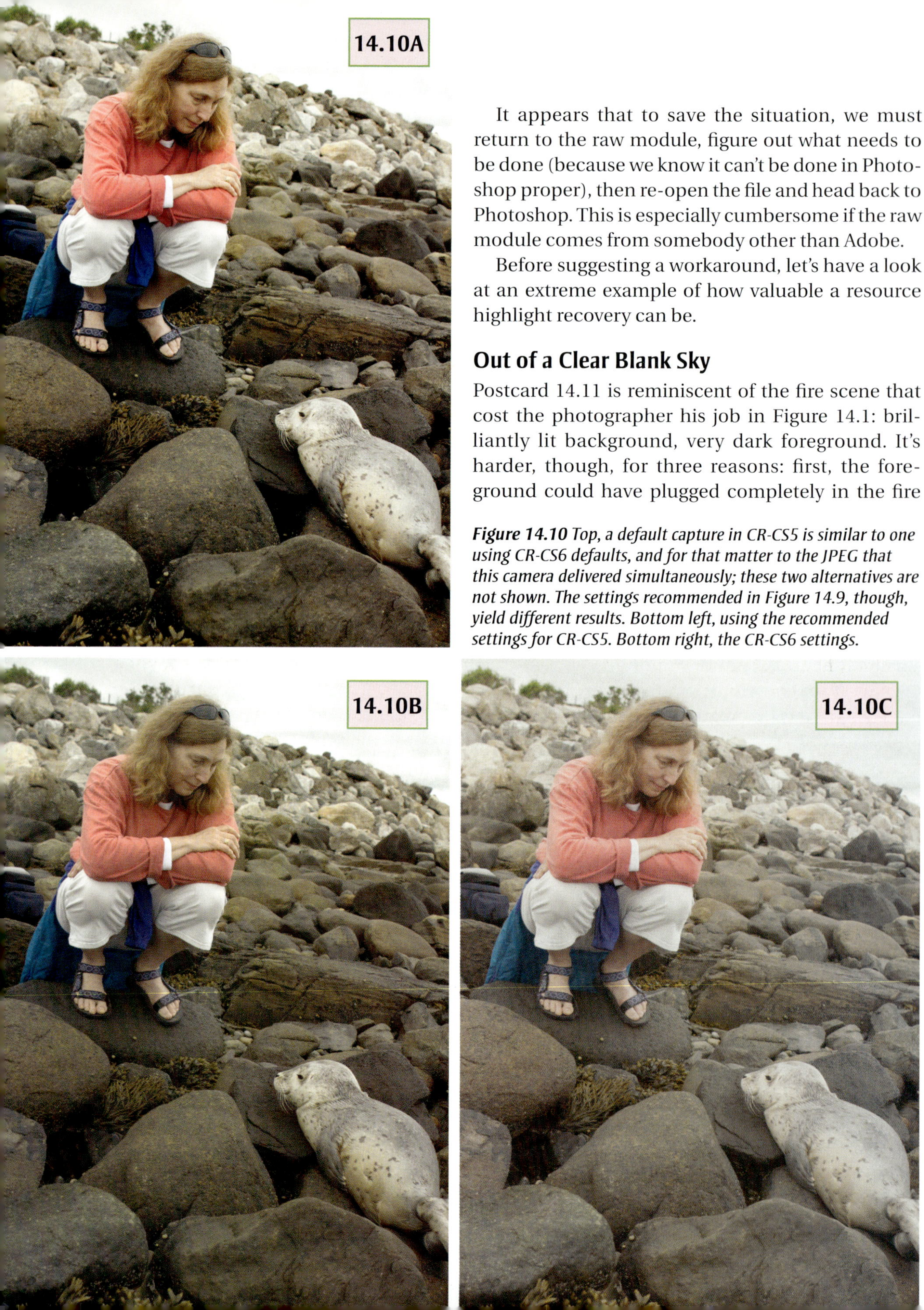

It appears that to save the situation, we must return to the raw module, figure out what needs to be done (because we know it can't be done in Photoshop proper), then re-open the file and head back to Photoshop. This is especially cumbersome if the raw module comes from somebody other than Adobe.

Before suggesting a workaround, let's have a look at an extreme example of how valuable a resource highlight recovery can be.

Out of a Clear Blank Sky

Postcard 14.11 is reminiscent of the fire scene that cost the photographer his job in Figure 14.1: brilliantly lit background, very dark foreground. It's harder, though, for three reasons: first, the foreground could have plugged completely in the fire

***Figure 14.10** Top, a default capture in CR-CS5 is similar to one using CR-CS6 defaults, and for that matter to the JPEG that this camera delivered simultaneously; these two alternatives are not shown. The settings recommended in Figure 14.9, though, yield different results. Bottom left, using the recommended settings for CR-CS5. Bottom right, the CR-CS6 settings.*

scene for all the photographer cared; here it has to hold detail. Second, the fire photographer got more detail in the background than he needed, whereas half the background in Figure 14.11 is blank. Third, the guy shooting the fire scene was a professional who knew which end of a camera was which.

Nevertheless something attractive can be salvaged. The original murky foreground should hold no terrors. We have more powerful tools than any raw converter for dealing with it. The background is a different story.

Two sliders in CR-CS5 and three in CR-CS6 address highlight enhancement. CR-CS5's Recovery has been replaced in CR-CS6 with a stronger implementation called Highlights, which did most of the work here. I also put in a Contrast setting of –100, which is so unusual that I will put off explaining why until the second half of the chapter.

The settings and their result are shown in Figure 14.12. From there to the final postcard should by now be a matter of routine:

- No initial color issue found.
- The background is so neutral that all three RGB channels look alike. In the foreground, however, the green has better detail because it is always lightest in trees. Therefore, on a duplicate layer, I replaced the others with it, and changed mode to Luminosity.
- I applied Shadows/Highlights, but not the Bigger Hammer.
- A strong false profile, multiplied, using a blurred copy of the original blue channel as a layer mask. The blue is the best choice because it is always the darkest in trees.
- The H-K action, to neutralize and darken the bluish areas of background, and especially to tone down certain greens, preparing for the next step.
- The MMM + Color Boost action could now be operated with a heavy hand. Without the previous H-K action there would not have been enough distinction between the greens for so much color to be credible.
- The sharpening action to be described in the next chapter, with an emphasis on Hiraloam Light.

I opened the chapter by blasting raw modules for being stuck in the past, and I meant it. This exercise, however, suggests otherwise. A scanner operator of 25 years ago could have gotten reasonable foreground trees if this disastrous original were in film. But there would have been no chance of getting anything usable out of the background sky, let alone something as detailed as Figure 14.12.

Now that we've shown a correction that is worthy of modern times, let's consider a workflow to match.

Cheap Storage And Its Advantages

In 1994, the time of my first book on color correction, hard disks cost about 10,000 times what they do today. RAM was a comparative bargain, only 5,000 times today's price.

Procedures that developed when it was not feasible to have lots of images open at once or to store multiple versions of them may no longer make sense in today's world.

Combine these ingredients, add the batch-processing capabilities of today's modules, and liberate yourself from a workflow dictated by yesterday's limitations.

* * *

Most people who work with raw images, I think, work with them in bunches. The assumption that we've been using—that only the current image is important, and there are no others—is therefore fallacious.

The following procedure works in most raw modules. For convenience, we'll talk about it in terms of Camera Raw, show an example of how it might help, and finally ask whether it's worth the investment of time.

The assumption that the settings shown in Figure 14.9 are usually best leaves a minority of files in which they aren't. When that's the case, what would be a better option, or at least a useful one to have available?

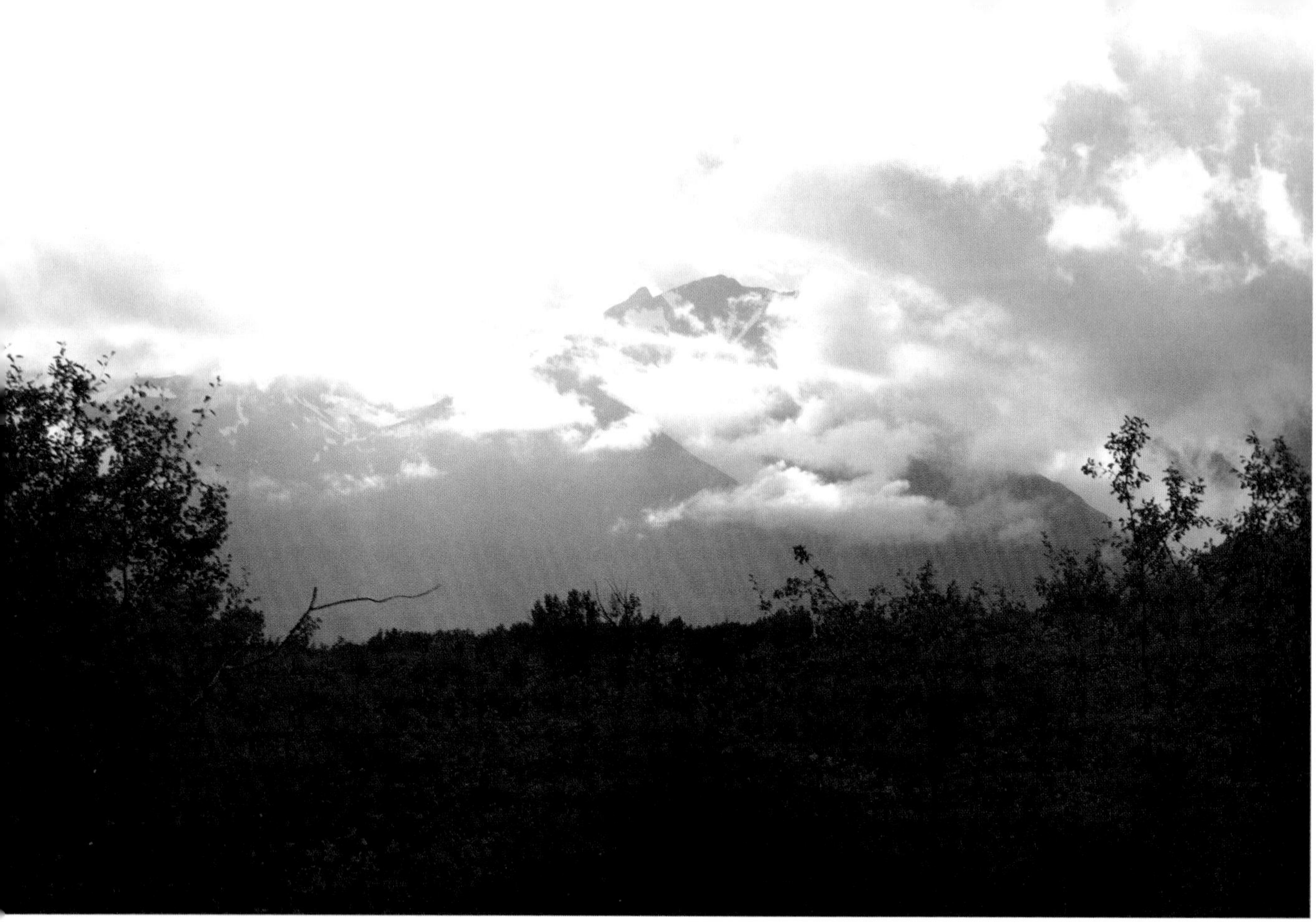

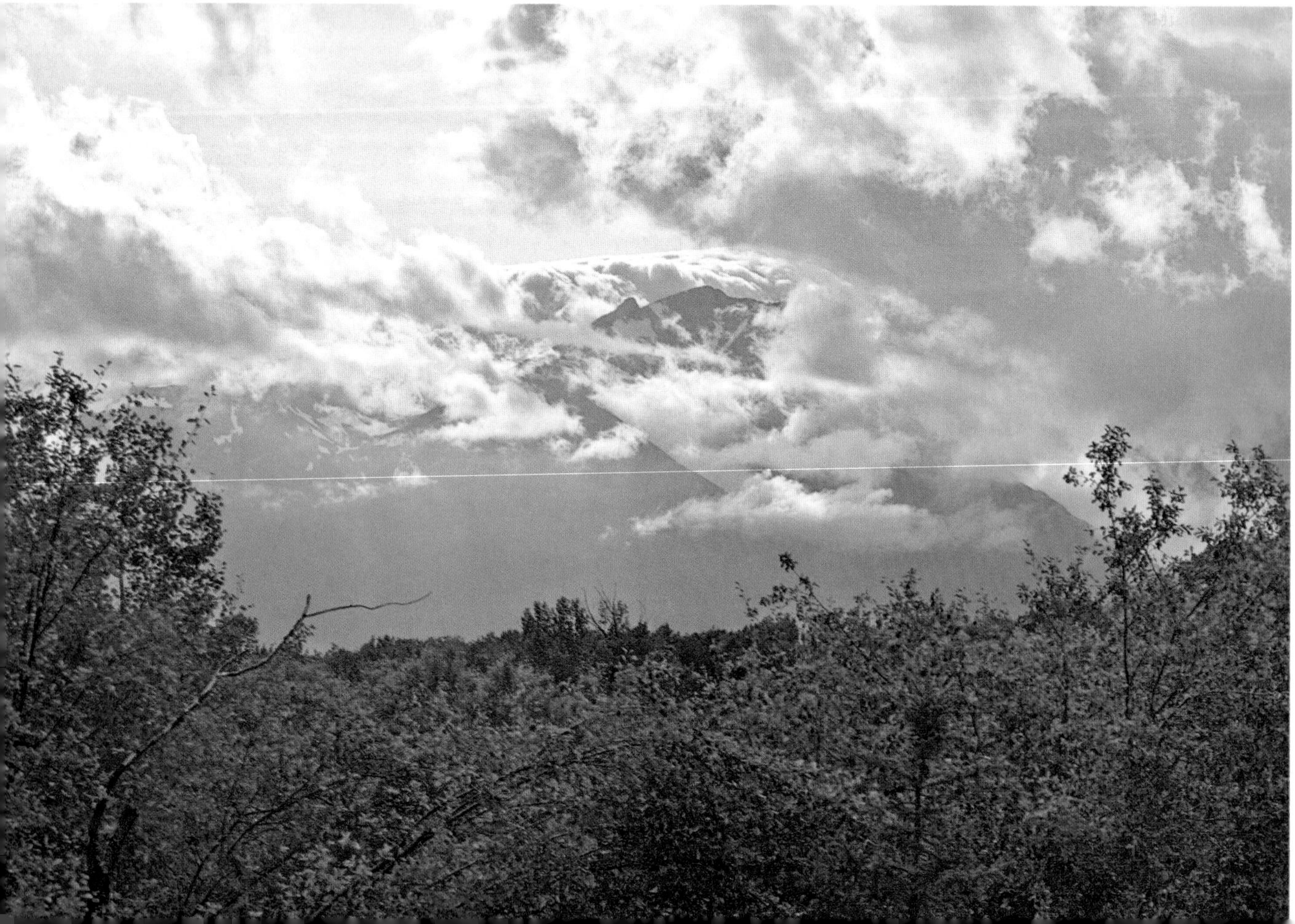

***Postcard 14.11** (opposite) Near Prince George, British Columbia, Canada.*

Once we agree on an answer, it's easy to set up a system that gives access to whatever we might need whenever we want it.

The answer depends on how far-fetched you want to be. It depends on how important these files are. And if we have any clue at all about the nature of the images other options may suggest themselves. But without knowing anything about what challenges may be forthcoming, I expect that at least two extra versions might be helpful:

- The Camera Raw defaults. As you know, these will produce—temporarily—something that looks better than a second version opened with the settings of Figure 14.9. We expect to be able to make something better still by working with something flatter. The question is, will it turn out better than the default *in every single respect?* Because if it doesn't, that default capture can be useful.
- A version with enhanced highlights won't rescue disasters like Postcard 14.11, which need custom settings. But a small percentage of files would benefit.

With three versions, I would expect to be able in certain cases to improve on what would otherwise be possible. On the other hand, making them may burn a lot of time.

It's only a waste of time, however, if it has to be done by hand on every image. Fortunately, today's software lets us automate; today's hard drive prices let us store multiple versions, and today's RAM prices let us have them open simultaneously.

A Raw Workflow for This Century

To start, we need to save at least one preset, perhaps more.

- Open any raw file. The Basic panel pops up. If you are using CR-CS5, change its values to those of Figure 14.9. If CR-CS6, you probably don't have to do anything, as Figure 14.9 shows the module's defaults.
- Right above the bar that says Basic, click the Tone Curve icon, second from left. You are shown the Parametric panel, which you don't want. Click Point instead. In CR-CS6, alter the curve to that of Figure 14.9, more or less—it need not be a perfect match. In CR-CS5 it looks like you don't have to do anything, but in fact the default is a curve called Medium Contrast. Change it to Linear.
- To avoid complexity, I omit a useful change to the next panel, Detail. An explanation of what the change is and why it is desirable is in the second half of the chapter.
- Click and hold the icon at the right of the function name bar to bring up a flyout. Choose

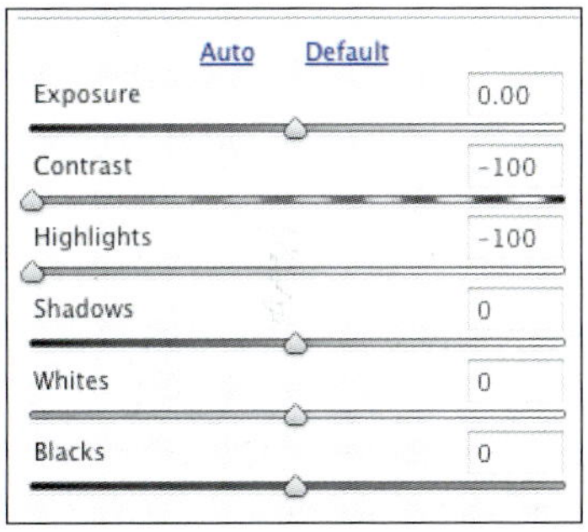

***Figure 14.12** These settings did most of the heavy lifting in Postcard 14.11.*

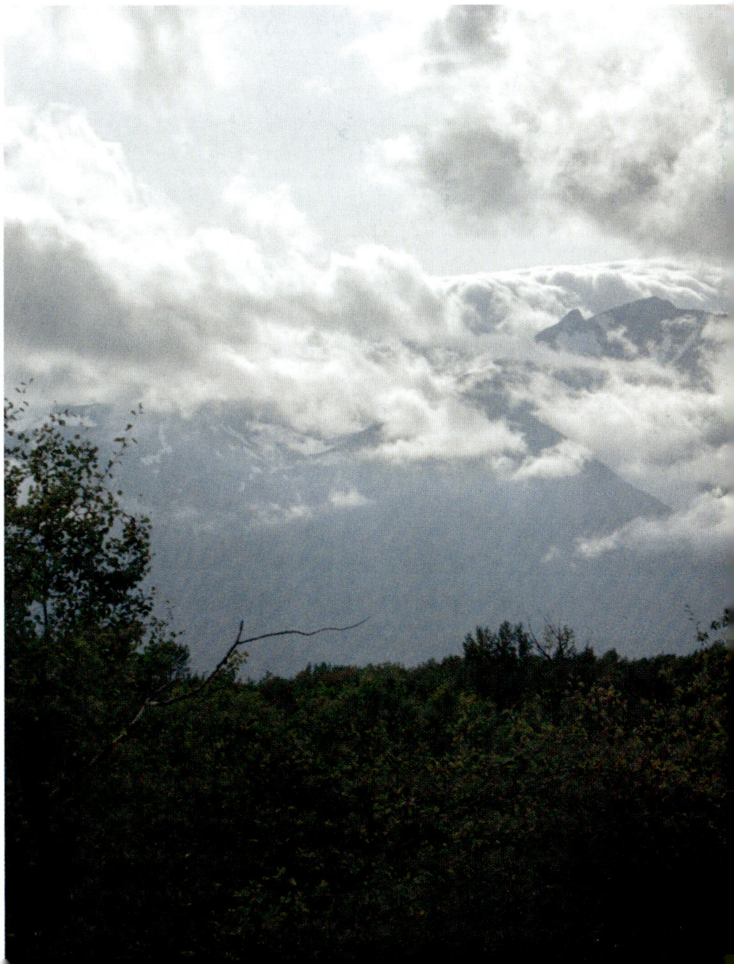

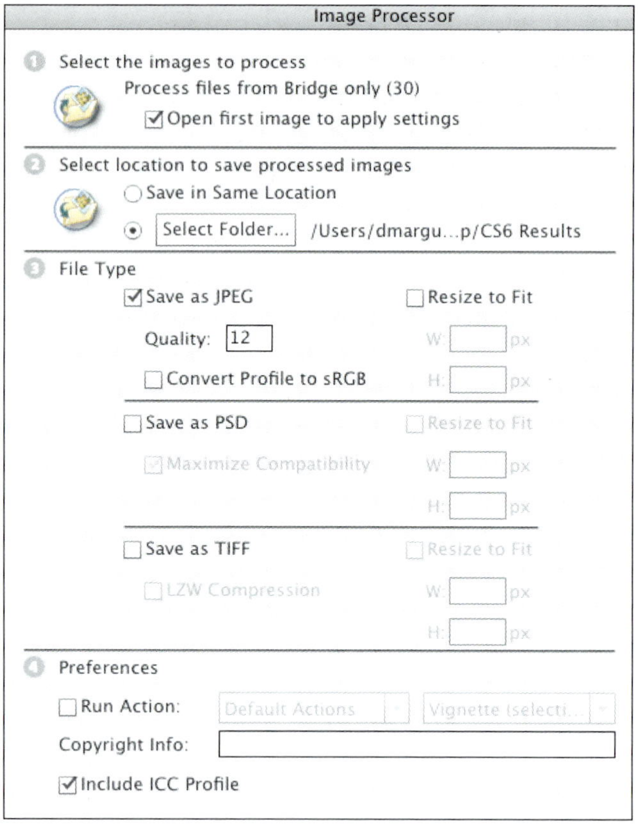

***Figure 14.13** The Image Processor dialog, accessible from Bridge through Tools: Photoshop.*

Save Settings. A dialog appears. Click Save. Photoshop now suggests that you use the name of the file as the name of the preset, a poor idea. Change it to something informative, like Dan's Recommendation. Click Save again. Photoshop assigns the suffix .xmp, and stores it in the appropriate folder.

- After saving the preset, click Cancel if you don't intend to apply it to the current file. When you open raw files in the future, you can apply it by calling up the flyout and clicking and holding Apply Preset. Whatever name you chose will be shown as an option.

You are now ready to process images. Let us say that you have just received fifty raw files, of which you intend to process some, but not all. No immediate crisis requires you to commence curving right now.

- Place the files in a folder by themselves.
- Open the folder in Bridge.
- Edit: Select All.
- Remembering that you are working in Bridge and not Photoshop, choose Tools: Photoshop>Image Processor. Figure 14.13's dialog appears.
- In Item 1, check Open first image to apply settings. In Item 2, decide whether to put the results in a different folder, as shown here, or within a subfolder in the current folder. Item 3 specifies the file type. Make sure that Run Action is not checked in Item 4. Click Run.
- The first file now opens into Camera Raw. If Default is not chosen, click it, or load a modified default if you have one. Either way, click Open Image.
- Go away. Or catch up on your tweeting. Your computer is still usable as Photoshop crunches fifty files in the background. It may take a while, but eventually you will find the finished files in a subfolder called JPEG, if that's the format you chose.
- When complete, return to Bridge, bring up Image Processor and click Run again.
- This time, when the first file reopens, if using CR-CS6, enter Highlights=–50. In CR-CS5, enter Recovery=50, Contrast=0.
- Click Open Image and the whole merry-go-round restarts. Come back half an hour later or whatever, and there will be fifty more files in the JPEG folder. They can't be mixed up: the first (default) files are named in the format filename.jpg; the second (enhanced highlights) are filename_1.jpg.
- Once finished, let the third time be the charm. Reopen the Image Processor dialog, click Run, and this time when the first image appears, choose Load Preset from the flyout, and choose Dan's Recommendations.

After the usual Open Image and background processing, you now have fifty filename_2.jpg files to join the other hundred.

How much time did all this take?

Well, assuming that you weren't twiddling your thumbs while the processing was taking place, almost none.

Why waste time pulling fifty versions with enhanced highlights, considering that you probably will only use five or so?

It is faster to apply a known setting once and later delete 45 worthless files, than to try to customize one, let alone five, settings for images that need highlight enhancement.

Is having so many extra versions worth anything?

The highlight version isn't needed that often but can be essential. CR-CS6 has an improved treatment, giving us more opportunities to use this version. Meanwhile, the default is poor for contrast but excellent for blending for color when our own technique falls short.

Three Fallacies From the Last Century

The procedure just discussed, and the highlight restoration of which Postcard 14.11 is an extreme example, are both examples of using today's capabilities to achieve better quality and efficiency. They show why you need to know how to use the raw module of your choice. Now I would like to talk about why you shouldn't use them more extensively.

In saying this, I snap my fingers at a publicity machine that cranks out testimonials and reasons for why doing as much as possible in raw is the only way to go. Sometimes they consist of digs at a competitive module, or at Photoshop itself when the raw module comes from someone other than Adobe. Such comments need not concern us.

These claims come in three basic forms. First, that you get better texture and fewer artifacts if you do the heavy work in raw. Second, that there is more flexibility because it is "nondestructive." Third, that this is the wave of the future, and all professionals are turning to it, and if you don't adopt it you are a Luddite and/or mentally deficient.

As to the first claim, I can't speak for non-Adobe products because I haven't run enough tests. With respect to Camera Raw, and I believe Lightroom would follow, not only is the claim false, but the reverse is true: you get more artifacting in these modules than if you did the work elsewhere. There's an illustration in the second half.

Moving on to the second claim is difficult because the buzzword *nondestructive* may have two meanings. The first is that we should not risk being unable to restore things to some previous state. Some are naive enough to proselytize that every move we make should be nondestructive, by the foregoing definition.

This is a solution in search of a problem. Anybody who's ever had the experience of losing irreplaceable steps already makes sure that all crucial stuff is backed up, or on adjustment layers, or something else equally flexible. As to what the proselytizers can do with their noncrucial items, or those that can be duplicated without undue sweat, my suggestion would be unlikely to survive the scrutiny of the beta readers. Instead, I will pass the buck to my friend and fellow author Matt Kloskowski, who had the integrity to stand up to the hype as follows:

> No! I am not telling you to go forth and destroy...I'm not saying that at all. All I'm saying is to think about it...Think about the type of work you're in and who your clients are. Do they often request changes? If you don't have clients (or your client is yourself) then consider how many times you actually go back and edit the images that you worked so hard to nondestructively change. This will vary for everyone and only you know the answer. But if that answer is "Never" or "Not very often" then at least consider whether it's worth the hassle and extra file size to try to do everything nondestructively.

The second meaning of *nondestructive* is more attractive. Camera Raw currently sports ten main panels. Some have multiple functions. Any setting you choose for any of them is tentative. You can return to it later after adjusting others. This is a good capability to have in principle; nothing gets set in stone until you decide it's time, and it allows experimentation with the panels' interactions.

The problem is that before the capability is useful, the panels have to be worth using.

The third claim antedates Photoshop; it has been used by graphic arts vendors for as long as I can remember. Attempting to shame users into adopting a product by suggesting that more sophisticated people are doing so invariably shows that the usual way of ensuring adoption—namely, making a product better than what was available in the past—has failed.

And before recoiling in horror at the thought of emerging from the raw module with something ugly, remember the photographer of the fire image of Figure 14.1. He wasn't shooting raw, but his strategy was very appropriate for our time. He made sure that what came out of the camera was something that could be corrected and *he did not care how bad it looked temporarily.* His bosses, alas, did not appreciate his logic.

The shrdlu Scorecard

More raw modules exist than I have time to test thoroughly, although I've played with a good many. Their capabilities change rapidly, too. I therefore can't endorse any of them. Generally, though, I would say that there's no reason not to embrace a raw workflow—other than the raw developers' failure to embrace progress.

I'm pleased to note, therefore, that a couple of freeware/shareware modules, largely the product of one person in each case, show a lot of original thinking and incorporate capabilities not typical of the past. I'm not telling you to go download them, because I can't vouch for their stability, speed, or reliability under intense production pressure. They can't run PPW just yet. But because they are so well thought out, and so unfettered by the past, I raise a glass to these independent modules, RPP (Raw Photo Processor) and RawTherapee.

Back to the real world. Let's run down the capabilities of raw converters in general to see to what extent they deliver what the Picture Postcard Workflow requires.

- Chapter 3: adjust for color inaccuracy. The assignment is easy and one would expect raw modules to have no difficulty with it. Adobe's Camera Raw and Lightroom, however, could not perform adequately in this area until 2012. At present, though, all raw modules hold their own unless the initial color problems are severe.
- Chapter 4: changes to contrast. This critical area is responsible for the added depth in many of the postcards we've looked at, the Grand Canyon of Postcard 4.1 being a striking example. It requires the use of channel blending and of curves that affect only contrast. To my knowledge no current raw module can do both of these things; I know of only one that can do either.
- Chapter 5: color enhancement. In principle the raw modules don't need this; they boost colors when they establish light and dark points, whereas PPW leaves them bland. However, our suggested strategy of creating something much too colorful and then backing off gracefully doesn't work well in raw modules, because they lack the full masking control of Photoshop. Also, strong color boosts in the Adobe products often create too much noise. It is unlikely that the quality of the enhancement can be matched in RGB. Some raw modules sensibly use LAB, although the Adobe products don't.
- Chapter 6: the MMM for color variation. This step creates much of the realism that is the signature of the PPW. No raw module has anything like it.
- Chapter 7: light use of the Shadows/

Highlights command. The Adobe products and several others have equivalents.

- Chapter 8: darkening of skies. Something like this capability is occasionally found in raw modules. Camera Raw can do as well as our action some of the time.
- Chapter 9: skin desaturation isn't necessary in a fully raw workflow the way that it is in the PPW. So although the raw modules don't have it, they don't need it.
- Chapter 10: the Bigger Hammer for heavy-duty highlight and shadow enhancement. Nothing as flexible is found in any raw module at present.
- Chapters 11-12: masked multiplications. This key step in uniting the light and dark halves into a harmonious whole is not emulated in any raw module as far as I know.
- Chapters 13: The H-K action to darken neutrals. I don't believe that any raw module can emulate this either.

Summing Up

The above comparison is not kind to raw modules. Of the ten items listed, the modules misleadingly called *modern* can't even touch more than half, and the rest only tenuously. Worse, I'd say that five categories are vital and the other five less so. Of the five biggies—initial color, contrast changes, color boost, MMM, and masked multiply—only the first is even addressed.

Though disappointing, that result is not surprising. The first step is the one that most closely resembles the way that things have always been done. All the others are newer. Things were never done that way because they couldn't have been.

Throughout military history, peacetime generals have been guilty of configuring their forces to win the last war and to defeat the last enemy. Time and again they are caught flatfooted when the next enemy deploys some new weapon or strategy. After a certain time, they catch up.

So let it be with the raw modules. I expect them to catch up, too. When they do, the advice of this chapter may be no more applicable than if I had told you to set text on a Linotype, or even a Compugraphic machine. The lessons of history, however, endure. Respect the proven techniques of the past. Ask yourself, though, what they proved themselves against. If things were done a certain way because no other way was technically possible, it's time to reconsider them.

Review and Exercises

✓In lightening the foreground of Postcard 14.11 while attempting to preserve what little was left of the light background, why was the green channel the best choice for blending?

✓The master curve recommended for use in CR-CS6, shown at the top of Figure 14.9, definitely hurts contrast. Explain why it also results in grayer colors.

✓Find some JPEGs that look good out of the camera. Choose three that have a colorful subject, and three that do not. To each, apply the flattening master curve shown at the top of Figure 14.9. Then, having made them look worse, recorrect them using the PPW. Compare to the original. Do you think this strategy works? In which group did it work better?

A Closer Look

We've had a hint of the power of opening multiple versions quickly. Here's an extension of that theme, followed by a discussion of the specifics of Camera Raw.

In 2011 I received a slew of raw files from a professional photographer. There was no rush to process them. The scenery was tropical, and a postcard look was desirable.

The photographer knew that such scenes look terrible if the coloring is even slightly too cool. Also, he feared that the strong sunlight might make it hard to hold lighter areas.

Recall the strategy of the photographer of Figure 14.1, who underexposed a sunset image with a view to later correction and paid for it with his job. This tropical photographer did not go as far. But he planned it so that his shots would more likely have problems with shadows plugging than with light areas washing out.

He changed the Camera Raw defaults and applied a new setting to everything. It overrode the camera's setting for white balance and substituted something slightly yellower. He also used the Fill Light slider (CR-CS5) to enhance shadow detail. And in that form, the files came to me. How should I proceed?

* * *

Batch-opening seems like a clear choice. Earlier I suggested three versions: the Camera Raw default, the settings of Figure 14.9, and a version with enhanced highlights. The photographer's own setting made a fourth variant.

The "original" shown in Postcard 14.14 is the CR-CS5 default. Nothing further was done with this variant. In fact, I never used the default for any of the corrections in the set, because the photographer's custom setting always gave something more suited to my need for a different, yet plausible, interpretation of the color.

I never used that fourth version (custom setting) as a start point, either. Instead, I used the Figure 14.9 settings unless there was important highlight detail. That happens to be the case here, so I started with a version that had Recovery=+50 and otherwise was the CR-CS5 default, minus sharpening and noise reduction. It will be shown later as Figure 14.17C.

In moving on, there was no initial color issue. I did some light blending in luminosity mode, false profile/multiply, and then H-K. The color increase was mostly MMM, in view of the need for variation in the water. The whole thing, therefore, took less than three minutes and produced Figure 14.15A. The file as opened with the photographer's settings is Figure 14.15B.

It is only to be expected that Figure 14.15A will be the better of the two, since I knew what the image looked like when correcting it and the photographer's settings did not. The question is whether it is better in every respect. It should be asked once for color, again for contrast.

I strongly prefer my version's dark greens. I also prefer the variation in the water, but am not sold on its underlying color. I consider the beach to be slightly red.

Evaluation of contrast is more one-sided in favor of my greenery, darker ocean, and especially the whitewater. On the other hand, I dislike the beach. Figure 14.15B portrays the sand reflecting the warm sun enticingly.

In short, Figure 14.15A is *not* better in every respect. The merit of having alternate images is that we can pick their best points. Occasionally we just split the difference. Figure 14.16A is a 50–50 blend. It doesn't seem to have helped.

Instead, we use masks, just as we commonly do with the MMM + Color Boost action. For color, it's easy. Everything I like about Figure 14.15B is light. Everything I dislike is dark. Therefore, Figure 14.15B goes as a layer on top of Figure 14.15A. The RGB composite, or the L of LAB, is loaded as a layer mask, minimizing the impact in darker areas. The layer is changed to Color mode, 50% opacity. The result is Figure 14.16B.

Postcard 14.14 *(opposite) A beach near Rincón, Puerto Rico.*

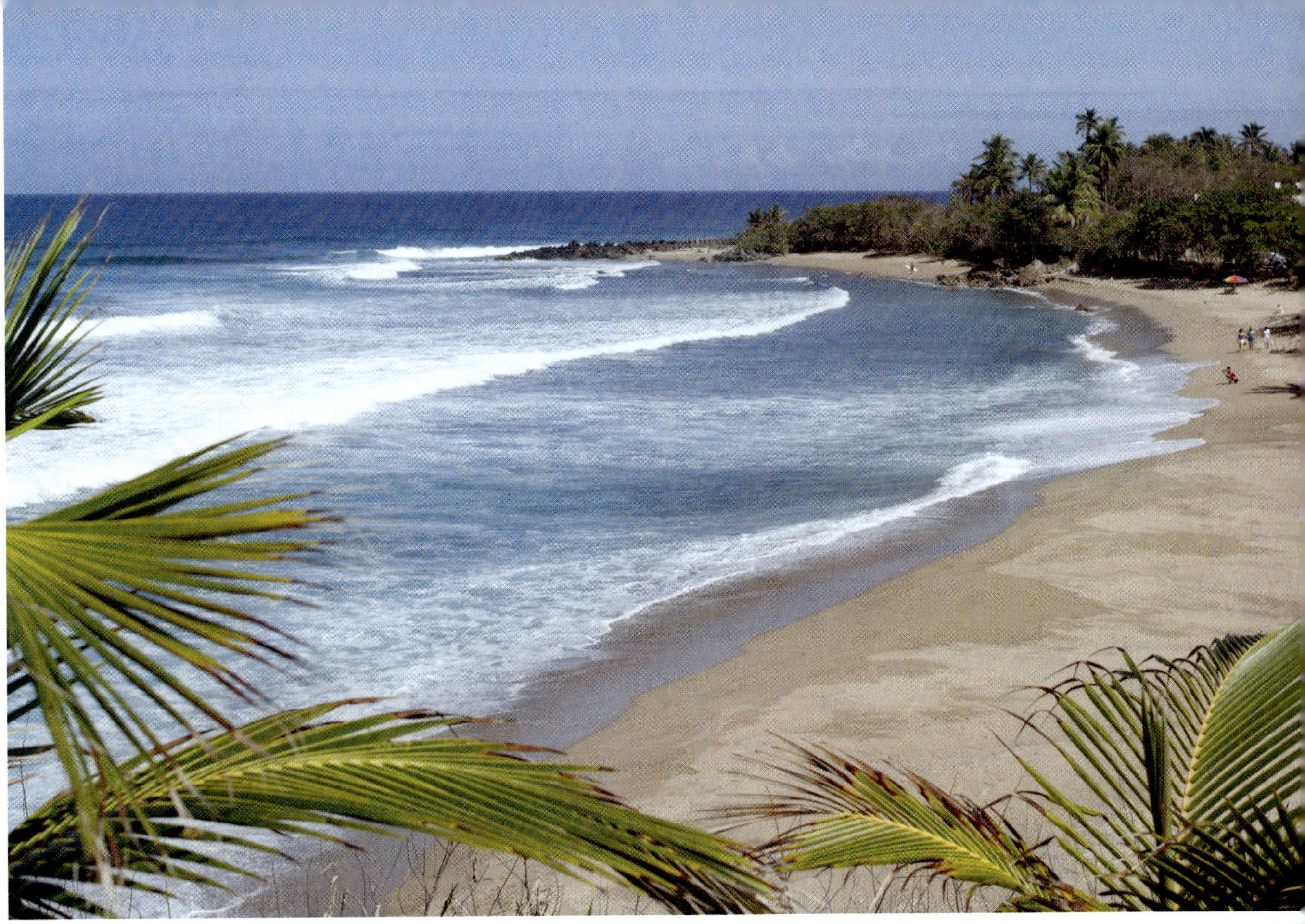
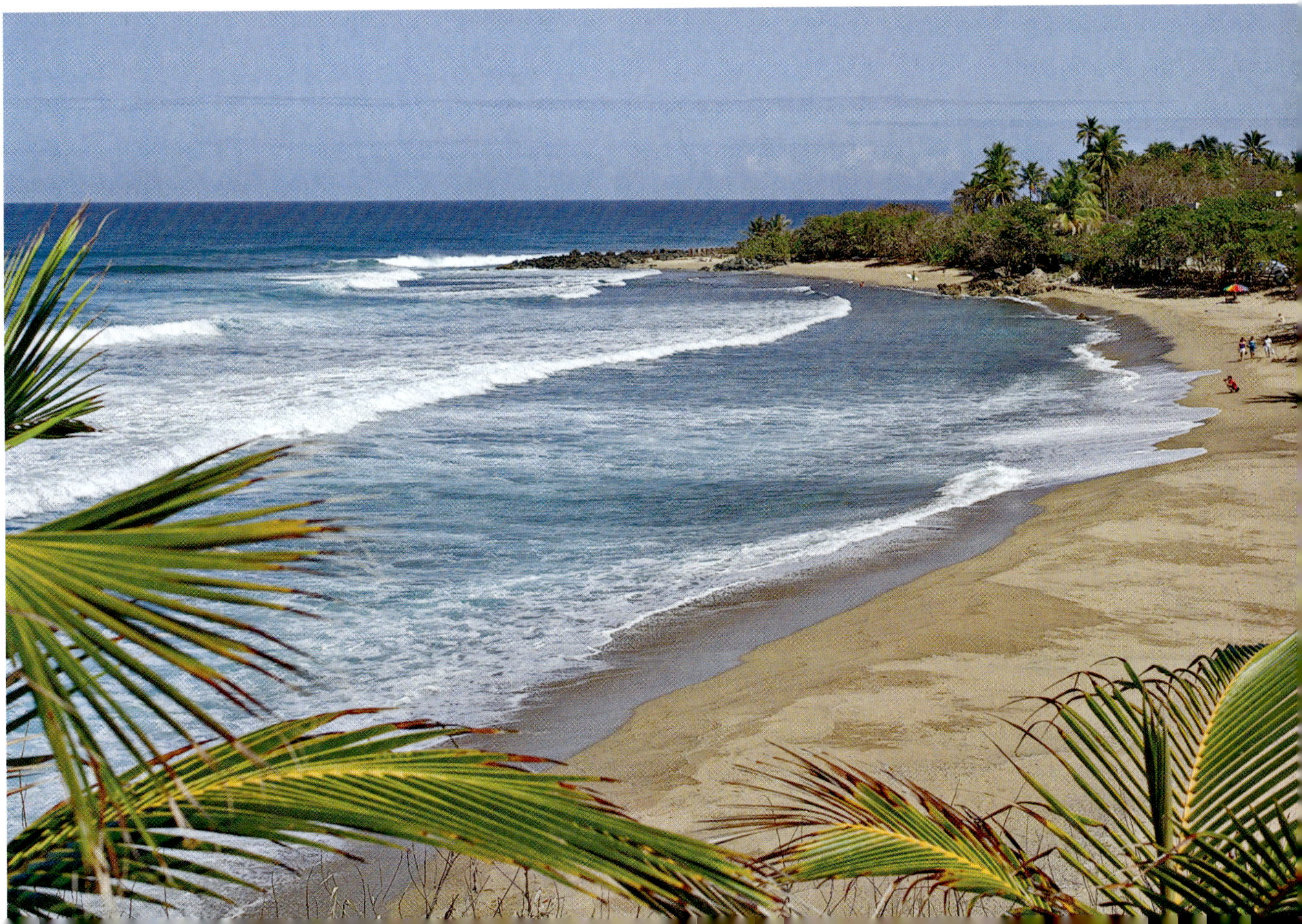

I now copy the color layer, mask and all, to a third layer, which gets set to Luminosity. This move, which is not shown, is less successful. The beach gets better, as planned, but the whitewater, being light, picks up the inferior detail of Figure 14.15B.

Since the beach is somewhat darker than the whitewater, yet not as dark as the trees, the solution is a U-shaped curve to the layer mask. The curve is shown next to the composite result, Figure 14.16C. You may wish to compare a similar U-curve way back in Figure 5.12B.

All this could have been done without Camera Raw, but it would have taken more time. To see where other opportunities may arise, let's go over the command structure, including the differences between CR-CS6 and CR-CS5.

Please keep in mind that I do not endorse Camera Raw over any other module. I write about it because it's the one we all have. And if you're thinking this is some subtle swipe at Camera Raw, it isn't. It's correct that I think that previous versions were woeful technically, and even the current version lags somewhat. However, I read online reviews of products that seem to spec out better, and find complaints that this module is too slow and has a dorky interface, and that one crashes frequently, and the other one sometimes delivers grotesque artifacts. None of these problems, in my opinion, currently exist in Camera Raw, and that counts for a lot.

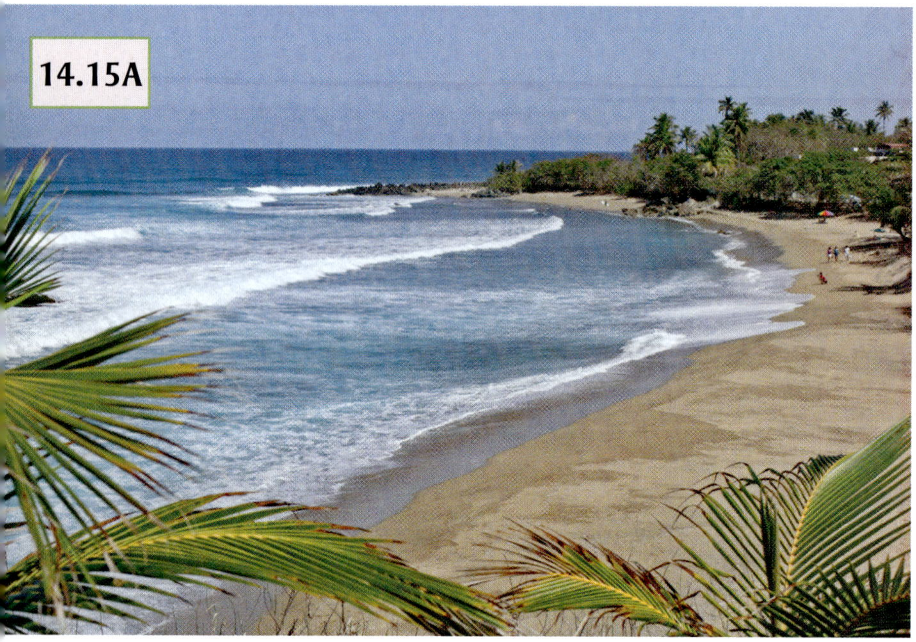

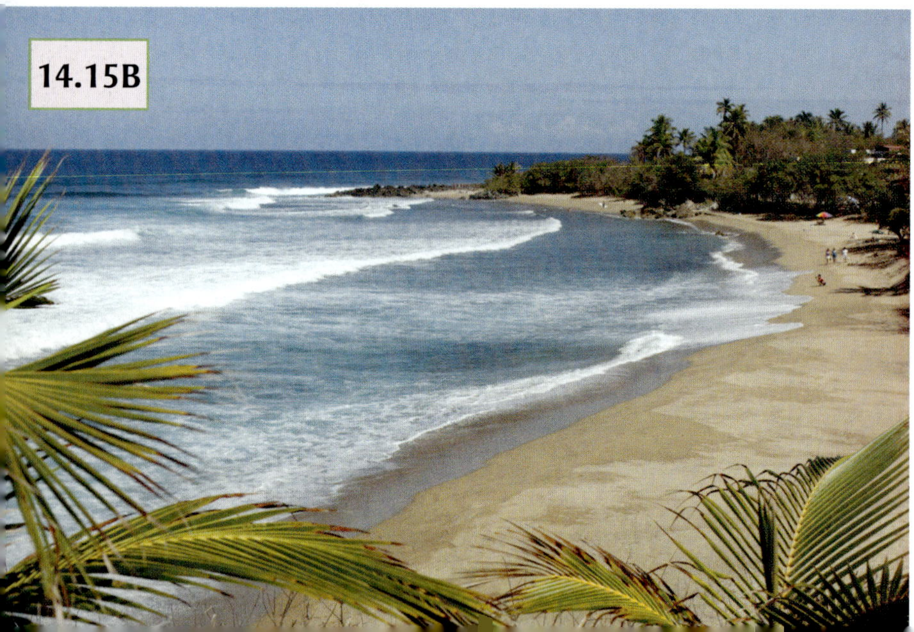

Tone Panel, Color Section

- **Temperature** and **Tint** (both versions) were the only ways to attempt to correct color casts in CR-CS5; CR-CS6 adds channel curves.

The two sliders compare roughly to the AB channels of LAB. Temperature, like the B, runs from yellow to blue. Tint, like the A, goes from green to magenta. Annoyingly, these sliders alter darkness, too. Moves toward green and yellow lighten and toward blue and magenta darken. The color changes affect all ranges although gamut issues limit the

***Figure 14.15** Top, a tentative correction, applying PPW to an initial capture based on CR-CS5 defaults plus highlight enhancement. Bottom, an uncorrected second acquisition in CR-CS5, overriding the White Balance setting in favor of something yellower.*

amount of the change in the highlights and shadows. There is no provision for limiting the effect to a certain tonal range, as with a mask.

Uses: Each file opens by default with settings called As Shot, meaning that the values are those suggested by the camera. Be cautious about changing them. The two exceptions: first, for artistic purposes it may help to add a slight artificial cast, as the photographer did in Figure 14.15B. Second, if the raw file has an extreme cast, something worse than, say, the hockey scene of Figure 3.12, an attempt to reduce without eliminating it can make a final correction easier.

Pictures with horrible casts, usually taken indoors under low light or strange illumination, are deceptive. You can correct them. And when you do, the audience

***Figure 14.16** Top, a 50–50 blend of Figure 14.15A and 14.15B. Middle, Figure 14.15B is still at 50% opacity, but its impact is restricted to lighter areas by a layer mask, and the mode is set to Color. Bottom, the color layer and its mask are duplicated. Mode is changed to Luminosity, and the curve below is applied to the layer mask.*

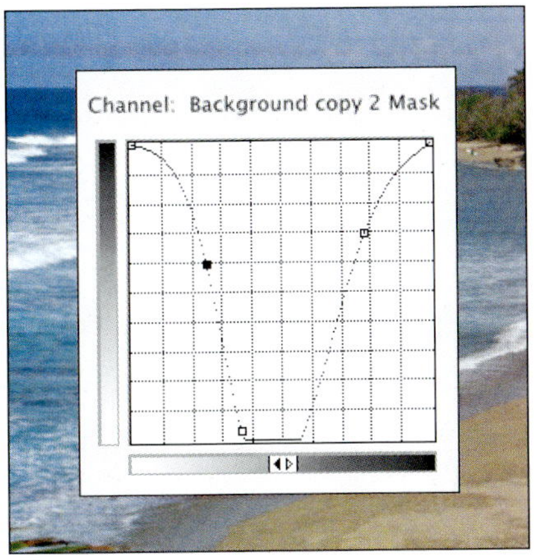

14.16A

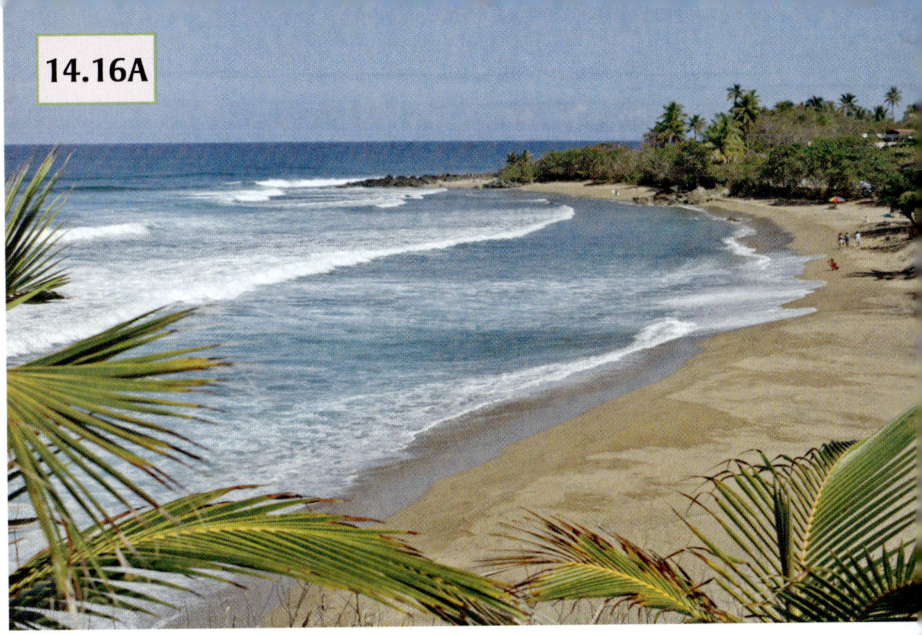

14.16B

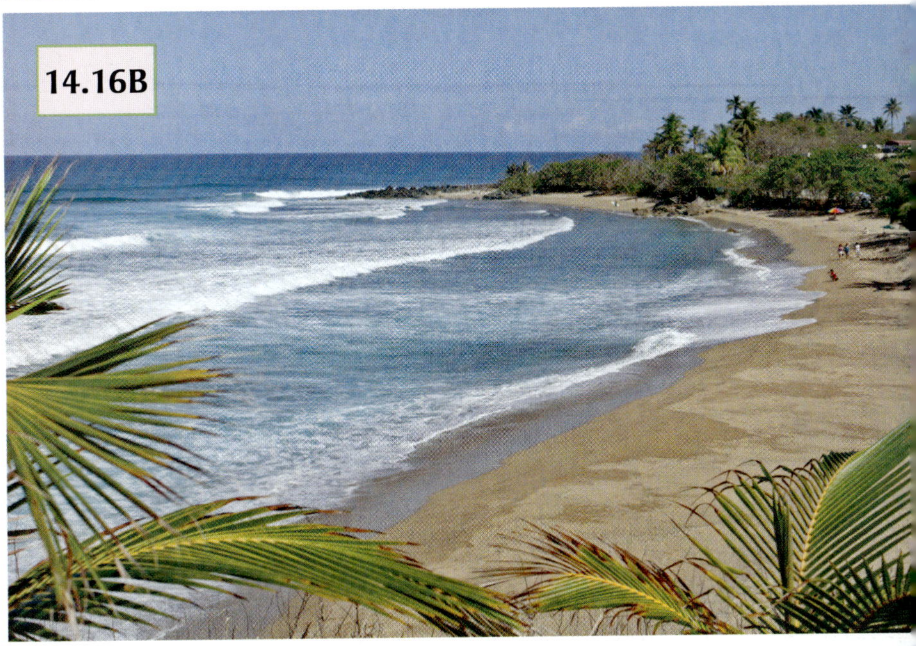

14.16C

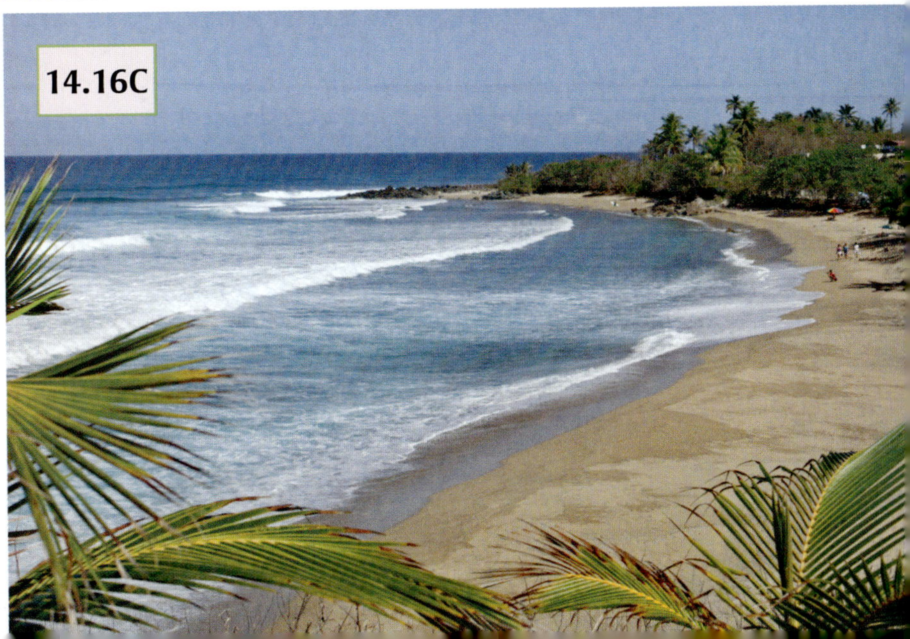

gasps. They can't believe the improvement. So naturally you feel appreciated and at peace with the wicked world.

Impressing laypeople is not a reliable measure of image quality. Ask yourself how the scene would have been perceived by people who were present when the photo was taken. This doesn't mean making the photo look like it was shot in sunlight. In fact, it's not clear what it does mean, other than the cast must be savagely slashed and probably the picture lightened overall.

The odds of getting something impressive out of a really poor original on your first try are excellent. The odds against achieving perfection are much higher.

The same strategy stressed throughout the book applies here. Use our standard workflow to correct a cast, no matter how severe. But if it's a bad one and it's worth the extra time, go back and do a second quick version, and choose a different approach. If your first attempt used RGB curves, do it the second time in LAB. Or try doing it entirely with Hue/Saturation. With even more time to kill, try out the opponent-color method illustrated way back in Figure 9.14. Or do any of these things at about half the strength you think is appropriate, correct contrast from there, and at the end go back and try to eliminate the cast that remains.

None of the above are recommendable if they are your only shot at the correction. But any of them, if applied in Color mode at a low opacity, is likely to improve your first effort. Here's why.

All methods of attacking strong casts have similar objectives, but in practice the results never are identical because the tools being used are too different. Nevertheless, all will have things in common. And if all the methods get the same result in a certain area, that area is likely right. The mistakes, if any, will be found where they vary. So a slight averaging of color is likely to pay dividends.

This long explanation left out one of the liest and most efficient ways to get an alternate color version: do it in Camera Raw by manipulating the Temperature and Tint sliders. Will the result be as good as with curves? Probably not. Will its color be credible? Yes. And if you blend it into your "final" file as described above, will you have something better than either version? Very likely. And if not, what do you have to lose?

If you decide to do it, you may as well go whole hog. The assumption is that the Camera Raw version will be used for its color only. In that case, it may pay to take a few seconds to use some of the contrast-related sliders discussed below, Clarity being a good start. The question again: what have you got to lose? It only takes a few seconds extra. You think the chances of using this contrast change are poor, but if it turns out otherwise, it will be one of life's happy little surprises.

The automated methods discussed earlier, plus the ability to create alternate versions to combat serious casts, are the current principal advantages that Camera Raw offers—and they aren't old-fashioned ones, either.

Tone Panel, Contrast Section

- **Exposure** (both versions; stronger and slightly different effect in CR-CS6) is the simplest slider. It lightens or darkens overall. Shadows and highlights are not protected and can vanish, although a change in the CR-CS6 algorithm affords a bit of protection. Color can change because all channels are affected equally.

  Uses: None that I would recommend.

- **Recovery** (CR-CS5) was replaced by **Highlights** and **Whites** in CR-CS6. All can unearth hidden highlights, but only the Highlights slider enhances them. Recovery and Whites do not add apparent crispness in the sense of the Bigger Hammer action or even of the Shadows/Highlights command in Photoshop proper.

To see the differences in approach, take a closer look at the whitewater in the tropical scene we just worked on. First, as a baseline, Figure 14.17A is the CR-CS6 default. Figure 14.17B is its counterpart in CR-CS5. To it, a Recovery setting of +50 is added in Figure 14.17C.

The image has gotten darker overall, up to about the three-quartertone. In principle this adds highlight and quartertone detail. However, these settings also darken the highlight, which costs contrast. To me, in spite of the need for more highlight detail, Figure 14.17C looks worse than either default. On the other hand, it can be fixed by forcing a light point back in.

Moving on to CR-CS6, Figure 14.17D shows Whites at a setting of −50. To some extent it has the same relationship to the default Figure 14.17A that the Recovery version does to its own default. However, it is not as ham-handed as Recovery because it does not reach as far into the midtones.

Figure 14.17E substitutes −50 Highlights for −50 Whites. The setting produces better water, for two reasons. First, the highlight was not permitted to darken. Second, Highlights uses a blurred-mask kind of routine to sharpen detail, while Whites does not.

Uses: In a Camera Raw-only workflow the Whites slider can help. If PPW techniques will be used, however, Highlights is never worse and often better. Unlike the earlier Recovery, Highlights can sometimes substitute for the Bigger Hammer. Like that action, it can provoke haloing. Unlike it, what's affected is determined by overall darkness, not that of a single channel. The Bigger Hammer, therefore, can be effective in strongly colored objects, such as the flowers we saw back in Figure 10.13. Also, if you're using the PPW panel, the Bigger Hammer has the enormous advantage of its options window, which allows previewing many different enhancement methods.

- **Fill Light** and **Blacks** (CR-CS5) were replaced by **Shadows** and **Blacks** in CR-CS6. The same considerations that we just discussed for highlights apply, but in reverse. CR-CS6 treats shadows exactly as it does highlights; the Shadows and Blacks sliders being mirror images of Highlights and Whites. This symmetry was not found in CR-CS5. Also, in CR-CS6 positive values in Whites and Highlights suppress highlight detail rather than enhancing it, something that wasn't explicitly possible previously.

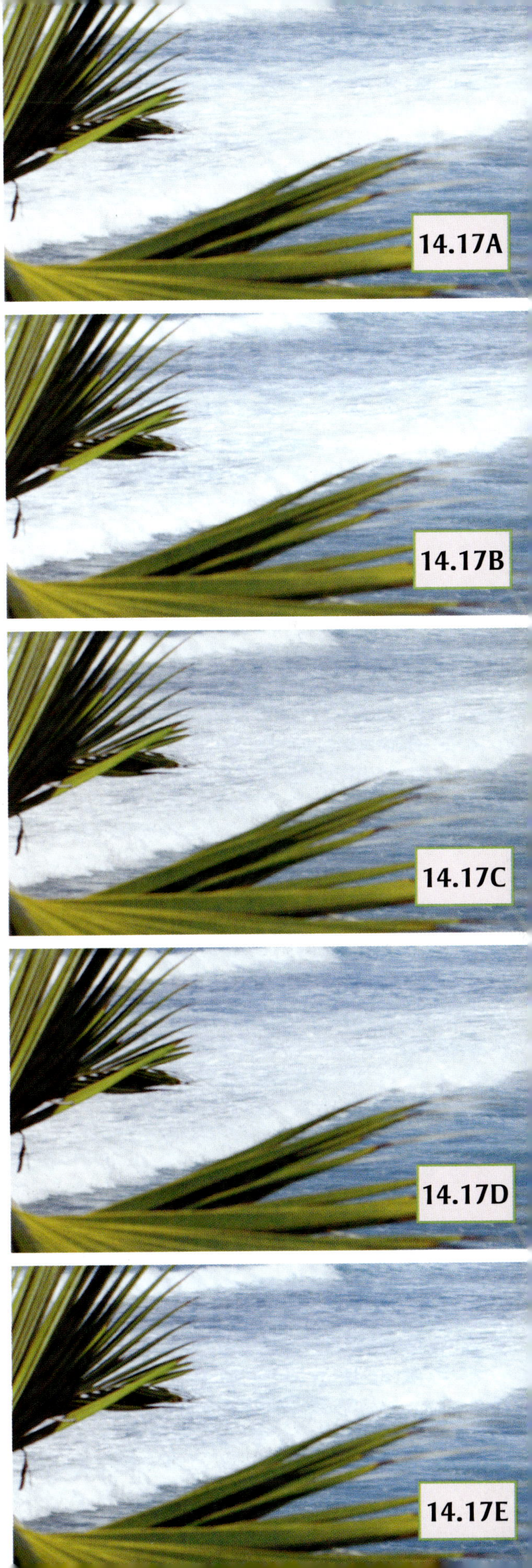

Figure 14.17 *The Highlights slider in CR-CS6 offers true highlight enhancement. Top to bottom, the CR-CS6 defaults; the CR-CS5 defaults; +50 Recovery (CR-CS5); –50 Whites (CR-CS6); and –50 Highlights (CR-CS6).*

Shadows were treated differently in CR-CS5. Fill Light was the opposite of Recovery. It could not be used to suppress shadows any more than Recovery could suppress highlights. However, it was apparently felt that there was a need for such a capability in shadows, although not in highlights. The CR-CS5 Blacks slider is, in fact, Fill Light in reverse. The CR-CS6 Blacks slider replaces both; it should probably have been renamed to avoid confusion.

The new CR-CS6 slider, Shadows, is to Blacks (CR-CS6) as Highlights is to Whites.

Uses: Shadow enhancement in a raw module is generally unnecessary, unlike highlights. Otherwise, the same comments apply. For our purposes Shadows is a better choice than Blacks.

- **Contrast** (same concept in both versions, stronger effect in CR-CS6) is an oldie but goodie. Quartertones and midtones are usually more important than highlights and shadows. We gain more range with which to portray them by short-changing the shadows and highlights without wiping them out completely. The higher the Contrast setting, the greater the suppression of the extremes.

This tactic works well in the melons of Figure 14.4 and the crouching woman of Figure 14.10. But it would do poorly in the current surf scene.

Uses: Don't use it for batch acquisitions, but consider adding Contrast to individual files if you can see that your highlights and shadows aren't important.

The trick I pulled in the blown-out sky exercise of Postcard 14.11 was a Contrast setting of −100, drastically decreasing midtone detail and assigning it to highlights and shadows. Don't hold your breath until you see another picture for which this move is appropriate.

- **Brightness** (CR-CS5, no explicit equivalent in CR-CS6) is responsible for the signature flaw in the work of Camera Raw aficionados. Although no longer visible by name, its mischievous legacy lives on.

No two modules agree on how to interpret what the camera actually saw. They do agree, however, that the most literal interpretation of the incoming data creates something too dark. The question is how to transform it into something presentable. Several right answers exist. The wrong answer is the way that it is done in Camera Raw.

The Brightness command applied the same adjustment to all channels, or to use the technical term, it was a master curve. Detail in strongly colored objects depends upon what's found in the lightest channel. Equal lightening of all channels damages this critical information.

There are other defects to this approach but the inability to hold detail in colored objects is the big one. We saw earlier in this chapter that even experts could not get optimal results from the bright flowers of Figure 14.8 once Camera Raw's algorithm had lessened their detail.

Bright colors that need detail are mose likely to be reds. And that's the signature defect referred to above. Hundreds of people show me their work. It's usually easy to tell which of them are making lavish use of an Adobe raw module: their reds tend to be blobs.

This may sound like beating a dead horse because the Brightness slider no longer exists in CR-CS6. The horse, however, is very much alive, though disguised as a bird of paradise.

Setting everything to 0 in the simplified interface of CR-CS6 now produces a nice-looking picture; previously it yielded something useful to the skilled but unattractive to everyone else.

To make zero-looks-good work requires lightening behind the scenes. CR-CS6 does that in the same quality-killing way. Go back to the brilliant flowers of Postcard 4.18. A convoluted procedure was shown to fix an original with almost no detail in its bright reds.

Although not mentioned at the time, the original was so terrible because it was opened with the zero-looks-good defaults of CR-CS6.

Uses: You're stuck with it. The question is how to minimize damage. Camera Raw's other tools can undo some of it but Photoshop's are more effective. In CR-CS5 the recommended settings of Figure 14.9 use Brightness conservatively enough to avoid major problems while strongly enough to make color adjustments easier. CR-CS6 doesn't have this option. I think it's better now just to apply a flattening curve after acquisition, which retains detail that Camera Raw shouldn't be losing in the first place.

Tone Panel, Final Section

- **Clarity** (both versions, but different algorithm and a stronger effect in CR-CS6) is a more sophisticated version of the Contrast slider with a little conventional sharpening thrown in. It increases contrast in the midtones, but the attendant loss in lighter and darker areas is handled more delicately and less detectably than is the case with Contrast.

  Uses: In a Camera Raw-only workflow this is often a quick path to improvement, one that would be a welcome addition to Photoshop proper. It should not be used on images whose character you would describe as being light or dark, because its impact would be to lighten or darken them further.

  Clarity should not be used in files destined for the PPW, however, because the type of sharpening it does inhibits better sharpening later.

- **Vibrance** and **Saturation** (both versions) attempt to boost color. Saturation does so overall. Vibrance tries to be more intelligent. It limits the boost in reds, thinking that they might be fleshtones. It darkens blues as well as intensifying them, also a correct decision for most images.

  Uses: In our workflow, none. MMM + Color Boost is stronger in all respects.

Other Panels

- **Tone Curve panel, parametric** (both versions) is aggravating. On the one hand, it repackages the curves dialog in a more intuitive way. On the other, it can only apply a master curve. This is like designing a race car that cannot shift out of first gear.

  Uses: None until the situation is corrected.

- **Tone Curve panel, point** (channel curves added in CR-CS6). Master curves—the use of one curve that applies equally to all channels—have been known to be an inferior method of setting range since the mid-1980s, when vendors of "high-end" equipment in that turtle-computing time considered using them to speed things up. They decided correctly that the quality hit was too severe. By the mid-1990s even color beginners were aware that using master curves for anything more than minor changes resulted in unacceptable detail losses.

  For the first dozen years of its existence, Camera Raw, unlike its competitors, offered no other alternative. Individual channel curves were finally introduced in CR-CS6. It is therefore now possible to correct images with more than one cast.

  The curves are applied in an RGB that is almost certainly different from the one in your own Color Settings. It employs sRGB gamma, but the color definitions of ProPhoto RGB. This is a dubious choice, but it's workable.

  Uses: In CR-CS5, none. In CR-CS6 the master channel curve is used in the suggested defaults shown in Figure 14.9. Otherwise, there are some minor disadvantages to using them on individual images. Unless you decide to acquire the image twice, the curves can't be applied in Color mode. If the curves are extreme the Camera Raw result will be marginally more noisy than doing it in Photoshop. Neither of these factors is a big deal.

- **Detail panel, sharpening** (both versions) Camera Raw's sharpening is no worse than Photoshop's USM filter—each is around thirty years behind the times. There is no excuse for such a technically feeble implementation in either, but at least in Photoshop we can write actions to work around the deficiencies.

  In any event, a raw module is the wrong place to apply sharpening, which should come near the end of the workflow. Otherwise, what looks good now may appear oversharpened later. The comment applies also to the practice of light sharpening (sometimes also known as input or capture sharpening) early, with stronger sharpening later in Photoshop. The idea is wrong-headed; an earlier light sharpen (barring one saved in the form of a halo map and imposed later) pre-empts better sharpening later. If you don't believe it, persuade yourself by acquiring a few files both sharpened and unsharpened. Then, apply the next chapter's action, and see whether any of its sophisticated tools can get as good of a final sharpen out of the presharpened version as is possible with the undamaged one. I predict you will find the white artifacting to be a daunting problem.

Uses: None. Set Amount to 0 and move on.

- **Detail panel, noise reduction** (both versions). Some considerations are similar to those for sharpening. The competition is Photoshop, whose noise reduction was fine for the last decade of the previous century but is pitiful for the second decade of ours. In principle, Camera Raw's implementation is better. On the other hand, while almost all images need sharpening, only a few need noise reduction. Any attempt to reduce noise risks softening the image, yet if noise gets magnified later in the process some may find it a nuisance to remove.

I personally keep noise reduction off but I don't advocate that you do the same without some thought. The default is unlikely to do much harm. It can, however, make it harder for a skilled person to take out noise later, because it attacks certain things that aren't really noise and thereby disguises the real target.

Uses: If you rarely find noise to be a problem, turn it off. If you never intend to reduce noise manually because you can't afford the time, leave it on. If you are confident in your ability to manage noise and are willing to take the time to do so when objectionable, turn it off.

- **HSL/Grayscale panel** (both versions) is a weak implementation of a strong idea. It tries to update Photoshop's antiquated Hue/Saturation command, but is noisy and lacks the control of the target colors that H/S has. Even without these factors, though, the raw module is the wrong place to apply such a command. We should assume that the workflow will produce a good result without this, H/S, Selective Color, or anything similar. If this assumption is proven false, then we can and should act. But doing so prematurely can limit future options.

Uses: None.

- **Split Toning panel** (both versions). The idea of allowing different moves for the dark and light halves of the picture, with the user defining the limits of the halves, is a good one. Unfortunately, the critical step of excluding the deepest shadows, which generally should remain neutral, was omitted. Otherwise, Split Toning would be a welcome addition to Photoshop.

Uses: None.

As to Noise, It's Mostly Noise

One of the marketing claims for raw modules is that their adjustments are somehow purer, which is commonly understood as "less noisy." Meanwhile, my recommendation for CR-CS6 is to flatten the image with a curve and then reopen it elsewhere. Such an execute-and-reverse strategy often produces noise.

Couple the two, and you may start to wonder whether you risk excessive artifacting by getting out of the raw module too early. For Camera Raw (and, I imagine, for Lightroom as well) the opposite is true. (As noted earlier, I haven't run similar tests on non-Adobe products.)

An up-front caution. Camera Raw is not noisy enough to have a practical impact except in extreme cases. The noise becomes worse the more that color is involved, but it can be seen, if you look hard enough, even with something as bland as the example we're about to study.

The scene needs more color and also must be lightened. Figure 14.18A is a CR-CS6 default capture. Figure 14.18B was acquired in CR-CS6 with the flattening curve shown in Figure 14.9. Figure 14.18C was acquired in CR-CS5 to an even flatter specification than recommended: it has a Brightness setting of 0 and otherwise the settings of Figure 14.9.

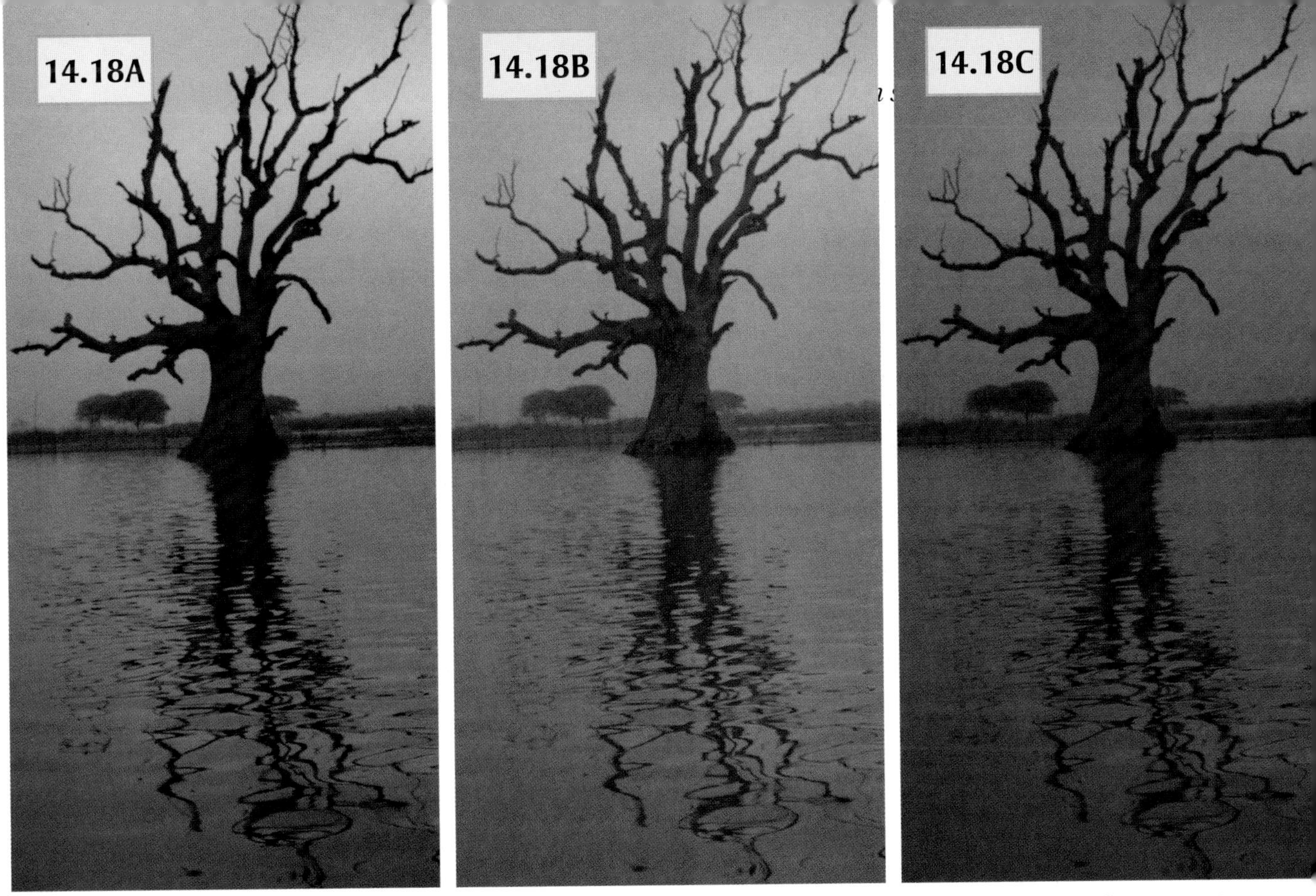

***Figure 14.18** Three start points for a torture test. Left, CR-CS6 default settings. Middle, the flattening curve of Figure 14.9 is added. Right, opened in CR-CS5 with the Figure 14.9 settings except that Brightness is set to 0.*

Once we correct for these things and try for the same look with each of the three, which would you guess will have the most noise?

* * *

Correcting within Camera Raw is noisier than dumping out a flatter file and correcting it in Photoshop. This is true for contrast but it is more true of color and it is especially true if the alternative is correcting the color in LAB. I have tested the proposition with a variety of methods and images.

The differences, though present, are minor enough that big enlargements are needed to see them. The following example is an extreme one but should make the point.

To get something where the extra noise is visible to the unaided eye requires a strong color boost. Unfortunately, the methods being tested are so different that an identical look is impossible. We have to settle for contestants close enough to draw conclusions about noise.

An intermediate step is not shown because its results, like those of the tests that do present seemingly similar versions, aren't dramatic enough. I added +100 Saturation to the CR-CS6 settings of Figure 14.18A. Then, I moved it into LAB. Figures 14.18B and 14.18C went into LAB immediately without the saturation boost. I used straight-line curves at equal angles in the A and B to boost color in them, and a customized L curve to try to match the Camera Raw result.

At this point all three versions were similar. If you looked hard enough and magnified the file, you could see that the version done entirely in Camera Raw was the worst of the three.

I continued by jacking up the color beyond all reason. All three files were now subjected to two applications of the Color Boost action, with opacity of each increased from the default 75% to 100%.

The original acquisition specified a resolution of 6 megapixels. The three Figure 14.18 versions and their Figure 14.19 counterparts have been downsized. The final six have not, so they are cropped as needed to show the effect. Figures 14.19A, 14.19D, and 14.19G are based on Figure 14.18A, in which the heavy work is done in Camera Raw. Figures 14.19B, 14.19E and 14.19H are based on the CR-CS6 capture with flattening curves, Figure 14.18B. And Figures 14.19C, 14.19F, and 14.19J derive from the ugliest start point, the zeroed-out CR-CS5 version of Figure 14.18C.

The test is fair. All three originals have had the same number of conversions. From additional testing, I can say that the problem is not in the Saturation slider. The same amount of artifacting is caused by either Vibrance or Curves.

Figure 14.19A may strike you as more colorful than its two opponents. Not true; tests show that they are equally vivid. The contrary impression is caused by color shifts. Note the wild redness in the tree trunk. If you don't believe that the two LAB competitors have been pushed just as hard, take a look at the sunny area in the upper right. The two LAB versions have pushed it so far out of gamut that Photoshop has no clue how to deal with it, resulting in artifacting that isn't found in the Camera Raw version. It's easily fixed, because at least the hue is accurate. It is not so easy to clean up a bright red tree.

The conventional wisdom says Figure 14.19A should be the cleanest because it is the one where the most range-setting occurred in the raw module, and Figure 14.19C the worst because it requires the most work outside of it.

Not so. The one with the least exposure to the Camera Raw range-opening algorithm also has the least noise in the final product.

Summing Up

Commands that aren't discussed here are mostly camera-specific, with the exception of a grain setting that is premature in Camera Raw but would be useful in Photoshop.

Figure 14.19 *The test continues, after intermediate steps described in the text. This page left, a CR-CS6 modification of Figure 14.18A. Middle and right, LAB modifications of Figures 14.18B and 14.18C, respectively. All have been downsized, as have their counterparts in Figure 14.18. At actual size of acquisition, opposite page, differences are more pronounced.*

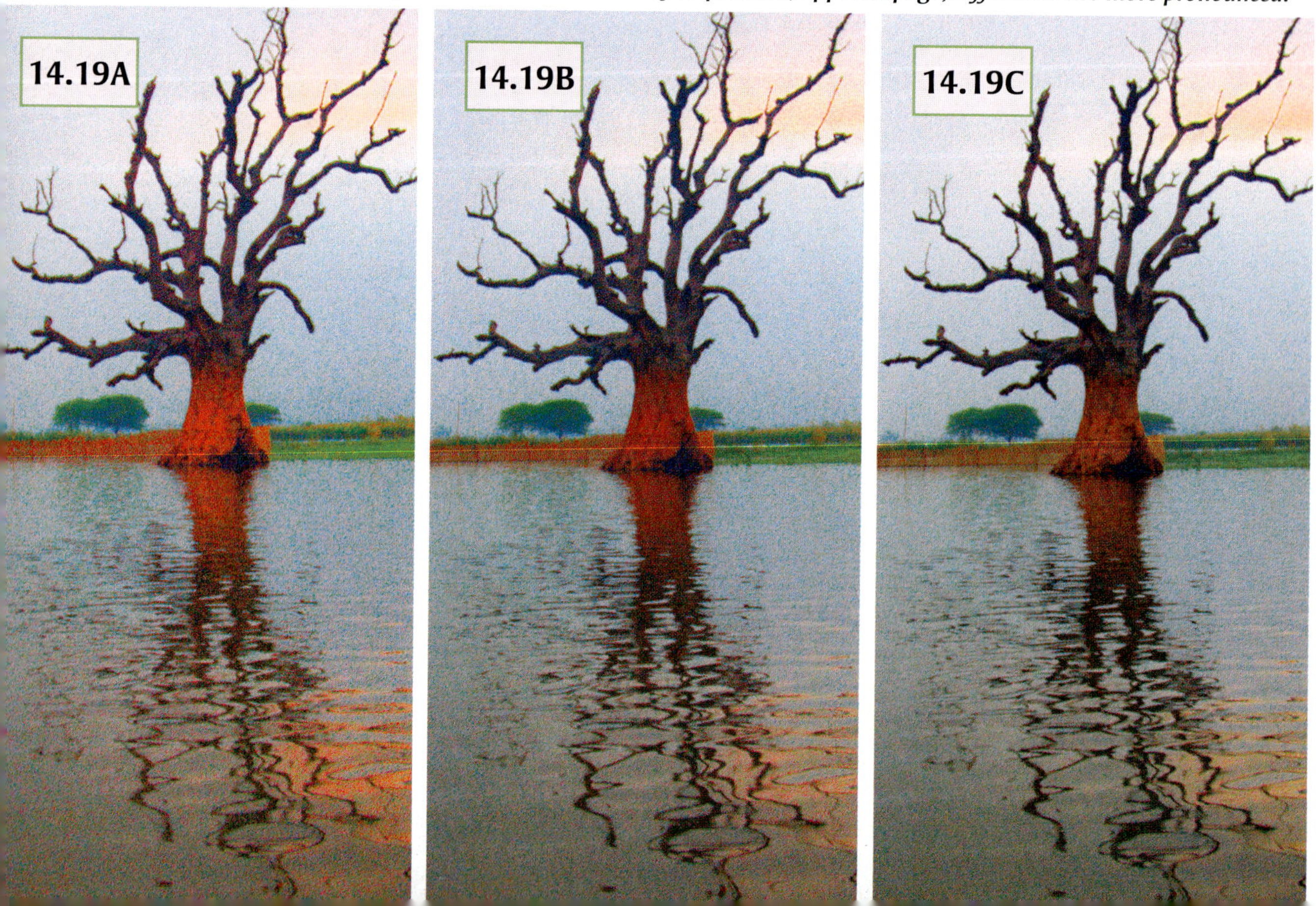

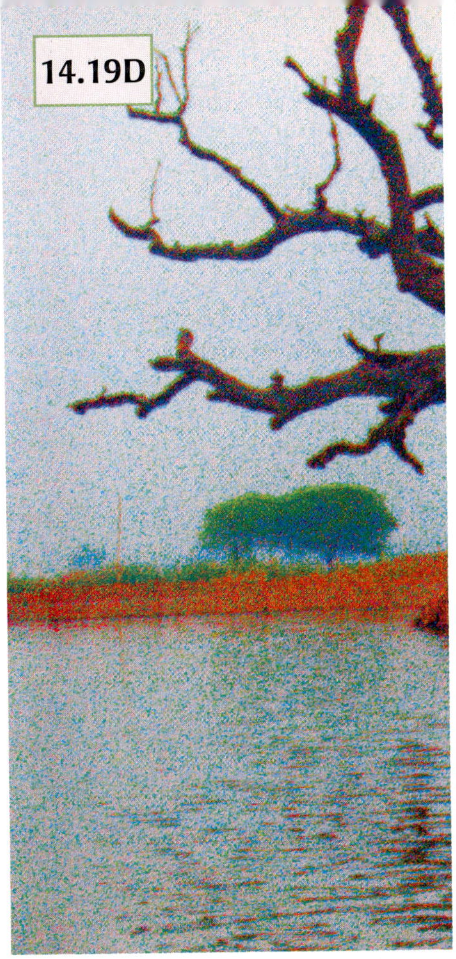

14.19D

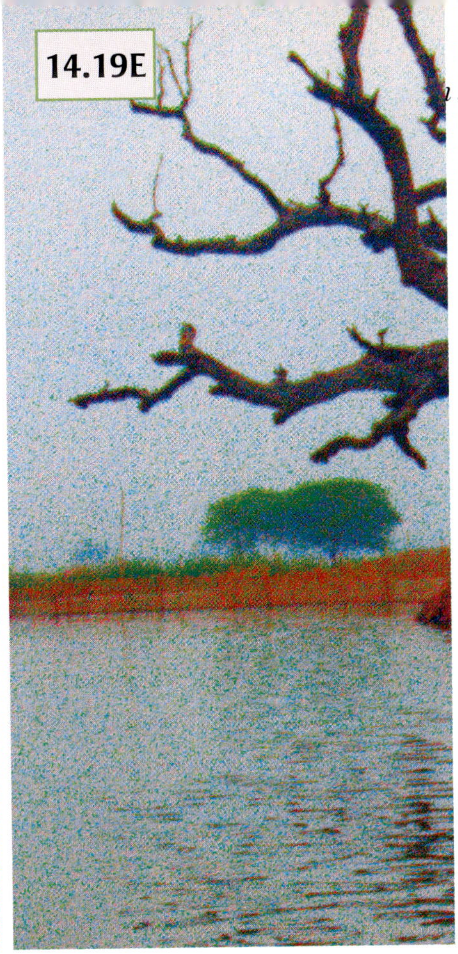

14.19E

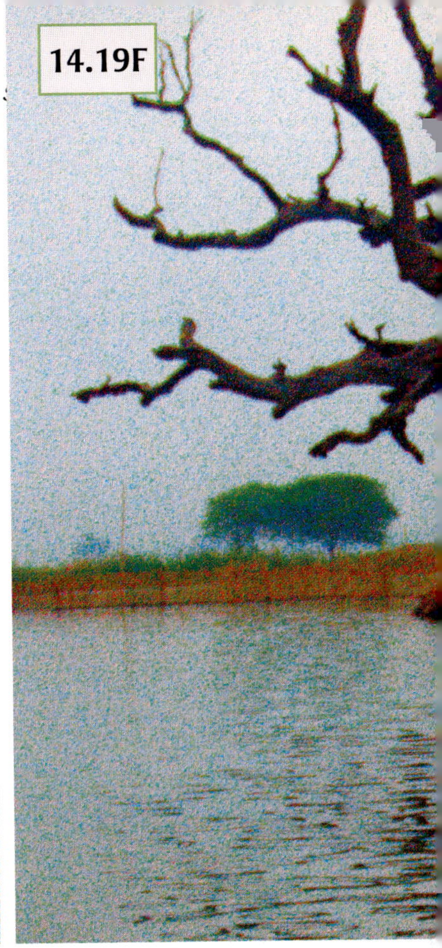

14.19F

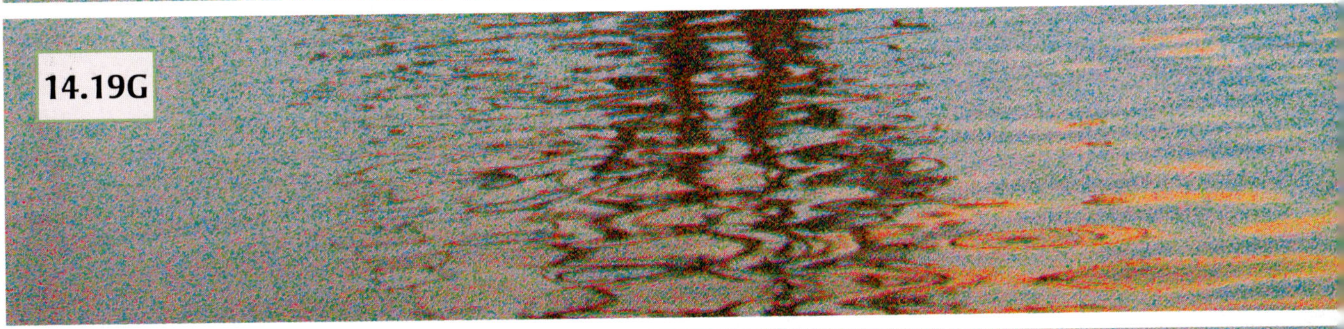

14.19G

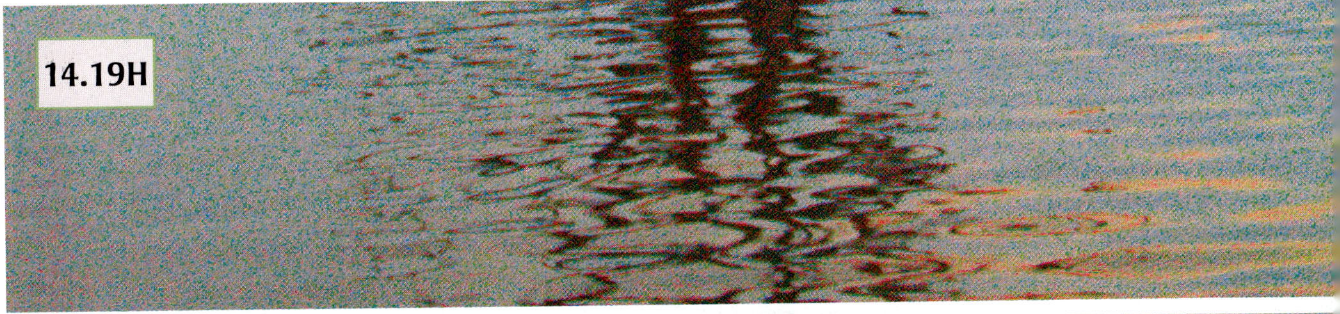

14.19H

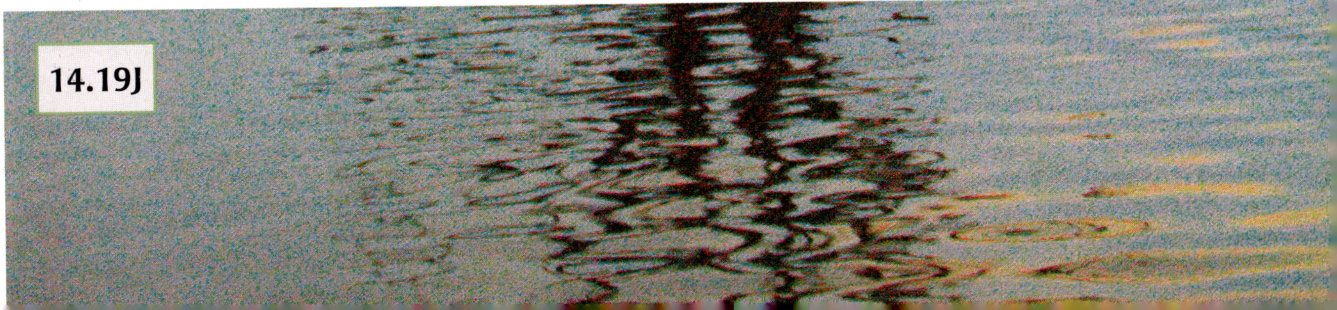

14.19J

This is one of several features in which Camera Raw's performance exceeds Photoshop's, almost as if the two products were competitors. The situation is challenging for the user, who must keep track of which is advancing faster.

We have only been processing pictures digitally for commercial purposes for thirty years. Workflows that developed early were primitive perforce, as anything more would have brought an extremely expensive computer to its knees. As time went on, workflows changed, not just because more complexity became possible but because the complexity gave better results.

Surprisingly, the pace has slowed in the last decade. Photoshop itself has become faster but not better; the entire PPW would have worked fine ten years ago had computers been fast enough. Camera Raw is better today but only because previous versions were so weak; the current iteration, except for a couple of improved algorithms, could, and should, have been released ten years earlier.

In future years raw modules will likely catch up. Accordingly it would be futile to pay much attention to the current state of their capabilities, which may change rapidly and without notice.

Studying the history of development in the graphic arts prevents one from being taken in. This chapter, for example, occasionally appears to snipe at workflows that happen to be old. Age, however, is a poor reason for rejection. Traditional workflows become traditional for good reasons. Linotypes were wonderful machines in their day. They were replaced not because they were old but because technology produced something clearly superior.

It is up to you to sift through the hype. I hope you will agree that things like the MMM action are useful not because they use technology unavailable in the past but because they make pictures look dramatically better. Similarly, the previous versions of Camera Raw were undesirable not because they were new but because they re-introduced problems that had long been solved by traditional workflows.

Such judgments will grow more difficult. Radical rethinking of traditional workflows could produce something faster and more effective than the PPW. Nothing is preventing the development of such alternatives today except lack of knowledge and/or enthusiasm for the project.

Although such a treasure chest is possible today, we end users haven't been given the keys. Tomorrow may be another story. But to have a happy ending we must consider yesterday, and resolve not to relive it. Unless yesterday happens to have been preferable.

The Bottom Line

This chapter discusses the best ways to acquire raw files for processing through the Picture Postcard Workflow. At present raw converters all use a workflow little modified from those of ten years or more ago. This calls for conservatism in acquiring the files. Opening tonal range in a raw module temporarily makes the file look better, but it can pre-empt superior moves that affect both color and contrast.

15

110 Steps to A Sharper Image

Sharpening technique has advanced rapidly. Faster computers allow more sophisticated maneuvers. The Picture Postcard Workflow doesn't require a specific sharpening method, but if you need a good one, here's an action that can be made as easy or as complex as you wish.

This final chapter discusses sharpening, also known as unsharp masking or USM. The color moves we've seen so far fit into a general, logical scheme with interacting parts. Sharpening is a necessary part of any workflow, but there's no need to use the methods I recommend to benefit from the rest of the PPW.

Why include this material at all, then? The biggest reason is the rate of change. Electronic sharpening has been around for forty years. Photoshop's filter is half that age. People used to apply that filter and call it quits. It wasn't until 1998 that practical, yet more sophisticated handling was proposed, keeping the traditional look but with greater realism. By the early part of the current century people were thinking of forms of sharpening that didn't resemble traditional methods at all.

More progress has therefore been made in understanding sharpening—and notice, I've never said what *sharpening* is—in the last five years than in the previous five hundred. Any of several intelligent suggestions made available in the last decade can make a difference as opposed to not sharpening at all or doing a bad job of it.

The action proposed here is modern because it has to be. It is so complex that it would have brought the computers of ten years ago to their knees. It's full of options that can solve almost any sharpening problem. It can also be used in a very simple way. That's how it will be shown in the first half of this chapter, followed by an in-depth look in the second.

Nobody likes complexity for its own sake. On the other hand, you should remember the lesson of the previous chapter. Traditional methods became traditional because they were good. They should be respected.

However, if it was not technically possible to do things a different way, it is time to reconsider them.

* * *

Ansel Adams summarized the whole issue as follows:

> Some photographic issues seem to defy precise explanation. Visual impressions are difficult to assess in verbal form, and we grope for words that encompass the qualities of the medium. One such elusive concept is sharpness. It is worthwhile...to consider sharpness and related concepts in physical terms, but in discussing mechanical or optical issues we must not lose sight of the much greater importance of image content—emotional, aesthetic, or literal. I believe there is nothing more disturbing than a sharp image of a fuzzy concept!

The philosophy is eloquently stated but difficult to implement. Sharpening is the most subjective area of color correction, the one where two people are most likely to disagree. It is hard to evaluate on screen. The reasons for sharpening in the first place are unclear; it definitely is effective, but the standard explanations as to why don't stand up to scrutiny.

The word means different things to different people. Ten years ago it would have referred only to the use of Filter: Sharpen>Unsharp Mask or something similar. Today many other routines, such as the Shadows/Highlights command or the Clarity slider of Camera Raw, are reasonably described as sharpeners. So is a multiplication through a blurred layer mask.

Enough of semantics. For now, we need to know only that almost all images need to be sharpened and that there are many ways to go about it.

Now, down to business. Make sure you're evaluating only the techniques I'm showing and not my taste. It's easy to back off (or increase) if you don't like my settings. But if you do decide that I've sharpened too much, remember that you're a biased observer. You *know* that these images have been sharpened. The casual observer does not. You will be more sensitive, because you know how to spot the artificiality that looks like added focus to most people.

When Is Automation Worthwhile?

All sharpening methods rely on trickery. The best sharpen is the one that does the most without making the trickery obvious.

It follows that sharpening needs to be done near the end of the correction process. This is particularly true in the PPW, which stresses files considerably. It may exaggerate artifacts to the point of becoming offensive. I am not so doctrinaire as to say that sharpening should always be the very last thing, but anything done afterward had best be minor.

OK. You have a file that has gone through the workflow described in previous chapters, or any other workflow, for that matter. Time now to sharpen. You have three options.

- Call up Filter: Sharpen>Unsharp Mask, enter numbers that suit you, and click OK.
- Use somebody else's method.
- Use the action I'm about to describe.

There is no reason to apologize for choosing one of the first two, and also no reason to continue reading this chapter. If you've decided to slog on, the first question is, why an action at all?

Suppose you have chosen the first alternative: a single application of the USM filter. It's one step. It can't be automated unless you are willing to lose the flexibility of entering your own numbers.

Let me suggest a superior way—not the way I recommend, but an improvement on USM alone. It requires four steps, not one.

- Make a duplicate layer.
- On it, apply USM at a setting stronger than you would normally like.

- Image: Apply Image, Source=same document, Layer=Background, Channel=RGB, Blending=Darken, Opacity=50%.
- Reduce layer opacity to taste.

If you don't believe that this is an improvement over USM alone, try it yourself on a few of your own files. Sharpening artifacts normally both lighten and darken around edges. The light artifacts are more offensive. The above procedure cuts that lightening in half.

Could the procedure be automated? Well, the final step certainly can't. You need to see the image before making the decision on opacity. And there's also a decision that requires attention during the second step.

That decision, however, is not as critical as the one in the fourth step. We *could* give that second step a standard value, something very high. The quality cost would be small. And then we could automate the first three steps. We could write an action that leaves us on the top layer, ready to make the opacity decision. The process would then be the following two steps, rather than four:

- Play the action.
- Reduce layer opacity to taste.

You would have to be doing a whole lot of sharpening to make it worthwhile to write the action and give up a certain amount of flexibility to save just two steps each time.

But what if, instead of saving two steps, you were saving 109?

Simpler Than It Sounds

The Sharpen action is the most complicated one in the PPW panel. It has around 110 steps, double that of the next most complicated, which is MMM + Color Boost.

So much for the question of whether to automate. Nobody in their right mind would do 110 manual steps on image after image. And so much for why you haven't seen such a behemoth action before. Even five years ago, playing such a thing would leave you time to step out for a beer before all the computing was done. Today, the action plays in close to real time except on large files.

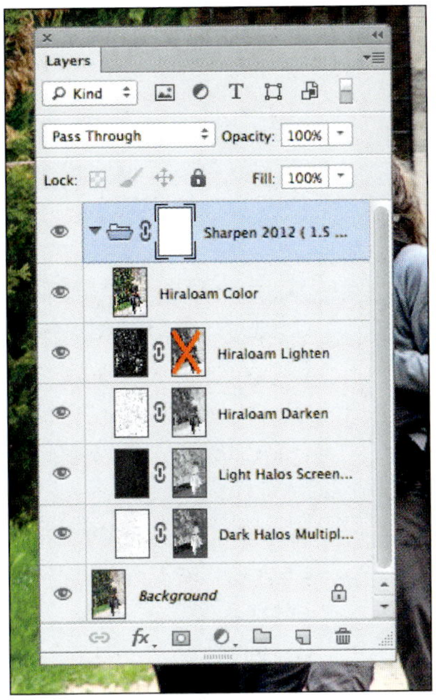

***Figure 15.1** The Sharpen action adds five layers, each for a different method. The top layer group can be adjusted to soften the overall effect.*

In our workflow the time for sharpening is right after the MMM + Color Boost action, which means we have an LAB document. Conveniently, the Sharpen action requires LAB, too. If you don't happen to have a flattened LAB file, it tries to produce one by flattening the file (if already in LAB) or asking your permission to convert and flatten it if in RGB or CMYK. When complete, the layer structure is that pictured in Figure 15.1.

Notice the similarities between this action and the hypothetical four-step one. You are not asked to enter any numbers until the end. At the end, you are presented with a layer that regulates the strength of the effect. This time it isn't a layer as such, but rather a layer group that incorporates all five of the sharpening layers beneath it. Reducing the group's opacity cuts back all of them.

I am not going to spell out each of the 110 steps, not even in the second half of the chapter. You do not need this information to use the action effectively. All you need to know is that if it produces a file that looks too sharp to you, adjust the opacity of the layer group to taste—essentially just as you would in the hypothetical example.

That's the easy way. It is now decision time. More flexibility is built into this action than in any other sharpening methodology I've seen. But fully exploiting it takes lots of study. The easy way of just adjusting the top opacity slider is plenty powerful.

Yes, if you go through the second half of this chapter you can get better sharpening. However, unless you have an interest in how sharpening works, I suggest you skip it, at least for now. Spending a lot of time sharpening leaves less time to do other things that might be more useful. And, even forgetting the study time, the first hundred or so times you use these other options it is likely to take several minutes to sharpen the picture. The sharpen will be slightly better, but you could have used the time to make a new version of the picture from scratch.

This action has five different sharpening passes, each on its own layer, some with their own masks. When the image looks oversharpened, it's often the fault of only one or two of these layers. Modifying or shutting off the offensive one is more effective than blending the unsharpened version into everything.

When one of the layers is misbehaving, it is generally due to something specific and unpredictable. To whet your appetite for the second half, though, let me tell you about one exception.

The layer named Hiraloam Darken does not always agree with faces. It exaggerates wrinkles and makes the person look older. Also, in blue skies, it can put a nasty dark halo around clouds. So, even if you've decided to use the simplified workflow of just adjusting the layer group's opacity, you should toggle off the Hiraloam Darken layer when you encounter such files.

I use this action on every image, incorporating the fancy options described in the second half. It doesn't take me any more time, because after running the action on tens of thousands of images I can look at something oversharpened and immediately know which layer is the culprit.

Getting to such a point is desirable, of course. But it involves a lot of work. Only you can decide whether it is worth it for a marginal gain over doing things the simple way.

At the close of the first half of nearly every chapter, I've said the same thing, describing what's in the next chapter should you choose to skip the second half of this one.

The next chapter will be one you must write yourself. If we part company here, I wish you a future of truly compelling images. If you adopt any part of the PPW (or any other modern workflow, for that matter) it should be because you have concluded that its benefits outweigh the time you have to spend on it. I hope you have reached a similar conclusion about this book.

Chapter Goals and Recap

Sharpening is a necessary part of any correction process. In the PPW, it is the final step and is independent of what happened previously. Therefore, any sharpening method you like can be substituted for the one described here.

This chapter describes a lengthy and sophisticated action that allows a fast, respectable sharpen with almost no effort. It also has almost any option that one might desire to customize the sharpen.

How Difficult Is It? If used as described in the first half, very easy. The second half's options are powerful—and complex.

How Often Is It Needed? Every image benefits from at least some form of sharpening.

A Closer Look

The PPW action incorporates five types of sharpening, all configurable separately. The rest of the chapter discusses how to use these options. Some illustrations are intentionally overdone because otherwise the differences may be too subtle to evaluate. First, though, we should look at some real-world examples. In Figures 15.2, 15.3, and 15.4 each version A has been corrected but not sharpened. It has been resampled to fit the page, so that the sharpening can be applied to a file of exactly the size intended for use.

Each version B is the straight default of the PPW Sharpen action. Each version C, instead, uses only Filter: Sharpen>Unsharp Mask. To make the comparison fair, the settings I chose were designed to leave some parts apparently sharper than version B and others less so.

Figures 15.2B and 15.2C remind us why all pictures need to be sharpened: either is better than Figure 15.2A. The differences between the two are less compelling.

Figure 15.2B has better definition in the clothing. It also seems more effective in the background building. The faces are distinctly more open. Figure 15.2C has sharper greenery.

But do you want each leaf and bristle so sharply defined? The action thinks not. It does not like to sharpen strongly colored objects. The added detail in Figure 15.2C distracts from the people. The greenery in Figure 15.2B is softer but at the same time a great improvement over the original.

***Figure 15.2** Left, a file that has been corrected and is awaiting sharpening. Center, the defaults of the Sharpen action are applied. Right, an attempt at a similar result using the Unsharp Mask filter.*

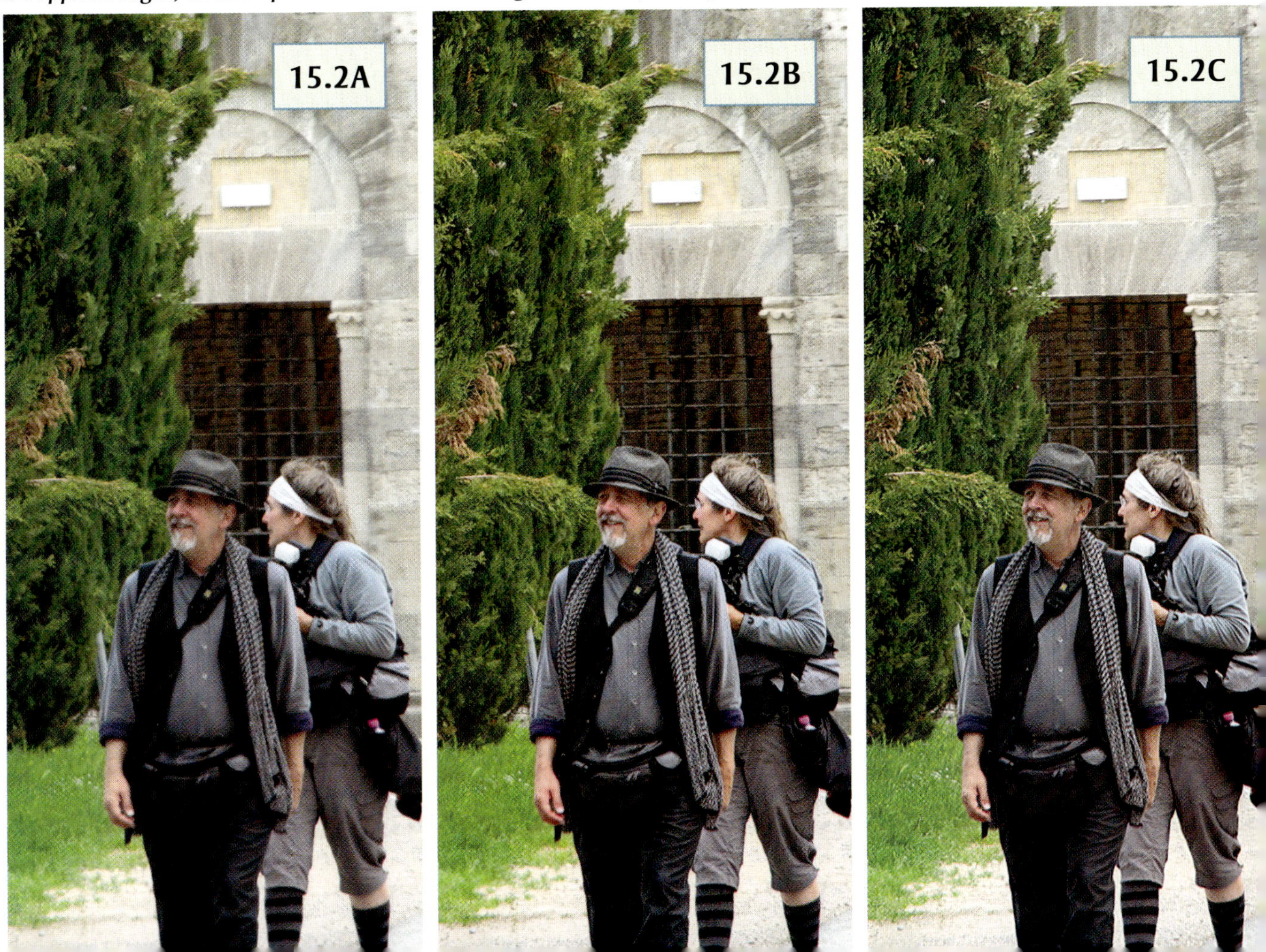

I am unpersuaded by the lighter faces, but I prefer the background, and strongly prefer the clothing in Figure 15.2B.

Five Sharpens Are Better Than One

In the next example the advantages are clearer. Figure 15.3B looks richer than 15.3C. The background is more convincing. The faces and the man's vest are more interesting, The action has avoided sharpening the bright flowers. They have more detail in Figure 15.4C, at the cost of color intensity. Not a good bargain, in my view.

Traditional methods might be expected to have an advantage in the woman's blouse. The fine detail there, with distinct edges, is ideal for a method whose artifacts are narrow. And indeed, the blouse is excellent in Figure 15.4C.

Beta reader Bevi Chagnon was not so sure. She wrote, "If this photo was to sell the blouse, yes, I agree. But this is a photo showing the interaction among three people. Version C has sharpened the blouse so much that I can't stop looking at it. It draws my eye away from the real action in the photo, which is the conversation between these friends. I find this quite common with fabric textures in photos, such as lace, dots, stripes, tweeds, and plaids. Although sharpening can make the fabric 'pop,' I might not want to make the fabric the center of attention."

Figure 15.3B enhances the fabric just as much, but in a way that meets Bevi's objection. The PPW action uses traditional narrow-artifact sharpening too, although not as much of it. The lighter lines aren't as light as in Figure 15.3C, but a different type of sharpen has made the rest of the blouse slightly darker, so the apparent contrast is about the same as in Figure 15.3B.

The consideration comes into play again in a portrait. Figure 15.4A is full of fine lines.

As in both previous examples, the dark clothing is better defined in Figure 15.4B than in 15.4C. The colored area of the dress shows the same defect in Figure 15.4C that we saw in the flowers of Figure 15.3C. In attempting to sharpen an area that the action wisely left alone, the USM filter wiped out the bright colors.

As against that, Figure 15.4C shows more detail in the glass, hair, and skin. This is a mixed bag. I definitely prefer its glass and suspect you do as well. I personally prefer the softer look of Figure 15.4B's hair, but I don't expect everyone would agree. And there would certainly be disagreement about the skin. I prefer Figure 15.4C because I happen to like natural skin texture as opposed to plastic.

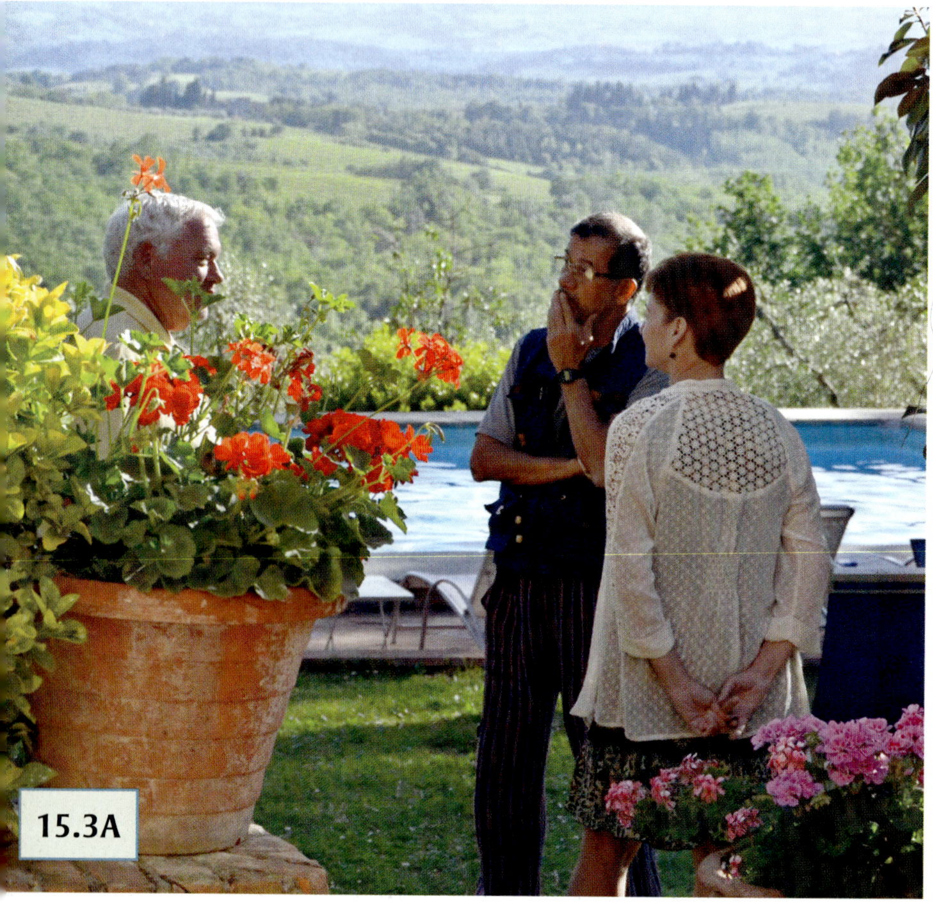

15.3A

Figure 15.3 Left, the original. Opposite, top, the PPW sharpen. Bottom, using the Unsharp Mask filter only.

This view puts me in a minority, at least in the professional graphic arts community. Also, most women, in my experience, do not care to have their wrinkles emphasized.

At the end of the first half of the chapter I pointed out that the Hiraloam Darken layer can add apparent age to skin. I therefore recommended disabling it in portraits, which was not done in Figure 15.4B. My improved version, Figure 15.4D, is a more sophisticated way of eliminating that layer's effects. In the first draft of this chapter, I described what I did, right here.

Certain experts among the beta readers, however, made me move it, because they saw ramifications that they had not previously considered. They requested a thorough explanation of a concept called a *halo map.* As that subject gets geeky fast, I prefer to return to it later.

You've just heard that if we start to dig more deeply we will find ourselves in a hole too deep for many experts. What does it mean for us, given the limited time we have available for studying?

How Much Do We Gain?

Review the last three examples. Compare each unsharpened version A, to each C, sharpened only with the USM filter. Then compare C to B, the result of the action. Which comparison shows the most improvement?

My answer is depressing. One contestant uses a method

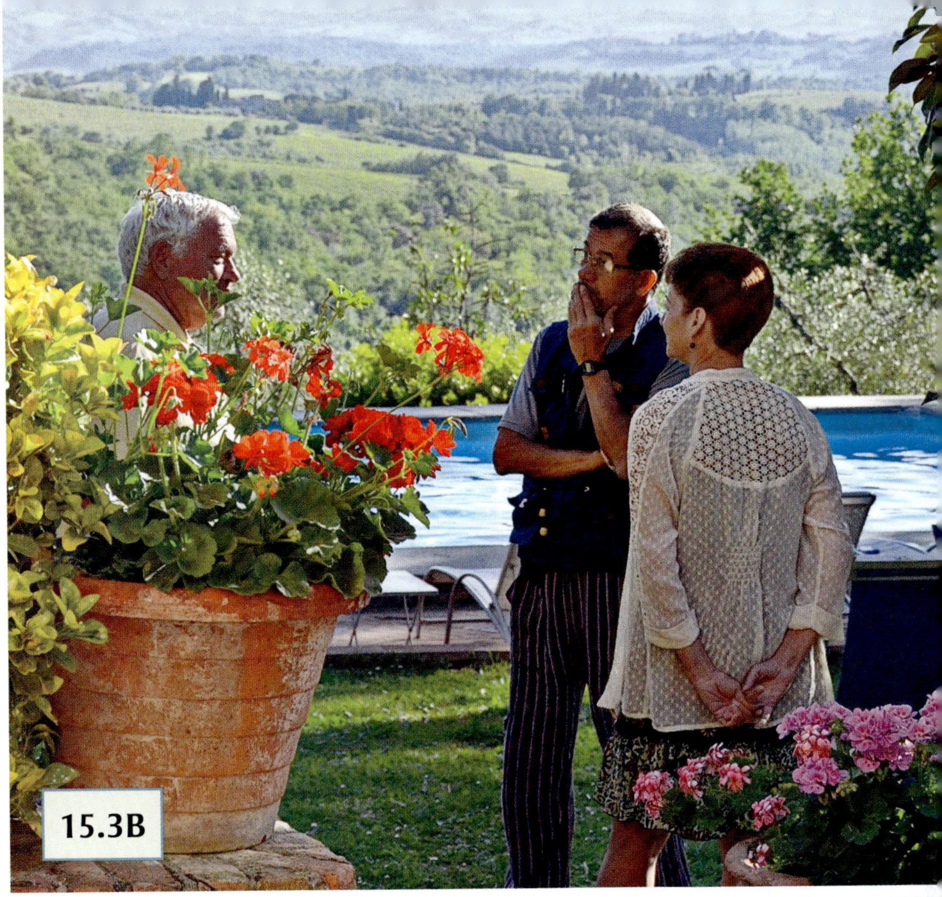

15.3B

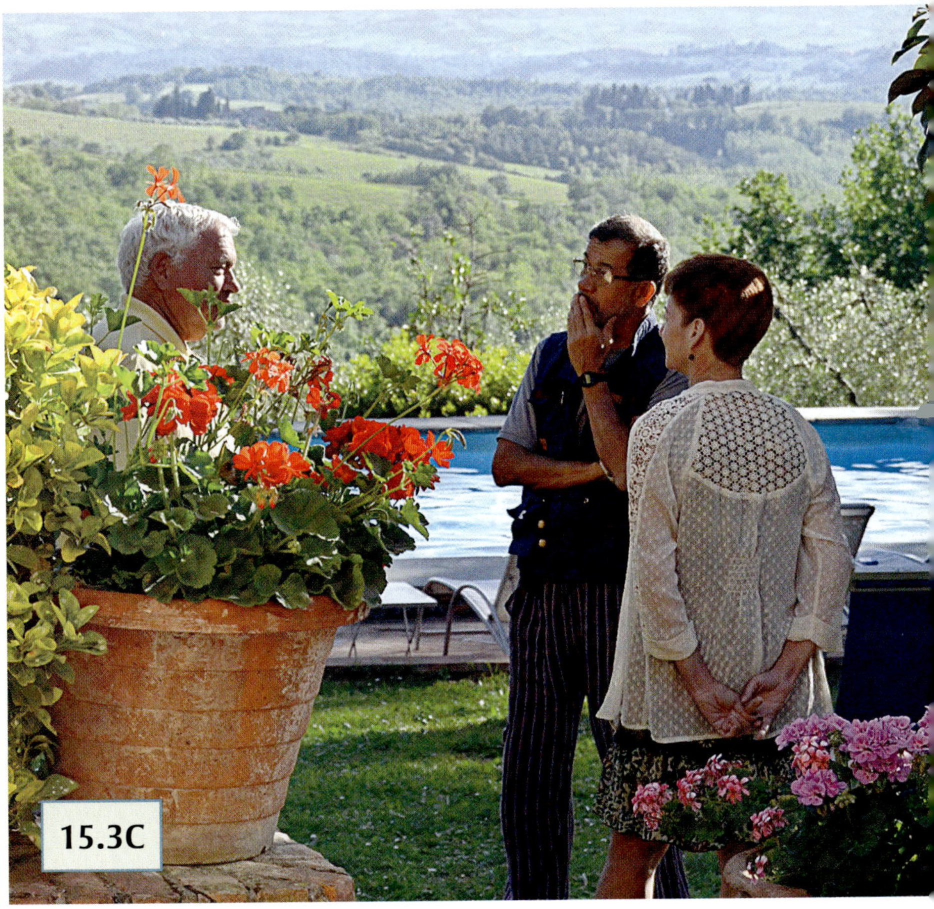

15.3C

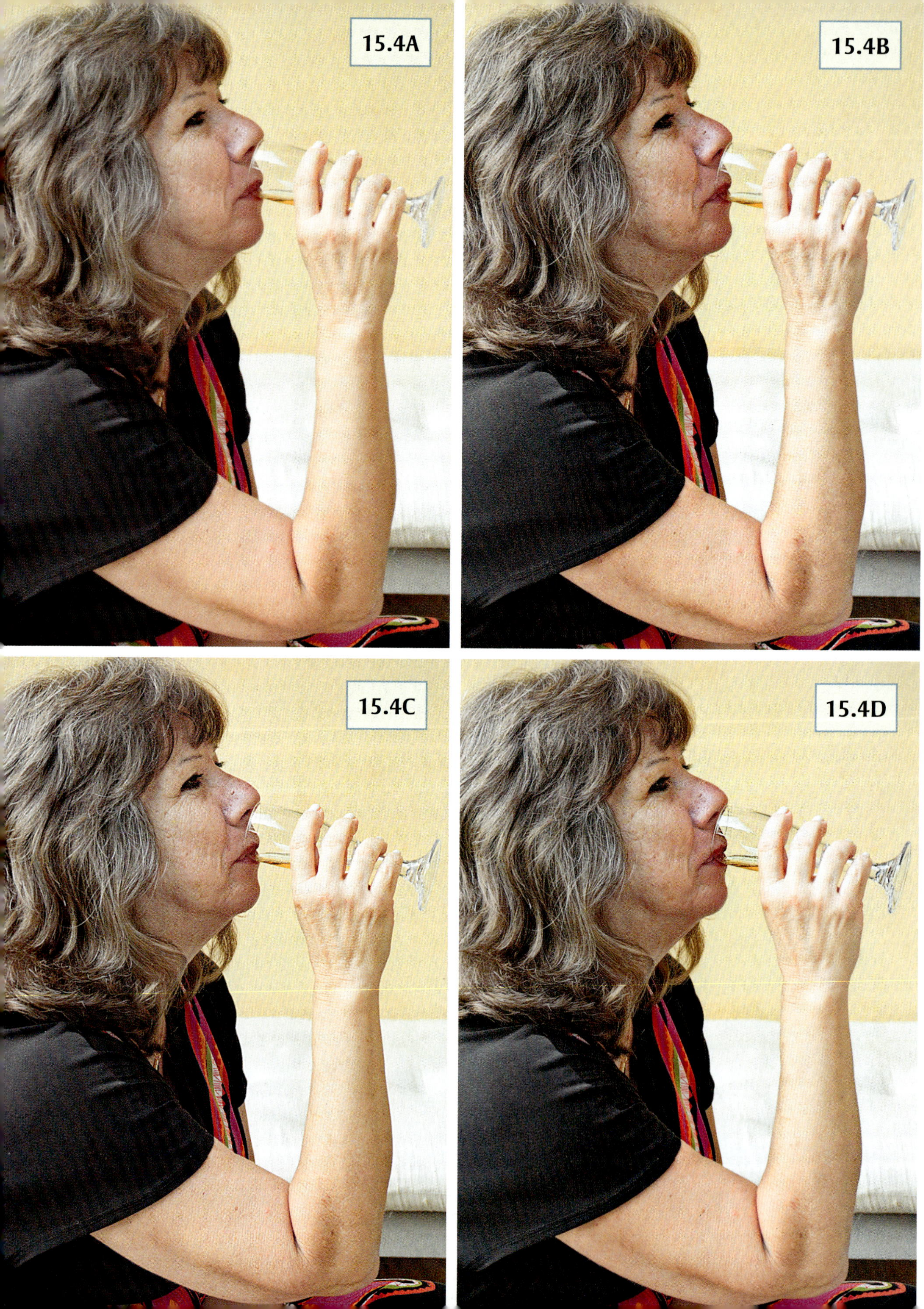
15.4A
15.4B
15.4C
15.4D

15.4E

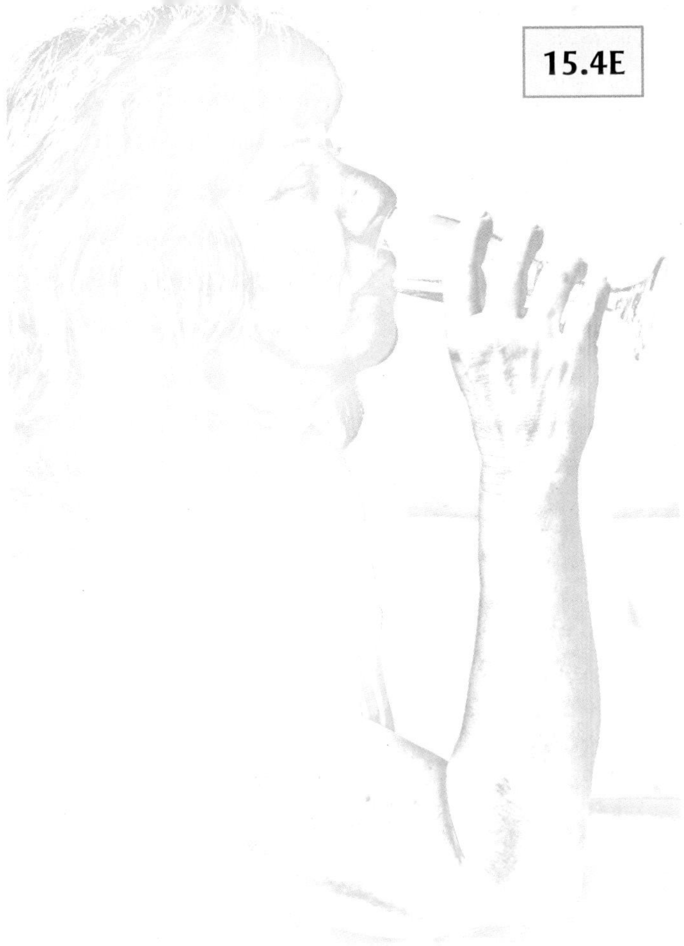

***Figure 15.4** Opposite, top left, the unsharpened file. Top right, the action default. Bottom left, the Unsharp Mask filter instead. Bottom right, the action defaults are modified with respect to the skin and the glass. Above, with contrast greatly intensified, the masked halo map used by the Hiraloam Darken layer.*

known to be inferior for more than a quarter of a century. The other not only corrects for the first one's defects, but incorporates several specialized subroutines in the course of using a thousand times as much computing power.

Given that, wouldn't you expect the quality difference to be greater? Something shockingly better? Because it's not happening. These comparisons show that it's more important to sharpen in the first place than it is to make the sharpening more sophisticated. There's been a quality gain, yes, particularly in the landscape scene of Figure 15.3, but not as much as one might expect.

For that matter, the competition could have been made closer. Recall my description of a hypothetical four-step action that would reduce the lightening effect of the USM. Coupled with an increase in the Amount setting of the filter, it would produce a slight but noticeable improvement on the C versions.

What are these slight improvements worth? Not all that much, unless the picture is very important. But, if nothing better were available, I would certainly urge writing this four-step action and using it every time you sharpen. True, it doesn't save much time—until you multiply it by the thousands of images you may be sharpening in the near future.

If you are committed to running an action to improve your sharpening, it hardly matters whether the action has four steps or 110. There is, however, an interesting benefit to the added complexity.

Many of us have to process large numbers of pictures in very little time. It is convenient, in such circumstances, to have the sharpening applied by batch processing, requiring no intervention from us. We'll talk about how to do that shortly, including a practical example from a beta reader.

Such a procedure only works when the sharpening is reliable. Any such action will do better on some pictures than on others, but we have to hope it doesn't make something look really stupid.

Bevi found fault with the conventionally sharpened Figure 15.3C because it oversharpened some fabric. A complex procedure is less likely to beget such defects because it does not put all its sharpening eggs in one basket. With so many subtle things going on, there is less chance that one of them will prove obnoxious.

This is, incidentally, more or less the same argument for making multiple versions of a correction rather than trying to fine-tune one. If you process one file using straight PPW, a second using LAB only, and a third entirely in Camera Raw, the three won't look alike. However, since they're all trying to do the same thing, they will have certain things in common. Those shared things represent correctness, which is why blending the multiple versions so often creates a better result than any of the three. Errors are reduced, righteous practices magnified.

Maps, Masks, and Madness

If you find the initial default sharpen excessive, the standard response should be to reduce the layer group's opacity, toning down everything. A more powerful approach is to identify which of the five layers are causing problems and reduce only their opacities. A third possibility, more potent yet, is to intervene in the layers with tools that go beyond the opacity slider.

If you're using the first method, you can ignore the individual layers. If you move to the second, you need to know what each layer is trying to do, but not necessarily how it does it. The third approach, however, requires understanding that these layers are tricky things.

First, three of the five have layer masks to limit their effect. The mask is specific to the type of sharpen. For example, Hiraloam Darken's mask protects shadows, which the method otherwise would often plug.

Second, all except Hiraloam Color are halo maps—the concept that was so tantalizing to the expert readers. A definition follows.

Any type of sharpening works by adding artifacts, commonly called halos. Some make the file lighter, others darker. USM and most other sharpening filters return a file into which these halos have already been integrated.

Suppose, however, the halos are somehow kept separately, and only incorporated into the file at the last minute. There would have to be at least two extra layers. One would presumably be a white layer that only gets darker where halos are intended to appear; it would be used to darken or multiply the unsharpened original. Then a second layer would operate in reverse to incorporate light halos when the time came.

I don't have a full list of the advantages of doing things this way but here's a start.

- Most sharpening algorithms exaggerate strong transition areas more than lesser ones. Therefore, sharpening a file that has already been sharpened is challenging, as it contains artificially strong transitions that may be blown out of all proportion by a second sharpen. A halo-map structure avoids this. The PPW action generates several sets of halo maps, true, but they are all based on the original file and are unaffected by the other maps.
- Lightening and darkening are completely independent as opposed to being symmetrical. In the PPW action, light conventional halos are much narrower and less pronounced than dark ones, although their masks are identical. Light and dark hiraloam behave in the opposite way, sharing settings but using different masks.
- Certain files react well to having the strongest sharpening effects reduced. On the other side of the coin, eliminating subtle areas of the halo map is an anti-noise move. Either thing is possible with curves to the halo map.
- If sharpening is obnoxious in a certain area, we can intervene by erasing or lightening the halo map, without affecting the base image. That, in fact, was the approach used to produce Figure 15.4D. The same thing works if you want to increase sharpening in a certain location only. Halo maps are so subtle that nobody will ever detect that you have selected a part of them.

And on and on. The advantages of separate halo maps are so compelling that you may wonder why they haven't been generally adopted, (Several other people have produced techniques that use halo maps effectively, but it's still an uncommon approach.)

The reason it's uncommon is that it isn't traditional. But the reason the traditional way became traditional was that there was no alternative. The Photoshop USM filter was fine in its era, which was one of eight megabytes maximum RAM and extremely slow virtual memory. I well recall when applying that USM filter to a moderate sized file required spending five to ten minutes staring at a progress bar. Effective use of halo mapping would have taken hours.

The Return to Figure 15.4D

Halo maps are hard things to show because they're so subtle. Figure 15.4E, hugely exaggerated, is the Hiraloam Darken halo map that got stamped into Figure 15.4B.

It is an attempt to add shape by subtly forcing darker areas away from their neighbors. Usually this is a good idea. If you doubt it, go back one example. The corresponding layer darkened the trees in Figure 15.3B, creating a more convincing background than that of 15.3C. The three faces in that picture are too small to be damaged.

The last sentence confused beta reader Russ Brown, who wrote, "It seems to me that the little, blobby trees in the distance are even smaller, so how is it that the faces are too small to be affected but the trees are not?"

The answer lies not in small faces, but in large ones like Figure 15.4. The halo map shown there unattractively intensifies heavier parts of the nose, the chin, and the sides of the arm. The skin is too smooth to hide these artifacts. A tree, being full of texture that disguises halos, is another story. And the face is a quartertone, to which we are especially sensitive. We are more prone to reject artificiality in objects falling in that range than in something as dark as a tree.

In other words, the answer to Russ's question is that the trees avoid damage not because they are small but because they are trees.

Back to Figure 15.4B. The facial damage is there, but the impact on the glass of wine is useful, and I personally like what's happening to the hair.

The solution is to lighten or delete the part of the halo map that covers the skin. The actual map is so amorphous that no telltale evidence of a botched selection can appear. I simply activated the Hiraloam Darken layer, made the world's sloppiest lasso selection of the general area of the face and arm, and filled it with white. Nobody can possibly tell that I picked up pieces of the hair and background as well. But you can see that between Figures 15.4B and 15.4D the darkening of the arm and face has vanished.

We now shift from maps to masks. Without the mask on the Hiraloam Darken layer, there would be a major problem in the dress, which is black with some strongly colored areas.

Notice how Figure 15.4E applies less of the effect to the dress than to either the hair or the skin. It's dangerous to further darken anything as heavy as this dress, because detail will likely vanish. The mask prevents it.

These masks can also come in handy if the desire is not to eliminate some of the sharpening, but to intensify it.

As noted earlier, the glass is better in the traditional version, Figure 15.4C, than in the action's 15.4B. To match the effect requires working on one or both of the layers that emulate conventional sharpening, namely Dark Halos Multiplied and Light Halos Screened.

These two layers, especially the first, would be stronger than the maximum current sharpening setting in Photoshop's USM filter, were they not restrained by masks. We don't need to look at either the layers themselves or their masks in the following correction, any more than we needed to look at Figure 15.4E's halo structure to delete the area we wanted to change.

Instead, Shift-click the mask icon on each layer to toggle it off. That shows whether there's enough potential improvement to continue. If there is, usually the best approach is to lighten the mask with a curve. This photo might be the exception, because of the taboo against accentuating wrinkles.

If you agree and would like to adjust the mask locally where it affects the glass, it's easy. Just set a paintbrush tool to white, 50% opacity or so. With the layer mask icon active, paint into the area you want to affect. I went overboard and used 100% opacity to produce Figure 15.4D, because I wanted there to be no doubt that a move has been made.

Let's now take an in-depth look at each layer, together with its merits and perils. We'll then move on to automated sharpening, before putting this book to bed.

Layer by Layer, Illustrated

The action was written for files roughly of 10-30 megabytes. No method can produce a perfect sharpen sight unseen; the question is whether it is "good enough" most of the time, and whether we can then modify it in the event that "good enough" isn't good enough for our purposes. That said, if your images are generally smaller or larger than the range just stated you may wish to make some modifications to the action's default behavior. The PPW panel offers several ways to do this; see its documentation for details.

The following example is intentionally too harsh so that we can visualize more clearly what the action does. The file was downsized to fit the page at 150 pixels per inch, lower than recommended for quality printing, and then the action was applied. The lower resolution exaggerates the impact of the sharpen.

Figure 15.5A is the unsharpened start point of an image that may seem familiar. Each succeeding variant adds one sharpening layer.

The first two layers employ what is usually called conventional sharpening, because it is similar to historic practice. The artifacts, or halos, that produce the impression of sharpness are tiny, but violent. One layer adds only artifacts that are darker than the unsharpened version, the other lighter ones. Figure 15.5B shows the impact only of the Dark Halos Multiplied layer; 15.5C adds Light Halos Screened.

The next two layers are also divided into dark and light halves, but they use a different type of sharpening. The halos are large, but subtle. This type of sharpening is often referred to by a name that shortens the descriptive phrase High Radius, Low Amount. So, Figure 15.5D adds Hiraloam Darken to 15.5C. Then, Hiraloam Lighten is tossed into the mix in Figure 15.5E.

Until recently people thought that sharpening should exclusively affect detail and not color. This turns out to be a misconception. The Hiraloam Color layer alters color only. Where two unlike colors meet, it forces them apart, without altering darkness.

You may find it difficult to distinguish Figure 15.5F, which adds it, from 15.5E.

You are unlikely to have that problem with Figure 15.5G. All three hiraloam layers have very low default percentages. It's deliberate, because their normal effect is so subtle that it's hard to see what they are doing, and without that knowledge it's hard to know whether to adjust them. The solution: move the opacity out to 100%. The result looks ludicrous, but it highlights what the layer is affecting.

Figure 15.5G, then, raises the Hiraloam Color opacity to 100% rather than the 20% of Figure 15.5F. It makes evident the emphasis on small patches of color.

This same image was used for a demonstration in Chapter 5. A beta reader complained then that the final version, Figure 5.14B, although attractive in the flowers, was excessively colorful elsewhere. By using a less strongly corrected start point, Figure 15.5A, and hiraloam color, we can answer that objection, obtaining prominent flowers on a subtler background.

Figure 15.5H teaches the relation of resolution to sharpening. Starting with an unsharpened file at 300 pixels per inch, the default action was applied and the file was then downsampled to 150. All other variants were downsampled first and sharpened afterward. Figure 15.15H is more subdued than its counterpart, Figure 15.15F, because its halos are only half the size.

Layer by Layer, Described

- **Dark Halos Multiplied** establishes a halo map on a white background. The layer is set to Multiply mode at 100% opacity. The layer mask emphasizes sharpening in near-neutral quarter- and midtones. In more colorful or significantly lighter or darker areas the mask restricts the effect. Color is unchanged.

Pluses and Pitfalls: This is the workhorse layer for conventional sharpening. It rarely creates disasters. It may, however, aggravate problems if the unsharpened base is noisy.

Solutions: Like each of the first four layers,

this one maps halos separately. They can be modified, intensified, or erased without doing anything to the underlying material. No great care needs to be taken because the maps are so vague that it's impossible to detect when they've been altered. For example, to exaggerate the sharpen in a certain area, you can lasso it and apply a darkening curve to the halo map.

To strengthen the layer's effect, try Shift-clicking its mask off. Or, apply a darkening curve to the layer itself, remembering that the white background must remain white.

When the layer makes the file look grainy (and you check to see whether it is really the culprit by toggling its visibility on and off), the solution is a curve that eliminates highlights, which is where the mildest artifacts are found. This is the equivalent of the Threshold field in the Unsharp Mask filter. However, you will not need to use it as often. Graininess is most offensive in colored areas, which the action already protects with a mask and the USM filter does not. If you read the documentation, you'll see that I had trouble locating an image that actually needed this treatment, and had to resort to sabotaging a file to get something in which the effect would be noticeable.

When a file has previously been sharpened, the opposite occurs. Areas that the action wants to sharpen strongly look bad, whereas more modest sharpens are still pleasing. If this occurs, curve the layer by lightening its shadow while placing a holding point nearer its highlight.

- **Light Halos Screened** is the counterpart of the previous layer, but it is not applied nearly as strongly. The light halos are both narrower and less intense than the ones on the Dark Halos Multiply layer beneath it. They appear as white lines on a black background. The layer is set to Screen mode, with a default opacity of 75%. It uses a copy of the same mask that Dark Halos Multiply employs.

Pluses and Pitfalls: Light narrow halos are more intrusive than dark ones. The action therefore makes them narrower and less pronounced than Dark Halos Multiplied. This layer is nevertheless more likely to do something bad—or something good—than its dark counterpart. So if you have decided to adjust layers rather than change opacity of the top layer group, keep a careful eye on Light Halos Screened.

For example, in portrait work these halos are often about the width of a strand of hair. If this layer is emphasized, strands of near-white will appear. Probably this is either very good or very bad depending on your agenda for the image.

Also, many cameras and raw modules attempt to spoil our day by doing some kind of pre-sharpen, usually without telling us. This would be a nuisance under the best of circumstances. One of the main reasons for the development of the PPW action was to find a means to compensate for such mischief.

Worse, the presharpening almost always makes equally strong and equally wide light and dark halos, a practice known as inferior for thirty years or so. If there has been such presharpening it may be necessary to turn off the Light Halos screened layer altogether.

To illustrate, Figure 15.6A was opened in Camera Raw's current defaults, which include a mild sharpen, not as damaging as those of certain cameras. A second version was opened with sharpening disabled but otherwise identical settings. There is no point comparing the two because they are visually quite close.

When the two are sharpened with the PPW action defaults, suddenly the defects are magnified. Figure 15.6B, based on the presharpened version, seems lighter, as those pesky halos have been intensified. I'm not saying this is a crisis, but then again I could have *provoked* one with stronger settings, or by choosing a noisier original. I just point out that Figure 15.6C, based on an unpresharpened capture, is likely to be a better point of departure.

Solutions: Because the halos are so thin there isn't much need for anything fancier than adjusting layer opacity. The trick is to recognize pictures that actually need more light sharpening.

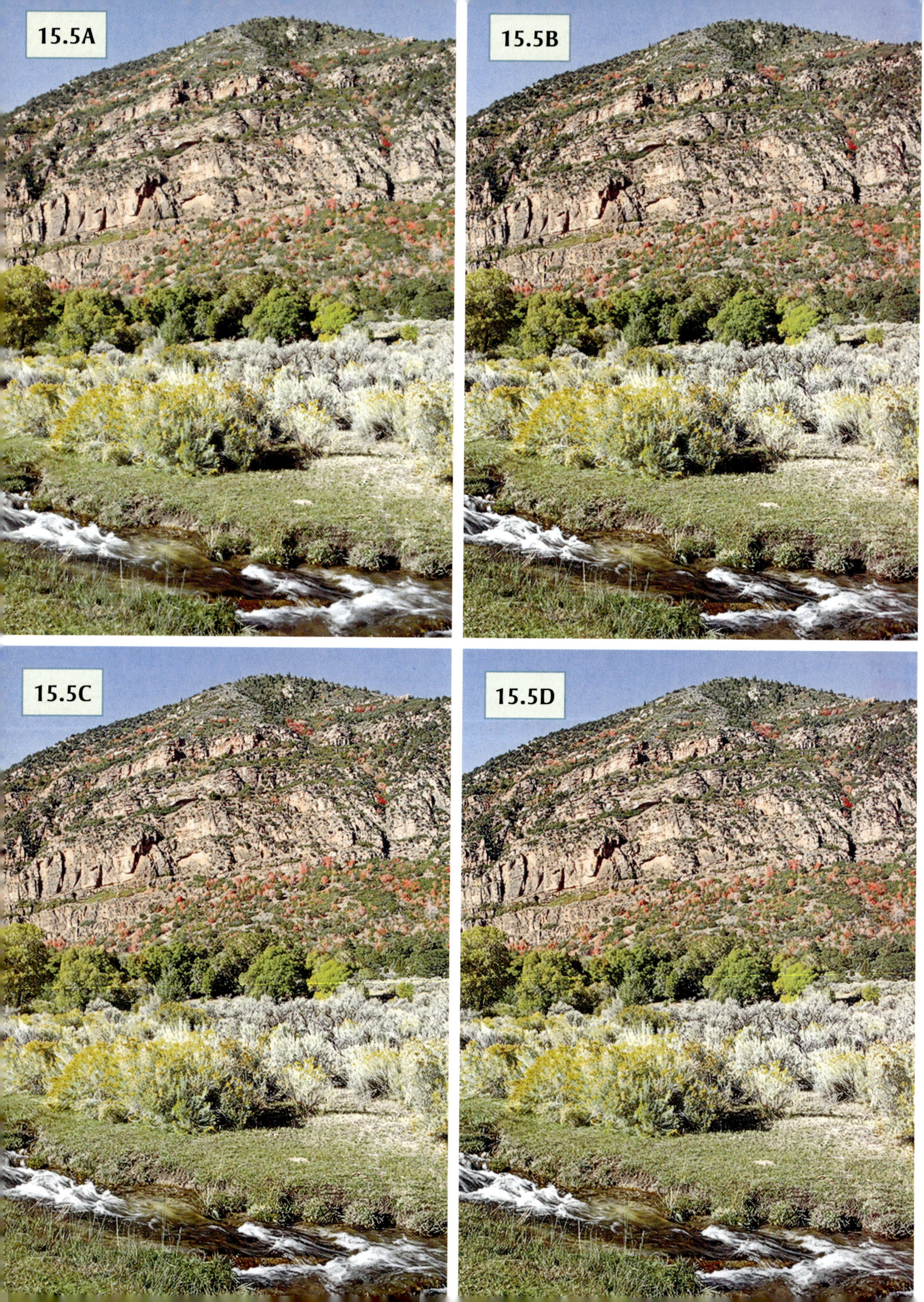
15.5A
15.5B
15.5C
15.5D

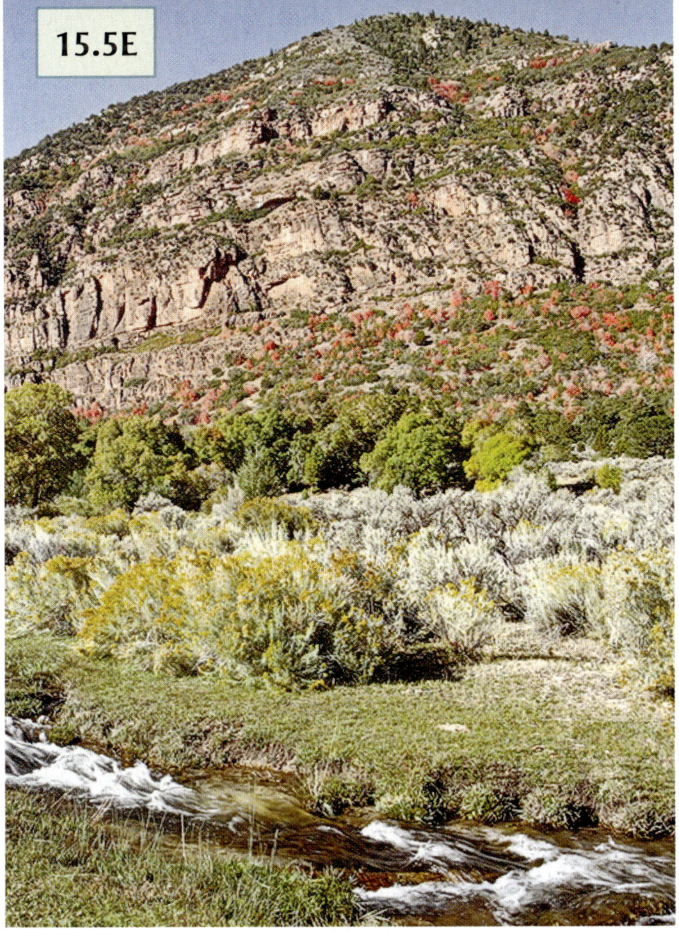

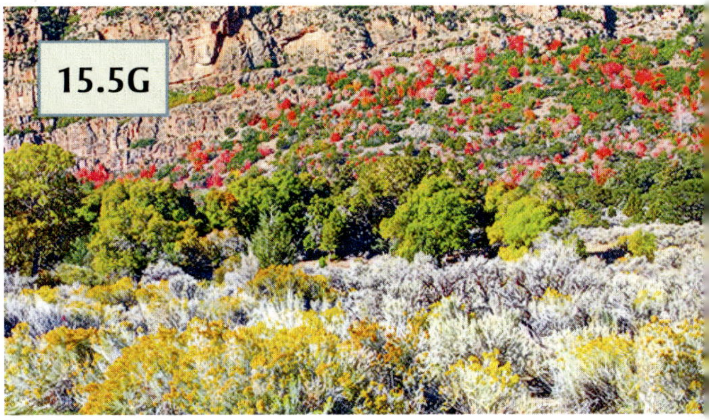

***Figure 15.5** All versions except the final one were sharpened and printed at a resolution of only 150 pixels per inch, exaggerating the effects of the action. Opposite page, top left, the original. Top right, default settings of the action, with only the Dark Halos Multiplied layer active. Bottom left, the Light Halos Screened layer is added. Bottom Right, the Hiraloam Darken layer is added. This page, top left, the Hiraloam Lighten layer is added. Bottom left, the Hiraloam Color layer is added. Above, a section of the file with Hiraloam Color increased to 100% opacity. Below, a default sharpen was applied when the resolution was 300 pixels per inch. The file was then downsized to 150 for printing.*

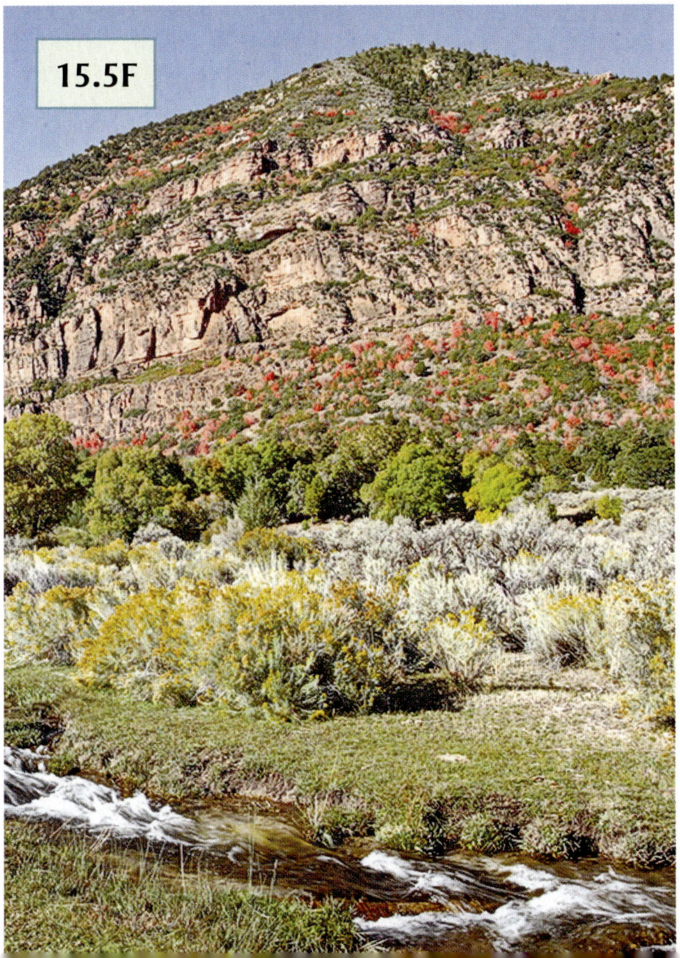

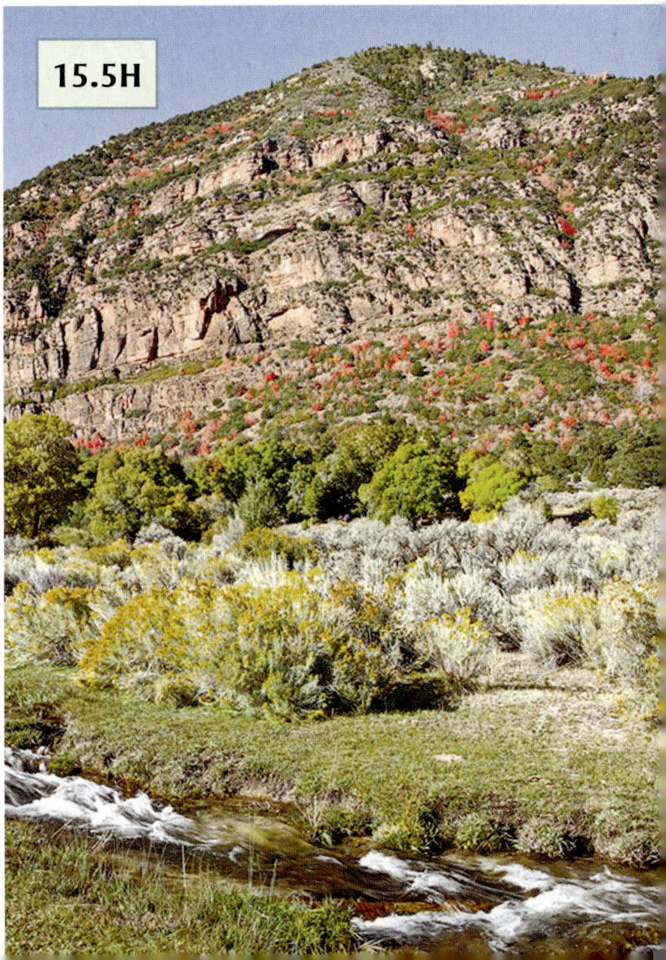

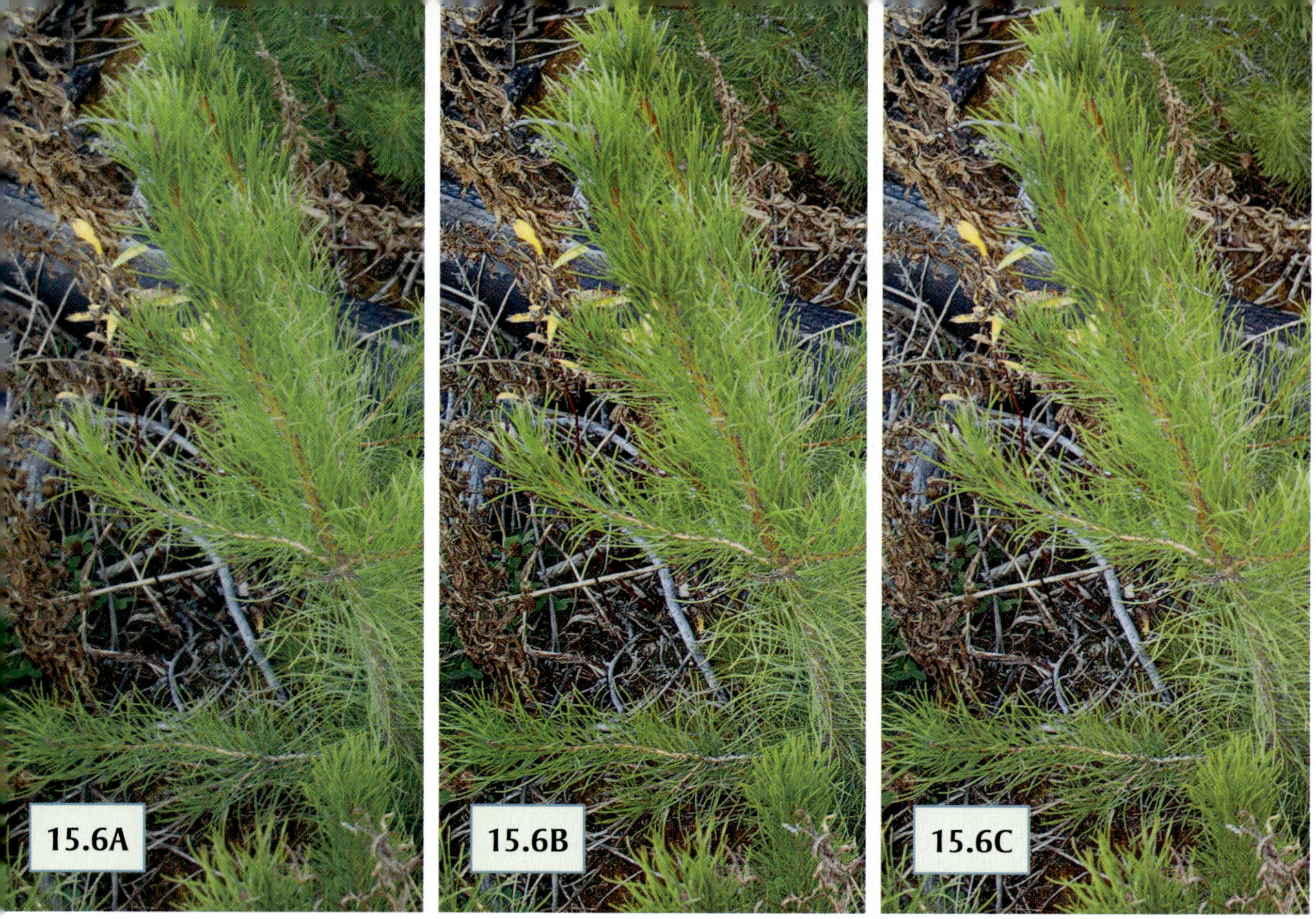

***Figure 15.6** Presharpening in a camera or raw module looks innocuous but has consequences down the line, generally in the form of excessive light haloing. Left, a default acquisition in today's Camera Raw. Middle, it is sharpened using PPW defaults. Right, a file using the same acquisition parameters except presharpening gets the same treatment.*

They aren't common, but they exist. Diagnose them by looking for thin light lines, such as the aforementioned strand of hair. Would you like it if they blew out completely and became pure white? Ordinarily no, but in Figure 15.7A the answer is yes. If the light lines in the instrument dials vanish completely, so much the better.

Figure 15.7B, the default PPW sharpen, is an improvement. But without touching the other layers, I then produced Figure 15.7C by increasing the opacity of the Light Halos Screened layer and also Shift-clicking away its mask. If what this does to the hair is objectionable I would just mask that part out.

- **Hiraloam Darken** establishes wide, diffuse dark halos on a white background. The layer is set to Multiply mode at a default opacity of 20%. A mask stops shadows from plugging.

Pluses and Pitfalls: Hiraloam Darken is the most volatile of the five layers. Sometimes the default is too low and sometimes too high. We looked at the actual halos back in Figure 15.4E. They're large. If they happen to fall in a smooth area, like a face or a sky, they become obvious, but they are insidiously effective when disguised by something textured.

Solutions: A previous version of this action had a default opacity twice as high for this layer. I changed it because although it was often useful, it was killing too many pictures. You should consider increasing layer opacity in the many cases in which it is useful. It doesn't hurt to yank the opacity slider out to 50% or so just to see the impact, and adjust afterward.

Figure 15.8A could be a problem for conventional sharpening because its thin lines might be exaggerated too much. On the other hand, it is so full of texture that nobody is going to be able to detect the hiraloam halos.

Figure 15.8B is the default sharpen. Figure

15.8C shakes things up by increasing the Hiraloam Darken layer to 80% opacity and eliminating the Dark Halos Multiplied layer. I also hiked opacity of the Hiraloam Color layer to emphasize the flowers. I will explain when we get to the discussion of that layer.

- **Hiraloam Lighten** can work magic on the right image. Its wide yet subtle halos appear on a black background, with layer mode set to Screen. Its layer mask is based on luminosity, but is disabled by default. (To enable it, Shift-click its icon). Default opacity is 18%.

Pluses and Pitfalls: If shadows are closed, raising the opacity of this layer can make a big difference. In all three of our first examples, Figures 15.2, 15.3, and 15.4, subjects wore dark clothing, sometimes with multiple tones. It came out decisively better in the versions done using the action. Default settings were in effect; in real life I would increase layer opacity.

At its default, Hiraloam Lighten occasionally lightens the darkest parts so much that we have to re-establish the shadow. At high opacities it can almost have the impact of lightening the midtone with a curve. This sometimes gives more life to a background than we might like, distracting attention from the main subject.

Solutions: There may be an occasion where you would like to see more of an effect in the midtones than the shadows. In this case you should raise opacity, but enable the layer mask. Remember also to keep an eye on shadow values; this layer may have lightened them and you will need to intervene.

- **Hiraloam Color** affects the AB channels only. It drives neighboring colors away from each other, without changing darkness. There is no mask. Default opacity is 15%.

Pluses and Pitfalls: Like Hiraloam Lighten, Hiraloam Color can be a lifesaver for the right kind of image, which comes in two categories, maybe more. The first contains objects that are identifiable only by their color.

Suppose that Figures 15.5 and 15.8 were both in grayscale. I doubt you would know they both feature small, distant flowers. There isn't enough detail to make them recognizable as such. As printed, however, you perceive splotches of color and your imagination provides the identification. Since distinguishing the color is key to knowing what these objects are, you should jack up Hiraloam Color to make them more perceptible against their backgrounds.

The second category is that of Figure 15.9A. Nobody cares what colors these fireworks deliver, as long as they're brilliant. Figure 15.9B, the action default, is a step in the right direction. But yanking Hiraloam Color out to 100% opacity seals the deal. Throwing restraint to the winds, I also took Hiraloam Darken to 100%, accentuating the contrast between the buildings and the sky. Between Figures 15.9A and 15.9C, then, the only difference is the sharpening.

Potential problems: In portraits, teeth and/or the whites of the eyes may be turned blue or green as they move away from the reddish skintone. Also, if you choose to increase the opacity of this layer in landscape shots, be wary of where the sky hits the horizon.

Solutions: Unless you run into one of the categories listed above, you can safely ignore this layer: its defaults have a mild positive effect on almost all other image classes. If you suspect this might be one of the exceptions, start by yanking the opacity slider out to 100%, as was done back in Figure 15.5G. That will tell you whether there's likely to be a benefit, and will show any nasty stuff that should be masked out if you decide to use a strong setting.

Sharpening and Survival

As far as I know, this is the first discussion of anything like Hiraloam Color in print. That it is so effective in certain cases opens up lines of speculation, a followup to a similar discussion about skintone in the second half of Chapter 9.

The human visual system evolved at a time when our foreparents were considered to be choice morsels by various beasts of prey. Many other species faced the same peril.

The other animals, however, had well-designed defenses that our ancestors lacked. Antelope can outrun tigers. Birds can outfly them. Our close relatives, the monkeys, can outclimb them. Rabbits can outdig them.

Predators like buffalo meat, too, and even bear, but even a very stupid lion would not attack an adult of these species, unless he felt like winning the Darwin Award.

Our ancestors, however, could not stand and fight. They could not run away, or climb trees, or crawl down a hole. They had no sharp teeth or claws, poor senses of smell and hearing, and a propensity to spend too much time surfing Facebook while predators were hunting. How, then, did they survive?

We don't have great night vision, like cats do, or great distance vision, like eagles. But we do have excellent color perception and the ability to pick up detail. Our ancestors therefore may have been able to identify certain threats visually before other potential victims could.

The threats, however, had the annoying tendency to resemble things to which we ourselves are a threat. Our ancestors had to make instantaneous decisions as to whether nearby animals were ones that humans like to eat, or ones that like to eat humans.

Neither would be colorful. Whether predator or prey, why advertise one's presence?

Consequently, our visual systems presumably are better equipped to make fine decisions about slightly warm grays than they would be about, say, the brilliant reds found in some flowers. In other words, where color serves to identify an object (or at least to eliminate it as a threat) we may not devote as much brainpower to resolve it as we would in trying to determine what type of large animal is confronting us.

Best sharpening practice caters to this principle. The more colorful an object is, the less it should be sharpened. Flowers should generally not be sharpened. Neither should blue skies. But neutrals and near-neutrals should. Faces are somewhere in the middle. They aren't neutral, but they aren't extremely colorful either, so the sharpening effect should, in my opinion, be toned down—not eliminated, but reduced. The PPW action does this.

Automation, Further Automated

I don't suggest that any automated process with fixed settings can sharpen better than a skilled person who knows the character of the image being worked on. It is, however, useful to inquire whether it can sharpen better than any other automated process that works sight unseen.

Why is this question important? Suppose that you, working alone, are given 500 files for which a pleasing color correction is desired. Sounds reasonable enough, until you learn that you will get them early one morning and they are due back 24 hours later.

A skilled PPW practitioner can put finished files out in an average of three minutes apiece. It is true that there is no rest for the wicked, so we assume no sleep. Even the wicked, however, have to eat and take bathroom breaks. A three-minute average while sitting at the computer will leave you about a hundred files short. Therefore, there will be some compression of the workflow, and I can tell you exactly what it will be.

Pulling all-nighters was a regular occurrence in my youth. I still do it occasionally but have no desire for color correction to be the cause. Rather than give up sleep, I would sacrifice everything except the MMM + Color Boost action.

I would make no initial color move. If the original had a huge cast I would run Image: Auto Color.

I would use the Shadows/Highlights command if appropriate because it takes zero time. I would not do any luminosity blending. I would use the Bigger Hammer or multiplying only where screamingly and utterly obvious.

This compression of the workflow should

Figure 15.7 *(opposite) Top, prior to sharpening. Middle, the PPW sharpening action defaults are applied. Bottom, the impact of the Light Halos Screened layer is drastically increased.*

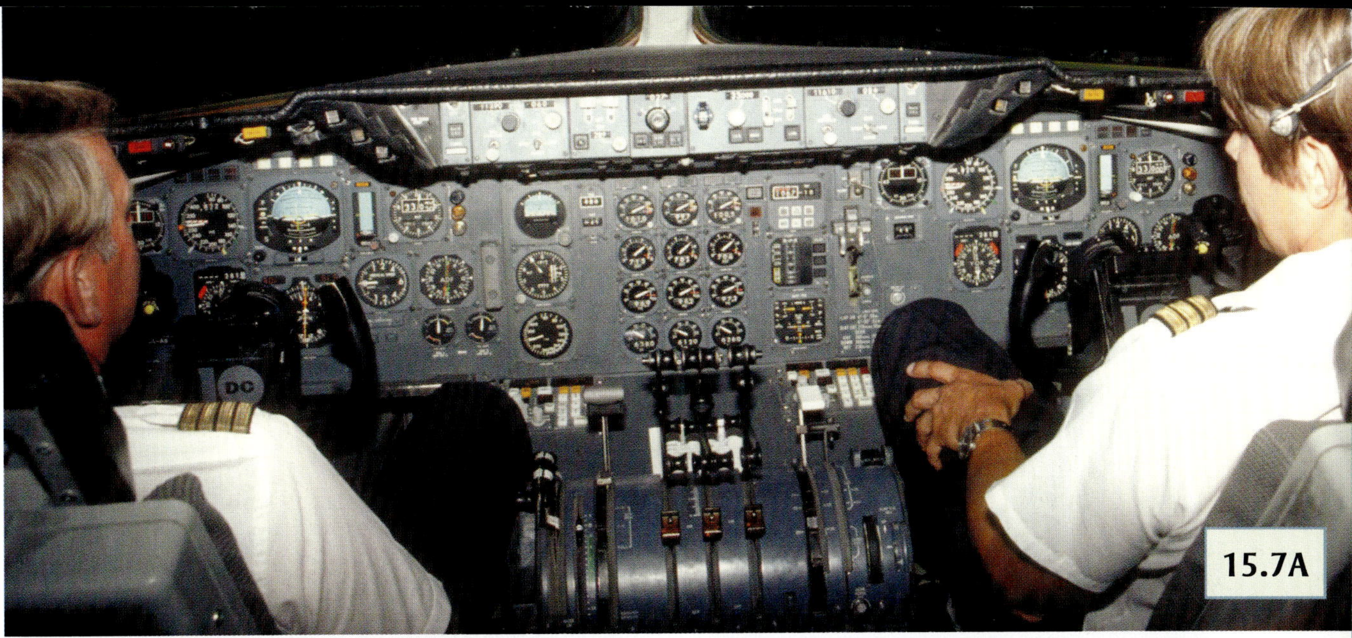

15.7A

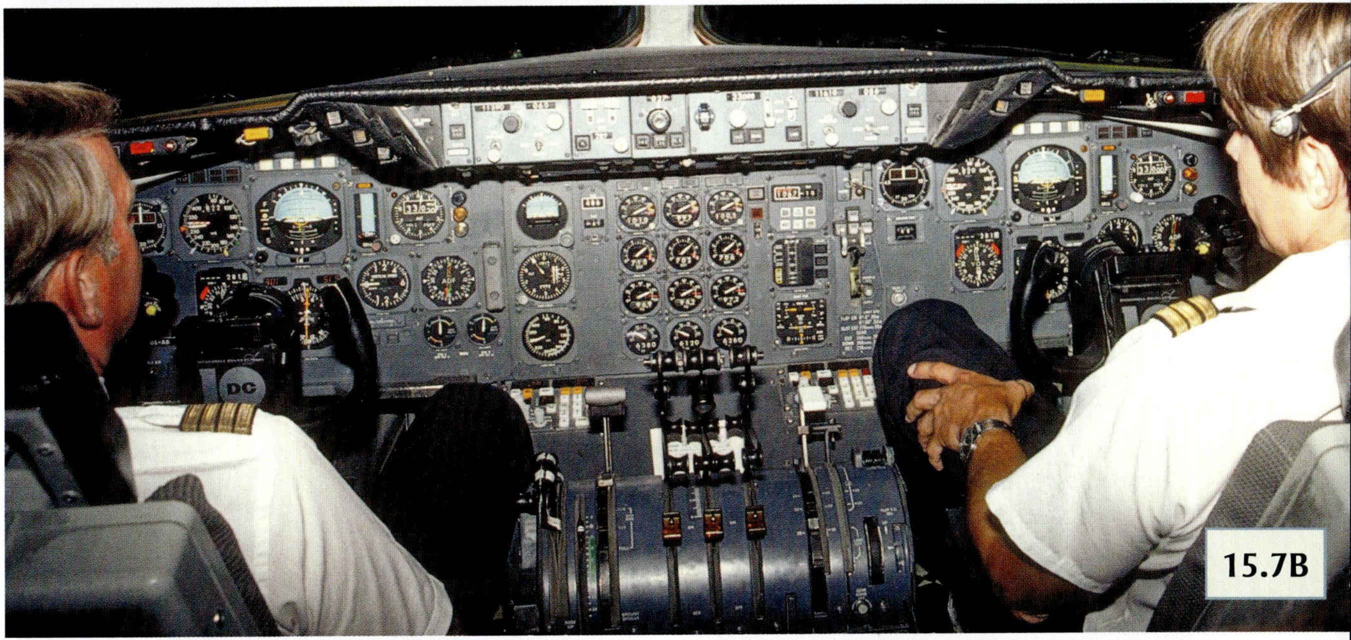

15.7B

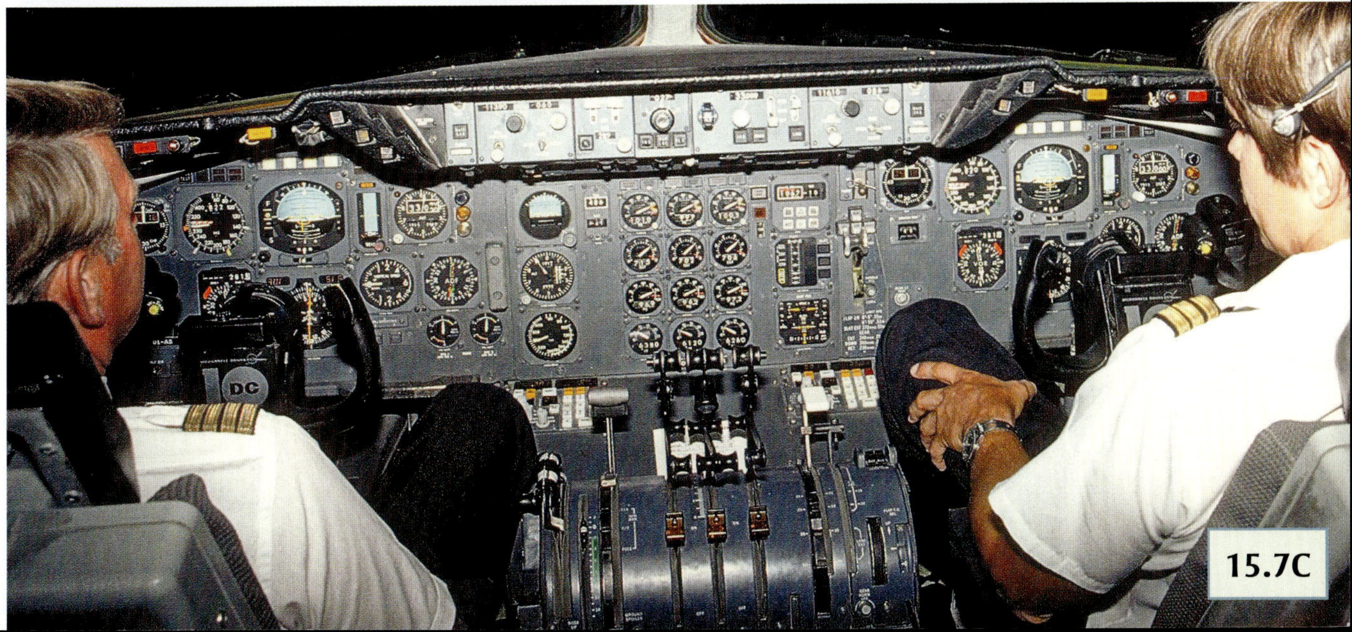

15.7C

leave 30 or 40 seconds with which to juggle MMM + Color Boost settings and still be able to churn these things out at better than one a minute. So, even with breaks, 500 pictures in ten hours seems reasonable. Pre-sharpening, that is.

Naturally I would not leave the pictures unsharpened. Instead, my finished files would go into a hot folder. I would open that folder into Bridge, select everything, go to Tools: Photoshop>Batch and order the Sharpen action applied to all 500 while I slept. In the morning I would review three random images to make sure that no disaster had occurred. The other 497 would go out as is, sight unseen.

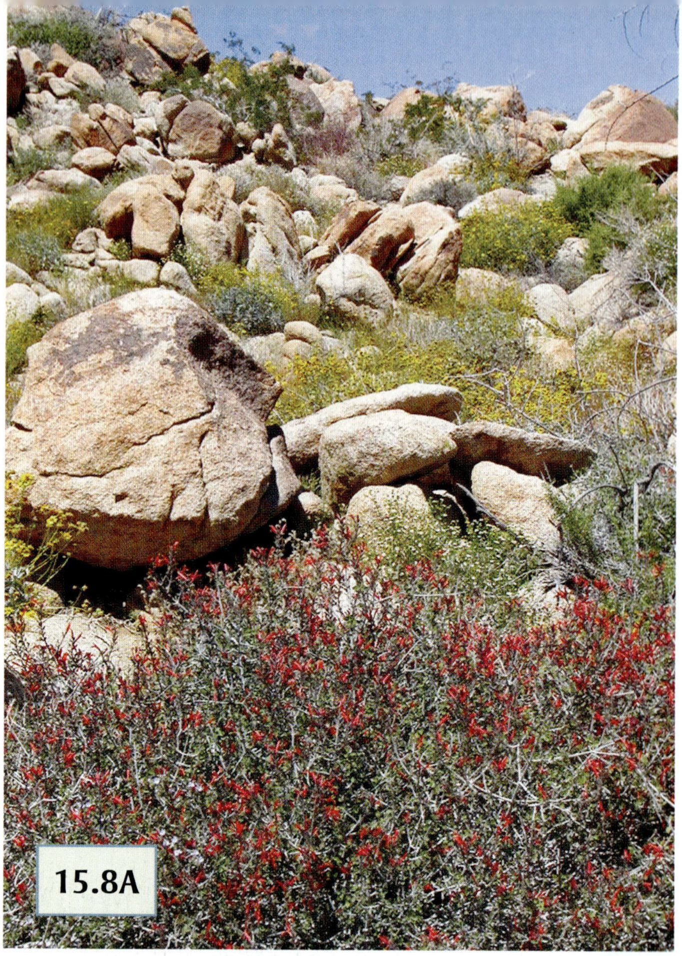
15.8A

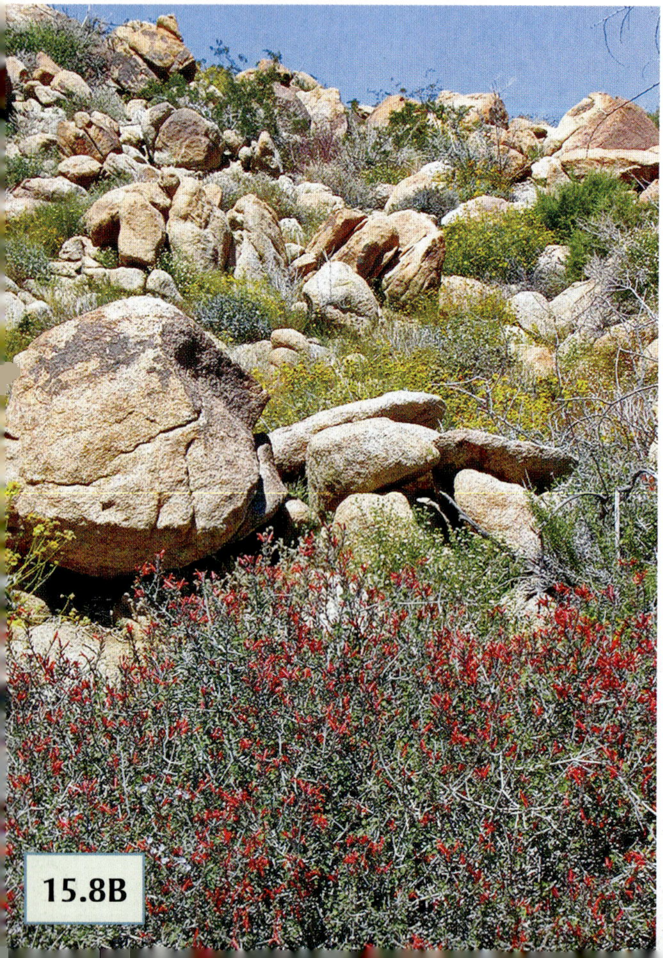
15.8B

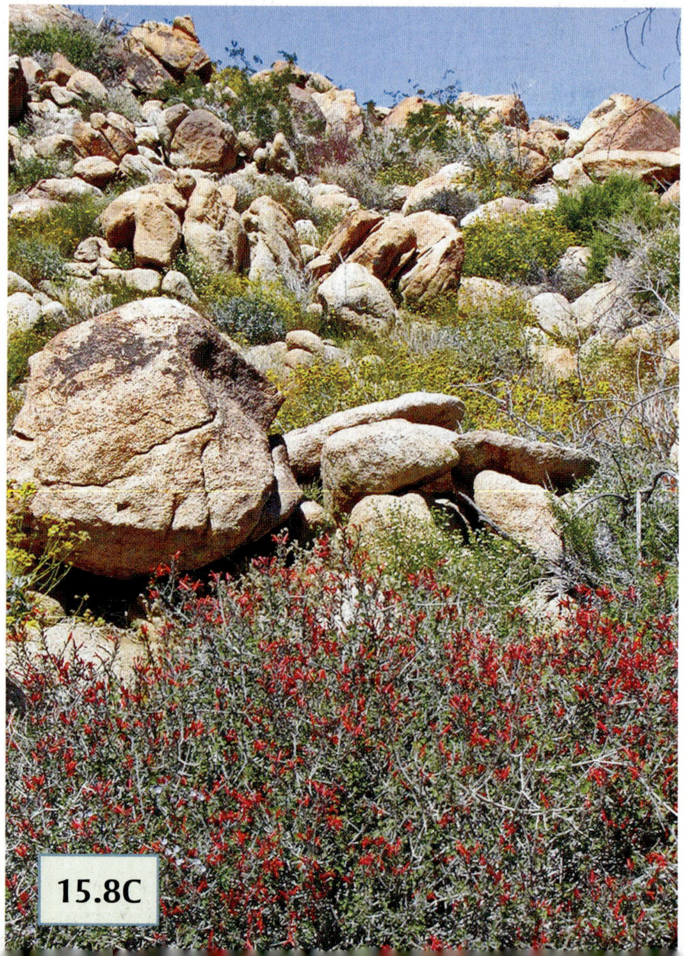
15.8C

***Figure 15.8** Top, before sharpening. Bottom left, the action's defaults. Bottom right, the Dark Halos Multiplied layer is eliminated, while opacity is increased for Hiraloam Darken and Hiraloam Color.*

Such an approach may not be as sloppy and low-quality as it sounds. Beta reader Clarence Maslowski describes a process where he modifies Hiraloam Darken to avoid using it in faces while retaining it elsewhere—in short, an automated version of the procedure shown earlier in Figure 15.4D. It's a complicated series of steps, but he only has to suffer through it one time, and then it can be reapplied to as many images as he likes, 80 in this case.

"I had to process about 40 mug shots and 40 full-length portraits of the same individuals last week," Clarence says. "Even using the PPW after the first three images, I was looking for efficiencies. To that end I copied and modified the Skin Desaturation action so that it generated a mask that could be applied to the existing mask of the Hiraloam Darken layer. Even with the manual fine-tuning it is a little faster than painting black onto the mask. It certainly is more precise, particularly when it comes to lips.

***Figure 15.9** Top, before sharpening. Bottom left, the action's default result. Bottom right, the Hiraloam Color and Hiraloam Darken layers are each increased to 100% opacity.*

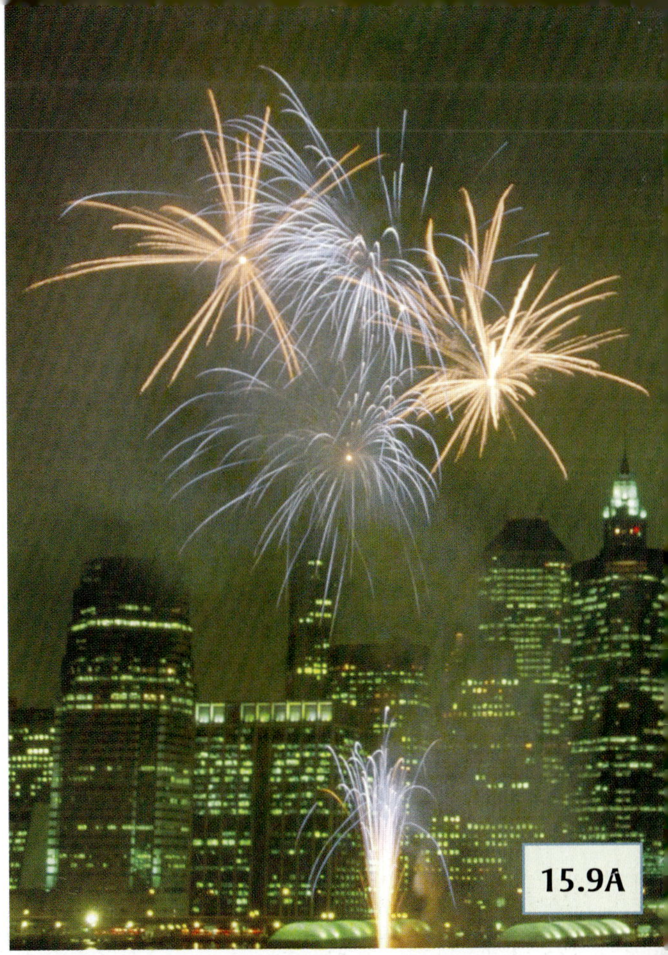

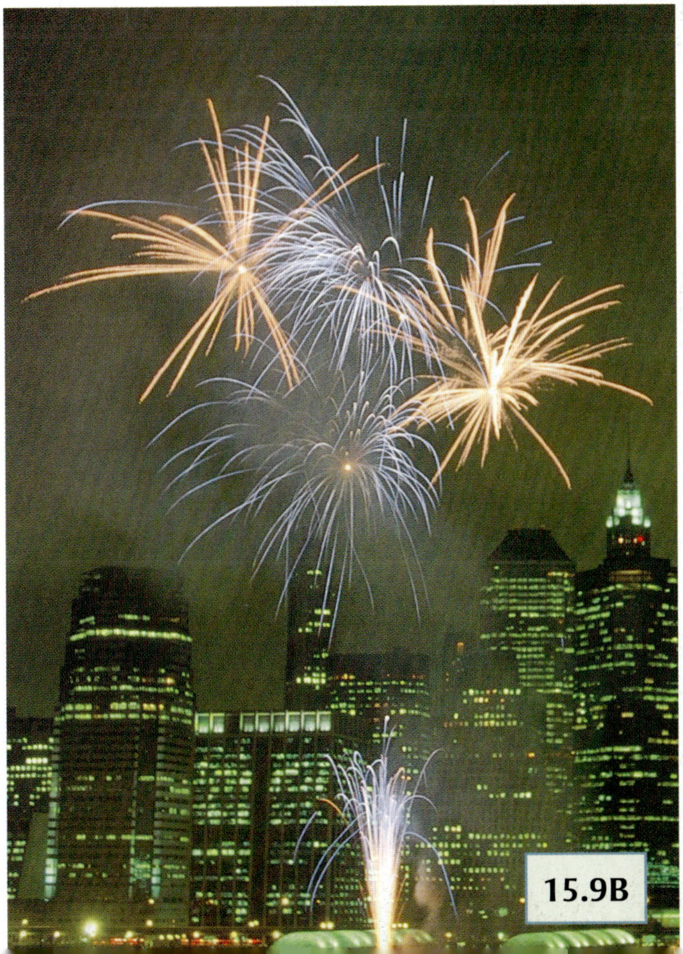

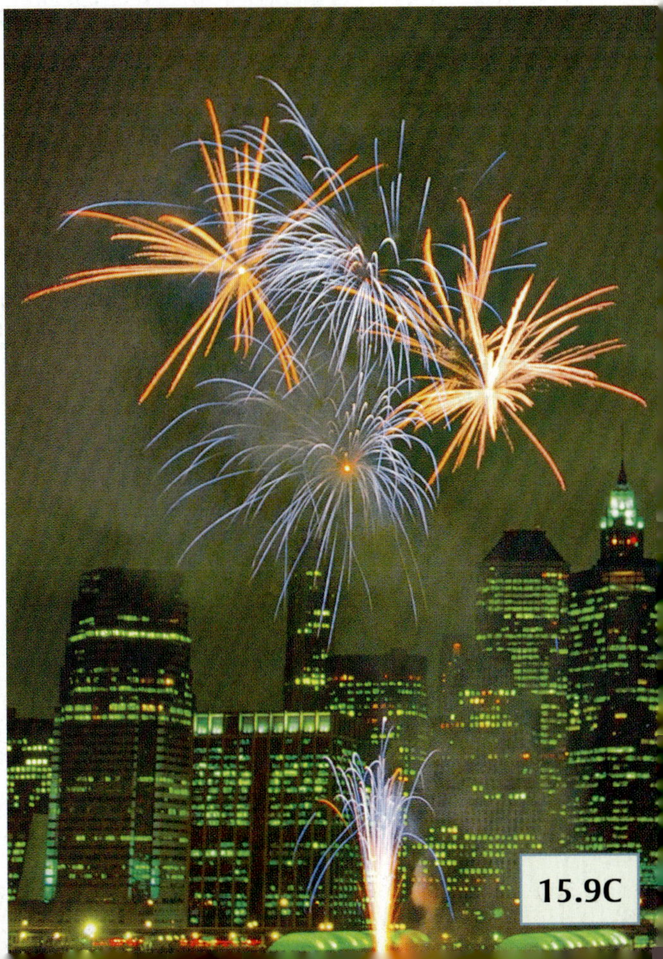

"Copy the original RGB file, run Skin Desaturation, return it flattened to RGB and put it onto the original file as a layer in Difference mode. Copy the blue channel and modify with steep curves, blurring, and invert. Go back to the Difference Skin Desaturation layer and change to Normal mode and flatten. Proceed with the remaining PPW until sharpening, where this alpha channel is applied to the Hiraloam Darken layer mask in Darken mode.

"This works well on faces. I have found that I usually prefer or am indifferent about Hiraloam Darken layer on skin other than a face. This situation is taken care of with a quick erasure before applying."

Summary, Strategies, Special Occasions

You shouldn't care what Ansel Adams would have thought of your sharpening, or what I would think. There is just too much room for differences in taste. The following items, however, are not matters of taste, but correct advice.

- Nobody is saying that you have to use this action; the chapter is more about sharpening principles than specifics. If you do decide to use it, sticking with adjusting the top layer group is a perfectly valid approach.
- All monitors exaggerate the impact of conventional sharpening. In print, the picture looks softer. People who prepare jobs for print for a living have adjusted to this fact of life. Less experienced folk commonly are buffaloed into cutting back on conventional sharpening too much. This doesn't contradict the earlier observation that sharpening is highly subjective. It is not to be expected that all professionals would agree with your sharpening decisions, or mine either. However, they shouldn't *all* disagree. If all professionals say that you're not sharpening enough, they're right.
- Just as people commonly underestimate how much conventional sharpening they can get away with, they can misjudge how much hiraloam it takes to be obnoxious. When halos appear in light areas, the monitor can dazzle us into underestimating how evil they will look in print. Conservatism is therefore in order when choosing the final opacity setting for the Hiraloam Darken or Hiraloam Lighten layers.
- Sharpening can add punch. But between *credible* methods of sharpening, there isn't that much difference. If you've got a good method already, you'll gain more by studying curves rather than sharpening.

The PPW sharpening action gives you whatever you need to bring your own pictures into sharp focus, provided that, as Adams wisely pointed out, you have sharp enough concepts to work with.

* * *

In the twilight of his career, Adams wrote:

> Very few photographic manufacturing technicians comprehend photography as an art form, or understand the kinds of equipment the creative person requires. The standards are improving in some areas, however: in my opinion modern lenses approach the highest possible levels of perfection, and today's negative and printing materials are superior to anything I have known and used in the past.

Every statement above is true in my opinion, and some of it is encouraging. In a way, though, it's sad. It means that Ansel Adams' influence is not what it might have been had he lived in a different time. I believe it is correct that today's lenses aren't drastically better than those of Adams' later career. The darkroom materials are

The Bottom Line

Almost all images benefit from some type of sharpening. The conventional wisdom has always been that sharpening belongs at or near the end of the process.

This chapter discusses an action that applies five different types of sharpening simultaneously. The first half suggests an easy way of using it; more complex methods are discussed in the second half.

irrelevant today. Adams himself foresaw that, and was licking his chops:

> I am sure the next step will be the electronic image, and I hope I shall live to see it. I trust that the creative eye will continue to function, whatever technological innovations may develop.

Adams did not get his wish. His life ended in 1984, barely into the age of drum scanning. That cost us dearly. If an intellect of his magnitude, with his capacity for experimentation, and his desire to empower the photographer had been around during the early digital days things would have turned out quite differently.

Adams lived, however, in a boring time. By the end of his career, photography was a very mature discipline. Equipment was stable and long-lived. There was no shortage of knowledgeable teachers. The advice being given to aspiring photographers was generally sound, and widely available. Many different companies competed to provide services.

Under these circumstances there were simply not going to be huge advances in how to expose a photograph, or how to develop and print it. Adams' influence is lasting, yet it is not as great as it would have proved had he been our contemporary.

What a difference a quarter of a century makes. Our field is *not* mature. Our appreciation of what can and should be done is rapidly changing, as is our taste. Equipment is improving so fast that anything we bought more than five years ago has already probably hit the recycling dump. We have many good teachers to learn from but are plagued by a godawful gang of hucksters. Most of us manipulate our images using products from a company with a monopoly position.

Stability, or challenge and frustration: which era would you pick?

We don't get to choose the world we live in, unfortunately. For what it's worth, I would choose today's. I like excitement.

* * *

The night before I wrote this, Giuliana Abbiati sent me the latest version of the PPW panel. Until then, the sharpening action required a flattened LAB file. That's still the default, unless you change it. You now have the option to retain your existing layer structure and add the various halo maps.

Such a capability might not sound like it would work. Suppose your top layer is an adjustment layer, how can it be sharpened?

The script knows how. It makes a composite layer, generates the halo maps, adds them to the file, and then throws the composite layer away. Thus, we could have a single file containing a Skin Desaturation layer, up to six MMM + Color Boost layers, and five halo maps, everything with appropriate masks.

On the one hand this gives more creative capability to alter an image than anything previously imagined. On the other, it qualifies more as post-modern than modern, because at the moment it is unduly stressful to our poor computers. Today, rather than watch the script progress, I'd prefer the "modern" approach of doing a second version from scratch. Two years, five years from now the decision will be different.

Much of what you've read here will be valid for several decades. Other parts will only be "modern" for a short time, to be replaced by better things. Call it evolution, call it progress, call it an eternal challenge. The expansion of our understanding of what makes a pleasing image has been improving for centuries. It's now up to you to see that the improvement continues.

Acknowledgments

People feel that a serious treatment of these topics is so important that many of them have volunteered to make tremendous efforts to help the cause. First, having read the book you can appreciate how much work it was for the beta readers, Alessandro Bernardi, Russ Brown, Mike Demyan, Adriano Esteves, James Gray, John Jacobs, Clarence Maslowski, Marco Olivotto, John Pavel, and Frederick Yocum. The group's administrator, Daniele Di Stanio, set things up so that we could pass things between one another smoothly. Bevi Chagnon and Jacob Rus contributed valuable input to parts of the book. Cathy Panagoulias, known in Italy as *la principessa,* as expert in editing as she is in managing her husband, gave the final drafts thorough reads.

More than a hundred photographers have supported my efforts over the years by allowing me to use their work—over a terabyte to choose from, at this point—for educational purposes. Many of their names are in the Notes & Credits section, but a special thanks is due to three of them.

When I first introduced the ancestor of this workflow around five years ago, my opinion about its quality, speed, and applicability was based on trying it out on hundreds of my own photographs. As I am not exactly a Vincent Versace when it comes to photography, I felt I ought to repeat the experiment with the shots of someone who was. Representing professional photographers, Vincent endorsed the idea and gave me hundreds of his images to work on. So did David Cardinal. I also wanted the work of a "prosumer", that is, somebody who can only be distinguished from a professional photographer by the fact that photography is not his primary source of income. Fred Drury filled this role.

If, like me, you save a mountain of time and add a lot of quality by using the free PPW panel, you owe immense gratitude to Giuliana Abbiati. I provided the initial actions and the first iteration of a panel that enabled one-click access to all of them. It was primitive next to the sleek, scripted model of today. Giuliana saw the need for more options, and did the development, scripting, and testing. She, Alessandro, Marco, and I prepared the massive documentation, in two languages.

I also thank my students around the world, and the members of my appliedcolortheory list, for their support and suggestions. Also, I thank my publishers Peachpit Press and Kelby Training for bringing my work to public attention, Adobe Systems for making it all possible, and Google for letting the world find out that I existed.

That world has reached out to me and changed my life. Partly this was due to a committed group of people who were determined to bring me to their countries to teach. They are Alessandro Bernardi (Italy); Michael Cervantes (Puerto Rico); Jane England (Canada); Carlos Garro (Costa Rica); Timo Kirves (Finland); Sterling Ledet (U.S.); Andrés Pérez (Ecuador); Valery Pogorely (Russian Federation); Daniel Rubinstein (U.K.); Eduardo Ruiz (Peru); and Werner Tschan (Switzerland).

More than that, I've always been a big traveler, but in the last decade and a half it's been an experience that others would have difficulty imagining. In every corner of the world I find readers, students, friends. Invariably they want not just to talk about color but to show me their country as it really exists. The extended international family that my work has provided is the greatest gift anyone could receive.

Notes & Credits

Almost all original images that appear in this book are available for download at our site moderncolorworkflow.com, along with many videos, the PPW panel, and some supplementary documentation.

The originals we have posted are for your private use in practicing and perfecting the techniques discussed here. You may manipulate the images however you like for your own edification, including printing them to test how well you did. However, these images are copyrighted. You may not publish them, post them, share them with others, or allow any reproduction other than what you yourself need for learning purposes.

Some files have been downsampled, which will not affect the exercises.

Below, chapter by chapter, are the credits for the images and miscellanea, a listing of the videos and other material that is planned for posting as of press time, and answers to the Review and Exercises questions found at the end of the second half of most chapters.

Introduction

The six photos used to illustrate the Introduction were taken by Andrey Khludeyev, Paco Márquez, Jill Smith, and Werner Tschan. Two are professional photographers of some distinction, one is an amateur who uses very fine equipment, and one person uses a camera that costs very little. There is no difficulty picking out which is which, is there?

● *What's planned for posting:* I made a video showing how to install the PPW panel. Also, the entire development team got together to talk about how it came about.

Chapter One

The Emerald Lake image is mine.

● *What's planned for posting:* The beta readers thought that the way this chapter was written would leave people with the idea that the correction took forever to execute. I've therefore redone it from scratch for the camera, with minimal explanations so that the speed can be evident.

Chapter Two

Both photographs in this chapter are by Giovanni Barbisan.

● *What's planned for posting:* Originally the second half of this chapter was written as a full explanation of how I unified eight takes on the swan image into a single superior version. The beta readers said that it required too much cross-referencing for anyone to follow and would be better shown in video form. So I have recorded it, but have also saved and posted the original pages that you have been spared from plowing through—just in case you want to go into that much depth.

Chapter Three

The scene of Lucerne, Switzerland, and of the man with the camera bag are mine. The cheetahs were photographed by Andreas Kahlau. The hockey image was provided by the *Knoxville News Sentinel.* The graveyard scene is by Marty Stock, and the studio shot of a camera by Darren Bernaerdt.

Columbo's exegesis of how little things cost him his appetite came during the episode *Ransom for a Dead Man.*

The technique of lowering opacity of the threshold adjustment layer to identify highlight was suggested a few years back by reader Brian Avery.

● *What's planned for posting:* Alessandro Bernardi talks about different curves dialogs in various Photoshop versions and how to reconcile them with what's shown in this book. I add videos showing how to apply the lessons of the chapter to two images.

Review and Exercises Section:

- Neutral objects have equal values in all three RGB channels, or 0^A0^B in LAB.
- The Info palette has two sides, each controlled by its own eyedropper. Most users leave the left side at its default, Actual Color. The right side can be changed to show LAB equivalents by clicking its eyedropper.
- Highlight and shadow are the lightest and darkest significant points, not necessarily the literally lightest and darkest.
- In the AB channels positive values denote warmth (magenta in A, yellow in B) and negatives coolness (teal-green in A, blue in B).
- The quiz answers: 1D, 2A, 3G, 4C, 5H, 6F, 7B, 8E. As usual, I waited until I had forgotten which was which, then made the following notes as I took the quiz myself.

I first looked for eccentric LAB values, like the extremely yellow 15^A71^B. The only listed object it could possibly describe is the taxi.

$(36)^A(15)^B$ is an unusual bright cyan. It must be the glacial lake.

Only one value, $(1)^A2^B$, is close to neutrality, which means that only one listed object can be basically gray. Clearly, it has to be the stone marker.

30^A5^B is a fairly bright, slightly red magenta. It must be the leopard's tongue.

Eliminating these four gimmes leaves four choices, two of which are warm (both AB channels positive); and one cool (both negative). The final value is A–negative and even more B–positive, which is the formula for natural greenery. That value therefore must describe the trees. Of the remaining three, the seawater is the only cool object, and must take the AB–negative value.

The two remaining objects, the sunny face and the fried chicken, are roughly of the same hue, both B>A>0. The question then is which is more intensely colored (less neutral). That one, the face, takes the higher values.

Chapter Four

The Grand Canyon shot is by Valery Pogorely. Wildlife specialist David Cardinal photographed the leopard. The red flowers whose detail was obliterated by poor acquisition was shot by Alessandro Bernardi, as was the picture of the New York Stock Exchange. The images of the pink hibiscus, the alligators, and the greenish lake are mine.

- *What's planned for posting:* Marco Olivotto presents a video on how the Apply Image command works. In another, I demonstrate how blending worked in the leopard image, and also show another image that is handled similarly to that of the alligators.

Review and Exercises Section:

- The green channel carries roughly twice the weight of the red and six times that of the blue.
- When an image features different strong colors its channels will show a lot of contrast, perhaps too much for blending purposes.
- If a layer is in Luminosity rather than Normal mode when you are working on it you will not get accurate views of what you are doing to each channel.
- The dull colors of the Grand Canyon look fuller when they are darker. The luminosity maneuvering lightened the reddish soil and the trees in the foreground, making them seem more subdued although technically the color did not change. The PPW solution is to enhance color later, retaining the extra snap.
- Chapter 4 is about adding detail. In faces, extra detail is often considered offensive as it makes the person seem older.

Chapter Five

The two Irish images are by David Xenakis. The elk and the Yellowstone thermal pool were both shot by Fred Drury. The stream photograph is by Bud Turner. The seated hiker and the Bow River scene are mine.

Marco Olivotto describes the following procedure to evaluate what Blend If affects:

1. Create an Invert adjustment layer just above the Color Boost layer. The image turns into a negative.

2. Create a clipping mask on the Invert adjustment layer. The parts affected by the Color Boost layer's Blend If settings turn to a grayish hue.

3. When you move the Blend If sliders on This Layer, the excluded parts look normal, the rest remain inverted. If you play with the Underlying Layer slider, the opposite will happen. This is useful to have an idea of what Blend If is doing in transition areas.

4. When done, remove the Invert adjustment layer.

- *What's planned for posting:* One quick video runs through the operation of the Color Boost action; a second shows the various options for it within the PPW panel.

Review and Exercises Section:

- The L channel of LAB can be loaded as a layer mask to the Color Boost layer if you believe that colors in darker parts of the image are too strong.
- If the mask icon in the Layers palette carries a border, the mask is active and will be the target if you decide to use Apply Image to copy the L or some other channel into it. If the layer is active and the mask icon isn't bordered, then the image itself would be the target. This also holds when applying curves to a mask: make sure the icon indicates that the mask and not the image is active.
- Endpoint values of 99^L (highlight) and 5^L (shadow) are aggressive; some would prefer 98^L and 8^L. It is undesirable to finalize shadow in LAB if the final destination of the file is CMYK. The reason: darkening the black curve in CMYK holds detail more effectively than darkening the L.

Chapter Six

The opening quotation is from *Maui Revealed* by Andrew Doughty. The photos of London's Tower Bridge and of San Francisco's Golden Gate Bridge were taken by Larry Efird. Stevenson's poem *Where Go the Boats?* is from *A Child's Garden of Verses.* The horses, the family with the white background, and the two women who appeared in PP4E were all photographed by Mark Laurie. The Navajo Dome scene is by Alessandro Bernardi. The Zulu woman was photographed by Andreas Kahlau. The Las Vegas night scene was shot by Andrey Khludeyev. The red flowers of the quiz are mine.

The two Hunt quotations are from *The Reproduction of Colour.*

- *What's planned for posting:* One video distinguishes the effects of the three components of the MMM + Color Boost action. A second shows the further options available within the PPW panel. In a third video, Alessandro Bernardi explores creative uses of the action in cases such as the fashion work in which he specializes.

Review and Exercises Section:

- In Figure 2.6E the MMM selection was of a green area. In an effort to spread it out, the action made everything that was originally *more* green (if it existed) greener still, and everything less green even less so, or, in other words, more purple. The white swan was less green than the selection, so it became more purple. This would not happen today because a mask now protects near-neutrals against such drastic hue changes.
- The MMM selection forces everything else away from it. Select dark objects, and the resulting picture will be lighter. In Figure 6.14A the selection was the lips, which are on average light and red. The result was a change toward dark green. Figure 6.14C used Select All, which included the dark green background and the black hair. The background and the face cancelled each other for color, but the result was nevertheless lighter than the other two versions.

Chapter Seven

The chickens image is by David Xenakis. The scene of new citizens taking the oath is from the *Knoxville News Sentinel.* The woman with the watery background, the church, the cavern, and the Pizarro statue are all mine.

- *What's planned for posting:* Because this chapter is simple, there is no review section and no video planned for posting. Instead, there is a page-long comment by Marco Olivotto, clarifying or taking issue with some of my comments about the Clip setting during the discussion of Figure 7.3.

Chapter Eight

The Arches National Park scene was photographed by Bud Turner. The freestanding clouds of Figure 8.3 are taken from a photo by Bruce Bohlen. The shot of Montreal's Olympic Stadium is from the Corel Professional Photos collection. The two shots of Roman arches are mine, as is the Ocean Drive scene.

About the curious fact that no language seems to have a word for the blue parts of skies, Marco Olivotto writes, "In Italian we say *il cielo* [the sky] *è azzurro* about 70 percent of the time. The rest of the time it is *blu.* We also have the word *celeste,* which indeed contains the root of *cielo* but is curiously never used for the sky, except in the expression *la volta celeste,* meaning "the celestial vault", i.e. the firmament. The word *celeste* denotes a color similar to that of the sky (The Virgin's vest is almost invariably *celeste,* in our iconography), but it has a religious root: *coro celestiale* is a choir sounding like angels, and a dress can be *celeste* but for some reason the sky never is. How weird."

- *What's planned for posting:* I have a video comparing the two Darken Sky actions.

Review and Exercises Section:

- A *selection* is a temporary isolation of a certain area for correction. The term *mask* is occasionally used to mean the same thing, but it normally describes a more sophisticated selection, often requiring hand modifications, and saved into an alpha channel (or supplementary grayscale document) for future use. A *layer mask* is a different animal; it limits what parts of a layer are applied to the rest of the document. An *alpha channel* does not affect printing; it can become a selection at any time through Select: Load Selection.
- An alpha channel increases document size. Also, a file containing an alpha channel cannot be saved in JPEG format.
- Adjustment layers do not survive conversions to another colorspace. If you try to convert a file containing an adjustment layer, Photoshop issues a warning and asks whether you wish to flatten the image first, or to discard the adjustment layer.
- The Darken Sky B action is best for complicated skies, those having a lot of interaction between blue and cloudy areas.
- If clouds aren't properly neutralized before running either Darken Sky action, the action may consider them part of the sky proper and make them heavier than we would like.

Chapter Nine

For the first three years of the PPW, I tried to deal with overly red fleshtones on an ad hoc basis during the application of the Color Boost action. I thank Stephen Marsh for suggesting the better alternative of a generalized action to desaturate fleshtones.

The striking portrait of the Vietnamese woman smoking is by Vincent Versace. The advertising photograph of the woman's hands is by Ric Cohn. The Tuscan breakfast scene is mine. The seated man was shot by Marco Diodato. The woman in the red hat was photographed by Mike Demyan. The woman with black hair is by Mark Laurie. The Engels quote is from "Stages of Prehistoric Culture" in *Origins of the Family.*

- *What's planned for posting:* A three-page discussion of how blurring can be used to emphasize certain objects and not others, using a real photo to which noise had been added artificially, appeared late in the second half of early drafts of this chapter. The beta readers and I agreed that it would appeal only to hard-core students of the subject and that if we left it in people would skip to the next chapter. So we pulled it, but that fragment of the last draft is posted for those interested.

I've made a video redoing the exercise of ruining the hand advertisement, and also demonstrating the Skin Desaturation action.

Review and Exercises Section:

- The chapter emphasizes the importance of deciding whether to add contrast—detail—to a face. If you decide it is not a good idea, then you should avoid Chapter 4's techniques of channel blending and curving, at least as they apply to the face. You also need to watch other common commands that may increase facial contrast. The Bigger Hammer action sometimes does it. The H-K Effect layer of the H-K action *always* does it. And the MMM and MMM + Color Boost actions each have a layer called MMM Luminosity, which normally also adds facial detail.
- In the rare case where you actually want less detail than found in the original, you should consider luminosity blends using the red channel as source. The red is poor in facial contrast, at least at the outset.

Chapter Ten

The girl paddling was photographed by Vincent Versace. The challenging picture of the house fire was furnished by the *Knoxville News Sentinel.* The day lily used in the quiz and the brooding clouds of Iceland are both by Vladimir Yelisseyev. The parking meter is from the ImageKit royalty-free collection. All other pictures in the chapter are mine.

Photoshop's formula for overlay computation, using BLP and TLP to stand for bottom and top layer pixel, FP for final pixel, and the 255–0 lightness-to-darkness scale, is as follows. If BLP>127.5 (in other words if it falls in the light half of the possible values), FP=TLP*[255–BLP]+255–(2*BLP); If BLP<127.5, FP=TLP*BLP/127.5. Personally I prefer to consider it as an S curve!

- *What's planned for posting:* One video is a general discussion of the Bigger Hammer action, showing the sorts of images illustrated in the chapter. A second concentrates on the options in the PPW panel, and how they open the possibility of using the action on many more image categories.

Review and Exercises Section:

- To toggle between before and after the Bigger Hammer, turn off the Overlay Layer.
- The Darkening Layer of the action lets you control the effect in the shadows.
- The Blend If sliders in Blending Options are split by Option-clicking them. The purpose is to establish a smooth transition zone that averages values from both layers, rather than totally excluding one.
- The red channel is likely a poor choice for an overlay if the image is a portrait or anything else featuring fleshtones. The red channel is always the lightest in skin, so using it as an inverted overlay would probably darken the skin inappropriately.

Chapter Eleven

Florence's Ponte Vecchio is by Haridimos Thravalos. The two Hawaii scenes are mine.

- *What's planned for posting:* A video demonstration of how to choose the proper masking channel for multiplication and why blurring is necessary.

Review and Exercises Section:

- The Layers palette puts a thin border around a layer mask's icon when it is the active channel (and thus the target of Apply Image). If the thin border instead is on the icon of the layer itself, Apply Image would alter the image proper.
- A layer mask must be heavily blurred when the two layers it unites differ greatly in darkness (contrast).

• The Bigger Hammer action produces somewhat similar results to the blurred multiply method of this chapter. It adds much more detail to the highlights and shadows, however. If these areas are critical to the image, use Bigger Hammer, but if they aren't, stick with multiplication.

Chapter Twelve

The palace in Seville's Alcázar is mine, as are the Khrushchev tomb from the Novodevichy Necropolis in Moscow, the man in the burnt-out redwood, and the two Italian women. The water break was photographed by Jim Richardson, the woman in sun and shadow by Valery Pogorely. The photograph of the Château d'Azay-le-Rideau is by David Cardinal, as is the image of elephants at the waterhole. The Burmese couple was photographed by Vincent Versace.

The formula for an Exposure>Gamma Correction setting that emulates a particular false profile is: Gamma Correction=current gamma (usually 2.2)/gamma of false profile.

• *What's planned for posting:* A theoretical discussion of creating one file for light areas, a second for darks, and unifying them through a blurred mask makes up one video. A second is a remake of the water break image, with the annoying result of a version better than the one shown here in the book.

Review and Exercises Section:

• If the blur to these layer masks were omitted the resulting merge would seem strangely lacking in contrast. The blur is unnecessary when there is little to no difference in contrast between the two layers, or when the masked layer is set to Color mode.

Chapter Thirteen

The tomatoes were captured by Vincent Versace. The woman with the Christmas decorations appeared in the *Knoxville News Sentinel.* The red wall in Capitol Reef National Park is by Alessandro Bernardi. The food platter was photographed by Paco Márquez. The alabaster eggs are by Jill Smith. The advertisement for sparkling wine is by Ric Cohn. The painter who ends the chapter was photographed by David Xenakis. The Swiss lake, the Pompeii scene, and the picture of Capitol Reef that starts the second half are all mine.

• *What's planned for posting:* A general video discussion of the H-K action and its various options.

Review and Exercises Section:

• The H-K Effect layer darkens, but it doesn't change color. The Color Only layer desaturates, with an emphasis on retaining strongly colored areas.

• Even images that are basically subdued, as the Pompeii shot is, benefit from small amounts of bright color. The H-K action makes it possible to include some without overwhelming the viewer with brilliance.

Chapter Fourteen

The Peruvians in red were photographed by Vincent Versace, as was the Burmese water scene used as a noise demonstration in the second half. Jim Bean shot the melons. The flowers used in the classroom exercise were photographed by David Xenakis. The woman with the seal is by Marty Stock. The original British Columbia clouds shot is so horrible that modesty prohibits me telling you who took it.

Matt Kloskowski's remarks were posted in 2008 on http://scottkelby.com.

• *What's planned for posting:* A lengthy video showing how the workflow described in this chapter would handle a boatload of incoming raws, culminating with a demonstration of how a raw module can be used in conjunction with the PPW to correct an indoor image with a nasty cast.

Review and Exercises Section:

• In Postcard 14.11 the background, being neutral, is about the same in all channels. The foreground trees, however, are lightest in the green channel, where they also show the most contrast. Attempts to get more detail into both areas should therefore benefit from more use of the green.

- Applying a master curve to flatten an image reduces color because contaminating channels are strengthened where they are light, and dominating channels weakened where they are dark.

Chapter Fifteen

The Adams aphorism on sharpening is from *The Camera.* His comment about the advent of digital files is from *Examples.*

The man and woman were shot by Andrey Khludeyev. The three people by the pool are by Machaele Heise. Paco Márquez photographed the woman drinking prosecco. The rocks and flowers shot, and the pine needles for the presharpening comparison are mine. The cockpit and the fireworks are both from the Corel Professional Photos library.

- *What's planned for posting:* By beta reader request, I recorded a video discussing the concept of a halo map. The method shown is not recommended, but it does demonstrate how the halos can be stamped into an unsharpened file, or partially erased if need be.

A Note on the Type

The text type was prepared for the first (1994) edition of my book *Professional Photoshop.* The letterforms are those of Utopia, designed by Robert Slimbach in 1990. I stripped out all the width and kerning information and substituted my own, because I believe in relatively large type and I write in a two-column format, a deadly typographic combination if the letterspacing isn't well controlled.

Ledet Training

My color correction courses in the United States have always been marketed by Ledet Training, originally a tiny Atlanta operation that has grown into one of the largest providers of graphic arts training services in North America, with classrooms in many major cities. Its extraordinarily deep course list is found at www.ledet.com.

Other Countries, Other Languages

As the pictures in the book indicate, I enjoy traveling the world. I have taught classes in many countries, in, so far, Spanish, German, and Italian as well as English. If you would like to arrange an engagement outside of the United States, contact me directly.

The Applied Color Theory Newsgroup

In 1999, Ledet Training launched a newsgroup to support those who had attended or were thinking of attending my color correction courses, or who are interested in my writings. It currently has 4,000 members. The emphasis is on discussions of practical applications of color knowledge using Photoshop.

Signup for the list is at http://tech.groups.yahoo.com/group/colortheory or at www.ledet.com/margulis.

Reaching the Author

My address is dmargulis@aol.com. While I do try to reply to all correspondence, a three- to six-week delay has regrettably become the norm. If you need a quicker answer to a technical question, I recommend joining and posting it to the Applied Color Theory group (details above).

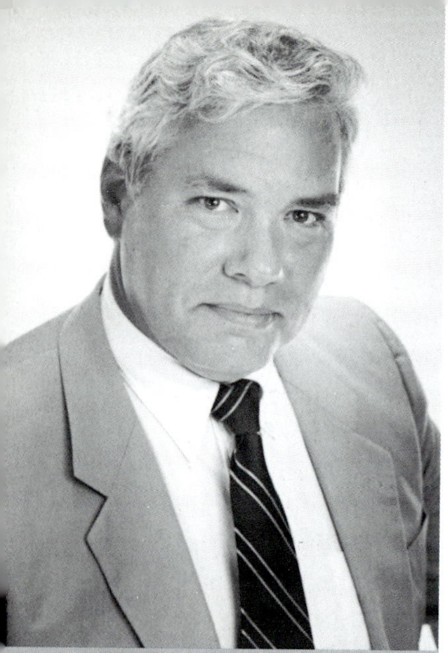

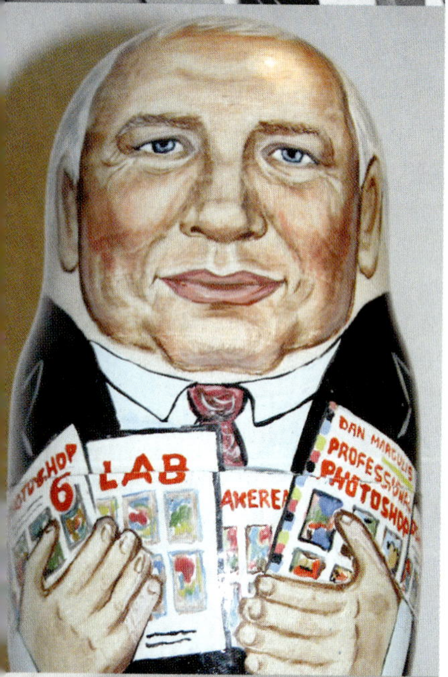

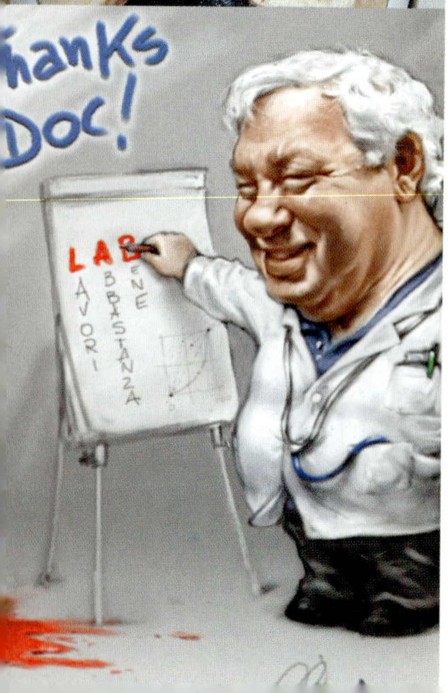

PARTNERS FOR TWENTY YEARS

Two decades ago, we were a small Atlanta company, offering courses in desktop graphic arts applications. Dan Margulis was running a Manhattan prepress house and writing a magazine column about desktop production.

The rapidly changing prepress industry was creating demand for serious color correction training. Dan's *Makeready* column proved he had the skills to deliver. So we asked Dan to put together a three-day, small-group, hands-on class, to be called Applied Color Theory. That first class quickly sold out, so we scheduled another. Then another.

Dan's first book came out the following year. His techniques improved and his audience expanded as photographers jumped on the bandwagon. We have presented Applied Color Theory over a hundred times in the United States. Dan has taken it to a dozen different countries, in four different languages.

The ahead-of-the-curve thinking that brought about Applied Color Theory has continued at Ledet Training. A focus on the real-world needs of professionals helped us grow into one of the most relied upon training companies in North America for marketing and communications software. Currently Ledet has seven training centers across the USA and is authorized by Adobe, Apple, Google, and Autodesk. Course offerings include all commonly used graphics software as well as modern communications technology such as mobile/tablet publishing and app development, web design and marketing, video production, eLearning, and social media advertising.

And yes, we still offer Applied Color Theory.

Dan has long been considered the leading authority on color correction in the world. We congratulate him on this book, which continues his tradition of introducing innovative, powerful techniques. We are proud to sponsor it.

http://www.ledet.com/subscribe *Cool Stuff* Our free email newsletter and mailing list (privacy guaranteed, easy one-click unsubscription).

http://www.ledet.com/events Our schedule of over 200 open-enrollment courses, including live online classes.

http://www.ledet.com/request/new Quote request for on-site training.

LEDET

http://www.ledet.com

877-819-2665 +1 770-414-5007

We teach the cool stuff!

http://www.ledet.com/margulisdiscount A **$50 DISCOUNT** for hands-on training, offered exclusively to readers of this book.

Pictured, top to bottom: Dan Margulis in 1994, when he began to teach Applied Color Theory for Ledet Training; traditional matryoshka nested doll presented to Dan by Russian students in 2004; an appreciation from Italian students in 2012.

Workflow Summary

The Picture Postcard Workflow (PPW) was introduced in April, 2007. Some of it is simple, but other parts are so complex as to be unworkable unless automated. Over the years I've released a series of actions and updated them as improvements suggested themselves. Adobe's introduction of Configurator enabled us to organize everything into a single panel that allowed us to access each one by a single click. I began using such a panel in my classes in 2010.

Many people volunteered to help develop it further. I enlisted the help and energy of three Italian colleagues, who felt that a more sophisticated variant was possible and desirable. The complicated scripting was done by Giuliana Abbiati. Most of the documentation within the panel is by me, but important articles were contributed by Alessandro Bernardi and Marco Olivotto.

I have been refining these actions for several years. In September, 2011, our group released a significant improvement: a scripted PPW panel that loads all the actions, which can then be run through the Actions palette or, more efficiently, with one click in the panel. It also provides ready access to certain commands commonly used in the workflow, such as blur filters. In March 2012 came PPW panel 2.0, with improved actions and many user-definable options. Release 3.0, with many new options, is being made available with this book in early 2013.

The panel is freeware. It contains extensive documentation of each action. Everything is loaded automatically by the installer. Photoshop CS5 or CS6 is required.

The action set is available as a separate download for those who do not have the requisite Photoshop version, as is the documentation. These actions are usable, as far as is known, in any version of Photoshop at least as far back as CS, and in any language. They do not, however, include many of the important scripted features of the panel.

The following is a current summary of workflow steps in their recommended order. The chapters in which they are explained are noted, as are the actions that pertain to them. Also, since some readers may have been exposed to earlier versions of the workflow, I highlight areas where my recommendations have changed. To aid in testing these methods I point out some files in the text that might help you see how they work.

For each step, I indicate the functions that the PPW panel adds to the base action. One major advantage isn't specific to any action, so I'll state it here: the panel sees each action as a single history state. Running the actions without the panel records each step. The translation: some of these actions are complex enough to flush your image history, making it difficult to revert back to a previous state. The panel has no such problem.

The Workflow Steps:

Correct Initial Color Problems

Chapter 3

Using the Info palette, examine the image for any colors that cannot possibly be correct. If none can be found, proceed to the next step. Otherwise, establish a curves adjustment layer to remove the objectionable colors.

Although this step takes place in RGB, it goes faster if you think in terms of LAB equivalents. Set the right-hand side of the Info palette to read LAB, and you'll only have to evaluate two channels for color, rather than three.

Change the mode for the curves layer from Normal to Color—even if it makes the image look flatter, worse. Since these curves are not intended to augment contrast, there is no point in pre-empting better moves later.

Use a threshold adjustment layer, if needed, to identify the lightest and darkest significant areas—as opposed to the areas that are literally lightest and darkest. Place a color sampler point in each for later use.

Actions provided: None.

PPW panel functionality: Clicking to add or edit an adjustment layer brings up the traditional curves dialog, not the one introduced for adjustment layers in Photoshop CS4.

Evolution of recommendations: If the original file is very flat, writing curves may be easier if this and the contrast step we're about to discuss are taken in reverse order.

Recommended exercise: This is the toughest step of the workflow because it requires discipline. One stumbling block is getting used to the idea of scrutinizing seemingly unimportant things when their color is more reliable than that of more significant objects. The Swiss scene of Postcard 3.3 is a good one for experimentation. It shows how moves to neutralize what seems to be a useless cloud can eliminate a nasty cool cast.

Improve Contrast
Chapter 4

Some of the PPW's most impressive results come from this step, which seeks depth, a sense of three dimensions. It adds as much detail as possible, ignoring any damage to the color, because the intent is to restore the color from the previous step. So,

- Flatten the image if necessary. Establish a duplicate layer.
- Examine the red, green, and blue channels to see if any is clearly superior to another or to both of the others. If it is, blend into or replace the bad channel(s) with the good one, using Lighten or Darken mode if appropriate. The RGB composite can also be used as a blend source.
- When finished with any blends, examine the red and green channels again (the blue contributes so little to contrast that you may as well ignore it.) If any curve is available that increases detail in the critical areas of the red and/or green, go for it, using the same layer.
- Change layer mode to Luminosity. Note: often there is more opportunity for improvement in the green channel than in the red. If this is the case, consider running two luminosity layers, or, more commonly, a straight luminosity layer with a curves adjustment layer, also set to Luminosity mode. While the first layer is still in Normal mode, adjust the green to be as light as possible consistent with holding highlight detail—normally a value of around 250^{G}. When the layer is set to Luminosity mode, this number will be recalculated because the other channels are currently darker, so the new green value will be lower (darker). It is now possible to further lighten the green with a curves adjustment layer, again changing to Luminosity mode afterward.

Actions provided: None.

PPW panel functionality: None.

Evolution of recommendations: Luminosity maneuvering has been around for a long time and the techniques are well understood. The big change has been the suggestion that this type of method is for every image and not just ones with problems.

Recommended exercise: The Grand Canyon of Postcard 4.1 and the alligators of Postcard 4.15 offer easy yet spectacular examples of the power of luminosity blending.

Shadows/Highlights
Chapter 7

Less effort is needed for this step than any other, because the PPW theory is that it isn't important enough to warrant custom treatment. The recommended settings, which are shown in Figure 7.1, almost never change.

At the end of this step, save a separate copy

of the image to hold in reserve for possible blending with the final result.

To start this step, flatten the image if necessary. Evaluate detail in the shadows and highlights and proceed as follows:

- If you are satisfied with what is there, save the separate copy as indicated above, and skip ahead to the Darken Sky actions.
- If you would be pleased with some improvement but it is not critical to the image, apply Shadows/Highlights at the conservative settings shown in the documentation, save a separate copy as indicated above, and skip to the Darken Sky actions.
- If highlight and/or shadow enhancement is vital, apply Shadows/Highlights at the conservative settings shown in the documentation, save a separate copy as indicated above, and go on to the Bigger Hammer.

Actions provided: S/H + OK is a two-step action that applies the default settings without opening a dialog. This saves no time unless you are using the PPW panel.

PPW panel functionality: Other than accessing the action with a single click, none.

Evolution of recommendations: I used to recommend this step before the previous (Improve Contrast) one if the image already had a full range, otherwise afterward. That's still the technically correct approach, but it was confusing to some. I don't think the theoretical advantage is big enough to warrant the bother. So, if you're comfortable with it, stick with the old approach.

Recommended exercise: On a full-range image, the effect is so mild that you can test it on any file you like. You should also try applying it to a flat-looking image to see the apparent gain in contrast (which the PPW recommends that you decline).

The Bigger Hammer
Chapter 10

This technique is for when you have decided that highlight (usually) and/or shadow detail is so critical to your image that Shadows/Highlights is inadequate. If you do not feel that this is so, move on.

The Bigger Hammer's impact comes from a blurred inverted overlay, which is on a layer by itself. It also returns a darkening layer above it that, by default, reduces impact in the shadows by half. The settings are good ones sight unseen, but they don't work well for fleshtone images. We can substitute others, but until 2012 doing so required pasting something new into the overlay layer and then blurring it, a cumbersome procedure. Now, however, panel options make investigating other possibilities easy.

The action's fourth layer, invisible by default, represents how the file would look if the overlay layer had never been blurred. It's hideous, but can be useful. Sometimes the action produces disagreeable-looking halos. The invisible layer has none, so it can be painted into the lower layer where halos are offensive.

Actions provided: The Bigger Hammer.

PPW panel functionality: Option-clicking the Bigger Hammer action accesses one of the most powerful panel features. A fully interactive preview shows the results of five different channels (red, green, blue, RGB, and RGB desaturated) as the overlay, as well as the ability to vary the blurring radius setting. Also, the algorithm can be altered to emphasize shadow enhancement, or to remain true to the original color. The flexibility in toggling through all these allows more frequent use of the Bigger Hammer, because now it should be tried whenever you have a suspicion, however slight, that it might work.

Evolution of recommendations: The addition of an unblurred layer to avoid haloing; the extended previewing options introduced in the PPW panel.

Recommended exercise: The waterfall of Postcard 10.1 is a straightforward introduction of highlight detail. If you'd like to put the

PPW panel's options dialog through its paces, try the flowers of Figures 10.13 and 10.14.

The Darken Sky Actions
Chapter 8

The blue areas of certain skies seem too light for the rest of the picture. If your sense of aesthetics calls for darkening them, two actions are supplied. Both create an alpha channel for skies and leave you a multiply layer with that channel as a layer mask. The primary action is called Sky Mask SC. If the sky is complex, with subtle interaction between clouds and blue, use Sky Mask B instead.

The action's alpha channel is retained in case it needs to be modified; it is also useful in the event that the sky needs to be blurred.

Actions provided: Darken Sky SC and Darken Sky B, both of which work in the same way but yield slightly different results.

PPW panel functionality: Nothing beyond the ability to choose either action.

Evolution of recommendations: No changes to speak of.

Recommended exercise: Any picture with a sky is suitable. I'd suggest the Icelandic scene of Figure 10.11 as an interesting experiment. It's not in the sky chapter, but it certainly could have been. Together with the Bigger Hammer action that it nominally illustrates, you should be able to come up with a big improvement over the original.

False Profile>Multiply>Blur Mask
Chapters 11–12

When a picture is partly in sun and partly in shade, the camera does not provide a starting point that we consider natural. A human observer tries harder to balance the two halves.

If you don't think that the image divides into distinct light and dark halves, forget this step. If you do decide to use it, you will need to lighten the image first to avoid plugging the shadows.

Assuming an RGB file, the lightening method of choice is a false profile. If that spooks you, a reasonable alternative is to apply Image: Adjustments>Exposure>Gamma Correction at a value of around 1.50. Either way, the picture will now look too light.

- Next, add a curves or other adjustment layer. Without entering new values, change layer mode to Multiply. The problem has now been reversed; the image looks too dark.
- Add a layer mask. If you see no obvious channel as a source, use the RGB composite as the mask. If you consider that the dark half of the picture is more important than the light, take the RGB composite from the multiplying layer; otherwise take it from the background layer.
- Blur the layer mask heavily. For files in the neighborhood of 15-30 megabytes, a Gaussian blur Radius of about 30 pixels is appropriate.

The PPW panel installs all needed false profiles and gives you scripts that apply them and generate a multiplying layer automatically. You will have to supply your own layer mask, however.

Whenever you use a false profile, remember that a conversion to another colorspace, such as LAB (or to your normal RGB workspace), is eventually required. That conversion makes the lightening effect permanent.

Actions provided: Technically, none. The PPW panel uses scripts, not actions, for this function because it must detect your RGB workspace, which an action cannot do.

PPW panel functionality: The PPW panel installs all needed profiles, and thereafter automatically permits you to assign profiles of 1.4 or 1.0 gamma. The primary values of your current workspace are assumed. Also, a supplementary free download permits you to specify almost any gamma you like.

Evolution of recommendations: Originally I recommended that the multiplication be done in LAB because it boosted colors attractively. Experience, though, has convinced me otherwise. Right after the multiplication, an LAB file looks better—but an RGB multiplication leaves more room for superior color techniques later.

Recommended exercise: Postcard 12.1's Alcázar and the water break of Figure 12.5 each offer dramatic gains with this method.

The CMYK Detour
Chapters 12–13

This is a variant of the previous step, aimed at accentuating bright colors at the same time as enhancing shadow detail. It has some similarities to the next step (H-K) but the effects can be more dramatic, especially if the file has sun-shade distinction.

- Apply a false profile as in the previous section. If you're using the PPW panel to do it, delete the multiply layer.
- Convert to Profile using a Medium GCR and a low black ink limit, or use the provided action. Either way "locks in" the false profile that was assigned in the last step. You now have a CMYK file that looks very light.
- Apply a sharp curve to the black channel only to establish a full shadow. If desirable, increase the quartertone setting for a stronger impact in near-neutral colors. The image now looks very strange. It seems washed out, but the weight of its shadows is correct. The image also looks too gray due to the addition of so much black.
- Re-convert the file to RGB. Then follow the instructions in the previous section for establishing a multiplying layer.

Actions provided: False CMYK.

PPW panel functionality: The panel installs the proper CMYK profile. The action is accessed by a single click.

Evolution of recommendations: As with the previous step, the original recommendation was to multiply in LAB rather than RGB. Also, this CMYK step is not as important as it used to be, due to the advent of the H-K action.

Recommended exercise: The lakeside scene of Figure 13.1 is a good one with which to compare this method to the H-K.

The H-K Action
Chapter 13

Many pictures benefit if neutral midtones are darkened. This is suggested by an anomaly of the human visual system known as the Helmholtz-Kohlrausch Effect. Other pictures benefit if near-neutrals are pushed even more toward gray, because doing this emphasizes the brighter colors that aren't affected by the action. That last concept is a bit more hit and miss. If you'd like to give either theory a try, an action called H-K does it. It runs in RGB and creates independent layers for color and for contrast.

The H-K Effect layer darkens quartertone and midtone in less saturated colors, without desaturating them. Often this gives a pleasing sense of overall depth that is difficult to achieve in other ways. It should be avoided in portraits, because it ages the subject. But there's never any harm in trying: either you will like what this layer does, or you won't.

The Color Only layer poisons all color, but the more saturated the original color, the less it is affected. This is helpful in images dominated by a single color, such as landscape shots that are dominated by greens. It is also somewhat helpful in fleshtones. Generally the file will look worse, temporarily, when this layer is active. However, the idea is that it will make subsequent color enhancement more effective by reducing competition to the brightest areas.

Actions provided: H-K.

PPW panel functionality: The action's Ersatz Black channel can be useful. By default it is discarded after use to reduce file size and permit saving as a JPEG. However, Option-clicking the action in the panel permits you to change this preference, or to retain the channel for this file only. The second half of Chapter 9 explains why you might want to.

Evolution of recommendations: The original version of this action unified luminosity and color changes into a single layer. This proved less than clever, because often we want one without the other.

Recommended exercise: The red cliff of Figure 13.11 offers a quick look at how effective this step can be. Then move on to the similar, but more difficult, tomatoes of Figure 13.4.

Skin Desaturation
Chapter 9

The PPW emphasizes bright, vivid, happy colors. Most of the time, this is what viewers and clients like, with one notorious exception. We are willing to accept landscapes with greens more vivid than those found in nature, but we reject skintones that are even slightly too red.

Acknowledging the probability that fleshtones will get too red as the result of subsequent steps, I now advocate desaturating them as a matter of course at this point.

Therefore, in all images involving flesh, I recommend playing an action that moves the file into LAB and, on an adjustment layer, desaturates colors it identifies as being in the skintone range. The layer's opacity can be altered as circumstances warrant.

Actions provided: Skin Desaturation.

PPW panel functionality: Nothing beyond a click for the action.

Evolution of recommendations: I originally recommended that fleshtones be treated like anything else: if subsequent steps made them too intense, use layer masks to control the effect. This advice wasted a lot of time.

Recommended exercise: Any portrait should do.

The Modern Man from Mars
Chapter 6

This complex action, aimed at creating believable variation in color, is the signature of PPW. It requires that you make a loose selection indicating the most important tonal/color ranges.

This selection is not actually used when the image is altered, but only as a guide to what's important. The final correction is applied in LAB to the entire file, without a selection.

The action delivers separate layers for luminosity and color changes. You can increase or decrease opacities to taste, or even discard a layer altogether.

This method is most effective when color variation is more important than fidelity to hue. It works in tandem with the Color Boost action to be discussed next. You have your choice of treating them as separate steps or as a single action.

Actions provided: MMM runs this procedure alone; MMM + Color Boost combines it with the next step. Reminder: A selection is required. If you are using the PPW panel, and you click either action without having first made a selection, a prompt will ask if you wish to use Select All.

PPW panel functionality: A powerful interactive preview lets you compare and toggle between results with up to four different selections. Note: for the MMM + Color Boost action, the panel only allows two selections.

Evolution of recommendations: The original Man from Mars Method was introduced in the early 2000s. It was based on curves and required an accurate choice of pivot point. It also did not separate contrast from color changes. The MMM action was introduced in 2010 and has been improved substantially since then. Most importantly, I now recommend that experienced PPW practitioners combine MMM and Color Boost within a single action.

Recommended exercise: Rather than experimenting with files from this one, I'd suggest going back a chapter and doing quick versions of Figures 5.7, 5.15, and 5.18. Each features a large body of water that gives the MMM an opportunity to shine.

The Color Boost
Chapter 5

At the time this step arrives the PPW has usually produced a bland-looking image, because traditional methods of enhancing color have been omitted. The Color Boost action goes to the opposite extreme: it deliberately makes things overly colorful, leaving to us the decision of how to back off.

Color Boost is simple, only a few steps as opposed to more than 50 for MMM. Like MMM, it runs in LAB. It delivers two adjustment layers, only one of which has an immediate impact. The Color Boost layer adds the fireworks; the Endpoint Adjustment layer is there in case you want to make some adjustment to the L channel, such as establishing a highlight or altering overall weight.

The real fun is in deciding how to tone down the excessive color imparted by the Color Boost layer. The obvious solution is to reduce opacity, but that isn't always the best way. Applying the L channel as a layer mask sometimes does just about the same thing, but often enough is decidedly better. Note: if you use a mask, you may have to consider increasing the layer's opacity so that more of its color can show through. Alternatively, you can consider establishing the layer mask by applying the L at something less than 100% opacity. Experience over a couple of years suggests that this is the method most likely to get the best result on a series of pictures—but not necessarily on each of them.

Many other options present themselves. The A and B channels of LAB are layer mask candidates, sometimes in combination with the L or one of the RGB channels.

Using the top (Endpoint Adjustment) layer is optional. Make sure, though, that you have proper highlight and shadow values—having gone to all this trouble to add drama, why settle for flatness? Also, make a final decision as to whether you like the overall weight of the image and if not, correct it.

Studying the overly colorful version desensitizes the eye, causing us sometimes to approve something that we will later consider too loud. Always compare your version not just to the original, but to the conservatively corrected image you saved early in the process. If necessary, blend part of it into what you have, usually in Color mode.

Actions provided: Color Boost alone, or MMM + Color Boost, which is the recommended choice for those comfortable with the workflow. Remember that MMM requires that you make a selection first.

PPW panel functionality: The action's defaults accentuate the A channel more than the B. This can be overridden either permanently or file by file. The MMM + Color Boost action can compare two different selections. Also, an MMM Saturation layer can be added. I recommend that expert users incorporate it as a new default.

Evolution of recommendations: Originally I did a lot of this color boosting with overlay blends in LAB. It was a lot better than trying to do it in RGB, but not as flexible or accurate as the Color Boost action, which came out in 2009. MMM was introduced later that year and the unified MMM + Color Boost action in 2011. The optional MMM Saturation layer was added by beta reader suggestion during the preparation of this book in 2012.

Recommended exercise: The action will pep up any picture you like. For an unusual mask treatment, try the green river of Figure 5.20.

Sharpening
Chapter 15

All workflows require sharpening at or near the end of the correction process. Nothing in the PPW requires the use of one method over another. Nevertheless, an action is provided to serve both those who need maximum sophistication, and those who are intent on getting sharpening out of the way as quickly as possible.

If you wish to fine-tune the settings, the action separates the sharpen onto five layers: light and dark halos at a low radius, light, dark, and color halos at a high one. All but the Hiraloam Color layer are halo maps that contain no image detail, and can be modified with curves, opacity reduction, layer masks, or even by erasing offending areas manually. Curving the halo maps can, for example, compensate for images that have previously been sharpened in-camera or upon acquisition in a raw module.

If speed is an issue, however, the action's defaults work well. If you feel they are too much for a certain image, a layer group on top of the stack combines all five of the underlying layers. Lowering its opacity is a quick way to reduce the effect overall.

Four of the five sharpening layers use masks that are specifically designed to minimize shortcomings of the particular method. Also, the amount of light conventional (narrow halo) sharpening is much less than dark conventional sharpening.

Actions provided: Sharpen 2013 and Sharpen Old. The two use slightly different haloing algorithms. On rare images Sharpen 2013 produces nasty artifacts that can't be reduced by simply changing opacities; in these cases one can revert to the older action.

PPW panel functionality: Option-clicking the Sharpen 2013 button gives you several preview options, and the ability to alter the Radius settings for any or all of the five sharpening layers, either as a permanent preference or for this file only.

Evolution of recommendations: The action's defaults have been changed several times in response to user experience.

Recommended exercise: If you intend to use the action in its simplest form (adjusting the layer group only) then you can try it out on whatever image you like. If you are going to adjust individual layers, all of the images in Chapter 15 are worth looking at. In evaluating the top layers, it can be very useful to take each one out to 100% opacity. It will look ugly, but you'll see what the layer is doing. Be particularly aware of Hiraloam Lighten and Hiraloam Color; these are the two that occasionally produce a really good effect that would be hard to equal with any other tool.

Index